POLICING

SAGE Text/Reader Series in Criminology and Criminal Justice

Craig Hemmens, Series Editor

Other Titles of Related Interest

POLICING
A Text/Reader

Carol A. Archbold
North Dakota State University

Los Angeles | London | New Delhi
Singapore | Washington DC

Los Angeles | London | New Delhi
Singapore | Washington DC

FOR INFORMATION:

SAGE Publications, Inc.
2455 Teller Road
Thousand Oaks, California 91320
E-mail: order@sagepub.com

SAGE Publications Ltd.
1 Oliver's Yard
55 City Road
London EC1Y 1SP
United Kingdom

SAGE Publications India Pvt. Ltd.
B 1/I 1 Mohan Cooperative Industrial Area
Mathura Road, New Delhi 110 044
India

SAGE Publications Asia-Pacific Pte. Ltd.
3 Church Street
#10-04 Samsung Hub
Singapore 049483

Printed in the United States of America

Library of Congress Cataloging-in-Publication Data

Archbold, Carol.
Policing : a text/reader / Carol A. Archbold.

p. cm.
Includes bibliographical references and index.

ISBN 978-1-4129-9369-2 (pbk.)

1. Police—United States—Study and teaching. 2. Community policing—United States. 3. Law enforcement—United States. I. Title.

HV8142.A73 2013
363.2′30973—dc23   2012023365

This book is printed on acid-free paper.

SUSTAINABLE FORESTRY INITIATIVE
Label applies to the text stock

Certified Sourcing
www.sfiprogram.org
SFI-00341

Acquisitions Editor: Jerry Westby
Associate Editor: Megan Krattli
Assistant Editor   Rachael Leblond
Editorial Assistant: MaryAnn Vail
Production Editor: Laureen Gleason
Copy Editor: Kim Husband
Typesetter: C&M Digitals (P) Ltd.
Proofreader: Gretchen Treadwell
Indexer: Gloria Tierney
Cover Designer: Edgar Abarca
Marketing Manager: Terra Schultz
Permissions Editor: Karen Ehrmann

12 13 14 15 16 10 9 8 7 6 5 4 3 2 1

Brief Contents

Detailed Contents

Readings

> This article describes an alternative to traditional policing. It requires
> police officers to look for the root cause of calls for service instead of responding
> to them in a reactive manner.

> Policing after 9/11 utilizes intelligence far more than it did prior to 9/11.
> This article provides a discussion of the main principles behind
> intelligence-led policing (ILP).

Section 3. The Scope of American Law Enforcement   85

Readings

Section 7. Patrol, Investigations, and Innovations in Technology 246

Readings

Foreword

Y ou hold in your hands a book that we think is a different approach. It is billed as a *text/reader*. What that means is that we have attempted to take the two most commonly used types of books, the textbook and the reader, and blend the two in a way that will appeal to both students and faculty, using the best parts of each format.

Our experience as teachers and scholars has been that textbooks for the core classes in criminal justice (or any other social science discipline) leave many students and professors cold. The textbooks are huge, crammed with photographs, charts, highlighted material, and all sorts of pedagogical devices intended to increase student interest. Too often, though, these books end up creating a sort of sensory overload for students and suffer from a focus on "bells and whistles" such as fancy graphics at the expense of coverage of the most current research on the subject matter.

Readers, on the other hand, are typically composed of recent and classic research articles on the subject matter. They generally suffer, however, from an absence of meaningful explanatory material. Articles are simply lined up and presented to the students with little or no context or explanation. Students, particularly undergraduate students, are often confused and overwhelmed.

This text/reader represents our attempt to take the best of both the textbook and reader approaches. This book is composed of research articles on policing. This text/reader is intended to serve either as a supplement to a core undergraduate textbook or as a stand-alone text. The book includes a combination of previously published articles and textual material introducing these articles and providing some structure and context for the selected readings.

The book is broken up into a number of sections. The sections of the book track the typical content and structure of a textbook on the subject. Each section of the book has an introductory chapter that serves to introduce, explain, and provide context for the readings that follow. The readings are a selection of the best recent research that has appeared in academic journals, as well as some classic readings where appropriate. The articles are edited as necessary to make them accessible to students. This variety of research and perspectives will provide the student with a grasp of the development of research as well as an understanding of the current status of research in the subject area. This approach gives the student the opportunity to learn the basics (in the text portion of each section) and to read some of the most interesting research on the subject.

In Section 1, there is an explanation of the organization and content of the book, providing context for the articles that follow. This will assist the student in understanding the articles. This section also includes the history of policing in the United States. Section 2 focuses on several alternative approaches to policing that have been used since the 1970s. Section 3 discusses the types and levels of law enforcement in the United States. The changing face of policing and police culture are featured in Section 4. The hiring, training, promotion, and retention of police officers are discussed in Section 5. Section 6 presents material based on police organizations and leadership. Section 7 includes information on police practices, while Section 8 discusses the level of effectiveness of police practices. Police liability and accountability are discussed in Section 9 of this text/reader. Section 10 highlights the sometimes complicated relationship between police officers and citizens, and Section 11 focuses on how the use of discretion by police officers can influence the police–citizen relationship. Section 12 features a thorough discussion of police deviance and ethics. And finally, Section 13 identifies some current issues facing American police officers and concludes with information that provides a glimpse into the future of policing in the United States.

Each section includes a summary of the material covered. There is also a set of discussion questions. These summaries and discussion questions should facilitate student thought and class discussion of the material.

It is our belief that this method of presenting the material is more interesting for both students and faculty. We acknowledge that this approach may be viewed by some as more challenging than that of the traditional textbook. To that we say Yes! It is! But we believe that if we raise the bar, our students will rise to the challenge. Research shows that students and faculty often find textbooks boring to read. It is our belief that many criminal justice instructors welcome the opportunity to teach without having to rely on a "standard" textbook that covers only the most basic information and lacks both depth of coverage and an attention to current research. This book provides an alternative for instructors who want to get more out of the basic criminal justice courses/curriculum than one can get from a basic textbook that is aimed at the lowest common denominator and filled with flashy but often useless features that merely serve to drive up the cost of the textbook. This book is intended for instructors who want to go beyond the ordinary, basic coverage provided in textbooks.

We also believe students will find this approach more interesting. They are given the opportunity to read current, cutting-edge research on the subject while also being provided with background and context for this research. In addition to including the most topical and relevant research, we have included a short entry, "How to Read a Research Article." The purpose of this entry, which is placed at the beginning of the book, is to provide students with an overview of the components of a research article. It also serves to help walk them through the process of reading a research article, lessening their trepidation and increasing their ability to comprehend the material presented therein. Many students will be unfamiliar with reading and deciphering research articles; we hope this feature will help them to do so. In addition, we provide a student study site on the Internet. This site has additional research articles, study questions, practice quizzes, and other pedagogical material that will assist the student in the process of learning the material. We chose to put these pedagogical tools on a companion study site rather than in the text to allow instructors to focus on the material while still giving students the opportunity to learn more.

We hope that this unconventional approach will be more interesting to students and faculty alike and thus make learning and teaching more fun. Criminal justice is a fascinating subject, and the topic deserves to be presented in an interesting manner. We hope you will agree.

Craig Hemmens
Carol A. Archbold

Preface and Introduction

Policing in the United States has evolved significantly since its inception. In the beginning, the police consisted of informal, volunteer-based watchman groups that were uneducated, untrained, and ineffective. Over time, the police have become more educated, better trained, and, depending on how you measure it, more effective. The face of policing has also changed, with more women and racial/ethnic minorities choosing this line of work for their careers. Technology continues to advance. Some would argue that this makes the police more efficient as they conduct their work. The book that you are holding contains information about all of the previously mentioned issues related to policing in America and more. It covers issues that are controversial (such as racial profiling and police misconduct) and interesting (including how police agencies are dealing with the downturn in the economy and the various ways that the media impacts the police).

When I sat down to write this book, I did so with the mind-set that this textbook would be different than other policing textbooks on the market. The difference between my textbook and the others is that I intentionally include information about racial/ethnic minority officers and female police officers whenever possible throughout the book. Other textbooks devote only a few pages to these issues. Most policing textbooks do not discuss issues related to small police agencies or those located in rural areas. I find this puzzling, as many of you reading this book will become police officers in areas that are rural or in agencies that consist of 10 or fewer employees. I also include information on gay and lesbian officers, as these groups are also often overlooked in policing textbooks. And finally, the impact of the media on policing in the United States is also discussed throughout this book. This is a significant topic, as most Americans get their information about the police from media sources; thus, it is important to acknowledge their influence and that the information provided to the public about the police is questionable and, in many cases, wrong. I also wanted to write a textbook that is easy to read and understand. By presenting the material in a clear and concise manner, it is my hope that students will *want* to read the textbook instead of feeling like they *have* to read the textbook. I recognize that this is a big (and some would argue impossible) task, but my objective was to write an engaging and informative book that students will enjoy.

The text/reader format used in this book is both innovative and unique. It provides students a traditional textbook format that includes authored sections that cover many of the major issues in policing, along with a reader portion that contains a mix of classic and contemporary research articles that complement the material presented in the authored sections. This blending of textbook and reader provides a more interesting learning experience for students and opens the door for class instructors to discuss research on a wide variety of policing topics. The articles included at the end of each section come from peer-reviewed journals and are written by policing scholars at various stages in their careers. The journal articles were edited in a way so that they are more user friendly to students at the undergraduate level. I also included book chapters from classic and contemporary books. These chapters were also edited with ease of reading and length in mind.

There are 13 sections in this book. Each section opens with "Section Highlights" to give you a preview of the topics covered in each section. After the authored text in each section, there are several key terms that identify some of the most important concepts and ideas presented in the authored material. There are also several questions that will challenge you to think more about the material you just read in each section. There are also suggested web resources to provide additional information on topics found within each section. And finally, there are two journal articles/book chapters included at the end of the authored material in each section. These articles/chapters focus on key issues that were presented in a more general manner in the authored text portion of the section.

Ancillaries

The ancillaries that accompany this text/reader are designed to be learning tools for students and helpful pedagogical resources for instructors of this course. A password-protected instructor teaching site, available at **www.sagepub.com/archbold**, contains PowerPoint slides, a test bank, and other helpful instructional tools. The student study site available at **www.sagepub.com/archbold** features eFlashcards, web quizzes, SAGE journal articles, and more.

Acknowledgments

In 2000, I remember creating a list of professional goals for myself when I was a doctoral student in the criminal justice department at the University of Nebraska–Omaha. One of the items on that list was to write a policing textbook before I retire. As I sit here more than a decade later writing the acknowledgments for this book, I cannot help but think about all of the people that have encouraged and inspired me to achieve all of the goals on that list.

I would like to thank three individuals that have given me endless amounts of professional advice and that have been fantastic mentors to me dating back to graduate school: Dr. Samuel Walker (University Nebraska–Omaha), Dr. Michael Meyer (University of North Dakota), and Dr. Dorothy Moses Schulz (John Jay College of Criminal Justice–CUNY). Without your guidance and support over the years, I would never have had the courage to take on this massive task.

I would like to thank my colleagues at North Dakota State University (especially Dr. Amy Stichman and Dr. Thomas Ambrosio) for their words of encouragement when I thought that I would never finish writing this book. Your support means a great deal to me.

I want to thank several of the graduate students that I work with at North Dakota State University (Ericka Wentz, Tod Dahle, and McKenzie Wood). I have had so much fun working with each of you. I appreciate how understanding all of you have been on those days when I was distracted by an impending deadline for this book. I look forward to watching the three of you create lists of professional goals for yourselves and ultimately achieve them in the future. A special thanks to Ericka Wentz for creating the ancillaries for this book and to Tod Dahle for creating the glossary for this book—I really appreciate your help.

I would also like to thank my parents (Clifford and Carol Erickson), my sister (Cheri Graff), and my niece (Amie Osborn). You are all a great support system. I appreciate how you all provide copious amounts of encouragement regardless of what I am working on and how much time it might take me to finish. I want to thank my two sons (Jackson and Braeden Archbold) for inspiring me and making me laugh every day. Thank you for being so understanding when I had to miss some of your soccer and hockey games to write this book. And last but certainly not least, I want to thank my husband, Jason Archbold. I don't know too many people that would sacrifice their weekends for nearly 2 years so that their spouse can write a book. You never once complained and have been nothing but supportive during this process. Thanks for helping me accomplish this goal and being such a fantastic friend and husband. I am lucky to have you in my life.

The completion of this book would not have been possible without the help of several people. I would like to thank Jerry Westby, Megan Krattli, and Mary Ann Vail at Sage for their support and encouragement through this process. I also want to thank Kimberly Husband for doing such a good job with the copy editing of this book.

Several people provided valuable feedback when they reviewed various sections of this book, including Lisa Bostaph (Boise State University), Max Bromley (University of South Florida), Tod Burke (Radford University), Kimberly Dodson (Western Illinois University), Frank Ferdick (University of South Carolina), Lisa Graziano (California State University–Los Angeles), John Hamilton (Park University), Stephen Hennessy (Saint Cloud State University), Gary M. Hoffman (SUNY, Albany), Richard Hough (University of West Florida), Larry Karson (University of Houston–Downtown), Kent Kerley (University of Alabama–Birmingham), Brandon Koi (Aurora University), Todd Lough (Western Illinois University), Edward Maguire (American University), Heather Melton (University of Utah), Kirk Miller (Northern Illinois University), Scott Phillips (Buffalo State College), Blake Randol (Washington State University), Joseph Schafer (Southern Illinois University), Julie Schnobrich-Davis (Central Connecticut State University), Ernest Scott (University of South Florida–Sarasota), and William Vizzard (California State University, Sacramento). Your suggestions for revisions have greatly improved this book.

Many of the photos from this book were collected with the help of Patty Swift of the Fargo Police Department. Thank you for being so helpful, Patty. I would like to thank Chief Keith Ternes of the Fargo Police Department for allowing me to use photos that truly enhance this textbook. I want to thank several people in the Fargo Police Department for giving me permission to use photographs of them in this book: Jess Homan, Susan Dealing, Michelle Voeltz, Tara Morris, Sarah Rasmussen, Travis Stefonowicz, Bill Ahfeldt, David Cochran, Jason Skalicky, Ross Renner, Mike Sanden, Dave Boe, Brad Boeddeker, Michael Bernier, Todd Wahl, Ryan Dorrheim, Steve Lynk, Shawn Gamradt, George Vinson (and of course, K9 Earl), Pat Claus, Dave Todd, Todd Osmundson, and Thorvald (Tod) Dahle.

I want to thank the Cass County Sheriff's Department (Sheriff Paul Laney, Judy Tollefson, Jonathan Partrick, Derek Hodges, Rick Hinton, and Amanda Brooks-Samek); the Bismarck Police Department (Chief Keith Witt, Dan Donlin, and Noah Lindelow); the Devil Lake Police Department (Chief Keith Schroeder and James Frank); the Lisbon Police Department (Chief Jeanette Persons); the West Fargo Police Department (Chief Arland Rasmussen, Michael D. Reitan, Duane Sall, Patrick Hanson, and Mile Orth); the North Dakota State Highway Patrol (Colonel James Prochniak, Jody Skogen, Rick Richard, and Thomas Iverson); the North Dakota Game and Fish Department (Chief Robert Timian, Jackie Lundstrom, and Amy Jo Brown); and the North Dakota State University Police and Safety Office (Chief Bill Vandal and Julie Hinkel).

John Hallberg of the Institute for Regional Studies and University Archives at North Dakota State University was instrumental in obtaining permission to use many of the historical photos featured in this book. Emily Schultz from the State Historical Society of North Dakota and Sharon Silengo from the North Dakota Heritage Center—State Historical Society of North Dakota helped me with several historical photos featured in the book as well.

I want to thank Michael Scott (Director of the Center for Problem-Oriented Policing in Madison, Wisconsin) for allowing us to use the illustration of the crime triangle in this book.

And finally, I want to thank Joe Kavlie, Hunter Panning, Ericka Wentz, Daryl Graff, Iris Wetsch, Cheri Graff, Clifford Erickson, Carol Erickson, Jason Archbold, and Jackson and Brady Archbold for appearing in the photos in this book.

I dedicate this book to my mom, Carol R. Erickson.
From you, I learned how to be a strong, independent, and confident woman.
Your strength, courage, and grace inspire me every day.
I am proud to share the same name with such a wonderful person.
I love you, Mom!
Carol Ann

Part I

Overview of the Police in the United States

—————————— ——————————

—————————— ——————————

Native American police officers—1883

The History of the Police

Section Highlights

- Examine the English roots of American policing.
- Understand evolution from watch groups to formalized police agencies.
- Look at the professionalization of the police through reform.

I t is important to examine the history of policing in the United States in order to understand how it has progressed and changed over time. Alterations to the purpose, duties, and structure of American police agencies have allowed this profession to evolve from ineffective watch groups to police agencies that incorporate advanced technology and problem-solving strategies into their daily operations. This section provides an overview of the history of American policing, beginning with a discussion of the English influence of Sir Robert Peel and the London Metropolitan Police. Next, early law enforcement efforts in Colonial America are discussed using a description of social and political issues relevant to the police at that time. And finally, this section concludes with a look at early police reform efforts and the tension this created between the police and citizens in their communities. This section is organized in a chronological manner, identifying some of the most important historical events and people who contributed to the development of American policing.

The Beginning of American Policing: The English Influence

American policing has been heavily influenced by the English system throughout the course of history. In the early stages of development in both England and Colonial America, citizens were responsible for law enforcement in their communities.[1] The English referred to this as *kin police* in which people were responsible for watching out for their relatives or kin.[2] In Colonial America, a watch system consisting of citizen volunteers (usually men) was in place until the mid-19th century.[3] Citizens that were part of watch groups provided social services, including lighting street lamps, running soup kitchens, recovering lost children, capturing runaway animals, and a variety of other services; their involvement in crime control activities at this time was minimal at best.[4] Policing in England and Colonial America was largely ineffective, as it was based on a volunteer system and their method of patrol was both disorganized and sporadic.[5]

Sometime later, the responsibility of enforcing laws shifted from individual citizen volunteers to groups of men living within the community; this was referred to as the **frankpledge system** in England.[6] The frankpledge system was a semistructured system in which groups of men were responsible for enforcing the law. Men living within a community would form groups of 10 called **tythings** (or tithings); 10 tythings were then grouped into *hundreds*, and then hundreds were grouped into *shires* (similar to counties).[7] A person called the *shire reeve* (sheriff) was then chosen to be in charge of each shire.[8] The individual members of tythings were responsible for capturing criminals and bringing them to court, while shire reeves were responsible for providing a number of services, including the oversight of the activities conducted by the tythings in their shire.[9]

A similar system existed in America during this time in which constables, sheriffs, and citizen-based watch groups were responsible for policing in the colonies. Sheriffs were responsible for catching criminals, working with the courts, and collecting taxes; law enforcement was not a top priority for sheriffs, as they could make more money by collecting taxes within the community.[10] Night watch groups in Colonial America, as well as day watch groups that were added at a later time, were largely ineffective; instead of controlling crime in their community, some members of the watch groups would sleep and/or socialize while they were on duty.[11] These citizen-based watch groups were not equipped to deal with the increasing social unrest and rioting that were beginning to occur in both England and Colonial America in the late 1700s through the early 1800s.[12] It was at this point in time that publicly funded police departments began to emerge across both England and Colonial America.

Sir Robert Peel and the London Metropolitan Police

In 1829, **Sir Robert Peel** (Home Secretary of England) introduced the Bill for Improving the Police in and Near the Metropolis (Metropolitan Police Act) to Parliament with the goal of creating a police force to manage the social conflict resulting from rapid urbanization and industrialization taking place in the city of London.[13] Peel's efforts resulted in the creation of the London Metropolitan Police on September 29, 1829.[14] Historians and scholars alike identify the **London Metropolitan Police** as the first modern police department.[15] Sir Robert Peel is often referred to as the father of modern policing, as he played an integral role in the creation of this department, as well as several basic principles that would later guide the formation of police departments in the United States. Past and current police officers working in the London Metropolitan Police Department are often referred to as *bobbies* or *peelers* as a way to honor the efforts of Sir Robert Peel.[16]

Peel believed that the function of the London Metropolitan Police should focus primarily on crime prevention—that is, preventing crime from occurring instead of detecting it after it had occurred. To do this, the police would have to work in a coordinated and centralized manner, provide coverage across large designated *beat areas*, and also be available to the public both night and day.[17] It was also during this time that preventive patrol first emerged as a way to potentially deter criminal activity. The idea was that citizens would think twice about committing crimes if they noticed a strong police presence in their community. This approach to policing would be vastly different from the early watch groups that patrolled the streets in an unorganized and erratic manner.[18] Watch groups prior to the creation of the London Metropolitan Police were not viewed as an effective or legitimate source of protection by the public.[19]

It was important to Sir Robert Peel that the newly created London Metropolitan Police Department be viewed as a legitimate organization in the eyes of the public, unlike the earlier watch groups.[20] To facilitate this legitimation, Peel identified several principles that he believed would lead to credibility with citizens including that the police must be under government control, have a military-like organizational structure, and have a central headquarters that was located in an area that was easily accessible to the public.[21] He also thought that the quality of men that were chosen to be police officers would further contribute to the organization's legitimacy. For example, he believed that men who were even tempered and reserved and that could employ the appropriate type of discipline to citizens would make the best police officers.[22] It was also important to Peel that his men wear appropriate uniforms, display numbers (badge numbers) so that citizens could easily identify them, not carry firearms, and receive appropriate training in order to be effective at their work.[23] Many of these ideologies were also adopted by American police agencies during this time period and remain in place in some contemporary police agencies across the United States. It is important to note that recently, there has been some debate about whether Peel really espoused the previously mentioned ideologies or principles or if they are the result of various interpretations (or misinterpretations) of the history of English policing.[24]

◪ Policing in Colonial America

Similar to England, Colonial America experienced an increase in population in major cities during the 1700s.[25] Some of these cities began to see an influx of immigrant groups moving in from various countries (including Germany, Ireland, Italy, and several Scandinavian countries), which directly contributed to the rapid increase in population.[26] The growth in population also created an increase in social disorder and unrest. The sources of social tension varied across different regions of Colonial America; however, the introduction of new racial and ethnic groups was identified as a common source of discord.[27] Racial and ethnic conflict was a problem across Colonial America, including both the northern and southern regions of the country.[28] Since the watch groups could no longer cope with this change in the social climate, more formalized means of policing began to take shape. Most of the historical literature describing the early development of policing in Colonial America focuses specifically on the northern regions of the country while neglecting events that took place in the southern region—specifically, the creation of **slave patrols** in the South.[29]

Slave patrols first emerged in South Carolina in the early 1700s, but historical documents also identify the existence of slave patrols in most other parts of the southern region (refer to the Reichel article included at the end of this section).[30] Samuel Walker identified slave patrols as the first publicly funded police agencies in the American South.[31] Slave patrols (or "paddyrollers") were created to manage the race-based conflict occurring in the southern region of Colonial America; these patrols were created with the specific intent of maintaining control over slave populations.[32] Interestingly, slave patrols would later extend their responsibilities to include control over White indentured servants.[33] Salley Hadden identified three principal duties placed on slave patrols in the South during this time, including searches of slave lodges, keeping slaves off of roadways, and disassembling meetings organized by groups of slaves.[34] Slave patrols were known for their high level of brutality and ruthlessness as they maintained control over the slave population. The members of slave patrols were usually White males (occasionally a few women) from every echelon in the social strata, ranging from very poor individuals to plantation owners that wanted to ensure control over their slaves.[35]

Slave patrols remained in place during the Civil War and were not completely disbanded after slavery ended.[36] During early Reconstruction, several groups merged with what was formerly known as slave patrols to maintain control over African American citizens. Groups such as the federal military, the state militia, and the Ku Klux Klan took over the responsibilities of earlier slave patrols and were known to be even more violent than their predecessors.[37] Over time, these groups began to resemble and operate similar to some of the newly established police departments in the United States. In fact, David Barlow and Melissa Barlow noted that "by 1837, the Charleston Police Department had 100 officers and the primary function of this organization was slave patrol ... these officers regulated the movements of slaves and free blacks, checking documents, enforcing slave codes, guarding against slave revolts and catching runaway slaves."[38] Scholars and historians assert that the transition from slave patrols to publicly funded police agencies was seamless in the southern region of the United States.[39]

While some regard slave patrol as the first formal attempt at policing in America, others identify the unification of police departments in several major cities in the early to mid-1800s as the beginning point in the development of modern policing in the United States.[40] For example, the New York City Police Department was unified in 1845,[41] the St. Louis Metropolitan Police Department in 1846,[42] the Chicago Police Department in 1854,[43] and the Los Angeles Police Department in 1869,[44] to name a few. These newly created police agencies adopted three distinct characteristics from their English counterparts: (1) limited police authority—the powers of the police are defined by law; (2) local control—local governments bear the responsibility for providing police service; and (3) fragmented law enforcement authority—several agencies within a defined area share the responsibility for providing police services, which ultimately leads to problems with communication, cooperation, and control among these agencies.[45] It is important to point out that these characteristics are still present in modern American police agencies.

Other issues that caused debate within the newly created American police departments at this time included whether police officers should be armed and wear uniforms and to what extent physical force should be used during interactions with citizens.[46] Sir Robert Peel's position on these matters was clear when he formed the London Metropolitan Police Department. He wanted his officers to wear distinguishable uniforms so that citizens could easily identify them. He did not want his officers armed, and he hired and trained his officers in a way that would allow them to use the appropriate type of response and force when interacting with citizens.[47] American police officers felt that the uniforms would make them the target of mockery (resulting in less legitimacy with citizens) and that the level of violence occurring in the United States at that time warranted them carrying firearms and using force whenever necessary.[48] Despite their objections, police officers in cities were required to wear uniforms, and shortly after that, they were allowed to

Urban police officers, 1890

carry clubs and revolvers in the mid-1800s.[49] In contemporary American police agencies, the dispute concerning uniforms and firearms has long been resolved; however, the use of force by the police is still an issue that incites debate in police agencies today.

⬙ Policing in the United States, 1800–1970

One way to understand the history of American policing beginning in the 19th century through the 21st century is to dissect it into a series of eras. Depending on which resource you choose, the number and names of those eras will slightly vary; however, there is a general agreement on the influential people and important events that took place over the course of the history of American policing. The article written by George Kelling and Mark Moore included at the end of this section provides three eras as the framework for an interesting and thorough discussion of the history and progression of policing in the United States. The remainder of this section will continue to identify important people and events that have shaped and influenced policing up through 1970.

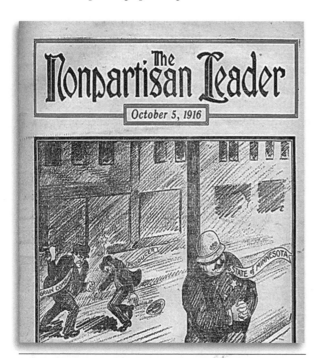
Police officers were viewed as an extension of politicians—1916.

Politics and the Police in America (1800s–1900s)

A distinct characteristic of policing in the United States during the 1800s is the direct and powerful involvement of politics. During this time, policing was heavily entrenched in local politics. The relationship between the police and local politicians was reciprocal in nature: politicians hired and retained police officers as a means to maintain their political power, and in return for employment, police officers would help politicians stay in office by encouraging citizens to vote for them.[50] The relationship was so close between politicians and the police that it was common practice to change the entire personnel of the police department when there were changes to the local political administration.[51]

Politicians were able to maintain their control over police agencies, as they had a direct hand in choosing the police chiefs that would run the agencies. The appointment to the position of police chief came with a price. By accepting the position, police chiefs had little control over decision making that would impact their employees and agencies.[52] Many police chiefs did not accept the strong political presence in their agencies, and as a result, the turnover rate for chiefs of police at this time was very high. For example, "Cincinnati went through seven chiefs between 1878 and 1886; Buffalo (NY) tried eight between 1879 and 1894; Chicago saw nine come and go between 1879 and 1897; and Los Angeles changed heads thirteen times between 1879 and 1889."[53] Politics also heavily influenced the hiring and promotion of patrol officers. In order to secure a position as a patrol officer in New York City, the going rate was $300, while officers in San Francisco were required to pay $400.[54] In regard to promoted positions, the going rate in New York City for a sergeant's position was $1,600, and it was $12,000 to $15,000 for a position as captain.[55] Upon being hired, policemen were also expected to contribute a portion of their salary to support the dominant political party.[56] Political bosses had control over nearly every position within police agencies during this era.

Due to the extreme political influence during this time, there were virtually no standards for hiring or training police officers.[57] Essentially, politicians within each ward would hire men that would agree to help them stay in office and not consider whether they were the most qualified people for the job. August Vollmer bluntly described the lack of standards during this era:

> Under the old system, police officials were appointed through political affiliations and because of this they were frequently unintelligent and untrained, they were distributed through the area to be policed according to a hit-or-miss system and without adequate means of communication; they had little or no record keeping system; their investigation methods were obsolete, and they had no conception of the preventive possibilities of the service.[58]

Mark Haller described the lack of training another way:

> New policemen heard a brief speech from a high-ranking officer, received a hickory club, a whistle, and a key to the callbox, and were sent out on the street to work with an experienced officer. Not only were the policemen untrained in law, but they operated within a criminal justice system that generally placed little emphasis upon legal procedure.[59]

Police services provided to citizens included a variety of tasks related to health, social welfare, and law enforcement. Robert Fogelson described police duties during this time as "officers cleaning streets . . . inspecting boilers . . . distributed supplies to the poor . . . accommodated the homeless . . . investigated vegetable markets . . . operated emergency vehicles and attempted to curb crime."[60] All of these activities were conducted under the guise that it would keep the citizens (or voters) happy, which in turn would help keep the political ward boss in office. This was a way to ensure job security for police officers, as they would likely lose their jobs if their ward boss was voted out of office. In other cities across the United States, police officers provided limited services to citizens. Police officers spent time in local saloons, bowling alleys, restaurants, barbershops, and other business establishments during their shifts. They would spend most of their time eating, drinking, and socializing with business owners when they were supposed to be patrolling the streets.[61]

There was also limited supervision over patrol officers during this time. Accountability existed only to the political leaders that had helped the officers acquire their jobs.[62] In an essay, August Vollmer described the limited supervision over patrol officers during earlier times:

> A patrol sergeant escorted him to his post, and at hourly intervals contacted him by means of voice, baton, or whistle. The sergeant tapped his baton on the sidewalk, or blew a signal with his whistle, and the patrolman was obliged to respond, thus indicating his position on the post.[63]

Sometime in the mid- to late 1800s, **call boxes** containing telephone lines linked directly to police headquarters were implemented to help facilitate better communication between patrol officers, police

Call boxes were the most common form of communication used by police officers during the political era.

supervisors, and central headquarters.[64] The lack of police supervision coupled with political control of patrol officers opened the door for police misconduct and corruption.[65]

Incidents of police corruption and misconduct were common during this era of policing. Corrupt activities were often related to politics, including the rigging of elections and persuading people to vote a certain way, as well as misconduct stemming from abuse of authority and misuse of force by officers.[66] Police officers would use violence as an accepted practice when they believed that citizens were acting in an unlawful manner. Policemen would physically discipline juveniles, as they believed that it provided more of a deterrent effect than arrest or incarceration. Violence would also be applied to alleged perpetrators in order to extract information from them or coerce confessions out of them (this was referred to as the **third degree**). Violence was also believed to be justified in instances in which officers felt that they were being disrespected by citizens. It was acceptable to dole out "street justice" if citizens were noncompliant to officers' demands or requests. If citizens had a complaint regarding the actions of police officers, they had very little recourse, as police supervisors and local courts would usually side with police officers.

One of the first groups appointed to examine complaints of police corruption was the Lexow Commission.[67] After issuing 3,000 subpoenas and hearing testimony from 700 witnesses (which produced more than 10,000 pages of testimony), the report from the Lexow investigation revealed four main conclusions:[68] First, the police did not act as "guardians of the public peace" at the election polls; instead they acted as "agents of Tammany Hall." Second, instead of suppressing vice activities such as gambling and prostitution, officers allowed these activities to occur with the condition that they receive a cut of the profits. Third, detectives only looked for stolen property if they would be given a reward for doing so. And finally, there was evidence that the police often harassed law-abiding citizens and individuals with less power in the community instead of providing police services to them. After the Lexow investigation ended, several officers were fired and, in some cases, convicted of criminal offenses. Sometime later, the courts reversed these decisions, allowing the officers to be rehired.[69] These actions by the courts demonstrate the strength of political influence in American policing during this time period.

Policing Reform in the United States (1900s–1970s)

Political involvement in American policing was viewed as a problem by both the public and police reformers in the mid- to late 19th century. Early attempts (in the 19th century) at police reform in the United States were unsuccessful, as citizens tried to pressure police agencies to make changes.[70] Later on in the early 20th century (with help from the Progressives), reform efforts began to take hold and made significant changes to policing in the United States.[71]

A goal of police reform included the removal of politics from American policing. This effort included the creation of standards for recruiting and hiring police officers and administrators instead of allowing politicians to appoint these individuals to help them carry out their political agendas. Another goal of police reform during the early 1900s was to professionalize the police. This could be achieved by setting standards for the quality of police officers hired, implementing better police training, and adopting various types of technology to aid police officers in their daily operations (including motorized patrol and the use of two-way radios).[72] The professionalization movement of the police in America resulted in police agencies becoming centralized bureaucracies focused primarily on crime control.[73] The importance of the role of "crime fighter" was highlighted in the Wickersham Commission report (1931), which examined rising crime rates in the United States and the inability of the police to manage this problem. It was proposed in this report that police officers could more effectively deal with rising crime by focusing their police duties primarily on crime control instead of the social services that they had once provided in the political era.[74]

In an article published in 1933, August Vollmer outlined some of the significant changes that he believed had taken place in American policing from 1900 to 1930. The use of the civil service system in the hiring and promotion of police officers was one way to help remove politics from policing and to set standards for police recruits. The implementation of effective police training programs was also an important change during this time. The ability of police administrators to strategically distribute police force according to the needs of each area or neighborhood was another change made to move toward a professional model of policing. There was also an improved means of communication at this time, which included the adoption of two-way radio systems. Many agencies also began to adopt more reliable record-keeping systems, improved methods for identifying criminals (including the use of fingerprinting systems), and more advanced technologies used in criminal investigations (such as lie detectors and science-based crime labs). Despite the heavy emphasis on crime control that began to emerge in the mid-1930s, some agencies began to use crime-prevention techniques. And finally, this era saw the emergence of state highway police to aid in the control of traffic, which had increased after the automobile was introduced in the United States.[75]

Vollmer stated that all of these changes contributed to the professionalization of the police in America.

O. W. Wilson was the protégé of August Vollmer. His work essentially picked up where Vollmer's left off in the late 1930s. He started out as police chief in Wichita, Kansas, and then moved on to establish the School of Criminology at the University of California.[76] Wilson's greatest contribution to American policing lies within police administration. Specifically, his vision involved the centralization of police agencies; this includes both organizational structure and management of personnel.[77] Wilson is also credited with creating a strategy for distributing patrol officers within a community based on reported crimes and calls for service. His book, *Police Administration,* published in 1950, became the "bible of police management" and ultimately defined how professional police agencies would be managed for many decades that followed.[78]

It is clear that the work of Vollmer and Wilson helped American policing advance beyond that of the

Radar "speed reader" in patrol car—1954

Police officers focused on order maintenance during war protests—1969.

Police reform resulted in police officers shifting their focus to crime control—1960.

political era; however, Harlan Haun and Judson Jeffries argue that police reforms of the 1950s and 1960s neglected the relationship between the police and the public.[79] The relationship deteriorated between the two groups because the citizens called for police services that were mostly noncriminal in nature, and the police responded with a heavy emphasis on crime control.[80] The distance between these two groups would become even greater as the social climate began to change in the United States.

The 1950s marked the beginning of a social movement that would bring race relations to the attention of all Americans. Several events involving African American citizens ignited a series of civil rights marches and demonstrations across the country in the mid-1950s. For example, in December 1955, Rosa Parks was arrested after she violated a segregation ordinance by refusing to move to the back of the bus. Her arrest triggered what is now referred to as the Montgomery bus boycott.[81] African American citizens carpooled instead of using the city bus system to protest segregation ordinances. Local police began to ticket Black motorists at an increasing pace to retaliate against the boycott. In one instance, Martin Luther King Jr. was arrested for driving 5 miles per hour over the posted speed limit.[82] Arrests were made at any type of sit-in or protest, whether they were peaceful or not. Research focused on the precipitants and underlying conditions that contributed to race riots during this time period identified police presence and police actions as the major conditions that were present prior to most of the race riots in the 1950s and 1960s.[83] In addition, the President's Commission on Civil Disorder (also known as the Kerner Commission) reported that "almost invariably the incident that ignites disorder arises from police action."[84]

Social disorder resulting from protests, marches, and rioting in the 1960s resulted in frequent physical clashes between the police and the public. It was during this time that people across the United States began to see photographs in newspapers and news reports on television that featured incidents of violence between these two groups. The level of violence and force being used by police officers was shocking to some citizens, as they had not been exposed to it through visual news media in the past. One of the most recognized examples of this type of violence was the clash between police and protesters at the Democratic National Convention in Chicago in August of 1968.[85] Graphic photos of the police hitting, pushing, and arresting protesters were featured on the national news and in many national printed publications. These types of incidents contributed to the public-relations problem experienced by American police during the 1960s.

Any police reform efforts taking place in the 1960s were based heavily on a traditional model of policing. Traditional policing focuses on responding to calls for service and managing crimes in a reactive manner.[86] This approach to policing focuses on serious crime as opposed to issues related to social disorder and citizens' quality of life. The traditional policing model places great importance on the number of arrests police officers make or how fast officers can respond to citizens' calls for service.[87] In addition, this policing strategy does not involve a cooperative effort between the police and citizens. Richard Adams and his colleagues described it best when they stated that "traditional policing tends to stress the role of police officers in controlling crime and views citizens' role in the apprehension of criminals as minor players at best and as part of the problem at worst."[88] The use of traditional policing practices coupled with the social unrest that was taking place during the 1960s contributed to the gulf that was widening between the police and citizens.

SUMMARY

- American policing was influenced by Sir Robert Peel and the London Metropolitan Police.
- Policing in Colonial America consisted of voluntary watch groups formed by citizens; these groups were unorganized and considered ineffective.
- Slaves patrols in the southern region of the United States were used to control slave populations and have been identified by some scholars and historians as the first formal police agencies in this country.
- Politics played a major role in American policing in the 1800s. Political involvement was believed to be at the core of police corruption present in the agencies at that time.
- Police reform was geared toward making the police more "professional."

KEY TERMS

call box	political era	slave patrols
frankpledge system	reform era	third degree
London Metropolitan Police	Sir Robert Peel	tything

DISCUSSION QUESTIONS

1. Why is Sir Robert Peel important to the development of policing in the United States?

2. Describe some of the duties associated with the early watch groups in the United States in the mid-19th century.

3. Identify several principles espoused by Sir Robert Peel as he began to assemble the London Metropolitan Police Department.

4. What was O. W. Wilson's main contribution to American policing?

5. Explain how the traditional model of policing contributed to the deterioration of the relationship between police and citizens in the United States during the 1960s.

WEB RESOURCES

- To learn more about Sir Robert Peel, go to http://www.bbc.co.uk/history/historic_figures/peel_sir_robert .shtml.
- To learn about some important dates in the history of American law enforcement, go to http://www.nleomf .org/facts/enforcement/impdates.html.
- To learn more about the history of police technology, go to http://www.police-technology.net/id59.html.

How to Read a Research Article

You will likely hear your instructor say, "According to the research . . ." or "The research tells us . . ." several times during class when he or she is presenting material from this book. All of the information contained in the authored sections of this text/reader is based on research. In addition, the journal articles included at the end of every section feature studies conducted by researchers. You might be asking yourself, "How do I read a journal article?" The following pages provide a brief description of the information that is typically included in peer-reviewed journal articles. I also provide a set of questions that you should be able to answer after you have finished reading a journal article. This information is intended to help you navigate your way through the journal articles included at the end of each section in this book.

Most research articles that are published in peer-reviewed, academic journals will have the following components: (1) introduction, (2) literature review, (3) methodology, (4) findings/results, and (5) discussion/conclusion section. It is important to note that the components found within journal articles will vary. Some journal articles may not contain all of the traditional components. In fact, some articles that outline the tenets of a proposed theory will not have any of the main components. This type of article is purely descriptive. The articles included at the end of the first section of this text/reader fall into the descriptive category. There are some articles in which the components are not clearly identified by the traditional subheadings (as they may use alternative subheading titles) but are discussed within the text of the article. In most cases, however, the five traditional components will be easy to identify if the author of the article has included them.

Introduction

Journal articles usually begin with an introduction section. The introduction identifies the purpose of the study. The introduction usually provides a broader context for the research questions or hypotheses being tested in the study. The reasons the study is important are also usually included in the introduction of a journal article.

Literature Review

Most journal articles provide an overview of the published literature related to the topic of the study. Some authors prefer to combine the literature review with the introduction section. The purpose of the literature review is to present studies that have already been conducted on the research topic featured in the journal article. By reviewing the literature, authors can highlight how their research will contribute to the existing body of research or explain how their study is unique when compared to previous studies.

Methodology

The methodology section describes how the study was conducted. This section usually includes information about who or what was studied, the research site(s), the type of data collected for the study, how long the study lasted, and how the data were analyzed by the researcher(s). The reader will usually be able to determine whether the study is quantitative, qualitative, or a combination of both after reading this section. The information included in this section should include enough detail so that the reader can understand exactly how the study was conducted. In addition, the high level of detail in this section allows other researchers to replicate the study in other research sites if they choose to do so.

 ## Findings/Results

The findings/results section explains what the researcher found when he or she analyzed the data. Research findings are expressed using numbers in a series of tables if the research is quantitative in nature. If the study utilized qualitative data, the research findings will consist of descriptions of patterns and themes that were discovered within the textual data. This section is important because the research findings tell the reader about the outcome of the study.

 ## Discussion/Conclusion

The discussion/conclusion section usually provides a brief recap of the purpose of the study and a general description of the main research findings. This part of the journal article explains why the research findings are important or what policy implications result from the research findings. This is also the point in the article at which the author points out the limitations of the study. And finally, this section usually contains several suggestions for future research on the topic featured in the study.

Now that you have an understanding of the parts of a journal article, I will use the article written by Weisheit, Wells, and Falcone in Section 3 of this text to demonstrate how you can apply the five components we just discussed above.

 ## Community Policing in Small Town and Rural America

By Ralph A. Weisheit, L. Edward Wells, and David N. Falcone

1. **What is the purpose of the study in this article?**

   The purpose of the study is mentioned at the end of the third paragraph of the paper—"This article examines the idea of community policing by considering the fit between the police practices in rural areas and the philosophy of community policing as an urban phenomenon." The authors also hypothesize that "... experiences in rural areas provide examples of successful community policing" and that their comparison "raises questions about the simple applicability of these ideas to urban settings."

2. **Do the authors present any literature that is directly or indirectly related to their study?**

   Yes. The authors begin with a section that discusses what community policing is so that the reader is familiar with this topic. Next, under the subheading "Existing Evidence," the authors state, "Although there have been no studies that directly examine the extent to which rural policing reflects many key elements of community policing, there are many scattered pieces of evidence with which one can make this case." In the paragraphs that follow, they present evidence from past studies that supports the idea that they hypothesized in the beginning of the paper.

3. **How was the study conducted? Specifically, how do the authors describe their research design/methodology and data analysis?**

Under the subheading "The Study," the authors describe the methodology/research design. They mention that the article is based on interviews that were conducted as part of a larger research project. Unstructured interviews were conducted with 46 rural sheriffs and 28 police chiefs in small towns. Some of the interviews were conducted face to face, while others were conducted over the telephone. The length of the interviews ranged from 20 minutes to 2 hours; the average interview lasted 40 minutes. The authors describe some of the questions covered during the interviews. The authors do not specifically explain *how* they analyzed the interview data; however, it appears as though they looked for themes in the interview data and compared them to findings from previous studies on community policing. This is a qualitative, exploratory study in which the authors are laying the groundwork for future studies on this topic. It is exploratory because no other studies have been conducted on this specific topic.

4. **What are the main research findings?**

After examining the interview data, the authors found several ways that rural policing mirrors community policing (the findings section begins under the heading "Observations"). First, they identify "community connections" as one of the ways that rural policing mirrors community policing. They describe how the two are similar and then provide quotes from the interview data to support this finding. They also identify "general problem solving" and "effectiveness" as two other similarities between rural policing and community policing. The authors then make a comparison between rural and urban policing when they interviewed chiefs of police and sheriffs that previously worked in an urban setting. The individuals with work experience in both settings reported a difference in the way they policed in both settings (once again this is supported by quotes from the interview data).

5. What does the article include in the conclusion/discussion section?

Under the subheading "Discussion," the authors provide a brief and general overview of the findings. They also provide further evidence of similarities between rural policing and community policing through the use of additional quotes. They conclude the article by stating that a more extensive study on rural policing is needed in order to state conclusively that rural policing and community policing are similar in operation and outcomes. The authors do not point out the limitations of their study in the conclusion section; instead, they state that this is an exploratory study that is only a portion of a larger study with a different focus.

As you work your way through this text/reader, you will notice how the journal articles included at the end of each section vary in their organization and presentation of content. If you do not find all (or any) of the five main components in some of the articles, keep in mind that the purpose of the article may not be to present a research study. Several of the articles are descriptive in nature: they present ideas about various topics in policing. Regardless of the format or presentation of information, the articles will provide valuable information that will help you further understand policing in the United States.

READING 1

In this article, Philip Reichel provides a comprehensive overview of slave patrols of the South. Slave patrols consisted of mostly White citizens who monitored the activities of slaves. Reichel asserts that modern policing has passed through various developmental stages that can be explained by typologies (i.e., informal, transitional, and modern types of policing).

Southern Slave Patrols as a Transitional Police Type

Philip L. Reichel

Accounts of the developmental history of American policing have tended to concentrate on happenings in the urban North. While the literature is replete with accounts of the growth of law enforcement in places like Boston (Lane, 1967; Savage, 1865), Chicago (Flinn, 1975), Detroit (Schneider, 1980) and New York City (Richardson, 1970), there has been minimal attention paid to police development outside the North. It seems unlikely that other regions of the country simply mimicked that development regardless of their own peculiar social, economic, political, and geographical aspects. In fact, Samuel Walker (1980) has briefly noted that eighteenth and nineteenth century Southern cities had developed elaborate police patrol systems in an effort to control the slave population. Walker even suggested these slave patrols were precursors to the police (1980: 59). As a forerunner to the police, it would seem that slave patrols should have become a well researched example in our attempt to better understand the development of American law enforcement. However, the regionalism of many existing histories has meant that criminal justicians and practitioners are often unaware of the existence of, and

the role played by, Southern slave patrols. This means our knowledge of the history of policing is incomplete and regionally biased. This article responds to that problem by focusing attention on the development of law enforcement in the Southern slave states (i.e., Alabama, Arkansas, Delaware, Florida, Georgia, Kentucky, Louisiana, Maryland, Mississippi, Missouri, North Carolina, South Carolina, Tennessee, Texas and Virginia) during the colonial and antebellum years. The particular question to be answered is: were Southern slave patrols precursors to modern policing?

Answering the research question requires clarification of the term *precursor*. The concept of a precursor to police implies there are stages of development preceding the point at which a modern police force is achieved. Several authors have looked at specific factors which influenced the development of police organizations in particular cities. Fewer have tried to make generalizations about police growth across the society. The latter group, which includes Bacon (1939), Lundman (1980) and Monkkonen (1981), draw on case studies of certain cities to hypothesize a developmental sequence explaining modernization of police

Author's Note: Historian Gail Rowe and two anonymous American Journal of Police *referees provided me with invaluable assistance and suggestions for which I am most grateful. This is an extensively revised version of a paper presented at the 1985 Annual Meeting of the Academy of Criminal Justice Sciences.*

in America. Lundman (1980), however, presents his ideas with the help of a typology of police systems.[1] The advantage of a historical typology is that it allows conceptualization of a developmental sequence and can therefore be most helpful in determining whether or not slave patrols can be viewed as a part of that sequence.

The Stages of Police Development

Lundman (1980) has suggested three types or systems of policing: informal, transitional, and modern. *Informal policing* is characterized by community members sharing responsibility for maintaining order. Such a system was typical of societies with little division of labor and a great deal of homogeneity. There existed among the people, a "collective conscience" which allowed them willingly to participate in the identification and apprehension of rule violators. As society grew, people had wider-ranging jobs and interests. Agreement as to what was right and wrong became less complete and informal police systems became less effective. Society's response was the development of *transitional policing* which served as a bridge between the informal and modern types. In that capacity, the transitional systems included aspects of the informal networks but also anticipated modern policing in terms of offices and procedures.

Identification of the point at which a police department becomes modern has not been agreed upon. Bacon, for example, cited six factors to be met: 1) city-wide jurisdiction; 2) twenty-four-hour responsibility; 3) a single organization in charge of the greater part of formal enforcement; 4) a paid personnel on a salary basis; 5) a personnel occupied solely with police duties, and 6) general rather than specific functions (1939: 6). At the other extreme is Monkkonen's (1981) suggestion that the decisive movement

to a modern police department occurs when the police adopt a uniform. Lundman follows Bacon but identifies only four distinctive characteristics of *modern policing* (1980: 17). First, there are persons recognized as having full-time police responsibilities. Also, there is 2) continuity in office as well as 3) continuity in procedure. Finally, for a system to be considered modern it must have 4) accountability to a central governmental authority.

Those four characteristics incorporate most of Bacon's suggestions but ignore Monkkonen's. Walker, however, found the use of uniforms as a starting point for modern policing to be "utter nonsense" (1982: 216), since the development process was not the same in every city and the new agencies varied so much in size and strength.[2] Instead, Lundman's characteristics seem appropriately chosen for present needs to identify the modern police type.

Existing histories of law enforcement provide significant information about informal (e.g. constables, day and night watches) and modern (e.g. London, New York City, Boston) types, but tend to ignore examples of what Lundman might call transitional. The implication is that modern policing was the result of simple formalization of informal systems. This article offers Southern slave patrols as an example of policing which went beyond informal but was not yet modern. Because few people are aware of them, the patrols will be described before being linked to transitional police types.

A Description of Southern Slave Patrols

A number of variables influence the development of formal mechanisms of social control. Lundman's review of the literature (1980: 24) identified four important factors: 1) an actual or perceived increase in crime; 2) public riots; 3) public intoxication; and 4) a need

---

[1]Lundman's typology of police systems is not to be confused with other typologies (e.g., Wilson's 1968 policing styles) which differentiate contemporary as opposed to the historical types Lundman addresses.

[2]Monkkonen's reasons for using uniforms as the starting date can be found in his book (1981: 39–45, 53) and in an article (1982: 577).

to control the "dangerous classes." Bacon (1939) in a comprehensive yet infrequently cited work, took a somewhat different approach. He identified three factors of social change influencing development of modern police departments: 1) increased economic specialization; 2) formation and increasing stratification of classes; and 3) increase in population size. As a result of these social changes Bacon argues there comes "an increase in fraud, in public disorders, and in legislation limiting personal freedom" which pre-existing forms of maintaining order (e.g. family, church, neighborhood) are unable to handle (1939: 782). Variations in enforcement procedures then occur which are "pointed at specific groups, economic specialists, and certain times, places, and objects" until eventually there is a "tendency for specialists to become unified and organized" (Bacon, 1939: 782–783).

Given the scholarly works identifying such numerous and intertwined variables affecting the development of police agencies, it is potentially misleading to concentrate on just one of those factors. However, historical accounts of social control techniques in the South seem to suggest that a concern with class stratification (Lundman's fourth factor and Bacon's second) played a primary role in the development of formal systems of control in that region. Although the conflicts presented by immigrants and the poor have been shown to be important in the development of police in London, New York, and Boston (Lundman, 1980: 29), the conflicts presented by slaves have received very little attention. Bacon compared slaves to Southern whites and found the folkways and mores of the two castes were so different that "continual and obvious force was required if society were to be maintained" (1939: 772). The continual and obvious force developed by the South to control its version of the "dangerous classes" was the slave patrol. Before discussing those patrols it is necessary to understand why the slaves constituted a threat.[3]

Slaves as a Dangerous Class

The portrayal of slaves as docile, happy, and generally content with their bondage has been successfully challenged in recent decades. We can today express amazement that slaveowners could have been unaware of their slaves' unhappiness, yet some whites were continually surprised that slaves resisted their status. Such an attitude was not found only among Southern slaveowners. In a 1731 advertisement for a fugitive slave, a New England master was dismayed that this slave had run away "without the least provocation" (quoted in Foner, 1975: 264). Whether provoked in the eyes of slaveholders or not, slaves did resist their bondage. That resistance generally took one of three forms: running away, criminal acts and conspiracies or revolts. Any of those actions constituted a danger to whites.

The number of slaves who ran away is difficult to determine (Foner, 1975: 264). However, it was certainly one of the greatest problems of slave government (Paterson, 1968: 20). Resistance by running away was easier for younger, English-speaking, skilled slaves, but records indicate slaves of all ages and abilities had attempted escape in this manner (Foner, 1975: 260). Criminal acts by slaves have also been linked to resistance. Foner (1975: 265–268) notes instances of theft, robbery, crop destruction, arson and poison as being typical. Georgia legislation in 1770 which provided the death penalty for slaves found guilty of even attempting to poison whites was said to be necessary because "the detestable crime of poisoning hath frequently been committed by slaves." A 1761 issue of the *Charleston Gazette* complained "the Negroes have again begun the hellish practice of poisoning" (both quoted in Foner, 1975: 267).

Possibly the most fear-invoking resistance however, were the slave conspiracies and revolts: Such action occurred as early as 1657, but the largest slave

---

[3]Some may find the explanation of slaves as a danger to be an exercise in the obvious, but Walker's (1982) comments provide a guiding principle. He suggests that "constructing a thesis around presumed existence of a dangerous class is…a sloppy bit of historical writing" unless we are told who composed the group, where they stood in the social structure and in what respect they are a danger (Walker, 1982: 215). While the "who" (slaves) and "where" (at the very bottom) questions have been addressed above and countless other places, the "what" question is less understood.

uprising in colonial America took place on September 9, 1739 near the Stono River several miles from Charleston. Forty Negroes and twenty whites were killed and the resulting uproar had important impact on slave regulations. For example, South Carolina patrol legislation in 1740, noted:

> FOREASMUCH as many late horrible and barbarous massacres have been actually committed and many more designed, on the white inhabitants of this Province, by negro slaves, who are generally prone to such cruel practices, which makes it highly necessary that constant patrols should be established (Cooper, 1938b: 568).

Neighboring Georgians were also concerned with the actuality and potential for slave revolts. The preamble of their 1757 law establishing and regulating slave patrols argues:

> it is absolutely necessary for the Security of his Majesty's Subjects in this Province, that Patrols should be established under proper Regulations in the settled parts thereof, for the better keeping of Negroes and other Slaves in Order and prevention of any Cabals, Insurrections or other Irregularities amongst them (Candler, 1910: 225).

Each of the three areas of resistance aided in slaves being perceived as a dangerous class. There was, however, another variable with overriding influence. Unlike the other three factors, this aspect was less direct and less visible. That latent variable was the number of slaves in the total population of several colonies. While

Table 1	Colonial, Populations by Race, 1680 to 1780[a] Percentages							
	South Carolina[b]		**North Carolina**[c]		**Virginia**[d]		**Georgia**[e]	
	White	**Black**	**White**	**Black**	**White**	**Black**	**White**	**Black**
1680	83	17	96	4	96	4	-	-
1700	57	43[f]	94	4	87	13	-	-
1720	30	70	86	14	76	24 (1715)	-	-
1740	33	67	79	21	68	32 (1743)	80	20 (1750)
1760	36	64 (1763)	79	21 (1764)	50	50 (1763)	63	37
1780	58	42 (1785)	67	33 (1775)	52	43	70	30 (1776)

[a]The sources used to gather these are many and varied. The resulting percentages should be viewed as estimates to indicate trends rather than indication of exact distribution. Slave free blacks and in the early years, Indian slaves, are not included under "black."

[b]1680, 1700, 1720 and 1740 from Simmons (1976: 125); 1763 and 1785 from Greene and Harrington (1966: 172–176).

[c]1680, 1700, 1720 and 1740 from Simmons (1976: 125); 1764 from Foner (1975: 208); 1775 from Green and Harrington (19666: 156–160).

[d]1680, 1715, 1743, 1763 and 1780 from Greene and Harrington (1966: 134–143); 1700 from Wells (1975: 161).

[e]Georgia was not settled until 1733 and although they were illegally imported in the mid-1740 slaves were not legally allowed until 1750 from Wells (1975: 170); 1760 from Foner (1975: 213); 1776 from Greene and Harrington (1968: 180–183).

[f]Wood (1974: 143) believes black inhabitants exceeded white inhabitants in South Carolina around 1708.

an interest in knowing the continuous whereabouts of slaves was present throughout the colonies, slave control by formal means (e.g., specialized legislation and forces) was more often found in those areas where slaves approached, or in fact were, the numerical majority. Table 1 provides population percentages for some of the Southern colonies/states. When considering the sheer number of persons to be controlled it is not surprising that whites often felt vulnerable.

The Organization and Operation of Slave Patrols[4]

Consistent with the earliest enforcement techniques identified in English and American history, the first means of controlling slaves was informal in nature. In 1686 a South Carolina statute said anyone could apprehend, chastise and send home any slave found off his/her plantation without authorization. In 1690 such action was made everyone's duty or be fined forty shillings (Henry, 1968: 31). Enforcement of slavery by the average citizen was not to be taken lightly. A 1705 act in Virginia made it legal "for any person or persons whatsoever, to kill or destroy such slaves (i.e. runaways)... without accusation or impeachment of any crime for the same" (quoted in Foner, 1975: 195). Eventually, however, such informal means became inadequate. As the social changes suggested by Bacon (1939) took place and the fear of slaves as a dangerous class heightened, special enforcement officers developed and provided a transition to modern police with general enforcement powers.

In their earliest stages, slave patrols were part of the colonial militias. Royal charters empowered governors to defend colonies and that defense took the form of a militia for coast and frontier defense (Osgood, 1957). All able-bodied males between 16 and 60 were to be enrolled in the militia and had to provide their own weapons and equipment (Osgood, 1957; Shy, 1980; Simmons, 1976). Although the militias were regionally diverse and constantly changing (Shy, 1980),

Anderson's (1984) comments about the Massachusetts Bay Colony militia notes an important distinction that was reflected in other colonies. At the beginning of the 18th century, Massachusetts' militia was defined not so much as an army but "as an all-purpose military infrastructure" (Anderson, 1984: 27) from which volunteers were drawn for the provincial armies. This concept of the militia as a pool from which persons could be drawn for special duties was the basis for colonial slave patrols.

Militias were active at different levels throughout the colonies. New York and South Carolina militias were required to be particularly active. New York was menaced by the Dutch and French-Iroquois conflicts while South Carolina had to be defended against the Indians, Spanish, and pirates. By the middle of the Eighteenth century the colonies were being less threatened by external forces and attention was being turned to internal problems. As early as 1721 South Carolina began shifting militia duty away from external defense to internal security. In that year, the entire militia was made available for the surveillance of slaves (Osgood, 1974). The early South Carolina militia law had enrolled both Whites and Blacks, and in the Yamassee war of 1715 some four hundred Negroes helped six hundred white men defeat the Indians (Shy, 1980). Eventually, however, South Carolinians did not dare to arm Negroes. With the majority of the population being black (see Table 1) and the increasing danger of slave revolts, the South Carolina militia essentially became a "local anti-slave police force and (was) rarely permitted to participate in military operations outside its boundaries" (Simmons, 1976: 127).

Despite their link to militia, slave patrols were a separate entity. Each slave state had codes of laws for the regulation of slavery. These slave codes authorized and outlined the duties of the slave patrols. Some towns had their own patrols, but they were more frequent in the rural areas. The presence of constables and a more equal distribution of whites and blacks made the need for the town patrols less immediate. In the rural areas,

---

[4]Information about slave patrols is found primarily in the writings of historians as they describe aspects of the slaves' life in the South. Data for this article were gathered from those secondary sources but also, for South Carolina and Georgia, from some primary accounts including colonial records, Eighteenth and Nineteenth century statutes and writings by former slaves.

however, the slaves were more easily able to participate in "dangerous" acts. It is not surprising that the slave patrols came to be viewed as "rural police" (cf. Henry, 1968: 42). South Carolina Governor Bull described the role of the patrols in 1740 by writing:

> The interior quiet of the Province is provided for the small Patrols, drawn every two months from each company, who do duty by riding along the roads and among the Negro Houses in small districts in every Parish once a week, or as occasion requires (quoted in Wood, 1974: 276 note 23).

Documentation of slave patrols is found for nearly all the Southern colonies and states[5] but South Carolina seems to have been the oldest, most elaborate, and best documented. That is not surprising given the importance of the militia in South Carolina and the presence of large numbers of Blacks. Georgia's developed somewhat later and exemplifies patrols in the late 18th and early 19th centuries. The history and development of slave patrol legislation in South Carolina and Georgia provides a historical review from colonial through antebellum times.

In 1704 the colony of Carolina[6] presented what appears to be the South's first patrol act. The patrol was linked to the militia yet separate from it since patrol duty was an excuse from militia duty. Under this act, militia captains were to select ten men from their companies to form these special patrols. The captain was to

> muster all the men under his command, and with them ride from plantation to plantation, and into any plantation, within the limits or

precincts, as the General shall think fitt and take up all slaves which they shall meet without their master's plantation which have not a permit or ticket from their masters, and the same punish (Cooper, 1837: 255).

That initial act seemed particularly concerned with runaway slaves, while an act in 1721 suggests an increased concern with uprisings. The act ordered the patrols to try to "prevent all caballings amongst negroes, by dispersing of them when drumming or playing, and to search all negro houses for arms or other offensive weapons" (McCord, 1841: 640). In addition to that concern the new act also responded to complaints that militia duty was being shirked by the choicest men who were doing patrol duty instead of militia duty (Bacon, 1939; Henry, 1968; McCord, 1841; Wood, 1974). As a result, the separate patrols were merged with the colonial militia and patrol duty was simply rotated among different members of the militia. From 1721 to 1734 there really were no specific slave patrols in South Carolina. The duty of supervising slaves was simply a militia duty.

In 1734 the Provincial Assembly set up a regular patrol once again separate from the militia (Cooper 1838a, p. 395). "Beat companies" of five men (Captain and four regular militia men) received compensation (captains $50 and privates $25 per year) for patrol duty and exemption from other militia duty. There was one patrol for each of 33 districts in the colony. Patrols obeyed orders from and were appointed by district commissioners and were given elaborate search and seizure powers as well as the right to administer up to twenty lashes (Cooper 1838a: 395–397).[7]

Since provincial acts usually expired after three years, South Carolina's 1734 Act was revised in 1737

---

[5]See Resc. (1976) for Alabama; O.W. Taylor (1958) for Arkansas; Flanders (1967) for Georgia; Coleman (1940) and McDougle (1970) for Kentucky; Bacon (1939), J.G. Taylor (1963) and Williams (1972) for Louisiana; Sydnor (1933) for Mississippi; Trexler (1969) for Missouri; Johnson (1937) for North Carolina; Patterson (1968) and Mooney (1971) for Tennessee; and Ballagh (1968) and Stewart (1976) for Virginia.

[6]In 1712 the northern two-thirds of Carolina was divided into two parts (North Carolina and South Carolina) while the southern one third remained unsettled until 1733 when Oglethorpe founded Georgia.

[7]The right to administer a punishment to slaves was given to patrols in other colonies and states as well. Patrols in North Carolina could administer fifteen lashes (Johnson, 1937: 516) as could those in Tennessee (Patterson, 1968: 39) and Mississippi (Sydnor, 1933: 78) while Georgia (Candler, 1910: 232) and Arkansas (O.W. Taylor, 1958: 210) followed South Carolina in allowing twenty lashes.

and again in 1740. Under the 1737 revision, the paid recruits were replaced with volunteers who were encouraged to enlist by being excused from militia and other public duty for one year and were allowed to elect their own captain (Cooper 1838b; 456–458). The number of men on patrol was increased from five to fifteen and they were to make weekly rounds. Henry (1968: 33) believed these changes were an attempt to dissuade irresponsible persons who had been attracted to patrol duty for the pay.

The 1740 revision seems to be the first legislation specifically including women plantation owners as answerable for patrol service (Cooper 1838b; 569–570). The plantation owners (male or female) could, however, procure any white person between 16 and 60 to ride patrol for them. In addition, the 1740 act said patrol duty was not to be required in townships where white inhabitants were in far superior numbers to the Negroes (Cooper 1838b; 571). Such an exemption certainly highlights the role of patrols as being to control what was perceived as a dangerous class.

At this point we turn to the Georgia slave patrols as an example of one that developed after South Carolina set a precedent. Georgia was settled late (1733) compared to the other colonies and despite her proximity to South Carolina she did not make immediate use of slaves. In fact while slaves were illegally imported in the mid 1740s, they were not legally allowed until 1750. Within seven years Georgians felt a need for control of the slaves. Her first patrol act (1757) provided for militia captains to pick up to seven patrollers from a list of all plantation owners (women and men) and all male white persons in the patrol district (Candler 1910: 225–235). The patrollers or their substitutes were to ride patrol at least once every two weeks and examine each plantation in their district at least once every month. The patrols were to seek out potential runaways, weapons, ammunition, or stolen goods.

The 1757 Act was continued in 1760 (Candler 1910: 462) for a period of five years. The 1765 continuation (Cobb 1851: 965) increased the number of patrollers to a maximum of ten, but left the duties and structure of the patrol as it was created in 1757. In the 1768 revision (Candler 1911: 75) the possession and use of weapons by slaves was tightened and a fine was set for selling alcohol to slaves. More interesting was the order relevant to Savannah only which gave patrollers the power to apprehend and take into custody (until the next morning) any disorderly white person (Candler 1911: 81). Should such a person be in a "Tippling House Tavern or Punch House" rather than on the streets the patrol bad to call a lawful constable to their assistance before they could enter the "bar." Such power was extended in 1778 when patrols were obliged to "take up all white persons who cannot give a satisfactory account of themselves and carry them before a Justice of the Peace to be dealt with as is directed by the Vagrant Act" (Candler, 1911: 119).

Minor changes occurred between 1778 and 1830 (e.g. females were exempted from patrol duty in 1824) but the first major structural change did not take place until 1830. In that year Georgia patrols finally began moving away from a direct militia link when Justices of the Peace were authorized and required to appoint and organize patrols (Cobb, 1851: 1003). In 1854 Justices of the Interior Courts were to annually appoint three "patrol commissioners" for each militia district (Rutherford, 1854: 101). Those commissioners were to make up the patrol list and appoint one person at least 25 years old and of good moral character to be Captain.

The absence of significant changes in Georgia patrol legislation over the years suggests the South Carolina experiences had provided an experimental stage for Georgia and possibly other slave states. Differences certainly existed, but Foner's general description of slave patrols seems accurate for the majority of colonies and states; patrols had full power and authority to enter any plantation and break open Negro houses or other places when slaves were suspected of keeping arms; to punish runaways or slaves found outside of their masters' plantations without a pass; to whip any slave who should affront or abuse them in the execution of their duties; and to apprehend and take any slave suspected of stealing or other criminal offense, and bring him to the nearest magistrate (1975: 206).

The Slaves' Response to the Patrols

The slave patrols were both feared and resented by the slaves.[8] Some went so far as to suggest it was "the worse thing yet about slavery" (quoted in Blassingame, 1977: 156). Former slave Lewis Clarke was most eloquent in expressing his disgust:

> (The patrols are) the offscouring of all things; the refuse,…the ears and tails of slavery;… the tooth and tongues of serpents. They are the very fool's cap of baboons,…the wallet and satchel of polecats, the scum of stagnant pools, the exuvial, the worn-out skins of slaveholders. (T)hey are the meanest, and lowest, and worst of all creation. Like starved wharf rats, they are out nights, creeping into slave cabins, to see if they have an old bone there; they drive out husbands from their own beds, and then take their places (Clarke, 1846: 114).

Despite the harshness and immediacy of punishment as well as the likelihood of discovery, slaves continued with the same behavior that brought about slave patrols in the first place. In fact, they added activities of specific irritation to the patrollers (or, as they were variously known, padaroe, padarole, or patteroller). Preventive measures like warning systems, playing ignorant and innocent when caught and learning when to expect a patrol were typically used. More assertive measures included building trap doors for escape from their cabins, tying ropes across roads to trip approaching horses, and fighting their way out of meeting places (Genovese, 1972: 618–619; Rose, 1976: 249–289). As have victims in other terrifying situations, the slaves occasionally resorted to humor as a source of strength. One version of a popular song makes that point:

> Run, nigger, run; de patter-roller catch you;
> Run, nigger, run, its almost day.

> Run, nigger, run; de patter-roller catch you;
> Run, nigger, run, and try to get far away.
> De nigger run, he run his best;
> Stuck his hand in a hornet's nest.
> Jumped de fence and run through de pastor;
> Marsa run, but nigger run faster.

> (Goodman, 1969: 83)

In an ironic sense the resistance by slaves should have been completely understandable to American patriots. Patrols were allowed search powers that the colonists later found so objectionable in the hands of British authorities (Foner, 1975: 221). Add to that the accompanying lack of freedoms to move, assemble, and bear arms, and the slave resistance seems perfectly appropriate.

Problems with the Slave Patrols

In addition to the difficulties presented by the slaves themselves, the patrols throughout the South experienced a variety of other problems. Many of these were similar to problems confronting colonial militia: training was infrequent; the elites often avoided duty; and those that did serve were often irresponsible (Anderson, 1984; Osgood, 1957; Shy, 1980; Simmons, 1976). In addition, the patrols had some unique concerns.

One of the first problems was the presence of free Blacks. Understandably, slaves caught by patrollers would try to pass themselves off as free persons. The problem was particularly bad in some of the cities where many free Blacks existed. In 1810, for example, the Charleston census showed 1,783 free Negroes (Henry, 1968: 50). Special acts eventually allowed the patrol to whip even free Negroes away from their home or employer's business unless they produced "free papers." In all but one of the slave states a Black person was presumed to be a slave unless she or he could prove differently. The sole exception to this procedure was

---

[8]Rawick (1972: 61–65) provides interesting recollections of patrols by ex-slaves in Alabama, Georgia, Louisiana, North Carolina, Tennessee and Virginia.

Louisiana where "persons of color are presumed to be free" (Louisiana supreme court quoted in Foner, 1983: 106) until proven otherwise.

Other problems centered on the apparently careless enforcement of the patrol laws in some districts. When all was quiet and orderly the patrol seemed to be lulled into inactivity (Henry, 1968: 39). But there seemed always to be individuals having problems with slaves and those persons often complained about the lax enforcement of patrol laws. Flanders (1967: 30) cites several examples from exasperated Georgians who complained that slaves were not being properly controlled. In 1770 South Carolina Governor Bull noted that "though human prudence has provided these Statutory Laws, yet, through human frailty, they are neglected in these times of general tranquility" (quoted in Wood, 1974: 276 note 23). Fifty years later the situation had not improved much as then Governor Geddes suggested in his annual message:

> The patrol duty which is so intimately connected with the good order and police of the state, is still so greatly neglected in several of our parishes and districts, that serious inconveniences have been felt… (quoted in Henry, 1968: 38).

Even when the patrols were active they did not avoid criticism. Genovese (1972: 618) quotes a Georgia planter who complained: "Our patrol laws are seldom enforced, and even where there is mock observance of them, it is by a parcel of boys or idle men, the height of whose ambition is to 'ketch a nigger'." Earlier it was noted that South Carolina in 1721 modified its patrol law because the "choices and best men" (planters) were avoiding militia duty by doing patrol duty. As Bacon (1939: 581) notes, service by such men was something of a rarity in police work anyway. However, it must have been a rarity in other slave states as well since the more typical opinion of the patrollers was that expressed above by the Georgia planter. As with militia duty in general, the elite members of the districts often were able to avoid patrol duty by either paying a fine or finding a substitute.

Where the "ketch a nigger" mentality existed, the patrols were often accused of inappropriate behavior. Complaints existed about patrollers drinking too much liquor before or during duty (Bacon, 1939: 587; Rose, 1976: 276; Wood, 1974: 276), and both South Carolina (Cooper, 1838b; 573) and Georgia (Candler, 1910: 233–234) had provisions for lining any person found drunk while on patrol duty.

More serious complaints (possibly linked to the drinking) concerned the harshness of punishment administered by some patrols. Ex-slave Ida Henry offered an example:

> De patrollers wouldn't allow de slaves to hold night services, and one night dey caught me mother out praying. Dey stripped her naked and tied her hands together and wid a rope tied to de handcuffs and threw one end of de rope over a limb and tied de other end to de pummel of a saddle on a horse. As me mother weighed 'bout 200, dey pulled her up so dat her toes could barely touch de ground and whipped her. Dat same night she ran away and stayed over a day and returned (quoted in Foner 1983, p. 103).

Masters as well as slaves often protested the actions of the patrol—on which the owners had successfully avoided serving (Genovese, 1972; 618). The slaves were, after all, an expensive piece of property which owners did not want damaged. Attempts to preserve orderly behavior of the patrollers took the form of a fine for misbehavior and occasionally reimbursement for damages (Henry, 1968: 37, 40). However, patrollers were allowed a rather free hand and many unlawful acts were accepted in attempts to uphold the patrol system. Henry saw this as the greatest evil of the system since "it gave unscrupulous persons unfair advantages and appears not to have encouraged the enforcement of the law by the better class" (1968: 40).

This review of the slave patrols shows them to have operated as a specialized enforcement arm. Although often linked to the militia, they had an autonomy and unique function which demands they be viewed as something more than an informal police type yet certainly not an example of a modern police organization. To identify the historical role and place of slave patrols we will turn to the concept of transitional police types.

✍ Discussion

By definition a transitional police type must share characteristics of both informal and modern systems. Drawing from his four characteristics of a modern type, Lundman says transitional systems differ from modern ones by: 1) reliance upon other than full-time police officers; 2) frequent elimination and replacement (i.e. absence of continuity in office and in procedure); and 3) absence of accountability to a central governmental authority (1980: 19–20). When slave patrols are placed against these criteria they can be shown to have enough in common to warrant consideration as a transitional police type. First, like informal systems, the slave patrols relied on the private citizen to carry out the duties. However, unlike the constable, watchman and sheriff, the patrollers had only policing duties rather than accompanying expectations of fire watch and/or tax collection. The identification of patrollers as "police" was much closer to a social status as we know it today. For example, when South Carolina planter Samuel Porcher was elected a militia captain he described himself as being "a sort of chief of police in the parish" (J. K. Williams, 1959: 65). Slave patrols relied upon private citizens for performance of duties, yet those patrollers came closer to being fulltime police officers than had citizens under informal systems.

As noted earlier, slave patrols were not always active and even when they were they did not always follow expected procedure. The periodic lapses and frequent replacement of patrols is expected under Lundman's idea of a transitional type. Since the patrols operated under procedures set down in the Slave Codes they did approximate continuity in procedure.

However, the South Carolina chronology of patrol legislation suggests those procedures changed as often as every three years.

The final criterion against which slave patrols might be judged is accountability to a control governmental authority. Lundman says such accountability is absent in a transitional system (1980: 20). It is at this point that slave patrols as a transitional police type might be challenged. The consistent link between slave patrols and militia units makes it difficult to argue against accountability to a central government authority. Even when the link to militia was not direct, there was a central authority controlling patrols. From 1734 to 1737 South Carolina patrols were appointed by district commissioners and obeyed orders of the governor, military commander-in-chief, and district commissioners (Bacon, 1939: 585; Wood, 1974: 275). In 1753, North Carolina justices of county courts could appoint three free-holders as "searchers" who took an oath to disarm slaves[9] (Patterson, 1968: 13). In 1802 the patrols were placed entirely under the jurisdiction of the country courts which in 1837 were authorized to appoint a patrol committee to ensure the patrol functioned (Johnson, 1937: 516–517). Tennessee, a part of North Carolina from 1693–1790, also used the "searchers" as authorized by the 1753 act. In 1806, ten years after statehood, Tennessee developed an elaborate patrol system wherein town commissioners appointed patrols for incorporated and unincorporated towns (Patterson, 1968: 38). Louisiana patrols (originally set up in 1807 by Territorial legislation) went through a period of confusion between 1813 and 1821 when both the militia and parish judges had authority over patrols. Finally, in 1821 parish governmental bodies were given complete authority over the slave patrols (J.G. Taylor, 1963: 170; E.R. Williams, 1972: 400). Slave patrols had first been introduced in Arkansas in 1825 and were apparently appointed by the county courts until 1853. After then appointments were made by the justice of the peace (O.W. Taylor, 1958: 31, 209) as was true in Georgia beginning in 1830 (Cobb, 1851: 1003). In 1831 the

---

[9]This oath read: "I, A.B., do swear that I will, as searcher for guns, swords and other weapons among the slaves of my district, faithfully, and as privately as I can, discharge the trust reposed in me, as the law directs, to the best of my power. So help me God" (Quoted in Patterson, 1968: 13 note 23).

incorporated towns in Mississippi were authorized to control their own patrol system and in 1833 boards of county police (i.e. county boards of supervisors) could appoint patrol leaders (Sydnor, 1933: 78). The Missouri General Assembly first established patrols in 1825 then in 1837 the county courts were given powers to appoint township patrols to serve for one year (Trexler, 1969: 182–183).

That review of patrol accountability in eight states suggests that slave patrols often came under the same governmental authority as formal police organizations. Or, as Sydnor pointed out in reference to the Mississippi changes: "the system was decentralized and made subject to the local units of civil government" (1933: 78). An argument can be made that the basis for a non-militia government authorized force to undertake police duties was implemented as early as 1734 when South Carolina patrols were appointed by district commissioners or in 1802 when North Carolina placed patrols under the jurisdiction of the county courts. What then does that mean for the placement of slave patrols as an example of a transitional police type? If the various governmental bodies mentioned above are accepted as being examples of "centralized governmental authority," it means two positions are possible. First, slave patrols must not be an example of a transitional type. This position is rejected on the basis of information provided here which shows the patrols to have been a legitimate entity with specialized law enforcement duties and powers.

The other possible position is that "absence of accountability to a centralized governmental authority" is not a necessary feature of transitional policing. This seems more reasonable given the information presented here. Since there has not been any specific example of a transitional police force offered to this point,[10] Lundman's characteristics are only hypothetical. As other examples of transitional police types are put forward we will have a firmer base for determining how they differ from modern police.

 Conclusion

As early as 1704 and continuing through the antebellum period, Southern slave states used local patrols with specific responsibility for regulating the activity of slaves. Those slave patrols were comprised of citizens who did patrol duty as their civic obligation, for pay, rewards, or for exemption from other duties. The patrollers had a defined area which they were to ride in attempts to discover runaway slaves, stolen property, weapons, or to forestall insurrections. Unlike the watchmen, constables, and sheriffs who had some non-policing duties, the slave patrols operated solely for the enforcement of colonial and state laws. The existence of these patrols leads to two conclusions about the development of American law enforcement. First, the law enforcement nature of slave patrol activities meant there were important events occurring in the rural South prior to and concurrently with events in the urban North which are more typically cited in examples of the evolution of policing in the United States. Because of that, it is undesirable to restrict attention to just the North when trying to understand and appreciate the growth of American law enforcement. Second, rather than simply being a formalization of previously informal activities, modern policing seems to have passed through developmental stages which can be explained by such typologies as that offered by Lundman who described informal, transitional, and modern types of policing.

While those conclusions are important, focusing attention on slave patrols and the South is desirable for reasons which go quite beyond a need to avoid regional bias in historical accounts or to describe a form of policing which is neither informal nor modern. For example, what implication does this analysis have on the usefulness of typologies in historical research? Further, how might typologies and the accompanying description of those types assist in generating a theory to explain the development of law enforcement?

---

[10]Lundman (1980: 20) only notes Fielding's Bow Street Runners, Colquhoun's River Police and mid-Nineteenth century Denver, as possible examples of transitional police.

If typologies are helpful as a historiographic technique, is Lundman's the best available or possible? Based on the usefulness of the typology for describing slave patrols and placing them in a specific historical context, it seems to this author that typologies are an excellent way to go beyond descriptive accounts and move toward the development of theoretical explanations. As greater use is made of typologies to conceptualize the development of American law enforcement, it seems likely that existing formulations will be modified. For example, slave patrols seem to exemplify what Lundman called the transitional police type except in terms of Lundman's proposed absence of accountability to a centralized governmental authority. Recall, however, that Bacon also suggested a developmental sequence (without specifying or naming "types") for police which described modern police as having general rather than specific functions (Bacon, 1939: 6). Combining the work of Lundman and Bacon, we might suggest that precursors to modern police are not necessarily without accountability to a centralized governmental authority, but do have specialized rather than general enforcement powers. In this manner, the characteristics of policing which precede the modern stage might be: 1) frequent elimination and replacement of the police type (Lundman); 2) reliance upon persons other than full-time police officers (Lundman); and 3) enforcement powers which are specialized rather than general (Bacon).

In addition to providing organized conceptualization, typologies also provide a basis for theoretical development. For example, there does not as yet appear to be an identifiable Northern precursor, like slave patrols, between the constable/watch and modern stages. Is that because the North skipped that stage, compressed it to such an extent we cannot find an example of its occurrence, or passed through the transitional stage but researchers have not described the activities in terms of a typology? While each of those questions is interesting, the first seems to have particularly intriguing implications for if it is correct it means there may not be a general evolutionary history for policing. For example, are modern police agencies necessarily preceded by a developmental stage comprised of a specialized police force? Is the progression in the developmental history of law enforcement agencies one of generalized structure with general functions, to a specific structure with specific functions, and finally a specific structure with general functions?

As an example of how this type of inquiry can fit with theoretical developments, we should note recent work by Robinson and Scaglion (1987). Those authors present four interdependent propositions which state:

1. The origin of the specialized police function depends upon the division of society into dominant and subordinate classes with antagonistic interests;

2. Specialized police agencies are generally characteristic only of societies politically organized as states;

3. In a period of transition, the crucial factor in delineating the modern specialized police function is an ongoing attempt at conversion of the social control (policing) mechanism from an integral part of the community structure to an agent of an emerging dominant class; and

4. The police institution is created by the emerging dominant class as an instrument for the preservation of its control over restricted access to basic resources, over the political apparatus governing this access, and over the labor force necessary to provide the surplus upon which the dominant class lives (Robinson and Scaglion, 1987: 109).

The development of law enforcement structures in the antebellum South would seem to support each of the propositions. Slave patrols were created only because of a master-slave social structure (proposition 1), existing as colonies became increasingly politically organized as states (proposition 2), and elites were able to convince community members to "police" the slaves (proposition 3), because control of those slaves was necessary to solidify elite positioning (proposition 4).

In order to respond with authority to these questions and implications, it will be necessary to continue research on the history of law enforcement. Detailed study of slave patrols in specific colonies and states is necessary as are research endeavors which assess the applicability of various typologies in different jurisdictions. Hopefully this initial effort will serve to both inform criminal justicians and practitioners about an important but little-known aspect of American police history as well as encourage research on non-Northern developments in the history of law enforcement. It has been argued here that most histories of the development of police have portrayed a regional bias suggesting that evolution was essentially Northern and urban in nature. In addition, existing information has covered the initial organizational stages of policing and the formation of modern police departments, but we are left with the impression that little activity of historical importance occurred between those first developments and the eventually modern department. Lundman has called that middle stage "transitional" policing and it is that concept which has been used here to: 1) debunk the portrayal of American law enforcement history as restricted to the urban North, and 2) provide an example of a form of policing more advanced than the constable/watch type but one which was not yet modern.

◪ References

Anderson, F. (1984) *A People's Army: Massachusetts Soldiers and Society in the Seven Years' War*. Chapel Hill, NC: University of North Carolina.

Bacon, S. (1939) *The Early Development of American Municipal Police: A Study of the Evolution of Formal Controls in a Changing Society*. Unpublished dissertation, Yale University. University Microfilms No. 66–06844.

Ballagh, J. (1968) *A History of Slavery in Virginia*. New York: Johnson Reprint Company.

Blassingame, J.W. (ed.) (1977) *Slave Testimony: Two Centuries of Letters, Speeches, Interviews, and Autobiographies*. Baton Rouge, LA: Louisiana State University Press.

Candler, A. (ed.) (1910) *The Colonial Records of the State of Georgia*, Vol. 18. Atlanta, GA: Chas. P. Byrd, State Printer.

———— (ed.) (1911) *The Colonial Records of the State of Georgia*, Vol. 19, Part 2. Atlanta, GA: Chas. P. Byrd, State Printer.

Clarke, L.G. (1846). *Narratives of Suffering*. Available on Library of American Civilization fiche #12812.

Cobb, T.R. (1851). *A Digest of the Statute Laws of the State of Georgia*, Athens, GA: Christy, Kelsea & Burke.

Coleman, J.W., Jr., (1940) *Slavery Times in Kentucky*. New York: Johnson Reprint Company.

Cooper, T. (ed.) (1837) *Statutes at Large of South Carolina*, Vol. 2, Part 1. Columbia, SC: A.S. Johnston.

———— (ed.) (1838a). *Statutes at Large of South Carolina*, Vol. 3, Part 1. Columbia, SC: A.S. Johnston.

———— (ed.) (1838b) *Statutes at Large of South Carolina*, Vol. 3, Part 2. Columbia, SC: A.S. Johnston.

Flanders, R.B. (1967) *Plantation Slavery in Georgia*. Cos Cob, CT: John E. Edwards, Publisher.

Flinn, J. (1975) *History of the Chicago Police from the Settlement of the Community to the Present Time*. Mountclair, NJ: Patterson Smith.

Foner, P.S. (1975) *History of Black Americans: From Africa to the Emergence of the Cotton Kingdom*. Westport, CT: Greenwood.

———— (1983) *History of Black Americans: From the Emergence of the Cotton Kingdom to the Eve of the Compromise of 1850*. Westport, CT: Greenwood.

Genovese, E.D. (1972) *Roll Jordon, Roll: The World the Slaves Made*. New York: Pantheon.

Greene, E. and Harrington, V. (1966) *American Population Before the Federal Census of 1790*. Gloucester, MA: Peter Smith.

Henry, H.M. (1968) *The Police Control of the Slave in South Carolina*. New York: Negro Universities Press.

Johnson, G.G. (1937) *Ante-bellum North Carolina: A Social History*. Chapel Hill, NC: University of North Carolina.

Lane, R. (1967) *Policing the City: Boston 1822–1885*. Cambridge, MA: Harvard University Press.

Lundman, R.J. (1980) *Police and Policing: An Introduction*. New York: Holt, Rinehart and Winston.

McCord, D.J. (ed.) (1841) *Statutes at Large of South Carolina*, Vol. 9, Part 2. Columbia, SC: A.S. Johnston.

McDougle, I.E. (1970) *Slavery in Kentucky 1792–1865*. Westport, CT: Negro Universities Press.

Monkkonen, E. (1981) *Police in Urban America, 1860–1920*. Cambridge, MA: Cambridge University.

———— (1982) "From cop history to social history: The significance of the police in American history." *Journal of Social History*, 15:575–592.

Mooney, C.C. (1971) *Slavery in Tennessee*, Westport, CT: Negro Universities Press.

Osgood, H.L. (1957) *The American Colonies in the Seventeenth Century*, Vol. 1, Gloucester, MA: Peter Smith.

Patterson, C.P. (1968) *The Negro in Tennessee, 1790–1865*. New York: Negro Universities Press.

Rawick, G.P. (1972) *The American Slave: A Composite Autobiography*. Westport, CT: Greenwood.

Richardson, J. (1970) *The New York Police: Colonial Times to 1901*. New York: Oxford University.

Robinson, C. and Scaglion, R. (1987) "The origin and evolution of the police function in society: Notes toward a theory." *Law & Society Review*, 21: 109–153.

Rose, W.L. (ed.) (1976) *A Documentary History of Slavery in North America*, New York: Oxford University.

Rutherford, J. (ed.) (1854) *Acts of the General Assembly of the State of Georgia*, Savannah, GA: Samuel T. Chapman.

Savage, E.A. (1865) *A Chronological History of the Boston Watch and Police, from 1631–1865.* Available on Library of American Civilization fiche #13523.

Schneider, J. (1980) *Detroit and the Problem of Order, 1830–1880: A Geography of Crime, Riot, and Policing.* Lincoln, NE: University of Nebraska.

Shy, J.W. (1980) "A new look at colonial militia." In P. Karsten (ed.). *The Military in America.* New York: Free Press.

Simmons, R.C. (1976) *The American Colonies.* New York: McKay.

Stewart, A. (1976) "Colonel Alexander's Slaves Resist the Patrol." In W.L. Rose (ed.) *A Documentary History of Slavery in North America.* New York: Oxford University.

Sydnor, C.S. (1933) *Slavery in Mississippi.* New York: Appleton-Century Company.

Taylor, J.G. (1963) *Negro Slavery in Louisiana.* New York: Negro Universities Press.

Taylor, O.W. (1958) *Negro Slavery in Arkansas.* Durham, NC: Duke University.

Trexler, H.A. (1969) "Slavery in Missouri: 1804–1865." In H. Trexler, *Slavery in the States: Selected Essays.* New York: Negro Universities Press.

Walker, S. (1980) *Popular Justice.* New York: Oxford.

——— (1982) "Counting cops and crime." Book Review, *Reviews in American History.* 10: 212.

Wells, R. (1975) *The Population of the British Colonies in America Before 1776: A Survey of Census Data.* Princeton, NJ: Princeton University.

Williams, E.R., Jr. (1972) "Slave patrol ordinances of St. Tammuny Parish, Louisiana, 1835–1838." *Louisiana History.* 13: 399–411.

Williams, J.K. (1959) *Vogues in Villainy.* Columbia, SC: University of South Carolina.

Wood, P.H. (1974) *Black Majority: Negroes in Colonial South Carolina.* New York: Knopf.

DISCUSSION QUESTIONS

1. Why is it important to recognize the existence and purpose of slave patrols in America?

2. Explain how modern policing has evolved through a series of developmental stages.

3. Given the historical presence of slave patrols, how could these impact police–community relationships in the southern region of the United States?

READING 2

In this article, George Kelling and Mark Moore examine the history of American policing over the course of three eras: political, reform, and community/problem-solving eras. More specifically, their historical overview of the police includes a look at the changes to the source of police legitimacy, police function, organizational design, relationships with citizens, sources of demands for service, tactics and technology, and measurements of police effectiveness over time.

The Evolving Strategy of Policing

George L. Kelling and Mark H. Moore *Read*

Policing, like all professions, learns from experience. It follows, then that as modern police executives search for more effective strategies of policing, they will be guided by the lessons of police history. The difficulty is that police history is incoherent, its lessons hard to read. After all, that history was produced by thousands of local departments pursuing their own visions and responding to local conditions. Although that varied experience is potentially a rich source of lessons, departments have left few records that reveal the trends shaping modern policing. Interpretation is necessary.

⊠ Methodology

This essay presents an interpretation of police history that may help police executives considering alternative future strategies of policing. Our reading of police history has led us to adopt a particular point of view. We find that a dominant trend guiding today's police executives—a trend that encourages the pursuit of independent, professional autonomy for police departments—is carrying the police away from achieving their maximum potential, especially in effective crime fighting. We are also convinced that this trend in policing is weakening *public* policing relative to *private* security as the primary institution providing security to society. We believe that this has dangerous long-term implications not only for police departments but also for society. We think that this trend is shrinking rather than enlarging police capacity to help create civil communities. Our judgment is that this trend can be reversed only by refocusing police attention from the pursuit of professional autonomy to the establishment of effective problem-solving partnerships with the communities they police.

Delving into police history made it apparent that some assumptions that now operate as axioms in the field of policing (for example that effectiveness in policing depends on distancing police departments from politics; or that the highest priority of police departments is to deal with serious street crime; or that the best way to deal with street crime is through directed patrol, rapid response to calls for service, and skilled retrospective investigations) are not timeless truths, but rather choices made by former police leaders and strategists. To be sure, the choices were often wise and far-seeing as well as appropriate to their

times. But the historical perspective shows them to be choices nonetheless, and therefore open to reconsideration in the light of later professional experience and changing environmental circumstances.

We are interpreting the results of our historical study through a framework based on the concept of "corporate strategy."[1] Using this framework, we can describe police organizations in terms of seven interrelated categories:

- The sources from which the police construct the legitimacy and continuing power to act on society.
- The definition of the police function or role in society.
- The organizational design of police departments.
- The relationships the police create with the external environment.
- The nature of police efforts to market or manage the demand for their services.
- The principal activities, programs, and tactics on which police agencies rely to fulfill their mission or achieve operational success.
- The concrete measures the police use to define operational success or failure.

Using this analytic framework, we have found it useful to divide the history of policing into three different eras. These eras are distinguished from one another by the apparent dominance of a particular strategy of policing. The political era, so named because of the close ties between police and politics, dated from the introduction of police into municipalities during the 1840's, continued through the Progressive period, and ended during the early 1900's. The reform era developed in reaction to the political. It took hold during the 1930's, thrived during the 1950's and 1960's, began to erode during the late 1970's. The reform era now seems to be giving way to an era emphasizing community problem solving.

By dividing policing into these three eras dominated by a particular strategy of policing, we do not mean to imply that there were clear boundaries between

---

[1]Kenneth R. Andrews, *The Concept of Corporate Strategy*, Homewood, Illinois, Richard D. Irwin, Inc., 1980.

the eras. Nor do we mean that in those eras everyone policed in the same way. Obviously, the real history is far more complex than that. Nonetheless, we believe that there is a certain professional ethos that defines standards of competence, professionalism, and excellence in policing; that at any given time, one set of concepts is more powerful, more widely shared, and better understood than others; and that this ethos changes over time. Sometimes, this professional ethos has been explicitly articulated, and those who have articulated the concepts have been recognized as the leaders of their profession. O. W. Wilson, for example, was a brilliant expositor of the central elements of the reform strategy of policing. Other times, the ethos is implicit—accepted by all as the tacit assumptions that define the business of policing and the proper form for a police department to take. Our task is to help the profession look to the future by representing its past in these terms and trying to understand what the past portends for the future.

The Political Era

Historians have described the characteristics of early policing in the United States, especially the struggles between various interest groups to govern the police.[2] Elsewhere, the authors of this paper analyzed a portion of American police history in terms of its organizational strategy.[3] The following discussion of elements of the police organizational strategy during the political era expands on that effort.

Legitimacy and Authorization

Early American police were authorized by local municipalities. Unlike their English counterparts, American police departments lacked the powerful, central authority of the crown to establish a legitimate, unifying mandate for their enterprise. Instead, American police derived both their authorization and resources from local political leaders, often ward politicians. They were, of course, guided by the law as to what tasks to undertake and what powers to utilize. But their link to neighborhoods and local politicians was so tight that both Jordan[4] and Fogelson[5] refer to the early police as adjuncts to local political machines. The relationship was often reciprocal: political machines recruited and maintained police in office and on the beat, while police helped ward political leaders maintain their political offices by encouraging citizens to vote for certain candidates, discouraging them from voting for others, and, at times, by assisting in rigging elections.

The Police Function

Partly because of their close connection to politicians, police during the political era provided a wide array of services to citizens. Inevitably police departments were involved in crime prevention and control and order maintenance, but they also provided a wide variety of social services. In the late 19th century, municipal police departments ran soup lines; provided temporary lodging for newly arrived immigrant workers in station houses;[6] and assisted ward leaders in finding work for immigrants, both in police and other forms of work.

Organizational Design

Although ostensibly organized as a centralized, quasi-military organization with a unified chain of command, police departments of the political era were nevertheless decentralized. Cities were divided into precincts, and precinct-level managers often, in concert with the ward leaders, ran precincts as small-scale

---

[2]Robert M. Fogelson, *Big-City Police*, Cambridge, Harvard University Press, 1977; Samuel Walker, *A Critical History of Police Reform: The Emergence of Professionalism*, Lexington, Massachusetts, Lexington Books, 1977.

[3]Mark H. Moore and George L. Kelling, "To Serve and Protect Learning From Police History," *The Public Interest*, 7, Winter 1983.

[4]K.E. Jordan, *Ideology and the Coming of Professionalism: American Urban Police in the 1920's and 1930's*, Dissertation, Rutgers University, 1972.

[5]Fogelson, *Big-City Police*.

[6]Eric H. Monkkonen *Police in Urban America*. 1860–1920. Cambridge, Cambridge University Press, 1981.

departments—hiring, firing, managing, and assigning personnel as they deemed appropriate. In addition, decentralization combined with primitive communications and transportation to give police officers substantial discretion in handling their individual beats. At best, officer contact with central command was maintained through the call box.

External Relationships

During the political era, police departments were intimately connected to the social and political world of the ward. Police officers often were recruited from the same ethnic stock as the dominant political groups in the localities, and continued to live in the neighborhoods they patrolled. Precinct commanders consulted often with local political representatives about police priorities and progress.

Demand Management

Demand for police services came primarily from two sources: ward politicians making demands on the organization and citizens making demands directly on beat officers. Decentralization and political authorization encouraged the first; foot patrol, lack of other means of transportation, and poor communications produced the latter. Basically, the demand for police services was received, interpreted, and responded to at the precinct and street levels.

Principal Programs and Technologies

The primary tactic of police during the political era was foot patrol. Most police officers walked beats and dealt with crime, disorder, and other problems as they arose, or as they were guided by citizens and precinct superiors. The technological tools available to police were limited. However, when call boxes became available, police administrators used them for supervisory and managerial purposes; and, when early automobiles became available, police used them to transport officers

from one beat to another.[7] The new technology thereby increased the range, but did not change the mode, of patrol officers.

Detective divisions existed but without their current prestige. Operating from a caseload of "persons" rather than offenses, detectives relied on their caseload to inform of other criminals.[8] The "third degree" was a common means of interviewing criminals to solve crimes. Detectives were often especially valuable to local politicians for gathering information on individuals for political or personal, rather than offense-related, purposes.

Measured Outcomes

The expected outcomes of police work included crime and riot control, maintenance of order, and relief from many of the other problems of an industrializing society (hunger and temporary homelessness, for example). Consistent with their political mandate, police emphasized maintaining citizen and political satisfaction with police services as an important goal of police departments.

In sum, the organizational strategy of the political era of policing included the following elements:

- Authorization—primarily political.
- Function—crime control, order maintenance, broad social services.
- Organizational design—decentralized and geographical.
- Relationship to environment—close and personal.
- Demand—managed through links between politicians and precinct commanders, and face-to-face contacts between citizens and foot patrol officers.
- Tactics and technology—foot patrol and rudimentary investigations.
- Outcome—political and citizen satisfaction with social order.

---

[7] *The Newark Foot Patrol Experiment*, Washington, D.C., Police Foundation, 1981.

[8] John Eck, *Solving Crimes: The Investigation of Burglary and Robbery*, Washington, D.C., Police Executive Research Forum, 1934.

The political strategy of early American policing had strengths. First, police were integrated into neighborhoods and enjoyed the support of citizens—at least the support of the dominant and political interests of an area. Second, and probably as a result of the first, the strategy provided useful services to communities. There is evidence that it helped contain riots. Many citizens believed that police prevented crimes or solved crimes when they occurred.[9] And the police assisted immigrants in establishing themselves in communities and finding jobs.

The political strategy also had weaknesses. First, intimacy with community, closeness to political leaders, and a decentralized organizational structure, with its inability to provide supervision of officers, gave rise to police corruption. Officers were often required to enforce unpopular laws foisted on immigrant ethnic neighborhoods by crusading reformers (primarily of English and Dutch background) who objected to ethnic values.[10] Because of their intimacy with the community, the officers were vulnerable to being bribed in return for nonenforcement or lax enforcement of laws. Moreover, police closeness to politicians created such forms of political corruption as patronage and police interference in elections.[11] Even those few departments that managed to avoid serious financial or political corruption during the late 19th and early 20th centuries, Boston for example, succumbed to large-scale corruption during and after Prohibition.[12]

Second, close identification of police with neighborhoods and neighborhood norms often resulted in discrimination against strangers and others who violated those norms, especially minority ethnic and racial groups. Often ruling their beats with the "ends of their nightsticks," police regularly targeted outsiders and strangers for rousting and "curbstone justice."[13]

Finally, the lack of organizational control over officers resulting from both decentralization and the political nature of many appointments to police positions caused inefficiencies and disorganization. The image of Keystone Cops—police as clumsy bunglers—was widespread and often descriptive of realities in American policing.

The Reform Era

Control over police by local politicians, conflict between urban reformers and local ward leaders over the enforcement of laws regulating the morality of urban migrants, and abuses (corruption, for example) that resulted from the intimacy between police and political leaders and citizens produced a continuous struggle for control over police during the late 19th and early 20th centuries.[14] Nineteenth-century attempts by civilians to reform police organizations by applying external pressures largely failed; 20th-century attempts at reform, originating from both internal and external forces, shaped contemporary policing as we knew it through the 1970's.[15]

Berkeley's police chief, August Vollmer, first rallied police executives around the idea of reform during the 1920's and early 1930's. Vollmer's vision of policing was the trumpet call: police in the post-flapper generation were to remind American citizens and institutions of

[9]Thomas A. Reppetto, *The Blue Parade*, New York, The Free Press, 1978.

[10]Fogelson, *Big-City Police*.

[11]Ibid.

[12]George L. Kelling, "Reforming the Reforms: The Boston Police Department," Occasional Paper, Joint Center For Urban Studies of M.I.T. and Harvard, Cambridge, 1983.

[13]George L. Kelling, "Juveniles and Police: The End of the Nightstick," in *From Children to Citizens, Vol. II: The Role of the Juvenile Court*, ed. Francis X. Hartmann, New York, Springer-Verlag, 1987.

[14]Walker, *A Critical History of Police Reform: The Emergence of Professionalism*.

[15]Fogelson, *Big-City Police*.

the moral vision that had made America great and of their responsibilities to maintain that vision.[16] It was Vollmer's protege, O.W. Wilson, however, who taking guidance from J. Edgar Hoover's shrewd transformation of the corrupt and discredited Bureau of Investigation into the honest and prestigious Federal Bureau of Investigation (FBI), became the principal administrative architect of the police reform organizational strategy.[17]

Hoover wanted the FBI to represent a new force for law and order, and saw that such an organization could capture a permanent constituency that wanted an agency to take a stand against lawlessness, immorality, and crime. By raising eligibility standards and changing patterns of recruitment and training, Hoover gave the FBI agents stature as upstanding moral crusaders. By committing the organization to attacks on crimes such as kidnapping, bank robbery, and espionage—crimes that attracted wide publicity and required technical sophistication, doggedness, and a national jurisdiction to solve—Hoover established the organization's reputation for professional competence and power. By establishing tight central control over his agents, limiting their use of controversial investigation procedures (such as undercover operations), and keeping them out of narcotics enforcement, Hoover was also able to maintain an unparalleled record of integrity. That, too, fitted the image of a dogged, incorruptible crime-fighting organization. Finally, lest anyone fail to notice the important developments within the Bureau, Hoover developed impressive public relations programs that presented the FBI and its agents in the most favorable light. (For those of us who remember the 1940's, for example, one of the most popular radio phrases was, "The FBI in peace and war"—the introductory line in a radio program that portrayed a vigilant FBI protecting us from foreign enemies as well as villains on the "10 Most Wanted" list, another Hoover/FBI invention.)

Struggling as they were with reputations for corruption, brutality, unfairness, and downright incompetence, municipal police reformers found Hoover's path a compelling one. Instructed by O.W. Wilson's texts on police administration, they began to shape an organizational strategy for urban police analogous to the one pursued by the FBI.

Legitimacy and Authorization

Reformers rejected politics as the basis of police legitimacy. In their view, politics and political involvement was the *problem* in American policing. Police reformers therefore allied themselves with Progressives. They moved to end the close ties between local political leaders and police. In some states, control over police was usurped by state government. Civil service eliminated patronage and ward influences in hiring and firing police officers. In some cities (Los Angeles and Cincinnati, for example), even the position of chief of police became a civil service position to be attained through examination. In others (such as Milwaukee), chiefs were given lifetime tenure by a police commission, to be removed from office only for cause. In yet others (Boston, for example), contracts for chiefs were staggered so as not to coincide with the mayor's tenure. Concern for separation of police from politics did not focus only on chiefs, however. In some cities, such as Philadelphia, it became illegal for patrol officers to live in the beats they patrolled. The purpose of all these changes was to isolate police as completely as possible from political influences.

Law, especially criminal law, and police professionalism were established as the principal bases of police legitimacy. When police were asked why they performed as they did, the most common answer was that they enforced the law. When they chose not to enforce the law—for instance, in a riot when police isolated an area rather than arrested looters—police justification for such action was found in their claim to professional

---

[16]Kelling, "Juveniles and Police: The End of the Nightstick."

[17]Orlando W. Wilson, *Police Administration*, New York: McGraw-Hill, 1950.

knowledge, skills, and values which uniquely qualified them to make such tactical decisions. Even in riot situations, police rejected the idea that political leaders should make tactical decisions; that was a police responsibility.[18]

So persuasive was the argument of reformers to remove political influences from policing, that police departments became one of the most autonomous public organizations in urban government.[19] Under such circumstances, policing a city became a legal and technical matter left to the discretion of professional police executives under the guidance of law. Political influence of any kind on a police department came to be seen as not merely a failure of police leadership but as corruption in policing.

The Police Function

Using the focus on criminal law as a basic source of police legitimacy, police in the reform era moved to narrow their functioning to crime control and criminal apprehension. Police agencies became *law enforcement* agencies. Their goal was to control crime. Their principal means was the use of criminal law to apprehend and deter offenders. Activities that drew the police into solving other kinds of community problems and relied on other kinds of responses were identified as "social work," and became the object of decision. A common line in police circles during the 1950's and 1960's was, "If only we didn't have to do social work, we could really do something about crime." Police retreated from providing emergency medical services as well—ambulance and emergency medical services were transferred to medical, private, or firefighting organizations.[20] The 1967 President's Commission on Law Enforcement and Administration of Justice ratified this orientation: heretofore, police had been conceptualized as an agency of urban government; the President's Commission

reconceptualized them as part of the criminal justice system.

Organizational Design

The organization form adopted by police reformers generally reflected the *scientific* or *classical* theory of administration advocated by Frederick W. Taylor during the early 20th century. At least two assumptions attended classical theory. First, workers are inherently uninterested in work and, if left to their own devices, are prone to avoid it. Second, since workers have little or no interest in the substance of their work, the sole common interest between workers and management is found in economic incentives for workers. Thus, both workers and management benefit economically when management arranges work in ways that increase workers' productivity and link productivity to economic rewards.

Two central principles followed from these assumptions: division of labor and unity of control. The former posited that if tasks can be broken into components, workers can become highly skilled in particular components and thus more efficient in carrying out their tasks. The latter posited that the workers' activities are best managed by a *pyramid of control*, with all authority finally resting in one central office.

Using this classical theory, police leaders moved to routinize and standardize police work, especially patrol work. Police work became a form of crimefighting in which police enforced the law and arrested criminals if the opportunity presented itself. Attempts were made to limit discretion in patrol work: a generation of police officers was raised with the idea that they merely enforced the law.

If special problems arose, the typical response was to create special units (e.g., vice, juvenile, drugs, tactical) rather than to assign them to patrol. The creation of these special units, under central rather than

---

[18]"Police Guidelines," John F. Kennedy School of Government Case Program #C14-75-24, 1975.

[19]Herman Goldstein, *Policing a Free Society*, Cambridge, Massachusetts, Ballinger, 1977.

[20]Kelling, "Reforming The Reforms: The Boston Police Department."

precinct command, served to further centralize command and control and weaken precinct commanders.[21]

Moreover, police organizations emphasized control over workers through bureaucratic means of control: supervision, limited span of control, flow of instructions downward and information upward in the organization, establishment of elaborate record-keeping systems requiring additional layers of middle managers, and coordination of activities between various production units (e.g., patrol and detectives), which also required additional middle managers.

External Relationships

Police leaders in the reform era redefined the nature of a proper relationship between police officers and citizens. Heretofore, police had been intimately linked to citizens. During the era of reform policing, the new model demanded an impartial law enforcer who related to citizens in professionally neutral and distant terms. No better characterization of this model can be found than television's Sergeant Friday, whose response, "Just the facts, ma'am," typified the idea: impersonal and oriented toward crime solving rather than responsive to the emotional crisis of a victim.

The professional model also shaped the police view of the role of citizens in crime control. Police redefined the citizen role during an era when there was heady confidence about the ability of professionals to manage physical and social problems. Physicians would care for health problems, dentists for dental problems, teachers for educational problems, social workers for social adjustment problems, and police for crime problems. The proper role of citizens in crime control was to be relatively passive recipients of professional crime control services. Citizens' actions on their own behalf to defend themselves or their communities came to be seen as inappropriate, smacking of vigilantism. Citizens met their responsibilities when a crime occurred by calling police, deferring to police actions, and being good witnesses if called upon to give evidence. The metaphor that expressed this orientation to the community was that of the police as the "thin blue line." It connotes the existence of dangerous external threats to communities, portrays police as standing between that danger and good citizens, and implies both police heroism and loneliness.

Demand Management

Learning from Hoover, police reformers vigorously set out to sell their brand of urban policing.[22] They, too, performed on radio talk shows, consulted with media representatives about how to present police, engaged in public relations campaigns, and in other ways presented this image of police as crime fighters. In a sense, they began with an organizational capacity—anticrime police tactics—and intensively promoted it. This approach was more like selling than marketing. Marketing refers to the process of carefully identifying consumer needs and then developing goods and services that meet those needs. Selling refers to having a stock of products or goods on hand irrespective of need and selling them. The reform strategy had as its starting point a set of police tactics (services) that police promulgated as much for the purpose of establishing internal control of police officers and enhancing the status of urban police as for responding to community needs or market demands.[23] The community "need" for rapid response to calls for service, for instance, was largely the consequence of police selling the service as efficacious in crime control rather than a direct demand from citizens.

Consistent with this attempt to sell particular tactics, police worked to shape and control demand for police services. Foot patrol, when demanded by citizens, was rejected as an outmoded, expensive frill. Social and emergency services were terminated or given to other agencies. Receipt of demand for police services was centralized. No longer were citizens

---

[21]Fogelson, *Big-City Police*.

[22]William H. Parker, "The Police Challenge in Our Great Cities," *The Annals* 29 (January 1954): 5–13.

[23]For a detailed discussion of the differences between selling and marketing, see John L. Crompton and Charles W. Lamb, *Marketing Government and Social Services*, New York, John Wiley and Sons, 1986.

encouraged to go to "their" neighborhood police officers or districts; all calls went to a central communications facility. When 911 systems were installed, police aggressively sold 911 and rapid response to calls for service as effective police service. If citizens continued to use district, or precinct, telephone numbers, some police departments disconnected those telephones or got new telephone numbers.[24]

Principal Programs and Technologies

The principal programs and tactics of the reform strategy were preventive patrol by automobile and rapid response to calls for service. Foot patrol, characterized as outmoded and inefficient, was abandoned as rapidly as police administrators could obtain cars.[25] The initial tactical reasons for putting police in cars had been to increase the size of the areas police officers could patrol and to take the advantage away from criminals who began to use automobiles. Under reform policing, a new theory about how to make the best tactical use of automobiles appeared.

O.W. Wilson developed the theory of preventive patrol by automobile as an anticrime tactic.[26] He theorized that if police drove conspicuously marked cars randomly through city streets and gave special attention to certain "hazards" (bars and schools, for example), a feeling of police omnipresence would be developed. In turn, that sense of omnipresence would both deter criminals and reassure good citizens. Moreover, it was hypothesized that vigilant patrol officers moving rapidly through city streets would happen upon criminals in action and be able to apprehend them.

As telephones and radios became ubiquitous, the availability of cruising police came to be seen as even more valuable: if citizens could be encouraged to call the police via telephone as soon as problems developed, police could respond rapidly to calls and establish

control over situations, identify wrong-doers, and make arrests. To this end, 911 systems and computer-aided dispatch were developed throughout the country. Detective units continued, although with some modifications. The "person" approach ended and was replaced by the case approach. In addition, forensic techniques were upgraded and began to replace the old "third degree" or reliance on informants for the solution of crimes. Like other special units, most investigative units were controlled by central headquarters.

Measured Outcomes

The primary desired outcomes of the reform strategy were crime control and criminal apprehension.[27] To measure achievement of these outcomes, August Vollmer, working through the newly vitalized International Association of Chiefs of Police, developed and implemented a uniform system of crime classification and reporting. Later, the system was taken over and administered by the FBI and the *Uniform Crime Reports* became the primary standard by which police organizations measured their effectiveness. Additionally, individual officers' effectiveness in dealing with crime was judged by the number of arrests they made; other measures of police effectiveness included response time (the time it takes for a police car to arrive at the location of a call for service) and "number of passings" (the number of times a police car passes a given point on a city street). Regardless of all other indicators, however, the primary measure of police effectiveness was the crime rate as measured by the *Uniform Crime Reports*.

In sum, the reform organizational strategy contained the following elements:

- Authorization—law and professionalism.
- Function—crime control.

---

[24]Commissioner Francis "Mickey" Roache of Boston has said that when the 911 system was instituted there, citizens persisted in calling "their" police—the district station. To circumvent this preference, district telephone numbers were changed so that citizens would be inconvenienced if they dialed the old number.

[25]*The Newark Foot Patrol Experiment.*

[26]O.W. Wilson, *Police Administration.*

[27]A.E. Leonard, "Crime Reporting as a Police Management Foot," *The Annals* 29 (January 1954).

- Organizational design—centralized, classical.
- Relationship to environment—professionally remote.
- Demand—channeled through central dispatching activities.
- Tactics and technology—preventive patrol and rapid response to calls for service.
- Outcome—crime control.

In retrospect, the reform strategy was impressive. It successfully integrated its strategic elements into a coherent paradigm that was internally consistent and logically appealing. Narrowing police functions to crime fighting made sense. If police could concentrate their efforts on prevention of crime and apprehension of criminals, it followed that they could be more effective than if they dissipated their efforts on other problems. The model of police as impartial, professional law enforcers was attractive because it minimized the discretionary excesses which developed during the political era. Preventive patrol and rapid response to calls for service were intuitively appealing tactics, as well as means to control officers and shape and control citizen demands for service. Further, the strategy provided a comprehensive, yet simple, vision of policing around which police leaders could rally.

The metaphor of the thin blue line reinforced their need to create isolated independence and autonomy in terms that were acceptable to the public. The patrol car became the symbol of policing during the 1930's and 1940's; when equipped with a radio, it was at the limits of technology. It represented mobility, power, conspicuous presence, control of officers, and professional distance from citizens.

During the late 1960's and 1970's, however, the reform strategy ran into difficulty. First, regardless of how police effectiveness in dealing with crime was measured, police failed to substantially improve their record. During the 1960's, crime began to rise. Despite large increases in the size of police departments and in expenditures for new forms of equipment (911 systems, computer-aided dispatch, etc.), police failed to meet their own or public expectations about their capacity to control crime or prevent its increase. Moreover, research conducted during the 1970's on preventive patrol and rapid response to calls for service suggested that neither was an effective crime control or apprehension tactic.[28]

Second, fear rose rapidly during this era. The consequences of this fear were dramatic for cities. Citizens abandoned parks, public transportation, neighborhood shopping centers, churches, as well as entire neighborhoods. What puzzled police and researchers was that levels of fear and crime did not always correspond: crime levels were low in some areas, but fear high. Conversely, in other areas levels of crime were high, but fear low. Not until the early 1980's did researchers discover that fear is more closely correlated with disorder than with crime.[29] Ironically, order maintenance was one of those functions that police had been downplaying over the years. They collected no data on it, provided no training to officers in order maintenance activities, and did not reward officers for successfully conducting order maintenance tasks.

Third, despite attempts by police departments to create equitable police allocation systems and to provide impartial policing to all citizens, many minority citizens, especially blacks during the 1960's and 1970's, did not perceive their treatment as equitable or adequate. They protested not only police mistreatment, but lack of treatment—inadequate or insufficient services—as well.

Fourth, the civil rights and antiwar movements challenged police. This challenge took several forms. The legitimacy of police was questioned: students resisted police, minorities rioted against them, and the public, observing police via live television for the first time, questioned their tactics. Moreover, despite police attempts to upgrade personnel through improved

---

[28]George L. Kelling et al., *The Kansas City Preventive Patrol Experiment: A Summary Report*, Washington, D.C., Police Foundation, 1974; William, Spelman and Dale K. Brown, *Calling the Police*, Washington, D.C., Police Executive Research Forum, 1982.

[29]*The Newark Foot Patrol Experiment*; Wesley G. Skogan and Michael G. Maxfield, *Coping With Crime*, Beverly Hills, California, Sage, 1981; Robert Trojanowicz, *An Evaluation of the Neighborhood Foot Patrol Programs in Flint, Michigan*, East Lansing, Michigan State University, 1982.

recruitment, training, and supervision, minorities and then women insisted that they had to be adequately represented in policing if police were to be legitimate.

Fifth, some of the myths that undergirded the reform strategy—police officers use little or no discretion and the primary activity of police is law enforcement—simply proved to be too far from reality to be sustained. Over and over again research showed that use of discretion characterized policing at all levels and that law enforcement comprised but a small portion of police officers' activities.[30]

Sixth, although the reform ideology could rally police chiefs and executives, it failed to rally line police officers. During the reform era, police executives had moved to professionalize their ranks. Line officers, however, were managed in ways that were antithetical to professionalization. Despite pious testimony from police executives that "patrol is the backbone of policing," police executives behaved in ways that were consistent with classical organizational theory—patrol officers continued to have low status; their work was treated as if it were routinized and standardized; and petty rules governed issues such as hair length and off-duty behavior. Meanwhile, line officers received little guidance in use of discretion and were given few, if any, opportunities to make suggestions about their work. Under such circumstances, the increasing "grumpiness" of officers in many cities is not surprising, nor is the rise of militant unionism.

Seventh, police lost a significant portion of their financial support, which had been increasing or at least constant over the years, as cities found themselves in fiscal difficulties. In city after city, police departments were reduced in size. In some cities, New York for example, financial cutbacks resulted in losses of up to one-third of departmental personnel. Some, noting that crime did not increase more rapidly or arrests decrease during the cutbacks, suggested that New York City had been overpoliced when at maximum strength. For those concerned about levels of disorder and fear in New York

City, not to mention other problems, that came as a dismaying conclusion. Yet it emphasizes the erosion of confidence that citizens, politicians, and academicians had in urban police—an erosion that was translated into lack of political and financial support.

Finally, urban police departments began to acquire competition; private security and the community crime control movement. Despite the inherent value of these developments, the fact that businesses, industries, and private citizens began to search for alternative means of protecting their property and persons suggests a decreasing confidence in either the capability or the intent of the police to provide the services that citizens want.

In retrospect, the police reform strategy has characteristics similar to those that Miles and Snow[31] ascribe to a defensive strategy in the private sector. Some of the characteristics of an organization with a defensive strategy are (with specific characteristics of reform policing added in parentheses):

- Its market is stable and narrow (crime victims).
- Its success is dependent on maintaining dominance in a narrow, chosen market (crime control).
- It tends to ignore developments outside its domain (isolation).
- It tends to establish a single core technology (patrol).
- New technology is used to improve its current product or service rather than to expand its product or service line (use of computers to enhance patrol).
- Its management is centralized (command and control).
- Promotions generally are from within (with the exception of chiefs, virtually all promotions are from within).
- There is a tendency toward a functional structure with high degrees of specialization and formalization.

---

[30]Mary Ann Wycoff, *The Role of Municipal Police Research as a Prelude to Changing It*, Washington, D.C., Police Foundation, 1982; Goldstein, *Policing a Free Society*.

[31]Raymond E. Miles and Charles C. Snow, *Organizational Strategy, Structure and Process*, New York, McGraw-Hill, 1978.

A defensive strategy is successful for an organization when market conditions remain stable and few competitors enter the field. Such strategies are vulnerable, however, in unstable market conditions and when competitors are aggressive.

The reform strategy was a successful strategy for police during the relatively stable period of the 1940's and 1950's. Police were able to sell a relatively narrow service line and maintain dominance in the crime control market. The social changes of the 1960's and 1970's, however, created unstable conditions. Some of the more significant changes included: the civil rights movement; migration of minorities into cities; the changing age of the population (more youths and teenagers); increases in crime and fear, increased oversight of police actions by courts; and the decriminalization and deinstitutionalization movements. Whether or not the private sector defensive strategy properly applies to police, it is clear that the reform strategy was unable to adjust to the changing social circumstances of the 1960's and 1970's.

 ## The Community Problem-Solving Era

All was not negative for police during the late 1970's and early 1980's, however. Police began to score victories which they barely noticed. Foot patrol remained popular, and in many cities citizen and political demands for it intensified. In New Jersey, the state funded the Safe and Clean Neighborhoods Program, which funded foot patrol in cities, often over the opposition of local chiefs of police.[32] In Boston, foot patrol was so popular with citizens that when neighborhoods were selected for foot patrol, politicians often made the announcements, especially during election years. Flint, Michigan, became the first city in memory to return to foot patrol on a citywide basis. It proved so popular there that citizens twice voted to increase their taxes to fund foot patrol—most recently by a two-thirds majority. Political and citizen demands for foot patrol continued to expand in cities throughout the United States. Research into foot patrol suggested it was more than just politically popular, it contributed to city life: it reduced fear, increased citizen satisfaction with police, improved police attitudes toward citizens, and increased the morale and job satisfaction of police.[33]

Additionally, research conducted during the 1970's suggested that one factor could help police improve their record in dealing with crime: information. If information about crimes and criminals could be obtained from citizens by police, primarily patrol officers, and could be properly managed by police departments, investigative and other units could significantly increase their effect on crime.[34]

Moreover, research into foot patrol suggested that at least part of the fear reduction potential was linked to the order maintenance activities of foot patrol officers.[35] Subsequent work in Houston and Newark indicated that tactics other than foot patrol that, like foot patrol, emphasized increasing the quantity and improving the quality of police-citizen interactions had outcomes similar to those of foot patrol (fear reduction, etc.).[36] Meanwhile, many other cities were developing programs, though not evaluated, similar to those in the foot patrol, Flint, and fear reduction experiments.[37]

---

[32]*The Newark Foot Patrol Experiment.*

[33]*The Newark Foot Patrol Experiment*; Trojanowicz, *An Evaluation of the Neighborhood Foot Patrol Program in Flint, Michigan.*

[34]Tony Pate et al., *Three Approaches to Criminal Apprehension in Kansas City: An Evaluation Report*, Washington, D.C., Police Foundation, 1976; Eck, *Solving Crimes: The Investigation of Burglary and Robbery.*

[35]James Q. Wilson and George L. Kelling, "Police and Neighborhood Safety: Broken Windows," *Atlantic Monthly*, March 1982: 29–38.

[36]Tony Pate et. al., *Reducing Fear of Crime in Houston and Newark: A Summary Report*, Washington, D.C., Police Foundation, 1986.

[37]Jerome H. Skolnick and David H. Bayley, *The New Blue Line: Police Innovation in Six American Cities*, New York, The Free Press, 1986; Albert J. Reiss, Jr., *Policing a City's Central District: The Oakland Story*, Washington, D.C., National Institute of Justice, March 1985.

The findings of foot patrol and fear reduction experiments, when coupled with the research on the relationship between fear and disorder, created new opportunities for police to understand the increasing concerns of citizens' groups about disorder (gangs, prostitutes, etc.) and to work with citizens to do something about it. Police discovered that when they asked citizens about their priorities, citizens appreciated the inquiry and also provided useful information—often about problems that beat officers might have been aware of, but about which departments had little or no official data (e.g., disorder). Moreover, given the ambiguities that surround both the definitions of disorder and the authority of police to do something about it, police learned that they had to seek authorization from local citizens to intervene in disorderly situations.[38]

Simultaneously, Goldstein's problem-oriented approach to policing[39] was being tested in several communities: Madison, Wisconsin; Baltimore County, Maryland; and Newport News, Virginia. Problem-oriented policing rejects the fragmented approach in which police deal with each incident, whether citizen- or police-initiated, as an isolated event with neither history nor future. Pierce's findings about calls for service illustrate Goldstein's point: 60 percent of the calls for service in any given year in Boston originated from 10 percent of the households calling the police.[40] Furthermore, Goldstein and his colleagues in Madison, Newport News, and Baltimore County discovered the following: police officers enjoy operating with a holistic approach to their work; they have the capacity to do it successfully; they can work with citizens and other agencies to solve problems; and citizens seem to appreciate working with police—findings similar to those of the foot patrol experiments (Newark and Flint)[41] and the fear reduction experiments (Houston and Newark).[42]

The problem confronting police, policymakers, and academicians is that these trends and findings seem to contradict many of the tenets that dominated police thinking for a generation. Foot patrol creates new intimacy between citizens and police. Problem solving is hardly the routinized and standardized patrol modality that reformers thought was necessary to maintain control of police and limit their discretion. Indeed, use of discretion is the *sine qua non* of problem-solving policing. Relying on citizen endorsement of order maintenance activities to justify police action acknowledges a continued or new reliance on political authorization for police work in general. And, accepting the quality of urban life as an outcome of good police service emphasizes a wider definition of the police function and the desired effects of police work.

These changes in policing are not merely new police tactics, however. Rather, they represent a new organizational approach, properly called a community strategy. The elements of that strategy are:

Legitimacy and Authorization

There is renewed emphasis on community, or political, authorization for many police tasks, along with law and professionalism. Law continues to be the major legitimating basis of the police function. It defines basic police powers, but it does not fully direct police activities in efforts to maintain order, negotiate conflicts, or solve community problems. It becomes one tool among many others. Neighborhood, or community, support and involvement are required to accomplish those tasks. Professional and bureaucratic authority, especially that which tends to isolate police and insulate them from neighborhood influences, is lessened as

[38]Wilson and Kelling, "Police and Neighborhood Safety: Broken Windows."

[39]Herman Goldstein, "Improving Policing: A Problem-Oriented Approach," *Crime and Delinquency*, April 1979, 236–258.

[40]Glenn Pierce et. al., "Evaluation of an Experiment in Proactive Police Intervention in the Field of Domestic Violence Using Repeat Call Analysis," Boston, Massachusetts, The Boston Fenway Project, Inc., May 13, 1987.

[41]*The Newark Foot Patrol Experiment:* Trojanowicz, *An Evaluation of the Neighborhood Foot Patrol Program in Flint, Michigan.*

[42]Pate et. al., *Reducing Fear of Crime in Houston and Newark: A Summary Report.*

citizens contribute more to definitions of problems and identification of solutions. Although in some respects similar to the authorization of policing's political era, community authorization exists in a different political context. The civil service movement, the political centralization that grew out of the Progressive era, and the bureaucratization, professionalization, and unionization of police stand as counterbalances to the possible recurrence of the corrupting influences of ward politics that existed prior to the reform movement.

The Police Function

As indicated above, the definition of police function broadens in the community strategy. It includes order maintenance, conflict resolution, problem solving through the organization, and provision of services, as well as other activities. Crime control remains an important function, with an important difference, however. The reform strategy attempts to control crime directly through preventive patrol and rapid response to calls for service. The community strategy emphasizes crime control *and prevention* as an indirect result of, or an equal partner to, the other activities.

Organizational Design

Community policing operates from organizational assumptions different from those of reform policing. The idea that workers have no legitimate, substantive interest in their work is untenable when programs such as those in Flint, Houston, Los Angeles, New York City, Baltimore County, Newport News, and others are examined. Consulting with community groups, problem solving, maintaining order, and other such activities are antithetical to the reform ideal of eliminating officer discretion through routinization and standardization of police activities. Moreover, organizational decentralization is inherent in community policing: the involvement of police officers in diagnosing and responding to neighborhood and community problems necessarily pushes operational and tactical decisionmaking to the

lower levels of the organization. The creation of neighborhood police stations (storefronts, for example), reopening of precinct stations, and establishment of beat offices (in schools, churches, etc.) are concrete examples of such decentralization.

Decentralization of tactical decisionmaking to precinct or beat level does not imply abdication of executive obligations and functions, however. Developing, articulating, and monitoring organizational strategy remain the responsibility of management. Within this strategy, operational and tactical decisionmaking is decentralized. This implies what may at first appear to be a paradox: while the number of managerial levels may decrease, the number of managers may increase. Sergeants in a decentralized regime, for example, have managerial responsibilities that exceed those they would have in a centralized organization.

At least two other elements attend this decentralization: increased participative management and increased involvement of top police executives in planning and implementation. Chiefs have discovered that programs are easier to conceive and implement if officers themselves are involved in their development through task forces, temporary matrix-like organizational units, and other organizational innovations that tap the wisdom and experience of sergeants and patrol officers. Additionally, police executives have learned that good ideas do not translate themselves into successful programs without extensive involvement of the chief executive and his close agents in every stage of planning and implementation, a lesson learned in the private sector as well.[43]

One consequence of decentralized decisionmaking, participative planning and management, and executive involvement in planning is that fewer levels of authority are required to administer police organizations. Some police organizations, including the London Metropolitan Police (Scotland Yard), have begun to reduce the number of middle-management layers, while others are contemplating doing so. Moreover, as in the private sector, as computerized information gathering systems reach their potential in police departments, the need for

---

[43]James R. Gardner, Robert Rachlin, and H.W. Allen Sweeny, eds., *Handbook of Strategic Planning*, New York, John Wiley and Sons, 1986.

middle managers whose primary function is data collection will be further reduced.

External Relationships

Community policing relies on an intimate relationship between police and citizens. This is accomplished in a variety of ways: relatively long-term assignment of officers to beats, programs that emphasize familiarity between citizens and police (police knocking on doors, consultations, crime control meetings for police and citizens, assignment to officers of "caseloads" of households with ongoing problems, problem solving, etc.), revitalization or development of Police Athletic League programs, educational programs in grade and high schools, and other programs. Moreover, police are encouraged to respond to the feelings and fears of citizens that result from a variety of social problems or from victimization.

Further, the police are restructuring their relationship with neighborhood groups and institutions. Earlier, during the reform era, police had claimed a monopolistic responsibility for crime control in cities, communities, and neighborhoods; now they recognize serious competitors in the "industry" of crime control, especially private security and the community crime control movement. Whereas in the past police had dismissed these sources of competition or, as in the case of community crime control, had attempted to coopt the movement for their own purposes,[44] now police in many cities (Boston, New York, Houston, and Los Angeles, to name a few) are moving to structure working relationships or strategic alliances with neighborhood and community crime control groups. Although there is less evidence of attempts to develop alliances with the private security industry, a recent proposal to the National Institute of Justice envisioned an experimental alliance between the Fort Lauderdale, Florida, Police Department and the Wackenhut Corporation in which the two organizations would share responses to calls for service.

Demand Management

In the community problem-solving strategy, a major portion of demand is decentralized, with citizens encouraged to bring problems directly to beat officers or precinct offices. Use of 911 is discouraged, except for dire emergencies. Whether tactics include aggressive foot patrol as in Flint or problem solving as in Newport News, the emphasis is on police officers' interacting with citizens to determine the types of problems they are confronting and to devise solutions to those problems. In contrast to reform policing with its selling orientation, this approach is more like marketing: customer preferences are sought, and satisfying customer needs and wants, rather than selling a previously packaged product or service, is emphasized. In the case of police, they gather information about citizens' wants, diagnose the nature of the problem, devise possible solutions, and then determine which segments of the community they can best serve and which can be best served by other agencies and institutions that provide services, including crime control.

Additionally, many cities are involved in the development of demarketing programs.[45] The most noteworthy example of demarketing is in the area of rapid response to calls for service. Whether through the development of alternatives to calls for service, educational programs designed to discourage citizens from using the 911 system, or, as in a few cities, simply not responding to many calls for service, police actively attempt to demarket a program that had been actively sold earlier. Often demarketing 911 is thought of as a negative process. It need not be so, however. It is an attempt by police to change social, political, and fiscal circumstances to bring consumers' wants in line with police resources and to accumulate evidence about the value of particular police tactics.

Tactics and Technology

Community policing tactics include foot patrol, problem solving, information gathering, victim counseling

---

[44]Kelling, "Juveniles and Police: The End of the Nightstick."

[45]Crompton and Lamb, *Marketing Government and Social Services.*

and services, community organizing and consultation, education, walk-and-ride and knock-on-door programs, as well as regular patrol, specialized forms of patrol, and rapid response to emergency calls for service. Emphasis is placed on information sharing between patrol and detectives to increase the possibility of crime solution and clearance.

Measured Outcomes

The measures of success in the community strategy are broad: quality of life in neighborhoods, problem solution, reduction of fear, increased order, citizen satisfaction with police services, as well as crime control. In sum, the elements of the community strategy include:

- Authorization—commonly support (political), law, professionalism.
- Function—crime control, crime prevention, problem solving.
- Organizational design—decentralized, task forces, matrices.
- Relationship to environment—consultative, police defend values of law and professionalism, but listen to community concerns.
- Demand—channelled through analysis of underlying problems.
- Tactics and technology—foot patrol, problem solving, etc.
- Outcomes—quality of life and citizen satisfaction.

 ## Conclusion

We have argued that there were two stages of policing in the past, political and reform, and that we are now moving into a third, the community era. To carefully examine the dimensions of policing during each of these eras, we have used the concept of organizational strategy. We believe that this concept can be used not only to describe the different styles of policing in the past and the present, but also to sharpen the understanding of police policymakers of the future.

For example, the concept helps explain policing's perplexing experience with team policing during the 1960's and 1970's. Despite the popularity of team policing with officers involved in it and with citizens, it generally did not remain in police departments for very long. It was usually planned and implemented with enthusiasm and maintained for several years. Then, with little fanfare, it would vanish—with everyone associated with it saying regretfully that for some reason it just did not work as a police tactic. However, a close examination of team policing reveals that it was a strategy that innovators mistakenly approached as a tactic. It had implications for authorization (police turned to neighborhoods for support), organizational design (tactical decisions were made at lower levels of the organization), definition of function (police broadened their service role), relationship to environment (permanent team members responded to the needs of small geographical areas), demand (wants and needs came to team members directly from citizens), tactics (consultation with citizens, etc.), and outcomes (citizen satisfaction, etc.). What becomes clear, though, is that team policing was a competing strategy with different assumptions about every element of police business. It was no wonder that it expired under such circumstances. Team and reform policing were strategically incompatible—one did not fit into the other. A police department could have a small team policing unit or conduct a team policing experiment, but business as usual was reform policing.

Likewise, although foot patrol symbolizes the new strategy for many citizens, it is a mistake to equate the two. Foot patrol is a tactic, a way of delivering police services. In Flint, its inauguration has been accompanied by implementation of most of the elements of a community strategy, which has become business as usual. In most places, foot patrol is not accompanied by the other elements. It is outside the mainstream of "real" policing and often provided only as a sop to citizens and politicians who are demanding the development of different policing styles. This certainly was the case in New Jersey when foot patrol was evaluated by the Police Foundation.[46] Another example is in

---

[46]*The Newark Foot Patrol Experiment.*

Milwaukee, where two police budgets are passed: the first is the police budget; the second, a supplementary budget for modest levels of foot patrol. In both cases, foot patrol is outside the mainstream of police activities and conducted primarily as a result of external pressures placed on departments.

It is also a mistake to equate problem solving or increased order maintenance activities with the new strategy. Both are tactics. They can be implemented either as part of a new organizational strategy, as foot patrol was in Flint, or as an "add-on," as foot patrol was in most of the cities in New Jersey. Drawing a distinction between organizational add-ons and a change in strategy is not an academic quibble; it gets to the heart of the current situation in policing. We are arguing that policing is in a period of transition from a reform strategy to what we call a community strategy. The change involves move than making tactical or organizational adjustments and accommodations. Just as policing went through a basic change when it moved from the political to the reform strategy, it is going through a similar change now. If elements of the emerging organizational strategy are identified and the policing institution is guided through the change rather than left blindly thrashing about, we expect that the public will be better served, policymakers and police administrators more effective, and the profession of policing revitalized.

A final point: the classical theory of organization that continues to dominate police administration in most American cities is alien to most of the elements of the new strategy. The new strategy will not accommodate to the classical theory: the latter denies too much of the real nature of police work, promulgates unsustainable myths about the nature and quality of police supervision, and creates too much cynicism in officers attempting to do creative problem solving. Its assumptions about workers are simply wrong.

Organizational theory has developed well beyond the stage it was at during the early 1900's, and policing does have organizational options that are consistent with the newly developing organizational strategy. Arguably, policing, which was moribund during the 1970's, is beginning a resurgence. It is overthrowing a strategy that was remarkable in its time, but which could not adjust to the changes of recent decades. Risks attend the new strategy and its implementation. The risks, however, for the community and the profession of policing, are not as great as attempting to maintain a strategy that faltered on its own terms during the 1960's and 1970's.

DISCUSSION QUESTIONS

1. According to this article, how has the legitimacy of the police changed over time?

2. How have the demands for police service changed over the course of the three eras?

3. Explain how the relationship between the police and public has changed, and identify some of the factors that influenced this change.

SECTION

2

More informal interaction with the public has changed the relationship between the police and citizens.

Progressing Beyond Traditional Policing

Section Highlights

- Problems associated with the traditional model of policing
- Overview of alternatives to traditional policing
- Shift in policing toward the use of intelligence after 9/11

T he traditional model of policing requires police officers to focus heavily on responding to calls for service and solving crimes in a reactive manner with virtually no input or cooperation from citizens. The social unrest in the 1960s coupled with the use of **traditional policing** practices created tension between police and citizens. Ironically, this policing strategy emerged during a time when American police agencies were attempting to become more "professional." This section outlines how policing in the United States has advanced beyond the traditional model of policing. More specifically, this section describes alternative approaches to traditional policing that have been used beginning in the 1970s up through today. These strategies include team policing, problem-oriented policing, broken windows, community policing, zero-tolerance policing, and intelligence-led policing. The effectiveness of these strategies on reducing crime and disorder and improving police–community relations is also discussed in this section.

⊠ Moving Beyond Traditional Policing

In response to the social turmoil of the 1960s, the President's Commission on Law Enforcement and the Administration of Justice (1967) challenged police agencies across the United States to be more responsive during a time when social change was occurring at a fast pace.[1] The desire to professionalize the police coupled with a troubled relationship with the public (specifically in African American communities) led some police administrators to question how they could reconnect with the public while effectively dealing with an increasing crime problem. Police administrators began to look for policing techniques beyond the traditional approach they had used in previous decades. Beginning in the late 1960s, police administrators began to experiment with various nontraditional policing strategies with the hope that it would improve their relationship with citizens and allow them to more effectively manage crime.

Team Policing

Team policing was one of the first alternative approaches used in place of traditional policing by some American police agencies in the late 1960s. The use of a team approach to policing was first suggested in 1967 by the President's Commission on Law Enforcement and the Administration of Justice and then later reiterated by the 1973 Commission on Standards and Goals.[2] It is difficult to define team policing, as it meant something different in every place that attempted to implement it.[3] There were, however, three elements of team policing that were common among most agencies that tried to adopt this approach: first, requiring permanent assignment of teams of officers in neighborhoods to strengthen their relationship with citizens and to help identify crime problems unique to each neighborhood; second, maximum interaction and communication among all officers assigned within an area (this includes officers both involved and not involved in team policing efforts); and finally, active and frequent communication among team police officers and citizens.[4]

There were several evaluations of the impact of team policing efforts across the United States. *Issues in Team Policing: A Review of the Literature* notes that a wide range of results was reported within team policing literature, with some evaluations indicating positive results; however, the validity of some of those evaluations is questionable.[5] Ultimately, team policing was viewed as a failure and quickly faded away in the mid-1970s.[6] So why did team policing fail? It failed because there was a lack of support by middle managers within police agencies, the dispatch technology at that time made it difficult for team policing officers to remain in assigned neighborhoods, and there was no clarification to officers on how their behavior and police role should differ from traditional policing.[7]

Despite the fact that police agencies were beginning to look for alternatives to traditional policing strategies, the early 1970s were a time when researchers began to focus on how various police activities impacted crime. More specifically, researchers examined the effectiveness of traditional police strategies including routine patrol, response time to calls for service, and criminal investigation. A national study conducted by the RAND Corporation found that crimes were not solved by investigators focusing primarily on gathering evidence from crime scenes; instead, they needed to interview and work with witnesses and victims in order to get enough information to clear cases.[8] Another study conducted in Kansas City examined how police response time impacts the likelihood of the apprehension of offenders. This study revealed that faster response times did not result in more arrests and that the immediacy of initial reporting by citizens played a much greater role in resulting arrests.[9] The Kansas City Preventive Patrol study conducted in 1972 to 1973 revealed that random police patrol does not deter crime.[10] The findings from these studies challenged the assumption that these traditional police activities had an impact on crime. In essence, the research findings suggested that police officers had to do more than just simply react to calls for police service.

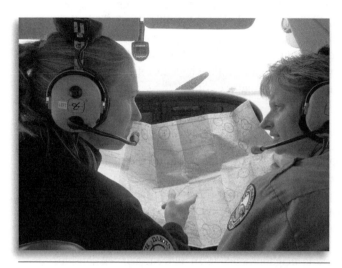

Problem solving requires police officers to communicate effectively and utilize analytical reasoning skills.

Problem-Oriented Policing

In 1979, Herman Goldstein introduced **problem-oriented policing** (POP) as an alternative to reactive, traditional policing. As previously mentioned, traditional policing consists of officers responding to a series of individual calls for service; once a call is completed, the officer moves on to the next call and so on. POP requires officers to look for patterns among individual calls for service to identify underlying causes of the problem or behaviors, locations, victims, and offenders that the calls may have in common.[11] In other words, "A problem is the basic unit of police work rather than a crime, a case, calls, or incidents."[12]

Officers use methodical problem-solving processes to respond to incidents of crime and disorder. One problem-solving methodology is the **SARA model**. This acronym represents a four-stage process that can be used by police officers as they attempt to solve problems.

1. *Scanning*—the identification of repeated problems by the police and the public

2. *Analysis*—an examination of underlying conditions or common factors unique to the identified problem

3. *Response*—research how the identified problem is handled in other places by other police agencies to help determine what response would be most effective

4. *Assessment*—determine if the response to the problem had any impact on the identified problem; the assessment should be an ongoing process in order to maintain desired outcomes[13]

Another technique used to identify issues related to crime and disorder is the "crime analysis triangle."[14] This approach to problem identification is derived from routine activities theory. Routine activities theory helps explain how and why crime occurs by identifying certain conditions related to offenders, victims/targets, and opportunity.[15] This theory is based on the idea that crime will occur if there is a motivated offender, a victim/target without a guardian present, and if an opportunity presents itself at that place at that particular time. The crime analysis triangle uses these three elements from routine activities theory to figure out how to control and manage the presentation of opportunities for crime to occur when offenders and victims come together in certain places at certain times (see illustration).[16]

The use of such problem-solving strategies has contributed to the overall success of POP in the United States. Beginning with one of the first POP evaluations in Newport News, Virginia, there is a growing body of research-based evidence that suggests that it can be an effective approach to policing.[17] The National Research Council reports that problem-solving techniques can reduce some types of crime, gun-related youth homicide, citizens' fear of crime, and several other types of disorder, including prostitution and drug dealing.[18] The reported benefits from using POP have contributed to the increasing use of this strategy in police agencies across the United States. According to Michael Scott of the Center for Problem-Oriented Policing,

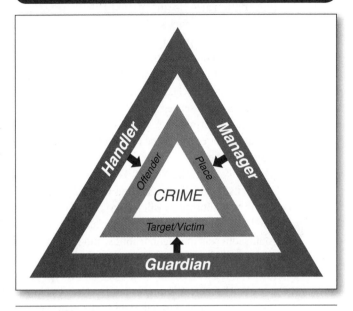

The Crime Analysis Triangle

Source: Center for Problem-Oriented Policing, www.popcenter.org.

there is no easy way to quantify the number of police agencies engaged in problem-oriented policing, much less to gauge the precise nature and quality of those efforts; it is safe to say that far more agencies claim to be engaged in problem-oriented policing today than at any other time.[19]

Despite claims of increased use by many American police agencies, Herman Goldstein asserts that the implementation and maintenance of POP can be difficult. He has identified several impediments to the full utilization and development of POP in police agencies across the United States.[20] First, police leaders have to understand that a long-term commitment to POP is necessary. This includes a commitment with allocation of resources, as well as continuity whenever there are changes in the police administration. Second, within most agencies, there is a lack of people with the skills that are required to analyze problems and to evaluate strategies used to deal with the identified problems. To correct this issue, police administrators should create a division or unit within the agency that is devoted solely to research, planning, and crime analysis. Once this division is created, it should be staffed with individuals that have skills related to research methods and criminological theories. Third, there is a lack of collaboration between police agencies and academicians. Police administrators need to allow researchers into their agencies to conduct research. Fourth, there is an absence of pressure by the public requesting that police agencies use problem-solving strategies. And finally, there is a lack of financial support to either implement or maintain POP within police agencies of various sizes; however, this is likely to be more difficult for smaller police agencies with very limited budgets. Even considering some of the issues related to the adoption and maintenance of POP, research suggests that there can be many benefits to communities when police agencies utilize this alternative to traditional policing. Herman Goldstein describes problem-oriented policing in greater detail in his article that is included at the end of this section.

Broken Windows

As crime continued to rise in the late 1970s, there was also an increase in citizens' fear of crime in the United States. Some police agencies tried to reduce citizens' fear of crime by reducing reported crimes in the area.[21] Others believed that putting police officers back on foot patrol would remind citizens of a time long ago when crime was not as bad, thus reducing their fear of crime.[22] This assertion was tested after the 1973 Safe and Clean Neighborhoods Act was passed by the New Jersey legislature. The primary goal of this legislation was to create safe and clean neighborhoods; the use of foot patrol was mandated as part of this legislation to increase police presence.[23] The Police Foundation conducted an evaluation of the impact of foot patrol on crime and fear of crime in Newark, New Jersey, from 1978 to 1979. The evaluation revealed that foot patrol did not have an effect on crime rates but did have a positive impact on citizens' attitudes toward crime and their fear of crime.[24]

The results from the Newark Foot Patrol study influenced the **broken windows theory** proposed by James Q. Wilson and George Kelling in 1982. Broken windows is based on the idea that visible decay or disorder in neighborhoods will lead to crime and other problems related to social disorder. Wesley Skogan identified two types of disorder: (1) social/human disorder—such as people hanging out on street corners and youths loitering in neighborhoods, and (2) physical disorder—such as graffiti, trash in the streets, and dilapidated cars and buildings.[25] If residents living within a neighborhood see evidence of disorder or decay and then become fearful, they might retreat indoors and the interaction between them, their neighbors, and the police will become minimal or nonexistent. The loss of the watchful eyes of citizens' contributes to crime moving into an area, as they will not be able to provide information to the police about incidents happening in their neighborhoods.[26]

Foot patrol plays a key role in broken windows. This is based on the notion that foot patrol officers will be able to identify patterns of disorder in neighborhoods and create a strong relationship with people living in those neighborhoods. Wilson and Kelling argue that this could not be accomplished in the same manner by officers in patrol cars.[27] The importance of foot patrol to broken windows theory was confirmed with the results of the Newark Foot Patrol study in 1972 to 1973, and then again several years later with the results of the Flint, Michigan, Foot Patrol study in 1979 to 1982. These two studies revealed that police officers on foot patrol can in fact reduce citizens' fear of crime.

Broken windows sounds good …but does it really work? The answer to this question is unclear, as the body of research on this topic is somewhat mixed. There are some studies that have found that broken windows has had an impact on a variety of crimes.[28] There are other studies that have found no empirical support for broken windows.[29] Additional research on this topic should be conducted in the future in order to better understand the impact of this particular policing strategy.

Community Policing

Throughout the reform era in American policing, the goal was to professionalize the police. This goal was based on good intentions, but ultimately it resulted in several unforeseen problems for the police. To begin with, the relationship between citizens and the police deteriorated with the introduction of motorized patrol and the focus on crimefighting adopted by most police agencies.[30] Motorized patrol reduced the amount of face-to-face contact between the police and citizens, and the interactions that did take place between the two groups became more impersonal and strained. This growing rift between the police and citizens contributed to the emergence of a police subculture in which there was an inherent distrust of citizens, the media, and police administrators.[31] These unforeseen problems marked the beginning of another phase of police reform that centered on trying to bridge the gap that had widened between the police and citizens in the 1960s.

Rumblings of a new community-based approach to policing began as early as the mid-1970s with the community-oriented policing project in San Diego, California,[32] and continued through the 1980s. **Community policing** became a popular topic among police administrators in the early 1990s and received additional attention with the passage of the 1994 Violent Crime Control and Law Enforcement Act.[33] Title I of this Act (Public Safety Partnership and Community Policing Act) placed great importance on fostering a relationship between police and citizens in addition to utilizing problem-solving skills as part of routine police work. This legislation was meant to encourage police agencies to adopt community policing across the United States.[34] This act also created the Office of Community Oriented Policing Services (COPS) to regulate and distribute the $8.8 billion allocated to programs derived from this legislation.[35]

What exactly is community policing? Community policing is not easily characterized; in fact, it may be defined and practiced in different ways by different police agencies.[36] The Office of Community Oriented Policing Services describes community policing as "a philosophy that promotes organizational strategies, which supports the systematic use of partnerships and problem-solving techniques, to proactively address the immediate conditions that give rise to public safety issues such as crime, social disorder, and fear of crime."[37] This approach to policing is different from traditional policing, as it promotes partnerships with citizens and places an emphasis on quality-of-life issues that are important to citizens. It is also important to note that community policing and problem-oriented policing are not the same thing. Jack Greene explains that "while community policing has a broad community building mandate, problem-oriented policing is more focused and, as its name implies, problem specific."[38]

Community partnerships, organizational transformation, and problem solving are three general components associated with community policing.[39] **Community partnerships** with citizens, other government and law enforcement agencies, community groups, and the media are important, as they help increase trust in the police and also aid in the identification and development of solutions to problems in communities. **Organizational transformation** occurs when police management, information systems, organizational structure, and police personnel come together to support community partnerships and proactive problem-solving efforts.[40] This requires police agencies to become less centralized or bureaucratic in nature and also to adopt management styles that allow more decision making to take place at the patrol level. And finally, **problem solving** involves the process of proactive and systematic identification of problems, as well as finding solutions to identified problems in communities. This involves the use of some systematic problem-solving approach such as the SARA model or the crime analysis triangle (discussed earlier in this section). These three components must be present in order for community policing to be fully implemented by police agencies.

Building a strong relationship with citizens is an important part of community policing.

The adoption of community policing by American police agencies has increased over time. A report by the Bureau of Justice Statistics stated that in 2007, 53% of police agencies included a community policing component in their mission statement compared to 47% of agencies in 2003.[41] More than half (56%) of all local police agencies provided community policing training to their newly hired police officers in 2007.[42] Nearly half (47%) of all local police agencies employed sworn officers that were working as community policing officers.[43] When comparing statistics from 1997 to those from 2007, there has been an increase in the reported adoption of community policing in the United States. The increase in reported implementation of community policing over time has been supported by grants provided by the Office of Community Oriented Policing Services (COPS). COPS grants provide local police agencies with resources to fund training, adoption of community-based programs, and other efforts that reflect the community-policing philosophy.[44]

Despite the increase in reported implementation by police agencies in the United States, there have been some criticisms of community policing. A book written by Jack Greene and Stephen Mastrofski, *Community Policing: Rhetoric or Reality,* identifies several problems related to community policing. The authors note that implementation would be difficult without a practical definition of community policing. Also, they write that community policing might just be "old wine in new bottles" or that it is a public relations attempt by police agencies to improve their legitimacy with the public. The book also discusses the extent to which community policing can actually fulfill the claims it makes regarding community impact. Other issues include limited resources and budgets (especially if COPS grants are no longer available to police agencies in the future) and the ability of police administrators to control police officer discretion after organizations become decentralized as a result of organizational change related to community policing.[45] Over the last three decades, research examining some of the previously mentioned problems has shed some light on the effectiveness of community policing in the United States.

Because definitions of community policing vary among police agencies in the United States, it has been difficult to assess as a general policing strategy.[46] As a result, police practices associated with community policing have been evaluated on an individual basis. For example, neighborhood watches, foot patrol, storefront offices, and community meetings have not been found to reduce crime, but they may influence citizen perceptions of disorder in their neighborhoods.[47] There is also some evidence that the community's level of fear is lowered when community policing efforts focus on increasing police–citizen interaction. Another part of community policing is making changes to the organizational structure of American police agencies. The National Research Council reports that it is difficult to form general conclusions about changes made to organizational structures nationwide due to wide variation across police agencies.[48] And finally, evaluations of problem-solving activities have shown that this approach to policing can be highly effective.[49] This body of research will be covered in greater detail in Section 8 when police effectiveness is discussed.

Community policing has been touted as one of the most significant changes made to American policing since police reform began long ago. This approach to policing emerged because of the growing divide between police and citizens and has since been recognized as an effective way for the police to reconnect with the public. Despite the success of community policing, some police agencies have begun to refocus their efforts toward aggressively targeting minor crimes and problems related to social disorder. In other words, some police agencies replaced building community partnerships with a form of "kick ass" policing.[50]

Zero-Tolerance Policing

The phrase *zero tolerance* suggests that no infraction (either big or small) will be tolerated within certain settings. This phrase was often used during the 1980s and 1990s during the war on drugs in the United

States. Zero tolerance was first applied to American policing in the early 1990s. Police Commissioner William Bratton and Mayor Rudolph Giuliani implemented a policing strategy that focused primarily on the control of social disorder and minor crimes in New York City in 1993. This strategy, referred to as **zero-tolerance policing**, requires police officers to strictly enforce laws and ordinances related to minor crimes and disorder (such as public drunkenness, panhandling, vandalism, loitering, prostitution, etc.).[51]

Zero-tolerance policing contains elements of both traditional policing and broken windows. Similar to traditional policing, zero-tolerance policing narrows the police role to strict enforcement of the law, with a heavy reliance on formal actions such as arrest and writing tickets.[52] Like broken windows, this strategy assumes that disorder and minor crimes can lead to more serious crimes if left unattended by the police.[53] This approach is also based on principles related to deterrence theory. The hope is that the aggressive enforcement of laws and ordinances related to minor crimes and disorder will send a message to criminals that the police will not tolerate any types of crime (neither minor or major), and as a result, people will be deterred from committing crimes in the future.[54]

Does zero-tolerance policing really work? The National Research Council examined studies focused on the impact of disorder policing on crime (*disorder policing* is a general term used for policing strategies that focus on the enforcement of laws and ordinances related to less serious crimes and disorder such as broken windows and zero-tolerance policing). The council asserts that enforcement practices (specifically arrest) applied broadly to the enforcement of minor crimes have not been supported by research.[55] They point out that a study by George Kelling and William Sousa did find a direct link between rate of arrests for minor crimes and crime rates in New York City precincts.[56] However, the validity of this study has been questioned due to several limitations with the data analyzed in the study.[57] Some argue that the reduction in crime in New York City after Bratton and Giuliani implemented zero tolerance policing cannot be attributed to this policing strategy, as crime was also dropping at a similar pace in several other major cities across the United States at that time.[58] Specifically, crime was dropping in cities that were using other types of policing strategies that were not based on zero tolerance (such as the San Diego Police Department using problem-oriented policing at that time).[59]

Aggressive policing tactics, such as zero-tolerance policing, often result in increased arrests.

Zero-tolerance policing has been the subject of criticism. Some argue that zero-tolerance policing may put the community back into a more passive role in crime and order maintenance (similar to that of the reform era) in favor of a more aggressive and active role on behalf of the police.[60] Lawrence Sherman argues that zero-tolerance policing can actually increase crime over time. He believes that people may become angry about being arrested more frequently for minor crimes, thus inciting them to lash out or participate in additional crimes.[61] Another criticism of zero-tolerance policing is that it puts police officers into a "wartime mentality" in which they use overly aggressive actions toward citizens and ultimately alienate themselves from the public (particularly minority citizens and citizens living in low-income, high-crime neighborhoods).[62] Evidence of this in New York City was an increase in both citizen complaints and lawsuits against the police based on allegations of police abuse and misconduct after zero-tolerance policing was implemented.[63] Critics of zero-tolerance policing assert that this aggressive approach directly conflicts with the goals of community policing. Further, critics argue that zero-tolerance policing could potentially undo any progress that has been made in communities in which the police have successfully rebuilt their relationship and trust with the public.

Zero-tolerance policing is viewed by some as taking a step backward in regard to police reform in the United States. It is believed that this policing strategy puts police officers in an adversarial position with the public. Still others view this approach to policing as an effective means of crime control. Despite this debate, American policing continues to adapt to demands placed on them by the public and changing social conditions.

Intelligence-Led Policing

The attack on the World Trade Center in New York City on September 11, 2001, highlighted the importance of intelligence as it relates to national security in the United States. After that day, police executives began to think about ways that they could incorporate intelligence more effectively in their work. This event in American history marks the beginning of increased interest in one of the most recent alternatives to traditional policing—**intelligence-led policing** (ILP). This approach has been used in other countries (including Australia, New Zealand, and countries within the United Kingdom) dating back to the 1990s.[64] The concept of ILP is not necessarily new to the United States; it just began to receive more attention from police executives after the terrorist attacks took place in 2001. The Carter and Carter article included at the end of this section provides a comparison of ILP in the United Kingdom and the United States.

The term *intelligence-led policing* does not have one standard definition and is used in different ways by police agencies across the United States.[65] Jerry Ratcliffe defines intelligence-led policing as

> a business model and managerial philosophy where data analysis and crime intelligence are pivotal to an objective, decision-making framework that facilitates crime and problem reduction, disruption and prevention through both strategic management and effective enforcement strategies that target prolific and serious offenders.[66]

Essentially, the goal of ILP is to collect intelligence on crime and criminals and then formulate the best way to respond to these problems.

But how does ILP work exactly? The **three-I model** (interpret, impact, influence) explains how ILP can be used in relation to crime reduction in policing.[67] There are three parts to this model. First, crime analysts need to *interpret* the criminal environment to look for significant or emerging threats. Next, crime analysts must use that intelligence to *influence* key decision makers within the organization. And finally, key decision makers need to provide resources to have an *impact* on the criminal environment.[68] All three components of the three-I model must be present in order for crime prevention and reduction to occur.[69]

Intelligence-led policing has been utilized in all types of police agencies in the United States. Marilyn Peterson provides several examples of the application of ILP in *The Basics of Intelligence Revisited*:[70]

- A county sheriff's office identifies narcotics control as its top priority and develops strategies accordingly. The office targets known offenders and groups, shuts down open-air drug markets and crack houses, and participates in school-based drug awareness programs to help prevent drug use.
- A statewide agency identifies vehicle insurance fraud as a top area for enforcement. The agency targets those involved in staged accidents, identifies communities in which insurance fraud is prevalent, looks for similar methods of operation that may indicate ongoing fraudulent activity, and mounts a public education campaign.

- A police agency in a small city makes safe streets a priority. The agency focuses on directed enforcement in identified hot spots. It also targets career criminals whose apprehension will significantly reduce the number of crimes being committed. Preventive measures include enhanced patrols, improved street lighting, and crime watch programs.

The sharing of intelligence among various types of law enforcement and government agencies is at the very core of ILP. The United States has recently developed fusion centers that provide information to police officials at various levels (from patrol up to the chief) and across various types of police agencies (from local to federal level agencies).[71] There are fusion centers in at least 25 states at the time of this writing, with several other states planning to implement them in the future.[72] Fusion centers not only include antiterrorism information but also provide information on a wide variety of crimes, including identity theft, money laundering, armed robbery, and insurance fraud, to name a few.[73]

Intelligence-led policing shares both similarities and differences with other policing strategies used in the United States. Traditional policing is similar to ILP, as the hierarchical structure of both approaches is from the top down or bureaucratic in nature, thus resulting in police management being primarily responsible for determining priorities of the organization.[74] These two policing approaches are different from one another, as the target of focus for traditional policing is crime detection, while ILP focuses on repeat offenders and other frequently occurring crimes.[75] ILP is compatible with problem-oriented policing (specifically the SARA model), as there is a similar process of identifying problems and applying solutions to those problems.[76] There are elements of community policing that are also similar to those found in ILP. For example, a major part of community policing involves officers getting to know the neighborhoods in which they patrol, requiring them to talk and interact with citizens. ILP is similar to this, as intelligence can only be collected if there is familiarity with a particular area, as well as the people and activities unique to that area.[77]

ILP has received criticism for both the means by which intelligence is collected and how the intelligence is used after it has been collected. The main criticism centers around issues related to the right to privacy. Critics argue that there is little accountability for the means by which the police gather intelligence on people or how this information is stored and later used as part of crime-reduction or -prevention strategies. Others argue that intelligence-led policing could be used as a tool for profiling citizens that are part of various racial and ethnic groups. There is only a scant amount of published research on ILP in the United States, as it is a strategy that has only recently been adopted by some police agencies across the country. As a result, there is no way to determine the effectiveness of this policing strategy in the United States at this point in time.

SUMMARY

- Police administrators began to look for alternatives to the traditional model of policing after the social unrest of the 1960s.
- Team policing was a strategy used to encourage police officers to get to know the neighborhoods to which they were assigned and to encourage them to get to know the residents of those neighborhoods.
- Herman Goldstein proposed that police officers take a more analytical approach to conducting police work by looking for underlying causes of problems instead of responding to all calls for service in the same way.
- Broken windows theory is based on the premise that the police need to take care of signs of disorder when they first appear; otherwise, the disorder will turn into more serious crime problems.
- Community policing focuses on the police and citizens working together in a collaborative effort to identify and manage crime and disorder.

KEY TERMS

broken windows theory	organizational transformation	team policing
community partnerships	problem-oriented policing	three-I model
community policing	problem solving	traditional policing
intelligence-led policing	SARA model	zero-tolerance policing

DISCUSSION QUESTIONS

1. Explain why police executives decided to look for alternatives to the traditional policing model in the early 1970s.

2. What are some of the reasons that team policing failed?

3. Compare and contrast community policing with team policing.

4. What are some of the criticisms of zero-tolerance policing?

5. How does intelligence-led policing differ from the traditional model of policing?

WEB RESOURCES

- To learn more about problem-oriented policing, visit the Center for Problem-Oriented Policing website at http://www.popcenter.org/about/.
- To learn more about intelligence-led policing, go to https://www.ncjrs.gov/pdffiles1/bja/210681.pdf.
- To learn more about community policing, go to http://www.cops.usdoj.gov/default.asp?item=36.

In this article, Herman Goldstein describes how traditional policing in the United States is based on a "means over ends" approach in which the police function in a reactive manner. He suggests that the police approach their work with an interest in finding the root cause of the problems identified by the public. Once the root cause(s) of problems have been identified, police officers should explore alternative ways to resolve them other than through the use of traditional formal actions (such as ticketing or arrest).

Improving Policing:
A Problem-Oriented Approach

Herman Goldstein

The police have been particularly susceptible to the "means over ends" syndrome, placing more emphasis in their improvement efforts on organization and operating methods than on the substantive outcome of their work. This condition has been fed by the professional movement within the police field, with its concentration on the staffing, management, and organization of police agencies. More and more persons are questioning the widely held assumption that improvements in the internal management of police departments will enable the police to deal more effectively with the problems they are called upon to handle. If the police are to realize a greater return on the investment made in improving their operations, and if they are to mature into a profession, they must concern themselves more directly with the end product of their efforts.

Meeting this need requires that the police develop a more systematic process for examining and addressing the problems that the public expects them to handle. It requires identifying these problems in more precise terms, researching each problem, documenting the nature of the current police response, assessing its adequacy and the adequacy of existing authority and resources, engaging in a broad exploration of alternatives to present responses, weighing the merits of these alternatives, and choosing from among them.

Improvements in staffing, organization and management remain important, but they should be achieved—and may, in fact, be more achievable—within the context of a more direct concern with the outcome of policing.

All bureaucracies risk becoming so preoccupied with running their organizations and getting so involved in their methods of operating that they lose sight of the primary purposes for which they were created. The police seem unusually susceptible to this phenomenon.

One of the most popular new developments in policing is the use of officers as decoys to apprehend offenders in high-crime areas. A speaker at a recent conference for police administrators, when asked to summarize new developments in the field, reported on a sixteen-week experiment in his agency with the use of decoys, aimed at reducing street robberies.

One major value of the project, the speaker claimed, was its contribution to the police department's public image. Apparently, the public was intrigued by the clever, seductive character of the project, especially by the widely publicized demonstrations of the makeup artists' ability to disguise burly officers. The speaker also claimed that the project greatly increased the morale of the personnel working in the unit. The officers found the assignment exciting and challenging, a welcome change from the tedious routine that characterizes so much of regular police work, and they developed a high esprit de corps.

The effect on robberies, however, was much less clear. The methodology used and the problems in measuring crime apparently prevented the project staff from reaching any firm conclusions. But it was reported that, of the 216 persons arrested by the unit for robbery during the experiment, more than half would not have committed a robbery, in the judgment of the unit members, if they had not been tempted by the situation presented by the police decoys. Thus, while the total impact of the project remains unclear, it can be said with certainly that the experiment actually increased the number of robberies by over 100 in the sixteen weeks of the experiment.

The account of this particular decoy project (others have claimed greater success) is an especially poignant reminder of just how serious an imbalance there is within the police field between the interest in organizational and procedural matters and the concern for the substance of policing. The assumption, of course, is that the two are related, that improvements in internal management will eventually increase the capacity of the police to meet the objectives for which police agencies are created. But the relationship is not that clear and direct and is increasingly being questioned.

Perhaps the best example of such questioning relates to response time. Tremendous resources were invested during the past decade in personnel, vehicles, communications equipment, and new procedures in order to increase the speed with which the police respond to calls for assistance. Much less attention was given in this same period to what the officer does in handling the variety of problems he confronts on arriving, albeit fast, where he is summoned. Now, ironically, even the value of a quick response is being questioned.[1]

This article summarizes the nature of the "means over ends" syndrome in policing and explores ways of focusing greater attention on the results of policing—on the effect that police efforts have on the problems that the police are expected to handle.

The "Means Over Ends" Syndrome

Until the late 1960s, efforts to improve policing in this country concentrated almost exclusively on internal management: streamlining the organization, upgrading personnel, modernizing equipment, and establishing more businesslike operating procedures. All of the major commentators on the police since the beginning of the century—Leonhard F. Fuld (1909), Raymond B. Fosdick (1915), August Vollmer (1936), Bruce Smith (1940), and O. W. Wilson (1950)—stressed the need to improve the organization and management of police agencies. Indeed, the emphasis on internal management was so strong that professional policing was defined primarily as the application of modern management concepts to the running of a police department.

The sharp increase in the demands made on the police in the late 1960s (increased crime, civil rights demonstrations, and political protest) led to several

---

[1]The recent study in Kansas City found that the effect of response time on the capacity of the police to deal with crime was negligible, primarily because delays by citizens in reporting crimes make the minutes saved by the police insignificant. See Kansas City, Missouri, Police Department, *Response Time Analysis*, Executive Security (Kansas City, 1997).

national assessments of the state of policing.[2] The published findings contained some criticism of the professional model of police organization, primarily because of its impersonal character and failure to respond to legitimate pressures from within the community.[3] Many recommendations were made for introducing a greater concern for the human factors in policing, but the vast majority of the recommendations that emerged from the reassessments demonstrated a continuing belief that the way to improve the police was to improve the organization. Higher recruitment standards, college education for police personnel, reassignment and reallocation of personnel, additional training, and greater mobility were proposed. Thus the management-dominated concept of police reform spread and gained greater stature.

The emphasis on secondary goals—on improving the organization—continues to this day, reflected in the prevailing interests of police administrators, in the factors considered in the selection of police chiefs and the promotion of subordinates, in the subject matter of police periodicals and texts, in the content of recently developed educational programs for the police, and even in the focus of major research projects.

At one time this emphasis was appropriate. When Vollmer, Smith, and Wilson formulated theft prescriptions for improved policing, the state of the vast majority of police agencies was chaotic: Personnel were disorganized, poorly equipped, poorly trained, inefficient, lacking accountability, and often corrupt. The first priority was putting the police house in order. Otherwise, the endless crises that are produced by an organization out of control would be totally consuming, without a minimum level of order and accountability, an agency cannot be redirected—however

committed its administrators may be to addressing more substantive matters.

What is troubling is that administration of those agencies that have succeeded in developing a high level of operating efficiency have not gone on to concern themselves with the end results of their efforts—with the actual impact that their streamlined organizations have on the problems the police are called upon to handle.

The police seem to have reached a plateau at which the highest objective to which they aspire is administrative competence. And, with some scattered exceptions, they seem reluctant to move beyond this plateau—toward creating a more systematic concern for the end product of their effort. But strong pressures generated by several new developments may now force them to do so.

1. The Financial Crisis

The growing cost of police service and the financial plight of most city governments, especially those under threat of Proposition 13 movement, are making municipal officials increasingly reluctant to appropriate still more money for police service without greater assurance that their investment will have an impact on the problems that the police are expected to handle. Those cities that are already reducing their budgets are being forced to make some of the hard choices that must be made in weighing the impact of such cuts on the nature of the service rendered to the public.

2. Research Findings

Recently completed research questions the value of two major aspects of police operations—preventive patrol and investigations conducted by detectives.[4]

---

[2]See President's Commission on Law Enforcement and Administration of justice, *The Challenge of Crime in a Free Society* (Washington, DC: Govt. Printing Office, 1967); National Advisory Commission on Civil Disorders, *Report of the National Advisory Commission on the Civil Disorders* (Washington, DC: Govt. Printing Office, 1968); National Commission on the Cases and Prevention of Violence, *To Establish Justice, to Insure Domestic Tranquility. Final Report* (Washington, DC: Govt. Printing Office, 1969); President's Commission on Campus Unrest, *Report of the President's Commission on Campus Unrest* (Washington DC: Govt. Printing Office, 1970); and National Advisory Commission on Criminal Justice Standards and Goals, Police (Washington, DC: Govt. Printing Office, 1972).

[3]See, for example, National Advisory Commission on Civil Disorders, Report, p. 158.

[4]George L. Kelling et al., *The Kansas City Prevention Patrol Experiment: A Summary Report* (Washington, DC: Police Foundation 1974); and Peter W. Greenwood et al., *The Criminal Investigation Process, 3 vols.* (Santa Monica, Calif.: Rand Corporation, 1976).

Some police administrators have challenged the findings;[5] others are awaiting the results of replication.[6] But those who concur with the results have begun to search for alternatives, aware of the need to measure the effectiveness of a new response before making a substantial investment in it.

3. Growth of a Consumer Orientation

Policing has not yet felt the full impact of consumer advocacy. As citizens press for improvement in police service, improvement will increasingly be measured in terms of results. Those concerned about battered wives, for example, could not care less whether the police who respond to such calls operate with one or two officers in a car, whether the officers are short or tall or whether they have a college education. Their attention is on what the police do for the battered wife.

4. Questioning the Effectiveness of the Best-Managed Agencies

A number of police departments have carried out most, if not all, of the numerous recommendations for strengthening a police organization and enjoy a national reputation for their efficiency, their high standards of personnel selection and training, and their application of modern technology to their operations. Nevertheless, their communities apparently continue to have the same problems as do others with less advanced police agencies.[7]

5. Increased Resistance to Organizational Change

Intended improvements that are primarily in the form of organizational change, such as team policing, almost invariably run into resistance from rank-and-file personnel. Stronger and more militant unions have engaged some police administrators in bitter and prolonged fights over such changes.[8] Because the costs in terms of disruption and discontent are so great, police administrators initiating change will be under increasing pressure to demonstrate in advance that the result of their efforts will make the struggle worthwhile.

Against this background, the exceptions to the dominant concern with the police organization and its personnel take on greater significance. Although scattered and quite modest, a number of projects and training programs carried out in recent years have focused on a single problem that the public expects the police to handle, such as child abuse, sexual assault, arson, or the drunk driver.[9] These projects and programs, by their very nature, subordinate the customary priorities of police reform, such as staffing, management, and equipment, to a concern about a specific problem and the police response to it.

Some of the earliest support for this type of effort was reflected in the crime-specific projects funded by the

---

[5]For questioning by a police administrator of the findings of the Kansas City Preventive Patrol Project, see Edward M. Davis and Lyle Knowles, "A Critique of the Report: An Evaluation of the Kansas City Preventive Patrol Experiment," *Police Chief*, June 1975, pp. 22–27. For review of the Rand study on detectives, see Daryl F. Gates and Lyle Knowles, "An Evaluation of the Rand Corporation's Analysis of the Criminal Investigation Process," *Police Chief*, July 1976, p. 20. Each of the two papers is followed by a response from the authors of the original studies. In addition, for the position of the International Association of Chiefs of Police on the result of the Kansas City project, see "IACP Position Paper on the Kansas City Preventive Patrol Experiment," *Police Chief*, September 1975, p. 16.

[6]The National Institute of Low Enforcement and Criminal Justice is sponsoring a replication of the Kansas City Preventive Patrol Experiment and is supporting further explorations of the criminal investigation process. See National Institute of Law Enforcement and Criminal Justice, *Program Plan, Fiscal Year 1978* (Washington, DC: Govt. Printing Office, 1977), p. 12.

[7]Admittedly, precise appraisals and comparisons are difficult. For a recent example of an examination by the press of one department that has enjoyed a reputation for good management, see "The LAFD: How good is it?" *Los Angeles Times*, Dec. 18, 1977.

[8]Example of cities in which police unions recently have fought vigorously to oppose innovations introduced by police administrations are Boston, Massachusetts, and Troy, New York.

[9]These programs are reflected in the training opportunities routinely listed in such public Hons [*sic*] as *Police Chief, Criminal Law Reporter, Law Enforcement News,* and *Crime Control Digest,* and by the abstracting service of the National Criminal Justice Reference Center.

Law Enforcement Assistance Administrations.[10] Communities—not just the police—were encouraged to direct their attention to a specific type of crime and to make those changes in existing operations that were deemed necessary to reduce its incidence. The widespread move to fashion a more effective police response to domestic disturbances is probably the best example of a major reform that has, as its principal objective, improvement in the quality of service delivered, and that calls for changes in organization, staffing, and training only as these are necessary to achieve the primary goal.

Are these scattered efforts a harbinger of things to come? Are they a mutual development in the steadily evolving search for ways to improve police operations? Or are they, like the programs dealing with sexual assault and child abuse, simply the result of the sudden availability of funds because of intensified citizens concern about a specific problem? Whatever their origin, those projects that do subordinate administrative considerations to the task of improving police effectiveness in dealing with a specific problem have a refreshing quality to them.

 ## What Is the End Product of Policing?

To urge a more direct focus on the primary objectives of a police agency requires spelling out these objectives more clearly. But this is no easy task, given the conglomeration of unrelated, ill-defined, and often inseparable jobs that the police are expected to handle.

The task is complicated further because so many people believe that the job of the police is, first and foremost, to enforce the law: to regulate conduct by applying criminal law of the jurisdiction. One commentator on the police recently claimed: "We do not say to the police: 'Here is the problem. Deal with it. We say: 'Here is a detailed code. Enforce it.'"[11] In reality, the police job is perhaps most accurately described as dealing with problems.[12] Moreover, enforcing the criminal code is itself only a means to an end—one of several that the police employ in getting their job done.[13] The emphasis on law enforcement, therefore, is nothing more than a continuing preoccupation with means.

Considerable effort has been invested in recent years in attempting to define the police function: inventorying the wide range of police responsibilities, categorizing various aspects of policing, and identifying some of the characteristics common to all police tasks.[14] This work will be of great value in refocusing attention on the end product of policing, but the fact that it is still going on is not cause to delay giving greater attention to substantive matters. It is sufficient, for our purposes here, simply to acknowledge that the police job requires that they deal with a wide range of behavioral and social problems that arise in a community—that the end product of policing consists of dealing with these problems.

By problems, I mean the incredibly broad range of troublesome situations that prompt citizens to turn to the police, such as street robberies, residential burglaries, battered wives, vandalism, speeding cars, runaway children, accidents, acts of terrorism, even fear. These and other similar problems are the essence of police work. They are the reason for having a police agency.

Problems of this nature are to be distinguished from those that frequently occupy police administrators, such as lack of manpower, inadequate supervision, inadequate training or strained relations with police

---

[10]See, for example, National Institute of Law Enforcement and Criminal Justice, Law Enforcement Assistance Administration, "Planning Guidelines and Program to Reduce Crime," Mimeographed (Washington, DC, 1977), pp. VI–XIII. For a discussion of the concept, see Paul K. Wormeli and Steve E. Kolodary," *Journal of Research in Crime and Delinquency*, January 1972, pp. 54–68.

[11]Ronald J. Allen, "The Police and Substantive Rulemaking, Reconciling Principle and Expediency," *University of Pennsylvania Law Review*, November 1976, p. 97.

[12]Egon Bittner comes close to this point of view when he describes police functioning as applying immediate solutions to an endless array of problems. See Egon Bittner, "Florence Nightingale in Pursuit of Willie Sutton," in *The Potential for Reform of Criminal Justice*, Herbert Jacob ed. (Beverly Hills, Calif.: Sage, 1974), p. 30. James Q. Wilson does also when he describes policing as handling situations. See James Q. Wilson, *Varieties of Police Behavior: The Management of Law and Order in Eight Communities* (Cambridge, Mass.: Harvard University Press, 1968), p. 31.

[13]I develop this point in an earlier work. See Herman Goldstein, *Policing a Free Society* (Cambridge, Mass.: Ballinger, 1977), pp. 30, 36–39.

[14]In the 1977 book, I presented a brief summary of these studies. Ibid., pp. 26–28.

unions. They differ from those most often identified by operating personnel, such as the lack of adequate equipment, frustrations in the prosecution of criminal cases, or inequities in working conditions. And they differ, too, from the problems that have occupied those advocating police reform, such as the multiplicity of police agencies, the lack of lateral entry, and the absence of effective controls over police conduct.

Many of the problems coming to the attention of the police become their responsibility because no other means has been found to solve them. They are the residual problems of society. It follows that expecting the police to solve or eliminate them is expecting too much. It is more realistic to aim at reducing their volume, preventing repetition, alleviating suffering, and minimizing the other adverse effects they produce.

 ## Developing the Overall Process

To address the substantive problems of the police requires developing a commitment to a more systematic process for inquiring into these problems. Initially, this calls for identifying in precise terms the problems that citizens look to the police to handle. Once identified, each problem must be explored in great detail. What do we know about the problem? Has it been researched? If so, with what results? What more should we know? Is it a proper concern of government? What authority and resources are available for dealing with it? What is the current police response? In the broadest-ranging search for solutions, what would constitute the most intelligent response? What factors should be considered in choosing from among alternatives? If a new response is adopted, how does one go about evaluating its effectiveness? And finally, what changes, if any, does implementation of a more effective response require in the police organization?

This type of inquiry is not foreign to the police. Many departments conduct rigorous studies of administrative and operational problems. A police agency may undertake a detailed study of the relative merits of adopting one of several different types of uniforms. And it may regularly develop military-like plans for handling special events that require the assignment of large numbers of personnel.[15] However, systematic analysis and planning have rarely been applied to the specific behavioral and social problems that constitute the agency's routine business. The situation is somewhat like that of a private industry that studies the speed of its assembly line, the productivity of its employees, and the nature of its public relations program, but does not examine the quality of its product.

Perhaps the closest police agencies have come to developing a system for addressing substantive problems has been their work in crime analysis. Police routinely analyze information on reported crimes to identify patterns of criminal conduct with the goal of enabling operating personnel to apprehend specific offenders or develop strategies to prevent similar offenses from occurring. Some police departments have, through the use of computers, developed sophisticated programs to analyze reported crimes.[16] Unfortunately, these analyses are almost always put to very limited use—to apprehend a professional car thief or to deter a well-known cat burglar—rather than serving as a basis for rethinking the overall police response to the problem of car theft or cat burglaries. Nevertheless, the practice of planning operational responses based on an analysis of hard data, now a familiar concept to the police, is a helpful point of reference in advocating development of more broadly based research and planning.

The most significant effort to use a problem orientation for improving police responses was embodied in the crime-specific concept initiated in California in 1971,[17] and later promoted with LEAA

---

[15]For an up-to-date description of the concept of planning and research as it has evolved in police agencies, see O. W. Wilson and Roy C. McLaden, *Police Administration*, 4th ed. (New York: McGraw- Hill, 1977), pp. 157–81.

[16]For examples, see National Institute of Law Enforcement and Criminal Justice, *Police Crime Analysis Unit Handbook* (Washington, DC: Govt. Printing Office, 1973), pp. 90–92, 113–31.

[17]For a brief description, see Joanne W. Rockwell, "Crime Specific…An Answer?" *Police Chief, September* 1972, p. 35.

funds throughout the country. The concept was made an integral part of the anticrime program launched in eight cities in January 1972, aimed at bringing about reductions in five crime categories: murder, rape, assault, robbery, and burglary.[18] This would have provided an excellent opportunity to develop and test the concept, were it not for the commitment that this politically motivated program carried to achieving fast and dramatic results: a 5 percent reduction in each category in two years and a 20 percent reduction in five years. These rather naive, unrealistic goals and the emphasis on quantifying the results placed a heavy shadow over the program from the outset. With the eventual abandonment of the projects, the crime-specific concept seems to have lost ground as well. However, the national evaluation of the program makes it clear that progress was made, despite the various pressures, in planning a community approach to the five general crime categories. The "crime-oriented planning, implementation and evaluation" process employed in all eight cities had many of the elements one would want to include in a problem-oriented approach to improving police service.[19]

Defining Problems With Greater Specificity

The importance of defining problems more precisely becomes apparent when one reflects on the long-standing practice of using overly broad categories to describe police business. Attacking police problems under a categorical heading—"crime" or "disorder," or "delinquency," or even "violence"—is bound to be futile. While police business is often further subdivided by means of the labels tied to the criminal code, such as robbery, burglary, and theft, these are not adequate, for several reasons.

First, they frequently mask diverse forms of behavior. Thus, for example, incidents classified under

"arson" might include fires set by teenagers as a form of vandalism, fires set by persons suffering [from] severe psychological problems, fires set for the purpose of destroying evidence of a crime, fires set by persons (or their hired agents) to collect insurance, and fires set by organized criminal interests to intimidate. Each type of incident poses a radically different problem for the police.

Second, if police depend heavily on categories of criminal offenses to define problems of concern to them, others may be misled to believe that, if a given form of behavior is not criminal, it is of no concern to the police. This is perhaps best reflected in the proposal of decriminalizing prostitution, gambling, narcotic use, vagrancy, and public intoxication. The argument made over and over again is that removing the criminal label will reduce the magnitude and complexity of the police function, freeing personnel to work on more serious matters and ridding the police of some of the negative side effects, such as corruption, that these problems produce. But decriminalization does not relieve the police of responsibility. The public expects drunks to be picked up, if only because they find their presence on the street annoying or because they feel that the government has an obligation to care for persons who cannot care for themselves. The public expects prostitutes who solicit openly on the streets to be stopped, because such conduct is offensive to innocent passersby, blocks pedestrian or motor traffic, and contributes to the deterioration of a neighborhood. The problem is a problem for the police whether or not it is defined as a criminal offense.

Finally, use of offense categories as descriptive of police problems implies that the police role is restricted to arresting and prosecuting offenders. In fact, the police job is much broader, extending, in the case of burglary, to encouraging citizens to lock their premises more securely, to eliminating some of the conditions that might attract potential burglary, to counseling burglary victims on ways they can avoid similar attacks

---

[18]The program is described in Eleanor Chelimsky. *High Impact Anti-Crime Program, Final Report, vol. 2* (Washington, DC: Govt. Printing Office, 1976), pp. 19–38.

[19]Ibid., pp. 145–50, 413–21.

in the future, and to recovering and returning burglarized property.

Until recently, the police role in regard to the crime of rape was perceived primarily as responding quickly when a report of a rape was received, determining whether a rape had really occurred (given current legal definitions), and then attempting to identify and apprehend the perpetrator. Today, the police role has been radically redefined to include teaching women how to avoid attack, organizing transit programs to provide safe movement in areas where there is a high risk of attack, dealing with the full range of sexual assault not previously covered by the narrowly drawn rape statutes, and— perhaps most important—providing needed care and support to the rape victim to minimize the physical and mental damage resulting from such an attack. Police are now concerned with sexual assault not simply because they have a direct role in the arrest and prosecution of violators, but also because sexual assault is a community problem which the police and others can affect in a variety of ways.

It seems desirable, at least initially in the development of a problem-solving approach to improved policing, to press for as detailed a breakdown of problems as possible. In addition to distinguishing different forms of behavior and the apparent motivation as in the case of incidents commonly grouped under the heading of "arson," it is helpful to be much more precise regarding locale and time of day, the type of people involved, and the type of people victimized. Different combinations of these variables may present different problems, posing different policy questions and calling for radically different solutions.[20]

For example, most police agencies already separate the problem of purse snatching in which force is used from the various other forms of conduct commonly grouped under robbery. But an agency is likely to find it much more helpful to go further—to pinpoint, for example, the problem of teenagers snatching the purses of elderly women waiting for buses in the downtown section of the city during the hours of early darkness. Likewise, a police agency might find it helpful to isolate the robberies of grocery stores that are open all night and are typically staffed by a lone attendant; or the theft of vehicles by a highly organized group engaged in the business of transporting them for sale in another jurisdiction; or the problem posed by teenagers who gather around hamburger stands each evening to the annoyance of neighbors, customers, and management. Eventually, similar problems calling for similar responses may be grouped together, but one cannot be certain that they are similar until they have been analyzed.

In the analysis of a given problem, one may find, for example, that the concern of the citizenry is primarily fear of attack, but the fear is not warranted given the pattern of actual offenses. Where this situation becomes apparent, the police have two quite different problems: to deal more effectively with the actual incidents where they occur, and to respond to the groundless fears. Each calls for a different response.

The importance of subdividing problems was dramatically illustrated by the recent experience of the New York City Police Department in its effort to deal more constructively with domestic disturbances. An experimental program, in which police were helped to use mediation techniques, was undertaken with obvious public support. But, in applying the mediation techniques, the department apparently failed to distinguish sufficiently those cases in which wives were repeatedly subject to physical abuse. The aggravated nature of the latter cases resulted in a suit against the department in which the plaintiffs argued that the police are mandated to enforce the law when any violation comes to their attention. In the settlement, the department agreed that its personnel would not attempt to

---

[20]For an excellent example of what is needed, see the typology of vandalism developed by the British sociologist Stanley Cohen, quoted in Albert M. William, for "Vandalism," *Management Information Service Report* (Washington, DC: International City Management Association, May 1976), pp. 1–2. Another excellent example of an effort to break down a problem of concern to the police—in this case, heroin––is found in Mark Harrison Moore, *Buy and Bust: The Effective Regulation of an Illicit Market in Heroin* (Lexington, Mass.: Lexington Books, 1977), p. 83.

reconcile the parties or to mediate when a felony was committed.[21] However, the net effect of the suit is likely to be more far reaching. The vulnerability of the department to criticism for not having dealt more aggressively with the aggravated cases has dampened support—in New York and elsewhere—for the use of alternates to arrest in less serious cases, even though alternatives still appear to represent the more intelligent response.

One of the major values in subdividing police business is that it gives visibility to some problems which have traditionally been given short shrift, but which warrant more careful attention. The seemingly minor problem of noise, for example, is typically buried in the mass of police business lumped together under such headings as "complaints," "miscellaneous," "noncriminal incident," or "disturbances." Both police officers and unaffected citizens would most likely be inclined to rank it at the bottom in any list of problems. Yet the number of complaints about noise is high in many communities—in fact, noise is probably among the most common problems brought by the public to the police.[22] While some of those complaining may be petty or unreasonable, many are seriously aggrieved and justified in their appeal for relief. Sleep is lost, schedules are disrupted, mental and emotional problems are aggravated. Apartments may become uninhabitable. The elderly woman living alone, whose life has been made miserable by inconsiderate neighbors, is not easily convinced that the daily intrusion into her life of their noise is any less serious than other forms of intrusion. For this person, and for many like her, improved policing would mean a more effective response to the problem of the noise created by her neighbors.

✖ **Researching the Problem**

Without a tradition for viewing in sufficiently discrete terms the various problems making up the police job, gathering even the most basic information about a specific problem—such as complaints about noise—can be extremely difficult.

First, the magnitude of the problem and the various forms in which it surfaces must be established. One is inclined to turn initially to police reports for such information. But overgeneralization in categorizing incidents, the impossibility of separating some problems, variations in the reporting practices of the community, and inadequacies in report writing seriously limit their value for purposes of obtaining a full picture of the problem. However, if used cautiously, some of the information in police files may be helpful. Police agencies routinely collect and store large amounts of data even though they may not use them to evaluate the effectiveness of their responses. Moreover, if needed information is not available, often it can be collected expeditiously in a well-managed department, owing to the high degree of centralized control of field operations.

How does one discover the nature of the current police response? Administrators and their immediate subordinates are not a good source. Quite naturally, they have a desire to provide an answer that reflects well on the agency, is consistent with legal requirements, and meets the formal expectations of both the public and other agencies that might have a responsibility relating to the problem. But even if these concerns did not color their answers, top administrators are often so far removed from street operations, in both distance and time, that they would have great difficulty describing current response accurately.

---

[21]See *Bruno v. Codd*, 90 Miss. Ed 1047,396 N.Y.S. 24 974 (1977), finding a cause of action against the New York City Police Department for failing to protect battered wives. On June 26, 1978, the city agreed to a settlement with the plaintiffs in which it committed the police to arrest in all cases in which "there is reasonable cause to believe that a husband has committed a felony against his wife and/or has violated an Order of Protection or Temporary Order of Protection." See Consent Decree, Bruno against McGuire, New York State Supreme Court. Index 821946/76. (Recognizing the consent decree, the New York Appellate Court, First Department, in July if 1970 (#5020) described an appeal in the case as most in so far as it involved the police department. From a reading of the court's reversals as to the other parts of the case, however, it appears that it would also have reversed the decision of the lower court in sustaining the action against the police department if there had not been a consent decree.)

[22]It was reported that, on a recent three-day holiday weekend in Madison, Wisconsin, police handled slightly more than 1,000 calls, of which 118 were for loud parties and other types of noise disturbances. See "Over 1,000 Calls Made to Police on Weekend," *Wisconsin State Journal* (Madison, Wisc., June 1. 1976).

Inquiry, then, must focus on the operating level. But mere questioning of line officers is not likely to be any more productive. We know from the various efforts to document police activity in the field that there is often tremendous variation in the way in which different officers respond to the same type of incident.[23] Yet the high value placed on uniformity and on adhering to formal requirements and the pressures from peers inhibit officers from candidly discussing the manner in which they respond to the multitude of problems they handle—especially if the inquiry comes from outside the agency. But one cannot afford to give up at this point, for the individualized practices of police officers and the vast amount of knowledge they acquire about the situations they handle taken together are an extremely rich resource that is too often overlooked by those concerned about improving the quality of police services. Serious research into the problems police handle requires observing police officers over a period of time. This means accompanying them as they perform their regular assignments and cultivating the kind of relationship that enables them to talk candidly about the way in which they handle specific aspects of their job.

The differences in the way in which police respond, even in dealing with relatively simple matters, may be significant. When a runaway child is reported, one officer may limit himself to obtaining the basic facts. Another officer, sensing as much of a responsibility for dealing with the parents' fears as for finding the child and looking out for the child's interests, may endeavor to relieve the parents' anxiety by providing information about the runaway problem and about what they might expect. From the standpoint of the consumers—in this case, the parents—the response of the second officer is vastly superior to that of the first.

In handling more complicated matters, the need to improvise has prompted some officers to develop what appear to be unusually effective ways of dealing with specific problems. Many officers develop a unique understanding of problems that frequently come to their attention, learning to make important distinctions among different forms of the same problem and becoming familiar with the many complicating factors that are often present. And they develop a feel for what under the circumstances constitutes the most effective responses. After careful evaluation, these types of responses might profitably be adopted as standard for an entire police agency. If the knowledge of officers at the operating level were more readily available, it might be useful to those responsible for drafting crime-related legislation. Many of the difficulties in implementing recent change in statutes relating to sexual assault, public drunkenness, drunk driving and child abuse could have been avoided had police expertise been tapped.

By way of example, if a police agency were to decide to explore the problem of noise, the following questions might be asked. What is the magnitude of the problem as reflected by the number of complaints received? What is the source of the complaints: industry, traffic, groups of people gathered outdoors, or neighbors? How do noise complaints from residents break down between private dwellings and apartment houses? How often are the police summoned to the same location? How often are other forms of misconduct, such as fights, attributable to conflicts over noise? What is the responsibility of a landlord or an apartment house manager regarding noise complaints? What do the police now do in responding to such complaints? How much of the police procedure has been thought through and formalized? What is the authority of the police in such situations? Is it directly applicable or must they lean on somewhat nebulous authority, such as threatening to arrest for disorderly conduct or for failure to obey a lawful order if the parties fail to quiet down? What works in police practice and what does not work? Are specific officers

---

[23]See, for example, the detailed accounts of police functioning in Minneapolis, in Joseph M. Livermore, "Policing," *Minnesota Law Review*, March 1971, pp. 849–728. Among the works describing the police officers' varying styles in responding to similar situations are Wilson, *Varieties of Police Behavior;* Albert J. Ress, Jr., *The Police and the Public* (New Haven, Conn.: Yale University Press. 1971); Jerome H. Skalaick, *Justice without Trial: Law Enforcement in Democratic Society* (New York: John Wiley, 1966); and Egon Bittner, *The Functions of the Police in Modern Society: A Review of Background Factors, Current Practices, and Possible Role Models* (Washington, DC: Govt. Printing Office, 1970).

recognized as more capable of handling such complaints? If so, what makes them more effective? Do factors outside the control of a police agency influence the frequency with which complaints are received? Are noise complaints from apartment dwellers related to the manner in which the buildings are constructed? And what influence, if any, does the relative effectiveness of the police in handling noise complaints have on the complaining citizen's willingness to cooperate with the police in dealing with other problems, including criminal conduct traditionally defined as much more serious?

Considerable knowledge about some of the problems with which the police struggle has been generated outside police agencies by criminologists, sociologists, psychologists, and psychiatrists. But as has been pointed out frequently, relatively few of these findings have influenced the formal policies and operating decisions of practitioners.[24] Admittedly, the quality of many such studies is poor. Often the practitioner finds it difficult to draw out from the research its significance for his operations. But most important, the police have not needed to employ these studies because they have not been expected to address specific problems in a systematic manner. If the police were pressured to examine in great detail the problems they are expected to handle, a review of the literature would become routine. If convinced that research findings had practical value, police administrators would develop into more sophisticated users of such research; their responsible criticism could, in turn, contribute to upgrading the quality and usefulness of future research efforts.

Exploring Alternatives

After the information assembled about a specific problem is analyzed, a fresh, uninhibited search should be made for alternative responses that might be an improvement over what is currently being done. The nature of such a search will differ from past efforts in that, presumably, the problem itself will be better defined and understood, the commitment to past approaches (such as focusing primarily on the identification and prosecution of offenders) will be shelved temporarily, and the search will be much broader, extending well beyond the present or future potential of just the police.

But caution is in order. Those intent on improving the operations of the criminal justice system (by divesting it of some of its current burdens) and those who are principally occupied with improving the operating efficiency of police agencies frequently recommend that the problem simply be shifted to some other agency of government or to the private sector. Such recommendations often glibly imply that a health department or a social work agency, for example, is better equipped to handle the problem. Experience over the past decade, however, shows that this is rarely the case.[25] Merely shifting responsibility for the problem, without some assurance that more adequate provisions have been made for dealing with it, achieves nothing.

Police in many jurisdictions, in a commendable effort to employ alternatives to the criminal justice system, have arranged to make referrals to various social, health, and legal agencies. By tying into the services provided by the whole range of other helping agencies in the community, the police in these cities have taken a giant step toward improving the quality of their response. But there is a great danger that referral will come to be an end in itself, that the police and others advocating the use of such a system will not concern themselves adequately with the consequences of referral. If referral does not lead to reducing the citizens' problem, nothing will have been gained by this

[24]See, for example, the comments of Marvin Wolfgang in a congressionally sponsored discussion of federal support for criminal justice research, reported in the U.S., House, Committee on the Judiciary, Subcommittee on Crime, *New Directions for Federal Involvement in Crime Control* (Washington, DC: Govt. Printing Office. 1999). Wolfgang claims that research in criminology and criminal justice has had little impact on the administration of justice or on major decision makers.

[25]For further discussion of this point, see American Bar Association, *The Urban Police Function, Approved Draft* (Chicago: American Bar Association, 1973), pp. 41–42.

change. It may even cause harm. Expectations that are raised and not fulfilled may lead to further frustration; the original problem may, as a consequence, be compounded; and the resulting bitterness about government services may feed the tensions that develop in urban areas.

The search for alternatives obviously need not start from scratch. There is much to build on. Crime prevention efforts of some police agencies and experiments with developing alternatives to the criminal justice system and with diverting cases from the system should be reassessed for their impact on specific problems; those that appear to have the greatest potential should be developed and promoted.[26] Several alternatives should be explored for each problem.

1. Physical and Technical Changes

Can the problem be reduced or eliminated through physical or technical changes? Some refer to this as part of a program of "reducing opportunities" or "target hardening." Extensive effort has already gone into reducing, through urban design, factors that contribute to behavior requiring police attention.[27] Improved locks on homes and cars, the requirement of exact fares on buses,[28] and the provision for mailing social security checks directly to the recipients banks exemplify recent efforts to control crime through this alternative.

What additional physical or technical changes might be made that would have an effect on the problem? Should such changes be mandatory, or can they be voluntary? What incentives might be offered to encourage their implementation?

2. Changes in the Provision of Government Services

Can the problem be alleviated by changes in other government services? Some of the most petty but annoying problems the police must handle originate in the policies, operating practices, and inadequacies of other public agencies: the scattering of garbage because of delays in collection, poor housing conditions because of lax code enforcement, the interference with traffic by children playing because they have not been provided with adequate playground facilities, the uncapping of hydrants on hot summer nights because available pools are closed. Most police agencies long ago developed procedures for relaying reports on such conditions to the appropriate government service. But relatively few police agencies see their role as pressing the changes in policies and operations that would eliminate the recurrence of the same problems. Yet the police are the only people who see and who must become responsible for the collective negative consequences of current policies.

3. Conveying Reliable Information

What many people want, when they turn to the police with their problems, is simply reliable information.[29] The tenant who is locked out by his landlord for failure to pay the rent wants to know his rights to the property. The car owner whose license plates are lost or stolen wants to know what reporting obligations he has, how he goes about replacing the plates, and whether he can drive his car in the meantime. The person who suspects

---

[26]Many of these programs are summarized in David E. Aaronson et al., *The Near Justice Alternatives to Conventional Criminal Adjudication* (Washington DC: Govt. Printing Office. 1977); and David E. Aaronson et al., *Alternatives to Conventional Criminal Adjudication: Guidebook for Planners and Practitioners*, Caroline S. Cooper, ed. (Washington, DC: Govt. Printing Office, 1977).

[27]The leading work on the subject is Oscar Newman, *Defensible Space, Crime Prevention through Urban Design* (New York, Macmillan, 1972). See also Westinghouse National Issue Center, *Crime Prevention through Environmental Design…A Special Report* (Washington, DC: National League of Cities, 1977).

[28]For summary of a survey designed to assess the effect of this change, see Russell Grindle and Thomas Acciluao, "Innovations in Robbery Control," in *The Prevention and Control of Robbery*, vol. I, Floyd Feenty and Adrianne Weir, eds. (Davis, Calif: University of California, 1973), pp. 315–20.

[29]In one of the most recent of a growing number of studies of how police spend their time, it was reputed that, of the 18,012 calls made to the police serving a community of 24,000 people in a four-month period, 59.96 percent were requests for information. Police responded to 66 percent of the calls they received by providing information by telephone. See J. Robert Lilly, "What Are the Police Now Doing?" *Journal of Police Science and Administration*, January 1978, p. 56.

his neighbors of abusing their child wants to know whether he is warranted in reporting the matter to the police. And the person who receives a series of obscene telephone calls wants to know what can be done about them. Even if citizens do not ask specific questions, the best response the police can make to many requests for help is to provide accurate, concise information.

4. Developing New Skills among Police Officers

The greatest potential for improvement in the handling of some problems is in providing police officers with new forms of specialized training. This is illustrated by several recent developments. For example, the major component in the family-crisis intervention projects launched all over the country is instruction of police officers in the peculiar skills required to de-escalate highly emotional family quarrels. First aid training for police is being expanded, consistent with the current trend toward greater use of paramedics. One unpleasant task faced by the police, seldom noted by outsiders, is notifying families of the death of a family member. Often, this problem is handled poorly. In 1976, a film was made specifically to demonstrate how police should carry out this responsibility.[30] Against this background of recent developments, one should ask whether specified training can bring about needed improvement in the handling of each specific problem.

5. New Forms of Authority

Do the police need a specific, limited form of authority which they do not now have? If the most intelligent response to a problem, such as a person causing a disturbance in a bar, is to order the person to leave, should the police be authorized to issue such an order, or should they be compelled to arrest the individual in order to stop the disturbance? The same question can be asked about the estranged husband who has returned to his wife's apartment or about the group of teenagers annoying passersby at a street corner. Police

are called upon to resolve these common problems, but their authority is questionable unless the behavior constitutes a criminal offense. And even then, it may not be desirable to prosecute the offender. Another type of problem is presented by the intoxicated person who is not sufficiently incapacitated to warrant being taken into protective custody, but who apparently intends to drive his car. Should a police officer have the authority to prevent the person from driving by temporarily confiscating the car keys or, as a last resort, by taking him into protective custody? Or must the officer wait for the individual to get behind the wheel and actually attempt to drive and then make an arrest? Limited specific authority may enable the police to deal more directly and intelligently with a number of compactable situations.

6. Developing New Community Resources

Analysis of a problem may lead to the conclusion that assistance is needed from another government agency. But often the problem is not clearly within the province of an existing agency, or the agency may be unaware of the problem or, if aware, without the resources to do anything about it. In such cases, since the problem is likely to be of little concern to the community as a whole, it will probably remain the responsibility of the police, unless they themselves take the initiative, as a sort of community ombudsman, in getting others to address it.

A substantial percentage of all police business involves dealing with persons suffering from mental illness. In the most acute cases, where the individual may cause immediate harm to himself or others, the police are usually authorized to initiate an emergency commitment. Many other cases that do not warrant hospitalization nevertheless require some form of attention. The number of these situations has increased dramatically as the mental health system has begun treating more and more of its patients in the community. If the conduct of these persons, who are being

---

[30]*Death Notification* (New York: Harper & Row, 1976).

taught to cope with the world around them, creates problems for others or exceeds community tolerance, should they be referred back to a mental health agency? Or, because they are being encouraged to adjust to the reality of the community, should they be arrested if their behavior constitutes a criminal offense? How are the police to distinguish between those who have never received any assistance, and who should therefore be referred to a mental health agency, and those who are in community treatment? Should a community agency establish services for these persons comparable to the crisis-intervention services now offered by specially organized units operating in some communities?

Such crisis-intervention units are among a number of new resources that have been established in the past few years for dealing with several long-neglected problems: detoxification centers for those incapacitated by alcohol, shelters and counseling for runaways, shelters for battered wives, and support services for the victims of sexual assault. Programs are now being designed to provide a better response to citizen disputes and grievances, another long-neglected problem. Variously labeled, these programs set up quasi-judicial forums that are intended to be inexpensive, easily accessible, and geared to the specific needs of their neighborhood. LEAA has recently funded three such experimental programs, which they call Neighborhood Justice Centers.[31] These centers will receive many of their cases from the police.

Thus, the pattern of creating new services that bear a relationship with police operations is now well established, and one would expect that problem-oriented policing will lead to more services in greater variety.

7. Increased Regulation

Can the problem be handled through a tightening of regulatory codes? Where easy access to private premises is a factor, should city building codes be amended to require improved lock systems? To reduce the noise problem, should more soundproofing be required in construction? The incidence of shoplifting is determined, in part, by the number of salespeople employed, the manner in which merchandise is displayed, and the use made of various anti-shoplifting devices. Should the police be expected to combat shoplifting without regard to the merchandising practices by a given merchant, or should merchants be required by a "merchandising code" to meet some minimum standards before they can turn to the police for assistance?

8. Increased Use of City Ordinances

Does the problem call for some community sanction less drastic than a criminal sanction? Many small communities process through their local courts, as ordinance violations, as many cases of minor misconduct as possible. Of course, this requires that the community have written ordinances, usually patterned after the state statutes that define such misconduct. Several factors make this form of processing desirable for certain offenses: It is less formal than criminal action; physical detention is not necessary; cases may be disposed of without a court appearance; the judge may select from a wide range of alternative penalties: and the offender is spared the burden of a criminal record. Some jurisdictions now use a system of civil forfeitures in proceedings against persons found to be in possession of marijuana, though the legal status of the procedure is unclear in those states whose statutes define possession as criminal and call for a more severe fine or for imprisonment.

9. Use of Zoning

Much [of] policing involves resolving disputes between those who have competing interests in the use made of a given sidewalk, street park, or neighborhood. Bigger and more basic conflicts in land use were resolved long ago by zoning, a concept that is now firmly established. Recently, zoning has been used by a number of cities to limit the pornography stores and adult movie houses in a given area. And at least one city has experimented

---

[31]The concept is described in Daniel McGillis and Joan Mullen, *Neighborhood Justice Center: An Analysis of Potential Models* (Washington, DC: Govt. Printing Office, 1977). See also R. F. Conner and R. Sureka, *The Citizen Dispute Settlement Program: Restoring Disputes outside the Courts—Orlando, Florida* (Washington, DC: American Bar Association, 1977).

with the opposite approach, creating an adult entertainment zone with the hope of curtailing the spread of such establishments and simplifying the management of attendant problems. Much more experimentation is needed before any judgment can be made as to the value of zoning in such situations.

Implementing the Process

A fully developed process for systematically addressing the problems that make up police business would call for more than the three steps just explored—defining the problem, researching it and exploring alternatives. I have focused on these three because describing them may be the most effective way of communicating the nature of a problem-oriented approach to improving police service. A number of intervening steps are required to fill out the process; methods for evaluating the effectiveness of current responses, procedures for choosing from among available alternatives, means of involving the community in the decision making, procedures for obtaining the approval of the municipal officials to whom the police are formally accountable, methods for obtaining any additional funding that may be necessary, adjustment in the organization and staffing of the agency that may be required to implement an agreed-upon change, and methods for evaluating the effectiveness of the change.

How does a police agency make the shift to problem-oriented policing? Ideally the initiative will come from police administration. What is needed is not a single decision implementing a specific program or a single memorandum announcing a unique way of running the organization. The concept represents a new way of looking at the process of improving police functioning. It is a way of thinking about the police and their function that, carried out over an extended period, would be reflected in all that the administrator does: in the relationship with personnel, in the priorities he sets in his own work schedule, in what he focuses on in addressing community groups, in the choice of training curriculums, and in the questions raised with local and state legislators. Once introduced, this orientation would affect subordinates, gradually filter through the rest of the organization, and reach other administrators and agencies as well.

An administrator's success will depend heavily, in particular, on the use made of planning staff, for systematic analysis of substantive problems requires developing a capacity within the organization to collect and analyze data and to conduct evaluations of the effectiveness of police operations. Police planners (now employed in significant numbers) will have to move beyond their traditional concern with operating procedures into what might be characterized as "product research."

The police administrator who focuses on the substance of policing should be able to count on support from others in key positions in the police field. Colleges with programs especially designed for police personnel may exert considerable leadership through their choice of offerings and through the subject matter of individual courses. In an occupation in which so much deference is paid to the value of a college education, if college instructors reinforce the impression that purely administrative matters are the most important issues in policing, police personnel understandably will not develop their interest beyond this concern.

Likewise, the LEAA, its state and local offspring, and other grant-making organizations have a unique opportunity to draw the attention of operating personnel to the importance of addressing substantive problems. The manner in which these organizations invest their funds sends a strong message to the police about what is thought to be worthwhile.

Effect on the Organization

In the context of this reordering of police priorities, efforts to improve the staffing, management, and procedures of police agencies must continue.

Those who have been strongly committed to improving policing through better administration and organization may be disturbed by any move to subordinate their interest: to a broader concern with the end product of policing. However, a problem-oriented approach to police improvement may actually contribute in several important ways to achieving their objectives.

The approach calls for the police to take greater initiative in attempting to deal with problems rather than resign themselves to living with them. It calls for tapping police expertise. It calls for the police to be more aggressive partners with other public agencies. These changes, which would place the police in a much more positive light in the community, would also contribute significantly to improving the working environment within a police agency—an environment that suffers much from the tendency of the police to assume responsibility for problems which are insolvable if ignored by others. And an improved working environment increases, in turn, the potential for recruiting and keeping qualified personnel and for bringing about needed organizational change.

Focusing on problems, because it is a practical and concrete approach, is attractive to both citizens and the police. By contrast, some of the most frequent proposals for improving police operations, because they do not produce immediate and specifically identifiable results, have no such attraction. A problem-oriented approach, with its greater appeal, has the potential for becoming a vehicle through which long-sought organizational change might be more effectively and more rapidly achieved.

Administrative rule making, for example, has gained considerable support from policy makers and some police administrators as a way of structuring police discretion with the expectation that applying the concept would improve the quality of the decisions made by the police in the field. Yet many police administrators regard administrative rule making as an idea without practical significance. By contrast, police administrators are usually enthusiastic if invited to explore the problem of car theft or vandalism. And within such exploration, there is the opportunity to demonstrate the value of structuring police discretion in responding to reports of vandalism and car theft. Approached from this practical point of view, the concept of administrative rule making is more likely to be implemented.

Long-advocated changes in the structure and operations of police agencies have been achieved because of a concentrated concern with a given problem. The focus on the domestic disturbance, originally in New York and now elsewhere, introduced the generalist-specialist concept that has enabled many police agendas to make more effective use of their personnel; the problem in controlling narcotics and the high mobility of drug sellers motivated police agencies in many metropolitan areas to pool their resources in special investigative units, thereby achieving in a limited way one of the objectives of those who have urged consolidation of police agencies; and the recent interest in the crime of rape has resulted in widespread backing for the establishment of victim-support programs. Probably the support for any of these changes could not have been generated without the problem-oriented context in which they have been advocated.

An important factor contributing to the successes is that a problem-oriented approach to improvement is less likely to be seen as a direct challenge to the police establishment and the prevailing police value system. As a consequence, rank-and-file personnel do not resist and subvert the resulting changes. Traditional programs to improve the police—labeled as effort to "change," "upgrade," or "reform" the police or to "achieve minimum standards"—require that police officers openly acknowledge their own deficiencies. Rank-and-file officers are much more likely to support an innovation that is cast in the form of a new response to an old problem—a problem with which they have struggled for many years and which they would like to see handled more effectively. It may be that addressing the quality of the police product will turn out to be the most effective way of achieving the objectives that have for so long been the goal of police reform.

DISCUSSION QUESTIONS

1. Explain what Herman Goldstein means by the "ends over means syndrome."

2. What are some of Goldstein's suggestions for alternative response to problems identified by police officers?

3. How does administrative rule making play a role in problem-oriented policing?

READING 4

The terrorist attacks on September 11, 2001, changed the lives of Americans. Policing in the United States has also changed significantly since 9/11. American policing agencies have begun to shift their attention to the collection and use of intelligence to help them as they conduct their work—this is called intelligence-led policing (ILP). This paper discusses the conceptual foundation for ILP and also examines policy developments that have influenced the adoption of ILP by American police agencies.

Intelligence-Led Policing

Conceptual and Functional Considerations for Public Policy

David L. Carter and Jeremy G. Carter

Policing in the post-9/11 environment has entered what may be referred to as the Homeland Security era (Ratcliffe, 2008b). Specifically with respect to intelligence-led policing (ILP), there are a number of public policy factors that are shaping this new paradigm. The authors will discuss the conceptual foundation for ILP as influenced by the British experience followed by an examination of significant policy developments in the United States that are influencing the adoption of ILP by American law enforcement agencies. Although concern has been expressed by police leaders that intelligence activities may undermine community policing initiatives, the authors argue that ILP is a complementary expansion of the community policing concept.

 ## British National Intelligence Model (NIM) and ILP[1]

When seeking to employ a new concept, policy makers often look to other models in an attempt to learn what works and adopt (or adapt) that practice. The British

have a long and more sophisticated legacy in criminal intelligence than U.S. law enforcement, hence the value of examining the British experience. All 43 provincial British constabularies, as well as the London Metropolitan Police, have had some form of fairly long-standing intelligence function to deal with organized crime, drugs, and other complex crimes unique to their jurisdictions.

At a national level, the National Drugs Intelligence Unit was created in the 1980s to deal with the significant increase in transnational drug trafficking and associated crime. In 1992, the drugs intelligence service was expanded and renamed the National Criminal Intelligence Service (NCIS) to deal with all forms of organized crime, not just illicit drugs. In particular, the NCIS evolved in response to the changing political environment associated with the European Union (EU), where, among other factors, immigration and customs checkpoints were eliminated for persons traveling between the EU member countries thereby making it easier for criminal enterprises to operate in Western Europe. In 2006, a new intelligence-led agency was created, the Serious Organised Crime Agency

[1]Much of the information in this section is based on the first author's experience in working with the British police for more than 20 years.

(SOCA), that integrated the NCIS along with a national investigative body, the National Crime Squad (NCS), and the drug enforcement functions of Her Majesty's Revenue and Customs (HMRC) Service. As will be seen, these changes were influenced by government-wide philosophical changes that occurred over the previous decade.

In the 1990s, the British government began implementing a business-plan philosophy for all elements of government service (Ratcliffe, 2002). This had two fundamental initiatives: either privatize portions of government service or apply a business model to remaining government services. This move had wide-ranging effects. For example, the British National Rail Service—BritRail—was sold in pieces to various private companies. Similarly, local governments privatized such functions as vehicle maintenance and janitorial services. The national police training function in England and Wales was also changed to a quasiprivate organization called Centrex, which has evolved once again to be part of the National Policing Improvement Agency (NPIA).[2] The point to note is that the mandate to use business processes permeated virtually every aspect of British government, including the police.

As part of this movement, in the late 1990s, the NCIS, with advice from Her Majesty's Inspectorate of Constabulary (HMIC),[3] developed the British NIM, which was initially released in 2000 and formally adopted in 2002 as accepted policy by the British Association of Chief Police Officers (ACPO), which is a national police policy-making body. The NIM followed the government policy of using a business process model to deal with crime control and employed the ILP philosophy to introduce intelligence into virtually all aspects of the policing business plan.

The adoption of the NIM by ACPO meant that the chief constables of the provincial police forces in England and Wales agreed to adopt the NIM and adapt it to meet the needs of their policing area—This change represented the transition between traditional intelligence processes to ILP.[4] The intelligence function within the provincial constabularies largely deals with violent crime, football hooliganism, nonserious (local) organized crime, and unique local recurring crime problems. At the national level, the intelligence function of SOCA is responsible for transnational organized crime, terrorism, and other criminal threats to Britain that emerge from outside the United Kingdom.

The British police adoption of ILP, as per the NIM, has not been easy. Many did not understand the concept; it required a reallocation of resources and added a significant analytic component to each police force. The NIM was criticized by many as being an esoteric model that created a great deal of data and new processes that were not providing good value for [the] money (Association of Chief Police Officers [ACPO], 2005). Its full implementation has been much slower than anticipated, and as one might assume, some of the police forces have embraced the concept much more broadly than others.

Despite these problems, there have also been important successes attributable to the NIM. There are many lessons learned from the British experience that can be adopted in the United States, and there is a unique body of model practices, including analytic models, that are available from the HMIC. However, American law enforcement agencies have a significantly different experience in law enforcement intelligence that prohibits wide-scale adoption of British ILP, with some notable exceptions in the predominantly larger

---

[2]National Policing Improvement Agency supports police service by providing expertise in areas as diverse as information and communications technology, support to information and intelligence sharing, core police processes, managing change, and recruiting, developing, and deploying people.

[3]The Her Majesty's Inspectorate of Constabulary (HMIC) is an organization in the British Home Office responsible for inspecting the British police forces to ensure they are efficient organizations employing good practice and providing good value for money in their service (Her Majesty's Inspectorate of Constabulary, 1997).

[4]England and Wales have 43 provincial constabularies, whose chief constable is responsible to the local police authority (somewhat akin to a board of police commissioners). The commissioner of the London Metropolitan Police reports to the British Home Secretary and has much broader authority and flexibility. Although British Association of Chief Police Officers (ACPO) policy is not binding on the London Metropolitan Police, it has also adopted the National Intelligence Model (NIM).

U.S. major urban areas. Some perspective will provide greater understanding.

The creation of Britain's 43 police forces was a product of amalgamating many smaller police agencies in the 1960s. The smallest of these constabularies has around 900 sworn constables who are policing sizeable geographic areas with both urban and rural characteristics. Most of the provincial police agencies have 1,200 to 1,600 sworn personnel. Although not a national police force, there are national standards that apply to all of the agencies for training, promotion, operations, and salary (Bayley, 1992). Indeed, personnel may laterally transfer between the constabularies.

Given the size of these police forces and their reasonable operating budgets,[5] all have the resources to hire analysts and the flexibility to reassign personnel to meet the needs of a comprehensive new initiative such as ILP. This is not meant to infer that the constabularies are flush with money and personnel; rather, one finds significantly more flexibility, resources, and diverse expertise in large agencies than in the small departments typically found in the United States. Moreover, having a solid history of sophisticated law enforcement intelligence, the British police service was able to adopt the NIM and, consequently, ILP with greater ease than in the United States.

The American Experience With Law Enforcement Intelligence

Historically, the vast majority of American law enforcement agencies have had no intelligence capacity or training on the intelligence process—Intelligence was typically viewed as something only needed by the largest agencies. For many American agencies that did have an intelligence capacity, the legacy has also been somewhat problematic. Early law enforcement initiatives typically had no analysis and essentially consisted of dossiers kept on individuals who were suspicious or were deemed to be threats of some sort, often based on intuitive, rather than empirical, threat

criteria (Carter, 2004). In the 1960s and 1970s, many agencies were sued under federal civil rights legislation for maintaining intelligence records on people who had not committed crimes but were engaged in expressive behaviors and ideologies that were deemed to be unconventional or un-American. Although these practices generally no longer exist, the legacy lives on, with many members of the public remaining suspicious of current law enforcement intelligence initiatives (German & Stanley, 2007).

Beyond the civil rights issues, the intelligence function was often ill-defined, typically remaining out of the mainstream of state and local law enforcement activities. There were few analysts and many of these were poorly trained, often inheriting the title of analyst as a result of longevity, not expertise. Hence, it was often difficult to distinguish what the intelligence unit, as an organizational component, contributed to the total law enforcement mission. Although there were certainly exceptions to this characterization, this was the status quo for many American law enforcement agencies. Although this has changed dramatically, history remains a difficult obstacle to overcome.

Comparing U.S. and U.K. Law Enforcement Intelligence

In comparison to the British police structure, the roughly 16,000 U.S. law enforcement agencies, most of which have 10 or fewer sworn officers, have diverse policing standards both between and within states. They often have limited budgets, all of which typically come from local funds with some exceptions in the form of short-term federal grants. Federal standards and recommendations are largely unenforceable unless tied explicitly to special conditions of a grant.

In light of these radical differences and the significantly different history of law enforcement intelligence, when one compares U.S. and U.K. policing, it is unreasonable to assume that the basic practices of the NIM, as found in the United Kingdom, and, by

---

[5]The British national budget, through the Home Office, provides 51% of the funding for each of the provincial police forces; 49% comes from local funds. This permits the Home Office to exert greater influence for national standards and priorities, although each chief constable retains significant autonomy in practice.

extension, ILP can be effectively implemented in the United States on a short-term wholesale basis. In the United States, law enforcement needs to start at a far more basic level. A functional model of ILP must be developed that has both the flexibility and applicability to the U.S. law enforcement landscape.

At the outset, ILP should be viewed as a philosophy, not a process (Ratcliffe & Guidetti, 2008). Indeed, American law enforcement agencies should rely on this philosophy to develop new intelligence-based processes that functionally balance each agency's jurisdictions, characteristics, and resources (Ratcliffe, 2005). The lessons learned from community policing can be a valuable guide (Carter, 2002). Developing ILP in a law enforcement agency requires two developmental activities. One activity is to devise the information collection framework to manage threats within a jurisdiction, and the other is to develop the organizational infrastructure to support the ILP initiative. The foundation for these two changes has been laid in post-9/11 intelligence developments.

 ## Post-9/11 Changes to Law Enforcement Intelligence

In the post-9/11 era, law enforcement intelligence experienced a rapid change. In October 2001, about 6 weeks after the 9/11 attacks, at the International Association of Chiefs of Police (IACP) annual meeting in Toronto, Ontario, Canada, the Police Investigative Operations Committee discussed the need for state, local, and tribal law enforcement (SLTLE) agencies to reengineer their intelligence function; for more law enforcement agencies to develop an intelligence capacity; and the need for national leadership to establish standards and direction for the intelligence process in these agencies. From this meeting, the IACP, with funding from the Office of Community Oriented Policing Services (COPS), held an Intelligence Summit in March 2002. The summit made a series of recommendations including development of a criminal intelligence sharing plan and the adoption of ILP (International Association of Chiefs of Police [IACP], 2002).

The Global Justice Information Sharing Initiative (Global), a formal advisory group funded by the Office of Justice Programs, was already in existence with the charge of developing processes and standards to efficaciously share information across the criminal justice system. In response to the IACP Intelligence Summit recommendations, Global created a new subgroup: the Global Intelligence Working Group (GIWG). The purpose of the GIWG was to move forward with the recommendations from the summit. The first GIWG product was the National Criminal Intelligence Sharing Plan (NCISP).

The intent of the NCISP was to provide SLTLE agencies (particularly those that did not have an established intelligence function) with the necessary tools and resources to develop, gather, access, receive, and share intelligence. To accomplish this, the plan established a series of national standards that have been formally recognized by the professional law enforcement community as the proper role and processes for the contemporary application of law enforcement intelligence (Carter, 2004). The plan is having a significant effect on organizational realignment, information sharing philosophy, and training in America's law enforcement agencies.

One of the key recommendations from the NCISP was for American law enforcement agencies to adopt ILP "to provide public safety decision makers the information they need to protect the lives of our citizens" (Global Intelligence Working Group [GIWG], 2003, p. v). Ironically, although the plan extensively discusses the need and importance of ILP, it neither defines the concept and identifies the components of ILP nor explains how the concept should be implemented.

At virtually the same time the NCISP was created, the Department of Homeland Security (DHS) was developing plans to meet its mission, mandated in Homeland Security Presidential Directive-8, "to prevent, respond to, and recover from threatened and actual domestic terrorist attacks, major disasters, and other emergencies" (Department of Homeland Security [DHS], 2003, p. h). A critical part of this initiative was to define critical knowledge, skills, abilities, and processes—that is, capabilities—that were necessary for law enforcement and emergency services personnel to perform these tasks. These capabilities have been articulated in detail in the Target Capabilities List (TCL). Intended to protect the nation from all hazards, "the TCL is a national-level, generic model of operationally ready capabilities defining all-hazards preparedness" (DHS, 2007, p. 1). The list is broken down into different areas associated with prevention and response. In the prevent mission area there are two specific intelligence-related target capabilities: information gathering and recognition of indicators, and warnings and intelligence analysis and production. The importance of these developments was that a new component of intelligence was added to the ILP mission: Homeland Security intelligence is defined as follows:

> [It is] the collection and analysis of information concerned with non-criminal domestic threats to critical infrastructure, community health and public safety for the purpose of preventing the threat or mitigating the effects of the threat. (Carter, in press)

These new intelligence responsibilities have emerged within the Homeland Security framework—that intelligence activities at the state, local, and tribal levels must assess threats posed by all hazards. Although there are certainly gray areas within this framework, the key challenge is for law enforcement agencies to focus on threats posed by hazards that have implications for public safety and order-maintenance responsibilities in addition to criminal threats. Thus, another component was entered into the ILP equation.

A final element in the evolution of law enforcement intelligence as related to the current discussion was the creation of the Information Sharing Environment (ISE) as required by the Intelligence Reform and Terrorism Prevention Act (IRTPA) of 2004. Although this legislation focused on the intelligence community, nearly one third of the action steps in the Information Sharing Environment Implementation Plan is also directed toward SLTLE agencies. The ISE seeks to "implement an effective, widespread culture of information sharing, balanced with a need for security and the protection of privacy and civil liberties" (Program Manager—Information Sharing Environment [PM-ISE], 2007, p. 63). The Implementation Plan provides a detailed process and action plan that indicate significant expectations for SLTLE to be participants in the ISE. The heart of information sharing and generation of raw information at the state, local, and tribal levels is intended to be via ILP.

The Concept of ILP

The ILP is envisioned as a tool for information sharing both within law enforcement agencies and between all participants in the ISE. The concept aids law enforcement agencies in identifying threats and developing responses to prevent those threats from reaching fruition in America's communities (IACP, 2002). Despite the demand for increased partnerships for information sharing among agencies being emphasized (McGarrell, Freilich, & Chermak, 2007), there remains a common misunderstanding of how this will be achieved. The challenge, however, is that there are differing views of the ILP concept and its application. Indeed, there is a movement toward the adoption of ILP without a universally accepted definition or operational philosophy. The intent of this discussion is to provide a perspective of ILP in the context of contemporary law enforcement intelligence developments in the Homeland Security era, integrating the more commonly accepted principles of community and problem-oriented policing.

It is clear that there is an expectation that SLTLE agencies will adopt ILP; however, the following question remains: How is this accomplished? There is no manual of practice for ILP because, like community policing (Carter, 2002; Manning, 1984), it must be tailored to the characteristics of each individual agency. The ILP may be characterized as follows:

> [It is] an underlying philosophy of how intelligence fits into the operations of a law enforcement organization. Rather than being

simply an information clearinghouse that has been appended to the organization, ILP provides strategic integration of intelligence into the overall mission of the organization. (Carter, 2004, p. 4)

Thus, the concept of ILP must be created through an inclusive development process that ensures it is integrated with an agency's goals and functions, its capabilities, and the characteristics of both the agency and the jurisdiction it serves. It is not an add-on responsibility to the agency but an adaptation to more efficiently and effectively deal with multijurisdictional threats and serious crime that touches communities. However, obstacles will be prevalent with this shift toward an intelligence led operations approach. Shifts in organizational decision-making and problem-solving approaches have been problematic for law enforcement agencies (Weisburd, Mastrofski, McNally, Greenspan, & Willis, 2003; Willis, Mastrofski, Weisburd, & Greenspan, 2003). There are no shortcuts in the process—It requires creativity, organizational introspection, and a willingness to adapt the organization.

Commitment to the ILP concept is not simply a macro- or microlevel decision, but it is a multilevel process. Given the nature of police organizations as highly bureaucratic and structured, successful policy implementation can often be difficult (O'Toole & Montjoy, 1984). As such, it is necessary for training programs to provide educational opportunities for personnel at all levels of law enforcement agencies. Chief executives often have a more comprehensive understanding of ILP as compared to line-level officers, similar to community policing (Kratcoski & Noonan, 1995). This lack of understanding among line-level officers with respect to ILP can be attributed to resistance to new policing methods (Ratcliffe, 2008a) or poor perceptions of outputs on behalf of sworn officers and civilian analysts (Cope, 2004). The principles of ILP are similar to those of community policing (Clarke, 2006), and—as such—educational training across all levels of the police organization explaining the benefits of ILP should yield positive results (Meese, 1993).

Defining ILP

There is no universally accepted definition of ILP, although the components of most definitions are the same or at least similar. The Bureau of Justice Assistance (BJA) produced an unpublished memorandum that was intended to guide the solicitation and review of violence reduction grants using ILP processes (Bureau of Justice Assistance [BJA], 2007). The conceptual foundation of ILP provided by BJA was articulated as building on the lessons from problem-oriented policing and CompStat, applying these principles to a threat-based environment of multijurisdictional complex criminality. The conceptual foundation embraces post-9/11 initiatives in law enforcement intelligence as previously discussed.

In the document, BJA (2007) stated, "ILP can be defined as a collaborative law enforcement approach combining problem-solving policing, information sharing and police accountability, with enhanced intelligence operations" (p. 1). Building on this conceptual foundation, the authors propose an operational definition of ILP:

> The collection and analysis of information related to crime and conditions that contribute to crime, resulting in an actionable intelligence product intended to aid law enforcement in developing tactical responses to threats and/or strategic planning related to emerging or changing threats.

Dissecting this definition provides further insight. An essential part of the intelligence process is collecting raw information that may be used in the analysis. Collection should be focused to identify and understand threats that emerge within a jurisdiction. This focus is often determined by an analyst, who will define intelligence requirements, and it is based on information received from both officers and citizens in the form of suspicious activity reports (SARs). The key point to note is that collection seeks raw information within defined threat parameters that is essential for effective analysis (Carter, 2004).

Analysis is the scientific approach to problem solving. It relies on deductive and inductive reasoning to define requirements and forecast threats (Ratcliffe, 2008a). Analysis may be quantitative, notably for strategic analysis, but it is frequently qualitative (for both tactical and strategic analysis). The Office of the Director of National Intelligence (ODNI) has explained that analysis is a process in the production of intelligence in which intelligence information is subjected to systematic examination to identify significant facts and derive conclusions (Ramsey, 2007). The analytic process is synergistic, providing integrated meaning and deriving knowledge from diverse raw facts. Moreover, analysis is used to define intelligence gaps and articulate requirements.

As ILP focuses on threats, it becomes essential to identify variables within a community and the surrounding region that support the generation and maturation of crime. These can be wide ranging: the emergence of organized criminal elements within the region who traffic in drugs or guns; the emergence of an extremist group that articulates hate or violence; conflict within a region that may be a breeding ground for violence between racial, ethnic, or religious groups; and a variety of unique characteristics that are idiosyncratic to a given community, such as proximity to an international border that contributes to criminal threats. It is important that the information collected provide insight on the existence of the conditions, factors that will exacerbate the conditions, and individuals who may be instrumental in exploiting the conditions to commit terrorism or crime.

Another critical element of the analytic process is to produce actionable intelligence. Paraphrasing public presentations by former FBI Executive Assistant Director for Intelligence Maureen Baginski, intelligence helps law enforcement officers make decisions. Essentially, for intelligence to be useful it must provide direction to develop and execute plans. A law enforcement agency must be able to take an intelligence report and implement some type of activity that will prevent or mitigate crime. This means that the intelligence produced by an analyst will drive operational responses and strategic planning for threats.

With actionable intelligence, a law enforcement agency has sufficient information to develop interventions to threats. The intelligence report may describe either imminent threats to a community or region, wanted persons who may pose threats, or threat methodologies about which law enforcement officers should be aware. The basic premise is this: The agency must be able to use the information in an operational manner. Moreover, actionable intelligence should ensure that the right information is placed into the hands of the people who can do something about the threat.

Building on the concept of intelligence being actionable is the provision of both tactical and strategic analysis. Depending on the nature of the threat, a wide array of tactical responses may be deemed appropriate, ranging from increasing mass transit security procedures to being aware of suspicious activities at a potential intelligence target. Intelligence from tactical analysis is all about prevention: Using information related to terrorism and crime threats for strategies that will eliminate or mitigate short-term and immediate threats (Kelling & Bratton, 2006). Tactical intelligence is epitomized by the following question: What type of operational response can be developed using this intelligence?

Threats within a community typically change over time. Strategic analysis is used primarily for planning and resource allocation to understand the changing nature of the threat picture. Information is provided to decision makers about the changing nature, characteristics, and methodologies of threats and emerging threat idiosyncrasies for the purpose of developing response strategies and reallocating resources. For example, if a community has never had a problem with right-to-life extremists and a new clinic opens providing abortion procedures, a strategic analysis may provide insight on whether the clinic and its personnel will be subject to any type of threat by extremist groups.

When strategic analysis is used, plans may be developed to either prevent a threat from maturing or mitigate the threat should it emerge. It is epitomized by the following question: What future plans and resources must be developed, and how must they be configured, to meet threats defined in the strategic analysis?

Community- and Problem-Oriented Policing and ILP

A common concern expressed by police executives is that the shift toward ILP—largely as a result of increased Homeland Security responsibilities—may require a shift of resources away from community policing. It becomes a question of how community policing and ILP are integrated. As will be seen, there are more commonalities between the two than one may intuitively expect. Indeed, new dimensions of ILP depend on strong community relationships. Crime will continue to be a critical responsibility for the police as will the need for community support. Moreover, with increased social tension as a result of Homeland Security initiatives (Moynihan, 2005), the need is even greater to maintain a close, interactive dialogue between law enforcement and the community.

Community policing has developed skills in many law enforcement officers that directly support new ILP responsibilities: Problem solving, environmental scanning, effective communications with the public, fear reduction, and community mobilization to deal with problems are among the important attributes community policing brings to this challenge (Haarr, 2001). The NCISP observed these factors:

> Over the past decade, simultaneous to federally led initiatives to improve intelligence gathering, thousands of community-policing officers have been building close and productive relationships with the citizens they serve. The benefits of these relationships are directly related to information and intelligence sharing: COP officers have immediate and unfettered access to local, neighborhood information as it develops. Citizens are aware of, and seek out COP officers to provide them with new information that may be useful to criminal interdiction or long-term problem solving. The positive nature of COP/citizen relationships promotes a continuous and reliable transfer of information from one to the other. It is time to maximize the potential for community-policing efforts to serve as a gateway of locally based information to prevent terrorism, and all other crimes. (GIWG, 2003, p. 4)

These factors precipitated the development of ILP as an underlying philosophy of how intelligence fits into the operations of a law enforcement organization. As one component of its philosophy, ILP employs community policing principles, building on tactics and methodologies developed during years of community-policing experimentation. The following comparisons illustrate this point. From an information management perspective, community policing utilizes information gained from citizens to help define the parameters of community problems whereas ILP relies on information input as the essential ingredient for intelligence analysis. Two-way communication with the public is essential for community policing as information is sought from the public about offenders while disseminating critical information to the public aids in crime prevention and fear reduction. In terms of ILP, communications from the public can provide valuable information for the intelligence cycle. When threats are defined with specific information, communicating critical information to citizens may help prevent a terrorist attack and, like community policing, will reduce fear (Moore, 1992). Scientific data analysis provides a critical crime analysis component in the CompStat process (Shane, 2004) and also serves as a key ingredient for intelligence-based threat management. Lastly, problem solving allows community policing to reconcile community conditions that are precursors to crime and disorder. Within ILP, this same process is used for intelligence to reconcile factors related to vulnerable targets of criminal extremists or the trafficking of illegal commodities by criminal enterprises.

Like community policing, ILP requires an investment of effort by all components of the organization as well as the community (Maguire, 1997).

Gone are the days when intelligence units operated in relative anonymity. Based on the precepts of the ILP philosophy and the standards of the NCISP, law enforcement intelligence is an organization-wide responsibility that relies on a symbiotic relationship with residents.

Comparing ILP and CompStat

The CompStat process, with its origins at the New York Police Department (Henry, 2003), has been an important tool for law enforcement agencies to effectively deal with crime trends on a timely basis by relying on effective analysis, relentless follow-up, and organizational accountability. The process has been adopted—in varying forms—by many law enforcement agencies across the United States and several foreign countries with consistent success. There has been a solid foundation of research supporting CompStat as a crime management tool that demonstrates the value of innovative approaches to law enforcement problems (Dorriety, 2005; Henry, 2003).

As law enforcement personnel grapple with understanding ILP, many have suggested that it is the same as CompStat (Wood & Shearing, 2007). Certainly, there are important similarities that will help in the adoption of ILP. However, there are also important substantive differences that must be similarly recognized. At the heart of the matter is this fact: CompStat and ILP are different based on a number of functional variables that are illustrated in Table 1. As can be seen, ILP is concerned with all crimes and all threats, not just terrorism. However, the nature of crime that ILP focuses on is typically multijurisdictional and often complex criminality, such as criminal enterprises.

The value of CompStat is the identification of a crime series or serious crime within a jurisdiction (i.e., hot spots) based on a timely analysis of incident reports. The analysis of data captured via crime reporting can provide important information—such as geographical parameters and modus operandi—that can be used to forecast a crime series in the immediate future, aid in problem solving and provide descriptive information, such as behaviors, targets, and criminal instruments that operational units may use to apprehend perpetrators, disrupt criminal activity, or alter crime-generating environments (McDonald, 2002).

Conversely, ILP focuses on threats rather than crimes that have occurred. The threat information may be derived from SARs filed by an officer, tips and leads submitted by community members, significant changes in sociodemographics within a region, or other indicators (some of which may be collateral crimes) that reasonably suggest the presence or emergence of a serious multijurisdictional crime problem. Rather than analyze information and evidence derived from incident reports, the intelligence analyst must define intelligence requirements consisting of information that the analyst needs to more definitively identify the threat and factors that are contributing to the threat's evolution (Carter, in press). Similarly, to be effective, both community policing and ILP require feedback on information analysis—whether it is crime analysis or intelligence analysis—to be consistently informed of potential problems or threats that may be encountered during the course of their shift (Carter, 2002).

In this regard, what types of information do street officers need from the intelligence function? Ideally, intelligence analysis should address four broad questions:

1. Who poses threats? This response identifies and describes behaviors of people in movements or ideologies who pose criminal threats to community safety.

2. Who is doing what with whom? This includes the identities, descriptions, and characteristics of conspirators or people who provide logistics in support of terrorism and criminal enterprises.

3. What is the modus operandi of the threat? Intelligence analysis seeks to identify how criminal enterprises operate. It also seeks to determine what criminal, terrorist, or extremist groups typically target and the common methods of attacking the targets.

4. What is needed to catch offenders and prevent crime incidents or trends? Intelligence requirements seek specific types of information that are needed to fully understand the threat environment.

Both CompStat and ILP are prevention oriented and are driven by an information flow coming from the line-level upward (Moore, 2003). Intelligence awareness training for street officers recognizes that officers on patrol have a strong likelihood of observing

Table 1 Comparison of CompStat and Intelligence-Led Policing

Similarities of CompStat and Intelligence-Led Policing[a]
Both have a goal of prevention
Commitment to the concept by the chief executive is essential
Analysis serves as the basis for operational responses
Processes for constant raw information flow for analysis must be in place
Community engagement is critical for reporting suspicious activities
Intervention activities are driven by definable evidence of crime and threats
Administrative and organizational flexibility are required
Research and lessons learned serve as the basis for creative intervention
Managers and supervisors are held demonstrably accountable

Substantive Differences of CompStat and Intelligence-Led Policing	
CompStat	*Intelligence-Led Policing*
Intrajurisdiction	Multijurisdiction
Incident driven	Threat driven
Analysis based on known facts from reported crime data and investigations	Analysis based on tips, leads, suspicious activity reports, and information collection
Focuses on crime sprees and incident trends with intent to apprehend specific offenders	Focuses on root causes and conditions that contribute to serious crime and terrorism
Relies on crime mapping, incident analysis, and modus operandi analysis	Relies on link analysis, commodity flow, transaction analysis, and association analysis
Time sensitive (24 hr feedback)	Strategic (inherently long term)
Predominant focus on street crime (burglary, robbery, homicide, assault, etc.)	Predominant focus on criminal enterprises (terrorism, organized crime, etc.)
Reported criminal incidents drive collection and analytic parameters	Intelligence requirements drive collection and analytic parameters

[a]There are important lessons learned from CompStat that can be applied to intelligence-led policing.

circumstances and people that may signify a threat or suggest the presence of a criminal enterprise. As previously mentioned, the patrol officer must be trained to regularly channel that information to the intelligence unit for input into the intelligence cycle for analysis. Like community policing, this requires new responsibilities for patrol officers and organizational flexibility to permit officers to explore new dimensions of crimes and community problems that traditionally have not been part of a patrol officer's responsibilities (Fleming & Lafferty, 2000). Although there are fundamental similarities, the methodology and focus of ILP is notably different—and more difficult—than CompStat because of the differences in the raw data.

Conclusions

The authors have argued that although the British experience with ILP has provided an important foundation for U.S. initiatives, there are important differences in legacy and functional responsibilities that limit the wholesale adoption of the British model. Among those limitations has been the array of post-9/11 federal standards for the American law enforcement intelligence process, including the new dimension of Homeland Security intelligence. Although the implementation of ILP will be a challenge for most U.S. law enforcement agencies, the authors argue that the experience and foundation of CompStat and community policing serve as important springboards for success. Although there are substantive differences in the concepts, the similarities serve as reliable policy experiences to make implementation of ILP a functional reality.

References

Association of Chief Police Officers. (2005). *Guidance on the National Intelligence Model.* Retrieved October 24, 2008, from http://www.acpo.police.uk/asp/policies/Data/nim2005.pdf

Bayley, D. H. (1992). Comparative organization of the police in English-speaking countries. *Crime and Justice, 15,* 509–545.

Bureau of Justice Assistance. (2007). *Intelligence-led policing and the Bureau of Justice.* Washington, DC: Author.

Carter, D. L. (2002). *The police and the community* (7th ed.). Englewood Cliffs, NJ: Prentice Hall.

Carter, D. L. (2004). *Law enforcement intelligence: A guide for state, local and tribal law enforcement agencies.* Available from www.intellprogram.msu.edu

Carter, D. L. (in press). *Law enforcement intelligence: A guide for state, local and tribal law enforcement agencies* (2nd ed.). Washington, DC: Office of Community Oriented Policing Services.

Clarke, C. (2006). Proactive policing: Standing on the shoulders of community-based policing. *Police Practice and Research, 7,* 3–17.

Cope, N. (2004). Intelligence led policing or policing led intelligence? Integrating volume crime analysis into policing. *British Journal of Criminology, 44,* 188–203.

Department of Homeland Security. (2003). *Homeland Security Presidential Directive-8.* Retrieved October 24, 2008, from http://www.ojp.usdoj.gov/odp/docs/Website_Stakeholder_List.pdf

Department of Homeland Security. (2007). *Targeted Capabilities List.* Retrieved October 24, 2008, from http://www.fema.gov/pdf/government/training/tcl.pdf

Dorriety, J. (2005). CompStat for smaller departments. *Law and Order, 53*(6), 100–105.

Fleming, J., & Lafferty, G. (2000). New management techniques and restructuring for accountability in Australian police organizations. *Policing: An International Journal of Police Strategies & Management, 23,* 154–168.

German, M., & Stanley, J. (2007). *What's wrong with fusion centers?* New York: American Civil Liberties Union.

Global Intelligence Working Group. (2003). *National criminal intelligence sharing plan.* Retrieved October 24, 2008, from http://www.it.ojp.gov/documents/National_Criminal_Intelligence_Sharing_Plan.pdf

Haarr, R. N. (2001). The making of a community policing officer: The impact of basic training on occupational socialization on police recruits. *Police Quarterly, 4,* 402–433.

Henry, V. E. (2003). *The CompStat paradigm: Management and accountability in policing, business, and the public sector.* Flushing, NY: Looseleaf Law Publications.

Her Majesty's Inspectorate of Constabulary. (1997). *Policing with intelligence.* London: Author.

International Association of Chiefs of Police. (2002). *Criminal intelligence sharing: A national plan for intelligence-led policing at the local, state and federal levels. Recommendations from the Intelligence Summit.* Retrieved October 24, 2008, from http://epic.org/privacy/fusion/intelsharerpt.pdf

Kelling, G. L., & Bratton, W. J. (2006). Policing terrorism. *Civic Bulletin, 15,* 12.

Kratcoski, P. C., & Noonan, S. B. (1995). An assessment of police officers' acceptance of community policing. In P. C. Kratcoski & D. Dukes (Eds.), *Issues in community policing* (pp. 169–185). Cincinnati, OH: Anderson.

Maguire, E. R. (1997). Structural change in large municipal police organizations during the community policing era. *Justice Quarterly, 14,* 547–563.

Manning, P. (1984). Community policing. *Journal of American Police, 3,* 205–227.

McDonald, P. P. (2002). *Managing police operations: Implementing the New York Crime Control Model—CompStat.* Belmont, CA: Wadsworth.

McGarrell, E. F., Freilich, J. D., & Chermak, S. (2007). Intelligence-led policing as a framework for responding to terrorism. *Journal of Contemporary Criminal Justice, 23,* 142–158.

Meese, E. (1003). Community policing and the police officer. *Perspectives on Policing, 15,* 2–15.

Moore, M. H. (1992). Problem-solving and community policing. *Crime and Justice, 15,* 99–158.

Moore, M. H. (2003). Sizing up CompStat: An important administrative innovation in policing. *Criminology & Public Policy, 2,* 469–494.

Moynihan, D. P. (2005). Homeland Security and the U.S. public management policy agenda. *Governance: An International Journal of Policy, Administration and Institutions, 18,* 171–196.

O'Toole, L. J., & Montjoy, R. S. (1984). Interorganizational policy implementation: A theoretical perspective. *Public Administration Review, 44,* 491–503.

Program Manager—Information Sharing Environment. (2007). *Information sharing environment implementation plan.* Retrieved October 24, 2008, from http://www.ise.gov/docs/ISE-impplan-200611.pdf

Ramsey, T. (2007). *Global maritime intelligence integration enterprise.* Washington, DC: Office of the Director of National Intelligence.

Ratcliffe, J. H. (2002). Intelligence led policing and the problems of turning rhetoric into practice. *Policing & Society, 12,* 53–66.

Ratcliffe, J. H. (2005). The effectiveness of police intelligence management: A New Zealand case study. *Police Practice and Research, 6,* 434–445.

Ratcliffe, J. H. (2008a). *Intelligence-led policing.* Cullompton, UK: Willan.

Ratcliffe, J. H. (2008b). Knowledge management challenges in the development of intelligence-led policing. In T. Williamson (Ed.), *The handbook of knowledge based policing: Current conceptions and future directions* (pp. 205–220). Chichester, UK: John Wiley.

Ratcliffe, J. H., & Guidetti, R. A. (2008). State police investigative structure and the adoption of intelligence-led policing. *Policing: An International Journal of Police Strategies & Management, 31,* 109–128.

Shane, J. (2004, April). CompStat process. *FBI Law Enforcement Bulletin, 73*(2), 12–23.

Weisburd, D., Mastrofski, S. D., McNally, A. M., Greenspan, R., & Willis, J. J. (2003). Reforming to preserve: CompStat and strategic problem solving in American policing. *Criminology & Public Policy, 2,* 421–456.

Willis, J. J., Mastrofski, S. D., Weisburd, D., & Greenspan, R. (2003). *CompStat and organizational change in the Lowell Police Department: Challenges and opportunities.* Washington, DC: Police Foundation.

Wood, J., & Shearing, C. (2007). *Imagining security.* Cullompton, UK: Willan.

DISCUSSION QUESTIONS

1. Compare and contrast the use of intelligence by the police in the United Kingdom compared to the police in the United States.

2. Explain how ILP is similar to CompStat.

3. How can ILP be viewed as an expansion of community- and problem-oriented policing?

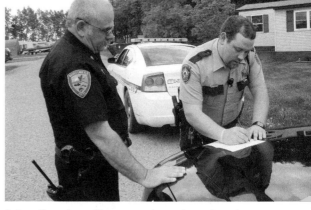

Police officers from different agencies work together when cases span several jurisdictions.

The Scope of American Law Enforcement

Section Highlights

- Review the levels of law enforcement.
- Compare rural and urban police agencies.
- Discuss fragmentation of police service and ways to manage it.

Policing in the United States is both complex and dynamic. There are several types of law enforcement agencies that provide a wide range of services to the public. This section discusses the scope of law enforcement in the United States by examining the various levels and types of agencies, services provided by these agencies, and how geographic location, specifically rural versus urban, impacts the manner in which these agencies function and interact with the public. This section also includes a discussion of the fragmentation of police service and how consolidation, coordination, and contracting of services among police agencies are ways to manage issues related to fragmentation.

Defining *Law Enforcement* and *Police*

Do the terms **law enforcement** and **police** mean the same thing? The answer to this question is no. People often use these two terms interchangeably; however, they have two very different meanings. Law enforcement is the job of making sure that people obey the law.[1] *Police* is defined as "A body of persons making up such a department, trained in methods of law enforcement and crime prevention and detection, and authorized to maintain the peace, safety, and order of the community."[2] This definition identifies law enforcement as one of many responsibilities of the police.

Gary Cordner and Elizabeth Perkins Biebel describe the difference between these two terms:

> . . . law enforcement, that is, using the criminal law, should be understood as one *means* of policing, rather than as the end or goal of policing. This tenet is much more than a subtle shift in terminology. It emphasizes that police pursue large and critically important societal goals—controlling crime, protecting people, reducing fear, and maintaining order. In every instance, police should choose those lawful and ethical means that yield the most efficient and effective achievement of these ends. Sometimes this may involve enforcement of criminal law and sometimes it may not. Thus, the words "policing" and "law enforcement" are not synonymous, and law enforcement is not the only or even necessarily the principal technique of policing.[3]

Law Enforcement Agencies in the United States

Recent statistics indicate that there are more than 18,000 law enforcement agencies in the United States.[4] This statistic reflects all local, state, and federal law enforcement agencies. The Law Enforcement Management and Administrative Statistics (LEMAS) survey is used to collect information on American law enforcement agencies. This survey asks questions related to agency operating expenditures, employee job functions, salaries, demographic characteristics of officers (such as race, age, sex, etc.), department policies, education and training requirements, computers and information systems, vehicles, special units, and community policing activities. This survey has been administered every 3 to 4 years since 1987. LEMAS is one of the most comprehensive data-collection efforts focused on law enforcement agencies in this country.

Police agencies receive the most government funding out of all criminal justice–related agencies. The most recent statistics indicate that expenditures related to police protection in the United States comprise 45.5% of the nation's total justice expenditure, while corrections received 32.6%, and legal and judicial services received 21.8%.[5] When examining the cost of police protection more closely, it appears that local governments provide the largest portion of funding for police protection.[6] An increase in employment within law enforcement helps explain why so many resources are provided for police protection in the United States. From 1982 to 2007, the number of employees (both sworn and civilian positions) in American law enforcement agencies increased from approximately 724,000 to 1.16 million.[7]

Levels of Law Enforcement

Many countries have national police organizations through which one federal agency manages all of the police services for that particular country. The structure of law enforcement in the United States is different from other countries, as it is based on the concept of federalism. Federalism is "the process by which two or more governments share power over the same geographic area."[8] In the United States, there are three core levels of law enforcement: local, state, and federal. These three levels vary in function, purpose, size, and training. The three levels are also unique, as they have varying jurisdictional boundaries. Variation in jurisdictional boundaries contributes to the problem of fragmentation as it relates to police service in the United States (fragmentation will be discussed in greater detail at the end of this section).

Local Level

Local-level agencies provide general law enforcement services to the public (with the exception of sheriffs' departments) and are operated by a unit of local government such as a town, city, township, or county.[9] **Municipal police** agencies are those that provide service to cities. **Sheriffs' departments** are considered part of local law enforcement; however, they are organized by county instead of by city. County police are similar in function to municipal police except their jurisdictional boundaries are countywide instead of citywide. They are unlike sheriffs' departments, as they do not provide services related to county jails and courts. Not every county in the United States has county police; those counties that do not usually have sheriffs' departments to provide service at the county level. There are also county constable offices in the United States. Not every state has county constable offices. Most (but not all) of the existing county constable offices are located in the state of Texas.[10] The duties of county constables vary across jurisdictions. Some responsibilities resemble those of sheriffs' deputies (such as serving warrants, seizing and selling property confiscated during arrests, and enforcing state laws).[11] The structures of county constables' offices are similar to those of sheriffs' departments, as they are both headed by elected officials (constables and sheriffs).

Municipal Police

Municipal police agencies provide a wide range of services to the public. They are responsible for controlling crime through law enforcement, maintaining social order within their communities, investigating crimes reported to them by citizens, controlling traffic within city limits, and, when needed, providing support in emergency or medical situations. Services provided by contemporary municipal police agencies should reflect the needs of the communities they serve.

Within the local level of law enforcement, municipal police agencies employ the most people (69.5% of all full-time sworn positions) and operate the highest number of agencies.[12] The Bureau of Justice Statistics reported that in 2008, there were 12,501 municipal police departments in the United States, employing a total of 593,013 full-time employees, with approximately 461,063 of those being sworn positions.[13] Sworn positions are those in which individuals received all required training and certification to perform law enforcement duties. Nonsworn positions do not require specific law enforcement training or certification and generally focus on administrative and community-based tasks (such as issuing parking tickets or handling animal control calls, to name a few). Employment by municipal police agencies increased by 27% (or 1.7% annually) from 1987 to 2003.[14] From 2004 to 2008, the number of full-time sworn personnel in municipal police agencies increased by 14,000 or 3.2%.[15] More than half (53%) of municipal police agencies in the United States employed fewer than 10 officers in 2008.[16] That means that the typical municipal police agency is quite small.

County Sheriff

Sheriffs' departments are considered part of local law enforcement. This type of agency is different from municipal agencies in several ways: First, jurisdictional boundaries for sheriffs' departments are countywide, while municipal police agencies have citywide boundaries. Sheriffs' departments are responsible for patrolling unincorporated or sparsely populated areas, as well as small towns that do not have their own municipal police agencies. Second, sheriffs' departments are headed by elected officials called sheriffs, while municipal police agencies are led by police chiefs (which, in most cases, are appointed by the mayor or city council). Third, sheriffs' departments provide services beyond the scope of law enforcement, while municipal police

Sheriffs' deputies manage inmates that are held in county jails.

agencies focus primarily on law enforcement-related activities. Sheriffs' departments are responsible for maintaining and staffing county jails. They process all individuals that have been arrested and taken into custody and then monitor inmates during the time that they are housed in jails. Sheriffs' deputies are also responsible for transporting individuals to and from court and also serve as bailiffs in courtrooms. In essence, sheriffs' departments provide services within all three areas of the criminal justice system (law enforcement, courts, and corrections).

Sheriffs' departments employ the second highest number of people within the local level of law enforcement (30.5% of all full-time sworn positions).[17] In 2008, there were 3,063 sheriffs' departments in the United States, employing 353,461 full-time employees, with approximately 182,979 of those being sworn positions.[18] From 1987 to 2003, employment by sheriffs' departments increased by 75% (or 4.7% annually). This rate of growth far exceeds that of municipal police agencies (27%) during the same time frame.[19] Employment of full-time sworn personnel in sheriffs' departments increased by 4% from 2004 to 2008.[20] Sheriffs' offices have grown because they are now performing contract policing to municipalities that have eliminated expensive police departments as a result of the downturn in the economy. Slightly less than half (48%) of all sheriffs' departments employ between 10 and 49 employees; this means that the typical sheriff's department is slightly larger than the typical municipal police agency.[21]

State Level

State-level law enforcement agencies began to emerge in the United States at the turn of the 20th century. The need for state police resulted from several factors:[22] First, in some states (specifically Pennsylvania and New York), local law enforcement agencies could no longer handle labor-related conflicts that were taking place at that time. As a result, these two states were among the first to create state-level police agencies to provide aid to municipal police agencies when incidents of social unrest would arise. Second, state-level police were needed to pursue suspects statewide when they attempted to flee local police. This especially became a problem after automobiles were introduced in the United States. Third, state police could help patrol roadways in rural areas in which there were no local police available to do so. By 1925, most states had established state police agencies.[23]

With the exception of Hawaii (which is classified as a special jurisdiction agency), all 49 states have state-level police agencies today.[24] In 2008, state law enforcement agencies employed 93,148 full-time employees.[25] These employees work in a variety of state police agencies, including state highway patrol, wildlife/game and fish management, fire marshal offices, attorney general investigators, and state tax or revenue units.[26] State police agencies provide a wide range of services, including enforcement of traffic laws on state highway systems, investigatory services for municipal police agencies that do not have investigative units, record keeping (specifically the maintenance of state crime databases), and crime laboratory services for municipal police agencies that do not have such facilities. They are also responsible for mandating statewide training standards for police training academies.

State Highway Patrol

One of the most visible state-level law enforcement agencies is the highway patrol. It is one of the most visible because its main responsibility is enforcing traffic laws while patrolling major roadways across the United States. State highway patrol provides a variety of other services to the public, such as providing help in emergency situations that occur on major roadways, investigating traffic accidents, inspecting commercial vehicles to ensure that they abide by state weight limits and the laws governing transportation of hazardous materials, reporting maintenance needs of roadways, and creating education-based information to encourage citizens to follow the rules of the road and operate their vehicles safely.[27]

State highway patrol has a visible presence on our nation's roadways.

Special Jurisdiction Agencies at Local and State Levels

Several agencies at the local and state levels of law enforcement are specialized based on jurisdictional boundaries, including transit authority, school district police, housing authority, airport police, harbor police, hospital police, wildlife/game and fish management, university campus police, and tribal police. This section will discuss three of these special jurisdiction agencies: university campus, natural resources, and tribal police. In 2008, there were 1,733 specialized local and state-level agencies employing 56,968 full-time sworn employees in the United States.[28] Of these specialized agencies, university campus and natural resource–based agencies employ the most people.

University Police

Yale University was the first university in the United States to create a police agency in reaction to violent interactions between Yale students and citizens of New Haven, Connecticut, in 1894.[29] The need for **university campus police** agencies continued during the 1960s and 1970s, when protests against war and other social inequities took place on university campuses, and when crime began to increase both on and off of university campuses across the country. The passage of the Crime Awareness and Campus Security Act of 1990 further emphasized the need for university police, as it requires colleges and universities to record and maintain crime statistics and to create plans for providing security to students and campus employees.[30]

University police officers provide security and respond to a variety of calls for service within the boundaries of their campuses. In addition, university police oversee events that take place on campus, enforce traffic laws, investigate crimes that take place on campus, and provide security to all campus buildings.[31] One benefit of having university police is that they can respond quickly because of their location on university and college campuses.[32]

Past research that has compared university and municipal police agencies has revealed that, in general, these two types of agencies are very similar in both the services they provide and the manner in which they provide those services.[33] The organizational structures of university and municipal police agencies are also similar.[34] Both types of agencies sometimes utilize nontraditional policing strategies, including community policing and problem-oriented policing; however, university police agencies are more likely to have formal community policing plans in place than are municipal police agencies.[35] The Bureau of Justice Statistics reported that 69% of university police agencies had formal community policing plans compared to 14% of municipal police agencies.[36]

In 2008, there were 508 university police agencies serving 4-year universities and colleges, with another 253 agencies serving institutions that grant 2-year degrees.[37] University police agencies located on 4-year university and college campuses employed 10,916 full-time sworn officers, while agencies serving institutions that grant 2-year degrees employed 2,648 full-time sworn officers.[38] Most (74%) 4-year colleges and universities with student populations of 2,500 or more have university police agencies serving them.[39] These agencies employ sworn personnel that have full arrest powers granted by local or state governments, and more than half (67%) of these agencies use armed patrol officers on campus. Private universities generally employ more nonsworn officers when compared to publicly funded universities.[40]

Wildlife Conservation/Game and Fish

Wildlife conservation/state game and fish are another type of state law enforcement agency. People working within this type of agency are referred to as game wardens, conservation officers, or wildlife officers. This

Responsibilities of game wardens/conservation officers center on wildlife management.

category of law enforcement is unique because of its focus on the enforcement of laws related to the hunting, fishing, and trapping of wild animals. Game wardens have a wide range of responsibilities, including the enforcement of license requirements for people who hunt and fish; investigation of wildlife crimes (including cases of animal poaching); assisting with wildlife management duties, including tracking and counting wildlife animals; and also instructing hunter safety classes for the public. The Bureau of Justice Statistics reported that in 2008, there were 246 agencies in operation and 14,571 employees working in jobs related to natural resources and parks and recreation.[41]

Individuals working in this type of agency have frequent encounters with people who carry firearms or other weapons. Conservation officers also frequently patrol areas that are isolated and sparsely populated, which means that it can be difficult to get immediate backup from fellow officers. It seems that these working conditions would increase the probability that game wardens would have to use force or would have force used against them more often than other types of law enforcement officers. Fortunately, research has found that this is not the case.[42]

In general, there has been limited research on wildlife conservation officers. The few studies that have been conducted on this topic focus on the use of force by and against game wardens, the implementation of community policing by wildlife conservation agencies,[43] and the use of discretion by game wardens.[44]

Tribal Police Agencies

Tribal police provide service to citizens residing on 510 American Indian reservations that are acknowledged by the United States federal government.[45] As of September 2008, American Indian tribes operate 178 law enforcement agencies.[46] These agencies employ a total of 3,462 full-time personnel, with more than half (67%) being sworn positions and 33% nonsworn positions. Approximately two-thirds of tribal police officers are Native American; however, only about 56% of these officers are members of the tribes that they serve.[47]

Policing on American Indian reservations is a complex issue, as there is variation in both law enforcement authority and jurisdictional boundaries. These complexities result from a series of laws that have been enacted over time. A consequence of these laws is that there are several types of law enforcement agencies operating on American Indian reservations today.[48] Eileen Luna identified five types of law enforcement agencies operating in Indian Country.[49] First, the Bureau of Indian Affairs Law Enforcement Services (BIA) is a federal-level agency responsible for law enforcement on 64 reservations across the United States. The BIA has very little (if any) accountability to tribal governments or councils. Second, there are approximately 90 tribes that have taken either complete or partial control over policing on their reservations from the BIA. These tribes were able to do so under Public Law 93-638 (1975 Indian Self-Determination and Education Assistance Act). Agencies operating under PL 638 must enter into an agreement with the BIA specifying law enforcement services that they will provide in exchange for federal funding. Third, there are approximately 60 tribal police agencies that are completely funded by individual tribes. These police agencies are controlled and held accountable to the tribal government; therefore, these police agencies operate however the tribe and its members see fit. Fourth, there are 25 self-governing agencies operating under the Indian Self-Determination Act of 1994, which allows tribes to take over policing responsibilities while also receiving some funding from the federal government. These agencies are different from agencies operating under PL 93-638, as they receive funding to enhance and strengthen them as opposed to relying solely on government funding for the operation. Fifth, there are state law enforcement agencies providing service on 39 American Indian reservations pursuant to Public Law 83-280 of 1953. Public Law 280 transferred law enforcement authority from the federal level to the state level in some states. In these jurisdictions, state and local governments provide law enforcement service to reservations; however, in some cases, tribes will also establish their own tribal police agencies to supplement whatever service is provided by state and local agencies.

It is important to point out that these five types of agencies are not mutually exclusive and can operate simultaneously within any given reservation.[50] This can result in major overlap of police services and invoke confusion over jurisdictional boundaries. Some agencies have created cross-deputization agreements to overcome jurisdictional confusion. Cross-deputization allows officers from state and tribal agencies to cross jurisdictional boundaries to deal with criminal cases.[51] There are some jurisdictions in which agreements have been made to allow officers from federal, state, county/local, or tribal agencies to arrest offenders whether they are Native American or not if the crime occurred on reservation land.[52]

There are both similarities and differences among tribal and local-level law enforcement agencies. In general, the services provided by tribal police are similar to those provided by municipal/county police agencies. These services include responding to calls for service by citizens; engaging in crime-prevention activities, enforcing traffic codes, serving warrants and other court-related documents, and providing security in courtrooms.[53] Differences emerge between these two types of agencies when one considers *how* policing is conducted. For example, the very nature of traditional policing puts officers in an adversarial position with citizens. This approach to policing does not work on American Indian reservations, as the Native American culture is based on the concept of community and people working together.[54]

Differences between these two types of police agencies can also be found in the types of crime that officers deal with while on duty. Tribal police officers encounter a high number of alcohol-related offenses, including liquor law violations, driving while intoxicated, and public drunkenness or misconduct resulting from alcohol consumption.[55] Officers working in local-level agencies also deal with alcohol-related offenses, but not to the same degree of frequency as tribal police officers. Another difference between these two types of agencies is the representation and experiences of female police officers. The Luna-Firebaugh article included at the end of this section discusses how the experiences of women working in tribal police agencies are different from those of women working in nontribal agencies.

Federal Level

Federal-level law enforcement agencies are subunits of the United States federal government. These agencies are housed in two departments found within the federal government system: the **Department of Homeland Security** and the **Department of Justice**. Prior to 2002, federal law enforcement was housed primarily in the Department of Justice (DOJ). The DOJ is responsible for enforcing laws and administering justice at the federal level. The terrorist attacks that took place on September 11, 2001, were the catalyst for changing the structure of federal law enforcement. This tragic event led to the creation of the Department of Homeland Security (DHS) in 2003. The mission of DHS is to protect the United States from attacks by foreign nations. The organization charts of both the DOJ and the DHS are complex (both provided in this section). Each department has many subdivisions containing several agencies that have specific purposes and functions.

Federal Law Enforcement and the Department of Justice

In 1870, the Department of Justice was established.[56] The DOJ is led by the attorney general. Individuals working in the DOJ participate in activities that are reflected in its official mission statement:

> To enforce the law and defend the interests of the United States according to the law; to ensure public safety against threats foreign and domestic; to provide federal leadership in preventing and controlling crime; to seek just punishment for those guilty of unlawful behavior; and to ensure fair and impartial administration of justice for all Americans.[57]

The DOJ is composed of several divisions with varying purposes and functions (see the chart on page 93). Not all of the divisions are directly responsible for providing law enforcement services similar to local and state law enforcement agencies. This section will discuss four federal-level law enforcement agencies, the Federal Bureau of Investigation; the Drug Enforcement Administration; the Bureau of Alcohol, Tobacco, Firearms and Explosives; and the United States Marshals Service.

Federal Bureau of Investigation (FBI). The FBI was established in 1908 during the presidency of Theodore Roosevelt.[58] This agency's mission is to protect the United States against terrorism and foreign intelligence threats, enforce criminal laws of the United States, and provide guidance and service to other federal, state, and local law enforcement agencies. This agency handles many types of crime, including cyber- or technology-based crimes, white collar crime, transnational crime, public corruption, and violations of citizens' civil rights.[59] The collection of crime statistics from state and local law enforcement agencies (the Uniform Crime Report) is another responsibility of the FBI. This agency has the widest jurisdiction of any federal law enforcement agency. In 2010, the FBI had a total of 35,525 employees—this includes 13,847 special agents working in the field and 21,678 support staff.[60]

Organization Chart for the Department of Justice

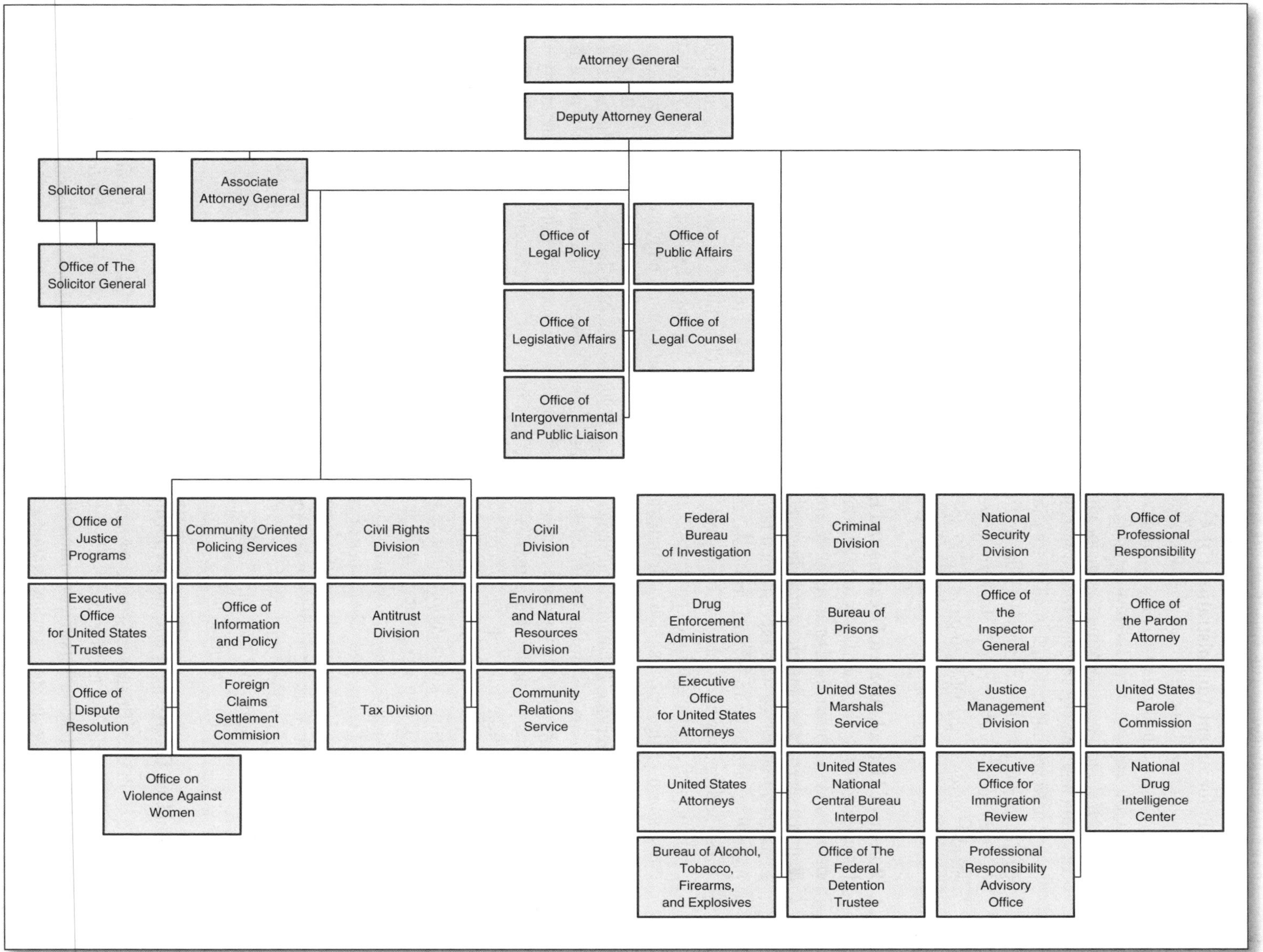

Source: See http://www.justice.gov/jmd/mps/manual/orgcharts/dojorg.pdf.

Drug Enforcement Administration (DEA). President Richard Nixon created the DEA through an executive order in 1973 to combat "an all-out global war on the drug menace."[61] Every aspect of the work of this agency centers on illegal drugs. This work involves drug-related crimes both within the United States and abroad. DEA agents aid in the investigation and preparation of criminal cases involving individuals and groups that have been identified as major violators of drug laws. This agency is also responsible for the collection and analysis of drug-related intelligence that is gathered within the boundaries of the United States; however, international intelligence is also collected, as a large portion of drug trafficking involves people residing in other countries. Collaboration with local, state, and international law enforcement agencies plays an important role in the management of the distribution and sale of illegal drugs in the United States. Currently, the DEA employs 5,235 special agents and manages 87 foreign offices in 63 countries around the world.[62]

Bureau of Alcohol, Tobacco, Firearms and Explosives (ATF). The ATF was formalized on July 1, 1972. Its historical roots can be traced back to 1789, when Congress first imposed a tax on imported alcohol and then created a unit within the Department of Treasury to collect those taxes.[63] Over the years, this agency acquired several additional responsibilities related to firearms and explosives and was also moved into the Department of Justice with other federal law enforcement agencies. Today, the ATF's mission centers on protecting citizens from "violent criminals, criminal organizations, the illegal use and trafficking of firearms, the illegal use and storage of explosives, acts of arson and bombings, acts of terrorism, and the illegal diversion of alcohol and tobacco products."[64] In 2009, the ATF employed 2,450 special agents, 789 industry operations investigators, and 1,769 administrative/professional/technical employees.[65]

U.S. Marshals Service. Established on September 24, 1789, the U.S. Marshals Service is the oldest federal law enforcement agency in the United States.[66] This agency serves as the enforcement arm of federal courts, and as a result, it is involved in nearly all federal law enforcement initiatives. The utility of this agency is reflected in the myriad activities that are part of its daily operations. For example, agents are responsible for protecting federal judicial officials (including judges, attorneys, and jurors). This group works in collaboration with other federal, state, local, and international law enforcement agencies when they conduct fugitive investigations that span across the country or international boundaries. The U.S. Marshals Service is also accountable for the management of the witness protection program. This program relocates, protects, and gives new identities to people that testify on behalf of the government in cases that involve organized crime and other types of criminal activities. Working with the Bureau of Immigration and Customs, the U.S. marshals also transport prisoners between judicial districts and to international locations.[67] Agents working within this agency are appointed by the president of the United States. The U.S. marshals can be found in 94 districts across the United States—one for each federal judicial district. Current statistics indicate that there are 3,340 deputy U.S. marshals and criminal investigators employed by this federal law enforcement agency.[68]

Federal Law Enforcement and the Department of Homeland Security

The Department of Homeland Security became operational on January 24, 2003.[69] President George W. Bush identified four missions to correspond with the main divisions within the DHS: (1) *border and transportation security*—control the borders and prevent terrorists and explosives from entering the country; (2) *emergency preparedness and response*—work with state and local authorities to respond quickly and effectively to emergencies; (3) *chemical, biological, radiological, and nuclear countermeasures*—bring together the country's best

Organization Chart of the Department of Homeland Security

Source: See http://www.dhs.gov/xlibrary/assets/dhs-orgchart.pdf.

scientists to develop technologies that detect biological, chemical, and nuclear weapons to protect citizens; and (4) *information analysis and infrastructure protection*—review intelligence and law enforcement information from all agencies of government and produce a single daily picture of threats against the United States.[70] This department is composed of many agencies (see organization chart), some of which do not directly provide law enforcement services "in the field" as state and local law enforcement agencies do.

U.S. Customs and Border Protection (CBP). Customs and Border Protection (CBP) was created in 2003 under the Department of Homeland Security; however, the history of this agency dates back to 1789, when Congress established Customs and its ports of entry.[71] The CBP was created as a result of the U.S. federal government responding to social changes that have occurred over time. The mission of the CBP is to secure and facilitate trade and travel across all borders of the United States while enforcing U.S. regulations and laws related to immigration and trade.[72] This agency plays a key role in anti–drug trafficking efforts by the U.S. federal government. Controlling terrorism within the United States by securing this nation's borders has also become a prominent part of its daily operations. Today, the CBP plays an integral role in monitoring both people and instruments of terrorism that attempt to enter into the United States at both the northern and southern borders.

According to 2009 statistics, this agency employs 44,783 CBP officers and border patrol agents.[73] A large workforce is needed, because on a typical day, the CBP processes 989,689 passengers and pedestrians and 57,761 truck, rail, and sea containers; executes 2,139 apprehensions for illegal entry into the United States; and seizes 6,643 pounds of narcotics.[74] This agency is unique, as it employs individuals with a variety of educational backgrounds and professional experiences, including trade specialists, intelligence analysts, and agricultural scientists. The use of airplanes, boats, and automobiles enables agents within CBP to protect and monitor 1,900 miles of border with Mexico and 5,000 miles of border with Canada.[75]

U.S. Immigration and Customs Enforcement (ICE). ICE was created in 2003 with the merging of the investigative and law enforcement elements of the U.S. Customs Service and the Immigration and Naturalization Service Agency.[76] This agency is composed of two principal units—Homeland Security Investigations (HSI) and Enforcement and Removal Operations (ERO). HSI is responsible for the investigation of immigration crimes, human rights violations, the smuggling of narcotics and weapons into the United States, financial and cyber crimes, and export enforcement issues.[77] ERO enforces immigration laws of the United States. This group is involved with the apprehension, arrest, and removal of convicted criminals that are not legal residents of the United States and individuals seeking refuge in the United States.[78] ICE is the largest investigative agency within the Department of Homeland Security.[79] This agency is the second largest within the Department of Homeland Security, as it employs more than 20,000 people in more than 400 offices across the United States and 46 foreign countries around the world.[80]

Federal Emergency Management Agency (FEMA). FEMA was formally established in 1979. This agency coordinates the federal government's efforts in preparing for, preventing, responding to, and recovering from both natural and man-made disasters (including acts of terrorism).[81] Prior to 1979, information and support provided before and after natural disasters came from several agencies within the U.S. federal government, including the Federal Insurance Administration, the National Fire Prevention and Control Administration, the National Weather Service Community Preparedness Program, the Federal Preparedness Agency of the General Services Administration, and the Federal Disaster Assistance Administration. The creation of FEMA streamlined these agencies into one large agency, as well as the process by which emergency management services can be procured. FEMA employs more than 3,700 full-time positions, with another 4,000 standby disaster assistance employees who are available after disasters occur.[82]

Transportation Security Administration (TSA). The TSA was created after the passage of the Aviation and Transportation Security Act on November 19, 2001, in response to the terrorist attacks that took place on September 11, 2001.[83] Originally housed in the Department of Transportation, the TSA was transferred into the Department of Homeland Security in March 2003.[84] The main focus of this agency is to strengthen the security of the transportation systems in the United States. TSA works closely with a variety of law enforcement and intelligence agencies to provide security for railways, airlines, and roadways. Activities associated with this agency are most visible in airports, where security officers screen both passengers and baggage for explosives and other types of contraband. The TSA employs approximately 48,000 transportation security officers in 457 airports across the United States.[85]

U.S. Coast Guard. The U.S. Coast Guard received its official name in 1915. Its history dates back to August 1790, when Congress authorized the construction of 10 vessels to enforce tariff and trade laws and to prevent smuggling by way of water.[86] This agency was housed in the Department of Treasury and the Department of Transportation prior to its inclusion in the Department of Homeland Security in 2003. The U.S. Coast Guard is the only military-based organization within the DHS. This organization protects United States maritime interests in the ports, at sea, and internationally. This includes responding to water-based search-and-rescue cases and screening transportation containers aboard both commercial and private vessels for drugs, instruments of terrorism, and other contraband that is a threat to the United States.[87] The U.S. Coast Guard employs 38,000 active-duty members, 8,000 reservists, and 35,000 auxiliary personnel.[88]

U.S. Secret Service. The U.S. Secret Service was created on July 5, 1865, as a branch of the United States Treasury Department to combat the counterfeiting of U.S. currency.[89] Today, the Secret Service faces crimes related to forgery and theft of U.S. Treasury checks and bonds, credit card fraud, telecommunications fraud, computer fraud, identity fraud, and other crimes involving federally insured financial institutions.

After the assassination of President William McKinley in 1901, the Secret Service was given an additional task: providing protection to presidents, vice presidents, and their immediate families.[90] Over time, this agency has expanded its responsibilities for providing security beyond that of the president. Today, this agency is required to provide protection to former presidents and their spouses (for no more than 10 years from the date they leave office); children of former presidents until the age of 16 years; visiting heads of foreign states or governments and their spouses; and major presidential and vice presidential candidates and their spouses within 120 days of a general presidential election.[91] There are approximately 3,200 special agents, 1,300 uniformed division officers, and more 2,000 technical, professional, and administrative support personnel working within the U.S. Secret Service.[92]

U.S. Citizenship and Immigration Services (USCIS). The USCIS officially took over responsibilities for the immigration service function of the U.S. federal government on March 1, 2003.[93] Prior to 2003, the Immigration and Naturalization Service division maintained control over most issues related to immigration. The passage of the Homeland Security Act of 2002 resulted in the dismantling of the Immigration and Naturalization Service and separated it into three divisions within the Department of Homeland Security: (1) U.S. Citizenship and Immigration Services (USCIS), which is responsible for national immigration services by exclusively focusing on the administration of benefit applications; (2) Immigration and Customs

Enforcement (ICE), which focuses specifically on immigration enforcement; and (3) Customs and Border Protection (CBP), which provides security to all borders of the United States.[94]

Today, the USCIS manages requests for U.S. citizenship, as well as requests from current residents to bring relatives to live and work in the United States.[95] This agency also manages several humanitarian programs that provide protection to individuals inside and outside the United States who are displaced or are forced to flee their countries. The USCIS is pivotal in the first stages of the adoption process for U.S. citizens who wish to adopt children from other countries. This agency also provides information and other services to new immigrants coming into the United States to help them integrate into American culture.[96] Currently, the USCIS employs 15,000 employees working in 250 field offices around the world.[97]

⬚ Private Security

Private security agencies have gradually assumed a larger role in the management of crime and crime prevention in the United States.[98] Private security is "the nongovernmental, private-sector practice of protecting people, property, and information, conducting investigations, and otherwise safeguarding an organization's assets."[99] There are several subsections within the private security industry, including whether the security agencies are proprietary or contractual in nature; the type of security provided to clients (such as physical, information, or employment-related); the nature of the services provided to clients (such as guarding property or part of armored transport); and the type of markets they serve (such as critical infrastructure and commercial venues).[100]

In many places, private security officers outnumber sworn police officers. According to the Bureau of Labor Statistics (2010), there were approximately 1.1 million private security officers in the United States in 2007 compared to 833,600 sworn police officers. The exact count of private security officers is unknown, as many private security agencies do not publish personnel information or make it available to the public. Further, in recent years, the line between private security and the police has become blurry, making it even more difficult to get an exact count. Private security agencies have become more involved in public policing activities as the economic downturn in the United States has forced some police agencies to contract out some of their work to private security agencies (this issue is discussed in greater detail in Section 13 of this book).

Private security officers have become more policelike in their appearance and operation. For instance, they often carry firearms, conduct surveillance and investigations, patrol in marked vehicles, and wear uniforms signifying the agencies by which they are employed. There are, however, several significant differences between these two groups. For instance, most security officers receive little training when compared to sworn police officers.[101] These groups are funded by different sources—private security agencies are paid by corporate entities, while police agencies are funded by the taxpayers in their communities. Further, the police focus primarily on crime prevention and crime management, while private security agencies are focused on making profits, as most businesses are.[102]

Private security agencies were perceived to be irrelevant to American police agencies in the 1960s and 1970s.[103] It was not until the 1980s that this relationship began to improve. Specifically, the introduction of problem-oriented and community policing encouraged increased collaboration among the police and private security agencies.[104] The importance of this relationship became even clearer after the terrorist attacks on 9/11. This event solidified the need for frequent exchange of critical information and the ability of these two groups to work together on homeland security issues. Despite an improved relationship, research suggests that there are still some issues—specifically, that police agencies have been reluctant to share information with private security agencies.[105] These problems will need to be resolved, as private security officers continue to have an increasing presence in American policing.

Law Enforcement in Rural America

Most research conducted on the police in the United States focuses on large agencies that are located in heavily populated urban areas. This is interesting, since most police agencies in the United States are quite small, with nearly half employing fewer than 10 employees.[106] Researchers have also paid little attention to police agencies operating in rural parts of the country. *Rural* in this case refers to areas with populations less than 2,500 people.[107] Recent statistics indicate that 40.6% of all local police agencies in the United States serve populations under 2,500.[108] It has been assumed that research findings from studies conducted in large, urban police agencies will be applicable to small, **rural police** agencies. The little research that has been done on rural agencies reveals that these agencies are quite different from large urban police agencies in many ways.

One difference between urban and rural police agencies is their organizational structure. Large, urban police agencies generally have a multitiered, bureaucratic organizational structure in which there is room for expansion, including the addition of specialized units and divisions. Rural police agencies usually have low bureaucratic hierarchy with very few positions between patrol officer and police chief.[109] In some rural areas, the chief of police will patrol the community alongside patrol officers, participating in many of the same activities. This is unlikely to occur in large, urban police agencies, as chiefs of police take on more of an executive role that focus primarily on the management of their organizations, similar to business executives working in the business world.

Another difference between urban and rural police agencies relates to police role. Rural police officers have to work as generalists—that is, they are responsible for a variety of administrative, public service, and law enforcement–based tasks.[110] The role of generalist is something that police officers working in rural agencies will experience over the course of their entire careers. In contrast, urban police agencies have several positions that are more focused and specialized (such as patrol officer, investigator, crime scene analyst, administrator, etc.). Specialization is something that is valued in large urban police agencies. In these urban agencies, police officers begin their careers working in patrol but have opportunities to advance through the ranks to more specialized positions if they choose to do so.[111]

The police–community relationship is also different for urban and rural police officers. In small, rural towns, it is likely that police officers know most of the people living and working in their communities. Because of this, rural police officers have to negotiate between having close ties with the

Rural police officers are considered "generalists," as they provide a wide range of services to the public.

community members that they serve and maintaining a level of professionalism. The Weisheit, Wells, and Falcone article included at the end of this section discusses the police–citizen relationship in a rural setting and describes how community policing plays a role in the relationship. This is very different from police officers working in urban settings, as larger populations reduce the likelihood that urban police officers will know everyone in their communities. Large urban police agencies often use rotating shift systems in which officers will only spend a certain amount of time working in one area before they rotate into a new area. The constant rotation of officers in and out of areas or neighborhoods does not provide them the opportunity to get to know the people living there. In addition, urban police agencies follow the "professional model," which imposes a clear distinction between police officers and the citizens they serve.[112] This model of policing would not be effective in small, rural settings, as close-knit relationships between citizens and police officers are highly valued.

Another difference between these two types of agencies is clearance rates for violent crime. David Falcone and his colleagues point out that "in urban jurisdictions police have lower clearance rates (i.e. fewer crimes known to police are solved or 'cleared' by arrest of suspected offenders) in all Part I crime categories than their small-town counterparts."[113] There are several possible explanations for why small, rural police agencies have higher clearance rates when compared to urban police agencies.[114] First, the flexibility that comes with the role of generalist allows rural police officers to more efficiently deal with community problems. Second, the "flat" bureaucratic structure of rural police agencies affords officers on patrol a wide range of discretion in their decision making. If additional advice or guidance is needed from higher-ranking officers, they can easily contact and communicate with that person(s). Third, the close-knit relationships that rural officers have with citizens in their communities can help them get information about criminal incidents more easily and probably more quickly than in large urban settings.[115]

There may also be a difference between urban and rural police officers and their involvement with acts of police misconduct and use of excessive force. Ralph Weisheit and his colleagues suggest that rural police officers have a higher level of scrutiny when it comes to the use of excessive force and acts of police misconduct. It is likely that rural police officers will know the person if they choose to use excessive force; this would likely not be the case for police officers working in urban settings.[116] Similarly, if rural officers are involved in acts of misconduct, they face a greater level of accountability to their communities because of the close-knit relationship between the two groups. Weisheit and his colleagues also note that it is possible that rural police officers might be more tempted to get involved in acts of misconduct that involve some type of personal gain because of their low salaries.[117] This is another topic, among several others, in which additional research is needed to fully understand police misconduct and accountability in rural police agencies.

And finally, rural police agencies face many challenges due to their size and geographic location that are not experienced in most large, urban settings. For example, many of these rural police agencies are located in areas with small tax bases, which consequently impact their operating budgets. With fewer resources, rural police agencies are limited in their ability to acquire new technology and advanced training for their officers. The lack of resources also impacts the salaries of police officers working in rural areas. According to recent statistics, the average starting salaries for entry-level local police officers ranged from $26,600 in the smallest jurisdictions to $49,500 in the largest jurisdictions.[118] In some cases, rural areas only have part-time police officer positions that pay very little. All of these challenges also make it difficult for rural agencies to recruit and retain officers from outside of their communities.

✂ Fragmentation of Police Service

Three levels of law enforcement were presented earlier in this section: local, state, and federal. When these three levels are combined, there are more that 18,000 individual law enforcement agencies across the United States.[119] One way to look at this multilevel policing system is that there is an abundance of police agencies to handle all types of calls for service from the public. On the other hand, because there are so many agencies, it is possible that resources are being wasted due to an overlap in services in some areas. Ronald Hunter describes **fragmentation** as "the responsibility for providing police services, which is borne predominantly by local agencies, is usually divided among several different agencies within an area. This often leads to problems with communication, cooperation and control among the agencies."[120]

How does fragmentation impact police service in the United States? There are two opposing responses to this question. Some argue that fragmentation is a problem and that it impacts the efficiency and effectiveness of the administration of police service.[121] Because there is often a lack of communication, and in some cases, competition among police agencies, services may not be provided in the most efficient or effective manner. Another response to this question is that fragmentation is not necessarily a problem. It has been argued that the current structure of American policing allows agencies to not only tailor police services to the needs of each community but also be certain that the needs of citizens are met, whether it is from one or multiple police agencies.[122]

Several strategies have been used to manage issues related to fragmentation: (1) contractual agreements among police agencies, (2) creation of cooperative task forces using resources from multiple police agencies, and (3) consolidation of police agencies. Elinor Ostrom and her colleagues found that some police agencies create agreements (either with formal contracts or more informal verbal agreements) regarding which police agency will provide certain services in a particular jurisdiction.[123] In other places, law enforcement agencies will form cooperative task forces to respond to specific types of crimes and incidents (such as a multijurisdictional special weapons and tactical team or SWAT unit). And finally, in some jurisdictions, several small police agencies will merge into one large agency to provide police service to an area while using fewer resources.[124] It is important to point out that while one strategy might be effective in one jurisdiction, it might not work in other jurisdictions. Police administrators need to work with community members to determine which strategies will work best for their communities.

SUMMARY

- Municipal police agencies employ the most sworn officers in the United States.
- Federal-level law enforcement agencies are housed within two departments: the Department of Justice and the Department of Homeland Security.
- Fragmentation of police service in the United States is the result of having various levels and types of law enforcement agencies. Fragmentation can occur with an overlap of police service in an area in which resources are seen as wasted, while fragmentation can also occur when there is not enough police service available.
- Rural police officers are different from urban police officers, as their role is as a generalist, while urban officers have more specialized and focused positions.

KEY TERMS

Department of Homeland Security
Department of Justice
fragmentation
law enforcement

municipal police
police
rural police
sheriff's department

tribal police
university campus police

DISCUSSION QUESTIONS

1. What is the difference between the terms *police* and *law enforcement*?

2. Identify similarities and differences among agencies found at the local, state, and federal levels.

3. What are some of the responsibilities of the U.S. Marshals Service?

4. Identify three ways that fragmentation of police service is managed in the United States.

5. Explain some of the ways that rural policing is both similar to and different from policing in urban settings.

WEB RESOURCES

- To learn more about municipal police, go to http://bjs.ojp.usdoj.gov/index.cfm?ty=tp&tid=71.
- To learn more about the Department of Homeland Security, go to http://www.dhs.gov/index.shtm.
- To learn more about tribal police, go to http://bjs.ojp.usdoj.gov/index.cfm?ty=tp&tid=75.

READING 5

The role of women in tribal police agencies is explored in this article written by Eileen Luna-Firebaugh. Using interview data, this study found that women working in tribal police agencies report very different experiences than women working in nontribal police agencies. The differences in experience are found at the patrol level as well as in promoted positions.

Women in Tribal Policing: An Examination of Their Status and Experiences

Eileen M. Luna-Firebaugh

Extensive research has been done on the role of women in policing. Studies have found that women in policing are somewhat disconnected from the traditional power structure within mainstream policing, and are viewed by police administrations and by themselves as bringing different values and gifts to the role of policing. Research has also found that women are generally outside power structures within policing and view themselves as hampered in their chosen profession.

This study focuses on the role of women in tribal policing. The findings indicate that women are more highly represented in tribal policing than in non-Indian police departments. Five times more women hold positions of supervision and command in tribal police departments than in non-Indian departments. Of great significance is the lack of gender-based hostility perceived by women in tribal police departments

Introduction

American Indian tribal police departments are a relatively new phenomenon. Prior to the last decade, policing on reservations was largely the business of the Bureau of Indian Affairs. Now, as tribes take over this critical role, they face the issue of effective and efficient provision of police services. They also face the challenge of recruitment, hiring, and retention of responsible police personnel.

In the non-Indian community, it took many years for law enforcement agencies to hire women as police officers. Often this hiring was a result of lawsuits filed by women who had been denied equal access. Rarely did law enforcement agencies perceive the varied skills that women bring to a job to be essential for their provision of police services. This has not been the case with tribal police departments, however, where, from the beginning, women have been hired and utilized as police officers.

Part of the reason that tribal police departments have been more open to the hiring and integration of women into law enforcement could be the fairly recent inception of tribal law enforcement, thus allowing these agencies to benefit from the changes that the field has gone through in general. Another reason could be the traditional positions of influence and authority of women in many Indian nations.

Tribal police departments face serious issues of violence, crime and criminality among reservation populations. The question that must be faced is how can tribal police departments address these issues in the most effective manner. The answer is crucial if crime rates in Indian Country are to be reduced.

Crime rates, particularly for violent crime, are significantly higher than in the non-Indian community. A study by the Bureau of Justice Statistics (BJS) in 1999 painted a bleak picture of the American Indian community (Greenfield & Smith, 1999). This study found that American Indians are victimized by crime at a rate that is more than double those of the U.S. population in general. Indian young adults, those between the ages of 18 and 24, were the victims of violence at the highest rate of any racial group, when considered by age, amounting to about one violent crime for every four persons.

The situation for American Indian women is equally bleak. The BJS study found that American Indian women are the victims of crime at a rate that is nearly 50% higher than that reported by Black males. Rates of sexual abuse against American Indian women are the highest in the nation. Seven Indian women out of 1,000 are victims of rape or sexual assaults compared with 3 per 1,000 among Blacks and 2 per 1,000 among Whites. Over 76% of American Indian women had a history of domestic violence as victims, and 69% of American Indian children reported exposure to violence.

American Indian women are more than twice as likely to report being stalked than women of other racial or ethnic backgrounds. Approximately 70% of restraining orders obtained by Indian women against stalkers were violated.

Another issue for American Indian tribal police is that American Indians are usually victims of crimes perpetrated by someone of another race. At least 70% of the crime experienced by American Indians is interracial, with the criminal perpetrator being White in 60% of the cases. Total 9 of 10 of the incidents of rape/sexual assault against AI women are committed by non-Indians, as compared with rates for White victims (70% of the perpetrators are White) and Black victims (81% of the perpetrators are Black). This issue creates a serious complication for tribal law enforcement, as tribes do not have jurisdiction over serious felonies committed by a non-Indian against an Indian. Crimes such as these are the responsibility of the Federal Bureau of Investigation,[1] or the state, where Public Law 280 is in effect.[2]

A predominant factor found in the BJS study was the effect of alcohol consumption. Almost half (46%) of all convicted American Indians in local jails had been under the influence of alcohol when they committed the offense for which they had been convicted. This percentage rises to 70% when only violent crimes are considered. This is in stark contrast with all other racial groups, where only a third or less was reported to be under the influence of alcohol during the commission of non-violent crimes and 41% for violent crimes.

Another critical issue in Indian Country is an extremely high rate of suicide. Reports issued by Federal government agencies over the last three decades substantiate extremely high suicide rates for Native American populations. Depression, poverty, alcoholism, and unemployment are rampant in Indian Country. These factors, coupled with the high number of adolescents on most reservations, exceeding 50% in many places, have resulted in extremely high rates of suicide.

One study, a 1973 report entitled "Suicide, Homicide, and Alcoholism Among American Indians," issued by the National Institute of Health, set the suicide rate for American Indians at twice the national average. The rates for Indian youth on some reservations were up to six times the national average at the time of that report. A later study, conducted nationwide in 1987, found that the suicide rates for Indian and Alaska Native youths, aged 10–24, were 2.8–2.3 times as high as general U.S. rates for similarly aged youth (May, 1987). How to deal with these questions and others frame the challenges facing American Indian tribal governments as they seek to control violence on reservations and to advance self-determination and sovereignty.

One significant approach to dealing with the crime rates and the widespread social anomie of the

---

[1]The Major Crimes Act, 23 Stat. 385 (1885).

[2]Public Law 280, 67 Stat. 588.

young has been the rapid development of tribal police departments. A national study of American Indian tribal police, conducted between 1996 and 2000, determined that, since 1995, there had been a very rapid growth in tribally funded police departments (Luna, 1997, 1998). In 1995, there were 114 tribal police departments. This number grew to 170 as of fall, 1996, a number that has continued to grow since that date. The primary question now facing these new departments is the appropriate format and style of policing for Indian Country.

In order to answer this fundamental question the author has examined different facets of tribal law enforcement. The questions addressed in this study of tribal law enforcement include the following:

1. What involvement do women have in tribal law enforcement in terms of participation and rank?

2. What reasons does tribal command staff give for the involvement of women in tribal law enforcement?

3. What do women police officers think about their role in tribal police departments?

⬛ Background

Bob Thomas, a Cherokee University of Arizona professor, said in conversation long ago, "Indians have relationships, Americans have roles." This is true in many instances, and nowhere more than in tribal policing. In the previously referenced study of American Indian tribal police, this became a truism. Tribal police administrators and personnel frequently stated that their department personnel saw themselves as "the community." These tribal employees saw their job as a relationship with the tribe, as an extension of the community. They were responsive to the needs of the community, and felt a level of responsibility to that community. In short, they saw themselves and their department in relationship to each other, not as separate, unlike most police in the non-Indian community who tend to view themselves as "hired guns," whose job it is to fight crime, rather than solve problems.

Given this relationship, what form of policing is most applicable to Indian country? For much of the 20th century, the policing in the non-Indian community was of the "professional" model. This model, with its emphasis on technology, specialized police activities, and restricted use of police discretion does not conform to the concept of peacekeeping; the style of policing most commonly used in traditional or rural communities.

Professional-style policing in the United States is rooted in the Anglo-American concepts of law and government that were brought to this country by the first English settlers. In brief, this legal tradition is highly individualistic, placing a high value on the rights of the individual vis-a-vis government. In this respect, it is different than the legal traditions that prevail in continental Europe, which give far greater weight to the powers of the state. The individualistic ethos is also quite different than the more communal and collective traditions of the American Indian community (Walker, 1998).

With respect to law enforcement institutions, the Anglo-American tradition emphasizes a strict separation between government officials and citizens. The rights of the latter enjoy the highest priority, and government officials are entitled to use only those powers that are expressly granted to them. Moreover, these powers are strictly limited, with these limits being codified in the Bill of Rights (with statutes and court decisions interpreting and amplifying the various provisions of the Bill of Rights). American legal culture has become even more rights-oriented in the last three decades (as in, for example, the development of such notions as a right to privacy and the rights of specific groups such as prisoners, students, and the poor) (Walker, 1999).

Law enforcement professionalism, as it has developed in the 20th century, has emphasized the impersonality inherent in the Anglo-American legal tradition (Walker, 1977). That is to say, the individual police officer, in dealing with an individual citizen, is expected to suppress all personal feelings about the citizen and his or her actions. The officer is expected to enforce the law with cold and impersonal efficiency.

Or, in the language of the cops themselves, the officer is expected to do it "by the book." This impersonality represents an attempt to ensure equal justice, one of the highest values of Anglo-American law, and to suppress personal factors that might represent bias against a particular group.

Finally, law enforcement professionalism has been pursued through bureaucratization, with police services delivered through large and complex organizations operating on the basis of written and impersonal rules (Walker, 1977). In short, the essential nature of American law enforcement, from basic legal principles to police organizational structures, is very much in conflict with the communal and informal aspects of American Indian culture.

The opposite of this "professional" approach to police services is the concept of community policing, an approach that is beginning to take hold in the non-Indian community. Community policing has, at its heart, the belief that the control of violence and criminality is best achieved with the full cooperation and assistance of the community. This approach to policing emphasizes the concepts of restorative justice, and the enhancement of community cohesion and action, ideas that fit well within Indian Country, and with many women police officers.

The community policing approach of pro-active "peace-keeping" rather than arrests and crime control after an incident fits tribal law enforcement well, as does an emphasis on responsibility and accountability of law enforcement to the community, rather than only to the department's chain of command (Luna, 1999). The devolution of power to, and community consultation with, a broad-based circle of responsible leaders is a common approach to decision-making regarding many issues in many Indian communities. This element alone could greatly enhance the work of police in Indian communities.

Given the problems of high incidents of violence, victimization, suicide, and substance abuse on reservations, it is essential that tribal police departments pursue a course that will enable them to use all available personnel to the best of their advantage. Low pay,

high turnover, and lack of qualified personnel hamper tribal police departments. The availability of women to fill and promote throughout police ranks is an opportunity that tribal police departments should not miss. This course, however, is one that would distinguish tribal police departments from non-Indian ones, where women officers are often victims of discrimination and lack of opportunity.

Methodology

During 1996–2000, this author conducted a national study of the 170 tribal police departments in the United States. A survey form was developed and mailed to all tribal police departments, in conjunction with the Police Executive Research Forum, the University of Nebraska, Department of Criminal Justice and the Harvard Criminal Justice Policy Program. Follow-up phone contacts were made to facilitate receipt of the surveys. Ultimately, 78 tribal police departments of the 170 returned the survey, a response rate of 45.8%. Of the tribal police departments that responded 66 (38.8%) indicated that they had women in their ranks.

Three police departments in Washington state, two of them tribal and one immediately adjacent to a reservation were chosen for interviews. The choices were made given their proximity to each other, the length of time women had been in the departments, and the ranks women had achieved. In depth, face-to-face, interviews were then conducted during the summer of 2001. A total of seven tribal police personnel, both male and female, of varying ranks were interviewed regarding the "fit" of women within tribal policing, and issues related to promotion and special assignments. The interviewees included two male Police Chiefs, one female Detective, one male Sergeant, one female and one male Patrol Officer and one female Reserve Officer.

The interviews were of an open-ended nature, conducted both on the job and away from the job site. While much of these data are not yet analyzed, some trends have already emerged. The most striking findings focus on the "fit" of women officers within tribal police departments and the full integration of women within tribal police ranks.

 ## Findings

While there has been little research into women tribal police officers, some has been done on the problems faced by women officers within non-Indian police departments. One of the most serious problems reported is the lack of success women officers have had for promotional opportunities in non-Indian police departments (Walker, Spohn, & DeLone, 1996). Women in non-Indian police departments make up approximately 14.1% (or a total of approximately 76,747) of the country's 544,309 officers. Women of color who are police officers comprise approximately 3.5% of the total (Martin, 1994).

Throughout the United States, there are approximately 1,459 tribal police officers, of which approximately 217 (14.8%) are women. This percentage compares favorably with the percentage of female officers in non-Indian police departments. The comparison becomes ever more dramatic when the percentage of women in supervisory and command ranks is considered.

Women have achieved limited success in attaining higher levels of supervision and command in non-Indian police departments. Women in non-Indian police agencies hold few mid-level managerial positions (Sergeant for example), and are virtually excluded from command positions (Turner, 1996). The number of women who held positions above the entry officer rank in non-Indian police departments totaled just 3.3% in 1986 (Martin, 1994).

It is here that tribal police departments markedly diverge from non-Indian police departments. The number of mid-level managerial and command positions held by women in tribal police departments is impressive. As represented by the tribes reporting pertinent information in this study, there are approximately 290 supervisory and command positions in tribal police departments. Women hold 33 (11.4%) of all tribal police supervisory and command positions. Women hold approximately 13% of the mid-level managerial positions in tribal police departments, including 24 Sergeant and 3 Lieutenant positions. Further, women hold three Captain and three Chief positions, approximately 6.7% of the command positions in tribal police departments.

A strong argument for the equality that is perceived by women in tribal policing might be made when the percentage of women holding the rank of supervisor and above is compared to that of men holding such ranks. Approximately 15.2% of women in tribal policing hold the rank of Sergeant and above, a rate that exceeds their representation in tribal police departments. Approximately 20.6% of men in tribal policing hold ranks of Sergeant and above. While the numbers are still somewhat unbalanced, the position of women within tribal police departments is strong, and significantly stronger than that of women in non-Indian police departments. This alone could account for the lack of gender-based hostility, and commitment to community policing, perceived by women tribal police. This empowerment of women officers to function fully as police may have a significant bearing on the ability of tribal police departments to contend successfully with the violence that is rampant on reservations.

The "Fit" of Women in Tribal Policing

Women fit well within tribal police departments. They have been hired in higher numbers, and have reached positions of supervision and command more quickly, and in greater numbers, than in non-Indian departments. The most striking finding was the repeated emphasis of the value of women to the tribal police departments, and the lack of gender-based, job-related issues, for women in positions of supervision and/or command.

Frequently, male tribal police chiefs spoke of their belief that tribal police departments treated women officers equally, and that they were seen by other officers, and by the tribal communities, as equal. The chiefs repeatedly stated their commitment to the recruitment and hiring of the best personnel available. This position was underscored by the emphasis placed on recruitment of women into police ranks and on the availability and encouragement of training opportunities.

In one tribal police department north of Seattle, a non-Indian reserve female officer was being given extensive police officer training, at the tribal, county and state levels, in order to enhance her ability to become a full time tribal police officer. This woman, while on the list for a full time officer position with an adjacent, non-tribal police department, expressed her decision to stay with the tribal department, even though the pay would be significantly lower than the other opportunity. She stated that she had been made to "feel welcome" from tribal members, and other tribal police personnel.

This officer was enthusiastic about working in a small department that emphasized community policing, which, while given lip service, was not really accepted or adhered to by the non-Indian police departments with which she was familiar. She asserted that being in on the ground floor of the development of a new tribal police department gave her opportunities for training, assignment, and advancement that would not be available elsewhere. Most importantly, this officer had perceived no gender-based bias against her from either the community or her co-workers.

The Chief of Police, an American Indian from a different tribe than the one he serves, seconded the perceptions expressed by this female officer. He stated that, given the size of the tribal police department (a total of seven) it was essential that the members of the department all work together in a flexible and amicable manner. This Chief of Police emphasized the community policing approach that he felt was essential to working successfully on the reservation. He has placed an emphasis on training, not just in appropriate practices, but also to simply "open the eyes" of the officers to issues and new ways of approaching situations. He articulated the need for officers "to be able to think" and to evaluate situations, and his commitment to amicable resolution of community disputes.

At another tribal police department in northern Washington State, the situation for women officers was similar. An Indian female detective, who is a member of a different tribe, had also been recruited by non-Indian police departments but had turned down these opportunities, even though the pay was significantly higher, in favor of staying with the tribal department. She asserted that she had remained due to the opportunities for training and promotion, and due to the lack of sexism she encountered on the job. She used as an example of these opportunities the fact that she had been promoted to Detective within a period of 5 years, over many male officers with significantly longer tenure in the department.

This Detective emphasized the flexibility of the department, and its emphasis on being a good parent as well as a good officer. She stated that the department is very community oriented, and that there is a lot of balance in the department between officers of all ranks and the tribal government. She echoed Professor Bob Thomas when she stated that "tribal police officers have roles, but they also have relationships with the community, and with each other," a situation which she contends enhances the ability of tribal police officers to work successfully at all levels.

The Chief of Police, an Indian from a different tribe, corroborated the perceptions of the female Detective interviewed above. He emphasized the belief that a tribal police department should be tied to the tribal community. He contends that the tribal police department should work with the tools they have as part of the tribal community, and not attempt to turn a tribal police department into a state police department. He further emphasized his commitment to community policing, and his belief that tribal police departments should do their own felony investigations, rather than simply turning them over to the FBI.

The comfort levels and commitment to their departments expressed by women in tribal policing were unfortunately not the case for an Indian woman officer working in an adjacent, non-Indian, police department. This officer expressed general dissatisfaction with her department and with her situation. Three other women officers have all left the department, two from policing itself, leaving her as the only female officer.

This officer contends that she is not viewed as an individual, but instead "lumped" with other female officers who were deemed unsatisfactory by the department and about whom negative comments were frequently made. She has been the recipient of comments of a sexist nature, and has heard anti-Indian comments made about members of the community, although these have not been directed toward her.

This officer has frequently requested advanced training opportunities, but has been refused, even though she had a college education and held seniority over others who were allowed to attend. She, and other newer officers, are trained and committed to the concept of community policing, but the command staff, and other, more senior, officers are not. She believes that this difference in ideology is at the heart of much of the conflict in the department.

This officer has come to believe that her future in this department is limited. She does not feel empowered to do her best work in combating crime and violence in the community and has decided that, although she is committed to law enforcement, she will leave this department. Given contacts she has made with other women tribal officers, this officer has begun to apply with tribal police departments.

⊠ Conclusion

Women Police Officers experience a hostile work environment at a high rate in the non-Indian community. In a recent study, 87% of women police officers reported having such an experience (Fletcher, 1995). Further studies indicate that two-thirds of 70 female officers interviewed reported at least one instance of sex discrimination, and 75% reported incidents of on the job sexual harassment (Martin, 1992). It can only be imagined the impact that such a situation can have on one's ability to do the job required of a police officer.

In this study, the author explored the involvement of women in tribal law enforcement and the perceptions that tribal command, fellow officers, and women tribal police themselves had of their contributions to the field. Women are highly regarded in the tribal police departments for which they work, as evidenced by the numbers of women who have been promoted into responsible positions, and by the testimony of those with whom they work.

From the limited number of interviews conducted in this study, it would appear that women officers do not perceive tribal policing as a hostile work environment. Rather they expressed the belief that they, their work, and their ideas, were valued and that they were treated as equals. It is further evident that their male colleagues and superiors do not support the idea that tribal policing is a hostile environment for women. Rather, they emphasized the value of women as tribal police officers and the idea [that] when [the] "best person for the job" is selected; it might well be a woman.

The question remains whether the promotion of women into positions of responsibility influences the workplace, both as to policing styles and to a reduction of the perception of hostility that many women in non-Indian police departments express. It would seem that the numbers of women in supervisory and command positions within tribal policing might have a direct bearing on the empowerment perceived by women tribal police. The fact that a woman had recently become a tribal Chief of Police in the State of Washington was given by two female officers as a reason to stay within tribal policing. An exploration of the impact of increased numbers of women in supervisory and command positions could be of value, and further, to what do women attribute their movement into the higher ranks of policing within a tribal content.

Yet another question is whether the matrilineality, or the culture and traditions of a given tribe affects the advancement of women in tribal police ranks. The traditional role of women in particular tribes, and the acceptance of women in peacekeeping or other roles of influence, could help to explain some of the differences for women in Indian policing, and it is these differences that make working in tribal policing so rewarding for so many women.

With the rate of crime within tribal communities, the style of policing is a serious consideration. Of significance, then, is how women who hold supervisory and command positions approach policing, how that approach influences those they supervise and command, how this style of policing is viewed by tribal police command, and, most importantly, how effective their style, whatever it might be, is in serving the community. These questions remain for additional study. But some evidence is clear. Women in tribal police departments hold positions of influence within tribal policing, and it may be their status within the field that helps to reduce crime and violence in Indian Country.

 # References

Fletcher, C. (1995). *Breaking and entering: Women cops talk about life in the Ultimate Men's Club*. New York: Harper Collins.

Greenfield, L. A., & Smith, S. K. (1999, February). *American Indians and crime*. NCJ 173386. Washington: U.S. Department of Justice, Office of Justice Programs, Bureau of Justice Statistics.

Luna, E. M. (1997, March/April). Community policing in Indian Country. *Church and Society Magazine*. Presbyterian Church, USA.

Luna, E. M. (1998). The growth and development of tribal police. *The Journal of Contemporary Criminal Justice, 14*(1). 75–86.

Luna, E. M. (1999). Law enforcement oversight to the American Indian community. *The Georgetown Public Policy Review, 4*(2), 149–164.

Martin, S. E. (1992). The changing status of women officers: Gender and power in police work. In I. L. Moyer (Ed.), *The changing role of women in the criminal justice system* (pp. 281–305). Prospect Heights, IL: Waveland.

Martin, S. E. (1994). "Outsider within" the station house: The impact of race and gender on Black women police. *Social Problems, 41*(3), 383–400.

Turner, S. (1996). Review of *Breaking and entering*, by C. Fletcher, *Wisconsin Women's Law Journal, 11* (Wis, Women's L.J.), 175.

Walker, S. (1977). *A critical history of police reform*. Lexington: Lexington Books.

Walker, S. (1998, September). *Achieving police accountability*. New York: The Center on Crime, Communities and Culture.

Walker, S. (1999). *The rights revolution*. New York: Oxford University Press.

Walker, S., Spohn, C., & DeLone, M. (1996). *The color of justice: Race, ethnicity, and crime in America*. Belmont: The Wadsworth.

DISCUSSION QUESTIONS

1. What are some of the challenges faced by tribal agencies in the United States?

2. Describe some of the differences in the workplace experiences of female tribal police officers compared to female officers working in agencies off of American Indian reservations.

3. What are some of the reasons given by Luna-Firebaugh that explain the differences in the workplace experiences of female police officers working in tribal agencies compared to nontribal agencies?

READING 6

Ralph Weisheit and his colleagues take a look at how policing in small towns and rural areas closely mirrors the principles and actions associated with community policing. The authors compare policing styles among rural and urban areas. In addition, the relationship between the police and citizens in rural areas is different from the relationship between police and citizens in urban areas.

Community Policing in Small Town and Rural America

Ralph A. Weisheit, L. Edward Wells, and David N. Falcone

In recent years, American policing has seen the emergence of a new vocabulary and, some would argue, a new philosophy of policing. The *idea* of community policing has swept the country, although in practice the term has been defined in many ways, some of them seemingly contradictory. At the heart of community policing is the idea that police departments must be more responsive and connected to the communities they serve, that policing is properly a broad problem-solving enterprise that includes much more than reactive law enforcement, and that individual line officers on the street and in the community should have a major role in this process.

Community policing by no means represents an isolated development. Rather, it seems to have emerged as a correlate of various social trends and movements, particularly the victim's rights and civil rights movements, each of which has organized citizens to demand that police be more accountable to the public (Karmen 1990). Similarly, such grassroots organizations as Mothers Against Drunk Driving (MADD) have focused on monitoring criminal justice agencies and have demanded that they be more accountable to the public for their decisions. The interest in community policing among police administrators also parallels general management trends that have emerged in the business world. Total quality management (TQM), for example, concerns itself with reducing layers of bureaucracy, empowering line employees, and increasing responsiveness to customers (e.g., Walton 1986)—ideas that have figured prominently in discussions of community policing. Health care and medicine have shown parallel developments, particularly in the growing trend toward medicine as proactive wellness production, rather than simply reactive disease treatment. The result is an emphasis on holistic, coproductive, general practitioner, and family practice medicine, as contrasted with segmented, specialty-oriented medicine. Given the developments in policing's recent past, the greater organization of citizens, and management

Authors' Note: This manuscript was prepared with the support of the National Institute of Justice (Grant No. 92-IJ-CX-K012). The views presented here are those of the authors and do not necessarily reflect those of NIL. An earlier version of this article was presented to the Academy of Criminal Justice Sciences' Annual Meeting in Chicago on March 10, 1994.

trends more generally, it would have been surprising if some form of community policing had *not* become a dominant philosophy among police administrators.

Although community policing clearly has roots in earlier police strategies, as an organizational philosophy, its boundaries, implications for specific programs, and the circumstances under which it might be effective are still being explored. This article examines the idea of community policing by considering the fit between police practices in rural areas and the philosophy of community policing as an urban phenomenon. We suggest that experiences in rural areas provide examples of successful community policing, but the comparison also raises questions about the simple applicability of these ideas to urban settings.

What Is Community Policing?

Although a relatively new idea, the concept of community policing has already generated a sizable and rapidly growing body of literature (e.g., Brown 1989; Goldstein 1987; Greene and Mastrofski 1988; Moore 1992; Trojanowicz and Bucqueroux 1990; Wilson and Kelling 1989). Although there is agreement on some broad dimensions of the concept, there is substantial variability in the types of program activities included under this conceptual umbrella and in the presumed central focus of the approach. Some discussions depict community policing as primarily a matter of reorganizing the nature of *police work,* from reactive law enforcement to proactive policing (in the classical sense of that term), order maintenance, and problem solving.

At other times, the emphasis is on the implications of community policing for the *organizational structure* of police agencies as formal organizations. These discussions suggest that community policing is primarily a move from segmented, hierarchical, paramilitary bureaucracies . . . to more participatory and flexible organizations. Still other discussions of community policing stress the *community* half of the term and center on the idea that social order is most effectively a coproduction by police and the community, where police-citizen connections and cooperation are essential to doing the job effectively and properly.

The focus here is not on the organizational structure of police departments, although the rural setting does provide opportunities to study the issue of formal organization variability. Most rural municipal police departments are small and have simple organizational structures; however, it is possible for sheriff's departments to be rather large and organizationally complex while still serving a predominantly rural area. Rather than organizational structures, this study focuses on the relationship between the community and the police in rural areas and how this relationship affects police practices.

It is possible to extract three broad themes from the literature on community policing that are relevant to the relationship. The first has to do with the police being *accountable* to the community as well as to the formal police hierarchy. The second is that police will become more *connected* with and integrated into their communities, which means that police will interact with citizens on a personal level, will be familiar with community sentiments and concerns, and will work *with* the community to address those concerns. A third and final theme requires that police will be oriented to *solving general problems,* rather than only responding to specific crime incidents. The discussion that follows reflects each of these broad themes and how it plays out in rural areas. First, however, we will describe the existing literature that can also be used to build our arguments.

Existing Evidence

We begin with the simple observation that community policing looks and sounds a great deal like rural and small town policing, as it has been practiced for a long time. Although there have been no studies that directly examine the extent to which rural policing reflects many key elements of community policing, there are many scattered pieces of evidence with which one can make this case.

In his study of tasks regularly performed by police in 249 municipal agencies of differing sizes, Meagher

(1985) found that small agencies were more concerned with crime prevention, medium-sized agencies showed the greatest concern for providing noncrime services, and large agencies focused on enforcing criminal laws and controlling crime through arrests. Similarly, Flanagan (1985) examined public opinion data about the police role. He found that the larger and more urban the community, the more citizens were likely to believe that police should limit their role to enforcing criminal laws. Conversely, people from smaller communities were more likely to want police to perform a wide variety of problem-solving and order-maintenance functions. Gibbons (1972) also saw evidence of this emphasis on order maintenance in his study of "crime in the hinterland." In the sheriff's department in rural Pine County (a pseudonym), Decker (1979) observed that

> the police were called upon and *expected* to render services for a wide variety of irregular occurrences, only a few of which were statutorily defined as law enforcement responsibilities. For example, the deputies complied with a request to inspect a boundary line between two farmers' property that was only accessible by tractor. In a related incident, the same mode of transportation was used to check on a foundered cow. Many instances required the symbolic presence of a sheriff's deputy to legitimate its occurrence in the citizen's eyes. (p. 104)

In many rural areas, police *must* provide a wide range of services because other social services are either nonexistent or are more remote than the police. Marenin and Copus (1991) observed that in rural Alaska, where all types of social services are scarce, traditional law enforcement is a relatively small part of the service police are expected to perform: "Village policing is not normal policing, in the sense of law enforcement or crime control, but is much more of a social work kind of job" (p. 16), which includes fire fighting, emergency medical services, and rescue operations.

A number of researchers have observed that styles of policing are partly a reflection of the relationship between police and the community. Although police in

many urban areas may be viewed as outsiders, in rural areas they are viewed as an integral part of the community (Decker 1979). In interviews with officers from one rural department and several urban departments, Kowalewski, Hall, Dolan, and Anderson (1984) found that whereas officers in rural and urban departments had many similar concerns, they differed in several interesting respects. Urban officers thought they were less respected and less supported by citizens, whereas police in rural communities felt more public support for being tough, particularly with juveniles. Dealing with juveniles is an important function for rural police because this is often a major concern for rural community members (Decker 1979).

Consistent with the greater informality of social interaction processes in rural areas, rural and urban officers believed they were given public respect for different reasons (Decker 1979). In urban areas, respect went to the *position,* the role, or the badge, and it was believed that a good way to improve public respect was through professionalizing the department. In contrast, respect was thought to be given to rural officers as *individuals,* who had to prove that respect was *personally* deserved. This was often done by establishing a reputation for toughness and fairness early in their career.

Given the nature of rural culture and of social interactions in rural areas, police-community relations probably will be very different in rural and urban departments. In rural areas, officers are likely to know the offenders, the victims, and their families, just as the officer and his family will be known by the community. Rural officers are also more likely to know and appreciate the history and culture of an area and to use that information in their work, something observed by Weisheit (1993) in his study of rural marijuana growers. Given the close social ties between police and the community, it should be expected that rural officers will use policing styles that are responsive to citizens in their area and that, in turn, local residents should be supportive of the police. In fact, a 1991 Gallup survey found measurable rural-urban differences in the support that citizens show for the local police. In urban areas, 54% of the citizens reported having a great deal of respect for the local police, contrasted to 61% of rural citizens. The differences were even more pronounced when asked about police brutality and the discretionary use of force by police. In the survey, 59% of urban residents thought that there was police brutality in their area, but only 20% of rural residents believed this to be the case ("Americans Say Police Brutality Frequent," 1991).

The same features of rural policing that compel officers to be more responsive to the public also mean that rural police may have relatively less discretion because their work is more visible to the public:

> A major explanation for the high degree of police discretion found in urban areas is the *low visibility* of police actions. In smaller communities the actions of police officers are known to most of the population thanks to the effectiveness and extensiveness of informal communication networks; there they are more highly visible. As a result, small town police enjoy less latitude in deviating from dominant community values. (Eisenstein 1982, p. 117)

Consistent with this idea, Crank (1990) found that organizational and community factors had a different impact on the adoption of a legalistic police style in rural and urban areas. In urban areas, characteristics of the police organization, such as the number of ranks or the ratio of administrators to sworn officers, were better predictors of police style than were characteristics of the community, such as percentage Black or level of economic distress. In rural areas, these relationships were reversed, with community factors being more important than organizational ones. As might be expected, Crank's data suggested that rural departments are more responsive to the local community, whereas urban departments may be more sensitive to the dynamics of the police organization. Or, as a publication of the International Association of Chiefs of Police (IACP) put it, "The urban officer answers to the police department. The rural or small town officer is held accountable for his actions by the community" (IACP, 1990, p. 9).

In many ways, rural departments are positioned to be the very embodiment of community policing. According to the IACP document,

> Rural and small town police are closer to their community than are urban police. Rural and small town police are a part of the local culture and community, whereas urban police tend to form a subculture and move apart from the community.... Urban police tend to be efficient; rural police tend to be effective. (IACP, 1990, p. 8)

These scattered pieces of evidence suggest it would be fruitful to more fully examine the link between rural policing and community policing. They also suggest that rather than modifying rural departments to fit an urban definition of good policing, or of community policing, urban departments might well look to rural areas for insights into policing in general and community policing in particular.

The Study

The information presented here is drawn from a larger study of rural crime and rural policing funded by the National Institute of Justice. The larger study involves collecting and reviewing relevant literature, conducting a focus group with rural sheriffs, locating and cataloging data sets relevant to rural crime, and, finally, interviewing officials familiar with rural crime and rural policing. This article is based on information from interviews conducted to date. The larger study was not specifically designed to study community policing but to consider rural crime and rural policing issues more generally. In the course of reviewing the literature and in interviews with rural police, we were continuously presented with ideas that paralleled those raised in discussions of community policing in urban areas. Thus what follows explores one dimension of a larger study which is itself exploratory. The purpose is not to reach definite conclusions but to stimulate thinking and suggest patterns that merit further study.

Although over 100 people from a variety of perspectives have been interviewed thus far, this discussion is based on interviews with 46 rural sheriffs and with 28 police chiefs in small towns. Of these 74 interviews, 13

(18%) were face-to-face, and the remainder were by telephone. Although we wanted to include jurisdictions of varying sizes, the focus was on the most rural jurisdictions. Among interviewed municipal chiefs, their community ranged in size from 900 to 50,000 people, with an average of 7,500 persons. Departments ranged in size from 1 to 66 uniformed officers, with an average of 17 officers. The departments of the interviewed county sheriffs ranged in size from 1 to 182 uniformed officers, with an average of 23 officers. This figure is a very rough approximation because sheriff department size is difficult to compute due to sometimes high numbers of part-time employees, jail staff who are sometimes also sworn officers, and some counties having a large number of reserves. The county populations served by these sheriffs ranged from 2,100 to 712,000 people, with only 8 of the 46 sheriffs working in a county of more than 50,000.

As an exploratory study, locating subjects for interviews focused on identifying individuals from the widest possible range of social and physical environments, rather than on studying "average" rural settings. Indeed, the differences across rural areas are so substantial that speaking of averages is probably misleading and is certainly of limited use for policy. Rural Montana and rural Delaware, for example, probably are as dissimilar as they are similar. To capture as much of this range as possible, we selected police officers from across the country, attempting to include every state, while giving particular attention to the 18 states identified as predominantly rural by the federal General Accounting Office (1990).

Because we are engaged in an exploratory study, we felt it important to use largely unstructured interviews. Appreciating rural variation, and always keeping it in mind, we were still interested in identifying common themes. Thus we used the available literature and information gathered from a series of preliminary interviews to develop a list of question areas to be covered in the course of the interviews, but we also encouraged subjects to explore other areas they thought were important. Question areas included crime concerns, police-citizen interactions, police practices, and the working relationship between police and other criminal justice agencies. The length of interview ranged from 20 minutes to 2 hours but was typically about 40 minutes long.

 ## Observations

There was general agreement among the interviewed rural police that their long-standing police practices fit well into what has been termed community policing. However, the concept of community policing is a broad one, encompassing a variety of ideas. Consequently, we focus here on more specific ways in which rural police practices seem to mirror the principles of community policing.

Community connections. A key element of community policing is police-citizen familiarity and interaction. For example, having officers walk through neighborhoods and talk with people means that more citizens will know officers personally, and, at the same time, officers will come to know many individuals in a neighborhood. The bonds between rural police and the community are also strengthened by the practice of hiring local citizens in police agencies. Thus the officers not only know the community and share many of the values of its members, they are also members of that community and are often involved in community activities. As Decker (1979) noted:

> All members of the sheriff's department had biographies not uncommon to those of the community. The sheriff and his three deputies were all born and educated in the county. Prior to joining the force, every member was involved in an agricultural form of employment, the dominant form of employment for the county. There is evidence of integration into the community in other ways. Each member participates in an important community function; i.e., the softball team, Jaycees, Rotary, Elk's Club, etc. (p. 105)

Many urban departments have recently tried, with varying degrees of success, to induce individual officers to live in their work area, sometimes even providing financial incentives for them to do so. Living in the areas they patrol, however, has been a long-standing practice in rural and small town agencies that has occurred naturally and without special effort. Through increased citizen-police interactions, it is believed that citizens will be more likely to cooperate with the police, and police, in turn, will be more sensitive to the community.

Sheriffs and chiefs with whom we spoke frequently saw what they had been doing in rural areas as community policing and believed they were well ahead of urban areas in this regard. One sheriff's comments are typical:

> Yes, there's far more community policing taking place in rural agencies than urban. We have been doing community policing since time began, I believe. We have always stopped and talked with the ranchers, the businessmen. We have walked the streets, rattled doors, and checked on sick folks. We know the various workers in the community and what they do. We see the kid delivering papers at 6:00 a.m. and talk with him. We have always done that. We are much closer to the people. Consequently, your whole mode of operation changes. Our method of gathering information derives from our personal contact on a day-to-day or minute-to-minute basis. In an urban setting, you're out "developing informants." We do that too, but the vast majority of our information comes from regular folks on a regular basis. I'm a believer in scanners. That would cause cardiac arrest in a lot of agencies. We have gotten more help from folks that have heard us out on a chase and we have lost the guy. They call up and say, "He's two blocks away going down this street." Plus, it tells them we are on the job, what we're doing.

This illustration shows how a strong bond between police and the community in rural settings is helpful in enforcing the law. It is also true, however, that rural police themselves act differently when such a bond exists:

You cannot call somebody an SOB on the street here because the next day you could be buying tires from him or going in to eat in his restaurant. You've got to know these people because you deal with them day after day. I worked in Fort Worth, Texas. You get into a row with some guy down there—he's smart mouthing you, bad mouthing you. You can give it right back because you're not going to see that man again, except in court. After court, you'll never lay eyes on him again. Here, he's the cousin of the deputy who works the night shift.

Knowing their citizens well also allows rural officers greater latitude in disposing of cases informally:

> The street officer sees ol' Joe on the street and waves to him. When Joe gets drunk and gets into a row, he can just grab him and stuff him into the car. If he doesn't need to go to jail, he can just take him home and turn him over to Martha. She's going to straighten him out.
>
> In smaller communities, particularly with juveniles, which is most of the crime problem in small communities, in my experience, the parents were not some faceless, mythical creatures from the middle of nowhere. I could grab up little Johnny by the scruff of his neck or whatever and we would go talk to Mommy and Daddy, who also knew me. We could work things out a lot easier, without having to get involved in the formal justice system. . . . The small communities, at least where I worked, generally if we had to make an arrest, it was the exception rather than the norm. We almost looked at arrests as a last resort. Everything else either has not worked or will not work. If I had to make an arrest, it was almost as if I'd done something wrong further back down the line.

These close personal interactions also mean that citizens expect more of their police, both in the range of services offered and in the personal attention that will be paid to individual cases:

The city residents expect the man in blue to come by and be very perfunctory, a Joe Friday. We're expected to do the follow-up and a lot more caring. People expect caring from rural law enforcement. We're not there to just take the reports of crimes; we also scoot the kiddies across crosswalks. It's an obligation. We have to wave at everybody we pass by. We have to be more caring.

We've had a lot of examples. An officer might go to a domestic one night and he'll stop by the next night and see how things are going. It's not uncommon for an officer, where a couple of juveniles have gotten into trouble, the next day he's got off to go get 'em and take them fishing. They try and get involved personally and make a difference.

In rural areas, police are highly visible members of the community, and it is not unusual for citizens to know individual officers by name. It also appears rather common for a citizen to consider a particular police officer *his* or *her* officer and to request him or her by name when problems arise. Although this also happens to some extent in urban areas, it appears to be far more common in rural communities.

These examples illustrate how close police-citizen interactions in rural areas shape the nature of police work in those areas. For the most part, the features of rural policing described above arise quite naturally and spontaneously and are not the result of formal policies or of specific community policing *programs.*

General problem solving. Another central characteristic of community policing is the focus on general problem solving, rather than more narrowly on reactive law enforcement. That is, officers not only respond to specific criminal incidents, but, more importantly, they recognize and respond to more general problems that set the stage for specific criminal acts. These problems are not limited to "crimes" and the solutions need not involve arrests.

This lady just recently passed away. We've changed light bulbs for people. She called up,

she's old, she's not very mobile, she's scared. The power went off, and now she's hearing things. Tell us the name, we know we're going to change a light bulb, talk to her for five or ten minutes and everything's fine. That is a service that fortunately we can still do—spend the time, especially on some of the older residents. Everything is OK, we're here. You call, we're going to be there.

When asked about the kinds of problems to which his department was expected to respond, one small-town chief responded:

Everything, including the kitchen sink. I've had people in here to counsel families on their sex life because they think I'm the Almighty and can do that. I've had people come in who are having problems making ends meet, and we intercede for them in getting assistance, helping them file for welfare. We do a lot of service-oriented work. I consider it non-law enforcement. Somebody needs a ride, like an elderly lady needs a ride to the doctor. We'll take her to the doctor or go get her groceries for her.

Because they are closer to the public they serve, and because they are often the only 24-hour service providers in rural areas, rural police receive calls for a wide range of services. If they respond to a wider variety of non-police problems than do urban police, it is not because they are required to do so by statute or because written departmental policies demand it. Rather, it is because they define police work differently, perhaps because the people they serve are neighbors and fellow community members, rather than nameless, faceless citizens. As such, it is not a conscious formal decision but a necessity arising from the social context.

Rural versus urban policing. We found some of the most telling evidence that rural and urban policing styles are very different in the experiences of rural sheriffs and chiefs who had previously worked outside of rural areas or who hired officers with such experiences:

> Their [police and citizens'] kids go to the same school. You see them on the street. You see them in the grocery store. It isn't like a city. In fact, I've worked with several cities and their officers are cold. They treat the good people the same way they treat the bad people. They are callous.
>
> If you hire somebody from a larger agency who has been in a situation where they specialized, they tend to look at a "hay seed" operation and say things need to be done in a different way . . . We've had some real problems with them having personality conflicts with the public in general because they are used to dealing with people as faces and not as neighbors or friends or relatives.
>
> I'm willing to be shown that I'm wrong, but it's a lot harder being a sheriff of a small rural county than it is to be the sheriff of [a city] with a population of 250,000 because everybody in that [rural] county—they want to be able to pick up that phone, whether it be Saturday night at 2:00 in the morning and they have a problem. They want to be able to pick up that phone and call that sheriff. They don't want to talk to a deputy, or the dispatcher. They want the sheriff, "I have a problem." It may be dogs barking.

One officer who had worked in an urban department and then moved to a rural part of Alaska declared:

> If there's a bar fight and I get involved, and somebody comes toward me with the intent of attacking me, I've had several bar patrons jump on them and take them down and even put their hands behind their back so I can handcuff them. It's not like a bar in the lower 48. You still have to watch your back, but we're a part of the community here more than you are there. In an urban area, the police officer is not part of the community. Here, a police officer is a part of the community. We live here, we work here, our kids run around with their kids, date their kids, and go to basketball games. I encourage my officers, and I do it by example, to participate as much as possible in all community functions. . . . But we just don't have problems that we can't take the time to sit down and talk it over with them. In the lower 48, I never had time. At the end of my shift, I was handing call cards out for burglaries in progress and rapes to the following shift. I had already worked 2 hours overtime and I couldn't get to all of them. But here, we have time to take care of the problems. I don't know if they would even use it [the time] if they had it in the lower 48.

Another chief who was asked if he thought rural police had to be more sensitive to the public than urban police responded:

> Absolutely. I come from a bigger agency. In the bigger agencies, you lose that personal day-to-day touch with the actual citizenry, unless you're there for a specific reason. Here, we're very close to these people. There's not too many of us, so they all get to know you. They come in all the time with their problems, and not just law enforcement-related problems. Yes, we're extremely sensitive. It's a very close-knit operation.

These comments repeat many of the contrasts between rural and urban policing noted in earlier sections. Routine personal contact between the police and the policed changes the relationship between the two. And the fact that many rural officers live in the communities they police seems to further strengthen the ties between the two groups.

Effectiveness. Aside from being good public relations, it has also been argued that community policing is more effective. The idea that rural departments may be more effective is not consistent with stereotypes of rural police, and there may be some disagreement about what constitutes effective. One bit of evidence about the relative effectiveness of rural police comes from the *Uniform Crime Reports,* which report the percentage of crimes cleared by arrest by size of the community served. As Table 1 shows, agencies in rural counties have consistently higher clearance rates than departments in cities of 250,000 or more. This pattern holds for every index crime except rape, for which the clearance rates are essentially the same.

The gap in clearance rates between rural and urban areas shown in Table 1 is particularly marked for violent crimes. Some of the rural-urban differences

Table 1 Percentage of Index Crimes Cleared by Arrest, 1992		
Crime Type	**Cities 250,000+**	**Rural Counties**
Violent	38.5	60.7
Murder	59.6	74.5
Rape	53.4	53.0
Robbery	21.4	38.1
Aggravated Assault	53.2	63.4
Property	14.3	18.4
Burglary	11.3	16.4
Larceny	16.9	18.3
Vehicle theft	10.3	32.4
Arson	9.2	21.8
All Index Crimes	18.8	23.0

Source: Uniform Crime Reports 1992, Table 25, Pp. 208–9.

might be attributable to differences in reporting and recording practices. Rural police might, for example, be less likely to write up a report on a larceny if there are no suspects. However, this cannot explain the very large rural-urban difference in clearance rates for homicides. Homicides will almost certainly be recorded regardless of whether there are suspects. It is also possible that the close social networks in rural areas make it easier to solve crimes. One police chief told us:

You've got a specific number of kids who are committing things and it's very easy after a crime to determine who did it here. The closeness of the community and the wide variety of MOs, when something happens they usually leave enough of a telltale sign that we know exactly who committed it. We only have one school that we have to listen to for rumors and things. We've got a lot of law-abiding kids that let us know what they are hearing. We solved almost every one of our crimes here. For every one of our thefts, burglaries, we know who has done it.

A county sheriff echoed this view by noting:

For example, my secretary's husband owns the tire store. His tire store got burglarized. People know him and they know her, so they come and tell me "I know who did it." All we have to do is prove it. In some place like Fort Worth [Texas], that's not going to happen— ever. The people on the street don't know the cop; the cop doesn't know the person on the street. They don't intermix too much.

Finally, when one chief was asked if knowing people in the community made his job easier, he replied:

Yeah, I'll give you an example. I live on a road, and when I heard on the squawk box here of a burglary at a neighbor's house three doors down, I immediately called my neighbor across the street, because I knew the two girls were home at that time. I just asked them, "Did you see anything?" They said, "Yeah, I saw this person that was passing around." We picked them up and recovered the goods. Because we are small, my neighbors saw the car and recognized the person, the thief. It happens with some frequency because of the fact that people know each other.

The circumstantial evidence presented here suggests that rural police are more effective than urban police, and that effectiveness may be related to the close bonds among community members and between the community and the police. This was also suggested by Cordner (1989), who found that rural departments were more effective investigators, and this was in part due to the close social networks in those areas:

Consider two small police departments, one located in a rural area and the other in a metropolitan area. Although the residential populations served by the two agencies may be the same size, the investigators in the rural departments have some natural advantages. They actually know, by name, by sight, and/or by reputation, a much greater proportion of the people in their jurisdiction and its surrounding area than the metropolitan agency investigators know of theirs. The witnesses that they deal with are much more likely to have recognized suspects they observed. Also, the rural investigator has only a few neighboring jurisdictions to keep in contact with, whereas the metropolitan investigator may have a dizzying array of other police departments in close proximity. (p. 153)

Factors in the rural environment that seem to make rural police more effective are those interpersonal networks that community policing tries to foster in urban areas. Thus a better understanding of how rural departments use these networks may have implications for community policing in urban areas.

Other issues. Looking at policing in rural areas leads one to think about community policing in other ways, particularly to adopt a more elaborate conception of *the community* than is common in discussions of community policing. For example, community policing discussions often allude to the community in terms of lay citizens or nonpolice agencies that might be helpful to citizens. In the rural environment, however, the community in which the police officer works includes not only citizens but other criminal justice officials as well. As one sheriff describes it:

I tell the guys, we are as much social workers as we are law enforcement officers—community policing. We are expected to work for solutions for these people—what brought them to our attention. When these cases are brought to court, myself, the state public defender, the chief deputy, the prosecutor, and the judge have all set [sic] around a table and discussed what actions we're going to do to this guy, what treatment program we can come up with to keep him from becoming a repeater. I think that's probably unusual, even in rural areas. We take an interest. At court time, it's not unusual for the officer working the case, the prosecutor, and the public defender to go over here to the restaurant and get in the back corner where you have some privacy, and try to work out a solution to the case. What's best for him and what's best for the community?

It is easy to see how this informal approach can be a two-edged sword. In many cases it can render justice in the very best sense of the word. At the same time, however, it is less clear what happens to justice when the defendant is an outsider, such as a migrant worker, or an insider who is simply disliked, or when rural officers do not use good sense or sound judgment.

Accordingly, it is easy to see why some critics are concerned that community policing can shift away from something that is *for* the good of the public to a technique for manipulating the public and doing things *to* it (see Bayley 1988). After all, the development of the formal, militarized style of modern urban police was itself a response to corruption and misbehavior by police, arising from informality that also meant a lack of control (Klockars 1988). Although our study was not designed to examine misconduct or corruption among rural police, such a study would provide insights into problems that arise when the police and the community are *too* close.

Policing in rural areas can also illustrate the idea of decentralizing police department activities. One municipal chief, who previously had been a police officer in a large city, suggested that as generalists, rural police do not simply involve themselves in a variety of nonpolice functions, but they also have to be generalists within policing:

In a rural area, you do everything yourself. You do the fingerprinting, the pictures, the interviews, the crime scene, everything. In a big department in an urban area, you specialize. As a patrolman in an urban area, I would simply secure the scene of a crime. Once the detective arrived, it was theirs. The detective called in whoever they [sic] needed. Here, there's one officer on duty; he's the primary officer. If he calls for a backup and I come out, he is still the primary officer. The future of policing is where a complete, mature, well-rounded police officer can step into a situation and handle it, or call for the necessary elements to handle it. The day will come in this country . . . where all police officers, no matter where they are stationed, they're it. . . . There won't be chiefs and things like that. There might be supervisors, but they'll be stationed in one place where they can respond to many, many officers from many, many areas.

Rural police practices also raise questions about the nature of police accountability to the public and highlight the difference between *formal* and *informal* accountability. Formal accountability is more explicit but less direct, being concentrated through specific established channels of communication and authority within the organization. In contrast, informal accountability is diffused through multiple channels spread throughout the community, which are also more direct. For example, under formal accountability, the officer is accountable through the organization, and citizens make their complaints through formal channels. Their complaints are processed and eventually fed back to the officer. In contrast, informal accountability means that officers are more directly and immediately aware of citizen concerns and may hear about those concerns from a variety of people, both inside and outside the police organization, in a variety of social settings.

We have argued throughout that as a result of close social ties between police and community in rural settings and in the absence of organizational buffers in small rural departments, rural police are more accountable and responsive to local citizens than are urban police. Although this appears to be true of rural police as a group, rural sheriffs with whom we spoke were emphatic that, as *elected* officials, they were compelled to be much more sensitive to citizen concerns than were municipal chiefs. *If* their perceptions are accurate, and *if* accountability to the public is a worthwhile goal, then it is interesting to speculate what might happen if municipal departments shifted to a system in which chiefs were elected officials.

Discussion

We have argued that modern community policing draws heavily on ideas and practices that have long been traditions in rural areas, although this link is rarely made explicit. It is important to understand the rural dimensions that matter most. What makes the rural community unique in the examples given here is not simply low population density, but also relatively dense social networks. Even among rural areas there is variation in the density of these networks, and it is possible to police rural areas without having the kinds of experiences described here. State police, for example, may operate in rural areas but have relatively little connection to local social networks. As one sheriff observed about his own prior experience as a state trooper:

> I was in 11 stations in 25 years with the state police. I worked all over the place. You see a group of young state troopers come in, they work there for a very short period of time, they go out, they don't care about the individual population. They're statistically oriented—A, B, C—so they are out to make numbers. I think your [sheriffs'] deputies are there for life. They develop a better relationship with the people, on the whole, where they are *their* cop.

Similarly, one may be an officer whose background and/or personality make it difficult for him or her to fit in with the local culture—and it is our experience that such officers have a particularly difficult time doing their work. Thus a rural area is not simply a physical place but a *social place* as well. This is something community policing advocates in urban areas recognize when they suggest that beats cover *natural* (i.e., social) neighborhood boundaries, rather than those created for bureaucratic expediency. Of course, the social characteristics of crime and policing in rural areas are shaped by the size of the population and the size of the department. We do not know the threshold size for either departments or communities, that is, the size at which they cease to be clearly *rural*. However, we did encounter a number of departments in which rapid population growth had transformed their rural conditions and eroded the police-community networks that once characterized their community:

> That is the one thing that I'm crying about. We are now responding to in excess of 3,000 calls for service in a year. We are losing some of that personal contact. [His city] and some of the urban areas are having to limit the types of calls they will respond to, such as whether they will do funeral escorts. It's a Catch 22; when you become incident driven, the community plays a less active role, and it's a downward spiral.

Although we have gone to great lengths to show themes common to community policing and rural policing, we would argue that community policing is *not* simply and invariably identical to rural policing. Rather, community policing is a formalized and rationalized version of small town policing—where the purpose is to introduce accountability and provide a measure of legal rationality to what, in rural areas, is a much more spontaneous and informal process. Thus community policing and rural policing are not identical. Community policing is small town policing set in a rational framework that attempts to formalize the spontaneous acts of good sense and good citizenship found in many rural officers into a *program* that can be taught and that can be monitored and evaluated. This observation suggests a fundamental paradox of community policing—in many ways it is the formalization of informal custom and the routinization of spontaneous events.

It is also true that rural policing is not homogenous across the country. One implication of this is that, to be effective, there can be no *one* program of community policing. Effective community policing must be tailored to the needs and wishes of each individual community, just as rural police tailor their activities to their local communities.

Further, what we have learned about community policing in rural departments suggests there are elements of the model that chiefs and line officers in urban departments might *not* find attractive or acceptable. For example, the closeness between citizens and police in rural areas may have many benefits for both groups, but it also comes at the expense of the privacy of rural chiefs and line officers. We have observed there are very few rural chiefs or rural sheriffs whose home telephone numbers are unlisted—and many reported that citizens were more than willing to call them at home at any hour, even regarding minor problems. In many communities, line officers could also expect to routinely be contacted at home on police business. One rural chief provided a particularly telling example, an example that is unlikely to be duplicated by any large urban chief:

> In a small town you lose your private life, too. It has taken a toll on my wife and our kids. Two years ago on Thanksgiving we had our family over and then we had a domestic that ended up on my front porch. The husband came over to tell me the problem and then she came over.... It was pretty embarrassing. I have since put a sign up on my porch that says this is not the police department, it is our home. Dial 911 if you have an emergency. It hasn't worked. The amount of calls that you get at your house, and ... if you get an unlisted number, they will come by your house. I would rather have them call me.

This chief, and a number of others, also observed that when off duty they could not have a beer at the local bar without starting rumors in the community. In such cases it is not unusual for chiefs, sheriffs, and their officers to go to nearby towns if they wish to have a quiet evening or if they wish to have a drink. How many urban chiefs and line officers are willing to "live" their jobs to this extent?

Another feature common to rural policing that may not be welcomed by urban officers is the high level of community involvement expected of rural officers. In most rural areas, officers live in the community in which they work. Beyond that, it is our impression that rural police are more involved in civic organizations than are urban police. In most rural communities this is voluntary. One sheriff was more explicit, expressing his philosophy this way:

> I tell them [deputies] before they are ever employed that I want my people involved in the community in some way. It may be a service club, a fraternal organization, your church—I don't care what it is. But I don't want you and your partner to just work together all day and drink together all night. When you deal with the rear end of society, and the majority of our work deals with those kinds of people, it's awful easy to build a negative, horrible attitude where everybody is a SOB or a jerk.... Some kind of community activity, but in some way to deal with real people, just like themselves and see that they are not all criminals. If they'll do that, then they try to make their community a better place rather than just through law enforcement.

In summary, rural policing presents an *ideal type* example of community policing. A more extensive study of rural policing should allow us to determine which aspects of the rural police experience can be applied to urban models of community policing. At the same time it is important to determine if there are key elements of successful rural policing that will *never* fit the urban setting. By improving our understanding of these contrasting areas, the study of rural policing can also provide a better understanding of community policing's potential and its limitations.

References

"Americans Say Police Brutality Frequent." 1991. *The Gallup Poll Monthly* 306:53–56.

Bayley, David H. 1988. "Community Policing: A Report From a Devil's Advocate." Pp. 225–37 in *Community Policing: Rhetoric or Reality,* edited by J. R. Greene and S. D. Mastrofski. New York: Praeger.

Brown, Lee P. 1989. *Community Policing: A Practical Guide for Police Officials.* Washington, DC: National Institute of Justice.

Cordner, Gary W. 1989. "Police Agency Size and Investigative Effectiveness." *Journal of Criminal Justice* 17:145–55.

Crank, John P. 1990. "The Influence of Environmental and Organizational Factors on Police Style in Urban and Rural Environments." *Journal of Research in Crime and Delinquency* 27:166–89.

Decker, Scott. 1979. "The Rural County Sheriff: An Issue in Social Control." *Criminal Justice Review* 4:97–111.

Eisenstein, James. 1982. "Research on Rural Criminal Justice: A Summary." Pp. 105–43 in *Criminal Justice in Rural America,* edited by S. Cronk, J. Jankovic, and R. K. Green. Washington, DC: U.S. Department of Justice.

Flanagan, Timothy J. 1985. "Consumer Perspectives on Police Operational Strategy." *Journal of Police Science and Administration* 13:10–21.

General Accounting Office. 1990. *Rural Drug Abuse: Prevalence, Relation to Crime, and Programs.* Washington, DC: U.S. General Accounting Office.

Gibbons, Don C. 1972. "Crime in the Hinterland." *Criminology* 10:177–91.

Goldstein, Herman. 1987. "Toward Community-Oriented Policing: Potential, Basic Requirements, and Threshold Questions." *Crime & Delinquency* 33:6–30.

Greene, Jack R. and Stephen D. Mastrofski, eds. 1988. *Community Policing: Rhetoric or Reality.* New York: Praeger.

International Association of Chiefs of Police (IACP). 1990. *Managing the Small Law Enforcement Agency.* Dubuque, I A: Kendall/Hunt.

Karmen, Andrew. 1990. *Crime Victims: An Introduction to Victimology,* 2nd ed. Pacific Grove, CA: Brooks/Cole.

Klockars, Carl B. 1988. "The Rhetoric of Community Policing." Pp. 239–58 in *Community Policing: Rhetoric or Reality,* edited by J. R. Greene and S. D. Mastrofski. New York: Praeger.

Kowalewski, David, William Hall, John Dolan, and James Anderson. 1984. "Police Environments and Operational Codes: A Case Study of Rural Settings." *Journal of Police Science and Administration* 12:363–72.

Marenin, Otwin and Gary Copus. 1991. "Policing Rural Alaska: The Village Public Safety Officer (VPSO) Program." *American Journal of Police* 10:1–26.

Meagher, M. Steven. 1985. "Police Patrol Styles: How Pervasive is Community Variation?" *Journal of Police Science and Administration* 13:36–45.

Moore, Mark Harrison. 1992. "Problem-Solving and Community Policing." Pp. 99–158 in *Modern Policing,* edited by M. Tonry and N. Morris. Chicago: University of Chicago Press.

Trojanowicz, Robert and Bonnie Bucqueroux. 1990. *Community Policing: A Contemporary Perspective.* Cincinnati, OH: Anderson.

Walton, Mary. 1986. *The Deming Management Method.* New York: Perigee.

Weisheit, Ralph A. 1993. "Studying Drugs in Rural Areas: Notes from the Field." *Journal of Research in Crime and Delinquency* 30:213–32.

Wilson, James Q. and George L. Kelling. 1989. "Making Neighborhoods Safe." *Atlantic Monthly* 263:46–52.

DISCUSSION QUESTIONS

1. What is community policing?

2. What kinds of services are provided by police officers in small towns or rural areas?

3. What is the main finding from this study?

SECTION

4

Police agencies have become more diverse since the 1960s.

Police Officers and Police Culture

Section Highlights

- Discuss police culture.
- Explore how demographics of police officers have changed over time.
- Examine how changes in police personnel have altered the police culture.

There are approximately 837,000 sworn police officers working in local, state, and federal law enforcement agencies in the United States.[1] The number of sworn law enforcement positions has continued to increase each year for the last two decades.[2] There does not appear to be any slowing in the growth of this occupation any time soon, as the Bureau of Labor Statistics recently reported that the rate of employment for police officers is expected to grow 10% from 2008 to 2018. This is as fast as the average growth for all other occupations.[3]

In addition to an increase in employment, the people working in American police agencies have also changed significantly since the 1960s. This section discusses how police officer characteristics, specifically sex, race, and sexual orientation, have begun to change a profession that has historically consisted of White males. This section examines how, if at all, these changes in personnel have impacted the way that police work is conducted, its impact on the relationship between police and citizens, and the extent to which it has altered the culture that exists within American police agencies.

Police Culture

The idea that police are somehow different from the rest of society suggests that a police culture exists. The word *culture* refers to the behaviors and beliefs that are characteristic of a particular group.[4] Egon Bitner argues that the most distinctive way that the police are different from nearly every other occupation is that they possess the ability to use force.[5] The excerpt from John Crank's book, "Understanding Police Culture," included at the end of this section describes some of the elements that are unique to police culture.

Police culture has been studied from two perspectives. First, police culture has been studied by focusing on similarities among police officers and how they function as a group. This approach is based on the idea that the police are a distinctive group that functions according to a unique set of rules, practices, beliefs, and principles that are accepted by all members. Second, research on police culture has also looked at differences among police officers and police organizations and how this might affect the group and its work. This approach examines how variation in organizations, rank, policing styles, and individual officers can result in divisions within the police culture.[6]

Similarities Among Police Officers

William Westley first proposed the idea of a police culture when he studied the police using observation-based data in Gary, Indiana, in 1950.[7] His case study revealed that the culture of policing is based on **solidarity** among its members, the use of violence as an acceptable means of doing police work, and secrecy between the police, the public they serve, and police supervisors. In 1966, Jerome Skolnick also examined police culture with an observational study of the police.[8] His study revealed that police officers develop a "working personality" to cope with stressors related to their work:[9]

> . . . the policeman's role contains two principal variables, danger and authority, which should be interpreted in the light of a constant pressure to appear efficient. The element of danger seems to make the policeman especially attentive to signs indicating a potential for violence and lawbreaking. As a result, the policeman is generally a "suspicious" person. Furthermore, the character of the policeman's work makes him less desirable as a friend, since norms of friendship implicate others in his work. Accordingly, the element of danger isolates the policeman socially from the segment of the citizenry which he regards as symbolically dangerous and also from the conventional citizenry with whom he identifies.

More recently, Eugene Paoline III constructed a traditional occupational police culture model. According to Paoline, police officers have two working environments: occupational environment and organizational environment.[10] *Occupational environment* consists of interactions between the police and citizens, with a specific focus on the dangers of police work and the use of coercive force by police officers. To cope with dangers related to the job, police officers are suspicious of anyone that is not a police officer (an "us versus them" mentality). This often leaves police officers feeling socially isolated when they are both on and off duty. The *organizational environment* consists of police officers' interaction with their supervisors—specifically, the scrutiny by their supervisors and the ambiguous nature of the police role. To cope with role ambiguity, police officers maintain a "crime fighter image." They also practice a method of **CYA** (cover your ass) or "laying low" to avoid problems with their supervisors. CYA encourages officers to avoid participating in activities that might bring unnecessary attention to them.[11] Police culture, then, can consist of similarities among police officers with respect to their shared acceptance of a unique set of rules, practices, beliefs, and principles.

Differences Among Police Officers

Another way to study police culture is to examine differences among police officers or within police organizations. In the past, researchers have examined differences in police culture according to rank within police agencies. Elizabeth Reuss-Ianni found that two cultures of policing exist among the ranks when she conducted a study in the New York City Police Department.[12] First, a "street cop culture" was revealed at the rank of patrol officer. This culture is based on an "us versus them" worldview (with "them" including both citizens and police supervisors) and secrecy and solidarity among patrol level officers. Second, the "management cop culture" is shared by people working in ranks above the level of patrol. This group believes that community relations, accountability to the public, productivity, and cost-effective approaches to police work are important. They are viewed by patrol officers as being more loyal to political and social groups in the community than to their colleagues working within the organization.[13] This approach to studying police culture suggests that there is not a general consensus among all police personnel—specifically, that there are divisions among the police by rank within police organizations.

Police culture has also been studied by examining different policing styles adopted by individual police officers. Individual officers may not view or conduct their work in the same manner as their colleagues, but they remain loyal to their organization. Variation in policing styles can result from direct and vicarious contact with citizens, varying interpretations of laws, officers' perceptions of how they believe the job should be done or how they believe that their supervisors expect them to do the job, the nature of the environment they work in, and officers' perceptions of what they believe the citizens expect from them. Several typologies related to police officer styles emerged during the 1970s (see "Research on Police Officer Styles" below).

Research on Police Officer Styles	
R.B. Coates (1972)—"*Dimensions of police-citizen interaction: A social psychological analysis*"	**Legalistic-abusive**—is extremely rigid and authoritarian, views people as either good or bad
	Community service—wants to help people (the oppressed), avoids a heavy-handed application of the law
	Task oriented—is concerned with rules and procedures, both egalitarian and nonauthoritarian
Susan O. White (1972)—"*A perspective on police professionalization*"	**Tough cop**—sees his or her job as "keeping the criminal element under control" and is very concerned with the outcome of his or her work
	Crime fighter—focuses heavily on the enforcement of laws and crime control
	Problem solver—is sympathetic and respectful to citizens in need of help, social worker
	Rule applier—operates "by the book" but is friendly and polite during encounters with citizens

(Continued)

(Continued)	
M.W. O'Neill (1974)— *"The role of the police: Normative role expectations in a metropolitan police department"*	**Crime fighter**—believes "real" police work consists of investigating serious crimes
	Social agent—views him- or herself as a problem solver
	Law enforcer—focuses on crime control (both serious and less serious crimes), believes in the concept of deterrence
	Watchman—tries to maintain a low profile and does as little as possible
William Kerr Muir Jr. (1977)—*"Police: Street corner politicians"*	**Professional**—works within the boundaries of the law but is not afraid to use coercion or force if necessary
	Enforcer—"super cop," focuses heavily on law enforcement, sees people as either good or bad
	Reciprocator—has a helping orientation toward citizens, seeks to effect change
	Avoider—avoids doing any kind of police work, viewed as a misfit in the police role
John Broderick (1977)—*"Police in a time of change"*	**Idealist**—is concerned with citizens' rights and maintaining order, is very thorough when doing his or her job
	Enforcer—is a cynical, authoritarian, and extreme crime-fighter, is unhappy on the job
	Optimist—is oriented toward people, not crime, tends to enjoy his or her work
	Realist—feels unappreciated by the public, maintains "the hell with it" attitude toward his or her job as a police officer

Another way to examine differences within police culture would be to look at some of the characteristics of individual police officers. Historically, policing has been a profession dominated by White males, and as a result, the police culture reflects the values and practices that are accepted by this particular demographic.[14] So how does the police culture impact the workplace experiences and assimilation of women, racial/ethnic minorities, and gay and lesbian police officers? The next part of this section answers this question by examining the history, assimilation, and workplace experiences of these groups.

 Women in Policing

The entrance of women into American policing began in the late 19th century with them working as police matrons.[15] Police matrons worked primarily with other women and children and did not have the authority to make arrests. It was not until the early 1900s that women were officially recognized as policewomen. This new title allowed them to work with *both* men and women and also granted them the authority to make arrests. Lola Baldwin and Alice Stebbins Wells are often identified as the first policewomen in the United States. Lola Baldwin was hired by the Portland (OR) Police Department in 1908.[16] Alice Stebbins Wells was hired by the Los Angeles (CA) Police Department in 1910.[17] Dorothy Schulz, a leading expert on women in policing, points out that Mary Owens was hired by the Chicago Police Department in 1893 but is often overlooked as the first policewoman in the United States because she was given the title of "policeman" when she first began her career.[18] It was not until the late 1960s that female police officers were allowed to patrol the streets alongside their male colleagues.[19] It was also around that time that the title "policewoman" began to disappear, and female officers were then referred to as "police officers."[20]

Today, the number of women working as police officers in the United States is the highest it has ever been. A series of Bureau of Justice Statistics (BJS) reports indicates that women comprise 11.3% of all sworn positions in municipal police agencies, 12.9% in sheriffs' departments,

Female police officer looking after a lost dog—1953

6% in state police agencies, 16% in federal agencies, 15% in tribal police agencies, and 17% in university police agencies.[21] Women are also more likely to work in large police agencies. The National Center for Women and Policing reports that women represented 12.7% of all sworn positions in large police agencies and 8.1% in small/rural police agencies in the United States in 2001.[22] Affirmative action programs are believed to be a driving force behind the increasing number of women entering the policing profession since the 1970s.[23]

These employment statistics suggest that there has been some progress in the hiring of female officers in the last four decades; however, this progress has been slow, as women have only gained an average of one half of a percentage point per year from 1972 to 1999.[24] There is also some evidence that the increasing presence of women in policing has stalled in recent years.[25] For example, women represented 14.4% of all sworn positions in large police agencies in 1999, 13% in 2000, and 12.7% in 2001.[26] A BJS report reveals a similar trend as the number of women filling sworn police positions increased only slightly during the 1990s and 2000s.[27]

There has been less progress in the advancement of women into police supervisory and management-level positions. The National Center for Women and Policing notes that "Within large police agencies, sworn women currently hold only 7.3% of top command positions (chiefs, assistant chiefs, commanders, and captains), 9.6% of supervisory positions (lieutenants and sergeants), and 13.5% of line operation positions (detectives and patrol officers)."[28] Approximately 2% of chief of police positions in the United States are filled by women.[29] In contrast, a recent study found that women are moving up through the ranks within federal law enforcement agencies despite the fact that the hiring of women by this particular type of agency has become stagnant in recent years.[30]

Workplace Experiences of Female Police Officers

With policing being a male-dominated profession, how easily do female officers assimilate into police organizations? In her classic study, Rosabeth Kanter discovered that women are sometimes viewed as *tokens* within organizations that have mostly male employees.[31] A token group is a subgroup within an organization that represents less than 15% of the overall organization and is in some way different from the rest of the group.[32] The women in Kanter's study reported feeling isolated from their male coworkers and that they had difficulty fitting in at work. While Kanter's theory of **tokenism** has been applied to women working in a variety of male-dominated occupations, there have only been a few studies related to tokenism and female police officers. Most of these studies have found that female officers experience tokenism at some point in their career.[33] A recent study by Cara Rabe-Hemp found that some female officers reported that they had experienced token-based treatment early on in their careers, but that they experienced it less over time.[34] One could argue that this is a sign of progress for the assimilation of women into policing.

Research dating back to the 1970s has found that some male officers hold negative views toward female officers.[35] These negative perceptions have made integration into this profession difficult for some women. One reason some male officers hold these negative perceptions is the belief that female police officers are not strong enough to do the job.[36] This is interesting, because studies focused on the competency of female police officers have found that women are just as competent at police work as men.[37] There is also some evidence that female officers do not provide support or feel a sense of camaraderie with other female officers that they work with.[38] Studies have found that African American female police officers face an especially difficult time at work, as they have to deal with discrimination based on both their race and gender.[39]

Female police officers cope with the difficulty of assimilation into police agencies in many ways. Some women alter their role within the police organization in an attempt to be accepted by their male colleagues. Susan Martin found that female police officers negotiate their roles in the workplace. More specifically, some women choose to take on roles that resemble traditional gender roles in order to get along with their male colleagues (**policeWOMEN**), while other women want to be treated like their male colleagues and hope to counter stereotypes that women are unable to perform the duties of a street patrol officer (**POLICEwomen**).[40] Patricia Remmington found that female police officers took on passive roles at work by allowing their male partners to always drive the patrol car and take control during interactions with citizens.[41] By allowing the male officers to take charge, female officers were not viewed as a threat to them. This approach to role negotiation might resolve conflict between male and female officers in the workplace at that time; however, it could be detrimental to women in the future if they choose to pursue promotion into positions that would require them to demonstrate leadership qualities.

Men and women work alongside each other, participating in similar activities, in police agencies today.

Despite the struggle that some women experience when attempting to integrate into police agencies, research findings are mixed when it comes to female officers experiencing greater levels of stress, lower levels of job satisfaction, greater levels of cynicism toward their work, and consideration of job change when compared to male police officers.[42] This means that some female police officers have negative workplace experiences while others do not.

A Comparison of Male and Female Police Officers

An interest in learning more about female police officers started when they began to engage in patrol duties alongside their male colleagues in the late 1960s. Female officers demonstrated early on that they are as competent at police work as male officers.[43] In fact, there are very few differences among male and female officers when it comes to their work. For example, research indicates that men and women have similar reasons for wanting to both pursue and maintain careers in policing.[44] The most common reasons given by both of these groups include wanting a job that provides a good salary and job security, being able to help other people, and wanting an exciting career that allows them to be outside of an office setting.[45] Another similarity between these two groups relates to their decision to pursue promotion. Female officers' attitudes toward the promotion process are influenced by their own perception of their leadership abilities, job satisfaction, negative experiences at work related to administration bias, and factors related to marriage, family, and children.[46] Male police officers gave similar responses, with the exception of having doubts about their leadership abilities and fear of bias of the administration.[47]

While research has revealed that female officers are just as competent at police work as male officers, some studies have found slight differences in *how* male and female officers do their jobs:

- Male officers generally issue more tickets and make more arrests than female officers.[48]
- Female officers use their firearms less often than male officers.[49]
- Male officers are more authoritarian than female officers.[50]
- Male officers are more likely to use controlling behaviors (such as physical restraints and verbal threats) than female officers.[51]
- Female officers are less likely to be named in complaints filed by citizens.[52]
- Female officers show greater empathy for victims of rape and domestic violence.[53]

✉ Racial/Ethnic Minority Police Officers

Policing in the United States has been a profession dominated by White males dating as far back as the mid-1800s.[54] Today, police officers across the United States are still predominantly White and male; however, some progress has been made in the racial/ethnic diversification of American police agencies. This progress initially began with the passing of the 1964 Civil Rights Act (Title VII), which prohibits employers from discriminating against individuals based on their race, color, religion, sex, or national origin. Several years later, the 1972 Equal Employment Opportunity Act extended protection against employment discrimination to state and local government agencies. Similar to the experience of women in policing, these two pieces of legislation provided opportunities for racial/ethnic minorities to enter the policing profession but did not guarantee them easy integration into this line of work.

African American Police Officers

According to W. Marvin Dulaney, the introduction of African Americans into American policing dates back to 1803 in New Orleans when "'free men of color' served on the city guard and constabulary forces."[55] Using census data and other historical records, Jack Kuykendall and David Burns also examined the history of the employment of African American police officers in the United States. They discovered that there were an

Employment of African American Police Officers in the United States	
Year	**% of African American Officers**
1890	2.7
1900	2.2
1910	.88
1920	1.2
1930	.97
1940	.90
1950	2.0
1960	3.5
1970	6.3
1987	9.3
2003	11.3
2007	11.9

estimated 74,629 watchmen, policemen, and firefighters in the United States in 1890 and that 2,019 of those workers were African American.[56] Their study indicates that the progress for hiring African American police officers was slow from 1890 to 1970, while more recent statistics provided by the Bureau of Justice Statistics indicate that the progress has continued to be slow from 1970 to 2007 (see table to the left).[57]

There is some evidence that progress has been made with African American police officers being promoted into supervisory or management-level positions within American police agencies. African American chiefs of police were leading half of the largest police agencies in the country during the 1980s.[58] In the 1990s, there were approximately 200 African American police executives.[59] In 1997, when the Police Executive Research Forum (PERF) surveyed police executives in the United States, 10.9% of the respondents identified themselves as African American chiefs of police.[60]

There has been little research conducted on the workplace experiences of African American police officers. The little research that has been conducted on this topic has revealed several barriers in the workplace, including the following:[61] (1) unfair evaluation during field training programs—this process can disqualify African American officers before they reach the end of their probationary period after the training academy; (2) unfair disciplinary practices—African American officers are more likely to receive some kind of formal disciplinary action when compared to White officers; this becomes problematic later on if they want to advance within the organization; and (3) blocked opportunities for promotion into either specialized or supervisory positions—African American officers are not included in the informal networking that plays an important role in the promotion process.

Hispanic Police Officers

It is difficult to trace the history of Hispanic police officers in the United States, as there has been very little research conducted on this group. Most of the research on diversity in American policing has focused on the experiences of African American officers.[62] Limited information on the employment of Hispanic police officers can be found in the histories of several police agencies across the southern region of the United States. For example, the San Diego Police Department hired its first Hispanic police officer in 1889.[63] Even earlier, Pablo de la Guerra Y Noriega was the first Hispanic U.S. marshal, working in Southern California from 1850 to 1854.[64] Outside of the historical accounts found on department websites, there is virtually no research on the history of Hispanic police officers in the United States.

Today, there is increased interest in this group, as the U.S. Census has identified Hispanics as the fastest growing racial/ethnic group in the country. According to figures from the 2010 Census, Hispanic citizens represent about 15.5% of the overall population in the United States and are expected to triple in number by 2050.[65] Statistics on Hispanic police officers also indicate an increase, as they represented 4.5% of all sworn positions in 1987, 9.1% in 2003, and 10.3% in 2007.[66] Cynthia Perez McCluskey and John McCluskey found that the degree of enhanced diversity in police agencies varies by the ethnic composition of the community; cities with large Hispanic populations are also more likely to increase Hispanic representation within their police force.[67] There appears to be limited Hispanic representation in police supervisory and management-level positions. Survey results from a 1997 police executive survey conducted by the Police Executive Research Forum reported that 4.7% of the surveys were filled out by executives that identified themselves as Hispanic.[68]

As the composition of police agencies has changed over time, workplace experiences of police officers have also changed.

Despite the increase in employment of Hispanic police officers, little research has been conducted on the workplace experiences of this group. One of the few studies focused on the experiences of Hispanic police officers was conducted in the mid-1980s. David Carter studied perceptions of discrimination among Hispanic police officers. Using survey and interview data, he found that Hispanic police officers felt that they are discriminated against in the workplace. The officers reported that they believe that Hispanic citizens living in their communities have also experienced discrimination from the police.[69] Interestingly, when Hispanic officers in this study reported that they had been treated in a discriminatory manner at work, they also stated that they believed that it was not done intentionally, but that it was "just the way that things worked in their department."[70] The workplace experiences of minority officers (including Hispanic officers) were recently explored in the Hassell and Brandl article included at the end of this section.

Asian Police Officers

Very little is known about Asian police officers working in the United States. There are two general reasons for the lack of research on Asian police officers.[71] First, there is an assumption based on stereotypes that Asian Americans are "model minorities" that do not experience employment discrimination like other racial/ethnic groups. Second, there are only a few police agencies across the United States that employ any measurable percentage of Asian officers to conduct research that results in generalizable findings. As a result, researchers will either ignore this group of officers or add them into the "other" category with various other racial groups.

Some of the important "firsts" for Asian police officers in the United States have been documented by newspapers and other media outlets. For example, Fred H. Lau is believed to be the first Asian American to head a major city's police force on the U.S. mainland. He served as chief of police for the San Francisco Police Department from 1996 to 2002.[72] Heather Fong is another pioneer for Asian police officers. She was the first Asian American woman to lead a police agency in a major metropolitan city (San Francisco, CA) in the United States.[73] Hired in 1977, she worked her way up through the ranks over the course of 27 years and was ultimately sworn in as police chief in 2004.[74]

Official statistics provided by the Bureau of Justice Statistics combine Asian, Pacific Islander, and American Indian officers into one large group. This group comprised 0.8% of all sworn police positions in 1987, 2.8% in 2003, and 2.7% in 2007.[75] Another data source reveals that only 1.6% of all sworn police officers in the United States are Asian.[76] It is unclear why there are so few Asian police officers. In an interview with the *New York Times*, Cochi Ho (an FBI agent in New Jersey) stated that "Being in law enforcement is considered a negative…in most Asian countries police officers are considered low jobs for uneducated people."[77] This statement suggests that there could be cultural barriers for police agencies to overcome if they are seeking to recruit Asian applicants for employment. Jean Reith Schroedel and her colleagues studied Asian American police officers in California. They believe that stereotypes about Asian Americans being timid and unassertive could explain why there are so few Asian Americans police officers. Also, during oral interviews conducted during the hiring process, there could be bias against the verbal accents of Asian applicants that influences whether or not they are hired.

Tea & Justice: NYPD's 1ˢᵗ Asian Women Officers, is a documentary that presents the workplace experiences of three Asian women who joined the New York Police Department during the 1980s.[78] This documentary features the careers of Officer Trish Ormsby and Detectives Agnes Chan and Christine Leung. The women share stories about their levels of satisfaction at work, how stereotypes related to the Asian culture have impacted them in their work environment, and how they have overcome those barriers over the course of their careers.[79] Similar to all other race/ethnic groups in American policing, there is a need for additional research on the workplace experiences of Asian police officers.

Gay and Lesbian Police Officers

The 1964 Civil Rights Act (Title VII) prohibits employers from discriminating against individuals based on their race, color, religion, sex, or national origin. Conspicuously absent from this list of characteristics is sexual orientation; however, today there are 20 states and more than 100 local jurisdictions in the United States that prohibit public employment discrimination based on sexual orientation.[80] It is difficult to judge how much progress has been made in the employment of gay and lesbian officers in the United States, as no national data have been collected on this group. Further, it is difficult to identify gay and lesbian officers unless they choose to reveal their sexual orientation. Unlike women and racial/ethnic minority officers, gay and lesbian police officers do not possess any visible attributes specifically identifying them as members of a minority group.

Some gay and lesbian police officers are making the decision to "come out" and identify themselves as gay or lesbian at work. A 1998 article in *The Advocate* describes how some police officers are choosing to disclose their sexual orientation at work to make it easier for other gay and lesbian officers to come out in the future.[81] Still, other gay and lesbian police officers are choosing not to reveal their sexual orientation at work, as they fear that their status will impede their ability to succeed at work. This article, along with a few published studies, reveals that there are difficulties that gay and lesbian officers have had to endure after they reveal their sexual orientation at work.

Workplace Experiences of Gay/Lesbian Police Officers

Policing is a profession dominated by a White, masculine, heterosexual ethos.[82] It is based on an image that places value on physical strength, aggressiveness, and authority. These valued characteristics have made it difficult for women, racial/ethnic minority, and gay and lesbian police officers to fully integrate into police organizations. There is some research that suggests that like in society, there are homophobic attitudes within some police agencies.[83] Phillip Lyons and his colleagues discovered that some police officers endorse homophobic statements. This was especially the case with police officers working in rural police agencies, as they reported the highest levels of homophobia when compared to officers working in urban areas.[84] It is important to note, however, that there is no existing research that has linked police officers' homophobic beliefs with discriminatory actions at work.

There are several reasons that some people oppose the idea of gays and lesbians working as police officers.[85] First, some people believe that the public would lose respect for the police or not view them as a legitimate group. There is also a concern that the employment of gay and lesbian officers would negatively impact morale within police departments and, in some cases, heterosexual officers might not provide backup or support for gay and lesbian officers in dangerous situations. And finally, there is concern that officers would be faced with unwanted sexual attention from gay and lesbian officers. It is important to point out that there is no research to support any of these assertions.

In contrast, people that support the hiring of gay and lesbian police officers believe that sexual orientation has nothing to do with being a competent police officer.[86] Further, some believe that gay and lesbian police officers could actually improve police–community relations. There is some evidence that gay and lesbian officers are often not as quick to judge people and are more compassionate toward citizens that are disenfranchised in society or that have a history of being treated poorly by the police.[87] Interestingly, gay and lesbian police officers assert that regardless of their sexual orientation, all police officers are trained the same way—essentially, this suggests that police training and socialization supersede any individual officer characteristics (including sexual orientation).

Research centered on the workplace experiences of either "closeted" police officers or officers that are "out" have found that there are some problems with integration. Gay and lesbian officers have reported that they have to manage their gay identities at work in order to fit in.[88] Some gay and lesbian police officers report that they feel like they need to prove that they are strong enough to do the job.[89] This group of police officers faces attitudinal barriers to equality at work including being the target of homophobic comments or jokes, being treated like outsiders by fellow officers (feeling socially isolated at work), or being identified as the token gay/lesbian for their police agency.[90] Despite feeling like outsiders at work, many gay and lesbian police officers reported that they are very committed and loyal to the policing profession.

Employment-based barriers faced by gay and lesbian police officers include problems related to promotion, officer assignment, and evaluations based on work performance.[91] There are two contrasting viewpoints on promotion opportunities for gay and lesbian officers. First, some officers believe that their chances of being promoted would be greatly reduced if they were "out" at work.[92] They feel that supervisors with a bias against gay men and lesbians would be less likely to support their advancement within police agencies. Other officers believe that their chances for promotion would greatly improve if their sexual orientation were known at work, as it would give police executives bragging rights about having diverse agencies and supporting the promotion of gay and lesbian officers.[93]

Despite some of the integration issues, several police agencies have made positive changes to alter the workplace environment to be more accepting of gay and lesbian officers. In 2002, a published case study on the integration of gay and lesbian personnel in the San Diego Police Department revealed that there has been a process of normalization with the acceptance of working alongside gay and lesbian officers.[94] Further evidence of progress is the creation and implementation of gay, lesbian, bisexual, and transgender (**GLBT**) units or liaison officers in some police agencies across the United States. GLBT liaison officers/units act as conduits between the police and gay and lesbian communities. And finally, there are several metropolitan police agencies that specifically recruit gay and lesbian officers, including Minneapolis, Boston, Portland, Seattle, Madison (WI), Atlanta, Philadelphia, San Francisco, Los Angeles, New York City, and Chicago.[95]

 Impact of Diversification of Police Agencies

When comparing the demographic characteristics of police officers four decades ago to those of officers working in contemporary police agencies, it is clear that there have been changes. The next logical question is: How have these changes in personnel influenced police agencies or how police work is conducted in the United States? David Sklansky asserts that there are two possible responses to this question.[96] One response is that the changes in police personnel have changed nothing—"blue is blue," or, in other words, "the job shapes the officer, the officer does not shape the job."[97] Another potential response would be that these changes in police personnel have had an effect on everything—including the competency of police officers, police–community relations, and effects on police organizations, specifically police culture.[98]

After reviewing research in all three areas, Sklansky concluded that, in general, there is no research evidence that suggests that minority police officers differ in behaviors at work when compared to White officers.[99] His assessment of the research on community effects resulting from diversification of police agencies revealed mixed findings, with only a few studies finding that changes to police personnel had an effect on police–community relations.[100] He notes that the culture within police agencies, along with police socialization and training, overrides any effect that changes to police personnel might have on either officer behavior or community relations.

More research is needed to understand exactly how the police culture has been changed by increased diversification.

Sklansky determined that the diversification of police personnel has had some effect on police organizations. There is evidence that one-on-one interactions between White and minority officers can produce positive changes in some police officers' attitudes. Police associations have also had an effect on police organizations, as they serve as both social and fraternal organizations for officers and also as collective bargaining agents and lobbying groups for various groups of officers.[101] Some examples of these organizations include the Fraternal Order of Police, National Black Police Association, the International Association of Women Police, National Asian Peace Officers' Association, Lesbian and Gay Police Association, and the National Latino Peace Officers Association.

And finally, Sklansky reports that diversification of police officers has produced *social fragmentation* within police agencies in the United States. Social fragmentation is when police officers divide into segmented groups within an organization based on certain characteristics (such as race/ethnicity, gender, and sexual orientation).[102] These divisions among police officers within police organizations have changed the nature of the police culture.

Despite an increase in the representation of women, racial/ethnic minorities, and gay and lesbian officers, progress is still needed on the integration of these groups into what has traditionally been a profession dominated by White males. By continuing to increase representation of these groups and providing opportunities for them to be in positions of leadership, much-needed changes in the police culture could take place in the future.

SUMMARY

- Women did not begin to patrol the streets with their male colleagues until the late 1960s.
- Both men and women report that they wanted to become police officers because it provides a good salary and job security, they are able to help other people, and they want careers that are exciting and allow them to be outside of an office setting.
- There is very little research focused on the workplace experiences of police officers from various racial and ethnic backgrounds.
- The police culture makes it difficult for some racial/ethnic minority, female, and gay and lesbian police officers to fully assimilate into some American police agencies.

KEY TERMS

CYA

GLBT

police culture

POLICEwomen

policeWOMEN

solidarity

tokenism

DISCUSSION QUESTIONS

1. Who were two of the first policewomen hired in the United States?

2. Explain the progress of female police officers being promoted within American police agencies.

3. How did the 1964 Civil Rights Act (Title VII) impact the hiring of both female and racial/ethnic minority police officers?

4. Describe some of the hurdles faced by gay and lesbian police officers.

5. David Sklansky presents two perspectives on the impact of the diversification of police agencies. Identify and explain both of these perspectives.

6. What is tokenism? How does it impact the workplace experiences of female and racial/ethnic minoriy officers?

WEB RESOURCES

- To learn more about women in policing, go to http://womenandpolicing.com/.
- To learn more about African American police officers, go to http://www.noblenational.org/.
- To learn more about Asian police officers, go to http://www.napoaonline.org/.

READING 7

The assimilation of women, racial/ethnic minorities, and gay and lesbian officers into American police agencies has not been without some difficulty. Kimberly Hassell and Steven Brandl examine the workplace experiences of these groups with the Milwaukee Police Department in Wisconsin. An analysis of the survey data reveals that these groups report different workplace experiences when compared to their White male colleagues. The findings in this study mirror others that have found that the workplace climate influences workplace stress.

An Examination of the Workplace Experiences of Police Patrol Officers: The Role of Race, Sex, and Sexual Orientation

Kimberly D. Hassell and Steven G. Brandl

Introduction

Historically, policing has been an occupation represented primarily by White males. Over the last several decades, however, a fundamental reform effort undertaken in police departments across the country has been to diversify the workforce, especially with regard to race, sex, and, most recently, sexual orientation of officers (National Research Council, 2004). To a large extent, these efforts have been prompted by equal opportunity law, in particular the Civil Rights Act of 1964, the 1972 Equal Employment Opportunity Act, affirmative action policies, and court orders (Alozie & Ramirez, 1999; Lewis, 1989).

Aside from the legal mandates, many arguments have been offered espousing the benefits of a more diverse police workforce. For example, it has been suggested that diversity in the workforce encourages tolerance in interactions with a diverse citizenry; that it encourages different styles of policing, promotes trust and fairness in policing, it encourages citizen support and cooperation with the police, and that diversity

encourages multiple viewpoints and ideas on how to go about doing "good" police work (e.g., see National Research Council, 2004; Skolnick & Fyfe, 1993).

Although police departments have increased the representation of racial minorities and women, research has demonstrated that the assimilation of these officers into workplace cultures has not been problem-free (Dodge & Pogrebin, 2001; Martin, 1994; Pike, 1985; Texeira, 2002). Indeed, a potentially significant impediment to the creation of a well-functioning diverse workforce is that individuals, or groups of individuals, may receive (or perceive) unequal treatment at work, in spite of equal employment opportunity laws. Unequal treatment may lead to many negative outcomes, including employee turnover, productivity and performance declines, absenteeism, and even civil claims, not to mention the individual consequences for workers (e.g., Anderson, Litzenberger, & Plecas, 2002; Brown, Cooper, & Kirkcaldy, 1996; Crank, Regoli, Hewitt, & Culbertson, 1995; Haarr & Morash, 1999). Perceptions of inequality at work may also be a major factor that deters some people from seeking employment in the occupation in the first place (Peak, 1997).

To create and maintain a diverse workforce that is hospitable, it is necessary to first be aware of officers' workplace experiences and problems. With this understanding, interventions may be developed to address these issues. In this article, we report the results of analyses that extend our understanding of the relationship between officers' characteristics and workplace experiences and we examine a potential consequence of negative workplace experiences. Specifically, we address three fundamental questions: First, do officers (considering differences in sex, race, and sexual orientation) have the same workplace experiences? Second, do officers differ in terms of their reported workplace stress? And third, do officers'[1] characteristics and/or workplace experiences influence officer stress?

In answering these questions, we address some of the shortcomings evident in prior research on the issue. Often, studies that examine the workplace experiences of officers are based on national or cross-departmental surveys and the corresponding data are analyzed without regard to differences across these departments (e.g., Morash & Haarr, 1995). Although formal police organizational structures tend to be similar (Crank, 2003; Maguire, 2002), the informal structures and organizational cultures of police departments tend to vary markedly (Hassell, 2006; Paoline, 2003). As a result, for example, White officers in predominately non–White police departments may have substantially different workplace experiences and problems than White officers in predominately White police departments. Simply stated, data collected from national studies, or studies including multiple departments, may mask important department level variation (National Research Council, 2004). In this study, we focus on the experiences of officers in a single police department.

In addition, many studies that examine the workplace experiences of police officers focus on *either* racial or sex differences (Bolton, 2003; Collins, 2004; Dodge & Pogrebin, 2001; Dowler, 2005; National Center for Women and Policing, 2002; Peak, 1997; Texeira, 2002; Wells, Wells, & Alt, 2005) and only a few studies examine the experiences of gay and bisexual officers (Belkin & McNichol,

2001; Bernstein & Kostclac, 2002; Buhrke, 1996; Burke, 1994; Leinen, 1993; Miller, Forest, & Jurik, 2003). In this study, we examine all three characteristics: race, sex, and sexual orientation. To the extent possible, we examine interaction effects among these characteristics as they may relate to workplace experiences and problems. Finally, unlike most other studies that have examined the workplace experiences of officers, we examine the relationship between officers' workplace experiences and a potential consequence of those experiences: stress. By extending the research in these ways, we cast additional light on the workplace experiences of police officers and the consequences of those experiences.

 ## Police Organizational Climate and Workplace Problems

To understand the behaviors, attitudes, and perceptions of police officers, one must be cognizant of the organizational context in which officers work. An important dimension of this context is the climate of the organization. Climate refers to the patterns and the nature of interactions among organizational members. It is how the context of the organization is actually perceived, experienced, and interpreted by its members. It affects members of the organization. As Dennison (1996) explained, "Climate refers to a situation and its link to thoughts, feelings, and behaviors of organizational members. Thus, it is temporal, subjective, and often subject to direct manipulation by people with power and influence" (p. 644). A climate characterized by negative interactions among members may create workplace problems for (some) members (Morash & Haarr, 1995). Workplace problems are negative and may have detrimental consequences, such as dysfunctional levels of stress and poor job performance.

The Workplace Problems of Police Officers

Research consistently shows that racial/ethnic minorities in policing experience workplace problems that differ from the problems of their White counterparts (Bolton, 2003; Dowler, 2005; Haarr & Morash, 1995, 1999; Peak, 1997). Morash and Haarr (1995) found that for racial/ethnic minorities, the sense of being "invisible" increased their occupational stress; the stigmatization based on appearance was related significantly to increased levels of stress. Haarr (1997) found that African Americans were more likely to report feelings of social distance than other officers.

More recently, Bolton (2003) examined the workplace experiences of Black police officers and found that there is a shared perception among Black officers that systematic barriers exist in agencies that limit their advancement and affect career longevity. Black officers reported lack of support networks and constant conflict and stress. Moreover, many of the Black officers interviewed explained that they were exposed to racial jokes, cartoons, name-calling, slurs, rudeness, and petty harassment. Dowler (2005) also found, in his study of 1,104 police officers in the Baltimore Police Department, that Black officers were more likely to perceive criticism from peers. We could find no published studies comparing the workplace experiences of Latino officers with officers of other races.

Research has also shown that women in policing encounter workplace problems that differ from men (Wexler & Logan, 1983). In particular, research shows that the most unique problem facing women in law enforcement is sexual harassment while on the job (Collins, 2004; Dodge & Pogrebin, 2001; National Center for Women and Policing, 2002; Texeira, 2002; Wells et al., 2005). A study undertaken by the City of Los Angeles found that policewomen experience sexual harassment at higher rates than other female city workers (City of Los Angeles Commission on the Status of Women, 1992; Texeira, 2002, p. 527). Not only did policewomen experience greater levels of sexual harassment but they also experienced the most extreme cases of overt harassment (City of Los Angeles Commission on the Status of Women, 1992). Studies also reveal that women police officers are more likely than male officers to encounter higher levels of overt hostility and other negative social interactions on the job, including negative attitudes of male officers, exposure to tragedy and trouble, group blame and rumors, exposure to profanity and sex jokes, and stigmatization due to appearance (Balkin, 1988; He, Zhao, & Archbold, 2002; Janus, Janus, Lord, & Power, 1988; Martin, 1980; National Center for Women and Policing, 1998; Timmins & Hainsworth, 1989).

Studies have also suggested that female officers' experiences vary by race and ethnicity (Collins, 2004; Martin, 1994; Morash, Haarr, & Gonyea, 2006; National Center for Women and Policing, 2001; Texeira, 2002; Zhao, Herbst, & Lovrich, 2001). In one of only a few studies of African American policewomen's experiences, Texeira (2002) found that African American women felt that harassment by their peers and supervisors was the most difficult force for them to overcome. Sexual harassment was also a problem; however, these women perceived that, "they are [sexually] harassed not because they are women but because they are African American women" (p. 525). Haarr and Morash (2004) also found that African American women were subjected to higher levels of sexual harassment than White female officers.

In addition, Texeira (2002) discovered that African American male officers were not always sympathetic to Black women officers; the harassment by African American male officers included verbally threatening and demeaning behaviors and was more covert than the harassment by White male officers. This finding is similar to Martin's (1994) finding that Black males use their masculinity to align themselves with the dominant majority of White males while extricating themselves from Black female officers. In addition, Pike (1985) found that White policewomen distance themselves from Black policewomen as a means of aligning themselves with the White majority. Dodge and Pogrebin (2001), in their study of Black female officers, found that many Black men are deliberately unsupportive of Black women due to their own minority status. Alozie and Ramirez (1999) argued that members of racial/ethnic groups in general found their greatest competition to be with White females. In essence, research suggests that race and sex are negotiated statuses in police organizations, with women who are racial/ethnic minorities falling at the "bottom of the police occupational stratification structure" (Dodge & Pogrebin, 2001, p. 552; Martin, 1994; Pike, 1995; Texeira, 2002).

Homosexuality differs from sex and race/ethnicity as a status in that homosexuality is not ascribed: Gays, lesbians, and bisexuals can choose to hide their sexual orientation (Burke, 1994; Leinen, 1993, p. 2; Miller et al., 2003). The empirical research, although scant, indicates that openly gay, lesbian, and bisexual officers face differential treatment on the job (Bernstein & Kostclac, 2002; Buhrke, 1996; Burke, 1994; Leinen, 1993; Miller et al., 2003). Research shows that gay, lesbian, and bisexual officers who choose to remain "closeted" do so due to fear of reprisal, fear of rejection, offensive jokes, pranks, and overt harassment and discrimination (Buhrke, 1993; Leinen, 1993; Miller et al., 2003).

 ## Consequences of Workplace Problems: Stress

A significant amount of research has examined stress among police officers. Not surprisingly, much of this research has come to the conclusion that policing is a stressful occupation (Dantzer, 1987; Eisenburg, 1975; Goodman, 1990; He, Zhao, & Archbold, 2002; Kroes, 1985; Liberman et al., 2002; Loo, 1984; Morash, Haarr, & Kwak, 2006; Reese, 1986; Selye, 1978; Violanti, 1985). Although the police role and responsibilities accompanying those roles (i.e., exposure to physical danger, observing human depravity, etc.) is stressful, research indicates that many stressors originate from *within* the police organization (Liberman et al., 2002; Haarr & Morash, 1999; Jaramillo, Nixon, & Sams, 2005; Morash & Haarr, 1995; Toch, 2002). Some of these internal organizational stressors include role ambiguity, role conflict, lack of supervisor support, lack of group cohesiveness and lack of promotional opportunities (Anderson et al., 2002; Jaramillo et al., 2005). Research has also uncovered that the stress inherent in the climate of law enforcement organizations is exacerbated by social factors such as race/ ethnicity, sex, and sexual orientation (Collins & Gibbs,

2003; Dodge & Pogrebin, 2001; Ellison, 2004; Ellison & Genz, 1983; Greene & Carmen, 2002; Haarr & Morash, 1999; Morash, Haarr, & Kwak, 2006; Morash, Kwak, & Haarr, 2006; Teaban, 1975).

Prior research suggests that workplace stress is a consequence of negative workplace experiences. High stress levels among enforcement officers have been linked to job dissatisfaction, absenteeism, "burnout," premature retirement and attrition and other work performance problems (Anderson et al., 2002; Brown, Cooper & Kirkcaldy, 1996; Crank et al., 1995; Gaines & Jermier, 1983; Territo & Vetter; 1987) in addition to physical and psychological ailments (Anderson et al., 2002; Liberman et al., 2002: Wester & Lyubelsky, 2005).

 ## Method

Study Site

The peculiarities and dynamics of the police organization affect officers' workplace experiences (Hassell, 2006; Martin, 1990). Accordingly, it is important to provide details regarding the setting of this study. As of 2004, the year in which data for this study were collected, the Milwaukee Police Department (MPD) employed 1,923 sworn officers (i.e., police officers, detectives, sergeants, lieutenants, etc.). Approximately 16% of sworn officers were female, 67% were White, 21% were African American, and 10% were Hispanic. Structurally, the department was divided into seven geographic districts, each district led by a captain. The department was organized in a traditional manner with a typical command structure. Collective bargaining applied to all civilian and sworn employees.

In 2004, the department was led by a White female police chief, the department's first female chief. At the time the data were collected, she had been in office for approximately 9 months. Prior to her appointment at the end of 2003, an African American male held the position of chief. He served as chief from 1996 to 2003, rising through the ranks from patrol. By many accounts, there was a contentious relationship between officers in the department and the chief. For instance, near the end of his term, a lawsuit was filed against him by 17

White male officers who alleged that he discriminated against White male officers in the promotional process to the rank of captain. Ultimately, these officers were awarded over US$2 million in damages. In addition, internal investigations during this chief's tenure increased from approximately 250 in 1996 to more than 1,200 in 2000. His tenure as chief has been referred to by many in the department as a "reign of terror," whereas the appointment of the new chief in 2003 was viewed as a "breath of fresh air."

According to the 2000 census, Milwaukee is the 19th largest city in the country with a population of 596,974. The largest proportion of the workforce in Milwaukee is involved in industrial manufacturing (22%). Fifty percent of the city's population is White, 37% is African American, and 12% is Hispanic or Latino. The median household income is $32,216, with just over 21% of persons below the poverty level. Approximately 55% of housing units in the city are renter occupied. Nearly 30% of the population is under the age of 18 and nearly 40% is 24 years of age or younger. Overall, Milwaukee residents are more likely to be younger and less well-off economically compared to national averages. The violent crime rate in Milwaukee is slightly higher, and the property crime rate is slightly lower than cities of similar size.

Data

The data for this study were collected using questionnaires administered to all police patrol officers employed in the Milwaukee Police Department in 2004.[3] The questionnaire was administered during mandatory in-service training sessions held at the MPD training academy during July and August of 2004. Prior to the administration of the survey, officers were shown a videotaped introduction to the survey that included information about the purpose of the project, the confidential and anonymous nature of the data, and instructions for completing the questionnaire. Once the respondents completed the questionnaire they were instructed to place their questionnaires in the provided unmarked envelopes and to deposit them in the designated box. Of the 1,388 police patrol officers who attended the training (all the patrol officers in the department), 1,191 completed the questionnaire (86.8% response rate).

The questionnaire used in this study was a modified version of the one used by Morash and Haarr (1995). For this study, the draft by Morash and Haarr (1995) was reviewed by several members of the MPD (including the chief), the Milwaukee Department of Employee Development and the lesbian, bisexual, gay, and transgender group within the department. As a result of these reviews, several questions were added, several were deleted, and numerous wording changes were made. The final questionnaire consisted of 63 questions. Space was provided on the questionnaire for additional comments if officers wished to provide any. Most of the questions asked respondents about their own experiences at the MPD within the last year. The questions related to a comprehensive array of workplace experiences, demographic information, stress, and the likelihood of leaving the MPD in the near future.[4] Similar to Morash and Haarr (1995), the questions that related to workplace experiences varied in their referents; that is, some questions asked about experiences in relation to coworkers, and some asked about experiences in relation to supervisors, and some asked generally about "people at work." All questions that related to workplace experiences used a Likert-type scale where respondents were asked to indicate whether they *strongly disagreed, disagreed, agreed* or *strongly agreed* with the statements.

Variables

Officer characteristics. Five individual-level officer characteristic variables were included in the analyses: race (White/non–White; White/African American/Latino/a); sex (male/female); sexual orientation (heterosexual/gay/lesbian, bisexual); educational level (completed high school/completed some college/completed college or more); and length of service (in years).

Workplace experience. As noted, the questionnaire asked about a comprehensive array of workplace experiences. Through factor analysis, seven statistically distinct groups of questions about workplace experiences were identified. In addition, two questions were included in the analyses to tap two additional workplace experiences (see Table 1). The workplace experience variables include (a) lack of support/influence/feedback, (b) lack of opportunity, (c) negative physical abilities, (d) uniform/equipment, (c) victim of theft/vandalism, (f) ridicule, setup, invisibility, (g) sexually offensive behaviors, (h) perceptions of bias, and (i) vulgar language/jokes. Each index was additive and standardized (i.e., values for each question were tallied and divided by the number of questions in the index). As a result, for each respondent, each workplace experience measure could assume a value of 1 to 4, with 1 being the most positive and 4 being the most negative. Given the coding scheme, higher scores on the indexes represent workplace experiences that are workplace problems.

Police workplace stress. Workplace stress was measured as an index of four items ($\alpha = .935$). Respondents were asked (a) if they experienced unwanted stress from their job, (b) whether the amount of unwanted stress from their job has had a negative effect on their physical well-being, (c) whether the amount of unwanted stress from their job has had a negative effect on their emotional well-being, and (d) whether unwanted stress has had a negative effect on their job performance. In the questionnaire, these questions were prefaced with the statement "Unwanted stress is defined as stress as a result of those offensive behaviors and/or conduct mentioned in the previous questions." As with the workplace experience indexes, the stress index was additive and standardized with higher scores indicating greater stress.

Table 1   Workplace Experience
Lack of support/influence/feedback: Measures the sense that the respondent has little or no ability to influence or change the way work is performed and a lack of recognition of good work (five items, $= \alpha$ .662)
Lack of opportunity: Measures the respondent's sense that opportunities for promotion and preferred assignments are limited compared to coworkers (two items, $\alpha = .492$)
Negative physical abilities: Refers to the respondent's sense that people at work underestimate the respondent's physical abilities to do the job (one item)
Uniform/equipment: Measures whether the respondent thinks that the equipment and uniform is not well-suited for his/her needs (one item)
Victim of theft/vandalism: Refers to whether the respondent had personal property vandalized or stolen at work (one item, $\alpha = .673$)
Ridicule, setup, and invisibility: Measures the sense that people at work set the respondent up for mistakes and dangerous situations, ridicule the respondent for mistakes at work, make offensive comments about respondent's looks and do not recognize respondent's presence (nine items, $\alpha = .870$)
Sexually offensive behavior: Measures whether people at work make unwanted advances for romantic, physical, and sexual relationships with or without threats and exposure to pornography (seven items, $\alpha = .940$)
Perception of bias at work: Measures of the sense that there is bias at work against people of respondent's sex, age, race, ethnic group, and sexual orientation (five items, $\alpha= 888$)
Vulgar language/unwanted comments: Measures unwanted comments about homosexuality, gay and lesbian persons and language that is deemed vulgar and offensive (nine items, $\alpha = .928$)

Results

The sample for this study includes 1,191 police patrol officers (see Table 2). Of the responding officers, approximately 80% are male; approximately 62% are White, 22% African American, and 11% Latino. Defined by race and sex, nearly 50% of the officers are White males, 17% are African American males, 10% are Latino males, 13% are White females, 5% are African American females, and just over 3% are Latina females. Just over 3% of the sample identified themselves as being gay, lesbian, or bisexual. The mean number of years that officers were employed in the department is 9.45, with a range of less than 1 year to 32 years. The overwhelming majority of

officers had either some college, or completed college, or more. Even though our sample is relatively large and the MPD is relatively diverse, some of the subgroups of our critical variables of interest (i.e., sex by race and sexual orientation) are relatively small. Given the purpose of the study, however, in most of the analyses we examine differences across these subgroups,

As noted below, the unstable estimates that may result from relatively small subgroup sample sizes, as well as the lack of statistical power in relatively small subsample sizes, need to be considered in interpreting the results of the analyses. Due to the nature of the data, we used ordered logistic regression, which is required for ordinal data where there are more than two

Table 2 Characteristics of Officers (N = 1,191)					
	N	**%**		**N**	**%**
Sex	1,149	100.0	Latino male	113	10.0
Male	920	80.1	Other male	33	3.1
Female	229	19.9	White female	148	13.0
Education	1,175	100.0	African American female	56	4.9
High school	68	5.8	Latina female	14	1.2
Some college	625	53.2	Other female	10	0.9
Comp college or more	482	41.0	Sexual orientation	1,169	100.0
Race	1,162	100.0	Heterosexual	1,133	96.9
White	724	62.3	Gay/Lesbian/Bisexual	36	3.1
African American	261	22.5	Years @ MPD	1,178	100.0
Latino	128	11.0	M	9.45	
Other	49	4.2	SD	6.67	
Race × Sex	1,135	100.0	Range	< 1–32	
White male	563	49.6	Natural log M	1.94	
African American male	198	17.4	Natural log SD	0.84	

Notes: Totals may not equal 100% due to rounding; missing data excluded from table.

outcomes. There were no issues with multicollinearity; all variance inflation factor scores were under 2.

Table 3 shows the aggregate responses for each of the workplace experiences and for the item that represents the potential consequences of negative workplace experiences. Once again, higher scores represent more negative workplace experiences and greater stress. As seen in Table 3, the workplace problem most frequently experienced by officers is "lack of support/influence/feedback" and the least commonly experienced problem is "sexually offensive behaviors" (sexually offensive behaviors is the least commonly experienced problem for men and women).

To examine differences in officers across the workplace experiences of interest, we estimate nine regression equations (Table 4). In each equation, the

workplace experience is the dependent variable; the primary independent variables of interest are race, sex, and sexual orientation. Race and sex are defined in terms of five dummy variables: whether officers are African American males, Latino males, African American females, or Latina females; for the analyses that are presented in tables, White male officers serve as the comparison group. Sexual orientation is defined as a single dummy variable (heterosexual/gay, bisexual, or lesbian). Education (high school/some college/college degree or more) and length of service (in years, logged) are included as controls.

Table 4 shows the results of these analyses. Although little of the variance in any workplace experience is explained by race, sex, or sexual orientation (or by education and length of service, for that matter),[5] all of the

Table 3 Workplace Experience of Officers (N = 1191) and Their Consequences				
	N	**Mean**	**SD**	**Range**
Workplace experiences of officers				
Lack of support/influence/feedback	1,161	2.52	.50	1–4
Lack of opportunity	1,771	2.28	.61	1–4
Negative physical abilities	1,181	1.85	.77	1–4
Negative uniform/equipment	1,151	2.13	.68	1–4
Victim of theft/vandalism	1,162	2.00	.78	1–4
Ridicule/set up	1,151	1.75	.47	1–4
Sexually offensive behaviors	1,162	1.34	.46	1–4
Perceptions of bias	1,161	2.07	.71	1–4
Perceptions of vulgar language/jokes	1,162	1.52	.56	1–4
Consequences of workplace experiences				
Stress from experiences	1,165	2.24	.82	1–4
Still at MPD in 1 year	1,158	1.14	.51	1–4
Still at MPD in 5 years	1,124	1.51	.95	1–4

Notes: Missing data excluded from table.

Table 4 Ordered Logic Regression Analyses of Workplace Experience

Regressors	Lack of support	Lack of opportunity	Negative physical abilities	Negative uniform	Victim of theft	Ridicule/set up	Sexually offensive behavior	Bias	Vulgar language
African American male	−.29 (−1.90)	.69** (4.40)	.46 (2.83)	−.64** (−3.55)	.63* (4.02)	.17 (1.14)	.19 (1.13)	1.85** (11.25)	.66(4.40)
Latino male	.09 (.47)	.50* (2.54)	54** (2.64)	−.44* (−1.96)	−.01 (−.03)	.24 (1.28)	.21 (1.00)	.67** (3.53)	.36 (1.85)
White female	.06 (.33)	−.04 (−.20)	.95* (5.06)	−.08 (−.40)	.13 (.72)	.25 (1.43)	.82** (4.42)	.95** (5.44)	.60**(3.32)
African American female	.59* (2.28)	.56 (−2.15)	.84** (3.10)	−.07 (−.22)	.86** (3.5)	.56* (2.15)	1.23** (4.76)	2.34** (8.72)	1.53**(5.62)
Latina female	.95* (2.0)	.63 (−.34)	1.35** (2.68)	.20 (.34)	.77 (1.61)	.55 (1.17)	1.54** (3.06)	2.29** (5.10)	2.29** (4.60)
Sexual orientation	−.07 (−.20)	−.47 (−1.28)	.34 (.90)	−.19 (−.47)	.22 (.66)	.29 (.84)	.40 (1.13)	.35 (1.01)	2.40** (6.10)
Education	.06 (.66)	.09 (.94)	.13 (1.27)	−.10 (−.89)	.06 (.59)	.25** (2.60)	.25* (2.38)	.16 (1.70)	.23* (2.35)
Length of service	.14* (2.13)	−.20** (−2.86)	−.16** (−2.21)	−.06 (−.73)	.20* (2.91)	−.05 (−.68)	.17* (2.32)	.01 (.18)	.18** (2.64)
Pseudo R²	.00	.00	.02	.01	.01	.00	.02	.04	.03
LR X²	18.08*	35.27*	49.47*	15.56*	39.68**	15.47*	57.22**	195.69	120.26**

Note: Entries are unstandardized coefficients with *z*-scores in parentheses.

$*p < .05. **p < .01.$

equations are significant. In addition, race and sex show several significant and differential effects across workplace experiences. In particular, African American male officers report significantly more negative workplace experiences than White male officers on 5 of the 9 dimensions (i.e., lack of opportunity, other officers underestimating their physical abilities, being a victim of theft or vandalism at work, perceptions of bias, and perceptions of vulgar/offensive language) and more positive experiences on only one dimension (i.e., uniform/equipment). Latino male officers report more negative workplace experiences than White male officers on 3 of the 9 dimensions (i.e., lack of opportunity, other officers underestimating their physical abilities, and perceptions of bias). White female officers report more negative workplace experiences than White male officers on 4 dimensions (i.e., negative physical abilities, perceptions of sexually offensive behaviors, perceptions of bias, and perceptions of vulgar/offensive language). African American female officers report more negative workplace experiences than White male officers on 8 of the 9 dimensions (negative uniform is the only dimension on which White male officers and African American female officers are similar). Latina female officers report more negative experiences than White male officers on five of the nine dimensions (i.e., lack of support, negative physical abilities, perceptions of sexually offensive behavior, perceptions of bias, and perceptions of vulgar/offensive language). In short, it appears that the workplace experiences of African American female officers are most unlike the workplace experiences of White male officers, followed by African American male officers, Latina female officers, and White female officers. The workplace experiences of Latino male officers are most similar to those of White males. With regard to sexual orientation, gay, lesbian, and bisexual officers report significantly more negative workplace experiences than heterosexual officers on only one dimension: perceptions of vulgar language.

To examine differences between other groups of officers, separate regression analyses were conducted (to save space, these results are not tabled). Analyses that include only male officers and use African American officers as the comparison group show that Latino male officers and African American male officers are significantly different on only two of the nine workplace experiences (i.e., victim of a theft or vandalism and perceptions of bias); on both dimensions, African American male officers report more negative experiences than Latino officers.

Parallel analyses were conducted with female officers, first using White female officers as the comparison group. Here, African American females differed significantly from White females on 5 of the 9 dimensions (i.e., lack of support/influence, lack of opportunity, victim of theft/vandalism at work, perceptions of bias, and perceptions of vulgar language); on each dimension, African American female officers report more negative experiences than White female officers. Latina female officers had significantly more negative experiences than White female officers on three workplace experiences (i.e., lack of support, perceptions of bias, and perceptions of vulgar language).[6] When African American female officers were used as the comparison group, Latina officers did not differ from African American female officers on any of the nine workplace experiences.[7]

Within each workplace experience, the differential effects of race and sex are also worthy of highlight (see Table 4). Specifically, African American female officers and Latina female officers (but not White female officers or any male officers) report significantly more negative experiences regarding "lack of support/ influence" in the organization compared to White male officers. Officers who are White and/or male perceive an ability to influence or change the way work is performed in the organization more so than officers who are minority *and* female. Regarding "lack of opportunity," officers who are Latino and African American males or African American females perceive fewer opportunities for promotion and preferred assignments compared to White male officers; Latina and White females do not differ from White male officers in this regard. As for "physical abilities," all race/sex groups report their physical abilities to do the job as being underestimated compared to White males. Here, being any "minority" (defined in terms of sex or race) carries with it more negative experiences. The only other workplace experience where this same pattern holds true is with "bias" relating to the officer's sex, race, age, ethnic group, or sexual orientation.

As for officers' experiences with "uniform and equipment," African American and Latino male officers report differences compared to White male officers; their experience with uniform-equipment is actually more positive than White male officers. With regard to being a "victim of a theft or vandalism," African American officers (male and female) report significantly more negative experiences compared to White male officers; the experiences of Latino officers (male and female) and White female officers do not differ significantly from White male officers on this dimension. African American females experience ridicule and report being set up more often than White males.

As for "sexually offensive behaviors" at work, not surprisingly, all female officers (White, Latina, and African American) report more negative experiences than White male officers. African American and Latino male officers do not differ from White male officers in this regard. Finally, as for vulgar and offensive language, all race and sex groups, with the exception of Latino males, report significantly more negative experiences compared to White males; gay, lesbian, and bisexual officers report significantly more negative experiences compared to heterosexual officers.

In summary, White male officers have the most positive workplace experiences. However, for male officers, "minority" status is not uniformly negative; Latino males have substantially similar (although not the same) workplace experiences as White male officers. This is not the case for African American male officers, who clearly have substantially more negative experiences than White male officers. For female officers, the same general pattern holds true, although it appears less pronounced; at the very least, it is fair to say that there are more differences between White female officers and African American female officers than there are between White female officers and Latina female officers, although the extent of these differences is greater with male officers than with female officers. In addition, as noted, the differential effects of race and sex and sexual orientation are evident in the individual

workplace experiences. Some workplace problems are largely a minority female phenomenon (i.e., lack of support), some are a minority phenomenon (i.e., lack of opportunity), some are an African American phenomenon (i.e., victim of theft/vandalism), some are an African American female phenomenon (i.e., ridicule and setup), some are an issue to just female officers (i.e., sexually offensive behaviors), some are largely a nonissue (i.e., negative uniform), whereas others appear to be largely universal problems (i.e., vulgar language, underestimates of physical abilities) compared to the experiences of White male officers.

To examine differences among officers in terms of reported stress, we estimate two regression equations. As for stress, it is seen that all race by sex officer groups report significantly higher levels of stress than White male officers, with the exception of White females and Latino males, who do not differ significantly from White males in this regard. Additional analyses (not tabled) reveal that African American females report significantly higher levels of stress than White female officers and Latino male officers but not African American male officers or Latina female officers. High levels of stress appear to be primarily a phenomenon among African American officers and Latina female officers. In addition, it is seen in Table 5 that length of service has a significant impact on reported stress levels; officers with more years of service report greater stress than officers with fewer years of service.

The next set of regression analyses examines the impact of workplace experiences as well as officers' background characteristics (as controls) on workplace stress (see Table 5). With regard to the workplace stress equation, it is seen that race and sex do not directly affect workplace stress. However, of the nine workplace experiences that are included in the equation[9] seven are significantly related to stress (lack of opportunity and negative physical abilities are the lone exceptions). Higher levels of lack of support/influence, negative feelings toward uniforms and equipment, theft/vandalism at work, ridicule and setup, bias, and vulgar language result in increased levels of workplace stress. Sexually offensive behaviors are also statistically related to stress but the relationship is again counterintuitive; officers

Table 5   Ordered Logic Regression Analyses of Workplace Stress: Officer Characteristics and Workplace Experience

Regressors	Stress	Stress	Regressors	Stress	Stress
African American male	0.40* (2.69)	0.01 (0.08)	Opportunity		0.18 (−.05)
Latino male	0.21 (1.13)	−0.08 (−0.38)	Physical abilities		0.17 (1.77)
White female	0.27 (1.53)	−0.04 (−0.23)	Negative uniform		0.23* (2.45)
African American female	0.80** (3.13)	−0.06 (−0.23)	Theft/vandalism		0.19* (2.27)
Latina female	0.99* (2.07)	0.30 (0.56)	Ridicule/setup		1.40** (7.32)
Sexual orientation	−0.04 (−0.11)	−0.62 (−1.66)	Sexually offensive behavior		−0.59* (−3.07)
Education	0.15 (1.51)	0.02 (0.19)	Bias		0.44** (4.43)
Length of service	0.29** (4.46)	0.32** (4.36)	Language/jokes		0.67** (3.62)
Support/influence/feedback		0.83** (5.88)	Pseudo R^2	0.01	0.10
			LR X^2	40.80**	4–8.20**

Note: Entries are unstandardized coefficients with *z*-scores in parentheses.

*$p < .05$. **$p < .01$.

who perceive greater levels of sexually offensive behaviors at work report lower levels of stress. In short, the results show that sex and race directly affect workplace experiences (Table 4), workplace experiences directly affect stress (Table 5), but sex and race do not directly affect workplace stress (Table 5).

 Conclusion

At the outset of the study, we asked three research questions. First, we asked whether different groups of officers (considering race, sex, and sexual orientation) have similar workplace experiences. This study clearly shows that different subgroups of officers have different experiences within the police department. Generally, those officers who have the greatest representation in the organization (White, male, heterosexual) have the most favorable workplace experiences, while those individuals who have the least representation (minority, female, gay/bisexual) have the least favorable workplace experiences. The study also shows that most subgroups of officers share many of the same concerns/problems (i.e., lack of support/influence/feedback), although these problems are more frequently experienced by members of some groups than by others. More specifically, our analyses indicate that with regard to workplace experiences, being female and being a racial/ethnic minority brings with it substantially (but not uniformly) different experiences on the job compared to male and White officers. Black females experience a greater number of workplace problems compared to all other race/sex combinations. Black males and Latino females also experience more workplace problems than White males, Latino males, and White females.

The most common workplace problem experienced by officers was lack of support/influence. The least common workplace problem was sexually offensive behaviors; this pattern holds for both male and female officers. This finding is interesting as most research on workplace experiences of female officers suggests that sexual harassment and/or sexually offensive behaviors on the job are widespread problems. One recent study on the dynamics of sexual harassment among female police officers, on the other hand, noted that many policewomen indicated that they had not experienced sexual harassment (Somvadee & Morash, 2008). In that study, some women did not view sexual attention as severe enough to warrant harassment, while others considered it a price of fitting in. Many of the women studied did not consider sexual harassment a "problem" because they handled the inappropriate language and/or behaviors within the workgroup, with many male colleagues backing down and even apologizing. It could be that the female officers we studied also handled sexually offensive behaviors within the workgroup, which could have empowered the women. This may explain the negative relationship between our measurement of sexually offensive behaviors and stress. Clearly, additional research is needed to clarify the dynamics of sexual harassment in the workplace.

Second, we asked whether officers differ in terms of their reported workplace stress. Again, our data indicate that both race and sex, separately and in interaction, are important considerations in understanding these relationships. In particular, Black female officers experience the greatest amount of stress, but all race/sex combinations experience greater levels of stress than White male and female officers, and Latino male officers. Finally, we asked whether officers' characteristics and/or workplace experiences influence officer stress. Officers of varying races/ethnicities, sexes, and sexual orientations do not have greater levels of stress based solely on their ascribed characteristics. On the other hand, our findings confirm previous research that workplace climate has an effect on workplace stress (Morash & Haarr, 1995). In other words, although race, sex, and sexual orientation do not directly influence stress, they do so indirectly. Nearly all of the dimensions of workplace climate considered here were related to workplace stress, which clearly highlights the importance of the immediate working environment in dealing with stress.[10]

Police managers can change the workplace climate through management, supervision, training, and mentoring. Clear policy statements, proper supervision, well-controlled investigations, and just use of sanctions will assist in this regard. Through training and reinforcement, police managers must communicate to officers that negative workplace experiences are not necessarily the equivalent of hurt feelings; in the written comments provided on the questionnaire, several officers made reference to hurt feelings being part of the job. According to one officer, "there seems to be too much time devoted to feelings…we have a tough job—do it or get out…too many people whine about things not being fair." In addition, research suggests that formal mentoring programs may reduce workplace stress (Hassell & Archbold, 2009). Work experiences do not have to be negative and unfair, especially as it relates to groups of individuals. The negative workplace experiences investigated in our study are not experienced randomly by a few individuals; they are experienced by certain groups of officers—primarily groups based on race and sex (and sexual orientation to a lesser degree).

Similarly, officers need to understand the power of words. The language of the workplace reflects the nature of the workplace. This is most evident with responses to the questions contained in four of the workplace experience indices: ridicule/setup, sexually offensive behaviors, perceptions of bias, and especially vulgar language/jokes. For some officers and supervisors, it might just be the way that cops talk, but it must be understood that negative/vulgar language creates an atmosphere of disrespect and exclusion (Fine, 1987). For those uncomfortable or offended with such language, it signals that the workplace is not their workplace and that they are outsiders. In these instances, language results in more than just hurt feelings; language is an expression of power that dissects the work environment, reducing solidarity and generating a negative workplace climate where stress can have deleterious effects for the department and communities it serves. Again, training and supervisory reinforcement can affect the language used in the workplace.

Finally, the issues that appear to be of most concern to personnel—lack of support/ influence and lack of opportunity—may be the most difficult to address. In the written comments, many officers voiced frustration regarding these matters. For example, one officer wrote, "I think patrol officers who do their jobs should be able to have input as to how things are done." Another officer added, "The best changes can be made by listening to the officers who do the job." Police departments have traditionally emphasized the command and control approach to management; however, some officers clearly expect to participate in decision making. Supervisors should seek input from patrol officers regarding day-to-day procedures and provide positive feedback about their work when appropriate. We also recommend that officers be given more discretion to identify and initiate responses to problems/ incidents. Such initiatives may go a long way in improving perceptions of the workplace climate, as long as personnel from all subgroups have equal participation and representation.

Although the findings of this study are important, they are not without limitation. The major weakness of this study is the relatively small sample sizes of certain subgroups (i.e., African American and Latina females; gay/lesbian/bisexual officers). Unfortunately, in most departments, these subgroups are undersized. Although our samples of these subgroups are small, we felt the benefit of including the interaction terms outweighed validity threats. As Daly and Tonry (1997, p. 208, italics in original; see also Holcomb, Williams, & Demuth, 2004, p. 884) argued, "the most interesting analytical and political questions center on the *intersections* of race and gender, not merely the separate categories of 'Black,' 'White,' 'male,' and 'female.'" Although it is important to note that the conclusions are tentative, the findings uncover the significance of investigating not only the interaction effects between sex and race but also the importance of moving beyond the use of a broad "non–White" category in criminal justice research. In this department, White, Latino, and African American officers have different workplace experiences. Furthermore, being female makes one vulnerable to negative workplace experiences; being female and a racial/ethnic minority, particularly an African American female, makes one even more vulnerable. The inclusion of sexual orientation as a variable of interest is also important as contemporary police departments seek to further diversify. In addition, we have restricted our analysis of the workplace experiences of officers to a quantitative analysis; an ethnographic study would further enhance our understanding of the working climate within the department. Future research should continue to investigate and clarify the relationship between race, sex, sexual orientation, and workplace climate in police organizations. The creation of well-functioning and diverse police departments may depend on it.

Notes

1. The larger study consisted of a survey of all police department personnel including detectives, supervisors, command staff, and civilians.

2. To help protect respondents' anonymity, certain identifying questions were not asked (e.g., work location, shift).

3. The purpose of these analyses is to examine the differential effects of the critical variables of interest on workplace problems, not to explain variation in workplace problems. As a result, the variance explained by each of the equations is of tertiary importance.

4. Although sample size concerns are relevant in these analyses, it is instructive to note that none of the other probability values for the White female and Latina female officer comparisons were less than 26.

5. Although sample size issues are also relevant in these analyses, it should be noted that none of the difference between Latina female officers and African American female officers approached a conventional level of statistical significance (i.e., the smallest probability value was 36).

6. Once again, our intent is not to explain variation in the dependent variables of interest but only to assess the impact of the included independent variables on the dependent variables.

7. Although the purpose of this study was not to identify the consequences of workplace stress, other research documents well the emotional, mental, physical, and performance-based toll stress has on officers and the department (e.g., Anderson et al., 2002; Anshel, 2000, Liberman et al., 2002; Webb & Smith, 1980; Wester & Lyubelsky, 2005).

References

Alozie, N. O., &. Ramirez, E. J. (1999). "A Piece of the pie" and more: Competition and Hispanic employment on urban police forces. *Urban Affairs Review, 34,* 456–475.

Anderson. G. S., Litzenberger, R., & Plecas, D. (2002). Physical evidence of police officer stress. *Policing: An International Journal of Police Strategies and Management, 25,* 399–420.

Balkin, J. (1988). Why policemen don't like policewomen. *Journals of Police Science and Administration, 16*(l), 29–36.

Belkin, A., & McNichol, J. (2001). *Pink and blue: Outcomes associated with the integration of openly gay and lesbian personnel in the San Diego police department.* Santa Barbara: Center for the Study of Sexual Minorities in the Military, University of California, Santa Barbara.

Bernstein, M., & Kostclac, C. (2002). Lavender and blue: Attitudes about homosexuality and behavior toward lesbians and gay men among police officers. *Journal of Contemporary Criminal Justice, 18,* 302–328.

Bolron, K., (2003). Shared perceptions: Black officer discuss continuing barriers in policing. *Policing: An International Journal of Police Strategies and Management, 26,* 386–399.

Brown, J., Cooper, C., & Kirkcaldy, B. (l996). Occupational stress among senior police officers. *Officer. British Journal of Psychology, 87,* 31–41.

Buhrke, R. A. (1996). *A matter of justice: Lesbians and gay men in law enforcement.* New York: Routledge.

Burke, M. F. (1994). Homosexuality as deviance: The case of the gay police officer. *British Journal of Criminology, 34,* 192–203.

City of Los Angeles Commission on the Status of Women. (1992). *Report of the City Of Los Angeles 1992 Sexual Harassment Survey.* Los Angeles: Commission on the Status of Women.

Collins, S. C. (2004). Sexual harassment and police discipline: Who's policing the police? *Policing: An International Journal of Police Strategies and Management, 27,* 512–538.

Collins, P. A., & Gibbs, C. C. (2003). Stress in police officers: A study of the origins, prevalence and severity of stress-related symptoms within a county police force. *Occupational Medicine, 53,* 256–264.

Crank. J. (2003). International theory of police: A review of the state of the art. *Policing: An International Journal of Police Strategies and Management, 26,* 186–207.

Crank, J. P., Regoli, R., Hewill J., & Culbertson, R. G. (1995). Institutional and organizational decedents of role stress, work alienation, and anomie among police executives. *Criminal Justice and Behavior, 22,* 152–171.

Daly, K., & Tonry, M. (1997). Gender, race and sentencing. In M. Tonry (Ed.), *Criminal and justice: A review of research* (pp. 201–252). Chicago: University of Chicago Press.

Dantzer, M. L. (1987). Police-related stress: A critique tor future research. *Journal of Police Criminal Psychology, 3,* 43–48.

Dennison, D. R. (1996). What is the difference between organization culture and organizational climate? A native's point view on a decade of paradigm wars. *Academy of Management Review, 21,* 619–654.

Dodge, M., &. Pogrebin, M. (2001). African American policewomen: An exploration of professional relationships. *Policing: An International Journal of Police Strategies and Management, 24,* 550–562.

Dowler, K. (2005). Job satisfaction, burnout and perception of unfair treatment: The relationship between race and police work. *Police Quarterly, 8,* 476–489.

Eisenburg, T. (l975). Job stress and the police officer: Identifying stress reduction techniques. In W. H. Kroes &. I. J. Harrell, Jr. (Eds.), *Job stress and the police officer: Identifying stress reduction techniques* (HEW Publication No. NIOSH 760187). Washington, DC: U.S. Government Printing Office.

Ellison, K. W. (2004). *Stress and the police officer* (2nd ed.). Springfield, IL: Charles C. Thomas.

Ellison, K. W., & Genz, J. L. (1983). *Stress and the police officer.* Springfield, IL: Charles C. Thomas.

Gaines, J., & Jermier, J. M. (1983). Emotional exhaustion in a high stress organization. *Academy of Management Journal, 26,* 567–586.

Goodman, A. M. (1990). A model for police officer burnout. *Journal of Business and Psychology, 5,* 85–99.

Greene, H. T., & Carmen, A. D. (2002). Female police officers in Texas: Perceptions of colleagues and stress. *Policing: An International Journal of Police Strategies and Management, 25,* 385–398.

Haarr, R. N. (1997). Patterns of interaction in a police patrol bureau: Race and gender barriers to integration. *Justice Quarterly, 14,* 15–85.

Haarr, R. N., & Morash, M. (1999). Gender, race and strategies of coping with occupational stress in policing. *Justice Quarterly, 16,* 303–335.

Haarr. R. N., & Morash, M. (2004). Police workplace problems, coping strategies and stress: Changes from 1990 to 2003 for women and racial minorities. *Law Enforcement Executive Forum, 4,* 165–185.

Hassell, K. D. (2006). *Police organizational cultures and patrol practices.* New York: LFB Scholarly.

He, N., Zhao, J., &. Archbold, C. A. (2002). Gender and police stress: The convergent and divergent impact of work environment work-family conflict and stress coping mechanisms of female and male police officers. *Policing: An International Journal of Police Strategies & Management, 24,* 687–708.

Holcomb, J. E., Williams, M., & Demuth, S. (2004). White female victims and death penalty disparity research. *Justice Quarterly, 21,* 877–902.

Janus, S., Janus, C., Lord, L., & Power, T. (1998). Women in police work: Annie Oakley or Little Orphan Annie? *Police Studies, 11,* 124–127.

Jaramillo, F., Nixon, R., & Sams, D. (2005). The effect of law enforcement stress an organizational commitment. *Policing: An International Journal of Police Strategies and Management, 28,* 321–336.

Klinger, D. A. (1997). Negotiating order in patrol work: All ecological theory of police response to deviance. *Criminology, 35,* 277–306.

Kroes, W. H. (1985). *Society's victim: The police officer.* Springfield, IL: Charles Thomas.

Leinen, S. (1993). *Gay cops.* New Brunswick, NJ: Rutgers University Press.

Lewis, W. G. (1989). Toward represents bureaucracy: Blacks in city police organizations, 1975-1955. *Public Administration Review, 49,* 257–267.

Liberman, A. M., Best, S. R., Metzler, T., J., Fagan, J. A., Weiss, D. S., & Marmar, C. R. (2002). Routine occupational stress and psychological distress in police. *Policing: An International Journal of Police Strategies and Management, 25,* 421–436.

Leo, R. (1984). Occupational stress in the law enforcement profession. *Canadian Mental Health, 32,* 10–13.

Maguire, E. R. (2002). *Organizational structure in American police agencies: Context, complexity and control.* Albany: State University of New York Press.

Martin, S. E. (1980). *Breaking and entering: Policewomen on patrol.* Berkeley: University of California Press.

Martin, S. E. (1990). *Women on the move? A report on the status of women in policing.* Washington, DC: Police Foundation.

Martin, S. E. (1994). Outsider within the station house: The impact of race and gender on Black women police. *Social Problems, 41,* 383–400.

Martin, S. E., Forest, K. B., & Jurik, N. C. (2003). Diversity in blue: Lesbian and gay police officers in a masculine occupation. *Men and Masculinities, 1,* 355–385.

Morash, M., & Haarr, R. N. (l995). Gender, workplace problems and stress in policing. *Justice Quarterly, 12,* 113–140.

Morash, M., Haarr, R. N., & Gonyea, D. P. (2006). Workplace Problems the Police Departments and Methods of Coping: Women at the Intersection. In C. M. Renznti, L. Goodstein, & S. L. Miller (Eds.), *Rethinking gender, crime & justice: Feminist readings* (Los Angeles, CA: Roxbury.

Morash, M., Haarr, R., & Kwak, D. (2006). Multilevel influences on police stress. *Journal of Contemporary Criminal Justice, 22*(1), 26–43.

Morash, M., Kwak, D., & Haarr, R. (2006). Gender differences in the predictors of police stress. *Policing: An International Journal Police Strategies and Management, 29,* 541–563.

National Center for Women and Policing. (1998). *Equality denied: The status of women in policing: 1998.* Columbia University, New York.

National Center for Women and Policing. (2002). *Equality denied: The status of women in policing: 2001.* Columbia University, New York.

National Center for Women and Policing. (2002). *Equality denied: The nature of Columbia: 2002.* Columbia University, New York.

National Research Council. (2004). *Fairness and Effectiveness in Policing: The Evidence.* Washington, DC: The National Academies Press.

Paoline, E. A. (2003). Taking stock: Toward a richer understanding of police culture. *Journal of Criminal Justice, 31,* 199–214.

Peak, K. (l997). African Americans in policing. In R. Dunham & G. Alpert (Eds.), *Critical issues in policing* (pp. 356–362). Prospect Heights, IL: Waveland Press.

Pike, D. L. (1985). Women in police academy training: Some aspects of organizational response. In L. I. Moyer (Ed.), *The changing roles of women in the criminal Justice system* (pp. 250–270). Prospect Heights, IL: Waveland Press.

Reese, J. T. (1986). Policing the violent society: The American experience. *Stress Medicine, 2,* 233–240.

Selye, I. L. (1978, December). The stress of police work. *Police Chronicle,* 14.

Skolnick, J. H., &. Fyfe, J. J. (1993). *Above the law: Police and the excessive use of force.* New York: Free Press.

Somvadee, C., & Morash, M. (2008). Dynamics of sexual harassment for policewomen working alongside men. *Policing: International Journal of Police Strategies and Management, 31,* 485–498.

Teahan, J. (1975). A longitudinal study of attitude shifts among Black and White police officers. *Journal of Social Issues, 31,* 47–55.

Territo, L., &. Vetter, H. J. (1981). Stress and police personnel. *Journal of Police Science and Administration, 9,* 195–203.

Texeira, M. T. (2002). Who protects and serves me? A case study of sexual harassment of African American women in one U.S. law enforcement agency. *Gender and Society, 16,* 524–543.

Timmins, W. M., & Hainsworth, B. E. (1989). Attracting and retaining females in law enforcement: Sex-based problems of women cops in 1988. *International Journal Offender Therapy and Comparative Criminology, 33,* 197–205.

Toch, H. (2002). *Stress in policing.* Washington, DC: American Psychological Association.

Violati, J. M. (1985). The police stress process. *Journal of Police Science and Administration, 13,* 106–110.

Webb, S. D., & Smith, D. L. (1980). Police stress: A conceptual overview. *Journal of Criminal Justice, 8.* 251–257.

Wells, S., Wells, S. K., & Alt, B. L. (2005). *Police women: Life with the badge.* Westport, CT: Praeger.

Wester, S. R., & Lyubelsky, J. (2005). Supporting the thin blue line: Gender-sensitive therapy with male police officers. *Professional Psychology: Research and Practice, 36*(1), 51–58.

Wexler, J. G., & Logan, D. D. (1983). Sources of stress among women police officers. *Journal of Police Science and Administration, 11,* 46–53.

Zhao, J., Herbst, L., & Lovrich, N. P. (2001). Environmental and institutional effects present in the employment of women police officers: Separating the predictors of minority and non-minority female officer hiring. *Journal of Urban Affairs, 23,* 243–257.

DISCUSSION QUESTIONS

1. Describe the workplace experiences of women, racial/ethnic minorities, and gay and lesbian police officers based on some of the previous studies conducted on this topic.

2. What are the main findings of this study?

3. How can police administrators use the findings from this study to make changes to the workplace climate for women, racial/ethnic minorities, and gay and lesbian officers?

READING 8

The excerpts from John Crank's book, *Understanding Police Culture,* provide a description of the term *culture* and how this relates to the police. Crank identifies the complex and interesting components found within the police culture that makes this group distinct from all other occupations. These excerpts also describe the police culture in the context of various environments.

Understanding Police Culture

John Crank

 ### Perspectives on Police Culture

"Its a Cop Thing. You Wouldn't Understand."

The quote above, displayed in large black letters, was on the front of a T-shirt worn by a heavily muscled off-duty police officer. I watched him as he casually walked to the back of the convenience store, a smile on his face. It was late June in Las Vegas, and the summer winds were already hot. Reaching into a cooler, he grabbed a quart of Gatorade.

My thoughts turned to the implied question— What *is* a cop thing? Trying to identify what that thing was became the basis for this book: understanding police culture and the powerful "thing" that moved it. The answer that I arrived at, though presented in an academic style in this book, also uses blunt non-academic images. This book is a stylistic blend, combining scholarly analysis with more plain writing that allows me to convey the vigor, taste and scrape of police work. I seek to capture the emotions that infuse police cultures, the zest, tragedy, and inevitable boredom that characterizes the job. The result is this book, an essay about culture that provides the emotions and values that infuse technical aspects of police work.

The things that give meaning to police work do not lie in technical evaluations of their activity, or in lists of bureaucratically driven command protocols. Being a cop is a state of mind, and it is that state of mind that I try to express in a way that also reproduces police culture for the reader. It is that element—what it feels like to be a cop—that I try to capture. It is in the meanings that move human sensibilities and mobilize behavior that cop culture can be glimpsed.

Police culture is at once more complex and elegant than suggested by a focus on dark elements of policing such as corruption, testimonial deception, and cynicism. The way in which culture uniquely characterizes the police does not reside primarily in these most publicly visible attributes of police work, but in the myriad details of occupational activity. Culture is a diffusion of the work-a-day world in which ways of doing work become habitual and habits become meaningful. Culture, like heaven and the devil, is sustained, celebrated and feared; in short, lived in the concrete minutia of everyday work.

Culture is not a simple term. It is what some writers call multivocal, which means that its use conjures many meanings simultaneously. I will use culture in different ways to try to capture this multivocality. Three ways of thinking about culture are listed below; I do not believe that any of the three is a better way of thinking about culture than any other—each simply expands the richness of the meaning of the idea. I mention these three because, when considered together, they begin to approximate the richness that lies in the world of the ordinary. Through culture, the work-a-day world transforms into a triumph of the spirit and the mind harmonized with others in occupational activity.

Culture Is a Confluence of Themes

First, I view culture as a confluence of themes of occupational activity. The word "confluence" is a metaphor suggesting the emptying of streams and rivers into a common body of water. At a confluence, the particular contributions of individual creeks and rivers are no longer clearly recognizable—the flow is a blend of them all. Police culture is like this. Diverse aspects of organizational activity merge into a whole united by commonly held values and shared ways of thinking. Culture cannot be wholly explained by the presence of any particular theme (though it may be clearly visible through the theme) but rather by the unique mix of them all in a particular occupational setting. The texture of police culture—the entire body of meaning or world-view of its celebrants—lies in the way in which these themes join together in some particular encounter, play off each other, motivate and justify behavior, and are expressed in some story a police officer tells another after a long shift.

Culture Is a Carrier of Institutionalized Values

Second, culture carries important values that are shared by members of a group. The idea that some ways of doing things become valued in themselves means that they have become institutionalized: we do them because we share a belief that they are the right things to do. Marriage between a man and a woman, for example, is the most common institutionalized form for propagating families between consenting adults in the United States—many people strongly believe in the formality of marriage and frown upon couples that are not heterosexual, that live together without formal marriage vows, and that have children out of wedlock. There are powerful, harsh terms for violations of these values: children out of wedlock are bastards, unmarried couples are

"living in sin," and homosexual couples are called "queers." This example, simple though it is, reveals the power with which values attach to and legitimize or stigmatize particular forms of behavior. It is very hard to think against the moral grain.

Organizations themselves are carriers of important institutional values. We tend to think of organizations as rational bureaucracies, but they are quite a bit more than this. Organizations also carry values and meanings that are important to society itself.

Culture Is How Police Express Emotions

Third, I try to capture the spice and magic that accompanies the work of street officers. Police work is not simply a set of rules that guide what officers do, carried by a municipal bureaucracy that organizes police work. Police work is something more than a set of organizational structures, formal policy, tactics, and strategy. The "something more" is the powerful personal sentiments that officers feel about what they do. To be meaningful, a study of police culture must somehow look beyond over-worked and tired ideas of organizational structure and look at the feelings police officers hold for each other and about their work. If police work is meaningful, then this study of police culture must tap some of the meanings and feelings that police work holds for officers. Accordingly, I strive to capture the unpredictability of the work, the seductions of street life, the efforts of officers to peer through the haze of the obvious, the bullshit of police administration, the ironic sense that works so well for officers in the field. In the writing, I occasionally capture a glimpse of the secret heart of police culture itself.

Culture and the Formation of Values

We are constantly engaged in a process of interacting with other people, and the meanings these interactions hold for us emerge in a practical, common-sense way from these interactions. According to this idea, we create meaning daily as an ongoing process of acting and reacting to other people and events in simple everyday life. Meaning emerges in the form of common sense, or what works as individuals together seek to solve routine problems (Geertz, 1973). These meanings tend to provide a sensibility out of which future action is conditioned.

Observers of culture have developed a diverse and colorful terminology to describe the interactive process: as shared typifications (Berger & Luckmann, 1966), as common-sense knowledge (Geertz, 1973), as figurative action (Shearing & Ericson, 1991), as documentary interpretation (Garfinkle, 1967), as a tool-kit (Swidler, 1986), and as a humanistic coefficient (Znaniecki, 1936). These descriptions share a common theme. Culture is a body of knowledge that emerges through the shared application of practical skills to concrete problems encountered in daily routines and the normal course of activities. This body of knowledge contains both information and values, and behavior tends to flow from this body of knowledge in ways that are self-confirming.

Drawing from various writers, I argue that particular police cultures are grounded in everyday activity of the police, and cannot be understood apart from the way in which they interact with their various environments. Values are grounded in preferred ways of responding to widely shared problems. For example, cops everywhere experience firsthand the legal system when they make an arrest, deal with the community media when they are involved in high-profile crime, have to write tickets to unhappy motorists, and complain bitterly about the seeming arbitrariness of departmental brass. Over time, ways of thinking about and working with these groups become taken for granted and are understood as common sense. We can thus begin to understand why police cultures are so similar across the United States—the problems they confront and the social and political environments they inhabit, except for variation in geography, are themselves remarkably similar.

The accumulation of common-sense meanings over time leads to ways of doing and thinking that are taken by group members as something larger, and sometimes more important than life—an example that comes to mind is the importance of risking one's life for one's partner. It is simply unthinkable that police officers would not place themselves in danger to protect a fellow officer.

In other words, ways of doing and thinking become institutionalized, accepted as larger than life, as valued in themselves (Selznick, 1949). This view is called an *institutional perspective*. Researchers and writers that use institutional perspectives seek to identify meanings that underlie ways of thinking and acting that are often taken for granted (DiMaggio, 1991:11). Institutions, it is argued, constrain rational decisionmaking vis-à-vis hidden assumptions and accepted practices (Douglas, 1986). Institutional theorists are consequently the great unmaskers; they seek to identify that which we take for granted and to move it into the realm of rational discourse. Values will tend to become institutionalized over time, but their meaning will always have a touchstone in everyday reality and a connection with real people. Values and meanings are part and parcel of what it means to act human, and are intrinsic elements of all cultures.

Grounded Aesthetics and Police Culture

In this section, I discuss in more detail the foundations of culture, that is, the way in which members of the rank-and-file find meaning in ordinary activity. This book takes the position that culture is socially constructed meaning, which simply means that ideas, information, and ways of doing and thinking about activities are found meaningful and shared by two or more people. Knowledge about how to act and how to think about work derives directly from real-world experiences shared by its members. Viewed through the lens of culture, the content of day-to-day activity becomes meaningful, collects value, and is understood in a vocabulary of common sense (Shearing & Ericson, 1991; Geertz, 1973). The constructed world is an everyday one, and cultural vocabularies that describe it are pragmatic (Willis, 1990).

Problem-solving is not a solitary exercise, but occurs in the sharing of problems concretely experienced (Berger & Luckmann, 1966). Many problems are similar, and come to be recognized, discussed, and shared as a common type of problem; to use the language of phenomenology, they are a typification. These pragmatic typifications or areas of similarly perceived experience are the building blocks of culture. When added together they become a store of "common knowledge" about how things work (Wuthnow et al., 1984:47).

Skolnick, for example, discusses the "symbolic assailant," a person whose clothes and mannerisms suggest that the person will cause trouble and is a likely candidate for a stop and frisk. Training officers teach recruits what to look for in terms of potential danger, and officers tell each other stories about things they have seen that mark individuals as dangerous—a type of tattoo, piece of clothing marking a gang member, or the like. Thus, typifications indicating the potential for trouble and danger arise from the concrete doing of police work, are shared by cops (and hence the phrase "shared typification") and become a part of the lore of a local police culture.

In time such typifications are regarded as common knowledge that carries common-sense value. Put sensibly, common knowledge is part of a cultural tool-kit for carrying out everyday activities (Swidler, 1986:275). This tool-kit is described by, she observes, "action and values" … "organized to take advantage of cultural competences." Common knowledge, with its roots in shared everyday experience, is a way of thinking about the world, of organizing information into typifications that enable an actor to do their work with the competency to know how events will unfold. In the case of police culture, culturally shared meanings represent how cops think about their working environment, and with the passage of time they indicate how cops think about their lives.

I believe that the idea of grounded aesthetics has much to offer to our understanding of the culture of policing. By thinking of the police in terms of grounded aesthetics, we can focus on concrete events, style of dress, forms of patrol, ways of talking, styles of weaponry, and rituals of celebration and of grieving; in short, the styles of behavior they choose to adapt to their various audiences. We can also think about stories that cops tell, those that are retold and become part of the cultural lore of an agency, both for the meanings they carry about the doing of police work and for the artistry that goes into their construction.

The artistry inherent in the idea of a grounded aesthetic suggests that members of the police culture are not simple dopes (Garfinkle, 1967) mindlessly responding to powerful environmental forces—the institution of crime control, the courts, or their own

organization. Cops are selecting modes of adaptation that they prefer, that they sometimes, to use a term uncommon to scholarly studies, simply *like*. The term aesthetics suggests an emotive element to how officers adapt to their audiences: they make choices that are pleasing to them, that make them feel good, or that at appropriate times make them angry.

Finally, the notion of grounded aesthetics provides insight into how some common cultural goods are transmitted across diverse agencies to increase similarities among police cultures—to contribute to a global "culture of policing" that transcends particular departments. Processes of media transmission provide for a common core of cultural symbols across organizations. Training films that discuss danger and show cops killed in action contribute to a shared, and particularly intense way of thinking about danger among the police. Magazines selling various products describe particular types of weapons available to the police and enable the selection of defenses—lead-lined gloves, baton, hand-weapons, shot-guns, knives, and the like—according to personal taste and skills of the officer. Television shows such as "Cops," where media ride along with officers in the hopes of gleaning a moment of excitement in the hum-drum of routine patrol, are talked about and provide a forum for thinking about good (and "stupid," as one cop described "Cops" to me) police behavior. In short, many elements of cop culture are available through forms of media, and provide an easily and widely accessible pool of cultural goods that cops select to enhance their self-image as tough enforcers (Kappeler, Blumberg & Potter, 1993).

 ## Culture and Cultural Themes

The term *cultural theme* represents the joining of two phenomena. First, themes are broad areas of shared activity. They represent activities that tend to be widely distributed, that is, common to all police departments. In this book, they are described in terms of the ordinary "doing" of police work, and derive their meaning from routine, ordinary police activity. However, a theme is more than an area of activity. It is also a way of thinking about that activity, the sentiment that is associated with the activity. Kappeler, Sluder, and Alpert (1994:108) use the term *dynamic affirmation* to describe the linkage of activity and sentiment. Put another way, police don't approach each aspect of their work as if they had never done it before—there are traditions and ways of thinking that are associated with their many activities. Nor are the themes rule-bound—they are predispositive, applying appropriate customs and taken-for-granted assumptions to, in Shearing and Ericson's (1991) colorful phrasing, provide the sensibility for thinking about particular routine activities.

That the police share a culture united by common themes has been noted by many observers—Manning, 1989, 1977; Reuss-Ianni, 1983; Shearing & Ericson, 1991; McNulty, 1994; and Bayley & Bittner, 1984, to name but a few. Shared cultural themes—of unpredictability (Skolnick, 1994), "Assholes" (Van Maanen, 1978), management brass (Ianni & Ianni, 1983), and the liberal court system (Niederhoffer, 1969) have been cited so frequently as to seem ubiquitous in literature on police culture. Yet there is little consensus on even what the boundaries of a culture are, let alone what themes are and how we distinguish among them.

Below are some general considerations of culture and its themes pertinent to police culture specifically. These considerations have to do with cultural boundaries, and how I developed the boundaries of police culture used in this book.

Boundaries

When we think about culture, we tend to think in imaginatively primitive terms, such as some small group geographically isolated from other groups, perhaps some remote Indian tribe deep in the Amazon rain forest. The principle of geographic remoteness does not apply for the police—they are embedded in and surrounded by other groups. How, then, can we describe boundaries for police culture so that we clearly know who it is that we are studying?

A boundary central to police culture is rank. That a police organization may contain multiple cultures has been suggested by various scholars (Gregory, 1983; Van

Maanen & Barley, 1982). Manning (1976) describes a three-tier image of police culture segmented by rank. Distinguishing cultural characteristics, he observes, can be noted at the ranks of line officers, at the middle-management ranks, and at the level of command. While granting that there are core values that mobilize all levels of the police, I will limit the focus of the current inquiry to elements associated with the segment at the bottom of the chain-of-command, line-officer culture. The audience of line-officer culture includes organizational management or "brass" as well as the courts, felons and misdemeanants, and the public. As I discuss in detail later, line officers routinely interact with these audiences, and the routines officers have and values and sentiments that correspond to their routines comprise cultural themes and circumscribe their culture.

The Selection of Cultural Themes

I have deliberately selected the most inclusive, but perhaps also the most undisciplined, means to answer this question, through the identification and discussion of themes identified by other researchers on the topic. This method suffers from problems of validity. Themes are described using writings both from quasi-scientific models of inquiry and from the anecdotal perceptions of police researchers or writings of former cops (see Van Maanen, 1978, for a description of this problem). Distinguishing fact from fancy is nearly impossible (and perhaps artificial). Consequently, I may at times be charged with mixing a fanciful blend of police anecdotes and researcher anecdotes together with more scientific research to create a story rather than to construct meaningful theory. I plead guilty to the charge, offering on my behalf the thin argument that police anecdotes may not be technically true in the sense that most accurately represents historical fact or reality. Nonetheless, they may be an accurate reflection of the sentiments and values that characterize police cultures. The study of culture is not simply a pursuit of historical truths, but a search for meanings, values, and traditions as they are sensed, believed, and acted out by particular groups. In this context, anecdotal stories are more than conversational entertainment, they are the carriers of cultural history. To overlook their importance is to neglect a central device of culture itself—its oral traditions and its bases for action.

The Inclusiveness of Themes

When a cultural theme is identified, can it be known if the theme represents only one particular culture in some particular organization, or if it is more inclusive, characterizing beat officers in municipal departments generally? In this book, I identify a diverse array of cultural themes associated with police culture. Yet the apparent pervasiveness of some of these themes undoubtedly derives from the process of academic reproduction of knowledge rather than from our knowledge of police culture in different settings. It is difficult to separate what we know about the police mystique from writings that reflect academic mystique of the police. I try to address this problem by citing a wide variety of materials to illustrate concepts and examples.

Thematic Overlap

To what extent are cultural themes discrete entities? In this book I will try to separate them analytically, yet do so with the caveat that in practice they seem to be more like unintegrated congeries than distinct elements (Spradley & McCurdy, 1975). Cultural logic is an astonishing process of circular reasoning encompassing fluid situations: police-citizen interactions that progress unpredictably and rapidly, danger anticipated and resolved in a context of hurried decisions, reactions to potential threats, use of force and applications of street justice, and how to act, to avoid action and corresponding responsibility, or to simply lie in the face of sharply incomplete and inconsistent information from the public, the courts, and from their own superiors. The rush and tedium of everyday phenomena becomes overlaid with cultural meanings and values, general principles and guides for behavior that apply to individual, concrete encounters. Thus, by identifying and analyzing as discrete that which is fluid and highly interrelated I may well be obscuring what was in practice uniquely cultural about them—like explaining a tree through a description of its chemical properties.

I argue that street cops everywhere tend to share a common culture because they respond to similar audiences everywhere. Put another way, at the municipal level they operate in similar institutional environments, where the expectations of important actors tend to be similar. By actors, I mean those groups with whom the police interact, and who have expectations about how the police are going to act around them. Police audiences—the public, criminals, lawyers, automobile drivers, the courts, and departmental administrators across the cities and towns of the United States have remarkably similar expectations of the police. These expectations provide the basis for large numbers of common elements among American police organizational cultures. In the following chapter I will discuss principal audiences of the police, and how they contribute to a common definition of police culture.

 Articulating Police Culture and Its Environments: Patterns of Line-Officer Interactions

Police Culture Is Embedded In and Bounded by Organizational Structure

This book adopts Reuss-Ianni's (1983) and Manning's (1989) perspective that culture is differentiated in police organizations. I focus on common culture among line-officers. I argue that culture arises in similar ways across police organizations in large part because the occupational organization of line officers—the squad—is itself similar in all organizations.

All departments, given sufficient organizational size, are organized at the line level into squads. Rubinstein's (1973:32–43) analysis of the organization of squads in Philadelphia could apply to any city in the United States. Squads worked a six-day week, and were assigned to work shifts at one of three times. Day work was normally from 8 a.m. to 4 p.m., while night work started at 4 p.m. and extended to midnight. The last shift, which Rubinstein called "last out," began at midnight and ended at 8 o'clock the following morning. With minor variation, this shift pattern is omnipresent across municipal police organizations today.

This working schedule, especially in departments where officers rotate across shifts, tends to isolate members of the squad from the public. Former non-police friends, who may work a normal 8-5 job, are unavailable for leisure activities. They frequently work weekends and holidays, and cannot commit themselves to outside engagements that might broaden their friendship networks. Officers are also isolated from most other police officers in the department. They are in contact with members of their squad, but less frequently have contact with officers working other squads and other shifts. Their circle of acquaintances and friends are limited to the fellow cops with whom they come into contact on a regular basis.

Squads are divided into platoons of around 25 officers, each of these directed by a sergeant. The sergeants are answerable to lieutenants, the highest-ranking officer with whom line-officers are likely to make contact. While squads are differentiated by shift, platoons are differentiated by geography. In Rubinstein's study, the platoons were assigned to the "east end" and the "west end," the informal division of the district. Each platoon had its own roll call, but members of the two platoons knew each other and were in frequent interaction during shifts and at the end of shifts.

The period at the end of the shift is a particularly fertile period in which to rehash the activities of the day, to pass on new information about problems, and to tell stories and exploits of particular officers. Pogrebin and Poole, studying a Colorado police department, noted the importance of end-of-shift discussion and interaction for officers. Officers remained well past the end of the shift to "'cool out' from a rough shift, …or to vicariously experience the highlights of fellow officers' calls…"

It also provided an opportunity to discuss department policies, politics, and personalities. Rumors made their rounds at this time—with a few being squelched, several being started, and many being embellished (Pogrebin & Poole, 1988: 188–189).

End-of-shift thus provided a fertile period for interactions that provided a basis for the emergence of police culture from the shared experiences that officers had encountered during their shifts.

Department-wide common culture emerges because officers are occasionally reassigned to new squads across the organization. Rubinstein noted the importance of the transfer of personnel across squads for the dissemination of common culture.

Occasionally a man transfers from one squad to another, bringing with him knowledge of ex-colleagues which he offers to his new colleagues, enriching their knowledge about co-workers who are frequently seen, greeted, chatted with, but rarely known in the personal way as are the (members of the) squad (Rubinstein, 1973:32).

The fundamental unit of local cop culture is the squad. However, because of transfers over time, and stemming from the inevitable gossip that characterizes the police locker-room, squad information is transmitted across the organization and provides a common basis for culture across the organization.

Cultural Themes Stem From the Everyday Interactions of the Police With Their Various Environments

The members of a squad are in contact on a regular basis with people in their working environments in ways that are governed by particular rules and procedures. By environments, I mean that cops regularly come into contact with particular groups in their everyday working conditions. Cops interact with courtroom personnel in the courthouse and occasionally in the station house, the public primarily on the streets in vehicular stops or at their houses in response to a call for service, and management in their offices when they are called to the office to be chastised, or on rare occasion at the scene of a crime after a particularly violent incident. These environments tend to be replicated in similar fashion across municipal districts. Moreover, the work and the organization of squads is similar across jurisdictions. Finally, media influences—radio, television, the movies, newspapers, training films—carry common notions of police values and behavior and thus contribute powerfully to the cultural similarity of police organizations. Police cultures thus tend to be more alike than would be suggested by the sheer diversity of city characteristics, sizes, and types of municipal governments in the United States.

The Street Environment Is the First and Most Salient Environment

This is the officers patrol beat where the powerful themes of territoriality, force, and uncertainty are played out. Officers are assigned to a particular area, and become responsible for the production of police activity in that area. In this environment, police behavior reflects the interaction of their personal temperament, the circumstances of the encounter, and the attitudes of the individuals involved in the encounter (Black, 1980). The particular way a police-citizen encounter is resolved is an aesthetic through which officers play out their roles as police. This environment can be separated into the following activity-types that give rise to and sustain police culture.

Citizen-Invoked Interactions

Citizen-invoked interactions occur when a citizen telephones a department or when an alarm is sounded, and a patrol car is dispatched to the source of the call. This type of interaction accounts for the bulk of police-citizen contacts. It is reactive style of policing, and powerfully shapes police-citizen relations. For property crimes, police can do little more than take a report. The likelihood of solving the crime is remote, and citizens know this. The police officer is often the verbal target of a citizen's frustration, and police are frustrated in their reactive role, locked into dealing with the problems caused by crime without being able to actually do something about the crime itself. Consequently, these encounters tend to be dispiriting for police and citizens alike; they tend to be perfunctory and ceremonial, satisfying the record-keeping requirements of crime reporting and the needs of insurance companies (Van Maanen, 1973).

Traffic Stops

Line officers also routinely come into contact with the citizenry through traffic stops. Perhaps because stops are so mundane in the sweep of police activity, observers of the police have paid them scant attention. However, traffic stops are integral to the patrol task. Through the presence of formal and informal quotas, they are semi-articulated—officers aren't assigned particular stops, but they often face departmental expectations that they will issue a certain number of citations. Public response to citations is less than friendly. Even in that rarest of traffic stops, when a citizen responds to the news of their violation and impending ticket with "You are absolutely right, officer. I deserve the ticket and will be more careful in the future," cops know that citizens are giving their best shot at appearing apologetic in the hopes that they will be forgiven.

Police-Citizen Interactions Are Articulated by the Organization

Contact with the public is articulated through the organization. The decision to intervene is at the discretion of the officer, but problems associated with intervention are enveloped in department policy. And if the intervention is followed by an arrest, a panoply of organizational linkages—paperwork, court appearances, and the like—come into play. Dispatchers tell officers where to go, messages are taped, and vast arrays of accountability mechanisms are activated when an officer is dispatched to a scene.

In spite of the seeming autonomy and low visibility of police attributed by many authors to contemporary patrol practices, police-citizen interactions are increasingly modulated through the organization. Consequently, much of what I describe herein as police culture—solidarity and loose coupling—stems from this extraordinary task ambiguity and the way in which administrators seek to control line officer-citizen encounters by controlling inputs and outputs through communications and dispatch.

Administrative Environment

The second environment is the organizational adminis-tration (Reuss-Ianni, 1983). Line officers are physically present at the police station during two periods each day, prior to and at the end of their shift. Pogrebin and Poole (1988:180) describe both the beginning and the conclusion of shift work, summarized as follows.

Roll Call

Prior to the beginning of the shift, officers arrive at the station house and go to their locker room to change into uniforms. They then go to a briefing room for assignments and for roll call. The briefing session lasts for 15 to 20 minutes, during which time officers receive information on the activities of the previous shift, on the focus of the current shift, and on any new policy. Shift sergeants may caution officers on particular dan-gers, praise them for particular accomplishments, or call attention to particular problems.

Roll call may contain mild rebukes of officers. During roll call, particular officers may be singled out for unpleasant duty, may be given disagreeable temporary partners, or otherwise be the recipient of administrative "bullshit." Jocular humor provides a way in which offi-cers maintain face when subjected to rebuke during roll call (Pogrebin & Poole, 1988). The time periods before and after roll call, when officers are on their way to or from their cars, provide time to talk and exchange infor-mation. Police on duty exchange information, meeting covertly away from supervisors. The most important information of the day is sometimes shared among officers on their way to their cars, out of the hearing range of superior officers but not yet in their cars where their conversation can be monitored by radio dispatch.

Shift End

At the end of the shift, officers return to the briefing room to complete their paperwork. Their reports are reviewed by their sergeants, and time is spent debrief-ing. As Poole and Pogrebin note, officers often spend more time than necessary here, relaxing and exchanging stories about shift activities. Shift end is consequently an environment for the types of interaction and story-telling that contributes to the generation of local cultural knowledge. Officers also may extend the end of the shift to the local pub or to an officer's house, further-ing interaction and story-telling—what some observers call bullshit sessions.

Sergeant Supervision

During the shift, sergeant supervision is somewhat informal, occurring prior to and during patrol activity. Sergeants are the first link in the chain-of-command above line officers, and are responsible for the supervi-sion of line officers during patrol. Though the sergeant is generally thought of as the most influential person over the day-to-day activities of officers (see, for exam-ple, Trojanowicz, 1980; Rubinstein, 1973), there is evi-dence that Sergeants exercise scant control over line personnel (Kappeler, Sluder & Alpert, 1994). Allen and Maxfield (1983), studying arrest, citation, and warrant behavior of officers, found that sergeants had no sub-stantive effects on officers' line activities, and only in a few cases did supervisor's emphasis on work quantity affect officers' total output. Surprisingly, even the per-ception that they worked under arrest quotas had scant impact on arrest practices. Implications were clear:

> The influence of first-line supervisors in direct-ing the behavior of officers is seriously limited. Even though supervisors emphasize a particu-lar performance criterion or suggest that a certain level of performance be met, officers under their command do not seem to respond positively to these cues. (Maxfield, 1983:82)

In other words, sergeants were themselves loosely associated with the police culture.

Internal Review

Officers are articulated to the organization through internal review procedures. Review may be mandatory, for example, when an officer fires a service weapon, or may occur under subpoena, when an officer is being investigated for wrongdoing or as a witness to other wrongdoing. This is the form of articulation that is most feared by officers (Perez, 1994). It has been hoped that internal review would penetrate police culture and curb its excesses. Unfortunately, internal review is often perceived by line officers as an arbitrary tactic used by management to "hang officers out to dry" rather than as a tool for the uncovering of wrongdoing. Police reformers have failed to recognize that internal review is the source of loose coupling and a powerful stimulus for the development of police culture.

Standard Operating Procedure

The rules binding line officers with the organizational administration are called standard operating procedure (SOP), intended to guide police encounters in specific circumstances. They are written by the administration, and may reflect state and municipal influences over police behavior. Standard Operating Procedure is a typically thick manual that defines the vast array of rules telling officers what they should not do in various circumstances, representing, quipped one officer, "100 years of fuckups." Representing the rules by which the organization seeks to coordinate its functions, the SOP provides little insight into the creative process officers use to deal with their most intransigent concerns—unpredictable police-citizen interactions. Officers recognize instinctively, or from experience if instinct does not provide insight soon enough, that SOP is a tool used punitively, always in retrospect, and by managers who seek to protect themselves from line-level mistakes. For many line officers, SOP represents the systematic formalization of department "bullshit."

The Courts

When line officers make an arrest, they have linked the police with another component of the criminal justice system. The third environment to which the police are articulated is the courts. This articulation is of several types. In the first type, police are articulated through the warrant process. If the police suspect that a crime has occurred, and that evidence for the crime exists, unless there are warrantless bases to obtain information they must seek a warrant. This can be a frustrating process, as Sutton (1991) noted in the following case where a

detective recreates his efforts to get an appointment to have a warrant signed:

Receptionist:	…if that's the case, you don't want to find just any attorney, you want a search warrant. Just a moment, let me check.
Officer:	(and I know what they're doing while I'm on hold.)
Attorney #1:	No. Can he come over at 2:00?
Attorney #2:	No. I can't cause I really got to go do this.
Receptionist:	Sorry, we don't have anybody right now (Sutton, 1991:435–436).

A variety of additional circumstances articulate police with the courts. If an officer has made a felony arrest, he or she will have to appear at a preliminary hearing. An officer may face cross-examination and direct examination. More frustrating to a line officer is that the case may be postponed, and an officer will have to reappear multiple times during this and subsequent proceedings. Both work and time off may be disrupted at the whim of the court.

During the pretrial phase, the defense has the right of discovery, to find out about all evidence that may be used against the defendant at the trial. The trial itself may demand precious off-duty time. All testimony is recorded and available for reference by the defense for future use. An officer's legitimacy will be measured by the police report, by transcripts of earlier proceedings, the D.A. interview, and by the quality of the evidence (officers sometimes simply forget to bring important evidence with them).

Police legitimacy in the courtroom, based on the legality of their behavior, may be at odds with their street behavior. While on patrol, officers may rely on the presence of a wide variety of subtle cues in deciding where and how to intervene in the affairs of a citizen. Instinct, as much as the presence of articulable cause, may guide their behavior. And arrest may represent a desire to bring justice to some asshole rather than a calculated estimate of the presence of probable cause (Van Maanen, 1978). On patrol, officers learn how to use personal authority to handle situations. In the courtroom legitimacy are issues of the quality of the evidence and demeanor in front of the judge, and officers have to express obeisance to the judge.

Media

The fourth area of articulation is with the media, members of which are in frequent interaction with the police. Newspaper reporters are social control agents whose influence can both negatively and positively affect the police. The police know this, and seek their sanction through co-optive strategies. As Ericson (1989) has observed,

> . . . the police try to incorporate the news media as *part of* the policing apparatus. They do so by giving journalists physical space within police buildings, by taking them into account in organizational charts, directives and planning, and by making them part of the everyday social and cultural practices in the police organization (Ericson, 1989:208).

News reporters, particularly the "inner circle," frequently carry scanners so that they, like police, can arrive at the scene of breaking crime events. These are often individuals who support the police and may have worked with them for years. Their values are the values of the police culture. At the scene of a criminal activity, police try to steer the flow of information to friendly reporters, and to avoid the release to others who might also look at the conduct of the police.

Police manage the release of friendly information through the inner circle when possible. They seek to otherwise tightly control the release of information that might ideologically disparage the organization. The strategic use of secrecy and silence enables them to control information to non-friendly press, while inner-circle reporters will censor themselves. Through articulating their relationship with inner-circle reporters, the police seek to assure the support of the media. The police avoid the release of much negative information in this way (Ericson, 1989).

Scandal ruptures the inner circle. Sometimes stories are too hot to be controlled by the inner circle, and public relations units cannot contain the sudden, massive investigation of what Ericson (1989) calls the "outer circle." The impact of scandal is massive and causes a dramatic loss of legitimacy for the police. Such events are periods of *uncontrolled articulation*, chaos personified, formal relations between the police and other groups yielding confusing and poorly regulated communications. Departments are swamped by persons seeking information, officers in different circumstances, ranks, and degree of involvement provide inconsistent accounts of the department, and the veil of secrecy is widely breached, as managers and line personnel alike seek to strategically cover their butts.

In summary, the relationship between line officers and these groups gives meaning to culture. The values, stories, metaphors, and meanings that give each police culture its unique identity stems from its relations with these groups. Because culture is grounded in the relations of line officers with these groups, culture had an immediacy and practicality often overlooked by students of culture. How police deal collectively with these groups, and pass that knowledge on to recruits, is what police culture is all about.

DISCUSSION QUESTIONS

1. What does John Crank identify as the "fundamental unit of local cop culture"?

2. Identify and describe the various environments that influence police culture.

3. Based on what you learned from the Crank excerpt, what are three words that you would use to describe police culture? Explain your choices.

Police officers begin their careers working on patrol.

Career Paths of Police Officers

Section Highlights

- Examine why people choose to become police officers.
- Review the three phases of training.
- Identify the factors that influence officers to seek promotion.

Police work is often presented as an exciting and challenging profession on popular television programs. Despite the fact that police work on TV has been edited to present some of the most interesting aspects of the job, many people are still drawn to this profession each year. Other than the excitement of the job, why do people choose to become police officers? And once they have made this career choice, what do they have to do to become police officers? This section begins with a discussion of some of the most common reasons that people choose to become police officers. Standard application and selection requirements are then covered to provide a general overview of the hiring process. This section also covers three types of police training that take place over the course of a typical policing career: police academy training, field training officer (FTO)/police training officer (PTO) program, and in-service training.

Choosing a Career in Policing

The career paths of individuals who choose to become police officers begin with them making the decision to apply. Research indicates that people choose careers in policing for an opportunity to help other people, a good salary and job security, a job that is exciting, and the prestige that comes with being a police officer.[1] Surprisingly, men and women give very similar responses when asked about their motivations for becoming police officers.[2] A recent study of police recruits in the New York City Police Department revealed that, in general, motivations for pursuing policing careers were also similar across all racial/ethnic groups.[3] Police cadets in the Los Angeles Police Department reported that they had decided to become police officers several years before they had actually applied for the job—they stated that it was something that they had always wanted to do.[4] There are other people that choose policing as a career as a result of recruitment efforts by police agencies.

Recruitment

Police agencies use a variety of recruitment techniques to attract the best applicants. Visiting technical schools, community colleges, and universities is a common recruiting practice used by police agencies. Potential applicants are also reached through career fairs, advertisements in newspapers, television and radio, and Internet recruiting websites. Some police agencies begin the recruitment process early by visiting local high schools. The **Explorers program** is another way to spark interest in a policing career early on in youth populations. The Explorers program gives youth a hands-on look at the profession by allowing them to participate in activities with officers from local police agencies. This is a program offered in cities across the United States.[5] All of these recruitment efforts are important, as they have a direct impact on the quality of police officers that are ultimately hired.

The Explorers program introduces young people to the policing profession.

The diversification of police agencies has become an important part of the recruitment process for American police agencies. Agencies specifically seeking female applicants highlight their family-friendly policies to attract women who might have otherwise believed that having a family would be a barrier to a career in policing.[6] Female police officers also attend career fairs to attract female applicants, and are able to give them first-hand accounts of what it is like to be women working in this profession. Similarly, agencies that are looking to expand racial/ethnic diversity within their organizations provide mentoring programs in which minority police officers share their experiences with minority citizens that are considering jobs in policing. Other police agencies conduct focus groups and community meetings in racially diverse neighborhoods to attract more diverse applicants.[7] Many police agencies have found that they need to go beyond traditional recruiting efforts if they want to attract a more diverse pool of applicants.

Standard Employment Requirements	
U.S. citizenship/driver's license	Residency requirements
Minimum age 21 years	Education—at least high school diploma
Height proportionate to weight	Vision—varies across agencies
Criminal record—no felonies	

What Are Some of the Common Requirements for Hiring Police Officers?

There are no national, standardized employment requirements imposed on police agencies in the United States. Requirements for employment vary from state to state and agency to agency. This variation in employment requirements explains why police agencies are so different from one another across the country. Most police agencies, however, do have standard employment requirements in the following areas:

U.S. Citizenship/Driver's License

Being a citizen of the United States is a nearly universal requirement that needs to be met in order to become a police officer in any state in the United States.[8] A valid driver's license is also a universal requirement to become a police officer.

Residency Requirements

Residency requirements vary from one police agency to the next. Some police agencies require their officers to live within the city limits of the communities they serve, while other agencies do not. Less restrictive residency requirements might allow their employees to live no further than a certain number of miles away from police headquarters. Residency requirements have been debated for some time and have even been contested in court. In general, residency requirements have been deemed constitutional by federal level courts as long as the employing agency can demonstrate that there is a rational basis for such a requirement.[9]

Reasons police officers should be required to live within the communities they serve include the idea that this will allow them to better understand the needs of their community; they will have a greater stake in serving the community; they will contribute to the local tax base; it could reduce absenteeism of officers; and it allows police officers to respond quickly if they are needed in emergency situations.[10] In contrast, there are many reasons to oppose residency requirements, including the idea that it could disqualify otherwise qualified applicants that live outside of the community; police officers will be able to provide quality services even if they do not live in the communities they serve; and officers should be given the choice to live wherever they want to live—housing in some cities is very expensive and could cause financial hardship for police officers forced to live there.[11] This requirement has become negotiable in some jurisdictions when police agencies have had difficulty attracting qualified applicants within the community.

Age

The minimum hiring age commonly used by police agencies in the United States is 21 years old.[12] Recently, there has been discussion about raising the minimum hiring age beyond 21 years old. Justification for increasing the **age requirement** is based on the idea that chronological age may not reflect an individual's maturity level; thus, raising the hiring age by a few years will give people more time to mature. The opposing side of this debate asserts that if the age is raised too high, it will reduce the overall size of the pool of applicants. On November 5, 2010, the Chicago Police Department announced that it had raised its minimum hiring age from 21 to 25 years old. Police Superintendent Jody Weis stated that this increase in the minimum hiring age was an effort to encourage a more mature police force.[13]

Education

Nearly all local police agencies in the United States have some kind of education requirement as part of their hiring standards.[14] A majority (82%) of local police agencies require that applicants have a high school diploma, while 6% require some college credits but no degree, 9% require a 2-year degree, and 1% requires a 4-year degree.[15] When these statistics are compared to those from previous decades, it is clear that police officers are becoming more educated in the United States over time. But does an increase in education requirements result in better police officers? This question has been studied extensively over the last four decades. In the Roberg and Bonn article included at the end of this section, the impact that higher education has on police officer attitudes and job performance is discussed in detail.

Height/Weight

Many police agencies in the United States used **height and weight requirements** as part of their selection process for hiring until the late 1970s.[16] Some agencies required that applicants weigh at least 150 pounds and measure 5'8" or taller.[17] This requirement had an exclusionary effect on women and some racial/ethnic minorities interested in becoming police officers. Under **Title VII of the 1964 Civil Rights Act**, the courts determined that this screening requirement was discriminatory, as it would disqualify a higher percentage of female applicants when compared to male applicants.[18] Further, the courts ruled that this requirement was not an accurate way to assess whether someone could do the job. Most agencies eliminated this requirement after the Supreme Court ruling in the case of *Dothard v. Rawlinson* (433 U.S. 321, 1977).[19] Today, some agencies use a modified version of this requirement by requiring that applicants' height is proportionate to their weight; however, most police agencies will assess whether someone is physically capable of doing police work by requiring them to complete a physical agility exam.[20]

Vision

Many police agencies have a vision requirement. The level of vision required by applicants varies from one agency to the next. In most agencies, peripheral vision must be normal and there cannot be a history of eye disease.[21] It is important to have good vision when performing most job-related tasks, but any problems with vision can jeopardize both a police officer and public safety in this particular line of work.

Criminal Record

According to recent statistics, all local police agencies in the United States conduct criminal record checks on all applicants as part of the hiring selection process.[22] Most police agencies will not hire people that have been convicted of felony charges, as most state Police Officer Standards and Training (POST) programs will not allow certification of people with such convictions.[23] There is great variation from one police agency to the next regarding the type of violations that will be allowed as part of the hiring process. Many police agencies have a list of the criminal violations that are either tolerated or not on their department website.[24]

In the past, when police agencies have lowered their hiring standards, the results have been disastrous. For example, in 1988, Congress required the District of Columbia to hire 1,500 new police officers within a 20-month time period or it would lose $430 million of aid. This rushed hiring process (which involved lowering hiring standards) resulted in more than half of the officers hired during that timeframe either being arrested or being brought up on criminal charges.[25] Similarly, many of the officers that were involved in the 1998 Rampart scandal in the Los Angeles Police Department were hired during a time when employment standards were lowered. Many of the Rampart police officers had been previously convicted of a variety of criminal acts, including selling marijuana, domestic violence, grand theft, and driving under the influence.[26] After investigating the police officers that were directly involved in this scandal, the Los Angeles Police Department concluded that

> While it is impossible to substantiate completely, it appears that the application of our hiring standards was compromised when these officers were hired during periods of accelerated hiring in the late 1980s and early 1990s. . . . Several employees were aware of the Department hiring people with prior gang affiliations, drug use and criminal histories.

These examples demonstrate the importance of maintaining high employment standards for police officers.

Selection Process

The process of becoming a police officer goes beyond filling out an application and meeting the minimum employment requirements. This process can be lengthy (6 months or longer) and requires applicants to demonstrate that they are both physically and mentally fit to be effective in this profession. The selection process varies from one police agency to the next, but there are some general steps used by most police agencies across the United States. The steps in the selection process also vary in the order of occurrence across police agencies.

Written Exam

Once it has been determined that the minimum standard requirements have been met by applicants, they will likely be asked to take a written examination. Most (80%) American police agencies serving populations of 25,000 or more require applicants to take a written aptitude exam.[27] Written exams measure reading comprehension, vocabulary skills, and, in some cases, analytical and problem-solving skills. The content of written exams varies from one agency to the next. Many police agencies tailor written exams to measure skills that they feel are important for police officers working in their communities. Exams are graded and

Applicants are required to demonstrate that they are physically able to do the job.

then rank ordered from the highest to the lowest score. Exam scores are often combined with other scored requirements for each applicant over the course the hiring process to determine each applicant's overall ranking in the pool of candidates.

Physical Agility Exam

Applicants will be asked to take a physical agility test to determine if they are capable of meeting the physical demands of police work. Most (90%) police agencies serving populations of 25,000 or more require applicants to complete a physical agility test.[28] Physical agility exams require applicants to do push-ups, do sit-ups, and run a specified distance to judge their cardiovascular endurance levels. Some police agencies also utilize obstacle courses to test an applicant's physical agility. There has been some controversy over the use of agility courses, as they often disqualify a high percentage of female applicants.[29] Research on this topic finds that physical agility courses do not reflect the skills that police officers actually need to be able to provide adequate services to the public.[30]

Oral Interview

Nearly all (99%) police agencies require their applicants to participate in an oral interview with a panel of professionals.[31] The composition of professional panels varies from one police agency to the next, but police executives, civil service representatives, human resource personnel, and, in some instances, citizens from the community could be part of this group. Like many of the other steps in the hiring process, the content of the questions asked during an oral interview will vary across agencies. Some general questions that could be asked may be related to why an applicant wants a job in that particular agency; why he or she wants a job in policing (in general); or how the person might respond to hypothetical situations (i.e., would you write your own mother a speeding ticket?). In some cases, applicants are asked questions regarding elements of crimes or criminal code for their jurisdiction.

Medical and Psychological Exams

Applicants will also be asked to take both medical and psychological examinations. Many police agencies leave these examinations for the end of the screening process because of the costs associated with such services. A majority (89%) of American police agencies require medical examinations to ensure that applicants are in good physical condition.[32] The examination includes elements of routine annual physical examinations conducted by physicians. In addition, audiograms (hearing), vision testing, pulmonary function testing (breathing), chest x-ray, electrocardiograms (heart function), and cardiopulmonary stress tests (heart and lungs) are sometimes included in medical exams.[33] Drug testing has become part of the medical examination in some agencies. In fact, most (83%) police agencies require drug testing prior to being hired.[34]

Psychological screening is used by many (72%) police agencies as part of the screening process.[35] The type of test used in psychological screening varies across police agencies; however, the **Minnesota Multiphasic Personality Inventory (MMPI)** is often used to assess the psychological state of applicants.[36] The MMPI screens for psychological issues, including paranoia, schizophrenia, depression, and manic behaviors.[37] The Inwald Personality Inventory is another test that is used during the screening process. This instrument is used to identify negative personality traits, including rigidity, loner mentality, emotional instability, impulsivity, antisocial attitudes, and difficulty with interpersonal relationships.[38] This "screening out" approach has been criticized because it focuses on identifying negative traits while failing to identify people who have positive traits that would be suitable for this profession.[39]

Record Checks/Background Investigation

Nearly all (99%) police agencies conduct a background check on applicants.[40] The depth of background checks varies across agencies, but in general, this usually involves telephone interviews with neighbors, teachers, personal references, and former employers. It is also at this stage in the process that applicants' driving, criminal, and credit records are examined. Recent statistics indicate that all police agencies check to see if applicants have criminal records, and nearly all (99%) agencies check driving records.[41] The inclusion of credit history as part of the background investigation is becoming common in police agencies. For example, 70% of police agencies serving populations of 25,000 or more looked at the credit scores of applicants in 2003; this increased to 83% in 2007.[42]

Polygraph Examination

Polygraph examinations are not used as frequently in the hiring process compared to some of the other screening techniques mentioned in this section. Only half (50%) of local police agencies require applicants to take a polygraph exam.[43] This practice has become less common over time, as it is expensive and the accuracy of this test has been challenged in court.[44] It has been suggested that if police agencies choose to use this screening approach, they should use it to deter lying instead of detecting lying.[45] In addition, the results of such an exam should not be weighted as heavily as other parts of the screening process, as the accuracy of its results is debatable.

Assessment Centers

An **assessment center** is a place applicants go to participate in a series of situational exercises that simulate responsibilities and working conditions of police officers.[46] The situational exercises are used to assess applicants' abilities to work in teams, their communication skills, and their ability to interact with the public.[47] They are another tool that is used to supplement (not replace) the traditional screening process used by police agencies. Slightly more than one-third (35%) of all local police agencies use assessment centers as part of their hiring process.[48] The high cost of using assessment centers prohibits some agencies from utilizing this tool in their screening process.[49] But are assessment centers better than traditional cognitive exams for predicting who will be good police officers? Joan Pynes and John

Bernardin conducted a study comparing the predictability accuracy of traditional cognitive exams (pen-and-paper format) and assessment center exercises.[50] This study revealed that traditional cognitive exams were better predictors of police academy performance, while assessment centers were better predictors of on-the-job performance.

If applicants successfully make it to the end of the selection process and are offered a job, they will be required to enroll in a police academy. In some places, people are not allowed to enter academy training until *after* they have been offered a job with a police agency.[51] People who have been offered a job prior to entering the police academy would be paid all or a portion of the salary they will receive once they are done with academy training, and the agency may also cover all or some of the costs of academy training. In contrast, some agencies require people to complete police academy training *before* they begin the screening process.[52] The drawback of entering police academy training before having a job offer is that the individual would be responsible for paying for his or her own police academy training.

Training

Police officers go through three stages of training over the course of their careers: police academy training, field training officer (FTO)/police training officer (PTO) program, and in-service training. Each phase of training provides officers with the information and skills that are necessary to be effective in this position.

Police Academy Training

Police academy training is the first phase of training for police officers. The purpose of academy training is to teach police cadets about what is expected of them once they become police officers and also the proper way to conduct police work. In 2006, there were 648 state and local law enforcement training academies providing basic training skills across the United States (98% of these academies were approved by state agencies).[53] The average police academy program lasts 19 weeks or 761 hours (not including field training requirements).[54] The average number of training hours (including both classroom and field training) is 1,370 hours.[55]

Police academy training has both a classroom and field training component. The topics covered in the classroom portion of academy training vary from one academy to the next; however, there are several topics that are covered by most police academies:[56]

- Criminal law (average of 36 hours)
- Constitutional law (average of 12 hours)
- Cultural diversity (average of 11 hours)
- Community policing (average of 8 hours)
- Mediation/conflict management (average of 8 hours)
- Report writing (average of 20 hours)
- Ethics (average of 8 hours)

Some police academies offer training on a variety of specialty topics, including domestic violence, interacting with juveniles, terrorism, hate crimes, and handling hazardous materials.

Training in the field is also part of police academy training. This type of training focuses on the physical aspects of police work. Some common topics covered in field training include:[57]

- Firearm skills (average of 60 hours)
- Self-defense skills (average of 51 hours)
- Health and fitness training (average of 46 hours)
- Patrol (average of 40 hours)
- Investigations (average of 40 hours)
- Emergency vehicle operation (average of 40 hours)
- Basic first aid skills (average of 24 hours)

Firearms training is just one of several practical applications covered in the academy.

Police academies have been criticized for not incorporating more training related to community policing and problem solving into their curricula.[58] The criticism comes from the idea that most police agencies claim to have adopted community policing and problem-oriented policing practices (which rely less on physical skills), but a large portion of police academy training is focused on the physical aspects of the job instead of skills related to community and problem-oriented policing. Another criticism is that the academy curriculum reinforces the idea that masculinity and aggressiveness are valued and necessary traits associated with being a police officer. An emphasis on such traits can make police academy training difficult for some women.[59]

FTO/PTO Programs

The **field training officer (FTO) program** was developed in San Jose, California, in 1972.[60] This stage of training requires newly sworn police officers to apply what they have learned in the police academy to real-life situations on the streets while being observed by field training supervisors. The FTO program also helps to determine who will be able to function effectively as police officers. There are several general phases included in most FTO programs:[61] (1) an introductory stage in which recruits learn about policies and procedure that are unique to their agency; (2) training and evaluation phases in which recruits are introduced to more difficult tasks associated with policing; and (3) the final evaluation phase in which recruits work independently while they are being critiqued by field training supervisors. FTO programs have been criticized because they do not contain elements of community or problem-oriented policing.[62]

A new postacademy training program, the **police training officer (PTO) program**, was created in the early 2000s through funding provided by the Office of Community Oriented Policing Services in Washington, DC.[63] The Reno, Nevada, Police Department worked in conjunction with the Police Executive Research Forum (PERF) to study the training needs of police agencies across the country. Based on findings from this study, the new PTO program was designed around the concept of problem-based learning. Problem-based learning is a process that helps officers develop problem-solving skills, the ability to be critical thinkers, and skills to work well in a team setting.[64]

The PTO program is composed of eight phases.[65] (1) *Orientation phase* provides information before trainees enter the field training program. (2) *Integration phase* teaches trainees about department resources, their agencies' administrative procedures, and the PTO process. (3) *Phase A* is the initial training, which emphasizes nonemergency incident responses. (4) *Phase B* is the second training experience, which focuses on emergency incident responses. (5) *Midterm evaluation* allows PTO supervisors to evaluate the progress of trainees at the midway point to determine if additional training is needed or if the trainee can move on to the next phase. (6) *Phase C* focuses on training related to patrol-related activities. (7) *Phase D* centers on training related to criminal investigations. (8) *Final phase* once again requires trainees to demonstrate their abilities in front of PTO supervisors. If trainees have difficulty with certain tasks, they will be allowed to go back for additional training. If trainees do not demonstrate appropriate levels of ability after they receive additional training, they will be terminated.

The PTO program is different from the FTO program, as it is emphasizes problem-based learning skills that enhance problem solving and critical thinking, while the FTO program focuses on developing mechanical repetition skills and rote memory capabilities.[66] The FTO program places great emphasis on applied skills, which include defensive tactics and shooting abilities, while the PTO places great emphasis on problem-solving and critical-thinking skills. The PTO program was designed to be flexible so that each individual agency can tailor the training to fit its individual needs, while the FTO program is structured in a more general manner based on the assumption that most police agencies function in the same way.[67] The PTO program is viewed as more reflective of both problem-oriented and community-based policing, while the FTO program is based on a more traditional policing model. Thus far, there has not been a nationwide adoption of the PTO program, but some police agencies are choosing PTO programs over FTO programs today.

In-Service Training

In-service training takes place over the course of police officers' careers once they have completed both academy and FTO/PTO training. Nearly all (92%) local police agencies in the United States require their officers to participate in some type of in-service training each year.[68] The type of training and the number of required hours varies from one agency to the next. Recent statistics indicate that the average number of in-service training hours required by American police agencies each year is 35.[69]

A wide range of topics can be included in this phase of training. Training in certain areas may be required of police officers each year (such as firearms or defensive tactics training); however, officers may also be able to choose from some elective topics. Some examples of elective training topics include problem-solving skills, computers, equipment (such as breathalyzers or nonlethal weapons), search and seizure, domestic violence, crime scene investigation skills, and interview and interrogation skills.[70] This type of training is important because it helps police officers stay current on any changes that may impact their work, and it allows them the opportunity to continually refine their policing skills.

⊠ Promotion

Promotion within police organizations is a way to facilitate organizational continuity and reward officers that demonstrate excellence at work. The promotion option also provides police officers the opportunity to learn new skills and take on additional responsibilities that can expand their roles within the organization. Promotional opportunities may also keep police officers from getting bored with their work and, as a result, increase their commitment to the job.[71] The availability of promotion opportunities differs from one agency to the next, with large police agencies providing more opportunities for advancement than smaller agencies with fewer positions overall.

But how does the promotion process work? Similar to the recruitment, hiring, and training of police officers, the promotion process varies across the country. Several general elements are included in the promotion process.[72] (1) *Written test*—the written exam is often used at the beginning of the promotion process to help rank order people based on their general knowledge of policing. (2) *Practical exercise*—officers are given tasks that mirror those that they may encounter once they are promoted. For example, each person might be asked to write a memo to the chief explaining how she or he believes a policy or procedure could be changed to be more effective. (3) **In-basket exercise**—this type of activity is used

Promotion allows police officers to take on new challenges and responsibilities.

to assess quick and effective decision making. A common in-basket exercise would require officers to respond to a series of e-mails (all of which pose a different set of problems) in an allotted amount of time. (4) *Oral interview board*—this assesses officers' attitude, judgment, leadership skills, and professional accomplishments. The composition of this board differs from place to place; however, it is common to have sworn police personnel and/or community representatives or a combination of both in this group. (5) *Review of performance evaluations*—the idea behind the review of performance evaluations is that past job performance can predict future job performance. Once officers have been scored using several means of assessment, they are rank ordered and placed on the promotion eligibility list. The chief of police then uses this list to choose who will be promoted.

So why do police officers choose to pursue promotional advancement? Thomas Whetstone found that officers pursue advancement because it is a personal goal they have set for themselves, because promotion allows for additional career opportunities, some people want to be in leadership roles, and because others in the department had encouraged them to do so.[73] Both male and female police officers gave these reasons, with slight variation in the order. There were some racial differences in motivations for pursuing promotion. White officers stated that they viewed promotion as a personal goal, while minority officers reported that promotion would allow them to be positive role models to youth in their community.[74]

Research has also explored the reasons officers choose *not* to pursue promotion. There are three general categories of reasons some police officers opt out of the promotion process.[75] First, there are personal reasons—these include a potential decrease in salary (they might lose opportunities for overtime if promoted), child care, and familial concerns, because a promotion may require a shift change, and they believe that they are not ready for the test. Second, officers cited professional reasons, including that they prefer their current shift and assignment, they are not interested in the promoted position (specifically the position of sergeant), and they feel that they are not ready to be promoted. And finally, officers reported several organizational reasons, such as perceptions of unfair testing practices, bias by the administration, not enough openings, and that they were not encouraged to do so by others/supervisors.

With a few exceptions, there is little variation in the reasons given for why male and female police officers choose not to pursue promotion.[76] In a recent study, female police officers reported both personal and organizational reasons for choosing not to pursue promotion (similar to those previously mentioned) but also stated that being married to male officers working within their organization hindered their ability to advance—hence, they paid a "marriage tax."[77] Tokenism is another factor that impacts the promotion of both racial minority and female police officers. A recent study by Carol Archbold and Dorothy Moses Schulz found that some women choose not to pursue promotion because they believe that their male colleagues will think that they were promoted because they are women and not because they are qualified to do the job.[78] Racial/ethnic minority police officers share similar experiences when they seek promotion within police agencies.[79]

⬛ Retention

The decision to leave the policing profession can take place at any time over the course of an officer's career. Joan Barker studied the occupational socialization of Los Angeles police officers and found that there are several stages in an officer's career at which he or she may question his or her career choice:[80]

1. *Hitting the streets*—this phase occurs during the first 3 years, including the time in the training academy and probationary period, and also the time that officers begin learning the realities of police work. During this stage, officers are trying to prove themselves, and their colleagues help them learn the ropes using both formal and informal practices unique to their department.

2. *Hitting their stride*—this is a 5-year phase in which officers are gaining confidence and developing their own style of policing. At this point in their careers, they begin to notice and express dissatisfaction with negative parts of their job.

3. *Hitting the wall*—this phase lasts roughly 4 years. Officers begin to question many aspects of their work and become disillusioned about their job.

4. *Regrouping*—this phase lasts until an officer makes the decision to retire or leave the job before retirement. This phase consists of officers re-evaluating their careers and deciding how to proceed. If they choose to remain in policing, they take time during this phase to figure out a strategy toward finishing their careers through retirement.

5. *Deciding to retire*—the final phase in an officer's career is when he or she decides to retire from policing. This is a hard decision for most officers, as many retire at a young age and are then faced with the task of finding another way to spend their time (in some cases finding another career).

Some of Barker's career phases identify times when officers may be more likely to think about leaving policing. For example, when officers are first exposed to the realities of police work in the hitting-the-streets phase, they could decide to leave before becoming too entrenched in the work. The hitting-the-wall phase is also a point in time at which some officers might become so disillusioned with their jobs that they decide to leave.

But why do some people choose to leave? Being unhappy with salaries and benefits (primarily in small agencies), frustration with police administration and the criminal justice system, and job and family stress are some reasons people choose to leave this line of work.[81] There is evidence that female police officers are more likely to leave policing compared to male officers.[82] Minority police officers are also more likely to drop out of policing when compared to White officers.[83] The article written by Robin Haarr that is included at the end of this section examines the reasons people (specifically racial/ethnic minorities and women) drop out of policing. Police administrators need to track individuals who choose to leave their agencies (perhaps by using exit surveys) to better understand why these individuals decided to leave. This information may then be used to implement changes within their organizations that could result in fewer people leaving in the future. In contrast, studies have also revealed that good salaries and benefits, job security, the challenge and excitement of the job, job satisfaction, an opportunity to work with people, and simply needing a job are some of the reasons people choose to remain police officers.[84]

SUMMARY

- Men and women give very similar reasons for wanting to pursue policing careers.
- Most police agencies have a minimum hiring age of 21 years.
- After submitting an application, most people will be required to take a written exam and participate in a physical agility test, an oral interview, and medical and psychological testing and agree to a background investigation.
- There are three stages of training that take place over the course of a police officer's career: police academy training, field training officer (FTO)/police training officer (PTO), and in-service training.

KEY TERMS

age requirement
assessment center
Explorers program
FTO/PTO program
height/weight requirement

in-basket exercise
in-service training
Minnesota Multiphasic Personality
   Inventory (MMPI)

residency requirement
Title VII (1964 Civil Rights Act)

DISCUSSION QUESTIONS

1. What are some of the ways that police agencies recruit applicants for police officer positions?

2. Discuss the history of the use of height/weight requirements by police agencies.

3. How are assessment centers used by some police agencies during the hiring process?

4. Why have some police training academies been criticized over the years regarding the substance of their training curricula?

WEB RESOURCES

- To learn more about the Explorers program, go to http://exploring.learningforlife.org/services/career-exploring/law-enforcement/.
- To learn more about law enforcement training academies, go to http://bjs.ojp.usdoj.gov/index.cfm?ty=tp&tid=77.
- To learn more about careers in policing, go to http://www.policecareer.com/careerassessment.htm.

READING 9

This article explores whether a college education is necessary for police officers working in modern police agencies in the United States. Roy Roberg and Scott Bonn explain the evolution of higher education in policing, as well as the debate over its importance to this profession. The authors believe that there is strong empirical evidence to support a college degree requirement for all police officers; however, they suggest that the requirement should be implemented at a slow, graduated pace.

Higher Education and Policing: Where Are We Now?

Roy Roberg and Scott Bonn

 ## Introduction

For nearly 100 years, there has been a debate over whether a college education for police officers is desirable or even necessary. In present-day society, with the ever-expanding complexity of the police role and the transition to community policing, this question is more important than ever. Interestingly, the initial requirement of a high school diploma to enter the field of policing occurred at a time when most of the nation's population did not finish high school. Thus, a requirement of a high school education actually identified individuals with an above average level of education.

Today, the high school diploma has essentially been replaced by a college degree as the above-average level of educational attainment in the USA. In fact, 24.4 percent of Americans age 25 and over have a four-year college degree or higher (US Census Bureau, 2000). Consequently, local police departments that have not raised their educational requirements for entry have failed to keep pace with their early tradition of employing people with an above-average education. It should be noted, however, that while police departments in general do not require a four-year degree, an increasing number of police officers do have them. Also, many local departments require a minimum two-year degree, or its equivalent in college units. Baro and Burlingame (1999, p. 60) argue, however, that while an increasing number of officers are completing college units, this could simply represent "degree inflation" as an associate's degree (two year) today may only be the equivalent of a high school diploma in the 1960s.

The evolution of higher education in policing, the long-term debate over its importance, social and technological changes, and the complexity of the contemporary police role provide the focus of this article.

 ## The History of Higher-Education Programs for Police

The debate over higher educational requirements for police officers is not new. Starting in the early 1900s, Berkeley, California, Police Chief August Vollmer called for the recruitment of officers who were not only trained in the "technology of policing" but who also understood "the prevention of crime or confrontation through [their] appreciation of the psychology and sociology of crime" (Carte, 1973, p. 275). Vollmer, known as the father of police professionalism, required his officers to attend classes at University of California at Berkeley and designed a series of courses there specifically to enhance their formal education. Because of his outspoken support of higher education, his officers became known as "Berkeley's college cops" (Carte, 1973).

Following Berkeley's lead, other programs emphasizing police education were developed at major universities during the 1920s and 1930s. Early programs laid the foundation for higher education in criminal justice, which was typically labeled police science, police administration, or law enforcement. Such curricula were developed in selected four-year institutions and many community colleges through the mid-1960s.

Even with the development of academic police programs, the concept of the college-educated police officer was strongly resisted by the majority of rank-and-file officers. In fact, it was not until the latter 1950s and early 1960s that a minimum requirement of a high school or general equivalency diploma (GED) was firmly established (Garner, 1999). Officers who either had a degree or were attending college were often viewed with suspicion and distrust by their peers and supervisors. Goldstein (1977, p. 284) aptly described their plight during this era:

> The term itself implied that there was something incourageous about an educated police officer. College graduates despite their steadily increasing number in the general population, did not seek employment with the police. The old but lingering stereotype of the "dumb flatfoot," the prevalent concept of policing as a relatively simple task, the low pay, and the limitations on advancement—all of these factors made it appear that a college education would be wasted in such a job.

Two significant and interrelated events, however, took place in the mid- to late-1960s that required the country to take a hard look at the level of professionalism and quality of US police forces as well as the rest of the criminal justice system. These two events played a major role in ushering in the "golden age" for higher education for the police (Pope, 1997). The first event was the enormous increase in the crime rate that began in the early 1960s; the second event was the ghetto riots, which occurred in the mid-1960s. The burning, looting, and general turmoil in many of the nation's major cities was the catalyst that spurred the public and the government into action. It was at this juncture that the "war on crime" began (Pope, 1987).

As a result of a heightened emphasis on crime prevention, the growth of law enforcement programs in both two-year and four-year schools during the 1960s and 1970s was dramatic. It has been reported that in 1954 there was a total of 22 such programs in the country (Deutsch, 1955), but by 1975 the numbers had increased to more than 700 in community colleges and nearly 400 in four-year schools (Korbetz, 1975). Southerland (2002) reported a total of 408 four-year criminal justice programs in the USA in 1999–2000.

Also playing a key role in the debate over higher education in policing, the President's Commission on Law Enforcement and Administration of Justice (1967) issued a comprehensive report titled *The Challenge of Crime in a Free Society* which documented the serious impact of crime on US society. The report identified the need for college-educated personnel (including the police) to address the increasing complexities of society. One of their most significant, and controversial, recommendations was that the "ultimate aim of all police departments should be that all personnel with general enforcement powers have baccalaureate degrees" (President's Commission, 1967, p. 109).

Shortly thereafter, Congress passed the Omnibus Crime Control and Safe Streets Act of 1968, which created the Law Enforcement Assistance Administration (LEAA). Through LEAA, the federal government poured billions of dollars into the criminal justice system—focusing on the police—in an attempt to improve their effectiveness and reduce crime. Under LEAA, an educational-incentive program, known as the Law Enforcement Education Program (LEEP), was established in the late 1960s, professedly to increase the educational standards of officers throughout the nation. In practice, it provided financial assistance primarily to in-service police personnel, rather than "civilians" who wished to pursue law enforcement as a career.

In 1973 a highly influential *Report on Police* by the National Advisory Commission on Criminal Justice Standards and Goals (1973), further advanced the higher-education recommendations made by the President's Commission. The *Report on Police* included a graduated timetable that would require all police officers, at the time of initial employment, to have completed at least two years of education (60 semester units) at an accredited college or university by 1975, three years (90 semester units) by 1978, and a baccalaureate degree by 1982 (National Advisory Commission on Criminal Justice Standards and Goals, 1973, p. 369).

Based on these reports and the federal government's educational-incentive program, a meteoric and unregulated increase in police science (law enforcement) programs ensued. Serious questions about their academic rigor and viability were soon raised. In order to capture their fair share of the LEAA funds, many schools hurriedly spliced together programs that were lacking in academic quality. These programs failed to meet the President's Commission's goals, that is, to provide a broad educational background that would help officers to meet the demands of their changing and increasingly challenging roles.

The National Advisory Commission on Higher Education for Police Officers spent two years conducting a national survey and documenting the problems of police education (Sherman and The National Advisory Commission on Higher Education for Police Officers, 1978). The report was extremely critical of the state of the art of police education at the time. The Commission found that many criminal justice college programs were "simply extensions of academy-based courses" (Garner, 1999, p. 90). It recommended significant changes in virtually all phases of police higher education, including institutional, curriculum, and faculty. Significantly, the Commission recommended that police should be educated prior to employment; this argument attacked the very basis of the LEEP program, which as previously noted, provided an overwhelming amount of its funds to in-service personnel. This recommendation started a serious debate on whether police departments should place more emphasis on "recruiting the educated" or on "educating the recruited." The commission concluded that the "occupational perspective" of full-time police work, "probably reduces the impact of college on students" (Sherman and The National Advisory Commission on Higher Education for Police Officers, 1978, p. 13).

Since the late 1960s and early 1970s, many police programs have broadened their focus, emphasizing criminal justice administration rather than technical training. As the LEEP program was eventually phased out, so too were most of the weaker police programs in higher education that had emerged largely to pursue federal funding. The stronger programs continued to recruit PhDs trained in criminal justice and other social sciences for their faculties, thus establishing a more scholarly approach toward teaching and research. These changes in higher education in criminal justice, including faculty quality, student body makeup and curricular content, have allowed the field to mature quite rapidly and gain academic respectability. As reported by Garner (1999, pp. 90–91), "many of the past decade's mistakes have resulted in a natural 'course correction' as a consequence of demanding increased standards and reduced discretionary funding."

 ## Higher Education Requirements for Police

Advances in raising educational requirements for police have been slow and sporadic. In fact, a four-year college degree requirement is still virtually nonexistent. A national study of approximately 3,000 state and local police departments serving communities of all sizes, conducted by the Bureau of Justice Statistics (BJS) (Hickmans and Reaves, 2003a), indicates that only 1 percent of departments required a college degree for employment in 2000. However, in some jurisdictions the number is considerably higher than 1 percent, for example, 6 percent for departments in cities serving between 500,000 and 1,000,000 residents. Interestingly, 0 percent of departments serving more than 1,000,000 residents require either a four-year or even a two-year degree. However, 33 percent of departments serving more than 1,000,000 residents do require some college. A total of 15 percent of departments had some type of college requirement, usually a two-year degree (8 percent). For sheriffs' offices, the BJS survey (Hickman and Reaves 2003b) reports that 12 percent of offices serving more than 1,000,000 residents require some college (while none require a degree); 6 percent of all offices require a two-year degree.

The BJS national survey (Hickman and Reaves, 2003a, p. 6) further reported that the percentage of officers employed by a department with some type of college requirement for new officers in 2000 was 32 percent, or about three time that of 1990 (10 percent). From 1990 to 2000, the percentage of officers employed by a department with a degree requirement increased from 3 percent to 9 percent; for Sheriffs' offices, the percentage with a degree requirement increased from 3 percent to 5 percent. These trends are encouraging, but there is clearly room for improvement.

Even though the development of formal educational requirements has been slow, some research suggests that approximately one quarter of officers in the field have a baccalaureate degree, most likely due to the increased number of colleges and universities offering criminal justice/criminology degrees. For instance, a 1994 national study of departments with more than 500 sworn officers (Sanders *et al.*, 1995) found that approximately 28 percent of the officers were college graduates. Data from another national study for the Police Executive Research Forum (PERF) of 485 state, county, and municipal police departments (Carter *et al.*, 1989a) indicated that 65 percent of police officers have completed at least one year of college and an additional 23 percent possess a four-year degree (as reported by Carter and Sapp, 1990b).

Just as the percentage of police officers holding college degrees has increased, so too has the number of police chiefs holding degrees. A study conducted by PERF (*Law Enforcement News*, 1998) of 358 city and county police chiefs in jurisdictions of 50,000 or more residents discovered that 87 percent held bachelor's degrees, almost 47 percent had master's degrees, and nearly 5 percent had law or doctoral-level degrees. This is

an important finding because it suggests that with highly educated police chief executives as role models, higher education may finally be emerging as an important part of the police culture. It is likely that these chiefs will begin to emphasize, and even require, higher education as part of their overall strategy to improve their departments, including promotional and hiring practices.

A study of 51 sheriff's departments and municipal police agencies in Colorado indicated that 22 percent had a written policy requiring a college degree for promotion (Nees, 2003). The PERF survey on higher education (Carter *et al*, 1989a) found a growing trend for departments to tie educational requirements to promotion. Some 20 percent of those responding indicated that they had either a formal or informal policy requiring some level of advanced education for promotion; 5 percent required a college degree (as reported by Carter and Sapp, 1992).

The Arlington, Texas, Police Department provides an example of what college degree requirements may look like in the future. Arlington, with approximately 600 sworn and 180 non-sworn personnel, began phasing in college degree requirements in 1986; currently, about 75 percent of Arlington officers hold a bachelor's degree (Bowman, 2002). Table 1 chronicles the development of the Arlington Police Department's emphasis on higher education.

As Table 1 indicates, by 1999, all new recruits in Arlington were required to hold a bachelor's degree. With respect to promotion, by 1991 a bachelor's degree was required for deputy-chiefs, and in 1995 for lieutenants. A master's degree requirement was instituted in 1990 for assistant chiefs; and in 2000, at least a four-year degree was required of officers seeking promotion.

 ## The Impact of Higher Education on Police Attitudes and Performance

Early research on the impact of college on police attitudes centered on comparing levels of authoritarianism of college-educated police to police with little or no college. For instance, it was shown that police with

Table 1 Development of higher education requirements in the Arlington, Texas, police department	
For entry	**For position**
1986, Bachelor's degree required for new recruits with no prior police experience. Associate's degree required for recruits with a minimum of two years' experience	1991, Bachelor's degree required for deputy chiefs
	1995, Bachelor's degree required for lieutenants
1994, Bachelor's degree required of all new recruits, regardless of experience	1999, Master's degree required for assistant chiefs
	2000, Bachelor's degree required of officers seeking promotion

Source: Bowman (2002)

some college (Smith *et al*, 1968) and those with college degrees (Smith *et al*, 1970) were significantly less authoritarian than their non-college-educated colleagues. Guller (1972) found police officers who were college seniors showed lower levels of authoritarianism than officers who were college freshmen and of similar age, socioeconomic background, and work experience, indicating that the higher the level of education, the more flexible or open one's belief system may be. Dalley (1975) discovered that authoritarian attitudes correspond with a lack of a college education and increased work experience. The author suggested that a more liberal attitude is more conducive to the discretionary nature of law enforcement. A number of other researchers have also found college-educated officers to be more flexible and less authoritarian (Parker *et al*, 1976; Roberg, 1978; Trojanovicz and Nicholson, 1976).

There is some evidence to indicate that college-educated officers are not only more aware of social and cultural/ethnic problems in their community, but also have a greater acceptance of minorities (Weiner, 1976), are more professional in their attitude (Miller and Fry, 1978) and ethical in their behavior (Tyre and Braunstein, 1992). In addition, college-educated officers are thought to be more understanding of human behavior, more sensitive to community relations, and hold a higher service standard (Miller and Fry, 1976; Regoli, 1976). This suggests that such individuals may be more "humanistic" police officers. Carian and Byxbe

(2000) conducted a study of undergraduate college students (235 criminal justice majors and 428 non-criminal justice majors) at three large southern universities in which subjects were asked to specify the prison sentence for a white or black convicted felon in one of two hypothetical cases. No significant differences were found in sentencing preferences between criminal justice majors and their non-criminal justice counterparts—suggesting that higher education appears to deliver a more humanistic candidate for police work— a good sign as the nationwide trend toward community policing continues. It has been argued that humanism is a valuable trait in departments that practice community policing because an officer's ability to empathize and communicate with local citizens is vital to its success (Meese, 1993).

Because police departments are so diverse, it is difficult to define performance measures. What is considered to be "good" or "poor" performance may vary from department to department. The criteria used to measure police performance are not clear-cut and are often controversial. Accordingly, research findings on police performance will usually be more useful if they are based on a wide variety of performance indicators. The research described next, on the relationship between higher education and police performance, is based on a number of different measures of performance.

Several studies have indicated that officers with higher levels of education performed their jobs in a more satisfactory manner than their less educated peers, as indicated by higher evaluation ratings from their supervisors (Finnegan, 1975; Roberg, 1978; Smith and Aamodt, 1597; Truxillo *et al.*, 1998). The Roberg (1978) study of 118 patrol officers in the Lincoln, Nebraska, Police Department, indicated that officers with "college degrees had the most open belief systems and the highest levels of job performance, indicating that college-educated officers were better able to adapt to the complex nature of the police role" (Roberg, 1978, p. 344). It was shown that age, seniority, and college major had no impact on the results, lending support to the notion that the overall university experience may be important in broadening one's perspectives. It is important to note that all of the college graduates were from a major land-grant state university that could be considered to have high-quality academic programs. Thus, the quality of the educational experience may also be an important variable in determining the impact of higher education.

The Smith and Aamodt (1997) study, which consisted of 299 officers from 12 municipal departments in Virginia, found that the benefits of a college education did not become apparent until the officers gained some experience. This finding is not surprising and suggests that higher education is simply another tool, along with training and experience, which allows officers to become more effective performers. Truxillo et al. (1989) studied a cohort of 84 officers in a southern, metropolitan police department over ten years and found that college education was significantly correlated with promotions as well as supervisory ratings of job knowledge.

Other researchers have found college to have a positive effect of a number of key, individual performance indicators. For example, several researchers have found college-educated officers to have fewer citizen complaints filed against them (Cascio, 1977; Cohen and Chaiken, 1972; Finnegan, 1976; Sanderson, 1977; Trojanowicz and Nicholson, 1976; Wilson, 1999; Lersch and Kunzman, 2001). Additional research has indicated that college educated officers tend to perform better in the academy (Sanderson, 1977), have fewer disciplinary actions taken against them by the department, have lower rates of absenteeism, receive fewer injuries on the job, and are involved in fewer traffic accidents (Cascio, 1977; Cohen and Chaiken, 1972; Sanderson, 1977). There is even some evidence that better-educated officers tend to use deadly force (i.e. fire their weapons) less often (Fyfe, 1988). In one recent study, citizen encounters involving inexperienced and less-educated officers resulted in increased levels of police force (Terrill and Mastrofski, 2002). Another study conducted in the state of Florida (*Law Enforcement News*, 2002), reported that police officers with just a high school diploma made up slightly more than 50 percent of all sworn law enforcement personnel between 1997 and 2002, yet they accounted for nearly 75 percent of all disciplinary actions issued by the state. Based on these findings, the International Association of Chiefs of Police (IACP) has commissioned a two-year national study on the correlation between higher education and disciplinary action against officers (*Law Enforcement News*, 2002). The goal of the national study is to provide empirical support to police administrators who want to implement college requirements in their departments.

Some interesting findings with respect to the evolution of police departments indicate that college-educated officers are more likely to attain promotions (Cohen and Chaiken, 1972; Polk and Armstrong, 2001; Roberg and Laramy, 1980; Sanderson, 1977; Whetstone, 2000), tend to be more innovative in performing their work (Trojanowicz and Nicholson, 1976), and are more likely to take leadership roles in the department and to rate themselves higher on performance measures (Coben and Chaiken, 1972; Trojanowicz and Nicholson, 1976; Weirman, 1978; Krimmel, 1996). Kakar (1998) indicated that these officers with higher education rated themselves higher in leadership, responsibility, problem-solving and initiative-taking skills in comparison to less educated officers.

Of course, not all of the research findings on higher education and policing are either positive or have significant findings. For example, in one large-scale reanalysis of survey findings in a 1977 study, Worden (1990) found that the effects of higher education on attitudes and performance were so small that they were not statistically significant. Nevertheless, he did discover that supervisors found educated officers to be more reliable employees and better report writers, and citizens found them to be exceptional in their use of good judgement and problem solving.

There is also evidence that college-educated officers become involved in cases of "individual liability significantly less frequently than non-college officers" (Carter and Sapp, 1989. p. 163), and that college-educated officers tend to have a broader understanding of civil rights issues from legal, social, historical, and political perspectives (Carter and Sapp, 1990a). Because lawsuits claiming negligence on behalf of police departments are on the increase (along with the amount of damages being awarded—often between $1 million and $2 million per case), this is an important area for future research. If a correlation between higher education and reduced liability risk can be established, the availability and cost of such insurance to police departments requiring higher education could be affected.

 ## Higher Education and Community Policing

One of the most important changes in police organizations over the past 20 years has been the evolution of community policing. According to Geller and Swanger (1995, p. 3), community policing involves a "strategic shift…toward the view that police can better help redress and prevent crime, disorder, and fear, through active, multifaceted, consultative, and collaborative relationships with diverse community groups and public and private-sector institutions." At the heart of community policing is the notion that "public safety [is] a community responsibility, rather than simply the responsibility of…the police." This change "transforms the police officer from an investigator and enforcer into a catalyst in a process community self help. Rather than standardized services, police services become "customized" to individual communities" (Osborne and Gaebler, 1993, pp. 50, 174).

The Bureau of Justice Statistics reports a substantial movement toward this approach. The BJS national

survey (Hickman and Reaves, 2003a) of approximately 3,000 state and local police agencies, serving communities of all sizes, reported in 2000 that 90 percent of all officers worked for a department with either a formal or informal community policing plan. The survey revealed that 60 percent of the nation's largest police agencies (serving 1 million or more residents) had a formal plan, while 40 percent had an informal plan, indicating that 100 percent of the nation's largest departments now have some form of community policing plan. In addition, the BJS national survey of the nation's sheriffs' offices (Hickman and Reaves, 2003b) reported that in 2000, 74 percent of all sworn personnel worked for an agency with either a formal or informal community policing plan. Even though the BJS data cannot tell us the degree to which such plans have usually been implemented, or how well they conform to community policing principles, it is nevertheless clear that a national, philosophical shift toward community policing has developed.

It has been argued that "the implementation of a community policing plan supports and empowers front-line officers, decentralizes command, and encourages innovative problem solving" (Hickman and Reaves, 2008b, p. 14). Vital to the successful application of community policing is a problem-solving orientation by its practitioners. As noted by Goldstein (1979, p. 236), a problem-oriented approach suggests that the police develop "a more systematic process for examining and addressing the problems that the public expects them to handle." Goldstein argued that the police have historically been too narrowly focused on specific incidents (i.e. they handle the same incidents time after time) and should instead became more involved with solving the problems that lead to these repeated incidents. Goldstein also believes that the community policing approach should improve the working environment for educated officers, who have much greater flexibility to take the initiative and be creative in solving problems. An improved work environment should lead to increased job satisfaction for the police and improved quality of police service provided to the community. Significant to the debate over higher education, a transition to community policing should more effectively utilize the potential of college-educated officers, "who have been smothered in the atmosphere of traditional policing" (Goldstein, 1987, p. 28).

Griffin *et al.* (1978) found that as education increases, sources of job satisfaction may be related to internal factors, such as control. Accordingly, they recommended that structural changes (i.e. decentralization) be implemented in police departments to allow for more control among lower-level officers. Likewise, Sherwood (2000, p. 210) states that job satisfaction may be linked to the "use of a variety of skills, the ability to follow the task through to a conclusion, freedom to make decisions, and knowledge of the effectiveness of one's efforts…" This is consistent with the less hierarchical structure and more autonomous style of community policing which, logically, should be most appealing to officers with higher education. Reinforcing the need for higher education to effectively implement community policing, Redelet and Carter (1994, p. 156) stated:

> Given the nature of this change, the issue of college education is even more critical. The knowledge and skills officers are being asked to exercise in community policing appears to be tailored to college preparation.

Perhaps most importantly, higher education can provide the skills necessary to analyze and to evaluate a range of nontraditional solutions to a problem. Worden (1990, p. 576) stated:

> Because college education is supposed to provide insights into human behavior and to foster a spirit of experimentation, college-educated officers are (hypothetically) less inclined to invoke the law to resolve problems, and correspondingly are inclined more strongly to develop extralegal solutions.

In turn, the freedom to exercise one's reasoning and analytical skills (i.e. the ability to "think outside of the box") should lead to increased job satisfaction among educated officers (Sherwood, 2000).

Higher Education, Community Policing and Terrorism

The threat of domestic terrorism will undoubtedly affect the police role. DeGuzman (2002), for instance, argues that patrol work in the post 9-11 USA will need to be "target-oriented" with greater emphasis placed on "event" analysis in addition to crime analysis. Target-oriented is the concept that officers assess likely targets in their districts; that is they should not only be watching over obvious places and persons who might be of danger, but also where disruption in "safe places" might occur. This suggests that the police should be able to "deconstruct the obvious" (Crank, 1999; Manning, 1979). In other words, they should attempt to determine the vulnerability of people and places and how they may become targets of terrorism. Event analysis suggests that the police should be aware of ideologies and cultural context, including important celebrations and event anniversaries of known activists, terrorists, or groups and attempt to determine whether these events may be connected to a possible terrorist act. Because one of the central themes of community policing is problem solving, many departments are already familiar with one method of analysis that could be used for this purpose, known as scanning, analysis, response and assessment (SARA). The SARA process would be appropriate for analyzing events in the community and their relationships to possible terrorist acts.

DeGuzman (2002) believes that the threat of terrorism will test officers' decision-making and communication skills, and provide a challenge to police legitimacy (i.e., belief that police are fair and equitable). The author suggests this will occur as a result of traffic enforcement being intensified to combat terrorism, it is believed that no-nonsense (or even "zero-tolerance") policies regarding traffic violations will limit the movement of terrorists. A number of Supreme Court decisions have expanded the use of traffic stops for the purpose of stopping, searching and investigating. Thus, it is suggested that the previously unreliable "hunch" or "sixth sense" by the police is slowly being acknowledged by the courts as legitimate grounds for police intervention. And, given the social climate of the time, it is not expected that the courts will be likely to strictly interpret the requirements of the exclusionary rule (against unreasonable searches and seizures) as originally set out in *Mapp v. Ohio* (1961)[I]. Of course, while such an approach may, at least on the surface, appear better able to track and investigate certain people, there are important constitutional issues with respect to "racial profiling," and perhaps just as importantly, police legitimacy. Recently, this type of "sixth sense discretion" and zero tolerance policies have led to distrust of the police by minority groups, with a concomitant loss of police legitimacy (Kennedy, 1997).

While undoubtedly more emphasis will need to be placed on anti-terrorist activities in the future, the police need to be careful not to develop a "we versus they" attitude with respect to these activities. Thus, it seems more crucial than ever to promote a community policing approach, where vital information can be gained through improved relationships with the community. In this way, the public plays an important role not only in helping to combat traditional criminal activity, but potential terrorist acts as well. Additionally, this should also lead to gains in police legitimacy, which, in turn, will lead to additional help and information from the public in preventing crime and terrorism. In fact, studies have indicated that police legitimacy among the public is highly correlated to a willingness to obey the law (Tyler, 1990) and that community policing facilitates police legitimacy (Skogan, 1994). The superior communication and problem-solving skills derived from higher education, implicitly required by community policing, would seem well suited to fostering legitimacy among citizens for law enforcement officers.

The unique and complicated challenges posed by the threat of terrorism will require police officers that are at once both analytical and socially aware. Being well versed in the latest crime fighting technology will not suffice, unless it is accompanied by an awareness of social context. Consistent with this line of reasoning, Goldstein (1987) believes that if the police are to improve operations and to mature as a profession, they need to focus more directly on the end product of their work (including the consequences), and to become

more sensitive to the community in which they operate. Logically, the analytical skills provided by higher education will prepare an officer to meet the complex challenges presented by terrorism, while exposure to the humanities and social sciences through higher education will produce a more sophisticated, "socially conscious" and culturally attuned officer.

Validating Higher Education for Policing

Given the increasing number of college-educated officers in the field, such slow progress in developing higher-education standards is perplexing, especially considering the evidence that, in general, college education has a positive effect on officer attitudes, performance, and behavior. With such support for higher education, why have standards not been significantly raised by most police departments? The PERF study (Carter *et al.*, 1989a) identified two common reasons.

1. Fear of being sued because a college requirement could not be quantitatively validated to show job relatedness.

2. Fear that college requirements would be discriminatory toward minorities.

Each of these important issues warrants discussion.

Higher Education as a BFOQ

As the PERF study of police executives reported (Carter *et al.*, 1989a), one of the primary reasons departments had not embraced higher-educational requirements more vigorously was the dilemma of not being able to validate such a requirements for the job, thus opening the department to a court challenge. Establishing higher educational requirements as a bona fide occupational qualification (BFOQ) for police work could be an important step in facilitating the use of advanced education as a minimum entry-level selection criterion. A brief discussion of higher education as a BFOQ for police work follows:

Interestingly, the courts in this country have continuously upheld higher educational requirements in policing to be job related. In *Castro v. Beecher* (1972)[2], the requirement of a high school education by the Boston Police Department was affirmed citing the recommendations of the President's Commission on Law Enforcement and Administration of Justice (1967) and the National Advisory Commission on Civil Disorders (1968). *Arnold v. Ballard* (1975, p. 73B)[3] supported the notion that an educational requirement can be quantitatively job validated in stating that such requirements "indicate a measure of accomplishment and ability which … is essential for…performance as a police officer." And, in *Davis v. City of Dallas* (1985)[4], the court upheld a challenge to the Dallas Police Department's requirement of 45 semester units (equivalent to one and one-half years of college) with a minimum of a C average from an accredited university.

In *Davis v. City of Dallas*[4] the court's decision was based partially on the complex nature of the police role and the public risk and responsibility that are unique to it. Such a decision indicates that higher standards of qualification can be applied to the job because police decision making requires an added dimension of judgement. This logic has been applied by the courts to other occupations such as airline pilots and health-related professions. Thus, the *Davis v. City of Dallas* (1985)[4] decision can be viewed as the next logical step in increasing police professionalism and may provide further support for police executives to require higher education (Carter *et al*, 1988, p. 10).

 ## Higher Education, Discrimination and Recruitment

A second area of concern reported to PERF by police executives was the potential impact the higher-education requirement might have on the employment of minorities. If minority-group members do not have equal access to higher education, such a requirement

could be held to be discriminatory by the courts. Not only that, but there are also obvious ethical and social issues raised. Any educational requirements for policing, then, must not only be job related but also nondiscriminatory.

In the *Davis v. City of Dallas*[4] case, the suit contended that higher-education requirements were discriminatory in the selection of police officers. According to Title VII of the Civil Rights Act, there cannot be employment barriers (or practices) that discriminate against minorities, even if they are not intended to do so. However, in *Griggs v. Duke Power Co.* (1971, p. 853)[5], the US Supreme Court held that if an employment practice is job related (or a "business necessity"), it may be allowed as a requirement, even though it has discriminatory overtones. Thus, courts must base decisions on the balance between requirements that are necessary for job performance and discriminatory practices. In *Davis v. City of Dallas*[4], the city of Dallas conceded that the college requirements did have a "significant disparate impact on blacks" (*Davis v. City of Dallas*, 1983, p. 207[4]). As noted above, the court nevertheless held that the complex requirements of police work (e.g. public risk and responsibility, amount of discretion) instigated against the discriminatory effects of a higher-education requirement.

In other words, if certain requirements for the job can be justified, even though they may discriminate against certain groups, the benefits of such requirements are judged to outweigh any discriminatory effects. Following this line of reassuring, if higher educational requirements can be shown to be a bona fide occupational qualification (BFOQ), then such a requirement would be considered a business necessity, and thus a legitimate requirement for successful job performance.

Some data, however, exist to suggest that requiring a bachelor's degree may have an adverse impact on race. Decker and Huckabee (2002) explored the effect of raising educational requirements to a bachelor's degree by analyzing recruit information from the Indianapolis Police Department over four years. They concluded that almost two-thirds (65 percent) of successful candidates overall would have been ineligible, and 77 percent (30 of 39) of African-American applicants did not have degrees. The researchers also looked at raising the age requirement to 25, and found that 25 percent of the traditionally successful applicants would not have been eligible, however, the age requirement would not have a disproportionately high effect on minorities as it would have eliminated only 18 percent of black applicants. While the research did not discuss whether any recruitment efforts were made to increase the pool of college educated minority applicants (unlikely), it is worth noting that nine of the 39 African American applicants did possess baccalaureate degrees.

While it appears, at least in this instance, that a college degree requirement had an impact on race, it also had an impact on the overall applicant pool, which is likely to occur when departments are attempting to improve the quality of their personnel by raising standards. There is little doubt that departments that raise their educational requirements will also need to significantly enhance their recruitment efforts, as other professional fields have done. For example, using multicultural recruiting task forces and employing broad-based recruitment efforts, including college campuses and reaching beyond city, county and state boundaries, have proven to be effective (*Law Enforcement News*, 1997).

Some police departments already aggressively recruit college graduates. For instance, in a study of 37 Texas police department (TELEMASP, 1996), it was found that the median number of recruiting trips to college campuses was six, that 21 departments (56 percent) have educational-incentive pay, providing additional pay for officers who have attained certain levels of higher education. In addition, some departments grant bonus points on hiring tests or use an accelerated career ladder for those with college education. Still others provide tuition-assistance programs and flexible duty shifts for officers who are still working on their degrees. One of the departments reported that it has had some success in recruiting college-educated officers through participation in a college internship program.

The PERF study (as reported by Carter and Sapp, 1992) found that most of the departments had developed one or more educational-incentive policies to encourage officers to continue their education beyond that required for initial employment. Some of these include tuition assistance or reimbursement, incentive pay, shift or day-off adjustments, and permission to attend classes during work hours. Another study of 72 Texas police departments, representing more than half of the police officers licensed in the state (Garner, 1998), indicated that 52 departments (72 percent) offered some type of incentive for obtaining a college education, 42 reported various forms of tuition reimbursement, while 32 provided higher pay for those with degrees. Other educational incentives offered by numerous departments included the use of vehicles for transportation to classes, time off to attend courses, and scheduling preferences to accommodate the college semester. Various departments used one or more of these incentives.

The preponderance of data indicates that a trend toward higher education exists in policing and appears not to have the negative impact on minority-officer recruitment that was initially feared. The fact that the proportion of minorities employed by state and local departments, especially in medium to large agencies, is approximately equal to proportions in the national population (Hickman and Reaves, 2003a; Hickman and Reaves, 2003b) is also encouraging. As Carter and Sapp (1992, pp. 11–13) argued:

> It appears that a college requirement is not impossible to mandate as evidenced by both the legal precedent and empirical data. A college educated police force that is racially and ethically representative of the community can be achieved. This only serves to make a police department more effective and responsive to community needs.

 ## Requiring a College Degree and Policy Implications

If college education is to become an entry-level requirement for policing, it is important that supporting policies also be established. As noted above, it is possible to offset the possible discriminatory effects of a higher-education requirement through an aggressive recruitment strategy. Additionally, of course, it is helpful to have a competitive salary scale, good employment benefits and high-quality working conditions. It is important to point out that over the past decade, many medium and large police departments have implemented highly competitive salary structures, in line with, and often substantially above the starting salaries for college graduates in most public-sector and many private-sector jobs. In addition, healthcare and retirement benefits are often very good at the local and state levels. Finally, in the long term, the implementation of a community policing paradigm will likely be necessary in order to significantly enhance police working environments, creating a more professional atmosphere where college graduates will feel comfortable and can flourish.

In the final analysis, it appears as though enough evidence (both empirical and experiential) has been established to support a strong argument for a college-degree requirement for entry-level police officers:

- The benefits provided by a higher education, combined with social and technological changes, the threat of terrorism (along with civil rights issues) and the increasing complexity of police work, suggest that a college degree should be a requirement for initial police employment.
- If educational and recruitment policies are appropriately developed, a higher-education requirement should not adversely affect minority recruitment or retention.

Recognizing that there are diverse types of police departments throughout the country, with differing styles of operation, levels of performance, and community needs, it is apparent that some can adapt to a college-degree requirement more readily than others.

Consequently, perhaps some type of graduated timetable for college requirements similar to those found in the National Advisory Commission's *Report on police* (1973) would be appropriate (as noted previously, the Commission recommended that all officers be required to have a baccalaureate degree by 1982).

A graduated timetable could be set up for phasing in first, a two-year degree requirement, and second, a baccalaureate degree for initial selection purposes. In fact, PERF called for a similar plan years ago (Carter *et al*, 1989b). At the same time, requirements could be established for supervisory and executive personnel, first at the baccalaureate level, and then, at least for executives, at the master's level. These requirements could also be tapered to account for different types of agencies; for example, larger agencies serving larger and more diverse populations could have the requirements phased in earlier. However, the bottom line would ultimately require any officer with general enforcement powers to have a degree, regardless of location or type of agency. For those departments or cities that feel they could not comply with such requirement, they could contract with a nearby agency that can meet the requirements. Such an arrangement is not without precedent, as many small and/or rural cities contract for local police services through larger municipal or county departments.

The quickest way for a police department to require higher education is for the chief to get squarely behind it. This process, however, has been limited to a very small number of departments over the past four decades, and it is clear that something more is needed. It is likely that in order for higher education to become entrenched throughout the field, a serious push will be needed from the federal government, perhaps along the lines of the Justice Department's community-oriented policing services (COPS) program, which has provided funds nationally to promote community policing (but with tighter strings attached). With respect to higher education, federal funding should be provided to police departments for achieving higher educational standards. Specifically, the funds could be used for:

- broad-based recruitment efforts;
- educational-incentive programs;
- the elimination of policies that restrict applicant searches (including residency requirements); and
- to promote the development of a written policy defining college education as a BFOQ as it relates to the department.

However, as persuasively argued by Sherman and the National Advisory Commission on Higher Education for Police Officers (1978), the focus should be on "recruiting the educated" rather than on "educating the recruited," so as not to repeat the mistakes made by LEEP over 30 years ago.

Although some "growing pains" are to be expected, the advantages of such a requirement in today's ever changing, more highly educated and diverse society, outweigh any potential disadvantages of waiting for additional "evidence" of its importance to accrue. Recognizing that nearly 25 percent of Americans have a four-year college degree or higher, the law enforcement field has simply not kept pace with societal trends in education. Therefore, the time has arrived to upgrade American policing and service to the community, through higher education requirements, thus, moving the occupation closer to a professional status.

 Notes

1. *Mapp v. Ohio* (1961), 367 U.S. 643.
2. *Castro v. Beccher* (1972), 549 F.2d 725.
3. *Arnold v. Ballard* (1975), 390 F. Supp., N.D. Ohio
4. *Davis v. City of Dallas* (1985), 777 F.2d 205.
5. *Griggs v. Duke Power Co.* (1971), 401 U.S. 432.

 References

Baro, A.L. and Burlingame D. (1998), "Law enforcement and higher education: is there an impasse?", *Journal of Criminal Justice Education*, Vol. 10 No. 1, pp. 57–78.

Bowman, T. (2002), "Educate to elevate", *Community Links*, August, pp. 11–13.

Carlan, P.E. and Byxbe, F.R. [2000], "The promise of humanistic policing is higher education living up to societal expectation?". *American Journal of Criminal Justice*, Vol. 24 No. 2, pp. 235–15.

Carte, G.F., (1973), "August Vollmer and the origins of police professionalism", *Journal of Police Science and Administration*, Vol. 1, pp. 274–81.

Carter, D.L. and Sapp. A.D. (1989), "The effect of higher education on police liability implications for police personnel policy", *Americans Journal of Police*, Vol. 8, pp. 153–66.

Carter, D.L. and Sapp, A.D. (1990a), "Higher education as a policy alternative to reduce police liability", *Police Liability Review*, Vol. 2, pp. 1–3.

Carter, D.L., and Sapp, A.D. (1990b), "The evolution of higher education in law enforcement preliminary findings from a national study", *Journal of Criminal Justice Education*, Vol. 1, pp. 59–86.

Carter, D.L., and Sapp, A.D. (1992), "College education and policing: coming of age", *FBI Law Enforcement Bulletin*, January, pp. 8–14.

Carter, D.L., Sapp, A.D. and Stephens, D.W. (1985), "Higher education as a bona fide occupational qualification (BFOQ) for police: a blueprint", *American Journal of Police*, Vol. 7, pp. 1–27.

Carter, D.L. Sapp, A.D. and Stephens, D.W. (1989a), *The State of Police Education: Policy Directions for the 21st Century*. Police Executive Research Forum, Washington, D.C.

Carter, D.L., Sapp, A.D. and Stephens, D.W. (1989b), *A Resolution of the Membership of the Police Executive Research Forum*, Police Executive Forum, Washington, DC.

Cascio, W.F. (1977), "Formal education and police officer performance", *Journal of Police Science and Administration*, Vol. 5, pp. 69–98.

Coben, B, and Chaiken, J.M. (1972), *Police Background Characteristics and Performance*, Rand Institute, New York, NY.

Crank, J.P. (1999), *Understanding Police Culture*, Anderson, Cincinnati, OH.

Dalley, A.F. (1975), "University and non-university graduated policemen: A study of police attitudes", *Journal of Police Science and Administration*, Vol. 3, pp. 458–68.

DeGuzman, M.C. (3002), "the changing roles and strategies of the police in time of terror", *Academy of Criminal Justice Sciences Today*, Vol. 12 No. 3, pp. 9–13.

Decker, L.K. and Huckabee, R.G. (2003), "Raising the age and education requirements for police officers: will too many women and minority candidates be excluded?" *Policing*, Vol. 25, pp. 789–801.

Deutsch, A. (1956). *The Trouble with Cops*, Crown Publishers, New York, NY.

Finnegan, J.C. (1976), "A study of relationships between college education and police performance in Baltimore, Maryland", *The Police Chief*, Vol. 34, pp. 60–2.

Fyfe, J.J. (1988), "Police use of deadly force, research and reform", *Justice Quarterly*, Vol. 5 No. 2, pp. 155–205.

Garner, R. (1995), "Community policing and education the college connection", *Texas Lute Enforcement Management and Administrative Statistic Program Bulletin*, January.

Garner, R. (1999), "College-educated cops: is the time now?" Sewell, J.D. (Ed.), *Controversial Issues in Policing*, Allyn and Bacon, Boston, MA, pp. 88–102.

Geller, W.A. and Swanger, G. (1995), *Managing Innovation in Policing: The Untapped Potential of the Middle Manager*, Police Executive Research Forum, Washington, DC.

Goldstein, H. (1977), *Policing of Free Society*, Ballinger, Cambridge, MA.

Goldstein, H. (1979), "Improving policing a problem-oriented approach". *Crime and Delinquency*, Vol. 25 No. 2, pp. 236–58.

Goldstein, H. (1997), "Toward community-oriented policing, potential, basic requirements, and threshold questions", *Crime and Delinquency*, vol. 33 No. 1, pp. 6–35.

Griffin, G.R. Dunbar, R.L.M. and McGill, M.E. (1978), "Factors associated with job satisfaction among police personnel", *Journal of Police Science and Administration*, Vol. 6, pp. 77–85.

Guller, I.R. (1972), "Higher education and policemen attitudinal differences between freshman and senior police college students", *Journal of Criminal Law, Criminology, and Police Science*, Vol. 63, pp. 396–401.

Hickman, M.J., and Reaves, B.A. (2003a), *Local Police Departments 2000*, Bureau of Justice Statistics, Washington, DC.

Hickman, M.J., and Reaves, B.A. (2003b), *Sheriffs' Offices 2000*, Bureau of Justice Statistics, Washington, DC.

Kakar, S. (1998), "Self-evaluation of police performance: an analysis of the relationship between police officers' education level and job performance". *Policing An International Journal of Police Strategies & Management*, Vol. 21, pp. 632–47.

Kennedy, R. (1997), *Race, Crime and the Law*, Pantheon, New York, NY.

Korbeiz, R.W. (1975), *Law Enforcement and Criminal Justice Education Directory, 1975–1976*, International Association of Chiefs of Police, Gaithersburg, MD.

Krimmel, J.T. (1996), "The performance of college-educated police a study of self-rated police performance measures", *American Journal of Police*, Vol. 15 No.1. pp. 85–96.

Law Enforcement News (1997), "Men and women of letters no BS: Tulsa PD rookies to need four-year degrees". *Law Enforcement News*, 30 November, p. 1.

Law Enforcement News (1998). "Survey says big-city chiefs are better-educated than outsiders", *Law Enforcement News*, 30 April, p. 7.

Law Enforcement News (2002), "For Florida police, higher education means lower risk of disciplinary action", *Law Enforcement News*, 31 October, p. 1–10.

Lersch, K.M. and Kunzman, L.L. (2001), "Misconduct allegations and higher education in a southern sheriff's department". *American Journal of Criminal Justice*, Vol. 25 No. 2. pp. 161–72.

Manning, P.K. (1979), "Metaphors of the field; varieties of organizational discoursed", *Administrative Science Quarterly*, Vol. 24, pp. 660–71.

Meese E. (1993). "Community policing and the police officer", *Perspectives on Policing*, Vol. 15, National Institute of Justice, Washington, DC and Harvard University, Boston, MA, p. xx.

Miller, J. and Fry, L. (1976), "Reexamining assumptions about education and professionalism. In law enforcement", *Journal of Police Science and Administration*, Vol. 4, pp. 187–96.

Miller J. and Fry, L. (1978), "Some evidence on the impact of higher education for law enforcement personnel", *The Police Chief*, Vol. 45, pp. 30–3.

National Advisory Commission on Criminal Justice Standards and Goals (1973), *Report on Police*, US Government Printing Office, Washington, DC.

Nees, H. (2003), "Education and criminal justice employees in Colorado", *Police Forum*, Vol. 1, pp. 59.

Osburne, D. and Guebler, T. (1993), *Reinventing Government*, Penguin, New York, NY.

Parker, L. Jr., Donnelly, J., Gerwitz, J., Marcus, J. and Kowalewski, V. (1976), "Higher education: its impact on police attitudes", *The Police Chief*, Vol. 43, pp. 33–6.

Polk, E. and Armstrong, D.A. (2001), "Higher education and law enforcement career paths: is the road to success waived by degree?" *Journal of Criminal Justice Education*, Vol. 12 No. 1, pp. 77–99.

Pope, C.E. (1987): "Criminal justice education: academic and professional orientations", in Mumskin, R. (Ed). *The Future of Criminal Justice Education*, Long Island University, Brookeville, NY.

President's Commission on Law Enforcement and Administration of Justice (1967). *The Challenge of Game in a Free Society*, US Government Printing Office, Washington, DC.

Radelet, L. and Carter, D. (1994), *The Police and the Community*, Macmillan, New York, NY.

Regoli, R.M. (1976). The effects of college education on the maintenance of police cynicism", *Journal of Police Science and Administration*, Vol. 4, pp. 340–5.

Roberg, R.R. (1978), "An analysis of the relationships among higher education, belief systems, and job performance of patrol officers", *Journal of Police Science and Administration*, Vol. 6, pp.336–44.

Roberg, R.R. and Lacany, J.E. (1990), "An empirical assessment of the criteria utilized for promoting police personnel; a secondary analysis", *Journal of Police Science and Administration*, Vol. 8, pp. 183–7.

Sauders, B. Hughes, T. and Langworthy, R. (1995), "Police officer recruitment and selection; a survey of major departments in the US", *Police Forum*, Academy of Criminal Justice Sciences, Richmond, KY.

Sanderson, B.B. (1977), "Police officers; the relationship of college education to job performance", *The Police Chief*, Vol. 44, pp. 52–3.

Sherman, J. W. and The National Advisory Commission on Higher Education for Police Officers (1978), *The Quality of Police Education*, Jossey-Bass, San Francisco, CA.

Sherwood, C.W. (2000), "Job design, community policing, and higher education: a tale of two cities", *Police Quarterly*, Vol. 3 No. 2, pp. 191–212.

Skogan, W. (1994), "The impact of community policing on neighborhood residents: a cross-site analysis", in Rosenbaum, D. (Ed.), *The Challenge of Community Policing: Testing the Promises*, Sage, Thousand Oaks, CA.

Smith, A.B., Locke, R. and Fenster, A. (1970), "Authoritarianism in policemen who are college graduates and non-college graduates", *Journal of Criminal Law, Criminology, and Police Science*, Vol. 61, pp. 313–5.

Smith, A.B., Locke, B. and Walker, W.F. (1968), "Authoritarianism in police college students and non-police college students", *Journal of Criminal Law, Criminology, and Police Science*, Vol. 59, pp. 440–3.

Smith, S.M. and Aamodt, M.G. (1997), "The relationship between education, experience, and police performance", *Journal of Police and Criminal Psychology*, Vol. 12, pp. 7–14.

Southerland, M.D. (2002), "Criminal justice curricula in the United States: a decade of change", *Justice Quarterly*, Vol. 19 No. 4, pp. 589–601.

TELEMASP (1996), "Recruitment practices", Texas Law Enforcement Management and Administrative Statistics Program, September.

Terrill, W. and Mastrofski, S.D. (2002), "Situational and officer-based determinants of police coercion", *Justice Quarterly*, Vol. 19 No. 2, pp. 215–18.

Trojanowicz, R.C. and Nicholson, T. (1576), "A comparison of behavioral styles of college graduate police officers v. non-college-going police officers", *The Police Chief*, Vol. 43, pp. 57–8.

Truxillo, D.M., Bennett, S.R. and Collins, M.L. (1998), "College education and police job performance: a ten-year study", *Public Personnel Management*, Vol. 27 No. 2, pp. 269–80.

Tyler, T. (1990), *Why People Obey the Law*, Yale University Press, New Haven, CT.

Tyre, M. and Braunstein, S. (1992). "Higher education and ethical policing", *FBI Law Enforcement Bulletin*, June, pp. 6–10.

US Census Bureau (2000), "Profile of selected social characteristics: 2000, DP-2", available at: www.factfinder.census.gov (accessed 25 May 2003).

Weiner, N.L. (1976), "The educated policeman", *Journal of Police Science and Administration*, Vol. 4, pp. 459–7.

Weirman, C.L. (1978), "Variances of ability measurement scores obtained by college and non-college educated troopers", *The Police Chief*, Vol. 45, pp. 34–6.

Whetstone, T.S. (2000), "Getting stripes: educational achievement and study strategy used by sergeant promotional candidates", *American Journal of Criminal Justice*, Vol. 24, pp. 247–57.

Wilson, H. (1999), "Post-secondary education of the police officer and its effect on the frequency of citizen complaints", *Journal of California Law Enforcement*, Vol. 33, pp. 3–10.

Worden, R.F. (1990), "A badge and a baccalaureate: policies, hypotheses, and further evidence", *Justice Quarterly*, Vol. 7, pp. 565–92.

DISCUSSION QUESTIONS

1. Identify some of the ways that police officers with college degrees behave differently than those without degrees.

2. Explain how higher education for police officers coincides with the tenets of community policing.

3. What are some of the policy implications for police administrators to consider before they implement the requirement of a college degree for police officers?

READING 10

Robin Haarr examines why police recruits "drop out" of police work. Using interview data, Haarr found that people drop out of police work by deciding to leave the profession themselves, they are asked to leave the police academy, or the department initiates termination. Close attention is paid to the reasons why both women and racial/ethnic minorities leave the policing profession.

Factors Affecting the Decision of Police Recruits to "Drop Out" of Police Work

Robin N. Haarr

Resignation of police officers is a significant concern among police executives because of the direct financial costs of recruiting, selecting, and training police personnel as well as the indirect costs related to disruption of services and organizational efficiency, time spent waiting for police recruits to achieve a "streetwise" competence, and providing fewer services to citizens (Gettinger, 1984; Harris & Baldwin, 1999; Manili & Connors, 1988; Webster & McEwen, 1992). The financial costs of premature resignation vary across police agencies; but, in 1999, Harris and Baldwin (1999) estimated the replacement cost for a single police officer to be approximately $14,300. If one considers that resignation often occurs during the earliest stages of a police officer's career, the replacement cost for an officer could be as high as $29,000.

Since the 1970s, police agencies have undertaken special initiatives to increase the recruitment and hiring of female and racial/ethnic minorities, yet the numbers of full-time sworn personnel in police departments serving populations of 250,000 or more remains low. In 2000, females represented only 16.3% of full-time sworn personnel (up from 12.1% in 1990), Blacks made up 20.1% (18.4% in 1990), Hispanics were 14.1% (9.2% in 1990), 2.8% were Asian/Pacific Islander (2.0% in 1990), and 0.4% were Native American (0.3% in 1990) (U.S. Department of Justice, 2000). Thus, the costs of premature resignation of female and racial/ethnic minority officers are not amenable to the same financial calculations provided by Harris and Baldwin (1999).

Despite high costs associated with resignation of police personnel, research into the reasons for resignation and turnover is sparse (Fielding & Fielding, 1987; Harris & Baldwin, 1999; James & Hendry, 1991; McDowell, 1971; Reiser, 1974; Seidel & Courtney, 1983; Sparger & Giacopassi, 1983; Wales, 1988). Moreover, virtually no research has explored the reasons for resignation of women and racial/ethnic minority officers (Doerner, 1995; Fry, 1983; Holdaway & Barron, 1997). This article is significant because it adds to the limited literature on police resignation and explores why female and racial/ethnic minority officers drop out of police work during the early stages of their careers.

◿ Theories of Resignation

A review of the limited literature on police resignation and turnover reveals four lines of inquiry, including job satisfaction, "burnout" theory, confluency theory, and cognitive dissonance theory. One of the earliest studies of police resignation (Wilson & McLaren, 1950) theorized that police officers who are dissatisfied with their job voluntarily resign from police work, whereas officers who have high levels of job satisfaction remain. Factors affecting job satisfaction included salary, rank, overtime compensation, insurance, length of work week, medical and safety programs, and retirement incentives.

Building on the concept of job satisfaction, Reiser (1974) proposed a theoretical link between police turnover and burnout caused by job stress. Adherents of burnout theory argue that police officers who voluntarily resign after relatively long periods of police service do so because they gradually experience a state of burnout that occurs due to inherently cumulative occupational and organizational dissatisfactions and stresses (DeLey, 1984; Favreau & Gillespie, 1978; Harris & Baldwin, 1999; Seidel & Courtney, 1983; Sparger & Giacopassi, 1983). In a study of Memphis police officers who voluntarily resigned from police work between 1975 and 1980, Sparger and Giacopassi (1983) concluded that veteran officers voluntarily resigned because of "burnout" resulting from the culmination of occupational frustrations and dissatisfactions related to traditional authoritarian management styles, organizational policies, departmental politics, lack of appreciation for their efforts, the system of internal discipline, pay and fringe benefits, relations with civic officials, court policies, and community expectations. Veteran officers who voluntarily resigned reported feeling stagnated in one's job (see also Seidel & Courtney, 1983; Singleton & Teahan, 1978).

More recently, Dick (2000) analyzed clinical data from therapy with police officers who were under stress and considering leaving the police force and described "epiphenal events" that resulted in emotional exhaustion and burnout. At the epiphenal event, officers reasoned that the organization stood in the way of their ability to make their desired, positive contribution through work. Dick presents the data as evidence of an officer's inability to cope in a way that allows continuation of work, whereas adherents of burnout theory contend that retention of officers requires an awareness of job satisfaction factors.

Harris and Baldwin (1999) tested confluency theory and eight variables associated with job satisfaction as predictors of turnover among officers who voluntarily left the Birmingham, Alabama, Police Department between 1992 and 1996. Confluency theory attributes police turnover to an absence of pre-employment job awareness and to incongruencies between job expectations and realities. Their findings failed, however, to support confluency theory and disagreed with conventional wisdom and the majority of turnover research findings (Hoffman, 1993; Phelan, 1991; Premack & Wanous, 1985; Seidel & Courtney, 1983; Sparger & Giacopassi, 1983; Wales, 1988).

Although job dissatisfaction and burnout theory are useful in explaining the resignation of veteran officers, it does not apply to the sample of police recruits in this study. Because police recruits in this study were tracked for a 16-month period, starting with recruits' entry into basic training, it is assumed that recruits would not experience a state of burnout; rather, recruits would experience problems of adjustment as they enter basic training and are socialized into their new role as police officer. Drawing on Festinger's (1957) theory of cognitive dissonance and prior research by McDowell (1971), Van Maanen (1975), and Fielding and Fielding (1987), I hypothesize that police recruits who "voluntarily resign" from police work within the early stages of police training and service experience problems of adjustment as a result of conflict between the version of policing embodied in their ideal, that projected in formal training, and the reality of policing in practice. Officers who experience adjustment problems and conflict within the early stages of their careers may respond to the psychological dissonance by altering and revising their belief systems and remaining in law enforcement or resigning from police work and relieving the painful psychological experience by preserving their idealized notion of the job (Fielding & Fielding, 1987). The decision to remain in or resign from police work is contingent on the recruits' stake in conformity to occupational and work group norms and commitment to the occupation and organization (Van Maanen, 1975).

Fielding and Fielding (1987) tested the use of cognitive dissonance theory in a longitudinal study of 125 police recruits who entered the Derbyshire Training Establishment, of which 28 (22%) resigned within 42 months of joining. They compared resigners to nonresigners on individual demographics and attitudes toward crime, law enforcement, and social and political issues. At induction into police work, resigners and nonresigners did not differ in their levels of instrumentalism (attitudes toward extrinsic aspects of the job: pay, status, or security); however, by the end of the first year, resigners reported greater instrumentality and less commitment to the police role. Resigners also expressed greater dissatisfaction with the amount of paperwork involved in the job, the social isolation associated with the job, and the public image of the police. Resigners were also more likely to advocate recriminatory action (use of corporal and capital punishment) against offenders, were less concerned with achieving fairness in assessing punishment, and were more concerned with punishing the offender. Fielding and Fielding concluded that those who were most likely to resign from police work within the first 4 years were those whose early idealism was soonest traded for the pragmatic instrumentalist perspective that overtook all police to some degree.

Cognitive dissonance theory of police resignation can be enhanced when coupled with the sociological concept of occupational socialization (Fielding & Fielding, 1987), which places emphasis on the formal and informal processes of socializing recruits to the fundamental features of the occupational culture, including team membership, acceptance of particular values and beliefs, stereotypical thinking, trust, forming of relationships through joke telling, and the manner of dealing with racial/ethnic minorities and other members of the public. Van Maanen (1975) contended that police officers are continually involved in the process of socialization, which begins prior to one's entry into police work (referred to as anticipatory socialization) and continues indefinitely forward to an officer's present position. Police officers experience their police careers in stages of career contingency, representing thresholds at which officers can decide to withdraw from further commitment or continuation in police work. The decision to resign is contingent, in part, on officers' stake in conformity and commitment to the occupation and organization.

 ## Female and Minority Officers' Resignation

A shortcoming of the police resignation and turnover research is that it reflects the experiences of Caucasian male police officers. Most resignation studies have failed to consider distinctive predictors of resignation among women and racial/ethnic minorities; rather, the tendency has been to present women's attrition from police organizations as related to family concerns (e.g., child care, unsupportive husbands) and personal failures in coping (Doerner, 1995; Seagram & Stark, 1992). This approach fails to consider the unique workplace problems for women in policing and a connection between these problems and resignation. For example, women in "male defined" occupations, such as policing, experience male coworkers and supervisors who are unsupportive and hostile toward females as well as sexual harassment and gender discrimination from peers, supervisors, and subordinates (Haarr, 1997; Lafontaine & Tredeau, 1986; Martin, 1980, 1990; Morash & Haarr, 1995; Texeira, 2002).

Research exploring the resignation of racial/ethnic minority officers from police work is virtually absent. The only systematic study of resignation among Black and Asian officers was conducted in Great Britain by Holdaway and Barron (1997) and revealed that Black and Asian officers were routinely excluded from full participation in the workforce and becoming a member of the occupational culture at various stages of their career. Minority officers who desired to be more integrated into the police force recognized the need to demonstrate their commitment to the dominant assumptions of the Caucasian occupational culture, which constructed racial prejudices and discrimination. Holdaway and Barron concluded that Black and Asian officers who resigned conveyed a

pride and integrity about their status as Black and Asian people, and resignation became a means to harmonize one's cultural and personal identities.

This study explores the reasons why police recruits drop out of police work within the first 16 months of their policing careers, including those reasons that may be salient for women and racial/ethnic minorities. This study also explores the usefulness of cognitive dissonance theory as an explanation for the voluntary resignation of police recruits from police work within the early stages of police training and service.

Method and Data

The sample of dropouts for this study was obtained as part of a larger longitudinal study of a panel sample of 446 police recruits who were followed through the 606.5-hour, 16-week Phoenix Regional Police Basic Training Academy Program and then to their respective police agencies, where they proceeded through field training and the completion of a 1-year probationary period. The panel sample of 446 police recruits was selected from 14 successive training academy classes that began between December 1995 and October 1996. On entering the training academy, police recruits were pretested (Time 1; see Table 1). The pretest measured police recruits' baseline attitudes toward police-public relations, policing philosophies and strategies, and problem-solving techniques. A 16-week lag existed between the pretest and the first posttest (Time 2), which was conducted during the final days of basic training. At Time 2, 389 recruits completed the posttest. A second posttest (Time 3) was conducted at or near the end of the recruits' field training process, 12 weeks after the first posttest. At Time 3, 356 police recruits completed the posttest. Finally, a third posttest (Time 4) occurred after recruits completed 1 year of employment in their respective police agency. At Time 4, 292 police recruits completed the survey (administered between March 1997 and February 1998). Twenty-five Arizona police agencies had police recruits in the final sample.

Table 1 Characteristics of the Panel Sample by Time (%)

Characteristics	Time 1: Enter Academy (*n* = 446)	Time 2: Exit Academy (*n* = 389)	Time 3: End Field Training (*n* = 356)	Time 4: End 1 Year (*n* = 292)
Gender				
Male	89.7	88.4	88.5	90.1
Female	10.3	11.6	11.5	9.9
Race/ethnicity				
Caucasian	76.8	79.4	79.5	81.4
Black/African American	3.2	3.7	3.9	3.4
Hispanic/Latina	12.8	12.0	11.0	10.3
Asian American	2.5	2.9	3.4	2.8
Native American	3.2	0.8	0.6	0.0
Other	1.6	1.3	1.7	1.7
Age				
20–25 years	47.7	45.2	42.9	31.3
26–30 years	32.3	34.1	36.2	44.1
31–35 years	12.3	13.7	13.0	14.8
36–40 years	4.1	3.4	4.2	5.2
41 years and older	2.9	3.6	3.7	4.5
Level of education				
High School/GED	9.0	5.9	5.4	4.8
Technical school	4.1	2.3	1.1	1.7
Some college	48.4	52.1	51.9	51.2
Bachelor's degree	35.1	37.4	37.6	40.6
Graduate degree	3.4	2.3	4.0	1.7
Police agencies				
Phoenix PD	54.5	56.9	57.2	58.5
Suburban Phoenix	23.6	24.3	25.2	28.2
Rural Arizona agencies	11.7	11.1	11.5	8.2
Indian tribal agencies	4.9	2.8	2.2	2.4
University agencies	2.2	2.3	2.8	2.7
Other agencies	3.1	2.6	1.1	0.0

Sample and Survey of Dropouts

Of the original sample of 446 police recruits, 113 (25.3%) dropped out of police work during the period of the research, which included the 16-month period starting with each recruit's entry into the basic training academy. A "dropout" is an officer who voluntarily decided to leave police work or was terminated from police work. Fifty-two (46%) of the 113 police recruits dropped out during basic training (between Time 1 and Time 2), 18 (15.9%) dropped out during the field training process (between Time 2 and Time 3), and 43 (38.1%) dropped out after they completed the field training process yet prior to the end of a 1-year probationary period (between Time 3 and Time 4).

On completion of the third posttest (Time 4) in February 1998, a one-page questionnaire and a letter requesting participation in a telephone interview was mailed, via certified mail, to the 113 police recruits who dropped out of police work between December 1995 and February 1998. To encourage dropouts' participation in a telephone interview, they were offered $20 as an incentive for returning the one-page questionnaire and participating in a telephone interview. Thirty-four (30.1%) of the 113 dropouts returned the one-page questionnaire and consented to participate in a telephone interview. The overall size of the sample should be placed within the context of the obstacles faced when attempting to contact dropouts via mail. One obstacle faced was that 33.6% ($n = 38$) of the initial mailings came back as undeliverable by the U.S. Postal Service because the most recent address of a dropout, provided by the training academy, was out of date. The lack of accurate information about the current address of resigners clearly reduced the sample. Finally, 1.8% ($n = 2$) of the dropouts refused to accept the certified letter and declined to be interviewed.

The final sample was made up of 34 dropouts: 44.1% ($n = 15$) dropped out during basic training, 26.5% ($n = 9$) during field training, and 29.4% ($n = 10$) after completing field training yet prior to the end of a 1-year probationary period. The sample of dropouts includes 19 (55.9%) Caucasian males, 4 (11.8%) Caucasian females, 5 (14.7%) Hispanic males, 1 (2.9%) Hispanic female, 3 (8.8%) Native American males, and 1 (2.9%) African American male. There is nothing to suggest that the resigners interviewed were atypical of dropouts.

The telephone interview schedule was premised on the view that a decision to resign from police work was rarely sudden or brought on by a single event but was part of a mental process of self-reflection that takes into account a variety of circumstances over a period of time (Holdaway & Barron, 1997). It was also developed to explore the usefulness of cognitive dissonance theory as an explanation for the voluntary resignation of police recruits from police work within the early stages of police training and service. Thus, the interview schedule consisted of a series of open-ended questions developed to tap eight information domains: reasons for entering police work, reasons for leaving police work, training academy experiences, experiences working in their police agency, expectations about police work, realities of police work that conflicted with their expectations, recommendations for changes to academy training, and recommendations for changes to field training. The telephone interviews, which lasted 15 to 45 minutes, were conducted to gain a descriptive understanding of dropouts' experiences in the training academy and the police department and their reasons for leaving police work.

 ## Data Analysis

The first step in the analysis was to use data collected from the Police Personnel Survey to compare dropouts to non-dropouts on individual characteristics. This analysis allows us to determine whether select individual characteristics were significant in differentiating police recruits who dropped out of police work within the first 16 months of their police careers from those who remained. Next, qualitative data, collected via telephone interviews with dropouts, were systematically analyzed and dominant themes identified. Analysis was based on point of dropout, reason for dropout, and the interactive effects of race and gender. Data analysis was guided by the recognition that a police recruit does not decide suddenly to resign from police work because resignation is a process of reflection and decision making (Holdaway & Barron, 1997). Thus, efforts were made to identify and understand those situations when doubts about remaining in police work were raised in the recruits' mind.

Results

Dropouts Versus Non-dropouts: Individual Characteristics

Using data collected from the Police Personnel Survey, dropouts were compared to non-dropouts on individual characteristics. Table 2 reveals that although the number of females ($n = 46$) entering police work is small, there was no statistically significant difference between males (25.3%) and females (28.3%) in the rate of dropout from police work.

Significant differences did emerge in rates of dropout among racial/ethnic minorities. One of the most interesting findings is that Native Americans had the highest rate of dropout at 85.7%. It is notable to point out that 91.6% ($n = 11$) of the Native Americans who dropped out did so during the 16-week basic training academy. Hispanics also experienced a high rate of dropout (38.6%), significantly greater than the dropout rate for Caucasians (22.0%).

Significant differences also emerged in rates of dropout among recruits who were separated or divorced (42.9%) on entering basic training versus those who were married (20.6%) or single (27.1%). In regard to level of education, recruits with a high school diploma/ GED (37.9%) or some graduate courses/graduate degree (36.8%) were more likely to drop out of police work than recruits with some college/college degree (21.8%). There were no significant differences in dropout rates based on age or prior military or law enforcement experience.

Table 2	Comparison of Dropouts to Non-Dropouts on Individual Characteristics			
Characteristics	**Dropouts ($n = 113$)**	**Non-Dropouts ($n = 333$)**	**Total ($N = 446$)**	χ^2
Gender				
Male	25.3	74.7	89.7	.69
Female	28.3	71.7	10.3	
Race/ethnicity				
Caucasian	22.0	78.0	76.8	37.07*
Hispanic/Latino	38.6	61.4	12.8	
Black/African American	14.3	85.7	3.214	
Native American	85.7	14.3	3.2	
Asian American	9.1	90.9	2.5	
Other	14.3	85.7	1.6	
Age group				
20–25 years	23.6	76.4	47.5	.89
26–30 years	25.9	74.1	32.1	
31–35 years	29.1	70.9	12.3	
36–40 years	27.8	72.2	4.0	
41 years and older	27.8	72.2	4.0	

Characteristics	Dropouts ($n = 113$)	Non-Dropouts ($n = 333$)	Total ($N = 446$)	χ^2
Marital status				
Single	27.1	72.9	49.9	7.22*
Married	20.6	79.4	43.8	
Separated/divorced	42.9	57.1	6.3	
Level of education				
High school/GED	37.9	62.1	13.1	9.80*
Some college/degree	21.8	78.2	78.4	
Some graduate courses/degree	36.8	63.2	8.6	
Prior military				
Yes	24.7	75.3	35.7	.09
No	26.0	74.0	64.3	
Prior law enforcement				
Yes	26.0	74.0	23.5	.02
No	25.3	74.7	76.6	

Note: All figures shown are percentages, except for those in the fourth column. $*p \leq .01. **p \leq .05$

Reasons for Dropping Out of Police Work

Analysis of qualitative data obtained via telephone interviews with dropouts revealed police recruits who dropped out of police work within the first 16 months of their careers could be grouped into three distinct categories: self-initiated resignations, academy-initiated terminations, and department-initiated terminations. Among the sample of 34 dropouts, 50% ($n = 17$) self-initiated resignation, 26.5% ($n = 9$) were terminated by training academy administrator, and 23.5% ($n = 8$) were terminated by their employing agency (see Table 3).

Table 3   Reasons for Dropout by Point of Resignation for the Sample of Dropouts (%)

Reason for Dropout	Time 1 to Time 2: Basic Training ($n = 15$)	Time 2 to Time 3: Field Training ($n = 9$)	Time 3 to Time 4: 1 Year ($n = 10$)	Total ($N = 34$)
Self-initiated resignation	17.6	17.6	14.7	50.0
Academy-initiated termination	26.5	—	—	26.5
Department-initiated termination	—	8.8	14.7	23.5
Total	44.1	26.5	29.4	100.0

Self-Initiated Resignation

The majority (88.2%, $n = 15$) of recruits who self-initiated resignation experienced a significant amount of stress and conflict when their beliefs and expectations about police work differed considerably from the actual practices and realities of police work. Police recruits who self-initiated resignation during the basic training program indicated that the conflict they felt when they realized their experiences in the training academy were inconsistent with or contradictory to their sense of self and their cognitions about what police work should be forced them to reconsider their decision to enter further into police work. One Caucasian male explained that within the first 4 days of basic training, he heard instructors lecture on "the cold reality of shooting someone." He recalled, "At the time, I struggled with the reality that I might have to shoot someone and wondered whether I would be able to, psychologically, cope with shooting another person." The act of shooting someone created a sense of internal conflict for him, and after discussing his internal conflicts with his wife, he decided to resign from police work. He explained, "I thought policing was the career for me. I spent 2 years going through the recruitment and hiring process and getting ready mentally and physically to go into police work." Within the first week of basic training, this recruit self-initiated resignation.

Police recruits who self-initiated resignation during basic training typically did not identify only one aspect of the academy experience that created conflict for them; rather, their decision to resign was based on a multitude of factors. The decision to resign was based largely on the realization that their attitudes toward police-public relations and interactions as well as appropriate and inappropriate work behaviors differed considerably from some of their classmates.

> I left police work because I was tired of my coworkers' attitudes, which were very different from mine. I wanted to do something for the community, but the other cops were unbelievable; some of them were egotistical maniacs. It was like if you're a moron in here, you must be a moron out there. …I guess maybe I just have a different approach to policing than some others do. A lot of them just like to go out there and kick ass. I like to talk. I liked actually being able to help people. (Hispanic male)

For some recruits, the recognition that their attitudes and values conflicted with their classmates was coupled with an aversion for the paramilitary nature of academy training. Under the paramilitary model, police recruits are expected to be obedient, obey orders, perform tasks in a precisely prescribed manner, and meet intellectual and physical demands in a highly structured environment with discipline and, in some cases, harassment. Considering that only 35.7% of the recruits who entered the training academy had prior military experience and 23.5% had prior law enforcement experience, it is not surprising that some recruits experienced conflict when exposed to and socialized into the paramilitary model of policing. The features of the paramilitary model that resigners found to be particularly stressful included the authoritarian style of management, the process of breaking down individuals in order to build them back up as police officers, the strict standards of physical fitness, and the stringent physical exercise regimen. One Caucasian female explained that the combination of experiences with classmates, training academy staff, and the paramilitary structure of the training academy culminated in her resignation.

> I left police work because I was discouraged with the system and lack of integrity. I witnessed cover-ups and officers not being truthful. I believe police officers are supposed to be held to a higher level of integrity than the general public, and I didn't see that [in the basic training academy]. I always thought police work was to uphold justice, and [I learned] that is not the case. … It was the atmosphere more than anything else. I also thought the training academy was too intense

considering what police work really is like once you get on the street. The training and physical aspects are understandable, but the same standards are not held after you leave the academy; you have overweight officers on the street where in the academy if you were one pound over they threatened to kick you out. It just seemed like a double standard. I understand the point of the training academy is to break you down so that they can build you back up, but they never build you back up. For example, we had uniform inspections every day and they would always flunk you. They would always find something and it seemed extreme, like lint. We already had to run miles and miles, and if you flunked the uniform inspection, you had to run even more miles. We're only human. Plus, we are not going to chase a suspect for 2 miles, not on foot. We are going to get in our car, get the helicopters out, and get back up. It was just excessive; I guess the experience opened my eyes to the real work of the police, and it is not what I perceived.

Once police recruits complete basic training, they return to their respective police agencies, where they undergo the field training process, which represents an important stage in the process of socialization into the organization and occupation as well as immersion into the real world of police work. The field training phase presents the first real opportunity for the police recruit to experience the police officer role, engage in actual police work, and experience the environment and culture of the organization. During this stage, recruits are assigned to one or more field training officers (FTOs), who are responsible for training them in formal policies and procedures, teaching them how to put the skills acquired in the training academy to use on the street, teaching them which people should not be trusted and need to be policed, and exposing them to the informal culture of the police agency.

Police recruits who resigned during the field training phase found that the cumulative and interactive effects of the field training process, their incompatible relationship with their FTO(s), factors of the organizational environment, and the informal culture of the police agency caused them a substantial level of stress and conflict, which created a state of dissonance and led to their decision to resign from police work. Aspects of police work and the organization that resigners maintained caused them stress and conflict included risks related to the job, problems with FTOs and supervisors, the phenomenon of running call-to-call, the immense amount of paperwork, organizational policies and procedures, politics that guide assignments and promotions, and the possibility of being sued for doing one's job. Rather than allowing the powerful forces of the organizational environment and informal occupational culture to reshape their attitudes and behaviors to be more congruent with those of their FTOs and coworkers or adjusting their expectations to be more compatible with the realities of police work, they chose to resign from police work. In the end, many resigners concluded policing was not the job for them.

I thought I knew what police work was all about. I enjoyed the academy, it was a different experience because I am not military, but once you get past that and get used to it, it was great. The academy taught [me] a lot, but you don't come out knowing all the things you need to know; the academy only teaches the basics. Field training is an incredible amount of information and you have no clue. In the academy, they tell you about the paperwork and how you will need to document details, but they don't tell you that paperwork is 99.5% of what you do and that only .5% will be contact with people and hands-on work. That was disappointing. I knew there was paperwork involved, but I didn't know how much. I don't enjoy paperwork. It isn't even the paperwork, but you are not even taught procedures for documenting. I came to field training and my FTO expected me to know policies and procedures. It was just too much information. I began to doubt myself and question my judgment. My FTO had me thinking that I was incompetent. …The field training process was a major part of my reason to quit police work. I always considered a police officer to be a public servant, but the majority of police work is the documentation of crime and not necessarily helping victims. I looked forward to helping victims. In the academy, the instructors preached community policing, but once you're working the streets, there is no chance of doing that. All you do is run call-to-call, and there is no opportunity to get out and talk to citizens. Even with victims, there is no time to assist them and say, "Here are some things you can do" or "These are your rights." It is so high volume that it prevents that kind of interaction. The reality of the work is show up, document, and leave. (Caucasian male)

When asked if there were any other reasons for leaving police work, he proceeded to explain,

The officers I worked with were abusive to me and citizens. A lot of times you are humiliated in front of other officers or citizens to get you to learn something. Field training is stressful. There are so many officers around you who are knowledgeable and have so much experience. There is enough anxiety in field training, it didn't help to escalate things and make a scene. I was humiliated in front of citizens and coworkers. Also, I saw other officers go out of their way to demean citizens they came in contact with. My FTO said it was to elicit more information, but I think it was to get a rise out of them and get them upset. It was like it turned him on to bad-mouth suspects on the scene and other things like that. He was not the only one who did it; there were others on the squad. I thought police work was getting to know the community and finding ways to

prevent crime. The reality is there is no time for community policing.

During the field training phase, FTOs and supervisors exert considerable power over police recruits. They can verify or negate a recruit's work performance, delay training progress, and interpret in formal communication and written records a recruit's motivations and abilities or lack thereof (Holdaway & Barron, 1997). Three Caucasian males recalled that their FTOs exerted considerable power over them in negative ways, which triggered feelings of self-doubt, self-consciousness, and depression.

After completing field training, recruits proceed to complete a 1-year probationary period during which they are expected to demonstrate that they possess the skills and knowledge necessary to maintain a satisfactory level of work and suitability for permanent employment. If a satisfactory level of work is not achieved during the probationary period, questions about a recruit's suitability for permanent employment will be raised and a permanent appointment may not be confirmed. Recruits are also expected to demonstrate the capacity to work with their colleagues, which implies an ascribed status as a member of the police team, which embodies the values and practices of the rank-and-file.

The five police recruits who self-initiated resignation during the 1-year probationary period revealed that they experienced continued conflict and a state of dissonance based on the realization that their attitudes about police work and police-public interactions differed from their coworkers. Even though many of these recruits were assigned to a single-person patrol car, they still found police work was not what they expected; in particular, they realized police work did not allow for the level of involvement in community policing activities they had expected. One Caucasian female explained,

I have always been interested in policing. I was an officer in a big city and I expected a small city to be different. I thought they (small town officers) would be more community-oriented and different in the way they treated their citizens, but they were very heavy-handed....I guess the agency's ideas about what crime is and how to interact with people is different from my philosophies.

Coupled with the lack of involvement in community policing, resigners from different police agencies reported feeling conflict as they witnessed their coworker use "heavy-handed policing" tactics. Several resigners felt that their coworkers acted and behaved in ways that provoked subjects to fight and resist arrest, resulting in an escalation of the use of force.

I didn't leave police work, I just left that police agency. I didn't like the department or the city. It was the politics and policies. I responded to a fight and when I got there, the subjects involved were separated. One of the subjects had been drinking so he was a little out of it, but the officers weren't going to talk to him. It was like they just pushed the subject until he was provoked enough to fight. I guess I saw too much of that. (Caucasian male)

It opened my eyes to the real police work and it is not what I perceived. I definitely like helping people, that was the most rewarding and fulfilling aspect of police work. The worst thing was having to stand by and watch officers conduct illegal searches. Like when they are searching women, they have them lift their bras. You can't do that. I had to stand by and do nothing; there was no way to stop it. If you say anything, then all the officers are against you. The problem with that is if you need backup, it is really slow. I was also surprised at the lack of supervision. (Caucasian female)

These data support the proposition advanced by Holdaway and Barron (1997, p. 29) that "decisions to voluntarily resign from police work are not sudden or dramatic; rather, the decision to resign is the end result of a consideration of incompatible experiences within the workplace and relationships with colleagues and supervisors."

Gender Discrimination and Self-Initiated Resignation

Policing is heavily influenced by gender and preserves a set of traditional Anglo American masculine values; as a result, it provides a social context that can often be uncomfortable for women. Texeira (2002) contended that the most difficult force for female officers to overcome is often not work, the community, nor their families but the antagonism and harassment of their peers and supervisors who are part of the male-dominated culture of policing (see also Haarr, 1997; Hunt, 1990; Martin, 1980, 1990; Morash & Haarr, 1995). Thus, it was not surprising that 3 of the 4 Caucasian female recruits (75%) who self-initiated resignation spoke of gender discrimination directed at them by their FTO(s) and supervisor(s). One Caucasian female explained,

I was not prepared it, for the bad neighborhoods and drugs. I also had problems with my training sergeant. I felt like I was discriminated against, not in the sexual sense, but I was not treated the way I should have been. I heard other female officers had similar problems. ...It was very different from the academy. There were not many females in the precinct I was working, and there were none on my training squad. So, it was intimidating. Plus, I heard some things about my training sergeant before I ever left the academy. They were not going to make it easy. It was a difficult transition, and there was not the support that I had at the academy. Also, I had to work with people who did not like me. It was negative because I was surprised that a department like that would have someone with such a bad reputation in a training position. Well, I figured if I could get through such a negative field training experience and work in a not-so-good neighborhood, then I can do just about anything.... Being new, I had no one to go to for help. I didn't feel like I had any support. It was the first time in my life I had no one supporting me in my professional life. I had my family and friends, but it is hard to tell them what you are going through.

The only female recruit who did not experience gender discrimination was a Hispanic female who was married to a veteran police officer working in the same policy agency. Similarly, Texeira (2002) found that African American women who were married to officers were less likely to be sexual harassed on the job.

Family Strain and Self-Initiated Resignation

Four male recruits (2 Caucasian, 1 Native American, and 1 Hispanic) and 1 Hispanic female maintained their decision to resign was based on a combination of personal and family stresses due to the demands and pressures of the training academy and police work. For the Native American male, the academic and physical demands of basic training were very challenging. He also spoke of difficulties related to attending a basic training academy that was more than 200 miles away from his home, family, and friends who were living on the Indian reservation. The pressures of traveling long distances to attend basic training and the impact of the job on one's sense of self caused tension within recruits' families, particularly among newly married recruits.

Two resigners revealed that their involvement in police work caused their children stress. One Hispanic male explained,

> I was very interested in law enforcement. The training academy was challenging, physically and mentally demanding. I thought police work would be good [for me], but I left because it was too stressful and risky. It was just too much. I needed to do what was best for my family.

Similarly, a Hispanic female who resigned during field training explained,

> Policing was something I always wanted to do. I liked that I was able to get out and help

people. The area I worked had a lot of needs. I also speak Spanish and was able to help in that respect. I decided to leave police work because my children were having a hard time adjusting. My husband is a police officer and has been for 8 years, and the kids were used to me being home when he worked nights. The kids were OK while I was working days, but when I switched to nights, my son began biting his nails and my daughter wasn't sleeping very well. ...I liked doing something other than caring for my kids.

Each of these recruits spoke to the dilemma of reconciling the "competing urgencies" of family and work (Hochschild, 1989).

Academy-Initiated Termination

Police recruits whose termination was initiated during basic training by academy administrators were terminated for three reasons: medical withdrawal, breaking academy rules, and academic failure. The most common reason was medical withdrawal due to injury. The majority (66.7%, $n = 6$) of these dropouts, 5 Caucasian males and 1 Hispanic male, injured themselves during the regimented physical training schedule, which includes running several miles each day on desert mountain trails, completing obstacle courses, and maintaining an advanced weight training program. Recruits who missed more than 5 conditioning days were given a medical withdrawal due to injury.

> I hit my heel while jumping the wall on the obstacle course. I tried to recuperate; however, I am still suffering from the injury. I was on crutches for a couple of days and then I was dismissed because I couldn't keep up with the program. It was injustice because I wasn't given the chance to go back. At the time, I was 48 years old; now I am 50. I don't feel like going back and starting over. They broke my dream. (Hispanic male)

Not all recruits were terminated due to physical injury. One Native American male was terminated by academy administrators after he was placed on academic probation for failing three academy tests. The other two academy-initiated dropouts, 1 African-American male and 1 Caucasian male, were terminated after they were caught breaking academy rules and regulations (i.e., holding a second job and sexual harassment).

Police recruits who were terminated from basic training by academy administrators did not experience preresignation conflicts related to police work, the work environment, or academy classmates. Rather, they expressed a high level of postresignation conflict surrounding their injury, the inability to complete the training academy, and being forced to leave police work unexpectedly and against their desires. Some recruits felt that their dream of being a police officer was broken and they were forced to move onto another job (55.6%, $n = 5$).

Department-Initiated Termination

Eight dropouts were terminated from police work by their employing police agency; 3 recruits were terminated during field training and 5 after completing field training yet prior to the end of a 1-year probationary period. These dropouts reported that they were terminated for inadequate performance (e.g., making mistakes on the job) and/or breaking departmental policies. One Caucasian female alleged her termination was due to a combination of inadequate performance and gender discrimination on the part of her immediate supervisor.

> My supervisor said I had an unsatisfactory probation. I was given the option to quit or be terminated and I chose to be terminated. I had a problem with report writing. My sergeant would give my reports harsh critiques. I submitted several memos requesting additional report writing training. The memos were completely unacknowledged. Then I had an on-duty accident. They tried to make it

look as though I fell asleep, [but] I didn't fall asleep. Then there was a report of another accident that disappeared or got lost; after 14 days, it reappeared. They said there was no way it could have just vanished and resurfaced and they believed I just turned it in. …I was disillusioned when I came here with the notion of equality. …The superiors there have been around for 20 years or more, and they felt women were supposed to be moms or housewives. I am confident in myself and my ability to do this job. I know I can be good backup, I will get in there and fight, but that bothered my supervisors who expected me to duck, hide and run.… I am filing a suit for wrongful discharge, I want my job back, I believe it was discrimination.

Police recruits terminated by their employing agency were similar to those terminated by academy administrators in the sense that they expressed post-termination conflict. Six of the eight recruits terminated by their employing agency were trying to enter back into police work.

◪ Discussion and Conclusion

The findings presented here demonstrate the usefulness of cognitive dissonance theory as an explanation for the voluntary resignation of police recruits from police work within the first 16 months of their careers. In keeping with the theory, police recruits who self-initiated resignation within the first 16 months of their police careers experienced conflict and a state of dissonance when their experiences in the training academy, field training, and police work were inconsistent with or contradictory to their sense of self and their cognitions about what police work should be. This conflict forced them to reconsider their decision to enter any further into or remain in police work.

At each stage of career development, recruits' decision to resign was based on a multitude of factors and experiences. During basic training, voluntarily resignation was based on the realization that one's attitudes and beliefs about police-public relations and interactions and appropriate and inappropriate work behaviors differed considerably from one's academy classmates. For some recruits, this realization was coupled with an aversion for the paramilitary nature of the training academy. At the field training phase, resigners found the cumulative and interactive effects of field training, their incompatible relationship with their FTO(s), factors of the organizational environment, and beliefs and practices of the rank-and-file caused them a substantial level of stress and conflict. Recruits who voluntarily resigned after completing field training, yet prior to the end of their 1-year probationary period experienced dissonance when watching their coworkers use "heavy-handed policing" tactics, realized that their attitudes about police-public relations differed from that of their coworkers. Rather than allowing the powerful forces of the organizational environment to reshape their attitudes and behaviors to be more congruent with those of the rank-and-file, or adjusting their expectations to be more compatible with the realities of police work, recruits chose to resign from police work. The decision to resign, however, was not typically sudden or dramatic or brought about by a single event; rather, the decision to resign is the result of a mental reflection that takes into account a variety of circumstances over a period of time (Holdaway & Barron, 1997).

These findings confirm Van Maanen's (1975) hypotheses that police recruits face stages of career contingency and development within the early stages of their police careers. The stages represent crucial points at which recruits may experience temporary states of conflict and dissonance, which forces some recruits to reconsider their place in the organization and their decision to remain a member of the organization and occupation. Recruits who resign from police work chose to withdraw from further continuation in the socialization process and conformity to the norms, beliefs, and practices of the rank-and-file. In contrast, police recruits who were terminated by academy administrators or their employing agency did not experience pretermination conflict and dissonance; rather, they experienced posttermination conflict and a state of dissonance surrounding their unplanned and unexpected termination.

There were some similarities in the reasons for resignation of men and women and Caucasians and racial/ethnic minorities from police work, but gender and racial/ethnic minority status did exert a unique influence. Workplace problems that are salient to women, particularly gender discrimination, were woven into female recruits' mental reflections and decisions to resign. This finding provides support for prior research (Morash & Haarr, 1995), which has established that women are affected not only by workplace problems and stressors that influence men but also by some that are unique to their status as women and minorities. In comparison, Native American and Hispanic recruits had the highest rate of dropout within the first 16 months of their police careers and maintained that personal and family stresses related to the demands and pressures of basic training and police work weighted heavily on their decision to resign. These findings are the basis for the conclusion that there needs to be a more systematic examination of the resignation of women and racial/ethnic minority officers from police work. If the issue of resignation of female and minority officers is to be wholeheartedly undertaken, it must not be separated from the gendered and racialized dimensions of the organization and occupation (Holdaway & Barron, 1997).

In conclusion, these findings have raised important policy issues about the field training phase, including the selection, training, and supervision of FTOs. Careful selection of FTOs is essential because FTOs have a significant impact on the training and socialization of recruits to the understandings and practices of policing held by rank-and-file officers. Selection standards for FTOs should include, but not be limited to, work performance and aptitude, interest in training officers, and a genuine commitment to the integration of women and racial/ethnic minorities into the organization. FTOs should be systematically trained, informed of equal opportunity policies and sexual and racial harassment policies, and supervised by supervisors who have been carefully selected and trained.

These findings are important, but one should consider that they are based on a small sample of police dropouts. These findings may also be placed in jeopardy by methodological problems, such as dropouts do not always have "good" memories and are not able to clearly articulate the timing and sequence of events that led up to their resignation, particularly when they feel distressed about their experiences and are relying on a retrospective account of what happened and particularly when they are recalling sensitive and hurtful experiences (Holdaway & Barron, 1997). Similar to Holdaway and Barron's (1997) findings, many dropouts offered lengthy and somewhat rambling accounts that move backwards and forwards from incident to incident and from specific matters to general situations. Also, some dropouts may have had poor performance records but were not willing to admit this during an interview and may have rationalized their resignation by focusing on other, more comfortable and acceptable subjects. Future research needs greater methodological rigor to help alleviate these problems. Replicating this study in another setting is important, as it would help to determine whether the findings are generalizable across training academies and police organizations.

 References

DeLey, W. W. (1984). American and Danish police "dropout" rates: Denmark's force as a case study in high job satisfaction, low stress, and low turnover. *Journal of Vocational Behavior, 25,* 58–69.

Dick, P. (2000). The social construction of the meaning of acute stressors: A qualitative study of the personal accounts of police officers using a stress counseling service. *Work and Stress, 14,* 226–244.

Doerner, W. G. (1995). Officer retention patterns: An affirmative action concern for police agencies? *American Journal of Police, 14*(3/4), 197–210.

Favreau, D. F., & Gillespie, J. E. (1978). *Modern police administration.* Englewood Cliffs, NJ: Prentice Hall.

Festinger, L. (1957). *A theory of cognitive dissonance.* Evanston, IL: Row-Peterson.

Fielding, N. G., & Fielding, J. L. (1987). A study of resignation during British police training. *Journal of Police Science and Administration, 15,* 1, 24–36.

Fry, F. L. (1983). A preliminary examination of the factors related to turnover of women in law enforcement. *Journal of Police Science and Administration, 11,* 149–155.

Gettinger, S. (1984). *Assessing criminal justice needs.* Washington, DC: National Institute of Justice, U.S. Department of Justice.

Haarr, R. N. (1997). Patterns of interaction in a police patrol bureau: Race and gender barriers to integration. *Justice Quarterly, 14,* 53–85.

Haarr, R. N. (2001). The making of a community policing officer: The impact of basic training and occupational socialization on police recruits. *Police Quarterly, 4*(4), 402–433.

Harris, L. M., & Baldwin, J. N. (1999). Voluntary turnover of field operations officers: A test of confluency theory. *Journal of Criminal Justice, 27,* 6, 483–493.

Hochschild, A. R. (1989). *The second shift, working parents and the revolution at home.* New York: Viking.

Hoffman, J. (1993). The plague of small agencies: Turnover. *Law and Order, 41*(6), 25–28.

Holdaway, S., & Barron, A. M. (1997). *Resigners? The experience of Black and Asian police officers.* London: Macmillan.

Hunt, J. (1990). The logic of sexism among police. *Women and Criminal Justice, 1,* 3–30.

James, S., & Hendry, B. (1991). The money or the job: The decision to leave policing. *Australian and New Zealand Journal of Criminology, 24,* 169–189.

Lafontaine, E., & Tredeau, L. (1986). The frequency sources, and correlates of sexual harassment among women in traditional male occupations. *Sex Roles, 15,* 433–442.

Manili, B., & Connors, E. (1988). *Police chiefs and sheriffs rank their criminal justice needs.* Washington, DC: National Institute of Justice, U.S. Department of Justice.

Martin, S. E. (1980). *Breaking and entering: Policewomen on patrol.* Berkeley: University of California Press.

Martin, S. E. (1990). *Women on the move? A report on the status of women in policing.* Washington, DC: Police Foundation.

McDowell, C. F. (1971). The police as victims of their own misconceptions. *Journal of Criminal Law, Criminology, and Police Science, 62,* 430–436.

Morash, M., & Haarr, R. N. (1995). Gender, workplace problems, and stress in policing. *Justice Quarterly, 12*(1), 113–140.

Phelan, M. (1991). Number of officers leaving a department for any reason other than retirement. *Law and Order, 39*(5), 40–42.

Premack, S. L., & Wanous, J. P. (1985). A meta-analysis of realistic job preview experiments. *Journal of Applied Psychology, 70,* 706–718.

Reiser, M. (1974). Some organizational stresses on policemen. *Journal of Police Science and Administration, 2,* 156–159.

Seagram, B. C., & Stark, A. C. (1992). Women in Canadian urban policing: Why are they leaving? *Police Chief, 59*(10), 120–128.

Seidel, A. D., & Courtney, M. (1983). *Why cops quit—factors influencing patrol officers' tenure, retention, and resignation.* Rockville, MD: National Institute of Justice.

Singleton, G., & Teahan, J. (1978). Effects of job-related stress on the physical and psychological adjustment of police officers. *Journal of Police Science and Administration, 6,* 355–361.

Sparger, J. R., & Giacopassi, D. J. (1983). Copping out: Why police leave the force. In R. R. Bennett (Ed.), *Police at work: Policy issues and analysis.* Beverly Hills, CA: Sage.

Texeira, M. T. (2002). Who protects and serves me? A case study of sexual harassment of African American women in one U.S. law enforcement agency. *Gender & Society, 16*(4), 524–545.

U.S. Department of Justice, Bureau of Justice Statistics. (2000). *Police departments in large cities, 1990–2000.* Washington, DC: Government Printing Office.

Van Maanen, J. (1975). Police socialization: A longitudinal examination of job attitudes in an urban police department. *Administrative Science Quarterly, 20,* 207–227.

Wales, J. A. (1988). Officer retention. *Law and Order, 36*(5), 37–40.

Webster, B. A., & McEwen, T. J. (1992). *Assessing criminal justice needs.* Washington, DC:

National Institute of Justice, U.S. Department of Justice. Wilson, O. W., & McLaren, R. C. (1950). *Police administration.* New York: McGraw-Hill.

DISCUSSION QUESTIONS

1. Describe how this study was conducted. Identify how data were collected and the location of this study.

2. What were the main reasons that women left the policing profession?

3. What can police administrators learn from the findings of this study?

Part II

Police Operations and Effectiveness

SECTION

6

Police administrators and officers work together to achieve the goals of their organization.

Police Organization and Leadership

Section Highlights

- Review some of the factors that influence organizational change.
- Examine the extent to which leadership and supervisory styles influence officer behavior.
- Understand how police supervisors often have to manage issues related to stress, job satisfaction, morale, and cynicism among patrol officers.

L egendary football coach Vince Lombardi once said, "The achievements of an organization are the results of the combined effort of each individual."[1] This quote provides an explanation of how organizations can be successful contingent on the motivation and actions of their members. This theory could be applied to nearly every type of organization, including police organizations. In this section, several theories are presented to help you better understand why police organizations function and structure themselves in certain ways and how this can influence whether they are able to successfully reach their goals. There is also a discussion of the factors that are believed to bring changes to police organizations when they adopt practices such as community policing and COMPSTAT and how civil service systems, police unions, and accreditation can also alter the workplace environment. Several issues related to police leadership are addressed in this section, including how supervisory styles can influence officer behavior, as well as the management of some common personnel issues, including stress, cynicism, job satisfaction, and morale.

⊠ The Evolution of Police Organizations

When Sir Robert Peel created the London Metropolitan Police Department in 1829, he believed that in order for the police to be viewed as a legitimate organization in the eyes of the public, it must be under government control and have a military-like organizational structure and operational style.[2] When formal police agencies began to emerge across the United States, many of them loosely followed Sir Robert Peel's ideas. As a result, American police agencies were created to be under government control such that local politicians had significant influence over the police. The police agencies also had paramilitary structure and style (see Section 1 for more information on the history of police.)

A **paramilitary** style is one that resembles or has characteristics similar to those of the military. Police organizations are considered paramilitary for many reasons:[3] First, they wear uniforms that serve as visible symbols that they are members of an organization. Similar to military uniforms, police uniforms project an image of solidarity, power, and authority. The symbolism of the police uniform is strong in the eyes of the public. In 1970, the Lakewood Police Department in Colorado discovered this when they designed their police uniforms to resemble business wear instead of traditional police uniforms. Their police uniforms consisted of gray dress slacks, light blue buttoned shirts, ties, and navy blue blazers. Some citizens scoffed at the nontraditional uniforms and complained that it was difficult to distinguish who was a Lakewood police officer. The citizens' negative reaction to the uniform led the agency to adopt a more traditional police uniform a few years later.[4]

Police organizations are also considered paramilitary because police officers are authorized to carry and use firearms, as well as other means of physical force. And finally, the police utilize a centralized, bureaucratic organizational structure similar to that used by the military. A bureaucratic organizational structure is believed to promote stability, efficiency, and effectiveness.[5]

Max Weber (1864–1920), a German sociologist, identified several characteristics of a **bureaucracy**, as follows:[6] (1) *a defined hierarchy of authority* that includes a chain of command, with subordination of the lower levels to the upper levels of the hierarchical structure; (2) *impersonal rules* that clearly define the duties, responsibilities, and procedures attached to each position within the organization; (3) *written rules of conduct* for people within the organization; (4) *promotion based solely on achievement* of individuals within the organization; and (5) *specialized division of labor* in which each position has a clearly defined set of tasks and responsibilities. Weber believed that these characteristics would increase the level of organizational efficiency.

The paramilitary nature of the police has not gone without criticism. It has been blamed for encouraging police officers to maintain a warlike mentality toward citizens. Some believe that the paramilitary approach promotes an "us versus them" perspective, and in some

Some of the equipment used in modern police agencies resembles that used by the military.

instances this leads to the use of physical force by the police when it may not be justified.[7] Bureaucratic organizational structures have also been criticized for being extremely rigid, having an excessive amount of rules, having difficulty responding to societal changes, stifling their members' creativity and not fully utilizing their talents and skills, as well as frequent failures in communication when information flows from the top of the organization down through its various levels.[8]

In 1950, Orlando W. Wilson presented his ideas about police administration and management in his book, *Police Administration*.[9] This book has been referred to as the bible of police management, as many American police agencies adopted the managerial approach it outlines. Wilson's book reinforces several classic managerial principles, such as having a distinct hierarchical organizational structure and centralization of command, in which decisions are made at the top of the organization (with the chief) and flow down to patrol officers working the streets. Wilson's approach to police management is often referred to as the professional or traditional model of policing.

Two decades later in the 1970s, police reformers began to urge police administrators to adopt a more democratic style of management. They believed that a military model of management is not appropriate for police officers, as it suppresses their ability to use discretion to make quick decisions while interacting with citizens.[10] In addition, this approach to policing had begun to drive a wedge between the police and the citizens they served. It was not until the 1990s that police reform efforts began to take hold in the form of community policing. The hope was that community policing could not only change the impersonal working relationship between police and citizens but also change the bureaucratic organizational structure of police agencies across the United States.

Organizational Theories: Understanding Structure and Function of Police Organizations

Police organizations do not exist in a vacuum. There are several factors *outside* of police organizations that can influence change in their structure and function. Organizational theories can help us understand why police organizations are structured and operate in certain ways and why some police organizations have to make changes in order to reach their goals—or, in some cases, survive.

Systems Theory

Systems theory is based on the premise that an organization is composed of several interrelated and interdependent parts combined to accomplish an overall goal.[11] Ongoing feedback among the various parts of the system is essential in order for it to accomplish its goals and to continue to function. If one part of the system breaks down, the very nature of the system can be changed and, in some cases, it will cause the organization as a whole to no longer function.[12]

This theory can be applied to police organizations. Divisions in police organizations such as patrol, investigations, training, and communications are both interrelated and interdependent with one another.[13] These divisions all function independently but need to communicate with each other in order for the organization to properly function. Changes made to any one of the divisions will impact the other divisions and, ultimately, the organization as a whole. For example, if the training division is incorrectly training newly hired officers entering the organization, it could have an effect on the other divisions (i.e., how officers conduct their work while on patrol). If someone identifies areas in which the training is flawed and brings them to the attention of the training division, they can be fixed and the organization will once again be able to properly function.

Contingency Theory

Contingency theory is based on the premise that organizations are rational entities seeking to maximize their levels of effectiveness and efficiency and are structured so as to be able to reach their goals.[14] To achieve their goals, they need to be able to adapt to changes in their task environment. Thus, the task environment heavily influences organizational change.[15] Organizations need to adapt themselves to their task environment when their goals are impacted by changes that occur in the task environment.[16] This might require that the organization change its goals as well as its manner of operation in order to accommodate changes in the task environment.

The structure and function of police organizations can be explained using contingency theory. Police organizations are sometimes required to make changes to the way that they conduct their business and alter their organizational goals in response to their task environment (in this case, the task environment would include other criminal justice agencies, citizens in the community, etc.). Police organizations also structure themselves in ways designed to achieve their goals and to achieve maximum efficiency. For example, if a police agency's goal is crime control, it will structure itself in such a way as to ensure that it can be efficient and effective in controlling crime. In addition, it is also likely that the organization will concentrate most of its resources on activities and efforts that are geared toward crime control.

Contingency theory is the dominant theoretical framework used to study practices, behaviors, and structures of police organizations in the United States.[17] This theory has also been utilized in studies of innovation in police organizations, specifically community policing.[18] John Worrall and Jihong Zhao applied this theory in their study of the role of the COPS office in community policing in the United States. They found that COPS funding is strongly associated with the extent to which police agencies reported having community policing programs in place. That means that the existence of community policing programs is heavily contingent on the availability of COPS grants.[19]

Systems Theory and Police Organization

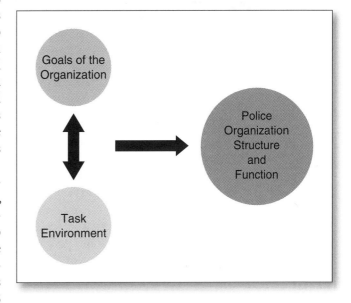

Contingency Theory and Police Organization

Institutional Theory

Institutional theory is based on the idea that an organization's goals and structural arrangement are influenced by the cultural and political elements found within its institutional environment.[20] Organizational legitimacy is an important part of this theory. *Legitimacy* refers to "the degree of cultural support for an organization—the extent to which the array of established cultural accounts provide explanations for its existence, functioning, and jurisdiction."[21] Legitimacy is not something that is automatically granted to organizations. They usually have to work hard to gain legitimacy from *sovereigns*.[22] Sovereigns are actors or groups found within an organization's institutional environment whose views of the organization are important in the acquisition of legitimacy.[23] Organizations sometimes find it necessary to incorporate institutional myths into their formal structures and activities in order for sovereigns in their institutional environments to perceive them as legitimate.[24] Organizations might adopt certain practices in order to achieve legitimacy within their institutional environments and to increase the likelihood of their survival or success. The adoption of these practices is not always connected to any direct increase in efficiency for the organization (this is part of institutional myths); however, the practices are hoped to increase the organization's legitimacy.

Institutional Theory and Police Organizations

Institutional Environment

Sovereigns

Police Organization Goals and Structure

Institutional theory was first used in police research in the 1990s.[25] John Crank used this theoretical perspective to describe the community policing movement.[26] This theory has also been used to examine police organizational structures and practices,[27] police chiefs' leadership styles,[28] vehicular stops related to profiling,[29] and the implementation of gang-suppression units in police agencies.[30]

Resource Dependency Theory

Resource dependency theory focuses on how external resources of organizations influence organizational behavior.[31] Resources that are needed by organizations to both function and survive come from and are controlled by other organizations (some politically based). This means that resources are a source of power.[32] Organizations that need resources can pool together or make agreements with other organizations to acquire necessary resources. This means that organizations need to be able to adapt to changes and be flexible in their process of seeking out resources. While institutional theory asserts that organizations look to their environment for legitimacy, resource dependency theory asserts that organizations look to their environment for resources. Resource dependency theory views the relationship between organizations and their environment as reciprocal, while institutional and contingency theories view the relationship as being more one sided (meaning that organizations are more dependent on their task and institutional environments).[33]

The manner in which police organizations are structured and function can be explained by resource dependency theory, as they rely heavily on resources from organizations in their external environments.

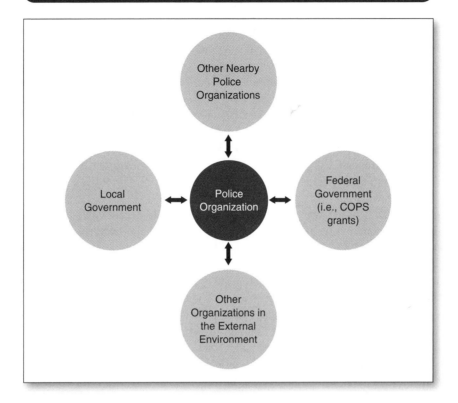

Resource Dependency Theory and Police Organizations

Police agencies have to be flexible and adaptive to be able to acquire resources. For example, if police agencies want to apply for COPS funding to implement community policing in their organizations, they need to restructure their organizations and change the way that they function in order to facilitate the adoption. As discussed in Section 13, some police agencies are forced to consolidate with other nearby agencies in order to acquire enough resources to survive or function.

◼ Altering Police Organizations

Previously in this section, several organizational theories were presented to help you understand why and how some police organizations change. It is also important to identify some of the factors that are believed to cause change in American police organizations.

Community Policing

In Section 2, community policing was identified as an alternative approach to traditional policing that was intended to modify police organizations and change the way that police officers deliver service to citizens.

In "Community Policing in America: Changing the Nature, Structure, and Function of the Police," Jack Greene describes how community policing is supposed to change police organizations:

> From the perspective of the police organization and service delivery system, community policing is a way of making police agencies less bureaucratic, specialized, and hierarchical. On the ground, police officers are seen as generalists, not specialists, a hallmark of the industrial organization from which police systems were modeled. Decentralized management and service delivery are cornerstones of the community policing movement, under the argument that the structure of traditional policing greatly inhibits the capacity of the police to deliver effective and efficient services to a visible and active clientele. The police organization under community policing is seen as being in a dynamic state, actively engaged with the environment and creating many boundary-spanning roles linking the organization to its immediate task environment as well as social, cultural and economic environments.[34]

Federal funding has been available to police agencies to help **decentralize** their patrol resources by using positions like community resource officers and creating neighborhood substations. Decentralization is meant to put police officers back into direct contact with citizens. Community policing uses a bottom-up approach that places an emphasis on police officers' abilities to use their judgment, training, and expertise in working with citizens to come up with solutions to problems that are occurring in their neighborhoods. This is a harsh contrast to the top-down approach used in the traditional policing model.

Have police organizations really changed as a result of community policing? This question is still being debated today among police scholars. For example, one study found mixed results for the idea that community policing has had an impact on changing American police organizations. Specifically, this study found that "large municipal police agencies experienced decreases in centralization and administrative intensity" . . . and that the 'flattening' of the police hierarchy did not occur . . . and the number of command levels did not change from 1993–1998."[35] Yet other studies have found that community policing has had minimal impact on police organizations.[36] Some have argued that the lack of organizational change is the result of police agencies not fully implementing community policing. Resistance from middle managers, patrol officers, and police unions, confusion about what community policing is, and concerns that community policing might make the police soft on crime are just a few of the reasons that police organizations have not fully adopted community policing.[37]

COMPSTAT

COMPSTAT (computer comparison statistics) has also been identified as a potential source of change in American police organizations. COMPSTAT was introduced in 1994 by Commissioner William Bratton of the New York City Police Department.[38] This is a goal-oriented management process that uses computer technology, operational strategy, and managerial accountability to structure the way that police agencies provide services related to crime control.[39] COMPSTAT-like processes have been adopted by several American police agencies but are sometimes referred to by a different name or acronym—COMPSTAT is not a universal term for this particular management approach.[40]

The COMPSTAT process is based on four principles: accurate and timely intelligence, rapid and focused deployment of personnel and resources, effective crime control tactics, and relentless follow-up, assessment, and accountability.[41] This process requires frequent meetings in which district or precinct supervisors appear before the highest levels of police management to report about crime problems in their areas, as well as their plans to solve the identified crime problems. It is supposed to change the structure of police organizations, as it requires all members of the organization to have input on how to best control crime in their districts. This means that every member of the organization is held accountable for crime problems in the areas that they work.

COMPSTAT sounds good, but how does it change police organizations? Some critics argue that COMPSTAT actually *reinforces* the hierarchical structure by requiring that each level of the organization be held accountable by the next level in the chain of command.[42] James Willis and his colleagues conducted a study on the adoption and operation of COMPSTAT in three cities (Lowell, Massachusetts, Minneapolis, Minnesota, and Newark, New Jersey). The findings of this study indicate that COMPSTAT was adopted and promoted by the police chiefs in all three cities. There was less success when the study examined changes to organizational structures and the work routines of police officers in all three cities. Willis and his colleagues concluded that "it will take profound changes in the technical and institutional environments of American police agencies for police departments to restructure in the ways anticipated by a technically efficient COMPSTAT."[43] The Willis article included at the end of this section examines how COMPSTAT and community policing influence decision making of first-line supervisors.

COMPSTAT requires police supervisors to take responsibility for crime that takes place in their beat areas.

Civil Service System

The **civil service system** is another mechanism that has altered police organizations and management over time. Specifically, it plays an important role in the employment practices of local, state, and federal government agencies. Civil service systems were originally adopted by government agencies to cut out corrupt political influence in the hiring, promotion, and firing of government workers.[44] Instead of political officials appointing individuals into specific government positions (such as police officer), the civil service system determines employment based on professional merit through the use of competitive examinations.[45] There was also hope that the civil service system would provide a level playing field for all individuals interested in government jobs by eliminating the influence of any potential biases based on gender or race/ethnicity.

Research on the impact of civil service on police organizations has found that this system may be partially responsible for the diversification of police agencies (specifically the increased hiring of racial/ethnic minorities and women).[46] In contrast, the civil service system has also been viewed as a barrier by some police executives that would like to make changes to police personnel policies. Some have argued that attempts to make changes to police personnel policies have been as difficult as "bending granite" as a result of the presence of civil service systems.[47] And finally, the civil service system has a disciplinary process that makes it difficult for police managers to weed out unsatisfactory officers.[48]

Police Unions/Associations

A union is an organization of workers formed for the purpose of advancing its members' interests in respect to wages, benefits, and working conditions.[49] Recent statistics indicate that police officers are represented by unions in approximately three-quarters of the 100 largest police agencies in the United States.[50] **Police unions** are common in most parts of the country, with the exception of the southern region of the United States. There are no police unions in North Carolina, South Carolina, Georgia, or Mississippi.[51]

Fraternal **associations** for police officers seek recognition and benefits for their members like police unions do, but they are also very different from police unions. Some fraternal organizations are tailored to specific types of officers based on their race/ethnicity, gender, or sexual orientation, while other fraternal organizations are open to all police personnel. Created in 1915, the Fraternal Order of Police (FOP) is one of the oldest organizations, representing more than 325,000 police officers in the United States.[52] The mission of the FOP is to "improve the working conditions of law enforcement officers and the safety of those we serve through education, legislation, information, community involvement, and employee representation."[53]

Police unions use **collective bargaining** when representing their members. Collective bargaining is the process of negotiations between employers and union representatives with the goal of reaching an agreement on the working conditions of their members.[54] Working conditions include wages and promotion, hours/assignments/shifts, employee training, health care and workplace safety, and grievance/disciplinary processes. The presence of police unions takes some of the power away from police chiefs, as both groups work together to create a safe and equitable work environment for police officers. The level of impact of police unions varies from state to state. In part, union power is determined by the size (number of members) and the longevity of unions. Unions that have been in place for long periods of time and that have many members will have more power than those with fewer members and that are less established.[55]

Through the use of collective bargaining, police unions are able to negotiate contracts that impact several management issues within police organizations, including the following:[56]

- *Personnel standards*—this includes mandatory drug testing and the maintenance of physical fitness standards for current police officers.
- *Assignment of police officers*—union contracts usually require that police officers be assigned to beat areas and shifts according to their level of seniority in the organization.
- *Discipline of police officers and accountability*—unions often reject the creation and use of civilian oversight boards and early-intervention systems (which identify problem police officers—these accountability mechanisms are discussed further in Section 9).
- *City or county finances/budgets*—unions are often successful at negotiating better salaries and benefits for police officers. A recent report by the Bureau of Justice Statistics revealed that the average salaries for newly hired sworn police officers were $10,900 (38%) higher in departments with collective bargaining than in agencies without it.[57] A study conducted by Steve Wilson and his colleagues also found that the average salaries for entry-level police officers that engage in collective bargaining were higher than those of their counterparts who did not have it; however, they concluded that the economic gains were relatively limited.[58]
- *Impact politics*—police unions have endorsed political candidates that most closely match their vision and goals. In addition, police unions attempt to influence the passage or blockage of certain ordinances related to the police in instances in which any change will impact their jobs or salaries.

Despite the lack of research on police unions and associations in the United States, it is clear that these groups have had an impact on the way that police organizations function and are managed.

Accreditation

In 1979, the Commission on Accreditation for Law Enforcement Agencies (**CALEA**) was created to serve as a credentialing agency for law enforcement agencies in the United States.[59] This agency was created through a collaborative effort involving the International Association of Chiefs of Police (IACP), National Organization of Black Law Enforcement Executives (NOBLE), National Sheriffs' Association (NSA), and the Police Executive Research Forum (PERF). The goals of accreditation include the ability to "strengthen crime prevention and control capabilities; formalize essential management procedures; establish fair and nondiscriminatory personnel practices; improve service delivery; solidify interagency cooperation and coordination; and increase community and staff confidence in the agency."[60]

The accreditation process outlined on the CALEA website includes five general steps: (1) a law enforcement agency enrolls in the program; (2) the agency conducts a self-assessment in which it is able to provide evidence that it is in compliance with all 463 standards required for accreditation; (3) CALEA representatives conduct an on-site assessment to ensure that the agency meets all of the standards; (4) CALEA commission members review information collected from the police agency and then makes a decision about whether it will be awarded accreditation; and (5) if an agency has been awarded accreditation, it must maintain compliance with CALEA standards and then participate in reaccreditation after 3 years.[61]

There have been many criticisms of police accreditation. This process has been criticized for only requiring evidence that police agencies have policies and procedures in place as required for accreditation but not requiring oversight mechanisms that ensure that the policies are enforced or followed by organization members.[62] It has also been criticized for not including elements of community policing in accreditation standards.[63] This is problematic, as community policing is the dominant policing strategy in the United States at this time. Police scholars have also been critical of the accreditation process, as they believe that the standards do not promote problem solving, as suggested by Herman Goldstein, and do little to actually improve the quality of leadership within police agencies.[64]

Given the concerns about the accreditation process, how does accreditation actually impact or change police organizations? Are accredited police agencies any different than police agencies that are not accredited? In a recent study, William G. Doerner and William M. Doerner found that the state accreditation process for Florida police agencies did not foster organizational change within the accredited agencies.[65] Kimberly McCabe and Robin Fajardo's study found that accredited agencies provide more field training to their officers, require higher minimum education requirements and mandatory drug testing for new officers, and are more likely to operate specialized units for the enforcement of drug and child abuse laws than nonaccredited agencies.[66] There were no differences between accredited and nonaccredited agencies with regard to organizations providing classroom-based training for their officers, starting salaries, employment of racial/ethnic minority and female police officers, and specialized units focused on domestic violence and gangs.[67] These research findings suggest that accreditation has some impact on issues within police organizations but provides no strong evidence that changes have taken place in their organizational structure.

Police Leadership

Police organizations are also shaped by leadership styles used by police administrators. Patrol officers working the streets will demonstrate policing styles that reflect their organization's style. James Q. Wilson first wrote about this issue in his book, *Varieties of Police Behavior: The Management of Law and*

Police executives shape the goals and objectives of police organizations.

Order in Eight Communities. According to Wilson, characteristics of the local population, government, and political culture influence police organizations' behavior. He found that the style of policing[68] used by police organizations would impact their organizational output (such as arrests). Wilson identified three styles of policing. First, he identified police officers with a *legalistic style* of policing as those who are focused on the enforcement of the law. Officers with this policing style do not excuse minor crimes and focus heavily on maintaining social order. Next, officers with a *watchman style* of policing focus on maintaining social order, usually ignore minor violations of the law, and use police intervention on an informal basis. And finally, officers with a *service style* focus on the needs of the community first and foremost. They take their jobs very seriously and work hard to provide social services to citizens they encounter on the job.

Because police administrators and their styles of supervision and leadership influence police organizations, it is important to discuss the role that they play within police organizations.

Police Chiefs

Chiefs of police are the main representatives of police organizations. They maintain control of the organization and make decisions that impact its ability to function and prosper. The size of a police organization influences the duties of a police chief. In medium- to large-sized agencies, police chiefs tend to focus their efforts on administrative tasks, while chiefs in small agencies will be responsible for administrative tasks as well as working the streets alongside patrol officers. This is common in rural organizations that employ only a few officers. Police chiefs can be individuals that have worked their way up through the ranks within organizations, or they can be hired as new employees by way of contracts. It is often the case that police chiefs are selected by mayors, city council members, or special panels that consist of police personnel, members of the local city government, and citizens. A study conducted by John Krimmel and Paul Lindenmuth found that police chiefs who receive positive performance and leadership ratings tend to be well educated, to be participants in the Federal Bureau of Investigation National Academy, to have been promoted to the position of police chief from within organizations in which they had already been employed, and to have worked in jurisdictions that had union presence.[69]

In the past few decades, the tenure of police chiefs has become quite short. The average length of employment for American police chiefs in large cities has ranged from 2.5 to 4.93 years.[70] There is debate about the impact that this short length of employment has on police organizations. Some argue that the short tenure of police chiefs can result in "organizational disruption, physical and financial costs to the community, and a lack of attention to the policy-making group's political agenda during the absence of the parting police chief."[71] In contrast, new police chiefs can create opportunities for growth and improvement of organizations and also rid organizations of stagnant leadership.[72]

Research has revealed that different types of leadership styles by police chiefs do in fact exist. Michel Girodo identified several management styles of police executives, including the following:[73]

- *Transformational-style leader*—serves as a source of motivation and support for members of her or his organization. This type of leader uses motivation to focus members of the organization on their tasks and rewards those that meet organizational goals. This type of leader works to change the culture within the organization. Ethics and morality play an important role in this leadership style.
- *Bureaucratic-style leader*—strictly enforces the rules of the organization. Uses an authoritarian approach to leadership and requires that members of the organization behave in a businesslike manner. Members of the organization move up through the ranks based on their ability to obey the rules.
- *Machiavellian-style leader*—gains influence with members of the organization through the use of deceptive and manipulative tactics. This leader's approach to reaching organizational goals is one of the end justifies the means. The use of coercion, instilling fear, and various reward techniques are characteristic of this type of leadership. This leadership approach results in a lack of trust within the organization among both members and their leaders.
- *Social contract-style leader*—achieves organizational success through the most efficient use of available resources. This leadership style reflects a cooperative relationship between leaders and employees in which leaders make a significant contribution to ensure success of their organization. This type of leader sees his or her role as being able to turn a group of employees into a cohesive, functional organization.

These leadership styles will not only impact the success of police organizations, they will also influence behaviors of individual police officers working on the streets.

Police Field Supervisors

Patrol officers are supervised by field supervisors. Field supervisors are individuals that hold ranks above patrol officers (such as sergeant and lieutenant) but are ranked below police executives, whose responsibilities are primarily administrative. Traditionally, field supervisors have been responsible for controlling the behavior of patrol officers while ensuring that officers use department policies and procedures as they interact with citizens. As police organizations have evolved over time, the role of field supervisors has also changed to reflect the principles of community and problem-oriented policing. Today, patrol officers are given more discretion to make decisions without the help of their supervisors. Supervisors are viewed as coaches or mentors by patrol officers. They are expected to rely less on their formal authority to supervise officers. Instead, they are to work in conjunction with patrol officers to come up with solutions to problems that are encountered while on patrol.[74]

Like police chiefs, the management style of police field supervisors varies. Using systematic observation and interviews, Robin Shepard Engel identified four distinct supervisory styles: traditional, innovative, supportive, and active.[75] *Traditional supervisors* value discipline and respect from patrol officers. They expect patrol officers to produce measurable outcomes (such as arrests) by which they can be evaluated. They also expect officers to approach their work in an aggressive manner. This type of supervisor resists new approaches to policing, including community and problem-oriented policing.

Innovative supervisors are likely to form relationships with the patrol officers they supervise. They appreciate and embrace new police innovations and encourage patrol officers to do the same. Being mentors and coaches to patrol officers they supervise is more important than enforcing department rules. *Supportive supervisors* serve as a buffer between patrol officers and higher-ranking police administrators; this includes protecting them from disciplinary actions or punishment. This type of supervisor encourages officers by giving them praise and is less concerned with the enforcement of department policies and regulations. And finally, *active supervisors* base their supervisory style on leading by example.[76] These supervisors work actively alongside patrol officers while also supervising their behavior. They generally have a positive view of the patrol officers they supervise but are unlikely to view themselves as coaches or mentors.

Robin Shepard Engel's study is important because it revealed that in some instances, supervisory styles did influence patrol officer behavior. She found that patrol officers with active supervisors were more likely to use force and engage in problem solving and community policing-related activities and less likely to spend time on administrative activities than were officers who had supervisors that were not classified as active.[77] It is important to point out, however, that collectively, the body of research on the influence of supervisors on patrol officers has produced mixed findings. There have been varied research findings for the influence of supervisors on the likelihood that patrol officers would make an arrest,[78] the length of time patrol officers spend with citizens,[79] and the use of officer discretion in a variety of encounters with citizens.[80]

Managing Personnel Issues

Police supervisors have to manage a variety of personnel issues that can affect both the quality of police service provided to the public and the success of their organizations. Many personnel issues are related to the health and well-being of police officers. In the last part of this section, we will cover several personnel issues, including stress, cynicism, job satisfaction, and morale, that can negatively affect police organizations.

Stress

Workplace stress is something that employees face in a variety of occupations. Policing is considered to be among the most stressful occupations in the United States.[81] Police officers face stress both within and outside of police organizations. Police work requires officers to be exposed to negative encounters with citizens and also to situations that involve danger, violence, and criminal behavior.[82] As discussed earlier in this section, most police organizations are structured and function in a bureaucratic manner. This type of organizational structure can repress police officers' sense of individuality and self-expression, which can result in stressful workplace conditions.[83] Other sources of stress found in police organizations include heavy workloads, frequent rotation of shifts, completion of paperwork and reports, and excessive department rules and regulations.[84]

It is important for police supervisors to monitor police officers' levels of stress, as studies have found that it can lead to divorce, suicide, and alcoholism.[85] Officers can also develop hypertension, ulcers, and cardiovascular disease from stress.[86] Stress that is not managed can also lead to burnout. Burnout is a prolonged response to continual emotional and interpersonal stressors in the work place.[87]

Frequent absences from work and lower levels of job satisfaction are additional negative consequences of police officer stress.[88] Supervisors can suggest several ways for police officers to manage their stress, including peer support groups, individual counseling, cognitive strategies, meditation, exercise, and making changes to their nutrition.[89]

Job Satisfaction

After decades of research, we are still asking questions about what job satisfaction means to police officers and how it might influence them in the workplace. Susette Talarico and Charles Swanson Jr. studied job satisfaction among police officers and found that several officer characteristics (including race, gender, and age) are related to job satisfaction. Other variables,

Stress felt by police officers can result from conditions found both within and outside of the workplace.

including pay and promotional opportunity, are identified as contributors to job satisfaction levels. The factor that was the most influential to job satisfaction in this study was police officers' perception of their organizations (including perceptions of the internal environment of the organization and the managerial style of operation used within their organization).[90]

Over a decade later, Jihong Zhao and his colleagues also found that a police agency's work environment is a principal source of job satisfaction.[91] Other studies have found that foot patrol and community policing enhance police officer job satisfaction.[92] There is some evidence that there is a relationship between officer cynicism and job satisfaction—specifically, that officers with greater levels of cynicism had lower levels of job satisfaction.[93]

Cynicism

Cynicism is "an attitude of contemptuous distrust of human nature and motives."[94] When people enter the policing profession, they have preconceived ideas about what it will be like. After time passes, the reality of the job becomes apparent and it often conflicts with their preconceived ideas about police work. The conflict between the reality of the job and idealism results in cynicism. The first study of police cynicism was conducted by Arthur Niederhoffer in 1967 when he studied the New York City Police Department. The findings of his research are presented in his book, *Behind the Shield: The Police in Urban Society* (an excerpt from this book is included at the end of this section).

Since Niederhoffer's study, there have been several studies focused on police officer cynicism. Researchers have examined the relationships between cynicism and characteristics of both individual officers and police organizations. There have been inconsistent findings in studies that examined cynicism and officer characteristics, including length of service, rank, and socio-economic status.[95] There is some evidence of a relationship between officers' cynicism and their relationship with fellow officers, police supervisors, and the public.[96] David Klinger asserts that officer cynicism toward citizens can influence the level of enforcement by patrol officers, which in some cases can result in acts of police brutality.[97] Others have argued that cynicism can also lead to the development of the "John Wayne syndrome," in which officers become emotionally withdrawn and overly serious about their work and develop authoritarian attitudes toward the public.[98]

Morale

Morale is defined as the mental and emotional condition (including enthusiasm, confidence, or loyalty) of an individual or group with regard to the function or tasks at hand. It is a sense of common purpose with respect to a group. It is the "esprit de corps" or the spirit of a group that makes its members want to succeed.[99] Scholarly interest in police morale dates as far back as 1945, when B. W. Gocke discussed why good morale is needed in police organizations:

> Among those things necessary for the proper functioning of a police department are: well selected and properly trained personnel, adequate equipment, and a soundly organized structure of administrative command and supervision. If these are present, the department has most of the essentials for success. For best results, however, the morale of the men also must be kept at a high level. All personnel should be eager and willing to do a good job; otherwise there is something wrong with the organization or its leadership.[100]

One might assume that there are volumes of studies focused on police officer morale given what we have learned in this section about the challenges associated with police work. Ironically, there has been very little published on this topic in academic journals. In 1967, J.Q. Wilson wrote about how the professionalization of the police has impacted police officers in both positive and negative ways. Police professionalism changed officer roles, police organizational structure, and the relationship between the police and the public. Low morale was identified as one of the negative consequences of police professionalism.[101]

SUMMARY

- Many police organizations both are organized and function in a paramilitary style.
- COMPSTAT, community policing, police unions, civil service systems, and accreditation are believed to change police organizations by way of organizational structure and the manner in which they function.
- Several organization-based theories can help us understand why the structure and function of police organizations change, including systems theory, contingency theory, institutional theory, and resource dependency theory.
- Police supervisors and administrators are required to manage several personnel issues, including stress, job satisfaction, cynicism, and morale among police officers.

KEY TERMS

bureaucracy
CALEA
civil service system
collective bargaining

COMPSTAT
contingency theory
cynicism
decentralized

paramilitary style
police unions/associations
systems theory

DISCUSSION QUESTIONS

1. What is COMPSTAT?

2. Identify some of the personnel issues that are influenced and often negotiated by police unions.

3. How does organizational legitimacy play a part in explaining police organizations according to institutional theory?

4. What are the management styles of police field supervisors according to Robin Shepard Engel?

5. What is a paramilitary style and how does this influence the structure of police organizations?

WEB RESOURCES

- To learn more about COMPSTAT, go to http://www.policefoundation.org/pdf/growthofcompstat.pdf.
- To learn more about the Fraternal Order of Police, go to http://www.fop.net/.
- To learn more about police accreditation, go to http://www.calea.org/.

READING 11

James J. Willis examines how COMPSTAT and community policing are used to guide the decision making of first-line supervisors. The main principles of both of these policing approaches are identified and discussed in the context of their impact on supervisors. Using data collected through focus groups, this study found that sergeants do not necessarily adopt the principles of either COMPSTAT or community policing.

First-Line Supervision and Strategic Decision Making Under Compstat and Community Policing

James J. Willis

Over the last quarter of a century, two of the most highly visible police reforms to have emerged in the United States are Compstat and community policing (Bratton & Knobler, 1998; Rosenbaum, 1994; Silverman, 1999; Silverman & O'Connell, 1999; Skogan, 2004, 2006a; Weisburd, Mastrofski, McNally, Greenspan, & Willis, 2003; Willis, Mastrofski, & Weisburd, 2007). Compstat is a highly focused strategic management system concentrating on reducing serious crime by decentralizing decision making to middle managers operating out of districts, by holding these managers accountable for performance, and by increasing the organization's capacity to identify, understand, and monitor responses to serious crime problems (Eterno & Silverman, 2006; Henry, 2002; Kim & Maurborgne, 2003; Maple & Mitchell, 1999; Silverman, 2006). Community policing is characterized by a variety of justifications: strengthening public support for the police, building social capital, achieving a more equitable distribution of police services, and reducing crime, disorder, and fear of crime by customizing solutions to local problems (Rosenbaum, 1994; Skogan, 2008a). Its methods are similarly diffuse, but often include community partnerships, problem solving, and the delegation of greater decision-making authority to

sergeants and their patrol officers at the beat level (Moore, 1992; Skogan, 2006a).

Both innovations have diffused rapidly throughout the United States and abroad (Skogan, 2006a, p. 5; Weisburd et al., 2003), and researchers are still trying to determine the effects of each of these reforms and their future prospects (Dabney, 2010; Weisburd & Braga, 2006). However, it is also important to know how these two reforms operate together when co-implemented in the same police agency. According to a 2006 national survey, 59% of large police agencies are pursuing both Compstat and community policing simultaneously suggesting how they work together has significant implications for how policing is done (Willis, Kochel, & Mastrofski, 2010).

This is the third article from a national assessment of this co-implementation issue. The first two used site-visit data to explain why Compstat and community policing operated largely independently and to make recommendations for their integration (Willis, Mastrofski, & Kochel 2010a, 2010b). The purpose of this article is narrower in scope. Its point of departure is the claim that both reforms are "strategic" or designed to heighten a police organization's capacity to identify problems in its crime environment, detect any changes, and respond effectively. This strategic focus is then examined from the perspective of one rank, first-line supervisors, whose decisions play a key role in converting policy into practice (Skogan, 2008b).

Although there is a small amount of research on co-implementation, it is generally within the broader context of organizational change (see Willis, Mastrofski, & Kochel, 2010b). In comparison, there is virtually no in-depth research on the decision making of first-line supervisors in co-implementing departments. This is a significant oversight as presumably these reforms' "big picture" approach toward handling an unstable environment should materialize in the kind of guidance that first-line supervisors receive from their superiors, in how they make decisions about crime and disorder problems, and in the kind of direction they give to the organization's largest resource—its patrol officers. Thus, using focus-group data from six police departments, this article asks, "How, if at all, did the co-implementation of Compstat and community policing influence the strategic decision making of first-line supervisors?"[1]

The answer to this question is important as studies often show significant slippage between the doctrines of particular reforms and how they operate in practice when implemented in a police organization (Clarke, 2004; Cordner & Biebel, 2005; Ratcliffe, 2002). Knowing how first-line supervisors said they adapted to the strategic components of these reforms can help identify where co-implementation problems are likely to occur and thus offer some direction on how they might be overcome. The next section describes how the key strategic elements of these reforms are supposed to work (at least according to their respective doctrines). This, then, acts as benchmark for making comparisons to how first-line supervisors said they made decisions within the context of these reforms.

First-Line Supervision in an Age of Reform

Before the emergence of community-oriented policing (COPS) in the early 1980s, patrol supervisors were described as performing traditional supervisory roles in organizations that were hierarchical, bureaucratic, and reactive (Engel, 2002, p. 52; Kelling & Moore, 1988). Sergeants were expected by their superiors to engage in preventive patrol, to ensure that their subordinates responded quickly and appropriately to individual incidents and calls for service, to check crime reports for inaccuracies, and to discipline officers who violated department rules (Allen, 1982; Manning, 1977; Rubinstein, 1973; Trojanowicz, 1980). This stress on internal control contributed to a supervisory system that was "essentially negative, relying primarily upon sanctions for non-compliance with police rules" (Weisburd & McElroy, 1988, p. 31).

Community policing and Compstat (which originated in the New York City Police Department in 1994) evolved in response to many of the bureaucratic pathologies associated with this traditional policing model (Bratton & Knobler, 1998; Reisig, 2010; Weisburd & Braga, 2006, pp. 11–12). Advocates for reform criticized police organizations for placing greater emphasis on "their organization and operation than on the substantive outcome of their work" (Goldstein, 1987, p. 236), for creating elaborate hierarchies and rules, for centralizing command and control, and for detaching themselves from the communities they served (Eck & Spelman, 1987; Trojanowicz & Bucqueroux, 1990).

To help overcome these challenges, reformers stressed the importance of refocusing the organization's energies on reducing and preventing crime and responding to concerns identified by those outside the department. The reform literature on Compstat (Silverman & O'Connell, 1999) and community policing (Skogan, 2006a; Trojanowicz & Bucqueroux, 1990) suggests that there are reform elements where they are similar and where they differ. Here four core elements of co-implementation are identified and assessed according to where the respective reform doctrines stand on each: (a) mission clarification; (b) decentralization of decision-making authority; (c) data-driven problem identification and assessment, and (d) innovative problem-solving tactics. These were selected because they appear most relevant to the strategic decisions of first-line supervisors.[2] Doctrines are essentially theoretical abstractions about how things are supposed to work and not how they actually do so. They are used here to help structure inquiry into how first-line supervision actually operated under these reforms.

One of the key distinguishing features of these reforms is their mission. Compstat's core mission is to reduce serious crime (McDonald, Greenberg, & Bratton, 2002). Indeed, its progenitors in New York City Police Department saw it as a way of getting back to the essential crime control element of the police (Timoney, 2010). In contrast, community policing encourages a substantial broadening of the police mission to a wider range of objectives which community members help identify as priorities. Crime reduction remains essential, but equally important are reducing fear of crime, responding to quality-of-life problems, and addressing minor problems and disorders (e.g., noise, abandoned cars, public drinking, graffiti; Skogan & Hartnett, 1997, p. 8).

An additional core element of both reforms is the decentralization of decision-making authority to make police organizations more flexible and responsive to local conditions, but so far, these reforms have pursued it to different degrees. Compstat has concentrated on the delegation of decision-making authority to middle managers, primarily at the district/precinct commander level. Community-policing approaches have been quite diverse, but, in general, there has been more interest in decentralizing decision making much further down the organization to the small area or beat level (Maguire, 1997). Opinions vary on whether community-policing responsibilities should be assigned to specialists working independently or in units, or to uniformed patrol, but generally community-policing reformers have stressed the benefits of despecialization (Bayley, 1994, p. 46).

As for data, both reforms emphasize crime analysis as a knowledge base for driving strategic responses to crime and social disorder. Where they differ is Compstat has tended to use a department's existing information systems (particularly police reports and computer-aided dispatch) and traditional measures of success (e.g., clearance rates and levels of reported crime). In contrast, community policing embraces nontraditional sources of information (e.g., community surveys and beat meetings) and additional performance measures (e.g., citizen fear levels and indicators of physical and social disorder) that are rarely captured in police databases (Peak & Glensor, 1999, pp. 94–96).

Finally, under Compstat and community policing, data are supposed to provide a basis for searching for and implementing innovative solutions. Police are expected to select responses that offer the best prospects of success, not because they are "what we have always done" but because a careful consideration of a number of alternatives showed them the most likely to be effective at reducing crime and disorder problems (Reisig, 2010; Silverman, 1999, pp. 123–124). These solutions may include law enforcement responses, such as arrest, but these should only be selected after a thorough assessment of alternatives.

Compared with the traditional model of policing, the full implementation of these reforms would seem to require significant changes in how first-line supervisors learn about crime and disorder problems and exercise their judgment in ways that are most likely to produce desired results. How, if at all, had first-line supervisors adapted to the major strategic elements of Compstat and community policing?

Method

In 2006, a national mail survey was administered to large municipal and county police agencies with 100 or more sworn officers according to the 2000 Census of State and Local Law Enforcement Agencies (excluding sheriff's departments). Of the 566 agencies in this sample pool, 355 (63%) responded to the survey. Respondents were asked to what extent their departments had adopted Compstat and/or community policing and what form they took. However, the survey instrument could not give in-depth insights on how this reform worked "on the ground." Consequently, the survey findings were used to identify seven large (>1,000 sworn), medium (500–999), and small (100–499) police agencies suitable for onsite fieldwork. The largest agency selected was the Los Angeles Police Department, California, followed by the Montgomery County Police Department, Maryland. The two medium agencies were the St. Louis County Police Department, Missouri, and Colorado Springs Police Department, Colorado. The three smallest were Overland Park, Kansas, Marietta, Georgia, and Cape Coral, Florida (see Appendix A for a profile of these departments).

Departments were asked to report on the implementation amount or "dosage" of each reform. For Compstat implementation, questions included to what extent the department concentrated on a single mission and used crime statistics to identify priorities and reallocate resources. Among community-policing items, departments reported on to what extent they gave community groups a say in establishing priorities and delegated authority to patrol officers to initiate projects.

Departments were selected for onsite visits that scored among the highest for both Compstat and community policing implementation and had been operating both reforms for at least 4 years. This helped ensure that visits were conducted at those departments where these reforms were a major part of daily operations and which had been operating long enough to overcome initial implementation problems. The validity problems associated with having a single respondent make broad generalizations about the level of implementation of a specific program are well known (Maguire & Mastrofski, 2000). Indeed, a systematic analysis of this project's fieldwork data suggested there was considerable variation in how each of these reforms was implemented across sites (Willis, Mastrofski, & Kochel, 2010b). Nonetheless, this assessment also confirmed that each department had either fully or moderately adopted nearly all the key elements of these reforms.

Five-day site visits were conducted between July 2006 and June 2007. The research activities included observing department activities, community meetings, and Compstat meetings at the department and district levels, and interviews. In addition, 2-hour focus groups were conducted with six (on average) first-line supervisors, any more would have been unwieldy (Krueger, 1994). Unfortunately one of the groups had to be cancelled due to scheduling issues[3] and so the data presented here are from six focus groups.

Given resource constraints, focus groups were chosen as an efficient method of gleaning multiple perspectives on the operational decision-making experiences of first-line supervisors within different agencies (Patton, 2002). Moreover, not only do focus groups allow for the surfacing of individual ideas, they are also a useful way for detecting where differences of opinion and consensus emerge (Krueger, 1994). To elicit thoughtful and in-depth insights on the nature of first-line supervision under these reforms, the department liaison who assisted with scheduling the on-site visit was asked to identify 6 to 10 first-line supervisors who were likely to be knowledgeable, perceptive, and articulate about Compstat and community policing, and who might be willing to participate in a focus group. As a variety of experiences were sought, the only additional stipulation was that the sergeants were not "cherry-picked" based on whether they were likely to express uniformly positive attitudes toward these reforms.

Of the final pool of 34 participants, the majority participants (23) were generalist patrol sergeants, 6 were assigned to community-policing units, 3 were assigned to traffic, and 2 were in administrative positions. The number of patrol officers supervised by generalist patrol sergeants also varied from as few as 5 to as many as 30 (although in this particular case, the sergeant was not in charge of a squad, but was a watch commander). As the focus groups were held on the last morning of the site visit (a Friday), day-shift sergeants were overrepresented in the sample. As the day shift is often regarded as the most desirable shift and generally assigned according to seniority, most of these sergeants would be considered veterans with 80% having upward of 15 years experience.

Given that the sample was small and not randomly selected, these findings are obviously not generalizable and should be interpreted with caution. It might be that those sergeants heard from were selected for reasons other than those that were stipulated or that the sergeants in the focus groups were less willing to adapt to the strategic elements of these reforms than less experienced supervisors who might be more receptive to change. Given these limitations, this research is best thought of as an exploratory study of strategic decision making by veteran first-line supervisors in co-implementing agencies.

An interview guide consisting of open-ended questions helped structure the focus group discussions to facilitate comparisons across sites (Morgan, 1997). Consistent with the literature on focus groups (Krueger, 1994; Morgan & Spanish, 1984), after a brief description about the purpose of the study, the focus group leader asked some introductory questions. Next was a transition to the study's main questions on how sergeants made decisions about specific crime and disorder problems. These were followed with some more general questions about the challenges of co-implementation and suggestions for how Compstat and community policing could be integrated more closely. Finally, the session ended with a summing up (to ensure an accurate representation of what was said) which also gave participants the opportunity to correct any errors or offer any final insights. In addition to covering a range of topics associated with strategic decision making, the focus group leader sought specificity by directing discussion to concrete examples and depth by way of several follow-up probes (Merton, Lowenthal, & Kendall, 1956; for a copy of the focus group instrument, see Appendix B). All of the focus groups were taped except for one which was not taped due to a technical difficulty. In this case, the focus group leader typed up his notes immediately after it ended to recall as much information as possible.

Each focus group tape was listened to at least twice and general themes were identified. Once this phase of the analysis was complete, the researcher looked for patterns, as well as any differences between them, to be sensitive to variations across sites. As the policing literature has not given much attention to the relationship between Compstat and community policing, this analysis was mostly inductive. Working back and forth between the data and the patterns in responses, the focus was on identifying the clear and consistent themes that emerged from this analysis (Patton, 2002).

The focus group guide provides the structure for the results section below so that sergeants' responses are not artificially detached from the context in which they arose. It focuses on two key questions: (a) What was the nature of the guidance that first-line supervisors received from their superiors on how to address a crime or neighborhood problem? and (b) What kind of direction did first-line supervisors give to their officers in terms of how these problems should be handled? In what follows, I begin by describing how strategic decision making should influence first-line supervision under Compstat and community according to the reform literature before examining how sergeants said it actually did operate.

⬥ Results

Guidance From Superiors to First-Line Supervisors on Crime and Neighborhood Problems

One of Compstat's principal objectives is to bend the performance of the organization to the chief executive's will, and to do this by empowering middle managers (or district commanders) to respond to the chief's direction (Weisburd et al., 2003). Regular Compstat meetings can be a powerful means of clarifying what is most valued by top leadership (reductions in serious crime) and for holding district commanders accountable for accomplishing the organization's crime control mission. To be consistent with this approach, pressure for results should show up in the kind of direction that first-line supervisors receive from their superiors. As the crime reduction efforts of district commanders are being frequently monitored and assessed, it seems reasonable to assume that they would issue specific directives about how a particular crime or neighborhood problem should be handled effectively and care about whether and how their commands were in fact implemented at the street level.

From the perspective of community policing, which devolves decision-making authority further, one would expect supervisors to receive some direction about which problems were most important to address (and many of these should be concerns identified by community members), but be given more autonomy than under Compstat (Skogan, 2006a).

There was a consensus among the focus group sergeants that the kind of guidance they received from above depended a great deal on a district commander's particular management style. However, the guidance they were most likely to receive routinely concerned the identification of a specific crime spike, trend, or pattern. On occasion, sergeants might also be told to address a community complaint, but this was less likely. Moreover, it was not customary to be given explicit instructions about how best to respond. One sergeant referred to patrol's knowledge and experience. He said that when the captain puts out a memo that says there has been a 43% increase in larcenies from autos:

> . . . he is saying, O.K. guys, you have one hundred years of experience between the three of ya' let's fix it. That is what he is doing: it is not a direct, "this is what we are going to do." He throws this thing out there. Put your heads together and figure out how we are going to resolve this issue.

In another focus group, a sergeant made a similar point about being left alone:

> The directive we get from our commander . . . when he has specific things he wants dealt with, he tells a lieutenant and it is passed down and these are usually things that are generated as a result of a complaint that he has gotten or a crime trend he has seen that he wants to make sure we are handling.

"Handling" could be as simple as the sergeant making sure that "fires were being put out," or working toward a more specific goal: "We've got 32 larcenies from autos, I want to see 18 next week." In both cases it was up to the sergeant to resolve the issue. The emphasis on addressing crime rather than disorder problems within the context of measurable results is certainly consistent with Compstat. However, the disinclination of district commanders to exert control over how first-line supervisors chose to respond is less consistent with Compstat doctrine, which seeks to harness the organization more

tightly to top management's objectives. Strengthening accountability for results is a key part of Compstat's design and how it was implemented at most of these sites. Nevertheless, research suggests that in practice Compstat encourages timely responses to crime problems, but top management is less concerned with the quality of those responses (Willis, Mastrofski, & Weisburd, 2007). Allowing sergeants to address crime problems any way they saw fit is consistent with these previous research findings. Sergeants were expected to respond to the concerns transmitted from above, but district commanders did not provide them with a carefully crafted plan about what to do because this was not a key feature of each department's Compstat's program: It was sufficient for sergeants to be doing something.

As for community policing, sergeants should be granted considerable discretion about how to mobilize but in ways that are structured to accomplish this reform's desired goals. The fact that community policing is distinguished by several objectives and approaches would seem to place an additional burden on district commanders to provide their sergeants with manageable choices, including instructions on how to judge which objectives or considerations were most important. Focus group participants did not report receiving this kind of guidance and expectations for community policing appeared much more diffuse than under Compstat (one sergeant exclaimed that he wished someone would tell him how community policing was actually defined).

Sergeants' comments suggested they were generally aware of the need to respond to community concerns, but they received little direction on the more strategic elements of this reform (e.g., problem solving and mobilizing local neighborhood resources) and their specific relationship to an overarching community-policing philosophy. Consequently, sergeants generally understood community policing as their having to demonstrate a commitment to the needs of the community and behaving courteously during individual encounters.

One of the most likely explanations for this rather limited conception was every department's decision to create specialist community-policing units rather than assigning community-policing responsibilities to all of uniformed patrol. Across sites, these specialist units comprised only a very small proportion of all officers assigned to patrol (approximately 5% to 10% in my assessment based on department records). Freed from answering 911 calls, community-policing officers were expected to respond to a wide range of minor crime problems or quality-of-life issues, thus freeing up patrol officers to respond to calls for service. Separate interviews with community-policing sergeants suggested they were much more familiar with the overall philosophy of this reform, particularly the idea that it was an organizational strategy that went beyond the kind of community relations described by the generalist patrol sergeants.

Although district commanders generally eschewed giving sergeants specific instructions on how they should mobilize, data were fundamentally important to shaping the decision of where and when to mobilize. Most important in this regard were officer reports on individual crime incidents with crime analysts paying particularly close attention to Part I crimes. Information on these data was generally disseminated electronically through reports, spreadsheets, and maps. Sergeants used these to identify which crimes were up or down and where they seemed to be concentrated. For example, one focus group member said:

> Our mall has been getting hammered pretty bad with larcenies. And just trying to remind people [her patrol officers] that this is out there, that we are getting hit pretty hard, that they are occurring between 1 and 4 o'clock in the afternoon ... get descriptions and pretty much set them on their way to go out and fight crime.

As none of these departments had implemented similarly sophisticated data systems to support community policing, sergeants did not mention receiving information that helped them systematically identify community problems, determine priorities, and document results. Consequently, sergeants tended to learn about those issues on a more ad hoc basis, such as

through communication with their district commanders and community-policing units, and by asking their patrol officers and individual citizens.

Guidance From First-Line Supervisors to Patrol Officers on Crime and Neighborhood Problems

As first-line supervisors are the "transmission belt" for translating policy into practice, it is important to know how decisions flowed down the chain-of-command (Skogan, 2008b, p. 25). One of the powerful forces shaping Compstat's inception as a crime-control approach was the concern that many patrol officers were too young and inexperienced to make decisions about how to tackle complex crime problems (Bratton & Knobler, 1998, p. 199). In contrast, community policing recognizes that the vast majority of police work is conducted by the rank and file who are regarded as a vital knowledge resource for rapidly identifying locally defined problems and helping develop local solutions (Skogan, 2006b, p. 38). What was the nature of the guidance that first-line supervisors offered to their patrol officers?

The most common theme that arose was how any form of strategic decision making among the lower ranks was strongly hindered by the demands of each department's 911 response system. Almost universally, focus group members stated that calls for service undermined their capacity to give strategic guidance to their patrol officers. As one sergeant said, "Unless there is a specific problem that has to be tackled at a particular time in a particular way, it is a matter of getting to deployment assignments when you can and between calls for service."

In response to a follow-up question, a sergeant in a different department said, "there is only so much you can do; you are tied to calls for service." Obviously when the calls were about violent crime, there was even more pressure to respond quickly. In one of the larger departments, a participant said,

> If you are in black-and-white you are going from violent crime to violent crime, to trying to handle radio calls as quickly as possible, to

going to violent crime. You don't have time to sit and just develop relationships with people all day.

Estimates of how much time the officers they supervised spent answering calls varied (approximately 40% to 50% of their time). Engaging in reactive or preventive patrol while responding to calls to intervene in those individual situations where "something-ought-not-to-be-happening and about which someone had better do something NOW!" are core features of the traditional policing model (Bittner, 1990, p. 249). Both reforms challenge this model by attempting to reallocate resources to those problems which are the most pressing. Rather than devoting substantial time and effort to dealing with all manner of citizen requests as they arise, officers should be targeting specific problems (Skogan et al., 1999, pp. 3, 35). Research in the 1970s and 1980s largely discredited the crime control benefits of this approach, but it remains a mainstay of American policing because citizens want to see patrol cars in their neighborhoods and receive timely service from police when they are summoned (Mastrofski & Willis, 2010).

The finding that Compstat's emphasis on rapid responses to crime problems that did little to promote creative solutions from district commanders or sergeants was reaffirmed when sergeants were asked to describe what kinds of approaches they expected their officers to adopt in response to crime and neighborhood problems. First-line supervisors did not mention using data to analyze problems and propose creative or innovative solutions. Rather, they wanted their officers to show that they were active or doing "something" to address crime problems and to stay busy. Just as district commanders wanted sergeants to show they were addressing the crime spikes or trends that they had identified, sergeants wanted the same from their officers.

Although it was possible that sergeants would encourage their officers to come up with creative problem-solving solutions, their comments suggested that it was more important that they engaged in activities that could be easily measured such as generating tickets and making arrests. When sergeants were asked what they wanted to see from their officers in terms of addressing specific crime problems, discussion invariably centered on a standard tool kit of law enforcement responses: location-directed patrol, traffic enforcement, and arrest. For example, in response to what he expected his officers to do to address his city's crime problems, a sergeant replied,

> Typically, I mean when you are talking about bar problems, construction area thefts, they don't demand an enormous amount of creativity in how you approach them ... you either want to be seen or you don't want to be seen. If you want to be seen, you want to patrol to increase visibility, do traffic enforcements, do bar checks.

This comment is indicative of those made by other respondents, but the context in which it is mentioned is also interesting because it reveals that these departments' focus on productivity to assess individual officer performance did little to promote problem solving. One of the challenges to community policing is that, unlike calls for service and reported crime, its accomplishments are not easily measured (Skogan, 2008a). In the focus groups, sergeants tended to emphasize traditional indicators that were easily captured by existing databases as measures of officer performance. Community-policing approaches often require that officers make artful judgments (e.g., resolving a long-standing neighborhood dispute), but, as one of the community-policing sergeants said, these are rarely documented and recorded and so are undervalued.

As mentioned earlier, from a community-policing perspective, traditional information systems of the kind used by Compstat are in many respects inadequate for the purpose of identifying and learning about many issues that concern citizens most. One means of learning about these and mobilizing accordingly is for officers to attend community meetings and work with local residents, business owners, and other neighborhood organizations to focus proactively and creatively on problems (Skogan, 2006a).

At none of the sites were patrol sergeants and their officers expected to attend regular community meetings and collaborate with community members or organizations to address neighborhood problems: this was the domain of community-policing units. As a result, first-line supervisors may have encouraged their officers to surface and respond to community problems, but this was only likely to occur on a desultory rather than a routine basis. Innovative problem solving was undermined by two additional factors: sergeants' many other responsibilities and the reluctance of each department to allow first-line supervisors to make key decisions about reallocating patrol resources.

Sergeants had to juggle their responsibility for ensuring public safety with myriad supervisory and administrative tasks. These included approving reports, cultivating morale, and helping officers advance their careers. These essential functions of first-line supervisors have not been lost on scholars or on sergeants themselves (the "boss" in Van Maanen's [1983] evocative terminology; p. 275). There was consensus among participants that sergeants were indispensable, with one capturing this sentiment when he said, "a sergeant is probably the most important position in the whole department." At the same time, these administrative burdens meant sergeants did not have time to innovate by drawing on knowledge gained in other departments and innovations in theory and research about crime control and prevention.

Another essential element of the problem-solving process is increasing a department's capacity to move resources to where a problem is and to change or disrupt department routines to do this. Although sergeants acknowledged that they had significant autonomy in deciding how to respond to problems in their beats, they also mentioned that this was not as extensive when it came to the reallocation of resources. Although they may have been allowed to approve overtime, any "special" or unusual requests (e.g., putting an officer in plainclothes, asking officers to work on their days off), or those that demanded a change to how resources were routinely allocated (e.g., coming up with an operational plan that required freeing several

officers from answering calls for service), required approval from the district commander.

In summary, at these sites a variety of factors conspired to limit the capacity of sergeants to engage in the kind of innovative problem solving that is regarded as a hallmark of both Compstat and community policing. Some of these were related to features of the programs as they had been implemented, such as Compstat's focus on rapid responses to crime and the absence of structured problem-solving partnerships with community members, but other factors were features of general police organization. Across sites, the traditional 911 service and existing performance systems did little to support innovation.

 Discussion

According to their supporters, both Compstat and community policing promise to transform police organizations radically, particularly in terms of making them respond strategically to crime and disorder problems. Given the central role that sergeants play in implementing these reforms at the street level, it would seem reasonable to expect to see significant changes at this rank. These focus groups, however, indicated a pattern of practices that did not readily fit with the idealized models of either Compstat or community policing. As these sergeants were purposively selected within departments that had assigned primary community-policing responsibilities to specialist units, these sites cannot represent the experiences of all co-implementing departments. However, the patterns described here provide some valuable insights into how these specific reforms operated and into police reform more generally.

The unevenness of co-implementation can be explained by each department continuing to stress features of police organizations that are most consistent with goals that have long been embraced by top police managers: fighting crime, centralizing decision-making authority, and responding to calls for service (National Research Council, 2004). Those elements of these reforms that represented the greatest departure from past management and supervisory ideals—community involvement in the production of police priorities and of responses to crime and neighborhood problems, devolving decision-making authority to the rank and file, and innovative problem solving—remained the least developed.

The most noticeable influence of these reforms on sergeants' decision making was guidance and the use of crime data for the rapid identification of serious crime problems. Sergeants were most likely to receive instruction from their superiors on crime trends and patterns. Moreover, sergeants also relied on these Compstat data to make decisions about where and when to focus patrol resources. Similar data systems were not in place for incidents of minor crime and social disorders, no doubt hampering sergeants' ability to conceive of community policing in more strategic terms, or as an approach designed to "address the causes and reduce the fear of crime and social disorder" (Scheider, Chapman, & Schapiro, 2009). Rather, sergeants tended to think of community policing as synonymous with the kind of "service-style" policing first identified by James Q. Wilson in the late 1960s (Wilson, 1968).

There was not an opportunity to observe these departments before Compstat and community policing were implemented, but based on respondents' comments during these site visits, these changes were significant. Crime analysis had come to play an integral role in police operations, particularly when it came to allocating resources to hot spots. Research shows that focusing patrol on areas where crime is concentrated can have significant crime reduction benefits (Braga & Weisburd, 2010). In addition, increasing the responsiveness of the police to the communities they serve has long been a core goal of community policing, and sergeants seemed to value the kind of customer service approach that this evokes (Mastrofski, 1999).

Despite the incorporation of these reform features into sergeants' decision-making routines, co-implementation had fallen short of its strategic promise. The reason for this is a mainstay of the literature on police organizational change (Maguire, 1997; Mastrofski, 2006; Mastrofski & Willis, 2010; Sadd & Grinc, 1994; Skogan, 2006a). Significant change requires

that police organizations go beyond programs and activities, by putting new organizational structures in place (Skogan, 2006a, p. 29). The sites here, however, were either unwilling or unable to do so, preferring to implement a specialist community-policing model which insulated them from making more radical changes. Envisioning what form these changes might have taken and their implications for first-line supervision is a useful way of assessing the lack of change that actually did take place. It also helps identify policy-relevant strategies for how first-line supervision could be harnessed more directly to the goals of these reforms. A recent article making recommendations for integrating Compstat and community policing is instructive here, because its suggestions are readily adapted to first-line supervision (Willis, Mastrofski, & Kochel, 2010a).

Creating performance measures at the organizational level to systematically identify and prioritize community concerns could help reinforce the fundamental importance of community policing's strategic mission to key decision makers, including sergeants. So, for example, departments might require that community-identified problems are routinely reported at Compstat meetings to focus the department on community-policing priorities (a practice we did not observe). Prioritizing and reporting community-policing concerns in this way would help focus and clarify their essential importance to the organization's core mission.

This approach could be further supported by an individual performance evaluation system that put less emphasis on traditional police responses and provides more incentives to engage in problem solving. Requiring sergeants to assess regularly the level of creativity of their officers in response to persistent crime and disorder problems, especially those identified by community members and not just those identified by the police, could help promote the kind of innovative thinking called for by both reforms.

Moreover, assigning patrol officers to permanent beat teams supervised by patrol sergeants and delegating responsibilities to these teams and not to community-policing units might increase accountability for community policing and problem solving across the organization. These teams could be made responsible for meeting with community members regularly and working with them to identify their most pressing concerns and figuring out the best ways to respond. Similar to Compstat's accountability mechanism, sergeants would experience accountability by having to demonstrate their understanding of the community's problems and the progress they were making in front of an audience of local residents and business owners directly invested in operational outcomes.

To be most effective, this would require that sergeants and patrol officers (and possibly community members) receive adequate training in the basic skills of problem solving. This would mean sergeants and their beat teams learning (a) when and how to identify a problem; (b) how to make reasonable suggestions for addressing it based on knowledge of the beat, conversations with stakeholders, and input from crime analysts; and (c) how to report on results of problem-solving efforts at community meetings. As part of this process, officers could be trained in the well-known SARA (scanning, analysis, response, and assessment) and crime triangle problem-solving models and could be introduced to other problem-solving resources, such as POP (problem-oriented policing) guides.

Perhaps most important for the successful realization of the strategic vision articulated by reformers would have been for departments to reorganize how daily work was assigned and managed by making changes to their 911 systems. Chicago, for example, assigns a team of officers to handle low priority calls thereby freeing up other officers that first-line supervisors can then reassign to tackle persistent crime or disorder problems (Skogan, 2006a, pp. 56–59). Such changes are costly and raise many other challenges, only one of which can be addressed here based on feedback from the focus groups. Would patrol sergeants have been interested in moving away from the specialist approach that characterized co-implementation in their agencies? Given that recent surveys of law enforcement organizations in the United States suggest that such a specialization approach is very popular, this is an important issue (Reaves, 2010, p. 27).

The sergeants in the focus groups were divided over whether primary responsibility for the implementation of community policing should fall to uniformed patrol or specialist officers. Generalist patrol officers were more likely than sergeants assigned to specialist community-policing units to support a specialist approach. Thus, we heard the following comments:

> The most effective way of community policing that we have ever done, is to generate specialist units to deal with the problem; when there are 1 or 2 folks available, they join in to be part of it ... If you have one or two officers free, do you feel like going off and tackling a problem by yourself ... no ... but if you have a group of officers, you kind of join in.

And,

> Retain traditional policing—clear chain-of-command, clear designation of supervision—*couple* that with specialized units to focus on problems: under-cover teams, specialist assignment teams. (Emphasis in original)

Alternatively, a sergeant assigned to a community-policing unit in another department, one that had disbanded a community-policing approach based on geographic decentralization, said: "What is lost is COPS. If I am deploying people out differently each day, there is no tie-in and development of relationships within the community, and ownership and even accountability to some degree."

If these comments are any indication of the sentiments shared by others in these departments and further afield, many officers' hearts and minds would have to be won for the successful implementation of a less specialized community-policing approach.

Conclusion

In closing, it might be useful to speculate whether these focus groups reveal a larger trend in U.S. policing where Compstat and community policing, despite the warnings of their supporters, are defined by their activities rather than as a fundamental transformation in how police departments operate (Silverman, 2006; Skogan, 2006a). Future research might examine this issue further, perhaps comparing first-line supervision in co-implementing departments with Compstat or community-policing-only agencies. If what was found in these focus groups characterizes U.S. policing more generally, reformers might consider experimenting with the recommendations described above that could strengthen strategic

decision making by first-line supervisors under both reforms. Of course, until these are tested there is no way to know if they would work as intended, but given that much hope and effort has been invested in these reforms, these suggestions might be worth considering. What is clearer is that in the absence of changes designed to work to the mutual benefit of Compstat and community policing, it seems likely that the strategic potential of co-implementation will remain more contingent upon the will and skill of individual sergeants than reformers might realize.

 ## Appendix A: Profile of Participating Police Departments

| Police department | Population[a] | Police officers[a] | | Part I crime statistics[a] | | Community indicators | | CP start date | CS start date |
		Sworn	Civilian	Violent crime	Property crime	Median household income[b]	% unemployed[c]		
Los Angeles, California	3,879,455	9,393	3,292	787	2,718	US$44,445	4.7	1990s	2003
Montgomery County, Maryland	932,131	1,211	440	231	2,484	US$87,624	3.7	1992	1995
Colorado Springs, Colorado	376,807	681	313	569	4,797	US$50,892	3.7	1992	2003
St. Louis County, Missouri	331,489[d]	753[d]	250[d]	124	1,054	US$53,186	4.5	1991	1991
Overland Park, Kansas	165,975	240	54	200	2,736	US$68,404	3.9	1995	2001
Cape Coral, Florida	142,371	209	124	285	3,447	US$54,026	3.3	2002	2002
Marietta, Georgia	63,228	136	32	633	4,147	US$40,645[e]	4.0	1997	2000

Note: CP = community policing; CS = Compstat.

a. Federal Bureau of Investigation (2006).

b. U.S. Census Bureau (2006). 2006 inflation-adjusted dollars.

c. Bureau of Labor Statistics, April 2007. For areas in a larger MSA area, these data are presented.

d. These data were collected from the St. Louis County Police Department Fact Sheet (2004). The population is for the jurisdictions served by the police department.

e. 2000 data; Marietta's 2006 data are unavailable.

Appendix B: Focus Group Guide

1. Introduction (Who we are, why we are visiting).

2. Goal: Learn from you—learn about how you make decisions and how you and your officers spend your time. Using a focus group because this allows us to hear a variety of perspectives on decision making within the department—it also allows us to hear many opinions in a short time.

3. Logistics: Informed consent—voluntary, no benefit, won't be identifying you in the final report, and will be taping.

4. Helpful ground rules:
   a. Please contribute, even if your perspective differs from others.
   b. There are no right answers here, so please feel free to speak your mind.
   c. It is helpful for me if you can provide specific examples of your experiences.

5. My role is to facilitate discussion—keep it on track and encouraging everyone to speak—I've got one shot at this, so my primary interest is getting as much information from you as possible.

6. To get things moving—would you complete the name tents by writing your name on one side and then writing your contact information on the back (shift, current assignment, how many officers you currently supervise, contact information). Once you have done that perhaps we could go round the table and you could:
   - Introduce yourself
   - Tell us your shift
   - No. of officers that work under your direct supervision
   - How long you've been with the PD
   - % of time on average shift that you estimate your officers spend on calls for service.

   - I know you have numerous administrative tasks like reading and signing reports, attending meetings, and giving advice to patrol officers but here I am interested in how you spend your time when dealing with crime and neighborhood/quality-of-life problems.

7. Perhaps you could think about the last time you got guidance or direction from a superior on how to deal with a crime or neighborhood problem. What was the nature of that guidance?
   a. What do you think caused your superior to give you guidance in this case?
   b. How detailed was the guidance? (Priority or degree of importance? Time? Place? Location?)

8. Over say, the past week, perhaps you could talk about a specific crime problem that you have been working on. How was this identified? What kinds of things have you been doing to deal with it?
   - What kinds of activities have you asked your officers to do?
     a. How often?
     b. What spurs?
     c. How detailed? (Priority/degree of importance? Time? Place? Location? How to respond?)

9. When not responding to calls, what kinds of things do you expect your officers to be doing in response to crime and neighborhood problems?

10. To what extent is crime analysis helpful in how you deal with crime problems?

11. In your mind, how well do CS and CP work together? What are some of the challenges that have arisen? What about the benefits?

12. Finally, what recommendations do you have for improving how these programs work together?

13. To finish let me summarize some of the main points—Is that accurate? Is there anything you would like to add or change?

Notes

1. The primary focus here is on first-line supervisors in charge of patrol officers. The terms *first-line/front-line/patrol supervisors* and *sergeants* are used interchangeably.

2. The research literature identifies an additional three elements of co-implementation: internal accountability, organizational flexibility, and external accountability. These are fully described elsewhere, including the main compatibility issues (Willis, Kochel, & Mastrofski, 2010). Some reference is made to these other elements in the Results section of this article, but they are not the main focus.

3. Colorado Springs Police Department, Colorado.

References

Allen, D. (1982). Police supervision on the street: An analysis of supervisor/officer interaction during the shift. *Journal of Criminal Justice, 10*, 91–109.

Bayley, D. (1994). *Police for the future*. New York, NY: Oxford University Press.

Bittner, E. (1990). Florence Nightingale in pursuit of Willie Sutton: A theory of police. In *Aspects of police work* (pp. 233–268). Boston, MA: Northeastern University Press.

Braga, A., & Weisburd, D. (2010). *Policing problem places: Crime hot spots and effective crime prevention*. New York, NY: Oxford University Press.

Bratton, W., & Knobler, P. (1998). *Turnaround: How America's top cop reversed the crime epidemic*. New York, NY: Random House.

Clarke, R. V. (2004). Defining police strategies: Problem solving, problem-oriented policing, and community-oriented policing. In Q. C. Thurman & J. Zhao (Eds.), *Contemporary policing: Controversies, challenges, and solutions* (pp. 18–38). Los Angeles, CA: Roxbury.

Cordner, G., & Biebel, E. (2005). Problem-oriented policing in practice. *Criminology & Public Policy, 4*, 155–180.

Dabney, D. (2010). Observations regarding key operational realities in a Compstat model. *Justice Quarterly, 27*(1), 28–51.

Eck, J., & Spelman, W. (1987). *Problem-solving: Problem-oriented policing in Newport News*. Washington, DC: Police Executive Research Forum.

Engel, R. (2002). Patrol officer supervision in the community policing era. *Journal of Criminal Justice, 30*, 51–64.

Eterno, J. A., & Silverman, E. B. (2006). The NYPD's Compstat: Compare statistics or compose statistics. *Policing: An International Journal of Police Science & Management, 12*, 426–449.

Federal Bureau of Investigation. (2006). *Crime in America*. Retrieved from http://www.fbi.gov/about-us/cjis/ucr/crime-in-the-u.s/2006/crime2006

Goldstein, H. (1987). Improving policing: A problem-oriented approach. *Crime & Delinquency, 25*, 236–58l.

Henry, V. E. (2002). *The COMPSTAT paradigm: Management accountability in policing, business, and the public sector*. Flushing, NY: Looseleaf.

Kelling, G. L., & Moore, M. H. (1988). From political to reform to community: The evolving strategy of police. In J. R. Greene & S. D. Mastrofski (Eds.), *Community policing: Rhetoric or reality* (pp. 3–26) New York, NY: Praeger.

Kim, W. C., & Mauborgne, R. (2003, April). Tipping point leadership. *Harvard Business Review*, 1–12. Retrieved from https://archive.harvardbusiness.org/cla/web/pl/product.seam?c=14017&i=14019&cs=61e2b53cc3609b79d96c08525d9b1a19

Krueger, R. (1994). *Focus groups: A practical guide for applied research*. Thousand Oaks, CA: SAGE.

Maguire, E. R. (1997). Structural change in large municipal police organizations during the community policing era. *Justice Quarterly, 14*, 547–576.

Maguire, E. R., & Mastrofski, S. D. (2000). Patterns of community policing in the United States. *Police Quarterly, 3*(1), 4–45.

Manning, P. K. (1977). *Police work: The social organization of policing*. Cambridge, MA: MIT Press.

Maple, J., & Mitchell, C. (1999). *The crime fighter: Putting the bad guys out of business*. New York, NY: Doubleday.

Mastrofski, S. D. (1999). *Ideas in American policing: Policing for people*. Washington, DC: Police Foundation.

Mastrofski, S. D. (2006). *Community policing: A skeptical view in Police Innovation: Contrasting Perspectives* (pp. 44–73). Cambridge, UK: Cambridge University Press.

Mastrofski, S. D., & Willis, J. J. (2010). Police organization continuity and change: Into the twenty-first century. In M. Tonry (Ed.), *Crime and justice: A review of research* (pp. 55–144). Oxford, UK: Oxford University Press.

McDonald, P., Greenberg, S., & Bratton, W. (2002). *Managing police operations: Implementing the New York crime control model—Compstat*. Belmont, CA: Wadsworth.

Merton, R. K., Lowenthal, M. F., & Kendall, P. L. (1956). *The focused interview: A manual of problems and procedures*. New York, NY: Free Press.

Moore, M. H. (1992). Problem solving and community policing. In M. Tonry & N. Morris (Eds.), *Modern policing* (pp. 95–158). Chicago, IL: University of Chicago Press.

Morgan, D. L. (1997). *Focus groups as qualitative research*. Thousand Oaks, CA: SAGE.

Morgan, D. L., & Spanish, M. T. (1984). Focus groups: A new tool for qualitative research. *Qualitative Sociology, 7*, 253–270.

National Research Council. (2004). Fairness and effectiveness in policing: The evidence. Committee to Review Research on Police Policy and Practices. In W. Skogan & K. Frydll (Eds.), *Committee on Law and Justice, Division of Behavioral and Social Sciences and Education*. Washington, DC: The National Academies Press.

Patton, M. Q. (2002). *Qualitative research and evaluation methods*. New York, NY: SAGE.

Peak, K., & Glensor, R. W. (1999). *Community Policing and Problem Solving: Strategies and Practices*. Upper Saddle River, NJ: Prentice Hall.

Ratcliffe, J. (2002). Intelligence-led policing and the problems of turning rhetoric into practice. *Policing & Society, 12*, 53–66.

Reaves, B. A. (2010). *Local police departments, 2007*. Washington, DC: Bureau of Justice Statistics.

Reisig, M. (2010). Community and problem-oriented policing. In M. Tonry (Ed.), *Crime and justice: A review of research* (pp. 1–53). Chicago, IL: University of Chicago Press.

Rosenbaum, D. (Ed.). (1994). *The challenge of community policing: Testing the promises*. Newbury Park, CA: SAGE.

Rubinstein, J. (1973). *City police*. New York, NY: Farrar, Straus, and Giroux.

Sadd, S., & Grinc, R. (1994). Innovative neighborhood oriented policing: An evaluation of community policing programs in eight cities. In D. P. Rosenbaum (Ed.), *The challenge of community policing: Testing the promises* (pp. 27–52). Thousand Oaks, CA: SAGE.

Scheider, M., Chapman, R., & Schapiro, A. (2009). Toward the unification of police innovations under community policing. *Policing: An International Journal of Police Strategies & Management, 32*, 694–718.

Silverman, E. B. (1999). *NYPD battles crime: Innovative strategies in policing*. Boston, MA: Northeastern University Press.

Silverman, E. B. (2006). Compstat's innovation. In D. Weisburd & A. Braga (Eds.), *Police innovation: Contrasting perspectives* (pp. 267–283). Cambridge, UK: Cambridge University Press.

Silverman, E. B., & O'Connell, P. (1999). Organizational change and decision making in the New York City Police Department: A case study. *International Journal of Public Administration, 22*, 217–259.

Skogan, W. G. (2006a). *Police and community in Chicago: A tale of three cities*. New York, NY: Oxford University Press.

Skogan, W. G. (2006b). The Promise of community policing. In D. Weisburd & A. Braga (Eds.), *Police innovation: Contrasting perspectives* (pp. 27–43). Cambridge, UK: Cambridge University Press.

Skogan, W. G. (2008a). An overview of community policing: Origins, concepts, and implementation. In T. Williamson (Ed.), *The handbook of knowledge-based policing: Current conceptions and future directions* (pp. 43–57). Chichester, UK: John Wiley.

Skogan, W. G. (2008b). Why reforms fail. *Policing & Society, 18*, 23–34.

Timoney, J. F. (2010). *From beat cop to top cop: A tale of three cities*. Philadelphia, PA: University of Pennsylvania Press.

Skogan, W. G. (Ed.). (2004). *Community policing: Can it work?* Belmont, CA: Wadsworth.

Skogan, W. G., & Hartnett, S. M. (1997). *Community policing: Chicago style*. New York, NY: Oxford University Press.

Skogan, W. G., Hartnett, S. M., DuBois, J., Comey, J. T., Kaiser, M., & Lovig, J. (1999). *On the beat: Police and community problem solving*. Boulder, CO: Westview.

Trojanowicz, R. (1980). *The environment of the first-line police supervisor*. Englewood Cliffs, NJ: Prentice Hall.

Trojanowicz, R., & Bucqueroux, B. (1990). *Community policing: A contemporary perspective*. Cincinnati, OH: Anderson.

U.S. Census Bureau (2006). www.census.gov

Van Maanen, J. (1983). The boss: First-line supervision in an American police agency. In M. Punch (Ed.), *Control in the police organization* (pp. 275–317). Cambridge, MA: MIT Press.

Weisburd, D., & Braga, A. (Eds.). (2006). Introduction. *Police innovation: Contrasting perspectives* (pp. 1–23). Cambridge, UK: Cambridge University Press.

Weisburd, D., Mastrofski, S. D., McNally, A. M., Greenspan, R., & Willis, J. J. (2003). Reforming to preserve: Compstat and strategic problem solving in American policing. *Criminology & Public Policy, 2*, 421–456.

Weisburd, D., & McElroy, J. (1988). Enacting the CPO role: Findings from the New York City Pilot Program in community policing. In J. R. Greene & S. D. Mastrofski (Eds.), *Community policing: Rhetoric or reality* (pp. 89–102). New York, NY: Praeger.

Willis, J. J., Kochel, T. R., & Mastrofski, S. D. (2010). *The co-implementation of Compstat and community policing: A national assessment* (Final report). Washington, DC: U.S. Department of Justice, Office of Community Oriented Policing Services.

Willis, J. J., Mastrofski, S. D., & Kochel, T. R. (2010a). Recommendations for integrating Compstat and community policing. *Policing: A Journal of Policy and Practice, 4*, 182–193.

Willis, J. J., Mastrofski, S. D., & Kochel, T. R. (2010b). The co-implementation of Compstat and community policing. *Journal of Criminal Justice, 38*, 969–980.

Willis, J. J., Mastrofski, S. D., & Weisburd, D. (2007). Making sense of COMPSTAT: A theory-based analysis of organizational change in three police departments. *Law & Society Review, 41*, 147–188.

Wilson, J. Q. (1968). *Varieties of police behavior*. Cambridge, MA: Harvard University Press.

DISCUSSION QUESTIONS

1. How are COMPSTAT and community policing similar? How are they different?

2. Why is it important to decipher the extent to which first-line supervisors adopt practices such as COMPSTAT and community policing?

3. How could the findings from this study influence the training of first-line supervisors?

READING 12

Arthur Niederhoffer discusses a variety of issues related to police officers working in the urban areas in his classic book, *Behind the Badge: The Police in Urban Society*. Several excerpts from his book are included in the following section; all of the excerpts focus on police cynicism. Niederhoffer explains the process by which officers become cynical, how cynicism impacts them at various stages in their careers, and some of the consequences of police officers becoming cynical toward members of the public. This is the first study of police cynicism conducted in the United States.

Anomie and Cynicism

Arthur Niederhoffer

Seventy years ago, Emile Durkheim introduced the term *anomie*. To the sociologist, *anomie* is a morbid condition of society characterized by the absence of standards, by apathy, confusion, frustration, alienation, and despair. Other behavioral sciences designate *anomie* as anomia, alienation, self-estrangement, forlornness, anxiety, cultural desolation, or noögenic neurosis.

Policemen with a philosophical or analytical bent are well aware of the threat of *anomie* in their world. They have their own idiosyncratic manner of describing it. One retired police officer, who was a supervisor in the Washington, D.C., Metropolitan Police Force, remarks:

> Among the problems that beset police officers, one concerns the emotional or psychological crisis which seems to come to every active and sincere policeman. . . .
>
> I have seen good men completely ruined by the hopeless feeling. I have seen many become worthless to their Department, to their community and to themselves. Worse yet, I have seen some few turn crooked. . . . I don't know how much can be done about this problem in writing about it rather than talking about it with the men who are in danger, so that they would recognize this mental— perhaps it might even be called spiritual

miasma that seems to hit too many good policemen. . . .

> The second phase of this problem is much more serious and much more widespread than the loss suffered by resignation. It is an insidious thing, all the more dangerous because it is not at once evident and apparent. It is similar to cancer.

The elements of this syndrome are loss of faith in people, of enthusiasm for the high ideals of police work, and of pride and integrity.

Anomie occurs particularly when the old values of a social system are being supplanted by a new code— exactly the case in the police organization. Seeking to wrest control from the old regime, the professionals are introducing a new ethic into the modern police force which is undermining old norms and loyalties. Caught between these contending forces, the policeman in the lower ranks feels uncertain of his position. The more professionalism becomes the predominant ethic, the greater each policeman's drive for advancement, and his disappointment at failure. There is also a parallel frustration when the public refuses to accord the force the professional status it desires.

According to Durkheim, the control exerted by law and morality creates a sense of social solidarity and is thus a safeguard against *anomie*. At first impression it would appear that above all other groups the police ought to be tied to the law, but because they learn to manipulate it, the law can become nothing but a means to an end. In performing his special role in the social system, the policeman realizes that for much of his time on duty he is above the law. Paradoxically, society has granted him the license to disregard the law in order to enforce it. He may kill [when] necessary, he may destroy property and invade privacy; he may make arrests merely on grounds of suspicion; he may disregard traffic regulations. The sense of power often corrupts him into a belief that he is superior to the law.

The policeman is also set apart because he has the power to regulate the life of others, a role symbolized by his distinctive weapons and uniform; likewise his constant dealing with crime may encourage him to view policemen as superior to the general race of men. As Westley indicates, it is difficult for policemen to keep faith in mankind:

> The policeman's world is spawned of degradation, corruption and insecurity. He sees men as ill-willed, exploitative, mean and dirty; himself a victim of injustice, misunderstood and defiled.
>
> He tends to meet those portions of the public which are acting contrary to the law or using the law to further their own ends. He is exposed to public immorality. He becomes cynical. His is a society emphasizing the crooked, the weak and the unscrupulous. Accordingly his morality is one of expediency and his self-conception one of a martyr.

 ## The Relation of Cynicism and Anomie

Robert K. Merton's widely acclaimed sociological model classifies the major types of adjustment to *anomie* as conformity, innovation, ritualism, retreatism, and rebellion. Another possibility prefigured by Nietzsche and Scheler, which Merton suggested in a footnote, is known as *ressentiment,* roughly translated as resentment, although in Merton's opinion, "no

English word fully reproduces the complex of elements implied by the word *ressentiment."*

This complex sentiment has three interlocking elements. First, diffuse feelings of hate, envy, and hostility; second, a sense of being powerless to express these feelings actively against the person or social stratum evoking them; and third, a continual re-experiencing of this impotent hostility. The essential point distinguishing *ressentiment* from rebellion is that the former does not involve a genuine change in values. *Ressentiment* involves a sour-grapes pattern which asserts merely that desired but unattainable objectives do not actually embody the prized values.

In the police system the typical adaptation to *anomie* is cynicism. Like *ressentiment* it consists of diffuse feelings of hate and envy, impotent hostility, and the sour-grapes pattern, and is used in this study to refer to a state of mind in which the *anomie* of the police organization as a whole is reflected in the individual policeman.

In the police world, cynicism is discernible at all levels, in every branch of law enforcement. It has also characterized police in other times and places. During the French Revolution and then under Napoleon, Joseph Fouche, the minister of police, concluded that with a few exceptions the world was composed of scoundrels, hypocrites, and imbeciles. Many years later, reviewing the American police scene in 1939, Read Bain found that policemen were committed to the belief that the citizen was always trying "to get away with something," and that all men would commit crimes except for the fear of the police.

In an interview conducted by the Center for the Study of Democratic Institutions, the late Chief William Parker of the Los Angeles Police Department was asked, "Are you inclined to be pessimistic about the future of our society?"

> I look back [he replied] over almost thirty-five years in the police service, thirty-five years of dealing with the worst that humanity has to offer. I meet the failures of humanity daily, and I meet them in the worst possible context. It is hard to keep an objective viewpoint. But it is also hard for me to believe that our society can

continue to violate all the fundamental rules of human conduct and expect to survive. I think I have to conclude that this civilization will destroy itself, as others have before it. That leaves, then, only one question—when?

A female store detective, with fifteen years of police experience to support her conclusions, states emphatically, "I am convinced that we are turning into a nation of thieves. I have sadly concluded that nine out of ten persons are dishonest."

As noted before, it is possible to distinguish between two kinds of police cynicism. One is directed against life, the world, and people in general; the other is aimed at the police system itself. The first is endemic to policemen of all ranks and persuasions—including the professionals. The second, common among patrolmen, is by definition excluded from the ideology of the professional policeman. The professional wants to transform and eventually control the system. This hope keeps him from cynicism.

Cynicism may be a by-product of *anomie* in the social structure; at the same time it may also prepare the way for personal *anomie* or anomia. Anxious over a personal failure, the individual policeman often disguises his feelings with a cynical attitude, and thus negates the value of the prize he did not attain. Frequently he includes in his cynicism all persons who still seek that prize or have succeeded in winning it, and, occasionally, deprecates the entire social system within which the failure occurred.

As the cynic becomes increasingly pessimistic and misanthropic, he finds it easier to reduce his commitment to the social system and its values. If the patrolman remains a "loner," his isolation may lead to psychological *anomie* and even to suicide.

Anomie is not the inevitable outcome of police cynicism. Instead a policeman may be absorbed by the "delinquent" occupational subculture, dedicated to a philosophy of cynicism. This group may be deviant, but it is not anomic. It has a code of values and a clear, consistent ideology that function well in the police world. The members may be alienated from their former groups and goals, but they can be completely incorporated into this new reference group.

The third adaptation to cynicism is to overcome it, to regain commitment to the ideal of a decent and honorable career within the police force. Typically, there are two critical points in the advanced career of a policeman when he may discard cynicism. One crisis occurs when he considers retrospectively the many risks his career has involved. Fearing investigation, he may surrender his disaffection and resolve to do his job to the best of his ability. The second opportunity for reassessment comes when a man who is near retirement seeks another job and is often rebuffed. When this happens, a policeman's present situation understandably will seem more attractive to him.

The process leading to cynicism and *anomie* may be viewed as a continuum stretching from commitment at one end to *anomie* at the other, with cynicism as the critical intervening stage. Since police professionals are committed to the highest ideals of police work, they belong at the commitment end; the cynics around the opposite pole. The following model illustrates the typical stages that succeed one another as the policeman moves from commitment to cynicism and *anomie*.

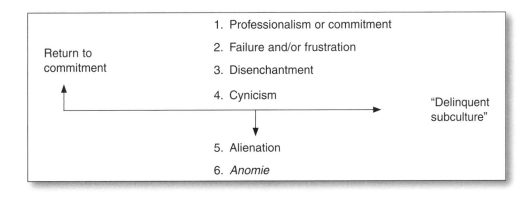

Differences in the patterns of cynicism are apparently related to a policeman's age and experience. The following classification scheme indicates that there is a succession of typical stages in the growth of cynicism that runs parallel to the occupational career.

The preliminary stage, pseudo-cynicism, is recognizable among recruits at the training school. This attitude barely conceals the idealism and commitment beneath the surface.

The second stage, romantic cynicism, is reached in the first five years of the police career. The most idealistic young members of the force are precisely the ones who are most disillusioned by actual police work, and most vulnerable to this type of cynicism.

The third stage, aggressive cynicism, depends on the conjunction of individual cynicism and the subculture of cynicism. It corresponds to *ressentiment* because resentment and hostility become obvious in this period, most prevalent at the ten year mark.

In the last few years of the police career, resigned cynicism replaces the former, more blatant type. This detachment may be passive and apathetic or express itself as a form of mellow if mild good will. It accepts and comes to terms with the flaws of the system.

Because these stages represent ideal types, there will probably be practical variations in style and degree.

Cynicism as an orientation to life depends for proof of its existence upon inferences drawn from human behavior. I have included descriptive material that indicates the likelihood of a correlation between police work and cynicism.

A more acceptable method is what Kenneth Clark has termed that of the "involved observer." Because I was a policeman for more than twenty years, and have read a large portion of the police literature, I am convinced that there is a great deal of cynicism among my former colleagues.

Although the study was completed toward the end of 1962, I believe that the tests of the following hypotheses are more than ever valid today.

1. For the first few years of a police career one's degree of cynicism will increase in proportion to his length of service, but it will tend to level off at some point between the fifth and tenth year of service. Generally, cynicism is learned as part of socialization into the police occupation, a process likely to take at least five years.

2. Newly appointed men will show less cynicism than more seasoned Police Academy recruits. In turn, the recruit group will be less cynical than the more experienced patrolmen: not only will the average degree of cynicism be lower, but there will be fewer cynics in the group.

3. Superior officers will be less cynical than patrolmen. According to our theory, cynicism is commonly a mode of adaptation to frustration. Cynicism should therefore vary positively according to the degree of failure and frustration. Men in the lower ranks have more reason to feel frustrated than do their superiors.

4. Among patrolmen, those with college educations will reveal a higher level of cynicism than other patrolmen because their expectations for promotion (still unfulfilled) were greater.

5. Patrolmen with preferred assignments (details) will be less cynical than other patrolmen.

6. Because foot patrolmen are of low status, they will be more cynical than patrolmen assigned to other duties.

7. Patrolmen who receive awards for meritorious duty will be less cynical. Patrolmen who are the subjects of departmental charges (complaints) will be more cynical.

8. Jewish patrolmen will be more cynical than non-Jewish patrolmen. Jewish tradition stresses that true success in life lies in becoming a professional man. A Jewish policeman

who remains a patrolman is thus a double failure: he did not become a doctor or lawyer, and he has been unable to rise from the low rank of patrolman.

9. When members of the force have served for seventeen or eighteen years, and are approaching retirement, they will exhibit less cynicism. When policemen near retirement search for employment outside the police system, they find opportunities distinctly limited. As a result, their appreciation of, and commitment to the police occupation revives.

10. Members of the Vice Squad will be more cynical than members of the Youth Division. The specific work situation within the organization plays its part in shaping attitudes.

11. Middle-class patrolmen will be less cynical than working-class patrolmen. Their receptivity to professionalism should insulate against cynicism. The middle-class ethic is more sympathetic to the ideas of professionalism than is the ideology of the working class.

The Sample

The sample consisted of 220 policemen. Thirty-four of them had been newly appointed and were, so to speak, a "naive" group that was used as a control. The next major segment was composed of 60 probationary patrolmen, referred to as recruits. They had two or three months of experience and were still attending the police training school. The rest of the sample included 84 patrolmen, 15 detectives, and 27 superior officers from the ranks of sergeant and lieutenant.

It is my belief that the sample represented a fair cross section of an urban police department. The responses were, if anything, weighted in favor of professionalism.

Findings

Of the eleven hypotheses, eight are supported by the data, several of them with statistically significant results. Three of them (5, 10, 11) could not be properly evaluated owing to insufficient information. The variables postulated as significant in the etiology of police cynicism affected the results in the predicted direction. These variables were length of service, degree of frustration, and Jewish background. Corollaries were promotion, education, and number of awards.

There were two striking unanticipated results, extraneous to the hypotheses. The first surprise was that the seven unmarried patrolmen scored highest of all. Do policemen's wives affect their husband's attitudes toward their occupation? Perhaps the degree of uxoriousness should be studied as a variable.

The other peculiar feature was the factor of age. In inter-group comparisons age did not show any consistent pattern of effects. In intra-group analysis, however, the younger half of every group scored higher in cynicism than the older half. Length of service was not a question because the same trend obtained in the control and recruit groups. Whatever the effect of the age factor was, it was subordinate to and controlled by the other variables upon which the hypotheses were constructed.

DISCUSSION QUESTIONS

1. What is cynicism?

2. What are some of the factors that influence the extent to which police officers become cynical?

3. What stage in a police officer's career was identified as the time when cynicism appears to peak?

Motorcycle patrol units are a popular and cost-efficient way conduct patrol.

Patrol, Investigations, and Innovations in Technology

P olice officers participate in a wide range of activities while providing service to the public. Many of these activities, including patrol and investigation, have been integral parts of American policing since the early 1900s. Any changes to police activities over time have been the result of advances in technology, individual agencies choosing to alter police procedures, changes that have been mandated as a result of court case outcomes, or changes to law. This section covers some of the police activities that take place on a typical shift; more specifically, this section examines how police officers spend their time. This section presents two activities that are central to policing in the United States: patrol and criminal investigation. Types of patrol (car, foot, etc.) and patrol strategies (routine preventive patrol, directed patrol, etc.) are discussed. The steps of the criminal investigation process are identified, in addition to factors that influence the effort and prioritization of criminal cases by investigators. Finally, advances in technology have provided police officers with additional tools to help them with their work. The adoption and potential problems related to such technologies are examined in this section.

What Do the Police Do With Their Time?

It is likely that the public's perception of what the police do with their time does not reflect what the police *actually* do on any given shift. This is especially the case if the public believes what is presented to them on reality television programs, such as *COPS*. This type of television program leads the public to believe that the police are constantly responding to calls for service, one after another, with little lag time in between calls, and that every call for service involves danger and excitement.

In reality, everyday police activities do not mirror those presented on television. In fact, what the police actually do with their time is quite different than what is often portrayed on television. Studies have found that during a typical shift, patrol officers have a substantial amount of time during which they are not responding to calls for service from the public (we will call this unassigned time). Recently, Stephen Mastrofski and his colleagues conducted a study on this topic in Indianapolis, Indiana, and St. Petersburg, Florida. They found that a patrol officer's typical shift includes 74% unassigned time.[1] Another current study using observational data from Baltimore, Maryland, found that patrol officers' shifts consist of 81% unassigned time.[2]

So, what do patrol officers do with the unassigned time they have during a typical shift? Christine Famega and her colleagues found that random patrol and providing backup for fellow patrol officers accounts for most of the unassigned time officers have when they are not responding to calls for service.[3] More specifically, this study found that officers spent on average 19% of total shift time responding to calls for service (1.5 hours), 5% on directed activities (24 minutes per shift), 47% on self-initiated activities (such as patrol and providing backup for fellow officers), and 29% of total shift time on other activities (such as administrative tasks and personal activities).[4] These research findings are significantly different from the way that police work is portrayed on television.

Patrol

Patrol is often referred to as the backbone of policing because it is the primary mechanism by which the police provide service to the public.[5] This activity can be conducted in a reactive manner (patrol officers respond to calls for service with direction from a dispatch system) and a proactive manner (patrol officers initiate contact with the public on their own).[6] Despite the current emphasis on community and problem-oriented policing, which encourage proactive policing, most American police agencies still conduct police activities in a reactive manner.

Historically, patrol has played an important role in policing in the United States. When looking back over time, it is easy to see how patrol methods have changed and how these changes have influenced various aspects of police work. In Section 1, we learned that in the political era of American policing, the primary type of patrol used by the police was foot patrol.[7] This type of patrol was used out of necessity, as motorized patrol was not accessible at that time. Foot patrol contributed to the police role being social service oriented, as it allowed officers more face-to-face interactions with the public.

In the reform era, the police switched from foot patrol to motorized patrol as part of their effort to become more professional.[8] They believed that by using motorized patrol, they could perform their job more efficiently and effectively, as they were able to move about more quickly and to respond to calls for service faster than they could have on foot. This shift from foot to motorized patrol also contributed to

Motorized patrol played a major role in police reform in the United States—1929.

their role becoming more focused on fighting crime. After the adoption of motorized patrol, patrol cars became physical barriers between the police and the public. This resulted in less face-to-face interaction between the two groups. The use of this type of patrol resulted in a strained relationship between the police and the public.

In the current **community/ problem-solving era**, the police utilize several types of patrol, including foot, bike, horse, and motorized patrol.[9] The range of patrol options complements the multifaceted role of contemporary police officers, which includes crime control, crime prevention, problem solving, and providing social services to the public.[10] Foot patrol has been reintroduced as part of community policing to provide more opportunities for the police to reconnect with citizens in their communities. Despite the wide array of patrol options available to police agencies, motorized patrol remains the dominant type of patrol used by police agencies today.

Motorized Patrol

In Section 1, August Vollmer was identified as an influential person in the professionalization of the police in the United States. He has been credited with developing some of the early college-level police education programs, promoting the use of science to detect and investigate crime, and endorsing the use of motorized patrol.[11] His police agency in Berkeley, California, became the first in the United States to use **motorized patrol**.[12] Soon after, police agencies across the country also began to adopt this type of patrol to replace foot patrol. Vollmer was passionate about the use of motorized patrol, as he believed that it would allow police officers to cover more ground within their communities and allow them to provide services more quickly and efficiently than they could by using foot patrol.

Patrol Strategies

Routine Preventive Patrol. Motorized patrol continued to be the dominant type of patrol used by American police agencies decades after Vollmer's endorsement in the early to mid-1900s. During this time, routine preventive patrol became a common patrol practice in many police agencies. Routine preventive patrol consists of police officers driving their squad cars around their designated beat areas or districts with the purpose of making their presence known to citizens. This patrol strategy is based on the premise that police presence will deter criminals from committing crimes for fear that the police will catch them as they randomly patrol the streets.

Specialized/Directed Patrol. According to Gary Cordner, directed or specialized patrol involves freeing some patrol officers from responding to calls for service so that they can focus their efforts in certain locations, toward specific offenders, or on certain crimes.[13] Directed patrol is composed of four basic characteristics: (1) It is proactive and aggressive in nature; (2) uncommitted/unassigned time of police officers is used to engage in directed law enforcement activities; (3) officers are instructed on how they should focus their directed patrol efforts; and (4) these instructions are based on information gleaned from crime analysis.[14] Crime analysis aids in the identification of problem places, offenders, and crimes that become the focus of specialized patrol efforts.

Location-Oriented Patrol Strategies. Ask any seasoned patrol officers where most crimes take place in their communities, and they will likely be able to point out crime-ridden areas with ease. Some police agencies utilize computer-based programs to identify locations in which most crime occurs and also the type of crimes that occur in certain locations. Lawrence Sherman labeled these locations "hot spots."[15] Hot spots are places in which the occurrence of crime is so frequent that it is highly predictable, at least for over a 1-year period.[16]

Another location-based patrol strategy in which police effort is focused on certain crimes in certain locations is **crackdowns**. Michael Scott describes a police crackdown as a sudden and dramatic increase in police presence, sanctions, and threats of apprehension either for specific offenses or for all offenses in specific places. This approach usually involves high police presence and numerous arrests.[17] Crackdowns are conducted sporadically and are usually a short-term patrol strategy. They are intended to increase the perceived risk of apprehension and increase the level of uncertainty about arrest.[18] This strategy can be used within individual neighborhoods, a couple of square blocks, public housing or apartment complexes, citywide, countywide, and, in some instances, statewide.[19] Crackdowns can also be used to target a variety of offenses, including drugs, prostitution, driving under the influence, robbery, burglary, gun-related crimes, and parking-related issues.[20]

Split-force patrol is another specialized patrol strategy. This approach requires the patrol force to be split into two groups: One group of officers is responsible for responding to calls for service from the public while the other group forms a specialized crime-suppression unit. The purpose of having a separate crime-suppression unit is to catch criminals in the act of committing crimes.[21] An 18-month study of the split-force patrol concept used by the Wilmington Police Department in Delaware found that routine calls were handled more efficiently and that

Crackdowns are often used by the police to target people that are driving under the influence of alcohol.

the quality of arrests had improved during this time frame.[22] Unfortunately, conflict developed between the two groups of patrol officers. Officers who were responsible for responding to calls for service believed that they had been demoted to a secondary function and that the crime-suppression unit was getting all of the interesting assignments.[23]

Offender-Oriented Patrol Strategies. This policing approach is based on the premise that there are individuals that commit a disproportionate number of crimes and that they should receive the most attention from the police. Offender-oriented policing is controversial, as some argue that it is a form of profiling based on extralegal factors, including race/ethnicity and socioeconomic status, to name a few.[24] The other side to this debate is that police work has always involved the profiling of suspicious people and that it is just a routine part of police work, not profiling.

The following three general patrol strategies are offender focused:[25]

- **Field interrogations**—function as a way to control crime and disorder. This long-standing technique consists of police officers questioning people they believe are suspicious or are likely to have been involved in criminal activities. The idea is that targeted individuals will be less likely to commit a crime if they know that the police are watching them or if the police make their presence known in the neighborhoods in which the targeted individuals reside.
- **Perpetrator-oriented patrol**—involves the surveillance of certain people suspected of committing multiple crimes or that have committed crimes that resulted in high levels of either property loss or damage or significant injury to people.
- **Repeat offender programs (ROP)**—focus on the identification and apprehension of high-risk repeat offenders. William Spelman found that roughly 10% of criminal offenders commit about 50% of all crimes; thus, most crimes are committed by a small percentage of offenders.[26] In the same study, Spelman found that there are three types of repeat offender programs, including: (1) prearrest targeting (patrol officers watch and then apprehend suspects before or while they are committing crimes), (2) warrant services (patrol officers track down parole and probation violators who have outstanding warrants for their arrest), and (3) postarrest enhancement (patrol officers help investigators build stronger cases against those who have already been arrested for certain crimes).

Foot Patrol

Foot patrol is the oldest form of police patrol.[27] This type of patrol was dominant in the political era of American policing, as there was limited access to motorized patrol at that time.[28] Foot patrol virtually disappeared during the reform era, as most police agencies were utilizing motorized patrol in their effort to become more professional.[29] Foot patrol was reintroduced in the early 1980s when police agencies across the country began to adopt community policing. The hope was that police officers on foot patrol would be able to have more face-to-face interaction with citizens, which would result in an improved relationship between the two groups.

Today, many police agencies use foot patrol. A recent Bureau of Justice Statistics report noted that more than half (55%) of all local police agencies in the United States use foot patrol in some capacity.[30] Foot patrol is a good option for police agencies trying to establish (or in some cases re-establish) their relationship and credibility with the community. In recent years, some police agencies have also been choosing to use foot patrol as a way to deal with rising gas prices (including agencies in Houston, Texas, and San Diego, California).[31] The high cost of gasoline has created budget crises in police agencies that rely primarily on motorized patrol. An increased use of foot patrol helps alleviate some of the extra costs resulting from high gas prices.

Other Types of Patrol

Besides motorized and foot patrol, some police agencies also use bike patrol. Similar to foot patrol, bike patrol was first used by the police in the late 1800s to early 1900s and then re-emerged with the introduction of community policing in the 1980s.[32] Recent statistics indicate that nearly one third (32%) of all local police agencies in the United States use bike patrol.[33] Despite the fact that bike patrol is becoming increasingly common, very little is known about the utility of this type of patrol.[34]

Mounted (horse) patrol is also used by some police agencies. This type of patrol has been touted as a good public relations tool for police agencies but is less common than bike patrol because of the costs associated with the maintenance of horses.[35] Approximately 1% of all local police agencies in the United States utilize horse patrol.[36] There is limited research on the use and impact of mounted patrol.[37]

Bike patrol facilitates more frequent interaction with citizens and is also cost effective at a time when gas prices are high.

One- Versus Two-Officer Patrol

How many officers should be assigned to a patrol car? This is a question that has been debated for decades. Police officers like the idea of having two officers per patrol car because they believe that it is safer to have someone to provide immediate backup when responding to calls for service. Police administrators prefer one-officer patrol units because they believe that it is more cost efficient than two-officer patrol units. A study conducted in San Diego found that one-officer patrol cars performed more safely, efficiently, and effectively when compared to two-officer patrol cars, and at almost half of the cost.[38] This study also found that one-officer patrol units received fewer complaints from citizens than two-officer patrol units.

The San Diego study was replicated in 1985 when David Kessler used data from the Kansas City Response Time Analysis Study. Findings from Kessler's study support the findings from the San Diego study that was conducted nearly a decade earlier. Today, it is common for police agencies to use one-officer patrol units as opposed to two-person patrol units.[39] The reason for this is primarily financial, as police executives are working with limited budgets.

Calls for Police Service and Police Patrol

A majority of requests for police service are directed through dispatch services connected to 911 and nonemergency numbers. This system results in most police actions being reactive in nature, and ultimately, the allocation of police services becomes based on telephone calls placed by citizens. Lawrence Sherman referred to this as the **dial-a-cop system**.[40] Some argue that the dial-a-cop system has conditioned police officers to do their job in a reactive manner as opposed to a proactive manner.[41]

Research on calls for police service indicates that people call the police for a wide variety of reasons. George Antunes and Eric Scott examined more than 26,000 calls for service from 24 police departments that served 60 neighborhoods.[42] The largest percentage of calls for service were those in which citizens wanted some kind of information, followed by calls concerning nonviolent crimes (such as burglary and larceny), requesting assistance with stray or wild animals, property checks, public nuisances (such as harassment and noise), and then traffic-related problems (such as accidents and vehicle violations).[43]

Lawrence Sherman found a similar pattern when he studied calls to the police in Minneapolis over the course of 1 year.[44] The top five most common types of calls for service in Minneapolis included: (1) conflict management—such as domestic disturbances, noise, and assault; (2) property-related crimes—such as theft, burglary, vandalism, and alarm calls; (3) traffic-related calls—such as enforcement issues, traffic accidents, and parking issues; (4) service-related calls—including lock-outs, medical emergencies, lost individuals, and fires; and (5) miscellaneous calls—such as calls inquiring about arrests and bookings.[45] Sherman's study also revealed that police work is concentrated in a small number of locations. He found that 5% of the 172,000 addresses in Minneapolis were the subject of 64% of 321,174 calls to the police.[46] About 60% of the addresses in the city of Minneapolis never called for police service, while of the remaining 40%, only half of the addresses called once for police service. The findings of this study justify the assignment of extra resources to these few locations as a way to reduce the overall total number of calls for police service (i.e., hot spot policing).

Who are the people requesting police services? Edem Avakame and his colleagues studied people that call the police by using data from the National Crime Victimization Survey (NCVS) from 1992 to 1994. They found that crime victims that are members of racial/ethnic minority groups, male, older, lower socio-economic status, unemployed, and live in urban settings are more likely to call the police than other crime victims.[47] George Antunes and Eric Scott analyzed more than 26,000 calls for service and discovered no major difference in the frequency of calls to the police among men and women; that African American citizens were twice as likely to call the police when compared to White citizens; and that business owners were more likely than private citizens to call for police service.[48]

Despite the criticism that dispatch or 911 systems condition the police to respond in a reactive manner, this centralized system allows citizens to easily contact the police. Dispatch systems are important, as they aid in the police being able to respond quickly when citizens need their help.

Civil Disobedience and Crisis Situations

Criminal investigation is another integral part of policing.

Police officers are also asked to respond to crisis situations and incidents of civil disobedience. In fact, they are often the first people to respond to such calls. These types of calls require the police to collaborate with people from other agencies and generally involve high levels of danger that can result in injury or death. This was the case for the police officers that responded to the World Trade Center after the terrorist attacks on 9/11. In 2005, the police played an important role in providing help to sick and injured people after Hurricane Katrina hit the central Gulf Coast states. And more recently, officers across the country have been called upon to deal with protestors associated with the Occupy Wall Street movement. Although most of the protests have been peaceful, there have been cases in which protestors became violent.[49]

⊠ Criminal Investigation

In addition to patrol, the police also investigate various types of crime. Criminal investigation has captured the attention of millions of Americans, as television programs such as *The First 48*, *Law & Order: Special Victims Unit*, and *CSI: Crime Scene Investigation* feature interesting cases being investigated (and ultimately solved) by savvy criminal investigators. Despite the plethora of television programs featuring criminal investigation, very little is known about this particular aspect of American policing. The lack of research on this topic is likely due to the fact that investigators and detectives only account for approximately 10 to 20% of sworn personnel in police agencies that have separate investigation divisions.[50] In smaller police agencies, criminal investigations are either conducted by police officers who are working the streets (that do not hold the official title of investigator), or state crime units or divisions are called upon to investigate reported crimes.

The Criminal Investigation Process

There are two phases in the criminal investigation process:[51]

1. *Preliminary investigation*—the first phase of the investigation process begins when police officers respond to crimes reported by citizens. Preliminary investigations are important, as they determine the likelihood that cases will be solved, and they also provide a foundation for cases that ultimately reach the courts. The purpose of preliminary investigations is to identify offenders, locate witnesses, collect evidence, and decipher what took place before the police were notified that a crime had occurred.

2. *Follow-up investigation*—the second phase of the investigation process occurs once the preliminary investigation is complete. Follow-up investigations usually take place when solvability factors are present. Solvability factors are pieces of information that help investigators increase the odds that they will solve a case. For example, a description of any vehicles present at the crime scene, property details, physical evidence, identification and location of witnesses, and information about offenders are all considered factors that contribute to the solvability of cases. Follow-up investigations often require investigators to move beyond the crime scene. They will interview witnesses (away from the crime scene) and look for additional information to answer the "who, what, why, where, and how" of each case.

Clearance of Criminal Cases

Despite what you might see on *CSI* or some of the other criminal investigation programs, not all cases are solved by investigators. In fact, less than half (47.2%) of violent crimes (murder, rape, robbery, and assault) and 18.3% of property crimes (burglary, larceny/theft, and motor vehicle theft) were cleared by arrest in 2010.[52] Each year dating back to 1929, the Federal Bureau of Investigations (FBI) has collected information on the clearance of serious crimes reported to law enforcement agencies across the United States.[53] This includes murder, forcible rape, robbery, aggravated assault, burglary, larceny-theft, motor vehicle theft, and arson. Recently, the FBI has begun to collect information on other less serious crime categories, as well as incidents that are defined as hate crimes. The FBI defines hate crimes as incidents motivated by race, religion, ethnicity, sexual orientation, or disability.[54] In general, crimes that involve physical harm to people have much higher **clearance rates** than crimes that involve the damage or disappearance of property (see table).

Crimes Cleared by Arrest, 2010	
Murder and nonnegligent manslaughter	64.8%
Forcible rape	40.3%
Robbery	28.2%
Aggravated assault	56.4%
Burglary	12.4%
Larceny-theft	21.1%
Motor vehicle theft	11.8%

Source: Data provided by the Federal Bureau of Investigations, www.fbi.gov.

Television programs that feature criminal investigation as the central theme often present the use of DNA evidence as a way that investigators can more easily solve cases. In reality, investigators do not always have DNA evidence to work with, and when they do have it, they do not always rely on it to solve their cases. David Schroeder and Michael White examined case files from homicides in New York City to determine how often investigators actually used DNA evidence in the course of their investigations.[55] In addition, they studied how the use of DNA evidence influenced the likelihood of case clearance. Findings from this study revealed that DNA evidence was hardly ever used by detectives and that the use of DNA evidence was not related to case clearance.[56]

Investigative Effort and Case Prioritization

One of the first empirical studies of criminal investigation was conducted by the RAND Corporation in the early 1970s.[57] This study examined criminal investigation practices and their impact on the clearance of cases. There were several findings from this study that lifted the shroud of mystery that surrounded criminal investigators at that time. For instance, differences in investigative training, staffing, workload, and procedures had no noticeable effect on crime, arrest, or clearance rates. More than half of all serious reported crimes received no more than superficial attention from investigators. The single most important determinant of whether a case would be solved is the information the victim supplies to the responding patrol officer, not the amount of effort by investigators. Detectives spend about 45% of their time involved with activities that are not focused on solving cases.[58]

A decade later, John Eck studied the investigation of burglaries and robberies and found some results that were slightly more favorable to detectives; specifically, he found that detectives and patrol officers contributed *equally* to the solution of these cases (the RAND study found that detectives spent very little time on cases when compared to patrol officers).[59] He also discovered that most of the cases rarely took more than 4 hours of effort. Most (more than three-fourths) of the cases were suspended within 2 days due to the lack of leads. This problem was the result of detectives relying too heavily on statements made by victims and not enough on information provided by witnesses, informants, colleagues, records, and evidence they had collected.[60] More recently, John Liederbach and his colleagues conducted a study that examines detective workload and found that detectives spend a great deal of time on "core investigative activities" (such as contacting victims, interrogating suspects, examining evidence, and preparing cases for court).[61] Similar to the earlier RAND study, this study found that investigators spend about one-third of their time involved in noncase-related activities such as entering time sheets, handling e-mails, and making database entries.[62]

How do investigators determine which cases are the most important? And how does this prioritization impact the amount of time spent on each case? There has been limited research on this topic; however, the little research that has been done has revealed two opposing perspectives on case prioritization and investigative effort. First, some argue that extralegal factors such as race and social class impact the amount of attention given to criminal investigations. Specifically, cases involving racial/ethnic minorities and individuals with low socioeconomic statuses will receive less attention than other cases involving White, middle- or upper-class individuals.[63] Kenneth Litwin found that cases with Latino victims are less likely to be cleared by arrest than those involving White victims. In addition, he found that cases are more likely to be cleared in communities that have higher homeowner rates when compared to others with lower homeowner rates. It is important to point out that Litwin's research findings may reflect the level of useful information provided by witnesses in those cases as opposed to investigators' use of discretion.[64]

The second perspective is based on the idea that all cases involving homicides or other violent crimes receive the most investigative effort based not on victim characteristics but on the seriousness of the crime and because investigators are pressured by their superiors to produce high clearance rates.[65] Most of the prior research on this topic has found that characteristics of the crime and *not* victim characteristics are the primary predictors of case clearance by investigators.[66] Additional research on this topic is needed in order to fully understand the complex nature of case prioritization and level of investigative energy spent on criminal investigation cases.

To date, there has been scant research on how demographic characteristics influence decision making when handling cases. The article by Megan Alderden and Sarah Ullman included at the end of this section examines gender differences among detectives in arrest decisions in sexual assault cases.

Technology and Police Activities

In the last three decades, technology has had a tremendous impact on policing. Over time, there have been changes in the way that police officers communicate with each other, their supervisors, and dispatch centers. The police have gone from using call boxes to two-way radios to cell phones.[67] The use of computers while on patrol has also helped patrol officers to be able to send and receive information more efficiently than in the past. In 2007, more than 90% of local police departments serving 25,000 or more residents reported using computers while in the field.[68]

Through the use of computers in their patrol cars, officers are able to access a plethora of automated information that helps them do their job each day. They are able to find

Computers in patrol cars allow police officers to access important information.

information related to vehicle and driving records, warrants and protection orders, calls for service history, criminal history records, crime maps, and other useful information available to them on the Internet.[69] On-board computers also help them share information with divisions or units within their own police agency (such as traffic units, sex crimes units, or gang-suppression units), as well as with other law enforcement agencies. Access to these types of information can presumably help patrol officers make more informed decisions when they interact with the public.

Computers are also helpful to the police as they track crimes in their communities. **Crime mapping** allows the police to plot crimes and incidents of social disorder on digitized maps. This type of technology aids police officers in problem-solving activities that are part of problem-oriented policing (see Section 2). Crime maps can be focused on blocks, neighborhoods, communities, cities, or regions. This technology allows police officials to compare and analyze plotted crimes with external data sources, including census data, city planning data, parks information, utilities information, and other types of data sources.[70] Crime mapping is essential for police agencies that use hot spot policing techniques that allow police administrators to focus patrol efforts in certain locations, focusing on certain crimes or offenders (see the discussion on hot spots policing earlier in this section). Crime mapping has been used to track many different types of crimes, including burglaries,[71] robberies,[72] homicides,[73] and juvenile crime.[74] The Chicago Police Department used crime mapping to define gang activity areas based on police records. This technique was useful in describing gang activity areas and in describing the spatial distribution of crime throughout the city.[75]

According to a recent Bureau of Justice Statistics report, most police departments serving populations of 25,000 or more used computers to gather intelligence, analyze patterns of crimes and other community problems, and map crime.[76] In 2007, about three out of four officers worked for a police department that used computerized crime mapping, compared to three out of five officers in 2003.[77] The article by Taylor, Kowalyk, and Boba included at the end of this section studies how crime mapping/crime analysts are perceived by police officers and how this technology fits within police organizations.

Recently, crime mapping has been used to predict where future crimes might occur (similar to how meteorologists attempt to predict the weather each week). This use of crime mapping is referred to as *predictive mapping*. Predictive mapping can aid police agencies in determining the deployment of officers in an effort to use their resources more efficiently. It could also help the police anticipate areas of potential crime displacement, which allows them to target broader geographic areas to reduce the likelihood that crime would occur in those areas. Predictive mapping can also be used to enhance any potential diffusion of benefits of police efforts in certain geographic locations (this is where there is a beneficial effect beyond the original locations that were targeted by police).[78]

Most police departments that attempt to forecast crime assume that the hot spots of the recent past are likely to be the hot spots of the near future. Very little research has tested this assumption. The few studies that have been conducted have found that the effectiveness of this approach is contingent upon the time frame of data used to make the prediction. One study found that using 1 month of crime data to predict future crimes is not enough to make an accurate prediction. Instead, using 1 year of crime data to make predictions is a much better idea, as the police will be able to predict future crimes with 90% accuracy.[79] This finding suggests that hot spots may heat up and then cool down over short periods of time, but ultimately stay in the same places over longer periods.

There have also been technological changes to the type of equipment that is used by police officers. One of the most notable changes would be the wide range of nonlethal weapons that have become available to police agencies across the United States. These nonlethal weapons include TASERS

(Thomas A. Swift's Electric Rifle), soft projectile guns that shoot bean bags or rubber bullets, and oleoresin capsicum (OC or mace).[80] Recent statistics indicate that 28% of all local police agencies use soft projectile weapons, while 8% use weapons that shoot rubber bullets.[81] The use of conducted energy devices (such as TASERS) increased from 47% of all local police agencies in 2003 to 75% of all agencies in 2007.[82] Despite the significant increase in the adoption of TASERS, very little is known about this device. Michael White and Justin Ready conducted a study on the use of TASERS that examined situations when this device is likely to be used, the prevalence of adoption by American police agencies, and the effectiveness of this technology. Results from their study reveal that in most cases, TASERs are used against violent/"emotionally disturbed" suspects in situations in which supervisors are present on the scene. Further, in a majority of cases (85%), the TASER was effective at incapacitating suspects and allowing the police to take them into custody.[83]

The adoption of new technology has not gone without criticism. For example, police officers' use of cell phones while on duty is controversial in jurisdictions in which citizens are banned from using their cell phones while driving their cars. Some believe that it sends the wrong message to the public when police officers write citations to citizens for using their cell phones while driving but are viewed by citizens when they are using cell phones themselves while driving. There is also the issue of accidents involving police officers that are distracted as they use cell phones while driving. Police executives are realizing that cell phone use is another form of potential liability for their agencies and have begun to create and enforce policies that restrict when and how patrol officers can use cell phones while they are at work.[84]

There is also increasing concern about litigation involving the police when citizens are seriously injured or killed as the result of some of the nonlethal weapons mentioned earlier. Kenneth Adams and Victoria Jennison reported that there have only been sporadic reports in the media of lawsuits involving TASER use by the police. They believe that lawsuits may be infrequent because serious injury or death is relatively rare or because lawyers are still trying to identify litigation strategies that will be successful in court.[85] Steve Hougland and his colleagues note that there has been a rise in the use of TASERS in police agencies in Florida and that this ultimately increases the chances that police agencies will be named in lawsuits.[86] The creation and enforcement of department policies that specify when and how these nonlethal weapons are to be used could result in a decline of police agencies being sued successfully by citizens that have suffered injuries. Ultimately, there has not been enough research on this topic to draw any meaningful conclusions about the extent to which police agencies are sued as a result of the use of these nonlethal weapons. Section 13 presents additional information on some of the cutting-edge equipment and technology only recently developed and made available to police agencies.

SUMMARY

- Patrol is considered the backbone of policing.
- Foot patrol has served different purposes over the course of the history of American policing.
- Only a small percentage of the population calls for police service.
- There are two steps in the criminal investigation process: (1) preliminary investigation and (2) follow-up investigation.
- Crime mapping is important for police agencies that utilize hot spot policing, as it identifies concentrated areas in which the most and certain types of crime occur.

KEY TERMS

clearance rates

community/problem-solving era

crackdowns

crime mapping

dial-a-cop system

field interrogations

foot patrol

motorized patrol

perpetrator-oriented patrol

repeat offender program

split-force patrol

DISCUSSION QUESTIONS

1. How has motorized patrol influenced the relationship between the police and citizens?

2. Describe the use of foot patrol over the course of the history of American policing.

3. Who is most likely to call for police service?

4. What do police officers do during the course of a typical shift?

5. Why is the preliminary investigation an important step in the investigation process?

WEB RESOURCES

- To learn more about the Newark Foot Patrol Experiment, go to http://www.policefoundation.org/docs/newark.html.

- To learn more about the Kansas City Preventive Patrol Study, go to http://www.policefoundation.org/pdf/kcppe.pdf.

- To learn more about criminal investigators, go to http://www.bls.gov/oes/current/oes333021.htm.

READING 13

This study explores the extent to which there are gender differences in detectives' arrest decisions in sexual assault cases. Using data from police case files, the authors studied victim, suspect, and detective characteristics from 328 criminal sexual assault cases. This study revealed that female detectives are less likely to arrest suspects in sexual assault cases when compared to male detectives.

Gender Difference or Indifference? Detective Decision Making in Sexual Assault Cases

Megan A. Alderden and Sarah E. Ullman

Research has consistently shown that police officers and prosecutors scrutinize sexual assault cases despite attempts to improve the processing of sexual assault cases through rape reform policy (Berger, Neuman, & Searles, 1994; Horney & Spohn, 1991). Victim, suspect, and incident characteristics continue to influence criminal justice practitioner decision making even if some of these characteristics are not legally required to prove a sexual assault occurred or meet evidentiary standards (see Beichner & Spohn, 2005; Frazier & Haney, 1996; Kerstetter, 1990; Kingsnorth, MacIntosh, & Wentworth, 1999; LaFree, 1981, 1989; Spears & Spohn, 1996, 1997; Spohn, Beichner, & Davis-Frenzel, 2001; Spohn & Holleran, 2001; Spohn & Horney, 1993; Spohn & Spears, 1996). Criminal justice practitioners use these factors to weed out those cases that they believe are not likely to move forward through the criminal justice system (Frohmann, 1991; Spohn et al., 2001). Those cases that do not meet a perceived set of standards are considered by criminal justice personnel to be a waste of time and resources. Therefore, the progression of such cases through the system is halted.

Past examinations of sexual assault processing decisions have focused only on the influence of victim, suspect, and incident characteristics on case outcomes and have failed to consider the characteristics of criminal justice personnel who are charged with making processing decisions. Criminal justice personnel are not passive participants. A defining aspect of their work is discretion; the high levels of discretion employed by criminal justice practitioners allow these employees some latitude in deciding which activities they are willing to engage in and how they should carry out their jobs (Lipsky, 1980). Because of this, one's identity, social position, and past experiences may all play significant roles in how individuals perform and value their work. It can also affect the types of choices being made. Therefore, simply examining the results of criminal justice practitioner decisions makes invisible the individuals making those choices and how these practitioners' own gender, race, age, and past experiences affect their judgments. This study sought to address this limitation in the sexual assault decision-making literature by exploring the influence of detective gender on decisions to arrest in sexual assault cases.

Police Officer Decision Making in Sexual Assault Cases

Police officers play an important role in the processing of sexual assault cases. Officers are charged with investigating and determining the "facts" about sexual assault cases, and they carry out this role with an immense amount of discretion. Officers have the discretion to decide which cases are worth investigating versus others that may be seen as a waste of time due to the circumstances surrounding the incident (i.e., rape involving an uncooperative victim or little evidence) or resources available to successfully investigate, arrest, and charge suspects. Their determination of which sexual assaults are worth investigating may also be influenced by their perceptions of what actually constitutes real rape (i.e., stranger rape) or who are legitimate victims (e.g., victims who were not engaged in morally questionable or risk-taking behavior at the time of the incident).

There are several decision-making points that sexual assault cases will go through that involve police officers. These processing points include the case founding decision, arrest, and presentation to the prosecution. Case founding refers to the initial determination by police officers that the reported incident actually constituted a criminal sexual assault as defined by state statute. This is the first step all cases must pass through once an official police report has been completed. Cases in which officers do not believe a crime occurred are unfounded or reclassified (generally to a lesser offense, such as assault), whereas cases in which officers do think a sexual assault occurred are founded. Officers continue working on those cases that are founded. Arrest occurs when the officer has enough probable cause to arrest and charge a suspect for a criminal sexual assault. In the jurisdiction studied, if the suspect has been identified and arrested, the officer can choose to seek felony charges by presenting the case to the prosecution for felony approval.[1] Each of these decision-making points represent occasions in which incident, victim, and suspect characteristics can influence case outcomes. They also represent instances

in which personal biases and attitudes can come into play because of the amount of discretion *individual* officers have when making decisions at each of these points. The individualistic nature of police decision making renders who is making the assessment just as important as the factors used by those officers.

Factors Known to Influence Officer Decisions

According to Martin (2005), one of the primary activities of police personnel is to "build their case" through documentation of facts. This often includes treating victims like witnesses to their own crimes. Research also indicates that the police officer role, which emphasizes close scrutiny of "facts" and identification of the "truth," results in officers becoming highly suspicious of sexual assault victims, which may influence how they interpret victim behaviors (Jordan, 2004). It is unknown, however, whether the tendency to be suspicious of sexual assault victims transcends gender or whether gender moderates this relationship. Those studies conducted thus far have either focused on victim, suspect, and case characteristics and case outcomes (see Frazier & Haney, 1996; Kerstetter, 1990; LaFree, 1989) or have focused on officer *perceptions* of rape scenarios, rape victims, and rape myths (see Brown & King, 1998; Campbell & Johnson, 1997; Feldman-Summers & Palmer, 1980; LeDoux & Hazelwood, 1985; Page, 2007, 2008a, 2008b; Schuller & Stewart, 2000).

Despite limitations, prior studies have been instrumental in helping us understand decision making by officers in sexual assault cases. It is now known, for example, that officers view inconsistencies in victim statements as a "red flag" that the sexual assault claims may be false (Jordan, 2004) and that the victim's moral character or risk-taking behavior prior to the incident significantly influences police decision making (Kerstetter, 1990; LaFree, 1989). It is also known that certain case characteristics, such as whether the suspect used a weapon (Kerstetter, 1990; LaFree, 1989), the victim reported resisting the attack (Kerstetter, 1990; LaFree, 1989), the victim sustained injuries (Frazier & Haney, 1996; Kerstetter, 1990), witnesses were present

(Frazier & Haney, 1996), victim–suspect relationship (Frazier & Haney, 1996; LaFree, 1989), and if the victim reported the incident in a timely manner (Jordan, 2004; LaFree, 1989) influence police officer decisions regarding whether they perceive victim claims to be legitimate and when to question and arrest suspects. Past research also indicates that different incident-based factors are significantly correlated with sexual assault case processing outcomes for stranger cases compared to known suspect cases (see Kerstetter, 1990; Kerstetter & Van Winkle, 1990). For instance, research indicates that evidentiary factors, such as the presence of a weapon, witness availability, and resistance, play a large role in arrest decision making in sexual assaults involving strangers, whereas victim credibility (e.g., the victim was not perceived as sympathetic) plays a large role in arrest decision making in cases involving known suspects (Kerstetter & Van Winkle, 1990).

 ## Gender and Blame Attribution

Some academics have argued that criminal justice agencies are less responsive when handling crimes involving predominately female victims, such as domestic violence and sexual assault, because male personnel dominate most criminal justice agencies or because these organizations have masculine characteristics (Martin, Reynolds, & Keith, 2002). This has led to calls for criminal justice agencies to hire more women; by hiring more female criminal justice practitioners it was believed that criminal justice organizations would be more sensitive to the needs of female crime victims (Caringella-MacDonald, 1988). The result of the "hiring mandate" has been more intentional recruitment of women, and such practices have resulted in a greater number of female police officers. In 1987, only 7.6% of police officers in the United States were female. By 2007, this percentage had increased to almost 12%. Large police departments were particularly successful in recruiting female officers. By 2007, women accounted for between 13% and 27% of sworn personnel in the 10 largest police departments (Langton, 2010).

Yet despite the increasing numbers of female police officers, little is still known about their decision-making practices in sexual assault and domestic violence cases. Most of the research to date has focused on officer perceptions. The idea that female officers may be more sensitive to victims of sexual assault is somewhat supported in the literature examining factors correlated with victim blaming. Attribution theory holds that individuals make blame determinations by examining causality and responsibility of the observed actors (Shaver, 1975). Individuals attribute responsibility by either attributing the behavior to the characteristics of the observed actor, some other external factors (Gray, Palileo, & Johnson, 1993), or both. The social position of the actor (i.e., his or her class, sex, race, or ethnicity), the location of the behavior (i.e., at home vs. in a dark alley), the observer's past experience, and psychological benefits associated with the allocation of blame can influence how and under what circumstances individuals will attribute responsibility (Shaver, 1975).

When applying attribution theory to sexual assault cases, researchers have focused on how victim, suspect, and incident characteristics play a role in how individuals attribute blame, in addition to how the characteristics, experiences, and personalities of those attributing blame also influence blame attribution. More important, respondent sex has been one of the most important predictors of blame attribution. In a meta-analysis of 65 reports on attitudes toward rape published between 1973 and 1993, Anderson, Cooper, and Okamura (1997) found that of the demographic factors examined by previous researchers, sex was the strongest predictor of rape myth acceptance; greater acceptance of rape myths was found in men than in women.

Studies that have examined officer perceptions of rape victims and rape myth acceptance have shown that officers are skeptical of rape victim claims (Jordan, 2004) and believe in some commonly held rape myths (Brown & King, 1998; Campbell & Johnson, 1997; Feldman-Summers & Palmer, 1980; LeDoux & Hazelwood, 1985; Page, 2007, 2008a, 2008b). The relationship between officer gender and officer perceptions is less clear. Some studies have found gender differences (see Brown & King, 1998; Page, 2007; Schuller & Stewart, 2000). For instance, Brown and King (1998) and Page (2007) found that women police officers were less accepting of rape myths than male police officers, whereas Schuller and Steward found that female officers were more likely than male officers to believe victims, attribute less blame to the victim, and believe that the suspects in hypothetical situations were guilty and should be charged. In contrast, Campbell and Johnson found no gender differences in officer definitions of sexual assaults. Caution, however, is needed when drawing strong conclusions between gender and officer perceptions. Page (2008a) notes that officers participating in research aimed at assessing rape myth acceptance may respond in socially desirable ways. This may result in research findings that underreport officer acceptance of rape myths or officers' negative perceptions of victims and suspects in certain rape scenarios (see also Lonsway, Welch, & Fitzgerald, 2001). The socially desirable responses may also mask existing gender differences in officer perceptions.

In summary, studies conducted to date have examined the influence of victim, suspect, and case characteristics on decision making (e.g., decision to arrest) or self-reported *perceptions* of sexual assaults and sexual assault victims, not how police officers actually behaved toward sexual assault victims while carrying out their jobs. No published studies have examined officer gender as a predictor of outcomes in sexual assault cases. Thus, it is unknown whether officer gender plays a role in decisions to arrest. One would expect, however, on the basis of past research on attribution theory and some evidence that female officers are more likely to believe victims and attribute less blame to the victim and that cases handled by female detectives will be more likely than cases investigated by male detectives to result in the arrest of the suspect after controlling for incident, victim, and suspect characteristics.

Present Study

This study examined detective arrest decisions for a sample of criminal sexual assault cases reported to a large Midwestern police department in 2003. This study focused on one main processing decision-making point:

arrest. The focus of this study is on the arrest decision because it represents a key decision-making point in the process in which the progress of a large number of cases is halted. For instance, though all of the cases handled by detectives examined for this study were founded, only 26.8% of cases resulted in an arrest.

Sample

The final sample for this study consisted of 328 criminal sexual assaults. The final sample was extracted from a database containing detailed information about 630 criminal sexual assault cases that occurred between January and August 2003. In this jurisdiction, individuals can be charged with criminal sexual assault if they sexually penetrate the victim by use of force or threat of force or the victim is unable to consent to penetration. The definition of criminal sexual assault employed by this Midwestern police agency is much broader than that used by the Federal Bureau of Investigation's Uniform Crime Reporting program in that the definition includes male victims, multiple forms of penetration, and the assaults in which the victim is unable to consent.

The original 630 cases included all sexual assaults in which the victim was female and 18 years or older. Although the original 630 cases included instances in which men or women were the alleged perpetrators, the final sample for this study was limited to instances in which the suspect was a man because there was only one case in which the alleged suspect was a woman. The final sample also excluded cases that were unfounded ($n = 40$) as these cases would not result in arrest; detectives only continue investigating cases that were originally founded. In addition, the final sample excluded cases in which multiple suspects or victims were present ($n = 132$) because cases involving multiple victims and/or multiple suspects are likely to be different (e.g., considered more serious) than those involving one suspect and one victim (he said/she said cases). Another 13 cases were excluded because no supplemental documentation could be found (only the original paper case report could be located).

Finally, cases in which multiple detectives were involved were excluded ($n = 109$) because the ability to accurately identify each individual and link that individual to his or her demographic characteristics and work experiences using the automated personnel database was not always possible. Although the automated personnel database was both accurate and complete, the unique employee identifier used to connect detectives to reports was only available for detectives who write up the supplemental reports in the system. In instances in which multiple detectives were involved in the case, only the detective who wrote up the reports could be definitively linked to his or her demographic characteristics via their unique employee identifier. Although attempts were made to link the other detectives involved in the case, the ability to do so consistently and with a high degree of accuracy was limited and, therefore, deemed unreliable.

It should be noted that there were some differences noted between those cases involving one detective and those involving multiple detectives. Most notable is that cases involving multiple detectives versus one detective were significantly more likely to involve weapons (34.9% vs. 21.5%, respectively) and victim injury (42.2% vs. 25.6%, respectively). Both of these factors suggest that more serious cases—those involving both weapon use and victim injury—were more likely to result in higher amounts of police resources devoted to the case. It was also found that cases involving multiple detectives were significantly more likely to result in the arrest of the suspects (59.4% vs. 23.8%, respectively), but review of the cases indicated that this higher frequency of suspect arrests was primarily due to the fact that many of the suspects were arrested on scene or quickly after the incident by patrol officers. The higher arrest frequency may also be a byproduct of assigning multiple detectives to more serious cases as noted previously. Although inclusion of cases involving multiple detectives would have been ideal, the reliability of doing so was not possible.

Data Collection

Data were collected from various paper and electronic files including the incident, arrest, and detective supplemental reports and an evidence-tracking database used to document and track all forensic evidence. Consistent with what Martin (2005) identifies as one of the primary activities of police personnel, these sources of data reflect the activities and information that police officers and detectives document as part of their efforts to "build their case." Although all of the information was documented in a manner that could be used in criminal court, it still was influenced by officer interpretations, attitudes, and beliefs about criminal sexual assaults, victims, and suspects.

Measures

As previously noted, several incident characteristics have been significantly predictive of officer decision making in sexual assault cases. These variables, in addition to detective gender, were examined to account for their relationship to the dependent variable: arrest. These variables included victim credibility, whether the victim sustained physical injuries, a weapon was used or implied, witnesses to the incident were present, the victim reported actively resisting the assault, the victim refused to submit to a rape kit, the rape was reported more than 6 hours later than the incident, and the incident involved strangers, acquaintances, or relatives or prior or current intimate partners.

For this study, *victim credibility* was operationalized in two ways: victim character and discrepancies in victim statements. The variable victim character was created to reflect whether the victim had questionable moral character as noted in the police reports reviewed. Questionable moral character was defined as an individual who was identified as a prostitute, drug or alcohol user, or had a prior arrest record. Information about the victim's moral behavior came from various sources, including officer knowledge of the victim (e.g., known prostitute), victim statements, witness statements, and in some cases, suspect statements. The second way in which victim credibility was measured pertained to the perceived truthfulness of victims when they reported the incident to the police. The variable was coded for whether discrepancy was noted by police officers or detectives.

Discrepancy was noted only if the police report indicated that the victim's story changed after questioning by police officers or detectives.

Analysis

Analyses for this study were conducted in three steps. First, frequencies and percentages were completed to describe the sample characteristics. Second, chi-square analyses were performed to clarify the relationship between the independent and dependent variables. The data were also partitioned by detective gender and additional chi-square analyses were performed to describe the relationship between incident, victim, and suspect characteristics and the dependent variable separately by detective gender. Bivariate correlations were also performed to identify any potential

problems with multicollinearity between the independent variables (data not shown, available on request from the first author). Finally, sequential logistic regression analysis was completed in which the control variables were first entered into a logistic regression model followed by detective gender. Sequential ordering of the variables allowed us to test whether detective gender had a statistically significant independent effect controlling for all other factors. The likelihood ratio test was used to test the difference between the model containing only incident, victim, and suspect characteristics and that including detective gender. Cases with missing data were excluded from the final model ($n = 21$). Logistic regression model diagnostics as well as the Hosmer and Lemeshow's (2000) goodness-of-fit test were performed to ensure the models were appropriate.

Table 1   Descriptive Statistics for the Independent and Dependent Variables

Variable	Frequency/n	%
Detective—female	121/328	36.9
Weapon used	67/328	20.4
Witness present	23/328	7.0
Resistance noted	92/321	28.7
Refused rape kit	55/311	17.7
Victim injured	83/328	25.3
Time reported—more than 6 hours	116/328	35.4
Discrepancy in victim statement	36/328	11.0
Character questioned	124/328	37.8
Victim/suspect—acquaintance/relative	112/326	34.4
Victim suspect—intimate partner	75/326	23.0
Suspect arrested	88/328	26.8

Note: N = 328.

Results

Table 1 presents the univariate descriptives for the variables examined. Overall, only 26.8% of the cases examined resulted in arrest. This means that almost 75% of cases that police officers believed met the legal definition of a criminal sexual assault were suspended pending additional evidence or arrest of the alleged suspect. Female detectives were assigned to investigate 36.9% of the cases examined. This percentage was slightly higher than the percentage of women among all sworn personnel in 2003 (36.9% vs. 22.9%, respectively). Although the police department studied does not have an official policy designating that more female officers be assigned to sexual assault cases, it does appear that female detectives from the violent crimes unit may have been assigned at a higher rate than expected given the overall percentage of female officers working for the department. Unfortunately, data on the total number of female detectives in 2003, or more specifically, the number of female detectives assigned to the violent crimes unit, were unavailable. Such data would have provided additional insight regarding whether female detectives were being assigned at a higher rate to sexual assault cases than their male counterparts.

The descriptive statistics also revealed that most cases did not involve a weapon (79.6%), witnesses (93.0%), resistance (71.3%), or victim injury (74.7%). In addition, a majority of cases were reported within 6 hours or less of the incident (64.6%), and in only 17.7% of cases did victims refuse to have a rape kit completed. In terms of victim credibility, in 37.8% of the cases detectives had noted information that questioned the victim's moral character and in 11.0% of cases the detectives had noted discrepancies in the victim statements. In terms of the victim–suspect relationship, 42.6% of cases allegedly involved strangers.

Five independent and control variables were significantly related to the arrest dependent variable at the bivariate level: detective gender, witness presence, resistance, rape kit refusal, and whether there were questions regarding victim character (Table 2). An additional three variables were significant at a more liberal $p \leq .20$: injury, discrepancy in victim statements, and victim–suspect relationship.

Table 2 Bivariate Relationship Between Control, Independent, and Dependent Variables

Variable	Male ($n = 207$)		Female ($n = 121$)		Total ($n = 328$)	
	No arrest ($n = 142$)	Arrest ($n = 65$)	No arrest ($n = 98$)	Arrest ($n = 23$)	No arrest ($n = 240$)	Arrest ($n = 88$)
Female detective	n/a	n/a	n/a	n/a	98 (40.8)	23 (26.1)
					$p = .015$	
Weapon present	32 (22.5)	15 (23.1)	15 (15.3)	5 (21.7)	47 (19.6)	20 (22.7)
	$p = .931$		$p = .455$		$p = .531$	
Witness present	7 (4.9)	12 (18.5)	4 (4.1)	0 (0.0)	11 (4.6)	12 (13.6)
	$p = .002$		$p = .324$		$p = .004$	
Resistance noted	32 (23.2)	24 (36.9)	24 (25.3)	12 (52.2)	56 (24.0)	36 (40.9)
	$p = .041$		$p = .012$		$p = .003$	

(Continued)

Table 2 (Continued)	Male (*n* = 207)		Female (*n* = 121)		Total (*n* = 328)	
Variable	No arrest (*n* = 142)	Arrest (*n* = 65)	No arrest (*n* = 98)	Arrest (*n* = 23)	No arrest (*n* = 240)	Arrest (*n* = 88)
Refused rape kit	28 (21.5)	6 (9.5)	18 (18.9)	3 (13.0)	46 (20.4)	9 (10.5)
	p = .040		*p* = .507		*p* = .039	
Victim injured	27 (19.0)	19 (29.2)	28 (28.6)	9 (39.1)	55 (22.9)	28 (31.8)
	p = .101		*p* = .323		*p* = .100	
Time reported > 6 hr	56 (39.4)	15 (23.1)	33 (33.7)	12 (52.2)	89 (37.1)	27 (30.7)
	p = .021		*p* = .099		*p* = .283	
Discrepancy noted	15 (10.6)	11 (16.9)	7 (7.1)	3 (13.0)	22 (9.2)	14 (15.9)
	p = .200		*p* = .355		*p* = .083	
Character questioned	44 (31.0)	30 (46.2)	38 (38.8)	12 (52.2)	82 (34.2)	42 (47.7)
	p = .035		*p* = .240		*p* = .025	
Victim–suspect relationship						
Stranger	67 (47.9)	20 (30.8)	44 (44.9)	8 (34.8)	111 (46.6)	28 (31.8)
Acquaintance/ relative	43 (30.7)	29 (44.6)	32 (32.7)	8 (34.8)	75 (31.5)	37 (42.0)
Intimate partner	30 (21.4)	16 (24.6)	22 (22.4)	7 (30.4)	52 (21.8)	23 (26.1)
	p = .058		*p* = .617		*p* = .052	

Note: Numbers in parentheses indicate percentage; n/a = not applicable.

Table 3 Logistic Regression Model Showing the Association Between Detective Gender and Suspect Arrest Controlling for Victim, Suspect, and Incident Characteristics

Variable	B	SE	P	OR	95% confidence interval	
					Lower	Upper
Detective gender	−0.70	0.30	.022	0.50	0.27	0.90
Resistance	0.82	0.31	.007	2.27	1.25	4.13
Rape kit completed	−0.84	0.42	.047	0.43	0.19	0.99
Victim character	0.70	0.30	.020	2.00	1.12	3.60
Acquaintance/relative	1.13	0.360	.002	3.08	1.52	6.25
Intimate partner	1.20	0.41	.004	3.29	1.46	7.41

Note: $\chi^2(11, 307) = 45.26, p < .001$; Nagelkerke $R^2 = .20$.

Table 3 shows the results from the final logistic regression model that included the control and independent variables. The model was statistically significant at the $p \leq .05$ level and review of the Hosmer and Lemeshow (2000) goodness-of-fit test indicated that the model was a good fit for the data. Detective gender did independently predict the probability of arrest even after controlling for all other variables, though the direction of the relationship was opposite to that hypothesized. Specifically, the odds that cases resulted in arrest increased 50% when the detective was male.

In addition to detective gender, several other variables were statistically predictive of arrest; that is, the odds that cases would result in arrest increased more than twofold when the victim reported resisting the attack and decreased by 57% when the victim refused to submit to a rape kit examination. Questionable moral character was also significantly predictive of the odds of arrest; the odds of arrest increased twofold in cases in which victims had questionable moral character. Finally, the odds of arrest also increased when the suspect was identified as an acquaintance or relative or if the suspect was an intimate partner. The odds of arrest for cases involving acquaintances or relatives were 3.1 times greater as compared to cases involving strangers and 3.3 times greater for cases involving intimate partners as compared to cases involving strangers.

 Discussion

It had been hypothesized that cases involving female detectives would be more likely to result in arrest based on the belief that women may be more sensitive to claims of sexual assault. However, the data examined for this study suggest otherwise. Rather, cases involving male detectives were significantly more likely to result in arrest. This finding was contrary to that expected given past research that indicates women are significantly less likely than men to attribute blame to sexual assault victims (see Anderson et al., 1997). These findings lead us to question assumptions of some researchers and feminists that hiring more female criminal justice practitioners will result in criminal justice

organizations becoming more sensitive to the needs of female crime victims (Caringella-MacDonald, 1988). In fact, these findings support other studies showing that creation of police units investigating sexual assaults comprised of mostly women do not necessarily result in better processing outcomes (LaFree, 1989) and that some women can be more harsh to sexual assault victims than men (Weir & Wrightsman, 1990). Martin (2005) argues that the selection of individuals to work with sexual assault victims solely on the practitioner's gender is risky because female practitioners are not necessarily more sensitive to sexual assault victims. This study's finding that female detectives were less likely to arrest suspects in sexual assault cases provides further support for Martin's warning. The belief that police agencies will be more sensitive to issues particular to women because more women are employed by those agencies assumes that being female has more influence on an individual's behaviors and attitudes than being a member of a criminal justice organization. It implies that women, as a group, have similar beliefs and perceptions about the world. Radical feminists and feminists of color have openly criticized such assumptions, arguing that women's experiences and perceptions about the world are conditioned by other factors, such as race, class, ethnicity, and education, not just gender (Crenshaw, 1993; Hurtado, 1996).

Arguments that women should be hired by police agencies based on the premise that women, as a group, will be more sensitive to female crime victims may do more harm than good. First, such arguments imply that there needs to be a valid reason why women should be considered as potential, viable employees. The need for validation has been a historical phenomenon that has plagued the criminal justice system. Scholars have long recognized that women's entry into criminal justice careers has been plagued with gender stereotyping, often resulting in women's professional roles being closely associated with traditional female characteristics such as nurturing and care-taking (Belknap, 2007). No such rationale has ever been provided or considered necessary for hiring men. Thus, female officers may be expected to engage in activities for which they have little interest or skills simply because they are female.

In terms of sexual assault cases, this may mean that female officers may handle higher volumes of sexual assault cases even if their treatment of such cases or victims is problematic.

Second, implying that female officers will be more able to deal with female crime victims may undermine efforts to improve victim outcomes. For years, victim advocates and feminist scholars have focused on ways to increase victim reporting to police and reduce secondary victimization following disclosure. Police agencies may simply believe that hiring a few female officers will fix the "problem." Yet the findings from this study and others suggest otherwise.

Other Notable Findings

This study also replicated findings from previous studies. For instance, resistance and willingness to submit to a rape kit were associated with an increased likelihood of arrest. The relationships between these variables and arrest were in the expected directions and are consistent with past research (see LaFree, 1989). Both resistance and rape kit submission are likely viewed by officers as evidence that the assault occurred. And though neither variable is statutorily required for police to prove a sexual assault occurred in this jurisdiction, police officers may still believe victim resistance and rape kit completion are markers of strong cases and use them to meet the probable cause standard required for arrest. Police officers may also feel that real sexual assault victims fight their attackers. Galton's (1975/1976) analysis of police processing of rape cases in Texas revealed that police investigators believed victims should resist attacks even if the suspect possessed a weapon or threatened the victim. These investigators held these beliefs despite the fact that statutorily resistance was not required to disprove consent in these circumstances. Galton concluded that these decisions, such as requiring victims to prove lack of consent via resistance despite no statutory requirements, results in police officers acting as rule makers versus rule enforcers. Similarly, detectives may also believe that only women who are real sexual assault victims would willingly submit to the rape kit examination that is both personal and invasive. Thus, though statutorily women do not have to submit to rape kits for their crimes to be real, detectives may use this as way to determine which cases are legitimate and worthy of further investigation.

Finally, cases involving known suspects (i.e., acquaintances, relatives, and intimate partners) were significantly more likely to result in arrest as compared to stranger cases. This finding is consistent with that reported by LaFree (1989). This finding likely reflects the greater ease of identifying known suspects and not necessarily more willingness of detectives to arrest persons known to the victim. For officers to make an arrest, they simply need to know who the suspect is and where that person can be located. Unlike stranger cases, in known suspect cases the identity of the suspect is no mystery. Therefore, officers can more easily clear these cases with arrest. However, this finding has serious limitations for the next steps in the processing continuum—prosecutor decisions to charge suspects and convictions. Past research has found that cases involving strangers are more likely to result in felony charges (Alderden & Ullman, in press; Beichner & Spohn, 2005, but not Spohn et al., 2001) and convictions (Spohn & Spears, 1996; Williams, 1981). Together these findings suggest that though sexual assault cases involving known suspects may have an increased likelihood of arrest than stranger cases, getting the suspect arrested may not necessarily increase the chances that the suspect will be charged and convicted.

In addition to the above variables, it was also found that victim character was also significantly predictive of arrest. This relationship is in the opposite direction than that reported in prior research (see LaFree, 1989). Although the positive relationship between victim character and arrest may seem counterintuitive, this finding may reflect the types of sources detectives used when documenting victim character. Specifically, a qualitative review of the data indicates that suspects were often sources of information that both discredited victim accounts of the incident as well as provided officers with additional details about victims' characters. The finding may also reflect greater willingness of detectives to make arrests in cases regardless of the victim's moral character. Such findings would suggest that efforts to reduce the influence of extralegal factors on decision making have been successful. Additional research is needed before strong conclusions can be drawn.

Limitations

This study was not without limitations. First, caution must be taken when generalizing the findings presented here to other jurisdictions because the study sample was limited to cases reported to one Midwestern police department. It is possible that gender differences in detective decision making are influenced by agency-level factors, including whether agencies provide special training to detectives or have specific policies and procedures for how sexual assault cases should be handled (thus, limiting variation in how individual officers investigate sexual assault). Moreover, officers may be influenced by the political and religious environments of the jurisdictions they serve. For instance, greater differences between male and female officer decisions may exist in more conservative regions (i.e., South) versus more liberal regions (i.e., West, Northeast) of the United States. Additional research that examines practitioner decision making by gender across jurisdictions that vary by size, sexual assault rates, region, and sexual assault investigation policies is, therefore, needed to help clarify the findings presented here.

Second, this study's sample was limited to adult female victims. It is unknown whether the gender difference noted here exists only for cases involving adult females. For instance, it is possible that male and female detectives behave similarly when investigating cases involving young children because children are perceived as undoubtedly innocent, but differently when investigating cases involving adults who may be perceived as being partially culpable in their victimizations. Thus, examination of sexual assault case decision making for cases that involve both men and women as well as individuals of all ages would help refine the relationship between victim demographic characteristics and detective decision making.

Finally, similar to other studies examining predictors of sexual assault case outcomes, this study relied on secondary data sources. Although all of the data examined were collected and documented as part of the case-building process and were documented with the

consideration that such information could ultimately be submitted as evidence during court proceedings, the data reflect the documentation of information that was deemed important by the persons working the cases. The information reflects *practitioners'* recollections and interpretations of various case-specific elements, including the victim and suspect statements. Access to actual victim and suspect statements may provide a more accurate understanding of what information is documented as part of the case-building process and the implications of selective documentation. Observations of detective interactions with victims as well as documentation of detective perceptions of sexual assault victim and case investigations may further illuminate differences between male and female detectives. This information combined could provide researchers with a better understanding of how criminal justice practitioners construct sexual assault cases and how practitioner personal backgrounds are related to decision making.

Conclusion

The purpose of this study was to expand on past research that has examined factors that are predictive of sexual assault outcomes by examining the influence of detective gender on arrest decision making. It was hypothesized that female detectives would be more likely [than] male detectives to arrests suspects in the sexual assault cases. Contrary to expectations, gender was significant but in the opposite direction. Male detectives were significantly more likely to arrest than female detectives. The findings further support the growing body of research that suggests women criminal justice practitioners may not be more sensitive to female victims (Martin, 2005), and in some cases, may be harsher toward sexual assault victims (Weir & Wrightsman, 1990).

Note

1. If the prosecuting attorneys refuse to approve felony charges, the charges may be downgraded to a misdemeanor (e.g., simple assault, domestic battery) or the suspect may be released without charging (i.e., the suspect is not formally charged and is free to leave the police station).

References

Alderden, M., & Ullman, S. (in press). Creating a more complete picture: Examining police and prosecutor decision making when processing sexual assault cases. *Violence Against Women.*

Anderson, K., Cooper, H., & Okamura, L. (1997). Individual differences and attitudes toward rape: A meta-analytic review. *Personality and Social Psychology Bulletin, 23*(3), 295–315.

Beichner, D., & Spohn, C. (2005). Prosecutorial charging decisions in sexual assault cases: Examining the impact of a specialized prosecution unit. *Criminal Justice Policy Review, 16*(4), 461–498.

Belknap, J. (2007). *The invisible woman: Gender, crime, and justice* (3rd ed.). Belmont, CA: Thomson Wadsworth.

Berger, R. J., Neuman, W. L., & Searles, P. (1994). The impact of rape law reform: An aggregate analysis of police reports and arrests. *Criminal Justice Review, 19*(1), 1–23.

Brown, J., & King, J. (1998). Gender differences in police officers attitudes towards rape: Results of an exploratory study. *Psychology, Crime & Law, 4*, 265–279.

Campbell, R., & Johnson, C. R. (1997). Police officers' perceptions of rape: Is there consistency between state law and individual beliefs? *Journal of Interpersonal Violence, 12*, 255–274.

Caringella-MacDonald, S. (1988). Parallels and pitfalls: The aftermath of legal reform for sexual assault, marital rape, and domestic violence victims. *Journal of Interpersonal Violence, 3*(2), 174–189.

Crenshaw, K. (1993). Demarginalizing the intersection of race and sex: A black feminist critique of antidiscrimination doctrine, feminist theory, and antiracist politics. In D. K. Weisbers (Ed.), *Feminist legal theory foundations* (pp. 383–395). Philadelphia: Temple University Press.

Feldman-Summers, S., & Palmer, G. C. (1980). Rape as viewed by judges, prosecutors, and police officers. *Criminal Justice and Behavior, 7*(1), 19–40.

Frazier, P. A., & Haney, B. (1996). Sexual assault cases in the legal system: Police, prosecutor, and victim perspectives. *Law & Human Behavior, 20*(6), 607–628.

Frohmann, L. (1991). Discrediting victims' allegations of sexual assault: Prosecutorial accounts of case rejections. *Social Problems, 38*(2), 213–226.

Galton, E. R. (1975/1976). Police processing of rape complaints: A case study. *American Journal of Criminal Law, 4*(1), 15–30.

Gray, N. B., Palileo, G. J., & Johnson, G. D. (1993). Explaining rape victim blame: A test of attribution theory. *Sociological Spectrum, 13*(4), 377–392.

Horney, J., & Spohn, C. (1991). Rape law reform and instrumental change in six urban jurisdictions. *Law and Society Review, 25*, 117–153.

Hosmer, D. W., & Lemeshow, S. (2000). *Applied logistic regression.* New York, NY: John Wiley.

Hurtado, A. (1996). *The color of privilege: Three blasphemies on race and feminism.* Ann Arbor: University of Michigan Press.

Jordan, J. (2004). Beyond belief? Police, rape and women's credibility. *Criminal Justice, 4*(1), 29–59.

Kerstetter, W. A. (1990). Gateway to justice: Police and prosecutorial response to sexual assaults against women. *Journal of Criminal Law & Criminology, 81*, 267–313.

Kerstetter, W. A., & Van Winkle, B. (1990). Who decides? A study of the complainant's decision to prosecute in rape cases. *Criminal Justice & Behavior, 17*(3), 268–283.

Kingsnorth, R., MacIntosh, R., & Wentworth, J. (1999). Sexual assault: The role of prior relationship and victim characteristics in case processing. *Justice Quarterly, 16*, 275–302.

LaFree, G. D. (1981). Official reactions to social problems: Police decisions in sexual assault cases. *Social Problems, 28*(5), 582–594.

LaFree, G. D. (1989). *Rape and the criminal justice: The social construction of sexual assault.* Belmont, CA: Wadsworth.

Langton, L. (2010). *Women in law enforcement, 1987–2008* (NCJ Publication No. 230521). Washington, DC: U.S. Department of Justice. Available from http://bjs.ojp.usdoj.gov/content/pub/pdf/wle8708.pdf.

LeDoux, J. C., & Hazelwood, R. R. (1985). Police attitudes and beliefs toward rape. *Journal of Police Science and Administration, 13*(3), 211–220.

Lipsky, M. (1980). *Street-level bureaucracy.* New York, NY: Russell Sage.

Lonsway, K. A., Welch, S., & Fitzgerald, L. F. (2001). Police training in sexual assault response: process, outcomes, and elements of change. *Criminal Justice and Behavior, 28*(6), 695–730.

Martin, P. Y. (2005). *Rape work: Victims, gender, and emotions in organizational and community context.* New York, NY: Routledge.

Martin, P. Y., Reynolds, J. R., & Keith, S. (2002). Gender bias and feminist consciousness among judges and attorneys: A standpoint theory analysis. *Signs, 27*(3), 665–701.

Page, A. D. (2007). Behind the blue line: Investigating police officers' attitudes toward rape. *Journal of Police and Criminal Psychology, 22*(1), 22–32.

Page, A. D. (2008a). Judging women and defining crime: Police officers' attitudes toward women and rape. *Sociological Spectrum, 28*, 389–411.

Page, A. D. (2008b). Gateway to reform? Policy implications of police officers' attitudes toward rape. *American Journal of Criminal Justice, 33*, 44–58.

Schuller, R. A., & Stewart, A. (2000). Police responses to sexual assault complaints: The role of perpetrator/complainant intoxication. *Law and Human Behavior, 24*, 535–551.

Shaver, K. G. (1975). *An introduction to attribution processes.* Hillsdale, NJ: Lawrence Erlbaum.

Spears, J. W., & Spohn, C. C. (1996). The genuine victim and prosecutor's charging decisions in sexual assault cases. *American Journal of Criminal Justice, 20*(2), 183–205.

Spears, J. W., & Spohn, C. (1997). The effect of evidence factors and victim characteristics on prosecutors' charging decisions in sexual assault cases. *Justice Quarterly, 14*(3), 501–524.

Spohn, C., Beichner, D., & Davis-Frenzel, E. (2001). Prosecutorial justifications for sexual assault case rejection: Guarding the gateway to justice. *Social Problems, 48*(2), 206–235.

Spohn, C., & Holleran, D. (2001). Prosecuting sexual assault: A comparison of charging decisions in sexual assault cases involving strangers, acquaintances, and intimate partners. *Justice Quarterly, 18*, 651–688.

Spohn, C., & Horney, J. (1993). Rape law reform and the effect of victim characteristics on case processing. *Journal of Quantitative Criminology, 9*, 383–409.

Spohn, C., & Spears, J. W. (1996). The effect of offender and victim characteristics on sexual assault case processing decisions. *Justice Quarterly, 13*(4), 649–679.

Weir, J. A., & Wrightsman, L. S. (1990). The determinates of mock jurors' verdicts in a rape case. *Journal of Applied Social Psychology, 20*, 901–919.

Williams, K. (1981). Few convictions in rape cases: Empirical evidence concerning some alternative explanations. *Journal of Criminal Justice, 9*, 29–39.

DISCUSSION QUESTIONS

1. What are some of the factors that influence whether an arrest will be made in sexual assault cases?

2. Why is it important to look for gender differences among male and female police officers?

3. What is the significance of using sexual assault cases as opposed to cases involving other types of crime?

READING 14

This study examines how crime analysts and patrol officers perceive each other. The function of crime analysts and how they fit within the police organization are another focus of this research. The findings of this study reveal that most crime analysts believe that police management is supportive of their work within the organization; however, they believe that patrol officers have less positive views of their role within the agency.

The Integration of Crime Analysis Into Law Enforcement Agencies: An Exploratory Study Into the Perceptions of Crime Analysts

Bruce Taylor, Apollo Kowalyk, and Rachel Boba

Throughout history, law enforcement agencies have looked to technology to enhance their effectiveness. Fingerprinting, two-way radios, and the use of automobiles are examples of technological innovation that have helped define the structure of police agencies and the function of their constituent units. With the advent of the information age, law enforcement once again has looked to technology to improve its functional capabilities. The [intelligence]-led policing (ILP) movement (see Anderson, 1997; Maguire, 2000; Ratcliffe, 2003) and its central driver, crime analysis, signify a commitment to the further development of an embedded analytical capability within police agencies across North America and the United Kingdom.

Crime analysis involves the systematic study of crime and disorder problems conducted within a police agency in order to assist in criminal apprehension, crime and disorder reduction, crime prevention, and evaluation (Boba, 2005; Bruce, Hick, & Cooper, 2004; Emig, Heck, & Kravitz, 1980; Gottlieb, Arenberg, & Singh, 1994; Vellani & Nahoun, 2001). Its potential contribution to law enforcement and ILP includes the examination of data and application of specific analytical techniques to focus police efforts toward more effective crime reduction strategies and greater managerial accountability.

Since the early 1990s, there has been a movement in state and local law enforcement agencies toward data-driven decision-making practices (Eck & LaVigne, 1994; Goldstein, 1990; Henry, 2002; Scott, 2000). Policing strategies such as COMPSTAT, technological innovations leading to the development of complex data warehousing systems and crime mapping techniques, and the hiring of individuals with specialized analytical skills have encouraged the transformation of police agencies into analytical organizations. Inexpensive and adaptable software applications have allowed law enforcement agencies to begin to produce analytical reports and maps to aid in the identification of crime problems and implementation of subsequent police responses (Boba, 2005; Clarke & Eck, 2005). Also, the influence of problem-oriented policing, combined with a greater appreciation for community-oriented programs and self-directed street-level initiatives, has generated substantial gains in the area of problem solving and analysis (Weisburd & Eck, 2004).

It should be pointed out that the use of analysts to synthesize and analyze crime data is not a radically new idea—law enforcement agencies have been poking pins into maps and reviewing crime reports for decades. However, early efforts to increase investigative capacity through the use of pin mapping were characterized by inefficiency and limited information sharing. As a result, pin maps are being replaced by geographic information system (GIS) technologies and crime mapping software in a widespread movement toward

increased efficiency. However, the application of crime analysis remains elusive as many administrative and operational difficulties continue concerning this emerging trend. While the incorporation of productive analytical practices is imperative, the law enforcement community is still developing an understanding of the usefulness and the "organizational fit" of analysts within the police organization.

The purpose of this article is exploratory and seeks to provide a depiction of how current analysts perceive patrol officers' and other sworn members' attitudes about the crime analysis function, its "organizational fit," as well as their own attitudes about sworn personnel. A preliminary examination of these issues was conducted through the use of a survey that was electronically distributed to a large number of law enforcement analysts in April 2006. It was intended to serve as a scan of the perceptions of analysts about various aspects of their involvement in everyday law enforcement practices. Questions centered on crime analysts' perceptions about the various functions of crime analysis, their work and products, their organizational placement and cultural acceptance, and their relationships with other agency personnel (with a special focus on patrol officers). Survey results were expected to help determine whether analysts believed that operational utility is currently being achieved within their units and whether they felt their skills and training were being used to full capacity. Based on these exploratory results, we make suggestions for further research that examine the unresolved issues of implementation, organizational placement, and usefulness of the crime analysis function.

Literature Review

Most of the literature in the area of crime analysis has been written on the mechanics of how to conduct various types of analyses with police agencies. The prevalence, characteristics, and effectiveness of crime analysis and crime mapping practice have received scant attention. Two national assessments, in addition to several specialized or qualitative studies, have been conducted over the last 10 years, most recently in 2000.

The first of these two national studies focused primarily on crime mapping. In 1997, the Crime Mapping Research Center (CMRC; later known as the Mapping and Analysis for Public Safety program, or MAPS) of the National Institute of Justice, conducted a nationwide crime mapping survey to gauge the use of GIS technology throughout the law enforcement community. The survey included a few questions about crime analysis. Of the 2,004 departments responding to the survey, a majority reported that they engaged in some form of crime analysis, with 73% conducting basic crime analysis to fulfill Uniform Crime Reporting guidelines and 52% producing statistical reports of criminal activity (Mamalian & LaVigne, 1999). Unfortunately, no further information was published from this survey about the nature and extent of crime analysis in the United States.

The second of these national studies focused specifically on crime analysis and was funded by the U.S. Department of Justice, Office of Community Oriented Policing Services. In 2000, O'Shea and Nicholls (2003) conducted a survey of all municipal police, sheriff's offices, and state law enforcement agencies with 100 or more sworn personnel. Of 859 possible respondents, 544 (63%) completed the survey (359 municipal, 159 sheriff, and 31 state agencies). Some of the study's findings indicate that the crime analysis function varies by police agency and is primarily specialized and centralized, with a typical analyst to police officer ratio of 1:100. The authors suggest that even though it is difficult to determine from the survey data how many analysts are civilian employees, their assertion is that "civilians constitute a strong presence in this aspect of policing...by all appearances, police executives feel comfortable with civilians performing the crime analyst function" (O'Shea & Nicholls, 2003, p. 248).

In addition, O'Shea and Nicholls (2003) found that although crime analysis is typically centralized within an administrative unit in the agency, the actual work of a crime analyst focuses more on tactical crime analysis (e.g., identifying patterns) rather than strategic crime analysis (e.g., examination of long-term trends). The authors also found that "bean counting" was a primary focus of crime analysis, despite technological advances in statistical analysis and GIS mapping capabilities.

This observation was partially attributed to training issues and a lack of understanding regarding the potential contribution of crime analysis. The authors claim that the limited nature of crime analysis can be attributed in part to the complexity of the requests made by police managers. That is, even when controlling for other factors such as budget expenditures, crime rates, and regional variation, the expectations of management are related to the quality of the crime analysis unit itself. The authors posit, "So, the interesting question is not 'Why do crime analysts continue to produce essentially counts of crime?' but 'Why does the demand from police executives continue to emphasize crime counts?'" (O'Shea & Nicholls, 2003, p. 249).

Other surveys of crime analysis and crime mapping have been conducted that examine issues of crime analysis certification (International Association of Crime Analysts, 1999) and the status of crime analysis in mapping in Florida (Watkins & Reynolds, 1999). While these studies attempted to determine job function, required skills and training, and the prevalence and quality of crime analysis, the scope of these two studies is too limited to generalize their respective findings to the discipline of crime analysis or to police agencies across the United States.

A qualitative study by Cope (2004) of two police forces in the United Kingdom provides some insight into crime analyst perceptions about their work and officers' perceptions. The researchers used participant observation and structured interviews with analysts, officers, and managers to collect their data. The findings of their research led them to two major conclusions. The first is that the analysts' products and contributions are limited because of data quality issues, lack of clarity regarding the impact of their work on operational efficiency, and the inability of analysts to accommodate a lack of analysis expertise among frontline police officers. The second conclusion addressed a perceived lack of integration between crime analysts and the police organization itself. The authors assert that it is not impossible to integrate analysis into policing, but only if sworn police officers/managers and analysts recognize, understand, and appreciate each other's unique skill sets and respective areas of expertise.

In summary, these studies indicate that crime analysts continue to face challenges in being incorporated fully into police agencies and providing management with effective products. The purpose of our research is to explore this topic further to begin to understand how crime and intelligence analysts in the United States perceive sworn members' attitudes about crime analysis, how analysts perceive the "organizational fit" of crime analysis, and analyst perceptions of sworn personnel. The existing body of research has not focused on these issues and/or is outdated in providing a portrayal of the current state of crime analysis in the United States. This article seeks to begin filling this gap by using exploratory research to develop hypotheses for more in-depth research.

 ## Method

The data for this research were collected with a cross-sectional survey of crime and intelligence analysts. In addition, we held a group discussion with police chiefs and sheriffs on the initial results of the survey to assist with developing the implications of our findings for this article. The study population was analysts serving in publicly funded law enforcement agencies in the United States that employ full-time sworn officers. The survey was completed by individuals who consider themselves "crime analysts," "intelligence analysts," or both.[1] Our sampling frame included analysts who were members of one of three listservers geared specifically toward the law enforcement analyst community (LEANALYST,[2] IACA,[3] and CRIMEMAP[4]).

In April 2006, the Police Executive Research Forum (PERF) created and executed an online survey of crime/intelligence analysts through three major crime analyst listservers. With limited resources available for this project, we focused on those analysts that participated in one of the three major analyst listservers with the idea that they would be the group most likely to be able to reflect on the organizational context for crime analytic work.[5] The survey was sent to all members of the listservers: LEANALYST (2,075 members), IACA (982 members), and CRIMEMAP (250 members).[6] The

goal of our survey was not to obtain a representative sample of all analysts in the country, but to access those knowledgeable members of the analyst community to identify for us the key issues that hinder the crime analysis function within law enforcement agencies, with particular attention paid to patrol-officer-related concerns. Additional discussions we held with many senior crime analysts provided anecdotal evidence that those analysts participating in these listservers were generally among the best informed and most engaged in the analysis field.

To maximize participation and elicit candid critical comments, our survey was voluntary and anonymous.[7] We wanted analysts to feel comfortable completing the survey and have full confidence that their individual responses would not be shared with members of their own agency or attributed to their agency. Of those individuals who consider themselves crime analysts or intelligence analysts, 238 responded and completed the survey online.

Our approach is not without its limitations. Our data do not necessarily represent the views of all analysts in the United States, and it is unclear if they even represent the views of the members of the three law enforcement analyst listservers.[8] Also, we are only obtaining analysts' perceptions and not those of sworn personnel in their agencies. While our design limits the generalizability of our results, the objective of our survey was not to obtain a representative sample of all analysts in the country, but to begin exploring the issues—as experienced analysts see them—of embedding crime analysis within law enforcement agencies, a fairly modest goal. We hope that future research will utilize our results to generate better informed survey items and test them with appropriate probability-based samples.

The survey was designed to elicit crime analysts' perceptions on the role of analysts in law enforcement agencies pertaining to the different functions of analysts, their work, and their relationships with other agency personnel. In order to provide context to these questions, the survey also included questions about the study participants' experience, skills, supervision, and their agencies' characteristics (such as size and organizational structure as it relates to crime analysis). The survey questions relating to perception were combined into four indices measuring the *analysts' perception* of (1) patrol officer attitudes toward crime analysis, (2) upper-management attitudes toward crime analysis, (3) the organizational fit of crime analysis within the agency, and (4) patrol officers' use of crime analysis products. Table 5 (in the results section) illustrates the survey questions listed in their respective indices. Survey items were generated by reviewing the literature and consulting crime analysts and law enforcement practitioners on the key elements of each of our content areas.

⊠ Results

Analyses of the 238 completed surveys are broken down into two topic areas. The first is a description of the sample including agency and analyst characteristics. The second is a presentation of the substantive results of the four indices measuring the analysts' perceptions. This section is followed by a discussion of the importance of these findings and suggestions for future research.

Description of the Sample

Agency characteristics. Most of the respondents were crime/intelligence analysts from city/municipal police departments (59.5%), sheriff's offices (17.3%), or state law enforcement agencies (11.0%). Smaller numbers of respondents were from county police departments (6.8%) and federal law enforcement agencies (5.5%). The vast majority of the respondents were from agencies with 100 or more sworn officers (81.8%) with 38.1% from agencies with between 100 to 499 officers and 29.7% from those with 1,000 or more (see Table 1 for full distribution).

The vast majority of the respondents were from agencies with 20 or fewer analysts (83.8%). The largest single category was respondents from agencies with 1 to 2 analysts (43.4%); 17% were from agencies with 3 to 5 analysts (see Table 2).

Analyst characteristics. Respondents were asked about how long they were employed as an analyst with

Table 1 Number of Sworn Law Enforcement Personnel Within the Agency (*N* = 238)

Number of Sworn Officers	Percentage
1–10	1.7
11–24	.8
25–49	2.1
50–99	13.6
100–499	38.1
500–999	14.0
1,000 or more	29.7
Total	100.0

Table 2 Number of Crime/Intelligence Analysts in the Law Enforcement Agency (*N* = 238)

Number of Analysts	Percentage
1–2	43.4
3–5	17.0
6–10	12.8
11–20	10.6
21–30	6.4
31–40	2.6
41–50	1.3
51	6.0
Total	100.0

their current agency. Our sample was diverse, with more than 70% having at least 3 years of experience. The breakdown of experience is in Table 3.

Respondents were asked about their primary analytical orientation. Most of the respondents conducted *both* crime mapping and offender pattern analysis (47.9%; offender pattern analysis focuses on repeat offenders as compared to crime mapping analysis that focuses on place and crime patterns). Others focus solely on crime mapping (19.2%) or offender pattern analysis (14.5%).

Additionally, others reported possessing another type of orientation (18.4%). Very few of the respondents identified themselves as solely an intelligence analyst (11.8%). Most of the respondents identified themselves as either solely a crime analyst (46.6%) or a combination of both crime and intelligence analysts (41.6%).

Respondents were asked about the rank of their direct supervisors. Although most (85.1%) of the respondents were not sworn members of their law enforcement agency, an overwhelming majority of their immediate supervisors were sworn members (75.8%). About one quarter reported their supervisors were sergeants, 22.2% lieutenants, 10% captains, 12.8% commanders/executives, and 30% another rank. Respondents were asked about their primary user group(s). Most of the respondents reported assisting detectives (44.3%) or law enforcement administrators/ upper management (21.1%). The remainder either assisted patrol officers (17.3%) or another user group (17.3%). These interactions with the primary user group were reported as occurring mostly on a daily (73.5%) or weekly basis (19.7%), with fewer than 7% of the respondents reporting monthly or less frequent interactions with their primary user group.

Table 3	Number of Years Employed as an Analyst With Their Current Agency ($N = 238$)
Years of Experience	**Percentage**
< 1	12.3
1–2	14.9
3–5	31.5
6–10	25.1
> 10	16.2
Total	100.0

Finally, analysts were asked about the location of their work space in the police building. Almost half of the respondents have a work space that is physically located in close proximity to the detective work space (46.2%), and 27.3% are located in an administrative unit. Only 18.5% of the respondents are located in close proximity to where patrol officers are based.

Indices for analyst ratings. Rather than relying on single survey items for the analysis, we developed four indices each containing a series of correlated question items to examine the four topics. The first two indices measure the analysts' perceptions of patrol officer attitudes about crime analysis and upper management attitudes about crime analysis. The second two indices measure the analysts' perceptions of the organization fit and acceptance of crime analysis in their agency and their attitudes toward patrol officers. They will be referred to as (a) "perceptions of officer attitudes," (b) "perceptions of management attitudes," (c) "organizational fit and acceptance," and (d) "attitudes toward patrol officers" throughout the remainder of the article.

Tables 4 and 5 contain the summary statistics for each of the four scales and the individual items used to measure each of these scales, respectively. Each of the indices (see Table 4) was scored with a scale from 1 to 5 (*strongly positive* = 1, *somewhat positive* = 2, *middle of the road* = 3, *somewhat negative* = 4, *strongly negative* = 5) and has satisfactory reliability (Cronbach's alpha scores over .70 are generally considered good), with the items within the scales showing strong interitem correlations.

Also, the data for each of the scales are normally distributed (all of the kurtosis statistics are below .20).

As seen in Table 4, most analysts felt that management was fairly supportive of their work (mean score of 2.3, between somewhat positive and middle of the road) and that organizational fit was not a problem (mean score of 2.4, between somewhat positive and middle of the road). However, the analysts' perceptions of patrol officers' perceptions of them only reached the middle of the road (mean score of 3), in contrast to the more positive attitudes expressed by analysts about

Table 4	Summary Statistics of the Analyst Ratings Index				
Index	**Measure**	**Cronbach's Alpha**	**Mean**	**SD**	**Kurtosis**
1	Perceptions of officer attitudes	.86	3.0	3.0	.16
2	Perceptions of management attitudes	.80	2.3	2.2	.16
3	Organizational fit and acceptance	.81	2.4	1.8	.15
4	Attitudes toward patrol officers	.70	1.7	1.5	.16

patrol officers (mean score of 1.7, between strongly positive and somewhat positive).

The analysis results for several of the individual items more specifically highlight the difference between how analysts think officers feel about them and vice versa. On survey question 11 (see Table 5), "Analysts are accepted within the 'police culture,'" less than half (45%) of the analysts "somewhat agreed" or "strongly agreed" with the statement. Furthermore, less than half (44%) of the analysts agreed that "patrol officers make effective use of crime analysts to solve crime and/or identify crime-related problems" (Question 14), and less than 18% agreed that "patrol officers believe it is important to understand the work of analysts"

(Question 22) or "patrol officers make an effort to understand the work of analysts" (Question 24).

In contrast, nearly all of the analysts (97.4%) felt that they make an effort to understand the work of patrol officers (Question 21). About two thirds of the analyst respondents felt that patrol officers do not have the time to work proactively and problem solve (Question 17—not in one of the four scales).[9] In addition to the concerns analysts have in working with patrol officers, only about one third of the analysts agreed that "generally speaking, law enforcement agencies make effective use of crime analysts to solve crime and/or process criminal intelligence" (Question 15—not in one of the four scales).[10]

Table 5	Police Executive Research Forum Survey of Crime Analysts—Analyst Ratings Index					
	Strongly Agree	**Somewhat Agree**	**Neither Agree nor Disagree**	**Somewhat Disagree**	**Strongly Disagree**	**Mean**
Index 1: Analyst perceptions of what patrol officers think of crime analysts						
1 Patrol officers/deputies appreciate the results of my work.	21.5%	51.1%	18.6%	6.3%	2.5%	2.17
14 Patrol officers make effective use of crime analysts to solve crime and/or identify crime-related problems.	7.6%	36.1%	29.4%	18.9%	8.0%	2.84
16 Frontline officers show an interest in crime analysis and problem solving.	4.6%	37.1%	30.4%	24.1%	3.8%	2.85

(Continued)

Table 5   (Continued)

	Strongly Agree	Somewhat Agree	Neither Agree nor Disagree	Somewhat Disagree	Strongly Disagree	Mean
22 Patrol officers believe it is important to understand the work of analysts.	5.1%	12.7%	37.6%	32.1%	12.7%	3.35
24 Patrol officers make an effort to understand the work of analysts.	2.1%	14.0%	36.4%	34.7%	12.7%	3.42
26 Patrol officers have succeeded in developing effective working relationships with analysts.	5.1%	34.2%	39.7%	18.1%	3.0%	2.80
Index 2: Analyst perceptions of what upper management thinks of crime analysts						
2 Upper management understands my role.	19.8%	44.7%	12.2%	14.8%	8.4%	2.47
3 Upper management appreciates the work that I do.	30.3%	41.0%	15.8%	10.7%	2.1%	2.13
4 My law enforcement agency provides me with the technology I require to complete the assigned tasks.	31.2%	32.1%	13.5%	16.5%	6.8%	2.35
7 My supervisor appreciates the contributions I make.	47.5%	40.3%	8.0%	3.4%	0.8%	1.70
19 Police executives believe analysts play an important role in law enforcement.	13.6%	42.8%	22.5%	16.5%	4.7%	2.56
Index 3: Analysts' own perceptions of their organization fit and acceptance within the agency						
8 My work is understood by my primary user group.	28.3%	47.3%	13.1%	9.3%	2.1%	2.10
9 My work is appreciated by my primary user group.	33.9%	50.8%	9.3%	5.9%	0.0%	1.87
10 My role and job function is properly placed within the organizational structure of my law enforcement agency.	23.9%	34.9%	13.9%	18.9%	8.4%	2.53
11 Analysts are accepted within the "police culture."	8.4%	36.6%	28.6%	19.7%	6.7%	2.80

	Strongly Agree	Somewhat Agree	Neither Agree nor Disagree	Somewhat Disagree	Strongly Disagree	Mean
12 I feel that my training and education are being put to good use.	22.4%	40.1%	15.6%	13.5%	8.4%	2.46
Index 4: Analyst attitudes toward patrol						
20 Police ride-along programs help analysts understand the needs of patrol officers.	38.0%	37.6%	21.9%	2.1%	0.4%	1.89
21 I believe it is important to understand the work of patrol officers.	66.9%	30.5%	2.1%	0.4%	0.0%	1.36
23 I make an effort to understand the work of patrol officers.	54.5%	40.4%	4.3%	0.9%	0.0%	1.51
25 I have succeeded in developing effective working relationships with patrol officers.	26.8%	46.8%	20.0%	6.0%	0.4%	2.06

Discussion

For this article, we conducted a cross-sectional survey of crime/intelligence analysts and held a group discussion with police chiefs and sheriffs on the results of the survey. The purpose of our exploratory project was to examine crime and intelligence analysts' perceptions of patrol officers' and other sworn members' attitudes about crime analysis, analysts' perceptions of the "organization fit" of crime analysis, and analysts' attitudes toward sworn personnel.

What we learned from our survey was that most analysts in our sample felt that management was fairly supportive of their work and that organizational fit was not a problem. However, the analysts' perceptions of what patrol officers thought of them only reached the middle-of-the-road level, contrary to the much more positive attitudes they expressed about patrol officers. Also, most of the respondents in our survey indicated that they work in specialized investigative units or administrative areas and have sworn personnel as supervisors. Although these analysts seem to find that their work is generally appreciated, the general level of interaction between analysts and frontline patrol officers seems to be limited at best and one sided (i.e., analysts seek to understand officers, but the reverse does not happen often). The significance of this finding should not be understated, as the capacity to develop effective street-level crime reduction strategies can sometimes depend on the ability of analysts to work with frontline officers to quickly turn crime data into "actionable intelligence."

As pointed out to the authors by an anonymous reviewer, our sample of analysts consisted of only a small group of respondents who were tactical analysts generating operational products (as evidenced by the challenges we uncovered in providing management with effective products, that only 17.3% of crime analysts reported assisting patrol officers, and only 18.5% of respondents were located close to where patrol officers are based). Tactical analysis benefits patrol officers and detectives, strategic analysis benefits managers, and intelligence analysis benefits organized crime investigators (Boba, 2005). One reason why our sample of crime analysts perceives patrol officers to hold "middle of the road" attitudes about their job function is that the latter group is not being directly served by the analytic product. The issue then may well be those of organizational placement, job description, work duties, and priority of function rather than any intrinsic reluctance to use crime analysis by operational patrol officers.

The results for several of the individual items when examined separately raise some additional concerns relating to whether the skills and training of analysts are being used to full capacity, whether analysts are being accepted within the police culture, whether agencies as a whole (and patrol officers in particular) are not using crime analysts to solve crimes, and whether patrol officers understand what analysts do. In addition, nearly all of the analysts felt that they make an effort to understand the work of patrol officers. An interesting issue to explore in future research is why the analysts feel they are making an effort but patrol officers are not. This divergent set of results is at least suggestive of a possible problem area. However, it is important to remember that our survey only presents the views of analysts, not the patrol officers' side. Our results should not be considered definitive. Future research will need to survey patrol officers to verify our results with analysts.

Another finding from the survey identified a perception among the vast majority of analyst respondents that patrol officers do not have enough time to engage in proactive investigations and problem-solving initiatives outside of their regular duties. Therefore, even if analysts could get patrol officers the ideal analytic products there is a concern about whether line-level patrol officers can find the time to act on the information. This concern, if valid, merits further consideration because it could have an effect on the implementation of an agency's ILP approach, often held out to be an alternative to the more common reactive model of police resource deployment.

While we feel that our survey achieved its goal of providing a glimpse into the field of crime analysis for establishing future research questions on the organizational fit of analysts, our survey had some methodological limitations. As discussed earlier, our data do not necessarily represent the nation of analysts and it is unclear if it even represents the views of the members of the three crime analyst listservers used for our sample. Despite these limitations, we believe our approach of surveying 283 active and knowledgeable members of the crime analyst community has been a useful approach for identifying the existence of problem areas in conducting crime analysis within law enforcement agencies.

Future Research

The purpose of our research was to provide specific ideas for future research into the area of increasing the effectiveness and inclusion of crime analysis within law enforcement agencies, based on experienced analysts' perceptions. Although there may be many other crime analysis topics to examine, this study indicates the following deserve attention:

- The effect crime analysis has had on the routine operation of police organizations, including whether crime analysis has become an ingrained aspect of allocation of patrol resources, criminal investigations, and other routine police operations. Future research can also explore whether the analytical function can become embedded within the police information system itself (e.g., CAD and RMS systems) and whether the productivity of individual officers can be increased through the use of crime analysis.
- Perceptions and attitudes of line-level officers and management personnel about crime analysis to confirm or refute the analysts' perceptions of sworn personnel and themselves.
- The nature and underlying characteristics of varying perceptions of management (e.g., crime analysts find them generally supportive) and line-level officers (e.g., crime analysts do not find them as supportive as management) about crime analysis.
- The reasons why patrol officers apparently do not seek to understand crime analysis when the reverse seems to be true.

- The reasons why patrol officers apparently do not effectively use analysts' products.
- The reasons why patrol officers may not have adequate time for problem solving activities.
- The specific nature of the role of civilian crime analysts in police culture.

Observation and interviews may be necessary to separate perceptions of exclusion and actual behavior.

 ## Conclusion

Central to the ILP movement is the crime analysis function, the primary means by which limited police resources can be deployed in a productive manner to better address community problems and ultimately reduce crime (Osborne & Wernicke, 2003). Although a large number of law enforcement agencies have hired analysts to advance their knowledge and effectiveness with limited resources, little research has been conducted to assess whether analysts have been *fully integrated* within the field of law enforcement and, if not, why not. If the function of crime analysis is ever to become broadly accepted and used within law enforcement agencies, we will need richer data on the successful process of embedding the crime analysis function itself. It is our hope that in this article we have provided some concrete concepts on which to base future research and provided a specific direction to understanding crime analysis within law enforcement—with the ultimate goal of making both crime analysis and policing in general more effective.

Notes

1. We used the following definition of crime analysts and intelligence analysts: Crime analysts help police agencies solve crimes, develop effective strategies and tactics to prevent future crimes, find and apprehend offenders, prosecute and convict offenders, improve safety and quality of life, optimize internal operations, prioritize patrol and investigations, detect and solve community problems, allocate resources, and plan for future resource needs. Intelligence analysts may do many of those same things and they study criminal relationships; link and chart suspects to criminal organizations or events to determine who is doing what with whom; work with intelligence officers who gather information by field observation, confidential information sources, and public records; establish criminal profiles that include prior crimes and criminal relationships to aid in making a connection between members and the organization; use telephone toll analysis to plot telephone activity to determine the size and location of criminal groups and individuals involved; and study the suspect's assets to determine the flow of money going in and coming from the targeted group.

2. LEANALYST is an Internet e-mail mailing list devoted to issues concerning law enforcement and the analysis of crime. The mailing list provides a place where law enforcement employees (sworn and nonsworn), academia, and businesses providing products or services to the law enforcement community can exchange information, methods, and ideas regarding the analysis of crime.

3. The International Association of Crime Analysts (IACA) was formed in 1990 to help crime analysts around the world improve their skills and make valuable contacts, to help law enforcement agencies make the best use of crime analysis, and to advocate standards of performance and technique within the profession itself. Within the past few years, IACA membership has hovered around 1,000. Members include crime analysts, intelligence analysts, police officers of all ranks, educators, and students. Their listserver serves their membership and is a conduit for information sharing about crime analysis work, resources, and administration.

4. CRIMEMAP is the National Institute of Justice, MAPS (Mapping and Analysis for Public Safety) program's listserver. CRIMEMAP serves as an information dissemination tool for crime analysts, researchers, geographers, software vendors, and other interested parties to communicate about crime mapping technologies related to criminal justice applications. The listserver enables subscribers to post and respond to questions, and also serves as a vehicle for MAPS staff to announce upcoming conferences and new publications.

5. An alternative approach would have been to capture a nationally representative sample of all crime analysts. However, this would have been much more costly and would have included many less-informed (and well-informed) analysts in our sample.

6. The totals come from the listserver managers. These numbers total 3,307, but it should be noted that many individuals belong to all three lists. Thus, at a minimum, 2,075 people were contacted.

7. Through the use of a password-protected survey operated from the Police Executive Research Forum's secured Web site, our team was able to offer the respondents full anonymity.

8. Due to the anonymous nature of our survey, we cannot test differences between those listserver members who did or did not complete the surveys. However, all analysts from these three listservers were given the opportunity to complete a survey.

9. Question 17 had the following distribution: 1.9% = *strongly agree*, 12.3% = *somewhat agree*, 19.9% = *neither agree nor disagree*, 54.1% = *somewhat disagree*, and 11.8% = *strongly disagree* (mean score of 3.6).

10. Question 15 had the following distribution: 2.3% = *strongly agree*, 30.9% = *somewhat agree*, 25.2% = *neither agree nor disagree*, 31.9% = *somewhat disagree*, and 6.7% = *strongly disagree* (mean score of 3.05).

 # References

Anderson, R. (1997). Intelligence-led policing: A British perspective. In A. Smith (Ed.), *Intelligence led policing: International perspectives on policing in the 21st century.* Lawrenceville, NJ: International Association of Law Enforcement Intelligence Analysts.

Boba, R. (2005). *Crime analysis and crime mapping.* Thousand Oaks, CA: Sage.

Bruce, C., Hick, S., & Cooper, J. (2004). *Exploring crime analysis: Readings on essential skills.* Overland Park, KS: IACA Press.

Cope, N. (2004). Intelligence led policing or policing led intelligence? *The British Journal of Criminology, 44,* 188–203.

Clarke, R. V., & Eck, J. (2005). *Crime analysis for problem solvers: In 60 small steps.* Washington, DC: U.S. Department of Justice, Office of Community Oriented Policing Services.

Eck, J., & LaVigne, N. (1994). *Using research: A primer for law enforcement managers.* Washington, DC: Police Executive Research Forum.

Emig, M., Heck, R., & Kravitz, M. (1980). *Crime analysis: A selected bibliography.* Washington, DC: U.S. National Criminal Justice Reference Service.

Goldstein, H. (1990). *Problem-oriented policing.* New York: McGraw-Hill.

Gottlieb, S., Arenberg, S., & Singh, R. (1994). *Crime analysis: From first report to final arrest.* Montclair, CA: Alpha.

Henry, V. (2002). *The COMPSTAT paradigm.* Flushing, NY: Looseleaf Law.

International Association of Crime Analysts. (1999). Online Survey.

Maguire, M. (2000). Policing by risks and targets: Some dimensions and implications of intelligence led crime control. *Policing and Society, 9,* 315–36.

Mamalian, C. A., & LaVigne, N. (1999). *Research preview: The use of computerized crime mapping by law enforcement: Survey results.* Washington, DC: U.S. Department of Justice, Office of Justice Programs.

Osborne, D., & Wernicke, S. (2003). *Introduction to crime analysis: Basic resources for criminal justice practice.* Binghamton, NY: Haworth Press.

O'Shea, T. C., & Nicholls, K. (2003). Police crime analysis: A survey of US police departments with 100 or more sworn personnel. *Police Practice and Research, 4,* 233–250.

Ratcliffe, J. H. (2003). Intelligence-led policing. *Trends and issues in crime and criminal justice* (248), Australian Institute of Criminology, Canberra, Australia.

Scott, M. (2000). *Problem-oriented policing: Reflections on the first 20 years.* Washington, DC: U.S. Department of Justice, Office of Community Oriented Policing Services.

Vellani, K. H., & Nahoun, J. (2001). *Applied crime analysis.* Boston: Butterworth-Heinemann.

Watkins, R. C., & Reynolds, K. M. (1999). *Crime analysis: Roles, responsibilities, and resources requirements of crime analysts in Florida.* Presentation at the 1999 American Society of Criminology Conference.

Weisburd, D., & Eck, J. (2004). What can police do to reduce crime, disorder and fear? *The Annals of the American Academy of Political and Social Science, 593,* 42–65.

DISCUSSION QUESTIONS

1. What is a crime analyst?

2. What is a reason that police agencies now believe that they need the services of crime analysts?

3. How can police administrators use the findings from this study to improve their organizations?

Police officer productivity is sometimes measured by the number of arrests officers make and citations they write in a specified period of time.

Police Effectiveness

Section Highlights

- Look at the history of police effectiveness over time.
- Examine police practices that are believed to be effective.
- Discuss how police effectiveness is measured today.

O n May 12, 1999, President Bill Clinton gave a speech in the Rose Garden of the White House in which he updated Americans on the progress that had been made since he signed the 1994 anti-crime bill. "When I signed the crime bill, I pledged to help communities all over our nation fund 100,000 community police officers by the year 2000.... In making America's thin blue line thicker and stronger, our nation will be safer."[1] But does adding more police officers to the streets really make us safer or have an impact on violent crime? This section discusses this issue and answers the question, "What works in policing?" This section begins with a discussion of how police effectiveness is defined and then provides a historical overview of the way that the effectiveness of the police has been measured over time. A discussion of the impact of several general and focused police practices on crime and citizens' fear of crime is also presented in this section.

What Is Police Effectiveness?

Efficiency and effectiveness are two concepts that are often used to measure the performance of public and private organizations.[2] Efficient organizations are those that can perform necessary tasks while using the least amount of resources (including time, personnel, and money). The level of effectiveness is often measured by the ability of organizations to perform critical tasks. Wesley Skogan defines an effective organization as one that "meets challenges put to them, satisfy demands for service or solve problems."[3] Thus, efficiency focuses on the resources used by organizations when completing tasks, while effectiveness centers on the ability of organizations to complete tasks. Using Wesley Skogan's definition of effectiveness as a guide, **police effectiveness** can be defined as the ability of police organizations to meet the challenges presented to them, to satisfy citizens' demands for service, and to solve problems within their communities.[4]

The manner in which police effectiveness is measured has changed significantly over time. Changes in the measurement of police effectiveness reflect changes in the goals and roles of police organizations and also priorities that are identified by citizens. George Kelling and Mark Moore described the change in the measurement of police effectiveness within the context of their three eras of policing. First, during the political era, measured outcomes of police work included the ability to control crime, maintain order, and provide relief to citizens faced with various social problems (including poverty and homelessness).[5] It was especially important for the police to be viewed as effective by political figures, as they were the primary source of job security for the police during this time. Next, during the reform era, crime control and the apprehension of criminals became the most important standards by which police organizations measured their effectiveness. Output measures of effectiveness during this era included the number of arrests made by police officers, the crime rate according to the Uniform Crime Report, the length of time it took police officers to respond to citizens calls for service (response time), and the level of police presence in the community (the number of officers patrolling the streets).[6] Today, during the community/problem-solving era, the measures of police effectiveness have expanded to include citizens' quality of life and police officers' abilities to solve problems and reduce citizens' fear of crime, maintain social order, increase citizens' satisfaction with police services, and manage crime.[7]

How Do the Police Impact Crime and Citizens' Fear of Crime?

Section 1 explains how crime control has been a major focus of policing in the United States from the time that formal police agencies began to emerge in the mid-1800s. Citizens' fear of crime has also become an important measure of whether police agencies are effective. Over time, the police have utilized a variety of strategies to manage crime and citizens' fear of crime in their communities. These strategies include more general police practices in which police actions are conducted with the purpose of providing crime control on a communitywide level and also more focused police practices in which the police concentrate their efforts on certain crimes, suspects, and locations within their community.

General Crime-Control Strategies

Police use several general practices to manage crime and fear of crime, including the addition of more police officers, the use of random preventive patrol, quickly responding to citizens' calls for service, and generalized arrest strategies.[8] In theory, these strategies seem like they would be effective at reducing crime and citizens' fear of crime, but decades of research have revealed some surprising results.

Adding More Police Officers

On October 28, 2010, the headline "More Police Officers to Patrol Washington Heights and Inwood to Fight Rise in Crime" was featured in a Manhattan newspaper.[9] The article states that there had been a recent increase in felony assaults, robberies, and grand larceny in Manhattan (New York) and that local political and police officials proposed adding more police officers in an effort to reduce these crimes. This news article presents a sentiment that is common in many communities that experience an increase in crime—more cops means less crime. In theory, this sounds like a good way to manage crime and to make people feel safer; however, research suggests that the addition of police officers might not be as effective as one might think.

John Eck and Edward Maguire examined existing research on this topic to see if there is any empirical evidence supporting the idea that hiring more police officers results in less crime.[10] They identified 27 studies focused on this issue dating back to the early 1970s. Most studies found that the number of police had no effect on crime. Other studies found that an increase in police resulted in an increase in crime. And only a few

There is a perception among some citizens that more police officers mean less crime in their neighborhoods.

studies found that more police resulted in less crime. Eck and Maguire conclude that there is no strong evidence that an increase in the number of police results in less crime. This conclusion suggests that it might not be the number of police officers patrolling the streets that matters, but instead, it is what police officers are doing while they are on patrol that counts.

Another way that some people assess police protection within a community is the police-to-population ratio. The **police–population ratio** is the number of sworn police officers per 1,000 citizens.[11] In 2008, the Bureau of Justice Statistics reported that the national average police–population ratio was 2.51 officers per 1,000 citizens—this figure includes police agencies in communities of all sizes.[12] Some argue that the police–population ratio is not a good way to measure safety in communities and that this is an arbitrary number. This argument is based on the fact that some cities with serious crime problems have more police officers or a higher police–citizen ratio than other cities of similar size that experience far less crime. The following table presents the 10 most safe and dangerous cities in the United States along with the police–population ratio for each city. Notice that in most cases, the cities that are ranked on the 10 most dangerous cities list have higher police–population ratios than the cities on the safest cities list. These numbers contradict the idea that more police officers mean safer communities or less crime. It is hard to determine if more police officers lead to more reported crime or more reported crime results in more police officers being hired by police departments; this is a classic case of "what comes first . . . the chicken or the egg?"

Routine Preventive Patrol

Another general crime-control strategy used by most American police agencies is **routine preventive patrol**. As mentioned in Section 7, routine preventive patrol consists of police officers randomly driving their patrol cars around their communities to make their presence known to citizens. This strategy is based on the idea that police presence will deter individuals from committing crimes out of fear that they

U.S. Cities With Populations of 500,000 or More			
Safest Cities*	**(Pol/Citizen Ratio)****	**Dangerous Cities***	**(Pol/Citizen Ratio)****
1. El Paso, TX	(1.8)	1. Detroit, MI	(3.5)
2. Honolulu, HI	(2.1)	2. Baltimore, MD	(4.7)
3. New York, NY	(4.3)	3. Memphis, TN	(3.1)
4. San Jose, CA	(1.5)	4. Washington, DC	(6.7)
5. San Diego, CA	(1.5)	5. Atlanta, GA	(3.4)
6. Austin, TX	(2.0)	6. Indianapolis, IN	(2.0)
7. Portland, OR	(1.9)	7. Philadelphia, PA	(4.7)
8. Los Angeles, CA	(2.5)	8. Milwaukee, WI	(3.4)
9. Seattle, WA	(2.2)	9. Houston, TX	(2.3)
10. Fort Worth, TX	(2.1)	10. Columbus, OH	(2.5)

* See http://os.cqpress.com/citycrime/2010/City_Crime_Rankings_bypop_2011-2011.pdf.

** Data drawn from the Bureau of Justice Statistics; see http://bjs.ojp.usdoj.gov/content/pub/pdf/lpd07.pdf.

will get caught. So does this mean that if there is more routine patrol in certain neighborhoods, there will be less crime when compared to neighborhoods that have lower levels of routine patrol? Several studies have addressed this question.

One of the earliest studies to examine the impact of routine preventive patrol on crime was Operation 25, conducted in New York City in 1954.[13] This study was conducted in one precinct in Harlem over the course of 4 months. During the study, the number of patrol officers was more than doubled from 188 to 440. The findings from this study revealed that there was a 55.6% decrease in reported felonies compared to a 4-month period during the previous year. This study was criticized for not having a comparison/control group, for relying solely on crime data generated by the police department, and for not checking to see if crime displacement had occurred in the surrounding areas.

More than a decade later in 1966, another study focused on the impact of increased patrol was conducted in the 20th Precinct in the New York City Police Department.[14] In this study, patrol was increased by 40% for 1 month. After relying on a before-after comparison design, there was a significant decrease in the number of robberies, grand larcenies, auto thefts, and other types of crime during this time frame. Unlike Operation 25, this study checked for crime displacement in three adjacent areas and found that it occurred in only one of the three areas near the 20th Precinct. This study was criticized for several reasons: (1) They could not compare crime data from the prior year, they had changed their reporting methods while the study was being conducted in 1966; (2) they relied solely on official crime data; (3) there was a lack of experimental design; and (4) it did not specify how extra patrol was deployed and what type of patrol activity was being used by those officers.

From 1972 to 1973, one of the most rigorous studies examining the impact of varying levels of patrol was conducted in Kansas City, Missouri. In this study, three areas had varying levels of controlled routine preventive patrol:[15] (1) the *reactive area* received no patrol—officers only went into the area when citizens called for service; (2) the *proactive area* had patrol levels that were two or three times more than normal; and (3) the *control area* received the normal level of preventive patrol (no change in patrol level). The research findings from this study found that regardless of the level of patrol, all three areas experienced no significant differences in crime, citizens' attitudes toward police service, fear of crime, response time, or citizens' satisfaction with response time. This study is regarded as one of the most important studies on police patrol, as its findings challenge the assertion that "more patrol is better." The results of this study also prompted police executives across the country to think not only about the allocation of patrol but also that focused patrol strategies might be a more effective alternative to traditional routine preventive patrol. While some departments have adopted focused patrol strategies since the time of the Kansas City Preventive Patrol study, routine preventive patrol remains a staple activity in most police departments across the country.

Rapid Response Time

Response time is the time that it takes from when dispatch first receives a call for police service from a citizen until a patrol car shows up on scene. Beginning in the reform era, police executives believed that **rapid response time** to citizens' calls would result in more arrests. They also believed that citizens would view the police as more professional and would have a more positive perception of them if police officers were able to respond to their calls more quickly.

One of the first studies focused on rapid response to calls for service was conducted in Kansas City, Missouri, in 1977.[16] The purpose of this study was twofold: (1) to determine the relationship of response time to on-scene criminal apprehension, availability of witnesses, citizen satisfaction, and the frequency of citizen injuries related to criminal and noncriminal incidents, and (2) the identification of problems and patterns in reporting crime and requesting police assistance. The results of the study indicate that response time is unrelated to the probability of making arrests or locating people who witnessed crimes. Reporting time by witnesses or crime victims was the strongest predictor of arrest and locating people who had witnessed the crimes. Citizens' satisfaction with police response was more closely related to their individual expectations and perceptions of response time than to actual police response time.

William Spelman and Dale Brown replicated the Kansas City response time analysis study using data from Jacksonville, Florida, Peoria, Illinois, Rochester, New York, and San Diego, California.[17] The findings of this study confirmed that citizen reporting time and not police response times most affect the possibility of arrest. The study also identified several issues related to why citizens delay or have difficulty when calling the police for help. For instance, some people reported that they were not sure whether a crime had been committed. Other people were busy trying to cope with the problems that the crime had created. Some people also stated that they had conflict with others about whether to call the police. There were several people that did not have a telephone available to make the call to the police. Some people said that they were unsure about where to call for police help, while others stated that they had difficulty communicating with the person taking their call for help.

Research conducted on rapid response by the police has revealed several important issues related to police response. First, rapid response to calls for service is not necessary for most calls because most crimes are discovered *after* they have been committed; thus, offenders have had time to escape or flee the scene. Second, rapid response does not increase the likelihood of arrest; what matters are the reporting habits of citizens. The faster that citizens call the police for help, the greater the chance that the police will apprehend suspects or find witnesses associated with the crime.

Generalized Arrest Strategies/Mandatory Arrest

The National Research Council identifies **mandatory arrest** laws as a **generalized crime-control strategy** used by the police, because arrest is used as a way to keep crime from occurring or recurring.[18] Research examining the impact of mandatory arrest by the police has centered on misdemeanor cases of domestic violence. Research findings on the deterrent effects of mandatory arrest have been somewhat mixed. Deterrent effects of arrest were found in studies conducted in Minneapolis, Miami-Dade County, and Colorado Springs County, but not in Omaha, Nebraska, Charlotte, North Carolina, and Milwaukee, Wisconsin. These findings suggest that contextual factors matter when assessing the impact of mandatory arrest; more specifically, the effects of arrest vary by city, neighborhood, and, in some cases, characteristics of offenders.[19] Lawrence Sherman and Richard Berk conducted the Minneapolis domestic violence experiment in 1981. This experiment is considered the first scientifically controlled test of the effects of arrest for any type of crime.[20] The experiment and its results are presented in an article at the end of this section. This study influenced the implementation of mandatory arrest policies in the United States.

Focused Crime-Control Strategies: Crimes, Places, and People

After the Kansas City Preventive Patrol study revealed that routine preventive patrol did not have an effect on crime or citizens' perceptions of crime, police administrators began to think about ways to focus their efforts to more effectively manage crime and fear of crime. Some of the most common types of focused crime-control strategies include hot spots policing, crackdowns, d-runs, and patrol tactics focused on specific people.

Hot Spots Policing

As previously mentioned in Section 7, Lawrence Sherman defined hot spots as places in which the occurrence of crime is so frequent that it is highly predictable, at least for over a 1-year period. Lawrence Sherman and David Weisburd conducted one of the first studies examining the effectiveness of hot spots policing in Minneapolis, Minnesota.[21] For 1 year, the police department increased the patrol dosage at 55 of 110 crime "hot spots," monitored by 7,542 hours of systematic observations. The experimental group received approximately twice as much observed patrol presence. The reduction in total crime calls ranged from 6% to 13%, and observed disorder was only half as prevalent in experimental areas as it was in the control areas. Sherman and Weisburd concluded that significant increases in police patrol presence can lead to modest reductions in crime, and even greater reductions occurred for observed disorder within the high-crime areas.

There have been several evaluations of the effectiveness of hot spots policing since the Sherman and Weisburd study. For example, Lorraine Green examined the impact of the SMART (Specialized Multi-Agency Response Team) program that used municipal codes and drug nuisance abatement laws to control drug and disorder problems in Oakland, California.[22] She found that the SMART program decreased drug crimes in the targeted locations. Lawrence Sherman and Dennis Rogan tested the effects of gun seizures on gun violence in hot spots located in Kansas City, Missouri, and found that gun crimes declined in the targeted areas by nearly half (49%), with no evidence of crime displacement in neighboring areas.[23] David Weisburd and Lorraine Green evaluated the impact of a drug-enforcement strategy in Jersey City and found that this strategy had a positive impact on drug crimes in 56 hot spots identified within the city. They also found no evidence of crime displacement but did find evidence of a "diffusion of benefits" around the experimental area (meaning that there were reductions in drug-related crimes in the areas surrounding the targeted areas or hot spots).[24] When considering the results of most of the evaluations of location-based policing, we can conclude that this policing strategy is effective.

Crackdowns

A crackdown is a sudden concentration of police presence in an area, often focused on reducing specific types of crimes. This police strategy is meant to increase the perceived risk of apprehension and the level of uncertainty of arrest for individuals.[25] In general, crackdowns have been found to have short-term benefits; therefore, when crackdown efforts subside, so do the benefits of this strategy.[26] Ideally, police agencies would continuously conduct crackdowns in order to produce more long-term benefits. The table below illustrates the types of crimes that have been the focus of crackdowns as well as the impact that this strategy has had on those crimes.

Police Crackdowns in the United States*			
Type of Offense	Location	Year	Level of Impact
Gang-related violence (Fritsch et al., 1999)	Dallas, TX	1996–1997	Significant reduction
Gun-related violence (Weiss & McGarrell)	Indianapolis, IN	1997	Significant reduction
Public disorder (Novak et al., 1999)	Anonymous	1992	No impact
Street drug markets (Smith, 2001)	Richmond, VA	1999	Significant reduction
Street prostitution (Weidner, 1999)	New York City, NY	1993	Significant reduction

* Information provided by Michael Scott, *Benefits and Consequences of Police Crackdowns* (Washington, DC: U.S. Department of Justice, 2003).

D-Runs

The New Haven Police Department in Connecticut created another type of specialized patrol called **d-runs** or crime-deterrent runs.[27] D-runs involve regular uniformed patrol units being given directed assignments to perform during their uncommitted patrol time. A preliminary examination of this strategy occurred over a 6-month period and revealed a decrease in reported crimes that were the focus of the d-runs conducted by patrol officers in the targeted areas.[28] An evaluation conducted by Gary Cordner in Pontiac, Michigan, looked at the impact of the integrated criminal apprehension program (ICAP).[29] ICAP included d-runs as part of the change made to patrolling strategies in the Pontiac Police Department. This evaluation revealed that when d-run officers used aggressive patrol tactics, there was a marked decrease in crime in the target areas; however, when d-run officers spent more time in the targeted areas, there were only minimal changes in arrests and deterrence effects.

Person-Focused Strategies

Some police agencies use crime-control strategies that involve focusing on people who are thought to have committed a crime or a series of crimes. The three main types of person-focused crime-control strategies include field interrogations, perpetrator-oriented patrol, and repeat-offender programs.

Field interrogations consist of the police questioning people they believe are suspicious or who are likely to have been involved in criminal activities. The idea is that targeted individuals will be less likely to commit a crime if they know that the police are watching them or if the police make their presence known in the neighborhoods in which the targeted individuals reside. A study was conducted on the impact of field interrogations in San Diego.[30] This study found that some level of field interrogation (as opposed to not having any field interrogations) can provide a deterrent effect on suppressible crimes in certain locations. Neither the frequency of field interrogations or amount of field interrogation training influenced citizens' perceptions of the police.

Perpetrator-oriented patrol involves the surveillance of certain people suspected of committing multiple crimes or who have committed crimes that resulted in high levels of property loss or damage or significant injuries to people. Past evaluations of perpetrator-oriented patrol strategies have found that this patrol technique results in an extraordinarily high number of arrests and also provides useful intelligence for other specialized units or patrol officers.[31] Unfortunately, one evaluation of this type of patrol found that members of the STRESS (Stop the Robberies—Enjoy Safe Streets) unit had an extraordinarily high rate of use of deadly force when compared to uniformed patrol officers.[32]

And finally, repeat-offender programs (ROP) focus on the identification and apprehension of high-risk repeat offenders. In general, evaluations of ROP programs have found that this patrol method results in quality arrests and that those arrested by ROP units had criminal records that were nearly twice the average of nonrepeat offenders.[33] An examination of the Phoenix Repeat Offender Program found no significant increase in conviction rates for the ROP cases but did find a significant increase in the likelihood of commitment to prison and in the length of sentences imposed on the ROP cases.[34] The Boston Gun Project—Operation Ceasefire—is a recent application of the repeat offender strategy. The goal of Operation Ceasefire is to reduce firearm-related homicides of youth (specifically African American youth). David Kennedy and his colleagues evaluated this program and discovered a 63% reduction in youth homicides.[35]

Community Policing

In Section 2, community policing was presented as an alternative to traditional policing. Although difficult to define, community policing can be described as an approach to policing that involves community–police partnerships and citizen involvement in the definition of crime and disorder problems, as well as the efforts aimed at reducing those problems.[36] Measuring the effectiveness of community policing requires researchers to go beyond simply examining crime rate trends. In addition to changes in crime and disorder, citizens' fear of crime is another way to measure the impact of community policing. Research has found that when community programs are based on increased community–police interactions, the level of fear within a community is significantly reduced.[37]

Because definitions of community policing have changed over time, it is impossible to know whether community policing (in general) "works." One way to assess the effectiveness of community policing is to look at some of the community policing–based programs that have been utilized over the past several decades. These programs include neighborhood watch, door-to-door visits, community meetings, storefront offices, and foot patrol programs.

Neighborhood Watch

Neighborhood watch is a program that teaches citizens how to identify and report suspicious activity to the police.[38] The goal of neighborhood watch is crime prevention based on neighbors watching out for each other and monitoring activities in their neighborhoods in a collaborative effort with local law enforcement.[39] There has only been limited research on neighborhood watch. These studies have found that this program does not reduce crime.[40] Wesley Skogan and Susan Hartnett found that neighborhood watch did have a positive impact on citizens' perceptions of disorder when they assessed Chicago's Alternative Policing Strategy (CAPS) program.[41]

Home Visits

Home visits are another type of community-based program aimed at reducing crime and disorder. Home visits include door-to-door canvassing of neighborhoods in which the goal is to gather information about neighborhood problems from citizens.[42] This approach is especially useful in identifying problems that have not yet been brought to the attention of the police. Door-to-door visits by the police are also used to

Police agencies often sponsor community picnics and other social events to encourage more positive police–citizen interactions.

inform residents about special police-based programs in their neighborhoods and to introduce residents to neighborhood beat officers.[43]

Evaluations of home visits by the police have revealed that this strategy lowers levels of social disorder.[44] It is important to note that there was variation in the impact of this program by citizen race. An assessment of Houston's community policing efforts (including home visits and storefront offices) revealed that African American residents were significantly less likely than White residents to know about the programs or report that they had any contact with the police in relation to these programs.[45] These findings suggest a need to pay close attention to racial composition of neighborhoods to ensure that residents of all races benefit from community-based programs.

Community Meetings

Increased interaction and communication between police officers and citizens is one of the cornerstones of community policing. This can be achieved by scheduling regular meetings for these two groups. Community meetings can be conducted either citywide or within individual neighborhoods. The purpose of holding these meetings is to allow citizens to share their concerns with the police and allow the police to articulate the efforts made to resolve problems identified by citizens.[46] Studies show that community meetings do not have a significant effect on crime; however, they do appear to influence citizens' perceptions of disorder.[47]

Storefront Offices

Police **storefront offices** are usually located within neighborhoods and business districts. They serve as alternative locations to centralized police headquarters where citizens can report problems of crime and disorder, acquire information about what is going on in their districts, or just talk to police officers working in their neighborhoods.[48] Storefront offices provide an opportunity for citizens and police officers to interact in a positive manner. This creates the foundation for these two groups to be able to work together to keep the neighborhood safe. Police organizations can become more decentralized in their organizational structure by utilizing storefront offices (see Section 2 for a detailed discussion of decentralization and community policing).

Research has found that community policing storefronts do not reduce crime; however, they do influence citizens' perceptions of disorder.[49] Wesley Skogan and Mary Ann Wycoff conducted an evaluation of storefront offices in Houston, Texas. Their evaluation found that citizens' level of fear decreased and their perceptions of their neighborhood and the police improved as a result of the adoption of storefront offices.[50]

Foot Patrol

Foot patrol was considered an important element of community policing in the 1980s but has not been considered as important in recent years.[51] American police agencies began to adopt foot patrol again when community policing first began to emerge in the late 1970s and early 1980s. Police executives hoped that it would allow more face-to-face contact between the police and citizens, which could result in better police–community relations. But does foot patrol actually improve police–community relations? Does it have an impact on crime or citizens' feelings of personal safety? There have been several studies that have sought answers to these questions. Unfortunately, research findings have been somewhat mixed with regard to the effect of foot patrol on crime and disorder.

One of the first foot patrol studies was conducted in Newark, New Jersey, from February 1978 through January 1979.[52] This study found that foot patrol had no effect on crime rates in Newark. Foot patrol did have an effect on Newark residents. Residents of the areas patrolled by officers on foot thought that crime was less of a problem than did residents living in areas where there was only motorized patrol. Citizens living in areas with foot patrol also reported that they felt safer and believed that they were less likely to be victimized in their neighborhoods. And finally, citizens residing in the foot patrol neighborhoods reported that they were more satisfied with police service in general. Several years later, additional studies conducted in Boston, Massachusetts, and Asheville, North Carolina, also found that foot patrol had no effect on crime.[53]

There are other studies that have found that foot patrol does have an impact on crime. This was the case with a study that took place in Flint, Michigan, between January 1979 and January 1982.[54] Interviews with community residents and foot patrol officers, as well as official crime reports, were used to assess the impact of foot patrol in 14 neighborhoods. Results of this study revealed a decrease in reported crimes. Most (70%) of the citizens who were interviewed for this study reported that they felt safer as a result of foot patrol in their neighborhoods. Similar findings were reported in a recent examination of a foot patrol program in Philadelphia, Pennsylvania (see article at the end of this section). This study is important because it is the first of its kind to examine the use of place-based policing (or hot spots policing) as it relates to foot patrol.

Finally, a study conducted in Nashville, Tennessee, revealed that the implementation of "walking patrol" actually *increased* some types of crime.[55] John Schnelle and his colleagues reported that the types of crime showing the most increase at the time of the walking patrol intervention were theft, simple assault, public drunkenness, and disorderly conduct. Major crime, such as murder, rape, and burglary, did not show such increases.[56] This increase in reported crime suggests that citizens will report more crime if they are in close proximity with police officers.

After reviewing the studies on foot patrol, we can conclude that the findings are mixed when considering its impact on crime. Several studies did find that foot patrol had a positive impact on citizens' perceptions of the police and their feelings of personal safety. And there is some evidence that it can result in greater reporting of crimes to the police.

⊠ Problem-Oriented Policing

Problem-oriented policing (POP) was presented as an alternative to traditional policing in Section 2. POP is based on the idea that police officers examine the causes of problems and then use tailor-made police practices to solve those problems.[57] Problems, in the context of problem-oriented policing, are recurring

Problem-oriented policing challenges officers to find the root cause of problems instead of just responding to each individual call.

sets of related harmful events in a community that members of the public expect the police to address.[58] This strategy requires police officers to go beyond using a "cookie cutter approach" when responding to citizens' calls for service, an approach in which all calls are handled in a similar manner. But does the use of problem solving by police officers really reduce crime and disorder problems?

The first evaluation of problem-oriented policing took place in Newport News, Virginia.[59] The **Newport News POP study** examined whether police officers in the Newport News Police Department could incorporate problem-solving techniques during their daily routines at work and the extent to which their problem-solving efforts were effective at reducing crime and disorder. Most police officers reported that they had attempted to use problem solving in their daily routines during their shifts. The use of problem solving also appeared to have an impact on crime and disorder. The evaluation revealed that burglaries had decreased by 35%, robberies decreased by 40%, and thefts from vehicles dropped by 55%. Over the years since the Newport News study, a wealth of studies have found that problem solving by police officers can reduce violent and property crime. Problem-oriented policing has also been effective at reducing prostitution,[60] drugs,[61] theft,[62] burglary,[63] and citizens' fear of crime.[64]

Police Strategies: What Is Effective?*	
Adding more police officers	Little or no evidence of effectiveness
Routine preventive patrol	Little or no evidence of effectiveness (early studies found that it worked, but these studies had methodological flaws)
Rapid response time	Little or no evidence of effectiveness (the time it takes for citizens to report crimes is more important than police response time)

(Continued)

(Continued)	
Generalized/mandatory arrest	Little or no evidence of effectiveness (mixed research findings for mandatory arrest of domestic violence offenders)
Hot spots policing	Moderate to strong evidence of effectiveness
Crackdowns	Moderate to strong evidence of effectiveness (short-term impact)
D-runs	Moderate to strong evidence of effectiveness
Person-oriented patrol strategies	Inconsistent evidence (mixed research results)
Community policing	
Neighborhood watch	No evidence of crime reduction
Door-to-door visits	Some evidence of crime and disorder reduction
Community meetings	Evidence that this strategy does not reduce crime but influences perceptions of disorder
Storefront offices	Evidence that this strategy does not reduce crime but influences perceptions of disorder
Foot patrol	Weak to moderate evidence of effectiveness (mixed research findings—does not reduce crime but reduces fear of crime)
Problem-oriented policing	Moderate to strong evidence of effectiveness

* Information for this table was taken from the National Research Council's "Fairness and Effectiveness in Policing: The Evidence" and also from *Preventing Crime: What Works, What Doesn't, What's Promising: A Report To the United States Congress* by L. Sherman, D. Gottfredson, D. MacKenzie, J. Eck, P. Reuter, and S. Bushway.

SUMMARY

- Citizen fear of crime has become an important way to measure police effectiveness.
- Adding more police officers to patrol the streets does not reduce violent crime.
- Research has revealed that in most cases, case clearance is not influenced by how fast police officers arrive on scene.
- Hot spots, crackdowns, and D-runs are considered focused crime control strategies.
- Problem-oriented policing has been effective in reducing crime and also citizens' fear of crime.

KEY TERMS

d-runs
generalized crime control
   strategies
mandatory arrest

neighborhood watch
Newport News POP study
police effectiveness
police–population ratio

rapid response time
routine preventive patrol
storefront offices

DISCUSSION QUESTIONS

1. Explain how police effectiveness has been measured over the course of the history of American policing.

2. Which strategies "work" when reducing crime and fear of crime?

3. Describe what the research has found on the impact of mandatory arrest for domestic violence.

4. Identify some of the community policing–based programs and whether they have been found to be effective.

5. What were the findings from the first evaluation of problem-oriented policing in the United States?

WEB RESOURCES

- To learn more about the police–citizen ratio, go to http://www.theiacp.org/LinkClick.aspx?fileticket=LF7xdW lltPk%3D&tabid=87.
- To learn more about Boston's Operation Ceasefire, go to https://www.ncjrs.gov/pdffiles1/nij/188741.pdf.
- To learn more about Chicago's CAPS program, go to https://portal.chicagopolice.org/portal/page/portal/ClearPath.

READING 15

The Minneapolis domestic violence experiment studied the effects of police responses to simple assaults. Police officers were randomly assigned to arrest, mediate, or order suspects to leave when they were involved in domestic assaults. Research findings revealed that suspects that were arrested (as opposed to receiving mediation or being asked to leave) were less likely to repeat the behavior after police intervention. The findings of this study influenced the mandatory arrest policies adopted by many jurisdictions across the United States.

The Specific Deterrent Effects of Arrest for Domestic Assault

Lawrence W. Sherman and Richard A. Berk with 42 Patrol Officers of the Minneapolis Police Department, Nancy Wester, Donileen Loseke, David Rauma, Debra Morrow, Amy Curtis, Kay Gamble, Roy Roberts, Phyllis Newton, and Gayle Gubman

The specific deterrence doctrine and labeling theory predict opposite effects of punishment on individual rates of deviance. The limited cross-sectional evidence available on the question is inconsistent, and experimental evidence has been lacking. The Police Foundation and the Minneapolis Police Department tested these hypotheses in a field experiment on domestic violence. Three police responses to simple assault were randomly assigned to legally eligible suspects: an arrest; "advice" (including, in some cases, informal mediation); and an order to the suspect to leave for eight hours. The behavior of the suspect was tracked for six months after the police intervention, with both official data and victim reports. The official recidivism measures show that the arrested suspects manifested significantly less subsequent violence than those who were ordered to leave. The victim report data show that the arrested subjects manifested significantly less subsequent violence than those who were advised. The findings falsify a deviance amplification model of labeling theory beyond initial labeling, and fail to falsify the specific deterrence prediction for a group of offenders with a high percentage of prior histories of both domestic violence and other kinds of crime.

Sociologists since Durkheim ([1893] 1972:126) have speculated about how the punishment of individuals affects their behavior. Two bodies of literature, specific deterrence and labeling, have developed competing predictions (Thorsell and Klemke, 1972). Durkheim, for example, implicity assumed with Bentham that the pains of punishment deter people from repeating the crimes for which they are punished, especially when punishment is certain, swift and severe. More recent work has fostered the ironic view that punishment often makes individuals more likely to commit crimes because of altered interactional structures, foreclosed legal opportunities and secondary deviance (Lemert, 1951, 1967; Schwartz and Skolnick, 1962; Becker, 1963).

Neither prediction can muster consistent empirical support. The few studies that allege effects generally employ weak designs in which it is difficult, if not impossible, to control plausibly for all important factors confounded with criminal justice sanctions and the rule-breaking behavior that may follow. Thus, some claim to show that punishment deters individuals punished (Clarke, 1966; F.B.I., 1967:34–44; Cohen and Stark, 1974:30; Kraut, 1976; Murray and Cox, 1979; McCord, 1983), while others claim to show that punishment increases their deviance (Gold and Williams, 1969; Shoham, 1974; Farrington, 1977; Klemke, 1978). Yet all of these studies suffer either methodological or conceptual flaws as tests of the effects of punishment (Zimring and Hawkins, 1973; Gibbs, 1975; Hirschi, 1975; Tittle, 1975), especially the confounding of incarceration with attempts to rehabilitate and the frequent failure to differentiate effects for different types of offenders and offenses (Lempert, 1981–1982).

Perhaps the strongest evidence to date comes from a randomized experiment conducted by Lincoln et al. (unpubl.). The experiment randomly assigned juveniles, who had already been apprehended, to four different treatments ranked in their formality: release; two types of diversion; and formal charging. The more formal and official the processing, the more frequent the repeat criminality over a two-year follow-up period. This study supports labeling theory for arrested juveniles, although it cannot isolate the labeling or deterrent effects of arrest per se.

In all likelihood, of course, punishment has not one effect, but many, varying across types of people and situations (Chambliss, 1967; Andenaes, 1971). As Lempert (1981–1982:523) argues, "it is only by attending to a range of such offenses that we will be able to develop a general theory of deterrence." The variables affecting the deterrability of juvenile delinquency, white-collar crime, armed robbery and domestic violence may be quite different. Careful accumulation of findings from different settings will help us differentiate the variables which are crime- or situation-specific and those which apply across settings.

In this spirit, we report here a study of the impact of punishment in a particular setting, for a particular offense, and for particular kinds of individuals. Over an eighteen-month period, police in Minneapolis applied one of three intervention strategies in incidents of misdemeanor domestic assault: arrest; ordering the offender from the premises; or some form of advice which could include mediation. The three interventions were assigned randomly to households, and a critical outcome was the rate of repeat incidents. The relative effect of arrest should hold special interest for the specific deterrence-labeling controversy.

⊠ Policing Domestic Assaults

Police have been typically reluctant to make arrests for domestic violence (Berk and Loseke, 1981), as well as for a wide range of other kinds of offenses, unless victims demand an arrest, the suspect insults the officer, or other factors are present (Sherman, 1980). Parnas's (1972) qualitative observations of the Chicago police found four categories of police action in these situations: negotiating or otherwise "talking out" the dispute; threatening the disputants and then leaving; asking one of the parties to leave the premises; or (very rarely) making an arrest.

Similar patterns are found in many other cities. Surveys of battered women who tried to have their domestic assailants arrested report that arrest occurred in 10 percent (Roy, 1977:35) or 3 percent (see Langley and Levy, 1977:219) of the cases. Surveys of police agencies in Illinois (Illinois Law Enforcement Commission, 1978) and New York (Office of the Minority Leader, 1978) found explicit policies against arrest in the majority of the agencies surveyed. Despite the fact that violence is reported to be present in one-third (Bard and Zacker, 1974) to two-thirds (Black, 1980) of all domestic disturbances police respond to, police department data show arrests in only 5 percent of those disturbances in Oakland (Hart, n.d., cited in Meyer and Lorimer, 1977:21), 6 percent of those disturbances in a Colorado city (Patrick et al., n.d., cited in Meyer and Lorimer, 1977:21) and 6 percent in Los Angeles County (Emerson, 1979).

The best available evidence on the frequency of arrest is the observations from the Black and Reiss study of Boston, Washington and Chicago police in 1966 (Black, 1980: 182). Police responding to disputes in those cities made arrests in 27 percent of violent felonies and 17 percent of the violent misdemeanors. Among married couples (Black, 1980:158), they made arrests in 26 percent of the cases, but tried to remove one of the parties in 38 percent of the cases.

An apparent preference of many police for separating the parties rather than arresting the offender has been attacked from two directions over the last fifteen years. The original critique came from clinical psychologists, who agreed that police should rarely make arrests (Potter, 1978:46; Fagin 1978:123–124) in domestic assault cases, and argue that police should mediate the disputes responsible for the violence. A highly publicized demonstration project teaching police special counseling skills for family crisis intervention (Bard, 1970) failed to show a reduction in violence, but was interpreted as a success nonetheless. By 1977, a national survey of police agencies with 100 or more officers found that over 70 percent reported a family crisis intervention training program in operation. While it is not clear whether these programs reduced separation and increased mediation, a decline in arrests was noted for some (Wylie et al., 1976). Indeed, many sought explicitly to reduce the number of arrests (University of Rochester, 1974; Ketterman and Kravitz, 1978).

By the mid-1970s, police practices were criticized from the opposite direction by feminist groups. Just as psychologists succeeded in having many police agencies respond to domestic violence as "half social work and half police work," feminists began to argue that police put "too much emphasis on the social work aspect and not enough on the criminal" (Langley and Levy, 1977:218). Widely publicized lawsuits in New York and Oakland sought to compel police to make arrests in every case of domestic assault, and state legislatures were lobbied successfully to reduce the evidentiary requirements needed for police to make arrests for misdemeanor domestic assaults. Some legislatures are now considering statutes requiring police to make arrests in these cases.

The feminist critique was bolstered by a study (Police Foundation, 1976) showing that for 85 percent of a sample of spousal homicides, police had intervened at least once in the preceding two years. For 54 percent of the homicides, police had intervened five or more times. But it was impossible to determine from the cross-sectional data whether making more or fewer arrests would have reduced the homicide rate.

In sum, police officers confronting a domestic assault suspect face at least three conflicting options, urged on them by different groups with different theories. The officers' colleagues might recommend forced separation as a means of achieving short-term peace. Alternatively, the officers' trainers might recommend mediation as a means of getting to the underlying cause of the "dispute" (in which both parties are implicitly assumed to be at fault). Finally, the local women's organizations may recommend that the officer protect the victim (whose "fault," if any, is legally irrelevant) and enforce the law to deter such acts in the future.

Research Design

In response to these conflicting recommendations, the Police Foundation and the Minneapolis Police Department agreed to conduct a randomized experiment. The design called for random assignment of arrest, separation, and some form of advice which could include mediation at the officer's discretion. In addition, there was to be a six-month follow-up period to measure the frequency and seriousness of domestic violence after each police intervention. The advantages of randomized experiments are well known and need not be reviewed here (see, e.g., Cook and Campbell, 1979).

The design only applied to simple (misdemeanor) domestic assaults, where both the suspect and the victim were present when the police arrived. Thus, the experiment included only those cases in which police were empowered (but not required) to make arrests under a recently liberalized Minnesota state law; the police officer must have probable cause to believe that a cohabitant or spouse had assaulted the victim within the last four hours (but police need not have witnessed the assault). Cases of life-threatening or severe injury, usually labeled as a felony (aggravated assault), were excluded from the design for ethical reasons.

The design called for each officer to carry a pad of report forms, color coded for the three different police actions. Each time the officers encountered a situation that fit the experiment's criteria, they were to take whatever action was indicated by the report form on the top of the pad. We numbered the forms and arranged them in random order for each officer. The integrity of the random assignment was to be monitored by research staff observers riding on patrol for a sample of evenings.

After police action was taken, the officer was to fill out a brief report and give it to the research staff for follow-up. As a further check on the randomization process, the staff logged in the reports in the order in which they were received and made sure that the sequence corresponded to the original assignment of treatments.

Anticipating something of the victims' background, a predominantly minority, female research staff was employed to contact the victims for a detailed face-to-face interview, to be followed by telephone follow-up interviews every two weeks for 24 weeks. The interviews were designed primarily to measure the frequency and seriousness of victimizations caused by the suspect after the police intervention. The research staff also collected criminal justice reports that mentioned the suspect's name during the six-month follow-up period.

⊠ Conduct of the Experiment

As is common in field experiments, implementation of the research design entailed some slippage from the original plan. In order to gather data as quickly as possible, the experiment was originally located in the two Minneapolis precincts with the highest density of domestic violence crime reports and arrests. The 34 officers assigned to those areas were invited to a three-day planning meeting and asked to participate in the study for one year. All but one agreed. The conference also produced a draft order for the chief's signature specifying the rules of the experiment. These rules created several new situations to be excluded from the experiment, such as if a suspect attempted to assault police officers, a victim persistently demanded an arrest, or if both parties were injured. These additional exceptions, unfortunately, allowed for the possibility of differential attrition from the separation and mediation treatments. The implications for internal validity are discussed later.

The experiment began on March 17, 1981, with the expectation that it would take about one year to produce about 300 cases (it ran until August 1, 1982, and produced 330 case reports.) The officers agreed to meet monthly with the project director (Sherman) and the project manager (Wester). By the third or fourth month, two facts became clear: (1) only about 15 to 20 officers were either coming to meetings or turning in cases; and (2) the rate at which the cases were turned in would make it difficult to complete the project in one year. By November, we decided to recruit more officers in order to obtain cases more rapidly. Eighteen additional officers joined the project, but like the original group, most of these officers only turned in one or two cases. Indeed, three of the original officers produced almost 28 percent of the cases, in part because they worked a particularly violent beat, and in part because they had a greater commitment to the study. Since the treatments were randomized by officer, this created no internal validity problem. However, it does raise construct validity problems to which we will later return.

There is little doubt that many of the officers occasionally failed to follow fully the experimental design. Some of the failures were due to forgetfulness, such as leaving the report pads at home or at the police station. Other failures derived from misunderstanding about whether the experiment applied in certain situations; application of the experimental rules under complex circumstances was sometimes confusing. Finally, from time to time there were situations that were simply not covered by the experiment's rules.

Whether any officers intentionally subverted the design is unclear. The plan to monitor randomization with ride-along observers broke down because of the unexpectedly low incidence of cases meeting the experimental criteria. The observers had to ride for many weeks before they observed an officer apply one of the treatments. We tried to solve this problem with "chase-alongs," in which the observers rode in their own car with a portable police radio and drove to the scene of any domestic call dispatched to any officer in the precinct. Even this method failed.

Thus, we are left with at least two disturbing possibilities. First, police officers anticipating (e.g., from the dispatch call) a particular kind of incident, and finding the upcoming experimental treatment inappropriate, may have occasionally decided to void the experiment. That is, they may have chosen to exclude certain cases in violation of the experimental design. This amounts to differential attrition, which is clearly a threat to internal validity. Note that if police officers blindly decided to exclude certain cases (e.g., because they did not feel like filling out the extra forms on a given day), all would be well for internal validity.

Second, since the recording officer's pad was supposed to govern the actions of each pair of officers, some officers may also have switched the assignment of driver and recording officer after deciding a case fit the study in order to obtain a treatment they wanted to apply. If the treatments were switched between driver and recorder, then the internal validity was again threatened. However, this was almost certainly uncommon because it was generally easier not to fill out a report at all than to switch.

Table 1 shows the degree to which treatments were delivered as designed. Ninety-nine percent of the suspects targeted for arrest actually were arrested, while only 78 percent of those to receive advice did, and only 73 percent of those to be sent out of the residence for eight hours were actually sent. One explanation for this pattern, consistent with the experimental guidelines, is that mediating and sending were more difficult ways for police to control the situation, with a greater likelihood that officers

might resort to arrest as a fallback position. When the assigned treatment is arrest, there is no need for a fallback position. For example, some offenders may have refused to comply with an order to leave the premises.

Such differential attrition would potentially bias estimates of the relative effectiveness of arrest by removing uncooperative and difficult offenders from the mediation and separation treatments. Any deterrent effect could be underestimated and, in the extreme, artifactual support for deviance amplification could be found. That is, the arrest group would have too many "bad guys" *relative* to the other treatments.

We can be more systematic about other factors affecting the movement of cases away from the designed treatments. The three delivered treatments represent a polychotomous outcome amenable to multivariate statistical analysis. We applied a multinominal logit formulation (Amemiya, 1981:1516–19; Maddala, 1983:34–37), which showed that the designed treatment was the dominant cause of the treatment actually received (a finding suggested by Table 1). However, we also found that five other variables had a statistically significant effect on "upgrading" the separation and advice treatments to arrests: whether police reported the suspect was rude; whether police reported the suspect tried to assault one (or both) of the police officers; whether police reported weapons were involved;

Table 1 Designed and Delivered Police Treatments in Spousal Assault Cases

Designed Treatment	Delivered Treatment			Total
	Arrest	Advise	Separate	
Arrest	98.9%	0.0%	1.1%	29.3%
	(91)	(0)	(1)	(92)
Advise	17.6%	77.8%	4.6%	34.4%
	(19)	(84)	(5)	(108)
Separate	22.8%	4.4%	72.8%	36.3%
	(26)	(5)	(83)	(114)
Total	43.4%	28.3%	28.3%	100%
	(136)	(89)	(89)	(314)

whether the victim persistently demanded a citizen's arrest; and whether a restraining order was being violated. We found no evidence that the background or characteristics of the suspect or victim (e.g., race) affected the treatment received.

Overall, the logit model fit the data very well. For well over 80 percent of the cases, the model's predicted treatment was the same as the actual treatment (i.e., correct classifications), and minor alterations in the assignment threshold would have substantially improved matters. Moreover, a chi-square test on the residuals was not statistically significant (i.e., the observed and predicted treatments differed by no more than chance). In summary, we were able to model the assignment process with remarkable success simply by employing the rules of the experimental protocol (for more details, see Berk and Sherman, 1983).

We were less fortunate with the interviews of the victims; only 205 (of 330, counting the few repeat victims twice) could be located and initial interviews obtained, a 62 percent completion rate. Many of the victims simply could not be found, either for the initial interview or for follow-ups; they either left town, moved somewhere else or refused to answer the phone or doorbell. The research staff made up to 20 attempts to contact these victims, and often employed investigative techniques (asking friends and neighbors) to find them. Sometimes these methods worked, only to have the victim give an outright refusal or break one or more appointments to meet the interviewer at a "safe" location for the interview.

The response rate to the bi-weekly follow-up interviews was even lower than for the initial interview, as in much research on women crime victims. After the first interview, for which the victims were paid $20, there was a gradual falloff in completed interviews with each successive wave; only 161 victims provided all 12 follow-up interviews over the six months, a completion rate of 49 percent. Whether paying for the follow-up interviews would have improved the response rate is unclear; it would have added over $40,000 to the cost of the research. When the telephone interviews yielded few reports of violence, we moved to conduct every fourth interview in person, which appeared to produce more reports of violence.

There is absolutely no evidence that the experimental treatment assigned to the offender affected the victim's decision to grant initial interviews. We estimated a binary logit equation for the dichotomous outcome: whether or not an initial interview was obtained. Regressors included the experimental treatments (with one necessarily excluded), race of the victim, race of the offender, and a number of attributes of the incident (from the police sheets). A joint test on the full set of regressors failed to reject the null hypothesis that all of the logit coefficients were zero. More important for our purposes, none of the t-values for the treatments was in excess of 1.64; indeed, none was greater than 1.0 in absolute value. In short, while the potential for sample selection bias (Heckman, 1979; Berk, 1983) certainly exists (and is considered later), that bias does not stem from obvious sources, particularly the treatments. This implies that we may well be able to meaningfully examine experimental effects for the subset of individuals from whom initial interviews were obtained. The same conclusions followed when the follow-up interviews were considered.

In sum, despite the practical difficulties of controlling an experiment and interviewing crime victims in an emotionally charged and violent social context, the experiment succeeded in producing a promising sample of 314 cases with complete official outcome measures and an apparently unbiased sample of responses from the victims in those cases.

 ## Results

The 205 completed initial interviews provide some sense of who the subjects are, although the data may not properly represent the characteristics of the full sample of 314. They show the now familiar pattern of domestic violence cases coming to police attention being disproportionately unmarried couples with lower than average educational levels, disproportionately minority and mixed race (black male, white female), and who were very likely to have had prior violent incidents with police intervention. The 60 percent suspect unemployment rate is strikingly high in a community with only about 5 percent of the workforce unemployed. The 59 percent prior arrest rate is also strikingly high, suggesting (with the 80 percent prior domestic assault rate) that the suspects generally are experienced lawbreakers who are accustomed to police interventions. But with the exception of the heavy representation of Native Americans (due to Minneapolis' unique proximity to many Indian reservations), the characteristics in Table 2 are probably close to those of

Table 2 Victim and Suspect Characteristics: Initial Interview Data and Police Sheets		
A. Unemployment		
Victims	61%	
Suspects	60%	
B. Relationship of Suspect to Victim		
Divorced or separated husband	3%	
Unmarried male lover	45%	
Current husband	35%	
Wife or girlfriend	2%	
Son, brother, roommate, other	15%	
C. Prior Assaults and Police Involvement.		
Victims assaulted by suspect, last six months	80%	
Police intervention in domestic dispute, last six months	60%	
Couple in Counseling Programs	27%	
D. Prior Arrests of Male Suspects		
Ever Arrested For Any Offense	59%	
Ever Arrested For Crime Against Person	31%	
Ever Arrested on Domestic Violence Statute	5%	
Ever Arrested On An Alcohol Offense	29%	
E. Mean Age		
Victims	30 years	
Suspects	32 years	
F. Education	**Victims**	**Suspects**
< high school	43%	42%
high school only	33%	36%
> high school	24%	22%
G. Race	**Victims**	**Suspects**
White	57%	45%
Black	23%	36%
Native American	18%	16%
Other	2%	3%

$N = 205$ (Those cases for which initial interviews were obtained)

domestic violence cases coming to police attention in other large U.S. cities.

Two kinds of outcome measures will be considered. One is a *police-recorded* "failure" of the offender to survive the six-month follow-up period without having police generate a written report on the suspect for domestic violence, either through an offense or an arrest report written by any officer in the department, or through a subsequent report to the project research staff of a randomized (or other) intervention by officers participating in the experiment. A second kind of measure comes from the *interviews with victims*, in which victims were asked if there had been a repeat incident with the same suspect, broadly defined to include an actual assault, threatened assault, or property damage.

The two kinds of outcomes were each formulated in two complementary ways: as a dummy variable (i.e., repeat incident or not) and as the amount of time elapsed from the treatment to either a failure or the end of the follow-up period. For each of the two outcomes, three analyses were performed: the first using a linear probability model; the second using a logit formulation; and the third using a proportional hazard approach. The dummy outcome was employed for the linear probability and logit analyses, while the time-to-failure was employed for the proportional hazard method.

Given the randomization, we began in traditional analysis of variance fashion. The official measure of a repeat incident was regressed on the treatment received for the subset of 314 cases (out of 330) that fell within the definition of the experiment. Compared to the baseline treatment of separation, which had the highest recidivism rate in the police data, the arrest treatment reduced repeat occurrences by a statistically significant amount ($t = -2.38$). Twenty-six percent of those separated committed a repeat assault, compared to 13 percent of those arrested. The mediation treatment was statistically indistinguishable from the other two. To help put this in perspective, 18.2 percent of the households failed overall.

The apparent treatment effect for arrest in this conventional analysis was suggestive, but there was a danger of biased estimates from the "upgrading" of some separation and advise treatments. In response, we applied variations on the corrections recommended by Barnow et al. (1980: esp. 55). In brief, we inserted instrumental variables in place of the delivered treatments when the treatment effects were analyzed. These instruments, in turn, were constructed from the multinomial logit model described earlier.

Table 3 shows the results of the adjusted models. The first two columns report the results for the linear probability approach. Again, we find a statistically

Table 3 Experimental Results for Police Data

Variable	Linear		Logistics		Proportional Hazard Rate	
	Coef	t-value	Coef	t-value	Coef	t-value
Intercept (separate)	0.24	5.03*	−1.10	−4.09*	−	−
Arrest	−0.14	−2.21*	−1.02	−2.21*	−0.97	−2.28*
Advise	−0.05	−0.79	−0.31	−0.76	−0.32	−0.88
	F = 2.01		Chi square = 5.19		Chi square = 5.48	
	P = .07		P = .07		P = .06	

$N = 314$

* $p < .05$, two-tailed test.

significant effect for arrest ($t = -2.21$). However, it is well known that the linear probability model will produce inefficient estimates of the regression coefficients and biased (and inconsistent) estimates of the standard errors. Significance tests, therefore, are suspect. Consequently, we also estimated a logit model, with pretty much the same result. At the mean of the endogenous variable (i.e., 18.2 percent), the logit coefficient for arrest translates into nearly the same effect (i.e., $-.15$) found with the linear probability model ($t = -2.21$).

One might still object that the use of a dummy variable outcome neglects right-hand censoring. In brief, one cannot observe failures that occur after the end of the experimental period, so that biased (and inconsistent) results follow. Thus, we applied a proportional hazard analysis (Lawless, 1982: Ch. 7) that adjusts for right-hand censoring. In this model the time-to-failure dependent variable is transformed into (roughly) the probability at any given moment during the six-month follow-up period of a new offense occurring, given that no new offenses have yet been committed. The last two columns of Table 3 indicate that, again, an effect for arrest surfaces ($t = -2.28$). The coefficient of -0.97 implies that compared to the baseline of separation, those experiencing an arrest were less likely to commit a new battery

by a multiplicative factor of .38 (i.e., e raised to the -0.97 power). If the earlier results are translated into comparable terms, the effects described by the proportional hazard formulation are the largest we have seen (see footnote 4). But the major message is that the arrest effect holds up under three different statistical methods based on slightly different response functions. Overall, the police data indicate that the separation treatment produces the highest recidivism, arrest produces the lowest, with the impact of "advise" (from doing nothing to mediation) indistinguishable from the other two effects.

Table 4 shows the results when self-report data are used. A "failure" is defined as a new assault, property destruction or a threatened assault. (Almost identical results follow from a definition including only a new assault.) These results suggest a different ordering of the effects, with arrest still producing the lowest recidivism rate (at 19%), but with advice producing the highest (37%).

Overall, 28.9 percent of the suspects in Table 4 "failed." Still, the results are much the same as found for the official failure measure. However, given the effective sample of 161, we are vulnerable to sample selection bias. In response, we applied Heckman's (1979) sample selection corrections. The results were virtually unchanged (and are therefore not reported).

Table 4   Experimental Results for Victim Report Data

Variable	Linear		Logistic		Proportional Hazard Rate	
	Coef	t-value	Coef	t-value	Coef	t-value
Intercept (advise)	0.37	5.54*	−0.53	−1.70	−	−
Arrest	−0.18	−2.00*	−0.94	−2.01*	−0.82	−2.05*
Separate	−0.04	−0.35	−0.15	−0.10	−0.27	−0.09
	F = 2.31		Chi-square = 4.78		Chi-square = 4.36	
	P = .10		P = .09		P = .11	

$N = 161$ (Those cases for which all follow-up interviews were obtained)

*$p < .05$, two-tailed test.

An obvious rival hypothesis to the deterrent effect of arrest is that arrest incapacitates. If the arrested suspects spend a large portion of the next six months in jail, they would be expected to have lower recidivism rates. But the initial interview data show this is not the case: of those arrested, 43 percent were released within one day, 86 percent were released within one week, and only 14 percent were released after one week or had not yet been released at the time of the *initial* victim interview. Clearly, there was very little incapacitation, especially in the context of a six-month follow-up. Indeed, virtually all those arrested were released before the first follow-up interview. Nevertheless, we introduced the length of the initial stay in jail as a control variable. Consistent with expectations, the story was virtually unchanged.

Another perspective on the incapacitation issue can be obtained by looking at repeat violence which occurred shortly after the police intervened. If incapacitation were at work, a dramatic effect should be found in households experiencing arrest, especially compared to the households experiencing advice. Table 5 shows how quickly the couples were reunited, and of those reunited in one day, how many of them, according to the victim, began to argue or had physical violence again. It is apparent that *all* of the police interventions effectively stopped the violence for a 24-hour period after the couples were reunited. Even the renewed quarrels were few, at least with our relatively small sample size. Hence, there is again no evidence for an incapacitation effect. There is also no evidence for the reverse: that arrested offenders would take it out on the victim when the offender returned home.

Table 5 Speed of Reunion and Recidivism by Police Action

Police Action	Time of Reunion			(N)	New Quarrel Within a Day	New Violence Within a Day
	Within One Day	More than One Day but Less Than One Week	Longer or No Return			
Arrested (and released)	38%	30%	32%	(N = 76)	(2)	(1)
Separated	57%	31%	10%	(N = 54)	(6)	(3)
Advised	–	–	–	(N = 72)	(4)	(1)

N = 202 (Down from the 205 in Table 2 due to missing data)

 ## Discussion and Conclusions

The experiment's results are subject to several qualifications. One caution is that both kinds of outcome measures have uncertain construct validity. The official measure no doubt neglects a large number of repeat incidents, in part because many of them were not reported, and in part because police are sometimes reluctant to turn a family "dispute" into formal police business. However, the key is whether there is *differential* measurement error by the experimental treatments: an undercount randomly distributed across the three treatments will not bias the estimated experimental effects (i.e., only the estimate of the intercept will be biased). It is hard to imagine that differential undercounting would come solely from the actions of police, since most officers were not involved in the experiment and could not have known what treatment had been delivered.

However, there might be differential undercounting if offenders who were arrested were less likely to remain on the scene after a new assault. Having been burned once, they might not wait around for a second opportunity. And police told us they were less likely during the follow-up period (and more generally) to record an incident if the offender was not present. For example, there would be no arrest forms since the offender was not available to arrest. If all we had were the official outcome measures, there would be no easy way to refute this possibility. Fortunately, the self-report data are *not* vulnerable on these grounds, and the experimental effects are found nevertheless.

It is also possible that the impact for arrest found in the official outcome measure represents a reluctance of *victims* to call the police. That is, for some victims, the arrest may have been an undesirable intervention, and rather than face the prospect of another arrest from a new incident, these victims might decide not to invoke police sanctions. For example, the arrest may have cost the offender several days' work and put financial stress on the household. Or the offender may have threatened serious violence if the victim ever called the police again. However, we can again observe that the self-report data would not have been vulnerable to such concerns, and the experimental effects were found nevertheless. The only way we can see how the self-report data would fail to support the official data is if respondents in households experiencing arrest became more hesitant to admit to *interviewers* that they had been beaten a second time. Since there was no differential response rate by treatment, this possibility seems unlikely. If the arrested suspects had intimidated their victims more than the other two treatment groups, it seems more likely that such intimidation would have shown up in noncooperation with the interviews than in differential underreporting of violence in the course of the interviews.

This is not to say that the self-report data are flawless; indeed there is some reason to believe that there was undercounting of new incidents. However, just as for the official data, unless there is differential undercounting by the experimental treatments, all is well. We can think of no good reasons why differential undercounting should materialize. In summary, internal validity looks rather sound.

The construct validity of the treatments is more problematic. The advice and separation interventions have unclear content. Perhaps "good" mediation, given consistently, would fare better compared to arrest. The more general point is that the treatment effects for arrest are only relative to the impact of the other interventions. Should their content change, the relative impact of arrest could change as well.

Likewise, we noted earlier that a few officers accounted for a disproportionate number of the cases. What we have been interpreting, therefore, as results from different intervention strategies could reflect the special abilities of certain officers to make arrest particularly effective relative to the other treatments. For example, these officers may have been less skilled in mediation techniques. However, we re-estimated the models reported in Tables 3 and 4, including an interaction effect to capture the special contributions of our high-productivity officers. The new variable was not statistically significant, and the treatment effect for arrest remained.

Finally, Minneapolis is hardly representative of all urban areas. The Minneapolis Police Department has many unusual characteristics, and different jurisdictions might well keep suspects in custody for longer or shorter periods of time. The message should be clear external validity will have to wait for replications.

Despite these qualifications, it is apparent that we have found no support for the deviance amplification point of view. The arrest intervention certainly did not make things worse and may well have made things better. There are, of course, many rejoinders. In particular, over 80 percent of offenders had assaulted the victims in the previous six months, and in over 60 percent of the households the police had intervened during that interval. Almost 60 percent of the suspects had previously been arrested for something. Thus, the counterproductive consequences of police sanction, if any, may for many offenders have already been felt. In labeling theory terms, secondary deviation may already have been established, producing a ceiling for the amplification effects of formal sanctioning. However, were this the case, the arrest treatment probably should be less effective in households experiencing recent police interventions. No such interaction effects were found. In future analyses of these data, however, we will inductively explore interactions with more sensitive measures of police sanctioning and prior criminal histories of the suspects.

There are, of course, many versions of labeling theory. For those who theorize that a metamorphosis of self occurs in response to official sanctions over a long period of time, our six-month follow-up is not a relevant test. For those who argue that the development of a criminal self-concept is particularly likely to occur during a lengthy prison stay or extensive contact with criminal justice officials, the dosage of labeling employed in this experiment is not sufficient to falsify that hypothesis. What this experiment does seem to falsify for this particular offense is the broader conception of labeling implicit in the prior research by Lincoln et al. (unpubl.), Farrington (1977) and others: that for every possible increment of criminal justice response to deviance, the more increments (or the greater the formality) applied to the labeled deviant, the greater the likelihood of subsequent deviation. The absolute strength of the dosage is irrelevant to this hypothesis, as long as some variation in dosage is present. While the experiment does not falsify all possible "labeling theory" hypotheses, it does at least seem to falsify this one.

The apparent support for deterrence is perhaps more clear. While we certainly have no evidence that deterrence will work in general, we do have findings that swift imposition of a sanction of temporary incarceration may deter male offenders in domestic assault cases. And we have produced this evidence from an unusually strong research design based on random assignment to treatments. In short, criminal justice sanctions seem to matter for this offense in this setting with this group of experienced offenders.

A number of police implications follow. Perhaps most important, police have historically been reluctant to make arrests in domestic assault cases, in part fearing that an arrest could make the violence worse. Criminal justice sanctions weakly applied might be insufficient to deter and set the offender on a course of retribution. Our data indicate that such concerns are by and large groundless.

Police have also felt that making an arrest was a waste of their time: without the application of swift and severe sanctions by the courts, arrest and booking had no bite. Our results indicate that only three of the 136 arrested offenders were formally punished by fines or subsequent incarceration. This suggests that arrest and initial incarceration alone may produce a deterrent effect, regardless of how the courts treat such cases, and that arrest makes an independent contribution to the deterrence potential of the criminal justice system. Therefore, in jurisdictions that process domestic assault offenders in a manner similar to that employed in Minneapolis, we favor a *presumption* of arrest; an arrest should be made unless there are good, clear reasons why an arrest would be counterproductive. We do not, however, favor *requiring* arrests in all misdemeanor domestic assault cases. Even if our findings were replicated in a number of jurisdictions, there is a good chance that arrest works far better for some kinds of offenders than others and in some kinds of situations better than others. We feel it best to leave police a loophole to capitalize on that variation. Equally important, it is widely recognized that discretion is inherent in police work. Simply to impose a requirement of arrest, irrespective of the features of the immediate situation, is to invite circumvention.

 # References

Amemiya, Takeshi 1981 "Qualitative response models: a survey." *Journal of Economic Literature* 19:1483–1536.

Andenaes, Johannes 1971 "Deterrence and specific offenses." *University of Chicago Law Review* 39:537.

Bard, Morton 1970 "Training police as specialists in family crisis intervention." Washington, D.C.: U.S. Department of Justice.

Bard, Morton and Joseph Zacker 1974 "Assaultiveness and alcohol use in family disputes—police perceptions." *Criminology* 12:281–92.

Barnow, Burt S., Glen G. Cain and Arthur S. Goldberger 1980 "Issues in the analysis of selectivity bias." Pp. 53–59 in Ernst W. Stromsdorfer and George Farkas (eds.), *Evaluation Studies Review Annual, Volume 5.* Beverly Hills: Sage.

Becker, Howard 1963 *The Outsiders.* New York: Free Press.

Berk, Richard A. 1983 "An introduction to sample selection bias in sociological data." *American Sociological Review,* 48:386–98.

Berk, Richard A. and Lawrence W. Sherman 1983 "Police responses to family violence incidents: an analysis of an experimental design with incomplete randomization." Unpublished manuscript, Department of Sociology, University of California at Barbara.

Berk, Sarah Fenstermaker and Donileen R. Loseke 1981 "Handling family violence: situational determinants of police arrest in domestic disturbances." *Law and Society Review* 15:315–46.

Black, Donald 1980 *The Manners and Customs of the Police*, New York: Academic Press.

Chambliss, William 1967 "Types of deviance and the effectiveness of legal sanctions." *Wisconsin Law Review* 1967:703–19.

Clarke, Ronald V. G. 1966 "Approved school boy absconders and corporal punishment." *British Journal of Criminology*: 6:364–75.

Cohen, Lawrence E. and Rodney Stark 1974 "Discriminatory labeling and the five-finger discount." *Journal of Research in Crime and Delinquency* 11:25–39.

Cook, Thomas D. and Donald T. Campbell 1979 *Quasi-Experimentation: Design and Analysis Issues for Field Settings*, Chicago: Rand McNally.

Durkheim, Emile [1893] 1972 *Selected Writings*. Edited with an Introduction by Anthony Giddens. [Selection from Division of Labor in Society, 6th edition, 1960 (1893)] Cambridge: Cambridge University Press.

Emerson, Charles D. 1979 "Family violence: a study by the Los Angeles County Sheriff's Department." *Police Chief* 46(6):48–50.

Fagin, James A. 1978 "The effects of police interpersonal communications skills on conflict resolution." Ph.D. Dissertation, Southern Illinois University Ann Arbor: University Microfilms.

Farrington, David P. 1977 "The effects of public labeling." *British Journal of Criminology* 17:112–25.

Federal Bureau of Investigation 1967 *Uniform Crime Reports*. Washington, D.C.: U.S. Department of Justice.

Gold, Martin and Jay Williams 1969 "National study of the aftermath of apprehension." *Prospectus* 3:3–11.

Gibbs, Jack P. 1975 *Crime, Punishment and Deterrence*. New York: Elsevier.

Heckman, James 1979 "Sample selection bias as a specification error." *Econometrica* 45:153–61.

Hirschi, Travis 1975 "Labeling theory and juvenile delinquency: an assessment of the evidence." Pp. 181–203 in Walter R. Gove (ed.). *The Labeling of Deviance*. New York: Wiley.

Illinois Law Enforcement Commission 1978 "Report on technical assistance project—domestic violence survey." (Abstract). Washington, D.C.: National Criminal Justice Reference Service.

Ketterman, Thomas and Marjorie Kravitz 1978 *Police Crisis Intervention: A Selected Bibliography*. Washington, D.C.: National Criminal Justice Reference Service.

Klemke, Lloyd W. 1978 "Does apprehension for shoplifting amplify or terminate shoplifting activity?" *Law and Society Review* 12:391–403.

Kraut, Robert E. 1976 "Deterrent and definitional influences on shoplifting." *Social Problems* 23:358–68.

Langley, Richard and Roger C. Levy 1977 *Wife Beating: The Silent Crisis*. New York: E.P. Dutton.

Lawless, Jerald F. 1982 *Statistical Models and Methods for Lifetime Data*. New York: Wiley.

Lemert, Edwin M. 1951 *Social Pathology*. New York: McGraw-Hill. 1967 *Human Deviance, Social Problems and Social Control*. Englewood Cliffs, NJ: Prentice-Hall.

Lempert, Richard. 1981–1982 "Organizing for deterrence: lessons from a study of child support." *Law and Society Review* 16:513–68.

Lincoln, Suzanne B., Malcolm W. Klein, Katherine S. Teilmann and Susan Labin unpubl. "Control organizations and labeling theory: official versus self-reported delinquency." Unpublished manuscript, University of Southern California.

Maddala, G. S. 1983 *Limited, Dependent and Qualitative Variables in Econometrics*. Cambridge: Cambridge University Press.

McCord, Joan 1983 "A longitudinal appraisal of criminal sanctions." Paper presented at the IXth International Congress on Criminology, Vienna. Austria, September.

Meyer, Jeanie Keeny and T. D. Lorimer 1977 *Police Intervention Data and Domestic Violence: Exploratory Development and Validation of Prediction Models*. Report prepared under grant #RO1MH27918 from National Institute of Mental Health. Kansas City, Mo., Police Department.

Murray, Charles A. and Louis A. Cox, Jr. 1979 *Beyond Probation*. Beverly Hills: Sage Office of the Minority Leader, State of New York 1978 *Battered Women: Part I (Abstract)*. Washington, D.C.: National Criminal Justice Reference Service.

Parnas, Raymond I. 1972 "The police response to the domestic disturbance." Pp. 206–36 in Leon Radzinowicz and Marvin E. Wolfgang (eds.), *The Criminal in the Arms of the Law*. New York: Basic Books.

Police Foundation 1976 *Domestic Violence and the Police: Studies in Detroit and Kansas City*. Washington, D.C.: The Police Foundation.

Potter, Jane 1978 "The police and the battered wife; the search for understanding." *Police Magazine* 1:40–50.

Roy, Maria (ed.) 1977 *Battered Women*. New York: Van Nostrand Reinhold.

Schwartz, Richard and Jerome Skolnick 1962 "Two studies of legal stigma." *Social Problems* 10:133–42.

Sherman, Lawrence W. 1980 "Causes of police behavior the current state of quantitative research." *Journal of Research in Crime and Delinquency* 17:69–100.

Shoham, S. Giora 1974 "Punishment and traffic offenses." *Traffic Quarterly* 28:61–73.

Thorsell, Bernard A. and Lloyd M. Klemke 1972 "The labeling process: reinforcement and deterrent." *Law and Society Review* 6:393–403.

Tittle, Charles 1975 "Labeling and crime; an empirical evaluation." Pp. 157–79 in Walter R. Gove (ed.), *The Labeling of Deviance*. New York: Wiley.

University of Rochester 1974 "FACIT—Family Conflict Intervention Team Experiment—Experimental Action Program." (Abstract). Washington, D.C.; National Criminal Justice Reference Service.

Wylie, P. B., L. F. Basinger, C. L. Heinecke and J. A. Reuckert 1976 "Approach to evaluating a police program of family crisis interventions in sex demonstration cities—Final report." (Abstract). Washington, D.C.: National Criminal Justice Reference Service.

Zimring, Franklin E. and Gordon T. Hawkins 1973 *Deterrence: The Legal Threat in Crime Control*. Chicago: University of Chicago Press.

DISCUSSION QUESTIONS

1. Explain how the experiment was designed and conducted (methodology).

2. What are some potential problems with the way that this study was designed?

3. Identify some unforeseen problems that could result from mandatory arrest policies.

READING 16

The Philadelphia foot patrol experiment represents a contemporary look at the effectiveness of foot patrol. This study is unique, as it uses GIS analysis, and it also examines the impact of foot patrol in violent crime hot spots. The findings from this study support the idea that targeted foot patrol in violent-crime hot spots can significantly reduce violent crime. This study contributes to the growing body of literature on place-based policing efforts.

The Philadelphia Foot Patrol Experiment: A Randomized Controlled Trial of Police Patrol Effectiveness in Violent Crime Hotspots

Jerry H. Ratcliffe, Travis Taniguchi, Elizabeth R. Groff, and Jennifer D. Wood

For most of the history of American policing, the role of foot patrols in public safety has been almost mythical. The growth of the night and rattle watches of the 1700s was the consequence of the assumed deterrence abilities of a patrolling, uniformed authority carrying the explicit threat of government intervention should social order unravel. To this day, we have a consistent public demand for foot patrols as a "proactive, non-threatening, community-oriented approach to local policing" (Wakefield, 2007: 343). Key questions yet remain. For example, do foot patrols achieve more than simply providing reassurance to the public? Does the enhanced visibility of officers on foot, instead of in cars, serve a significant and measurable deterrent effect? The evidence to date on these questions has been mixed, despite that the police have long been assumed to provide a deterrence function. This assumption can be traced back to the writings of both Bentham (1948[1789]) and Beccaria (1963[1764]) who argued for the need to influence the calculus of would-be criminals, for society to ensure that the costs of committing a crime would be outweighed by any potential benefits. Beccaria argued that the central mechanisms for adjusting this calculus are certainty of detection, severity of punishment, and celerity (or swiftness of punishment) (see Nagin and Pogarsky, 2001). The very origins of the police institution rest on this view. Sir Robert Peel established his police in London, U.K., as a means of providing an "unremitting watch" (Shearing, 1996: 74) through visible patrol. Citizens would be deterred through this system of surveillance, knowing that their chances of being caught and punished would be high.

Yet, despite the longevity of the deterrence doctrine, the evidence on whether the practice of foot patrol *actually* deters crime has been weak. Following the Kansas City preventative patrol experiment finding that vehicle-based patrol had no significant impact on crime rates (Kelling et al., 1974), the Newark foot patrol experiment did much to cement the view among many criminologists that varying the dosage of uniformed patrol has no quantifiable impact on crime (Kelling, 1981). Varying foot patrol levels across 12 Newark, NJ, beats resulted in no significant differences between treatment and control beats for recorded crime or arrest rates, although treatment areas did show improvements in community fear of crime (Pate, 1986).

Additional studies followed, ranging in magnitude and scope. For example, four foot patrol officers in a business district of Asheville, NC, had the same, apparently negligible, impact on recorded crime as the 300 officers moved to foot patrol as part of the Boston Police Department's 1983 Patrol Reallocation Plan (Bowers and Hirsch, 1987; Esbensen, 1987). Notwithstanding this lack of evidence, foot patrol became "the most popular and widely implemented component of community policing" (Rosenbaum and Lurigo, 1994: 303) even if many police departments adopted foot beats more to address community relations and fear of crime than for any direct crime deterrence benefits (Cordner, 1986; Jim, Mitchell, and Kent, 2006). The National Research Council (2004) review of police policy and practices summarized foot

patrol as an unfocused community policing strategy with only weak-to-moderate evidence of effectiveness in reducing fear of crime.

Since these early foot patrol studies, criminologists have gained a more nuanced understanding of criminal behavior within spatial and temporal contexts. For instance, both routine activity theory (Felson, 1987) and crime pattern theory (Brantingham and Brantingham, 1984) identify *place* as a fundamental component of the requirements of a crime, the centrality of which environmental criminologists have adopted as a potential avenue along which to promote crime-control opportunities. It is now widely understood that crime clusters within highly-specific geographic locations, commonly termed "hotspots." A crime hotspot is the accepted term for what was originally described as a cluster of addresses (Sherman and Weisburd, 1995), widened to include the possibility of street intersections and public space (Buerger, Cohn, and Petrosino, 1995). The term is now generally defined as a "geographical area of higher than average crime . . . an area of crime concentration, relative to the distribution of crime across the whole region of interest" (Chainey and Ratcliffe, 2005: 145–6). With the growth of crime mapping, crime hotspots have become significant *loci* for focused police activity.

With a refocusing on place, location-specific crime prevention can add to general offender deterrence with options to prevent potential offenders from committing crime at a specific location. Nagin (2010: 313) recently pointed out that effective deterrence stems from a tangible and direct prospect of detection, and that focused policing at crime hotspots "is probably effective because it tangibly and directly increases apprehension risk at the hot spot by substantially increasing police presence."

Although the National Research Council's (2004) review lamented the paucity of quality studies on the benefit of proactive police activity such as field interrogations and traffic enforcement, we have long had general support from Wilson and Boland's (1978) study of 35 cities to suggest that even some unfocused proactive police activity can have a reductive effect on robbery. A more extensive study of 171 American cities and the proactive drink/drive and disorder activities of police again found a similar dampening effect on robbery (Sampson and Cohen, 1988), and a recent update with a more fully specified statistical model again found a significant negative association between robbery rates and proactive policing across a similar number of U.S. cities (Kubrin et al., 2010). Focusing on gun violence, studies including the Kansas City gun intervention (Sherman, Shaw, and Rogan, 1995) and the Indianapolis directed patrol project (McGarrell, Chermak, and Weiss, 2002) led Koper and Mayo-Wilson (2006) to conclude that directed patrols targeted to the carrying of illegal weapons had a suppressive effect on gun violence at high-risk places and times.

A strong evidence base has similarly emerged in relation to the positive effects of the related strategy, *hotspots policing*. Echoing the findings of previous studies (such as Braga and Bond, 2008; Sherman, Gartin, and Buerger, 1989; Weisburd and Braga, 2006), both the National Research Council (2004) and Braga's (2007) systematic review concluded that focused hotspots policing works. Previous hotspots experiments have to date examined problem-oriented policing rather than foot patrol per se (Braga et al., 1999), or where foot patrol strategies were mixed with other interventions such as vehicle patrols (Sherman and Weisburd, 1995; Weisburd and Green, 1995). A rare exception is the British study in Hull, Humberside, where additional foot patrols in the city center reduced personal robbery during the course of a year by 16 percent while regional and national rates increased (Jones and Tilley, 2004). Given this new evidence, we suggest it is timely to reexamine the question of whether foot patrol, as a specific hotspots intervention, holds promise as an approach to reducing crime, and especially violent crime, which is a leading cause of death and injury in the United States (see Miller, Cohen, and Rossman, 1993).

In light of the theoretical advances discussed, and the development of new techniques in spatial analysis, one can revisit the research designs of earlier foot patrol studies with fresh eyes. Sherman and Weisburd (1995) already have pointed out that many of these early studies suffered from statistical and measurement problems, namely, a statistical bias across area-based studies toward the null hypothesis, and the measurement issue of an often inappropriate study area. The latter problem addresses the question of whether to organize a project by police districts, police beats, or other areas. Even if hotspots policing was part of the lexicon at the time, the ability to achieve a microspatial focus traditionally has been hampered by the need to measure and organize police resources by larger administrative regions.

This issue has to some extent been resolved with the development of geographic information systems (GIS) and the accompanying field of geographic information science (GISc), although as Rengert and Lockwood (2009: 110) pointed out, many crime analysts simply accept the "bounded space that is available to them rather than construct their own boundaries." GIS and GISc together provide both a tool and an analytical regime to approach spatially customized target areas for crime prevention activities. Thus, more recent police effectiveness research projects have been able to concentrate on crime hotspots.

The ability over time to move down through the cone of resolution (Brantingham, Dyreson, and Brantingham, 1976) from studying large administrative areas to smaller and smaller spatial units has enabled crime researchers to now explore crime hotspots at *micro units of place*, which are defined as addresses, street segments, or clusters of these microspatial units (Weisburd, Bernasco, and Bruinsma, 2009: 4). A focus on smaller places can address dosage concerns; concerns that foot patrol officers assigned to replace vehicle-based patrol in large geographic areas will be spread too thin, thereby diminishing any deterrence effect that could have been created by their presence.

Spatially oriented crime-control programs have actively addressed the redesignation of places that provide crime opportunities, looking to a locational focus to create constraints on criminality. Weisburd and Green (1995: 731) employed a randomized control design to examine a 7-month operation to reduce drug activity at drug hotspots in Jersey City, NJ, and found "consistent, strong effects of the experimental strategy on disorder-related emergency calls for service." Taking the cone of resolution to individual properties and corners, Green (1995) found an Oakland, CA, program that combined traditional enforcement with third-party interventions targeted at nuisance drug locations not only reduced drug problems but also demonstrated a diffusion of benefits to nearby locations.

The potential diffusion impact of crime prevention strategies at specific locations raises the question of how interventions such as foot patrols can prevent crime. General and specific deterrence may occur if the presence of a police officer is sufficient to increase an offender's perceived risk of apprehension (Nagin, 2010). A second potential mechanism is "proactive policing" (Kubrin et al., 2010), whereby the activity of a police officer, such as stopping and questioning suspects, performing a *stop-and-frisk* (also known as a *Terry stop*), or (with probable cause) conducting a full search of a suspect, may increase the chances that police will identify a fugitive or find illegal weapons or items and increase the arrest rate. The visible enforcement of minor infractions and disorder offenses may be perceived by offenders as indicative of a change in the apprehension risk, according to Sampson and Cohen (1988). Therefore, deterrence can potentially occur through officer *presence*, or where specific *activities* of police officers either increase the arrest-offense ratio or the perception that it has increased (Kubrin et al., 2010).

Spatial diffusion of benefits may occur if offenders perceive that officers patrolling a nearby hotspot may be able to intervene quickly should the alarm be raised about a crime, or if patrol boundaries are not known to offenders. A spatial diffusion could also occur if deterrence can serve to discourage the carrying of crime-enabling items, a change that can affect the offender both inside and outside the target area.

Conversely, place-based interventions can theoretically displace crime to nearby areas if officers never patrol nearby areas, and if the boundaries of the target area are known to local offenders. Yet even in these scenarios, displacement may be beneficial. Offenders may move to spaces that are less inviting or less familiar to them, resulting in a reduction of their

activity. Specific behaviors like drug market activity could be displaced to less public spaces, away from children, recovering drug addicts, and everyday people such that these groups are less exposed to the harms associated with dealing and selling (Caulkins and Reuter, 2009). The social harm outcomes of proactive police activity can therefore be theoretically beneficial in either a diffusion or a displacement regime. Displacement can move criminal activity to less optimal (Taniguchi, Rengert, and McCord, 2009) or less public locations, whereas a diffusion of benefits could mean reduced exposure to violence overall, which is a crime reduction outcome that also has been associated with improved public health outcomes (Guerra, Huesmann, and Spindler, 2003).

At the outset we should note that disentangling specific deterrence effects of officer presence versus officer (proactive) activity is beyond the reach of this study; however, within the broad research literature outlined earlier, our current study of officers walking patrol areas concentrated at crime hotspots can be characterized as a study of both foot patrol as well as hotspots policing. The remainder of this article reports on what the authors believe is the first large-scale, randomized controlled experiment of the effectiveness of foot patrol to reduce violence in crime hotspots.

Experimental Design

Background to the Philadelphia Experiment

Philadelphia is the fourth largest police department in America, with more than 6,600 police officers, These officers police a city of nearly 1.5 million people, recently ranked the 30th most dangerous in the United States (Morgan, Morgan, and Boba, 2010). Violence, recognized as one of the worst public health threats both nationally and locally (Centers for Disease Control and Prevention, 2010), remains a problem in the city. In 2008 (the year before this study's intervention), 331 homicides took place in the city, and since the year 2002, Philadelphia has experienced more than 100 shootings per month (Ratcliffe and Rengert, 2008).

Although the city had witnessed a gradual reduction in violent crime levels for a couple of years, a noticeable and consistent seasonal cycle of increases in violent crime has been occurring during the summer months (figure 1). A pilot study of 43 foot beats patrolled during the summer of 2008 indicated a modest reduction in violence in the target areas, with a slight diffusion of benefits to a buffer area of approximately 1,000 feet around target sites (Ratcliffe and Taniguchi, 2008).

With the availability of two waves of new recruits emerging from the police academy in March and late June 2009, we were provided with an opportunity to conduct a larger study. Police Commissioner Charles Ramsey expressed a desire to focus the new recruits emerging from the police academy toward small, targeted foot patrols in high violent crime areas primarily to reduce summer violent crime.

Figure 1   Weekly Violent Crime Counts, 2006 to October 2009, Philadelphia, PA

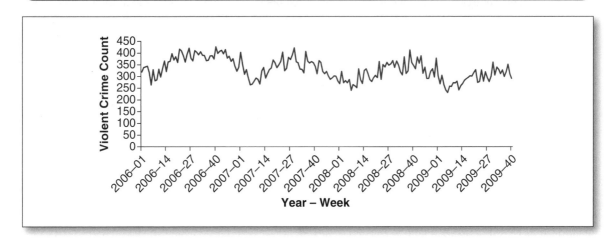

Selection of Random Assignment Hotspots

We followed a multistep process to identify the most dangerous places in Philadelphia. During January and February 2009, violent crime reports were drawn from the incident (INCT) database of the Philadelphia Police Department for 2006, 2007, and 2008. Violent crime was defined as homicide, aggravated assault, and robberies not occurring indoors (the outdoor selection of offenses being in line with the approach of Sherman and Weisburd, 1995). These categories of serious violent crime are typically not affected by issues with crime reporting or police discretion (Gove, Hughes, and Geerken, 1985). Crime events were weighted so events from 2008 counted 1.00, 2007 crimes counted .50, and 2006 crime events counted .25. In this way, more recent events had greater relevance in the creation of the target locations for 2009, but the area values could retain a portion of the long-term hotspot component, given many urban locations have long-term crime trajectories (Weisburd et al., 2004). These weighted values were summed for homicide, aggravated assault, and robbery, and then these events were mapped and aggregated to spatial units called Thiessen polygons to create a Voronoi network of spatial units. A Voronoi network consists of areal units created by using lines to divide a plane into areas closest to each of a set of points (in our case, street intersections) such that the space within each polygon is closer to the specific point within than to any other point (Chrisman, 2002). For points, we chose the nearly 22,000 intersections in the city. The Voronoi network as a unit of analysis is very similar to the "epicenter" (Sherman and Weisburd, 1995) and "intersection area" approaches (Braga et al., 1999; Weisburd and Green, 1995) used in previous place-based experiments. Those experiments either included the entire blocks associated with an intersection (Braga et al., 1999; Weisburd and Green, 1995) or a more subjective measure of "as far as the eye could see from sidewalk corners" in each direction (Sherman and Weisburd, 1995: 633).

Polygons greater than one million square feet were excluded, and a map of weighted violent crime totals for each polygon are presented to the two Philadelphia Regional Operations Commanders (ROC North and ROC South), with the top 220 violent crime corner polygons highlighted. This top 1 percent of corners (approximately, based on the 3-year weighted values) contained 15 percent of the 2008 robberies, 13 percent of 2008 aggravated assaults, and more than 10 percent of all 2008 homicides. The top 5 percent of corners accounted in 2008 for 39 percent of robberies, 42 percent of aggravated assaults, and 33 percent of homicides.

Police commanders informed us that they would have sufficient personnel to cover 60 foot patrols for 16 hours a day, 5 days a week, so the ROCs were asked to identify at least 120 potential foot patrol areas of roughly equivalent size, where each patrol area must contain at least 1 of the top 220 violent crime corners in the city. To aid the creation of patrol areas, we mapped the results of a local Moran's I spatial autocorrelation test (Anselin, 1995; Moran, 1950). Local Moran's I is one of a range of local indicators of spatial association (LISA) statistics available to crime scientists that can indicate clustering of high crime values (Anselin, 1996; Getis and Ord, 1992, 1996; Unwin, 1996). Mapping polygons with high violence counts that were among high violence neighbors enabled police commanders to see where the hottest corners were surrounded by other high crime areas and, from this information, to construct more effective foot patrol areas.

Commanders drew 129 potential foot beats they felt were the most important to pursue. The authors

examined the patrol areas and adjusted some that were overlapping or deemed too large as originally drawn. During this process, some of the original foot beats were split and others were combined, which left us with a total of 124 foot beats. The final areas were on-screen digitized, and a point-in-polygon GIS operation was used to reaggregate the weighted crime points from 2006 to 2008 to the new spatial units. The four lowest crime foot beats were dropped from consideration to leave 120 potential foot patrol areas.

To test the intervention of foot patrols, we employed a randomized block design. In some regards, this approach has some comparable components to a complete block design (Braga and Bond, 2008). Block designs have the advantage of minimizing the effects of variability by allowing for the comparison of similar cases (Mazerolle, Kadleck, and Roehl, 1998). An aggregate total of 2006–2008 temporally weighted violent crime (as discussed earlier) was used to rank all 120 areas from highest to lowest. The foot patrol areas were ranked such that the first couple contained the 1st and 2nd highest ranked areas, the second couple contained the 3rd and 4th highest areas, and so on to the 60th couple, which contained the 119th and 120th ranked locations. A quasi-random number generator was used to assign one member of each couple as a target area (which would receive foot patrol officers) or a control area (which would receive no foot patrol policing). This randomization process was done without regard to the spatial location or proximity of the treatment and control groups, or to the similarity of any other characteristic; randomization was solely a function of the temporally weighted violent crime counts for the 3 years preceding the experiment. In this way, we could use data from 2006 to 2008 to generate a group of target areas for the summer of 2009 that we anticipated would be collectively equivalent in terms of crime intensity as an equivalent group of control areas. Police district commanders were not provided with detailed information on the control locations. The target and control areas are shown in figure 2.

Data from 2006–2008 were employed to determine the hotspot areas because the police required sufficient lead time to set up officer allocation and assignment

Figure 2   Map of Philadelphia, PA with Target and Control Areas

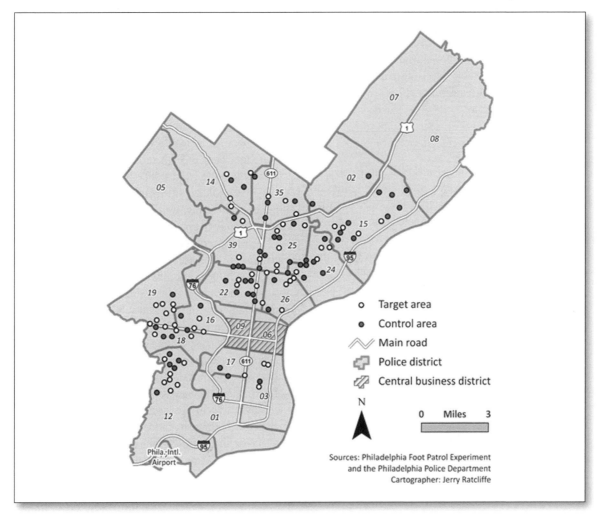

Sources: Philadelphia Foot Patrol Experiment and the Philadelphia Police Department
Cartographer: Jerry Ratcliffe

orders. As would be expected with a randomized design, no difference between treatment and control groups was found; however, when the experiment began in late spring of 2009, for currency we used the immediate 3 months of crime data prior to the start of the experiment for the pretreatment measure. Independent samples t test indicated no significant difference between treatment (mean = 5.98; standard deviation [SD] = 4.04) and control groups (mean = 4.93; SD = 3.34) on pretreatment violent crime counts, $t(118) = -1.55$, $p > .10$ (two tailed).

An a priori power analysis was conducted to determine the power of the experimental design (Faul et al., 2007). Given a two-tailed test, with an a level of .10, 60 cases in the treatment group and 60 cases in the control group power were found to be adequate (> 80 percent) when the effect size was large (> .80) or medium (.50). Power was low when effect size was small (.10)—a problem common to place-based randomized trials (Boruch et al., 2004)—but power would be higher than conventionally acceptable levels (greater than .80) given an effect size greater than .40 when using the parameters listed earlier.

Treatment

The target and control areas included an average of 14.7 street intersections (SD = 5.30) and 1.3 miles of streets (SD = .40). Each target area was patrolled by two pairs of officers recently graduated from the police academy. They received a 1-week orientation at the police district of their specific foot patrol location, and then they spent an initial period of a few weeks in and around their beat with an experienced officer. Because none of these orientation activities were required to remain in the foot patrol area, the evaluation date started the week after the final orientation. The officer pairs were assigned either a morning (10 A.M. to 6 P.M.) or an evening shift (6 P.M. to 2 A.M.) that they policed Tuesday through Saturday nights. The pairs alternated morning and evening shifts every other week. This meant that the areas were not assigned foot patrols from 2 A.M. to 10 A.M. each day, and from 2 A.M. Sunday right through to 10 A.M. Tuesday each week.

Officers were assigned from the academy in two phases. Phase 1 commenced on March 31, 2009, with officers in 24 foot patrol areas, and continued to September. Phase 2 commenced on July 7, 2009, and lasted for 12 weeks. There were 36 patrolled areas in Phase 2. This theoretically provided for 57,600 hours of foot patrol activity during the initial 12 weeks of both phases. District captains were instructed to ensure the foot beats were fully staffed over the experimental period. All patrol officers were provided with an initial criminal intelligence brief on their foot patrol area by the criminal intelligence unit, as well as whatever information about the area they gleaned from their initial orientation. They did not receive specific instructions on policing style from police headquarters; however, some officers did report being briefed on the expectations of their respective district commanders (at the rank of captain in the Philadelphia Police Department).

Field observations by trained researchers found considerable variation in activity. Some officers engaged in extensive community-oriented work, speaking to community members and visiting child care centers and juvenile hangouts, whereas others were more crime oriented, stopping vehicles at stop signs and intersections, and interviewing pedestrians. Some officers reported receiving a considerable level of supervision and interest from their immediate supervisors, whereas others reported being largely left to their own devices. Field observers reported that only a few foot patrol boundaries were rigidly observed; several officers—either through boredom or a perception that they were displacing crime to nearby streets—would stray for a time if they were aware of areas of interest just beyond the foot patrol area.

Table 1 Descriptive Statistics for Counts of Violent Events by Time Period, Experimental and Control Areas

Status (Time Period)	Sum	Mean	Median	Standard Deviation	Minimum	Maximum	Skewness
Target (Before, t_0)	359	5.98	5.00	4.04	1	18	.96
Target (During, t_1)	306	5.10	5.00	3.08	0	15	.77
Control (Before, t_0)	296	4.93	4.50	3.34	0	14	.79
Control (During, t_1)	327	5.45	5.00	4.26	0	21	1.63

Outcome Measure

The outcome measure for the experiment was reported violent crime. The crime data were drawn from the INCT database of the Philadelphia Police Department, a database containing all police incidents occurring in the city. The database records a Uniform Crime Reports (UCR) classification as used by the national reporting mechanism administered by the Federal Bureau of Investigation (FBI) and premises and nature codes that indicate the type of location and the origin of the incident. Violent crime is defined here as criminal homicide, all robberies (except cargo theft), and a majority of aggravated assaults. We excluded violent crime incidents that were deemed unlikely that a patrolling officer could be expected to prevent, such as rape (largely an indoor activity) and some aggravated assaults in specific categories such as against a student by a school employee or against a police officer. School assaults would largely take place on school premises, and assaults against police may increase artificially as a result of the increased presence of police officers. The INCT database incidents were drawn from roughly 3 months of each phase (the operational period) and the 3 months immediately preceding each phase (the pretreatment period). INCT records were drawn at the end of the overall experiment period. The Philadelphia system automatically geocodes crime events with a success (hit) rate in excess of 98 percent, well above an empirically derived minimum acceptable geocoding rate of 85 percent (Ratcliffe, 2004). Descriptive statistics are provided in table 1.

 Results

Table 1 shows change in reported crime in the 60 control and 60 target areas for the 3 months before and during the implementation dates for the operational phases. The inverted odds ratio for the crime reduction was .77, which when converted to a percentage change for the target areas relative to control sites indicate a relative reduction of 23 percent.

A simple approach to assessing the significance level of the effect of the intervention is to calculate a change score, the difference between t_0 and t_1. These scores are then subjected to an independent samples t test to determine whether the change between preoperation and operational time periods was significantly different for treatment and control areas. A significant difference between treatment (mean $= -.88$ SD $= 4.32$) and control (mean $= .52$, SD $= 3.44$) groups was found [$t(118) = 1.96, p = .05$], which suggests that treatment areas had significantly lower change scores (indicating a greater reduction of crime or smaller increases) than their control counterparts. Substantial limitations, however, exist in assessing the effects of treatment through a simple change score analysis. As change scores only measure the relative change from t_0 and t_1, they do not properly account for the starting point of each area.

Numerous methods exist to assess the statistical significance of the change between the preoperational and operational time periods (Twisk and de Vente, 2008). Given the randomization process employed in this study, the most direct method of evaluating change would normally be to conduct an independent samples t test to compare the count of events in the treatment and control groups during the operational period. Unfortunately this approach, much like the change score analysis presented earlier, fails to control adequately for short-term changes in violent crime. Not considering the differences between treatment and control groups creates a situation where regression toward the mean could threaten the internal validity of the study. In other words, failing to account for the starting point of each area (indicated by the "before" crime count) could lead to overestimation or underestimation of the treatment effect (Galton, 1886; Twisk and de Vente, 2008) where areas with very high or very low crime at t_0 will naturally migrate toward more moderate crime levels at t_1.

Therefore, to explore the impact of foot patrols on violent crime levels while capturing extraneous influences such as regression to the mean, a limitation of the typical t test, we employed linear regression models (Frison and Pocock, 1992; Twisk and Proper, 2004; Twisk and de Vente, 2008). The dependent variable was the count of violent crime during the 3-month operational phase, and the independent variable was a dummy variable representing treatment or control status. Pretreatment scores for the 3 months prior to the intervention were entered as a covariate, effectively controlling for natural regression to the mean. Table 2 (model 1) presents the results of a linear regression model predicting the violent crime count during the operational phase with the violent crime count during the preoperational phase and a dummy variable representing treatment status.

There was a strong relationship between pretreatment violent crime count and the violent crime count during the operational period. Treatment status was found to be nonsignificant. When differences between the starting violent crime levels in the foot patrol areas were properly accounted for, treatment and control areas showed no significant differences in the violent crime level during the operational period; however, one assumption underlying regression models is that the relationship between the covariate (here the pretreatment violent crime level) and the dependent variable (the crime level during the operational period) is the same for each group. Put simply, the treatment and control areas are assumed to have a similar relationship between the pretreatment violent crime count and the violent crime count during the operational

period. Exploratory analysis of the regression slopes fitted for each group suggested treatment and control areas had substantially different slope values. This suggested that an interaction term between treatment and the pretreatment violent crime count would be informative on both theoretical and statistical grounds. Table 2 (model 2) presents the results of a linear regression model including a pretreatment count and treatment status interaction term.

The significance of the interaction term suggests that it would be inappropriate to refer to the effectiveness of the treatment in reducing violent crime without also specifying the level of pretreatment violence. That is, the slope of the pretreatment violent crime level varied by treatment and control groups. Visual inspection of a scatter plot between violence preoperation and violence during the operation suggested that treatment may have little effect for areas starting and ending with low violent crime counts but may have a larger effect for areas with higher preoperation and during-operation counts. To explore these trends in more detail, adjusted mean crime counts for the operational period were calculated for preoperational violent crime scores corresponding to the 20th, 40th, 60th, 80th, and 90th percentiles. The differences in expected violent crime count for target and control areas were then

Table 2 Linear Regression Models Predicting Violent Crime Counts[a]

Variables	Model 1			Model 2		
	B	Standard Error	t	B	Standard Error	t
Constant	3.240***	.594	5.453	1.585*	.738	2.148
Pretreatment violent crime count	.448***	.083	5.404	.783***	.124	6.310
Treatment status	−.820	.616	−1.332	2.209[a]	1.045	2.114
Pretreatment violent crime count × treatment status				−.565	.161	−3.507

[a] $N = 120$.

* $p < .05$; ** $p < .01$; *** $p < .001$.

Table 3 Treatment-Control Differences in Counts of Violent Offenses, by Pretreatment Violent Crime Count

Pretreatment Violent Crime Count (Percentile)	Target Area Estimate During the Operational Period	Control Area Estimate During the Operational Period	Difference (Target Area-Control Area)	F	Significance
3.0 (20th)	4.449	3.936	.514	.538	.465
4.5 (40th)	4.667	4.719	−.052	.007	.935
6.0 (60th)	5.104	6.286	−1.182	3.919	.050
8.0 (80th)	5.540	7.852	−2.312	10.148	.002
11.0 (90th)	6.195	10.202	−4.008	13.705	< .001

assessed to determine under what pretreatment crime levels treatment had a significant impact. These results can be found in table 3.

These results suggest that there were no differences between treatment and control groups in the 20th and 40th percentiles. At the 60th percentile and higher, target areas had less violent crime than their control counterparts, a finding significant at $p < .05$. This difference became more noteworthy in higher percentiles. It is worth reiterating at this point that because pretreatment violent crime counts were entered into the regression model, the differences observed here represent impacts above and beyond what would be expected based on regression to the mean. In other words, even after accounting for natural regression to the mean, target areas in the top 40 percent on pretreatment violent crime counts had significantly less violent crime once the operational period was under way than their control counterparts. This finding has potential implications for deploying scarce resources and is discussed in the following section.

Variables broadly indicative of police activity can illuminate these results. For example, a *pedestrian stop* is recorded whenever a police officer conducts a field interview, stop-and-frisk, or search of a suspect in the street.

Table 4 Treatment-Control Differences in Counts for Various Incident Types by Time Period

Incident Type	Control Areas		Treatment Areas			
	Preoperation	During Operation (Percent)	Preoperation	During Operation (Percent)	Foot Patrol (Percent)	Percent Contribution to Increase
Pedestrian stops	5,965	5,985 (< 1)	7,366	12,103 (64)	4,282 (35)	90
Vehicle stops	5,600	4,862 (−13)	5,922	6,339 (7)	799 (13)	192
Disturbances	3,600	4,033 (12)	3,980	5,856 (47)	1,480 (25)	79
Narcotics	397	370 (−7)	464	535 (15)	119 (22)	168
Disorder	249	288 (16)	336	528 (57)	157 (30)	82
Arrests	1,395	1,361 (−2)	1,684	1, 905 (13)	398 (21)	180

Similarly a *vehicle stop* is recorded when this is conducted with occupants of a vehicle. Also, some types of police activity are largely the result of proactive policing rather than a response to calls from the public. For instance, *disturbances* can include incidents such as disorderly crowds or small gatherings that can be identified and dispersed by police officers as well as rowdy behavior in and around liquor establishments; *narcotics* incidents are largely the result of proactive police work; and *disorder* incidents such as prostitution, public drunkenness, loitering, and violation of city ordinances often are largely left to police to initiate, especially in higher crime areas. *Arrests* are likely a combination of reactive policing (responding to a call from the public) and proactive activity.

Table 4 shows that the frequency of all of these incident types increased during the police operation and that the foot patrol officers (as identified by their radio call signs) contributed substantially to the rise observed in treatment areas. Using the pedestrian stops example, although stops increased less than 1 percent in control areas, they increased by 64 percent in treatment areas. Foot patrol officers conducted 4,282 pedestrian stops, amounting to 35 percent of all pedestrian stops in the treatment areas during the

operation, and contributing 90 percent of the increase in the treatment sites. The additional vehicle stops and narcotics incidents handled by foot patrol officers in the treatment areas offset and added to a decrease in these activities by other (vehicle-bound) officers. This situation is the same as for the total number of arrests in the treatment areas. Non-foot-patrol-officer arrests declined slightly in both treatment and control areas; however, the additional nearly 400 arrests by foot patrol officers increased the overall arrest count by 13 percent.

When these additional activities are disaggregated even more, it can be observed that foot patrol officers in the top 20 percent of highest crime areas were engaged in significantly more work than patrol officers in the lower volume crime hotspots. Table 5 shows little substantial difference among average activity levels for crime hotspots at lower percentiles; however, activity across all measures increases considerably for the top 12 foot patrol areas, with, for example, officers conducting on average 115 pedestrian stops during the 3-month operational period compared with only 57 in the lowest pretreatment crime areas. They also conducted more vehicle stops, dealt with more disturbances and narcotics incidents, and made substantially more arrests.

Table 5   Mean Counts of Incidents Handled by Foot Patrol Officers During Experiment, by Pretreatment Violent Crime Count

Pretreatment Percentile	Pedestrian Stops	Vehicle Stops	Disturbances	Narcotics	Disorder	Arrests
0–20	57.3	11.3	18.9	1.1	1.3	3.2
20–40	61.8	13.7	23.6	1.5	2.7	6.3
40–60	44.9	7.5	22.3	.8	3.0	4.7
60–80	77.4	13.8	22.2	1.9	2.1	6.9
80–100	115.4	20.3	36.4	4.6	4.1	12.2

Limitations

We are cautious in saying that the crime reduction outcome in the foot patrol areas was entirely the result of foot patrol officers. Like many places, the Philadelphia Police Department does not employ crime analysts, and centrally generated spatial crime intelligence disseminated to district patrol officers and supervisors is fairly sparse (see Ratcliffe, 2008). Although knowledge of foot patrol locations was not formally disseminated beyond the necessary districts, neither were the sites exactly a secret, and in the absence of little other guiding information, it is possible that officers not involved in the experiment were called in to periodically assist foot officers, or used the known foot beat areas as indicative of crime hotspots to which they should also pay attention. Table 4 would suggest, however, that this was not a significant issue.

We also should caution that in terms of violent crime count, the numbers examined in this article are small. Although the aggregate crime counts are greater than 300 for the target areas, the effect becomes diluted when distributed across all target areas. At an individual foot patrol area level, the effect represents a net improvement of less than two violent crimes per foot patrol area, and this drops to less than one when the total net effect of changes in the displacement area is factored. This result is to be expected given that violent crime levels often are less than the public imagine, and especially given the constrained spatial units employed by the experiment. It is at least partially responsible for the low observed power found in this experiment. For this reason, we are reluctant to report results for individual police districts or foot patrol areas where one or two violent offenses either way could have an impact on an area's individual effectiveness.

We could not support sufficient field research time to generate robust measures of patrol time within each foot patrol area because of financial limitations. Graduate students observed foot patrol officers in each of the 60 treatment areas for approximately 2 hours for each day shift and 2 hours for each night shift, totaling 240 hours of observation time. This observational period is insufficient from which to extrapolate and develop an estimate of the total time spent by officers in

their beats. During observations, officers likely focused on showing researchers around their assigned beats. Even if officers went beyond beat boundaries in the presence of observers, we had no way of measuring how long they stayed and worked in such areas during the course of an (unobserved) shift of 8 hours. Foot patrol officers did conduct a few official activities in control areas, but this accounted for less than 4 percent of all incidents within the control areas. It is anticipated that analysis of both field notes as well as post-experiment interviews with foot patrol officers may in the future enable a more nuanced understanding of officer staffing and officer compliance with patrol boundaries.

This issue of potential crime displacement or diffusion of benefits is therefore addressed in our research. We recognize that our findings may overestimate the degree of displacement and, thus, are conservative with regard to the benefits of the intervention.

We also report descriptive output statistics on the differences between treatment and control areas with regard to several official indicators of proactive police activity. The data reported are official data only, the limitations of which are well known. As Durlauf and Nagin (2011) pointed out, measures of apprehension risk based on official records of crime or enforcement are incomplete because they cannot incorporate the risk of apprehension for opportunities overlooked by offenders as the risk was too high. Although these data suggest a component of the violent crime reduction may have its origins in proactive policing, disentangling specific deterrence effects of mere presence versus officers' proactive activity was beyond the reach of this article. It is acknowledged that we cannot parse the observed crime reduction into an officer *presence* component and an *activity* component, thereby limiting our study to a partial test of deterrence. Articulating the dimensions of this distinction would be an excellent avenue for future research.

 Discussion

We found that violent crime hotspots that were recipients of foot patrol officers for up to 90 hours per week had a reduction in violence of 90 offenses (with a net effect of 53 offenses once displacement is considered), outperforming equivalent control areas by 23 percent; however, the benefits were only achieved in areas with a threshold level of preintervention violence. When that threshold was achieved (in our study, an average of 6 violent crimes in the 3-month preintervention), these target areas in the top 40 percent on pretreatment violent crime counts had significantly lower levels of violent crime during the operational period, even after accounting for natural regression to the mean.

Our findings therefore raise the possibility that the Newark foot patrol experiment and subsequent follow-up studies are not necessarily the last word on foot patrol effectiveness. In theoretical terms, our study suggests that the foot patrols operated as a "certainty-communicating device" within the micro-spatial contexts of the hotspot areas. As our analysis focused on outdoor crimes, the data suggest that the police had the capacity to influence more behaviors in the target areas with high thresholds of pretreatment violence. As Stinchcombe (1963) pointed out long ago, police activity is structured by the location of crimes in terms of whether they occur in public space or within the "institutions of privacy." In dense urban settings with high levels of outdoor criminal behavior, more police-initiated activity in the form of enforcement and order maintenance is likely to occur. From this perspective, spatially focused foot patrol may communicate an increased level of certainty that crimes will be detected, disrupted, and/or punished. This perceived risk of detection might be especially high for individuals "on the run," such as those with arrest warrants who may seek to minimize the chances of police encounters in public spaces (see Goffman, 2009). Overall, this theoretical explanation is consistent with the conclusion of deterrence researchers that certainty of apprehension plays a stronger role than severity of punishment as a mechanism of general deterrence (Durlauf and Nagin, 2011; Nagin, 2010; Nagin and Pogarsky, 2001).

The overall crime reduction in foot patrol areas is not trivial, and the reduction represents a net outcome of 53 fewer crime victims in a city wrestling, like many American cities, with the individual and public health impact of violence. If, as we suggest, that deterrence is

highly localized, one possible explanation for the difference in crime outcome from Newark to Philadelphia may be an issue of spatial dosage. The Newark experiment began with existing foot beats, some of which were commercial corridors up to 16 blocks in length. The chances that patrolling officers would soon return to an intersection once perambulated would be slim. Benefiting from the application of GIS, in collaboration with senior commanders at the Philadelphia Police Department, we designed foot patrol areas that averaged just 1.3 miles in total street length. It is likely that if foot patrols are only effective because of a certain spatial concentration, then larger foot patrol areas become ineffective. When the local police department in Flint (MI) expanded its foot patrol areas against the wishes of the research team (in one case up to 20 times the original area), crime reduction effectiveness decreased substantially (Trojanowicz, 1986). If dosage, either in terms of spatial foot beat extent or the number of officers assigned to a given area, is fundamental to the effectiveness of foot patrols as a violent crime reduction tool, our research represents an important first step rather than the final word. We say a first step because we acknowledge that, as a result of the speed with which the operation was conceived and implemented, we had no time to find the funds necessary to enable a robust measure of dosage. This limitation should be considered by researchers looking to replicate this study.

A second potential distinction between Newark and Philadelphia relates to an operational difference. In Newark, several foot beats had existed for at least 5 years, and part of the experimental design used random selection to either retain or drop these beats. If some Newark beats had been patrolled for several years, the possibility exists that patrolling officers had become jaded or tired of the assignment, resulting in crackdown decay (Sherman, 1990). Equally possible, offenders had learned the rhythm of the foot patrols and adjusted to the conditions, finding new opportunities to commit crime in the target area in different ways. With regard to the Newark experiment, Pate (1986) also raised the issue of internal validity; because of the mechanism that had been used to select preexperiment foot beats, the selective assignment of new beats to nonequivalent groups was possible. These distinctions between the foot patrol experiments in Newark and Philadelphia reinforce the assertion of Durlauf and Nagin (2011:31) that "police-related deterrent effects are heterogeneous; they depend on how the police are used and the circumstances in which they are used."

The change score analysis provides an overall assessment of the outcome, but the linear regression incorporating the interaction term of treatment status with violence preintervention may provide the most significant finding from both an operational and a theoretical perspective. The lack of statistical significance for hotspots with a lower level of preintervention violence suggests that foot patrols are not a silver bullet to the problem of violence. Only when a preintervention violence count of six crimes (the 60th percentile in table 3) was achieved did the intervention become successful. The broader implication is that foot patrols may only be able to deter violent crime once a threshold of violence exists. In the future, police organizations may benefit from a more situational approach that is tailored to neighborhood characteristics and crime levels (Nolan, Conti, and McDevitt, 2004). For instance, police departments may want to target their foot patrol resources in only the highest crime places to improve overall security and maximize the chance of success, whereas other solutions, such as the targeted application of a problem-oriented policing approach, may be more suitable to neighborhoods with a lower threshold of violence and greater community capacity.

A situational approach may help address the concerns of some researchers of hotspots policing that their findings could be interpreted as providing carte blanche for a more aggressive policing stance (e.g., Sampson and Cohen, 1988; Sherman, 1986). We definitely concur. The data shown in table 5 indicate a substantial jump in proactive activity for foot patrol officers in the highest quintile crime areas of the experiment; however, we are reluctant to suggest that proactive policing alone resulted in the crime reduction found in this experiment. Being unable to gauge the level of informal community contacts during the foot patrols, we cannot state categorically that these formal activities alone were able to communicate the increased certainty of police intervention, which is essential to deterrence. Mere presence, or (unmeasured) community interactions, may have contributed equally to the crime reductions observed in the foot patrol areas. Proactive police work resulting in more traffic tickets, more pedestrian field interviews, and more arrests can run the risk of alienating the local community. Furthermore, increased police activity could potentially increase other public health risks. For example, increased enforcement of drug-related behavior may deter drug users from seeking services at a syringe exchange program (Davis et al., 2005). Thus, although our results suggest that foot patrols were effective in the higher crime hotspots, this may be too high a price for community–police relations in some areas and certainly more work needs to be conducted to examine the potentially harmful outcomes of focused police efforts (Durlauf and Nagin, 2011; National Research Council, 2004; Weisburd and Braga, 2006).

At least in Philadelphia, both anecdotal feedback from police commanders and documented field observations indicated that no noticeable public backlash occurred in response to additional police activity in the target areas. Rather, community figures in many areas complained when the summer foot patrol experiment finished and officers were reassigned. This should not read as a mandate to promote complacency in community relations. Our study was a largely *pro bono* venture to assist our local police department, and the limited funding we garnered in a short time was not sufficient to provide the resources to assess the community impact of the intervention in full. It is to be hoped that any replication in other jurisdictions will be able to examine the impact of foot patrols for a longer time period, as well as the broader impacts on community relations and public health.

Additional potential negative consequences relate to the increase in arrests and other enforcement. Many cities are facing overcrowded jails and prisons, as well as criminal justice systems straining under the weight of too few resources to address too many needs. Given that target area arrests increased 13 percent relative to the control areas, significant consequences on the criminal justice system in terms of increased criminal processing time or increases in the number of fugitives may ensue (Goldkamp and Vîlcică, 2008). Furthermore, we did discover some displacement of violent crime and this is obviously of concern to residents of areas surrounding police intervention sites. That the operation in question was an overall success and knowing that any displaced crime was of a lower volume than the crime prevented through the Philadelphia foot patrol experiment would be of little comfort to a crime victim in a surrounding area. This leaves police commanders with somewhat of a conundrum. They could plan enforcement operations for neighborhood-wide areas that demonstrate action to a wider community but potentially be unsuccessful at measurably reducing crime, or they could focus scarce resources in a small area and show effectiveness but have to accept the possibility of some collateral damage to nearby areas. It is to be hoped that if this experiment is repeated, either in Philadelphia or elsewhere, that the displacement observed here was anomalous and that future outcomes demonstrate the more common diffusion of benefits observed in many other studies (Hesseling, 1994; Ratcliffe and Makkai, 2004).

Finally, patrolling officers did little to address the underlying causes or social determinants of violence (World Health Organization, 2002). Environmental criminology theory stresses the importance of the situational and contextual moment of a crime event, and any deterrent capabilities of the police were likely place based but transitory. In a recent randomized experiment, the tactic of saturation patrol in police cars was found to underperform problem-oriented policing interventions (Taylor, Koper, and Woods, 2011). It may be that not only are vehicle-bound patrol officers unable to impact crime levels significantly, but also that foot patrol officers develop greater situational knowledge. A useful future direction with any foot patrol studies would be to develop in officers an appreciation for the merits of a problem-solving/problem-oriented policing approach that could leverage their local knowledge developed over months of foot patrol into a long-term problem reduction strategy.

 ## Conclusion

This research has been a response to an identified need to discover which specific hotspots strategies work best in particular types of situations (National Research Council, 2004; Weisburd and Braga, 2006). Foot patrols have until now been written off as unsuccessful in combating crime, and especially violent crime, which is a view largely emanating from the Newark foot patrol experiment of more than 25 years ago. We estimated that police foot patrols prevented 90 crimes in violent crime hotspots, although displacement of 37 of these crimes apparently occurred to nearby areas; thus, the net crime prevention effect from the foot patrol experiment was 53 crimes prevented. This crime reduction was most likely achieved through a combination of community contacts and interaction, alongside more proactive enforcement and field investigations. This additional level of police activity may seem overly aggressive in the eyes of some members of the community, but with others, there may be considerable relief that the police are having a more active presence in their neighborhoods. Community surveys or some other form of societal litmus test could help police find a state of equilibrium with effective and proactive enforcement on the one hand and community approval, or at least reluctant tolerance, on the other. If these findings can be replicated, and a suitable balance can be struck between police intervention and community perception, it may be that police are able to reap the crime reduction and public health outcomes of the focused foot patrol intervention examined here, while retaining the community support reported many years ago in Newark.

 ## References

Anselin, Luc. 1995. Local indicators of spatial association—LISA. *Geographical Analysis* 27:93–115.

Anselin, Luc. 1996. The Moran scatterplot as an ESDA tool to assess local instability in spatial association. In *Spatial Analytical Perspectives on GIS,* eds. Manfred Fischer, Henk J. Scholten, and David J. Unwin. London, U.K.: Taylor & Francis.

Barr, Robert, and Ken Pease. 1990. Crime placement, displacement, and deflection. In *Crime and Justice: An Annual Review of Research,* vol. 12, eds. Michael Tonry and Norval Morris. Chicago, IL: University of Chicago Press.

Beccaria, Cesare. 1963 (1764). *On Crimes and Punishments,* translated by H. Paolucci. Upper Saddle River: Prentice-Hall.

Bentham, Jeremy. 1948 (1789). *An Introduction to the Principles of Morals and Legislation.* New York: Kegan Paul.

Bohrnstedt, George W. 1969. Observations on the measurement of change. *Sociological Methodology* 1:113–33.

Boruch, Robert, Henry May, Herbert Turner, Julia Lavenberg, Anthony Petrosino, Dorothy de Moya, Jeremy Grimshaw, and Ellen Foley. 2004. Estimating the effects of interventions that are deployed in many places: Place-randomized trials. *American Behavioral Scientist* 47:608–33.

Bowers, Kate J., and Shane D. Johnson. 2003. Measuring the geographical displacement and diffusion of benefit effects of crime prevention activity. *Journal of Quantitative Criminology* 19:275–301.

Bowers, William J., and Jon H. Hirsch. 1987. The impact of foot patrol staffing on crime and disorder in Boston: An unmet promise. *American Journal of Police* 6:17–44.

Braga, Anthony A. 2007. *Effects of Hot Spots Policing on Crime: A Campbell Collaboration Systematic Review.* http://www.aic.gov.au/campbellcj/reviews/titles.html.

Braga, Anthony A., and Brenda J. Bond. 2008. Policing crime and disorder hot spots: A randomized controlled trial. *Criminology* 46:577–607.

Braga, Anthony A., David L. Weisburd, Elin J. Waring, Lorraine Green Mazerolle, William Spelman, and Francis Gajewski. 1999. Problem-oriented policing in violent crime places: A randomized control experiment. *Criminology* 37:541–80.

Brantingham, Paul J., and Patricia L. Brantingham. 1984. *Patterns in Crime.* New York: Macmillan.

Brantingham, Paul J., Delmar A. Dyreson, and Patricia L. Brantingham. 1976. Crime seen through a cone of resolution. *American Behavioral Scientist* 20:261–73.

Buerger, Michael E., Ellen G. Cohn, and Anthony J. Petrosino. 1995. Defining the "hot spots of crime": Operationalizing theoretical concepts for field research. In *Crime and Place*, eds. John E. Eck and David Weisburd. Monsey, NY: Criminal Justice Press.

Caulkins, Jonathan P., and Peter Reuter. 2009. Towards a harm-reduction approach to enforcement. *Safer Communities* 8:9–23.

Centers for Disease Control and Prevention (CDC). 2010. *Violence Prevention: A Timeline of Violence as a Public Health Issue.* http://www.cdc.gov/ViolencePrevention/overview/timeline.html.

Chainey, Spencer, and Jerry H. Ratcliffe. 2005. *GIS and Crime Mapping.* New York: Wiley.

Chrisman, Nicholas. 2002. *Exploring Geographic Information Systems.* New York: Wiley.

Clarke, Ronald V., and John E. Eck. 2005. *Crime Analysis for Problem Solvers—In 60 Small Steps.* Washington, DC: Center for Problem Oriented Policing.

Clarke, Ronald V., and David L. Weisburd. 1994. Diffusion of crime control benefits. In *Crime Prevention Studies*, ed. Ronald V. Clarke. Monsey, NY: Criminal Justice Press.

Cordner, Gary W. 1986. Fear of crime and the police: An evaluation of fear reduction strategy. *Journal of Police Science and Administration* 14: 223–33.

Davis, Corey S., Scott Burris, Julie Kraut-Becher, Kevin G. Lynch, and David Metzger. 2005. Effects of an intensive street-level police intervention on syringe exchange program use in Philadelphia, PA. *American Journal of Public Health* 95:233–6.

Durlauf, Steven N., and Daniel S. Nagin. 2011. Imprisonment and crime: Can both be reduced? *Criminology & Public Policy* 10:13–54.

Eck, John E. 1993. The threat of crime displacement. *Criminal Justice Abstracts* 25:527–46.

Esbensen, Finn-Aage. 1987. Foot patrols: Of what value? *American Journal of Police* 6:45–65.

Faul, Franz, Edgar Erdfelder, Albert-Georg Lang, and Axel Buchner. 2007. G*Power 3: A flexible statistical power analysis program for the social, behavioral, and biomedical sciences. *Behavior Research Methods* 39:175–91.

Felson, Marcus. 1987. Routine activities and crime prevention in the developing metropolis. *Criminology* 25:911–32.

Frison, Lars, and Stuart J. Pocock. 1992. Repeated measures in clinical trials: Analysis using mean summary statistics and its implications for design. *Statistics in Medicine* 11:1685–704.

Galton, Francis. 1886. Regression towards mediocrity in hereditary stature. *The Journal of the Anthropological Institute of Great Britain and Ireland* 15:246–63.

Getis, Arthur, and J. Keith Ord. 1992. The analysis of spatial association by use of distance statistics. *Geographical Analysis* 24:189–206.

Getis, Arthur, and J. Keith Ord. 1996. Local spatial statistics: An overview. In *Spatial Analysis: Modeling in a GIS Environment*, eds. Paul Longley and Michael Batty. London, U.K.: GeoInformation International.

Green, Lorraine. 1995. Cleaning up drug hot spots in Oakland, California: The displacement and diffusion effects. *Justice Quarterly* 12: 737–54.

Goffman, Alice. 2009. On the run: Wanted men in a Philadelphia ghetto. *American Sociological Review* 74:339–57.

Goldkamp, John S., and Rely E. Vîlcic . 2008. Targeted enforcement and adverse system side effects: The generation of fugitives in Philadelphia. *Criminology* 46:371–409.

Gove, Walter R., Michael Hughes, and Michael Geerken, 1985. Are uniform crime reports a valid indicator of the index crimes? An affirmative answer with minor qualifications. *Criminology* 23:451–502.

Guerette, Rob T. 2009. *Analyzing Crime Displacement and Diffusion.* Washington, DC: Center for Problem Oriented Policing.

Guerette, Rob T., and Kate J. Bowers. 2009. Assessing the extent of crime displacement and diffusion of benefits: A review of situational crime prevention evaluations. *Criminology* 47:1331–68.

Guerra, Nancy G., L. Rowell Huesmann, and Anja Spindler. 2003. Community violence exposure, social cognition, and aggression among urban elementary school children. *Child Development* 74:1561–76.

Hesseling, R. 1994. Displacement: A review of the empirical literature. In *Crime Prevention Studies*, vol. 3, ed. Ronald V. Clarke. Monsey, NY: Criminal Justice Press.

Jim, Julia, Fawn Ngo Mitchell, and Douglas R. Kent. 2006. Community-oriented policing in a retail shopping center. *Policing: An International Journal of Police Strategies & Management* 29:145–57.

Jones, Bethan, and Nick Tilley. 2004. *The Impact of High Visibility Patrols on Personal Robbery*. Research Findings, 201. London, U.K.: Home Office.

Kelling, George L. 1981. *The Newark Foot Patrol Experiment*. Washington, DC: Police Foundation.

Kelling, George L., Anthony M. Pate, Duane Dieckman, and Charles E. Brown. 1974. *The Kansas City Preventative Patrol Experiment: A Summary Report*. Washington, DC: Police Foundation.

Koper, Christopher S., and Evan Mayo-Wilson. 2006. Police crackdowns on illegal gun carrying: A systematic review of their impact on gun crime. *Journal of Experimental Criminology* 2:227–61.

Kubrin, Charis E., Steven F. Messner, Glenn Deane, Kelly McGeever, and Thomas D. Stucky. 2010. Proactive policing and robbery rates across U.S. cities. *Criminology* 48:57–97.

Mazerolle, Lorraine Green, Colleen Kadleck, and Jan Roehl. 1998. Controlling drug and disorder problems: The role of place managers. *Criminology* 36:371–403.

McGarrell, Edmund F., Steven Chermak, and Alexander Weiss. 2002. *Reducing Gun Violence: Evaluation of the Indianapolis Police Department's Directed Patrol Project, Reducing Gun Violence.* Washington, DC: National Institute of Justice.

Miller, Ted R., Mark A. Cohen, and Shelli B. Rossman. 1993. Victim costs of violent crime and resulting injuries. *Health Affairs* 12:186–197.

Moran, P. A. P. 1950. Notes on continuous stochastic phenomena. *Biometrika* 37:17–23.

Morgan, Kathleen, Scott Morgan, and Rachel Boba. 2010. *City Crime Rankings 2010–2011*. Washington, DC: CQ Press.

Nagin, Daniel S. 2010. Imprisonment and crime control: Building evidence-based policy. In *Contemporary Issues in Criminological Theory and Research: The Role of Social Institutions (Papers from the American Society of Criminology 2010 Conference)*, eds. Richard Rosenfeld, Kenna Quinet, and Crystal Garcia. Belmont, CA: Wadsworth.

Nagin, Daniel S., and Greg Pogarsky. 2001. Integrating celerity, impulsivity, and extralegal sanction threats into a model of general deterrence: Theory and evidence. *Criminology* 39:865–91.

National Research Council. 2004. *Fairness and Effectiveness in Policing: The Evidence*, eds. Wesley G. Skogan and Kathleen Frydl. Washington, DC: Committee to Law and Justice, Division of Behavioral and Social Sciences and Education.

Nolan, James J., Norman Conti, and Jack McDevitt. 2004. Situational policing: Neighbourhood development and crime control. *Policing & Society* 14:99–117.

Pate, Anthony M. 1986. Experimenting with foot patrol: The Newark experience. In *Community Crime Prevention: Does it Work?* ed. Dennis P. Rosenbaum. Newbury Park, CA: Sage.

Ratcliffe, Jerry H. 2004. Geocoding crime and a first estimate of an acceptable minimum hit rate. *International Journal of Geographical Information Science* 18:61–73.

Ratcliffe, Jerry H. 2008. *Intelligence-Led Policing*. Cullompton, Devon, U.K.: Willan.

Ratcliffe, Jerry H., and Toni Makkai. 2004. Diffusion of benefits: Evaluating a policing operation. *Trends & Issues in Crime and Criminal Justice* 278:1–6.

Ratcliffe, Jerry H., and George F. Rengert. 2008. Near repeat patterns in Philadelphia shootings. *Security Journal* 21:58–76.

Ratcliffe, Jerry H., and Travis Taniguchi. 2008. A preliminary evaluation of the crime reduction effectiveness of the PPD footbeat program. Unpublished internal report for the Philadelphia Police Department.

Ratcliffe, Jerry H., Travis Taniguchi, and Ralph B. Taylor. 2009. The crime reduction effects of public CCTV cameras: A multi-method spatial approach. *Justice Quarterly* 26:746–70.

Rengert, George F., and Brian Lockwood. 2009. Geographic units of analysis and the analysis of crime. In *Putting Crime in its Place: Units of Analysis in Geographic Criminology*, eds. David L. Weisburd, Wim Bernasco, and Gerben J. N. Bruinsma. New York: Springer.

Rosenbaum, Dennis P., and Arthur J. Lurigo. 1994. An inside look at community policing reform: Definitions, organizational changes, and evaluation findings. *Crime & Delinquency* 40:299–314.

Sampson, Robert J., and Jacqueline Cohen. 1988. Deterrent effects of the police on crime: A replication and theoretical extension. *Law & Society Review* 22:163–9.

Shadish, William R., Thomas D. Cook, and Donald T. Campbell. 2002. *Experimental and Quasi-Experimental Designs for Generalized Causal inference*. Boston, MA: Houghton Mifflin.

Shearing, Clifford. 1996. Reinventing policing: Policing as governance. In *Privatisierung Staatlicker Kontrolle: Befunde, Konzepte, Tendenzen*, eds. F. Sack, M. Voss, D. Frehsee, A. Funk, and H. Reinke. Baden-Baden, Germany: Nomos Verlagsgesellschaft.

Sherman, Lawrence. 1986. Policing communities: What works? In *Communities and Crime* eds. Albert J. Reiss, Jr. and Michael Tonry. Chicago, IL: University of Chicago.

Sherman, Lawrence. 1990. Police crackdowns: Initial and residual deterrence. In *Crime and Justice: An Annual Review of Research*, vol. 12, eds. Michael Tonry and Norval Morris. Chicago, IL: University of Chicago Press.

Sherman, Lawrence, Patrick Gartin, and Michael E. Buerger. 1989. Hot spots of predatory crime: Routine activities and the criminology of place. *Criminology* 27:27–55.

Sherman, Lawrence, James W. Shaw, and Denis P. Rogan. 1995. *The Kansas City Gun Experiment*. Washington, DC: National Institute of Justice.

Sherman, Lawrence, and David L. Weisburd. 1995. General deterrent effects of police patrol in crime "hot spots": A randomized, controlled trial. *Justice Quarterly* 12:625–48.

Stinchcombe, Arthur L. 1963. Institutions of privacy in the determination of police administrative practice. *American Journal of Sociology* 69: 150–60.

Taniguchi, Travis A., George F. Rengert, and Eric S. McCord. 2009. Where size matters: Agglomeration economies of illegal drug markets in Philadelphia. *Justice Quarterly* 26:670–94.

Taylor, Bruce, Christopher S. Koper, and Daniel J. Woods. 2011. A randomized controlled trial of different policing strategies at hot spots of violent crime. *Journal of Experimental Criminology* 7:149–181.

Trojanowicz, Robert C. 1986. Evaluating a neighborhood foot patrol program: The Flint, Michigan, Project. In *Community Crime Prevention: Does it Work?* ed. Dennis P. Rosenbaum. Newbury Park, CA: Sage.

Twisk, Jos W. R. and Karin Proper. 2004. Evaluation of the results of a randomized controlled trial: How to define changes between baseline and follow-up. *Journal of Clinical Epidemiology* 57:223–8.

Twisk, Jos W. R., and Wieke de Vente. 2008. The analysis of randomized controlled trial data with more than one follow-up measurement: A comparison between different approaches. *European Journal of Epidemiology* 23:655–60.

Unwin, David J. 1996. GIS, spatial analysis and spatial statistics. *Progress in Human Geography* 20:540–51.

Wakefield, Alison. 2007. Carry on constable? Revaluing foot patrol. *Policing: A Journal of Policy and Practice* 1:342–55.

Weisburd, David L., and Anthony A. Braga. 2006. Hot spots policing as a model for police innovation. In *Police Innovation: Contrasting Perspectives*, eds. David L. Weisburd and Anthony A. Braga. New York: Cambridge University Press.

Weisburd, David L., Wim Bernasco, and Gerben J. N. Bruinsma. 2009. Units of analysis in geographic criminology: Historical development, critical issues, and open questions. In *Putting Crime in its Place: Units of Analysis in Geographic Criminology,* eds. David L. Weisburd, Wim Bernasco, and Gerben J. N. Bruinsma. New York: Springer.

Weisburd, David L., Shawn D. Bushway, Cynthia Lum, and Sue-Ming Yang. 2004. Trajectories of crime at places: A longitudinal study of street segments in the City of Seattle. *Criminology* 42:283–321.

Weisburd, David L., and Lorraine Green. 1995. Policing drug hot spots: The Jersey City drug market analysis experiment. *Justice Quarterly* 12: 711–35.

Weisburd, David L., Laura A. Wyckoff, Justin Ready, John E. Eck, Joshua C. Hinkle, and Frank Gajewski. 2006. Does crime just move around the corner? A controlled study of spatial diffusion and diffusion of crime control benefits. *Criminology* 44:549–91.

Welsh, Brandon C., and David P. Farrington. 2009. *Making Public Places Safer*. Oxford, U.K.: Oxford University Press.

Wilson, James Q., and Barbara Boland. 1978. The effect of the police on crime. *Law & Society Review* 12:367–90.

World Health Organization (WHO). 2002. World report on violence and health. http://www.who.int/violence_injury_prevention/violence/world_report/en/.

DISCUSSION QUESTIONS

1. How is the Philadelphia foot patrol experiment different from the Newark foot patrol experiment discussed earlier in this section?

2. How do the findings of this study impact police executives' decisions regarding patrol deployment of patrol officers?

3. Identify some of the practical implications for violence reduction based on the findings of this study.

Police officers frequently encounter situations that expose them to liability.

Police Liability and Accountability

Section Highlights

- Review the positive and negative aspects of police liability.
- Provide a historical look at police accountability.
- Examine some contemporary accountability mechanisms.

In July 2011, the Chicago City Council Finance Committee approved a settlement of $6.5 million to be distributed to the families of an 8-year-old boy (deceased) and an 11-year-old girl (seriously injured) who were hit by an unmarked police car as it pursued a fleeing vehicle.[1] The police officer was held liable in this case because he did not have his lights and sirens on while he pursued the vehicle and he did not get approval from his supervisor to engage in the pursuit. The intention of this police officer was to pursue and catch someone that he believed posed imminent danger to the public; however, his actions were deemed negligent because he did not follow department pursuit policies, and his decision resulted in the injury and death of two innocent bystanders. It is cases like this one in Chicago that illustrate the complex nature of police work. Police officers are exposed to liability risks every day when they make decisions about how to respond (or not respond) to incidents. Sometimes they make the right decision, and other times their decision results in death or harm to others. The exposure to liability can result in police officers and police agencies being named in liability claims and lawsuits.

This section discusses the nature of police liability as well as the negative and positive consequences associated with police liability. This section also discusses how the threat of litigation impacts police officers, the types of incidents that most commonly result in police-involved lawsuits, and the financial impact that litigation has on police agencies. Recently, some police agencies have adopted accountability systems as a way to prevent or decrease future liability incidents. Several police accountability programs/mechanisms and the potential benefits resulting from such mechanisms are also presented in this section.

✉ Understanding Police Liability

Liability is the legal responsibility for one's actions or errors. Failure of persons or agencies to meet their responsibilities leaves them open to being named in a lawsuit for any resulting damages.[2] Liability can also apply to alleged criminal acts in which defendants may be responsible for their actions, which also happen to constitute a crime.[3] After reading this description of liability, it is easy to understand how this term applies to the policing profession, as many of the activities that police officers engage in expose them to potential liability. This is one of the most pressing issues faced by police executives, as it has consequences that are financial and that can impact the relationship between the police and citizens.[4]

Liability-based litigation involving the police can be filed in both state- and federal-level courts. Civil lawsuits can be filed in federal court in cases when people believe that the police have violated some constitutional or federally protected statutory right.[5] A common provision of the law used in cases of liability involving the police is **Title 42 United States Code, Section 1983**.[6] Some common types of police-related

Despite being very helpful to the police, K-9 dogs can also be a liability to police agencies.

Section 1983 claims include allegations regarding excessive force, false arrest, and unreasonable search of one's person, home, or vehicle. The number of Section 1983 cases has increased since the 1980s.[7] According to research, plaintiffs (citizens) win their cases in approximately half of the Section 1983 cases.[8]

Lawsuits can also be filed in state courts under state tort laws.[9] *Tort* is defined as "a wrongful act other than a breach of contract for which relief may be obtained in the form of damages or injunctions."[10] There are three general categories of torts under state laws, including strict liability tort, intentional tort, and negligence tort.[11] **Strict liability tort** involves behavior that is so dangerous that the likelihood that injuries or damages could result is great. This type of tort is generally not applied to police officers, as many of the duties they are tasked with are inherently dangerous.[12]

Intentional tort involves intentional behavior that results in someone getting hurt or some other type of damages. This type of tort does not mean that the police officer intended to inflict injury or damages, only that the police officer intended to behave in a way that ultimately resulted in injuries or damages.[13] An example of this would be when a police officer chooses to use a K-9 dog to help pursue a suspect. In some instances, the K-9 dog will injure (usually bite) a suspect when trying to subdue or stop the person. The police officer's intention was not to use the dog to injure the suspect; it was to stop the person from fleeing so that he or she could be apprehended. Wrongful death, false arrest, false imprisonment, and assault and battery are some common types of intentional torts involving police officers.[14]

Negligence tort involves actions that are careless or unreasonable or, in some cases, choosing not to take action, which results in damages or injury.[15] For example, if a police officer drives at an unnecessary high rate of speed when responding to a non–life-threatening call for service and hits a pedestrian in the process, the officer's actions could be considered negligent because it was not necessary for him or her to drive that fast. There are several forms of negligence that involve police officers and police administrators, including negligent operation of emergency vehicles; negligent failure to discipline or investigate; negligent failure to arrest; negligent failure to render assistance; negligent failure to protect; negligent police supervision and direction; negligent hiring, selection, and retention; and negligent entrustment and assignment.[16]

Lawsuits Filed Against the Police

Litigation involving the police has increased significantly since the 1970s.[17] Despite this increase, there has been limited research on this topic. The limited research is a result of methodological problems associated with the sensitive nature of the topic.[18] It is difficult to get police administrators to fill out surveys or agree to interviews in which they are asked questions about their agencies' involvement with litigation. Court records can be difficult to access in some jurisdictions, and in the instances when they are accessible, a significant portion of the cases are settled out of court, with part of the settlement agreement requiring that the court records be sealed from the public. Newspaper accounts of police-involved lawsuits can provide helpful details; however, this data source suffers from *selective reporting*. Selective reporting is when newspapers choose to only report cases or stories that involve extraordinary circumstances and that are not a reflection of typical cases.[19] Ironically, newspapers are one source that most often reports on litigation involving the police and are also where most citizens hear about police-involved lawsuits.

Despite the difficulty in studying police-involved litigation, we have learned several things from past studies. One study found that men and racial/ethnic minorities are most likely to file lawsuits against the police.[20] Another study discovered that lawsuits based on allegations of racial and gender discrimination comprised nearly one-third (30%) of all lawsuits filed against the police in Los Angeles, New York, and Chicago from 1993 to 2003.[21] There is also evidence that a large portion of lawsuits filed against police agencies are filed by police employees (these cases are often based on claims of discrimination or harassment).[22] Studies have also revealed that police officers that have been named in lawsuits generally do not receive any kind of discipline (regardless of the seriousness of the allegations in the lawsuits).[23] Michael Vaughn and his colleagues reported that only 10% of Texas police chiefs stated that they always discipline police officers that have been named in lawsuits.[24]

Impact of Litigation on Police Officers

Virtually every aspect of police work exposes police officers to some level of liability. This is the case for police officers working in agencies of all sizes.[25] Since there is so much exposure to liability that can lead to litigation, how does this impact police officers and the manner in which they conduct their work? This question has been examined by researchers dating back several decades. One study examined the level of

litigaphobia (*litigation* + *phobia*) experienced by police officers.[26] Most police officers in this study made statements indicating that they view the possibility of being sued by citizens as an inevitable and unavoidable part of their job. This study revealed that most police officers only *moderately* worry about work-related lawsuits filed by citizens. More than half (69%) of the police officers stated that they take specific actions in their daily work activities to prevent lawsuits being filed against them, including treating people fairly and doing their job "by the book."[27]

A recent study conducted by Michael Vaughn and his colleagues found limited evidence of litigaphobia among Texas chiefs of police.[28] Surveys were distributed to Texas police chiefs during a leadership and management training conference. The surveys inquired about their perceptions of civil litigation, fear of litigation, and other police liability issues. More than half (61%) of the police chiefs believe that the threat of litigation has little to no effect on the way that their departments function.[29]

▨ Impact of Litigation on Police Organizations

Exposure to liability can lead to liability claims and lawsuits filed against both police officers and police organizations. Litigation can tarnish the image of the police in the eyes of the public. If citizens frequently hear about their local police agency being named in lawsuits or having to pay out for liability claims, this could lead to a perception that there is something wrong with the police officers and the police agency. This could especially be the case if the liability claims and lawsuits are based on accusations of police misconduct or officer negligence. A tarnished image for a police agency can be problematic during a time when community policing is the dominant strategy in American policing.

Lawsuits and liability claims can also become a heavy financial burden for some police agencies. *City Pages* has tracked litigation involving officers in the Minneapolis Police Department for several decades. In 1994, this publication presented an article that featured the 10 most expensive police officers in the Minneapolis Police Department. During that decade, those officers had cost the department $5.8 million in settlement payouts and court costs.[30] Again in 2005, *City Pages* reported that the Minneapolis Police Department had settled 190 cases for about $10.9 million from 1995 to 2005.[31] From 2004 to 2009, the MPD paid out about $9.5 million in 80 police misconduct settlements. *City Pages* noted that this payout amount is almost as much as the city paid in the preceding 10 years, but in half of the time.[32]

The Los Angeles Police Department has also paid out a significant amount of money as a result of lawsuits. Interestingly, a large portion of the lawsuits is filed by their own employees. A recent article in the *Los Angeles Times* reported that from 2001 to 2011, 16 police officers won jury verdicts or settlements from the city for $1 million or more per lawsuit.[33] These employment lawsuits were based on accusations of sexual harassment, racial discrimination, retaliation, and other workplace problems. Records also show that from 2005 to 2010, LAPD officers have sued the department over workplace-related problems more than 250 times.[34] In 45 of those cases, the city paid settlements or verdicts totaling more than $18 million, while the city of Los Angeles has won approximately 50 cases. The remaining cases that are still active could result in tens of millions of dollars in potential liability payouts.[35] This recent trend has earned the LAPD the title of "one of the most litigious police departments in the United States."[36]

Other police agencies across the United States also face financial costs associated with liability. In 2010, the city of Chicago paid approximately $1.7 million to settle "small cases" (cases that cost less than $100,000) filed against Chicago police officers.[37] This amount is small compared to the $9 million in payouts

Increased supervision over patrol officers is one way to increase police accountability.

and settlements involving Chicago police officers in 2007 and 2008.[38] The recent drop in lawsuits against the Chicago Police Department is believed to be a result of the city fighting these cases in court instead of quickly settling these cases outside of court (which was done with most lawsuits in previous years). Like the Chicago Police Department, many police agencies are beginning to adopt strategies to reduce the amount paid out in police-related lawsuits or attempt to prevent them all together. This is especially important during a time when police organizations are working with limited budgets. Many of the strategies involve making changes within police agencies, such as improving or increasing police officer training, increasing supervision of patrol-level officers, changing police department policies and procedures, and increasing the level of police officer accountability.

⊠ Police Accountability

As odd as it might sound, there is a positive outcome that can result from police liability—an increase in the level of accountability placed on police officers and police agencies. *Police accountability* means "holding both individual police officers and law enforcement agencies responsible for effectively delivering basic services of crime control and maintaining order, while treating individuals fairly and within the bounds of law."[39] Police accountability has been supported and encouraged by the United States Department of Justice (USDOJ). In a 2001 report, the USDOJ stated that police organizations across the country should adopt practices and strategies that increase police officer accountability. Specifically, the report suggested several accountability practices such as (1) increased supervision over police officers—specifically involving the use of force and search-and-seizure activities, (2) acquiring feedback on police services from citizens and community groups, (3) creating and implementing mechanisms through which citizens can participate in evaluating police services—such as civilian review boards or oversight agencies, and (4) implementing information management systems (such as early warning/early intervention systems) to track the activities of police officers that can lead to costly liability claims or lawsuits.[40] Several of these practices will be discussed later in this section.

The presence of police accountability has changed over the course of the history of American policing. In the political era, police officers were held accountable by the political leaders that had helped them acquire their policing positions.[41] There were few repercussions for police officers when accusations of abuse and misconduct were made against them by citizens during this time.[42] During the reform era, citizens started to become more aware of acts of police misconduct as a result of publicized events that were presented by the media (such as pictures and video taken during the Democratic National Convention in Chicago in 1968—see Section 1). It was also during this era that the number of lawsuits filed against the police began to increase in the United States.[43] This increase in litigiousness suggests that citizens who believed that they were mistreated or abused by the police began to look for ways to hold police officers accountable for their actions. Several Supreme Court case decisions during this era also increased the level of police accountability by imposing more stringent standards on how police officers conduct routine police work. And finally, in the community/problem-solving era, police accountability is at an all-time high. Easy access to technology (such as cell phones that come equipped with cameras and video recorders) allows citizens to record their interactions or other people's interactions with the police. Pictures and videos make it easier for citizens to prove that police misconduct has occurred compared to the past, when it was a citizen's word against that of a police officer. In addition to the availability of technology, a variety of accountability mechanisms are found both within and outside of American police agencies that help police executives track and monitor the actions of police officers.

Accountability Within Police Organizations

Police accountability begins within police organizations. It can be enhanced through the efforts of police administrators and various oversight mechanisms and programs. Some of those efforts include increased supervision over patrol officers, mandatory reporting of critical incidents, rigorous performance evaluations, thorough investigations of allegations of police misconduct, and the monitoring and alteration of department policies, procedures, and officer training.

Supervision

The bureaucratic manner in which many police organizations are structured results in the direct supervisions of police officers, as everyone working within the organization has someone else watching over him or her. Patrol officers working the streets are monitored by first-line supervisors that are also working the streets. First-line supervisors answer to those that work in middle-management positions. And finally, middle management is watched over by the highest-ranking police executives (such as assistant chiefs and chiefs of police). Thus, the level of accountability within police organizations is contingent on the quality of oversight provided by those who supervise others. Presumably, if supervisors are not paying attention to what patrol officers are doing while on patrol, this leaves the door open for exposure to liability risks, as well as for acts of misconduct and abuse to occur. In contrast, if police supervisors are watching patrol officers closely, there should be less of a chance that acts of misconduct and abuse will occur and that they will be exposed to liability risks.

In addition to field supervisors, some police agencies utilize forms of virtual supervision. An example of this is the use of early warning/intervention systems (EW/EI). EW/EI systems are data-driven computer programs that monitor the performance of police officers.[44] Computer databases help supervisors identify patterns of problematic officer behavior. Police agencies use a variety of indicators to watch for potential problems. Some common indicators used in EW/EI systems include reported incidents of use of force, use of firearms, citizen complaints, liability claims and lawsuits, sick leave, off-duty employment, pursuit incidents, and damages to department vehicles.[45]

The word *early* in the title of this program suggests that the purpose of such systems is to identify problematic officer behavior *before* it results in some negative outcome (such as improper use of force resulting in injuries or death and the filing of citizen complaints or lawsuits, to name a few). Once a pattern of behavior is flagged by the EW/EI system, police supervisors can intervene to correct that issue or problem. Interventions can include a review by the officer's immediate supervisor, individual or group counseling with upper-level supervisors, and retraining or additional training.[46] After the intervention, police officer activities are monitored for a specified length of time to make sure that they do not revert to problematic behaviors.

The use of EW/EI systems is not widespread. According to a Bureau of Justice Statistics report, as of 2003, one-third (33%) of large police departments had a functioning computer-based personnel performance monitoring system.[47] For police agencies that want to become accredited or maintain their accreditation, it is now a requirement that they implement an EW/EI system.[48] The article written by Samuel Walker and his colleagues that is included at the end of this section provides additional information on the use of early warning systems by the police.

Performance Evaluations

Employees in both the private and public sectors participate in regular performance evaluations. The purpose of performance evaluations is to identify and reward desirable performance, to identify and seek to correct performance shortcomings, and to terminate employees whose performance is substandard.[49] This type of evaluation can enhance police officer accountability, as it will require that every police officer be reviewed on a regular basis, not allowing any officer that may not being doing his or her job to slip between the cracks. Police supervisors can use this regular performance assessment as a way to meet with police officers that they might otherwise have limited contact with. In theory, regular performance evaluations can work in a manner similar to EW/EI systems, as officers are informed about problematic performance issues and are given direction on how to fix those issues. One difference between EW/EI systems and regular performance reviews is that EW/EI systems are continuously evaluating police officer performance, while regular performance evaluations are usually conducted once during a specified time period (say, annually). It is important to note that some of the research conducted on regular performance evaluations of police officers has revealed that this type of assessment does not always adequately reflect officer performance.[50]

Investigations of Police Misconduct

According to a recent report, more than 26,000 citizen complaints were filed against police officers working in large state and local police agencies that were based on allegations of use of force.[51] Only about 8% of the complaints were sustained (meaning that there was sufficient evidence found after an investigation to justify disciplinary action against the officer/officers named in the complaint).[52] It is important to note that in most cases, citizen complaints that are filed against the police are investigated by police personnel working in Internal Affairs (IA) or Professional Standards (PS) divisions (Section 12 will present a more detailed discussion of citizen complaints). The low number of cases that are found in favor of citizens can be explained in a couple of ways: Either there is an extremely high rate of false reporting going on by citizens, or the investigations of the complaints are not done in a thorough and fair manner. To further complicate this issue, many of the internal investigations become personnel matters, which restricts the release of information from the investigation due to privacy regulations in some jurisdictions. According to Samuel Walker, there have been no studies on the effectiveness of IA or PS divisions that have met social science research standards.[53] There is anecdotal information in both newspaper articles and investigative reports that suggests that these divisions are often understaffed and underfunded, which could explain why some complaints of police misconduct are not thoroughly investigated.[54] Others argue that if the police are policing themselves, there is great potential for bias to influence these investigations.[55]

Department Policies

Standard operating procedures (SOP) manuals contain formal department policies for police agencies. SOPs serve as references for police officers to seek direction and guidance on how to handle situations that they encounter when interacting with the public. Because police officers look to SOPs for guidance on how to respond, it is important that department policies are clearly stated and easy to understand. Most of the research that has been conducted on the influence of department policies has focused on serious incidents such as use of deadly force and police pursuits. Research on both of these topics has revealed that department policies that restrict police officer discretion in the handling of such cases can reduce negative outcomes (such as citizen complaints or police-involved litigation).[56] This empirical evidence suggests that department policies can in fact enhance police accountability (especially for serious incidents in which officer discretion is restricted).

Equally important to having clearly stated department policies is ensuring that police officers are following those policies. One way to monitor police officer compliance with department policies is requiring mandatory reporting of critical incidents. Creating a paper trail provides another layer of accountability for both police officers and their supervisors.[57]

Police pursuits can result in serious injury or even death, and can become costly to police agencies.

Risk Management

Risk management is a tool that can help identify and manage potential risks and liability problems within organizations. Organizations adopt risk management because of increasing costs associated with liability claims and litigation, to reduce the risk of harm to their clients and their employees, and to provide a higher quality of service to their clientele.[58] Risk management is used in a variety of professional settings, including medicine, athletic training, psychology, social work, banking and finance, engineering and architecture, and schools and universities.[59]

Research on the use of risk management by police agencies in the United States can best be described as scant. Most of the published literature on this topic has been written by professionals that have experience working with police agencies that use risk management, but it is not based on scientific research.[60] Only within the last decade has any discussion of risk management emerged in the academic literature. In his book *Police Accountability: The Role of Citizen Oversight,* Samuel Walker reports that "one of the most notable failures of both police departments and other city officials has been their neglect of modern concepts of risk management and in particular their refusal to examine incidents that result in litigation and seek to correct the underlying problems."[61] The first study on the use of risk management by police agencies did not appear in print until 2004.[62] This study utilized interview and survey data from a national sample and also in-depth case studies of four police agencies that had reported using risk management to control police liability.[63] The Archbold article included at the end of this section features part of the national study on the use of risk management by American police agencies.

Police Accountability Mechanisms Outside of Police Organizations

In addition to accountability efforts within police organizations, there are also several mechanisms found outside of police organizations that are meant to enhance police accountability. Some of these external mechanisms include accreditation, citizen-based groups, the media, the court system (including civil lawsuits, pattern of practice suits, consent decrees, and court-appointed monitors) and civilian review boards.

Accreditation

As discussed in Section 6, the Commission on Accreditation of Law Enforcement Agencies (CALEA) is an organization that awards accreditation to law enforcement agencies after they have met a lengthy list of requirements. The official CALEA website states that its organizational goals are "to improve the delivery of public safety services primarily by maintaining a body of standards developed by public safety practitioners covering a wide range of up-to-date public safety initiatives; establishing and administering an accreditation process; and recognizing professional excellence."[64] In addition to these goals, CALEA also notes that accreditation can strengthen police accountability both within and outside of police agencies. Specifically, the CALEA website reports that accreditation heightens accountability for all of its clients and, in doing so, also encourages greater accountability within municipalities and the communities they serve.[65] It is important to point out that there has not been any empirical evidence found to support this statement. To date, there have not been any evaluations of the impact of CALEA accreditation on police accountability.

Citizen Groups

As previously mentioned in this section, citizens have begun to recognize and take action when they witness what they believe to be acts of police misconduct. The increase in accessibility to recording devices (specifically on cell phones) has helped citizens gather visual evidence of such instances. Today there are several citizen-based groups whose mission is to monitor the activities of the police. COP WATCH is a national network of citizen groups that monitor police and citizen encounters.[66] Their mission is based on one of deterrence; if the police know that COP WATCH is watching them, it may prevent police misconduct from occurring. These groups also organize public events to inform citizens about cases of misconduct that occur in their communities and instruct citizens on what they can do if they feel they have been victims of police abuse.[67] These groups often provide video footage of police–citizen encounters to media outlets to inform the public of incidents of police misconduct. Some additional examples of citizen-based groups that act as an accountability mechanism include Communities United Against Police Brutality,[68] Citizens Against Police Brutality & Misconduct,[69] and the Detroit Coalition Against Police Brutality.[70]

There have been criticisms of citizen-based groups (including COP WATCH). Police officials have stated that they are concerned that videotaping police–citizen encounters can create problems for police officer safety. There is concern that videotaping will act as a distraction to officers and, as a result, they could end up getting hurt or killed.[71] In some cases, these groups have acted as instigators to protests and rioting that can spin out of control.[72] Others argue that citizen-based groups often manipulate or edit video clips in a way that does not depict what actually happened during citizen–police encounters. Some police departments have begun to try and work with citizen-based groups like COP WATCH instead of continuing an adversarial relationship with them.[73]

Media

Most (70%) Americans report that they use television as a main source for national and international news.[74] In fact, the average American home had 2.93 TV sets in 2010.[75] Earlier in this section, the media (including the Internet, television, and newspapers) were identified as a source from which many citizens get information about police-involved litigation and police misconduct. If media sources did not present information about incidents of police misconduct or police-involved litigation, where would this information come from? How would citizens become aware of such incidents that occur in their communities? The media serve as external sources for police accountability because they provide information on this topic to citizens. One could argue that the media only present the most extraordinary cases of police misconduct or police-involved lawsuits.[76] Despite this criticism, citizens still learn about police activities taking place in their communities that they may not have otherwise heard about.

Police officers are cognizant that they are more closely watched by citizens today than ever before.

Courts

The court system in the United States has played a major role in reformation of the police in America. The court system has also served as an external accountability mechanism for the police in several ways. As discussed earlier in this section, citizens can file lawsuits against police officers and police organizations in both state and federal courts when they believe that the police acted in ways that have caused injury or death or violated their constitutional rights. The court system also holds police officers accountable by restricting their use of discretion in critical incidents. This is accomplished when court case outcomes provide specific guidance on how the police should and should not conduct official police business (such as outcome of *Tennessee v. Garner* [1985] and the use of deadly force). More recently, the American court system has held the police accountable through the use of various oversight mechanisms including pattern or practice lawsuits, consent decrees, and court-appointed monitors.

The **Violent Crime Control and Law Enforcement Act of 1994** prohibits government agencies and agents from engaging in a "pattern or practice" of conduct by law enforcement officials that deprives persons of rights, privileges, or immunities protected by the United States Constitution.[77] If the U.S. attorney general has reason to believe that a violation has occurred, the Department of Justice is authorized to sue police agencies in an effort to eliminate any such practice. **Pattern or practice** is a phrase that means that an act has occurred more than in just one isolated incident. This phrase suggests that this act is more of an organizational practice and is used more often than it is not.[78] According to the Department of Justice website,

> as of January 31, 2003, pattern or practice investigations of 14 agencies are ongoing. In general we do not announce the initiation of a pattern or practice investigation; however, the jurisdictions we are investigating often make that information public, particularly when the jurisdiction has requested the investigation. Our investigations in the following jurisdictions are public: Charleston, WV; Cleveland, OH; Detroit, MI; Eastpointe, MI; City of Miami, FL; New Orleans, LA; New York City, NY (two investigations: one regarding use of force, one regarding the street crimes unit and stop and frisk practices); Portland, ME; Prince George's County, MD; Providence, RI; Riverside, CA; Schenectady, NY; and Tulsa, OK.[79]

Police departments that are under pattern-or-practice investigations have the option to settle their court case instead of being tried in open court. The police departments that agree to settle also agree to be bound by **consent decrees**. Consent decrees are enforceable legal agreements that are usually overseen by court-appointed monitors and federal judges.[80] The content of consent decrees varies from one agency to the next, as they identify problems unique to each police agency and also identify changes that need to be made within police agencies to remedy the problems. Consent decrees often require changes to take place in police officer training, supervision of officers, discipline of officers, and complaint procedures that citizens use when they want to file complaints about mistreatment by police officers.[81] A major benefit of choosing to settle under consent decrees is that police agencies will follow court-ordered reforms of police management practices instead of paying monetary damages for their actions. Department of Justice investigations of police agencies can also result in a **memorandum of agreement (MOA)**. MOAs are more conciliatory than consent decrees, as they do not require any judicial monitoring like consent decrees often do.[82]

A common requirement of consent decrees is that police agencies will be watched by court appointed monitors. **Court-appointed monitors (CAMs)** are individuals responsible for tracking the progress made by police agencies that are under consent decrees. CAMs are also required to produce a report (usually on a quarterly basis) detailing how the police agency is (or is not) fulfilling its obligation of making changes.[83] Despite being court ordered to make changes, some police agencies do not comply very quickly (and in some cases they do not comply at all). For example, on January 15, 2010, the court-appointed monitor overseeing the Detroit Police Department says that the department had failed to keep track of police officers use of force incidents.[84] The CAM said that "there was a 50 percent drop in reports of force after Detroit police switched to computers in August 2008 and stopped logging them by hand."[85] In addition, the CAM also stated that the department has only complied with 29% of the changes outlined in the two consent decrees it has been operating under since 2003.[86] This is one example in which it is obvious why court-appointed monitors are a necessary and important part of police accountability for police agencies that are operating under consent decrees.

Civilian Review Boards

The investigation of citizen complaints filed against police officers has long been a topic of debate among police personnel and citizens. It has been the center of debate, as some citizens have a hard time believing that it is possible for police personnel to investigate complaints filed against their colleagues in an unbiased manner. National statistics on the number of sustained citizen complaints add to this debate. One study found that approximately 10% to 13% of all complaints filed against police officers are found in favor of the citizen (sustained).[87] This statistic could leave citizens feeling as though their complaints are not being heard or being taken seriously by police executives. Civilian review boards emerged as a way to allow citizens to become part of the process of investigating citizen complaints against the police.

Civilian review boards have developed in numerous cities across the United States. Each jurisdiction fashions its board to reflect the needs of the community, thus resulting in a variety of different types of civilian review boards. Peter Finn identified four types of civilian review boards in his manual, *Citizen Review of Police: Approaches and Implementation*, as described in the following table.[88]

Four Types of Civilian Review Boards
Type 1: Citizens investigate allegations of police misconduct and recommend findings to the chief or sheriff.
Type 2: Police officers investigate allegations and develop findings; citizens review and recommend that the chief or sheriff approve or reject the findings.
Type 3: Complainants may appeal findings established by the police or sheriff's department to citizens, who review them and then recommend their own findings to the chief or sheriff.
Type 4: An auditor investigates the process by which the police or sheriff's department accepts and investigates complaints and reports on the thoroughness and fairness of the process to the department and the public.

The idea behind the adoption of civilian review boards is that the investigation process of citizen complaints against the police would be fairer if citizens were involved. Research on this topic has found that civilian review boards do not sustain a higher rate of citizen complaints when compared to police internal affairs units (the division within police agencies that is usually responsible for investigating citizen complaints against police officers).[89] It is important to point out that more research is needed in this area, as there has been very little empirical exploration of this topic.

After reviewing a wide variety of police accountability mechanisms found both within and outside of police agencies, which type of mechanism is the most effective? According to Samuel Walker, an expert on police accountability, a mix of both internal and external accountability mechanisms is ideal.[90] Requiring oversight by both police executives and citizens or groups within the community puts a system of checks and balances into the process.

SUMMARY

- Lawsuits involving the police have continued to increase since the 1970s.
- Police officers are exposed to liability risks every day.
- Police accountability has increased over the course of the history of policing in the United States.
- Consent decrees are court-ordered mandates that outline changes that need to be made within police organizations that have been identified by pattern or practice lawsuits.
- Citizen groups, media, the court system, and citizen oversight boards are all police accountability mechanisms found outside of police agencies.

KEY TERMS

consent decree
court-appointed monitor
   (CAM)
intentional tort
litigaphobia

memorandum of agreement
   (MOA)
negligence tort
pattern or practice
strict liability tort

Title 42 United States Code,
   Section 1983
Violent Crime Control and Law
   Enforcement Act of 1994

DISCUSSION QUESTIONS

1. Explain how police liability and police accountability are related.

2. Describe how police accountability has changed over the course of the history of American policing.

3. Identify and then explain several police accountability mechanisms found outside of police departments.

4. Explain how both police officers and police agencies can be held liable for their actions or, in some cases, inaction.

5. Identify and explain the various types of civilian review boards that exist in the United States.

WEB RESOURCES

- To learn more about Section 1983 cases, go to http://www.fjc.gov/public/pdf.nsf/lookup/Sect1983.pdf/$file/Sect1983.pdf.
- To learn more about police accountability, go to http://samuelwalker.net/.
- To learn more about pattern or practice lawsuits, go to http://www.policeforum.org/library/police-evaluation/Executive%20Summary.pdf.

READING 17

This study explored the use of risk management in large municipal and county law enforcement agencies in the United States. In addition, this study identified factors and perceived impact associated with the adoption of risk-management programs by police agencies. Data analysis revealed that very few large police agencies use risk management in their effort to control the frequency and costs associated with police liability.

Managing the Bottom Line: Risk Management in Policing

Carol A. Archbold

Introduction

Since July 2000, Prince George's County, MD has paid out $7.9 million in jury awards and settlements in lawsuits that involved police misconduct and excessive force (*Washington Post*, 2003). In 2001, a jury awarded more than $7 million to a family whose 17-year-old son (unarmed) was fatally shot by a Baltimore Housing Authority police officer (*The Baltimore Sun*, 2001). In December 2002, the city attorney's office in Los Angeles provisionally agreed to pay $2.5 million in a settlement with a woman who lost her eye when a police officer shot her with a beanbag projectile because he mistakenly thought she was reaching for a weapon (*Los Angeles Times*, 2002).

These examples represent a small fraction of the multi-million dollar payouts resulting from the use of improper procedures by police officers in the last two years. The increasing costs resulting from payouts in police litigation cases and liability claims, coupled with increased pressure from public insurance pools to cut losses, are a few of the reasons that some US law enforcement agencies are beginning to implement risk management programs.

Risk management is a process used to identify and control exposure to potential risks and liabilities in both private and public organizations. In the past 20 years, risk management has been transformed from an insurance-based technical tool to a broad, policy-oriented managerial technique (Young, 2000). A wide variety of organizations adopt risk management practices to avoid increasing threats of litigation, reduce the risk of physical harm to their clients and themselves, and provide a higher quality of service to their clients (Wong and Rakestraw, 1991). With police managers facing similar issues, risk management appears to be a logical fit with police liability management in most police organizations.

To date, there is no published research that examines the use of risk management in American police agencies. The purpose of this study is to explore the use of risk management in some of the largest municipal and county law enforcement agencies in the USA. This study also identifies some of the factors associated with the adoption of risk management programs by law enforcement agencies, as well as the perceived impact of such programs on police liability from the perspective of risk managers and police officials. A discussion of some of the potential barriers to the implementation of risk management programs in law enforcement agencies is also included.

What Is Risk Management?

Risk management is a process that is used to identify potential risks and liabilities that could result in some kind of loss for both public and private organizations (monetary, property, etc.). Risk management strategies vary depending on the nature of the organization, including management style and organizational goals (Conrow, 2000). However, there are five basic steps in the risk management process that are applicable to most types of organizations (Wong and Rakestraw, 1991; Ashley and Pearson, 1993):

1. *Identify risk, frequency of exposure to risks, and the severity of losses resulting from exposure to risks*: to do this, organizations use data on the history of organizational loss including past lawsuits, complaints, and payouts resulting from liability claims.

2. *Explore methods to handle exposure to identified risks*: this step includes a thorough review of organizational policies and procedures, training, and supervision of employees.

3. *Choose appropriate treatment or response to manage exposure to risks*: this step includes making changes to department policies, training, and/or supervision to reduce exposure to liability incidents.

4. *Implement risk treatment*: implement all changes made to department policy, procedure, and/or training.

5. *Continuously evaluate risk treatment applied to organizational risks*: the risk management process is not over after steps 1–4 have been completed. The process is ongoing because organizational risks change over time and require continuous evaluation.

Today, risk management practices are used in a wide variety of professional settings including medicine (Armitage and Knapman, 2003; Ladebauche, 2001), athletic training (Osborne, 2001), psychology (Baerger,

2001), social work (Reamer, 1995; Gelman, 1992), banking and finance (Baxter, 2003), engineering and architecture (Paleologos and Lerche, 2002; Ichniowski, 1995), and schools and universities (Harshfield, 1996; Dise, 1995). Additionally, the use of risk management programs in the public sector is among the fastest growing segments of the risk management profession (Esenberg, 1992).

Risk Management in Municipal Government Agencies

It has long been a belief that the philosophies and practices of risk management are not applicable to public or municipal agencies (Esenberg, 1992). This is not the case as most municipal agencies can function more effectively with the maximum amount of resources available to them. Vincent (1996) notes that public organizations are usually held accountable more publicly than their private counterparts because they are entrusted with a budget that derives in large part from the community (taxpayers). The idea behind using risk management in local government agencies is that by identifying risks that can lead to organizational loss, as well as make changes to avoid or reduce future organizational loss, government agencies will be able to spend more resources on services to the community instead of liability claims and litigation.

There is not one single best risk management process that is suggested to be used universally or for specific types of organizations.

> No two local governments have exactly the same risks, and the risks change as the jurisdiction and legal climate changes. (Wong and Rakestraw, 1991, p. 1)

However, most municipal agencies adopt risk management practices due to the increasing insurance costs and in some cases, unavailable insurance coverage and loss control of existing resources available to government agencies (Neville, 1978).

Local government agencies are exposed to risk that could increase the probability of loss of organizational assets. Young (2000) identifies three general categories of assets that local government agencies are responsible for managing, including:

1. Physical assets.

2. Human assets.

3. Financial assets.

Physical assets include vehicles, buildings, computer equipment and other technological equipment. If physical assets are damaged or lost, the organization must absorb the cost of not only replacing the item, but also the time that is lost in replacing such items. For example, if a law enforcement vehicle is damaged or considered a complete loss, the police agency will have to pay to replace or fix the vehicle. In addition, there will [be] a period of time where the agency will be without one police vehicle available for patrol.

Human assets in local government agencies include elected officials, managers, and other workers employed within local government agencies (Young, 2000). These individuals are at risk for both physical and economic harm while on the job. For example, due to the nature of their work, both police and fire personnel are at risk for becoming injured or deceased while on the job. In addition to injury, these individuals could suffer economically if they are unable to return to work after an injury.

And finally, financial assets within local government agencies include any financial resource that is available to municipalities that have a direct impact on how agencies are able to function or perform expected duties/tasks (Young, 2000). The most important financial asset within police agencies includes resources that are part of annual budgets. Law enforcement agencies are at risk of losing financial assets due to budget cuts and also unanticipated payouts resulting from liability claims and litigation involving police personnel. The study presented in this paper is based on the idea that by incorporating risk management into police liability management

efforts the exposure to risks that could result in a loss of human, physical, and financial assets of police agencies could be reduced.

 ## Risk Management and Police Liability

Almost all of the basic duties of police work expose police officers to liability incidents on a daily basis (Gallagher, 1990b; Wennerholm, 1985). One aspect of police work that makes it unique to all other professions is the ability of police officers to use lethal and non-lethal force (Bittner, 1970). This unique aspect of police work also contributes to police officer exposure to high levels of risk, which could lead to litigation, liability claims or citizen complaints. It has been reported that improper use of lethal and non-lethal force by police officers during arrest and improper service of due process are two incidents in which damages are most likely sought, and that settlements are paid out to citizens (Blalock, 1974; del Carmen, 1991; Newell *et al.*, 1993).

Liability Assessment and Awareness International (LAAW) (Ashley and Pearson, 2001) suggests that police executives could manage liability related to use of force through close supervision of patrol officers. The group also suggests that police department policies should be created and maintained to keep the use of force under control. Also, by applying the highest standards to the use of force by police officers, as well as the review process of all misuse of force cases, law enforcement agencies can get a handle on use of force liability incidents (Ashley and Pearson, 2001). This assertion by the LAAW parallels the findings of most of the research on the use of lethal and non-lethal force, which suggests that policies and mandatory reporting of use of lethal/non-lethal force harnesses police officer behaviors and activities (Alpert and Fridell, 1992; Culliver and Sigler, 1995; Fyfe, 1979, 1981; Geller and Scott, 1992; Pate and Fridell, 1993; Pate and Fridell, 1995; Sparger and Giacopassi, 1992).

Another high risk liability incident often resulting in litigation for police agencies is law enforcement vehicle operation. High-risk liability incidents involving law enforcement vehicles include high speed pursuits, how and where police vehicles are parked, whether or not emergency lights/equipment are used while police vehicles are parked, where police officers place people and all involved vehicles during the investigation of traffic stops, and the misuse or nonuse of vehicle occupant restraints (Ashley and Pearson, 2001).

Alpert discusses several ways to identify and respond to exposure to risks related to emergency vehicle operations within police agencies including:

- a review of historical loss data;
- a review of both past and pending litigation cases against the police agency; and
- surveying patrol officers about some of the issues that arise from operating law enforcement vehicles (Alpert *et al.*, 2000, p. 154).

Because the operation of police vehicles is a necessary part of modern policing, identifying and then managing the risks associated with police vehicle operation also becomes a necessary task for police executives. Additional research on police pursuits suggests that both clarification of police pursuit policies, mandatory reporting, and consistent monitoring of pursuit activities by police management will reduce the overall number of pursuits, and in turn, will reduce the number of injuries and accidents resulting from police pursuits (Alpert and Fridell, 1992; Crew *et al.*, 1995; Crew *et al.*, 1994).

Existing literature on the use of risk management within police agencies identifies the oversight and management of department policies, training, recruitment/hiring standards, and supervision over line officers as a primary duty of risk management personnel (Gallagher, 1990a, b; Gallagher, 1992). Risk managers deal with high risk incidents (such as use of force and police pursuits) by tracking and identifying incidents that have resulted in some loss for their organization, and ultimately make changes to policies, training, and supervision of officers to reduce officer exposure to such risks. The benefit of using risk management as part of a police liability management strategy is three-fold (Young, 2000):

1. To increase the safety of both police officers and citizens.

2. Increase the quality of police services provided to the public.

3. Financial management of the costs associated with police-involved liability incidents resulting in liability claims or litigation.

Risk Management and US Law Enforcement Agencies

There are several agencies that encourage the use of risk management in law enforcement agencies by providing risk assessment tools and other resources that illustrate the potential benefits of risk management. For example, the Public Risk Management Association or PRIMA (a professional trade association of risk managers) provides a police liability assessment guide that outlines some of the areas of potential risks in police work. Some of the risks identified by PRIMA include the use of firearms and other non-lethal weapons (both on and off duty), pursuit driving, use of force, defensive tactics, and hostage situations. PRIMA suggests adequate training in those high-risk incidents, along with department policies that clearly outline proper police procedures in high-risk incidents as a first step to maintain control over police liability (PRIMAfile online, 2000).

The International Association of Chiefs of Police (IACP) provides a "critical incident protocol—a public and private partnership" that outlines a plan that law enforcement agencies can use to manage critical incidents through collaboration with other public and private agencies. Each chapter in this report describes how public and private organizations can use risk management practices (such as risk assessment and responding to identified risks) to take action in high risk or critical situations in a safe and cost efficient manner (International Association of Chiefs of Police, 2003). Several lessons on establishing partnerships, conducting evaluations of risk factors, developing emergency plans for response to critical incidents, and improving training are also included in this report. Even with the encouragement of these agencies, the findings of the current study reveal that very few law enforcement agencies use risk management to control police officer exposure to risk.

To date, there has been very little literature published on the use of risk management by law enforcement agencies. Most of the literature on risk management and law enforcement has been published in magazines geared toward police practitioners. For example, in June 1990, *The Police Chief* featured two articles that discuss police liability and risk management. Both of these articles highlight the importance of implementing risk management programs in police agencies by identifying changes that can be made to department policies, procedure, and training (Gallagher, 1990a, b). The articles also mention that risk management has the potential to bolster the level of professionalism within police organizations (Gallagher, 1990a,b). Gallagher (1990b) presents a "six-layered liability protection system" approach to risk management that includes the examination of department policies and procedures, disciplinary practices, police training, supervision, continuous review and revision process of operations, and the aid of legal support and services (p. 40). This six-layered approach helps police agencies identify risks, make changes to exposure to those risks, and ultimately, reduce costs associated with police liability incidents. Gallagher elaborates on his "six-layered liability protection system" in his book, *Risk Management Behind the Blue Curtain: A Primer on Law Enforcement Liability* (Gallagher, 1992).

Several articles on risk management and law enforcement also appear in *Business Insurance* magazine, *National Underwriter* magazine, and *Public Risk* magazine, which are publications geared toward risk managers and insurance professionals. These articles note that very few law enforcement agencies actually have in-house risk management departments (Ceniceros, 1998), and that risk management programs can help police managers identify patterns of problematic behavior and incorrect use of procedures by officers that can lead to litigation, citizen complaints, and liability claims (Heazeltine, 1986; Wojcik, 1994; Ceniceros, 1998; Katz, 1998; Lesh, 2002). All of these articles are based on the work experiences of risk managers and other insurance related professionals, not on any systematic, empirical research.

Only in recent years has risk management emerged in the academic literature. In *Police Accountability: The Role of Citizen Oversight,* Samuel Walker asserts that both police departments and other city officials have neglected the use of risk management in their liability management efforts (Walker, 2001). One exception to the neglect of risk management is the Los Angeles Sheriff's Department. Walker recognizes the impact of risk management in the Los Angeles Sheriff's Department (LASD), as that organization has managed to reduce litigation judgments and settlements from $15.5 million (between 1989 and mid-1992) to an average of about $2 million a year since 1992 (Walker, 2001, p. 101). Special Counsel Merrick Bobb monitors the activities of the LASD risk management unit and generates semiannual reports outlining the impact that this unit has on the costs associated with liability incidents.

A discussion of risk management is also included in the journal article "The new paradigm of police accountability: the US Justice Department 'Pattern or Practice' suits in context" (Walker, 2003). The ultimate goal in the new paradigm of police accountability is to achieve accountability on an organizational level (Walker, 2003, p. 51). Walker describes three characteristics of the new paradigm of police accountability including:

1. The integration of policies and procedures into a comprehensive accountability program using early intervention systems (early warning systems) as the foundation.

2. The collection and analysis of data on police department performance to identify problems that can be handled through intervention.

3. Then making intervention more proactive in nature instead of reactive as it has been in the past (Walker, 2003, pp. 29–30).

Risk management fits into the new paradigm of police accountability since its core objective is to identify organizational risks, apply some type of corrective action (such as changing department policies or training), and then monitor the impact of the corrective action.

Alpert *et al.* (2000) devote a chapter to civil liability and risk management in their book, *Police Pursuits: What We Know*. Alpert and colleagues describe risk management in the context of a "plan of action" to prevent costly payouts and injuries associated with police pursuits. The authors discuss the implementation of risk management in terms of taking a proactive or "front-end" approach instead of a reactive approach. The "front-end" approach to risk management is based on the idea that police agencies implement risk management practices before a major liability incident occurs (Alpert *et al.*, 2000, p. 156). This chapter provides a comprehensive overview of the principles and potential benefits of risk management, as well as suggestions for applying risk management practices to control liability related in police pursuits.

A review of the literature reveals that there has been no systematic research conducted on the use of risk management by law enforcement agencies in the US. The present study will contribute to this body of literature by providing a descriptive account of the use of risk management by police agencies in regard to police liability management. More specifically, this study will address the following research questions:

- What is the prevalence of the use of risk management by municipal and county law enforcement agencies in the US?
- What are some of the factors associated with the decision to adopt risk management programs by law enforcement agencies?
- What are some of the role(s) and duties of risk managers in the context of police organizations?
- How do risk managers and police officials explain the impact of risk management on police liability efforts within their organizations?

⊠ Methodology

To explore this topic, all municipal and county law enforcement agencies that employ 200 or more sworn police officers in the US are included in the sampling frame of this study. The Bureau of Justice Statistics report, "Law Enforcement Management and Administrative Statistics, 1999: Data for Individual State and Local Agencies With 100 or More Officers" (LEMAS report), identified 354 municipal and county law enforcement agencies employing 200 or more sworn officers (Reaves and Hart, 1999). Contact information for the administrative offices of all 354 police agencies was collected using the website www.officers.com. After identifying the law enforcement agencies that would be used in this study, data collection was conducted in two stages from February to August 2001.

Stage 1—Telephone Interviews

The first stage of data collection consisted of telephone interviews with agency representatives at all 354 law enforcement agencies identified in the LEMAS report. Agency representatives include police managers, risk managers, police legal advisors, and in some cases, staff from Internal Affairs divisions. Representatives from all 354 agencies responded to the telephone interview questions. Telephone interviews consisted of the following questions:

- What person(s) or group is responsible for liability management in your police agency?
- Does your police agency use risk manager(s) or police legal advisor(s) in its effort to control liability involving police personnel?
- If risk managers and/or police legal advisors are used by your agency, how do these positions fit into the police organizational structure?

Data from the telephone interviews is used to assess the prevalence of the use of risk management by police agencies, as well as details on how some of the largest US law enforcement agencies deal with their police liability issues.

Stage 2—Surveys

The second stage of data collection involved a survey of the law enforcement agencies that reported some use of risk management during initial telephone interviews. The survey data provides descriptive information about the purpose, organizational structure, role, and the perceived impact that risk management has on police liability within each police agency.

Only 14 of the 354 law enforcement agencies contacted by telephone reported the use of risk management in their agencies. Surveys were sent directly to the person(s) in charge of risk management for each of the 14 police agencies. A second round of surveys and follow-up letters was mailed to the police agencies that had not responded within three weeks of receiving the initial survey. Ten of the 14 police agencies (71 percent) returned completed surveys, while three police agencies did not respond. One police agency was in the process of setting up its risk management program when the survey was distributed; therefore, the newly hired risk manager felt that their program was "too new" to respond to the survey.

The survey instrument contained several open-ended questions organized into four categories:

1. *Origin/history of the use of risk management*: what was the reason(s) for implementing risk management? What person or group initiated the implementation of risk management? What year was risk management adopted by your organization?

2. *Characteristics of the risk management program*: what is the total number of personnel focused on risk management efforts? Describe the training or professional experience of risk management personnel in your organization. Where is risk management physically housed? (either in-house or outside of the police agency)

3. *Role(s) and duties of risk management within the police organization*: what are some of the main duties of the risk manager/management program? Explain the extent to which risk management influences department policies, police training, and the supervision of line officers.

4. *Perceived impact of risk management on police liability*: based on your experience, how does risk management impact police liability in your organization?

Data analysis for this study includes a qualitative analysis using Microsoft Access 2000 as a data management tool. This computer program allows the responses from open-ended survey questions and telephone interview notes to be analyzed simultaneously, which allows for easy identification of thematic categories within both qualitative data sources.

Findings

Prevalence of the Use of Risk Management by US Law Enforcement Agencies

Telephone interviews reveal that 14 of the 354 (0.039 percent) law enforcement agencies identified risk management as one of several tools they use to control police-related liability within their organizations. No agency reported that they use only risk managers to manage police liability issues. Nearly half (163 of 354) of all agencies reported that they use only police legal advisors in their liability management efforts. The remaining police agencies (177 of 354) reported that they rely solely on city/county attorneys to handle liability issues involving law enforcement personnel. The lack of specialized attention given to police liability issues is surprising given that costs associated with police liability incidents and litigation have increased substantially in the last three decades (del Carmen and Smith, 1997; Kappeler, 2001; Scogin and Brodsky, 1991).

The 14 law enforcement agencies that reported using risk management as part of their liability management efforts are dispersed across every region of the US (five agencies in the southwest, three agencies in south/southeast, three in the mid-west, two in the northeast, and one in the northwest). Five of the agencies are sheriffs' departments, while the other nine agencies are municipal police agencies. Most of the police agencies (11 out of 14) serve populations ranging in size from 500,000–3.6 million people (the other three agencies serve populations ranging from 198,000–478,000). All but one of the 14 police agencies employs 1,000 + full time sworn employees.

Characteristics Associated With the Adoption of Risk Management by Police Agencies

Of the small number of agencies using risk management, over half (60 percent) of the police agencies adopted risk management from 1993–1999, while the remaining agencies adopted such practices between 1973–1986. The chief of police or sheriff was identified as being responsible for initiating the adoption of risk management by 80 percent of the police agencies. This finding is significant because it suggests that some police managers are recognizing liability problems within their organizations, and then are ultimately taking steps to secure fiscal responsibility within their organizations. The other 20 percent of the agencies identified city and county attorneys, and other local government officials as the parties responsible for initiating the adoption of risk management.

The number of employees working within risk management divisions in police agencies ranged from 2–67 employees. The education and professional experience of risk management personnel varies including those with legal experience, training in risk management, accounting, insurance assessment/adjustment, and prior experience in law enforcement. Most of the police agencies (90 percent) reported that their employees have had some kind of specialized training in risk management. The specialized training is described as daylong seminars offered sporadically by risk managers that have had professional experience in risk management in both private and public organizations. The risk managers surveyed for this study indicated that their risk management training seminars ranged in length from eight hours to two days. Over half of the police agencies (60 percent) reported that their risk management employees have had training in both risk management and in practicing law. Another 40 percent of police agencies reported employing risk managers with prior experience in law enforcement. One third of the police agencies specifically mentioned that one or more individuals working in their risk management division has had prior experience with risk assessment and insurance liability claims prior to their employment within police agencies.

An analysis of the survey data also reveals a variety of factors regarding the decision of police agencies to adopt risk management practices. The most common factor reported by police agencies was adopting risk management "out of necessity." A majority of the police agencies (eight of ten) reported that an increase in lawsuits (and payouts resulting from those lawsuits) prompted them to implement risk management liability programs.

> There was an increase in third party lawsuits, which made the sheriff concerned. The sheriff wanted to become more proactive instead of using some of the reactive responses that had taken place in the past.

> We adopted an in-house legal advisor because of the costs of outside claims management. A private law firm was handling all liability claims for the sheriff's office. Cost was reduced by 50 percent when the risk management department was established.

> The chief of police was concerned about risk and liability issues among police managers, and instituted a plan for quality assurance that involves risk management.

A second factor reported in the adoption of risk management stems from the changes in the legal and social environment in which police officers work. In the current study, 70 percent of the agencies reported that risk management has become necessary because of the complex changes in laws that have occurred in the past three decades.

> The sheriff realized that as more and more laws were passed, it was becoming difficult to comply with and ensure compliance. The basis for creating any position was to assist deputies in enforcing the law and to aid in complying with law governing our employees.

To help officers understand statutes, ordinances, search and seizure, and civil liability issues. Also, forfeiture litigation and legislation.

There was a significant need to have an in-house risk manager and police legal advisor for the police department in order to ensure timely and appropriate responses to law enforcement legal issues.

A third factor reported for adopting risk management is negative media publicity of controversial incidents involving police liability. This was the case with some of the agencies (40 percent) responding to the survey, as they reported that several highly publicized police-related incidents prompted the hiring of risk managers.

The risk management program was implemented when the police department began self-criticism and evaluation in the wake of an incident that resulted in the beating death of a citizen by the police. The police department's top management recognized the need for change in the police department's approach to police misconduct and the management of risks.

There was concern over consent decrees in other cities. Also, there were two large payouts in civil suits over a police shooting and fatal traffic accident.

The three most common factors reported by police agencies for adopting risk managers can be categorized as a reactive response to increased losses from litigation and liability claims. This finding suggests that risk management is adopted primarily for the benefit of police organizations. However, survey data indicate that three out of the ten police agencies added risk management to their organization in hopes of improving the quality of police services provided to citizens. These three police agencies identified reduced costs associated with litigation and liability claims as a major benefit for local taxpayers

(citizens), and also a safer environment, as police procedures would be performed to ensure the safety of both citizens and police officers.

Role and Duties of Risk Management Within Police Organizations

Data analysis reveals that the primary role of risk managers within police organizations involves a direct influence on police liability management efforts. More specifically, risk managers initiate the reform of department policies, police officer training, and the supervision of patrol officers by police managers.

Changes in police department policies. The importance of keeping police department policies and procedures current to the standards required by state and federal law is a common theme that emerges from the survey data. It is also clear from the survey responses that the maintenance of department policies and procedures is one of the best ways to prevent future litigation for cases involving officers using out-dated techniques during field contacts with citizens (including arrest, search and seizure of property, and physical restraints). Risk managers can identify policies that have resulted in payouts for liability claims and civil suits involving police officers, and work with police legal advisors and/or local city attorneys to make changes to department policies in an effort to decrease organizational loss.

A majority of the police agencies using risk management (90 percent) reported that risk management has a direct and significant impact on any changes made to police department policies. The type of department policies that are most often influenced by risk managers can be categorized into two groups:

1. Inter-organizational police issues.

2. Citizen-related department policies.

The survey data indicates that risk managers make changes that impact liability costs associated with work-related injuries and motor vehicle incidents involving employees, loss or damage to department property, as well as sexual harassment and discrimination suits filed by employees within law enforcement agencies. There are also separate units or people within police organizations that handle employee-related liability incidents, such as fleet managers who handle all motor vehicle-related incidents, or risk specialists that focus on the costs of work injuries, and settlements or payouts from lawsuits filed against police agencies by their own employees.

> Almost all of the general orders in our policy and procedures manual, which is about 3 inches thick, are reviewed by me. I make many changes. Often the changes involve labor laws to reduce suits against the department by our own employees.

> There have been positive changes in our work related injuries and motor vehicle accident/incident and loss of property since the risk management program has been up and running.

Policies that impact people outside of the police organization (such as citizens) are also a major concern of risk managers. Some of the most common policies that were mentioned in the surveys include policies on use of force, field contacts with mentally ill or disabled persons, vehicular pursuits, searches and frisks, property seizures, arrest and custody procedures, and most recently racial profiling policies.

> We have made changes to our policies on use of force and police pursuits. Also the risk management division headed up CALEA accreditation, and we re-wrote the entire policy manual three times during my tenure.

> Our risk management section will occasionally suggest procedural changes to general orders to facilitate timely reporting and tracking. These changes are generally subtle and of little consequence to the daily operation of the sheriffs office. Upon occasion we

may be asked to look at specific operational policies to suggest improvement for the sake of reducing a particular type of loss. For example, we were asked to look at the emergency response policy, which required agency units responding to a call to adhere to state law regarding intersections. State law requires the exercise of "due care" when approaching an intersection with a red light or stop sign. We recommended a change requiring our units to come to a full stop under these conditions and ensure all traffic had stopped before proceeding. Our intersection collisions under emergency response mode dropped significantly after this change.

> I review or write policies to minimize high-risk incidents. Also, I changed the policy so that there is no shooting from moving vehicles, no strip searches without a warrant consent or arrest, and no racial profiling.

Changes to police training. Most police agencies responding to the survey (70 percent) indicate that police training is an integral part of risk managers' roles within police organizations. Data analysis reveals that each stage of police training is affected by the work of risk managers in relation to police officer exposure to liability, beginning in the academy and continuing all the way through to in-service training seminars.

> We teach classes at the local and regional training academics to new recruits and within our agency to experienced officers. We also endeavor to keep our officers current on the law through regular issuance of legal bulletins and similar updates.

> Extensive changes in our field training officer (FTO) program have been made to reflect a variety of state and federal law changes such as police hot pursuits and use of force, both non-lethal and lethal.

Risk management routinely receives the training schedule for all training (basic to advanced) for the police department. Suggestions are routinely made which are acted upon to change or improve every stage of police officer training.

Some of the training topics that are influenced by risk managers across all phases of training include (but are not exclusive to) incidents related to workmen's compensation and employee injury, defensive driving training, search and seizure of property, vehicular pursuits, racial profiling, civil rights, cultural diversity, and sexual harassment training, custody and arrest practices, handling domestic violence situations, and use of force.

An important relationship among the primary duties of risk managers emerged from the qualitative survey data, specifically in regard to altering department policies and police officer training. Essentially, any changes made to department policies result in changes to police department procedures, which also usually requires some additional modifications to police training.

Changes to the supervision of police officers by police supervisors. Less than half of the police agencies (40 percent) reported that risk management has some level of impact on the supervision of line officers by police managers. Those agencies posit that their risk managers provide additional training tailored to police managers to ensure adequate supervision of line officers. A common topic of supervisory training mentioned in the surveys includes civil liability-related issues (such as the importance of recording all incidents that could end up in litigation in the future, and how to prepare for trial if you are named as a defendant in a civil liability case). Other training topics include Section 1983 liability, sexual harassment, use of force, search and seizure, racial profiling, forced entries, and recording and protecting evidence. Risk managers rely on police supervisors to ensure that all line officers receive, understand, and put into practice any changes they make to department policies.

Supervisors receive training and education which enhances their ability to provide direction on report writing and completion of contact cards. Training is provided to sergeants, lieutenants, and watch commanders prior to their moving into a new position.

Nearly all program changes are reviewed by our office. The office also initially reviews civil suits and disciplinary proceedings. Police supervisors call us 24 hours a day when they encounter legal issues.

We train new supervisors proactively and on an ongoing basis. Supervisors often call us from the scenes of potential liability incidents. We also initiate change upon the review of all forced entries and use of force incidents. It is our job to spot potential problems.

Perceived Impact of Risk Management on Police Liability

The survey instrument also contained questions about the perceived impact of employing risk managers within police agencies to manage police liability issues. It is important to note that the perceived financial impact is based solely on the survey responses of police administrators, risk managers, and other police personnel directly involved with police liability management, and not on any official financial documents or third party evaluations.

Data analysis reveals that 60 percent of the police agencies surveyed believe that their risk management programs have some impact on the liability-related monetary payouts of their police organizations. Several of these agencies provide examples of their impact on financial payouts by their police organizations.

Yes, by denying frivolous lawsuits. The sheriff's office now has three in-house attorneys and a risk manager. This alone has reduced our costs by 30 percent.

The number of civil suits within the last six years or so has been significantly reduced. The major part of the fact was at the time we elected a new sheriff who has implemented and reinforced training of supervisors and on-line officers which has greatly reduced the number of incidents giving rise to civil suits.

We have been instrumental in early claims resolution saving literally millions of dollars. We are on 24-hour call and roll on to shootings, accidents, and other incidents for early liability assessment. Those are the kind of things that help us save money.

Several police agencies also point out that they believe that there is an incalculable aspect of the impact of risk management due to all of the lawsuits and liability claims that were prevented due to risk management efforts.

Proactive claims as well as earlier and better investigations have helped lead to fewer lawsuits, claims, and infractions. While we can document a marked decrease in collisions during emergency pursuits, we are unable to quantify the number of collisions that have been prevented.

Our program has significantly reduced payouts by better managing the cases. Prior to our arrival, everything was shipped immediately to an attorney. This method caused our department to pay more for claims because the people handling those claims were making a high hourly wage. By handling everything in-house, we have reduced the initial costs and improved our ability to respond quickly to situations. As a result, minor problems are solved immediately and are prevented from becoming major problems.

A majority of prevented liability incidents result from teaching police agents new laws, how to avoid claims of false arrests, by training police agents concerning new court decisions, and also about avoiding unconstitutional searches and seizures.

Three ways that risk managers can track their financial impact on police liability within their agencies are:

1. Examining trend data over a specified length of time.

2. Making comparisons of liability with similar law enforcement agencies.

3. Examining fluctuations in specific high-risk liability incident categories (such as use of force, false arrest, police pursuits, etc.).

These methods could provide some evidence of an impact on the frequency and costs of liability incidents resulting in payouts, as well as costly civil suits filed against their agencies.

It is important that law enforcement agencies that have risk managers on staff at least attempt to keep records of their efforts of liability management. Since police liability will always be a concern for police agencies, it will be necessary for the people that are tasked with handling police liability incidents to provide some kind of evidence that they are taking steps to manage liability within their agencies. Maintaining records of progress would also be a good way to justify hiring additional staff to help with liability management efforts. And finally, the records could be useful in determining some of the organizational factors that increase the probability that police personnel will be named as defendants in lawsuits.

The Los Angeles Sheriff's Department (LASD) in California provides a good example of how to track and publish the impact of risk managers on liability incidents. In June 1993, Merrick J. Bobb was appointed to be the Special Counsel in the Board of Supervisors. The Special Counsel is responsible for monitoring and reporting the progress of the LASD's efforts to make changes to the use of force against citizens, sensitivity of deputies, and the handling of citizen's complaints filed by citizens against the LASD.

Since October 1993 the semi-annual reports written by Merrick Bobb and his staff have detailed the efforts made by the LASD to improve police services provided to citizens, police accountability, and police professionalism. Each semi-annual report provides detailed information on the number of lawsuits and claims that were filed against the LASD, and also the various programs and training efforts implemented by the LASD to reduce the number of lawsuits and claims involving LASD employees. The report specifically identifies the work of both the risk management and legal advisory unit within the LASD. The semi-annual reports are accessible in paper form, and are also available to the public on the Los Angeles County web site (Los Angeles County, 2003).

 Discussion

The most significant finding presented in this paper is that very few (0.039 percent) of the largest US law enforcement agencies use risk management in their effort to control the frequency and costs associated with liability within their organizations. This finding is surprising given the increase in costs associated with settlements/payouts for police-involved litigation and liability claims over the past few decades. This finding is also surprising given that the nature of police work exposes police officers to risk incidents on a daily basis. In addition, risk management has been identified as a police liability management tool by two agencies that are influential in reform focused on police liability management and exposure to risk, including PRIMA and the International Association of Chiefs of Police (IACP).

There are several factors that could explain why so few US law enforcement agencies use risk management in their liability management efforts. First, there is limited formal training available for risk management that is specifically geared toward law enforcement liability management. Private parties that have had prior professional experience applying risk management practices in both private and public organizations provide most of the risk management training that is currently available. The problem is that these risk management training seminars last anywhere from a few hours up to a few days. To date, there is no

standardized risk management training that results in some kind of certification aimed specifically at law enforcement liability issues. Future research should examine the content of existing risk management training seminars geared specifically toward law enforcement agencies.

A lack of available resources to adopt such positions or programs within police agencies could be another reason that so few police agencies utilize risk management programs. Other law enforcement programs, such as community-oriented policing, have government grants readily available for police agencies that are interested in implementing these kinds of programs. Perhaps risk managers would be more common in police organizations if financial resources were available to them to contribute to the costs of adopting such programs.

A third factor that could contribute to the lack of risk management within US police agencies would be the paucity of available information or literature on the topic. If police scholars and practitioners are not frequently researching and publishing literature on risk management, there is not going to be any type of manual or "how-to" guide that explains the benefits of having such programs, or how to proceed in setting up such programs within police agencies. The lack of information available on risk management in law enforcement is apparent, as the topic is not discussed in most of the leading books on police administration and police management. In the few books that do discuss risk management, it is usually in relation to the specific types of liability incidents related to police work, not in the context of liability management or risk assessment within police organizations. Furthermore, the telephone interviews conducted in the first stage of data collection for this study revealed that police managers, city/attorneys, and other individuals involved in police liability management are interested in learning more about risk management, but recognize that there is limited published information available to them.

This paper can serve as a basic resource for police scholars and practitioners, city/county attorneys, risk managers, and various other city/county agents that are interested in learning about risk management as a way to manage police liability. However, there are several research topics in risk management and law enforcement that should be explored in the future. First, police scholars could evaluate the impact or effectiveness of risk managers on police liability incidents (both the frequency of incidents and monetary losses resulting from those incidents). Evaluation-based studies could be conducted as longitudinal studies in one or a few sites, or a comparison of several sites could be useful in measuring the effectiveness or impact of such programs in police agencies. Second, future research could also explore the reasons why so many of the largest law enforcement agencies in the US do not employ risk managers. This line of research could also include comparisons of the effectiveness of police liability management in law enforcement agencies that use and do not use the expertise of risk managers in liability management. And third, future research could explore how the characteristics of local city government or political culture are associated with the use of risk management by law enforcement agencies. Additional research on this topic is important, as police liability management will continue to be a top priority for police managers in the future.

 # References

Alpert, G. and Fridell, L. (1993), *Police Vehicles and Firearms: Instruments of Deadly Force*, Waveland Press, Prospect Heights, IL.

Alpert, G.P., Kenney, D.J., Dunham, R.G. and Smith, W.C. (2000), *Police Pursuits: What We Know*, Police Executive Research Forum, Washington, DC.

Armitage, G. and Knapman, H. (2003), "Adverse events in drug administration: a literature review," *Journal of Nursing Management*, Vol. 11, pp. 130–41.

Ashley, S. and Pearson, R. (1993), *Fundamentals of Risk Management*, Liability Assessment & Awareness International, Inc., available at: www.laaw.com

Baerger, D.R. (2001), "Risk management with the suicidal patient: lessons from case law," *Professional Psychology: Research and Practice*, Vol. 32, pp. 359–67.

Baltimore Sun (2001), "Jury finds against officer $7 million awarded to estate of teen slain by housing policeman," *Baltimore Sun*, May 30, pp. 1B.

Baxter, T.C. Jr (2003), "Governing the financial or bank holding company: how legal infrastructure can facilitate consolidated risk management," *Current Issues in Economics and Finance* Vol. 9, pp. 1–8.

Bittner, E. (1970), *The Functions of the Police in Modern Society*, National Institute of Mental Health, Washington, DC.

Blalock, J. (1974), *Civil Liability of Law Enforcement Officers*, Charles C. Thomas Publisher, Springfield, IL.

Ceniceros, R. (1998), "Policing their own risks: formal risk management growing in law enforcement," *Business Insurance*, Vol. 32, pp. 10–13.

Conrow, E.H. (2000), *Effective Risk Management: Some Keys to Success*, American Institute of Aeronautics and Astronautics, Inc., Reston, VA.

Crew, R. Jr, Kessler, D. and Fridell, I. (1991), "Changing hot pursuit policy: an empirical assessment of the impact on pursuit behavior," *Evaluation Review* Vol. 18, pp. 678–88.

Crew, R. Jr, Fridell, L. and Pursell, K. (1995), "Probabilities and odds in hot pursuits: a benefit-cost analysis," *Journal of Criminal Justice*, Vol 23, pp. 417–24.

Culliver, C. and Sigler, R. (1995), "Police use of deadly force in Tennessee following *Tennessee v. Garner*," *Journal of Contemporary Criminal Justice*,, Vol 11, pp. 187–95.

del Carmen, R. (1991), *Civil Liabilities in American Policing: A Test for Law Enforcement Personnel*, Prentice-Hall, Inc., Englewood Cliffs, CA.

del Carmen, R.V. and Smith, M.R. (1997), "Police, civil liability, and the law" in Dunham, R.G. and Alpert, G.P. (Eds), *Critical Issues in Policing: Contemporary Readings*, 3rd ed., Waveland Press, Prospect Heights, IL, pp. 225–42.

Dise, J.H. Jr (1995), "School held liable for textbooks selection: the risk of educational malpractice," *School & College*, Vol. 34, pp. 46–8.

Esenberg, R.W. (1992), "Risk management in the public sector," *Risk Management*, Vol. 39, pp. 72–5.

Fyfe, J.J. (1979), "Administrative interventions on police shooting discretion: an empirical examination," *Journal of Police Science and Administration*, Vol. 9, pp. 309–22.

Fyfe, J.J. (1981), "Who shoots? A look at officer race and police shooting," *Journal of Police Science and Administration*, Vol. 9, pp. 367–82.

Gallagher, G.P. (1990a), "The six-layered liability protection system for police," *The Police Chief*, June, pp. 40–4.

Gallagher, G.P. (1990b), "Risk management for police administrators," *The Police Chief*, pp. 18–29, June.

Gallagher, G.P. (1992). *Risk Management Behind the Blue Curtain: A Primer on Law Enforcement Liability*, Public Risk Management Association, Arlington, VA.

Gelman, S.R. (1992), "Risk management through client access to case records," *Social Work*, Vol. 37, pp. 73–80.

Geller, W. and Scott, M. (1992), *Deadly Force: What We Know: A Practitioners Desk Reference on Police-involved Shootings,* Police Executive Research: Forum, Washington, DC.

Harshfield, J.B. (1996), "Liability issues of using volunteers in public schools,", *NASSP Bulletin,* Vol. 80, pp. 61–6.

Heazeltine, H. (1986). "Case study: a risk audit of law enforcement," *Risk Management*, Vol. 10, pp. 60–3.

Ichniowski, T. (1995), "There's not claims crisis now, but new challenges loom," *Architectural Record*, Vol. 183, pp. 22–9.

International Association of Chiefs of Police. (2003), "IACP website report" available at: www.theiacp.org.

Kappeler, V.E. (2001), *Critical Issues in Police Civil Liability*, 3rd ed., Waveland Press. Prospect Heights, IL.

Katz, D.M. (1998), "LA cops lop $10M off tort costs," *National Underwriter*, Vol. 102 No. 26, pp. 11–12.

Ladebauche, P. (2001), "Lessons in liability for pediatric nurses," *Pediatric Nursing*, Vol. 27, pp. 581–8.

Lesh, D. (2002), "A blueprint for reducing lawsuits against police," *Public Risk*, Vol. 16, pp. 14–17.

Los Angeles County (2003), "Los Angeles County website" available at: www.co.la.ca.us/bobb.html

Los Angeles Times (2002). "City may pay $2.5 million to woman who lost eye," *Los Angeles Times*, December 17.

Neville, H.G. (1976), "Municipal risk management: an idea whose time has come," *Rough Notes*, Vol. 121, pp. 101–2.

Newell, C., Pollock, J. and Tweedy, J. (1993), "Financial aspects of police liability," International City/County Management Association Baseline Report, International City/County Management Association, Vol. 24, pp. 1–8.

Osborne, B. (2001), "Principles of liability for athletes trainers: managing sport-related concussion," *Journal of Athletic Training*, Vol. 36, pp. 316–22.

Paleologos, E.K. and Lerche, J. (2002), "Option coverage techniques for environmental projects," *Journal of Management in Engineering*, Vol. 18, pp. 3–7.

Pate, A. and Fridell, L. (1993), *Police Use of Force: Official Records, Citizen Complaints, and Legal Consequences*, Police Foundation, Washington, DC.

Pate, A. and Fridell, L. (1995). "Toward the uniform reporting of police use of force results of a national survey," *Criminal Justice Review*, Vol. 20, pp. 123–45.

PRIMAFILE Online. (2000), "Police liability assessment guide" *PRIMAFILE Online*, on file with author.

Reamer, F.G. (1995), "Malpractice claims against social workers; first facts," *Social Work*, Vol. 40, pp. 595–602.

Reaves, B. and Hart, T. (1999), *Law Enforcement Management and Administrative Statistics 1999: Data for Individual State and Local Agencies with 100 or More Officers*, Bureau of Justice Statistics, United States Department of Justice, Washington, DC.

Scogin, F. and Brodsky, S.L. (1991), "Fear of litigation among law enforcement officers," *American Journal of Police*. Vol. 10 No. 1, pp. 41–5.

Sparger, J.R. and Giacopassi, D.J. (1992). "Memphis revisited a reexamination of police shootings after the Garner decision," *Justice Quarterly*, Vol. 9, pp. 211–25.

Vincent, J. (1996), "Managing risk in public services a review of the international literature," *The International Journal of Public Sector Management*, Vol. 9, pp. 57.

Walker, S. (2001), *Police Accountability: The Role of Citizen Oversight*, Wadsworth Publishing, Belmont, CA.

Walker, S. (2003), "The new paradigm of police accountability: the US Justice Department 'pattern or practice' suits in context," *Saint Louis University Public Law Review*. Vol. 22, pp. 3–52.

Washington Post (2003), "Police abuse suits cost Pr. George's $7.9 million" *Washington Post*. January 3, pp. A01.

Wennerbolm. R.W. (1985), "Officer survival recommendations new civil liability concerns" in Wasserman, N. and Phelus, D.G (Eds), *Risk Management Today: A How-to Guide for Local Government*, Public Risk and Insurance Management Association and International City Management Association, Washington, DC.

Wojcik, J. (1994), "Liability lawsuits rise again for LAPD," *Business Insurance*, Vol. 28, pp. 20–2.

Wong, K.S.R. and Rakestraw, K.M. (1991), *The A, B, C's of risk management*, International City/County Management Association, Washington, DC.

Young, P.C. (2000), *Risk Management: A Comprehensive Approach*, International City/County Management Association, Washington DC.

DISCUSSION QUESTIONS

1. What are some of the reasons police agencies have chosen not to adopt risk management as part of their liability management efforts?

2. What are some of the reasons that a few American police agencies have adopted risk management programs?

3. Explain how early warning or early intervention systems can be used as part of a risk management program in police agencies.

READING 18

In this article, Samuel Walker and his colleagues describe how early warning systems are used within police agencies across the United States. They also describe how early warning systems enhance police officer accountability. And finally, this article explains some of the barriers to the adoption and implementation of early warning systems in police agencies.

Early Warning Systems for Police: Concept, History, and Issues

Samuel Walker, Geoffrey P. Alpert, and Dennis J. Kenney

Early warning (EW) systems have emerged as a new law enforcement administrative tool for reducing officer misconduct and enhancing accountability. EW systems are data-driven programs designed to identify officers whose behavior appears to be problematic and to subject those officers to some kind of intervention, usually in the form of counseling or training designed to correct the problematic behavior. Because of their potential for providing timely data on officer performance and giving police managers a framework for correcting unacceptable performance, EW systems are consistent with the new demands for performance evaluation raised by community policing (Alpert & Moore, 1993) and for the effective strategic management of police departments (Moore & Stephens, 1991).

The purpose of this article is to explore the concept of EW systems, the history of EW systems in American policing, and issues related to the program elements of EW systems. It reports the initial findings of a national evaluation of EW systems (Walker, Alpert, & Kenney, 1999). The evaluation involved a mail survey; municipal and county law enforcement agencies serving populations more than 50,000

people; and case studies of EW systems in three large, urban police departments.

The basic concept of EW systems is that law enforcement agencies should use data on problematic officer performance (e.g., citizen complaints, use-of-force incident reports, etc.) to identify those officers who appear to be having recurring problems or apparent problems interacting with citizens. As a retrospective, performance-based approach, an EW system is not designed to prospectively predict officer performance based on officer characteristics (Stix, 1994). An EW system is "early" in the sense that it attempts to identify officers before their performance results in more serious problems (e.g., civil litigation, police-community relations crisis, etc.). An EW system itself does not involve formal discipline (although an officer may be disciplined for particular actions that led to identification by the system); rather, it is an attempt to warn an officer and/or correct his or her behavior. Some EW systems explicitly state that their purpose is to help officers improve their performance (New Orleans Police Department, 1998).

The intervention phase of EW systems generally consists of individual counseling by a supervisor or in a training class. It is informal in the sense that as explained above, it is not defined as a discipline within the terms of the agency's personnel procedures or collective bargaining agreement. Generally, no record of participation in an EW program per se is placed in an officer's personnel file, although the incidents that originally identified the officer (e.g., citizen complaints, use-of-force reports) do remain in the officer's file and can be considered for discipline. A separate record of participation in the EW system is generally maintained by the internal affairs or professional standards unit of the police department.

EW systems have been endorsed by the U.S. Commission on Civil Rights (1981), the International Association of Chiefs of Police (1989), private consultants on police internal investigations (Reiter, 1998), and the 1996 Justice Department conference on Police Integrity (U.S. Department of Justice, 1997a). An EW system is incorporated in the consent decree negotiated by the Civil Rights Division of the Justice Department and the City of Pittsburgh (*United States v. City of Pittsburgh,* 1997). By 1999, an estimated 27% of all municipal and county law enforcement agencies serving populations greater than 50,000 had EW systems in place, and another 12% were planning to implement one (Walker et al., 1999).

The EW concept represents a departure from traditional police practice in which departments have been seen as punishment oriented, with innumerable rules and regulations that can be used against an officer (Westley, 1970, pp. 24–30) but with few procedures for rewarding good conduct. Alpert and Moore (1993, p. 129) argued that under community policing, police departments must develop performance measures that identify and reward "exemplary service to the community and the reduction or diffusion of violence," actions that have been essentially ignored by traditional performance evaluation systems. Apart from employee assistance programs designed to address substance abuse or family problems, police departments have done relatively little in a formal way to correct problem behavior. In the private sector, by comparison, personnel issues have become defined in terms of human resource development, with a specific emphasis on helping employees correct behavior that is not consistent with the organization's goals (Mathis & Jackson, 1999, p. 102).

The Problem Police Officer

Empirical Evidence

Interest in EW increased in response to growing evidence that in most law enforcement agencies, a small percentage of officers are responsible for a disproportionate share of citizen complaints, use-of-force incidents, or other problematic incidents. The phenomenon of the "problem officer" who receives a high rate of citizen complaints was first recognized in the 1970s. Toch, Grant, and Galvin (1975) developed a program in which Oakland, California, police officers with records of use-of-force incidents were counseled by peer officers. Goldstein (1977, p. 171) cited this program in a discussion of the need for identifying officers with a propensity for wrongdoing.

The U.S. Commission on Civil Rights (1981) published data indicating that a small group of Houston, Texas, police officers received extraordinarily high numbers of citizen complaints. In the aftermath of the 1991 Rodney King incident in Los Angeles, the Christopher Commission (1991) identified 44 problem officers in the Los Angeles Police Department (LAPD) with extremely high rates of citizen complaints. The commission commented that these officers were "readily identifiable" on the basis of existing LAPD records.

Investigative journalists have found the problem officer phenomenon in other police departments. In Kansas City, Missouri, 2% of the sworn officers were responsible for 50% of citizen complaints ("Kansas City Police," 1991). In Boston, 11% were responsible for 61.5% of complaints ("Wave of Abuse," 1992), and in Washington, D.C., a small number of officers were responsible for a large proportion of multiple discharge of firearms ("DC Police," 1998). With the exception of Kansas City, all of these reports found that police managers ignored patterns of repeated involvement in critical incidents and failed to take any kind of action against the officers with the worst records.

From Informal Knowledge to Management Tool

The concept of EW is consistent with the basic principles of personnel management and human resource development (Mathis & Jackson, 1999; Poole & Warner, 1998). Employers recruit, select, and train employees to serve effectively the goals and objectives of the organization. Effective personnel management assumes that employee performance is assessed and evaluated on a regular basis, and that the organization collects and analyzes performance data relevant for that purpose. It is also assumed that on an informal basis, each employee's immediate supervisor is familiar with the quantity and quality of the subordinate's performance (Mathis & Jackson, 1999, p. 102). Presumptively, systematic performance evaluations and supervisors' firsthand knowledge of employees is sufficient to identify those employees whose performance does not meet the organization's standards (Redeker, 1989).

Identifying problematic employees is a legitimate management goal as organizations seek to enhance the quality of the service they deliver and maintain positive relations with clients and customers. This is particularly important in human service organizations such as the police that routinely engage in a high level of interactions with citizen-clients (Bittner, 1970; Reiss, 1971). Alpert and Moore (1993, p. 130) argued that the goals of community policing require police departments to develop personnel evaluation systems that reward officers who avoid using force without justification (and by implication identify and properly discipline those who use excessive force).

Police personnel evaluation systems, however, have generally failed to provide meaningful assessments of performance. As Westley (1970, pp. 24–30) noted, police departments have been punishment oriented, with few formal programs for helping individual officers improve performance and little organizational focus on officers with recurring performance problems. Standard in-service training programs are generally directed at all sworn officers and not just officers with special performance problems. Employee assistance programs (EAPs), meanwhile, are generally

voluntary and directed toward officers with marital, psychological, or substance abuse problems, not officers with on-the-street performance problems (Ayers, 1990; Finn & Tomz, 1997). Thus, for example, an overly aggressive officer who receives a high rate of citizen complaints but has no off-the-job personal problems would fall outside the scope of standard EAPs.

A review of police personnel evaluation systems nearly 25 years ago found that they had serious deficiencies. In particular, the formal categories for performance assessment were vague and global (e.g., "initiative," "dependability") (Landy, 1977). A more recent report, reflecting the concerns of community policing, rendered an equally critical assessment. Oettmeier and Wycoff (1997) concluded that "most performance evaluations currently used by police agencies do not reflect the work officers do" (p. 5). In particular, they fail to address the most critical aspects of police work, notably the exercise of discretion under conditions of uncertainty and stress, with the most important decisions involving the use of deadly or physical force. The neglect of these aspects of the job is particularly important because of the unique role of the police (Bittner, 1970). And, as Alpert and Moore (1993) argued, community policing creates the need for even more comprehensive and sophisticated performance evaluation systems.

The historic failure to address problem officers is particularly notable because, as Goldstein (1977) observed, those officers "are well known to their supervisors, the top administrators, to their peers, and to the residents of the areas in which they work"; nonetheless, "little is done to alter their conduct" (p. 171). Insofar as law enforcement agencies took any kind of action, anecdotal evidence suggests that they "dumped" problem officers on racial minority neighborhoods (Reiss, 1971, pp. 167–168).

Two recent examples illustrate the extent to which some contemporary police departments have failed to collect, much less utilize, relevant data on potential officer misconduct. Prior to the 1997 consent decree with the U.S. Department of Justice (*United States* v. *City of Pittsburgh*, 1997), the Pittsburgh Police Bureau did not have a comprehensive department-wide database on citizen complaints, use-of-force incidents, and other problematic behavior. Similarly, prior to 1999, the LAPD did not ensure that all citizen complaints brought to the attention of the department were in fact officially recorded and eventually forwarded to a centralized office (Office of the Inspector General, 1997).

 ## History of the EW Concept

Emergence of the Concept

The first EW programs appear to have developed independently in a number of different departments in the late 1970s. The process of development was ad hoc and experimental, without the guidance of recommended or model programs. And because these initial programs appear to have been short lived, few records survive. Several departments began using indicators of activities to monitor officers' involvement in citizen contacts that involved use of deadly force and in response to growing public concern about that particular issue (Milton, Halleck, Lardner, & Albrecht, 1977). These initial approaches included review of arrest reports and identification of situations that involved the use of force by officers.

In Oakland, for example, records were kept on individual officers to determine whether any officers showed early signs of trouble. In addition, computers were used to determine whether any officer characteristics such as age, length of service, or education correlated with their use of force (Milton et al., 1977, p. 96). Toch et al. (1975) developed an experimental peer-counseling program directed toward officers with recurring performance problems.

In New York City, information on each officer's use of force, use of firearms, complaints, discipline, sick leave, and off-duty employment was used to determine whether that officer needed further monitoring or intervention. Officers who entered the information into the files were responsible for noting trends in behavior or activities and reporting them to a supervising officer (Milton et al., 1977, p. 96).

The Kansas City Police Department, meanwhile, cross-referenced officers with their supervisors "on the

theory that particular supervisory officers may be tolerating abusive behavior" (Milton et al., 1977, p. 97). The department also participated in a Police Foundation experiment in peer counseling designed to improve the performance of officers with recurring problems (Pate, McCullough, Bowers, & Ferrara, 1976).

The concept of EW systems received its first official endorsement in 1981 by the U.S. Commission on Civil Rights in its report *Who Is Guarding the Guardians?* The report was based largely on hearings with regard to police misconduct in Philadelphia, Memphis, and Houston. It included data on Houston police officers indicating that a small percentage of officers received a disproportionate share of complaints. The commission recommended that police departments create and utilize early warning systems, arguing that

> the careful maintenance of records based on written complaints is essential to indicate officers who are frequently the subject of complaints or who demonstrate identifiable patterns of inappropriate behavior. Some jurisdictions have "early warning" information systems for monitoring officers' involvement in violent confrontations. The police departments studied routinely ignore early warning signs. (U.S. Commission on Civil Rights, 1981, p. 159)

 ## The First Permanent EW Systems

The initial experiments with EW systems appear to have been short lived, and none of those identified by Milton et al. (1977) have survived to the present. The first EW systems known to have been maintained from their inception to the present were created in the Miami Police Department and in the Miami-Dade Police Department in the late 1970s.

Miami Police Department

The Miami Police Department became concerned with its officers' behavior that generated citizen complaints in 1979, in response to a major police–community relations crisis (Porter, 1984; U.S. Commission on Civil Rights, 1984). In a May 29, 1979, memorandum to the chief, the commander of the internal security unit suggested an EW system based on the principle of organizational development. That is, the development of the organization's capacity to provide better service to the public and to reduce both citizen complaints and the perception of poor service required attention to those officers and/or department practices that created real or perceived problems with the public. This memorandum proposed a "cyclical model where the problem is diagnosed, outside professionals are consulted, strategies are developed, programs are implemented and evaluated, and results are fed back to begin the cycle again" (Ross, 1979, p. 1).

To demonstrate his idea, Commander John S. Ross had identified a list of officers, by assignment, who had two or more citizen complaints during a 2-year period (1976–1978). Ross also compiled a list of officers who had received five or more civilian complaints during that period. Armed with those data and the internal security monthly activity reports, Ross computed some interesting statistics. He found that the average number of complaints filed against a Miami police officer was .65 per year and 1.3 complaints for 2 years. He found that 5% of the officers accounted for 25% of all complaints. He noted, "If this group were suddenly removed from our department, our complaint picture could be reduced by as much as one-fourth. Obviously, this group should warrant some special attention, if we are to reduce our complaint incidence" (Ross, 1979, pp. 2–3).

At the midpoint in the study, the average Miami police officer was 32 years old with 8 years of service. The officers with five or more complaints were 27.5 years old with 4.2 years of service. The officers with the most complaints were disproportionately assigned to midnight shift. The complaint of excessive force made up 9% of complaints against all officers, but for those with two to four complaints, the complaint of excessive force made up 13% of complaints, and for those with five or more complaints, the figure increased to 16%. A similar relationship was found with complaints for harassment.

Ross (1979) suggested that commanders and supervisors should be systematically provided with information "that can be used to identify problem officers" (p. 7). He also noted that off-duty employment, including rock concerts, wrestling matches, and football games, generates a high number of citizen complaints. He reasoned that fatigue may "heighten an officer's opportunity to react in an aggressive manner" (p. 10). Ross suggested that the department should respond to these officers before they become involved in self-destructive activities or develop a trend of violating departmental orders. His proposal included more intensive supervision, counseling by outside professionals, and training in tactics and strategies. Ross (1979) concluded,

> The problem will not vanish, but it can be reduced through constant attention. The solutions will not be cheap, they will be time consuming, and may be difficult to implement. However, the potential is there to make a significant impact on the citizen complaint's [sic] against police officers. (p. 12)

The Miami EW system evolved into one of the more comprehensive approaches to monitoring police officers in the United States. Most important, it currently uses a broader range of performance indicators than other EW systems, many of which rely solely on citizen complaints as performance indicators (Walker et al., 1999). As officers are identified by the system, their supervisors are notified by official memorandum. The supervisor is then responsible for meeting with the officer and determining whether he or she needs any assistance, counseling, training, or other intervention.

The Miami EW system uses four categories of behavior as selection criteria for identifying officers (Departmental Order 2, Chap. 8). These data, which are routinely collected by the department and entered into a department-wide database, include the following:

1. Complaints—A list of all officers with five or more complaints, with a finding of sustained or inconclusive, for the previous 2 years

2. Control of persons (use of force)—A list of all officers involved as principals in five or more control-of-persons incidents for the previous 2 years

3. Reprimands—A list of all employees with five or more reprimands for the previous 2 years

4. Discharge of firearms—A list of all officers with three or more discharges of firearms within the previous five years.

An officer who is identified by the EW system is subject to a performance review by his or her supervisor. The internal affairs unit provides the supervisor with a report of each incident that caused the officer to be placed on the EW system. The supervisor evaluates these reports to determine whether the officer's behavior was consistent with professional standards (e.g., use of force justified by the circumstances, citizen complaint without merit) or whether there are behavior problems (e.g., unjustified use of force) that require attention. In this respect, the EW system is discretionary and not mandatory. Not all officers identified by the performance indicators will be referred for intervention.

In the case of officers requiring formal intervention, the supervisor then writes a memorandum recommending one of the following: reassignment, retraining, transfer, referral to an employee assistance program, fitness-for-duty evaluation, or dismissal pursuant to civil service rules and regulations. The supervisor's memorandum goes to the commander of internal affairs through the chain of command. Each reviewing supervisor must agree or disagree with the recommendation. It is important to note that, unlike some other EW systems, a number of supervisors are involved in decisions related to potential problem officers, with the result that these decisions represent a consensus of opinion.

Miami-Dade Police Department

Several events took place in the Miami area during the late 1970s that created problems for police officers in the Miami-Dade Police Department, formerly the Metro-Dade Police Department, and Dade County Sheriff's Office. The beating of an African American school teacher and the beating death of another African American (insurance agent Arthur McDuffie) by Miami-Dade officers aggravated existing racial tensions in the Miami area. On May 17, 1980, the four officers accused of the death of McDuffie were acquitted by an all-White jury in Tampa. Upon notification of the verdict, 3 days of riots broke out that resulted in civilian deaths and millions of dollars in property damage (Porter, 1984; U.S. Commission on Civil Rights, 1982).

As a result of the problems, the Dade County Commission enacted local legislation that made public the internal investigations conducted by the Miami-Dade Police Department. In addition, an employee profile system was adopted to track formally all complaints, use-of-force incidents, commendations, discipline, and disposition of all internal investigations. As an offshoot of the employee profile system, the Miami-Dade Police Department implemented the early identification system (EIS) under the supervision of the Internal Review Bureau. This system was created because early signs of potential problems are often not apparent to officers and may be missed by some supervisors. It is not clear what role the city of Miami's EW system had in the development of the system for the Metro-Dade Police Department.

In 1981, a system of quarterly and annual EIS reports was instituted. Quarterly reports listed officers who had received two or more complaints that had been investigated and closed, or who were involved in three or more use-of-force incidents during a 3-month reporting period. Annual reports listed employees who had been identified in two or more quarterly reports. The requirement that complaints be investigated and closed before they would qualify to be included in the quarterly report created a timing problem, because many complaints would take months before they were investigated and closed. Because of this problem, monthly reports were issued in 1992, which listed employees who had received two or more complaints during the past 60 days (regardless of disposition). It is these monthly reports that have identified officers with the most recent complaints or behavioral concerns. Major Dan Flynn (n.d., p. 2) reported that

> patterns of certain kinds of officer behavior, such as serious disputes with citizens and/or co-workers, or an above-average rate of using force, can be very predictive of more serious stress-related episodes to follow. Even though not all complaints and disputes are the fault of the involved officer, a process that enables a review of those events is invaluable. It makes it possible to reach officers who may be experiencing an escalating level of stress, before it gets out of hand and results in serious misconduct.

The monthly, quarterly, and annual reports are disseminated to the supervisors of the listed officers. The information on the list is "utilized by supervisors as a resource to determine if job stress or performance problems exist. They are designed as a resource in evaluating and guiding an employee's job performance and conduct" (Charette, n.d., p. 5). The information included in these reports is used by supervisors as one resource about an officer's performance and in conjunction with other information to provide a comprehensive picture of that officer's performance.

The immediate supervisor of any officer identified by the system receives a report on that officer. The supervisor then discusses the report with the officer and determines what further action is needed. The options include no further action or referral to departmental or outside programs, including psychological services, stress abatement programs, and specialized training programs. In 1981, 150 employees were identified in the two initial reports. In 1982, 46 employees were identified in all four quarterly reports. This decline is due to a number of factors, including the improved recruitment and selection procedures in the agency, not just the EIS. Between 1981 and 1992, departmental strength increased approximately 96%, but complaints remained at an average of approximately 300 per year.

Charette (n.d.) concluded his report by noting: "A department's ability to monitor and control its employees [sic] conduct in a formalized tracking system, instills confidence in the employees, the organization, and the public it serves" (p. 12).

 ## Issues Related to EW Systems

The national evaluation of EW systems found that they are complex administrative tools, with a number of different goals, program elements, and potential impacts (Walker et al., 1999). There is presently no consensus of opinion among professionals with regard to any of these issues. EW systems are also high-maintenance operations requiring careful planning and a high level of ongoing administrative attention. The following section discusses the various issues related to the development and ongoing administration of EW systems.

Program Goals

EW systems are widely understood to be directed toward so-called problem officers, with the goal of reducing on-the-street police misconduct (U.S. Commission on Civil Rights, 1981). The national evaluation, however, found that the goals of EW systems must be understood in broader terms. This interpretation follows developments in private sector employment where human resource development is seen as operating at three levels: individual, group, and organization (Poole & Warner, 1998, p. 93). Consistent with that approach, law enforcement EW systems can be understood to have separate program goals related to individual officers, supervisors, and departments as a whole.

Individual Officers

EW systems are directed in part toward individual rank-and-file officers. The anticipated impact on an individual officer involves learning theory, deterrence theory, or some combination of the two.

Many EW systems are officially conceptualized as a means of helping officers. The New Orleans Professional Performance Enhancement Program (PPEP), for example, explicitly states that it is designed to help and not punish officers. The intervention phase includes a stress reduction component and a training session designed to help officers understand how to handle potentially volatile situations without incurring citizen complaints. In this respect, the anticipated impact of EW systems on officers may be characterized in terms of a learning effect.

At the same time, an implicit assumption of EW systems is that they will deter future misconduct. That is, the intervention phase will communicate to subject officers the threat of punishment in the future if their present behavior continues (Zimring & Hawkins, 1973). There is also an implicit assumption that an EW system will have some general deterrent effect on officers not subject to the system. The system theoretically communicates the threat of punishment should their performance warrant placement on the EW system.

In at least one observed police department, the EW system had a labeling effect, and officers were observed to refer to themselves as "bad boys" and to the program as "bad boys school" and "politeness school" (Walker et al., 1999). Thus, one of the dangers of EW systems is that through a labeling process (Schur, 1972), they will reinforce undesirable attitudes (and perhaps undesirable performance) among subject officers.

Deterrence theorists point out that deterrence is a communication system and that research to date has not adequately explored the extent to which a threat of punishment is perceived by its intended audience (Nagin, 1998). The same problem applies to EW systems, whether conceptualized in terms of deterrence, learning, or labeling. Thus, it is possible that some officers will be readily deterred by an EW system, some will learn from the counseling or training they receive, and some will not be affected by either process. By the same token, some officers may embrace the label of bad boy whereas others will not.

The national evaluation found that EW systems in three sites are effective in reducing citizen complaints and use-of-force reports among officers subject to intervention. The data are reported in Walker et al. (1999).

Supervisors

EW systems also have some impact on supervisors. This goal was explicitly acknowledged in two of the sites in the national evaluation (Miami-Dade and New Orleans), although in different ways, but not in the third (Minneapolis, Minnesota). The New Orleans PPEP requires the supervisor of a subject officer to monitor that individual for 6 months and to file performance evaluations every 2 weeks. Thus, the system has a formal mechanism for holding supervisors accountable for their behavior. New Orleans officials responsible for the PPEP expressed their belief that some supervisors would aggressively urge subject officers to improve their performance because further indicators of poor performance would reflect badly on them (Walker et al., 1999).

In Miami-Dade, several officials associated with the EW system explained that it "keeps things from slipping through the cracks." That is, the formal requirements of the program help ensure that a supervisor will pay closer than normal attention to an officer who is having performance problems and recognize that without such a safeguard the necessary attention may be lost in the rush of normal day-to-day work. The Minneapolis EW system paid little explicit attention to the behavior of supervisors (but see the subsequent changes in the program discussed below).

The potential impact of EW systems addresses an important issue in police management. Moore and Stephens (1991, p. 92) argued that one "particularly troubling deficiency" of traditional police management has been the lack of systems for monitoring the performance of supervisors. EW systems offer one potential remedy for that deficiency by defining specific activities related to holding officers under their command accountable. As is the case with the impact of EW systems on individual officers, however, there are a number of important but unresolved issues related to the impact of an EW system on supervisors. It is not known whether a formal monitoring process has a positive effect on supervisors or whether it is counterproductive because of the paperwork demands and a perceived intrusion into a supervisor's autonomy.

Departments

EW systems also have some impact on the organizations in which they function. Organizational development is seen as one of the key goals of human resource management (Mathis & Jackson, 1999, pp. 98–102; Poole & Warner, 1998, p. 93). The national evaluation, however, found that this was the least well-articulated aspect of EW systems. In theory, an EW system improves the overall quality of police service to the extent that it effects improvements in the behavior of individual officers. At the same time, to the extent that an EW system changes the behavior of supervisors, it has some broader impact on the department. Finally, to an unknown extent, the existence of an EW system communicates a general message about a department's values, indicating that misconduct will not be tolerated. From this perspective, an EW system can be conceptualized as one means of controlling police department use of authority in the service of a comprehensive strategic management of police departments (Moore & Stephens, 1991).

With respect to organizations, the national evaluation found that instead of affecting organizations, EW systems are more likely to be affected by the organization in which they operate. At one extreme, an EW system is not likely to be effective in a police department that has no serious commitment to accountability and integrity and where serious forms of misconduct are not punished. In this context, the EW system may well become little more than a formal bureaucratic procedure, empty of meaningful content. The potential contributions of an EW system will simply be overwhelmed by the failure of the department to investigate alleged misconduct and discipline officers appropriately. It is also possible that a poorly managed EW system will generate hostility and cynicism among officers to the extent that it harms the larger organizational environment (Omaha Police Union, 1992).

At the other end of the continuum, an EW system is most likely to be effective in a department that has high standards of accountability and, as a part of that commitment, has in place a personnel data system that captures the relevant data on police officer performance. In one of the sites in the national evaluation (Miami-Dade), the EW system was found to be simply one part of a larger personnel data system that, in turn, is part of a broader commitment to accountability. In this context, the EW system functions as a management tool that converts the data into a usable form.

The vast majority of police departments undoubtedly fall somewhere in the middle of this continuum. In many of those instances, the EW system has the potential for helping to change the organizational culture and enhancing standards of accountability. Investigating the impact of EW systems on organizations was not part of the design of the national evaluation, and no systematic data on this issue exist (Walker et al., 1999). Further research is needed on this subject.

Program Components

EW systems consist of three basic components: selection criteria, intervention, and post-intervention monitoring. The national evaluation found considerable variation in each of these components. There is also at present no consensus of opinion among law enforcement specialists as to the ideal components of an EW system.

Selection Criteria

EW systems operate on the basis of a set of formal criteria for identifying problem officers and selecting them for intervention. The national evaluation found considerable variation in the selection criteria currently being used and a lack of consensus within the law enforcement community with regard to the appropriate set of criteria.

Some EW systems rely solely on citizen complaints (e.g., Minneapolis), whereas others rely on a broad range of performance indicators (e.g., Miami-Dade and New Orleans). The indicators include but are not limited to official use-of-force reports, involvement in civil litigation, and violations of administrative rules (e.g., neglect of duty).

The use of multiple indicators provides a broader base of information about an officer's performance compared with reliance on citizen complaints alone. Citizen complaints are highly underreported (Walker & Graham, 1998) and therefore are unlikely to lead to the identification of officers whose behavior legitimately requires intervention. In a number of law enforcement agencies, citizen complaints are received by an independent citizen oversight agency (Walker, 2000). In these jurisdictions, it is not necessarily the case that the law enforcement agency receives timely or complete reports on all complaints filed.

Multiple indicators are more likely to identify officers whose performance is genuinely problematic and in need of some official intervention. Departmental use-of-force reports are widely used by EW systems, but their reliability depends on the scope of a department's reporting requirements, the extent of officer compliance with those requirements, and the existence of a data system that ensures that all relevant reports are entered into the EW database.

In sum, there are a number of unresolved issues related to selection criteria, including the best set of performance indicators to be used and the management infrastructure necessary to ensure that the relevant data are entered into the EW system. The national evaluation drew no conclusions with regard to the relative effectiveness of different selection criteria.

Intervention

The intervention phase of an EW system may consist of either an informal counseling session between the officer and his or her immediate supervisor or a training class involving a group of officers (e.g., New Orleans).

With respect to individual counseling sessions, there are a number of issues related to the delivery and content of the counseling. In Minneapolis, for example, the requirement that supervisors document the counseling session was abolished after a few years. In the absence of documentation and close supervision, there is no guarantee that counseling sessions will in fact occur, that supervisors will deliver the appropriate message, or that counseling sessions will be consistent across supervisors. It is entirely possible that some supervisors simply tell their officers not to worry about it, with the result being that the goals of the EW system are undermined. Some EW systems involve higher ranking command officers (e.g., commander of professional standards or internal affairs unit) in the counseling sessions, thereby ensuring consistency and guarding against the delivery of inappropriate messages.

Group training sessions, such as the PPEP classes in New Orleans, have the advantage of ensuring consistency of content. At the same time, however, a group approach inhibits the delivery of the appropriate message to officers who may have very different performance problems. The group approach also runs the risk of creating solidarity among officers in the class, causing them to embrace the bad boys label and reinforcing inappropriate attitudes (Schur, 1972). This effect occurred in at least one known instance (Omaha Police Union, 1992).

The national evaluation was not able to determine whether one form of intervention is more effective than other forms (Walker et al., 1999). More research on this issue is needed.

Postintervention Monitoring

Extreme variations are found among EW systems with respect to postintervention monitoring of subject officers. At one extreme are highly formal systems with considerable required documentation. At the other extreme are highly informal systems with no documentation.

The New Orleans PPEP represents a highly formal system. Subject officers are monitored for 6 months following intervention. Supervisors are required to observe subject officers on duty and to file a signed evaluation of officers' performance every 2 weeks (New Orleans Police Department, 1998). As noted above, this approach has the effect of putting supervisors on notice that their behavior is being monitored. Whether this approach has a positive effect on supervisors or is dysfunctional because of the increased paperwork requirements is not known.

Informal postintervention monitoring approaches rely on supervisors to monitor subject officers' performance and, in the event of further indicators of poor performance (e.g., citizen complaints), take whatever steps they deem necessary. In the absence of documentation or close supervision by higher ranking officers, however, there is no guarantee that the expected informal monitoring will occur.

One of the unresolved issues related to post-intervention monitoring involves striking the proper balance between a formal bureaucratic approach designed to hold supervisors accountable and an informal approach designed to enhance efficiency and flexibility.

Program Administration

The national evaluation found that EW systems are complex, high-maintenance operations, requiring a significant investment by the department in planning, personnel, data collection, and administrative oversight.

The national evaluation found that in two of the sites (Miami-Dade and New Orleans), the EW system was established with considerable initial planning and ongoing administrative attention, whereas in the third site (Minneapolis), the EW system had received little in the way of administrative attention. Yet, in that third site, developments subsequent to the evaluation period indicate that considerable new attention has been given to the EW system and that it has been substantially strengthened as a result.

The administrative demands of an EW system are illustrated by the New Orleans Police Department's PPEP, the most elaborate EW system of the three case studies in the national evaluation. The department's Public Integrity Division employs one full-time (non-sworn) data analyst and uses part of the time of two other full-time employees (one of whom is sworn) for the purpose of data entry. The Miami-Dade EW system, meanwhile, is an integral part of a sophisticated data system on police officer performance that has been developed over the course of two decades.

Conclusion

EW systems have emerged as a popular remedy for police misconduct. The national evaluation has found that EW systems exist in slightly more than one fourth of all law enforcement agencies and are spreading rapidly. The national evaluation also found that EW systems vary considerably in terms of their formal program content, specifically with respect to selection criteria, the nature of the intervention, and post-intervention follow-up. There are many unresolved issues related to these program elements, however, and it is not possible at present to specify any one approach that is the most effective.

EW systems are a potentially important management tool for the control of police officer misconduct and for promoting standards of accountability within a law enforcement agency. The national evaluation found, however, that EW systems are expensive, complex, high-maintenance operations, requiring a significant investment of administrative resources. There is evidence that some EW systems are essentially symbolic gestures with little substantive content. There is also some preliminary evidence that well-run EW systems are effective in reducing the number of citizen complaints and problematic behavior.

An EW system is no panacea for problems of misconduct and a lack of accountability. An EW system should be seen as one part of a system of accountability. In a law enforcement agency without effective accountability measures in place, it is unlikely than an EW system will have much, if any, effect. At the same time, in an agency that has made a commitment to accountability, an EW system can serve as one of several management tools designed to curb misconduct and raise the quality of services delivered to the public.

References

Alpert, G., & Moore, M. H. (1993). Measuring police performance in the new paradigm of policing. In *Performance measures for the criminal justice system.* Washington, DC: Government Printing Office.

Ayers, R. M. (1990). *Preventing law enforcement stress: The organization's role.* Washington, DC: Government Printing Office.

Bittner, E. (1970). *The functions of the police in modern society.* Washington, DC: National Institute of Mental Health.

Charette, B. (n.d.). *Early identification of police brutality and misconduct.* Unpublished manuscript, Metro-Dade Police Department, Miami, FL.

Christopher Commission. (1991). *Report of the independent commission on the Los Angeles* Police Department. Los Angeles: City of Los Angeles.

DC police lead nation in shootings. (1998, November 15). *The Washington Post*, p. 1.

Finn, P., & Tomz, J. E. (1997). *Developing a law enforcement stress program for officers and their families*. Washington, DC: Government Printing Office.

Flynn, D. (n.d.). *Reducing incidents of officer misconduct: An early warning system*. Unpublished manuscript, Metro-Dade Police Department, Miami, FL.

Goldstein, H. (1977). *Policing a free society*. Cambridge, MA: Ballinger.

International Association of Chiefs of Police. (1989). *Building integrity and reducing drug corruption in police departments*. Washington, DC: Government Printing Office.

Kansas City police go after their "bad boys." (1991, September 10). *The New York Times*, p. i.

Landy, F. (1977). *Performance appraisal in police departments*. Washington, DC: Police Foundation.

Mathis, R. L., & Jackson, J. H. (Eds.). (1999). *Human resource management: Essential perspectives*. Cincinnati, OH: Southwestern College.

Milton, C, Halleck, J., Lardner, J., & Albrecht, G. (1977). *Police use of deadly force*. Washington, DC: Police Foundation.

Moore, M. H., & Stephens, D. W (1991). *Beyond command and control: The strategic management of police departments*. Washington, DC: Police Executive Research Forum.

Nagin, D. (1998). Criminal deterrence research at the outset of the twenty-first century. In M. Tonry (Ed.), *Crime and justice: A review of research* (Vol. 23). Chicago: University of Chicago Press.

New Orleans Police Department. (1998). *Professional Performance Enhancement Program (PPEP)*. New Orleans, LA: Author.

Oettmeier, T. N., & Wycoff, M. A. (1997). *Personnel performance evaluations in the community policing context*. Washington, DC: Police Executive Research Forum.

Office of the Inspector General. (1997). *Six-month report*. Los Angeles: Los Angeles Police Commission.

Omaha Police Union. (1992, April). Bad boy/girl class notes shared. *The Shield*, p. 1.

Pate, T., McCullough, J. W, Bowers, R. A., & Ferrara, A. (1976). *Kansas City peer review panel: An evaluation*. Washington, DC: Police Foundation.

Poole, M., & Warner, M. (1998). *The IEBM handbook of human resource management*. London: International Thomson Business Press.

Porter, B. (1984). *The Miami riot of 1980*. Lexington, MA: Lexington Books.

Redeker, J. (1989). *Employee discipline: Policies and practices*. Washington, DC: Bureau of National Affairs.

Reiss, A. J. (1991). *The police and the public*. New Haven, CT: Yale University Press.

Reiter, L. (1998). *Law enforcement administrative investigations* (2nd ed.). Tallahassee, FL: Louo Reiter and Associates.

Ross, J. S. (1979, May 29). Citizen complaints against police officers (Memorandum from Commander John S. Ross to Chief Kennith I. Harms).

Schur, E. (1972). *Labelling deviant behavior*. New York: Harper & Row.

Stix, G. (1994, December). Bad apple picker: Can a neural network help find problem cops? *Scientific American*, 44–45.

Toch, H. J., Grant, D., & Galvin, R. T. (1975). *Agents of change*. New York: John Wiley.

United States v. City of Pittsburgh (W. D. P.A., 1997).

U.S. Commission on Civil Rights. (1981). *Who is guarding the guardians?* Washington, DC: Author.

U.S. Commission on Civil Rights. (1984). *Confronting racial isolation in Miami*. Washington, DC: Government Printing Office.

U.S. Department of Justice. (1997a). *Police integrity: Public service with honor*. Washington, DC: Government Printing Office.

U.S. Department of Justice. (1997b). *Police use of force: Collection of national data*. Washington, DC: Government Printing Office.

Walker, S. (2000). *Police accountability: The role of citizen oversight*. Belmont, CA: Wadsworth.

Walker, S., Alpert, G. P., & Kenney, D. (1999). *Responding to the problem police officer: A national evaluation of early warning systems*. Interim final report, National Institute of Justice.

Walker, S., & Graham, N. (1998). Citizen complaints in response to police misconduct: The results of a victimization survey. *Police Quarterly, 1*, 65–90.

Wave of abuse claims laid to a few officers. (1992, October 4). *The Boston Globe*, p. 1.

Westley, W. A. (1970). *Violence and the police*. Cambridge, MA: MIT Press.

Zimring, R. E., & Hawkins, G. J. (1973). *Deterrence: The legal threat in crime control*. Chicago: University of Chicago Press.

DISCUSSION QUESTIONS

1. Why might some police officers dislike the idea of their agency adopting an early warning system?

2. How do early warning systems help police officers?

3. What are some of the ways that police administrators intervene when police officers are identified by the early warning system after displaying problematic behaviors?

Part III

Police and Society

Citizens' perceptions of the police are partially influenced by the nature of their interaction.

Citizens and the Police

Perceptions and Interactions

- Examine variation in citizens' perceptions of the police.
- Review the relationship between police and citizens over the course of the three eras of policing.
- Explore some of the ways that the police try to improve their relationship with citizens in their communities.

"The police are the public and the public are the police—the police being only members of the public who are paid to give full time attention to duties which are incumbent on every citizen in the interests of community, welfare, and existence." This statement by Sir Robert Peel reflects his belief that the police need to operate under the guise that they are part of the community that they serve. The police–community relationship is important, as it can impact how easy or difficult it is for police officers to conduct their work, and it can also impact the quality of police service that is provided to the public. This section discusses the history of the relationship between police and citizens in the United States, as well as some of the factors that influence citizens' perceptions. A discussion focused on police officers' perceptions of citizens is also included in this section. And finally, this section closes with a discussion of some of the ways that the police use community-based programs to try and improve their relationships with citizens in their communities.

The History of the Police–Citizen Relationship

The relationship between police officers and citizens has evolved significantly over time. Modifications to this complex relationship result from changes in technology, the social and political climate within communities, and changes to the role that police officers have assumed over the course of the history of American policing.

Beginning in the political era, police officers were very involved with citizens in their communities. Kelling and Moore assert that the political influence during this era had both positive and negative consequences.[1] First, the police were very responsive to crime and disorder, as most police officers worked in the same neighborhoods they lived in. This meant that they had a personal stake in keeping crime and disorder under control. The problem was that they would become *too* entrenched in their neighborhoods, which resulted in them becoming involved in corrupt activities. They would also discriminate against people that would wander into the neighborhood but did not actually live in the neighborhood—or to put it another way, strangers were not welcome.[2] Second, their close ties with local political bosses meant that they were expected to provide a variety of social services to the public to keep them happy. Keeping the citizens happy meant that they would likely remain loyal to the politicians that were in charge at that time, and, in turn, this would provide job security for police officers appointed by local politicians.[3] And finally, police officers had plenty of opportunity to have face-to-face contact with citizens, as their primary mode of patrol was on foot. Citizens could request police service by flagging down police officers that were walking the streets in their neighborhood. Even though the lack of technology encouraged face-to-face interaction among police and citizens, it also meant that the police were not as efficient as they could have been with motorized patrol and more sophisticated communication systems.[4]

In the reform era, Kelling and Moore describe the relationship between the police and citizens as professionally remote. The distance between the police and the public was the result of police reform efforts taking place at that time. Specifically, the police were trying to become less involved with local politicians and wanted to show the public that they were professionals by taking a more formal approach to their work.[5] In addition, many police agencies began to get rid of foot patrol and utilize only motorized patrol in an effort to provide faster, more efficient service to the public. The drawback of adopting motorized patrol was that it significantly reduced face-to-face interactions between the two groups, which resulted in tension between them. Citizens could no longer ask police officers for help in person; instead, they had to call central headquarters to request police service. It was during this era that the "thin blue line" emerged between the police and citizens. The thin blue line is an imaginary line that separates police officers from citizens.[6]

And finally, in the community/problem-solving era, the police utilize community-based programs in an attempt to repair the strained relationship that developed during the reform era. Community policing has become a priority for police agencies, as they have tried to create partnerships with local businesses and citizens. Reintroducing foot patrol is a strategy that is used to increase face-to-face interactions between police and citizens.[7] Another way that the police have tried to rebuild their relationship with citizens is to use long-term assignments of police officers in neighborhoods, which allows them to become familiar with the residents. Kelling and Moore assert that the goal of police agencies in this era of policing is to create a more consultative relationship with the public they serve.

Citizens' View of the Police

Every year, Gallup polls Americans from all 50 states regarding their level of confidence in various American institutions. Since 1993, the police have enjoyed a high level of confidence from Americans when compared to other institutions in the United States.[8] Every year since 1993, more than half (50%) of the people participating in this poll reported that they have "a great deal" or "quite a lot" of confidence in the police. From 1993 to 2011, citizens' level of confidence in the police ranged from a low of 52% in 1993 to a high of 64% in 2004 and has averaged 57.89% during this period of time.[9]

Gallup's Confidence in American Institutions poll, 2011*			
	Great Deal/Quite a Lot	**Some**	**Very Little/None**
The military	78	16	3
Small business	64	26	8
The police	56	30	13
The church	48	29	22
Medical system	39	35	26
U.S. Supreme Court	37	41	20
Presidency	35	28	36
Public schools	34	38	27
Criminal justice system	28	42	29
Newspapers	28	40	31
Television news	27	40	32
Banks	23	40	36
Organized labor	21	39	37
Big business	19	41	39
HMOs (health insurance)	19	39	39
Congress	12	40	48

*This information came from Gallup; see http://www.gallup.com/poll/148163/americans-confident-military-least-congress.aspx.

Despite the fact that Gallup polls are criticized for being less than scientifically rigorous, the findings from this poll reflect the findings from empirical studies that focus on citizens' perceptions of the police. For example, in 1998, a study on criminal victimization and perceptions of community safety was conducted by the Bureau of Justice Statistics in 12 cities across the United States. This study revealed that most citizens (80%) across the 12 cities reported that they were either "satisfied" or "very satisfied" with the police.[10] This high level of citizen satisfaction toward the police is not unique to this study. In fact, a high level of citizen satisfaction has been reported each decade dating as far back as the 1960s.[11]

Citizens' perceptions of the police can be measured by using either global questions (the level of general satisfaction with the police) or more specific questions (the level of satisfaction with the police in regard to specific incidents or events).[12] There is evidence that both types of questions result in similar levels of satisfaction toward the police.[13] Research has also shown that global attitudes toward the police can influence perceptions of the police in specific contact situations.[14]

David Easton developed the concepts of diffuse support and specific support in his study of political institutions.[15] Easton defines **diffuse support** as an evaluation of what an organization is or what it represents, while **specific support** is based on citizens' evaluations of an organization's output or performance. When Easton's concepts have been utilized in research focused on citizens' perceptions of the police, most studies have found that specific support for the police is often lower than diffuse support for the police.[16] Robert Kaminski and Eric Jefferis conducted a study of the impact of a televised violent arrest of an African American youth by local police on Cincinnati residents' perception of the police.[17] Easton's theoretical perspective on diffuse and specific support was used to explain the findings of this study. This research revealed that although there were substantial differences among racial/ethnic minority and White citizens' levels of support for the police, most indicators of diffuse support were not influenced by the controversial televised arrest. Regardless of *how* you measure citizens' perceptions of the police, it is important to know that multiple factors can influence people's perceptions and that all of these factors should be considered when studying this topic.

Factors That Influence Citizen Perception of the Police

Research dating back more than four decades has revealed several categories of factors that influence citizen perceptions of the police. These factors include a variety of citizen characteristics, the frequency and type of police–citizen contact, and neighborhood characteristics. Over time, studies have shown that various combinations of these factors influence the way that citizens view the police working in their communities.

Citizen Characteristics

Earlier in this section, it was noted that most citizens (in general) have a positive view of the police. Variations in perceptions of the police emerge when individual characteristics of citizens are closely examined. For example, several studies have revealed a relationship between age and attitudes toward the police. Young people are more likely to report less satisfaction with the police when compared to older people.[18] Young people are more likely to engage in activities that grab the attention of the police, which means that they are also more likely to have contact with the police. Older citizens are concerned with their personal safety, which means that they support the police as a way to help keep their neighborhoods safe.[19] There have been inconsistent findings in the research on differences in perception of the police among men and women. Some studies have found that females have more positive perceptions of the police than males,[20] while other studies have found the opposite.[21] Overall, the findings for this particular citizen characteristic have been mixed.

Factors associated with citizen socioeconomic status also influence their perceptions of the police. Education level, employment status, income, homeownership, and length of time living at their place of residence are some of the ways that citizen socioeconomic status has been measured in past studies. Citizens with lower incomes, lower levels of education, and who rent their homes are likely to view the police more negatively than citizens with higher incomes, higher levels of education, and home ownership.[22] Most research has found that the impact of socioeconomic status on citizen attitudes toward the police is heavily influenced by their race.

A factor that has been most consistently found to influence citizen perceptions of the police is citizen race/ethnicity. Nearly every study on citizen perceptions of the police has found that African American citizens view the police more negatively than White citizens do.[23] The 12 cities study conducted by the Bureau of Justice Statistics found that 90% of White citizens were satisfied with police, while 76% of African American citizens and 78% of citizens in the "other" race/ethnic categories reported satisfaction with the police.[24] One reason that some African American citizens have negative views of the police is because they believe that they are targeted or profiled by the police (racial profiling is discussed in greater detail in Section 11).[25] African American citizens' attitude toward police may also be influenced by conditions in the cities where they live. Wesley Skogan found that African American citizens living in Chicago, Los Angeles, St. Louis, and Philadelphia rated the police more negatively than White citizens did, but found only a few differences in ratings between African American and White citizens in Atlanta and Denver.[26]

Studies show that Hispanic citizens have more positive views of the police when compared to African American citizens but have less favorable views when compared to White citizens.[27] A recent study revealed that Arab Americans have a positive view of the police.[28] Asian citizens have perceptions of the police that most closely resemble those of White citizens.[29] Yuning Wu and her colleagues found that most Chinese immigrants rated the police positively in their performance, effectiveness, integrity, and demeanor.[30] To date, only one study has found racial minorities reporting more positive views of the police compared to White citizens (the "Detroit exception" study). Using telephone survey data from Detroit, James Frank and his colleagues discovered that African American citizens held more favorable attitudes toward the police than did White citizens. These findings suggest that the social and political context of cities matters when it comes to citizen's attitudes toward the police (in this case, African American citizens held many prominent positions in the community, including the local government).[31]

Researchers have found that race effects are less influential when other variables are included in studies. For example, race has less of an impact when studies also include factors related to citizen socio-economic status.[32] Race also becomes less significant in citizens' perceptions of the police when neighborhood characteristics are considered.[33] Robert Sampson and Dawn Bartusch found that African American citizens' views of the police become more similar to those of White citizens when neighborhood economic disadvantage is considered.[34] This study found that in neighborhoods that experience high rates of violent crime, there were no racial differences in regard to attitudes toward the police.

Police–Citizen Contact

Citizen perceptions of the police are also influenced by direct and indirect contact they have with the police.[35] People who have had direct contact with the police are more likely to have negative perceptions of them when compared to citizens that have had no contact.[36] The type of interaction between the two groups is also important. If citizens have direct, positive interactions with the police, this can result in positive views of the police. In contrast, if citizens have direct negative experiences with the police, it could result in negative views of the police.[37] Research suggests, however, that negative interactions with the police could have a much stronger impact than positive interactions.[38]

Perceptions of the police are also influenced by who initiated the contact between these two groups. Citizens who experienced voluntary contact with the police generally report more positive perceptions of the police compared to citizens who experienced police-initiated contact.[39] Frequency of direct contact with the police also influences citizens' perceptions of the police. Citizens that interact with the police frequently are more likely to report negative perceptions of the police compared to people who have less contact.[40] And finally, if police officers are courteous and friendly to citizens during interactions, this is also a strong predictor of citizens' perceptions of the police.[41]

Studies that focus on citizen–police contact are limited by the fact that most citizens in the United States do not have direct contact with the police. A study by the Bureau of Justice Statistics reported that approximately 20% of the citizens that participated in their study had contact with the police at least one time during the previous year.[42] Only 4% of the people reported that they had contact with the police more than one time during the prior year. And in most of those cases, people had contact with the police for either routine traffic stops or when they had requested police service. Since most people never have direct, face-to-face contact with the police, their perceptions of the police can be influenced by other indirect sources of information.

Researchers have begun to examine how indirect contact with the police can shape citizens' perceptions of the police.[43] Indirect contact with the police is also referred to as **vicarious contact**. Vicarious contact has been measured in a variety of ways, including what citizens see during interactions between the police and other people in their neighborhood, what they heard happened to other people when they interacted with the police (from friends, family, neighbors, or the media), and hearing about incidents of police misconduct (from their friends, family, neighbors, or the media).[44]

A recent study found that citizens' perceptions of contact between the police and other people in their neighborhood significantly influenced their perceptions of the police. Ericka Wentz and Kristyn Schlimgen discovered that citizens' perceptions of contact between the police and other people in their neighborhood was the most significant predictor of citizens'

The nature of the interaction between police officers and citizens influences how citizens view them.

perceptions of the police out of all of the variables included in her study.[45] Another study revealed that people who personally witnessed or heard of incidents of police misconduct from other people reported more negative views of the police.[46] Joel Miller and his colleagues examined vicarious police contact by using experiences of family and friends that involved contact with the police. Their study found that negative vicarious contact through family and friends produced a negative effect on individual opinions of the police and that positive vicarious contact did not result in positive opinions.[47]

Media presentation of the police has also been identified as a factor that influences people's perceptions of the police. Sarah Eschholz and her colleagues focused on the effects of reality-based police programs on citizen attitudes toward the police.[48] This study used reality-based programs that show actual footage of law enforcement activities from the perspective of the police. Results indicate that in general, viewers that watched this type of programming reported having confidence in the police. There was a difference in confidence levels of the police when citizen race was considered. Specifically, White viewers showed significant increases in their level of confidence of the police with increased viewing of the reality programs, but there was no change in confidence levels of African American viewers. This finding could be caused by the fact that these reality programs often present a disproportionate number of African Americans as criminals, while the police officers that are presented are usually White. In addition, it is possible that there

The media can influence how citizens view the police in their communities.

was a "floor effect" in which African American viewers already had such a negative view of the police before they watched this type of program that their perceptions could not get any worse after watching these shows.[49]

Research on publicized incidents of police misconduct has revealed that media coverage can have a negative effect on attitudes toward the police;[50] however, some studies have found that the impact of negative media coverage does not appear to be permanent or long lasting.[51] Richard Fox and Robert Van Sickel examined the impact of highly publicized cases involving the police in the 1990s (including the trials of O.J. Simpson, Louise Woodward, William Kennedy Smith, the Menendez brothers, the police officers involved in the beating of the late Rodney King, the impeachment trial of Bill Clinton, and the criminal investigation of the Jon Benet Ramsey case).[52] In four of the five tabloid cases analyzed in this study, the pattern of responses indicated that there was a reduction in citizen confidence levels of the police. The O.J. Simpson trial had the biggest impact out of all five of the tabloid cases, as more than half (62%) of the respondents in the study reported a loss of confidence in the police. When considering the impact of all five tabloid cases combined, 23% of the survey respondents reported a decline in confidence in the police. Despite having some methodological limitations, the results of this study provide some insight into the power of influence that the media has over people's perceptions of the police.[53]

The media are also strong predictors of youth perceptions of the police. In a recent study that surveyed middle school students in the Midwest, it was discovered that kids who listen to music and watch television programs that portray the police in a negative manner were also more likely to report negative perceptions of the police.[54] In addition, when kids heard their parents, peers, and neighbors talk negatively about the police, they were also more likely to have negative perceptions of the police. The findings of this study are important because they suggest that parents can influence their children's view of the world around them (including their perceptions of the police) by monitoring what they say to their children, who their children socialize with, and the type of media that their children consume.

Past studies have shown that both direct and indirect contact variables are important when it comes to factors that shape citizens' perceptions of the police. Recently, however, research has revealed that when neighborhood characteristics are included in studies, the effects of citizen characteristics and police–citizen contact variables are reduced or become insignificant.[55]

Location/Community/Neighborhood Context

The geographic location in which people live has also been identified as an important predictor of citizens' perceptions of the police. People living in suburban areas have better attitudes toward the police than people living in urban areas do.[56] Also, people living in rural areas are more likely to have positive perceptions of the police when compared to people living in urban areas.[57] The article at the end of this section by Stacey Nofziger and L. Susan Williams is a recent study of citizens' perceptions of the police in a rural setting. Like so many other issues related to rural policing, additional research is needed on this topic, as there have only been a few studies of this kind over the last four decades.

Looking more closely at location, researchers have discovered that the characteristics of a neighborhood can influence citizen perceptions of the police. In general, researchers have identified two categories of neighborhood effects: (1) **neighborhood culture** includes the norms, behaviors, and qualities that are unique to a neighborhood, and (2) contextual or **quality-of-life factors** such as actual or perceived levels of crime and disorder in the neighborhood.[58] Studies

Neighborhood culture and quality-of-life factors can influence citizens' perceptions of the police.

that have utilized neighborhood characteristics have revealed that this type of factor can be a strong predictor of citizens' perceptions of the police. Residents living in disadvantaged neighborhoods are less likely to be satisfied with the police than are residents living in neighborhoods that have better socioeconomic conditions.[59] People who perceive their neighborhoods as high-crime areas are also more likely to have negative perceptions of the police.[60] People who are fearful of crime in their neighborhoods more often have negative views of the police when compared to people who feel safe in their neighborhoods.[61] Some of the visual cues that make people feel unsafe in their neighborhood include dilapidated buildings and cars, graffiti, litter in the streets, visible drug sales, people loitering, presence of gangs, and other types of public disorder.[62] The variation of perceptions of the police from one neighborhood to the next is most likely the result of different neighborhoods having different needs and also different expectations of the police.[63]

Researchers have also looked at the impact of police presence in neighborhoods on citizen perceptions of the police. One of the most cited studies that measured citizens' fear of crime and attitudes toward the police is the Kansas City Preventive Patrol study (see Section 8 for details of this experiment). This study found that the level of routine preventive patrol (a measure of police presence) had no influence on citizens' fear of crime or perceptions of the police.[64] In contrast, other studies have found a modest increase in satisfaction with the police and a reduction in citizens' fear of crime when police presence increased in their neighborhoods.[65]

Over time, we have learned that citizens' perceptions of the police are influenced by a wide range of factors. Some of these factors can have an impact on their own (individually), while others become less influential when additional types of factors are considered. It is critical that police administrators take the time to learn about citizens' perceptions of the police, as this will allow them to come up with better strategies to try and build a strong relationship with the communities they serve.

▧ Police View of Citizens

So far we have learned that there are several factors that influence how the public views the police. But what about the police? How do they view the citizens that they encounter while they are on duty? Past research on this topic sheds some light on how police officers viewed citizens before the emergence of community policing in the early 1980s. Many of these landmark studies identify police culture as a source of influence on how police officers interacted with the public during this time.

In 1951, William Westley's pioneering study in Gary, Indiana, was one of the first to examine how the police interact with members of the community.[66] Westley's study provides an understanding of police attitudes toward law-abiding citizens, the "slum dwellers" (the people that the police see as a direct source of the problems that they encounter), and the local media/press. This study highlights the negative perceptions that the police had toward the community. Westley argued that the hostile view of citizens in the community led some officers to use violence when it was not justified. Further, he asserts that the use of violence on citizens by police officers was not only accepted by officers, but in some instances it was expected.

Jerome Skolnick also explored police–citizen encounters in his observational study of the police in "Westville."[67] He first studied the **working personality** of police officers. The working personality is shaped by characteristics of police officers' work environment—specifically, the elements of danger related to the job, being in a position of authority, and working efficiently. These characteristics influence police officers' level of suspicion toward citizens, as well as the use of violence on citizens. Police officers also learn to identify **symbolic assailants**. These are people that the police believe are (or could potentially be) sources of danger to them. Skolnick observed what he described as a tumultuous relationship between the police and various racial/ethnic groups in Westville. In this study, police officers' perceptions of minority citizens were based on stereotypes, which in turn were reflected in the prejudicial manner in which the police would interact with them.

Using direct observation of the police, these two landmark studies identified a complicated relationship between the police and the public at that time. John Van Maanen also conducted a study based on participant observation with the Union Police Department in the 1970s that serves as the basis for his now classic paper titled "The Asshole." After observing Union police officers for 1 year, Van Maanen concluded that their occupational world consists of three categories of citizens: (1) *suspicious persons*—people that the police believe have been involved in criminal activity or are likely to become involved in criminal activity; (2) *assholes*—people that are unwilling to accept the police officer's definition of the situation; and (3) *know-nothings*—people that do not fit into the first two categories and are not police officers; thus, they know nothing about the police and what they do.[68] The type of interaction/exchange that takes place between police officers and citizens is determined by which category police officers place citizens into upon first interacting with them. Van Maanen's study provides another look at how the police viewed citizens on the streets before community policing became part of American policing. The article written by John Crank and Michael Caldero included at the end of this section is a contemporary look at how police officers view themselves as "angels," or guardians of right, while citizens are viewed as assholes.

Early studies of police officer perceptions of the public generally found that the police were highly suspicious of citizens. Or to put it another way, they had an "us" versus "them" worldview that influenced their interactions with the public. But is this how the police view citizens today? Have police officers' perceptions of the public changed? The advent of community policing in the early 1980s is considered a turning point by some in the relationship between the police and the public (Section 2 describes community policing in greater detail).[69] Community policing is centered on the idea that the police should view citizens as their partners. This is in stark contrast to the relationship between the two groups as it was described by Westley, Skolnick, and Van Maanen a decade earlier. It is still unclear how community policing has impacted this relationship, as the research on this subject has produced mixed results (an in-depth look at the research is included at the end of this section).

Recent studies on police perceptions of the public have identified specific factors that influence police officers' behavior toward citizens. For example, using observation-based data, Stephen Mastrofski and his colleagues found that citizens' behavior toward the police (such as citizens having a negative demeanor, physically resisting officers, refusing to obey police commands, and appearing to lack self-control) is the most powerful predictor of whether the police will act disrespectful toward them. Citizen gender/sex (male), age (younger), race/ethnicity (African American and Hispanic), income (lower), and degree of neighborhood disadvantage (lower income) are also important factors that determine how the police will respond to citizens.[70] These research findings suggest that there may only be a slight difference in the way that the police view citizens today compared to the research findings from more than five decades ago.

Some of the most common police operations can cause tension between the police and the public, including arrests, conducting searches, use of force, and routine traffic stops.[71] Police officers are required to enforce laws, maintain order, and manage crime; therefore, when they encounter people that have been involved in illegal activities, the interaction is based on a negative set of circumstances and has a great chance of resulting in some kind of negative outcome (such as a traffic ticket, an arrest, or use of force). Police officers are also called to help crime victims. The basis for this particular interaction is also negative, as someone has been victimized and is likely unhappy about it. The negative aspects of police work can result in police officers having a skewed view of the people that they interact with and can also develop into an "us" versus "them" mentality.[72] This negative view can impact the relationship that the police have with citizens in their communities.

Police officers' skewed perceptions are largely the result of **selective contact** and **selective perception**.[73] Selective contact is when police officers have more frequent contact with the criminal element in society and less contact with law-abiding citizens, which can result in the police viewing all citizens in a negative way. Selective perception is based on the idea that the police, like others in our society, are likely to remember unpleasant encounters with citizens more often than positive encounters.[74] Community-based programs such as PAL (Police Athletic/Activities League)[75] and citizen police academies provide police officers opportunities to interact with the public in a positive manner more frequently than in the past, when such programs did not exist. Despite the lack of research supporting the notion that these programs improve or change police officers perceptions of the public, they do provide more frequent positive interaction between these two groups, which is a good thing.

Consequences of a Strained Police–Citizen Relationship

Several negative consequences can result from a strained relationship between the police and the public. Incidents of police misconduct involving members of the public can result in citizens' questioning the integrity of the police.[76] This is significant because community support influences the legitimacy of American police agencies.[77] Further, if citizens do not trust the police, they will be less likely to contact or provide them with information about criminal activities, thus hindering police officers' ability to effectively manage crime.[78] Social unrest, riots, and protests are also potential results of a strained relationship between the police and the public. Steven Cox and Jack Fitzgerald report that most of the urban riots that occurred in the last half of the century were the result of negative attitudes toward the police resulting from police actions.[79] Research also suggests that a bad relationship between these two groups can result in citizens filing complaints and initiating litigation against police officers and police organizations.[80]

⚔ Improving the Police–Community Relationship

After considering the potential negative outcomes that can result from a fractured police–community relationship, it makes sense that police administrators would want to make changes. The first step in improving this relationship is for police administrators to examine how citizens perceive their organization and the delivery of police services by their officers. This can be accomplished through the use of community surveys. In an effort to help police agencies, the United States Department of Justice created handbooks that outline several ways that police agencies can survey citizens in their communities.[81] Community surveys can be used to assess police officer performance, quality of police services, and (in general) the state of the police–community relationship. Results from community surveys can help police executives select how to best utilize their resources, rank their priorities as an organization, identify problems in their community or individual neighborhoods, and help determine if community policing programs are effective.[82]

Once citizens have been surveyed, police administrators can begin to make changes within their agencies to improve their connection with citizens in their communities. For example, police agencies that have not implemented community-policing programs might want to consider doing so. Specifically, they should explore the use of community and police collaborations and partnerships. It is important to point out, however, that the research on the impact of community policing on police–community relations has produced mixed findings. Some studies have found that community policing significantly improves citizens' perceptions of the police, the image of the police, the perception that officers are concerned about citizens' needs, and the overall quality of police performance.[83] Other researchers have found that community policing does little to generate public support or improve the police–community relationship.[84] One thing that is certain is that community-policing programs offer the police more opportunity to interact with citizens in a positive manner. These opportunities for positive interactions might lessen police officers' selective perception and selective contact involving citizens.

Another way to improve police–community relations is for police administrators to require that all police personnel conduct themselves in a professional and courteous manner when interacting with the public. Police officers that use profanity during their interactions with citizens are often perceived as less friendly and less professional by citizens compared to police officers that do not use profanity.[85] Police administrators need to stress the importance of professionalism to officers, conducting fair and thorough investigations of citizen complaints by internal affairs/professional standards bureaus, and developing strict policies to minimize inappropriate behaviors. In instances in which police officers are not courteous, police agencies need to have transparent practices in place to deal with conflicts involving citizens—specifically the handling of citizen complaints that involve allegations of police misconduct. Verbal discourtesy and the handling of citizen complaints against police officers are discussed in greater detail in Section 12 of this book.

Negative interactions between police officers and racial/ethnic minorities have been discussed in several sections of this book. The relationship between the police and racial/ethnic minorities is at best described as strained in some cities across the United States. A common solution that is often suggested to remedy this problem is to increase diversity within police agencies by hiring more racial/ethnic minority police officers. This is a solution that is endorsed by some police administrators and citizens, and, in theory, sounds like it could work.[86] However, most of the research conducted on this issue has found that increasing the number of minority police officers does *not* improve racial minorities' attitudes toward the police or the relationship between these two groups.[87] It has also been discovered that the percentage of Black officers in a police department has no effect on the rate of citizen complaints filed against police officers.[88] These research findings should not be interpreted to suggest that police agencies should *not* continue to strive toward a more diverse workplace, because diversity is important for all organizations. It is important to understand, however, that increased diversity within police agencies does not result in improved relationships among the police and minority citizens.

There are also changes that can be made outside of police agencies to improve police–community relationships. One way to do this is to tailor police services to meet the varying needs of individual neighborhoods. This will require increased communication between the police and residents living in these neighborhoods. More frequent communication can be facilitated through the use of routine community and police meetings to discuss issues and concerns of citizens.

Some police agencies sponsor **citizen police academies** as a way for citizens to learn more about the

Positive interactions between officers and racial/ethnic minorities can help bridge the gap that exists between these two groups in some cities.

police and how they do their job. Citizen police academies are short programs that are sponsored by municipal and county police agencies that allow citizens the opportunity to learn about the police, how they are trained, and what they do. There is some exploratory research that suggests that these programs are useful as communication tools with the public.[89] It is important to point out that these programs have also been criticized for targeting people that already have a positive view of the police, not the citizens that are most likely to have negative views of them.[90]

Another approach to improving the relationship between the police and the community is the adoption of programs that would target groups that most often have negative perceptions of the police, including youth and minority populations. This would require police agencies to adopt programs that provide opportunities for these groups to have more frequent, positive contact with the police. These programs should be designed such that people can learn about the police and be able to ask questions about the police in order to view them in a more positive way.[91] An example of this includes the use of school resource officers. School resource officers are permanently assigned to middle schools and high schools so that they can maintain a constant, positive presence in youths' lives and have frequent, positive interactions with youth populations. Some police agencies also sponsor annual community picnics that include residents from all neighborhoods (including high-crime and predominately minority neighborhoods). Again, this allows the police and citizens more frequent, positive interactions.

Finally, police agencies should try to cultivate good relationships with their local media.[92] Television and newspaper reporters will develop and present news stories that involve the police with or without their cooperation. One way to provide the media with detailed accounts of police-involved activities is to have police personnel who are trained in media relations.[93] This is especially important in cases in which there has been some allegation of police misconduct. If the police fail to respond to media questions regarding incidents of alleged police misconduct, some citizens could view that as the police trying to be evasive or trying to cover up acts of wrongdoing.[94] Studies have found that publicized incidents of police misconduct can negatively influence citizens' attitudes toward the police.[95] Police agencies should encourage the local media to cover police-sponsored events and programs that show them interacting with the public in a positive manner. To date, the impact of positive media coverage of the police on citizens' perceptions has not been studied, but one can assume that the presentation of the police in a positive manner could not hurt them.

SUMMARY

- Most citizens are satisfied with the police in the United States.
- Citizen characteristics, police–citizen contact, and neighborhood context variables have been used to study citizen's perceptions of the police.
- Police officers sometimes have selective perception in regard to citizens because their contact with citizens is usually under negative circumstances.
- Observation-based data are a good way to study police officers' perceptions of citizens.
- Should police executives decide to try and improve their relationship with their community? Several programs and techniques can help them with this issue.

KEY TERMS

citizen police academy
diffuse support
neighborhood culture
quality-of-life factors

selective contact
selective perception
specific support
symbolic assailant

vicarious contact
working personality

DISCUSSION QUESTIONS

1. Describe the police–citizen relationship over the course of the three eras of policing.

2. Identify a recent controversy involving the police and citizens that you viewed on television. How does the information presented in this section relate to that incident?

3. What are some of the ways that researchers can study police–citizen interactions?

4. What is the relationship like between the police and citizens in your neighborhood? How do you think that this relationship could be improved or changed?

5. Discuss whether the diversification of police agencies improves the relationship between the police and citizens.

WEB RESOURCES

- To learn more about citizens' police academies, go to http://www.nationalcpaa.org/.
- To learn more about projects that have been implemented to enhance police–community relationships, go to http://www.parc.info/projects.chtml.
- To learn more about how community policing plays a role in the relationship between the police and citizens, go to http://www.ncvc.org/ncvc/AGP.Net/Components/documentViewer/Download.aspxnz?DocumentID=45695.

READING 19

The study presented in this paper examines how perceptions of police influence citizens' feelings of safety. Using survey data from a small community, this study revealed that citizen confidence in the police is influenced by positive interactions with the police and by the perception that crime has decreased in the community. Or to put it another way, citizen confidence in the police increases their feelings of personal safety.

Perceptions of Police and Safety in a Small Town

Stacey Nofziger and L. Susan Williams

Police departments face many new challenges in American society. Although crime rates are currently at their lowest point since 1978 (Uniform Crime Reports, 2000, p. 6), significant percentages of the population indicate that they are afraid to walk at night in areas near their own homes (Gallup, 1997), and crime is considered by most of the country to be a "serious social problem" (Ferraro, 1995, p. 2). In addition, police departments face greater scrutiny than ever before with regular reports of corruption (Cohen, 1998; K. Johnson, 1998; Sterngold, 2000; Witkin, 1995) and police brutality or misuse of force (Fyfe, 1988; Morrow, 1991; Roane, 2000). These challenges make it increasingly important to understand the impact of police on local communities.

Since the 1960s, many researchers have attempted to examine the relationship between citizens and local police. Although some studies have focused on the factors that influence the nature of police encounters with citizens (Black & Reiss, 1970; Lundman, Sykes, & Clark, 1978; Piliavin & Briar, 1964; Smith & Visher, 1981), many others have examined the attitudes of citizens toward police (Albrecht & Green, 1977; Boggs & Galliher, 1975; Parker, Onyekwuluje, & Murty, 1995; Peek, Lowe, & Alston, 1981; Sampson & Bartusch, 1999; Stoutland, 2001; Tuch & Weitzer, 1997; Weitzer & Tuch, 1999).

Although the literature on citizen attitudes toward police is fairly extensive, there are two main limitations. First, the majority of past studies have focused on very specific populations. In particular, urban samples of African Americans or comparisons between groups of urban Caucasians and African Americans dominate the literature. Second, the literature on fear of crime and perceptions of community safety, which is arguably an important measure of confidence in police, has largely focused on broader contextual issues such as media influence (Heath & Gilbert, 1996; P. Williams & Dickinson, 1993), the social organizational patterns in the neighborhood (Scott, 2001), or past victimization (Baba & Austin, 1989; Keane, 1995). Such studies have not examined how perceptions of the police may influence feelings of safety in the community.

This study addresses the lack of attention to community-level relationships by examining feelings of safety within a small midwestern community, a largely overlooked and informative context for assessing the impact of police–citizen interaction. We hypothesize that positive perceptions of the police, in the form of confidence in the local police force's ability to enforce laws and solve or prevent crimes, will increase citizens' perception of their town as a safe place.

Perceptions of Police

Inner cities and urban areas more generally have been assumed to have poor relations between citizens and police. Possibly because of this assumption, a great number of studies of attitudes toward police have been conducted in urban areas (Borrero, 2001; Parker et al., 1995; Sampson & Bartusch, 1999; Stoutland, 2001; Weitzer, 2000). In a review of studies on police–community relations, D. Johnson and Gregory (1971) described the urban police as being "perceived as soldiers of a White occupation army in a bitterly hostile country" (p. 95). Even though studies do often find that citizens in these areas have relatively negative perceptions of the police, there are also findings of some positive views. For example, Stoutland (2001) found that residents in high-crime Boston neighborhoods report feeling that the police do not show them respect or share their same priorities but do believe that the police are competent and dependable.

Another reason that urban areas have been the target of a great deal of this research is that such locations are likely to have greater social problems, such as poverty and high crime rates, which may contribute to negative attitudes toward police. Several studies have specifically examined the role that the immediate community environment plays in producing negative attitudes toward police. One consistent finding is that high crime rates produce more negative attitudes toward police (Parker et al., 1995; Priest & Carter, 1999). One proposed explanation of this negative assessment of the police is partly due to the fact that "citizens of high-crime neighborhoods are more likely to view themselves and the police as natural adversaries" (Parker et al., 1995, p. 406).

Although many studies indicate some consistent influences on perceptions of police, several findings demonstrate that not all urban neighborhoods are alike in their attitudes toward police. For example, Weitzer (2000) compared three very diverse Washington D.C. neighborhoods. This study found that the Black middle-class neighborhood had significantly different assessments of police than neighborhoods consisting of middle-class Whites or lower-class Blacks. Such findings imply that different elements related to the context or environment of the neighborhood may be an important predictor of attitudes toward the police.

One very important consideration in studies of police–citizen interactions and attitudes is the racial composition of the neighborhood. Since the 1960s, one of the most consistent findings is that race is a stronger predictor of attitudes than most other demographic characteristics such as sex, age, or socioeconomic status (for a review, see Peek et al., 1981, p. 362). These studies have consistently found that African Americans report less favorable attitudes toward police than Whites (Block, 1971; Gamson & McEvoy, 1970; Hadar & Snortum, 1975; Halim & Stiles, 2001; Hindelang, 1974; Jacob, 1972; Parker et al., 1995; Peek et al., 1981).

However, several studies have found that various contextual factors moderate the effect of race on attitudes. For example, Sampson and Bartusch (1999) found that controlling for the level of economic disadvantage in the neighborhood of residence produced similar attitudes among Caucasian and African American groups. In addition, a variety of demographic and contextual variables have been found to affect attitudes toward police within racial groups. For example, Boggs and Galliher (1975) compared attitudes of African Americans from a household population with a "street population" within one urban police district. These street respondents were 20- to 40-year-old men who had lived in three or more places in the past year and had held no steady job within the past year (Boggs & Galliher, 1975, p. 395). Although both samples reported dissatisfaction with the police, the street respondents were significantly more likely to hold negative views of police service than the household sample. In other studies comparing groups of African Americans, attitudes toward the police have been found to be affected by socioeconomic status (Parker et al., 1995; Peek et al., 1981), neighborhood crime rates (Parker et al., 1995), age (Boggs & Galliher, 1975; Gamson & McEvoy, 1970), sex (Peek et al., 1981), the type of initiation of police contacts (Boggs & Galliher, 1975), and recent publicized events of police brutality (Tuch & Weitzer, 1997).

These studies have contributed to our understanding of what influences perceptions of police in urban settings, but very few studies have examined citizen perceptions in nonurban areas. This type of urban ethnocentrism in research (Weisheit, 1993) ignores the fact that what may be true in urban areas may not generalize to other types of communities. As a whole, the literature on perceptions of police has ignored the possibility that citizens in nonmetropolitan areas may be influenced by different concerns than their urban counterparts. One exception is a study by Albrecht and Green (1977), who compared rural and nonrural areas in Utah. Their findings indicated that urban poor and minority groups have the least favorable attitudes, whereas rural and urban middle-class respondents have the most positive views of the police. However, the urban area in this study encompassed a population of only 70,000, with only about 11% of the population being either Black or Mexican American. Therefore, this "urban" sample was much smaller and had fewer minorities than most studies of attitudes toward police in urban settings. However, the implication that rural community members hold more positive attitudes toward police necessitates further research on nonurban settings.

Perceptions of Safety

Fear of crime has been a topic of research for more than 30 years, but recent scholarship has questioned the ways studies have conceptualized fear. Scott (2001) reviewed this conflict and argued that there is a definite "lack of consensus among scholars of what fear of crime actually means" (p. 30). Examinations of studies of fear reveal that this literature has primarily measured feelings of safety from risk of personal victimization. The most typically used measures do not ask about fear of specific crimes or the likelihood of actual victimization, although they claim they are measuring fear of crime. Some studies have measured perceived crime risk through questions designed to indicate how likely the respondents feel that they will be victimized by a specific type of crime within a given time (Ferraro, 1995; LaGrange & Supancic, 1992). Most commonly, studies have used variations of questions from the National Crime Survey (NCS) or the General Social Survey (GSS) that ask respondents how safe they feel in their neighborhoods or whether there are areas near their home that they consider unsafe at night.

Because the current study is most interested in how perceptions of police influence respondents' assessments of their community safety, measures such as those from the NCS and GSS are examined. However, the literature employing a wide variety of measures of fear and safety is reviewed to determine how past studies may inform the current research.

Studies on fear of crime and feelings of safety have focused on a variety of predictors, including the impact of media representations of crime (Heath & Gilbert, 1996; P. Williams & Dickinson, 1993) and past criminal victimization (Baba & Austin, 1989; Keane, 1995). Neighborhood disorder or general neighborhood environment has also been a regular focus of research on fear of crime (Ackah, 2000; Akers, La Greca, Sellers, & Cochran, 1987; Baba & Austin, 1989; Burby & Rohe, 1989; Chiricos, Hogan, & Gertz, 1997; Lee & Ulmer, 2000; Will & McGrath, 1995; Wilson-Doenges, 2000).

During the 1970s, the main thrust of this work looked at fear of crime as a response to having directly experienced criminal events (Lewis & Salem, 1986, p. 6). It was assumed that those who lived in high crime areas, or who had past experience with criminal victimization, would express high levels of fear about crime. Studies have found that perceived risk of victimization is correlated with official measures of crime in an area (Ferraro, 1995, p. 49). In comparison with those who had not been actual victims of crime, Craig (2000, p. 109) found that elderly respondents who had been victims reported being more fearful of further victimization and also reported lower feelings of safety in their community. However, several studies (Boggs, 1971; Conklin, 1971; Hindelang, 1974) actually found that such past experience was not directly related to fear of criminal victimization. Therefore, other explanations of assessments of risk and fear are needed.

One area of exploration has been to examine the impact of the level of disorganization in a neighborhood on feelings of fear and safety. If the community is not able to exert sufficient control over members, feelings of safety are likely to diminish. Lewis and Salem (1986, p. 99) found that fears of crime increased when "local residents are no longer sure that the behavior of their neighbors will conform" to agreed on acceptable standards of behavior. Minor indications of lack of order in an area, such as noisy neighbors, deteriorated buildings, or trash on the streets, can be seen as a sign that more serious violations of norms are possible (Scott, 2001, p. 46). Although studies on community disorganization have been largely conducted in inner city areas, the relationship between feelings of safety and perceptions of neighbors as trustworthy has also been found in rural areas (Mullen & Donnermeyer, 1985).

From these studies, it is clear that the community environment has a substantial impact on a variety of measures of crime- and victimization-related concerns. One important element of the community is whether the area studied is urban or rural. Several studies in the 1970s compared rates of fear of crime in urban and rural areas and found that rural areas had lower levels of fear. However, more recent studies have produced mixed results (see Weisheit, Falcone, & Wells, 1999, pp. 37–38 for review). In addition, a substantial portion of studies in rural areas is limited to groups that are perceived as particularly vulnerable, such as the elderly (Craig, 2000; Meithe & Lee, 1984; Mullen & Donnermeyer, 1985).

The literature on fear of crime and perceptions of safety provides an extensive list of studies on how the public views crime. However, these studies have largely neglected the impact of citizen perceptions of the local police on feelings of community safety. The very few studies that have included measures of attitudes toward police have been based on Black urban samples (Scott, 2001), have focused only on negative images of police and victimization fears (Baumer, 1985), or have evaluated how changes in police policy affect fear of crime (Skogan, 1994). These studies fail to consider how confidence in police can affect citizens' feelings of safety in their community.

The lack of research on perceptions of police and perceptions of safety in nonurban settings ignores the fact that a substantial portion of the population lives in such communities. Nearly one quarter of the U.S. population resides in rural areas (Bachman, 1992), and 88% of the incorporated communities and townships in the U.S. have fewer than 10,000 residents (Weisheit & Wells, 1996). In addition, the experiences of crime in these types of areas remain substantially different from

urban settings. In spite of data indicating a convergence of self-reported juvenile participation in crime, urban juveniles are still more likely than their rural counterparts to be arrested (L. Williams, 2001), and official crime rates remain significantly higher in urban areas (Uniform Crime Reports, 2000). However, due to the concentration of research in inner city and metropolitan areas, we know almost nothing about perceptions of safety or attitudes toward police in rural and small town populations. The current study addresses this lack in the literature by examining the impact of respondents' perceptions of the police on feelings of safety in a small town in the midwestern United States.

Data and Methods

The Community

The community under investigation in this study is distinct in many ways from samples used by most studies of attitudes toward police or perceptions of safety. The primary difference is that this sample is drawn from a county that consists of 14 small towns or hamlets. According to the 2000 U.S. census, the total population of this county is less than 63,000 and is 84.8% White. The largest minority group is African Americans, who make up only 6.9% of the entire county. These data are fairly consistent with the state figures of 86.1% White and only 5.8% Black but significantly different from national data indicating that only 75.1% of the population is White and more than 12% is Black.

In addition, this county has a high rate of renter-occupied housing units (only 47.2% owner-occupied and 52.8% renter-occupied), compared to 69.2% of the households in the state and 66.2% nationally being owner-occupied. Other indicators of economic well-being also indicate that this county is somewhat lower than state and national figures. The median income of this county is slightly less than $34,000 compared to nearly $36,500 for the state and $37,000 nationally. The poverty rate in the county is also slightly higher than the national rate (14.1% vs. 13.3%), even though the state as a whole only has a poverty rate of 10.9%.

However, somewhat contrary to these indicators, this county has a higher percent of college graduates than either the state or nation (16.7%, 12.3%, and 11.5%, respectively).

One reason for the unique demographic nature of the county is the presence of a state university located in the county seat. The university serves just less than 22,000 students, more than 18,000 of whom are classified as undergraduates. The majority of these students, more than 91%, come from within the state, but only 18.9% originated from within the host county (Fact Book, 2001). The presence of the university most likely influences not only the percentages of renters and college graduates but also the age distribution of the area. The median age of the county is 23.9, but only 18.8% of the population is younger than 18, compared to 26.5% younger than 18 in the state (U.S. Census Bureau, 2003). A common pattern for university students is that they move into the county during their college years and then move away after graduation. Therefore, the high percentage of the county that is made up of university students influences the average age of the county. In this case, 37.5% of the entire county is within the 15- to 24-year-old categories, the ages that are most likely to include college students.

The data for this study were collected as part of a county citizen survey conducted in October 2001 as part of an accrediting process for the local county police department. A total of 301 telephone interviews were completed with two different randomized samples, one of the general population of county residents and one of university students (see L. Williams & Schwery, 2002 for detailed description of collection methods).

The sample mirrors the larger community in many ways. Table 1 provides a breakdown of the sample by key demographic variables. First of all, the percentage of minorities is low, with 78.1% of the sample being White and the largest minority group, Black, only representing 6.6% of the sample. In addition, the sample is very young, with 51.5% reporting that they fall into the lowest age category of 18 to 29. Therefore, this sample is overwhelmingly young and White. Likely due to the youth of the sample, a significant portion also rent their place of residence (50.5%).

Table 1 Demographic Characteristics of Sample

	Frequency	Percentage[a]
Sex		
Male	122	40.5
Female	164	54.5
Race		
White	235	78.1
Black	20	6.6
Hispanic	12	4.0
Asian	5	1.3
Other	13	4.3
Age		
18–29	155	51.5
30–39	38	12.6
40–49	30	10.0
50–59	18	6.0
60–69	20	6.6
70–plus	31	10.3
Rent		
No	134	44.5
Yes	152	50.5

a. The total N of the sample is 301. Percentages do not total to 100 due to missing data.

 Dependent and Control Variables

Perceptions of Police

Perceptions about the police were measured with items designed to indicate the level of confidence that the respondents have in the police. Respondents were asked how well they thought the local police were able to solve and prevent crimes and how well the police would be able to respond to a major crisis (see Table 2 for description of dependent variables). Overall, respondents reported a high level of confidence in the police. For the three items asking about police ability to solve and prevent crime, from 61% to nearly 77% of respondents reported that they were satisfied or very satisfied with the local police. There was slightly less confidence in police ability to handle a major crisis, with only 23.6% indicating the top two levels of confidence and an additional 36.9% indicating that they believed the local police would do "somewhat well" in handling a major crisis.

A total of 195 cases have complete data for the measure of confidence in police.

Perceptions of Safety

The second key dependent variable of this study is how safe the respondents feel in their community. Two items were designed to measure respondents' perceptions of community safety. One measure was included to represent an overall assessment of safety, and a second was designed to determine whether there are any specific locations where the respondent does not feel safe. These two items are similar to those used by the GSS and Gallup Polls to assess fear and safety perceptions in the general population.

Overall, this sample indicates that they perceive their community to be safe. A total of only 16 respondents reported that they did not feel safe in the community. However, 72 reported that there was a specific area in their community where they did not feel safe. Only a very small percentage, a total of 10 respondents or 3.3% of the entire sample, indicated very low feelings of safety by responding that they felt there were unsafe areas and that they did not feel safe in the community. For the purposes of these analyses, the measure of perceived safety was coded as 0 if respondents reported feeling unsafe in the community in general or if they indicated that there was a specific place where they did not feel safe and coded as 1 if they did not fit these limitations. A total of 78 respondents, representing 25.9% of the sample, indicated at least some concern for their safety in the community.

Control Variables

In addition to standard demographic controls, such as age, race, sex, and rent, these analyses also included a number of control variables that have been found to be predictors of either perceptions of police or safety in past studies. Specifically, past direct victimization has been shown to consistently affect levels of fear or perceptions of safety. Therefore, we included in the analyses a measure asking whether the person had been a victim of crime in the past year. A total of 38 respondents, 12.6% of the sample, reported having been a victim in the past year. Another type of variable that could impact perceptions of safety is the assessment of whether crime is increasing or decreasing. A total of 117 respondents (38.9%) reported that they felt that crime has decreased in the community over the past year. Therefore, although direct victimization is low, the majority of the sample does not feel that crime is decreasing.

In predictions of satisfaction or perceptions of police, one very consistent finding is that having contact with police can substantially alter respondents' views. Therefore, several items were included in the analysis to assess the impact of having contact with police and, for those who did have contact, the quality of the contact. A total of 139 respondents had personal contact with a local police officer within the past year. For those who reported such contact, three items were used to assess whether this contact was positive or negative. Respondents were asked whether the officer seemed willing to help in the situation, if he or she was able to provide guidance or a solution to the situation, and if he or she was polite and courteous. The mean for this item (2.43 in a scale from 0 to 3) indicated that most of the respondents who had interacted with the police felt that these experiences were positive.

 Findings

Past studies have determined that perceptions of police are consistently different between different groups, particularly Black and non–Black populations.

The literature on safety also indicates that older respondents and women report higher levels of fear of general victimization or personal crime (Lewis & Salem, 1986; Scott, 2001). To determine whether perceptions of police or safety vary by groups in our sample, both variables were examined for the four major demographic characteristics of sex, race, age, and whether the person rents as a rough proxy for class. Because this sample includes a large percentage of young people, we compare the youngest age category to the rest of the population. Two sets of analyses are presented. The first considers mean differences in the full sample, and the second limits the sample to those who had contact with the police. Based on past research, it is expected that these two samples may have different perceptions of police and community safety.

All four demographic variables of age, sex, race, and "rent" vary significantly for the measure of confidence in police but not for feelings of safety in the full sample. The youngest group has a mean confidence in police that is lower than the rest of the population. Another group that is a substantial portion of this sample is renters. Renting is closely associated with age, but it also could be seen as a proxy for socioeconomic status because those who are unable to afford their own homes must rent. In this sample, those who own their own house have significantly higher confidence in the police. Another group with higher confidence in the police is females. The final demographic variable that is considered in this analysis is the race of the respondent. Although only 15 respondents in the full sample are Black, they do have a significantly lower mean confidence then [sic] the rest of the sample. Collectively, these analyses indicate that there is lower confidence in police among the younger, Black, male population who are renters.

Substantially different findings are produced when examining only those who have had contact with the police in the past year. In these analyses, the only mean difference that retains significance is for the comparison of Blacks to non–Blacks. A total of 11 Black respondents remain in the analysis from the 15 who had complete data for the measure of police confidence. This indicates that there is a high level of contact with police for the

Black respondents in the full sample. Having contact with the police actually lowers confidence among the Black population.

For the full sample, perceptions of the police are significantly correlated to all the variables in the analysis. The highest associations with feelings of confidence in the police are between age and feeling that there is less crime in the community than a year ago. The measure of perceptions of safety, in contrast, is only significantly correlated with two items, feeling that there is less crime in the community and perceptions of police.

Two other correlations that are important, given past research, is that being Black and having had contact with the police are both negatively associated with confidence in police. These findings appear consistent with past research indicating that African Americans have the least favorable attitudes toward police. Studies have also found that if the contact is initiated by the police, the perceptions about the police are more negative (Cheurprakobkit, 2000). Because there is not a clear indication in this study of who initiated police contact, looking at the assessment of the quality of the contact for those who interacted with the police in the past year is important in determining the impact that such contact may have on confidence in police.

Among those who did have contact with police, many similar items to the full sample are significantly correlated. Being Black remains correlated negatively with perceptions of confidence in police, but having had positive contact is very highly and positively correlated with confidence in police. Therefore, the content of the contact, not just contact itself, must be examined. In addition, having had positive experiences during contact with the police is the only item that is significantly correlated with perceptions of safety.

To determine how various demographics and experiences influence perceptions of the local police, two separate OLS regressions were conducted. The first model uses the full sample and includes controls for demographic characteristics, whether the person had been a victim of crime in the past year, their perception of current rates of crime, and whether they had contact with the police in the past year. The second model limits the sample to those who had contact with the police to determine whether the quality of this contact helps to predict perceptions of the police.

In Model 1, only one item, believing that there is less crime now than 1 year ago, significantly predicts perceptions of the police. Those respondents who think that there is less crime have more positive views of the police. However, having had direct contact with police or having been a victim of crime did not significantly mediate these perceptions. In addition, unlike many past studies, being Black did not significantly affect perceptions. However, the lack of statistical significance may well be due to the small number of African Americans in the sample. The coefficient for the effect of being Black is in the expected direction, with Blacks reporting lower confidence in police.

According to this model, being Black and the quality of the contact both predict confidence in police. These results indicate that the context of the contact with police, more than simply having contact, has an important influence on how the public views the police.

For the full sample, perceptions of the police positively and significantly predict feelings of safety, even when controlling for all the other key variables. Therefore, the key hypothesis in this study is supported. The perceptions that the community holds about the police do have a direct impact on feelings of safety. This relationship is found even when controlling for key predictors of feelings of safety such as age and race.

The predicted relationship between confidence in police and feelings of safety is not supported for the analysis that is limited to those who had contact with the police over the past year. The key variables of having had a positive experience with the police and having confidence in the police are both in the expected direction of increasing the likelihood of feeling safe.

Conclusion

Police departments across the United States have faced many challenges over the past four decades. Changes in our economy, schools and families, as well as waves

of intense racial conflict, have complicated the role of the police in our society. Police officers are not just enforcers of law but also serve as educators to children, liaisons between the citizenry and the state, and role models and neighbors in the community. Due to the increasing complexity of policing, understanding how the police are viewed in their communities and how these perceptions impact citizens' views of crime is essential.

By examining the connections between public confidence in police and feelings of safety, this article provides insights that can be useful to informing police policy. First, especially within smaller communities, it appears that the quality of the interaction between officers and citizens, not simply contact, has a significant impact on confidence in police. Although quality of contact is expected to be important in all interactions, it may be that both positive and negative interaction with police in small communities becomes especially salient. In nonurban settings, where informal ties are much closer, such involvement may have a greater impact than in urban communities. Even small changes in interaction characteristics may affect overall perceptions. For example, ensuring that police focus on being "polite" in every encounter with citizens may improve perceptions of police being helpful, whether or not they are actually successful in solving the problem. Such perceptions are very important because having confidence in the local police also substantially improves the perceptions of how safe the community is, regardless of whether the citizens have ever had contact with the police. Therefore, improving confidence in the local police is one way of ultimately improving the sense of safety within the community.

The overwhelming trend in this study is that the public have a great deal of confidence in the police and do feel safe in their community. There are several possible interpretations of this finding. First, it is possible that the police in this community are doing a very good job and that this confidence is earned. It is also possible that citizens feel safe because of the relatively low crime rates in this community. This community has a crime index of 56% that of the national average (Chamber of Commerce, 2002). Therefore, this area is relatively free of the crime problems that plague metropolitan areas of the country.

A third possibility is related to the timing of this survey. This survey was conducted between October 13, 2001, and October 26, 2001, just following the terrorist attacks on the World Trade Center and the Pentagon. In this time period, so soon after the September 11 events, there was a high level of nationalism across the country and a great deal of emphasis on the heroic efforts of firefighters and police in New York City. This sense of the nation pulling together to support each other in times of crisis may have generated higher scores on confidence than would have existed prior to September 11. However, it is interesting to note that the lowest levels of confidence were reported for the question asking how well the local police could handle a major crisis. This item was specifically added to the survey after the September 11 events. In spite of the response categories being skewed to indicate confidence in police (only one category allowed the respondent to have a choice of indicating the police would not handle a crisis well), the respondents were more cautious about indicating that the local police would respond "extremely" or "very" well to a major crisis. This could indicate that the community is confident in their police department's ability to handle everyday problems and crimes but that a crisis on the scale of September 11 may be perceived as beyond the capabilities of this small-town police department.

Although this study finds a high level of confidence in police and perceptions of community safety, it does suggest that police departments have an opportunity to improve relations with specific groups. In particular, relations between African Americans and police should be a key focus. Although there were very few African Americans in this sample, there were significant differences between Blacks and non–Blacks in mean levels of confidence in police. Furthermore, Blacks who had recent contact with police were also significantly less likely to indicate that they had confidence in police. Future research should determine variations in how police officers respond to African Americans in ways that could be modified to improve the quality of

contact between these groups, even in relatively small and nonurban populations.

The other key group that should be studied further is the younger population. Because the university plays a key role in this town and because students are a substantial portion of the population, the fact that young people report lower confidence in police may be an indicator that the police department needs to redouble their efforts to generate a more positive relationship with this population.

The importance of how special populations, such as a university, may impact perceptions of police and safety in a community needs to be further explored. Studying how such groups respond to the police can suggest new forms of community involvement or sensitivity training to police departments in such communities.

This study has contributed to understanding how confidence in police is related to perceptions of safety and suggests that communities need to continue efforts to enhance interactions between police and citizens. Increasing the positive experiences that citizens have with local police will not only improve the image of police in the community but also serves to decrease fear of crime. If community members feel more confident of their safety in the community, this may increase involvement in neighborhood activities, thus serving to improve the level of trust and organization within the area and ultimately decreasing further problems of crime.

 References

Ackah, Y. (2000). Fear of crime among an immigrant population in the Washington, DC, metropolitan area. *Journal of Black Studies*, *30*(4), 553–574.

Akers, R. L., La Greca, A. J., Sellers, C., & Cochran, J. (1987). Fear of crime and victimization among the elderly in different types of communities. *Criminology*, *25*, 487–505.

Albrecht, S. L., & Green, M. (1977). Attitudes toward the police and the larger attitude complex: Implications for police–community relationships. *Criminology*, *15*, 67–86.

Baba, Y., & Austin, D. M. (1989). Neighborhood environmental satisfaction, victimization, and social participation as determinants of perceived neighborhood safety. *Environment and Behavior*, *21*, 763–780.

Bachman, R. (1992). Crime in nonmetropolitan America: A national accounting of trends, incidence rates, and idiosyncratic vulnerabilities. *Rural Sociology, 57*(4), 546–555.

Baumer, T. L. (1985). Testing a general model of fear of crime: Data from a national sample. *Journal of Research in Crime and Delinquency, 22*, 239–255.

Black, D. J., & Reiss, A. J. (1970). Police control of juveniles. *American Sociological Review, 35*(1), 63–77.

Block, R. L. (1971). Fear of crime and fear of the police. *Social Problems, 19*, 91–101.

Boggs, S. L. (1971). Formal and informal crime control: An exploratory study of urban, suburban and rural orientations. *Sociological Quarterly, 12*, 319–327.

Boggs, S. L., & Galliher, J. F. (1975). Evaluating the police: A comparison of Black street and household respondents. *Social Problems, 22*, 393–406.

Borrero, M. (2001). The widening mistrust between youth and police. *Families in Society: The Journal of Contemporary Human Services, 82*, 399.

Burby, R. J., &. Rohe, W. M. (1989). Deconcentration of public housing: Effects on residents' satisfaction with their living environments and their fear of crime. *Urban Affairs Quarterly, 25*, 117–141.

Chamber of Commerce. (2002). *Lifestyle*. Retrieved from http://ks-manhattaned.civicplus.com/documents/Site%20Selection%20Data/MarketingLifestyle.pdf

Cheurprakobkit, S. (2000). Police–citizen contact and police performance: Attitudinal differences between Hispanics and non–Hispanics. *Journal of Criminal Justice, 28*, 325–336.

Chiricos, T., Hogan, M., & Gertz, M. (1997). Racial composition of neighborhood and fear of crime. *Criminology, 35*, 107–132.

Cohen, W. (1998, February 2). The feds make a cop drug bust. *U.S. News & World Report*, p. 36.

Conklin, J. (1971). Dimensions of community response to the crime problem. *Social Problems, 18*, 373–385.

Craig, M. D. (2000). *Fear of crime among the elderly: A multi-method study of the small town experience*. New York: Garland.

Fact Book. (2001). *Reports and historical information*. Retrieved from the Kansas State University Web site: http://www.k-state.edu/pa/statinfo/factbook/

Ferraro, K. F. (1995). *Fear of crime: Interpreting victimization risk*. New York: State University of New York Press.

Fyfe, J. J. (1988). Police use of deadly force: Research and reform. *Justice Quarterly, 5*, 165–205.

Gallup, G. H. (1997). *The Gallup poll: Public opinion 1996* (p. 204). Wilmington, DE: Scholarly Resources.

Gamson, W. A., & McEvoy, J. (1970). Police violence and its public support. *Annals of the American Academy of Political and Social Science, 391*, 97–110.

Hadar, I., & Snortum, J. R. (1975). The eye of the beholder: Differential perceptions of police by the police and the public. *Criminal Justice and Behavior, 2*, 37–54.

Halim, S., & Stiles, B. L. (2001). Differential support for police use of force, the death penalty, and perceived harshness of the courts. *Criminal Justice and Behavior, 28*(1), 3–23.

Heath, L., & Gilbert, K. (1996). Mass media and fear of crime. *American Behavioral Scientist, 39*, 378–395.

Hindelang, M. H. (1974). Public opinion regarding crime, criminal justice and related topics. *Journal of Research in Crime and Delinquency, 11*, 106–116.

Jacob, H. (1972). Contact with government agencies: A preliminary analysis of the distribution of government services. *Midwest Journal of Political Science, 16*, 123–146.

Johnson, D., & Gregory, R. J. (1971). Police–community relations in the United States: A review of recent literature and projects. *Journal of Criminal Law, Criminology, and Police Science, 62*, 94–103.

Johnson, K. (1998, January 22). 42 law officers arrested in sting. *USA Today*, p.3

Keane, C. (1995). Victimization and fear: Assessing the role of offender and offence. *Canadian Journal of Criminology, 37*, 431–455.

LaGrange, R. L., & Supancic, M. (1992). Perceived risk and fear of crime. *Journal of Research in Crime and Delinquency, 29*, 311–344.

Lee, M. S., & Ulmer, J. T. (2000). Fear of crime among Korean Americans in Chicago communities. *Criminology, 38*(4), 1173–1204.

Lewis, D. A., & Salem, G. (1986). *Fear of crime: Incivility and the production of a social problem*. New Brunswick, NJ: Transaction Books.

Lundman, R. J., Sykes, R. E., & Clark, J. P. (1978). Police control of juveniles: A replication. *Journal of Research in Crime and Delinquency, 15*, 74–91.

Meithe, T. D., & Lee, G. R. (1984). Fear of crime among older people: A reassessment of the predictive power of crime-related factors. *Sociological Quarterly, 25*, 397–415.

Morrow, L. (1991, April 1). Rough justice. *Time*, pp. 16–17.

Mullen, R. E., & Donnermeyer, J. F. (1985). Age, trust, and perceived safety from crime in rural areas. *The Gerontologist, 25*, 237–242.

Parker, K. D., Onyekwuluje, A. B., & Murty, K. S. (1995). African Americans' attitudes toward the local police: A multivariate analysis. *Journal of Black Studies, 25*, 396–409.

Peek, C. W., Lowe, G. D., & Alston J. P. (1981). Race and attitudes toward local police: Another look. *Journal of Black Studies, 11*, 361–374.

Piliavin, I., & Briar, S. (1964). Police encounters with juveniles. *American Journal of Sociology, 70*(2), 206–214.

Priest, T. B., & Carter, D. B. (1999). Evaluations of police performance in an African American sample. *Journal of Criminal Justice, 27*, 457–465.

Roane, K. R. (2000, February 7). Are police going too far? *U.S. News & World Report*, p. 25.

Sampson, R. J., & Bartusch, D. J. (1999). Legal cynicism and subcultural tolerance of deviance: The neighborhood context of racial differences. *Law and Society Review, 32*, 777–804.

Scott, Y. M. (2001). *Fear of crime among inner-city African Americans*. New York: LFB Scholarly Publishing.

Skogan, W. G. (1994). The impact of community policing on neighborhood residents: A cross-site analysis. In D. P. Rosenbaum (Ed.), *The challenge of community policing: Testing the promises* (pp. 167–181). Thousand Oaks, CA: Sage.

Smith, D. A., & Visher, C. A. (1981). Street-level justice: Situational determinants of police arrest decisions. *Social Problems, 29,* 167–177.

Sterngold, J. (2000, February 11). Police corruption inquiry expands in Los Angeles. *New York Times,* p. A16.

Stoutland, S. E. (2001). The multiple dimensions of trust in resident/police relations in Boston. *Journal of Research in Crime and Delinquency, 38,* 226–256.

Tuch, S. A., & Weitzer, R. (1997). The polls—trends: Racial differences in attitudes toward the police. *Public Opinion Quarterly, 61,* 642–663.

Uniform Crime Reports. (2000). *Crime in the United States.* Washington, DC: Federal Bureau of Investigation, U.S. Department of Justice. Retrieved from the FBI Web site: www.fbi.gov/ucr/00cius.htm

U.S. Census Bureau. (2003). *State and county quick facts from Population Estimates, 2000 Census of Population and Housing.* Retrieved from http://quickfacts.census.gov/qfd/ states/20000.html

Weisheit, R. A. (1993). Studying drugs in rural areas: Notes from the field. *Journal of Research in Crime and Delinquency, 30,* 213–232.

Weisheit, R. A., Falcone, D. N., & Wells, L. E. (1999). *Crime and policing in rural and small-town America* (2nd ed.). Prospect Heights, IL: Waveland.

Weisheit, R. A., & Wells, L. E. (1996). Rural crime and justice: Implications for theory and research. *Crime & Delinquency, 42*(3), 379–397.

Weitzer, R. (2000). Racialized policing: Residents' perceptions in three neighborhoods. *Law and Society Review, 34,* 129–155.

Weitzer, R., & Tuch, S. A. (1999). Race, class and perceptions of discrimination by the police. *Crime & Delinquency, 45*(4), 494–508.

Will, J. A., & McGrath, J. H. (1995). Crime, neighborhood perceptions, and the underclass: The relationship between fear of crime and class position. *Journal of Criminal Justice, 23,* 163–176.

Williams, L. S. (2001). City kids and country cousins: Rural and urban youths, deviance, and labor market ties. In R. T. Michael (Ed.), *Social awakening: Adolescent behavior as adulthood approaches* (pp. 379–413). New York: Russell Sage Foundation.

Williams, L. S., & Schwery, P. (2002). *Citizens survey: Technical report for Riley County Police Department.* Manhattan, KS: Riley County Police Department.

Williams, P., & Dickinson, J. (1993). Fear of crime: Read all about it? The relationship between newspaper crime reporting and fear of crime. *British Journal of Criminology, 33,* 33–56.

Wilson-Doenges, G. (2000). An exploration of sense of community and fear of crime in gated communities. *Environment and Behavior, 32,* 597–612.

Witkin, G. (1995, September 11). When the bad guys are cops. *Newsweek,* pp. 20–22.

DISCUSSION QUESTIONS

1. What are some of the factors that influence how citizens view the police?

2. How could police executives use the findings from this study to improve citizens' perceptions of the police?

3. Why is it important to conduct a study of this nature in a small rural setting as opposed to a large urban area?

READING 20

In this article, the authors explain how the police view themselves as "angels" and protectors despite the fact that some of them use questionable ways to conduct their work. In contrast, the police identify the people that they encounter as "assholes" because they are requiring the police to spend their time on them when they could be using it some other way. The process by which the police identify citizens as assholes is also discussed in this article.

Angels and Assholes: The Construction of Police Morality

John Crank and Michael Caldero

We both deal with the evil in life—but the difference is, with priests, there's a big distancing from evil. Priests only hear about it in the confessional and the office. For the priest, it loses about nine-tenths of its impact and its, its *wham*.

But with the police officers, with their experience of evil, there's an immediacy. They stand in it. They touch it . . . they taste it . . . they smell it . . . they hear it . . . they have to handle it. The priest only knows about evil intellectually; the cop knows it in his gut (Fletcher, 1991:5).

I n his vocabulary of good and evil, a priest accustomed to working with the police describes similarities between his and their work. Though police may describe their work in grittier terms than such eloquent abstractions of good and evil, the sense of righteousness is present and clearly visible to those who work with and around them.

By morality, I mean that police see themselves as representatives of a higher morality embodied in a blend of American traditionalism, patriotism, and religion. As moral agents, police view themselves as guardians whose responsibility is not simply to make arrests but to roust out society's trouble-makers (Sykes, 1986). They perceive themselves to be a superior class (Hunt & Magenau, 1993), or as Bouza notes (1990:17), people "on the side of angels." Morality is the sentiment that transforms cops' territories to dominions.

Cops' morality sometimes carries with it a judgment of citizens as different and sometimes childlike. Klein provides an example of an encounter that begins with a challenge to the authority of the police, and concludes with the moral authority of the police reasserted. The challenge begins during a normal tour of duty as a desk lieutenant.

One quiet Sunday afternoon I was the desk lieutenant on duty on a West Side precinct when a popinjay of a man of about 60 years of age came bounding into the station and up to the desk. "I want to file a complaint against Patrolman Santos," he announced. Before the man could continue, I interrupted with "Just a moment, please," reached for my scratch pad, and then asked the man for his name and address, noting the time above the date on my pad. The man became livid, and the next few words he uttered were accompanied by an openhanded pounding on the desk that practically made them inaudible. . . . Fearing that the man was working up to a heart attack, I resorted to my most unctuous manner in an effort to calm him. That only seemed to infuriate him more, so I picked up the big 'blotter' that lay before me, brought it down with a resounding crash on the desk, and yelled, "SHUT UP!" at the top of my voice. It worked.

The story continues with a discussion of the alleged brutality carried out by patrolman Santos, in which it is apparent that the patrolman did his utmost to resolve an argument between the complainant, his girlfriend, and a rescuer.

After getting this part of the story, I told Mr. Serene he should be grateful to the officer, not complaining against him, for after all hadn't Santos saved him from a likely beating at the hands of the would-be rescuer?

"Grateful! He took my girl away from me! I called her up this morning, and she says she never wants to see me again! Santos made me look like a bum, hauling me away in the police car!"

The officer informs the complainant that, under the circumstances he saw no basis for a complaint and was not going to file one, further inflaming Mr. Serene.

As Mr. Serene continued, fortissimo grosso, I walked out from behind the desk, grabbed him by the elbow, and propelled him toward the door, repeating firmly, "You will have to leave; you are interrupting and interfering with our duties."

At this point in the encounter, Mr. Serene refuses to accept this outcome, thereby elevating the encounter to a new level.

I will not leave; you can't make me. Where's Santos? He made me lose my girlfriend; I won't leave until you bring him in. I know the law; you can't make me leave.
    I took him up on the last declaration, trying a new tack: "You're absolutely right: I can't make you leave. But if you don't leave, I'll arrest you for causing a disturbance and preventing the orderly business of the precinct." The discourse ended a few minutes later with the arrest of my would-be complainant, who remained adamant to the bitter end, which consisted of an escorted ride in the patrol wagon to Night Court.

The story concludes with the acceptance of the moral authority of the police by the complainant.

Some weeks later, a very chastened Mr. Serene signaled a general release before a magistrate, and received a suspended sentence after apologizing to the sergeant, the detective, the clerical patrolman, Patrolman Santos, and this writer, all of whom had to appear in court before the judge could be convinced that this apparently sane man had caused so much trouble just because he had been embarrassed in front of his lady friend (Klein, 1968:37–38).

This story serves not only as an example of the assertion of police moral authority over a particular individual but of a particular *kind* of individual—the person who complains about the *way* in which police do their work. It is a story with archetypal dimensions—a citizen complain about the behavior of a cop, and a police officer uses both his formal and personal authority to reassert his authority, to make the malcontent acknowledge his uninformed and inappropriate behavior. The behavior of the citizen is shown to be child-like and in temper misdirected. The officer is wholly vindicated.

Morality as Dramaturgy: High-Mindedness

This narrative will, indeed, be one of progress. Starting from beginnings as humble as those of the infant city itself, it will, by an unbroken series of steps, arrive at a breadth and perfection of system commensurate with the modern glories of the American metropolis. This will be the most remarkable feature of the story, that—speaking broadly—there is neither defeat, failure, nor stagnation to be chronicled (Costello, 1972:1).

In these clear, simple terms Costello begins his chronicle of the history of the New York City police department. First written in 1885, 15 years before the turn of the twentieth century, the spirit is non-critical, supportive without question. His 572-page history does not mention the rampant corruption that characterized police practices in New York City in this era, nor does he discuss the electioneering violence carried on by police throughout this period. The mood he conveys is not complicated, not disturbingly realistic. Its ardor is that of rallying around the flag, of the celebration of Fourth-of-July patriotism. It is 100 percent pure high-minded morality.

Morality is sometimes viewed in non-critical, categorical ideas of right and wrong. In its simplest form, the evilness of those in the wrong—the *other*, evil—is under attack by the purity of the *us*, the angels (or vice versa). Possible taint of that which is good is not considered: if good is questioned, the credibility of the complainant is challenged. Fussell (1989), developing the idea of "high-mindedness," captures the clear and wonderful simplicity of high-minded morality in his description of the non-judgmental public declarations of support for the allies in the Second World War:

> If elementary logic—the only kind that war-time could accommodate—required the enemy to be totally evil, it required the allies to be totally good—all of them. The opposition between this black and this white was clear and uncomplicated, untroubled by subtlety or nuance, let alone irony or skepticism (Fussell, 1989:164).

Fussell referred to this uncritical perception of forces of good and evil as the quality of "high-mindedness," that is, a belief in the "successful pursuit of uncomplicated High Purpose." High-mindedness satisfied the wartime need of the home front to justify the slaughter of British troops on behalf of the "good cause." Literary repositories of high-mindedness, he noted, tended to become so uncritical as to be banal in their simplistic acceptance of the virtue of the troops. In the press, the rhetoric of military leaders, and among the civilian population, the moralistic dualism was "total, without shading or complexity" (Fussell, 1989:164)

The thin art of high-minded rhetoric is often present in public descriptions of the police and their adversaries. It typifies the often uncritical way in which the police are presented to the outside world as good guys, waging a war against the bad guys, criminals, or whoever fails to unequivocally support the police. The common-place term "bad guy" reveals this high-mindedness. Lawbreakers are rarely perceived to be ordinary people that have committed bad behavior: they are themselves wicked. The label is harsh and uncompromising.

The high-mindedness that we witness so frequently, coming from legislators, from police executives, from other police representatives, from telephone salesmen for the police charity ball for handicapped children, and from city mayors and council, is dramaturgy. It is a way to gain the support of the police for groups and individuals who want or need their support. That high-minded rhetoric is vapid is not a weakness when one considers its intent. It is pure high-purpose uncomplicated by shades of moral uncertainty—a show of unwavering support.

Morality is more than a dramaturgy of high-mindedness. Morality is also acted out daily by cops on the beat. The expectation that the police will control crime at the societal level is enacted at the individual level as the ability of the police officer to control his or her beat. The beat of an officer is thus transformed into a moral responsibility, the officer's dominion. The notion of beat control is an imperative with a powerful moral thrust. Only an asshole could disagree with how a police officer does his or her job (Van Maanen, 1978).

The moral dimension of police practice is the heart of police culture (Caldero, 1995). Morality is the first theme of solidarity; it is the theme that energizes and makes imperative the aesthetic of coercive territorial control. It justifies all that police do to control their turf, including righteous abuse of suspects and malcontents.

That the moral mandate and the use of coercive violence are inexorably interwoven in the same social fabric—territorial control—is beyond question. The relationship between morality and coercion, however, is perceived differently by the police and their various audiences. There has been an embarrassing though predictable tendency—sometimes less pronounced among the police themselves than among their political advocates—to exploit the high-minded aspects of police morality to justify the misuse of coercion and the abuse of police authority for political gain. The media are guilty of this (Ericson, 1991). Crime re-enactment television "which combine news films of events, re-enactment, voice-over narration by actors and actresses, and grainy video filming with hand-held cameras" profess to simulate reality. In pure high-mindedness we see television shows with titles such as "America's Most Wanted: America Fights Back" and "Cops." Nowhere, of course, is mentioned the moral dilemmas engendered by the use of police violence in a democratic society (Manning, 1995:376). Media constructions are inevitably high-minded, offering simple contrasts between good and evil, black and white (literally and figuratively), us and them.

The police are implicated in the media's narrow vision, of course, in that they tend to manipulate the flow of information to develop the good–bad contrast, revealing particular aspects of their work and obscuring others (Ericson, 1989: 139–140). The police may manipulate the image of their work to fit supportive social sentiments.

> Because society has come to learn that drug use is dangerous; that drug dealers are well organized and heavily armed; that certain deviant segments of society are less deserving of the full protections of the law; and that undefined "others" present a threat to the social and moral order, casting police actions within the context of fighting these groups makes the concrete actions of police, even deviant actions, more acceptable to the audience . . . For the larger public, the victim of police violence must be cast in terms of dangerousness versus the stereotypic depiction of the police as the "thin blue line" between order and anarchy (Kappeler, Sluder & Alpert 1994:106).

Kappeler and his colleagues suggested that police condone the perpetuation of such high-mindedness to obscure a closer inspection of rough and brutal police behavior in police–citizen interactions. High-mindedness, with its hidden stigmatization of classes of citizens as bad guys, justifies over-aggressive police behavior and provides the police with retrospective justification for reprehensible behavior. Who can question heavy-handed police behavior when it's against

some scumbag that probably deserves it anyway and just might think twice next time? Not considered is whether the scumbag actually did something that broke the law, threatened the public peace, whether the law itself should be questioned, or if the police should have free-wheeling authority to use violence at whim.

Police executives, speaking to a public audience and to the troops themselves, frequently implore such high-mindedness. Through moralistic exhortations, they try to show that they're "one of the boys." Consider former Chief (of the Los Angeles Police Department) Daryl Gates' speech to graduating recruits.

> "I have chiefs all over the country with these badge collections," says Daryl Gates, now nearly shouting as he reaches the apex of his address. "And they're forever coming up to me and saying, "Hey! Can I get a badge from the LAPD? It's the only one I don't have." And I tell them proudly, "That's the only one you're not going to get. Unless," says Daryl Gates, pounding the podium, "you wanna go through the Los Angeles Police Academy—If-You-Are-Qualified-Chief! . . . If you are qualified" (Domanick, 1994:17).

Such exhortations are not wholly innocent of underlying motive. That chiefs have limited control over the day-to-day behavior of line officers has been widely cited. As Chief Gates was to discover in early March of 1991, when the first news of the Rodney King police brutality case splashed across the nation's airwaves, the way a chief finds out about what officers are doing is often like the rest of us—through the newspapers. Control over the behavior of line personnel during field duty is meager at best, and the wide influence of police labor representation has given them a means to resist bureaucratic oversight. Chiefs have to display their loyalty to the troops in appropriate ways to insure support:

> The modernizing chief is constrained, therefore, to make at least symbolic obeisance to police solidarity by demonstrating that (he) is

a "cop's" cop, as well as a devotee of systems analysis . . . One of the ways he does this is by emphasis in his dress and bearing—the policeman's chief social tool—the ability to command personal respect (Bordua & Reiss, 1986:34).

 ## Muir: Maturity in the Face of Paradox

In spite of the high-mindedness of police advocates, the police themselves wrestle with a morality substantially more complex than good-guy bad-guy distinctions. Morality is easy in the abstract and in the extreme case, when the bad-guys are known and what they have done is clearly reprehensible. Such post-hoc arm-chair moralizing, however, is no prescription for the bulk of police-citizen encounters. Police-citizen encounters are not characterized by certainty, but uncertainty. Offenders do not advertise their identity to the police. Police-citizen interactions, in which the citizen may also be an offender, are characterized by secrecy, suspicion, and unpredictability.

Most bad guys are not heavyweight predators, but bantam-class misdemeanants and, to use Van Maanen's (1978) terminology, viewed as "assholes" whose culpability lies in an officer's interpretation of vague laws such as interfering with an officer or creating a public nuisance. In such encounters, where and when is the use of coercion morally justified? This is a more difficult question, yet an everyday one that defines much of the police culture. To ponder morality at this level is to begin to understand what the police are about.

Muir (1977) has put forth an eloquent model of police morality. Muir recognized that police confronted situations that did not fall neatly into fixed moral categories. Simple ideas of good and bad provided little direction for officers, who frequently had to balance their moral convictions against the ordinary problems that overwhelmed many of the people with whom they came into contact. Categoric codes of right and wrong, conceptualized as officer safety, might justify the use of deadly force in a confrontation with an armed bank robber, but such principles provided little insight into, for example, more common family beefs, where outcomes were unpredictable and simple ideas of right and wrong provided scant direction on what to do. A more complex idea of morality was needed to help cops think about such encounters.

Muir created a model of police use of force that he called the extortionate transaction. In a brilliant epiphany, he manipulated the model into four incongruities he named the "paradoxes of coercion." The first of these is the paradox of dispossession. "The less one has, the less one has to lose." The paradox in an antagonistic encounter is that the victim with nothing is less vulnerable to coercive threats: "In bargaining, weakness is often strength" (Muir, 1977:38–39).

The second, "the paradox of detachment," states that "the less the victim cares about preserving something, the less the victimizer cares about taking it hostage." This paradox deals with the victim and reveals the problematic nature of unfolding contingencies in an encounter: A victimizer "can't always perceive clearly what value a victim places on his own possessions" (Muir, 1977:40–41).

The third is the paradox of face: "the nastier one's reputation, the less nasty one has to be." This paradox is "elementally psychological. The successful practice of coercion is not to injure but to employ the threat to injure." Paradoxical is that violence is effective, not in its presence, but in its absence. All is threat and bluster. The risk, of course, is that someone will call the bluff. Unfortunately, this can destroy either party: to save face in the calling of a bluff "is to manifest malevolence and respond cruelly and destructively, even if it means risking one's own destruction" (Muir, 1977:42). The paradox is based on the threat of behavior that, if carried out, destroys the extortionate transaction.

The fourth is the paradox of irrationality: "The more delirious the threatener, the more serious the threat: the more delirious the victim, the less serious the threat." The paradox is that "being sensible and appearing so may be a liability in an extortionate world, and not knowing enough to know better may be an asset" (Muir, 1977:43).

Muir observed that these four paradoxes turn conventional ideas of morality on their head. Categoric ideas of right and wrong became problematic. Where is morality to be found, if the simple use of coercion to achieve good ends is thwarted by circumstances that contradict its effectiveness? Morality was to be found in an officer's talent in manipulating coercive authority to achieve good ends, without being overwhelmed by either the passionate pursuit of good ends or by an overwhelming sensitivity that he called perspective and that turned all issues of right and wrong into shifting shades of uncertainty. Passion, he argued, enabled officers to integrate coercion into their morals. The limits of moral passion were in the unprincipled abandonment of ethical concerns of civilized life. Without guilt, he noted there could be no conscience. Officers, he admonished, also needed to develop perspective, "a comprehension of the suffering of each inhabitant of the earth, and a sensitivity of man's yearning for dignity . . ." (Muir, 1977:50). The principled balance of passion and perspective promoted maturity, a moral balance that reflected an officer's ability to reconcile themselves to the use of force without being overwhelmed by its corrupting effects.

The strength of Muir's formulation is linking the four paradoxes to his adaptation of Weber's professional political model. The use of paradox was an eloquent statement of the unpredictability in police-citizen contacts. One of Muir's underlying themes, the ability to envision outcomes precisely the opposite than intended, was a skill that enabled an officer to adapt to the cascading contingencies that characterize many police-citizen encounters. Muir's paradoxes were ironies. They implicitly asked "Is there a way in which what I am doing is going to have precisely the opposite effect than what I intend?"

Morality flows from police officer's abilities to adjust their use of coercion to these paradoxical encounters. Morality, like heaven, is in the details, in the moment-by-moment adjustment to changing circumstances, without losing control in an explosion of coercive force. Morality is played out as gamesmanship, and officers develop strategies to minimize their use of force in order to maximize their effectiveness.

Muir's model is a powerful heuristic, strong medicine for advising future officers about the corrupting effects of power. It is also an admonition for cops to sharpen their senses for ambiguity, misunderstandings, the unpredictable, and the ironic. Ultimately, however, Muir's model fails as a guide for understanding police culture. His model is intended to teach officers how to think about their use of coercion in terms different from simple ideas of right/wrong, moral superiority, good guy/bad guy imagery. But the morality is post hoc, constructed in the replay of events past. When officers approach an ambivalent encounter, their behavior is not conditioned by paradoxical ideas of morality. It is conditioned by edge control, minimizing threats to personal danger, resolving the encounter, avoiding excessive paperwork, and getting on with something more interesting. Police work is more righteous than Muir's typology suggests, as Van Maanen (1978) recognized in the following article on a topic of eternal police interest: what to do about assholes. Muir sought an ideally moral officer, comfortable yet hesitant to use force when other solutions would achieve the same goal. Van Maanen (1978) recognized the ritualistic aspects of the use of force, and gained a better understanding of police culture.

Van Maanen: Righteousness and the Asshole

Van Maanen's classic paper titled "The Asshole" (1978) represented a fundamental rethinking of police use of coercive force. Van Maanen challenged the prevailing belief at the time that police use of force was directed primarily at criminal suspects. In his analysis of police overuse of coercion, he noted that police tended to focus, not on suspects, but on big-mouths, individuals who had not committed a legal violation but who in their behavior displayed resentment about the intrusion of the police into their affairs. His seminal paper captured the moral dimension of the use of coercion—police believe that they exist, in part, to protect the world from assholes.

Assholes, Van Maanen argued, represented a type of individual that organized a great deal of police activity. But a cop could not know who an asshole was until he encountered him or her. The process of labeling someone an asshole emerged in concrete encounters with citizens. The consequence of the label was an increased likelihood of street justice.

Van Maanen argued that the label "asshole" arose in the context of immediate situations, and was tied to observable social action. These situations were everyday police-citizen encounters. The stigmatization process—by which individuals were stigmatized as assholes, had three phases. The first phase was called *affront* and occurred when a police officer's authority was questioned by a citizen. A beer-guzzling citizen in a city park that responds to a police order to pour out the beer by pouring it over the officer's shoes, for example, has initiated a process that carries the risk of being labeled an asshole. This is a critical juncture in the labeling process:

> any further slight to a[n] officer, however subtle, provides sufficient evidence that he may be indeed be dealing with a certifiable asshole, and the situation is in need of rapid clarification (Van Maanen, 1978:229).

The second stage, *clarification*, represents the officer's effort to determine what sort of individual they are dealing with. Clarification involves the resolution of two implicit questions: (1) does the citizen know what they are doing? and (2) could they have acted differently under the circumstances? If the answer to both of these questions was yes, the person risked being labeled sub-human in a scatologically specific way, and became vulnerable to street justice. The third stage, *remedy,* was a typology of police behavioral responses that flowed from the clarification of the incident. Those that were labeled assholes were the most likely recipients of street justice, by which Van Maanen meant placement under questionable arrest, violence, and other rude attention-getting behaviors.

The asshole, Van Maanen argued, was a term that contained a great deal of meaning for the police. The label emerged from the need to maintain control in street encounters, and from a moral imperative to assert the authority of the state when it was questioned. The asshole thus organized much police work, and provided police with an expressive outlet in the absence of so-called "real" police work.

The term *asshole* may be the most ubiquitous celestial body in a cop's gritty cosmology. A major city in the southwest maintains a list of individuals that are perceived to be troublemakers on police calls for service. This list is located in the filing cabinet under the letter "A." Can you guess why? Bouza (1990) also noted the special utility of disorderly conduct statutes for those whom the police have defined as "assholes." One would be hard-pressed to encounter officers from any city in the United States that did not share a common vision of who assholes were.

I have frequently described to students Van Maanen's (1978) vision of the concrete way the label "asshole" arises in street encounters. I have been as frequently chastised by student-cops for failing to understand the term. I now suspect that Van Maanen, while providing an excellent (and titillating) example of ethnography, subtly missed an important aspect of the labeling process. Van Maanen's ideas of the process by which citizens are labeled assholes makes perfect sense, but only under the condition that an officer begins an encounter with a naive or neutral state of mind. Officers, however, don't do this. When they enter into a situation involving a citizen, they already have a pretty good idea about who is an asshole; more than likely they had this idea before they became cops. Nor are police-citizen encounters neutral events; police talk to citizens because something has gone sour and the police want something they think the citizen has; witness testimony or criminal involvement, for example.

Van Maanen, I think, overlooked the way in which police culture reinforces a common moral sensibility in a circular logic of asshole identification and subsequent retaliatory action that verifies that the individual was indeed an asshole. Some cops may wait and see what citizens do before labeling them in some way. However, after thousands of encounters cops have a pretty good read of citizens. Many citizens are labeled assholes before the encounter even begins, and a self-fulfilling logic will verify at some point in the encounter that they indeed are assholes.

Van Maanen suggested that wrongdoers weren't necessarily assholes; they frequently wanted to minimize problems with the police. Yet the police frequently treat lawbreakers roughly, justifying abusive treatment of suspects in terms of police officer safety. Anyone that has witnessed a police bust of a so-called drug house could not conclude that the police were treating inhabitants any kinder than Van Maanen's police treated assholes. What Van Maanen missed is that all lawbreakers are assholes, not just those that disagree with an officer's definition of a situation. Since an offender has violated the law, they have pretty much established that they have a different idea of appropriate behavior than the legal ideal cops are expected to uphold.

As a colleague pointed out, "people don't end up being assholes. Everyone starts out as an asshole, and cops will let some people off the hook, depending on their behavior." In other words, Van Maanen (1978) had the labeling process backwards. Within a few years after joining the force, some cops will see all citizens as assholes. Every situation is confronted with the presumption that an officer is dealing with an asshole. One of Fletcher's confidants captures this sentiment in the following comment:

> People lie to us eight hours a day. Everybody lies to us: offenders, victims, witnesses. They all lie to the police. It gets so bad, you go to a party, somebody comes up to talk to you. You're thinking, "Why is this guy saying this to me? What's his game?" You can't turn it off (Fletcher, 1991:278).

Before long, other police officers are assholes too. You're at roll call and hear your buddy make the same wisecrack for the 1000th time, and you think "Jeez that guy's an asshole." One morning you look at yourself in a mirror and you realize that there's an asshole looking back at you. At this point the term *asshole* becomes so universal that it loses all meaning. Even the angels are assholes. So what.

DISCUSSION QUESTIONS

1. Why do the police view citizens that they encounter as assholes?

2. Explain the process by which the label of *asshole* is applied to citizens.

3. At the very end of the paper, the authors assert that over time, police officers will begin to see other police officers as assholes and not angels. Why does this occur?

Police officers use discretion every time they interact with the public.

Discretion and the Police

Section Highlights

- Discretion allows police officers to make decisions on their own without any input from supervisors.
- Use of discretion is influenced by officer characteristics, situational characteristics, organizational variables, and environmental factors.
- Control mechanisms to regulate officer discretion are found both within and outside of police organizations.

Police officers make decisions every time they interact with the public. Their decision-making involves situations that are relatively minor (such as deciding whether to issue someone a ticket) to situations that involve some level of danger or potential physical harm (such as deciding whether to use a nonlethal weapon on a suspect). These decisions are guided by many formal factors, including laws, officer training, and department policies, along with several informal factors (such as the presence of onlookers or the citizen's demeanor). This section discusses police officer use of discretion and the myriad factors that influence the decisions they make each time they have contact with citizens. In addition, this section examines some of the ways discretion is used by police administrators, including how they allocate department resources and monitor department policies, procedures, and officer training. Abuse of police discretion and mechanisms used to control officer discretion are also discussed.

What Is Discretion?

Discretion is an official action taken by a criminal justice official based on the individual's judgment about the best course of action.[1] It is important to note that discretion involves both the decision to take action and *not* take action. Research conducted by the American Bar Foundation in the 1950s was among the first to reveal that agents working within the criminal justice system actually use discretion. Police discretion, then, is the freedom that police officers have to decide the best course of action each time they interact with the public.[2] William Westley observed discretion as it relates to the police in a study he conducted in 1951. This study was later published as a book, *Violence and the Police: A Sociological Study of Law, Custom and Morality,* in 1970.[3] His study revealed that police officers use both legal and extrale-gal factors when they decide how to respond to citizens (specifically the decision to use violence). Some of these factors are discussed later in this section.

Police officers are often referred to as the gatekeepers of the criminal justice system because they serve as the public's first point of contact with the criminal justice system. It is important to understand that the decisions made by the police impact other parts of the criminal justice system (i.e., courts and corrections). For example, if the police conduct crackdowns on specific types of crime, which results in an increase of arrests, a consequence of their actions could be increased caseloads for the courts and possibly an increase in jail populations. In turn, decisions made by court and corrections officials also impact the police. Thus, if the courts decide to dismiss or give lenient sentences or fines for certain types of crimes (such as prostitution or minor drug offenses) or if the local jail releases people early due to overcrowding, this could presumably impact the likelihood that the police will interact with those individuals again in the future. This shifting of discretionary power is referred to as the **hydraulic effect**. When one agency or one part of the criminal justice system increases its use of discretion, it will impact the other two parts of the system.[4] The illustration above provides a visual example of the hydraulic effect concept: when one agency exercises its discretion (represented by the arrows pointing upward), the other two agencies' use of discretion becomes restricted (represented by the arrows pointing down).

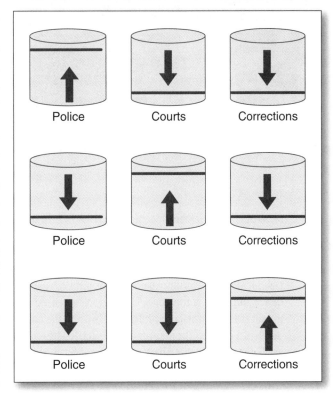

Discretion and the Criminal Justice System Hydraulic Effect

Police   Courts   Corrections

Police   Courts   Corrections

Police   Courts   Corrections

◪ Use of Discretion by Police Administrators

A vast majority of the research on police discretion centers on decision making by patrol-level officers, with little attention paid to police administrators.[5] Police administrators use discretion when they choose to alter or implement department policies, procedures, and officer training. Any alterations made to these three items directly impact how patrol officers conduct their work. So, if police executives choose to implement a stringent policy that outlines when officers can use nonlethal weapons, officers will need to receive training to understand the procedures related to the new "use of nonlethal weapons" policy. If police administrators fail to provide proper training for their officers, they could be held liable if officers improperly use nonlethal weapons and it leads to injury or death (see Section 9 for more on police liability).[6]

When police administrators make changes to department policies and procedures that include specific directives on how officers should respond in certain situations, this can significantly restrict officer discretion. Some argue that it is wise for police administrators to restrict officer discretion in situations that could potentially result in serious injury or death to both officers and citizens.[7] Situations such as automobile pursuits, use of nonlethal defensive tactics, hostage situations, and the use of lethal force are instances in which patrol offi-

Police administrators use discretion when they create, alter, and enforce department policies.

cers could benefit from specific directives to help them make the right decision.[8] When patrol officers make the wrong choice in these high-risk situations, they put themselves and their agencies at risk for liability claims and litigation.[9]

Several negative repercussions can result when patrol officers make the wrong decision during high-risk incidents, including an erosion of public trust and a lack of confidence in the police. The lack of confidence and trust in the police can end in increased complaints filed by citizens, litigation, and acts of social unrest (such as riots and protests). This was the case in Cincinnati, Ohio, after the police-involved shooting death of Timothy Thomas on April 7, 2001. The 4 days of rioting that took place after the Thomas shooting are believed to be the largest urban disorder in the United States since the Los Angeles riots in 1992.[10] The rioting in Cincinnati did not result from the Thomas shooting alone; it was the Thomas shooting coupled with the shooting deaths of 14 other African American men by Cincinnati police officers from 1995 to 2001.[11] This series of shootings not only eroded the public's trust in the Cincinnati Police Department but also fueled accusations that African Americans were the target of racial profiling by local police. It has been estimated that the cost resulting from the Cincinnati riots in 2001 was $13.7 million.[12] The costs are far greater when you consider how difficult it will be to rebuild the relationship between the police and the public in that community.

Police administrators also use discretion when they decide how to allocate resources within their organization. Ideally, these decisions reflect the goals and objectives of each police agency. For instance, police agencies that have incorporated community policing into their organizational goals would likely choose to use their resources on community-based programs, such as the implementation of a citizens' police academy or sponsoring an annual community picnic. Today, it is important for police administrators to use their resources in the most efficient manner, as many agencies across the United States are experiencing shrinking budgets as a result of hard economic times. The impact of economic conditions on the police is discussed further in Section 13.

Police administrators can also influence the quality of discretionary decision making by patrol officers.[13] First, administrators need to set high standards for hiring. If an agency sets high standards for hiring, it can increase the likelihood that its officers will make good decisions. Second, administrators need to ensure that their police officers are trained in a way that helps them make good decisions. This means that training should be available to refresh police officers on issues that they deal with on a frequent basis (such as conducting proper and legal searches and arrests), as well as new issues that arise (such as handling the abuse and illegal sale of prescription drugs). Third, clear and understandable department policies are essential in guiding patrol officers in their decision making. Fourth, administrators need to take corrective action when officers do not follow department policies and procedures (either intentionally or by mistake). This means holding police officers accountable for their decisions and actions. Corrective actions include retraining, additional training, or disciplinary action when warranted (i.e., suspension or termination). And fifth, police administrators should provide feedback to officers after they have made critical decisions (whether they were good or bad decisions). This not only informs officers about the consequences of their decisions but can also serve as an opportunity for police executives to provide positive feedback when officers have made good decisions.[14]

⬗ Use of Discretion by Police Officers

Discretion is used in nearly every facet of police work. Over the last five decades, research has examined police officer use of discretion during traffic stops,[15] arrests,[16] use of deadly force,[17] police pursuits,[18] searches,[19] and the handling of domestic violence cases,[20] to name a few. During this time, four broad categories of factors have been examined to determine their level of influence on police officer behavior: officer characteristics, situational/contextual factors, police organization characteristics, and environmental factors.

Officer characteristics include police officer gender, race/ethnicity, education level, and years of experience. In general, research has revealed that officer characteristics are not a major influence on police officer decision making;[21] however, there are some interesting research findings for each of these individual officer characteristics. Early research found that male officers were more likely to make arrests and use deadly force than female officers,[22] while more current research has revealed that in general, there are few differences between these two groups.[23]

The research is also mixed on officer race/ethnicity and officer behavior. Some studies that have examined the use of deadly force have found that African American officers are overrepresented in shootings involving citizens.[24] It is important to point out that African American officers are more likely to be deployed in high-crime areas where they are more likely to have to use deadly force compared to officers working in areas with less crime. This finding explains why African American police officers are more likely to use force than their White colleagues. The National Research Council concludes that overall, there is no strong evidence that police officer race/ethnicity influences police behavior.[25]

Studies have found mixed results for education level and officer behavior. One study found that college-educated officers are more likely to provide supportive actions to citizens (such as providing comfort and reassurance) than officers without a college education.[26] Other studies have found that officers' education level did not influence their behavior in any way.[27] Mixed research findings have also emerged from the research focused on officers' years of experience and police behavior. Research has found that officers with less experience are likely to make more arrests than officers with more experience.[28] Other studies have found no difference in behavior based on officers' years of experience.[29]

Egon Bittner highlighted the importance of **situational factors/contextual factors** in policing when he stated that "the role of the police is best understood as a mechanism for the distribution of non-negotiable coercive force employed in accordance with the dictates of an intuitive grasp of situational exigencies."[30] Situational factors are those that are unique to each police–citizen encounter.

Research shows that individuals with lower socioeconomic status and that project a negative or hostile demeanor toward the police are more likely to face formal police actions.[31] In contrast, complainants

that are polite to the police often get their wishes for police action when compared to complainants that are uncooperative or rude.[32] Some studies have shown that racial/ethnic minorities and women are treated differently from White and male citizens, although the research findings in these two areas are somewhat mixed.[33] The article by Geoffrey Alpert and his colleagues included at the end of this section examines some of the factors involved with police officer decision making and how these factors contribute to their decision to make traffic stops.

The relational distance between suspects and complainants has also been identified as an important contextual factor. Specifically, formal police action is more likely to occur when the two parties are strangers as opposed to being acquaintances.[34] The location at which police–citizen interactions takes place matters, as police

Studies have revealed that the number of police officers present on the scene influences officer decision making.

officers are more likely to take formal police action if there are other people around observing the interaction.[35] The number of officers present on the scene has also been found to influence police officer behavior. Studies have found that when there are greater numbers of police officers present on scene, there is a greater chance that force will be used by the police.[36] The seriousness of the crime, the presence or use of weapons by suspects, physical attack of police officer by citizens, and the weight of the evidence present on scene have all been found to influence the actions of police officers.[37]

Organizational factors are characteristics found *within* police agencies that can influence officer behavior. For example, the philosophy that a police agency follows can influence officer behavior.[38] If a police agency has incorporated community policing into its organizational goals and objectives, officers working within that agency are likely to respond to citizens in a manner that reflects ideologies associated with community policing.[39] Some research suggests that the size of police agencies also influences officer behavior. Stephen Mastrofski and his colleagues found that officers in large, bureaucratic police agencies are less likely to make arrests for driving under the influence than officers working in small police agencies.[40]

The degree of supervision over police officers, as well as the level of accountability within police agencies, can also impact officer behavior.[41] And finally, the culture found within police agencies can also influence officer behavior. As previously mentioned in Section 4, the police culture is made up of informal rules and norms that are both accepted and practiced by its members.[42] William Westley found evidence of this long ago when he revealed that members of the police culture share the acceptance of the use of violence against citizens. He stated that "the policeman uses violence illegally because such usage is seen as just, acceptable, and, at times, expected by his colleague group and because it constitutes an effective means for solving problems in obtaining status and self-esteem which policemen as policemen have in common."[43] The influence of organizational factors on officer behavior has received the least amount of attention from researchers when compared to the other three categories of factors.

Environmental factors are those that influence officer discretion from sources found *outside* of police agencies. This type of factor can be divided into two categories: community-/neighborhood-level characteristics and direct external efforts to control police behavior.[44] The racial composition, social economic class, and political culture found within neighborhoods influence the likelihood that formal actions will be used by the police (such as arrest and use of force).[45] James Wilson and Barbara Boland defined political culture as the widely shared expectations about how issues will be raised, governmental objectives defined, and the administration of public affairs conducted within a community.[46] Studies have revealed that the police are more likely to take formal police action in neighborhoods that are of low socioeconomic status, predominantly populated with racial/ethnic minority residents, and have a local political culture that supports aggressive policing tactics.[47]

Neighborhoods with high rates of violent crime also influence the behavior of the police.[48] David Klinger created an ecological-based theory focused on the idea that police officers' level of vigor when they exercise formal action will be influenced by characteristics found within the districts in which they work. He suggests that police officers working in districts in which deviance levels are high are less vigorous when taking formal police action. The level of deviance in a district also impacts officers' workloads and resource constraints for dealing with deviance. Police officers' perceptions of crime that is "normal," their perceptions of victim deservedness, and their level of cynicism about the effectiveness of formal social controls also determines the level of vigor used when they take formal police action. More specifically, police officers working in high-crime districts will be cynical about citizens living in the district, view crime that happens in high-crime districts as "normal," perceive crime victims in these neighborhoods as less deserving, and have less time to spend responding to citizens' calls for service.[49] To date, empirical tests of Klinger's theory have only found partial or limited support.[50]

Changes in law and court case rulings can also impact police officer behavior.[51] Court case rulings such as *Miranda v. Arizona* (1966) and *Mapp v. Ohio* (1961) have had a significant impact on when police officers are to inform citizens of their rights and have access to legal representation, as well as their right not to be subjected to unlawful searches and seizures.[52] These two cases, as well as numerous other court cases, have had a significant impact on police officer behavior.

A review of the existing body of research reveals that there are many types of factors that influence the behavior of police officers as they conduct their work. Given the level of complexity involved with police discretion, additional research is needed to fully understand the process by which police officers make decisions.

Abuse/Misuse of Discretion

Despite some of the positive aspects of police discretion (such as making decisions with limited resources in mind and also providing individualized justice for each case), there is also potential for misuse or abuse of discretion. The use of discretion by officers makes it difficult to track their activities, as there is often no paperwork that details why an interaction took place or why officers decided not to take any formal action during interactions with citizens.[53] Because there often is no paper trail, misuse or abuse of discretion is difficult to detect. Some have argued that police officer use of discretion interferes with the due process of law.[54] Also, the argument has been made that it erodes any potential deterrent effect if citizens know that there is a possibility that they will not be punished for breaking the law.[55] There is also the position that police officer discretion can result in differential treatment of citizens based on extralegal factors such as race/ethnicity, socioeconomic status, age, and gender.[56]

Racial profiling is an example of police officer abuse of discretion. In the last decade, racial profiling has been defined in a variety of ways;[57] however, in general, racial profiling is the use of race/ethnicity as a key factor in deciding whether to take formal police action against someone. Racial profiling can occur in any setting in which police and citizen interactions take place. Most research focuses on racial profiling that takes place during routine traffic stops. This is the case because this particular activity allows patrol officers a great deal of discretionary power, and they also have a significant amount of autonomy during this activity.

Deborah Ramirez and her colleagues identified two levels of police discretion related to traffic and pedestrian stops.[58] **Low-discretion stops** are those in which police officers have little discretion *not* to stop a vehicle or person. An example could include a police officer witnessing a car running through a red light at a dangerously high speed. Since the speeding car poses a direct threat to public safety, the police officer is left with few options. This could also include a situation in which someone is spotted carrying a weapon in a threatening manner in a public place. Low-discretion stops comprise between one-quarter and one-third of police stops.[59]

High-discretion stops are those that involve minor infractions of the law. Examples include situations in which drivers take a wide turn or do not properly signal before making the turn or somehow look suspicious to the police. The decision in the 1968 court case of *Terry v. Ohio* resulted in police officers being given the authority to investigate situations in which someone looks suspicious to them; this includes the ability

Accusations of racial profiling often result from police–citizen interactions during traffic stops.

to conduct a *stop and frisk*. A stop and frisk is when the police stop someone they believe is acting suspicious. Once a police officer stops someone for suspicious behavior, he or she has the right to frisk or pat down the person for weapons or contraband and also question that person about his or her behavior.[60] High-discretion stops allow police officers a great deal of discretionary power. This great allowance of discretion opens the door for potential abuse or misuse of police discretion. Thus, if police officers believe stereotypes regarding racial/ethnic minorities and their involvement in criminal behavior, high-discretion stops allow them opportunities to take action based on their personal biases.

There is also the position that racial profiling is simply a myth.[61] Heather MacDonald of the Manhattan Institute asserts that racial profiling is a myth that was created and maintained by anti–law enforcement groups in the United States. She argues that existing research on racial profiling is severely flawed and that it should not be used as evidence that racial profiling exists. Others have made similar statements about racial profiling. In 1999, Tommy Thompson (then governor of Wisconsin) refused to support a budget that included resources to collect demographic data (including race/ethnicity of drivers) on traffic stops because he believed that there is no evidence that racial profiling exists.[62] That statement made by Governor Thompson, along with several other public officials publicly denying that racial profiling exists, prompted David Barlow and Melissa Barlow to conduct a study on this issue in Milwaukee, Wisconsin. Their study is featured in an article included at the end of this section. This study provides a unique look at racial profiling, as it is the first of its kind to ask African American police officers if they have used racial profiling while on duty and if they have ever been victims of racial profiling themselves while off duty.

Controlling Discretion

When the American Bar Foundation study (ABF) revealed that criminal justice agents use discretion in their decision making, police officials were hesitant to admit that this was in fact the case.[63] Before this study, it was assumed that police officers enforced the law in every instance in which they were made aware that a crime had been committed—this is referred to as *full enforcement*. Full enforcement is the belief that laws are enforced by the police consistently and equally all of the time.[64]

The findings of the ABF study sparked debate about whether criminal justice officials should be able to use discretion. In fact, some people have argued that the use of discretion by all criminal justice agents should be stopped, essentially abolishing discretion all together.[65] The use of discretion within the criminal justice system was endorsed by the President's Commission on Law Enforcement and the Administration of Justice in 1967.[66] The support of the President's Commission made it easier for police executives to be more forthcoming about the fact that police officers do not make arrests or write tickets every time that they could legally do so. It is important to point out that if police officers did not exercise discretion and ticketed or arrested every person they encountered, the criminal justice system would collapse due to congestion. Officer discretion impacts the overall workload of the criminal justice system.

Since it is unlikely that the use of discretion will be abolished from the criminal justice system, there are several ways to control officer discretion. Mechanisms found both within and outside of police organizations can influence officers' use of discretion while also increasing the level of accountability for officer decision making.

Controlling Discretion Within Police Organizations

Supervision

The role of field supervisors is to manage the actions of patrol officers. The extent to which they do this has been studied by researchers dating back several decades. Some of the earliest research found that supervisors do influence patrol officers' behavior. William Muir discovered that patrol officers looked at their supervisors as mentors (unfortunately, for both good and bad behaviors).[67] Similar findings were reported by John Van Maanen several years later, as he found that patrol officers' supervisors would use informal rewards and punishments as a way to influence officer behavior.[68] More recently, Robin Shepard Engel studied the effects of supervisory styles on police behavior (specifically arrests, use of force, and issuing citations).[69] She found that police supervisors that demonstrated high levels of participation in both patrol and supervisory activities while in the field had a small effect on officer behavior. In contrast, she found that the mere presence of police supervisors (regardless of their supervisory style) increased the likelihood that patrol officers would make an arrest. Richard Johnson found that supervisor influence through the use of informal rewards and behavior modeling influenced the extent to which patrol officers issued traffic tickets.[70] This body of research suggests that supervision can in fact influence how police officers conduct their work.

Early Warning Systems/Early Intervention Systems

Some agencies use "virtual supervisors" to track and monitor police officers' use of discretion that result in some negative outcome (such as citizen or supervisor complaints filed against officers). An early warning system/early intervention system (EWS/EIS) is a data-driven computerized program used by police administrators to identify police officers that demonstrate a pattern of problematic behavior (Section 9 discusses EWS/EIS in greater detail). This system is designed to identify problem officers early enough to be able to intervene and provide retraining, additional training, or some other form of counsel with the hope that there will be a change in future behavior. This type of oversight mechanism is based on the concept of deterrence—specifically, that police officers will make better decisions if they know that their behavior (specifically bad behavior) is being tracked by an early warning system. EWS/EIS interventions are supposed to help police officers make better decisions; however, there has not been any research conducted on this topic as it relates specifically to the control of police officer use of discretion.

Training

Theoretically, one could assume that police officers that receive the most hours of training as well as the highest-quality training would do a better job using discretion than police officers that receive fewer hours and lower-quality training. Research has found that this is not necessarily the case for training police officers to properly use discretion.[71] Most police training materials do not focus specifically on discretion; instead, they center on explaining rules and procedures as they are laid out in formal department policies and operational procedures manuals. There is usually no *philosophical* discussion of the rules or procedures in police training.[72] This includes talking about situations that could occur and how use of discretion could change based on varying situational factors. It is impossible for police academies to train police cadets on every possible situation that they will encounter when they begin patrolling the streets; therefore, newly hired police officers are frequently required to make quick decisions based on factors other than their training. In addition, there are very few opportunities for additional training on the use of discretion after police recruits leave the academy. As a result, rookie police officers rely on informal decision-making instructions from senior-level police officers that they work with each day.

As discussed in Section 5, some police agencies have adopted police training officer (PTO) programs to replace field training officer (FTO) programs. What makes PTO programs different from the older FTO programs is that they are based on problem-based learning. Problem-based learning is a training method that presents rookie police officers with real-life problems that have no easy solutions.[73] The issues of proper use of discretion are addressed frequently throughout the modules associated with the PTO program. Standards- and problem-solving-based training require police officers to examine their actions and think about the possible consequences of their use of discretion. The hope is that when police officers are faced with situations in which they could use several conflicting alternatives, their PTO training will guide them in making decisions that are in compliance with professional standards outlined by their employing agencies. At this point in time, there have not been any empirical examinations of the impact of PTO training on officer use of discretion.

So, has there been any research that looks at how police training influences police officer use of discretion? To date, there has been scant research focused specifically on police training and officer use of discretion.[74] Some early studies found that training influences both the reporting behavior and quality of reports written by police officers,[75] but no recent studies have centered on how training impacts officer use of discretion.[76]

Officer training and department policies can serve as guides for officer decision making.

Department Policies

There has been some research on the impact of department policies on police officer behavior. Studies focused on use-of-deadly-force policies indicate that police officer-involved shootings decrease when department policies become more restrictive.[77] Similar findings have been uncovered when policies on police pursuits have been examined by researchers. When police agencies place greater restrictions on police pursuits, the number of pursuits dropped significantly.[78] Studies show that department policies can influence police officer behavior when they restrict officers' ability to use discretion in situations in which serious injury or death is a possible outcome of police actions. Clearly stated policies that have articulated consequences (or policies with "teeth") and consistent enforcement of department policies are two ways that police administrators can increase the likelihood that police officers will follow guidelines provided by department policies. Ultimately, the decision to follow department policies (or not) is determined by individual police officers.

Controlling Discretion Outside of Police Organizations

Several additional mechanisms exist outside of police agencies that can influence police officer use of discretion. Several external control mechanisms are discussed in the remaining part of this section.

Court Case Outcomes

Decisions made by the courts have had a significant impact on police officer use of discretion dating back many decades. Several court case outcomes control or restrict police officer use of discretion. For example, *Hudson v. Michigan* (2006) resulted in the "knock and announce" rule for police officers who wish to enter a private home.[79] **Tennessee v. Garner** (1985) restricts police officer use of deadly force when pursuing fleeing suspects. The outcome of this court case requires that police officers only use deadly force when they have probable cause to believe that a suspect poses a threat of death or serious physical injury to the officer or the public.[80]

Decisions made by courts can also provide greater latitude in the use of discretion by police officers. As explained earlier, the legal guidelines defining when police officers can stop and frisk someone resulted from the outcome of *Terry v. Ohio* (1968). This court decision gives police officers more discretion, as they can stop and frisk suspects without probable cause to arrest if they have "reasonable suspicion" that someone has committed a crime, is in the process of committing a crime, or is going to commit a crime. Legally speaking, *reasonable suspicion* is defined as "an objectively justifiable suspicion that is based on specific facts or circumstances that justifies stopping and sometimes searching (frisking) a person thought to be involved in criminal activity at the time."[81] It could be argued that the vague definition of reasonable suspicion opens the door for police officer abuse of discretion to occur.

Whren v. United States (1996) determined that any traffic offense committed by drivers give the police the legal right to stop them. Some believe that the *Whren* decision has given the police unlimited authority to stop and search any vehicle they want—even for the most minor traffic infractions, including failure to signal before turning a corner and taking a turn that is too wide, to name a few. In essence, "traffic code becomes a police officer's best friend," because if an officer follows someone long enough, he or she is likely to see the person make a mistake (regardless of how minor it may be).[82] Thus, if some police officers use racial profiling practices, they could identify minority drivers and then follow them until they make a minor traffic-related mistake. It is for this reason that some people argue that the *Whren* decision has given police officers a green light to use racial profiling practices.

It is clear from our discussion that both positive and negative consequences can result from alterations made to police officer discretion. The restriction of officers' discretion can reduce their involvement in situations in which they or someone else could be seriously injured or killed; however, the restriction also gives them fewer options when deciding how to respond to various situations. In addition, when officers are given more discretion, it can provide them with greater opportunities to abuse their discretionary power; however, it can also give them more options when interacting with citizens, which means they can provide more individualized justice.

Legislative Actions

Another way that police discretion can be controlled outside of police agencies is through legislative action. Legislation can increase, restrict, or, in some cases, attempt to eliminate police officer discretion. Recently, some states have adopted immigration laws that have changed the level of involvement of local and state police officers in immigration enforcement. Historically, the enforcement of immigration laws has been handled primarily by federal-level law enforcement. Today, local and state police officers in states such as Arizona and Alabama are required to check the status of people they encounter for a criminal offense and who they suspect may be in the United States illegally. This mandate dictated by state legislation has increased police officer discretion as it relates to handling immigration issues; however, it has also increased claims of racial profiling against police officers that are required to check immigration status as a result of the newly adopted legislation.[83] Section 13 discusses some of the additional issues police officers face as a result of the new immigration legislation that is being adopted across the country.

Another example of legislation that impacts police officer use of discretion is mandatory arrest legislation for domestic violence cases. Prior to the early 1980s, police officers often avoided taking any kind of formal action when they responded to calls involving domestic violence.[84] At that time, domestic violence was viewed as a private matter, not a criminal matter that should involve the police. From 1981 to 1982, Lawrence Sherman and Richard Berk conducted the first scientifically controlled test of the effects of arrest on domestic violence in Minneapolis, Minnesota.[85] This study revealed that arrest was the most effective method (as opposed to counseling the two parties or sending someone away from the premises) police can use to reduce domestic violence. After this study, many states began to push for legislation that required police officers to make an arrest in cases in which there were clear signs of injury to one or both parties as a way to prevent domestic violence. The adoption of mandatory arrest legislation began to spread across the United States after the Minneapolis experiment. From 1985 through 1990, the National Institute of Justice funded several replications of Sherman and Berk's experiment. Replications in Omaha, Nebraska,[86] Charlotte, North Carolina,[87] and Milwaukee, Wisconsin,[88] all found no evidence of a deterrent effect of arrest on recidivism of domestic violence. In Colorado Springs, Colorado, the research revealed no deterrent effect for arrest when analyzing official records; however, researchers did find a deterrent effect when they analyzed interview data from domestic violence victims.[89] A replication in Metro-Dade, Florida, revealed significant deterrent effects of arrest on domestic violence cases.[90] Unfortunately, the findings from the replication study conducted in Atlanta, Georgia, were never published.

Many have argued that mandatory arrest laws not only tie the hands of police officers but also disempower victims of domestic violence by not allowing them to have a say in what happens to their abusers.[91] Further, several studies have found that police officers working in some pro-arrest jurisdictions fail to arrest abusers despite the mandatory arrest laws in their state.[92] Despite the findings of the research conducted on mandatory arrest laws and domestic violence, many jurisdictions have continued to use mandatory arrest laws to handle cases of domestic violence.

Civilian Review of the Police

Civilian review of the police is a procedure by which citizen complaints filed against the police are reviewed by a board that consists of citizens or a combination of citizens and police instead of a panel consisting solely of police personnel (such as police investigators working in internal affairs or professional standards units).[93] Although there have not been any empirical studies examining their impact on police officer discretion, the idea is that civilian review boards will act as an accountability mechanism for police officer behavior. If police officers are making decisions that prompt citizens to complain, presumably these boards will be able to identify problematic behavior and then recommend corrective actions to police agencies to encourage those officers to make good decisions based on department policies, training, and, of course, laws.

Public Scrutiny

The level of public scrutiny of the police has increased in the last decade with the technological advancements made in personal communication devices (i.e., cell phones that come equipped with cameras and video recorders). It has become easier for citizens to capture images of police misconduct, as greater access to these electronic devices allows more frequent recordings of police and citizen interactions. But does an increased level of public scrutiny impact police officer behavior? There has been virtually no published research on this topic, so it is not known what kind of impact public scrutiny has on police behavior. In theory, we could assume that police officers will make good decisions if they know the public is watching them closely, but at this point in time, there is no empirical evidence to support this assertion.

Lawsuits Against the Police

Does the fear of being sued influence police officer behavior? Research focused on lawsuits and the police has found that litigation has little to no influence on police officer behavior. A detailed discussion of the research focused on lawsuits involving the police is presented in Section 9.

Additional research is needed to better understand all of the factors that influence officer decision making as well as the mechanisms that control police officers' use of discretion. This topic is important because the decisions made by police officers impact the rest of the criminal justice system as well as the lives of citizens that they encounter each day.

Controlling Police Officer Discretion (Internal and External Control Mechanisms)

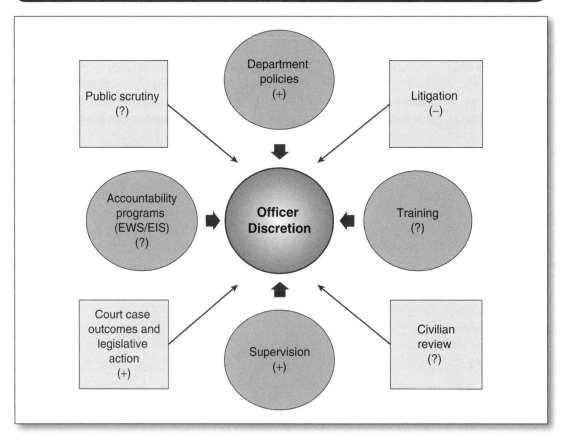

Notes:
+ indicates that there is an influence on police discretion
– indicates that there is no influence on police discretion
? indicates that there is no research suggesting an influence on discretion

SUMMARY

- Discretion is an official action taken by a criminal justice official based on the individual's judgment about the best course of action.
- Police administrators use discretion to implement or change policies, training, and procedures, as well as deciding how to allocate department resources.

- Decisions made by the police influence the other two parts of the criminal justice system (courts and corrections).
- Some people believe that racial profiling is a myth, while others have found empirical evidence that it does in fact exist.
- Officer characteristics, organizational factors, environmental factors, and situational/contextual factors have all been studied over the last four decades to determine their influence on police officer behavior.

KEY TERMS

alphabetical order
environmental factors
high-discretion stops
hydraulic effect

low-discretion stops
Mapp v. Ohio (1961)
Miranda v. Arizona (1966)
officer characteristics

organizational factors
situational/contextual factors
Tennessee v. Garner (1985)
Terry v. Ohio (1968)

DISCUSSION QUESTIONS

1. Explain why William Westley's 1950 study is important when examining police officer use of discretion.

2. Why is it important to understand how police administrators use discretion?

3. Discuss the significance of the racial profiling study conducted by David Barlow and Melissa Barlow.

4. Which of the four types of factors has found the most empirical support regarding having an impact on police officer use of discretion? What has the research found, exactly?

5. Describe low- and high-discretion stops. Which type of stop provides the most opportunity for patrol officers to abuse their use of discretion? Why?

WEB RESOURCES

- To learn more about broken windows and police discretion, go to https://www.ncjrs.gov/pdffiles1/nij/178259 .pdf.
- To learn more about racial profiling, go to http://www.racialprofilinganalysis.neu.edu/.
- To learn more about controlling police officer discretion, go to http://skogan.org/files/Lawful_Policing.pdf.

READING 21

The focus of this study is to observe the factors that lead police officers to become suspicious about a person or car. Using observational data, this study found that several factors were associated with the likelihood that an officer would make traffic stops based on suspicion. A surprising finding is that suspect characteristics were not found to be an important factor in becoming suspicious. This means that suspect race, gender, age, and perceived socioeconomic status did not influence officer suspicion.

Police Officers' Decision Making and Discretion: Forming Suspicion and Making a Stop

Geoffrey P. Alpert, Roger G. Dunham,
Meghan Stroshine, Katherine Bennett, and John MacDonald

Executive Summary

The majority of past research on police behavior has employed observational methodology to focus on actions taken by officers following contact with a citizen. This past research has largely concentrated on whether or not an arrest or other formal intervention follows a stop or other police-citizen interaction. The research at hand examines police officers' decisions before an initial contact is made. This study therefore focuses on the formation of suspicion and the decision to stop and question a citizen. Additionally, we analyze the outcomes of these stops.

It is important to note that observational studies have generally been designed to collect information on the actions and reactions of the police and citizens during an encounter, and that the common limitation of such studies lies in an assessment that focuses on the interaction process after the contact with a citizen has been made. While this method does produce data capable of answering many important questions about police behavior, it does not address why an officer selects a particular individual for a stop, thereby transforming some citizens into suspects at the expense of other citizens who are ignored. Our research, therefore, focuses on the vitally important decisions made prior to an initial police-citizen contact, answering questions about forming suspicion and making the decision to stop a citizen. These observations, read in conjunction with the outcome of these stops, provide a useful insight into how the decision to make a stop can affect police-citizen interactions.

Methodology

The present endeavor attempts to fill some of the gaps in the previous research. Our methodology integrates quantitative and qualitative data collection in an effort to improve the value of the data. Our quantitative data includes the routine information necessary to conduct a case study of a police department, including officer behavior and the independent variables that theoretically affect police behavior. The qualitative data were collected by using the general principles of observation and content analysis with a special emphasis on protocol analysis. Unlike the previous research, we are interested in the formation and creation of cognitive suspicion, as well as in formal actions (e.g. stops) taken by the police.

During the summer and fall of 2002, field observers accompanied officers in each of the four precincts and on all three shifts in Savannah, Georgia. Observers went on 132 tours with officers. Observers were trained to focus on how the officers spent their discretionary time. They were trained not to record any activities that were generated by radio calls, other officers, or situations in which they served as a backup officer. Observers were instructed to watch the interactions between the officer and suspect(s), to document what they saw and to note the sequence of events as they unfolded. They were provided structured questionnaires that included language for their questions and space to record officer responses.

Observers were trained to take note of occasions when officers appeared to notice a suspicious person or incident but ultimately decided not act upon it; in such instances observers were instructed to question the officer about his or her behavior at an opportune time. For example, if the observer noticed an officer do a "double-take," the observer would bring that to the officer's attention after the event and ask what he or she was thinking at the time. In other words, the observer would ask what caught the officer's eye and what made the officer proceed without acting. Observers also recorded the interactions between an officer and a citizen when suspicion actually led to a stop. In these instances observers were trained to complete a questionnaire concerning the officer and his or her patterns of behavior, a task undertaken when the officer was not engaged with a citizen.

There are two units of analysis in this study, each based on a stage in the officer's decision-making process: (1) the officer becoming suspicious of an individual, and (2) the officer making a stop based on the suspicion. First, we examine the decision to form a suspicion in relation to the characteristics of the areas patrolled, the persons encountered, the days and times suspicion was formed, and finally, the characteristics of officers. We next analyze the officer's decision to stop a citizen in relation to our independent variables. Lastly, we discuss factors associated with the various alternative outcomes of a stop (e.g. use of force, searches, tickets, and arrests).

 Findings

Officers formed suspicion when they observed something unusual, became curious or otherwise distrustful of an individual. During 132 tours where officers were accompanied by observers, officers formed suspicion 174 times. On average, an officer would form suspicion once during a tour of duty (or shift). Officers did not form suspicion on 60 of these tours. However, on one tour, an officer formed seven suspicions. In the majority of cases, individuals were driving vehicles, opposed to being on foot, at the time suspicion was formed or stops were made (70% and 73.8%, respectively). The majority of persons who aroused the suspicion of officers, or who were stopped by police, were male (74%) minority group members (71%) who averaged thirty-two years of age. However, blacks constituted a slightly higher percentage of suspicions (71.0%) than stops (68.9%), while whites had an inverse pattern (they constituted 29.0 % of the suspicions and 31.1 % of the stops).

Bases for Suspicion

When an officer was curious about a citizen or became suspicious, observers asked the officer to provide them with the reason(s) for this concern. The reasons provided by observers were coded according to the following categories: (1) appearance, (2) behavior, (3) time and place, and (4) information. "Appearance" refers to the appearance of an individual and/or vehicle, and can refer to things such as distinctive dress, indicators of class, vehicle type, color, condition, and the like. "Behavior" refers to any overt action taken by an individual or vehicle that seemed inappropriate, illegal, or bizarre. "Time and place" refers to an officer's knowledge of a particular location (e.g., park, warehouse district) and what activities should or should not be expected there after a particular time (e.g., after hours). Finally, "Information" refers to information provided by either a dispatcher or fellow officer (e.g., BOLO).

The main reason for forming suspicion was the behavior of the suspect(s). In the overwhelming majority of cases (66%), the officer told the observer that the behavior of the suspect(s) was the primary reason for forming suspicion. An analysis of observer descriptions of behavior revealed that the most likely behavioral reasons for forming suspicion of an individual/vehicle were traffic violations (e.g., running a red light, driving with expired plates), avoiding officers (e.g. turning around and walking the other way, hiding face), and looking nervous in the presence of the officer.

More than 18% of the suspicions were stimulated by information provided by either a dispatcher or fellow officer. This usually involved "Be on the Lookout" bulletins, or other information provided by the department or fellow officers concerning characteristics of suspects, crimes, or vehicles thought to be related to specific crimes. An analysis of observer descriptions of the types of information officers used revealed that the most likely types of information used for forming suspicion of an individual/vehicle were descriptions of personal characteristics, clothing, or descriptions of vehicles that were either stolen or thought to have been used in a crime.

Nearly ten percent of the reasons given for becoming suspicious of a person were related to time and place. These cases involved an officer drawing on his or her knowledge of a particular location (e.g., park, warehouse district) and what activities should or should not be expected there after a particular time (e.g., after hours). An analysis of the observers' descriptions of the situations which caused officers to become suspicious revealed a wide variety of situations, including a car parked near a school in the woods at night, a car driving slowly in a warehouse district late at night, and passengers in a car who do not match the ethnicity of the neighborhood they are driving in (especially at night).

Finally, nearly six percent of the reasons given by the officers for becoming suspicious were related to the appearance of the person(s). This criteria involved distinctive dress, indicators of class, vehicle type, color, and condition. An analysis of the observers' descriptions, as to which characteristics led officers to become suspicious, revealed characteristics such as a vehicle with heavily tinted windows, a dirty or damaged vehicle, an individual wearing gang colors, or an individual looking "strung out" like a drug addict.

Overall Patterns of Officer's Decision-Making Concerning Suspicion

To obtain an assessment of each officer's overall decision-making style, observers recorded the factors which the officer took into account when forming suspicion. It should be noted that this was an overall assessment of the officer, and not an assessment of the officer with regard to any one particular incident.

"Appearance," referring to things such as distinctive dress, indicators of class, and the like, appeared to be an important factor for the majority of officers, with most officers rating appearance with a medium priority rather than high priority. Observers' explanations of these ratings were qualitatively analyzed to provide some insight into the reasons officers considered appearance important or unimportant. The following are some explanations given by officers who rated appearance as a medium or high priority:

- Despite ethnicity, if someone is wearing all black clothing, this is an indication that they are up to no good.
- Officer is well acquainted with people and places in his beat; he can tell based on appearance who "doesn't belong"
- Person who looks "different" raises suspicion (e.g., white person in black neighborhood).

In contrast, officers who rated appearance to be of low priority typically provided one of two explanations: (1) that most people encountered looked similar enough to render appearance meaningless as a factor that might arouse suspicion, or, (2) that they did their best not to judge people based on their appearance.

Most officers described behavior as playing a significant role in their decision-making. Nearly half of the officers reported that behavior was a high priority and an additional one-third stated that behavior was a medium priority in forming suspicion. Again, observers' explanations of their ratings were qualitatively analyzed to provide some insight into the importance of behavior in forming suspicion. The following are examples of comments provided by officers who treated behavior as being of medium or high importance in forming suspicion:

- Police officer stated that he watches out for the "felony stare" (i.e., getting nervous when they see a police car, making every effort to avoid the police).
- Police officer said that behavior is very important to him because he can tell when a person is lying to him. He can tell this by the way they act.
- Police officer said he can tell if someone has done something just by how they respond to him.
- "It is very important to tell if they are fidgeting."

Analyses conducted on the importance of time and place in officer decision-making revealed that, in a little over one-quarter of cases, time and place were irrelevant to whether officers formed suspicion. For the majority of officers observed in this study, time and place was either of medium or high priority. Most often, this was related to people/vehicle(s) being out of place in a particular location at a given time. For instance, officers often relied on their knowledge of a particular location (e.g., park, warehouse district) and what activities should or should not be expected there after a particular time (e.g., after hours) to form suspicion. For example:

- People who look out of place (e.g., white person in black neighborhood) get stopped in places that have higher incidence of crime
- People can use the dark to their advantage to aid them committing crimes, therefore more attention paid at night
- People who look out of place are very suspicious, especially white people in a black neighborhood

- People who were where they shouldn't be (e.g., juveniles on a school playground at night) got stopped

Observers were also asked to rank the importance that information might have in determining the decision-making of police officers. A small number of observers believed that information rarely played a role in whether officers formed suspicion. In contrast, observers believed that the great majority of officers treated information as high priority.

Factors Correlated with the Decision to Stop a Suspected Individual/Vehicle

Now we will change our focus from the first unit of analysis (an officer becoming suspicious of a citizen) to the second unit of analysis (an officer making a decision to stop the citizen, based upon suspicion). It is important to note that "forming suspicion" did not necessarily result in stopping an individual. However, officers did stop the individual under suspicion the majority of the time ($n = 103$ or 59%). In cases where no stop was made, the officer's continued observation of the suspect(s) convinced him/her that the original concern was unwarranted. Furthermore, since officers formed suspicion a total of 174 times and made a total of 103 stops, we can calculate that officers made an average of less than one stop per ride on the basis of suspicion.

A correlation was computed for each of the independent variables and the decision to stop a person under suspicion. It is interesting that none of the suspect characteristics examined significantly influenced the likelihood of a stop. In other words, once the officers became suspicious of an individual they were equally as likely to stop the person whether or not the person was male or female, African-American or white, young or old, or perceived to be of a low or high socioeconomic status. The type of area in which the observation was made did have a significant effect on whether a stop was made by the officer. Suspicions were significantly less likely to result in stops in residential areas (46% of the time) when compared to the other types of areas, which ranged from 72% to 80% of the time.

Stops were significantly related to whether the observation occurred during the weekend or not. Suspicions resulted in actual stops 69% of the time during the weekdays, but only 41% of the time during the weekend (Friday and Saturday nights). It is quite likely that weekend nights are generally far busier times for law enforcement and officers cannot follow up on suspicious behaviors they observe as often as during the less busy time periods.

The nature of the suspicion also was influential in determining the relative likelihood that an officer would make a stop. Officers were significantly more likely to make stops when they had formed suspicion on the basis of the suspect's behavior (75% of the time), but significantly less likely to make a stop if they had formed suspicion on the basis of time and place (29%) or information (34%).

Finally, two officer characteristics were associated with making a stop of an individual. Older officers and officers with a high school education were significantly more likely to make stops than younger and more educated officers. Officers with a high school education made stops in 70% of the incidents which they defined as suspicious, a significantly higher percentages [sic] than that of educated officers. The mean age of officers making stops after forming suspicion is 34.5 years, which is significantly older than the mean of officers forming suspicion but not making a stop (31.3 years).

Officer and Suspect Demeanor throughout the Interaction

Observers recorded the demeanor of suspects and officers at various points during the encounter. Overall, officers acted more positively toward suspects than suspects did towards officers. Suspect and officer demeanor changed at approximately the same rate during their interaction, and in roughly one-fourth of all cases, the officer and suspect changed their demeanor during the course of the encounter.

The nature of an officer's and/or suspect's change in demeanor was evenly divided between changes for the better and for the worse. Officers tended to hold more positive attitudes toward suspects than suspects did towards officers. Regardless of whether an officer's demeanor changed for the better or worse, officers appeared overwhelmingly to be responding to the attitude/demeanor displayed by the suspect.

Very few officers were disrespectful toward the person they stopped. Of the four cases where an officer was disrespectful to the citizen, only one was assessed as being unprovoked; in the remaining instances officers were reacting to disrespect exhibited by the citizen. While the overall percentage of suspects who displayed disrespect to the police was also relatively low, suspects were disrespectful at over twice the rate of officers.

Factors Associated with the Outcome of a Stop

A correlational analysis was performed on a number of variables (area, time, individual characteristics of the actors, and reasons for becoming suspicious) that may have an impact on selected outcome measures (resistance, frisked, coercion used, being searched, issued a warning, ticket or being arrested). We discuss important relationships that emerge from this analysis in the sections below.

Characteristics of the Area

Characteristics of the area had an impact on whether or not the suspect was frisked. Suspects were more likely to be frisked if the area was private and when the area was residential. Further, suspects stopped in commercial areas were more likely to be issued a ticket (45%) than suspects stopped in residential areas (25%). There were two characteristics of areas that did not make a difference on any of the stop results: the racial makeup of the area and areas the officer thought were "trouble spots." Also, neither time measure—stops made after dark and stops made on weekend nights—affected stop outcomes.

Suspect Characteristics

Only one suspect characteristic was not related to any of the seven outcome variables: the race of the suspect did not affect the measured outcome of stops. Gender was related to the likelihood of being frisked and receiving a ticket. There was a five times greater likelihood of males being frisked than females. However, females who were stopped were nearly twice as likely as males to be issued a traffic ticket. Age was related to the likelihood of being frisked and of the vehicle being searched. Younger persons were significantly more likely to be frisked or have their vehicle searched than older individuals.

The perceived social class of the suspect was related to only one outcome variable, but the one which is the most severe: being arrested. Stopped suspects perceived by the officer to be lower class were arrested 25% of the time, while suspects perceived to be middle class were arrested only 6% of the time. Only four suspects were perceived to be in the upper class, and none were arrested. The reason for the greater likelihood of arrest of lower-status suspects is unclear. It may be due to a higher offending rate of lower-status citizens.

The suspect characteristic most consistently related to the results of stops was whether the suspect was under the influence of alcohol or drugs at the time of the stop. When this was the case, the suspect was significantly more likely to resist the officer, to be frisked, to have force used against him/her, to have their vehicle searched, and also to be arrested. More specifically, suspects under the influence of alcohol or drugs were approximately ten times more likely to resist (33%) than suspects not under the influence (3%). Further, suspects under the influence were about five times more likely to be patted down (75%) than other suspects (15%), and more than twelve times (25%) more likely to have force used against them during the encounter with the police than suspects not under the influence (2%). Police officers decided to search the vehicles of 50% of the suspects under the influence of alcohol or drugs, but only 5% of the vehicles of other suspects, a ten times greater likelihood. Finally, the suspects under the influence of alcohol or drugs were fourteen times more likely to be arrested (42%) than suspects not under the influence (3%).

A Brief Look at Outcomes and the Source of Suspicion

When the reason for forming suspicion was behavior (versus appearance, time and place, or information), suspects were significantly less likely to resist, to have force used against them, or to be frisked. However, they were significantly more likely to be issued a ticket. More specifically, only 2% of the suspects who were selected by the officer for observation because of their behavior ended up resisting the officer. Compare this figure to the 45% of suspects who resisted when the officer began observing them because of specific information received by the officer about the situation. There were too few cases involving suspicion based on appearance or time and place to allow valid comparisons with these categories. Pat downs were more likely to result when the officer had specific information (e.g. BOLO) that led him/her to become suspicious (82%) when compared to all the other reasons for forming suspicion. Suspicions formed strictly on the behavior of the suspects only resulted in pat downs 16% of the time. Officer use of force occurred most frequently when officers had specific information that led them to become suspicious (4 out of the 5 instances of force). Issuing tickets, on the other hand, came mostly from suspicions formed because of the behavior of the suspects (41%). This finding is logical as the behavior that the officer observed most often was a traffic violation. When information was the basis of suspicion, suspects were significantly more likely to resist, have force used against them, or to be frisked and arrested. When information led officers to become suspicious of an individual, the suspect was significantly less likely to be issued a ticket.

Characteristics of the Officer

In a perfect world, staffed with perfectly trained officers who follow specified policies and procedures to the letter, we would expect officer characteristics not to factor significantly in officer decision-making. In this study, only two officer characteristics influenced the results of stops, and each influenced only one outcome. The first is the officer's race, which influenced the likelihood of suspects receiving a ticket. White officers were more than twice as likely to issue tickets during their stops as were other officers.

The second officer characteristic to have an influence on the outcome of stops is an officer's length of tenure in the police department. Officer tenure was correlated with the resistance offered by suspects: officers with longer tenure were more likely to have a suspect offering resistance. Either the more senior officers are handling cases with a greater likelihood of suspect resistance or they are doing something that creates more resistance from the suspects (e.g. rougher treatment, less patience).

Reasons for Stopping Suspects

As with the previous analysis, we examined the descriptions of the officers' rationale for making a stop. The narrative descriptions of these cases indicate that the probability of stopping a citizen was greatly influenced by officers observing citizens committing traffic-related offenses. Importantly, these narrative descriptions reveal further evidence that the reasons for non-behavioral suspicion differ from those that cause the police to stop citizens.

 Conclusions

Research on the police has relied on observational strategies to develop rich and important information on the behavior of police and the public they serve in a natural setting. Our study, undertaken in cooperation with the Savannah Police Department, is based upon the ideas and data-collection instruments developed in earlier research efforts. One of the major differences in the methodology used in this study is the selection of police-citizen interactions used for analyses. Our unit of analysis is the formation of officer suspicion and the stops that are pursuant to that suspicion. Relying on the general principles of observational research and content analysis, we incorporated Staged Activity Analysis and Protocol Analysis into a hybrid methodology. This approach to collecting the data was successful in that ride-along observers were accepted by the police, thereby establishing the rapport

necessary to collect the required information. From our descriptive analyses, several conclusions emerged:

1. Officers formed suspicions quite infrequently. Most officers only formed one suspicion per shift, but the average was 1.3 per shift. It was very unusual for an officer to form more than three suspicions per shift.

2. For the most part officers formed suspicions using legitimate criteria. In the majority of cases, the officer told the observer that the behavior of the suspect(s) was the primary reason for forming suspicion. An analysis of the observers' descriptions of behavior revealed that the most likely behavioral reason for forming suspicion of an individual/vehicle was a traffic violation (e.g., running a red light, driving with expired plates).

3. Forming a suspicion did not necessarily result in a stop. Stops were made a majority of the time (less than one per shift); however there were instances when continued observation of the suspect(s) convinced the officer that the original concern was unwarranted.

4. While deployment patterns were not part of the analyses, it is likely that they are an important factor in explaining where most suspicions and stops occurred. The characteristics of areas where most suspicions were formed and where most stops were made are as follows: the majority of suspicions were formed in residential areas, and the greatest percentage of stops occurred in commercial areas. While the majority of the suspicions and stops were made in areas that were not considered particularly dangerous, they did occur in predominantly African-American areas.

5. The demographic characteristics of the citizen about whom officers formed suspicion, or who were stopped, were young minorities. However, Blacks constituted a slightly higher percentage of suspicions than stops, while

whites had a slightly higher percentage of stops than suspicions.

6. During the course of stops, officers acted more positively toward suspects than suspects did towards officers. Suspects were nearly three times more likely than officers to be negative and twice as likely to be disrespectful at the beginning of an encounter. Only a handful of officers had a negative initial demeanor or acted disrespectfully towards the citizen. Suspect and officer demeanor changed at approximately the same rate during their interaction, with half turning more negative and the other half turning more positive. Officers appeared to be responding to the attitude/demeanor displayed by the suspect. According to this measure, citizens being disrespectful were nearly twice as likely to be ticketed or arrested compared to citizens showing respect to the officer.

7. Officers were significantly more likely to make stops when they had formed suspicion on the basis of the suspect's behavior, rather than on the basis of time and place, information, or appearance. Suspect characteristics, such as gender, ethnicity, socio-economic status, and age, did not significantly influence the likelihood of a stop after a suspicion was formed. However, non-behavioral suspicions were most common when a suspect and an officer were both Black and least common when an officer and suspect were white.

8. Only two officer characteristics, age and education, were important determinants of the decision to make a stop. Older officers and officers with a high school education were significantly more likely to make stops than younger and more educated officers. Interestingly, white officers were more than twice as likely to issue tickets during their stops as other officers.

9. Suspects under the influence of alcohol or drugs negatively influenced the interaction.

Suspects under the influence of alcohol or drugs at the time of the stop were significantly more likely to resist the officer, to be frisked, to have force used against him/her, to have their vehicle searched, and to be arrested.

10. Most officers reported that they had working rules to help them identify suspicious persons or to determine how to handle a particular situation.

11. While most of the officer decisions were based on behavioral criteria, decisions based on the non-behavioral criteria were also important. In contrast to officer decisions based on behavioral criteria, the small percentage of decisions based on non-behavioral criteria can be explained by suspect and officer demographic variables. For example, officers were significantly more likely to form a non-behavioral suspicion when the suspect was Black and the officer had longer tenure.

12. Most of the stops were routine and resulted in no consequence for the citizen. When there was a consequence, the most common was a warning or a ticket. An arrest was made in less than 10% of the stops. Further, coercion against the citizen was seldom used and citizen resistance was uncommon. Frisking or searching suspects was more common than force, but most often came subsequent to an arrest or following suspect resistance. Coercion was never used unless the suspect offered resistance.

These conclusions are significant in several respects. First, to the best of our knowledge, this is the first attempt to assess officer decision-making before the actual stop is made, i.e., when officers are in the initial stages of forming suspicion. Second, our findings do not support the speculation that it is during this pre-stop stage of decision-making that major levels of discrimination are likely. In our analysis of the observations, very few problematic attitudes and behaviors surfaced. As in other observational research, most of the officers' time was spent in routine activities with routine outcomes. The Savannah study failed to uncover any serious or major flaws in how the police managed their interactions with citizens. However, in any organization, there is always room for improvement. We did uncover some stops based on non-behavioral criteria, and it is from these few potentially problematic interaction patterns that our policy suggestions are based.

 ## Policy Implications and Future Research

Our findings and conclusions have important policy implications regarding the management of police officer discretionary time, and for the development of officers' decision-making skills. The policy implications of our research are in many ways similar to findings in other observational studies: changing police officers' attitudes alone will not change their behavior on the street. It is clear that if changes are desired, managers must provide data-based training to educate officers about their actions. This training must be supported by close supervision to assure that the desired behavior is taking place.

Since officers form suspicions relatively infrequently, it may be necessary to create a workload analysis to determine how officer discretionary time is used. We did not record the time officers spent responding to radio calls and other service, so it may be that very little time exists for discretionary stops and the formation of suspicions. However, managers may be able to encourage officers to use their available time more efficiently, effectively, and productively.

As our research is the first to address the formation of suspicion, it is difficult to determine the value of these decisions. Our data show that not all suspicions resulted in an official response. This could mean that some of the criteria used by officers to form suspicion are proper and valuable, while using other criteria is unfounded and inefficient. Clearly, more attention and research needs to be done in this area, but our preliminary findings can guide future researchers and police managers.

Officers formed the majority of their suspicions in function of a citizen's behavior. However, there were some times when officers became suspicious about citizens based on non-behavioral criteria. Since these are the most problematic, officers need to understand their likely outcome and consequences. In other words, people are more likely to be angry and resentful of a police officer who becomes suspicious without behavioral cues. Training and role-play could help officers and managers understand the process of forming suspicion. In addition, special attention should be focused on managing intoxicated citizens as they are the most likely to have a bad attitude and resist an officer's actions. We learned the prevalent nature of working rules that govern officer behavior: it is vital that police managers be aware of these "rules" and that they ensure such rules remain consistent with both departmental policy and its mission statement.

DISCUSSION QUESTIONS

1. Why is observational data collection appropriate to study this topic?

2. What are some of the main findings in this study?

3. How can police training be modified or altered based on the findings of this study?

David Barlow and Melissa Barlow surveyed African American police officers in Milwaukee, Wisconsin, to study racial profiling. The officers were asked about their personal experiences of having been racially profiled while off duty and also whether they used racial profiling themselves while on duty. The findings from this study provide evidence that racial profiling does in fact exist.

Racial Profiling: A Survey of African American Police Officers

David E. Barlow and Melissa Hickman Barlow

After being arrested for a crime he witnessed someone else commit, a young Black law student at Harvard University wrote a "Bill of Rights for Black Men" (Bain, 2000). On *60 Minutes,* the young man described his experience of "Walking While Black" and why he believes that the U.S. Bill of Rights does not apply to young Black men in America, whom he claims are regularly subjected to a police practice that has become known as *racial profiling*. Bryonn Bain is not alone in believing that Black men are often stopped, questioned, and even arrested by police because of their race. A poll conducted by the American Institute of Public Opinion indicated that 60% of Americans aged 18 and older believe that the practice of racial profiling is widespread. The percentage of Whites who reported believing that racial profiling is common was 56%, whereas 76% of African Americans said they believed it to be a common practice of police (Kurlander, 2000). Even President George W. Bush, in his first message to Congress, indicated that he had asked Attorney General John Ashcroft to develop recommendations to end racial profiling.

What is racial profiling? Definitions vary, and it is important to know what definition is being used to know what to make of such high-profile statements regarding the practice. Indeed, the strongest denouncements of

racial profiling have often come from those who define the practice so narrowly (i.e., race as the *only* reason for stopping, questioning, or arresting someone) that we can imagine only the most extreme bigots engaging in it. Using such a definition, racial profiling is easy to both denounce and deny. The real question is how public officials and politicians respond to racial profiling as described by the many individuals who, like Bryonn Bain, believe that their rights have been violated—that their race has been used by police to deny them the protection against unreasonable search and seizure promised by the Fourth Amendment to the U.S. Constitution.

In fact, many government officials dismiss the testimony of Black and Brown Americans who claim that race has been used by police to determine their potential criminality. The personal experiences of people of color who have been victims of racial profiling are often rejected as being anecdotal, uninformed, or overly sensitive. Even leaders in law enforcement who are seriously committed to putting an end to racial profiling lack confidence in the ability of the general public to identify it. For example, the President of the International Association of Chiefs of Police, Chief Ron Neubauer, has stated that any officer who uses racial profiling should be removed from police work. "The IACP recommends zero tolerance ... the officers who still commit racial profiling need to be weeded out of the force" (as quoted in Strandberg, 1999, p. 65). However, Neubauer and other police executives attempting to address the problem of racial profiling suggest that many incidents are simply problems of perception because the public does not understand the intricacies, strategies, and techniques of law enforcement. Neubauer stated, "What appears to be racial profiling to the general public may be nothing of the sort" (as quoted in Strandberg, 1999, p. 62).

Racial Profiling and the Law

Despite claims by some that civil rights for racial minorities have been fully achieved in the United States, racial disparities in the criminal justice process remain and appear to be expanding (Leadership Conference on Civil Rights, 2001). Racial disparities exist at each phase of criminal justice processing, and it is the police who are the gatekeepers to that process (Barlow & Barlow, 2000; Chambliss, 2001; Cole, 1999; Mauer, 1999; Miller, 1996). As a result of decades of Supreme Court decisions limiting restrictions on law enforcement, police have tremendous discretion with respect to search and seizure in the context of traffic stops (see, for example, *Maryland v. Wilson,* 1997; *New York v. Belton,* 1981; *Ohio v. Robinette,* 1996; *Pennsylvania v. Mimms,* 1977; *United States* v. *Ross,* 1982; *Whren v. United States,* 1996; *Wyoming v. Houghton,* 1999). With the *Whren* decision, the Supreme Court enhanced the extensive power of police to detain individual citizens under the banner of the war on drugs by allowing pretext stops through the "objective" standard. Police officers who wish to stop a car for purposes of drug enforcement need not articulate reasonable suspicion that persons in the car are engaged in drug crimes. They need only show probable cause to stop for a traffic violation (Bast, 1997; Harris, 1997, 1999).

The standard that prevailed prior to the movement toward the objective standard now sanctioned by *Whren* was the "reasonable officer" standard. This standard required that an officer stop a vehicle for a traffic violation only if a reasonable officer would have made the stop. The reasonable officer standard prohibited police officers from using a minor traffic infraction as an excuse to stop a car for other purposes, such as to search for drugs. The intent of the officer was very important. In the face of a claim that a stop was made for reasons other than traffic enforcement, such as racial bias, previous policing patterns could be reviewed to determine whether the officer was enforcing the law without bias. The *Whren* decision's objective standard opens the door for police subterfuge. In the *Whren* case, it did not matter to the Court that the officers lied about their intent, that they were violating departmental policy to make the stop, or that they really wanted to stop this car because it contained two African American men who sat at a stop sign for 20 seconds in an area known for drug dealing. Under the objective standard, the motivation of the officer and previous enforcement patterns become irrelevant (Bast, 1997; Harris, 1997, 1999).

Whren clearly opens the door for racial profiling because it allows police officers to stop anyone they want without reasonable suspicion or probable cause, thus providing a mechanism for circumventing the Fourth Amendment requirements of the U.S. Constitution. Because minor traffic violations are numerous, to limit stops to the observation of a traffic violation is no limitation at all. If a police officer wants to stop a car, but does not have the legal authority to do so, all the officer has to do is to follow it until the driver gets nervous and at some point turns right without a turn signal, drifts across the center line, or simply fails to come to a complete stop at a stop sign. Ironically, if a police officer follows a car for a long time and the driver fails to make any driving error, then the driver fits the old established criminal profile of driving too cautiously. In this case, the police officer can stop the car for excessively careful driving, such as using the right turn signal every time, never crossing the center line, or always coming to a complete stop. Upon observing a minor traffic violation—or the suspicious absence of any minor traffic violation—the police officer can stop the driver and attempt to pressure him or her into giving consent for the car to be searched. This technique has long been used by police, but now the Supreme Court has legitimized the procedure. It is clear that the Supreme Court knew full well the implications of the *Whren* decision because Justice Scalia went to great lengths in his majority opinion to state that selective enforcement of the law based on race remains unconstitutional. Nevertheless, the Court has systematically removed nearly every tool available to determine whether selective enforcement is racially motivated (Bast, 1997; Harris, 1997, 1999).

Police Perspectives on Racial Profiling

Many police officers view racial profiling as an appropriate form of law enforcement. Although they might not use the term *racial profiling* to describe what they do, police officers participate in this practice because they believe it is precisely what their supervisors and the majority public wants them to do. In a cultural diversity awareness training class for police officers conducted by one of the authors, a police officer explained why he stops Black people who are driving through his suburban community even though it makes him uncomfortable. Although most officers presumably justify their stops based on presumed criminality, this officer stated that he stops and questions African Americans because it is precisely what his supervisors want him to do. He stated, "When someone from a $350,000 home calls the police and wants us to stop someone, we are going to do it and the chief is going to make sure we do it." The officer went on to ask, "Now, how do I stop that person without him thinking I'm a racist?"

As long as the courts do not take an active role in putting a stop to this practice or at least make it uncomfortable for them, police will continue to feel that it is condoned. Racial profiling is not a case of a few bad apples or rogue cops. It is a systematic strategy, often rationalized by a false belief that racial minorities are more criminal and more likely to use illegal drugs than White people. Some police officers defend racial profiting, maintaining that it is based on probabilities. They believe that it is a statistical reality that young men of color are disproportionately likely to commit crimes (Harris, 1999; Hughes, 2000). Disturbingly, the courts have frequently supported this viewpoint, primarily through allowing drug courier profiles to stand in for reasonable suspicion. As Cole (1999) noted, some profiles explicitly include race whereas others implicitly encourage reliance on racial characteristics. Cole cited numerous cases and reviews of court decisions indicating that drug courier profiles result in the disproportionate targeting of racial minorities as suspects. Courts have ruled that although stops based solely on race would violate the equal protection clause of the Constitution, race can be one of several factors used by officers in determining whom they choose to stop and search (see, for example, *United States v. Avery,* 1997; *United States v. Travis,* 1995). Kennedy (2000) noted that the rationale provided in support of such decisions is that the burden of brief detentions on law-abiding citizens of color is a minor and necessary inconvenience in the war on crime, suggesting that little damage is done by the practice of racial profiling. This perspective fails to acknowledge that these brief detentions grow into regular occurrences, breeding resentment and anger both in the citizens who are stopped and the police officers who confront hostility arising out of the realization that just because race is couched within other factors does not mean there is no racial discrimination (Kennedy, 2000).

When police officers use race as a factor in criminal profiling based on presumed statistical probabilities, they contribute to the very statistics upon which they rely (Hams, 1999; Hughes, 2000; Leadership Conference on Civil Rights, 2001). Therefore, police officers justify profiling, stopping, searching, and thus arresting African Americans disproportionately precisely because African Americans are profiled, stopped, searched, and arrested disproportionately. The vicious cycle continues as more minority arrests and convictions perpetuate the belief that minorities commit more crimes. The reasoning employed by police officers who use racial profiling for drug enforcement is particularly flawed because Whites use illicit drugs at a rate similar to the rate for Blacks and higher than that of Latinos. Recent estimates indicate that Whites account for nearly 70% of drug users (Substance Abuse and Mental Health Services Administration, 2001). Although African Americans comprise only 12% of drug users, they account for

35% of those arrested for drug abuse violations (U.S. Department of Justice, 2000).

The major problem with arrest statistics, then, is that they do not reflect the reality of crime as much as they reflect patterns in policing. Chambliss (1994) conducted ride-along research in which he observed that police officers stopped a large number of cars containing racial minorities, often using minor traffic infractions as a pretext to stop drivers whom they suspected of involvement with drugs. Officers routinely used manipulation or intimidation to convince drivers to submit to searches of their cars. Most of the drivers were then released, often with no ticket and no record. In a small fraction of the stops, drugs were found and individuals arrested. Because Whites were not stopped and searched to the same extent as Blacks, African Americans accounted for most of the arrests resulting from these encounters.

There is evidence that a similar dynamic is at work on our nation's highways. As Kurlander (2000) has pointed out, racial profiling is mandated by official and published guidelines, such as the 1985 guidelines for the Florida Highway Patrol. Within these guidelines, the profile for drug couriers included "the use of rental cars, scrupulous obedience to traffic laws, drivers wearing 'lots of gold,' drivers who do not 'fit the vehicle,' and *'ethnic groups associated with the drug trade'* [italics added]" (p. 148). Along these same lines, evidence in a 1992 class action suit filed by the Maryland American Civil Liberties Union (ACLU) included a Maryland State Police memorandum instructing officers to be on the lookout for drug dealers and couriers, described as "predominantly black males and black females" (*Wilkins v. Maryland State Police,* 1992).

Administrative directives such as those described above suggest the role of police leadership in racial profiling. Police administrators provide much of the impetus for racial profiling by encouraging and rewarding drug arrests. As Chambliss (2001) noted, drug arrests in poor urban communities, often largely populated by racial minorities, are easier to make than in most other contexts because of the open street-market dealing characteristic of these communities. Ease of arrest is also enhanced by the fact that residents of impoverished communities generally lack the political and economic

clout to resist aggressive police practices. Police departments come to rely on federal funds tied to their ability to demonstrate success in the area of drug enforcement, and large numbers of drug arrests are offered up as evidence that a police department is successfully winning the hopeless war against drugs.

Another contribution of police administrators to racial profiling is how they manage their departments and discipline their officers. One of the authors, a former police officer, worked for police administrators who would discipline officers for eating lunch outside the patrol area, driving over the speed limit, speaking rudely to someone, being late to work, or not wearing one's hat when outside the patrol car; but would take no action at all if an officer violated someone's civil and human rights. In fact, if an illegal stop and search led to an arrest for drug possession, the only punishment was that the evidence might be thrown out as inadmissible. Suggesting the degree to which drug arrests result from either unsubstantiated or illegally obtained evidence, Miller (1996) noted that a 1993 study by the California State Assembly found that 92% of Black men arrested by police on drug charges were subsequently released for lack of evidence or inadmissible evidence. Aware of the large percentage of drug arrests that do not result in conviction, officers who make such arrests say, "You may beat the rap, but you can't beat the ride." If the person subjected to an illegal stop and search is ultimately arrested for disorderly conduct or resisting arrest because they become agitated in the face of a gross injustice, this individual will not beat the rap or the ride.

 Empirical Research on Racial Profiling

As a result of legal challenges and increasing public discourse surrounding racial profiling, there are a number of ongoing empirical investigations designed to measure the extent of this phenomenon. Currently, these studies involve efforts to gather data on racial disparities in traffic stops by police. A recent report by the U.S. General Accounting Office (2000) identified five quantitative analyses, the cumulative results of which suggest that minority motorists, and African Americans in particular, are more likely than Whites to be stopped by police. The extent to which Blacks are disproportionately represented among traffic stops in comparison to their representation among motorists is evidenced by a statistical analysis mandated as a result of litigation in Maryland. This study showed that between 1995 and 1997, Black motorists made up more than 70% of those stopped by Maryland State Troopers along the Interstate 95 corridor, though they made up only 17% of motorists in the same time period (Russell, 1999). A recent report by the New Jersey attorney general provided evidence of racial disparities in traffic stops on New Jersey's roadways as well (Verniero & Zoubek, 1999).

A study currently being conducted in North Carolina attempts to address a number of key questions in the investigation of racial profiling through the use of a multimethod research design (Zingraff, Smith, & Tomaskovic-Devey, 2000). This study combines analysis of official data, baseline estimates of driving behaviors, a statewide citizen survey, focus groups of state troopers and supervisors, and citizen focus groups. Recognizing the complex nature of the phenomenon of racial profiling, the North Carolina investigators are exploring what officers do and why they do it, perceptions of racial profiling among the general public, and the experience of African Americans with regard to traffic stops (Zingraff et al., 2000).

The difficulty with gathering scientific data in this area is that it is nearly impossible to measure whether stops are racially motivated. Racially motivated stops are usually predicated on some other justification or pretext or the racial factor is conspicuously, and often skillfully, left out of police reports. Nonetheless, efforts to quantify racial disparities in traffic stops should continue. In the meantime, other methods for investigating racial profiling, such as the one described here, can further the agenda of adding social science knowledge to the shared personal knowledge amassed from the lived experiences of African Americans and other racial minorities in the United States. The importance of such research cannot be overstated. As Russell (1999) put it, "individual cases can be explained, dismissed and justified.

In their aggregate, the stream of anecdotal cases which suggest that Blackness can be equated with criminality has social consequences" (p. 721).

✖ Context for the Study

In the past 2 years, we have become involved with the National Association for the Advancement of Colored People (NAACP), the ACLU, and Milwaukee's Angela Davis Chapter of CopWatch in their respective endeavors to gather information about racial profiling in Milwaukee and Wisconsin as part of a broader effort to put an end to this practice. One of the major stumbling blocks in this struggle has been the denial by prominent government officials, most notably by former Wisconsin governor Tommy Thompson, that racial profiling occurs. In October 1999, then-Governor Thompson vetoed a budget item that would have appropriated money to gather demographic data on traffic stops to investigate the problem of "Driving While Black or Brown" stops. He stated that the extra time standing out in the road to write down the information would put police officers at too great a risk. Furthermore, Governor Thompson stated that because there is no evidence that racial profiling exists, there is no need to collect data on it. In support of this veto, Milwaukee Police Chief Arthur Jones, who is African American, and Milwaukee County Sheriff Lev Baldwin, who is White, denied that their departments engage in racial profiling. Governor Thompson further said that state law enforcement, almost as one voice, raised concerns over the costs involved in recording a driver's age, gender, race, or ethnicity; the nature of the search of the vehicle; and whether a citation or warning was issued. In lieu of providing for data collection that might shed light on the practice, Governor Thompson appointed a Task Force on Racial Profiling.

Official denials of the practice of racial profiling are in direct opposition to what members of the African American and Latino communities in Milwaukee have to say. Indeed, it is difficult to find a person of color who cannot relate at least one experience in his or her life of having been profiled based on race. There have been several public forums in Milwaukee during the past few years in which citizens have come forward to describe their experiences of having their civil rights violated by police. In addition, whenever the topic of a local Black radio station's morning talk show focuses on police, listeners call in to express their frustration about the frequency with which they are stopped by police because of their race. People describe feeling excluded from certain areas of the county because they are Black. Young African American men give accounts of being stopped and searched on a regular basis, usually with no ticket or citation being issued. For example, one young man reported that he had been stopped by police 18 times in a 6-month period. Employers in suburbs complain that they cannot keep employees from the inner city because they are continually stopped on their way to and from work and called on to explain their presence and show proof of employment. Mothers testify about their fear of their young sons turning 16 years old, because they know this is when it all begins.

On a panel on racial profiling at the December 1999 Big Ten Police Chiefs Conference in Madison, Wisconsin, there were 4 African Americans who averaged more than 20 years of law enforcement experience. Each of these law enforcement veterans stated at the outset that they themselves had been racially profiled on numerous occasions. The discussion among the 40 police chiefs in the room immediately proceeded from talking about whether racial profiling takes place to exploring strategies to put an end to this practice. Discussing the matter further over lunch, the veteran Black officers spoke about how saddened they were by the fact that they have to teach their own children how to survive an encounter with a police officer because of their race. The fact that these were experienced law enforcement officers stating that there is no question that racial profiling takes place was an extremely powerful indictment against those who deny the reality of this phenomenon.

It is difficult to reject the accounts of police officers who have been subjected to racial profiling as being uninformed or overly sensitive or to challenge their interpretations of events. Police officers, after all, well understand the intricacies, complexities, and dangers of law enforcement. It is for this reason that we set out to explore racial profiling by conducting a survey of African American police officers. African American police officers as respondents to a survey such as ours have conflicting interests. As African Americans, they have a vested interest in exposing the practice of racial profiling to bring an end to it and protect themselves and their communities from mistreatment by the police. On the other hand, as police officers, they have a vested interest in protecting the integrity of their profession and, thus, not perpetuating the perception that the police are engaged in this discriminatory practice. In fact, a few officers contacted us to express their concern that the survey might project a negative image of themselves as police officers, of the police department for which they work, or of policing in general. Each officer who telephoned emphatically stated that he or she had never been racially profiled or participated in the practice of racial profiling. Because it is natural to want to protect one's chosen profession from criticism, statements by African American police officers substantiating the reality of racial profiling are especially powerful.

Method of Investigation

The names and work addresses of Milwaukee police officers who were identified in official records as Black were provided by the Milwaukee Fire and Police Commission. An anonymous survey was mailed to these officers that asked them about their personal experiences of having been racially profiled by police. A definition of racial profiling was stated at the top of the survey, defining it as "when race is used by a police officer or a police agency in determining the potential criminality of an individual." The letter emphasized that we were not conducting an investigation of the Milwaukee Police Department but, rather, an investigation of the extent to which individual police officers who are African American have been victims of racial profiling by any police officer or agency.

The Milwaukee Police Department was selected because of the relatively large number of African American police officers in that department and because the Milwaukee Fire and Police Commission agreed to provide us with the names and districts of officers for the purpose of mailing the survey. According to the Fire and

Police Commission, the Milwaukee Police Department employs approximately 2,100 sworn personnel, 414 of whom are designated as Black. Each of the 414 Black officers was sent a survey with a cover letter explaining the project in detail. Three weeks later, a follow-up letter and survey were sent out to each person on the list to ensure as high a response rate as possible.

 ## Findings

The Respondents

Of the 414 African American police officers in the Milwaukee Police Department to whom we sent the survey, 167 responded, producing a response rate of 40%. A complete summary of responses to the questions about racial profiling, and the number of respondents who answered each question, can be found in Appendix B. Ninety-nine percent of the respondents indicated being 25 or older and having been a sworn police officer for at least 1 year. The percentage of male respondents is 83, whereas the percentage of female respondents is 17. These percentages are nearly identical to the proportions of male and female officers on the list of Black police officers provided by the Milwaukee Fire and Police Commission. Respondents were asked to identify themselves with regard to skin tone. Forty-one percent identified themselves as "dark-skinned," 31% as "light-skinned," and 28% as "other."

The Reality of Racial Profiling

The findings from this study of African American police officers substantiate what numerous citizens of Milwaukee have stated in public hearings and on radio talk programs—that racial profiling is a reality. Table 1 demonstrates that more than two thirds (69%) of the officers who responded to the survey believe that they have been stopped as a result of racial profiling at some point in their lives. Roughly half of the respondents indicated that they have been questioned as a result of racial profiling. Eighteen percent have been subjected to a search, and 22% were ticketed in an encounter attributed to racial profiling. Seven percent of respondents said that they had been arrested as a result of racial profiling. The large gap between the percentage stopped and the percentage arrested in a racial profiling encounter is consistent with other accounts, indicating that such stops are generally made without reasonable suspicion (Chambliss, 1994; Cole, 1999; Miller, 1996). In essence, stops based on racial profiling are "fishing expeditions" in which officers hope to obtain consent to search the person or vehicle, find some justification for a search, or identify some probable cause for an arrest. When these expectations are not fulfilled, which is most often the case, the officer initiating the stop lets the person go, with very little evidence (such as a ticket or an arrest report) left behind that the stop even occurred.

Table 2 demonstrates that racial profiling is not just a thing of the past. Forty-three percent of respondents said that they had been stopped as a result of

Table 1	Police Officers Who Have Experienced Racial Profiling		
	Yes (%)	**No (%)**	*n*
Stopped	69	31	166
Questioned	51	49	166
Searched	18	82	165
Ticketed	22	78	166
Arrested	7	93	166

Note: The table shows answers to the following question: "In your professional opinion, do you believe that you have ever been stopped, questioned, searched, ticketed, or arrested as a result of racial profiling as defined above? Please check all the boxes that apply."

Table 2	Police Officers Who Have Experienced Recent Racial Profiling (in percentages)			
	Past 5 Years ($n = 165$)		**Past 12 Months ($n = 164$)**	
	Yes	No	Yes	No
Stopped	43	57	26	74
Questioned	26	74	12	8S
Searched	7	9.1	1	99
Ticketed	5	95	2	98
Arrested	3	97		99

Note: The table shows answers to the following question: "In your professional opinion, do you believe that you have ever been stopped, questioned, searched, ticketed, or arrested as a result of racial profiling in the past 5 years? In the past 12 months? Please check all boxes that apply."

racial profiling in the past 5 years. One in four said they had been subjected to racial profiling in the past year. Every one of the officers who stated that they were subjected to racial profiling in the past year was a sworn police officer at the time of the incident. As would be expected, the percentages for having been searched, ticketed, and arrested are smaller than the percentages for having been stopped and questioned.

Does It Happen in Wisconsin?

One of the primary purposes of this survey was to gather data relevant to statements made by government officials, including Wisconsin's governor, the Milwaukee County sheriff, and the Milwaukee chief of police, that racial profiling is not practiced in the state of Wisconsin, the county of Milwaukee, or the city of Milwaukee. The information in Table 3 contradicts these statements, indicating that racial profiling is a current reality in Milwaukee and Wisconsin.

In the past 5 years, 43% of respondents were subjected to racial profiling in Wisconsin, 39% in Milwaukee County, and 38% in the city of Milwaukee. In the 12 months prior to the survey, 23% were racially profiled in Wisconsin and 20% were racially profiled in Milwaukee County. Perhaps most disturbing is that

nearly one of five police officers who responded to our survey were subjected to racial profiling in the past year in the city where they serve as law enforcement officers.

The Black Male

Of particular importance to understanding the phenomenon of racial profiling are the societal stereotypes that plague young Black men in the United States. Researchers have suggested that racial stereotypes and fears about Black men as being more criminal, more involved in illegal drugs, and more violent than other social groups penetrate the social consciousness of much of our society (Anderson, 1990; Hall, 1996; Russell, 1998). It is also widely agreed that the attitudes of police officers reflect the stereotypes and prejudices found throughout the rest of society and that young African American men are often perceived as symbolic assailants or as potential threats to the police (McConahay, 1986; Sears, 1988; Walker, Spohn, & DeLone, 2000). Much police research has established that although many racial/ethnic groups have had a history of confrontation with police, the group most consistently involved in conflict with the police is African American men (Barlow & Barlow, 2000). Thus, there is much to suggest that Black men are more likely than other groups to experience racial profiling at the hands of the police.

Table 3   Police Officers Who Have Experienced Racial Profiling in Wisconsin, the County of Milwaukee, and the City of Milwaukee

	Past 5 Years			Past 12 Months		
	Yes (%)	No (%)	*n*	Yes (%)	No (%)	*n*
State of Wisconsin	43	57	164	23	77	164
County of Milwaukee	39	61	164	20	80	164
City of Milwaukee	38	62	165	IS	S2	163
In another state	20	80	162	10	90	163

Note: The table shows answers to the following question: "In your professional opinion, do you believe that you have ever been stopped, questioned, searched, ticketed, or arrested as a result of racial profiling in the past 5 years or in the past 12 months in the state of Wisconsin, the county of Milwaukee, or the city of Milwaukee? Please check all the boxes that apply."

The only other group with which our data provide a basis for comparison to African American men is African American women. The findings in Table 4 appear to support the expectation that Black men are more likely to be victims of racial profiling by the police than Black women. Among respondents, male officers were more likely to report having been racially profiled than female officers in each of the time frame categories. Nearly 3 out of every 4 male respondents (74%) said that they had been subjected to racial profiling at some time in their lives, compared with 45% of female respondents. Almost half of the males (48%), compared with one fifth of the females (21%), said that they had been racially profiled in the past 5 years. Nearly 1 of every 3 male respondents (29%) reported having

been racially profiled in the in past 12 months, whereas the rate for female respondents in the same period was 1 in 10 (10%).

Skin Tone

Georges-Abeyie's (1989) theory of social distance suggests that discriminatory treatment of persons of color by police and other criminal justice personnel results in part because of the social distance created by differences in skin color between racial minorities and the White majority. Social distance theory suggests that discrimination will be greatest against those whose skin color is most different from the light skin tones of the majority. Tatum (2000), in an excellent discussion

Table 4   Police Officers Who Have Experienced Racial Profiling by Gender (in percentages)

	Ever Been Racially Profiled (*n* = 160)		Racially Profiled Past 5 Years (*n* = 165)		Racially Profiled Past 12 Months (*n* = 164)	
Gender	Yes	No	Yes	No	Yes	No
Male	74	26	48	52	29	71
Female	45	55	21	79	10	90

Note: The table shows answers, by gender, to the following question: "In your professional opinion, do you believe that you have ever been stopped as a result of racial profiling? In the past 5 years? In the past 12 months?"

of the literature on race and skin color, concludes that dark-skinned African Americans experience the greatest social distance from the White majority of any subgroup of the American population. Based on this literature, it is reasonable to expect that dark-skinned Blacks are victimized by racial profiling at a higher rate than Blacks with lighter skin tones.

Table 5 demonstrates that respondents who described themselves as "dark-skinned" reported having been racially profiled in the highest percentages for each of the three time periods (ever, in the past 5 years, and in the past 12 months). When considering the lower percentages of having been racially profiled for those who identified themselves as "light-skinned" and as "other," it should be noted that respondents who selected the category "other" generally described themselves as having medium, brown, or tan skin tones.

The Use of Racial Profiling

The final quantitative question in the survey asked respondents about their personal use of racial profiling in the performance of their job as a sworn police officer in the Milwaukee Police Department. The findings indicate that 90% of the respondents stated that they do not use racial profiling when they police and that they do not believe it to be a necessary and legitimate tool for police officers to use. However, considering the widespread condemnation of the practice of racial profiling by police executives, the International Association of Chiefs of Police, and the National Organization of Black Law Enforcement Officials, along with the historical fact that racial profiling is an oppressive form of control of African Americans and other people of color, it is somewhat surprising to find that 1 in 10 respondents stated that they use racial profiling and that 1 in 10 stated that they believe racial profiling is a necessary and legitimate tool for police officers.

Descriptions of Specific Cases

The final item on the survey was open-ended and asked respondents who have been subjected to racial profiling to describe the most recent time they had experienced such an encounter. Seventy of the respondents wrote nothing in the space provided. Fourteen used the space to state that they had not experienced racial profiling. One used the space to tell us that our time would be better spent examining the comparative lack of police protection for African Americans. One respondent indicated an unwillingness to share the details due to the possibility of repercussions. One gave a phone number, stating that the experience was too long to write about. Eighty respondents did provide a written description of the most recent time they were subjected to racial profiling.

Although we plan to discuss the qualitative portion of the survey in a separate article, it is worth mentioning here that the descriptions provided by the police officers in our study are dramatic. Many describe

Table 5	Police Officers Who Have Experienced Racial Profiling by Skin Tone (in percentages)					
	Ever Been Racially Profiled (*n* = 165)		Racially Profiled Past 5 Years (*n* = 164)		Racially Profiled Past 12 Months (*n* = 163)	
Skin Tone	Yes	No	Yes	No	Yes	No
Dark-skinned	75	25	50	50	34	66
Light-skinned	67	33	39	6!	22	78
Other	62	38	38	62	19	81

Note: The table shows answers, by skin tone (as self-identified by respondents), to the following question: "In your professional opinion, do you believe that you have ever been stopped as a result of racial profiling? In the past 5 years? In the past 12 months?"

the first words uttered by the officers who stopped them as abrupt and offensive questions, such as, "What are you doing here?" "Is this car stolen?" "Do you work here?" "Do you have a job?" When respondents asked why they had been stopped, they were told, "It's my job to ask the questions, not yours," "You were speeding," or "You fit the description of a suspect." Shortly after such statements, the respondents identified themselves as police officers. At this point, in many of the encounters described in the narrative accounts, the police officer initiating the contact quickly backed off and released the respondent. When the respondent attempted to continue the conversation and obtain clarification regarding the reason for the stop, the police officer was not able to give a reasonable justification and quickly left the scene. In one case, after the respondent requested that the officer provide his name and badge number and send for his supervisor, the police officer turned, ran back to his patrol car, and drove away.

⬙ Discussions and Conclusions

The purpose of this investigation was to provide data on the experience of racial profiling that cannot easily be dismissed by those who regard the accounts of ordinary citizens as unreliable and based on a lack of understanding of police work. Although some law enforcement leaders lack confidence in the ability of the general public to identify racial profiling, it could also be argued that denials of the reality of racial profiling by White authorities are unreliable and based on a lack of understanding of being Black in America. African American police officers have the unique vantage point of having the lived experience of being Black in America along with the professional knowledge and experience that comes with being police officers.

More than two thirds of the officers in our study reported having been on the receiving end of racial profiling at some point in their lives. Indicating that racial profiling is not just a thing of the past, 43% of respondents said that they had experienced racial profiling in the past 5 years, and 1 in 4 reported having been racially profiled in the past year. The degree to which racial profiling is a particular problem for Black

men is indicated by the fact that nearly 3 out of every 4 of the male respondents to our survey said that they had been subjected to this practice. Suggesting that dark-skinned African Americans are targeted to an even greater degree than those with light or medium skin tones, respondents who identified themselves as "dark-skinned" reported the highest percentages of having been racially profiled. Finally, despite having obvious reasons to oppose racial profiling, 1 in 10 of the officers in our survey reported that they engage in racial profiling themselves and believe it is a necessary tool of law enforcement.

The responses of the African American police officers in this survey must be added to the growing body of evidence of racial disparities in traffic stops and to the stream of first-person accounts by African Americans from all walks of life showing that racial profiling is a reality. Unfortunately, the obstacles faced by those who wish to bring an end to racial profiling include a context in which this practice is both denied and condoned. Even as police administrators deny the reality of racial profiling, they reward officers for effective use of drug courier profiles that rely on racial stereotypes. Even as the Supreme Court claims to guarantee equal protection for all citizens, it has all but condoned racial profiling by allowing police to use the pretext of traffic enforcement to stop anyone they want. Despite claims by some that civil rights for racial minorities have been achieved in the United States, racial discrimination continues to contaminate the criminal justice process. Though police officers are the gatekeepers to that process, they do not create their own marching orders. Bringing an end to racial profiling will require strong leadership dedicated to putting an end to racially biased policing in all its forms. Because of the failure of the Supreme Court to take decisive action to end racial profiling, police administrators must aggressively develop clear and direct policy guidelines that severely restrict police discretion when it comes to the use of race as a factor in determining potential criminality. These guidelines should be strictly enforced with disciplinary procedures for their violation. There must be an unequivocal message that racially biased policing will not be tolerated.

References

Anderson, E. (1990). *Streetwise*. Chicago: University of Chicago Press.

Bain, B. (2000, April 26–May 2). Walking while Black: The bill of rights for Black men. *Village Voice Online*. Retrieved October 25, 2000, from http://www.villagevoice.com/issues/0017/bain.shtml

Barlow, D. E., & Barlow, M. H. (2000). *Police in a multicultural society: An American story*. Prospect Heights, IL: Waveland.

Bast, C. M. (1997). Driving while Black: Stopping motorists on a subterfuge. *Criminal Law Bulletin, 33*, 457–486.

Chambliss, W. J. (1994). Policing the ghetto underclass: The politics of law and law enforcement. *Social Problems, 41*(2), 177–194.

Chambliss, W. J. (2001). *Power, politics and crime*. Boulder, CO: Westview.

Cole, D. (1999). *No equal justice: Race and class in the American criminal justice system*. New York: New Press.

Georges-Abeyie, D. (1989). Race, ethnicity, and the spatial dynamic: Toward a realistic study of Black crime, crime victimization, and criminal justice processing of Blacks. *Social Justice, 16*(4), 35–54.

Hall, R. (1996). Impact of skin color upon occupational projection: A case for Black male affirmative action. *Journal of African American Men, 1*(4), 87–94.

Harris, D. A. (1997). "Driving while Black" and all other traffic offenses: The Supreme Court and perpetual traffic stops. *Journal of Criminal Law and Criminology, 87*(2), 544–582.

Harris, D. A. (1999). Driving while Black: Racial profiling on our nation's highways. *American Civil Liberties Union Online*. Retrieved October 25, 2000, from http://www.aclu.org/profiling/report/index.html

Hughes, J. (2000). Some straight talk on profiling. *Law Enforcement News, 26*(530), 15.

Kennedy, R. (2000). Suspect policy. In Joseph L. Victor (Ed.), *Annual editions: Criminal justice* (24th ed., pp. 102–106). Guilford, CT: McGraw-Hill.

Kurlander, N. (2000). Software to track traffic stop data. *Law Enforcement Technology, 27*(1), 148–153.

Leadership Conference on Civil Rights. (2001). Justice on trial: Racial disparities in the American criminal justice system. *Leadership Conference Education Fund*. Retrieved October 25, 2000, from http://www.civilrights.org/publications/cj

Maryland v. Wilson, 519 U.S. 408 (1997).

Mauer, M. (1999). *Race to incarcerate*. New York: New Press.

McConahay, J. (1986). Modern racism, ambivalence, and the modern racism scale. In J. Dovidio & S. Gaertner (Eds.), *Prejudice, discrimination, and racism: Theory and research*. New York: Academic Press.

Miller, J. G. (1996). *Search and destroy: African-American males in the criminal justice system*. New York: Cambridge University Press.

New York v. Belton, 453 U.S. 454 (1981).

Ohio v. Robinette, 519 U.S. 33 (1996).

Pennsylvania v. Mimms, 434 U.S. 106 (1977).

Russell, K. K. (1998). *The color of crime: Racial hoaxes, White fear, Black protectionism, police harassment, and other macro aggressions*. New York: New York University Press.

Russell, K. K. (1999). "Driving while Black": Corollary phenomena and collateral consequences. *Boston College of Law Review, 40*(3), 717–731.

Sears, D. (1988). Symbolic racism. In P. Katz & D. Taylor (Eds.), *Eliminating racism*. New York: Plenum.

Strandberg, K. W. (1999). Racial profiling. *Law Enforcement Technology, 26*(6), 62–66.

Substance Abuse and Mental Health Services Administration. (2001, June). *National household survey on drug abuse, population estimates 2000*. Washington, DC: Substance Abuse and Mental Health Services Administration.

Tatum, B. (2000). Deconstructing the association of race and crime: The salience of skin color. In M. W. Markowitz & D. D. Jones-Brown (Eds.), *The system in Black and White: Exploring the connections between race, crime, and justice* (pp. 31–46). Westport, CT: Praeger.

United States v. Avery, 128 F.3d 974 (6th Cir. 1997).

United States v. Ross, 456 U.S. 798 (1982).

United States v. Travis, 62 F.3D 170 (6th Cir. 1995).

U.S. Department of Justice. Federal Bureau of Investigation, (2000). *Crime in the United States, 1999*. Washington, DC: Government Printing Office.

U.S. General Accounting Office. (2000). *Racial profiling: Limited data available on motorist stops*. Washington, DC: National Institute of Justice.

Verniero, P., & Zoubek, P. H. (1999). *Interim report of the state police review team regarding allegations of racial profiling*. Newark: New Jersey Office of the Attorney General.

Walker, S., Spohn, C., & DeLone, M. (2000). *The color of justice* (2nd ed.). Belmont, CA: Wadsworth/Thomson Learning.

Whren v. United States, 517 U.S. 806 (1996).

Wilkins v. Maryland Slate Police, CA. No. MJG-93-468 (D. Md. 1992).

Wyoming v. Houghton, 526 U.S. 295 (1999).

Zingraff, M. T., Smith. W. R., & Tomaskovic-Devey, D. (2000). North Carolina highway traffic and patrol study: "Driving while Black." *The Criminologist, 25*(3), 1–4.

DISCUSSION QUESTIONS

1. Why is this study unique?

2. What did the study find regarding skin tone and racial profiling?

3. If an African American police officer has been racially profiled while off duty, how do you think that this would impact her or his workplace experiences?

Ethics training is important, as police officers are presented with opportunities to become involved in deviant acts while on duty.

Police Deviance and Ethics

Section Highlights

- Review the various types of police deviance.
- Examine some of the factors that can lead to officers becoming involved in deviant acts.
- Explore how police ethics plays a role in controlling police officer behavior.

"Virginia Commonwealth University police sergeant was suspended after being arrested on distribution of child pornography charges." "Houston Texas police officer was convicted on federal corruption charges for using his police cruiser to escort what he believed was a shipment containing seven kilograms of cocaine." "Milwaukee Police Sergeant suspended for concocting a fake crime to cover up injuries that another officer sustained while he was sledding on duty."[1] Headlines in the media that feature scandals involving police officers quickly capture the attention of the public. All of the activities described in the previous news stories are acts of police deviance.

This section examines the extent to which police deviance occurs in the United States today and in the past. Several types of police deviance are identified and are accompanied by examples that have made the headlines in recent years. Factors that are believed to contribute to police officers becoming involved in acts of wrongdoing are discussed, along with some of the approaches used by police administrators to control such activities. Negative consequences that result from publicized incidents of police deviance are also highlighted. And finally, this section closes with a look at police ethics—more specifically, how ethics training impacts police officer behavior and the integrity of police organizations.

Definition of Terms

People often use the terms *police misconduct*, *police corruption*, and *police deviance* interchangeably when describing incidents of wrongdoing that involve police officers. It is important to note that each of these terms has varying definitions. For example, when police officers are involved in activities or behaviors that are inconsistent with accepted norms, values, or ethics associated with the policing profession, they are engaged in acts of **police deviance**.[2] There are two types of police deviance: (1) occupational deviance and (2) abuse of authority.[3] Police *occupational deviance* is the criminal and noncriminal acts that take place during the course of normal work activities and that are committed under the authority that police officers are granted in their positions.[4] Police corruption and police misconduct are two subsets of occupational deviance (see illustration). Acts that are committed by police officers during the course of work that result in some kind of personal gain or gain for others are acts of **police corruption**.[5] An example of this would be when police officers take money from crime scenes for their own personal use instead of logging the money into evidence as part of their criminal investigation. **Police misconduct** includes acts committed by police officers that violate department policies and procedures.[6] This includes cases in which police officers use physical force when it is not warranted according to guidelines provided by department policies and officer training.

In addition to occupational deviance, abuse of authority is another type of police deviance. *Abuse of authority* involves "any actions by a police officer without regard to motive, intent, or malice that tends to injure, insult, tread on human dignity, manifest feelings of inferiority, and/or violates an inherent legal right of a member of the police constituency."[7] This type of police deviance includes *physical abuse* (police brutality and police violence), in which officers use more physical force than is necessary during interactions with citizens; *psychological abuse,* in which police officers verbally assault, ridicule, discriminate against, or harass someone or threaten to take formal police action that is not justified against that person; and *legal abuse,* in which police officers violate an individual's constitutional, federally protected, or state-protected rights.[8]

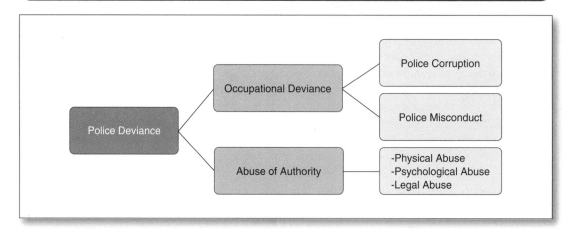

Understanding Police Deviance: Definition of Terms

History of Police Deviance in the United States

Acts of wrongdoing by police officers have occurred since the inception of policing in the United States.[9] In the political era, police deviance was a serious problem stemming from intense political involvement in American policing.[10] Police officers were handpicked by local politicians in an effort to help them maintain their positions.[11] In exchange for police officer positions, politicians would receive sums of money from the men that they hired to serve in these positions. Acts of wrongdoing by police officers in this era included the receipt of money, goods, and services from business owners under the agreement that the police would provide additional security to their businesses. It was also common for police officers to ignore vice crimes such as prostitution, illegal gambling, and the illegal sale of alcohol if they were given some of the profits that resulted from these activities. They would also use their discretionary power in questionable ways when interacting with immigrants and impoverished residents, which often included acts of brutality. Political involvement in policing is believed to be the driving force behind police corruption during this time.

In the reform era, changes to the police were centered on cutting the politics out of policing and making the police more professional.[12] Despite the police reform efforts that were taking place during this era, the Wickersham Report criticized the police for using the "third degree." This was a common course of action when the police tried to get information or confessions from people they believed were involved in crimes. The third degree involves questioning suspects for extended periods of time without food, water, or sleep; using bright lights and threats during interrogations; and using physical force to get people to provide them with information. During this era, police officers' use of excessive force against racial/ethnic minority citizens was reported by the media. This was especially the case during the civil rights movement that took place during the latter part of this era. Officers were involved in burglaries, briberies, and protection of illegal vice activities such as gambling and prostitution. Toward the end of this era, the media spotlight focused on widespread police corruption in the New York City Police Department (NYPD). Corruption problems in the NYPD were revealed when Frank Serpico (police officer) reported that police officers were involved in vice racketeering and other illegal activities.[13] When he refused to accept money from vice operations, he was treated as a "rat" or outcast by his colleagues.[14] The Knapp Commission was formed to investigate police corruption in the NYPD as a result of the Serpico case. This commission concluded that police deviance was not the result of a few "bad apples" in the NYPD; instead, they found evidence of widespread corruption throughout the police department.

Today, in the community/problem-solving era, police corruption scandals continue to be exposed in cities across the United States. Recently, several New Orleans police officers were convicted of charges related to the shooting of an unarmed man during Hurricane Katrina and then writing a false report to cover up their actions.[15] The NYPD has also been at the center of several scandals in the past few decades. In 1997, NYPD officers physically assaulted and sodomized Abner Louima with a toilet plunger in a police station house.[16] A few years later, four NYPD plain clothed officers shot Amadou Diallo 41 times; he was unarmed.[17]

It is clear that police deviance still occurs in American police agencies today; however, it is difficult to determine exactly how prevalent it is. It is difficult because many police agencies do not track incidents of police deviance (they are not required to keep track), and those that do keep track may be reluctant to provide that information to the public. In most cases, the public learns of occurrences of police deviance from the media.

One of the most comprehensive efforts to track incidents of police deviance is conducted by the National Police Misconduct Statistics and Reporting Project (NPMSRP). This nongovernment, nonpartisan project tracks media accounts of police deviance across the country in order to provide an estimate of the extent of this problem. Each year, this group publishes an annual report in an effort to raise public awareness of this issue. The 2010 annual report reveals that from January through December 2010, 4,861 individual cases of police misconduct were presented by the media. These cases involved 6,613 sworn law enforcement officers and 6,826 alleged victims. There were fatalities in 247 of these cases. And finally, the NPMSRP estimates that these acts cost $346,512,800 in civil judgments and settlements (this figure does not include settlements in sealed cases, court costs, or attorney fees).[18] The major drawback of using media reports is that there is no way to account for acts of police deviance that have not yet come to the attention of the media. In addition, media outlets may choose to report only the most egregious cases that come to their attention.

Types of Police Deviance

So what kinds of activities are categorized as police deviance? As mentioned earlier in this section, *police deviance* is a broad term that is used to describe actions and behaviors of police officers that are inconsistent with accepted norms, values, or ethics associated with the policing profession. These activities and behaviors generally fall into two categories: (1) activities that result in some personal gain for police officers, and (2) activities that do *not* result in any gain for police officers. Julian Roebuck and Thomas Barker identified several categories of police deviance that usually result in some material or monetary gain. Roebuck and Barker's categories of police deviance are presented in the following paragraphs and are accompanied by recent examples drawn from the news.[19]

Deviance That Results in Personal Gain

Corruption of Authority

The *corruption of authority* is the acceptance of free or discounted meals/liquor, services, or property/goods by police officers. Geoffrey Alpert and Roger Dunham reported that the acceptance of free meals and/or gifts was the most common form of police corruption in their study.[20] There is disagreement over whether police officers should be allowed to accept free meals and gifts. Some business owners see it as a gesture to show their appreciation to the local police, while others believe that it can lead to more serious forms of police deviance. One example that supports the latter argument occurred in 2008. A lieutenant major in the Daytona Beach Florida Police Department visited a local Starbucks up to six times during his shift and demanded free coffee. Starbucks usually offers free brewed coffee to police officers; however, the lieutenant major demanded free white mochas and specialty iced teas. When a Starbucks employee refused to give the specialty drinks for free, the lieutenant threatened that the response time to their business would be slow if they ever needed police service in the future. He was discharged from his position after he failed a polygraph test when asked about these allegations.[21]

Kickbacks

Kickbacks are instances in which police officers accept gifts, money, goods, or services for referring people to specific businesses (towing companies, ambulances, bail bonds, etc.). In 2011, a Baltimore police officer admitted to accepting $1,500 in kickbacks from the owners of an auto repair shop. The officer recommended the auto repair shop to motorists who had been in car accidents or that needed repairs, promising that the owners of the shop would waive their towing fees and help them file claims with their insurance companies. There is speculation that up to 50 additional Baltimore police officers were involved in this scam.[22]

Protection of Illegal Activities

Protection of illegal activities occurs when police accept money from vice operations or legitimate businesses operating in an illegal manner. In 2000, 11 West New York, New Jersey, police officers were sentenced for their involvement in the protection of illegal gambling and prostitution operations, extortion, and accepting bribes for over a decade. The former chief of police in West New York was sentenced to 4 years in prison for admitting that he had collected $2 million through loansharking and payoffs from illegal gambling operations.[23]

Opportunistic Thefts

Opportunistic thefts happen when police officers commit theft from arrestees, victims, crime scenes, and unprotected property. In 2011, a District of Columbia police officer was arrested on theft charges for stealing money

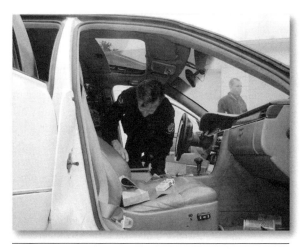

Opportunistic thefts can occur when officers conduct searches in vehicles or houses and on suspects they encounter while on duty.

from an elderly woman she met during a fraud investigation. The sergeant is accused of forging the signature of an 85-year-old woman on checks that totaled more than $43,000. The officer then deposited the elderly woman's money into her own personal bank account.[24]

Traffic Fix

A *traffic fix* takes place when police officers dispose of traffic tickets in exchange for money or some other kind of material reward. In 2007, a Westfield, Indiana, police lieutenant was accused of accepting cash in lieu of writing traffic tickets or taking people to jail. The lieutenant was stopping Hispanic drivers with the intent of making deals with them so that they could avoid being arrested or ticketed.[25] More recently, several police officers from the NYPD were indicted on a large-scale ticket-fixing scheme.[26] It is believed that this ticket-fixing scheme has resulted in the city losing between $1 million and $2 million in revenue.[27]

Misdemeanor Fix

A **misdemeanor fix** occurs when police officers quash misdemeanor court proceedings or misdemeanor citations for money or some other type of material reward. This also includes tampering with evidence and giving false testimony that eventually leads to the "fix" of misdemeanor cases or citations. In 2011, a 17-year veteran of the West Bloomfield, Michigan, Police Department was accused of soliciting more than a thousand dollars from a resident who was involved in a minor traffic accident. This example of a misdemeanor fix came to light after the resident complained about being asked for money in exchange for having his traffic citations dismissed.[28]

Felony Fix

A *felony fix* is the "fixing" of felony-level cases for money or other forms of material reward. This also includes tampering with evidence and giving false testimony in court proceedings to influence the outcome of felony court cases. In 2010, two Tulsa, Oklahoma, police officers were charged with perjury, civil rights violations, drugs, tampering with witnesses in felony cases, and coercing others to commit perjury with threats of retaliation.[29] Several people are now asking for their past convictions to be dismissed because of the corrupt behavior of the police officers involved in their cases.[30]

Direct Involvement in Criminal Activities

Direct involvement in criminal activities describes police officers' engaging in felonies such as burglary, robbery, and larceny for some kind of monetary or material reward. In 2010, a 22-year veteran officer from the Conroe, Texas, Police Department was convicted of robbing a bank at which he had previously worked as a security guard for several years.[31] In 2011, a police officer in Mount Washington, Kentucky, pled guilty to burglary and assault charges. The officer is accused of threatening and breaking into the home of his ex-girlfriend, who also happens to be a police officer.[32]

Internal Payoffs

Internal payoffs are made when one officer sells days off, holidays, or work assignments to another officer, or when an officer provides payments or favors in exchange for promotions. This type of police deviance is not very common today, as most police agencies allow police officers to choose their work assignments and shifts using a bidding system based on seniority. In addition, police unions monitor these processes closely to ensure fairness and equity to their members. Many police agencies use promotion processes that include both a test and an interview component that typically involves civil service and human resource employees. The representatives from these two groups are used in the process to ensure that it is conducted in a fair manner. Some jurisdictions choose to use alternative processes for both the assignment and promotion of police officers. In 2009, a Paramus, New Jersey, police captain denied that he traded political favors to advance through the ranks in his police department. He had been accused of selling fund-raising tickets for local politicians with the hope that it would lead to a future promotion.[33]

Shakedowns

Shakedowns happen when police officers take money or other valuable items from traffic offenders or criminals that are caught in the act of committing crimes. In 2004, a Newark police officer was charged with conspiracy, official misconduct, and theft. He was accused of taking cash, drugs, and weapons from drug dealers, criminal suspects, and others by shaking them down. He was also accused of planting drugs on people in order to increase his number of arrests. He then attempted to cover up his actions.[34]

Thomas Barker identified six categories of police deviance that do *not* result in any material or monetary gain to police officers. All six categories, as well as recent examples of each type of deviance, are presented in the following section.[35]

Deviance That Does Not Result in Personal Gain

Perjury

Perjury takes place when police officers lie or withhold information while under oath. Perjury is often used to cover up police officers' illegal behaviors.[36] **Testilying** is a slang term used for police officers giving false testimony against defendants in criminal trials.[37] This act of police deviance erodes the credibility of police officers in the courtroom. It can also impact the outcome of court cases in which innocent citizens face the possibility of being sentenced to jail or prison. In 2011, a Barre, Massachusetts, police officer was convicted of committing perjury while testifying before two grand juries in 2010 and, more recently, to a jury that was deliberating the trial of his girlfriend.[38]

Sleeping While on Duty

Sleeping while on duty refers to police officers who sleep or take naps during their scheduled shifts. This type of police deviance may appear to be harmless to some people. The problem is that police officers are not able to provide necessary services to the public if they are sleeping on the job—this would be especially important if they are needed in cases of emergencies when response time is critical. A study conducted in 2004 revealed that more than 30% of the police officers that were surveyed stated that they have witnessed fellow officers sleeping while on duty.[39] In 2011, a Cincinnati resident took cell phone video footage of a police officer sleeping on the job. The resident stated that he witnessed the officer sleeping while her patrol car lights were flashing when she was supposed to be securing the scene of a fallen tree.[40]

Sex While on Duty

Sex while on duty refers to police officers who engage in sexual acts during their scheduled shifts. There are several types of police sexual misconduct: (1) nonsexual contact (sexual harassment, flirting while on duty); (2) voyeuristic contact (watching other people have sex in public places); (3) contact with crime victims (sexual harassment); (4) contact with offenders (inappropriate body searches, frisks, and pat downs); (5) contact with juveniles offenders (sexual harassment and sexual contact); (6) sexual shakedowns (officers demand sex from prostitutes or others that are involved in criminal activities); and (7) citizen-initiated contact (consensual sex between police officers and citizens).[41] Research suggests that police sexual misconduct is more common among male police officers than female officers.[42] Studies have also revealed that both police officers and police chiefs believe that police sexual misconduct is common; however, they believe that the less serious forms of police sexual misconduct occurs the most (including consensual sex or flirting while on duty).[43] In 2011, a Phoenix police officer (the son of the mayor of Phoenix) was suspended for 4 days for inappropriately touching one woman and also for having sex twice while on duty with another woman.[44]

Consuming Drugs or Alcohol While on Duty

Consuming drugs or alcohol while on duty refers to police officers who consume these substances shortly before or during the course of their shifts. Peter Kraska and Victor Kappeler studied drug use by officers in a police agency in the Southern region of the United States. They found that there was a significant use of marijuana and nonprescription drugs by police officers in this department. They also found that most of the drug-using officers had 4 to 9 years of police experience and had track records of good performance at work.[45] In 2010, a Platteville, Wisconsin, police officer was arrested for maintaining a crack house and smoking crack several times while on duty. An informant stated that he had seen the police officer smoke crack on at least six occasions, including several times when she was in her police uniform and carrying her firearm.[46]

Police officer use of alcohol while on duty is also dangerous. Research suggests that some police officers consume alcohol as a way to deal with the stress associated with their job.[47] One study found that more than two-thirds (67%) of the police officers surveyed admitted to drinking while on duty or just before their shifts began.[48] In 2011, a Fort Wayne, Indiana, police officer was suspended for 6

The autonomous nature of police work lends to the opportunity for acts of police brutality to occur.

months without pay for coming to work with alcohol in his system. When he arrived at work, he had a blood-alcohol content of 0.03%. He admitted that he had consumed 12 or more beers within 12 hours of the start of his shift. It was the second time in 3 years that the police officer came to work with alcohol in his system.[49]

Police Brutality

Police brutality occurs when police officers use abusive language, intimidation, and threats toward citizens (including threats with weapons); conduct unwarranted stops and searches; and also use nonlethal physical force on citizens when it is not justified. There is no consensus among researchers regarding the prevalence of police brutality in the United States. A study using police–citizen traffic stop encounters revealed that the police used or threatened the use of physical force in approximately 1% of all police–citizen encounters.[50] Robert Worden asserts that (overall) police officers do not use force in most instances, but when they do use force, a substantial portion of that force seems to be excessive or unnecessary.[51] Others believe that police brutality is more common. Human Rights Watch examined police brutality in 14 large cities across the country and concluded that police brutality is persistent in all of the cities they included in their study.[52] The difficulty in deciphering the exact frequency of police brutality is that it is "a difficult-to-define and hard-to-observe phenomenon."[53] Often the only time that the general public hears about police brutality cases is when these incidents are brought to light by the media. In 2009, a Milwaukee resident was awarded $3 million from a police brutality lawsuit settlement (the largest in Milwaukee history). The settlement resulted from an incident in which two Milwaukee police officers broke the citizen's spine when they threw him to the floor and then slammed his head into the wall during an arrest. He became a quadriplegic as a result of the incident.[54]

Deadly Force

Police officers sometimes use *deadly force* when it is not warranted. Past research indicates that while police–citizen interactions are numerous, police officer use of deadly force is rare in the United States.[55] Some believe that police use of deadly force has decreased in the last few decades in part because of greater access to nonlethal weapons (such as TASERS),[56] as well as more restrictive deadly force policies adopted by police agencies.[57] Despite the reported decline in deadly force shootings, any incident of police officers using deadly force when it is not justified attracts the attention of the public. This is especially the case when White police officers shoot racial/ethnic minority citizens.[58] In 2001, a White Cincinnati police officer shot and killed an unarmed African American man who was fleeing to avoid being arrested on misdemeanor charges (unpaid traffic tickets). The shooting sparked several days of rioting, as the Cincinnati police had also shot 14 other Black men in the previous 6-year time period.[59]

Levels of Involvement

When a scandal involving police deviance is brought to the public's attention, it is common for police chiefs to blame the misconduct on one or a few *bad apples*. A bad apple is one or a few police officers that are involved in acts of wrongdoing. Bad apples are believed to be unlike or unrepresentative of the rest of the police organization.[60] This explanation suggests that the police agency can easily fix the problem by simply removing the bad apple(s) from the barrel. The **rotten apple theory** is an accurate depiction of some police scandals. There are many instances in which one or two officers are responsible for acts of wrongdoing while the rest of the police officers in the organization are doing a good job. Criticisms of the rotten apple(s) theory include that it does not account for the long history of police corruption in some police agencies and it also does not explain the absence of police deviance in other police agencies. Further, this theory does not explain why some police officers begin their careers as "good cops" but end up becoming "bad cops" or rotten apples.

There are also *rotten pockets* in which groups of police officers are working together when they are involved in acts of deviance.[61] *Rotten branches* are subunits within police organizations (such as specialized units—gang-suppression units, vice squads, etc.) that are involved in corrupt activities.[62] A growing body of research suggests that rotten apples are not individuals that enter the policing profession with some personal defect or deficiency; instead, it may be the stressful policing profession itself that provides fertile ground for bad apples to grow.[63] Maurice Punch takes the levels of police deviance a step further with his concept of a *rotten orchard*. A rotten orchard is when "systems become the contexts for widespread and institutionalized rule-bending and illegality . . . a wider system failure . . . The system includes the police organization, the criminal justice system and the broader socio-political context."[64]

There are other typologies that have been used to describe the levels of officer involvement in police deviance. Lawrence Sherman identified three levels of involvement. First, there are rotten apples and rotten pockets (as previously discussed). Second, there is *unorganized corruption* in which a majority of police officers are corrupt but are not working together. And third, *pervasive organized corruption* is an organized level of corruption that is systematic and reaches the highest levels in police departments.[65]

The Knapp Commission investigation revealed widespread corruption in the New York City Police Department in the 1970s. Specifically, the investigation uncovered two types of corrupt officers: (1) *Grass eaters* are police officers who accept payoffs and gratuities from which the circumstances of police work might develop, and (2) *meat eaters* are police officers who misuse their power and position to exploit situations for large payoffs in a premeditated manner.[66] The investigation revealed that a number of police officers that were grass eaters had learned this behavior from other veteran officers working within the organization. The commission suggested that the removal of veteran officers who were grass eaters was one way to prevent new police officers from becoming corrupt, as they would no longer have anyone modeling this type of behavior for them. The findings from the investigation discredit the rotten apple theory, as it found that the police culture within the New York City Police Department had directly contributed to the widespread involvement of officers in deviant activities.

 ## Causes of Police Deviance

What causes police officers to become involved in acts of deviance? Unfortunately, this is a question that does not have just one simple answer. It is a question that is frequently debated among police scholars and practitioners, as they have differing views on what causes police officers to become involved in acts of deviance. As mentioned earlier, police administrators often use the rotten apple theory to explain why acts of police deviance occur within their agencies. This theory suggests that there is something about the individual police officer involved in the misconduct that has caused him or her to be led astray, including poor decision making, impulsivity, immorality, or some other personality flaw. This explanation proposes that the cause of police deviance can be found within individual police officers.

Researchers have examined several causes of police deviance that come from within police organizations. It has been suggested that some police officers will become involved in misconduct as a result of low pay or inadequate salaries,[67] as well as a lack of opportunity for advancement and promotion (which can ultimately lead to additional pay).[68] Officers that earn low salaries may seek out additional money through illegitimate or illegal means (shakedowns, briberies, robberies, etc.). Another option for low-paid officers is taking on second jobs or "moonlighting."[69] Some police agencies have found that moonlighting can become problematic, as there are people who will not be able to perform their duties as police officers as a result of being tired from working a second job.[70] This has led some police agencies to either restrict the number of hours worked at a secondary job or not allow it at all. Some police agencies also restrict the type of businesses in which police officers are allowed to work at for a second job. Police officers are often not allowed to work at certain businesses such as bars or liquor stores, dance clubs, and strip clubs, as these places can provide easy access to illegal activities,[71] and sometimes the unsavory reputations of these businesses do not mirror the same image that is viewed as desirable by police administrators.

The nature of police work has also been identified as a contributing factor to police deviance. At the end of this section, the article "The Dirty Harry Problem," written by Carl Klockars, discusses how police work places officers in situations in which they may choose to use illegal or "dirty" means to complete their work. Because police officers have a high level of discretion associated with their job, they have the ability to make decisions without the input of others (including supervisors).[72] The ability to make decisions on their own can result in instances in which police officers make the wrong decision and choose to participate in deviant acts. Police work also provides plenty of opportunities for police officers to become involved in misconduct, as officers frequently interact with people who are involved in criminal activities. Ample opportunity coupled with a high degree of autonomy makes it easy for deviant acts to take place and also to go undetected. A lack of supervision or inadequate oversight of police officers also allows acts of police deviance to go unnoticed.[73]

It has been suggested that the socialization process that police officers experience is another potential cause of police deviance. The police socialization process is the primary way that officers learn their occupational values and morals. Steven Ellwanger suggests that there are two ways to think about the socialization process (specifically, how officers acquire police values).[74] First, we can think about it from a *value-predisposition perspective*. This is the idea that people bring with them a set of broader societal values when they enter police organizations. The societal values that match those that are valued by police agencies are reinforced, while the societal values that conflict with those valued by police agencies are ultimately replaced or changed during the processes of professionalization and culturalizaton.[75] *Professionalization* is the formal process through which police officers learn the norms and values of the profession through training and practice.[76] *Culturalization* is the informal process experienced by police officers as they learn the norms and values of the profession through interactions with their field training supervisor, "war stories" told by more seasoned police officers with whom they work, and personal experiences on the job.[77] And a second way to explain how police values are acquired is from a *values-learned perspective*. This is the idea that police values are learned through the socialization and culturalization processes that take place when people enter the policing profession.

It could be argued that the police socialization process can sometimes translate into deviance if certain conditions are present. For example, new police officers may begin their careers being trained by seasoned officers that may be involved in deviant activities.[78] As a result of the socialization process, some officers will continue to participate in such activities over the course of their careers. Police deviance may become an accepted practice by police officers if there is a presence of corruption in the community or local government.[79] If there is corruption among other prominent people within a community (such as prosecutors, politicians, and other community leaders), police officers may use that as an excuse to justify their own behavior.[80] If deviance is tolerated within local city government, there is also a chance that police deviance would be tolerated by police organizations.[81] Ultimately, if deviance is accepted or tolerated within a police agency, officers hired to work within that agency will learn this during the socialization process.

The Impact of Police Deviance on the Community and Police Organizations

Regardless of the causes of police deviance, this type of activity has several potential negative outcomes. Acts of deviance can lower citizens' confidence in the police and erode the relationship between these two groups.[82] There may also be an increase in citizen complaints filed against the police after citizens become aware of incidents of police misconduct in their community.[83] It can also cost taxpayers money in the form of settlements and payouts for litigation that can result from such acts.[84]

Police deviance can also undermine the efforts of police agencies that are committed to community policing. As discussed in Section 2, community policing is based on the premise that the police will partner with citizens to manage crime and maintain order in the community. If community members do not trust their local police as a result of known police misconduct, it is likely that they will not want to partner with them. Without support and help from the public, police officers could have a hard time doing their job.[85] Police deviance also encourages some police officers to be dishonest, as they may be put in positions in which they are asked or expected to cover up the deviant actions of fellow police officers.[86] And finally, it can lower the morale among police officers.[87] If some police officers within an organization are involved in acts of wrongdoing and the public becomes aware of those acts, the police officers that are *not* involved in those activities will be subjected to higher levels of scrutiny and lower levels of trust from the public. This can have a negative impact on how police officers view their work and how they believe that citizens view them.

When considering the negative effects that police deviance can have on communities, police officers, and police organizations, it is no surprise that community leaders and police administrators take steps to reduce or prevent these acts from occurring.

Controlling Police Deviance

Police deviance is a multifaceted issue that is difficult to control. Herman Goldstein identified four organizational and occupational dimensions that provide a context for understanding the complexity of this problem: (1) *organizational rules*—how organizational rules that govern police corruption are established, communicated, and understood by police personnel; (2) *the code* or *blue curtain*—the notion that police officers do not report fellow officers that are involved in acts of misconduct, which means that police agencies will need to "pull back the blue curtain" in an effort to control deviant officer behavior; (3) *public expectations*—the dimension that acknowledges the influence that the social, economic, and political environments have on the manner in which police organizations function; and (4) *prevention and control mechanisms geared toward police deviance*—the dimension found both within and outside of police agencies.[88]

External Control Mechanisms

Citizen involvement in the oversight of the police is one external mechanism that is used to control police deviance. Samuel Walker defines *citizen oversight* as "a procedure for providing input into the complaint process by individuals who are not sworn officers."[89] Citizen oversight increases the level of accountability of police officers and no longer allows the police to police themselves. Citizen involvement increases the likelihood that any police misconduct problems will be identified and handled in an appropriate manner. The adoption of citizen oversight programs in the United States has continued to increase over the last four decades.[90]

Police auditors are another type of external control mechanism. These individuals monitor citizen complaint processes within police agencies, along with several other police operations.[91] They have access to internal police documents to help them with their auditing process. Auditors publish annual reports providing details about the happenings within police agencies, along with specific recommendations to correct any problems that may have been identified. These reports also detail the efforts that police agencies have made to correct problems that auditors had previously identified.

The media are another external control mechanism for police deviance. As mentioned earlier in this section, it is often the media that present cases of police deviance to the public. When this happens, police administrators are put in positions in which they have to respond to the allegations made against their officer(s). The ease of access that citizens have to technology furthers the impact of the media on police deviance, as citizens will turn over recorded video footage of police officers involved in acts of misconduct to media outlets. When the media airs this type of footage, the general public becomes aware of the recorded events. A recent example of this is the video footage from the Occupy Wall Street protests that have taken place in cities across the United States. Videos of police officers using pepper spray and physical force on Occupy protesters grabbed the attention of the public and created a greater level of scrutiny of the police during these events.[92]

Federal government agencies that have the authority to conduct special investigations into police misconduct are another source of external control of police misconduct. As outlined in Section 9, special investigations conducted by the Department of Justice[93] and special commissions that are created to investigate allegations of police wrongdoing (i.e., the Knapp Commission) provide another layer of accountability that is found outside of police agencies. Court proceedings, including the criminal prosecution of police misconduct and the ability of citizens to file lawsuits naming both police officers and police agencies, are another external control mechanism for police deviance.[94] Section 9 of this book provides a detailed description of litigation involving the police.

Internal Control Mechanisms

There are several ways that police leaders can try to control police officers' involvement in acts of deviance. First, chiefs of police and other high-ranking police officials need to project a zero-tolerance attitude toward officer involvement in deviant acts. This means that clearly stated policies (and enforcement of those policies) should be implemented to support a zero-tolerance attitude.[95] It is also important that first-line police supervisors who are monitoring police officer activities on the streets also have a zero-tolerance attitude toward misconduct. Attentive supervisors can identify problems early on and then intervene with corrective actions to take care of any issues.[96]

Another way to control police deviance is through the use of effective recruitment and employment screening tools. Police recruiters can weed out individuals that have a greater chance of becoming problem officers *before* they are hired. Background checks,[97] in-depth psychological screening,[98] and maintaining high employment standards can help ward off high-risk applicants that are likely to become problem officers after they are hired.[99] Jack Greene and his colleagues discovered that prior traffic offenses, suspended or revoked licenses, and contact(s) with the criminal justice system are good predictors of future involvement in police misconduct.[100] Steps can be taken to identify potentially problematic officers by examining their performance in the police academy. The identification of individuals that performed poorly in the police academy (either in academy classes or that received discipline while in the academy) has been found to have some predictive value that could possibly direct early intervention efforts.[101]

Several police agencies across the United States use integrity tests to identify problem officers.[102] Integrity tests are staged situations that present opportunities for police officers to become involved in misconduct.[103] For example, some agencies will use undercover police officers who pretend that they are citizens with hostile attitudes toward the police to see if officers will handle these situations in an appropriate manner. Another common integrity test includes leaving money or property out in plain view at crime scenes to see if police officers will collect it as evidence or take it for their own personal use.[104] Integrity tests are conducted with no prior announcement or warning to police officers. Police supervisors are generally supportive of the use of integrity tests to both uncover and deter police misconduct in their organizations.[105] Police unions and some police officers, however, believe that integrity tests are a form of entrapment and should not be used to monitor officer behavior.[106]

It has also been suggested that police agencies shift their focus from the "bad cops" to the "good cops" by rewarding police officers that turn in fellow officers that are involved in police deviance.[107] This means that police officers will have to break their "code of silence." The code of silence is based on the idea that police officers will never tell on their colleagues, even if they are involved in corrupt activities. Gary Rothwell and Norman Baldwin conducted a study on whistleblowers within police agencies. This study found that two variables were consistent predictors of whistle blowing in police agencies: the presence of a mandatory reporting policy for police misconduct and supervisory status.[108]

Police agencies can increase their ability to control police deviance by having a functioning **internal affairs** division (IAD) or professional standards bureau (PSB). IADs and PSBs are divisions within police agencies that are responsible for investigating allegations of police misconduct filed by citizens and police personnel.[109] These divisions are often criticized for not doing fair and thorough investigations of complaints of police misconduct. Some argue that it is not appropriate for the police to be policing themselves. A national study by the Police Foundation revealed that police departments sustain only 10% of the complaints filed against police officers.[110] More recently, the Bureau of Justice Statistics reported that only 8% of the 26,556 citizen complaints filed against police officers in 2002 were sustained or found in favor of the citizen.[111] These statistics support the argument that the police should not be policing themselves, and can leave citizens feeling as though their complaints were not taken seriously.[112]

A handful of police agencies are using an alternative method to process citizen complaints filed against the police—**mediation**. Mediation is a form of alternative dispute resolution in which two parties resolve conflict through face-to-face dialogue with a trained mediator present.[113] The goal of mediation is for both parties to come to an understanding (not an agreement) about the conflict in which both sides are able to voice their opinions and concerns. Samuel Walker and Carol Archbold explored the use of mediation to handle citizen complaints against the police.[114] This study found that in the 14 cities where active mediation programs exist, only a few cases were actually being referred to mediation. Most citizen complaints continued to be handled using the traditional investigative process.

And finally, police agencies incorporate ethics into various stages of police officer training as a way to control officer involvement in misconduct. *Ethics* are "the rules of conduct recognized in respect to a particular class of human actions or a particular group, culture, etc."[115] Individuals that belong to a particular group use the rules of conduct or ethics that are applicable to their group as a way to guide their decision making and actions. Many occupations are bound to ethical guidelines unique to the profession, including medical doctors, social workers, teachers, researchers, real estate agents, nurses, journalists, librarians, and coaches, to name a few. Ethics are often incorporated into training of various professions with the hope that they will help individuals make the right decisions and do the right things (according to a set of morals and values that are deemed important by certain groups) as they conduct their work.

⊠ Police Ethics

A report by the International Association of Chiefs of Police (IACP) states that "ethics is our greatest training and leadership need today and into the next century."[116] Police executives have taken the IACP's statement on **police ethics** seriously, as all state and local law enforcement training academies now incorporate ethics into their curricula.[117] The Office of Community Oriented Policing Services (COPS office) has also developed "The ethics toolkit: Enhancing law enforcement ethics in a community policing environment."[118] This training toolkit has made it easier for police administrators to weave ethics into various phases of officer training.

Ethics play an important role in the perceived integrity and reputation of police organizations.

But does ethics training make a difference? Does ethics training influence police officer behavior? Only a few studies have attempted to answer these questions. One study that surveyed police officers from the southern region of the United States found that officers that were older, female, college educated, and had received some form of ethics training made more ethical decisions on how to handle ethics-based scenarios presented to them by researchers.[119] George Felkenes studied this issue using a sample from police agencies in Southern California. He found that nearly all (97%) of the police officers surveyed reported that the requirements for professional honesty were clearly presented to them by their respective agencies. This study also revealed that many police officers (75%) relied on their own personal ethics instead of law enforcement ethics to guide them in their professional activities.[120] Additional research is needed on this topic in order to fully understand the impact of ethics training on police officer behavior.

Another way to study police ethics is to measure a police agency's **culture of integrity**. Culture of integrity is the presence of clearly understood and implemented policies and rules within a police agency.[121] Carl Klockars and his colleagues created an instrument to measure the culture of integrity. The survey instrument includes 11 hypothetical scenarios that range from simple conflicts of interest to more serious events (see table on page 451). Respondents were asked seven questions in relation to each of the 11 scenarios. These questions focused on officers' perceptions of the seriousness of the activities presented in the scenarios, severity of discipline meted out in response to the activities in the scenarios, the willingness of police personnel to report the misconduct in the scenarios, and whether the behaviors in the scenarios violate department policies. Klockars and his colleagues administered the survey instrument to a sample of 3,235 police officers from 30 American police agencies.[122] Their study revealed that the more serious the officers perceived the scenario to be, the more likely they were to think that harsh discipline would be appropriate, and that they would be more likely to report their colleagues' behavior to their supervisors. The study also found that police officers believe that they have stronger integrity than their peers. It was not surprising to learn that there were significant differences in the culture of integrity among the 30 police agencies in their study.

Klockars's police integrity scale has been utilized in several studies. Joseph Schafer and Thomas Martinelli used Klockars's scale to study the perceptions of police integrity of first-line supervisors in the Sunnyville Police Department. This study revealed that the supervisors viewed the behaviors in the vignettes as more serious than the national sample of police officers used by Klockars and his colleagues several years earlier. Similar to Klockars's study, the supervisors also reported that they believe that they have greater integrity than their peers. The article written by Gennaro Vito and his colleagues included at the end of this section extends this line of research by using the Klockars's scale to measure the integrity of both first line police supervisors and middle managers.

The extent to which police deviance can be controlled or prevented has yet to be determined. The reason for this is the difficulty in identifying these acts, as well as the lack of reporting of such incidents by both citizens and police officers. Additional research focused on police ethics will be helpful in directing future police training efforts in the right direction.

Scenarios From Klockars's Police Integrity Scale

Case 1	A police officer runs his own private business in which he sells and installs security devices, such as alarms, special locks, etc. He does this work during his off-duty hours.
Case 2	A police officer routinely accepts free meals, cigarettes, and other items of small value from merchants on his beat. He does not solicit these gifts and is careful not to abuse the generosity of those who give gifts to him.
Case 3	A police officer stops a motorist for speeding. The officer agrees to accept a personal gift of half of the amount of the fine in exchange for not issuing a citation.
Case 4	A police officer is widely liked in the community, and on holidays, local merchants and restaurant and bar owners show their appreciation for his attention by giving him gifts of food and liquor.
Case 5	A police officer discovers a burglary of a jewelry shop. The display cases are smashed and it is obvious that many items have been taken. While searching the shop, he takes a watch worth about 2 days' pay for that officer. He reports the watch had been stolen during the burglary.
Case 6	A police officer has a private arrangement with a local auto body shop to refer the owners of cars damaged in accidents to the shop. In exchange for each referral, he receives payment of 5% of the repair bill from the shop owner.
Case 7	A police officer who happens to be a very good auto mechanic is scheduled to work during upcoming holidays. A supervisor offers him these days off if he agrees to tune up his supervisor's personal car. Evaluate the supervisor's behavior.
Case 8	At 2:00 a.m., a police officer who is on duty is driving his patrol car on a deserted road. He sees a vehicle that has been driven off the road and is stuck in a ditch. He approaches the vehicle and observes the driver is not hurt but is obviously intoxicated. He also finds that the driver is a police officer. Instead of reporting this accident and offense, he transports the driver to his home.
Case 9	A police officer finds a bar on his beat that is still serving drinks a half-hour past its legal closing time. Instead of reporting this violation, the police officer agrees to accept a couple of free drinks from the owner.
Case 10	Two police officers on foot patrol surprise a man who is attempting to break into an automobile. The man flees. They chase him for about two blocks before apprehending him by tackling him and wrestling him to the ground. After he is under control, both officers punch him a couple times in the stomach as punishment for fleeing and resisting.
Case 11	A police officer finds a wallet in a parking lot. It contains an amount of money equivalent to a full day's pay for that officer. He reports the wallet as lost property but keeps the money for himself.

SUMMARY

- Acts of police deviance have occurred dating as far back as the inception of policing in the United States.
- There are two categories of police deviance: acts that result in some kind of personal gain and acts that do not result in any personal gain.
- There are several control mechanisms used within police agencies and outside of police agencies to control police deviance.

- The rotten apple theory is commonly used by police executives when they respond to allegations of police deviance occurring within their police organizations.
- There are several factors both within police agencies and outside of police agencies that can cause police officers to become involved in acts of police deviance.

KEY TERMS

culture of integrity	misdemeanor fix	police misconduct
internal affairs	police corruption	rotten apple theory
kickbacks	police deviance	testilying
mediation	police ethics	

DISCUSSION QUESTIONS

1. What are some of the acts of police deviance that result in personal gain?

2. Explain why it is difficult for the public to know about the extent of police deviance in the United States.

3. What are police integrity tests? How is this particular control mechanism viewed by police officers and police executives?

4. Describe some of the ways that police leaders attempt to control police deviance within their agencies.

5. What was the last police scandal you heard about? Using the information presented to you in this section, explain the perceived cause of this deviant act and also ways that police executives could avoid similar acts from taking place in the future.

WEB RESOURCES

- To learn more about police misconduct, go to http://www.injusticeeverywhere.com/.
- To learn more about police corruption from a global perspective, go to http://www.usip.org/files/resources/SR%20294.pdf.
- To learn more about police ethics, go to http://www.theiacp.org/PoliceServices/ProfessionalAssistance/Ethics/tabid/140/Default.aspx.

READING 23

Carl Klockars examines the "Dirty Harry problem" in this article. Named after the 1971 movie, the Dirty Harry problem refers to police officers' use of "dirty" means in order to achieve the ends that are set by their supervisors. Klockars discusses how the nature of policing frequently puts officers in moral dilemmas. Some police officers ultimately lose their moral compass and become cynical when it comes to their work.

The Dirty Harry Problem

Carl B. Klockars

When and to what extent does the morally good end warrant or justify an ethically, politically, or legally dangerous means for its achievement? This is a very old question for philosophers. Although it has received extensive consideration in policelike occupations and is at the dramatic core of police fiction and detective novels, I know of not a single contribution to the criminological or sociological literature on policing which raises it explicitly and examines its implications.[1] This is the case in spite of the fact that there is considerable evidence to suggest that it is not only an ineluctable part of police work, but a moral problem with which police themselves are quite familiar. There are, I believe, a number of good reasons why social scientists have avoided or neglected what I like to call the Dirty Harry problem in policing, not the least of which is that it is insoluble. However, a great deal can be learned about police work by examining some failed solutions, three of which I consider in the following pages. First, though, it is necessary to explain what a Dirty Harry problem is and what it is about it that makes it so problematic.

The Dirty Harry Problem

The Dirty Harry problem draws its name from the 1971 Warner Brothers film *Dirty Harry* and its chief protagonist, antihero Inspector Harry "Dirty Harry"

Callahan. The film features a number of events which dramatize the Dirty Harry problem in different ways, but the one which does so most explicitly and most completely places Harry in the following situation. A 14-year-old girl has been kidnapped and is being held captive by a psychopathic killer. The killer, "Scorpio," who has already struck twice, demands $200,000 ransom to release the girl, who is buried with just enough oxygen to keep her alive for a few hours. Harry gets the job of delivering the ransom and, after enormous exertion, finally meets Scorpio. At their meeting Scorpio decides to renege on his bargain, let the girl die, and kill Harry. Harry manages to stab Scorpio in the leg before he does so, but not before Scorpio seriously wounds Harry's partner, an inexperienced, idealistic, slightly ethnic, former sociology major.

Scorpio escapes, but Harry manages to track him down through the clinic where he was treated for his wounded leg. After learning that Scorpio lives on the grounds of a nearby football stadium, Harry breaks into his apartment, finds guns and other evidence of his guilt, and finally confronts Scorpio on the 50-yard line, where Harry shoots him in the leg as he is trying to escape. Standing over Scorpio, Harry demands to know where the girl is buried. Scorpio refuses to disclose her location, demanding his rights to a lawyer. As the camera draws back from the scene Harry stands on Scorpio's bullet-mangled leg to torture a confession of the girl's location from him.

As it turns out, the girl is already dead and Scorpio must be set free. Neither the gun found in the illegal search, nor the confession Harry extorted, nor any of its fruits—including the girl's body—would be admissible in court.

The preceding scene, the heart of *Dirty Harry*, raises a number of issues of far-reaching significance for the sociology of the police, the first of which will now be discussed.

 ## The Dirty Harry Problem I: The End of Innocence

As we have phrased it previously, the Dirty Harry problem asks when and to what extent does the morally good end warrant or justify an ethically, politically, or legally dangerous means to its achievement? In itself, this question assumes the possibility of a genuine moral dilemma and posits its existence in a means–ends arrangement which may be expressed schematically as follows:

		MEANS	
		MORALLY GOOD (+)	MORALLY DIRTY (−)
E N D S	Morally good (+)	A + +	B − + The Dirty Harry Problem
	Morally dirty (−)	C + −	D − −

It is important to specify clearly the terms of the Dirty Harry problem not only to show that it must involve the juxtaposition of good ends and dirty means, but also to show what must be proven to demonstrate that a Dirty Harry problem exists. If one could show, for example, that box B is always empirically empty or that in any given case the terms of the situation are better read in some other means–ends arrangement, Dirty Harry problems vanish. At this first level, however, I suspect that no one could exclude the core scene of *Dirty Harry* from the class of Dirty Harry problems. There is no question that saving the life of an innocent victim of kidnapping is a "good" thing nor that grinding the bullet-mangled leg of Scorpio to extort a confession from him is "dirty."[2]

There is, in addition, a second level of criteria of an empirical and epistemological nature that must be met before a Dirty Harry problem actually comes into being. They involve the connection between the dirty act and the good end. Principally, what must be known and, importantly, known before the dirty act is committed, is that it will result in the achievement of the good end. In any absolute sense this is, of course, impossible to know, in that no acts are ever completely certain in their consequences. Thus the question is always a matter of probabilities. But it is helpful to break those probabilities into classes which attach to various subcategories of the overall question. In the given case, this level of problem would seem to require that three questions be satisfied, though not all with the same level of certainty.

In *Dirty Harry,* the first question is, Is Scorpio able to provide the information Dirty Harry seeks? It is an epistemological question about which, in *Dirty Harry,* we are absolutely certain. Harry met Scorpio at the time of the ransom exchange. Not only did he admit the kidnapping at that time, but when he made the ransom demand, Scorpio sent one of the girl's teeth and a description of her clothing and underwear to leave no doubt about the existence of his victim.

Second, we must know there are means, dirty means and nothing other than dirty means, which are likely to achieve the good end. One can, of course, never be sure that one is aware of or has considered all possible alternatives, but in *Dirty Harry* there would appear to be no reason for Scorpio in his rational self-interest to confess to the girl's location without being coerced to do so.

The third question which must be satisfied at this empirical and epistemological level concedes that dirty means are the only method which will be effective, but asks whether or not, in the end, they will be in vain. We know in *Dirty Harry* that they were, and Harry himself, at the time of the ransom demand, admits he believes that the girl is already dead. Does not this possibility or likelihood that the girl is dead destroy the justification for Harry's dirty act? Although it surely would if Harry knew for certain that the girl was dead, I do not think it does insofar as even a small probability of her being saved exists. The reason is that the good to be achieved is so unquestionably good and so passionately felt that even a small possibility of its achievement demands that it be tried. For example, were we to ask, If it were your daughter would you want Harry to do what he did? [I]t would be this passionate sense of unquestionable good that we are trying to dramatize. It is for this reason that in philosophical circles the Dirty Harry problem has been largely restricted to questions of national security, revolutionary terrorism, and international war. It is also why the Dirty Harry problem in detective fiction almost always involves murder.

Once we have satisfied ourselves that a Dirty Harry problem is conceptually possible and that, in fact, we can specify one set of concrete circumstances in which it exists, one might think that the most difficult question of all is, What ought to be done? I do not think it is. I suspect that there are very few people who would not want Harry to do something dirty in the situation specified. I know I would want him to do what he did, and what is more, I would want anyone who policed for me to be prepared to do so as well. Put differently, I want to have as police officers men and women of moral courage and sensitivity.

But to those who would want exactly that, the Dirty Harry problem poses its most irksome conclusion. Namely, that one cannot, at least in the specific case at hand, have a policeman who is both just and innocent. The troublesome issue in the Dirty Harry problem is not whether under some utilitarian calculus a right choice can be made, but that the choice must always be between at least two wrongs. And in choosing to do either wrong, the policeman inevitably taints or tarnishes himself.

It was this conclusion on the part of Dashiell Hammett, Raymond Chandler, Raoul Whitfield, Horace McCoy, James M. Cain, Lester Dent, and dozens of other tough-guy writers of hard-boiled detective stories that distinguished these writers from what has come to be called the "classical school" of detective fiction. What these men could not stomach about Sherlock Holmes (Conan Doyle), Inspector French (Freeman Wills Crofts), and Father Brown (Chesterton), to name a few of the best, was not that they were virtuous, but that their virtue was unsullied. Their objection was that the classical detective's occupation, how he worked, and the jobs he was called upon to do left him morally immaculate. Even the most brilliant defender of the classical detective story, W.H. Auden, was forced to confess that that conclusion gave the stories "magical function," but rendered them impossible as art.[3]

If popular conceptions of police work have relevance for its actual practice—as Egon Bittner and a host of others have argued that they do[4]—the Dirty Harry problem, found in one version or another in countless detective novels and reflected in paler imitations on countless television screens, for example, "Parental Discretion is Advised," is not an unimportant contributor to police work's "tainted" quality. But we must remember also that the revolution of the tough-guy writers, so these writers said, was not predicated on some mere artificial, aesthetic objection. With few exceptions, their claim was that their works were art. That is, at all meaningful levels, the stories were true. It is this claim I should next like to examine in the real-life context of the Dirty Harry problem.

 ## The Dirty Harry Problem II: Dirty Men and Dirty Work

Dirty Harry problems arise quite often. For policemen, real, everyday policemen, Dirty Harry problems are part of their job and thus considerably more than rare or artificial dramatic exceptions. To make this point, I will translate some rather familiar police practices, street stops and searches and victim and witness interrogation, into Dirty Harry problems.

Good Ends and Dirty Means

The first question our analysis of street stops and searches and victim and witness interrogation must satisfy is, For policemen, do these activities present the cognitive opportunity for the juxtaposition of good ends and dirty means to their achievement? Although the "goodness" question will be considered in some detail later, suffice it to say here that police find the prevention of crime and the punishment of wrongful or criminal behavior a good thing to achieve. Likewise, they, perhaps more than any other group in society, are intimately aware of the varieties of dirty means available for the achievement of those good ends. In the case of street stops and searches, these dirty alternatives range from falsifying probable cause for a stop, to manufacturing a false arrest to legitimate an illegal search, to simply searching without the fraudulent covering devices of either. In the case of victim or witness interrogations, dirty means range from dramaturgically "chilling" a *Miranda* warning by an edited or unemphatic reading to Harry's grinding a man's bullet-shattered leg to extort a confession from him.

While all these practices may be "dirty" enough to satisfy certain people of especially refined sensitivities, does not a special case have to be made, not for the public's perception of the "dirtiness" of certain illegal, deceptive, or sub-rosa acts, but for the police's perception of their dirtiness? Are not the police hard-boiled, less sensitive to such things than are most of us? I think there is no question that they are, and our contention about the prevalence of Dirty Harry problems in policing suggests that they are likely to be. How does this "tough-minded" attitude toward dirty means affect our argument? At least at this stage it seems to strengthen it. That is, the failure of police to regard dirty means with the same hesitation that most citizens do seems to suggest that they juxtapose them to the achievement of good ends more quickly and more readily than most of us.

The Dirty Means Must Work

In phrasing the second standard for the Dirty Harry problem as "The dirty means must work," we gloss over a whole range of qualifying conditions, some of which we have already considered. The most critical, implied in *Dirty Harry,* is that the person on whom dirty means are to be used must be guilty. It should be pointed out, however, that this standard is far higher than any student of the Dirty Hands problem in politics has ever been willing to admit. In fact, the moral dilemma of Dirty Hands is often dramatized by the fact that dirty means must be visited on quite innocent victims. It is the blood of such innocents, for example, whom the Communist leader Hoerderer in Sartre's *Dirty Hands* refers to when he says, "I have dirty hands. Right up to the elbows. I've plunged them in filth and blood. But what do you hope? Do you think you can govern innocently?"[5]

But even if cases in which innocent victims suffer dirty means commonly qualify as Dirty Harry problems, and by extension innocent victims would be allowable in Dirty Harry problems, there are a number of factors in the nature and context of policing which suggest that police themselves are inclined toward the higher "guilty victim" standard. Although there may be others, the following are probably the most salient.

1. The Operative Assumption of Guilt. In street stops and searches as well as interrogations, it is in the nature of the police task that guilt is assumed as a working premise. That is, in order for a policeman to do his job, he must, unless he clearly knows otherwise, assume that the person he sees is guilty and the behavior he is witnessing is evidence of some concealed or hidden offense. If a driver looks at him "too long" or not at all or if a witness or suspect talks too little or too much, it is only his operative assumption of guilt that makes those actions meaningful. Moreover, the policeman is often not in a position to suspend his working assumption until he has taken action, sometimes dirty action, to disconfirm it.

2. The Worst of all Possible Guilt. The matter of the operative assumption of guilt is complicated

further because the policeman is obliged to make a still higher-order assumption of guilt, namely, that the person is not only guilty, but dangerously so. In the case of street stops and searches, for instance, although the probability of coming upon a dangerous felon is extremely low, policemen quite reasonably take the possibility of doing so as a working assumption on the understandable premise that once is enough. Likewise the premise that the one who has the most to hide will try hardest to hide it is a reasonable assumption for interrogation.

3. The Great Guilty Place Assumption. The frequency with which policemen confront the worst of people, places, and occasions creates an epistemological problem of serious psychological proportions. As a consequence of his job, the policeman is constantly exposed to highly selective samples of his environment. That he comes to read a clump of bushes as a place to hide, a roadside rest as a homosexual "tearoom," a sweet old lady as a robbery looking for a place to happen, or a poor young black as someone willing to oblige her is not a question of a perverse, pessimistic, or racist personality, but of a person whose job requires that he strive to see race, age, sex, and even nature in an ecology of guilt, which can include him if he fails to see it so.[6]

4. The Not Guilty (This Time) Assumption. With considerable sociological research and conventional wisdom to support him, the policeman knows that most people in the great guilty place in which he works have committed numerous crimes for which they have never been caught. Thus when a stop proves unwarranted, a search comes up "dry," or an interrogation fails, despite the dirty means, the policeman is not at all obliged to conclude that the person victimized by them is innocent, only that, and even this need not always be conceded, he is innocent this time.

Dirty Means as Ends in Themselves

How do these features of police work, all of which seem to incline police to accept a standard of a guilty victim for their dirty means, bear upon the Dirty Harry problem from which they derive? The most dangerous reading suggests that if police are inclined, and often quite rightly inclined, to believe they are dealing with factually, if not legally, guilty subjects, they become likely to see their dirty acts, not as means to the achievement of good ends, but as ends in themselves—as punishment of guilty people whom the police believe deserve to be punished.

If this line of argument is true, it has the effect, in terms of police perceptions, of moving Dirty Harry problems completely outside of the fourfold table of means–ends combinations created in order to define it. Importantly as well, in terms of our perceptions, Dirty Harry problems of this type can no longer be read as cases of dirty means employed to the achievement of good ends. For unless we are willing to admit that in a democratic society a police arrogates to itself the task of punishing those who they think are guilty, we are forced to conclude that Dirty Harry problems represent cases of employing dirty means to dirty ends, in which case, nobody, not the police and certainly not us, is left with any kind of moral dilemma.

The possibility is quite real and quite fearsome, but it is mediated by certain features of police work, some of which inhere in the nature of the work itself and others, imposed from outside, which have a quite explicit impact on it. The most important of the "naturalistic" features of policing which belie the preceding argument is that the assumption of guilt and all the configurations in the policeman's world which serve to support it often turn out wrong. It is precisely because the operative assumption of guilt can be forced on everything and everyone that the policeman who must use it constantly comes to find it leads him astray as often as it confirms his suspicions.

Similarly, a great many of the things policemen do, some of which we have already conceded appear to police as less dirty than they appear to us—faked probable cause for a street stop, manipulated *Miranda* warnings, and so forth—are simply impossible to read as punishments. This is so particularly if we grant a hard-boiled character to our cops.

Of course, neither of these naturalistic restrictions on the obliteration of the means–ends schema is or should be terribly comforting. To the extent that the first is helpful at all assumes a certain skill and capacity of mind that we may not wish to award to all policemen. The willingness to engage in the constant refutation of one's working worldview presumes a certain intellectual integrity which can certainly go awry. Likewise, the second merely admits that on occasion policemen do some things which reveal they appreciate that the state's capacity to punish is sometimes greater than theirs.

To both these "natural" restrictions on the obliteration of the means–ends character of Dirty Harry problems, we can add the exclusionary rule. Although the exclusionary rule is the manifest target of *Dirty Harry,* it, more than anything else, makes Dirty Harry problems a reality in everyday policing. It is the great virtue of exclusionary rules—applying in various forms to stops, searches, seizures, and interrogations—that they hit directly upon the intolerable, though often, I think, moral desire of police to punish. These rules make the very simple point to police that the more they wish to see a felon punished, the more they are advised to be scrupulous in their treatment of him. Put differently, the best thing Harry could have done for Scorpio was to step on his leg, extort his confession, and break into his apartment.

If certain natural features of policing and particularly exclusionary rules combine to maintain the possibility of Dirty Harry problems in a context in which a real danger appears to be their disappearance, it does not follow that police cannot or do not collapse the dirty means–good ends division on some occasions and become punishers. I only hold that on many other occasions, collapse does not occur and Dirty Harry problems, as defined, are still widely possible. What must be remembered next, on the way to making their possibility real, is that policemen know, or think they know, before they employ a dirty means that a dirty means and only a dirty means will work.

Only a Dirty Means Will Work

The moral standard that a policeman know in advance of resorting to a dirty means that a dirty means and only a dirty means will work, rests heavily on two technical dimensions: (1) the professional competence of the policeman and (2) the range of legitimate working options available to him. Both are intimately connected, though the distinction to be preserved between them is that the first is a matter of the policeman's individual competence and the second of the competence of the institutions for which (his department) and with which (the law) the policeman works.

In any concrete case, the relations between these moral and technical dimensions of the Dirty Harry problem are extremely complicated. But a priori it follows that the more competent a policeman is at the use of legal means, the less he will be obliged to resort to dirty alternatives. Likewise, the department that trains its policemen well and supplies them with the resources—knowledge and material—to do their work will find that the policemen who work for them will not resort to dirty means "unnecessarily," meaning only those occasions when an acceptable means will work as well as a dirty one.

While these two premises flow a priori from raising the Dirty Harry problem, questions involving the moral and technical roles of laws governing police means invite a very dangerous type of a priori reasoning:

> Combating distrust [of the police] requires getting across the rather complicated message that granting the police specific forms of new authority may be the most effective means for reducing abuse of authority which is now theirs; that it is the absence of properly proscribed forms of authority that often impels the police to engage in questionable or outright illegal conduct. Before state legislatures enacted statutes giving limited authority to the police to stop and question persons suspected of criminal involvement, police nevertheless stopped and questioned people. It is inconceivable how any police

agency could be expected to operate without doing so. But since the basis for their actions was unclear, the police—if they thought a challenge likely—would use the guise of arresting the individual on a minor charge (often without clear evidence) to provide a semblance of legality. Enactment of stopping and questioning statutes eliminated the need for this sham.[7]

Herman Goldstein's preceding argument and observations are undoubtedly true, but the danger in them is that they can be extended to apply to any dirty means, not only illegal arrests to legitimate necessary street stops, but dirty means to accomplish subsequent searches and seizures all the way to beating confessions out of suspects when no other means will work. But, of course, Goldstein does not intend his argument to be extended in these ways.

Nevertheless, his a priori argument, dangerous though it may be, points to the fact that Dirty Harry problems can arise wherever restrictions are placed on police methods and are particularly likely to do so when police themselves perceive that those restrictions are undesirable, unreasonable, or unfair. His argument succeeds in doing what police who face Dirty Harry problems constantly do: rendering the law problematic. But while Goldstein, one of the most distinguished legal scholars in America, can follow his finding with books, articles, and lectures which urge change, it is left to the policeman to take upon himself the moral responsibility of subverting it with dirty and hidden means.

Compelling and Unquestionable Ends

If Dirty Harry problems can be shown to exist in their technical dimensions—as genuine means–ends problems where only dirty means will work—the question of the magnitude and urgency of the ends that the dirty means may be employed to achieve must still be confronted. Specifically, it must be shown that the ends of dirty means are so desirable that the failure to achieve them would cast the person who is in a position to do so in moral disrepute.

The two most widely acknowledged ends of policing are peace keeping and law enforcement. It would follow, of course, that if both these ends were held to be unworthy, Dirty Harry problems would disappear. There are arguments challenging both ends. For instance, certain radical critiques of policing attempt to reduce the peace-keeping and law-enforcing functions of the police in the United States to nothing more than acts of capitalist oppression. From such a position flows not only the denial of the legitimacy of any talk of Dirty Harry problems, but also the denial of the legitimacy of the entire police function.[8]

Regardless of the merits of such critiques, it will suffice for the purpose of this analysis to maintain that there is a large "clientele," to use Albert Reiss's term, for both types of police function.[9] And it should come as no surprise to anyone that the police themselves accept the legitimacy of their own peace-keeping and law-enforcing ends. Some comment is needed, though, on how large that clientele for those functions is and how compelling and unquestionable the ends of peace keeping and law enforcement are for them.

There is no more popular, compelling, urgent, nor more broadly appealing idea than peace. In international relations, it is potent enough to legitimate the stockpiling of enough nuclear weapons to exterminate every living thing on earth a dozen times over. In domestic affairs, it gives legitimacy to the idea of the state, and the aspirations to it have succeeded in granting to the state an absolute monopoly on the right to legitimate the use of force and a near monopoly on its actual, legitimate use: the police. That peace has managed to legitimate these highly dangerous means to its achievement in virtually every advanced nation in the world is adequate testimony to the fact that it qualifies, if any end does, as a good end so unquestionable and so compelling that it can legitimate risking the most dangerous and dirtiest of means.

The fact is, though, that most American policemen prefer to define their work as law enforcement rather than peace keeping, even though they may, in fact, do more of the latter. It is a distinction that should not be allowed to slip away in assuming, for instance, that the policeman's purpose in enforcing the law is to keep the peace. Likewise, though it is a possibility, it will not do to assume that police simply enforce the law as an end in itself, without meaning and without purpose or end. The widely discretionary behavior of working policemen and the enormous underenforcement of the law which characterizes most police agencies simply belie that possibility.

An interpretation of law enforcement which is compatible with empirical studies of police behavior—as peace keeping is—and police talk in America—which peace keeping generally is not—is an understanding of the ends of law enforcement as punishment. There are, of course, many theories of punishment, but the police seem inclined toward the simplest: the belief that certain people who have committed certain acts deserve to be punished for them. What can one say of the compelling and unquestionable character of this retributive ambition as an end of policing and policemen?

Both historically and sociologically there is ample evidence that punishment is almost as unquestionable and compelling an end as peace. Historically, we have a long and painful history of punishment, a history longer in fact than the history of the end of peace. Sociologically, the application of what may well be the only culturally universal norm, the norm of reciprocity, implies the direct and natural relations between wrongful acts and their punishments.[10] Possibly the best evidence for the strength and urgency of the desire to punish in modern society is the extraordinary complex of rules and procedures democratic states have assembled which prevents legitimate punishment from being administered wrongfully or frivolously.

If we can conclude that peace and punishment are ends unquestionable and compelling enough to satisfy the demands of Dirty Harry problems, we are led to one final question on which we may draw from some sociological theories of the police for assistance. If the Dirty Harry problem is at the core of the police role, or at least near to it, how is it that police can or do come to reconcile their use of—or their failure to use—dirty means to achieve unquestionably good and compelling ends?

Public Policy and Police Morality: Three Defective Resolutions of the Dirty Harry Problem

The contemporary literature on policing appears to contain three quite different types of solution or resolution. But because the Dirty Harry problem is a genuine moral dilemma, that is, a situation which will admit no real solution or resolution, each is necessarily defective. Also, understandably, each solution or resolution presents itself as an answer to a somewhat different problem. In matters of public policy, such concealments are often necessary and probably wise, although they have a way of coming around to haunt their architects sooner or later. In discovering that each is flawed and in disclosing the concealments which allow the appearance of resolution, we do not urge that it be held against sociologists that they are not philosophers nor do we argue that they should succeed where philosophers before them have failed. Rather, we only wish to make clear what is risked by each concealment and to face candidly the inevitably unfortunate ramifications which must proceed from it.

Snappy Bureaucrats

In the works of August Vollmer, Bruce Smith, O. W. Wilson, and those progressive police administrators who still follow their lead, a vision of the perfect police agency and the perfect policeman has gained considerable ground. Labeled "the professional model" in police circles—though entirely different from any classical sense of profession or professional—it envisions a highly trained, technologically sophisticated police department operating free from political interference with a corps of well-educated police responding obediently to the policies, orders, and directives of a central administrative command. It is a vision of police officers, to use Bittner's phrasing, as "snappy bureaucrats,"[11] cogs in a quasi-military machine who do what they are told out of a mix of fear, loyalty, routine, and detailed specification of duties.

The professional model, unlike other solutions to be considered, is based on the assumption that the policeman's motives for working can be made to locate within his department. He will, if told, work vice or traffic, juvenile or homicide, patrol passively or aggressively, and produce one, two, four, or six arrests, pedestrian stops, or reports per hour, day, or week as his department sees fit. In this way the assumption and vision of the professional model in policing is little different from that of any bureaucracy which seeks by specifying tasks and setting expectations for levels of production—work quotas—to coordinate a regular, predictable, and efficient service for its clientele.

The problem with this vision of *sine ira et studio* service by obedient operatives is that when the product to be delivered is some form of human service—education, welfare, health, and police bureaucracies are similar in this way—the vision seems always to fall short of expectations. On the one hand the would-be bureaucratic operatives—teachers, social workers, nurses, and policemen—resent being treated as mere bureaucrats and resist the translation of their work into quotas, directives, rules, regulations, or other abstract specifications. On the other hand, to the extent that the vision of an efficient and obedient human service bureaucracy is realized, the clientele of such institutions typically come away with the impression that no one in the institution truly cares about their problems. And, of course, in that the aim of bureaucratization is to locate employees' motives for work within the bureaucracy, they are absolutely correct in their feelings.

To the extent that the professional model succeeds in making the ends of policing locate within the agency as opposed to moral demands of the tasks which policemen are asked by their clients to do, it appears to solve the Dirty Harry problem. When it succeeds, it does so by replacing the morally compelling ends of punishment and peace with the less human, though by no means uncompelling, ends of bureaucratic performance. However, this resolution certainly does not imply that dirty means will disappear, only that the motives for their use will be career advancement and promotion. Likewise, on those occasions when a morally sensitive policeman would be compelled by the demands of the situational exigencies before him to use a dirty means, the bureaucratic operative envisioned by the professional model will merely do his job. Ambitious

bureaucrats and obedient timeservers fail at being the type of morally sensitive souls we want to be policemen. The professional model's bureaucratic resolution of the Dirty Harry problem fails in policing for the same reason it fails in every other human service agency: it is quite simply an impossibility to create a bureaucrat who cares for anything but his bureaucracy.

The idealized image of the professional model, which has been responded to with an ideal critique, is probably unrealizable. Reality intervenes as the ideal type is approached. The bureaucracy seems to take on weight as it approaches the pole, is slowed, and may even collapse in approaching.

Bittner's Peace

A second effort in the literature of contemporary policing also attempts to address the Dirty Harry problem by substituting an alternative to the presently prevailing police ends of punishment. Where the professional model sought to substitute bureaucratic rewards and sanctions for the moral end of punishment, the elegant polemics by Egon Bittner in *The Functions of Police in Modern Society* and "Florence Nightingale in Pursuit of Willie Sutton: A Theory of the Police" seek to substitute the end of peace. In beautifully chosen words, examples, and phrasing, Bittner leads his readers to conclude that peace is historically, empirically, intellectually, and morally the most compelling, unquestionable, and humane end of policing. Bittner is, I fear, absolutely right.

It is the end of peace which legitimates the extension of police responsibilities into a wide variety of civil matters—neighborhood disputes, loud parties, corner lounging, lovers' quarrels, political rallies, disobedient children, bicycle registration, pet control, and a hundred other types of tasks which a modern "service" style police department regularly is called upon to perform. With these responsibilities, which most "good" police agencies now accept willingly and officially, also comes the need for an extension of police powers. Arrest is, after all, too crude a tool to be used in all the various situations in which our peace-keeping policemen are routinely asked to be of help. "Why should," asks Herman Goldstein, in a manner in which Bittner would approve, "a police officer arrest and charge a disorderly tavern patron if ordering him to leave the tavern will suffice? Must he arrest and charge one of the parties in a lovers' quarrel if assistance in forcing a separation is all that is desired?"[12] There is no question that both those situations could be handled more peacefully if police were granted new powers which would allow them to handle those situations in the way Goldstein rhetorically asks if they should. That such extensions of police powers will be asked for by our most enlightened police departments in the interests of keeping the peace is absolutely certain. If the success of the decriminalization of police arrests for public intoxication, vagrancy, mental illness, and the virtually unrestricted two-hour right of detention made possible by the Uniform Law of Arrest are any indication of the likelihood of extensions being received favorably, the end of peace and its superiority over punishment in legitimating the extension of police powers seem exceedingly likely to prevail further.

The problem with peace is that it is not the only end of policing so compelling, unquestionable, and in the end, humane. Amid the good work toward the end of peace that we increasingly want our police to do, it is certain that individuals or groups will arise who the police, in all their peace-keeping benevolence, will conclude, on moral if not political or institutional grounds, have "got it coming." And all the once dirty means which were bleached in the brilliant light of peace will return to their true colors.

Skolnick's Craftsman

The third and final attempt to resolve the Dirty Harry problem is offered by Jerome Skolnick, who in *Justice Without Trial* comes extremely close to stating the Dirty Harry problem openly when he writes:

> … He (the policeman) sees himself as a craftsman, at his best, a master of his trade … [he] draws a moral distinction between criminal law and criminal procedure. The distinction is drawn somewhat as follows: The substantive law of crimes is intended to control the behavior of people who willfully injure persons or property, or who engage in behaviors having such a consequence, such as the use of narcotics. Criminal procedure, by contrast, is intended to

control authorities, not criminals. As such, it does not fall into the same *moral* class of constraint as substantive criminal law. If a policeman were himself to use narcotics, or to steal, or to assault, *outside the line of duty,* much the same standards would be applied to him by other policemen as to the ordinary citizen. When, however, the issue concerns the policeman's freedom to carry out his *duties,* another moral realm is entered.[13]

What is more, Skolnick's craftsman finds support from his peers, department, his community, and the law for the moral rightness of his calling. He cares about his work and finds it just.

What troubles Skolnick about his craftsman is his craft. The craftsman refuses to see, as Skolnick thinks he ought to, that the dirty means he sometimes uses to achieve his good ends stand in the same moral class of wrongs as those he is employed to fight. Skolnick's craftsman reaches this conclusion by understanding that his unquestionably good and compelling ends, on certain occasions, justify his employment of dirty means to their achievement. Skolnick's craftsman, as Skolnick understands him, resolves the Dirty Harry problem by denying the dirtiness of his means.

Skolnick's craftsman's resolution is, speaking precisely, Machiavellian. It should come as no surprise to find the representative of one of the classic attempts to resolve the problem of Dirty Hands to be a front runner in response to Dirty Harry. What is worrisome about such a resolution? What does it conceal that makes our genuine dilemma disappear? The problem is not that the craftsman will sometimes choose to use dirty means. If he is morally sensitive to its demands, every policeman's work will sometimes require as much. What is worrisome about Skolnick's craftsman is that he does not regard his means as dirty and, as Skolnick tells us, does not suffer from their use. The craftsman, if Skolnick's portrait of him is correct, will resort to dirty means too readily and too easily. He lacks the restraint that can come only from struggling to justify them and from taking seriously the hazards involved.

In 1966, when *Justice Without Trial* first appeared, Skolnick regarded the prospects of creating a more morally sensitive craftsman exceedingly dim. He could not imagine that the craftsman's community, employer, peers, or the courts could come to reward him more for his legal compliance than for the achievement of the ends of his craft. However, in phrasing the prospects in terms of a Dirty Harry problem, one can not only agree with Skolnick that denying the goodness of unquestionably good ends is a practical and political impossibility, but can also uncover another alternative, one which Skolnick does not pursue.

The alternative the Dirty Harry problem leads us to is ensuring that the craftsman regards his dirty means as dirty by applying the same retributive principles of punishment to his wrongful acts that he is quite willing to apply to others! It is, in fact, only when his wrongful acts are punished that he will come to see them as wrongful and will appreciate the genuine moral—rather than technical or occupational—choice he makes in resorting to them. The prospects for punishment of such acts are by no means dim, and considerable strides in this area have been made. It requires far fewer resources to punish than to reward. Secondly, the likelihood that juries in civil suits will find dirty means dirtier than police do is confirmed by police claims that outsiders cannot appreciate the same moral and technical distinctions that they do. Finally, severe financial losses to police agencies as well as to their officers eventually communicate to both that vigorously policing themselves is cheaper and more pleasing than having to pay so heavily if they do not. If under such conditions our craftsman police officer is still willing to risk the employment of dirty means to achieve what he understands to be unquestionably good ends, he will not only know that he has behaved justly, but that in doing so he must run the risk of becoming genuinely guilty as well.

 A Final Note

In urging the punishment of policemen who resort to dirty means to achieve some unquestionably good and morally compelling end, we recognize that we create a Dirty Harry problem for ourselves and for those we urge to effect such punishments. It is a fitting end, one

which teaches once again that the danger in Dirty Harry problems is never in their resolution, but in thinking that one has found a resolution with which one can truly live in peace.

 Notes

1. In the contemporary philosophical literature, particularly when raised for the vocation of politics, the question is commonly referred to as the Dirty Hands problem after J. P. Sartre's treatment of it in *Dirty Hands* (Les Maines Sales, 1948) and in *No Exit and Three Other Plays* (New York: Modern Library, 1950). Despite its modem name, the problem is very old and has been taken up by Machiavelli in *The Prince* (1513) and *The Discourses* (1519) (New York: Modern Library, 1950); by Max Weber, "Politics as a Vocation," (1919) in *Max Weber: Essays in Sociology,* eds. and trans. H. Gerth and C. W. Wills (New York: Oxford University Press, 1946); and by Albert Camus, "The Just Assassins," (1949) in *Caligula and Three Other Plays* (New York: Alfred A. Knopf, 1958). *See* Michael Walzer's brilliant critique of these contributions, "Political Action: The Problem of Dirty Hands," *Philosophy and Public Affairs,* 2(2) (winter 1972). Likewise the Dirty Hands/Dirty Harry problem is implicitly or explicitly raised in virtually every work of Raymond Chandler, Dashiell Hammett, James Cain, and other *Tough Guy Writers of The Thirties,* ed. David Madden (Carbondale, IL: Southern Illinois University Press, 1968), as they are in all of the recent work of Joseph Wambaugh, particularly *The Blue Knight, The New Centurions,* and *The Choirboys.*

2. "Dirty" here means both "repugnant" in that it offends widely shared standards of human decency and dignity and "dangerous" in that it breaks commonly shared and supported norms, rules, or laws for conduct. To "dirty" acts there must be both a deontologically based face validity of immorality and a consequentiality threat to the prevailing rules for social order.

3. W. H. Auden, "The Guilty Vicarage," in *The Dyer's Hand and Other Essays* (New York: Alfred A. Knopf, 1956) pp. 146–58.

4. Egon Bittner, *The Functions of Police in Modern Society* (New York: Jason Aronson, 1975) and "Florence Nightingale in Pursuit of Willie Sutton," in *The Potential For Reform Of the Criminal Justice System,* vol. 3, ed. H. Jacob (Beverly Hills, CA: Sage Publications, 1974) pp. 11–44.

5. Sartre, *Dirty Hands,* p. 224.

6. One of Wambaugh's characters in *The Choirboys* makes this final point most dramatically when he fails to notice that a young boy's buttocks are flatter than they should be and reads the child's large stomach as a sign of adequate nutrition. When the child dies through his mother's neglect and abuse, the officer rightly includes himself in his ecology of guilt.

7. Herman Goldstein, *Policing a Free Society* (Cambridge, MA: Ballinger Publishing, 1977), p. 72.

8. *See,* for example, John F. Galliher, "Explanations of Police Behavior: A Critical Review and Analysis," *The Sociological Quarterly,* 12:308–18 (summer 1971); Richard Quinney, *Class, State, and Crime* (New York: David McKay, 1977).

9. Albert J. Reiss, Jr., *The Police and the Public* (New Haven, CT: Yale University Press, 1971), p. 122.

10. These two assertions are drawn from Graeme Newman's *The Punishment Response* (Philadelphia: J. B. Lippincott Co., 1978).

11. Bittner, p. 53.

12. Ibid., p. 72.

13. Jerome Skolnick, *Justice Without Trial,* 2nd ed. (New York: John Wiley & Sons, 1975), p. 182.

DISCUSSION QUESTIONS

1. Describe a situation that police officers might encounter that would put them in a situation categorized as a moral dilemma.

2. The Klockars article was published in 1980. Do you think that police officers face the same Dirty Harry problems today? Why or why not?

3. How could police executives modify police officer training to help reduce the number of Dirty Harry problems that police officers become involved in?

READING 24

The current study uses the Klockars scale to explore the ethical views of police managers regarding their perceptions of police corruption. Surveys completed by police managers attending the Administrative Officers' Course at the Southern Police Institute at the University of Louisville were analyzed for this study. The research findings indicate that the police managers surveyed acknowledge the existence of a questionable moral climate within police agencies, and also that there appears to be a level of tolerance for misconduct in some of these agencies.

Police Integrity: Rankings of Scenarios on the Klockars Scale by "Management Cops"

Gennaro F. Vito, Scott Wolf, George E. Higgins, and William F. Walsh

Police officers are the "first responders" of the criminal justice system. They are responsible for enforcing laws, protecting the public from dangers, and ensuring that citizens' rights are upheld. However, with these duties comes an opportunity for corrupt, deviant, or inappropriate behaviors to take place. Policing is a highly discretionary, coercive activity that routinely takes place in private settings, out of the sight of supervisors and witnesses and is thus an occupation that is ripe with opportunities for misconduct of many types (Klockars, 1999, p. 208). Close contact with the public, the monitoring and control of vice activities, and the discretionary power exercised by officers make policing a "morally dangerous occupation" (Barker, 2006, p. 5). Because police officers are charged with such important responsibilities in our society, their behavior must be monitored in some fashion. Barker and Carter (1991) argue that what police officers do and how they do it affects the public's perceptions of the fairness and honesty of the entire criminal justice system. Consequently, police corruption is an important research subject in criminal justice. Identifying the extent of police corruption and offering ways to control it will lead to enhanced public safety while ensuring that the rights of citizens are protected. This study examines police supervisor perceptions of police corruptions through their responses to the Klockars scale with comparisons to data from previous studies on this subject (Klockars, 1999; Kutnjak Ivkovic, 2005b).

✄ Police Corruption Defined

Police corruption is difficult to define because of jurisdictional differences in legal statutes and the multitude of behaviors that can be included under a definition. Police corruption involves illegal behaviors as well as acts that are not always illegal but considered inappropriate behavior for officers (e.g., receiving free meals). Police corruption can involve organizational/rule violations such as gratuities and sexual misconduct, money corruption, and abuse of authority such as use of force and noble cause injustice (Barker, 2002). Kutnjak Ivkovic (2005a, p. 16) argues for a definitive definition that transcends jurisdictional boundaries and states that police corruption is

> ... an action or omission, a promise of action or omission, or an attempt by a police officer or a group of police officers, characterized by a police officer's misuses of the official position, motivated in significant part by the achievement of personal gain.

Law, policy, and procedures may attempt to regulate the discretionary power of police officers, but the nature of patrol makes autonomy an essential part of the officers operational milieu. Police officers on a daily basis engage in low-visibility decisions, in isolated locations, out of the public view. These facts make uncovering police corruption a very difficult task to accomplish.

Controlling police corruption is difficult, if not impossible, largely due to a strong reluctance by police officers to report fellow officers in what is often referred to as the "Blue Curtain" (Klockars, Kutnjak Ivkovic, & Haberfeld, 2006). In her observational study of police precincts in the Bronx and Manhattan, Reuss-Ianni (1983, pp. 13–16) indicated, this curtain exists at two levels in policing. Part of the "street cops" code is to not "give up" (inform on) fellow officers and be secretive about their on-the-job behavior. The traditional, pragmatic work place culture of the "street cops" was characterized by their self-image as crime fighters. These officers felt that their line experience, dealing with the daily realities of life on the street, gave them a much more realistic picture of police work than the management bureaucrats who have lost touch with the job. Their views are an example of an occupational culture: "a product of the various situations and problems which all vocational members confront and to which they equally respond" (Paoline, 2003, p. 200). As a result, "street cops" tended to distrust policy decisions made by the "management cops" who they believe traded in their experience for the physical comforts of office work as well as rank and positional power. They were also suspicious of the motives of their supervisors. The "street cops" viewed them as primarily interested in their own career and political advancement in the agency rather than making decisions based on the realities of the situation.

However, "management cops" felt that they had a more realistic view of the organization in all of its aspects—social, political, and operational. They believed that their administrative roles gave them a different perspective based on professionalism. They were primarily concerned with issues of "command and control" especially over the activities of the "street cops" (Reuss-Ianni, 1983). Therefore, they were interested in enforcing the rules of the organization, establishing and maintaining discipline and consistency of operations. In particular, middle managers tend to use management themes to serve as a buffer between the "street cops" and the top level, police commanders (Paoline, 2003, p. 206). Their views are an example of an organizational culture whose values are defined by top-level leaders. Yet, the "street cops" are likely to view their actions as "unpredictable and punitive supervisory oversight" (Paoline, 2003, p. 201). As a result, rule enforcement by police supervisors can lead "street cops" to engage in "lay low" or "Cover Your Ass" behavior that is unlikely to bring attention to themselves and thus avoid censure (Manning, 1995; Silverman, 1999).

The Klockars Scale

Several researchers have attempted to diminish the bias created by investigating police misconduct through survey research using hypothetical scenarios involving police integrity. "Using the organizational/occupational culture approach . . . modern social science can much more readily measure the ability of police officers to recognize misconduct, how seriously police officers regard misconduct, how amenable they are to supporting its punishment, and how willing they are to tolerate misconduct in silence" (Klockars & Kutnjak Ivkovic, 2004, p. 6). These scenarios were developed by Klockars (1999, pp. 210–211) and include 11 hypothetical situations involving police officers engaging in activities that appear to be conflicts of interest.[1] The scenarios are then accompanied by a series of six questions. Two questions ask about the seriousness of the act, two about discipline, and two about willingness to report. All of the questions attempt to measure the same organizational phenomenon: police integrity (Klockars & Kutnjak Ivkovic, 2004). Police integrity is defined by Klockars and Kutnjak Ivkovic (2004) as "the normative inclination to resist temptations to abuse the rights and privileges of their occupation" (p. 5). The advantage of using scenarios of police integrity is discussed by Klockars (1999, pp. 209–212):

> The major propositions of the idea that controlling corruption is an organizational

rather than an individual problem are questions of fact and opinion that can be explored directly and without anything like the resistance that direct inquiries about corrupt behavior are likely to provoke. It is, for example, possible to ask factual questions about officers' knowledge of agency rules, opinions about the seriousness of their violation, and the punishment they deserve or are likely to receive, and their estimates of officers' willingness to report such behavior, without asking them directly about their own or others' corrupt behavior.

What has become known as the "Klockars Scale" allows researchers to investigate the issue of police integrity rather than actual instances of police corruption (Klockars, 1999, pp. 210–211). Although this does not remedy the problem of measuring the true rate of corruption, it allows agencies to evaluate the integrity of their officers, whether their officers are willing to report unethical behavior, and whether current punishment practices appear to be effective. With information from such research, administrators can attempt to alleviate problem areas with advanced training programs aimed at increasing police integrity and by reevaluating policies regarding police misconduct. Rather than worrying about what the rate of corruption is within a department, administrators can use data gleaned from such a methodology to "think of ways in which their organizations can behave to enhance integrity" (Klockars, 1999, p. 212). This can be done without alienating officers through internal affairs investigations, media coverage, or outside researchers probing them to discuss their own or others' corruption.

Redefining the problem of police corruption as a problem of police integrity allows researchers to overcome the difficulties inherent in attempts to measure corruption (Klockars et al., 2000; Klockars & Kutnjak Ivkovic, 2004). The use of the Klockars scale (1999, pp. 210–211) makes it possible to address research questions that were previously impossible to consider. Additionally, it provides direct implications for practical police administration use.

If officers do not know whether certain conduct violates agency policy or what disciplinary threats the agency makes, administrators have a clear responsibility to communicate this information to officers. If officers do not regard certain misconduct as sufficiently serious, if they regard discipline as too severe or too lenient, or if they are willing to tolerate the misconduct of their police peers in silence, administrators have an obvious obligation to find out why. A police administrator can take specific actions to deal with each of these problems. (Klockars et al., 2000, p. 9)

The Klockars scale (1999, pp. 210–211) has been the basis of several studies. Klockars, Kutnjak Ivkovic, Harver, and Haberfeld (2000) sampled 3,235 officers from 30 U.S. police agencies. They demonstrated that the more serious a particular behavior was considered by police officers, the more severely it should and would be punished and the more willing they were to report it. The results of this study yielded important information for individual agencies and provided evidence that integrity issues were a serious problem in certain situations.

In her cross-cultural study of police misbehavior, Kutnjak Ivkovic (2005b) surveyed police officers (both line officers and supervisors) in the United States ($N = 3,235$), Croatia ($N = 1,649$), and Finland ($N = 378$) using the Klockars scale (1999, pp. 210–211). She then made comparisons to the scenario rankings by rank as well as country. For the entire sample of police officers, supervisors only ranked the acceptance of gratuities (Cases 2 and 4) as more serious than the line officers (Kutnjak Ivkovic, 2005b, p. 555). She attributed these differences to the supervisors' role in the organization—their heightened knowledge of institutional rules, positional power and authority, and an increased "stake in conformity" to official policy.

Across countries, the officers from Croatia and Finland were more likely than their American counterparts to view off-duty employment (Case 1) as a serious problem. Official policy in those countries discourages such work by officers (Kutnjak Ivkovic, 2005b, p. 557).

The Croatian officers were more troubled by the acceptance of free meals and services (Cases 2 and 4) than either the officers from Finland and the United States. The officers in the United States and Croatia viewed the case involving the cover-up of a police driving under the influence (DUI) accident case as less serious than the Finnish officers (Case 8). The U.S. and Finnish officers were more troubled by the excessive use of force against a car thief (Case 10) than the Croatian officers. The acceptance of a kickback (Case 6) and protection of a bar serving after hours (Case 9) in return for free drinks were ranked higher on the seriousness scale by the Croatian officers than by the U.S. and Finnish officers (Kutnjak Ivkovic, 2005b, p. 559). Thus, the rankings made by the officers were more heterogeneous across the three countries in the least serious cases but more homogeneous across the more serious cases. These findings will be used as a point of comparison for this study.

While officers on the line are an important group to address because they have direct contact with the public, first line supervisors (sergeants) and middle managers (lieutenants and above) in police departments are equally as important. Sergeants have the most direct contact with line officers of any supervisory level. Middle managers are important to understand because they are in a position to make and direct the implementation of policies. Managers at this level are responsible for organizing, coordinating, and controlling departmental resources and personnel (Sparrow, Moore, & Kennedy, 1990). Kelling and Bratton (1993) contend that they are primary control agents of a department's internal environment and operations. Thus, the police corruption or ethical issues that occur may be noticed, encouraged, or even discouraged by line and middle managers before they reach upper management (i.e., chief) level.

⊠ The Current Study

The purpose of the current study is to further explore the ethical views of police managers regarding police corruption. Extending the ethical views of police managers may provide information that will allow for the reduction of police corruption and the expressed values of the police organization regarding this problem. Therefore, the results of our study may provide a framework to develop policy to reduce police misconduct. Comparisons to previous findings on the Klockars scale (1999, pp. 210–211) could serve to determine whether views of what constitutes police corruption among officers and supervisors can be extended beyond the limits of the sample under analysis.

 Method

The survey respondents were police managers attending the Administrative Officers' Course of the Southern Police Institute at the University of Louisville during the years 2005–2007 ($N = 208$: Sergeants = 109, Middle Managers = 99).[2] The survey was voluntary and the respondents were guaranteed anonymity (response rate = 72.2%). The survey was not administered in the classroom. Students downloaded the scale from the course website, filled it out, and returned it to the instructor's mailbox.

The questionnaire consisted of seven demographic questions: sex, current age in years, race/ethnicity (1 – *Caucasian*, 2 – *African American*, 3 – *Asian*, 4 – *Hispanic*, 5 – *Other*), level of education (1 – *High School Diploma*, 2 – *Some College or Tech School*, 3 – *College degree*, 4 – *Graduate degree*), military service (0 – *No*, 1 – *Yes*), current rank, and number of years as a sworn officer in current department. In addition, there were 11 one paragraph scenarios with 7 response items (total number of response items: 84). Ten of the case scenarios involved police corruption issues while one (Case 10) is a description of police misuse of force. The scenario response items were scaled in Likert-type fashion (1 – *lowest* to 5 – *highest*) with the following response categories (1 – *Not at all serious* to 5 – *Very serious*). The reporting of the behaviors described in the scenarios was coded as: 1 – *Definitely No* and 5 – *Definitely Yes* with numbers 2–4 unlabeled. When asked about the departmental response or view of the behavior in question, the response categories were 1 – *None*, 2 – *Verbal reprimand*, 3 – *Written*

Table 1 Klockars Scenarios—Violations of Official Policy in Your Agency? ($N = 208$)	
Scenario	**Official Policy?**
1. Off-duty security system business	Definitely not (58.5%)
2. Free meals, discount on beat	Definitely yes (62.6%)
3. Bribe from speeding motorist	Definitely yes (98.5%)
4. Holiday gifts from merchants	Definitely yes (56.6%)
5. Crime scene theft of watch	Definitely yes (99.6%)
6. Auto repair shop 5% kickback	Definitely yes (90.9%)
7. Supervisor: holiday for tune-up	Definitely yes (73.1%)
8. Cover-up of police DUI accident	Definitely yes (61.3%)
9. Drinks to ignore late bar closing	Definitely yes (99.2%)
10. Excessive force on car thief	Definitely yes (92.3%)
11. Theft from found wallet	Definitely yes (99.2%)

reprimand, 4 – *Period of suspension without pay*, 5 – *Demotion in rank*, and 6 – *Dismissal*.

The average police manager in this study is a White male 43 years of age, with 17 years of service in a medium size municipal police agency. The majority of the respondents came from Southern states (65.3).[3] Thus, the respondents represent a nonrandom, convenience sample and they therefore may not be representative of the population of police managers.[4] For example, these officers are selected by their departments to attend the course. They are interested in career development and advancement. Thus, their views may not be typical of the population of police managers.

Results

The officers were given the 11 scenarios from the Klockars scale (1999, pp. 210–211) to rate. Table 1 demonstrates that only one of these scenarios (Case 1 – *Off Duty Security Business*) was considered as "definitely not" a violation of official departmental policy by a majority of the respondents (58.5%). All of the 10 remaining scenarios were considered by a majority of the respondents as a definite violation of existing departmental regulations, ranging from 99.6% for the Crime Scene Theft of a Watch (Case 5) to 61.3% for the Cover-Up of a Police DUI Accident (Case 8). Thus, these "management cops" clearly acknowledge the existence of official rules and regulations that attempt to control these behaviors. Furthermore, these police managers have both the authority and the responsibility to carry out these sanctions to control misbehavior.

Table 2 presents the seriousness rankings of the scenarios by the mean scale value given by Sergeants and Middle Managers. Also added are data from the Kutnjak Ivkovic (2005b) study, particularly the mean value of responses by the U.S. Line Officers. The level of seriousness for the scenarios (5 was the top level of seriousness) was consistently ranked by the members of each of these groups.

Scenarios that received the highest ranking by all three groups were the Crime Scene Theft of a Watch, Bribe from a Speeding Motorist, and Theft from Found Wallet (two opportunistic thefts and an acceptance of a bribe). The next level of seriousness gauged by both groups ranged from Drinks to Ignore a Late Bar Closing to Excessive Force on a Car Thief. The acceptance of drinks, kickback from a repair shop, and the supervisor's acceptance of a tune-up from an employee for a day off are all forms of bribery.

Table 2 Klockars Scale Scenario Mean Value Rankings: Sergeant, Middle Managers, and U.S. Line Officers

Case Description	Sergeant	Middle Manager	U.S. Line Officer[a]
Crime scene theft of watch	4.99 (1)	5.00 (1)	4.95 (1)
Bribe from speeding motorist	4.97 (2)	4.97 (2)	4.92 (2)
Theft from found wallet	4.95 (3)	4.97 (2)	4.84 (3)
Drinks to ignore late bar closing	4.77 (4)	4.74 (5)	4.49 (4)
Auto repair shop 5% kickback	4.76 (5)	4.85 (4)	4.43 (5)
Supervisor: holiday for tune-up	4.62 (6)	4.49 (7)	4.08 (6)
Excessive force on car thief	4.56 (7)	4.72 (6)	3.98 (7)
Cover-up of police DUI accident	3.81 (8)	3.76 (8)	2.94 (8)
Holiday gifts from merchants	3.30 (9)	3.62 (9)	2.71 (9)
Free meals, discount on beat	3.16 (10)	3.60 (10)	2.42 (10)
Off-duty security system business	1.64 (11)	1.91 (11)	1.43 (11)

Note. Spearman's *r* value: Sergeant to Middle Manager = 0.98. Spearman's *r* value: Sergeant to U.S. Line Officer = 1.0. Spearman's *r* value: Middle Manager to U.S. Line Officer = 0.98.

[a] U.S. line and supervisor ratings from Kutnjak Ivkovic (2005b, p. 556).

The beating of the car thief (after a chase) was ranked lower than the bribery cases. The three cases that had a mean value in the 3 range for the Sergeants and Middle Managers (Cover-Up of Police DUI Accident, Holiday Gifts from Merchants and Free Meals, and Discount on Beat) are offenses (abuse of authority and acceptance of gratuities) characterized by police corruption expert Tom Barker (2006, pp. 33–46) as "major law enforcement ethical violations" yet they were plainly discounted by this group of police supervisors and received even lower mean scores from the U.S. Line Officers.

Table 3 presents the mean score scenario rankings for the Sergeants, Middle Managers, USA, Croatia and Finland supervisors. Here, the Spearman correlations were highest for the Sergeants and Middle Managers with their counterparts in the United States ($r = 0.98$). They were slightly lower for the Sergeants and Middle Managers with the Croatia Supervisors ($r = 0.90$). This same value was registered between the rankings of the U.S. Supervisors and the Croatia Supervisors ($r = 0.90$). The rankings for the Sergeants and Middle Managers with the Finland Supervisors were somewhat lower ($r = 0.81$). The lowest Spearman rank correlations were registered by the U.S. to Finland Supervisors ($r = 0.74$) and the Croatia to Finland Supervisors ($r = 0.65$). These findings indicate that these attitudes toward different elements of police corruption are widely held among police supervisors from different departments and countries.

Table 3 Klockars Scale Scenario Mean Value Rankings: Sergeant, Middle Managers, and U.S., Croatia, and Finland Supervisors

Case Description	Sergeant	Middle Manager	U.S. Supervisor[a]	Croatia Supervisor	Finland Supervisor
Crime scene theft of watch	4.99 (1)	5.00 (1)	4.96 (1)	4.68 (1)	4.99 (1)
Bribe from speeding motorist	4.97 (2)	4.97 (2)	4.95 (2)	4.44 (3)	4.97 (2)
Theft from found wallet	4.95 (3)	4.97 (2)	4.92 (3)	4.51 (2)	4.78 (4)
Drinks to ignore late bar closing	4.77 (4)	4.74 (5)	4.73 (5)	3.78 (5)	4.78 (4)
Auto repair shop 5% kickback	4.76 (5)	4.85 (4)	4.77 (4)	3.78 (5)	4.72 (7)
Supervisor: holiday for tune-up	4.62 (6)	4.49 (7)	4.57 (6)	4.04 (4)	4.08 (8)
Excessive force on car thief	4.56 (7)	4.72 (6)	4.33 (7)	2.97 (7)	4.78 (4)
Cover-up of police DUI accident	3.81 (8)	3.76 (8)	3.35 (8)	2.75 (9)	4.88 (3)
Holiday gifts from merchants	3.30 (9)	3.62 (9)	3.40 (9)	2.09 (11)	4.04 (9)
Free meals, discount on beat	3.16 (10)	3.60 (10)	3.27 (10)	2.95 (8)	3.41 (10)
Off-duty security system business	1.64 (11)	1.91 (11)	1.58 (11)	2.50 (10)	2.41 (11)

Note: Spearman's *r* value: Sergeant to U.S. Supervisor = 0.98

Spearman's *r* value: Sergeant to Croatia Supervisor = 0.90

Spearman's *r* value: Sergeant to Finland Supervisor = 0.81

Spearman's *r* value: Middle Manager to U.S. Supervisor = 0.98

Spearman's *r* value: Middle Manager to Croatia Supervisor = 0.90

Spearman's *r* value: Middle Manager to Finland Supervisor = 0.81

Spearman's *r* value: U.S. Supervisor to Croatia Supervisor = 0.90

Spearman's *r* value: U.S. Supervisor to Finland Supervisor = 0.74

Spearman's *r* value: Croatia Supervisor to Finland Supervisor = 0.65

[a] U.S., Croatia, and Finland supervisor ratings from Kutnjak Ivkovic (2005b, p. 556).

Police managers, like all other human beings, acquire their attitudes through personal experience and social learning through association with significant others. When attitudes that are formed as the result of association and/or the vicarious learning process are integrated into a mutually reinforcing cluster of values and attitudes, they become elements of organizational culture. This transnational response set may reflect the universality of elements of the police culture. These respondents represent different national groups but they share a common occupation, organizational position, and common occupational experiences. Perhaps, this explains the universality of their attitudinal constructs.

Table 4 presents findings on how the Sergeants and Middle Managers felt that the offenses would be reported (either by themselves or other officers in their department). Between Sergeants and Middle Managers, there was a high level of correspondence in the reporting of

Table 4 Klockars Scenarios by Reporting Behavior[a]

Scenario	You Would Not Report	Officers Would Not Report	Scenario	You Would Not Report	Officers Would Not Report
Sergeants (N = 109)			Middle managers (N = 99)		
Off-duty security system business	79.8%	88.1%	Off-duty security system business	74.7%	85.9%
Free meals, discount on beat	46.8%	63.3%	Free meals, discount on beat	36.4%	55.6%
Cover-up of police DUI accident	43.1%	49.5%	Cover-up of police DUI accident	31.3%	55.6%
Holiday gifts from merchants	36.7%	58.7%	Holiday gifts from merchants	26.3%	47.5%
Excessive force on car thief	8.3%	26.9%	Supervisor: holiday for tune-up	7.1%	17.2%
Drinks to ignore late bar closing	4.6%	14.7%	Excessive force on car thief	5.1%	28.3%
Supervisor: holiday for tune-up	3.7%	13.8%	Drinks to ignore late bar closing	4.0%	11.1%
Auto repair shop 5% kickback	2.8%	4.6%	Auto repair shop 5% kickback	3.0%	7.1%
Theft from found wallet	2.8%	1.8%	Theft from found wallet	1.0%	3.0%
Bribe from speeding motorist	0.9%	2.8%	Bribe from speeding motorist	0%	3.0%
Crime scene theft of watch	0%	0.9%	Crime scene theft of watch	0%	1.0%

Note. Spearman's $r = .97$ (Sergeant to Middle Manager, Sergeant to Officers Who Would Not Report, and Middle Managers to Officers Who Would Not Report).

[a] Here, we assume that the police managers are speaking for the manner in which all officers in their department would respond in the cases posed by these scenarios.

these incidents. Their reporting behavior clearly matches the severity rankings given to these same incidents in Table 2. These police managers would report the behaviors that they felt were the most serious as indicated in the scenarios. In addition, they felt that their fellow officers would be likely to report such incidents. In fact, a majority of these police managers stated that they would report all of the incidents with the exception of the case of the Off Duty Security Business. As compared to their assessment of what their fellow officers would do, the majority of these police managers said that they would be more likely to report all of the scenarios with the exception of the first three (Crime Scene Theft of a Watch, Bribe from a Speeding Motorist, and Theft from Found Wallet) than "street cops." Overall, these responses indicate that the "management cops" feel that they take their supervisory role more seriously in terms of reporting violations of departmental policy.

Table 5 presents the modal discipline recommendations for the scenarios. The Sergeants and Middle

Table 5 Klockars Scenarios by Discipline Recommendations by Highest Percentage		
Scenario	**Discipline that *Should* Follow**	**Discipline that *Would* Follow**
Sergeants (N = 109)		
Off-duty security system business	None (76.1%)	None (76.1 %)
Free meals, discount on beat	Verbal reprimand (37.6%)	Verbal reprimand (33.9%)
Bribe from speeding motorist	Dismissal (67.0%)	Dismissal (62.4%)
Holiday gifts from merchants	Verbal reprimand (34.9%)	Written reprimand (31.2%)
Crime scene theft of watch	Dismissal (95.4%)	Dismissal (91.7%)
Auto repair shop 5% kickback	Dismissal (51.4%)	Dismissal (48.1 %)
Supervisor holiday for tune-up	Demotion in rank (36.5%)	Demotion in rank (35.2%)
Cover-up of police DUI accident	Suspension without pay (31.2%)	Suspension without pay (33.3%)
Drinks to ignore late bar closing	Suspension without pay (43.5%)	Suspension without pay (42.1 %)
Excessive force on car thief	Suspension without pay (51.9%)	Suspension without pay (46.7%)
Theft from found wallet	Dismissal (88.9%)	Dismissal (88.9%)
Middle Managers (N = 99)		
Off-duty security system business	None (71.1%)	None (71.1%)
Free meals, discount on beat	Verbal reprimand (37.4%)	Verbal reprimand (34.7%)
Bribe from speeding motorist	Dismissal (64.6%)	Dismissal (56.1 %)
Holiday gifts from merchants	Written reprimand (36.4%)	Written reprimand (34.3%)
Crime scene theft of watch	Dismissal (92.9%)	Dismissal (89.8%)
Auto repair shop 5% kickback	Dismissal (58.2%)	Dismissal (49.0%)
Supervisor holiday for tune-up	Demotion in rank (35.9%)	Demotion in rank (31.2%)
Cover-up of police DUI accident	Suspension without pay (38.1 %)	Suspension without pay (40.2%)
Drinks to ignore late bar closing	Suspension without pay (55.1%)	Suspension without pay (49.0%)
Excessive force on car thief	Suspension without pay (61.2%)	Suspension without pay (55.7%)
Theft from found wallet	Dismissal (82.1%)	Dismissal (74.7%)

Managers gave their opinion of what should happen and also what they felt would happen in their agency. Overall, there was a high level of correspondence between how the Sergeants and Middle Managers made these determinations. Overall, a majority of both the Sergeants and the Middle Managers felt that four offenses should warrant dismissal, in order of their percentage rating: Crime Scene Theft of a Watch, Theft from a Found Wallet, Bribe from a Speeding Motorist, and Auto Repair Shop 5% Kickback. Again, note that these offenses also had the highest mean rankings for seriousness for these "management cops" (with the exception of Drinks to Ignore Late Bar Closing, see Table 2). In terms of their perceptions that dismissal would be likely to follow such incidents, only the Kickback case registered less than a 50% likelihood of occurrence.

These "management cops" felt that three offenses would result in suspension without pay: Excessive Force on Car Thief, Drinks to Ignore Late Bar Closing, and Cover-Up of Police DUI Accident. A majority of both the Sergeants and the Middle Managers felt that Excessive Force on Car Thief should lead to such a decision but only a majority of the Middle Managers felt that the after-hours drinking incident should and would.

Both groups of officers felt one offense would result in a demotion in rank—a supervisor trading automobile service for a day off. They would also give a verbal reprimand to the officer in the case of Free Meals, Discount on Beat. Sergeants would extend this sanction to accepting Holiday Gifts from Merchants but the Middle Managers would make this a target for a written reprimand. The installation of security devices on off duty hours would not result in any discipline that should or would follow the offense.

⊠ Conclusion

The purpose of the current study was to provide an understanding of the police managers (i.e., "management cops") views on police corruption. Klockars (1999) noted that policing is an occupation rife with opportunities for misconduct. Corruption and violation of ethical standards by police personnel have existed since the origin of policing. These respondents were responsible for setting and controlling the ethical climate of their departments. The control of corruption is plainly impossible when police managers fail to report the unethical and often illegal behavior of their peers and thus fail to maintain an ethical climate in their organizations. This study examines potential police corruption by comparing management officers' responses to scenarios to line officers and international officers' views of the seriousness of the incidents. In addition, our respondents addressed the scenarios in the context of official policy, seriousness, reporting behavior, and discipline.

Seriousness of the corruption was similar among our "management cops" and U.S. line officers. For instance, the Sergeants, Middle Managers, U.S. Line Officers, and U.S. and international supervisors (i.e., Croatia and Finland) all agreed that theft of a watch from a crime scene was the most serious offense. This may hinder the clearing of a specific case. It also constitutes a crime (larceny-theft) as defined in state penal codes. In addition, it could force on-lookers to become a party to a conspiracy or to give up one of their own. This may provide officers with a psychological test or strain of their integrity and personal views on corruption. In a larger sense, all are agreed that tampering with potential evidence at a crime scene is unacceptable.

"Management cops" reported whether the scenario was a violation of official policy. From the responses, one scenario ranking plainly stands out. The Sergeants and Middle Managers each felt that driving an officer home following their involvement in a drunk-driving accident was the eighth ranked event in terms of seriousness—even though a majority of them (61.3%) stated that such an event was definitely a violation of departmental policy. Yet, such an incident would not be reported by 31.3% of the Sergeants and 41.3 of the Middle Managers. They also believed that a majority of the officers in their departments would not report this offense.

In the previous research, the USA (eighth – 3.35) and Croatian (ninth – 2.74) supervisors as well as the U.S. Line Officers (eighth – 2.94) also discounted the seriousness of this incident. Only the Finland supervisors (third – 4.88) felt that this scenario represented a grievous ethical error. This scenario is an example of a seriously corrupt practice—the protection of illegal activity via cover-up (Barker, 2006, p. 55). Yet, the failure to report it is consistent with one particular element of the "street cops" code—*Don't give up another cop* (Reuss-Ianni, 1983, p. 14). The fact that the view of this incident was similar for every sample of respondents except the Finland supervisors indicates that acceptance of such an ethical violation may be a widely held view among police officers.

Reporting behavior is important because it gives the sense of what needs to be done for a management cop or their perception of other officers to "give up another cop." In other words, reporting behavior is a direct examination of the "line" that the officers will take in a given situation. Between the "management cops" and the sergeants, the high correlation and those similar percentages indicate that they have similar "lines" when it is likely that they will "give up another cop." For instance, sergeants and "management cops" are likely to give up a cop when they tamper with a crime scene by theft of a watch. However, they are less likely to give up an off-duty cop that is operating a security system business.

Discipline for performing seemingly corrupt behavior is rather consistent across sergeants and "management cops." On one hand, no discipline should or would follow a sergeant or "management cop" that is operating an off-duty security system business. On the other hand, crime scene theft of a watch *should* and *would* result in a dismissal for both groups. This indicates that sergeants and management cops maintain similar views on discipline for these acts.

The findings from the current study suggest that police corruption is a behavior that has limits and is similar across levels (i.e., line officers, sergeants, and middle managers, and national and international officers). These results are tempered by the limits of the current study. First, the sample is a convenience sample of "management cops" from around the world. This reduces the generalizability of the results. However, the correlation of the majority of our results is high with line officers and management cops from other countries suggesting that our results are relatively stable. Second, the measure of police corruption is based on scenarios. Scenarios have two common problems: artificial and priming. Scenarios only provide life like

hypothetical situations. It is possible that a management cop's behavior will be different when entangled in a real situation. Scenarios also prime a response. That is, without an opportunity for an open-ended response, scenarios force a respondent to give a preset answer. These two factors reduce the veracity that scenarios provide definitive results. Regardless, many have used this format to elicit police corruption data and they provide the respondent an opportunity to respond in a more truthful manner (See Kutnjak Ivkovic, 2005a). Such scenarios provide information about decision making that may not be captured in any other method. Third, the data are cross-sectional and the research findings cross-national in nature. It is possible that the results may change over time, but the correlations between the results in the current study with those that have taken place previously suggest that not much change is likely.

Despite these limitations, these respondents control the professional environment of their departments. As "management cops," the procedures they develop and the actions they take in dealing with subordinates define and reinforce these sanctions as well as establish the core cultural values of their departments. These core values should serve as the basis for a moral compass in the department. They let officers know what is and what is not accepted behavior in the practice of day-to-day policing. Some of these respondents clearly would bend the rules when it comes to protecting another officer. This inquiry cannot identify to what extent rules are ignored but it does indicate that they are and by the very people responsible for the integrity of the organization. It is obvious that in some of the departments represented in this study, there is a set of bifurcated moral standards that serve to protect organizational members and lessen the integrity of the department. The unanswered questions are: where does such managerial behavior stop? What standards do you apply to decide to cover up one action and not another? and How then does an organization maintain a climate of integrity and ethical conduct when the discretionary decisions of individuals accountable for maintaining that climate is based on a misguided sense of loyalty to other members of their department?

Notes

1. This research is based on the scale originally published by Klockars (1999, pp. 210–211).

2. The Sergeants ($N = 109$) accounted for 53.4% of the sample. Middle Managers comprised the remaining 46.6% ($N = 99$): By far, lieutenants were the bulk of the Middle Manager group ($N = 96$ [96.9%]) with one chief and two majors.

3. In terms of department location, the remaining breakdown was Midwest (23.3%), Midwest (6.3%), and East (5.1%). These demographic descriptions represent the universe of AOC attendees during this time period. Other than rank, these variables were not obtained for each respondent to maintain anonymity of the responses.

4. Although this was a nonrandom availability sample, some of the demographic percentages for police officers are similar to those reported in the Federal Bureau of Investigation's (FBI) Uniform Crime Reports, 2004. It notes that nationally, most officers were male (73.1%). LEMAS data report that the majority of law enforcement officers in roughly the same time period were White (71%). Although both the UCR and the LEMAS refer to all officers in an agency and not just police managers, the percentages from both samples on these demographic variables are similar enough to assume that our AOC/SPI availability sample is roughly representative of the background of U.S. law enforcement agencies. Yet, difference between our respondents and LEMAS data remain in terms of location. The majority of our respondents were from Southern states (over 65%) (Reaves & Hickman, 2004).

References

Barker, T. (2002). Ethical police behavior. In K. M. Lersch (Ed.), *Policing and Misconduct*. Upper Saddle River, NJ: Prentice Hall.

Barker, T. (2006). *Police ethics: Crisis in law enforcement*. Springfield, IL: Charles C Thomas.

Barker, T., & Carter, D. L. (1991). A typology of police deviance. In T. Barker & D. L. Carter (Eds.), *Police Deviance*. (2nd ed.). Cincinnati, OH: Anderson Publishing.

Federal Bureau of Investigation. (2004). *Crime in the United States*. Retrieved May 23, 2010, from http://www. fbi.gov/ucr/cius_04/documents/CIUS_2004_Section6.pdf

Kelling, G. L., & Bratton, W. J. (1993). *Implementing community policing: The administrative problem. Perspectives on policing*. Washington, DC: National Institute of Justice.

Klockars, C. B. (1999). Some really cheap ways of measuring what really matters. In R. H. Langworthy (Ed.), *Measuring what matters: Proceedings from the policing research institute meetings* (pp. 195–214). Washington, DC: National Institute of Justice.

Klockars, C. B., & Kutnjak Ivkovic, S. (2004). Measuring police integrity. In M. Hickman, A. R. Piquero, & J. R. Greene (Eds.), *Police integrity and ethics* (pp. 3–20). Belmont, CA: Wadsworth.

Klockars, C. B., Kutnjak Ivkovic, S., & Haberfeld, M. R. (2006). *Enhancing police integrity*. New York, NY: Springer.

Klockars, C. B., Kutnjak Ivkovic, S., Harver, W. E., & Haberfeld, M. R. (2000). The measurement of police integrity. *National Institute of Justice: Research in Brief*. Washington, DC: U.S. Department of Justice.

Kutnjak Ivkovic, S. (2005a). *Fallen blue knights: Controlling police corruption*. New York: Oxford Press.

Kutnjak Ivkovic, S. (2005b). Police (mis)behavior: A cross-cultural study of corruption seriousness. *Policing, 28*, 546–566.

Manning, P. K. (1995). The police occupational culture in Anglo-American societies. In W. Bailey (Ed.), *The encyclopedia of police science* (pp. 472–475). New York, NY: Garland Publishing.

Paoline, E. A. (2003). Taking stock: Toward a richer understanding of police culture. *Journal of Criminal Justice, 31*, 199–214.

Reaves, B. A., & Hickman, M. J. (2004). *Law enforcement management and administrative statistics, 2000: Data for individual state and local agencies with 100 or more officers*. Washington, DC: U.S. Department of Justice, Bureau of Justice Statistics.

Reuss-Ianni, E. (1983). *Two cultures of policing: Street cops and management cops*. New Brunswick, NJ: Transaction Books.

Silverman, E. B. (1999). *NYPD battles crime: Innovative strategies in policing*. Boston, MA: Northeastern University Press.

Sparrow, M. K., Moore, M., & Kennedy, D. (1990). *Beyond 911: A new era of policing*. New York, NY: Basic Books.

DISCUSSION QUESTIONS

1. What types of questions are included in the Klockars scale?

2. How could the findings from this study help police leaders reduce police misconduct in their agencies?

3. What are some things that police supervisors can do to reduce the level of tolerance of misconduct among police officers?

In the future, officers will need to tailor police service to the needs of the growing elderly population in the United States.

Policing in the Present and Future

Section Highlights

- Cover several contemporary issues facing the police today, including their ability to serve populations with specialized needs.
- Examine some of the challenges faced by police agencies as they deal with shrinking budgets and fewer resources.
- Discuss changes in future police personnel and the use of cutting-edge technology.

Winston Churchill once said, "To improve is to change, to be perfect is to change often."[1] This quote embodies the evolution that American policing has experienced since its inception in the 1800s. As we learned in the previous sections of this book, changes in policing result from the efforts and ideas of innovators, and also as a response to the changes that occur in society. This section covers several issues that the police face today as a result of fluctuations in the economy, laws, the populations they serve, and conditions that threaten the safety of American citizens. This section discusses the myriad ways that police agencies have made alterations to their operations in response to the downturn in the economy. Police officers also serve more diverse populations that have specialized needs, including the elderly, the homeless, and the mentally ill. This section also covers deviations in policing related to changes in immigration laws and the focus on homeland security since the terrorist attacks on

September 11, 2001. This section closes with a discussion of the future of policing as it relates to hiring, personnel issues, and technology that is being developed for future use by police.

 ## The Police and the Economic Downturn

Recently, Americans have been experiencing some of the most difficult economic challenges since the Great Depression.[2] Government budgets have been severely cut at the local, state, and federal levels. These cuts have impacted the manner in which police agencies across the United States are able to operate. Bernard Melekian, director of the Office of Community Oriented Policing Services (COPS), recently explained how the economic downturn has forced police agencies to reprioritize their delivery of service to their communities:[3]

> Police service delivery can be categorized into three tiers. The first tier, emergency response, is not going to change. Tier two is non-emergency response; where officers respond to calls after the fact, primarily to collect the information and statements necessary to produce reports. These calls, while an important service, do not require rapid response—the business has already been vandalized, the bike already stolen. Tier three deals with quality of life issues, such as crime prevention efforts or traffic management duties. They help make our communities better places to live, but they are proactive and ongoing activities. The second and third tiers have always competed for staffing and financial resources, but as local budgets constrict, that competition becomes fiercer. The public expects that both tiers are addressed, and agencies with shrinking payrolls are faced with finding new ways to make sure that can happen.

The COPS office released a report detailing some of the ways that police agencies have responded during hard economic times in recent years. This report indicates that staffing within police agencies has been affected by budget cuts.[4] Some agencies have been forced to lay off police officers. At the end of April 2011, the San Jose Police Department in California laid off 106 police officers and were threatening to lay off another 155 police officers if the police union did not agree to a 10% cut in pay and benefits for their members.[5] Other agencies have used mandatory furloughs (temporary unpaid leave for employees) or hiring freezes to reduce labor costs within police organizations.[6]

Many police agencies have also had to reduce or eliminate some of the services they provide to their communities. For example, in some jurisdictions, the police will no longer respond to motor vehicle thefts, burglar alarms (unless a burglary is in progress), noninjury accidents, property crimes, financial crimes, computer crimes, and other nonviolent crimes.[7] Some agencies now require citizens to process incidents that are usually handled by sworn police officers. There are police departments that do not dispatch officers to noninjury traffic accidents and require the citizens involved in the accident to file their own accident reports.[8]

Another option is to hire more civilian employees to complete tasks that are usually completed by sworn officers.[9] **Civilianization** is the hiring of nonsworn personnel to replace or supplement sworn police forces—this is usually done to reduce costs within police organizations and, in some cases, to improve service.[10] Civilians can be hired to work as communication specialists, computer specialists, crime scene technicians, lawyers (legal advisors), planning and research specialists, budgeting and finance specialists, and to handle parking and traffic violations. The Bureau of Justice Statistics reported that the growth rate for civilian personnel was more than double that of sworn police personnel from 1992 to 2008.[11] According to one source, civilian employees cost anywhere from one-third to one-half as much as sworn police officers.[12]

In an effort to continue police service at a level that is expected by citizens and to reduce costs, some police agencies choose to collaborate with private security companies.[13] Over the last three decades, the number of private security personnel has increased three times more than the number of sworn police officers (see Section 3 for more information on private security).[14] Private security agents or companies are hired to help with video surveillance, traffic control, computer and communication systems maintenance, laboratory services, dispatch services, and training.[15] It is common for private security companies to be hired to monitor and maintain closed-circuit television systems and light-based intervention systems (both of which can act as eyes and ears for the police when they are not able to be present).[16] Using technology as a "force multiplier" is becoming increasingly common, as the cost to use such equipment is significantly less than paying the salaries of several sworn police officers.[17]

Another approach that is used to save money and maintain levels of police service is the use of volunteers.[18] Citizen volunteers working within police agencies have increased significantly from 2004 to 2010. According to statistics provided by the International Association of Chiefs of Police (IACP), American police agencies use approximately 245,000 citizen volunteers.[19] One of the most organized groups of citizen volunteers is **Volunteers in Police Service (VIPS)**. According to the official VIPS website, the purpose of this group is to

> provide support and resources for agencies interested in developing or enhancing a volunteer program, and for citizens who wish to volunteer their time and skills with a community law enforcement agency. The program's ultimate goal is to enhance the capacity of state and local law enforcement to utilize volunteers.[20]

Some police agencies use citizen volunteers to aid in the process of conducting criminal history checks, the enforcement of handicap parking regulations, conducting phone surveys to determine citizen satisfaction with police service, fingerprinting, photography, and data entry, to name a few areas.[21] The obvious benefit of using citizen volunteers is that there are no costs to police agencies.

Consolidation is another cost-saving approach used by some police agencies.[22] Consolidation includes situations in which two or more police agencies combine their resources, when two or more agencies merge to form a single agency, when a number of agencies within a region combine their resources to cover an entire geographic area instead of individual jurisdictions, or the contracting of services from nearby jurisdictions or regional agencies.[23] It is common for small, rural municipalities to contract with sheriffs' departments to provide police service instead of paying to maintain a local police agency.

Several advantages and disadvantages are associated with consolidation:[24] Some of the benefits include that it can be cost effective; it can provide smaller police agencies access to resources that were previously not available to them; and it can reduce the amount of overlap of police services in some areas. There are also several drawbacks associated with the consolidation of police agencies. For example, if a small agency collaborates with a larger agency, the smaller one may not have as much input or influence due to its lack of size. Partnering with other police agencies can result in individual police agencies losing some of their autonomy. Sometimes citizens reject the idea of consolidation because they fear that they will not get the same amount and quality of police service. Despite these drawbacks, many jurisdictions have been forced to consider consolidation as an option in order to alleviate resource deficits in their police agencies.

It is clear that the downturn in the American economy has altered the function and operation of police agencies. It has been predicted that many police agencies will continue to feel the effects of smaller budgets for several years to come.[25] American police agencies will have to continue to adapt and change in response to an unpredictable economy in the future.

Policing and the Elderly Population

The population of the United States is changing not only in terms of racial/ethnic diversity but also by age. The 2010 Census revealed that more people are 65 years and older than in any other previous census.[26] This segment of the population requires specialized services geared toward health care, social services, and other quality-of-life needs. As the elderly population continues to increase in the future, it is likely that the police will be called to respond to more cases of **elder abuse**. Elder abuse refers to "any intentional or neglectful acts by a caregiver or trusted individual that leads to, or may lead to, harm of a vulnerable elder."[27]

Types of Elder Abuse
Physical abuse—use of force to threaten or physically harm an elderly person.
Emotional abuse—verbal attacks, threats, isolation, or demeaning acts that cause or could cause mental anguish, pain, or distress to an elderly person.
Sexual abuse—any sexual contact with an elderly person that is forced, tricked, threatened, or nonconsensual.
Exploitation—theft, fraud, misuse, or neglect of authority and use of undue influence as a lever to gain control over an elderly person's money or property.
Neglect—failure or refusal of a caregiver to provide for an elderly person's safety and physical and emotional needs.
Abandonment—when a caregiver deserts an elderly person for whom he or she is responsible.
Self-neglect—the inability to understand one's own actions or inaction, which leads to or could lead to harm or endangerment to others.

Source: The National Center on Elder Abuse[28]

The prevalence of elder abuse in the United States is unknown[29] because there are varying definitions of elder abuse, there is no national standardized reporting system, and many elderly victims cannot report their victimization.[30] A 2003 report released by the National Research Council Panel to Review Risk and Prevalence of Elder Abuse and Neglect estimates that between 1 and 2 million Americans age 65 years or older have been injured, exploited, or mistreated by someone whom they depend on for care and protection.[31]

Many police agencies have responded to the aging population by implementing specialized training. This training includes teaching police officers various techniques for interviewing elderly crime victims, suggestions for how to approach elderly citizens that suffer from dementia, and the proper way to investigate and identify cases of elder abuse.[32] Illinois and Colorado are two states that have developed POST- (Police Office Standards and Training) approved curriculums for police officers focused on how to respond to the elderly.[33]

The Alzheimer's Association estimates that 5.4 million Americans are currently living with Alzheimer's disease.[34] This number is expected to climb to 16 million people by the year 2050.[35] Many state Alzheimer's Associations have created training material geared toward police officers and have donated it to state and local law enforcement agencies with the hope that they will incorporate it into their officer training programs.[36] This training includes dealing with unsafe driving by the elderly who are suffering from Alzheimer's, shoplifting, inappropriate behavior in public places, the identification of neglect and abuse of Alzheimer's patients, and responding to cases in which Alzheimer's patients have wandered from their homes. Some states have created partnerships between law enforcement agencies and security or tracking companies (such as Safe Return[37] and Project Lifesaver[38]) as a way to keep Alzheimer patients safe.[39] With a substantial portion of the aging population facing Alzheimer's disease and other dementia-related diseases, it is imperative that police agencies prepare to deal with this particular issue in the future.

Some police agencies have also created specialized units that specifically serve elderly crime victims. For example, the Milwaukee Police Department created the senior citizen assault prevention unit—referred to as the **Gray Squad**. The purpose of this unit is to investigate and prevent crimes against the elderly.[40] An evaluation of the Gray Squad revealed that elderly victims that were processed by members of the Gray Squad were more satisfied with the efforts of their local police when compared to elderly crime victims who had not received specialized service.[41] Another recent study looked at the impact of having senior services officers (SSOs) responding to elderly victims of domestic violence in Chicago. This research found that elderly domestic violence victims who received service from an SSO were more likely to have sought out help and other protective measures compared to elderly domestic violence victims that received traditional police service.[42] As the population continues to age, police agencies across the country will have to continue to adopt practices tailored for this segment of the population and their specialized needs.

Policing the Mentally Ill

It has been reported that nearly 10% of the people that the police suspect of criminal activity have a serious mental illness.[43] Interactions between the police and people with mental illness (**PWMI**) have increased as a result of these cases being processed through the criminal justice system instead of the mental health system—this is sometimes referred to as the "criminalization of the mentally ill."[44] Deinstitutionalization (shifting the focus of care from psychiatric hospitals to local community mental health centers) and more restrictive mental health codes have also contributed to the increased contact between PWMI and the police.[45]

Police officer interactions with PWMI result in some formal or informal response. Formal responses can include arrest or hospitalization.[46] It has been argued that arresting PWMI is not the ideal way to manage the underlying issues that may be driving the criminal or disruptive behavior. A report released in 2000 by the National Institute of Justice noted that once a mentally ill person is arrested for disorderly conduct or some other minor criminal offense, that person will likely be arrested again in the future and will then be labeled as criminal instead of receiving proper mental health treatment.[47] Hospitalization is not always an option for PWMI, as there are only a limited number of beds or spaces available in local mental health facilities.[48] The lack of formal options can leave police officers frustrated and in the position of having to resolve these situations using informal means.

Informal handling of PWMI usually depends on how police officers characterize the people that they encounter.[49] Some PWMI are categorized as *neighborhood characters*. These individuals display out-of-the-ordinary behaviors in public and are usually well known to the police and the people living in that particular area. Neighborhood characters are usually not arrested or hospitalized; instead, the police will talk with them and attempt to calm them down. *Troublemakers* are mentally ill individuals that act out in the presence of the police. Their actions are not necessarily violent but more of a nuisance to the police and the public. Troublemakers are also rarely arrested or hospitalized. And finally, there are mentally ill persons that are categorized as *quiet, unobtrusive "mentals."*[50] Linda Teplin describes this group as individuals that "offend neither the populace nor the police with obvious manifestations of their illness, and their symptoms are not considered serious enough to warrant hospitalization. Moreover, quiet 'mentals' are considered more disordered than disorderly and so are unlikely to provoke arrest."[51] Informal handling of PWMI occurs because there are instances when formal responses are not warranted or are simply not an option (specifically with regard to hospitalization).

Research focused on the interaction between the police and the mentally ill reveals that some police officers are frustrated by the lack of professional help available to this group.[52] In one study, police officers reported that the most appropriate disposition for cases involving mentally ill persons is taking them to a mental health service facility; however, most of them stated that they end up taking them to a general hospital or arresting them because there is a lack of space available at local mental health facilities.[53] Arresting PWMI does not provide the kind of mental health treatment that is needed by this segment of the population. Instead, the criminal justice system begins to act as a revolving door: the same PWMI are arrested, let go, and then re-arrested again in the future. An unfortunate consequence of this revolving door is that PWMI become viewed as criminals.

Specialized training focused on the identification of signs and symptoms of mental illness, as well as the proper management and referral of PWMI cases, is needed for police officers. This training should include informing police officers about all possible services available to PWMI. This training should become part of both academy and in-service training programs.[54] While most police agencies offer some kind of training focused on dealing with mentally ill persons, the training is often limited.[55] Further, police agencies should have formal policies and procedures in their operations manual detailing how such cases should be handled by police officers.

Highly publicized cases of PWMI committing violent crimes lend to the perception that they are more likely to be involved in violent crimes than the rest of the general population. The shooting of Arizona Congresswoman Gabrielle Giffords on January 8, 2011, by Jared Lee Loughner (who has since been diagnosed as schizophrenic) is an example of such a case.[56] The National Institute of Justice reports that "three percent of the variance in violent behavior in the United States is attributable to mental disorders."[57] Current studies have revealed that schizophrenia does not influence the prevalence of involvement in violent crimes unless that person is using alcohol or illegal drugs.[58] Ironically, statistics show that PWMI are more often the victims of crime, not the offenders. PWMI are 11 times more likely than the general population to become crime victims.[59] The likelihood for criminal victimization increases significantly if PWMI also happen to be homeless.

Policing the Homeless

The National Alliance to End Homelessness estimates that on any given evening, about 643,067 people do not have proper shelter or housing in the United States.[60] About half of the homeless population suffers from some type of mental illness, with one-quarter of this group having serious mental illnesses such as chronic major depression, bipolar disorder, and various types of schizophrenia.[61] Mental illnesses can impact one's ability to maintain steady employment and also stable relationships with other people. These issues can result in no resources to pay for housing and no support system for the mentally ill.

Nearly half of the homeless population suffers from some type of mental illness.

When police encounter the homeless, it is usually the result of citizens calling to report a homeless person to the police, police officers seeing homeless people in difficult situations, or business owners who call the police to have them move the homeless away from their businesses.[62] The homeless have high arrest rates that usually involve minor, nonviolent crimes (such as loitering, panhandling, disorderly conduct, etc.).[63] They are often viewed by the police as more of a public nuisance than a threat to public safety.[64]

There has been some research on police experiences with the homeless. A national study conducted by David Carter and Allen Sapp found that nearly half (49.8%) of police executives do not view homelessness as a police problem. Instead, they view it as a social problem that can be taken care of through social services.[65] Many (68%) police executives stated that the police do not have a clearly defined responsibility in dealing with noncriminal problems of the homeless. There are social services provided to the homeless by local agencies. The problem is that the police are usually the first and sometimes the only immediate resource available to respond and help the homeless. The article written by William King and Thomas Dunn included at the end of this section explains how some police officers transport and then "dump" what they view as troublesome persons (including homeless and mentally ill people) in other jurisdictions as an informal way of dealing with this particular segment of the population.

Studies have found that some homeless people do not trust the police, as they feel that they have been mistreated by police in the past. The lack of trust in the police can result in significant health issues for homeless individuals, as they are less likely to go to the police for help if they are injured as a result of crime victimization or some illness.[66] Homeless people have a greater chance to become ill, as they have limited access to proper nutrition and are also frequently exposed to extreme weather conditions, as well as unsanitary living conditions.[67]

Since some studies indicate that police executives and officers do not view homeless people as a policing problem, it is not surprising that many police agencies do not have specialized training centered on this segment of the population.[68] In the police agencies that do have specialized training, it is often limited to supervisors providing police officers with information about where they can give referrals to the homeless for services related to substance abuse, mental illness, and shelter. Some agencies have created multi-agency intervention units or liaisons focused on aiding the homeless. This is the case in Santa Monica, California,[69] Pinellas Park, Florida,[70] and New Orleans, Louisiana,[71] to name a few. If the economy in the United States continues to decline or is slow to improve, the number of Americans facing homelessness could increase. This means that local police agencies will have to become better equipped to deal with this issue. This will require them to forge partnerships with social service agencies and other local outreach centers that provide food and shelter for the homeless.

⊠ Policing and Immigration

Alabama has been in the headlines recently for its adoption of what is being touted as the most strict immigration laws in the country.[72] **Alabama HB 56** (the Beason-Hammon Alabama Taxpayer and Citizen Protection Act) was signed into law in June 2011.[73] Among other things, this law requires police officers to verify the legal status of people they suspect are in the United States illegally during routine traffic stops and other encounters. It also allows the police to hold people they believe are in the country illegally without bond. Arizona also has stringent immigration laws, specifically **Arizona SB 1070** or the Support Our Law Enforcement and Safe Neighborhoods Act, which was passed in April 2010.[74] This law requires that police officers attempt to determine someone's immigration status during traffic stops, detentions, or arrests when there is reasonable suspicion that the person is an illegal immigrant.

These strict immigration laws spark heated debates among citizens, politicians, and law enforcement personnel. Traditionally, the federal government has been in charge of enforcing immigration laws. In the past few decades (and especially since the terrorist attacks on 9/11), local law enforcement agencies have been asked to engage in immigration enforcement. Some jurisdictions have decided that their local police will not assume any role in immigration enforcement and that they will continue to leave immigration enforcement up to federal agencies.[75]

Some police agencies collaborate with federal immigration agencies through the **ICE 287 (g) program**. The United States Immigration and Customs Enforcement's ICE 287 (g) program that was passed in 1996 "allows federal officials to enter into written agreements with state and local law enforcement agencies to carry out the functions of immigration officers, including investigation, apprehension and detention."[76] As of September 2, 2011, ICE has 287 (g) agreements with 69 law enforcement agencies in 24 states and has certified more than 1,500 state and local police officers to enforce immigration laws within their jurisdictions.[77] The ICE training program is 4 weeks long and is held at the Federal Law Enforcement Training Center ICE Academy in Charleston, South Carolina.[78] The official ICE website also notes that "the 287 (g) program is credited with identifying more than 217,300 potentially removable aliens (mostly from jails) since January 2006."[79]

There is no consensus among police executives regarding the involvement of local and state law enforcement agencies in immigration enforcement. Some police leaders and associations oppose such laws,[80] while others are vocal supporters of the enforcement of strict immigration laws.[81] A 2008 report by the Police Executive Research Forum (PERF) identified some of the top concerns that chiefs of police and sheriffs from across the country have when it comes to their involvement in immigration enforcement. Many police leaders were worried about having an insufficient number of officers (65%), that their involvement in immigration enforcement would undermine the trust between their agencies and immigrant citizens in their communities (61%), insufficient resources (60%), insufficient jail space (51%), that immigration enforcement will distract from their department's core mission (49%), the inability of ICE to assist them in their efforts (38%), and that they would face additional civil liability issues as a result of becoming involved in immigration enforcement (29%).[82] Their involvement in immigration enforcement might also undermine community policing efforts that were adopted to bring them closer to the citizens in their communities—especially racial/ethnic citizens.[83] Perceptions of racial profiling would also become a problem for local police if they participate in enforcement of immigration laws.[84]

Guadalupe Vidales and her colleagues examined the influence of local police and immigration enforcement on Latino(a) citizen's perceptions of the police after the mayor of Costa Mesa, California, encouraged local police to engage in immigration enforcement.[85] This event drew national media attention because

Costa Mesa was one of the first cities to pursue this type of initiative. This study revealed that Latino(a) residents reported more negative views of the local police, found the police to be less helpful to them, and were less likely to report crimes after local police began to participate in immigration enforcement. The article written by Mary Romero included at the end of this section further highlights potential problems that result from local police enforcing immigration laws. This article uses the controversial Chandler Roundup incident as an example of negative consequences that can result from the enforcement of immigration law by local police. The fact that immigration enforcement by local and state law enforcement agencies has become part of the political arena increases the likelihood that it will continue to be an issue that police executives wrestle with in the future.

Policing and Terrorism

The United States Department of Defense defines *terrorism* as "the calculated use of unlawful violence or threat of unlawful violence to inculcate fear; intended to coerce or to intimidate governments or societies in the pursuit of goals that are generally political, religious, or ideological."[86] Acts of terrorism have occurred within the United States dating back more than a century.[87] The terrorist attacks that took place on September 11, 2001 (9/11), claimed the lives of nearly 3,000 people and caused many Americans to feel vulnerable to future attacks.[88] After that day, terrorism has become the focus of many government agencies, including the police.

Willard Oliver identifies 9/11 as the beginning of a new era of policing—the **homeland security era**.[89] This new era follows the political, reform, and community/problem solving eras that were discussed in the first section of this book. Using the framework provided by George Kelling and Mark Moore, Oliver predicts the direction of the homeland security policing era.[90] In this era, he believes that the police will receive authorization or legitimacy from national and international threats of terrorism, the law (intergovernmental), and professionalism. The police function will center on crime control—specifically, anti- and counterterrorism efforts—by using intelligence gathering and intergovernmental information sharing. The organizational design of American police agencies will become more centralized due to information sharing with other agencies, but it will also be decentralized as police officers working the streets will largely determine how services will be executed. Demands for police service will become centralized as a result of the centralized organizational design of police agencies. The relationship between the police and citizens will be professional as a result of the centralized nature of demand for service, organizational design, and function; however, the police will not isolate themselves from the public as they did in the reform era. Instead, they will work closely with the public in order to gather information and intelligence. The use of risk assessments, intelligence gathering/analyzing, and organizing large-scale crisis response plans will be the focus of police tactics and technology in this new era. And finally, Oliver believes that the outcome measures used in this new era of policing will include some from previous eras (such as crime control, citizen satisfaction, and quality-of-life issues) but will also emphasize citizen safety (specifically, the prevention of terrorist attacks through the use of antiterrorism efforts). Because Oliver's new era of policing was only recently presented to the world, only time will tell if American policing will move in the direction that he is predicting.

Some people believe that the shift toward homeland security and antiterrorism efforts by local and state police will lead to a more traditional model of policing that is akin to that proposed by August Vollmer and O. W. Wilson (see Sections 1 and 2 for a discussion of the traditional/professional model of policing).

There is some concern that this shift would erode any progress that has been made by police agencies that adopted community policing years ago.[91] It has also been suggested that policing has become more aggressive since 9/11 and that this more forceful approach counters the basic principles of community policing.[92] Further, some people worry that the police will become so focused on homeland security and the use of military-like tactics/technology that the lines between policing and the military will become blurred, leaving community policing by the wayside.[93]

Comparing the Four Eras of American Policing*				
Elements	**Political Era**	**Reform Era**	**Comm/Prob Era**	**Homeland Security Era**
Authorization	Politics & law	Law & professionalism	Community support, law, & professionalism	National/international threats, law, & professionalism
Function	Broad social services	Crime control	Broad, provision of service	Crime control, antiterrorism/counter-terrorism, intelligence gathering
Organizational design	Decentralized	Centralized	Decentralized, task forces	Centralized decision making, decentralized execution of services
Relationship to environment	Intimate	Professionally remote	Intimate	Professional
Demand	Decentralized, to patrol and politicians	Centralized	Decentralized	Centralized
Tactics and technology	Foot patrol	Preventive patrol and rapid response to calls for service	Foot patrol, problem solving, etc.	Risk assessment, police operations centers, information systems
Outcome measures	Citizen & political satisfaction	Crime control	Quality of life and citizen satisfaction	Citizen safety, crime control, antiterrorism

*Table from Willard Oliver, "The Fourth Era of Policing: Homeland Security," *International Review of Law Computers & Technology* 20 (2006): 52. Copyright © 2006 Routledge. Reprinted with permission.

A recent case study by RAND found that the Long Beach, California, Police Department had become focused on tactical concerns (including counterterrorism and patrol) and less concerned with community policing efforts such as foot patrol, involvement within schools (specifically the DARE program), and the division that was created for community relations.[94] David Thacher also examined this issue using Dearborn, Michigan, as his research site. Dearborn is an appropriate site for a study of this nature because it is home to one of the largest Arab populations in the United States. Thacher identified two specific burdens placed on cities that attempt to shift toward a homeland security approach: (1) there will be considerable damage to their overall reputation (since police surveillance implies that its objects are not trustworthy) and (2) there will be damage to the legitimacy and reputation of local police (since new surveillance may undercut the trust between police and the community).[95] Clearly these are issues that most police agencies would want to avoid.

In contrast to the previous studies, Jason Vaughn Lee analyzed national survey data from 2003 to examine the relevance of community policing at a time when homeland security has become a top priority.[96] This

Homeland security has become part of policing at the local, county, state, and federal levels.

study revealed that homeland security efforts can occur within police agencies that have adopted community policing without *replacing* community policing— or, put another way, the two approaches can be used together. Similarly, Allison Chappell and Sarah Gibson found that police chiefs from Virginia who employed community policing in their organizations were less likely to view it as being replaced by a focus on homeland security and perceived the two approaches to be simpatico.[97]

Some studies have found that police agencies have changed very little or have conducted their "business as usual" since 9/11. One study found that police agencies have undergone very little organizational change because they do not have the resources to do so.[98] Essentially, the only police organizations that have been able to make any meaningful organizational changes are those that have received financial support. Christopher Ortiz and his colleagues found evidence that police agencies in their study made little effort to move toward a homeland security focus in recent years.[99] The only significant change identified in this study was an increase in cooperation with federal agencies and an increase in information sharing.

Similar to the evolution and adoption of community policing, only time will tell if American police agencies will leave an era that is marked by the principles of community policing for one that concentrates solely on homeland security and terrorism.

Future of Policing in the United States

This book has covered the history and evolution of American policing and has also presented several contemporary issues faced by police officers today. But what about the future of policing in the United States . . . what will it be like in the years to come? Is it possible to predict what policing will be like in the future? In 1986, William Tafoya completed his dissertation titled "Delphi Forecast of the Future of Law Enforcement" at the University of Maryland.[100] Tafoya's work is the first to attempt to predict what the future of policing might be like in the United States. The following are a few of his predictions:[101]

- By 1990, computer-related crime will emerge as a threat to our economy and national security.
- By 1995, the involvement of the average citizen in policing will be the norm.
- By 1995, terrorism is expected to emerge as a major problem in the United States, much of it attributed to retaliation from the U.S. involvement in the affairs of other nations.
- By 2000, massive urban unrest and civil disorder will occur similar to what was experienced in the 1960s.

- By 2000, local law enforcement could be overwhelmed by sophisticated crime and may be reduced to taking preliminary reports.
- By 2000, computer-based training will be the standard for training in law enforcement but is unlikely to have any significant effect on the incidence of high-tech crime.
- By 2025, the majority of all law enforcement executives will have abandoned traditional autocratic management for a proactive, goal-oriented style.
- By 2035, private security agencies will assume a significant role in all law enforcement responsibilities.

Not only are these predictions interesting, but it could also be argued that many of Tafoya's predictions have turned out to be quite accurate so far.

Today, there are two groups whose work centers on the future of policing. First, the Society of Police Futurists International (PFI) was established in 1991 by William Tafoya (the person who made the predictions mentioned in the preceding paragraph).[102] This group "uses futures research (long-range planning and forecasting) to anticipate and prepare for the evolution of law enforcement ten, twenty, and even fifty years into the future."[103] A second group was formed in 2002; the Futures Working Group (FWG) consists of a partnership between the FBI and the PFI. The purpose of this group is "to develop and encourage others to develop forecasts and strategies to ethically maximize the effectiveness of local, state, federal, and international law enforcement bodies as they strive to maintain peace and security in the 21st century."[104] Individuals affiliated with FWG and PFI have published two pieces of literature that could be useful to police leaders: "Policing 2020: Exploring the Future of Crime, Communities and Policing"[105] and "The Future of Policing: A Practical Guide for Police Managers and Leaders."[106] The work conducted by these two groups can guide police executives as they plan the future direction of their agencies.

Numerous issues will challenge the police in the future. If you attend any professional law enforcement or academic conference, many of these issues are studied, presented, and discussed. The topics covered in the first half of this section (the impact of the economy on police agencies, their response to homeland security and terrorism, interacting with special segments of the population, and immigration enforcement) are issues that the police are currently dealing with and will likely continue to grapple with in the coming decade. Because it is not possible to cover *all* future issues that police executive and officers will face in this book, two topics are covered here that police executives will likely have to manage in the future in the remaining pages of this book.

Issues Related to Hiring and Personnel

The United States Department of Labor predicts that employment for police officers will continue to increase as fast as the average for all other occupations through 2018.[107] Employment in this profession is expected to grow 10% from 2008 through 2018. The easiest positions to attain will be in local police departments that offer low salaries or those in urban areas with higher crime rates.[108] Applicants with military experience, that are bilingual, or that have college training will have the best opportunities to be hired by local- and state-level agencies.[109] Federal-level positions will be more difficult to acquire (when compared to local or state agencies), as there is greater competition for fewer available positions. The Department of Labor notes that applicants that are bilingual, have a 4-year degree (and in most cases an advanced degree—either master's or law degree), and several years of law enforcement or military experience will have the best opportunities to be hired by federal agencies.

In addition to meeting the traditional hiring standards covered in Section 5 of this book, some police agencies are now beginning to look more closely at applicants' preservice behavior. Several police agencies now examine applicants' digital and online behavior.[110] Many police agencies will look at applicants' accounts on social networking sites (such as Facebook, MySpace, etc.), their personal blogs, or personal webpages for any information that might reveal that they are not desirable candidates for a policing position. A recent study conducted by the International Association of Chiefs of Police (IACP) found that more than one-third (37%) of the 728 departments that were surveyed reported that they review social media profiles of applicants before deciding to hire them.[111]

Some agencies are also starting to restrict officers' use of social media and other digital technology when they are off duty.[112] If police officers are posting inappropriate pictures or posting blogs or other online information that presents their personal opinions that may be biased (race, class, or gender bias) or that conflicts with their police organization's standards of professionalism, they may be fired or receive some type of discipline. A recent example of this involves a case in which three sheriff's deputies and their wives engaged in videotaped group sex, which was later made available for sale on the Internet. The sheriff fired the deputies on the basis that these acts could be considered officer misconduct. His decision was upheld by both the Federal District Court and the United States Court of Appeal.[113] Cases involving off-duty behavior of police officers have only recently begun to make their way through the court system. As a result, police executives have little guidance on how to create and implement policies regulating the off-duty behaviors of police officers. As technology continues to advance, it is possible that police executives will continue to encounter problems with its use by police employees in the future.

The diversification of police agencies in the United States will continue to be important in the future. Despite the progress that has been made in hiring minority and female police officers in the last few decades, this effort needs to continue (see Section 4 for a detailed discussion of minority and female police officers).

Research statistics indicate that the hiring of women in policing has hit a plateau.

The IACP has reported that many police agencies have experienced difficulty recruiting and hiring minority applicants since 9/11, as many potential applicants are lost to military reserve call-ups and activation and because of budget cuts in agencies across the country.[114]

There is also evidence that the hiring of female police officers has stalled in recent years. In a study published in 2011, Gary Cordner and AnnMarie Cordner point out that "the female proportion of sworn local police increased by more than 40% from 1987 to 1997 but has increased by less than 10% since then."[115] Using surveys completed by female officers and chiefs of police in Pennsylvania, the researchers found three reasons agreed upon by both police chiefs and female police officers for the stall in the hiring of female officers: (1) women have other employment opportunities that are more attractive than what police agencies can offer; (2) women are simply not interested in working as police officers; and (3) many women that were interested in this career were eliminated from the process by physical fitness tests.[116]

It is important to mention that this study also revealed that the three most common reasons for stalled hiring of female officers identified *only* by female police officers include: (1) the culture within police agencies is dominated by males and is not welcoming to women; (2) police agencies are not proactive enough at recruiting women; and (3) many agencies lack family-friendly policies geared toward pregnancy, child care, and other family-related issues.[117] The findings from this study reveal that there are still barriers that women have to overcome in order to be hired as police officers; however, many of these barriers can be eliminated by actions taken by police executives. It is clear that police executives still have many challenges ahead when it comes to the recruitment and hiring of racial/ethnic minority and female police officers.

Police Technology

"Policing Jetson-style" is an 8-minute animated video found on the Discoverpolicing.org website (sponsored by the U.S. Department of Justice Bureau of Justice Assistance and the IACP). This video provides a brief look at what a day in the life of a police officer might resemble in the future.[118] The video features several technological gadgets that could be used by the police of the future (including jet packs and armband computers sewn into officer uniforms), as well as some technology that is being used by a handful of agencies today (such as Segways, hot-spot mapping, automatic vehicle location, and license plate recognition).[119] Despite the fact that this video is meant for entertainment, it provides a glimpse of how American policing will continue to utilize advanced technology in the future.

Video recording devices have improved over time by becoming more compact in size, and also by producing higher-quality video recordings. The use of video cameras in patrol cars is now common in police agencies across the country. Recent statistics indicate that more than half (61%) of local police departments used video cameras in their patrol cars in 2007—this has increased since 2003, when 55% of local agencies used video cameras in squad cars.[120] Some innovative police agencies have figured out new ways to use video recording devices to help them with their work. Officers in Fort Smith, Arkansas, Cincinnati, Ohio, San Jose, California, and Aberdeen, South Dakota, are testing a new video camera device that attaches near officers' ears that allows them to record every encounter they have with citizens.[121]

Computers are commonly used by police officers today. Onboard computers (in squad cars) are used by most (90%) police agencies across the United States.[122] The Bureau of Justice Statistics reported that in 2007, about three in four police officers worked for departments that use computers as part of their crime mapping efforts. In addition, more than half (60%) of U.S. police departments use computers to transmit incident reports and other important electronic information.[123] Computers have become so compact that some police agencies have begun to use them outside of patrol cars. The Louisville Police Department now outfits its horse patrol officers with small, portable computers that attach to the horses' breast collars.[124] As computers continue to become smaller and more portable, it is likely that police officers will continue to use them in various aspects of their work.

Computers allow the police to access important information that helps them do their job. Social networking sites have become a treasure trove of information for the police, as they are able to get information that they might not otherwise have access to and, in some instances, are able to contact people that are otherwise difficult to reach. The limited research on the use of social networking sites by the police has revealed that many police agencies use these sites to provide information to citizens in their communities.[125] Some of this information includes safety tips, crimes occurring in the community, missing person information, recruitment for police agencies, and other public relations–based information.[126] Social networking sites have been used as part of community policing efforts by police agencies, as they are able to stay connected to citizens in their community in a virtual manner.

Computers will also be necessary tools for the police as they continue to deal with cybercrime in the future. Cybercrime is any crime that is committed against people, property, or the government using the Internet. Some of examples include identity theft, embezzlement, fraud, breaching government and business security, using the Internet to bully or threaten people, consumption of child pornography, and using viruses to damage information systems, to name a few. This type of crime can be quite costly, as businesses reported a loss of $867 million in 2005 as a result of being victims of cybercrime.[127] Other sources have reported that cybercrime across the globe costs roughly $50 billion annually.[128]

The extent to which cybercrime is a problem is not completely clear. There is some evidence that people and businesses do not report being victims of cybercrime to the police.[129] In 2008, the Bureau of Justice Statistics reported that only 15% of the 7,818 businesses that responded to the National Computer Security Survey reported incidents of cybercrime to the police.[130] Some businesses did not report because they believed that there was nothing to be gained by reporting it to the police, they did not think to report it, or they did not know whom to contact. Further, some businesses did not report their victimization to the police because they believed that it was outside the jurisdiction of the local police.[131]

Many police agencies would have a hard time responding to calls for service that involve cybercrimes because they do not have the resources, or, in some cases, they may not have the right equipment or trained personnel to respond to such calls.[132] Collaborations between police agencies and institutions of higher education is one way that the police can have access to training, expertise, and, in some cases, the much-needed equipment to better manage cybercrime.[133] In 1998, the National Institute of Justice funded a study to identify the needs of state and local law enforcement agencies to help them combat cybercrime. This study produced a list of 10 needs most commonly mentioned by police agencies, including (1) a public awareness campaign to educate the public about cybercrime; (2) comprehensive data that help to establish the extent and impact of cybercrime; (3) officer certification and training courses; (4) assistance in developing computer investigation units; (5) updated laws and regulations that are on pace with current types of cybercrimes; (6) cooperation and assistance from the high-tech industry, as the police are not experts in this area; (7) publications and resources focused on cybercrimes; (8) awareness and support from senior police executives and local political figures; (9) access to investigative and forensic tools and equipment that can be used by police agencies to fight cybercrime, and (10) structuring and implementing a computer crime unit to help police agencies respond to incidents of cybercrime in their communities.[134]

After listing all of the resources that are not available to the police for them to adequately deal with cybercrime, it is no surprise that many agencies do not view cybercrime as a major priority.[135] In fact, some police agencies believe that cybercrime should be enforced at the federal level of law enforcement. Ronald Burns and his colleagues conducted a national study focused on cybercrime and the police and learned that 93% of the police agencies they surveyed felt that cybercrime should be handled by federal-level police agencies.[136] It has been predicted by some that cybercrime will become a much larger problem in the future, as more people are using and have access to the Internet.[137] It is for this reason that resources and training must become more readily available to police agencies to help them adequately control cybercrime.

Some agencies are beginning to utilize technology that some would argue is an invasion of personal privacy. For example, the Michigan police have been using data-extraction devices (DEDs) since 2006. These devices have the ability to connect to citizens' cell phones to retrieve phone numbers, text messages, call history, photos, and video.[138] Other jurisdictions use passive alcohol sensors as part of their DUI enforcement efforts.[139] Passive alcohol sensors come in many forms, but a common form is a device that is attached to a flashlight. Flashlights with this technology attached can be used to test the air in vehicles during traffic stops and at DUI sobriety checkpoints to check for the presence of alcohol.[140] License plate recognition computers can read several thousand license plates in an hour in all types of weather conditions and at night.[141] These cameras are attached to patrol cars and have the ability to run license plates through databases to check for stolen vehicles or individuals with warrants for their arrest. The obvious complaint about this type of technology is that there could be serious violations to citizen privacy.

GPS (global positioning system) is also becoming a popular tool in law enforcement. Police officers can use GPS devices to track vulnerable populations if they wander away from their guardian or home (including elderly persons with dementia or children with special needs).[142] This technology is also used to track and monitor the whereabouts of patrol cars and patrol officers. The ability to track patrol cars and officers using GPS enhances officer safety.[143] GPS can help police officers locate individuals who have committed crimes.[144] **GPS tracking darts** allow police officers to shoot a small, sticky dart containing a GPS tracker from the grille of their patrol car onto a suspect's vehicle.[145] And finally, GPS can help criminal investigators build their cases when conducting investigations that will likely end up in court later on (such as tracking cell phone use to determine the locations of suspects at certain points in time).

X-ray technology has now been installed in police vehicles (specifically unmarked vans). Police vans containing x-ray equipment similar to that used in airports are already being used in some jurisdictions. This technology allows the police to see inside of vehicles, houses, and other structures.[146] Some agencies use this equipment to scan cars, campers, semi trucks, and other types of transportation for illegal drugs, guns, and human tracking.[147] This type of technology faces the same criticisms as the x-ray machines that are used in airport screening.

The previous examples of new technology represent only a small sample of the innovative tools being created for police officers and law enforcement agencies. There are clear advantages for police officers when they are able to use this type of technology; however, there are many legal and ethical issues to consider as well. It is likely that as technology continues to advance in the future, additional problems will also arise with the adoption of these tools.

Predicting what policing might look like in 2020, 2050, or even 2100 is challenging because several economic, political, and social factors are out of the control of police executives. This does not mean that police scholars and practitioners should not try to forecast what the future might entail for this profession; it simply means that there are many things to consider. Despite the potential difficulties, one thing is certain: policing in the United States will continue to be an important, challenging, and rewarding career well into the future.

SUMMARY

- Police agencies have had to make alterations to their organizational structure and operations to adapt to recent budget cuts.
- The hiring of civilians and use of volunteers is becoming more common in police agencies today as a "force multiplier" and as a way to cut costs.
- Due to the increasing elderly population in the United States, the police will likely respond to more cases of elder abuse and seniors involved in criminal activity.
- Changes in immigration laws and the terrorist attacks on 9/11 have placed local and state police agencies in a unique position in which they are being asked to enforce immigration laws. This has traditionally been the responsibility of the federal government.
- The adoption of new technology in the future will bring with it both advantages for police officers as well as many ethical and legal issues for police executives to manage.

KEY TERMS

Alabama HB 56
Arizona SB 1070
civilianization
consolidation

elder abuse
GPS tracking darts
Gray Squad
homeland security era

ICE 287 (g) program
PWMI
Volunteers in Police Service

DISCUSSION QUESTIONS

1. Explain Willard Oliver's new era of policing and how it is similar to and different from the current era of policing.

2. Why are the police encountering more people with mental illness today than in the past?

3. Explain the connection between the mentally ill and homeless populations.

4. Using the Internet, find one example of new police technology that was not mentioned in this book. Discuss the advantages and disadvantages of using the device.

5. Identify some of the potential problems that local and state law enforcement might face if they choose to enforce immigration laws in their communities.

WEB RESOURCES

- To learn more about how the police help the elderly with Alzheimer's, go to http://www.theiacp.org/LinkClick .aspx?fileticket=T0ZLYjhpVas%3d&tabid=392.
- To learn more about police and immigration, go to http://www.policeforum.org/library/immigration/ PERFImmigrationReportMarch2011.pdf.
- To learn more about the future of police technology, go to http://blog.discoverpolicing.org/uncategorized/ policing-jetson-style/.

Mary Romero looks at the enforcement of immigration laws in Arizona by local police agents. More specifically, this study critically analyzes a 5-day immigration raid that took place in 1997—this is often referred to as the "Chandler Roundup." This study is important because it identifies some of the potential negative consequences associated with this type of police behavior.

Racial Profiling and Immigration Law Enforcement: Rounding Up of Usual Suspects in the Latino Community

Mary Romero

"Where are you from?"

I didn't answer. I wasn't sure who the agent, a woman, was addressing.

She repeated the question in Spanish, "*¿De dónde eres?*"

Without thinking, I almost answered her question—in Spanish. A reflex. I caught myself in midsentence and stuttered in a nonlanguage.

"*¿Dónde naciste?*" she asked again . . .

She was browner than I was. I might have asked her the same question . . . "Are you sure you were born in Las Cruces?" she asked again.

I turned around and smiled, "Yes, I'm sure." She didn't smile back. She and her driver sat there for a while and watched me as I continued walking . . .

"Sons of bitches," I whispered, "pretty soon I'll have to carry a passport in my own neighborhood." . . . It was like a video I played over and over—memorizing the images . . .

Are you sure you were born in Las Cruces? ringing in my cars. (Sáenz 1992: xii)

The personal and community cost of racial profiling to Mexican Americans who are treated as outside the law does not appear in official criminal justice statistics. Benjamin Alire Sáenz captures the racial-affront experience when Immigration and Naturalization Service (INS) agents use racial profiling. He emphasized the irony when Mexican-American INS agents interrogate other Mexican Americans about their citizenship. Citizenship appears embodied in skin color (that is, brown skin absent a police or border patrol uniform) serving as an indicator of illegal status. Carrying a bodily "figurative border" (Chang 1999), "Mexicanness" becomes the basis for suspecting criminality under immigration law. Mexican Americans and other racialized Latino citizens[1] and legal residents are subjected to insults, questions, unnecessary stops, and searches. Surveillance of citizenship,

---

[1] Unlike the census categories, which make a distinction between race and ethnicity for the category "Hispanic," and restricting race to black and white, law enforcement clearly uses the ethnic descriptors of Mexican and Hispanic to identify an individual's physical characteristics. Therefore, this study makes a distinction between Latinos who can racially pass as white and those who are socially constructed (but nevertheless have real consequences) as racially distinct from whites or blacks (Romero 2001).

relentless in low-income and racialized neighborhoods along the border and in urban barrios, increases the likelihood of discrimination in employment, housing, and education. Latinos (particularly dark complected, poor, and working class) are at risk before the law. The following article uses a case study approach to identify the use of racial profiling in immigration law enforcement and to document the impact on US citizens and legal residents.

 # Domestic Function of Immigration Policy

Conquest of the Southwest subliminally grafted Mexicans to "the American psyche as a 'foreigner,' even though the land had once belonged to Mexico" (Romero 2001:1091). Following the Mexican-American War, special law-enforcement agencies were established to patrol the newly formed border and to police Mexicans who remained in occupied territory, as well as later migrants across the border. The most distinct form of social control and domination used by the US in this occupation was the creation of the Texas and Arizona Rangers. Maintaining the interests of cattle barons in Texas, the Texas Rangers treated Mexicans living along the border as cattle thieves and bandits when they attempted to reclaim stolen property from cattle barons. Similarly, the Arizona Rangers protected capitalist interests by protecting strikebreakers against Mexican miners. Following a parallel pattern, the INS rarely raided the fields during harvest time and scheduled massive immigration roundups during periods of economic recession and union activity (Acuña 2000). Remembering the policing functions of the Texas and Arizona Rangers and the Border Patrol (including the current militarization at the border) is crucial in recognizing the social functions accomplished by racialized immigrant raids, sweeps, and citizenship inspections (Acuña 2000; Andreas 2000; Dunn 1996; Nevins 2002). Under Operation Wetback, for example, only persons of Mexican descent were included in the campaign and thus were the only group to hear the burden of proving citizenship (Garcia 1980). Militarized sweeps of

Mexicans maintained the community in "a state of permanent insecurity" in the 1950s; in response a petition was submitted to the United Nations charging the USA with violating the Universal Declaration of Human Rights (Acuña 2000:306).

A number of recent studies unveil the hypocrisy of US border policies that manage to allow enough undocumented immigrant labor in to meet employers' demands while at the same time increasing INS and Border Patrol budgets (Andreas 2000; Massey et al. 2002; Nevins 2002). Longitudinal studies comparing INS efficiency and increased budget prior to the 1986 Immigration Reform and Control Act (IRCA) to late-1990s immigration law reforms suggest that the cost of detaining unauthorized border crossers has increased (Massey et al. 2002). Immigration researchers (Chavez 2001; Massey et al. 2002) claim that we are paying for the illusion of controlled borders while politicians make a political spectacle, pandering to alarmist public discourse about a Mexican immigrant invasion, the breakdown of the US-Mexico border, and increased crime resulting from immigration (Chavez 2001). Operation Blockade and Operation Gatekeeper failed to deter extralegal immigration from Mexico. US employers continue to have access to a vulnerable, cheap labor force created by assigning workers an "illegal" status. The worst costs of these failed policies are the increasing loss of human lives as migrants are forced to cross the border in the most desolate areas of the desert (Cornelius 2001; Eschbach et al. 1999).

In what follows, I demonstrate that more than "illusion" or "political capital" is gained. Meeting employers' demand for cheap labor while appearing to deter immigration includes a cost borne by Mexican Americans and other racialized Latinos. Immigration research tends to ignore the political, social, and economic costs paid by Mexican Americans and other Latinos who are implicated by immigration policies. Racialized citizens and legal residents become subjects of immigration stops and searches, and pay the cost of increased racism—sometimes in the form of hate crimes or the decrease of government funding and services to their communities (Chang and Aoki 1997; Johnson 1993; Mehan 1997). Both Operation Blockade and Operation Gatekeeper provided impetus to anti-immigration policies that not only decreased public funding assisting low-income Latino communities in general (regardless of citizenship status) but also fueled racism and anti-affirmative action policies (Chavez 2001; Lee et al. 2001). This article explores the ways that immigration raids function as a policing practice to maintain and reinforce subordinated status among working-class US citizens and legal residents of Mexican ancestry.

Critical Race Theory and Immigration Law Enforcement

Using a critical race theory framework, I examine racial- and class-based micro- and macro-aggressions that result from the use of racial profiling in immigration law enforcement. Citizens sharing racial and cultural similarities with "aliens" targeted by immigration law enforcement agents have been, and continue to be, treated as "foreigners" and denied equal protection under the law. Racialized immigration law enforcement not only places darker Mexican Americans at risk, but threatens members of the community who are bilingual speakers, have friends or family members who are immigrants, or who engage in certain cultural practices. Critical race theory "challenges ahistoricism and insists on a contextual/historical analysis of the law" (Matsuda et al. 1993:6). It aims to illuminate structures that create and perpetuate domination and subordination in their "everyday operation" (Valdez et al. 2002:3). Applying a critical race theory perspective to immigration, legal scholar Kevin Johnson (2002:187) argues that, "exclusions found in the immigration laws effectuate and reinforce racial subordination in the United States." A history of immigration laws based on racial exclusions reinforces stereotypes that Mexicans and other third-world immigrants are inferior and "alien" (Hing 1997;

Johnson 1997). Conceptualizing racial profiling practices in immigration law enforcement as micro- and macro-aggressions a petit apartheid—helps recognize the discriminatory functions that policing and inspections have on citizenship participation and the rights of Mexican Americans, Mexican immigrants, and other racialized Latinos, particularly the poor and working class.

Building on the work of psychologist Chester Pierce, critical race theorists have found the concept of micro-aggressions useful in describing the form of policing common in communities of color: "subtle, stunning, often automatic, and non-verbal exchanges which are 'put downs' of blacks by offenders" (Pierce et al. 1978:66).[2] In her research on race and crime, Katheryn Russell distinguished between racial assaults on a personal level or micro-aggressions, and "face group affronts" or macro-aggressions. The latter type of affront is "not directed toward a particular Black person, but at Blackness in general" and may be made "by a private individual or official authority" (Russell 1998:139). Macro-aggressions reinforce stereotypes of racialized groups as "either criminals, illiterates, or intellectual inferiors" (Russell 1998:140).[3] Dragan Milovanovic and Katheryn K. Russell (2001: vii) argued that both micro- and macro-aggressions work as "a cycle which sustains hierarchy and harms of reductions and repression." "Harms of reduction occur when offended parties experience a loss in their standing ... or restriction, preventing them from achieving a desired position or standing" (Henry and Milovanovic 1999:7–8). Harms of reduction and repression are detrimental because "they belittle, demean, ridicule or subordinate on the one hand, and on the other, they limit access to equal opportunities and fair dealings before the law" (Milovanovic and Russell 2001:xvi).

Daniel Georges-Abeyie's (2001:x) theoretical paradigm of grand and petit apartheid links current practices of racial profiling with other "negative social factors and discretional decision-making by both

---

[2]An example is assuming that a Mexican American cannot speak English or that she is the secretary, rather than a faculty member in the department.

[3]Richard J. Hermstein and Charles Murray's (1994) claims of Blacks' mental inferiority espoused in their book, *The Bell Curve*, is a prime example of a macro-aggression that has received extensive news coverage.

criminal justice agents and criminal justice agencies." Georges-Abeyie's theoretical work outlines a continuum of petit apartheid discriminatory practices ranging from the covert and informal to the overt and formal. Petit apartheid has been used to explain racial profiling in the war against drugs (Campbell 2001; Covington 2001), regulating and policing public space (Bass 2001; Ferrell 2001b), under-representation of persons of color interested in law enforcement (Ross 2001), and the use of racial derogation in prosecutors' closing arguments (Johnson 2001).

Petit apartheid relates to concerns about struggles over access to urban public space, freedom of movement, the processes of capital investment, political decision-making, and policing first theorized by Henri Lefebvre (1996 [1968]) and others (see Caldeira 2000; Ferrell 2001a; Harvey 1973, 1996; Holston 1999; Mitchell 2003). Images and perceptions of public space are used to encourage, discourage, or prohibit use and movement. Exclusionary models of public life are most noted for privileging middle-class consumers. Surveillance, stops, and searches maintain a landscape of suspicion and reinforce white, middle-class citizens' suspicions of racial minorities and protect their access to public space. When citizenship is racially embodied through law-enforcement practices that target Mexican-American neighborhoods and business areas, then Henri Lefebvre's (1996 [1968]:174) statement about urban space is actualized: "The right of the city manifests itself as a superior form of rights; right to freedom, to individualization in socialization, to habitat and to inhabit."

Immigration law enforcement assists such exclusionary use of urban public spaces and limits freedom of movement. However, the INS is in the position of having to negotiate an adequate flow of undocumented labor to meet urban capitalist needs while maintaining the appearance of controlling immigration. Consequently, immigration law enforcement in US cities is not structured around systematic or random checking of identification but rather a pattern of citizenship inspection that maintains the landscape of suspicion. Given the class and racial segregation perpetuated by exclusive residential zoning, the INS targets ethnic cultural spaces marked by Mexican-owned businesses, agencies offering bilingual services, and neighborhoods with the highest concentration of poor and working-class Latinos. Within these areas, INS agents engage in "typing" suspected aliens (Heyman 1995; Weissinger 1996) that embodies a "figurative border" (Chang 1999). In the process of typing Mexicans as suspects, Americans are "whitened."

The 1975 Supreme Court decision that "Mexican appearance" "constitutes a legitimate consideration under the Fourth Amendment for making an immigration stop" (Johnson 2000:676) legalized micro- and macro-aggressions inflicted upon Mexican Americans. Micro- and macro-aggressions, as well as petit apartheid, are experienced by Mexican Americans when they are caught within a racially profiled dragnet in which INS agents operate with unchecked discretion. Harms of reductions and repression occur when Latinos are subjected to racially motivated (and frequently class-based) stops and searches and race-related INS abuse (Arriola 1996 97; Benitez 1994; Lazos 2002; Vargas 2001). Micro-aggressions are racial affronts on a personal level, experienced when an individual Mexican American is stopped and asked to prove citizenship status; macro-aggressions are group affronts because they are directed towards "Mexicanness" in general. Macro-aggressions target dark complexions and physical characteristics characterized as "Mexican" or "Latino;" speaking Spanish, listening to Spanish music, shopping at Mexican-owned businesses or any other cultural practices that can bring on racially motivated stops.

The Case of the Chandler Roundup

INS data provide statistics on the number of individuals apprehended, but the agency does not collect data on the number of individuals stopped and searched who were citizens or legal residents. Consequently, the impact of racialized immigration law enforcement on communities of color is rarely visible in legal reporting procedures. However, every once in awhile, community protests against raids gain sufficient media attention to require public officials to respond by conducting investigations into allegations of law-enforcement wrongdoings. In these rare instances it becomes possible to uncover "more covert, hidden forms of discrimination" (Georges-Abeyie 2001:xiv) in the documentation by law-enforcement and public officials responding to allegations of civil-rights or human-rights violations. Formal investigations reveal the groups and communities targeted and the ways that public and private space is regulated under the auspices of immigration law enforcement. These institutional practices are "relations of ruling" and unravel the everyday management of social control and domination (Smith 1990, 1999).

In order to identify micro- and macro- aggressions and petit apartheid accomplished by immigration raids, I analyzed data from two official investigations into a five-day immigration raid in Chandler, Arizona. The raid was the third of its kind conducted by the Chandler Police during the summer of 1997 (Fletcher 1997). The immigration sweep came to be known as the "Chandler Roundup," reinforcing both the cowboy legacy of law enforcement in Mexican-American communities and the notion that Mexicans are "strays." On July 27, 1997, the Chandler Police Department and Border Patrol agents from Casa Grande Station and the Tucson area began a five-day immigration raid as a joint operation in the most highly populated Latino section of the city. Over the five days, 432 suspected undocumented Mexicans were arrested. The Chief Patrol Agent's *Summary Report of the Border Patrol Operations in Chandler, AZ* cited in the Arizona Attorney General's report (Office of the Attorney General Grant Wood 1997:15–17) outlined the daily activities as follows:

Day 1—July 27, 1997: "Within three hours ... more than 75 arrests out of approximately 100 contacts" were made through "casual contacts ... along the streets in and around public areas." A total of 83 arrests were made that day (82 Mexicans and 1 Guatemalan).

Day 2—July 28, 1997: The target area was "expanded to one square mile of the downtown Chandler area" and "nearly all contacts occurred outside dwellings" and "the exceptions were the result of specific information or probable cause." On this day, they arrested 102 Mexicans.

Day 3—July 29, 1997: Working with Chandler Police between 4:00 AM and 8:00 AM, they arrested 69 (ethnicity not noted). Bicycle patrols working public areas and trailer parks arrested an additional 49.

Day 4—July 30, 1997: A total of 77 illegal aliens were arrested.

Day 5—July 31, 1997: 52 arrests were made.

Immigrant advocates and Mexican-American residents in Chandler began organizing and held several community meetings with the police chief, Chandler City Council members, and the State Attorney General's staff. As a consequence of the public outcry, the investigations and lawsuits that followed produced government documentation of law-enforcement practices that detail the use of micro- and macro-aggressions towards Mexican Americans and other Latinos racially profiled as criminal, unauthorized, or extralegal. The primary focus of the investigations was police misconduct and violation of civil rights. A secondary issue concerned the role of local police departments participating in joint operations with the INS.

The State Attorney General's office immediately responded to complaints and began collecting eyewitness accounts from individuals willing to be interviewed. The Office of the Attorney General Grant Woods issued a report, *Results of the Chandler Survey,* in December 1997. Data collected and analyzed in the report included: minutes of meetings with the Latino community in Chandler, interviews with citizens and legal residents stopped during the five-day operation, minutes of City Council Meetings with community members, newspaper articles, memoranda between city officials, review of Chandler Police radio dispatch audio tapes, police field notes, and witness testimonies. The Attorney General's report is organized into the following sections: background information,[4] summary of the survey,[5] summary of the commission on Civil Rights Report, and an evaluation of claims of civil-rights violation and recommendations.

The following summer, the City of Chandler paid for an independent investigation (Breen et al. 1998). The final product was the three-volume report. Volume 1, *Report of Independent Investigation Into July 1997 Joint Operation Between Border Patrol and Chandler Police Department,* includes a mission statement, narrative[6] and summaries of interviews conducted with public officials.[7] Volume II, *Complainants,* is the independent investigators' direct response to the descriptive accounts of civil-rights violations documented in the Office of the Attorney General's *Survey.* Incidents reported in Volume II include only complaints formally filed with the Chandler Police, the Office of the Attorney General, or the Mexican Consultant's office. Volume III, *Appendices to Report of Independent Investigation,* includes four maps (the Tucson sector of the Border Patrol, Chandler and Vicinity, Area of Operation Restoration, and areas covered in the joint operation), excerpts from policy and procedure handbooks,[8] a survey of policies regarding illegal aliens in 14 cities in border states, a survey of how media learned of the 1997 joint operation, the Chandler Police Department's Community-Oriented Policing Programs, and 89 records of Border Patrol Forms I-213 (Deportable Alien) produced during the Joint Operation.

The summary section of each report differs in the perspective taken. In the State Attorney General's report, *Results of the Chandler Survey,* the construction of immigration as a problem in Chandler is presented from the community's perspective and supported by official documents, whereas the *Report of Independent Investigation Into July 1997 Joint Operation Between Border Patrol and Chandler Police Department* privileges the INS and police's documentation of a growing immigration problem and presents the "roundup" as the official response. Witness accounts cited in the *Survey* were collected immediately following the five-day immigration sweep. Each of the civil-rights violations from witness accounts noted in the Attorney General's report was investigated a year later by the independent investigators; however, only those violations corroborated by police officers' interviews, field notes, or arrest records were deemed legitimate in the *Report of Independent Investigation.* Defining validity with criteria that privileged police interviews and records (as well as INS official documentation) assured that the independent investigators' report minimized the violation of civil rights and was more favorable to the Chandler Police Department than was the Attorney General's report.

This study is an analysis of the official reports. While these data were obtained from legal documents constructed within a specific political, social, and economic context, the variety of documents produced presents diverse perspectives, including interested community members, citizens and legal residents stopped and searched, police officers participating in the raid, and City Council members. Clearly, the data

---

[4]Background information is based on media coverage from local newspapers, community meetings, and the minutes from Chandler City Council Meeting.

[5]The summary of the survey includes a detailed description of the Chandler Redevelopment Initiative developed by the City Council. The survey describes the Initiative's efforts and its connection on the joint operation carried out in areas with the highest concentration of Latino residents; INS protocols for joint operation; description of day-to-day activities based on Border Patrol documents; summary of witness accounts regarding children and schools, home contacts, and contacts around businesses, because these were areas that the police and public officials claimed were not included in the raid; and descriptions of the types of request made for proof of citizenship.

[6]The narrative offers a history of the City of Chandler and describes the development of immigration issues as a social problem that led to the joint operation. A description of the operation and the aftermath of community meetings, complaints, and lawsuits is also included.

[7]Interviews were conducted with the police who participated in the joint operation, supervisors and officers involved with processing illegal aliens, Border Patrol agents, City Council members, and Chandler city officials.

[8]Excerpts describe the duties of city officials and the Chandler Police Department, a summary of line of authority in the city, and a description of the structure and duties of the US Border Patrol.

analyzed do not include a complete profile of all the stops that were made during the five-day operation. However, the two reports provide a rare insight into strategically planned immigration law enforcement targeting low-income areas highly populated by Mexican Americans.

Complainants (Volume II of the *Report of Independent Investigation*) contained the following data: a profile of the type of individuals stopped and searched, activities by these individuals that warranted "reasonable suspicion," the type of documents these individuals are expected to carry, and the outcomes of stops. A few of the complaints include a brief summary of the incident in question. Not all complaints recorded by the government officials are complete, but as documentary practices of agencies of control, the data reveal everyday processes of ruling apparatus in low-income Latino communities (Smith 1990, 1999). Although only 71 individuals made formal complaints, 91 complaints were filed because each incident was documented as a separate complaint—a number of individuals were stopped more than once. I coded each of the 91 complaints, looking for patterns of immigration enforcement, including ethnicity of complainant, age, citizenship status, sex, activity engaged in at the time of the stop, request for identification, and outcomes of the stop.

Narratives are also an important source of data for identifying micro- and macro-aggressions and petit apartheid restricting citizenship rights, freedom of movement, and use of public and private urban space. Two types of narratives were coded. First, the narrative of the report itself. This included setting up the story of the Chandler Roundup (what is the context selected as background information to the raid?), an explanation of Mexican immigration requiring a joint operation between Chandler Police Department and the INS (how is the problem defined?), and, the justification for using racial profiling (why were low-income Mexican Americans stopped and searched?). The second type of narrative appears in the Attorney General's Report. These are summaries of witness accounts and detailed descriptions of incidents documented by the police in their radio-dispatch reports. Witness accounts were coded for verbal and non-verbal racial affronts against individuals and against "Mexicanness" in general. Radio-dispatch reports were coded for incidents of racial profiling and regulation of movement and activity. In order to explore micro- and macro-aggressions and the existence of processes and structures of petit apartheid in immigration raids, witness accounts and police records were coded for discriminatory practices ranging from the covert and informal to the overt and formal.

My analysis focuses first on identifying the distinct differences in each report for explaining the occurrence of a Joint Operation between the Chandler Police and the INS. I begin with the *Report of Independent Investigation's* narration of Mexican immigration as a problem requiring the immediate attention of the Chandler Police. Next, I contrast this with the community's depiction of Mexican immigration as a problem constructed by the Chandler City Council's urban-renewal project, Operation Restoration. I then turn to a quantitative analysis of data from the complaints complied in Volume II of the *Report of Independent Investigation*. A qualitative analysis of witness accounts from the Attorney General's Report follows. Here, I analyze the ways that citizenship is policed and the impact this form of policing has on freedom of movement and use of urban space.

Narrating Mexican Immigration as a Problem

Considering that the USA acquired Arizona as a result of the Mexican-American War, and that the Chandler area is the homeland of the Tohono O'Odham Nation, the version of history narrated in the *Report of Independent Investigation's* (Breen et al. 1998:1) is clearly biased and self-serving: "Chandler, Arizona is a city of about 160,000 that has blossomed in slightly more than a century from a seed planted by Alexander Chandler, who came to Arizona in 1887 as territorial veterinary surgeon." The first mention of Mexicans in the narrative describes their presence as workers and Anglos as employers:

> In the first years after the town's founding, cotton became the crop of choice for central Arizona farmers. These were the years of the Mexican Revolution, and thousands of Mexicans streamed northward to escape the violence spawned by it. Labor-intensive cotton farming provided a way for those fleeing the revolution to earn a living. Thus began a marriage between Chandler and those of Hispanic heritage that has lasted till the present day. (Breen et al. 1998:1)

This seeming "marriage" involved Mexicans providing the labor and Americans (read whites) providing the land from which the cotton was to be harvested. Mexican presence is also noted during WWII in reference to the Bracero Program: "the Arizona Farm Bureau approved the importation of Mexican workers, who found themselves harvesting cotton alongside German prisoners of war in the labor-starved market" (Breen et al. 1998:2).

The narrative continues by describing the "streams" that turn into the present "hordes" of Mexican immigrants entering the area. "Ron Sanders, chief patrol agent for the Border Patrol's Tucson sector, calls Chandler 'the most notorious hub for alien smuggling in the United States of America'" . . . until "literally thousands" of illegal aliens were in Chandler (Breen et al. 1998:2). INS intelligence in Dallas is the source for citing Chandler "as a major smuggling area as far south as Honduras and El Salvador" (Breen et al. 1998:2). The narrative continues with a litany from a handful of growers who complained about garbage, use of water, stolen fruit, and violence. To reinforce immigration as a social problem, the report lists six "homicides allegedly committed by illegal aliens" dating back to 1982 (Breen et al. 1998:10). In 1997, the Casa Grande Border Patrol station began targeting operations in groves. According to the Chandler Police, complaints about harassment of

citizens and an increase in crime led to a series of joint actions in the summer of 1997. No doubt the federal government's Operations Gatekeeper, Hold-the-Line, and other steps in militarizing the USA-Mexico border, gave local authorities in Chandler tacit approval to engage in the Joint Operation.

However, the Attorney General's *Survey* argues that another chain of events led up to the Joint Operation. Based on community protests voiced at meetings and interviews given to the media, the beginning of the "immigration problem" is not dated to the founding of the city but rather to the City of Chandler's 1995 urban-renewal project, Operation Restoration. City Council members began Operation Restoration by creating a task force to study issues affecting residents. The Neighborhood Empowerment Team conducted several mail-in surveys and held neighborhood meetings. Their final report found that residents were concerned about broken streetlights, uncollected garbage, trash in the streets, and unkempt alleys. From its inception, Operation Restoration targeted four older neighborhoods in the city located next to the newly developed downtown area. The targeted areas had the highest percentage of Latinos and low-income residents in the City. Claiming the Joint Operation was about redevelopment, City Council member Martin Sepulveda argued that the Mayor's dream of transforming Chandler into "'The jewel of the East Valley' would push out poor Hispanics" (Office of the Attorney General 1997:5). Operation Restoration was perceived by the Mexican-American community as urban renewal to create high-income real estate and zoning for strip malls, which would dislocate residents and raise land value beyond the reaches of local businesses.

In response to the community's accusation that the immigration sweep was a Mexican-American removal program, the *Report* stated that the Chandler Police involvement was merely "to undertake intensive zoning code enforcement and . . . step up patrol of the area" (Breen et al. 1998:14). Although the independent investigators acknowledged that the Neighborhood Empowerment Team's report was limited to repairing and cleaning the surrounding area, they accepted the police department's claim that the Joint Operation with the INS was conducted as their part in implementing Operation Restoration. Since Operation Restoration had already targeted "the downtown redevelopment zone, ranging from an eight-block to a four square mile area," using similar parameters for the roundup was justified and did not discriminate against Latinos.

The Attorney General's Office refuted this claim and argued that the Task Force's final report did not include reference to or recommendations about undocumented immigrants. Importantly, the Office of the Attorney General (1997:14) found that the area targeted for the raid was "without specific articulated criminal activity." Drawing from community meetings, the Attorney General's *Survey* includes the community standpoint primarily from Latinos. They perceived the redevelopment of the downtown area as the major incentive behind the raid. Operation Restoration became a defining moment in their memory of Chandler's history when "Mexicanness" was perceived as undesirable, even as cheap labor.

The careful selection of terms used in the documents evokes associations, meanings, and images supporting political spectacle (Edelman 2001). In order to establish undocumented Mexican immigration as an increasingly dangerous problem, the independent investigators erased Mexican Americans (and the Tohono O'Odham people) from local history. Restricting Mexican presence to discussions of "immigrants," "laborers," and "criminals" made American citizens of Mexican ancestry invisible. The terms "streams" and "hordes" found in the *Independent Investigation Report* in reference to the movement of people crossing the USA-Mexico border is consistent with the alarmist terminology noted by a number of immigration scholars (Chavez 2001; Santa Ana 2002). Mexican Americans are not mentioned in the *Report* as citizens or as long-term residents in the area but rather in the non-human category of "alien" (Johnson 1997). In the *Report,* Mexican Americans are always referred to in the present tense and only as "Hispanic." *Mexican* is always used as a term for the unauthorized, extralegal, or undocumented.

 ## Policing Citizenship, Movement and the Use of Urban Space

The policing of citizenship by the Chandler Roundup exemplifies procedures used to determine status and urban spaces that require regulation. The focus on policing was the redevelopment area targeted under Operation Restoration; that is, the cultural space inhabited by the large Latino population, low-income residents, and a commercial area serving a Spanish-speaking clientele. However, the image of citizenship visible in the discretionary stops suggests that beyond geography, the landscape of suspicion was embodied in particular behavior and appearance. Complaints made against the Chandler Police make visible the type of persons suspected as unauthorized and thus requiring surveillance. Requests for various types of identification reveal surveillance and restraint of movement in public areas. Embedded in witness accounts are the aesthetics of authority that enforce exclusionary use of public urban space, remaking the Mexican cultural space into white space. The material consequences of policing reinforce the vulnerability of undocumented workers in the local economy; place low-income, racialized citizens at risk before the law; and legitimate discriminatory behavior towards persons under surveillance.

 ## Complainants Analysis

Analysis of the data in the 91 complaints indicates specific patterns of racial and ethnic typing used in the Joint Operation. Data show that cultural and class behavior or activity was only monitored in targeted locations. The dominant feature of identifiable complainants was their racial ethnic background; all were of Mexican ancestry or Latino.[9] Fourteen of the complainants were stopped more than once during the five-day raid. Complainants ranged in age from 16 to 75; 49 were

---

[9]Citizenship status is not recorded for 29 complainants (involved in 41 stops).

male and 22 were female. The majority of males were between 18 and 39 years old and the majority of females were between the ages of 30 and 49. Complaints for 42 complainants contained the following information: 11 were US citizens of Mexican ancestry, 15 were Latino legal residents, 1 was a permanent resident, 3 had work permits, 1 had a green card, and 11 were undocumented. There is no documentation in the reports or in the newspaper coverage of a white person stopped during the raid. Ironically, one newspaper quoted a blond, blue-eyed, undocumented Irish immigrant employed at a local law firm as stating that she had never been asked to show proof of her citizenship status: "I don't have to worry. I blend in very well" (Amparano 1997:A1).

The phrase "driving while black" became familiar in debates over racial profiling, similarly the experience of "walking/driving/biking/standing while brown" is common for Mexican Americans in the vicinity of an immigration raid or during national sweeps, such as Operation Wetback in 1954 (Calavita 1992) or Operation Jobs in 1995 (US Attorney General Report 1995). The activities recorded in the complaints are accurately captured in the media's initial reporting of Mexican Americans' experience during the five-day immigration raid: "As they walked down sidewalks, drove cars or walked outside their homes" they were stopped by the police (Amparano 1997). Based primarily on interviews with police officers assigned to the target area during the operation (few Border Patrol agents agreed to be interviewed), the independent investigators found that illegal aliens were arrested in residential areas, in front of stores (especially the local Circle K), in trailer courts, and driving between 4:00 and 6:00 AM (the time many workers are traveling to construction sites during the summer).

The wide net that was cast made it inevitable that citizens and legal residents would be stopped by the police. The complaints indicate that, when proof of citizenship status was requested by law-enforcement agents, 33 of the 91 were driving, 24 were walking in their neighborhood or to a nearby store, 17 were at home, 10 were shopping (most were approached in the parking lot or in front of stores), 3 were riding bikes, and 2 were using public telephones. Significantly, only 2 were approached at their place of employment, suggesting the tacit desire to protect employers from possible sanctions. Specific activities are significant when class-based racial profiling is occurring. As in most urban areas, being a pedestrian is a sign of poverty. Middle and upper classes rarely walk or bike in Arizona heat unless they are engaged in exercise and dressed in special "work-out" clothes. They might be observed walking if a leashed dog is attached to their bodies. Using a public telephone is a similar sign of poverty when most homes in the US have several phones as well as cell phones.

After the stops were made, investigators documented only 33 outcomes for the 91 incidents. Of the 33 outcomes documented in the complaints, 23 were detained. Three of the people detained were illegal and 20 were legal. Four of those detained were handcuffed, including one US citizen. The period that the 23 were detained ranged from five minutes to four hours. Some of those detained for long periods of time reported that they stood in the 100+ degree weather common in July. After they showed proof of legal status, three complainants were issued citations for minor traffic violations (e.g., a rolling stop at a stop sign, a broken windshield, a missing headlamp, or a turn into the wrong lane).

Eighty-six claims involved law enforcement agents requesting proof of citizenship status. However, the kinds of documents requested were inconsistent, at times vague, and confusing to US citizens who had never been stopped before—51 incidents involved officers requesting to see the person's "papers" or *papeles,* 2 incidents involved requests for immigration papers, 13 incidents requested driver's license, 9 were asked to show "an identification," 10 were asked specifically for their green cards, and 1 officer requested to see "a card." Birth certificates, Social Security cards, green cards, or drivers licenses were produced by the claimants before the police allowed them to leave. In some cases, particularly for children and adolescents, family members assisted in obtaining documents.

Witness Accounts Analysis

Based on the writings of immigration-critical race legal scholars (i.e., Benitiez 1994; Chang and Aoki 1997; Johnson 2000, 2004; Vargas 2001), I identified five patterns of immigration law enforcement that placed Mexican Americans at risk: (1) discretionary stops based on ethnicity and class; (2) use of intimidation to demean and subordinate persons stopped; (3) restricting the freedom of movement of Mexicans but not others in the same vicinity; (4) reinforced stereotypes of Mexican as "alien," "foreign," inferior and criminal; and (5) limited access to fair and impartial treatment before the law. Recurring expressions that witnesses used to describe stops and searches were pain and humiliation, frightened, fearful, nervous, scared, embarrassed, violated, and mortified. Witness accounts offer descriptive narratives of the micro- and macro-aggressions occurring in immigration law enforcement.

Embedded in all the accounts is the recognition that they were stopped, questioned, and inspected by the police because their physical appearance was classified by law enforcement agents as "Mexican" and, thus, they were assumed to be unauthorized to be in the US. Skin color is used in the everyday immigration law-enforcement practice of operationalizing "reasonable suspicion":

> T was stopped and questioned by Chandler police and INS/Border Patrol when he stopped at a Circle K . . . The Chandler Police were stopping every "Mexican-looking" person as they entered or exited the store. "Non Mexican-looking" people entered and exited without being stopped. (Office of Attorney General Wood 1997:22)

An excerpt from witness account "D" demonstrates community members' recognition of INS and police officers' "discretion," as well as their power to violate civil rights.

> All the people shopping at this shopping center appeared to be Hispanic and many were being stopped and questioned by the officers. D and his uncle were conversing in Spanish and leaving the store with a package when they were approached by a Chandler police officer and an INS/Border Patrol agent on bicycles. The INS/Border Patrol agent asked

them in Spanish for their papers. The uncle, who had just become a United States citizen, had his citizenship papers with him and showed those to the officer. D had only a social security card and a driver's license . . . D took his wallet from his pocket to get his identification; the INS/Border Patrol officer then asked him for the wallet and examined everything in it. D feared that if he did not give the officers his wallet he would be arrested. Neither officer wrote any information down or kept anything from the wallet. No explanation was given for the stop (Office of Attorney General Wood 1997:21).

Although "D" is a US citizen, he understood that he does not have the same rights as whites and has limited access to fair dealings before the law. He was intimidated by the INS officer extending the citizenship inspection beyond his driver's license and Social Security card and into his personal belongings without a search warrant or a basis for probable cause.

"U" provided a description of an incident involving a person who questioned stops without probable cause and police discretion.

> U has a permit to work in the United States and is here legally . . . he and his cousin stopped at a Circle K . . . While they were parking their car, they were approached by a Chandler police officer on a bicycle who asked, in Spanish, for their papers. The cousin said that the police had no right to ask for papers and the Chandler police officer asked if they wanted him to call Immigration. They said yes and INS/Border patrol agents soon appeared. The cousin showed the agents his papers but U did not have his on him and when he showed them his social security card, there was a discrepancy in the computer and they were told the number had been canceled. The INS/Border Patrol agent said "I'm tired of this, everybody lies and says they have papers when they don't." The officers put U in handcuffs, searched him and took him to the

Chandler Police Station where he was detained. He asked them to give him a chance to call his home and have his wife bring his papers but they refused. He was held until about 11:30 (from 7 p.m.) until his cousin and his wife brought his papers to the police station. U was afraid that the Chandler police were going to take his green card away or that he was going to be separated from his family (Office of Attorney General Wood 1997:23).

"U" assumed protection and rights that his work permit grants and distinguished between city police officers and the INS. However, his attempt to assert his rights resulted in the use of excessive force and he was treated like a violent criminal requiring physical restraint. His account points to extensive discretionary power given to immigration law enforcement; the incident exemplifies intimidation, excessive force, and the lack of probable cause in the police stop.

Since the downtown redevelopment zone targeted in the roundup was not completely racially segregated, discretionary stops of persons of Mexican ancestry who appear to be poor or working class became visible. Public areas like stores, phone booths, and gas stations produced a spectacle for white gaze and allowed the immigration inspectors to employ stereotypes of Mexicans as foreign, alien, and criminal. However, appearances of class and citizenship can be deceiving as the following witness testimony reveals.

C is the highest ranked left handed golfer in Arizona. C is a large, dark completed, Hispanic, and native born Arizonan ... Returning from a golf match in July, he stopped ... for a cold drink and saw Chandler police officers talking to different people of apparent Mexican descent. At the time he was wearing an old tee shirt and a baseball cap. As he tried to exit the market, he was barred exit by a Chandler Police officer who asked if he was a local, if he had papers, and whether he was a citizen. C told the officer that he was a citizen and was leaving and the officer told him "No, you are not."

C then walked around the officer and went over to his car which was a 1997 Acura. The officer followed him but when he saw what car he was driving, permitted him to drive off. ... (Office of Attorney General Wood 1997–21)

Clearly "C" assumed "class privilege," challenging the officer's attempt to stop and search without probable cause. This account demonstrates the significance of class in immigration law enforcement. Once middle- and upper-middle-class status is identified by officers, police are less likely to violate civil rights.

In response to the extraordinary policing, community members avoided public areas. Witnesses reported that elderly neighbors feared the police, asking for assistance in obtaining food and medication so they could remain home, behind closed doors. Law enforcement agents' treatment of Mexicans thus deterred civic participation and shaped the field of action that Latinos perceived as available to them (Davis et al. 2001; Nelson 2001). By the fifth day of the operation, the community avoided local grocery stores and gas stations that had been heavily patrolled by the police and INS. Mexican shop owners complained that they lost revenue during the raid because their customers feared shopping in the area. In the absence of people in the streets and shopping areas, the police developed alternative strategies that included homes and construction sites.

Alongside stores with the largest number of Latino customers, the second major target areas were apartment complexes and trailer courts occupied by low-income Mexican Americans and Mexican immigrants. In a newspaper interview with a Chandler police officer, the claim was made that they did not bust "down doors in search of illegal immigrants." Witness accounts provide a counter narrative. Not only were neighborhoods in the targeted area searched house by house but apartment and trailer court managers assisted Chandler Police by identifying residents of Mexican descent. The following testimony describes the intimidation and demeaning actions used by law enforcement agents.

On July 28, 1997, at approximately 11 P.M., B and his family were sound asleep in a trailer owned by his brother-in-law ... The family was awakened by a loud banging on the front door and bright lights shining through the windows. When B looked around, he saw two Chandler police officers, with an INS/Border patrol agent behind them. All officers were bicycle officers. The officers demanded to be allowed into the trailer and when B asked if they had the right to come in, he was told "We can do whatever we want; we are the Chandler Police Department. You have people who are here illegally." Although B denied that there were any undocumented aliens there, the officers insisted on entering the trailer, rousing everyone from bed. The family members were all in their sleep clothes, but the officers refused to allow them to dress. None of the children were United States citizens, and except for the brother-in-law, all the rest were legal aliens; the brother-in-law had entered the country legally but his visa had expired and he was in the process of getting it renewed. When the officers discovered that he [sic] brother-in-law did not have proper papers, they called a Chandler Police Department backup vehicle and took him away in a patrol car. B attempted to give his brother-in-law street clothes when the officers were taking him away, but the officers would not allow this and took him away in his sleep clothes. He was later readmitted to the United States with the renewed visa he had been awaiting. The others were detained in the trailer for approximately ninety minutes; they were not searched but they were questioned even after they showed the papers demonstrating that they were legally in the United States. The police told B that they had spoken with the park manager and he had given them permission to search the trailers, had given them a map, and had marked on the map where Hispanic residents lived. The four children involved in the this [sic] incident are still fearful when someone knocks at the door of the

trailer, and continue to be nervous when they see police officers on the street ... Most of the police visits occurred between 10 p.m. and 11 p.m. and were precipitated by police banging on doors and windows and shining lights through the windows ... Every night someone else was taken away. (Office of Attorney General Wood 1997:19–20)

Home searches conducted in the presence of children serve as powerful socialization, teaching them about their lack of rights, inferior status, and unequal access to protection under the law. For many children, the house searches were probably their first encounter with a police officer, and they witnessed their parents, grandparents, and other family elders humiliated and treated as criminals. Witnessing stops and searches serves as an important lesson for children that the law distinguishes between family and neighbors on the basis of immigration status rather than criminal activity that harms others. Unlike stops made at shopping centers, house-to-house searches conducted on private property concealed civil and human rights violations from public view.

In addition to the house-to-house searches conducted, apartment complexes and trailer courts were also targeted for traffic enforcement. Several officers' interview summaries acknowledged that, outside of special D.U.I. enforcement, the Chandler Roundup was the first time they used traffic enforcement with a sporter. Vehicles leaving specific housing units that appeared to contain "migrant workers" were followed. Several officers reported that they "were to follow them and if probable cause was established" the vehicle was stopped. Officers were "instructed to issue a citation for the probable cause in case there was a question in reference to the stop." A summary of radio-dispatched transcripts for July 29, 1997, demonstrated that laborers driving to work were targeted as vehicles left apartment complexes housing low-income Mexican Americans and Mexican immigrants.

The vehicles were described by make, model and/or color, as well as direction of travel.

A total of forty-three (43) vehicles were specially singled out in a two hour period of time from 4:00 to 6:00 A.M. The officers identified seven (7) vehicles because of known violations of law warranting a stop. However, of the remaining thirty-six (36) vehicles called in, seven (7) calls describing vehicles were made despite the officers stating that there was no probable cause to believe that violations of the law had occurred. The other twenty-nine (29) vehicles were singled out without articulation of what, if any, violation of law may have been observed by the reporting officer. (Office of Attorney General Wood 1997:10)

Both the *Survey* and *Report* note that the Chandler Roundup extended to construction sites and permission from supervisors at the construction site was obtained before entering the areas to question employees. Even though the police arrested undocumented workers at construction sites, neither report cited employers' violation of the law. IRCA includes employer sanctions designating penalties for employers who hire immigrants not authorized to work in the United States. While citizenship and movement of laborers were clearly documented in both reports, there is a glaring absence of enforcement of employers' compliance with IRCA. Although questioning workers at a construction site resulted in 52 arrests, no employer suffered legal sanctions for IRCA violations. Nowhere in the Attorneys General's *Survey,* or in the independent investigator's *Report,* is there a mention of employers at construction sites being investigated.

 Conclusion

While legal scholars, civil rights advocates, and the general public denounced federal law enforcement practices towards Muslims and persons of Middle-Eastern descent under the Patriot Act, racialized immigration stops and searches, abuse, and harassment are ongoing processes honed over a century of citizenship inspections of Mexicans. Immigration policing is based

on determining that citizenship is visibly inscribed on bodies in specific urban spaces rather than "probable cause." In the Chandler Roundup, official investigations found no evidence that stops and searches were based on probable cause of criminal activity. The conclusion drawn by the Attorney General's investigation underscores the harms of micro- and macro-aggressions and the use of petit apartheid:

> . . . there were no other warrants, charges, or holds for these individuals that in any way indicated other criminal activity or that required extraordinary security or physical force. The issue raised by this type of treatment is not whether the arrest and deportation is legal, but whether human beings are entitled to some measure of dignity and safety even when they are suspected of being in the United States illegally. (1997:28–9)

The Chandler Roundup fits into a larger pattern of immigration law-enforcement practices that produce harms of reduction and repression and place Mexican Americans at risk before the law and designate them as second-class citizens with inferior rights. Latino residents in Chandler experienced racial affronts targeted at their "Mexicanness" indicated by skin color, bilingual speaking abilities, or shopping in neighborhoods highly populated by Latinos. During immigration inspections, individuals stopped were demeaned, humiliated, and embarrassed. Stops and searches conducted without cause were intimidating and frightening, particularly when conducted with discretionary use of power and force by law enforcement agents.

Like other metropolitan areas surrounding Phoenix, Chandler depends heavily upon low-wage, non-union, undocumented Mexican workers for their tourism and construction industries. These powerful business interests are influential at the state level, and cooperative efforts are made to assure seasonal labor needs are met. Both official investigations into the Chandler Roundup demonstrate complete disregard for enforcing sanctions of employers under IRCA. Yet the ability to clearly identify the everyday work patterns of immigrants and to use these circumstances to arrest immigrants as undocumented workers indicates that employers operate with complete immunity to IRGA provisions. The case of the Chandler Roundup demonstrates how INS enforcement practices not only favor and protect employers' access to an exploitable labor force, but remove or relocate workers as specific industries' needs warrant. Enforcement is structured specifically at eliminating and relocating undocumented workers from areas no longer relevant to the local economy or redevelopment plans. The Chandler Roundup was intended to remove a low-income population to allow for urban renewal, by creating a hostile environment for citizens, violating their civil rights through immigration law enforcement employing micro- and macro-aggressions. Racialized immigration stops establish, maintain, and reinforce second-class citizenship and limit civil, political, economic, and cultural rights and opportunities. In urban barrios, the costly enterprise of selected stops and searches, race-related police abuse, and harassment results in deterring political participation, in identifying urban space racially, in classifying immigrants as deserving and undeserving by nationalities, and serves to drive a wedge dividing Latino neighborhoods on the basis of citizenship status.

 References

Acuña, Rodolfo 2000 *Occupied America.* New York, NY: Longman.

Amparano , Julie 1997 "Brown Skin: No Civil rights? July Sweep on Chandler Draws Fire." *Arizona Republic* August 15:B1.

Andreas, Peter 2000 *Border Games, Policing the U.S.-Mexico Divide.* Ithaca, NY: Cornell University Press.

Arriola, Elvia R. 1996–97 "LatCrit Theory, International Human Rights, Popular Culture, and the Faces of Despair in INS Raids." *University of Miami Inter-American Law Review* 28:245–62.

Bass, Sandra 2001 "Out of Place: Petit Apartheid and the Police." Pp. 43–54 in *Petit Apartheid in the U.S. Criminal Justice System, The Dark Figure of Racism,* edited by Dragan Milovanovic and Katheryn Russell. Durham, NC: Carolina Academic Press.

Benitez, Humberto 1994 "Flawed Strategies: The INS Shift from Border Interdiction to Internal Enforcement Actions." *La Raza Law Journal* 7:154–79.

Breen, Thomas, Sergio Murueta, and John Winters 1998 *Report of Independent Investigation Into July 1997 Joint Operation Between Patrol and Chandler Police Department.* Vol. I, II, and III, Chandler, Arizona: The City of Chandler.

Calavita, Kitty 1992 *Inside the State, The Bracero Program, Immigration, and the I.N.S.* New York, NY: Routledge.

Caldeira, Teresa P.R. 2000 *City of Walls: Crime, Segregation, and Citizenship in São Paulo.* Berkeley, CA: University of California Press.

Campbell, Jackie 2001 "Walking the Beat Alone: An African American Police Officer's Perspective on Petit Apartheid." Pp. 15–20 in *Petit Apartheid in the U.S. Criminal Justice System, The Dark Figure of Racism,* edited by Dragon Milovanovic and Katheryn Russell. Durham, NC: Carolina Academic Press.

Chang, Robert S. 1999 *Disoriented: Asian Americans, Law, and the Nation-State.* New York, NY: New York University Press.

Chang, Robert S. and Keith Aoki 1997 "Centering the Immigrant in the Inter/National Imagination." *California Law Review* 85:1395–1447.

Chavez, Leo R. 2001 *Covering Immigration, Popular Images and the Politics of the Nation.* Berkeley, CA: University of California Press.

Cornelius, Wayne A. 2001 "Death at the Border: Efficacy and Unintended Consequences of US Immigration Control Policy." *Population and Development Review* 27(4):661–85.

Covington, Jeanette 2001 "Round Up the Usual suspects: Racial Profiling and the War on Drugs." Pp. 27–42 in *Petit Apartheid in the U.S. Criminal Justice System, The Dark Figure of Racism,* edited by Dragan Milovanovic and Katheryn Russell. Durham, NC: Carolina Academic Press.

Davis, Robert C., Edna Erez, and Nancy Avitabile 2001 "Access to Justice for Immigrants who are Victimized: The Perspectives of Police and Prosecutors." *Criminal Justice Policy Review* 12(3):183–96.

Dunn, Timothy J. 1996 *The Militarization of the U.S.-Mexico Border,* Austin, TX: CMAS Books, University of Texas at Austin.

Edelman, Murray 2001 *The Politics of Misinformation.* New York, NY: Cambridge University Press.

Eschbach, Karl, Jacqueline Hagan, Nestor Rodriguez, Rúben Hernandez-león, and Stanley Bailey 1999 "Death at the Border." *International Migration Review* 33(2):430–54.

Ferrell, Jeff 2001a *Tearing Down the Streets: Adventures in Urban Anarchy,* New York, NY: Palgrave Macmillan. 2001b "Trying to Make Us a Parking Lot: Petit Apartheid, Cultural Space, and the Public Negotiation of Ethnicity." Pp. 55–68 in *Petit Apartheid in the U.S. Criminal Justice System, The Dark Figure of Racism,* edited by Dragan Milovanovic and Katheryn Russell. Durham, NC: Carolina Academic Press.

Fletcher, Michael A. 1997 "Police in Arizona Accused of Civil Rights Violations; Lawsuit Cites Sweep Aimed at Illegal Immigrants." *Washington Post* August 20:A14.

Garcia, Juan Ramon 1980 *Operation Wetback: The Mass Deportation of Mexican Undocumented Workers in 1954.* Westport, CT: Greenwood Press.

Georges-Abeyie, Daniel E. 1990 "Criminal Justice Processing of Non-White Minorities." Pp. 25–34 in *Racism, Empiricism and Criminal Justice,* edited by Brian D. MacLean and Dragan Milovanovic. Vancouver, BC: The Collective Press.

Harvey, David 1973 *Social Justice and the City.* Baltimore, MD: John Hopkins University Press.

1996 *Justice, Nature, and the Geography of Difference.* Oxford, UK: Blackwell.

Henry, Stuart and Dragan Milovanovic 1999 *Constitutive Criminology.* London: Sage Publications.

Herrnstein, Richard J. and Charles Murray 1994 *The Bell Curve: Intelligence and Class Structure in American Life.* New York, NY: Free Press.

Heyman, Josiah McC. 1995 "Putting Power in the Anthropology of Bureaucracy: The Immigration and Naturalization Service at the Mexico-United States Border." *Current Anthropology* 36(2):261 87.

Hing, Bill Ong 1997 *To Be An American.* New York, NY: New York University Press.

Holston, James (ed.) 1999 *Citizens and Citizenship.* Durham, NC: Duke University Press.

Johnson, Kevin 1993 "Los Olvidados: Images of the Immigrant, Political Power of Noncitizens, and Immigrant Law and Enforcement." *Binghamton Young University Law Review* 1993:1139–1241.

1997 "Racial Hierarchy, Asian Americans and Latinos as 'Foreigners,' and Social Change: Is Law the Way to Go?" *Oregon Law Review* 76(2):347–67.

2000 "The Case Against Race Profiling in Immigration Enforcement." *Washington University Law Quarterly* 78(3):676–736.

2002 "Race and the Immigration Laws: The Need for Critical Inquiry." Pp. 187–98 in *Crossroads, Directions, and a New Critical Race Theory,* edited by Francisco Valdez, Jerome McCristal Culp, and Angela P. Harris. Philadelphia, PA: Temple University Press.

2004 *The "Huddled Masses" Myth: Immigration and Civil Rights.* Philadelphia, PA: Temple University Press.

Johnson, Sheri Lynn 2001 "Racial Derogation in Prosecutors' Closing Arguments," Pp. 79–102 in *Petit Apartheid in the U.S. Criminal Justice System, The Dark Figure of Racism,* edited by Dragan Milovanovic and Katheryn Russell, Durham, NC: Carolina Academic Press.

Lazos Vargas, Sylvia R. 2002 "'Latina/o-ization' of the Midwest: *Cambio de Colores* (Change of Colors) as *Agromaquilas* Expand into the Heartland." *Berkeley la Raza Law Journal* 13(113):343–68.

Lee, Yueh-Ting, Victor Ottati, and Imtiaz Hussain 2001 "Attitudes Towards "Illegal Immigration into the United States: California Proposition 187." *Hispanic Journal of Behavioral Sciences* 23(4):430–43.

Lefebvre, Henri 1996 "The Right to the City." Pp. 63–181, in *Writings on Cities,* edited and translated by E. Kofman and E. Lebas. Oxford, UK: Blackwell.

Massey, Douglas S, Jorge Durand, and Nolan J. Malone 2002 *Beyond Smoke and Mirrors: Mexican Immigration in an Eva of Economic Integration.* New York, NY: Russell Sage Foundation.

Matsuda, Mari J., Charles R. Lawrence III, Richard Delgado, and Kimberlé W. Crenshaw 1993 *Words That Wound; Critical Race Theory, Assaultive Speech, and the First Amendment.* Boulder, CO: Westview Press.

Mehan, Hugh 1997 "The Discourse of the Illegal Immigration Debate: A Case Study in the Politics of Representation," *Discourse & Society* 8(2):249–70.

Milovanovic, Dragan and Katherine Russell (eds.) 2001 *Petit Apartheid in the U.S. Criminal Justice System, The Dark Figure of Racism.* Durham, NC: Carolina Academic Press.

Mitchell, Don 2003 *The Right to the City: Social Justice and the Fight for Public Space.* New York, NY: The Guilford Press.

Nelson, Hilde Lindemann 2001 *Damaged Identities, Narrative Repair,* Ithaca, NY: Cornell University Press.

Nevins, Joseph 2002 *Operation Gatekeeper, The Rise of the "Illegal Alien" and the Making of the U.S.—Mexican Boundary.* New York, NY: Routledge.

Office of the Attorney General Grant Wood 1997 *Results of the Chandler Survey.* Phoenix, State of Arizona.

Pierce, Chester M., Jean V. Carew, Doama Pierce-Gonzalez, and Deborah Willis 1978 "An Experiment in Racism: TV Commercials." Pp. 62–88 in *Television and Education,* edited by Chester Pierce. Beverly Hills, CA: Sage Publications.

Romero, Mary 2001 "State Violence, and the Social and Legal Construction of Latino Criminality: From Bandido to Gang Member." *Denver University Law Review* 78(4):1081–1118.

Ross, Lee E. 2001 "African-American Interest in Law Enforcement: A Consequence of Petit Apartheid?" Pp. 69–78 in *Petit Apartheid in the U.S. Criminal Justice System, The Dark Figure of Racism,* edited by Dragan Milovanovic and Katheryn Russell. Durham, NC: Carolina. Academic Press.

Russell, Katheryn K. 1998 *The Color of Crime: Racial Hoaxes, White Fear, Black Protectionism, Police Harassment and Other Macroaggressions.* New York, NY: New York University Press.

Sáenz, Benjamin Alire 1992 *Flowers for the Broken: Stories.* Seattle, WA: Broken Moon Press.

Santa Ana, Otto 2002 *Brown Tide Rising, Metaphors of Latinos in Contemporary American Public Discourse.* Austin, TX: University of Texas Press.

Smith, Dorothy E. 1990 *Texts, Facts, and Femininity: Exploring the Relations of Ruling.* New York, NY: Routledge.

1999 *Writing the Social; Critique, Theory, and Investigations.* Toronto, ON: The University of Toronto Press.

U.S. Attorney General's Office 1995 "Securing America's Borders," 1995 Annual Report of the Attorney General of the United States. Retrieved January 4, 2004 (http://www.usdoj.gov/ag/annualreports/ar95/chapter3.htm).

Valdez, Francisco, Jerome McCristal Gulp and Angela P. Harris (eds.) 2002 *Crossroads, Directions, and a New Critical Race Theory.* Philadelphia, PA: Temple University Press.

Vargas, Jorge A. 2001 "U.S. Border Patrol Abuses, Undocumented Mexican Workers, and International Human Rights." *San Diego International Law Review* 2(1):1–92.

Weissinger, George 1996 *Law Enforcement and the INS, A Participant Observation Study of Control Agents.* New York, NY: University Press of America.

DISCUSSION QUESTIONS

1. Describe the events that took place during the Chandler Roundup.

2. How do you think that this type of event impacts citizens' perceptions of the police?

3. Explain how liability became an issue for the police after the Chandler Roundup.

READING 26

In this article, William King and Thomas Dunn study police-initiated transjurisdictional transport (PITT) of troublesome persons, or as it is sometimes called, "dumping." This paper describes PITT, explores possible causes of PITT, and proposes several ways to control PITT.

Dumping: Police-Initiated Transjurisdictional Transport of Troublesome Persons

William R. King and Thomas M. Dunn

Street-level interactions between police officers and various categories of disenfranchised, problematic, or disorderly persons have long concerned observers of the police. During the past 35 years, research interests in police-citizen interactions have concentrated primarily on police use of coercive actions (e.g., arrest and use of force) against problematic citizens (for review, see Riksheim & Chermak, 1993). This trend has continued with the most recent examinations of police behaviors (Engel, Sobol, & Worden, 2000; Klinger, 1994, 1996; Mastrofski, Worden, & Snipes, 1995). Given the severity of the consequences for citizens associated with formal coercive actions, the concentration on arrest and use of force is certainly important. This focus, however, does not adequately reflect the majority of police-citizen encounters. Many of the early qualitative observations of police behavior

suggested that officers very rarely use arrest or force to handle situations—rather, the majority of these encounters are handled informally (Bittner, 1967; Muir, 1977; Reiss, 1971; Rubinstein, 1973; Wilson, 1968).

Policing has evolved considerably since the 1960s to 1970s when much of this early qualitative research was conducted. In the past 20 years, many American police organizations have adopted community policing and/or aggressive order maintenance policies. The adoption of these policies has slightly different implications for officers' behavior at the street level. Some have suggested that community-policing policies will lead to greater use of informal handling of problematic situations encountered by officers (H. Goldstein, 1990; Trojanowicz & Bucqueroux, 1990). In fact, the emphasis of community-policing strategies is to encourage officers to respond to problematic situations in ways other than traditional, formal responses such as arrest and use of force (H. Goldstein, 1990; Trojanowicz & Bucqueroux, 1990). In contrast, aggressive order maintenance policies encourage officers to use formal coercive action toward citizens for even minor offenses that had been traditionally handled informally. Aggressive order maintenance entails using the threat of enforcing public order laws, such as curfews and loitering ordinances, as a way to control troublesome populations and, many claim, to control violent crime (Kelling & Coles, 1996). The recent passion with aggressive order maintenance as a crime control technique stems in part from the broken windows theory (Wilson & Kelling, 1982) and from claims that New York City's recent crime drop can be attributed to aggressive order maintenance (Eck & Maguire, 2000). These two dissimilar police tactics may lead officers to dump troublesome persons either in the interests of handling such situations informally (COP) or in the name of order maintenance.

Unfortunately, our knowledge of police interactions with troublesome persons has not kept pace with the changes in policing philosophies and strategies. This article expands our knowledge of police behavior, order maintenance, and troublesome persons in two unique ways. First, it concentrates on a type of informal handling of special populations that has received scant descriptive and/or empirical attention by police scholars: police-initiated transjurisdictional transport (PITT) of troublesome persons. Although the informal policy of transporting troublesome persons to another location—or police "dumping" of problematic citizens—is generally acknowledged by police practitioners, it has rarely been discussed in the policing literature or systematically studied. Second, this article expands the category of troublesome persons beyond the homeless and mentally disordered, who are traditionally studied by researchers, by including the informal handling of juveniles, prostitutes, and people under the influence of alcohol and drugs.

This exploration of a police response to troublesome persons is timely given the recent emphasis on community policing and aggressive order maintenance by the police. Although proponents of these policies certainly do not advocate dumping troublesome

persons in other jurisdictions, it is reasonable to suspect that some officers may resort to such tactics as the most expedient way of handling troublesome persons.

This examination of transjurisdictional transport of troublesome persons unfolds in four parts. First, the notion of PITT is described and its consequences explained. Second, three general information sources (empirical and nonempirical social scientific writings, general research on police behavior, and journalistic accounts) are explored in an effort to better describe and examine the use of PITT by police officers. Third, we discuss the possible explanations for this type of informal handling of citizens and we offer suggestions for preventing it. Finally, this article concludes with four possible research strategies for studying the incidence of PITT.

Defining PITT

Dumping or PITT is a low-visibility police activity that stands outside the legal and moral norms of policing. PITT occurs when a police officer interacts with a mentally disturbed person, a person who is homeless, a prostitute, a juvenile, a drunk, or a person under the influence of drugs, the officer views this person as "troublesome," and the officer resolves the situation by transporting that troublesome person out of that officer's (or the department's) jurisdiction and releases that person into his or her own recognizance. To qualify as PITT, the officer does not have to transport the person but can arrange transportation instead (e.g., by placing the person on a bus or train or by using another departmental vehicle, such as a patrol wagon). PITT does not include instances in which an officer transports someone to another location where they are released into the custody of another "capable guardian" (such as a mental hospital, jail, or the troublesome person's home). PITT only involves instances in which the troublesome person is released, unsupervised, somewhere else (but not instances in which the police refuse to transport someone from a dangerous area; see Kappeler, 1997). For example, an officer may give a homeless individual a ride to their jurisdiction's boundary, release the individual, and instruct them to not return. Similarly, arranging transport, such as buying a bus ticket for a mentally ill person to send him or her to another city, exemplifies dumping. Generally, the jurisdiction into which the troublesome person is released does not know about or approve of the arrival of the troublesome person. In some larger areas, PITT involves transporting people to another part of the jurisdiction but not out of that department's jurisdiction.

PITT is analogous to other punishments imposed by the criminal justice system, such as banishment (Walker, 1998). Some courts have used "sundown parole" in which petty criminals were told to leave town or face imprisonment. PITT has also been referred to by a number of different terms. Transportation that involves buying troublesome people bus tickets to facilitate their removal has been called "diesel therapy." Indians in Saskatoon, Canada, have referred to PITT as a "scenic tour," a "starlight tour," or a "ride in the country" (Brass, 2001).

Transporting and dumping people who may be under duress may lead to three adverse outcomes. First, the dumped persons may be harmed or may harm others when they arrive at their destinations. In some cases, the dumped persons are free to wander and may become crime victims or may victimize others. It is plausible that behaviors that attract police attention in one jurisdiction will not cease when the people are moved to other jurisdictions because the cause of their behavior has not been addressed. In some situations, dumped persons may succumb to exposure to the elements, such as by freezing to death or suffering heat stroke, or they may be struck by vehicles. Second, moving troublesome people to unfamiliar surroundings may aggravate their behavior and separate them from their social support networks and, in the case of mentally disturbed persons, perhaps their medication. Finally, it is possible that people such as juvenile runaways, persons who are homeless, and people who are mentally ill will end up in jurisdictions where they are easily overlooked (e.g., a large city) and will therefore be denied attention and possible treatment.

 # Examples of PITT in Prior Literature

Despite the relevance of dumping to contemporary policing, especially given the recent emphasis on community policing and aggressive order maintenance, there has been little systematic attention given to this matter. The prior literature on policing troublesome populations can be divided into three categories: empirical and nonempirical social scientific writings, more general research on police behavior, and journalistic accounts.[1] Accounts of PITT are sometimes incidentally caught by police researchers, but overall, the best accounts of PITT come from journalistic accounts.

Social scientific writings about troublesome persons are usually drawn from the observations, experiences, or thoughts of police researchers. In some cases, these writings are driven by some type of quantifiable data and in other cases, they are not. For example, Aaronson, Dienes, and Musheno (1984) relied on various police records to see how changes in local alcoholism laws affected police arrests of drunks. Similarly, William Muir's (1977) qualitative observation of police officers in one U.S. city led him to note how different police officers dealt with the inhabitants of skid row. Although Muir's research is more concerned with officer behavior in general and not interactions with troublesome persons, it is still an example of research that directly addresses troublesome persons and the police. Other examples of research in this category include discussions of how street police officers handle homeless people (Bittner, 1967), inhabitants of skid row (Muir, 1977), people who are mentally ill (Teplin, 1984), juveniles (Black & Reiss, 1970), or all these groups (Kelling & Coles, 1996; Wilson & Kelling, 1982). Some of these accounts also suggest how the police should deal with these groups (e.g., Kelling & Coles, 1996). Unfortunately, the empirical and nonempirical social scientific literature has rarely mentioned PITT. One exception is noted by Kappeler, Sluder, and Alpert (1994) and involves a case in which a police officer, "drove a young mugger far out of the precinct, forced the offender to strip to his shorts, and left him to make his own way back home" (p. 193). Generally, early observers of the police were more interested with informal ways of handling troublesome persons or police officers' use of arrest or physical force.[2]

A second body of research investigates the behavior of police officers on the street via systematic observation of police officers. This research is usually concerned with how police officers behave in general, not just when dealing with troublesome persons.[3] Research in this second category uses trained observers who accompany police officers on patrol and record officers' actions. These data are not collected to observe police interactions with troublesome persons per se but rather to study police officer behavior in general. The larger of these studies have produced rich data sets that have been subsequently used by researchers for years after collection (e.g., the Black and Reiss data collected in 1965, Reiss, 1971; the Police Services Study data collected in 1977, Caldwell, 1978; and the Project on Policing Neighborhoods (POPN) data collected in 1996–1997, Parks, Mastrofski, DeJong, and Gray, 1999). Most often, these data have been used to explore the correlates of officers' decision to arrest, use physical force, investigate, and provide service to people (for reviews of most of these studies, see Riksheim & Chermak, 1993; Sherman, 1980).

The data from systematic observations sometimes provide information about possible cases of PITT; unfortunately, these data are of little use to explorations of PITT if observers did not collect information about citizens' housing situation, youth, occupation in prostitution, mental stability, or blood-alcohol content. Sometimes, however, discussions of these data have provided accounts of dumping. For instance, an account drawn from the Black and Reiss data (collected in 1965) describe a disturbing example of dumping in which two officers were flagged down by a man and woman who claimed that a Black man "was causing trouble inside the public transport station from which they had just emerged" (Reiss, 1973, p. 276).

> With that, they ran into the station and grabbed the Negro man who was inside. Without questioning him, they shoved him into a phone booth and began beating him with their fists and a flashlight. They also hit him in

the groin. Then they dragged him out and kept him on his knees. He pleaded that he had just been released from a mental hospital that day and, begging not to be hit again, asked them to let him return to the hospital. One policeman said: "Don't you like us, nigger? I like to beat niggers and rip out their eyes." They took him outside to their patrol car. Then they decided to put him on a bus, telling him that he was returning to the hospital; they deliberately put him on a bus going in the opposite direction. Just before the Negro boarded the bus, he said, "You police just like to shoot and beat people." The first policeman replied, "Get moving, nigger, or I'll shoot you." The man was crying and bleeding as he was put onto the bus. Leaving the scene, the younger policeman commented, "He won't be back." (Reiss, 1973, p. 276)

Two studies using observational data of police response to troublesome persons deserve discussion. In 1980 to 1981, Linda Teplin trained graduate students to ride with officers in two Chicago precincts and record officer reactions to people who were believed to be mentally ill (see Teplin, 1984). Overall, Teplin's (1984) data led her to conclude that police officers are more likely to arrest people who are mentally ill compared with people who showed no signs of being mentally ill. Simply put, this conclusion supports the criminalization hypothesis, which posits that since deinstitutionalization in the late 1960s, mentally ill people are more likely to be arrested and processed through the criminal justice system. On the other hand, Engel and Silver (2001) found that police officers were less likely to arrest citizens exhibiting mental disorders (using observational data of the police collected in 1977 and 1996–1997). Unfortunately, neither Teplin nor Engel and Silver report on PITT or discuss it at length. Simply, there is a dearth of research on and discussion of PITT from quantitative data sets of police officer behavior.

Finally, the newsprint media reports occasionally on PITT. This article located instances of PITT in five cities (Cleveland, Ohio; Miami, Florida; Washington, D.C.; Schenectady, New York; and Saskatoon, Canada).

Allegedly, Cleveland police officers sometimes picked up homeless men and transported them to other parts of the city during 1992 and 1993.

> The city engaged in illegal dumping in an effort to "sanitize" downtown Cleveland. The ACLU began investigating the issue after receiving a tip that police were removing homeless people against their will from downtown shopping districts and dumping them in remote places. (Grant, 1997, p. 1B)

In February 1997 Cleveland settled a resulting lawsuit brought by the ACLU.

The city of Miami, Florida, was supposedly a popular homeless dumping area for local municipalities. During 2001, downtown Miami businesses and the Miami police accused other local police agencies of transporting their homeless to the Miami city limits or even to downtown Miami. In some cases, the homeless were allegedly transported across jurisdictional boundaries and left at downtown Miami homeless centers. In another instance, an ex–Key Biscayne police officer claimed she was ordered by her superiors to transport homeless people over a bridge and dump them at the Miami city limits (Corsa, 2001).

A similar incident occurred in July 1989 when Washington, D.C., metro police officers herded 24 prostitutes across the 14th Street Bridge from Washington into Arlington at 1:30 in the morning. The officers abandoned their forced march when a photographer and reporter from the *Washington Post* arrived. One prostitute stated, "They said they were taking us to Virginia, that we could work over there. They said we'd go to jail if we stopped" (Byrd, 1989). Surprisingly, an Arlington police officer claimed he had been instructed to dump troublesome people in Washington, D.C.

> I was told by a supervisor to take one guy to the D.C. line and basically deal with the problem that way. He was put at the end of the bridge and we told him, that way is D.C. Go over there. (Goldberg & Dedman, 1989)

More recently, allegations surfaced that officers of the Schenectady, New York, police dumped people (Barry, 2001). A Schenectady resident accused two officers of taking him 11 miles outside the city, removing his boots (which were thrown into the woods), and leaving him in the woods. One of the officers later stated under oath that such relocations were "common practice." A sworn deposition taken from another Schenectady officer stated

> that Schenectady officers would sometimes drop an alcohol-addled person at the doorstep of another community's police department and say there was a party inside with "free food and girls." Other departments would often return the favor with a different drunk or drug addict . . . . "you did it as a joke, and it went back and forth." (Barry, 2001, p. B1)

The final instance of PITT found in media accounts came from Saskatoon, Canada (Roberts, 2000). Two Saskatoon police officers were fired and later charged and convicted (of unlawful confinement) for dumping an aboriginal man outside the city on the night of January 28, 2000. The two officers had picked the man up for causing a disturbance but drove the man to a power station outside the city and released him with instructions to never return. The officers allegedly took the man's coat, although the temperature that night was below negative 22 degrees Celsius (Foss, 2001). The resulting trial raised other allegations of dumping, especially among local aboriginals. The bodies of five other men had been found outside Saskatoon between 1990 and 2000. Aboriginals alleged that the dead men were victims of police dumping, whereas others claimed they had been dumped by Saskatoon officers (Brass, 2001).

Overall, it appears that PITT is a method police officers employ sometimes to handle troublesome persons. Without further study, however, it is not possible to state definitively how often officers use it or what factors are related to its use because print-media accounts are not a representative sample of police officer behavior. Drawing from the larger literature of what influences police officer behavior, however, it is possible to hypothesize about the causes of PITT.

 # Causes of PITT

This article divides the hypothesized causes of PITT into three types: organizations, communities, and situational factors. Briefly, an officer's decision to dump a troublesome person is most likely influenced by a range of organizational, community, and situational characteristics. This categorization of the causes or correlates of officer behavior is in accord with prior reviews of police officer behavior (Riksheim & Chermak, 1993; Sherman, 1980).

Organizational Factors

Officers' decisions to dump people are likely related, in part, to certain organizational characteristics. First is the presence of a departmental emphasis on aggressive order maintenance (or zero tolerance) policing, departmental implementation of COP, and how widely implemented these policies are. The positive relationship between aggressive order maintenance and PITT is expected because of some departments' inducement that officers handle troublesome persons in a manner designed to quickly reduce disorder (as opposed to getting troublesome persons help or putting them under criminal justice control). The positive relationship between aggressive order maintenance and PITT differs based on how aggressively and how widely (geographically) departments implement zero-tolerance policing. It is likely that some departments will reserve certain areas of their jurisdiction for containing troublesome people (e.g., a skid row or a red-light district). Other departments, however, may eradicate all geographic areas for troublesome persons and hence will be more likely to engage in PITT (provided other facilities do not exist for holding troublesome people). Departments will vary in the temporal dimensions of their aggressive order maintenance. For example, departments embodying a strict, 24-hour aggressive policing stance are probably more likely to dump. These statements about aggressive

policing are based partially on the assumption that PITT results because officers become frustrated with alternative methods of handling troublesome people such as arresting them or taking them to a shelter.

The geographic and temporal aspects of PITT also apply to departments implementing COP. Because COP increases police officer discretion and emphasizes informal solutions to problems, it is also likely that departments with COP will see increased incidence of PITT. Again, this predicted relationship is related to how widely COP is implemented organizationally (e.g., is COP a special unit or departmental wide? Is the entire jurisdiction covered by COP officers or just certain neighborhoods?). This relationship is also influenced by the presence or absence of attractive alternatives available for officers who deal with troublesome persons.

The likelihood of PITT is also related to departmental culture. PITT is more likely if it is viewed by police officers as an accepted (but perhaps not departmentally condoned) way of handling problems. PITT is a low-fuss way of making bad people disappear, and police culture (or subtypes of police culture; see Paoline, 2001) rewards creative, common-sense ways of handling problems (Crank, 1998).

Finally, it is expected that officers are more likely to use PITT on troublesome people if they have either seen or heard of PITT in their areas. This includes officers who become the victims of PITT by other agencies when the other agencies dump troublesome persons in their jurisdiction. PITT is expected to be more prevalent in departments in which officers can learn how to dump and where officers see that PITT is not punished. Departments in which PITT is more widely practiced are expected to more readily educate officers about how to dump (through social learning).

Community Factors

The prevalence of PITT is also related to various community characteristics, such as the presence of suitable dumping areas, easy access to transportation, and the presence of suitable alternative placements. First, suitable dumping areas need to both retain dumpees and be low visibility for the officers initiating the dump and for the dumpees. Dumping areas can retain troublesome persons either through some form of "trap" or via their attractiveness for dumpees. Some dumping sites trap troublesome persons (i.e., prevent their quick return) by being distant, such as when people are transported by interstate bus lines. Other dumping areas limit dumpees' returns, for example, by forcing a dumpee to make a long walk over a bridge on a cold winter night. It seems likely that few dumpees would bother to make the cold, long return walk and risk being arrested upon their return. Other dumping grounds retain dumpees by their attractiveness for dumpees.

These dumping grounds are in areas, for example, with less police presence, that are warmer, or with easier access to alcohol or drugs.

Suitable dumping grounds must also be low visibility for both the officers dumping the persons and the dumpees. Officers who release dumpees on a journey to a dumping ground partially avoid being spotted directly dumping people (e.g., by taking them to the city limits and telling them to start walking or by placing dumpees on buses or transit lines). Dumping areas must also be low visibility for the dumpees so their arrival and presence are not noticed. Dumpees who call attention to themselves may also receive the attention of other police agencies, which may lead the dumpees to recount their tales of dumping. It is because of visibility that it is expected that suburbs are more likely to dump troublesome persons in neighboring cities than cities are to dump in the suburbs.

PITT is also related to easy access to transportation. Officers can usually opt to transport the persons themselves. However, transporting dumpees a great distance is a good way of ensuring they will not return, and such long-distance transport is best accomplished via transportation companies (such as bus lines, public transits, and so forth). Thus, the incidence of PITT is probably related to how much transport (bus lines and public transports) is readily available to officers. In some cases, officers may be able to enlist the assistance of other police agencies, which will transport troublesome persons a greater distance.[4]

The likelihood of PITT is also related to the availability of alternative placements for troublesome persons. These alternatives to PITT are "appropriate" (yet unsupervised) areas for such troublesome persons within jurisdictions (such as a skid row or a red-light district) or social service agencies where troublesome persons are supervised. Because the definition of troublesome persons posited here encompasses a wide range of people, the appropriate alternative placements would also need to be broad to deter dumping. Telling someone to get back to skid row is a simple if unsophisticated alternative to PITT. Of course, troublesome persons are then left unsupervised. Social service alternative placements are places officers can bring troublesome persons where they will be supervised by professionals. These include hospital psychiatric units, alcoholism and substance abuse shelters, homeless shelters, shelters for prostitutes, and youth curfew centers. The mere presence of a suitable placement will not prevent PITT. Some homeless shelters will not accept people who are under the influence of alcohol or drugs. Some substance abuse shelters will not take involuntary placements. Shelters are sometimes full. It is expected that in such circumstances, officers who have exhausted their options will be more likely to dump the persons. Officers in areas with few or no shelters and alternative placements will be more likely to resort to PITT.

Situational Factors

Past studies indicate the three best predictors of the police decision to arrest are all situational factors (the suspect's demeanor, a victim or complainant's preference for either arrest or leniency, and the seriousness of the alleged offense; Riksheim & Chermak, 1993; Smith & Visher, 1981). It is also likely that various attributes of both interactions between officers and troublesome persons and attributes of the troublesome persons influence officers' decisions to dump. For instance, people with a suitable place to go (such as a home or a friend's apartment) are more likely to be told to "go home" as opposed to being dumped. Likewise, troublesome persons who are compliant with officers' commands to leave an area are less likely to experience

PITT as compared with people displaying recalcitrance or poor demeanor. Even factors such as personal hygiene (or lack thereof) probably influence the decision to dump. Most police officers treat their cruisers as offices with four wheels and are unwilling to transport people who smell or may vomit or defecate in their cars. Under such circumstances, officers may opt for ordering the people to walk from the area or may arrange some form of alternative transport (such as public transit).

It should be obvious from this discussion that officers' decision to use PITT is not a simple decision. Rather, like all decisions made by police officers on the street, it is a solution influenced in part by certain agency, community, and situational attributes. Understanding the causes of PITT also helps guide possible ways of decreasing its occurrence.

 ## Controlling PITT

Preventing police officers from engaging in PITT is best thought of in light of the larger literature on controlling the discretionary decisions of criminal justice actors. Since the early 1960s, reformers have suggested and implemented various techniques to control discretionary decision making by criminal justice actors, including the police.

Generally, the following four ways of controlling criminal justice discretion have been offered: checking, structuring, confining, and using alternatives (Davis, 1969). Briefly, checking involves the review of criminal justice actors' actions either before or after the acts. For example, police officers must obtain search warrants from a judge (who presumably checks that the officers have sufficient cause for warrants). Some police departments require that a supervisor be dispatched to certain, sensitive calls (such as calls involving the mentally ill) to ensure that responding officers handle the situation properly. Structuring involves the use of rules and guidelines to direct actors' behavior and to tell actors what factors to account for and how much to weigh them in decision making (Gottfredson & Gottfredson, 1988). Some police departments have structured their

officers' decisions to engage in vehicle pursuits by asking officers to account for factors such as the suspected violation, traffic density, and road conditions before deciding to pursue. Structuring does not require that a decision maker adhere to a rule. Rather, guidelines can be disregarded provided the actors provide justification for why the guidelines were not followed. Third, decisions can be confined with concrete rules, which cannot be violated by actors even with justification. These "thou shalt nots" make it clear that some behaviors are absolutely inappropriate for criminal justice actors no matter what the justification. Confining discretion has been particularly successful in limiting police use of deadly force (Walker, 1993; White, 2001). Finally, adding discretionary options to a decision maker's repertoire can control discretion (Walker, 1993).

However, these four discretionary controls are only successful in certain circumstances. The following three key factors help explain why some discretionary reforms have been successful, whereas others have failed: visibility of decisions or acts, whether the decisions are reviewed and the actors are held accountable, and putting controls close to those who make decisions. First, highly visible decisions and actions are easier to control because actors are more likely to believe they are being observed (certainty) and actors' superiors are more likely to see and review the decisions (J. Goldstein, 1960). Thus, police shootings of citizens are highly visible and hence more amenable to control by police supervisors, other criminal justice actors (e.g., attorneys), or external, watchdog groups. It is hard to hide dead bodies or bullet holes in suspects (Fyfe, 1995). Actors are less likely to adhere to guidelines or rules during less visible actions, because these actions are less likely to be observed and hence less likely to be reviewed (J. Goldstein, 1960), or when the results of officers' actions can be explained away.[5]

Controls have often relied on review of officers' actions and holding officers accountable. Departments that have implemented a review procedure for officers who discharge their firearms appear to have been successful at controlling the number of citizens killed by police firearms (Fyfe, 1988; Walker, 1993; White, 2001). Naturally, reviews work best when the behavior is visible. Reviews must also be conducted if they are to work. The presence of review procedures that are never used will not deter inappropriate behaviors (see, in particular, White, 2001). Successfully controlling discretion also relies in part on holding actors accountable for their actions. Again, the efforts to control police shootings appear to work because officers are held accountable for improper firearms discharges. Finally, controls work best when they are enacted close to the actors they seek to control. Walker (1993) suggested that rules created by individual police departments (e.g., deadly force policies) probably control officers better than do rules made by legislators (e.g., mandatory arrest laws for perpetrators of domestic violence).

Rules and Regulations

With these two related streams of thought (discretionary controls and the elements of effective controls) in mind, we suggest that police agencies first create clear policies to ban officer dumping. Administrative rule making has long been suggested as a way to control discretion (Davis, 1969; Walker, 1993). However, effective rules require that controlled behaviors are visible, that violations are reviewed, that officers violating policies are held accountable, and that attractive alternatives to dumping exist for officers.

Increasing Visibility

Second, departments can work to increase the visibility of interactions between police officers and troublesome persons. Increasing visibility will work best to ensure that rules are followed and enforceable. There are two broad ways to do this: via paperwork or by involving other police personnel in police interactions with troublesome persons.

Some departments require that their officers complete a form anytime officers interact with mentally ill persons. Some departments require that dispatchers dispatch a supervisor whenever calls involve mentally ill persons. Both these techniques increase the visibility and facilitate the review of police interactions. Officers can choose to not complete or submit a form,

an action that thwarts later attempts to review their actions. As far as we know, completing paperwork and dispatching supervisors have only been used in departments for dealing with the mentally ill, not other troublesome people. Increasing the scope of paperwork to include a form completed for any persons with whom officers interact is one of the methods some departments are using to compile statistics on traffic stops in order to address the possibility of racial profiling. As such, if done properly, it may not be overly burdensome to use a form to record officer interactions with citizens. Of course, this method of increasing visibility will only work if officers comply with it. It is easy for officers to "forget" to complete an interaction form when they dump people. The annals of police research are replete with stories of the creative ways officers thwart the best-laid plans of managers and researchers (Petrocelli & Smith, 2000; Reuss-Ianni, 1983). It is likely that dispatching supervisors to all calls with troublesome persons would prove too burdensome for most departments.

One way to increase the visibility of police interactions with troublesome persons that also thwarts officers' attempts to transport the persons themselves is to require that officers use patrol wagons (and not their cruisers) to transport prisoners. Some police agencies already have such policies in place. If the transport officers in patrol wagons must log all their transports on paper and with a dispatcher, the likelihood of PITT decreases. Officers who are observed with someone in the back of their cruisers would have to explain why they were violating departmental policy. Using patrol wagons does not, however, keep officers from telling troublesome people to go elsewhere or from arranging their transport via another form of transportation.

Alternative Placements

A third possible way to decrease PITT is to use and increase the attractiveness of social service placements for troublesome persons. For example, detoxification centers, homeless shelters, shelters for prostitutes, psychiatric units at hospitals, and juvenile curfew drop-off centers all provide officers with alternatives to PITT.

However, officers will only use such alternatives if they find them attractive. Unfortunately, some shelters will not take homeless people who are also drunk. Some psychiatric units will not accept people who are mentally disturbed and acting violent. Sometimes, the closest shelter is many miles away. In such circumstances, it is little wonder that officers resort to PITT. It is important then that options to PITT are available and that these options are attractive to officers.

Related to the use of social service placements is the use of social service crisis response teams. Generally, such social service crisis response teams have been created to assist the police in their interactions with the mentally ill. Among the most notable of these crisis response teams has been one created in Memphis to deal with the mentally ill (Vickers, 2000). It is possible to create other response teams to deal specifically with certain categories of troublesome people. Officers could call for such response teams, or these teams could work independently on removing troublesome persons (such as curfew violators). It seems likely that in some circumstances in which officer did not wish to arrest, the response teams not only would increase the visibility of the interaction but also could transport the persons to suitable placements. In this manner, the burden of dealing with troublesome persons is removed from officers.

◢ Discussion

PITT has eluded systematic study by police researchers who heretofore have been interested in studying more visible police behaviors (such as arrest and use of force). Although overlooked, it is a serious, extralegal police action that has resulted in lawsuits and the death of dumpees. Recent trends toward COP and aggressive order maintenance make it likely that PITT will become more prevalent. Ironically, this increase in PITT will occur at the same time that police scholars have begun to advocate "policing for people" (that is, policing that focuses on being responsive to citizens and treating them fairly) (Mastrofski, 1999). Public knowledge of PITT undermines public confidence in the legitimacy of the police. In sum, although dumping is a serious problem, it is almost invisible to observers of the police, and thus we know remarkably little about it.

For these reasons, PITT is worthy of study in its own right. Unfortunately, PITT is also a low-visibility behavior that is easily altered when officers think they might be observed. It also produces little or no "trail" of permanent social artifacts (i.e., paper work or dispatch records) with which to study it. These attributes make it a particularly difficult social event to study (Reiss, 1992). Studying PITT, however, will allow us to estimate the incidence of PITT in various locales and explore its causes (and possible solutions). There are four research strategies that could be employed to study this problem: interviews, participant observations, systematic social observations, and vignettes.

First, high-risk populations (such as prostitutes, the homeless, juveniles, and the mentally ill) and their guardians (i.e., shelter directors and workers and mental health workers) could be interviewed. Interviews may reveal overall trends in dumping, including preferred dumping areas and the modes of transportation used. Likewise, officers could be interviewed or surveyed about their experiences with PITT (either firsthand or vicariously). We have found officers to be mixed in their responses to questions about dumping. Some officers have been forthcoming in talking about PITT, whereas others have not. Both methods of probing PITT are imperfect (i.e., fraught with telescoping, fabrication, and embellishment by interviewees). The absence of research on this topic, however, means that interviews will yield useful information.

Second, because officers are recalcitrant discussing PITT with outsiders, it would probably be fruitful to enlist the help of officers. Hundreds of police officers are currently pursuing master's degrees in criminal justice and related disciplines. It is probable that officers could explore the extent of PITT in their agencies, the reasons provided for dumping, and what changes might decrease its incidence (such as streamlining admissions to homeless shelters).

The experiences of these officers represent an imperfect receptacle of memories of PITT, and these experiences should be tapped. Furthermore, using officers to collect these observations potentially solves the problems of respondent reactivity to talking about PITT with outsiders.

Third, systematic social observation has become a popular albeit expensive way of observing what police officers do (Parks et al. 1999; Reiss, 1971). In the past, observers have been trained to record officer response to mentally ill individuals (Teplin, 1984). It would be easy to train observers to also record incidents of PITT while they gather other relevant data. Finally, vignettes have been used to study the ways in which officers exercise their discretion (Mastrofski, Ritti, & Hoffmaster, 1987). Vignettes would allow us to explore the organizational and environmental determinants of officers' propensities to engage in dumping as opposed to other solutions to troublesome persons.

 Notes

1. Cases of dumping have also appeared in the legal literature. One case involved PITT to another state (*Ketchum v. City of West Memphis, Arkansas*, 1992), and one case involved a "deportation" from Hemet, California (*Klock v. Cain*, 1993).

2. A unique perspective is offered by noted criminologist Hans Mattick. Professor Mattick reported being dumped repeatedly by the New Orleans police during the late 1930s. See John Laub's (1983) interview with Professor Mattick.

3. An exception is Teplin's (1984) research, which is reviewed later in the article.

4. A noted police scholar recounted (to one of the authors) that while assigned as a military police officer at his base's front gate, he encountered a mentally ill veteran who wished to enter the base. The military police's commanding officer summoned the local sheriff and instructed the sheriff's deputy to take the veteran to the county limits and release him.

5. Fyfe (1995) noted that although bullet holes in suspects are hard to explain, officers can explain bruised and bloodied suspects by saying they fell down.

 References

Aaronson, D. E., Dienes, C. T., & Musheno, M. C. (1984). *Public policy and police discretion*. New York: Clark Boardman.

Barry, D. (2001, August 17). A force in trouble: Inquiry exposes police misdeeds. *The New York Times*, p. B1.

Bittner, E. (1967). Police discretion in emergency apprehension of mentally ill persons. *Social Problems, 14*, 278–292.

Black, D., & Reiss, A. (1970). Police control of juveniles. *American Sociological Review, 35*, 63–77.

Brass, M. (2001). *Starlight tours*. Retrieved December 8, 2001, from http://www.cbc.ca/news/national/magazine/starlight/index.html.

Byrd, L. (1989, July 27). Prostitutes trail of tears: VA. Not amused by forced march from D.C. *Washington Post News Service*. Available from http://www.lexis-nexis.com/ universe

Caldwell, E. (1978). Patrol observation: The patrol encounter, patrol narrative, and general shift information forms (Police Services Study Methods Report, MR-02). Bloomington, IN: Workshop in Political Theory and Policy Analysis.

Corsa, L. (2001, May 17). Finally a solution to the homeless problem: Just put them in your patrol car and take them to Miami. *The New Miami Times*. Available from http://www. miaminewtimes.com

Crank, J. (1998). *Understanding police culture*. Cincinnati, OH: Anderson.

Davis, K. C. (1969). *Discretionary justice: A preliminary inquiry*. Urbana: University of Illinois Press.

Eck, J. E., & Maguire, E. R. (2000). Have changes in policing reduced violent crime? An assessment of the evidence. In A. Blumstein & J. Wallman (Eds.), *The crime drop in America* (pp. 207–265). New York: Cambridge University Press.

Engel, R. S., & Silver, E. (2001). Policing mentally disordered suspects: A reexamination of the criminalization hypothesis. *Criminology, 39*, 225–252.

Engel, R. S., Sobol, J. J., & Worden, R. E. (2000). Further exploration of the demeanor hypothesis: The interaction effects of suspects' characteristics and demeanor on police behavior. *Justice Quarterly, 17*, 235–258.

Foss, K. (2001, September 24). Natives struggle with fallout from trial. *Globe and Mail*, p. A16.

Fyfe, J. (1988). Police use of deadly force: Research and reform. *Justice Quarterly, 5*, 165–205.

Fyfe, J. (1995, March 11). *Training to reduce police violence*. Paper presented at the annual meeting of the Academy of Criminal Justice Sciences, Boston.

Goldberg, J., & Dedman, B. (1989, July 27). Prostitutes trail of tears: VA. Not amused by forced march from D.C. *Washington Post News Service*. Available from http://www.lexis-nexis.com/universe

Goldstein, H. (1990). *Problem-oriented policing*. New York: McGraw-Hill.

Goldstein, J. (1960). Police discretion not to invoke the criminal process: Low-visibility decisions in the administration of justice. *Yale Law Journal, 69*, 543–594.

Gottfredson, M. R., & Gottfredson, D. M. (1988). *Decision making in criminal justice: Toward the rational exercise of discretion*. New York: Plenum.

Grant, A. (1997, February 19). Cleveland settles with homeless; Suit accused police of "dumping" people. *The Plain Dealer*, p. A1B.

Kappeler, V. E. (1997). *Critical issues in police civil liability*. Prospect Heights, IL: Waveland.

Kappeler, V. E., Sluder, R. D., & Alpert, G. P. (1994). *Forces of deviance: Understanding the dark side of policing*. Prospect Heights, IL: Waveland.

Kelling, G., & Coles, C. (1996). *Fixing broken windows*. New York: Free Press.

Ketchum v. City of West Memphis, Arkansas, 974 F. 2d 81 (8th Circuit 1992).

Klinger, D. (1994). Demeanor or crime? Why "hostile" citizens are more likely to be arrested. *Criminology, 32*, 475–493.

Klinger, D. (1996). More on demeanor and arrest in Dade County. *Criminology, 34*, 61–82.

Klock v. Cain, 813 F.Supp. 1430 (Central District of California, 1993).

Laub, J. (1983). *Criminology in the making: An oral history*. Boston: Northeastern University Press.

Mastrofski, S. D. (1999). *Policing for people. Ideas in American Policing*. Washington, DC: Police Foundation.

Mastrofski, S. D., Ritti, R. R., & Hoffmaster, D. (1987). Organizational determinants of police discretion: The case of drinking-driving. *The Journal of Criminal Justice, 15*, 387–402.

Mastrofski, S. D., Worden, R. E., & Snipes, J. B. (1995). Law enforcement in a time of community policing. *Criminology, 33*, 539–563.

Muir, W. K. Jr. (1977). *Police: Streetcorner politicians*. Chicago: University of Chicago Press.

Paoline, E. A., III. (2001). *Rethinking police culture: Officers' occupational attitudes*. New York: LFB.

Parks, R. B., Mastrofski, S. D., DeJong, C., & Gray, M. K. (1999). How officers spend their time with the community. *Justice Quarterly, 16*, 483–518.

Petrocelli, M., & Smith, M. R. (2000). The implementation of a use of force study: Lessons learned for practitioners and researchers. *Police Forum, 10*, 1–3.

Reiss, A. J. (1971). *The police and the public*. New Haven: Yale University Press.

Reiss, A. J. (1973). How much "police brutality" is there? In S. M. David & P. E. Peterson (Eds.), *Urban politics and public policy: The city in crisis* (pp. 269–286). New York: Praeger.

Reiss, A. J. (1992). Trained incapacities of sociologists. In T. C. Halliday & M. Janowitz (Eds.), *Sociology and its publics: The forms and fates of disciplinary organization* (pp. 297–315). Chicago: University of Chicago Press.

Reuss-Ianni, E. (1983). *Two cultures of policing: Street cops and management Cops*. New Brunswick, NJ: Transaction Publishing.

Riksheim, E. C., & Chermak, S. M. (1993). Causes of police behavior revisited. *Journal of Criminal Justice, 21*, 353–382.

Roberts, D. (2000, April 12). Officers charged in alleged abandonment. *The Globe and Mail*, p. A8.

Rubenstein, J. (1973). *City police*. New York: Ballantine.

Sherman, L. W. (1980). Causes of police behavior: The current state of quantitative research. *Journal of Research in Crime and Delinquency, 19*, 69–100.

Smith, D. A., & Visher, C. A. (1981). Street-level justice: Situational determinants of police arrest decisions. *Social Problems, 29*, 167–177.

Teplin, L. (1984). Criminalizing mental disorder: The comparative arrest rates of the mentally ill. *American Psychologist, 39*, 794–803.

Trojanowicz, R., & Bucqueroux, B. (1990). *Community policing: A contemporary perspective*. Cincinnati, OH: Anderson.

Vickers, B. (2000). *Memphis, Tennessee, police department's crisis intervention team*. Washington, DC: Bureau of Justice Administration, Office of Justice Programs.

Walker, S. (1993). *Taming the system: The control of discretion in criminal justice, 1950–1990*. New York: Oxford University Press.

Walker, S. (1998). *Popular justice: A history of American criminal justice* (2nd ed.). New York: Oxford University Press.

White, M. (2001). Controlling police decisions to use deadly force: Reexamining the importance of administrative policy. *Crime & Delinquency, 47*, 131–151.

Wilson, J. Q. (1968). *Varieties of police behavior: The management of law and order in eight communities*. Cambridge, MA: Harvard University Press.

Wilson, J. Q., & Kelling, G. (1982). Broken windows: Police and neighborhood safety. *Atlantic Monthly, 249*, 29–38.

DISCUSSION QUESTIONS

1. Why is it important to study police-initiated transjurisdictional transport of troublesome persons?

2. Which agencies could police departments partner with to attempt to deal with this problem?

3. Why is this topic so difficult to study? What are some issues related to data collection?

Glossary

Age requirement: The minimum hiring age commonly used by police agencies in the United States is 21 years old. Most local police agencies do not have maximum age limits; however, federal-level agencies do have a maximum age limit.

Alabama HB 56: Law requiring police officers to verify the legal status of people they suspect are in the United States illegally during routine traffic stops and other encounters. It also allows the police to hold people they believe are in the country illegally without bond.

Arizona SB 1070: Law requiring that police officers attempt to determine someone's immigration status during traffic stops, detentions, or arrests when there is reasonable suspicion that the person is an illegal immigrant.

Assessment center: Where applicants participate in a series of situational exercises that simulate responsibilities and working conditions of police officers. They are frequently used in promotional processes.

Broken windows: A theory developed by James Q. Wilson and George Kelling based on the idea that visible decay or disorder in neighborhoods will lead to crime and other problems related to social disorder.

Bureaucracy: An organization with a defined chain of command, impersonal rules, specific expectations for conduct, with clear responsibilities for its members. Often considered to be rigid, stifling creativity, and overly rule oriented.

CALEA (Commission on Accreditation for Law Enforcement Agencies): An organization created in 1979 to serve as a credentialing agency for law enforcement agencies in the United States.

Call box: Use began in the mid- to late 1800s. They were communication devices placed strategically in a city containing telephone lines linked directly to police headquarters. They were implemented to help facilitate better communication between patrol officers, police supervisors, and central headquarters.

Citizen police academy: Short programs sponsored by municipal and county police agencies that allow citizens the opportunity to learn about the police, how they are trained, and what they do.

Civilianization: The hiring of nonsworn personnel to replace or supplement sworn police forces. This is usually done to reduce costs within police organizations and, in some cases, to improve service.

Civil service system: Originally adopted by government agencies to cut out corrupt political influence in the hiring, promotion, and firing of government workers, it determines employment based on professional merit through the use of competitive examinations.

Clearance rates: A method of measuring the effectiveness of police departments that is generally based on the percentage of crimes solved by arrest.

Collective bargaining: The process of negotiations between employers and union representatives with the goal of reaching an agreement on the working conditions of the union's members. Working conditions include wages and promotion, hours/assignments/shifts, employee training, health care and workplace safety, and grievance/disciplinary processes.

COMPSTAT (computer comparison statistics): A goal-oriented management process that uses computer technology, operational strategy, and managerial accountability to structure the way police agencies provide services related to crime control.

Community partnerships: Collaborative efforts between police and the public working to increase trust in the police and improve responsiveness to problems in the community.

Community policing: A policing philosophy that promotes organizational strategies, which supports the systematic use of partnerships and problem-solving techniques to proactively address the immediate conditions that give rise to public safety issues such as crime, social disorder, and fear of crime.

Community/problem-solving era: Beginning in the 1970s, an era of policing focusing on community-oriented and problem-oriented strategies to break down the separation from the public created during the reform era. Closer community involvement became a key focus, with a reinvigoration of foot patrol and other techniques to increase police–public interaction.

Consent decree: Enforceable legal agreements with police departments that are usually overseen by court-appointed monitors and federal judges. They identify problems unique to each police agency and also identify changes that need to be made within police agencies to remedy the problems.

Consolidation: A cost-saving approach in which two or more police agencies combine their resources; when two or more agencies merge to form a single agency; when a number of agencies within a region combine their resources to cover an entire geographic area instead of individual jurisdictions; or the contracting of services from nearby jurisdictions or regional agencies.

Contingency theory: A theory based on the premise that organizations are rational entities seeking to maximize their levels of effectiveness and efficiency and structured so as to be able to reach their goals.

Court-appointed monitor: Individual responsible for tracking the progress made by police agencies that are under consent decrees.

Crackdowns: A location-based patrol strategy in which police effort is focused on certain crimes in certain locations. It generally involves the use of a large number of officers working as a team for a short time to increase enforcement on a specific type of crime.

Crime mapping: Criminal incidents mapped geographically to assist in predicting where future crimes might occur. It can aid police agencies in determining the deployment of officers in an effort to use their resources more efficiently.

Culture of integrity: The presence of clearly understood and implemented policies and rules within a police agency.

CYA (cover your ass): Police officers "laying low" to avoid problems with their supervisors. The attitude encourages officers to avoid participating in activities that might bring unnecessary attention to them.

Cynicism: Police officers becoming distrustful of the public and question the motives of citizens. It is an attitude that develops with disillusionment toward what actual police work is like, frustrations with intrusive supervision, and frequent contact with the negative aspects of police work.

Decentralized: Commonly associated with community policing, police agencies using neighborhood substations and putting more officers back on the street to increase contact with citizens. Additionally, decision-making authority is pushed to lower levels of the organization, allowing officers more discretion in solving problems.

Department of Homeland Security: Created in 2003, one of two departments in the federal government housing federal-level law enforcement agencies. Its mission is to protect the United States from attacks by foreign nations.

Department of Justice: Established in 1870, one of two departments in the federal government housing federal-level law enforcement agencies. This includes the FBI, DEA, ATF, and Marshals Service.

Dial-a-cop system: The allocation of police services based on telephone calls placed by citizens. Some argue it has conditioned police officers to do their job in a reactive manner as opposed to a proactive manner.

Diffuse support: An evaluation of what an organization is or what it represents.

D-runs: A specialized type of patrol that involves regular uniformed patrol units being given directed assignments to perform during their uncommitted patrol time.

Elder abuse: Refers to an intentional or neglectful act by a caregiver leading to harm or potential harm to a vulnerable elder.

Environmental factors: Characteristics that influence officer discretion from sources found outside of police agencies.

Explorers program: A program that gives youths a hands-on look at the profession by allowing them to participate in activities with officers from local police agencies.

Field interrogations: A policing technique in which police officers question people they believe are suspicious or are likely to have been involved in criminal activities. The idea is that targeted individuals will be less likely to commit a crime if they know that the police are watching them or if the police make their presence known in the neighborhoods in which the targeted individuals reside.

Foot patrol: Police officers assigned an area to patrol on foot, a common tactic in both the political and community/problem-solving eras. It allows more face-to-face interaction with citizens, which could result in an improved relationship between police and citizens.

Fragmentation: Police services provided on the local level that may overlap each other. This potentially leads to communication problems and competition between agencies, leading to a waste of resources. It may also allow for the tailoring of police services to better meet the needs of each community.

Frankpledge system: A semi-structured system in England in which groups of men were responsible for enforcing the law.

FTO/PTO program (field training officer/police training officer): A stage of on-the-job training after completing the police academy in which new officers train with more experienced officers. The training typically lasts 3 months or more.

Generalized crime control strategies: Policing strategies or tactics applied to certain situations. Examples would be mandatory arrest policies and preventive patrol.

GLBT (gay, lesbian, bisexual, and transgender): Some police agencies employing GLBT units or liaison officers to act as conduits between the police and gay and lesbian communities.

GPS tracking darts: A small, sticky dart containing a GPS tracker shot from the grille of a patrol car onto a suspect's vehicle.

Gray Squad: A unit specifically designed to investigate and prevent crimes against the elderly.

Height/weight requirement: Part of the selection process used for hiring until the late 1970s. Under Title VII of the 1964 Civil Rights Act, the courts determined that this screening requirement was discriminatory, as it would disqualify a higher percentage of female applicants when compared to male applicants.

High-discretion stops: Those stops by police officers that involve minor infractions of the law. Examples include situations in which drivers take a wide turn, do not properly signal before making the turn, or somehow look suspicious to the police.

Homeland security era: A proposed new era of policing following the 9/11 terrorist attacks in which local agencies focus on cooperating more with federal law enforcement and intelligence agencies and paying more attention to what are perceived as terrorist targets. Driven by drastic increases in federal funding, some critics suggest it has lessened the focus on traditional policing activities.

Hydraulic effect: A shifting of discretionary power when one agency or one part of the criminal justice system increases its use of discretion, impacting the other two parts of the system.

ICE 287 (g) program: A program that allows federal officials to enter into written agreements with state and local law enforcement agencies to carry out the functions of immigration officers, including investigation, apprehension, and detention.

In-basket exercise: A common element in promotional processes, used to assess quick and effective decision-making.

In-service training: Periodic training provided to police officers on a wide range of subjects. Firearms, defensive tactics, and legal update training are common examples.

Intelligence-led policing: A strategy of policing in which police activities are led by criminal intelligence and data analysis. The goal is to more effectively address problems and reduce crime by managing resources in a more strategic manner.

Intentional tort: Involves intentional behavior resulting in someone getting hurt or some other type of damages. This type of tort does not mean the police officer intended to inflict injury or damages, only that the police officer intended to behave in a way that ultimately resulted in injuries or damages.

Internal affairs: Police personnel assigned to investigate citizen complaints and officer performance issues.

Kickbacks: Instances in which police officers accept gifts, money, goods, or services for referring people to specific businesses.

Law enforcement: The job of making sure people obey the law. It is just one of many responsibilities of the police.

Litigaphobia: A combination of the words *litigation* and *phobia* describing police officers that view the possibility of being sued as inevitable and unavoidable.

London Metropolitan Police: Recognized as the first modern police department. Led by the efforts of Sir Robert Peel, it was created on September 29, 1829.

Low-discretion stops: Those stops in which police officers have little discretion *not* to stop a vehicle or person. An example could include a police officer witnessing a car running through a red light at a dangerously high speed.

Mandatory arrest: A crime-control strategy requiring police officers to make an arrest in certain circumstances. It is commonly used in the enforcement of domestic violence laws.

Mapp v. Ohio (1961): A landmark Supreme Court decision that determined evidence obtained by the police in violation of the Fourth Amendment to the Constitution protecting against unreasonable search and seizure could not be used in court against a defendant.

Mediation: A form of alternative dispute resolution in which two parties resolve conflict through face-to-face dialogue with a trained mediator present.

Memorandum of agreement: A result of Department of Justice investigations, MOAs are more conciliatory than consent decrees, as they do not require any judicial monitoring like consent decrees often do. They are meant to identify and deal with problems in a police agency.

Minnesota Multiphasic Personality Inventory (MMPI): A psychological screening test that is often used to assess the psychological state of applicants. It screens for psychological issues including paranoia, schizophrenia, depression, and manic behaviors.

Miranda v. Arizona (1966): A landmark Supreme Court ruling that requires police officers to inform suspects who are being interrogated while in custody of their rights to counsel and against incriminating themselves in a crime.

Misdemeanor fix: Police officers quashing misdemeanor court proceedings or misdemeanor citations for money or some other type of material reward.

Motorized patrol: First used in Berkeley, California, in the early 1900s, when police officers began using cars and motorcycles to allow them to cover more ground within their communities and provide services more quickly and efficiently than they could by using foot patrol.

Municipal police: Responsible for controlling crime through law enforcement, maintaining social order within their communities, investigating crimes reported to them by citizens, controlling traffic within city limits, and, when needed, providing support in emergency/medical situations.

Negligence tort: Involves actions that are careless or unreasonable or, in some cases, choosing not to take action, which results in damages or injury.

Neighborhood culture: Includes the norms, behaviors, and qualities that are unique to a neighborhood.

Neighborhood watch: A program that teaches citizens how to identify and report suspicious activity to the police. The goal is crime prevention based on neighbors watching out for each other and monitoring activities in their neighborhoods in a collaborative effort with local law enforcement.

Newport News POP study: The first evaluation of problem-oriented policing looking to see if officers could effectively incorporate problem-solving techniques in their daily work. The study showed there appeared to be an impact on crime and disorder.

Officer characteristics: Includes police officer gender, race/ethnicity, education level, and years of experience.

Organizational factors: Characteristics found within police agencies that can influence officer behavior.

Organizational transformation: Police management, information systems, organizational structure, and police personnel coming together to support community partnerships and proactive problem-solving efforts.

Paramilitary style: An organizational style commonly followed by policing agencies that has characteristics similar to those of the military. In addition to wearing uniforms, titles like sergeant, lieutenant, and captain are commonly used, similar to titles in military organizations.

Pattern or practice: An act has occurred more than in just one isolated incident. This phrase suggests this act is more of an organizational practice and is used more often than it is not.

Perpetrator-oriented patrol: A policing approach involving the surveillance of certain people suspected of committing multiple crimes or that have committed crimes that resulted in high levels of either property loss or damage or significant injury to people.

Police: A body of persons making up a department, trained in methods of law enforcement and crime prevention and detection, and authorized to maintain the peace, safety, and order of the community.

Police corruption: Acts committed by police officers during the course of their work that result in some kind of personal gain or gain for others.

Police culture: The idea police are somehow different from the rest of society as a distinctive group who function according to a unique set of rules, practices, beliefs, and principles accepted by all members.

Police deviance: Refers to police involvement in activities or behaviors inconsistent with accepted norms, values, or ethics associated with the policing profession.

Police effectiveness: The ability of police departments to solve problems in their communities and satisfy the public. Measures may include arrest rates, crime rates, and response time to calls.

Police ethics: The rules of behavioral conduct expected of police officers.

Police misconduct: Acts committed by police officers that violate department policies and procedures.

Police–population ratio: The number of sworn police officers per 1,000 citizens in a particular jurisdiction.

Police unions/associations: An organization of police employees formed for the purpose of advancing its members' interests in respect to wages, benefits, and working conditions.

PoliceWOMEN: Female police officers that choose to take on roles that resemble traditional gender roles in order to get along with their male colleagues.

POLICEwomen: Female police officers that want to be treated like their male colleagues and hope to counter stereotypes that women are unable to perform the duties of a street patrol officer.

Political era: A time of policing in the United States during the 19th and early 20th centuries that was heavily entrenched in politics. Politicians maintained close control in police agencies, controlling the selection and promotion of personnel. Virtually no standards were used in hiring or training. Significant problems with police misconduct and corruption were common.

Problem-oriented policing: Requires officers to look for patterns among individual calls for service to identify underlying causes of the problem or behaviors, locations, victims, and offenders that the calls may have in common.

Problem solving: The process of proactive and systematic identification of problems, as well as finding solutions to identified problems in communities.

PWMI (people with mental illness): A group of people the police are having more frequent contact with as a result of these cases being processed through the criminal justice system instead of the mental health system.

Quality-of-life factors: Issues concerning residents relating to actual or perceived levels of crime and disorder in the neighborhood.

Rapid response time: The time it takes from when dispatch first receives a call for police service from a citizen until a patrol car shows up on scene. Reform-era police executives believed rapid response to citizens' calls would result in more arrests and citizens would see the police as more professional.

Reform era: A time of policing in the United States during the 1900s to 1970s, which occurred in response to the intrusive involvement of politics. Efforts were made in the to create standards for recruiting and hiring police. Training and technology were incorporated in an attempt to professionalize policing and promote the role of police officers as crime fighters.

Repeat offender program: A policing technique that focuses on the identification and apprehension of high-risk repeat offenders.

Residency requirement: A department or city policy creating restrictions on where officers can live. Some police agencies require their officers to live within the city limits of the communities they serve. Less restrictive residency requirements might allow employees to live no further than a certain number of miles away from police headquarters.

Rotten apple theory: Instances when one or two officers are responsible for acts of wrongdoing while the rest of the police officers in the organization are doing a good job.

Routine preventive patrol: Police officers driving their squad cars around their designated beat areas or districts with the purpose of making their presence known to citizens. This patrol strategy is based on the premise that police presence will deter criminals from committing crimes for fear that the police will catch them as they randomly patrol the streets.

Rural police: Police agencies covering areas with populations of less than 2,500 people. These agencies make up about 40% of local police agencies.

SARA (scanning, analysis, response, assessment) model: A four-stage problem-solving methodology used in problem-oriented policing.

Selective contact: When police officers have more frequent contact with the criminal element in society and less contact with law-abiding citizens, which can result in the police viewing all citizens in a negative way.

Selective perception: Based on the idea the police, like others in our society, are likely to remember unpleasant encounters with citizens more often than positive encounters.

Sheriff's department: Considered a part of local law enforcement with countywide jurisdictional boundaries. They are responsible for patrolling unincorporated or sparsely populated areas, as well as small towns that do not have their own municipal police agencies. They may also maintain and staff a county jail.

Sir Robert Peel: Often referred to as the father of modern policing. He played an integral role in the creation of the London Metropolitan Police.

Situational/contextual factors: A characteristic of a police–citizen encounter that is unique to each circumstance.

Slave patrols: The first publicly funded police agencies in the American South, created with the specific intent of maintaining control over slave populations.

Solidarity: A feeling of "us versus them" in which secrecy and unity are emphasized. Police officers are expected to be loyal to each other above the public and even the department administrators.

Specific support: An evaluation based on citizens' impressions of an organization's output or performance.

Split-force patrol: Policing approach requiring the patrol force to be split into two groups: One group of officers is responsible for responding to calls for service from the public while the other group forms a specialized crime-suppression unit. The purpose of having a separate crime-suppression unit is to catch criminals in the act of committing crimes.

Storefront offices: An alternative location to centralized police headquarters where citizens can report problems of crime and disorder, acquire information, or talk to police officers working in their neighborhoods. They are usually located within neighborhoods and business districts.

Strict liability tort: Involves behavior so dangerous the likelihood that injuries or damages could result is great. This type of tort is generally not applied to police officers, as many of the duties they are tasked with are inherently dangerous.

Symbolic assailant: A person the police believe is or could potentially be a source of danger to them.

Systems theory: A theory based on the premise that an organization is composed of several interrelated and interdependent parts combined to accomplish an overall goal.

Team policing: An alternative approach used in place of traditional policing by some police agencies in the late 1960s. It consisted of three elements: permanent assignment of officers to neighborhoods, maximum interaction and communication among the officers, and frequent communication with citizens.

***Tennessee v. Garner* (1985):** A Supreme Court decision that restricts police officer use of deadly force when pursuing fleeing suspects. Police officers may only use deadly force when they have probable cause to believe that a suspect poses a threat of death or serious physical injury to the officer or the public.

***Terry v. Ohio* (1968):** A Court decision that gives police officers more discretion, as they can stop and frisk suspects without probable cause to arrest if they have "reasonable suspicion" that someone has committed a crime, is in the process of committing a crime, or is going to commit a crime.

Testilying: A slang term used for police officers giving false testimony against defendants in criminal trials.

Third degree: Refers to when violence would be applied to alleged perpetrators in order to extract information from them or coerce confessions out of them.

Three-I (interpret, impact, influence) model: A model explaining how intelligence-led policing can be used in relation to crime reduction in policing.

Title VII (1964 Civil Rights Act): A court decision that determined height and weight requirements in police selection processes were discriminatory toward women and some racial/ethnic minorities. Also, the requirements are not an accurate way to assess whether someone can do the job.

Title 42 United States Code, Section 1983: A common provision of law used in liability cases involving the police. Some common types of claims include allegations regarding excessive force, false arrest, and unreasonable search of one's person, home, or vehicle.

Tokenism: A subgroup within an organization representing less than 15% of the overall organization that is in some way different from the rest of the group. Female police officers are sometimes viewed as token officers in a male-dominated organization.

Traditional policing: An approach whereby police officers focus heavily on responding to calls for service and solving crimes in a reactive manner with virtually no input or cooperation from citizens.

Tribal police: A policing agency providing service to citizens residing on American Indian reservations acknowledged by the United States federal government.

Tything: Men living in England within a community who formed groups of 10, in which members were responsible for capturing criminals and bringing them to court.

University campus police: Officers providing security and responding to a variety of calls for service within the boundaries of their campuses. In addition, they oversee events that take place on campus, enforce traffic laws, investigate crimes that take place on campus, and provide security to all campus buildings.

Vicarious contact: Indirect contact with the police that can be measured by what citizens see during interactions between the police and other people in their neighborhood, what they heard happened to other people when they interacted with the police, and hearing about incidents of police misconduct.

Violent Crime Control and Law Enforcement Act of 1994: Prohibits government agencies and agents from engaging in a "pattern or practice" of conduct by law enforcement officials that deprives persons of rights, privileges, or immunities protected by the United States Constitution.

Volunteers in Police Service (VIPS): A group of people who assist police agencies that are developing or that have existing volunteer programs.

Working personality: A concept described by Jerome Skolnick regarding the personality police officers develop to cope with stressors related to their work. It is shaped by elements of danger related to the job, being in a position of authority, and working efficiently.

Zero-tolerance policing: Requires police officers to strictly enforce laws and ordinances related to minor crimes and disorder. The theoretical expectation is that this aggressive enforcement will send a message to criminals that no crime will be tolerated, thus deterring the commission of future crimes.

Endnotes

 ## Section 1

1. E. Monkkonen, "History of Urban Police," *Crime and Justice* 15 (1992): 547–80.

2. C. Reith, *A New Study of Police History* (London: Oliver and Boyd, 1956).

3. M. Moore and G. Kelling, "To Serve and Protect—Learning From Police History," *Public Interest* 70 (Winter 1983): 49–65.

4. Ibid.

5. Ibid.

6. W. Morris, *The Frankpledge System* (New York: Longmans, Green and Co., 1910).

7. Ibid.

8. Ibid.

9. Ibid.

10. C. Uchida, "Development of the American Police: An Historical Overview," in *Critical Issues in Policing: Contemporary Readings*, ed. R. Dunham and G. Alpert, (Long Grove, IL: Waveland Press, 1989), 14–30.

11. Monkkonen, 1992.

12. Moore and Kelling, 1983; W. Miller, *Cops and Bobbies: Police Authority in New York and London, 1830–1870* (Chicago: University of Chicago Press, 1977).

13. J. Lyman, "The Metropolitan Police Act of 1829: An Analysis of Certain Events Influencing the Passage and Character of the Metropolitan Police Act in England," *Journal of Criminal Law, Criminology, and Police Science* 55 (Mar., 1964): 141–54.

14. T. Critchley, *A History of Police in England and Wales: 1900–1966* (London: Constable, 1978).

15. Critchley, 1978; Miller, 1977; Monkkonen, 1992; S. Walker, *Popular Justice—A History of American Criminal Justice* (New York: Oxford University Press, 1980).

16. Critchley, 1978; Miller, 1977.

17. Miller, 1977.

18. J. Wade, *A Treatise on the Police and Crimes of the Metropolis* (Montclair: Patterson Smith, 1972).

19. Lyman, 1964.

20. Ibid.

21. Miller, 1977.

22. Ibid.

23. Ibid.

24. S. Lentz and R. Chaires, "Invention of Peel's Principles: A Study of Policing Textbook History," *Journal of Criminal Justice* 35 (2007): 69–79.

25. Monkkonen, 1992.

26. Monkkonen, 1992; R. Fogelson, *Big-City Police* (Cambridge, MA: Harvard University Press, 1977).

27. Miller, 1977; P. Reichel, "The Misplaced Emphasis on Urbanization in Police Development," *Policing and Society* 3 (1992): 1–12.

28. Uchida, 1989.

29. P. Reichel, "Southern Slave Patrols as a Transitional Police Type," *American Journal of Police* 7 (1988): 51–77.

30. Reichel, 1988; K. Turner, D. Giacopassi, and M. Vandiver, "Ignoring the Past: Coverage of Slavery and Slave Patrols in Criminal Justice Texts," *Journal of Criminal Justice Education*, 17 (2006): 181–95.

31. Walker, 1980.

32. Turner, Giacopassi, and Vandiver, 2006; D. Barlow and M. Barlow, "Political Economy of Community Policing," *Policing: An International Journal of Police Strategies and Management* 22 (1999): 646–74; S. Hadden, *Slave Patrols: Law and Violence in Virginia and the Carolinas* (Cambridge, MA: Harvard University Press, 2001).

33. Hadden, 2001, 22.

34. Hadden, 2001.

35. Turner, Giacopassi, and Vandiver, 2006.

36. Hadden, 2001.

37. Ibid.

38. Barlow and Barlow, 1999, 648.

39. Barlow and Barlow, 1999.

40. Moore and Kelling, 1983.

41. See http://www.nyc.gov/html/nypd/html/home/home.shtml.

42. See http://www.slmpd.org/history.html.

43. See https://portal.chicagopolice.org/portal/page/portal/ClearPath/About%20CPD/History.

44. See http://www.lapdonline.org/history_of_the_lapd/content_basic_view/1107.

45. R. Hunter, "Three Models of Policing," *Police Studies* 13 (Fall 1990): 118–99 (see specifically 118–24).

46. D. Johnson, *American Law Enforcement—A History* (St. Louis, MO: Forum Press, 1981).

47. Miller, 1977.

48. Johnson, 1981; Monkkonen, 1992.

49. Fogelson, 1977.

50. G. Kelling and M. Moore, *Evolving Strategy of Policing* (Washington, DC: U.S. Department of Justice, 1988).

51. A. Vollmer, "Police Progress in the Past Twenty-Five Years," *Journal of Criminal Law and Criminology* 24 (May–Jun., 1933): 161–75.

52. Fogelson, 1997, 22.

53. Fogelson, 1997, 23.

54. Fogelson, 1997, 28.

55. Fogelson, 1997, 29.

56. M. Haller, "Historical Roots of Police Behavior: Chicago, 1890–1925," *Law and Society Review* 10 (Winter 1976): 306–7, 311, 316–17 (see 307).

57. R. Lane, "Urban Police and Crime in Nineteenth-Century America," in *Modern Policing*, ed. M. Tonry and N. Morris (Chicago, IL: University of Chicago Press, 1992), 1–50 (see 13).

58. Vollmer, 1933, 161.

59. Haller, 1976, 303.

60. Fogelson, 1997, 16.

61. Fogelson, 1997, 31.

62. Uchida, 1989, 1989.

63. Vollmer, 1933, 166.

64. Haller, 1976, 318.

65. Kelling and Moore, 1988.

66. Fogelson, 1977; Haller, 1976, 318.

67. Fogelson, 1977, 1–2.

68. Fogelson, 1977, 3–4.

69. Fogelson, 1977, 5.

70. Kelling and Moore, 1988.

71. Ibid.

72. Kelling and Moore, 1988.

73. Walker, 1980, 131.

74. National Commission on Law and Observance and Enforcement, *Wickersham Commission Report* (Washington DC: Government Printing Office, 1931).

75. Vollmer, 1933.

76. Walker, 1980, 172.

77. O. W. Wilson, *Police Administration* (New York: McGraw-Hill, 1950).

78. Walker, 172.

79. H. Hahn and J. Jeffries, *Urban America and Its Police. From the Postcolonial Era Through the Turbulent 1960s* (Boulder: University Press of Colorado, 2003).

80. Ibid.

81. S. Barkan, "Legal Control of the Southern Civil Rights Movement," *American Sociological Review* 49 (Aug., 1984): 552–65 (see 555).

82. Ibid.

83. R. Fogelson, "From Resentment to Confrontation: The Police, the Negroes, and the Outbreak of the Nineteen-Sixties Riots," *Political Science Quarterly* 83 (Jun. 1968): 217–47; H. Haun and J. Feagin, "Riot-Precipitating Police Practices: Attitudes in Urban Ghettos," *Phylon* 31 (2nd Qtr. 1970): 183–93; S. Lieberson and A. Silverman, "The Precipitants and Underlying Conditions of Race Riots," *American Sociological Review* 30 (Dec. 1965): 887–98.

84. National Advisory Commission on Civil Disorders, *Report of the National Advisory Commission on Civil Disorders* (Washington: Government Printing Office, 1968), 93.

85. J. Robinson, "Public Reaction to Political Protest: Chicago, 1968," *Public Opinion Quarterly* 34 (1970): 1–9.

86. M. Sparrow, *Implementing Community Policing* (Monograph). (Washington, DC: National Institute of Justice, 1988).

87. Ibid.

88. R. Adams, W. Rohe, and T. Arcury, "Implementing Community-Oriented Policing: Organizational Change and Street Officer Attitudes," *Crime & Delinquency* 48 (2002): 399–430 (see 401).

✉ Section 2

1. President's Commission on Law Enforcement and the Administration of Justice, *Task Force Report: The Police* (Washington, DC: Government Printing Office, 1967).

2. W. Gay, J. Woodward, H. Day, J. O'Nell, and C. Tucker, *Issues in Team Policing: A Review of the Literature* (Washington. DC: Government Printing Office, 1977).

3. L. Sherman, C. Milton, and T. Kelly, *Team Policing—Seven Case Studies* (Washington, DC: Police Foundation, 1973).

4. Ibid.

5. Gay, Woodward, O'Nell, and Tucker, 1977.

6. S. Walker, *Taming the System: The Control of Discretion in Criminal Justice, 1950–1990* (New York: Oxford University Press, 1993).

7. Sherman, Milton, and Kelly, 1973.

8. P. Greenwood and J. Petersilia, *The Criminal Investigative Process Volume 1: Summary and Policy Implications* (Santa Monica: Rand Corporation, 1975).

9. W. Bieck and D. Kessler, *Response Time Analysis* (Kansas City, MO: Board of Police Commissioners, 1977).

10. G. Kelling, T. Pate, D. Dieckman, and C. Brown, *The Kansas City Preventive Patrol Experiment: A Technical Report* (Washington, DC: The Police Foundation, 1974).

11. M. Scott, *Problem-Oriented Policing: Reflections on the First 20 Years* (Washington, DC: COPS Office, 2000).

12. See www.popcenter.org.

13. J. Eck and W. Spelman, *Problem-Solving: Problem-Oriented Policing in Newport News* (Rockville, MD: Police Executive Research Forum, 1987).

14. See www.popcenter.org.

15. L. Cohen and M. Felson, "Social Change and Crime Rate Trends: A Routine Activity Approach," *American Sociological Review* 44 (August) (1979): 588–608.

16. See www.popcenter.org.

17. Eck and Spelman, 1987.

18. National Academy of Sciences, *Fairness and Effectiveness in Policing: The Evidence* (Washington, DC: National Academy Press, 2004), 245.

19. Scott, 2000, 2.

20. H. Goldstein, "On Further Developing Problem-Oriented Policing: The Most Critical Need, the Major Impediments, and a Proposal," *Crime Prevention Studies* 15 (2003): 13–47.

21. A. Pate, M. Wycoff, and L. Sherman, *Reducing Fear of Crime in Houston and Newark—A Summary Report* (Washington DC: Police Foundation, 1986).

22. Police Foundation, *The Newark Foot Patrol Experiment* (Washington, DC: Author, 1981).

23. Ibid.

24. Ibid.

25. W. Skogan, *Disorder and Decline* (Berkeley: University of California Press, 1990).

26. J. Wilson and G. Kelling, "The Police and Neighborhood Safety: Broken Windows," *Atlantic Monthly* 127 (1982): 29–38.

27. Ibid.

28. Skogan, 1990; Y. Xu, M. Fielder, and K. Flaming, "Discovering the Impact of Community Policing: The Broken Windows Thesis, Collective Efficacy, and Citizens' Judgment," *Journal of Research in Crime and Delinquency* 42 (2005): 147–86.

29. B. Brown, D. Perkins, and G. Brown, "Incivilities, Place Attachment and Crime: Block and Individual Effects," *Journal of Environmental Psychology*, 24 (2004): 359–71; E. Kurtz, B. Koons, and R. Taylor, "Land Use, Physical Deterioration, Resident-Based Control and Calls for Service on Urban Streetblocks," *Justice Quarterly* 15 (1998): 121–49; R. Sampson and S. Raudenbush, "Systematic Social Observations of Public Spaces: A New Look at Disorder in Urban Neighborhoods," *American Journal of Sociology* 105 (1999): 603–51; P. Wilcox, N. Quisenberry, D. Cabrera, and S. Jones, "Busy Places and Broken Windows? Toward Defining the Role of Physical Structure and Process in Community Crime Models," *Sociological Quarterly* 45 (2004): 185–207.

30. S. Walker, *A Critical History of Police Reform: The Emergence of Professionalism* (Lexington, MA: Lexington Books, 1977).

31. Ibid.

32. J. Boydstun and M. Sherry, *San Diego Community Profile: Final Report* (Washington, DC: Police Foundation, 1975), 83.

33. W. Skogan, *Community Policing: Can it Work?* (Belmont, CA: Wadsworth Publishing Co, 2004).

34. Ibid.

35. See www.cops.usdoj.gov.

36. W. Skogan and S. Hartnett, *Community Policing, Chicago Style* (New York: Oxford University Press, 1997).

37. See www.cops.usdoj.gov.

38. J. Greene, "Community Policing in America: Changing the Nature, Structure, and Function of the Police," in *Criminal Justice 2000: Policies, Processes, and Decisions of the Criminal Justice System,* ed. J. Horney (Washington, DC: National Institute of Justice, 2000), 299–370.

39. Ibid.

40. See www.cops.usdoj.gov.

41. M. Hickman and B. Reaves, *Local Police Departments, 2007* (Washington, DC: Bureau of Justice Statistics, 2010).

42. Ibid.

43. Ibid.

44. See www.cops.usdoj.gov.

45. Ibid.

46. National Research Council, 2004.

47. Ibid.

48. Ibid.

49. Ibid.

50. Wilson and Kelling, 1982.

51. J. Greene, "Zero Tolerance: A Case Study of Police Policies and Practices in New York City," *Crime and Delinquency*, 45 (1999): 171–87.

52. Greene, 2000.

53. Greene, 2000.

54. Greene, 2000.

55. National Research Council, 2004.

56. G. Kelling and W. Sousa, Jr., *Do Police Matter? An Analysis of the Impact of New York City's Police Reforms* (Manhattan Institute Civic Report, December 2001). Available at http://www.manhattan-institute .org/pdf/cr_22.pdf.

57. A. Blumstein. "Disaggregating Violence Trends," in *The Crime Drop in America,* ed. A. Blumstein and Joel Wallman (New York: Cambridge University Press, 2000). See also J. Fagan and G. Davies, "Street Stops and Broken Windows: Terry, Race, and Disorder in New York City," *Fordham Urban Law Journal* 28 (2001): 457–504.

58. J. Eck and E. Maguire, "Have Changes in Policing Reduced Violent Crime? An Assessment of the Evidence," in *The Crime Drop in America,* ed. Alfred Blumstein and Joel Wallman (New York: Cambridge University Press, 2000).

59. Greene, 1999.

60. Greene, 2000.

61. L. Sherman, D. Gottfredson, D. MacKenzie, J. Eck, P. Reuter, and S. Bushway, *Policing for Crime Prevention, Preventing Crime: What Works, What Doesn't, What's Promising* (Washington, DC: U.S. Department of Justice, 1997).

62. Peter Manning, "Theorizing Policing: The Drama and Myth of Crime Control in the NYPD," *Theoretical Criminology* 5 (2001): 315–44.

63. Greene, 1999.

64. J. Ratcliffe, *Intelligence-Led Policing* (Canberra, Australia: Australian Institute of Criminology Trends and Issues in Crime and Criminal Justice, 2003).

65. J. Ratcliffe, *Intelligence-Led Policing* (Portland, OR: Willan Publishing, 2008).

66. Ratcliffe, 2008, 89.

67. Ratcliffe, 2003, 3.

68. Ratcliffe, 2003, 3.

69. Ibid.

70. M. Peterson, *The Basics of Intelligence Revisited in Turnkey Intelligence: Unlocking Your Agency's Intelligence Capability* (Richmond, VA: International Association of Law Enforcement Intelligence Analysts, Law Enforcement Intelligence Unit, and National White Collar Crime Center, 2002).

71. M. Peterson, *Intelligence-Led Policing: The New Intelligence Architecture* (Washington, DC: Bureau of Justice Assistance, 2005).

72. Ibid.

73. Ibid.

74. Ratcliffe, 2008.

75. Ibid.

76. Peterson, 2005.

77. Ibid.

⊠ Section 3

1. See http://www.macmillandictionary.com/dictionary/ american/law-enforcement.

2. See http://www.thefreedictionary.com/police.

3. G. Cordner and E. Perkins Biebel, "Problem Oriented Policing in Practice," *Criminology and Public Policy* 4, 2 (2005): 155–80.

4. B. Reaves, *Census of State and Local Law Enforcement Agencies, 2008* (Washington, DC: Bureau of Justice Statistics, 2011); B. Reaves, *Federal Law Enforcement Officers, 2004* (Washington, DC: Bureau of Justice Statistics, 2006).

5. T. Kyckelhahn, *Justice Expenditures and Employment, FY 1982–2007—Statistical Tables* (Washington, DC: Bureau of Justice Statistics, 2011).

6. Ibid.

7. Ibid.

8. See http://usgovinfo.about.com/od/rightsandfreedoms/a/ whatisfederalism.htm.

9. See http://bjs.ojp.usdoj.gov/index.cfm?ty=tp&tid=71.

10. Ibid.

11. See http://www.wilco.org/CountyDepartments/ Constables/tabid/217/Default.aspx.

12. Reaves, 2011.

13. Ibid.

14. Ibid.

15. Reaves, 2008.

16. Ibid.

17. Ibid.

18. Ibid.

19. Ibid.

20. Ibid.

21. Ibid.

22. H. O'Rourke, "State Police," in *Encyclopedia of Law Enforcement Volume 1* (Thousand Oaks, CA: Sage, 2005), 439–40.

23. Ibid.

24. Reaves, 2008.

25. Ibid.

26. Ibid.

27. D. Torres, *Handbook of State Police, Highway Patrols, and Investigative Agencies* (Westport, CT: Greenwood Publishing Group, 1987).

28. B. Reaves, *Census of State and Local Law Enforcement Agencies, 2004* (Washington, DC: Bureau of Justice Statistics, 2007).

29. J. Powell, *Campus Security and Law Enforcement* (Woburn, MA: Buttersworth, 1981).

30. D. Hummer, "Campus Policing," in *Encyclopedia of Law Enforcement volume 1* (Thousand Oaks, CA: Sage, 2005), 40–42.

31. See http://bjs.ojp.usdoj.gov/index.cfm?ty=tp&tid=76. See also K. Peak, E. Barthe, and A. Garcia, "Campus Policing in America: A Twenty-Year Perspective," *Police Quarterly*, 11 (2008): 239–60.

32. B. Reaves, *Campus Law Enforcement, 2004–05* (Washington, DC: Bureau of Justice Statistics, 2008).

33. M. Bromley and B. Reaves, "Comparing Campus and City Police Operational Practices," *Journal of Security Administration*, 21 (1998): 41–54.

34. E. Paoline III and J. Sloan, "Variability in the Organizational Structure of Contemporary Campus Law Enforcement Agencies: A National Analysis," *Policing: An International Journal of Police Strategies and Management,* 26 (2003): 612–39.

35. M. Lanier and D. Beer, "Policing the Contemporary University Campus: Challenging Traditional Organizational Models," *Journal of Security Administration*, 23 (2000): 1–20.

36. See http://bjs.ojp.usdoj.gov/index.cfm?ty=tp&tid=76.

37. Reaves, 2008.

38. Ibid.

39. Reaves, 2008.

40. Ibid.

41. Reaves, 2008.

42. S. Eliason, "Throwing the Book Versus Cutting Some Slack: Factors Influencing the Use of Discretion by Game Wardens in Kentucky," *Deviant Behavior* 24 (2003): 129–52.

43. R. Patten, "Policing in the Wild: The Game Wardens' Perspective," *Policing: An International Journal of Police Strategies and Management* 33 (2010): 132–51.

44. T. Carter, "Police Use of Discretion: A Participant Observation of Game Wardens," *Deviant Behavior* 27 (2006): 591–627.

45. E. Luna, "The Growth and Development of Tribal Police: Challenges and Issues for Tribal Sovereignty," *Journal of Contemporary Criminal Justice* 14 (1998): 75–86.

46. See http://bjs.ojp.usdoj.gov/index.cfm?ty=tp&tid=75.

47. S. Wakeling, S. Jorgenson, S. Michaleson, and M. Begay, *Policing on American Indian Reservations* (Washington, DC: U.S. Department of Justice, 2001).

48. Luna, 1998.

49. Ibid.

50. Ibid.

51. See http://bjs.ojp.usdoj.gov/index.cfm?ty=tp&tid=75.

52. Ibid.

53. Ibid.

54. Luna, 1998.

55. M. Hickman, *Tribal Law Enforcement, 2000* (Washington DC: Bureau of Justice Statistics, 2003).

56. See http://www.justice.gov/jmd/mps/manual/overview .htm.

57. Ibid.

58. See www.fbi.gov/about-us/history/brief-history.

59. See www.fbi.gov/about-us.

60. Ibid.

61. See www.justice.gov/dea/history.htm.

62. Ibid.

63. See www.atf.gov/about/history.

64. Ibid.

65. Ibid.

66. See http://www.justice.gov/marshals/.

67. Ibid.

68. Ibid.

69. See http://www.dhs.gov/xabout/history/gc_129796390 6741.shtm.

70. Ibid.

71. See www.cbp.gov/xp/cgov/about.

72. Ibid.

73. See http://www.cbp.gov/xp/cgov/about/.

74. Ibid.

75. Ibid.

76. See www.ice.gov/about/overview.

77. Ibid.

78. Ibid.

79. See http://www.ice.gov/doclib/news/library/factsheets/ pdf/day-in-life-ero.pdf.

80. See www.ice.gov/about/overview.

81. See http://www.fema.gov/about/history.shtm.

82. Ibid.

83. See http://www.tsa.gov/who_we_are/what_is_tsa .shtm.

84. Ibid.

85. Ibid.

86. See http://www.uscg.mil/history/.

87. Ibid.

88. Ibid.

89. See http://www.secretservice.gov/history.shtml.

90. Ibid.

91. Ibid.

92. Ibid.

93. See http://www.uscis.gov/portal/site/uscis/menuitem .eb1d4c2a3e5b9ac89243c6a7543f6d1a/?vgnextoid=e00c0b89284a 3210VgnVCM100000b92ca60aRCRD&vgnextchannel=e00c0b892 84a3210VgnVCM100000b92ca60aRCRD

94. Ibid.

95. Ibid.

96. Ibid.

97. See http://www.uscitizenship.info/us-citizenship-and-immigration-services-uscis.html.

98. Rick Ruddell, Matthew Thomas, and Ryan Pattern, "Examining the Roles of the Police and Private Security Officers in Urban Social Control," *International Journal of Police Science & Management* 13 (2011): 54–69.

99. ASIS International, *International Glossary of Security Terms.* See http://www.asisonline.org/library/glossary/index.xml.

100. K. Strom, M. Berzofsky, B. Shook-Sa, K. Barrick, C. Daye, N. Horstmann, and Susan Kinsey, *The Private Security Industry: A Review of the Definitions, Available Data Sources, and Paths Moving Forward* (Research Triangle Park, NC: RTI International, 2010).

101. J. Manzo, "Security Officers' Perceptions on Training," *Canadian Journal of Criminology and Criminal Justice* 51 (2009): 381–410.

102. C. Shearingand P. Stenning, "Modern Private Security: Its Growth and Implications," in *Crime and Justice: An Annual Review of Research, Volume III,* ed. M. Tonry N. Morris (Chicago: University of Chicago Press, 1981), 193–245.

103. A. Youngs, "The Future of Public/Private Partnerships," *FBI Law Enforcement Bulletin,* 73 (2004): 7–11.

104. Ibid.

105. A. Morabito and S. Greenberg, *Engaging the Private Sector to Promote Homeland Security: Law Enforcement–Private Security Partnerships* (Washington, DC: U.S. Department of Justice, 2005). See http://www.ncjrs.gov/pdffiles1/bja/210678.pdf.

106. Reaves, 2010.

107. See http://www.census.gov/population/censusdata/urdef .txt.

108. Reaves, 2010.

109. D. Falcone, E. Wells, and R. Weisheit, "The Small-Town Police Department," *Policing: An International Journal of Police Strategies and Management,* 25 (2002): 371–84.

110. Ibid.

111. Ibid.

112. Ibid.

113. Ibid., 375.

114. Ibid., 376–77.

115. Ibid., 377.

116. R. Weisheit, D. Falcone, and E. Wells, *Crime and Policing in Rural and Small Town America, 3rd ed.* (Long Grove, IL: Waveland Press, 2006), 123.

117. Ibid., 123.

118. Reaves, 2010.

119. Reaves, 2008.

120. R. Hunter, "Three Models of Policing," *Police Studies,* 13 (1990): 118–24; see 119.

121. P. Murphy and T. Plate, *Commissioner: A View from the Top of American Law Enforcement* (New York: Simon and Schuster, 1977), 71–72.

122. E. Ostrom, R. Parks, and G. Whitaker, "Do We Really Want to Consolidate Urban Police Forces? A Reappraisal of Some Old Assertions," *Public Administration Review* 33 (1973): 423–32.

123. Ibid.

124. J. Krimmel, "The Northern York County Police Consolidation Experience: An Analysis of the Consolidation of Police Services in Eight Pennsylvania Rural Communities," *Policing: An International Journal of Police Strategies and Management* 20 (1997): 497–507.

⊠ Section 4

1. B. Reaves, *Local Police Departments, 2007* (Washington, DC: Bureau of Justice Statistics, 2010); B. Reaves, *Federal Law Enforcement Officers, 2004* (Washington, DC: Bureau of Justice Statistics, 2006).

2. B. Reaves, *Census of State and Local Law Enforcement Agencies, 2004* (Washington, DC: Bureau of Justice Statistics, 2007).

3. See http://www.bls.gov/oco/ocos160.htm#projections_ data.

4. See http://dictionary.reference.com/browse/culture.

5. E. Bittner, *The Functions of Police in Modern Society* (Washington DC: National Institute of Mental Health, 1970).

6. E. Paoline III, "Taking Stock: Toward a Richer Understanding of Police Culture," *Journal of Criminal Justice* 31 (2003): 199–214.

7. W. Westley, *Violence and the Police: A Sociological Study of Law, Custom, and Morality* (Cambridge, MA: MIT Press, 1972).

8. J. Skolnick, *Justice without Trial* (New York: John Wiley & Sons, 1975).

9. J. Skolnick, "A Sketch of the Policemen's Working Personality," in *Justice without Trial: Law Enforcement in Democratic Society,* 3rd ed., Jerome Skolnick (New York: Wiley, 1994), 41–68.

10. Paoline III, 2003.

11. M. Brown, *Working the Streets: Police Discretion and the Dilemmas of Reform* (New York: Russell Sage Foundation, 1988).

12. E. Reuss-Ianni, *Two Cultures of Policing: Street Cops and Management Cops* (New Brunswick, NJ: Transaction Publishers, 1993).

13. Ibid.

14. Penny Dick and Devi Jankowicz, "A Social Constructionist Account of Police Culture and its Influence on the Representation

and Progression of Female Officers," *Policing: An International Journal of Police Strategies & Management* 24, 2 (2001): 181–99.

15. D. Schulz, "From Policewoman to Police Officer: An Unfinished Revolution," *Police Studies* 16, (1993): 90–98.

16. See http://www.portlandpolicemuseum.com.

17. See http://www.lapdonline.org/history_of_the_lapd/content_basic_view/833.

18. Schulz, 1993.

19. D. Schulz, "Police Women in the 1950s: Paving the Way for Patrol," *Women and Criminal Justice* 4 (1993): 5–30.

20. D. Schulz, *From Social Worker to Crime Fighter: Women in United States Municipal Policing* (Westport, CT: Praeger, 1995).

21. B. Reaves, *Federal Law Enforcement Officers, 2004* (Washington, DC: Bureau of Justice Statistics, 2006); B. Reaves, *Campus Law Enforcement, 2004–05* (Washington, DC: Bureau of Justice Statistics, 2008); Bureau of Justice Statistics, *Law Enforcement Management and Administrative Statistics, 2000: Data for Individual State and Local Agencies with 100 or More Officers* (Washington, DC: U.S. Department of Justice, 2004); B. Reaves, *Local Police Departments, 2003* (Washington, DC: Bureau of Justice Statistics, 2006); M. Hickman and B. Reaves, *Sheriff's Offices, 2003* (Washington, DC: Bureau of Justice Statistics, 2006).

22. National Center for Women and Policing, *Hiring & Retaining More Women: The Advantages to Law Enforcement Agencies* (Beverly Hills, CA: National Center for Women and Policing, 2003).

23. S. Martin, "Outsider within the Station House: Impact of Race and Gender on Black Women Police," *Social Problems* 41 (1994): 383–400. See also T. Sass and J. Troyer, "Affirmative Action, Political Representation, Unions and Female Police Employment," *Journal of Labor Research* 4 (1999): 572–90; R. Warner and B. Steel, "Affirmative Action in Times of Fiscal Stress and Changing Value Priories: The Case of Women in Policing," *Public Personnel Management* 18 (1989): 291–338; J. Zhao, L. Herbst, and N. Lovrich, "Race, Ethnicity, and the Female Cop: Differential Patterns of Representation," *Journal of Urban Affairs* 23 (2001): 243–57.

24. Ibid.

25. G. Cordner and A. Cordner, "Stuck on a Plateau? Obstacles to Recruitment, Selection and Retention of Women Police," *Police Quarterly* 14 (2011): 207–26.

26. Ibid.

27. L. Langton, *Women in Law Enforcement, 1987–2008* (Washington, DC: Bureau of Justice Statistics, 2010).

28. National Center for Women and Policing, *Equality Denied: The Status of Women in Policing: 2001* (Los Angeles: National Center for Women and Policing, 2002).

29. D. Schulz, *Breaking the Brass Ceiling: Women Police Chiefs and Their Paths to the Top* (Westport, CT: Praeger, 2004).

30. D. Schulz, "Women Special Agents in Charge: The First Generation," *Policing: An International Journal of Police Strategies and Management* 32 (2009): 675–93.

31. R. Kanter, *Men and Women of the Corporation* (New York: Basic Books, 1977).

32. Ibid.

33. C. Archbold and D. Schulz, "Making Rank: The Lingering Effects of Tokenism on Female Police Officers' Promotion Aspirations," *Police Quarterly* 11 (2008): 50–73; J. Belknap and J. Shelley, "The New Lone Ranger: Policewomen on Patrol," *American Journal of Police* 12 (1992): 47–75; J. Gustafson, "Tokenism in Policing: An Empirical Test of Kanter's Hypothesis," *Journal of Criminal Justice* 36 (2008): 1–10; J. Krimmel and P. Gormley, "Tokenism and Job Satisfaction for Policewomen," *American Journal of Criminal Justice* 28 (2003): 73–88; A. Stichman, K. Hassell, and C. Archbold, "Strength in Numbers? A Test of Kanter's Theory of Tokenism," *Journal of Criminal Justice* 38 (2010): 633–39; T. Wertsch, "Walking the Thin, Blue Line: Policewomen and Tokenism Today," *Women and Criminal Justice* 9 (1998): 23–61.

34. C. Rabe-Hemp, "Survival in an 'All Boys Club': Policewomen and Their Fight for Acceptance," *Policing: An International Journal of Police Strategies and Management* 31 (2008): 251–70.

35. P. Bloch and D. Anderson, *Policewomen on Patrol: Final Report* (Washington, DC: Police Foundation, 1974); J. Balkin, "Why Policemen Don't Like Policewomen," *Journal of Police Science and Administration* 16 (1988): 29–36. P. Harrington, "Advice to Women Beginning a Career in Policing," *Women & Criminal Justice* 14, 1 (2002): 1–13.

36. E. Koenig, "An Overview of Attitudes toward Women in Law Enforcement," *Public Administration Review* 38 (1978): 267–75; M. Vega and I. Silverman, "Female Police Officers as Viewed by Their Male Counterparts," *Police Studies* 5 (1982): 31–39.

37. S. Kakar, "Gender and Police Officers' Perceptions of Their Job Performance: An Analysis of the Relationship between Gender and Perceptions of Job Performance," *Criminal Justice Policy Review* 13 (2002): 238–56.

38. R. Haarr, "Patterns of Interaction in a Police Patrol Bureau: Race and Gender Barriers to Integration," *Justice Quarterly* 14 (1997): 53–85; S. Martin, "Outsider within the Station House: Impact of Race and Gender on Black Women Police," *Social Problems* 41 (1994): 383–400.

39. M. Dodge and M. Pogrebin, "African-American Policewomen: An Exploration of Professional Relationships," *Policing: An International Journal of Police Strategies and Management* 24 (2001): 550–62; Haarr, 1997, 53–85; S. Martin, 1994, 383–400.

40. Susan E. Martin, "POLICEwomen and policeWOMEN: Occupational Role Dilemmas and Choices of Female Officers," *Journal of Police Science and Administration* 7, 3: 314–23.

41. P. Remmington, "Women in the Police: Integration or Separation," *Qualitative Sociology* 6 (1983): 118–35.

42. K. Hassell, C. Archbold, and D. Schulz, *Women and Policing in America: Classic and Contemporary Readings* (Frederick, MD: Aspen Publishing, 2011).

43. Ibid.

44. D. Lester, "Why Do People Become Police Officers: A Study of Reasons and Their Predictions of Success," *Journal of Police Science and Administration* 11 (1983): 170–74; E. Poole and M. Pogrebin, "Factors Affecting the Decision to Remain in Policing: A Study of Women Officers," *Journal of Police Science and Administration* 16 (1988): 49–55; S. Meagher and N. Yentes, "Choosing a Career in Policing: A Comparison of Male and Female Perceptions," *Journal of Police Science and Administration* 14 (1986): 320–27.

45. Ibid.

46. C. Archbold and K. Hassell, "Paying a Marriage Tax: An Examination of the Barriers to the Promotion of Female Police Officers," *Policing: An International Journal of Police Strategies and Management* 32 (2009): 56–74.

47. T. Whetstone, "Copping Out: Why Police Officers Decline to Participate in the Sergeant's Promotion Process," *American Journal of Criminal Justice* 25 (2001): 147–59; T. Whetstone and D. Wilson, "Dilemmas Confronting Female Police Officer Promotional Candidates: Glass Ceiling, Disenfranchisement or Satisfaction?" *International Journal of Police Science and Management* 2 (1999): 128–43.

48. Bloch and Anderson, 1974.

49. J. Eterno, "Gender and Policing: Do Women Accept Legal Restrictions More Than Their Male Counterparts?" *Women & Criminal Justice* 18 (2006): 49–78; P. Hoffman and E. Hickey, "Use of Force by Female Police Officers," *Journal of Criminal Justice* 33 (2005): 145–51.

50. D. Bell, "Policewomen: Myths and Realities," *Journal of Police Science and Administration* 10 (1982): 112–20; S. Grennan, "Findings on the Role of Officer Gender in Violent Encounters with Citizens," *Journal of Police Science and Administration* 15 (1987): 78–85.

51. C. Rabe-Hemp, "Female Officers and the Ethic of Care: Does Officer Gender Impact Police Behaviors?" *Journal of Criminal Justice* 36 (2008): 426–34.

52. K. Lersch, "Exploring Gender Differences in Citizen Allegations of Misconduct: An Analysis of a Municipal Police Department," *Women & Criminal Justice* 9 (1998): 69–79.

53. A. Robinson and M. Chandek, "Philosophy into Practice? Community Policing Units and Domestic Violence Victim Participation," *Policing: An International Journal of Police Strategies and Management* 28 (2000): 280–302; J. Snortum and J. Byers, "Patrol Activities of Male and Female Officers as a Function of Work Experience," *Police Studies* 6 (1983): 36–42.

54. J. Kuykendall and D. Burns, "The Black Police Officer: An Historical Perspective," *Journal of Contemporary Criminal Justice* 1, (1980): 4–12.

55. W. Dulaney, *Black Police in America* (Bloomington: Indiana University Press, 1996), preface.

56. Kuykendall and Burns, 1980.

57. B. Reaves, *Local Police Departments, 2007* (Washington, DC: Bureau of Justice Statistics, 2010).

58. A. Thompson, *Career Experiences of African American Police Executives: Black in Blue Revisited* (New York: LFB Scholarly Publishing, 2003).

59. K. Osbourn, "Leading the Top Cops," *Black Enterprise* (December, 1990), 18.

60. See http://www.policeforum.org/library/police-management/Police%20Executive%20Research%20Forum.pdf.

61. K. Bolton and J. Feagin, *Black in Blue: African American Police Officers and Racism* (New York: Routledge Publishing, 2004).

62. L. Herbst and S. Walker, "Language Barriers in the Delivery of Police Services: A Study of Police and Hispanic Interactions in a Midwestern City," *Journal of Criminal Justice* 29 (2001): 329–40.

63. See www.policechiefmagazine.org/magazine/index.cfm?fuseaction=display_arch&article_id=1612&issue_id=92008.

64. See http://www.justice.gov/marshals/monitor/215-0402.pdf.

65. See http://www.census.gov/population/www/socdemo/hispanic/files/Internet_Hispanic_in_US_2006.pdf.

66. Reaves, 2010 .

67. C. Perez McCluskey and J. McCluskey, "Diversity in Policing: Latino Representation in Law Enforcement," *Journal of Ethnicity in Criminal Justice* 2 (2004): 67–81.

68. See http://www.policeforum.org/library/police-management/Police%20Executive%20Research%20Forum.pdf.

69. D. Carter, "Hispanic Police Officers' Perceptions of Discrimination," *Police Studies* 9 (1986): 204–10.

70. Ibid.

71. J. Schroedel, S. Frisch, R. August, C. Kalogris, and A. Perkins, "The Invisible Minority: Asian-American Police Officers," *State and Local Government Review* 26 (1994): pp. 173–80.

72. See http://www.equalrights.org/publications/reports/aabook/fred.asp.

73. See http://www.asianweek.com/2009/08/10/chinese-american-heroine-heather-fong/.

74. Ibid.

75. Reaves, 2010.

76. See http://query.nytimes.com/gst/fullpage.html?res=9D03E1DD113FF932A35756C0A9609C8B63.

77. Ibid.

78. See http://teaandjustice.com/about/synopsis.html.

79. Ibid.

80. R. Colvin, "Shared Perceptions among Lesbian and Gay Police Officers: Barriers and Opportunities in the Law Enforcement Work Environment," *Police Quarterly* 12 (2009): 86–101.

81. E. Meers, "Good Cop Gay Cop: From the Beat Patrol to the Precinct House, Gay and Lesbian Police Officers Are Shattering the Blue Wall of Silence," *The Advocate* (March 3, 1998), cover story.

82. J. Messerschmidt, *Masculinities and Crime: Critique and Reconceptualization of Theory* (Lantham, MD: Rowan & Littlefield, 1993).

83. M. Bernstein and C. Kostelac, "Lavender and Blue: Attitudes about Homosexuality and Behavior toward Lesbians and Gay Men among Police Officers," *Journal of Contemporary Criminal Justice* 18 (2002): 302–28.

84. P. Lyons, C. Anthony, K. Davis, K. Fernandez, A. Torres, and D. Marcus, "Police Judgments of Culpability and Homophobia," *Applied Psychology in Criminal Justice* 1 (2005): 1–14.

85. S. Miller, K. Forest, and N. Jurik, "Diversity in Blue: Lesbian and Gay Police Officers in a Masculine Occupation," *Men and Masculinities* 5 (2003): 355–85.

86. Ibid.

87. Ibid.

88. K. Myers, K. Forest, and S. Miller, "Officer Friendly and the Tough Cop: Gays and Lesbians Navigate Homophobia and Policing," *Journal of Homosexuality* 47 (2004): 17–37.

89. Ibid.

90. Colvin, 2009.

91. Ibid.

92. Ibid.

93. Ibid.

94. A. Belkin and J. McNichol, "Pink and Blue: Outcomes Associated with the Integration of Open Gay and Lesbian Personnel in the San Diego Police Department," *Police Quarterly* 5 (2002): 63–95.

95. Miller, Forest, and Jurik, 2003.

96. D. Sklansky, "Not Your Father's Police Department: Making Sense of the New Demographics of Law Enforcement," *Journal of Criminal Law & Criminology*, 96 (2006): 1209–44.

97. Dulaney, 1996.

98. Sklansky, 2006.

99. Ibid.

100. Ibid.

101. Ibid.

102. R. Haarr, "Patterns of Interaction in a Police Patrol Bureau: Race and Gender Barriers to Integration," *Justice Quarterly* 14 (1997): 53–85.

✉ **Section 5**

1. P. Foley, C. Guarneri, and M. Kelly, "Reasons for Choosing a Police Career: Changes Over Two Decades," *International Journal of Police Science and Management* 10, no. 1 (2008): 2–8.

2. M. Meagher and N. Yentes, "Choosing a Career in Policing: A Comparison of Male and Female Perceptions," *Journal of Police Science and Administration* 14, no. 4 (1986): 320–27.

3. A. Raganella and M. White, "Race, Gender, and Motivations for Becoming a Police Officer: Implications for Building a Representative Police Department," *Journal of Criminal Justice* 32, no. 6 (2004): 501–13.

4. H. Slater and M. Reiser, "Comparative Study of Factors Influencing Police Recruitment," *Journal of Police Science and Administration* 16, no. 3 (1988): 168–76.

5. For an example of this program, see http://phoenix.gov/police/explor1.html.

6. K. Hassell, C. Archbold and D. Schulz, *Women and Policing in America: Classic and Contemporary Readings* (Frederick, MD: Aspen Publishing, 2011).

7. U.S. Department of Justice, *Innovations in Police Recruitment and Hiring: Hiring in the Spirit of Service* (Washington, DC: U.S. Department of Justice: Office of Community Oriented Policing Services, 2006).

8. P. Bradley, "21st Century Issues Related to Police Training and Standards," *The Police Chief* 72, no. 10 (October 2005).

9. B. Nash, *Residency Requirements: Sometimes a Litigation Issue, More Often a Legislative One.* See http://www.fop.net/programs/research/residency.pdf.

10. Ibid.

11. Ibid.

12. A. Pearsall III and K. Kohlhepp, "Strategies to Improve Recruitment," *The Police Chief* 77 (April 2010): 128–30.

13. See http://www.suntimes.com/news/metro/2844192,new-police-requirements-102810.article.

14. B. Reaves, *Local Police Departments, 2007* (Washington, DC: Bureau of Justice Statistics, 2010).

15. Ibid.

16. K. Lonsway, 'Tearing Down the Wall: Problems with Consistency, Validity and Adverse Impact of Physical Agility Testing in Police Selection," *Police Quarterly* 6 (2003): 237–77.

17. R. Warner and B. Steel, "Affirmative Action in Times of Fiscal Stress and Changing Value Priories: The Case of Women in Policing," *Public Personnel Management* 18, no. 3 (1989): 291–338.

18. Ibid.

19. T. Sass and J. Troyer, "Affirmative Action, Political Representation, Unions and Female Police Employment," *Journal of Labor Research* 20, no. 4 (1999): 571–87.

20. Reaves, 2010.

21. See http://florida.aoa.org/documents/Recommended VisionStandardsPoliceOfficers.pdf.

22. Reaves, 2010.

23. See http://www.cga.ct.gov/2000/rpt/2000-R-0383.htm.

24. See http://www.dps.alaska.gov/Ast/recruit/statutestandards.aspx.

25. D. Bradford, "Police Officer Candidate Background Investigation: Law Enforcement Management's Most Effective Tool for Employing the Most Qualified Candidate," *Public Personnel Management* 27, no. 4 (1998): 423–45.

26. See http://www.ci.la.ca.us/oig/rirprpt.pdf.

27. Reaves, 2010.

28. Ibid.

29. C. Michael, "Women in Policing: The Physical Aspects," *Journal of Police Science and Administration* 10, no. 2 (1982): 194–205.

30. P. Harrington and K. Lonsway, "Current Barriers and Future Promise for Women in Policing," in *The Criminal Justice System and Women*, ed. B. R. Price and N. Sokoloff (New York: McGraw Hill, 2004).

31. Reaves, 2010.

32. Reaves, 2010.

33. An example of medical exams for police testing can be found at http://passthepolicetest.com/police-fitness-test/police-medical-exam-what-to-expect-what-does-it-mean.

34. Ibid.

35. Reaves, 2010.

36. E. Metchik, "An Analysis of the Screening Out Model of Police Officer Selection," *Police Quarterly* 2, 1 (1999): 79–95.

37. Ibid.

38. Ibid.

39. Ibid.

40. Reaves, 2010.

41. Ibid.

42. Ibid.

43. Ibid.

44. D. DeCicco, "Police Officer Candidate Assessment and Selection," *FBI Law Enforcement Bulletin* 69, no. 12 (2000): 1–6.

45. Ibid.

46. Ibid.

47. Ibid.

48. G. Coulton and H. Feild, "Using Assessment Centers in Selecting Entry-Level Police Officers: Extravagance or Justified Expense?" *Public Personnel Management* 24, no. 2 (1995): 223–43.

49. Ibid.

50. J. Pynes and H. Bernardin, "Entry-Level Police Selection: The Assessment Center is an Alternative," *Journal of Criminal Justice* 20, no. 1 (1992): 41–52.

51. See the Milwaukee Police Department website at http://city.milwaukee.gov/jobs/PO.

52. See http://www.alextech.edu/en/Students/Programs/LawEnforcement/LawEnforcementAS.aspx.

53. M. Hickman, *State and Local Law Enforcement Training Academies, 2006* (Washington, DC: Bureau of Justice Statistics, 2009).

54. Ibid.

55. Ibid.

56. Ibid.

57. Ibid.

58. D. Bradford and J. Pynes, "Police Academy Training: Why Hasn't It Kept Up with Practice?" *Police Quarterly* 2, no. 3 (1999): 283–301.

59. A. Prokos and I Padavic, "There Outta Be a Law against Bitches: Masculinity Lessons in Police Academy Training," *Gender, Work and Organization* 9, no. 4 (2002): 439–59.

60. M. Campbell, *Field Training for Police Officers: State of the Art* (Washington, DC: National Institute for Justice, 1987).

61. Ibid.

62. S. Pitts, R. Glensor and K. Peak, "The Police Training Officer (PTO) Program: A Contemporary Approach to Post-Academy Recruit Training," *The Police Chief* 74 (2007): 8.

63. Ibid.

64. Ibid.

65. Ibid.

66. Ibid.

67. Ibid.

68. Hickman, 2009.

69. Ibid.

70. See http://www.cityoffargo.com/CityInfo/Departments/Police/AboutFargoPolice/AdministrativeServicesDivision/Training/In-ServiceTraining/.

71. M.L. Dantzker, "An Issue for Policing: Education Level and Job Satisfaction," *American Journal of Police* 12, 2 (1993): 101–18.

72. D. Kurz, "A Promotional Process for the Smaller Police Agency," *The Police Chief* 73 (2006): 10.

73. T. Whetstone, "Copping Out: Why Police Officers Decline to Participate in the Sergeant's Promotional Process," *American Journal of Criminal Justice* 25, no. 2 (2001): 147–59.

74. Ibid.

75. Ibid.

76. Ibid.

77. C. Archbold and K. Hassell, "Paying a Marriage Tax: An Examination of the Barriers to the Promotion of Female Police Officers," *Policing: An International Journal of Police Strategies & Management* 32, no. 1 (2009): 56–74.

78. C. Archbold and D. Schulz. "Making Rank: The Lingering Effects of Tokenism on Female Police Officers' Promotion Aspirations," *Police Quarterly* 11, no. 1 (2008): 50–73.

79. F. Jollevet II, "African American Police Executive Careers: Influences of Human Capital, Social Capital, and Racial Discrimination," *Police Practice and Research: An International Journal* 9, no. 1 (2008): 17–30.

80. J. Barker, *Danger, Duty, and Disillusion: The Worldview of Los Angeles Police Officers* (Prospect Heights, IL: Waveland Press, 1999).

81. R. McIntyre, *Why Police Officers Resign: A Look at the Turnover of Police Officers in Vermont* (Washington, DC: U.S. Department of Justice, 1990).

82. Ibid.

83. R. Haarr, "Factors Affecting the Decision of Police Recruits to Drop Out of Police Work," *Police Quarterly* 8, no. 4 (2005): 431–53.

84. E. Poole and M. Pogrebin, "Factors Affecting the Decision to Remain in Policing: A Study of Women Officers," *Journal of Police Science and Administration* 16, no. 1 (1988): 46–55.

✉ Section 6

1. See http://www.brainyquote.com/quotes/authors/v/vince_lombardi_3.html.

2. W. Miller, *Cops and Bobbies: Police Authority in New York and London, 1830–1870* (Chicago: University of Chicago Press, 1977).

3. J. Auten, "The Paramilitary Model of Police and Police Professionalism," *Police Studies* 4 (1981): 67–78.

4. See http://www.lakewoodsfinest.org/history.htm.

5. J. Q. Wilson, *Bureaucracy* (New York: Basic Books, 1989).

6. M. Weber, *Economy and Society*, ed. and trans. G. Roth and C. Wittich (Los Angeles: University of California Press, 1921/1968), 956–58.

7. P. Kraska and V. Kappeler, "Militarizing American Police: The Rise and Normalization of Paramilitary Units," *Social Problems* 44, no. 1 (1997): 1–18.

8. Wilson, 1989.

9. O. W. Wilson, *Police Administration* (New York: McGraw-Hill, 1963).

10. Egon Bittner, *The Functions of the Police in Modern Society* (Chevy Chase, MD: U.S. National Institute of Mental Health, Center for Studies of Crime and Delinquency, 1970).

11. F. Luthans, *Introduction to Management: A Contingency Approach* (New York: McGraw-Hill, 1976).

12. Ibid.

13. R. Roberg, J. Kuykendall, K. Novak, *Police Management, 3rd ed.* (Los Angeles: Roxbury Publishing, 2002).

14. L. Donaldson, *American Anti-Management Theories of Organization: A Critique of Paradigm Proliferation* (Cambridge, MA: Cambridge University, 1995).

15. P. Lawrence and J. Lorsch, *Organization and Environment* (Homewood, IL: Richard D. Irwin, Inc., 1967).

16. J. Hauge and M. Aiken, *Social Change in Complex Organizations* (New York: Random House, 1970).

17. C. Katz, E. Maguire, and D. Roncek, "The Creation of Specialized Police Gang Units: A Macro-Level Analysis of Contingency, Social Threat, and Resource Dependency Explanations," *Policing: An International Journal of Police Strategies and Management* 25, no. 3 (2002): 472–506.

18. J. Zhao, *Why Police Organizations Change: A Study of Community Oriented Policing: A Contingency Approach* (Washington, DC: Police Executive Research Forum, 1996).

19. J. Worrall and J. Zhao, "The Role of the COPS Office in Community Policing," *Policing: An International Journal of Police Strategies and Management* 26, no. 1 (2003): 64–87.

20. J. Meyer and B. Rowan, "Institutionalized Organizations: Formal Structure as Myth and Ceremony," *American Journal of Sociology* 83, no. 2 (1977): 340–63.

21. J. Meyer and R. Scott, "Centralization and the Legitimacy Problems of Local Government," in *Organizational Environments: Ritual and Rationality,* ed. J. Meyer and W. Scott (Beverly Hills, CA: Sage, 1983), 199–215.

22. Meyer and Rowan, 1977.

23. J. Crank and R. Langworthy, "An Institutional Perspective of Policing," *Journal of Criminal Law and Criminology,* 83, no. 2 (1992): 338–63.

24. Meyer and Rowan, 1977.

25. J. Crank, "Institutional Theory of Police: A Review of the State of the Art," *Policing: An International Journal of Police Strategies and Management* 26, no. 2 (2003): 186–207.

26. J. Crank, "Watchman and Community: Myth and Institutionalization in Policing," *Law and Society Review* 28, no. 2 (1994): 325–51.

27. Crank and Langworthy, 1992; J. Crank and R. Langworthy, "Fragmented Centralization and the Organization of the Police," *Policing and Society* 6, no. 3 (1996): 213–29.

28. R. Hunt and J. Magenau, *Power and the Police Chief: An Institutional and Organizational Analysis* (Newbury Park, CA: Sage, 1993).

29. J. Crank and L. Rehm, "Reciprocity Between Organizations and Institutional Environments: A Study of Operation Valkyrie," *Journal of Criminal Justice* 22, no. 5 (1994): 393–406.

30. C. Katz, "The Establishment of a Police Gang Unit: An Examination of Organizational and Environmental Factors," *Criminology* 39, no. 1 (2001): 37–74.

31. J. Pfeffer and G. Salancik, *The External Control of Organizations: A Resource Dependence Perspective* (New York, Harper and Row, 1978).

32. L. Donaldson, *American Anti-Management Theories of Organization: A Critique of Paradigm Proliferation* (Cambridge, MA: Cambridge University Press, 1995).

33. Pfeffer and Salancik, 1978.

34. J. Greene, "Community Policing in America: Changing the Nature, Structure, and Function of the Police," in *Criminal Justice 2000: Policies, processes, and decisions of the criminal justice system,* ed. J. Horney (Washington, DC: National Institute of Justice, 2000), 299–370, 314.

35. E. Maguire and Y. Shin, "Structural Change in Large Police Agencies During the 1990s," *Policing: An International Journal of Police Strategies and Management* 26, no. 2 (2003): 251–75, 270.

36. G. Gianakis and G. Davis III, "Reinventing or Packaging Public Services? The Case of Community-Oriented Policing," *Public Administrative Review* 58 (1998): 485–98; J. Zhao, *Why Police Organizations Change: A Study of Community-Oriented Policing* (Washington, DC: Police Executive Research Forum, 1996).

37. J. Zhao, Q. Thurman, and N. Lovrich, "Community-Oriented Policing Across the U.S.: Facilitators and Impediments to Implementation," *American Journal of Police* 14, no. 1 (1995): 11–28.

38. J. Willis, S. Mastrofski, and D. Weisburd, "Making Sense of COMPSTAT: A Theory-Based Analysis of Organizational Change in Three Police Departments," *Law & Society Review* 41, no. 1 (2007): 147–88.

39. W. Walsh, "COMPSTAT: An Analysis of an Emerging Police Managerial Paradigm," *Policing: An International Journal of Police Strategies and Management* 24, no. 3 (2001): 347–62.

40. D. Weisburd, S. Mastrofski, R. Greenspan, and J. Willis. *The Growth of COMPSTAT in American Policing* (Washington, DC: Police Foundation, April 2004); see http://www.policefoundation.org/pdf/growthofcompstat.pdf.

41. Ibid.

42. D. Weisburd, S. Mastrofski, A. McNally, R. Greenspan, and J. Willis, "Reforming to Preserve: COMPSTAT and Strategic Problem Solving in American Policing," *Criminology and Public Policy* 2, no. 3 (2003): 421–56.

43. Ibid.

44. P. Tolbert and L. Zucker, "Institutional Sources of Change in the Formal Structure of Organizations: The Diffusion of Civil Service Reform, 1880–1935," *Administrative Science Quarterly* 28, no. 1 (1983): 22–39.

45. Ibid.

46. H. Locke, *Impact of Affirmative Action and Civil Service on American Police Personnel Systems* (Washington, DC: National Institute of Justice, 1979).

47. D. Guyot, "Bending Granite: Attempts to Change the Rank Structure of American Police Departments," *Journal of Police Science and Administration* 7, no. 3 (1979): 253–84.

48. G. Cordner and R. Sheehan, *Police Administration, 4th ed.* (Cincinnati, OH: Anderson Publishing, 1999).

49. See http://www.merriam-webster.com/dictionary/labor+union.

50. Office of Community Oriented Policing Services, *Police Labor–Management Relations: Perspectives and Practical Solutions for Implementing Change, Making Reforms, and Handling Crises for Managers and Union Leaders, 2 vols.* (Washington, DC: U.S. Department of Justice, 2006).

51. S. Walker, "The Neglect of Police Unions: Exploring One of the Most Important Areas of American Policing," *Police Practice and Research* 9, no. 2 (2008): 95–112.

52. See http://www.fop.net/.

53. Ibid.

54. United States Department of Labor, http://www.bls.gov/bls/glossary.htm#C.

55. H. Juris and P. Feuille, *Police Unionism—Power and Impact in Public-Sector Bargaining* (New York City: Lexington Books, 1973).

56. Walker, 2008.

57. Reaves, 2010.

58. S. Wilson, J. Zhao, L. Ren, and S. Briggs, "The Influence of Collective Bargaining on Large Police Agency Salaries: 1990–2000," *American Journal of Criminal Justice* 31, no. 1 (2006): 19–34.

59. See http://www.calea.org/content/commission

60. Ibid.

61. Ibid.

62. S. Mastrofski, "Police Agency Accreditation: The Prospects of Reform," *American Journal of Police* 5 (1986): 45–81.

63. G. Cordner and G. Williams, "Community Policing and Accreditation: A Content Analysis of CALEA (Commission on Accreditation for Law Enforcement Agencies) Standards," in *Quantifying Quality in Policing,* ed. Larry T Hoover (Washington, DC: Police Executive Research Forum, 1996), 243–61.

64. Mastrofski, 1986.

65. W. Doerner and W. Doerner, "The Diffusion of Accreditation Among Florida Police Agencies," *Policing: An International Journal of Police Strategies & Management* 32, no. 4 (2009): 781–98.

66. K. McCabe and R. Fajardo, "Law Enforcement Accreditation: A National Comparison of Accredited vs. Nonaccredited Agencies," *Journal of Criminal Justice* 29, no. 2 (2001): 127–31.

67. Ibid.

68. J. Wilson, *Varieties of Police Behavior—The Management of Law and Order in Eight Communities* (Cambridge, MA: Harvard University Press, 1968).

69. J. Krimmel and P. Lindenmuth, "Police Chief Performance and Leadership Styles," *Police Quarterly* 4, no. 4 (2001): 469–83.

70. F. Rainguet and M. Dodge, "The Problems of Police Chiefs: An Examination of the Issues in Tenure and Turnover," *Police Quarterly* 4, no. 3 (2001): 268–88.

71. Ibid., 270.

72. Ibid., 270.

73. M. Girodo, "Machiavellian, Bureaucratic, and Transformational Leadership Styles in Police Managers: Preliminary Findings of Interpersonal Ethics," *Perceptual and Motor Skills* 86, no. 2 (1998): 419–27.

74. H. Goldstein, *Problem-Oriented Policing* (New York: McGraw-Hill, 1990).

75. R. Shepard Engel, "Supervisory Style of Patrol Sergeants and Lieutenants," *Journal of Criminal Justice* 29, 4 (2001): 341–55.

76. Ibid.

77. Ibid.

78. D. Smith, "The Organizational Context of Legal Control," *Criminology* 22, no. 1 (1984): 19–38; R. Engel and R. Worden, "Police Officers' Attitudes, Behavior, and Supervisory Influences: An Analysis of Problem Solving," *Criminology* 41, no. 1 (2003): 131–66.

79. D. Allen, "Police Supervisions on the Street: An Analysis of Supervisor/Officer Interaction During the Hift," *Journal of Criminal Justice* 10, no. 2 (1982): 91–109; D. Allen and M. Maxfield, "Judging Police Performance: Views and Behavior of Patrol Officers," in *Police at Work: Policy Issues and Analysis,* ed. R. Bennett (Beverly Hills, CA: Sage, 1983), 65–86.

80. M. Brown, *Working the Street: Police Discretion and the Dilemmas of Reform* (New York: Russell Sage Foundation, 1988).

81. J. Violanti and F. Aron, "Ranking Police Stressors," *Psychological Reports* 75, no. 2 (1994): 824–26.

82. Ibid.

83. J. Crank and M. Caldero, "The Production of Occupational Stress in Medium-Sized Police Agencies: A Survey of Line Officers in Eight Municipal Departments," *Journal of Criminal Justice* 19, no. 4 (1991): 339–49.

84. J. Wexler and D. Logan, "Sources of Stress Among Women Police Officers," *Journal of Police Science and Administration* 11, no. 1 (1983): 46–53.

85. J. Violanti, J. Marshall, and B. Howe, "Stress, Coping, and Alcohol Use—The Police," *Journal of Police Science and Administration* 13, no. 2 (1985): 106–10.

86. J. Dash and M. Reiser, "Suicide Among Police in Urban Law Enforcement Agencies," *Journal of Police Science and Administration* 6, no. 1 (1978): 18–21.

87. W. McCarty, J. Zhao, and B. Garland, "Occupational Stress and Burnout Between Male and Female Police Officers: Are There Any Gender Differences?" *Policing: An International Journal of Police Strategies and Management* 30, no. 4 (2007): 672–91.

88. M. Morash, D. Kwak, and R. Haarr, "Gender Differences in the Predictors of Police Stress," *Policing: An International Journal of Police Strategies & Management* 29, no. 3 (2006): 541–63.

89. Katherine Ellison, *Stress and the Police Officer, 2nd ed.* (Springfield, IL: Charles C. Thomas Publisher, 2004).

90. Ibid.

91. J. Zhao, Q. Thurman and N. He, "Sources of Job Satisfaction Among Police Officers: A Test of Demographic and Work Environment Models," *Justice Quarterly* 16, no. 1 (1999): 153–73.

92. R. Trojanowicz and B. Bucqueroux, *Community Policing: A Contemporary Perspective* (Cincinnati, OH: Anderson Publishing, 1990); W. Skogan and S. Hartnett, *Community Policing, Chicago Style* (New York: Oxford University Press, 1997).

93. B. Regoli, J. Crank, and G. Rivera, "Construction and Implementation of an Alternative Measure of Police Cynicism," *Criminal Justice and Behavior* 17, no. 4 (1990): 395–409.

94. R. Dorsey and D. Giacopassi, "Assessing Gender Differences in the Levels of Cynicism Among Police Officers," *American Journal of Police* 5, no. 1 (1986): 91–112.

95. R. Bennett and E. Schmitt, "The Effect of Work Environment on Levels of Police Cynicism: A Comparative Study," *Police Quarterly* 5, no. 4 (2002): 493–522.

96. Regoli et al., 1990.

97. D. Klinger, "Negotiating Order in Police Work: An Ecological Theory of Police Response to Deviance," *Criminology* 35, no. 2 (1997): 277–306.

98. E. Chandler and C. Jones, "Cynicism—An Inevitability of Police Work? *Journal of Police Science and Administration* 7, no. 1 (1979): 65–68.

99. See http://www.merriam-webster.com/dictionary/ morale.

100. B. Gocke, "Morale in a Police Department," *Journal of Criminal Law and Criminology* 36, no. 3 (1945): 215–19.

101. J.Q. Wilson, "Police Morale, Reform and Citizen Respect: The Chicago Case," in *The Police: Six Sociological Essays,* ed. D. J. Bordua (New York: John Wiley & Sons, 1967), 137–61.

◈ Section 7

1. S. D. Mastrofski, R. B. Parks, A. J. Reiss, R. E. Worden, C. DeJong, and J. B. Snipes, *Systematic Observation of Public Police: Applying Field Research Methods to Policy Issues* (Washington, DC: National Institute of Justice, 1998).

2. C. Famega, J. Frank, and L. Mazerolle, "Managing Police Patrol Time: The Role of Supervisor Directives," *Justice Quarterly* 22, no. 4 (2005): 540–59.

3. Ibid., 550.

4. Ibid., 550.

5. O.A.W. Wilson, *Police Administration* (New York: McGraw-Hill, 1950).

6. G.W. Cordner, "Police Patrol Work Load Studies: A Review and Critique," *Police Studies* 2, no. 2 (1979): 50–60.

7. G. Kelling and M. Moore, *The Evolving Strategy of Policing* (Washington, DC: U.S. Department of Justice, 1988).

8. Ibid.

9. Ibid.

10. Kelling and Moore, 1988, 13.

11. N. Douthit, "August Vollmer: Berkley's First Chief of Police and the Emergence of Police Professionalism," *California Historical Quarterly* 54 (1975): 101–24.

12. Ibid.

13. G.W. Cordner, "The Effects of Directed Patrol: A Natural Quasi-Experiment in Pontiac," in *Contemporary Issues in Law Enforcement,* ed. J. Fyfe (Beverly Hills, CA: Sage, 1981).

14. J. Warren, M. Forst, and M. Estrella, "Directed Patrol: An Experiment that Worked," *Police Chief* (1979): 48, 49, 78.

15. L. Sherman and D. Weisburd, "General Deterrent Effects of Police Patrol in Crime 'Hot Spots': A Randomized, Controlled Trial," *Justice Quarterly* 12, no. 4 (1995): 625–48.

16. L. Sherman, "Hot Spots of Crime and Criminal Careers of Places," in *Crime and Place: Crime Prevention Studies: 4,* ed. John E. Eck and David Weisburd (Monsey, NY: Willow Tree Press, 1995).

17. M. Scott, *The Benefits and Consequences of Police Crackdowns* (Washington, DC: U.S. Department of Justice, 2004).

18. L. Sherman, "Police Crackdowns: Initial and Residential Deterrence," *Crime and Justice: A Review of Research. Volume 12*, in M. Tonry and N. Morris (Chicago, IL: University of Chicago Press, 1990).

19. Scott, 2004, 5.

20. Ibid.

21. National Research Council, 2004, 123.

22. J. Tien, J. Simon, and R. Larson, *Alterative Approach in Police Patrol—The Wilmington Split-Force Experiment* (Washington, DC: United States Department of Justice, 1978).

23. National Research Council, 2004, 123.

24. D. Harris, *Good Cops: The Case for Preventive Policing* (New York: The New Press, 2005). See also D. Harris, *Profiles of Injustice: Why Racial Profiling Cannot Work* (New York: The New Press, 2002).

25. G. Cordner, L. Gaines, and V. Kappeler, *Police Operations: Analysis and Evaluation* (Cincinnati, OH: Anderson Publishing, 1996), 119–22.

26. W. Spelman, *Repeat Offender Programs for Law Enforcement* (Washington, DC: Police Executive Research Forum, 1990).

27. See http://www.cops.usdoj.gov/html/dispatch/February_2009/foot_patrol.htm.

28. Kelling and Moore, 1988.

29. Ibid.

30. Bureau of Justice Statistics, *Local Police Departments, 2007* (Washington, DC: Bureau of Justice Statistics, 2010).

31. See http://www.cops.usdoj.gov/html/dispatch/February_2009/foot_patrol.htm and also http://www.nytimes.com/2008/07/20/us/20patrol.html.

32. C. Menton, "Bicycle Patrols: An Underutilized Resource," *Policing: An International Journal of Police Strategies and Management* 31, no. 1 (2008): 93–108.

33. Bureau of Justice Statistics, 2010.

34. Ibid.

35. S. Doeren, "Mounted Patrol Programs in Law Enforcement," *Police Studies* 12, no. 1 (1989): 10–17.

36. Bureau of Justice Statistics, 2010.

37. M. Roth, "Mounted Police Forces: A Comparative History" *Policing: An International Journal of Police Strategies and Management* 21, no. 4 (1998): 707–19.

38. J. Boydstun, M. Sherry and N. Moelter, *Patrol Staffing in San Diego—One- or Two-Officer Units* (Washington, DC: Police Foundation, 1977).

39. M. Estep, "*Patrol, Types and Effectiveness of,*" in *Encyclopedia of Police Science,* ed. J. Greene (New York: Routledge, Taylor and Francis Publishing, 2007), 898–904.

40. L. Sherman, *Repeat Calls to Police in Minneapolis* (Washington, DC: National Institute of Justice, 1987).

41. Ibid.

42. G. Antunes and E. Scott, "Calling the Cops: Police Telephone Operators and Citizens Calls for Service," *Journal of Criminal Justice* 9, no. 2 (1981): 165–79.

43. Ibid.

44. Sherman, 1987.

45. Ibid.

46. Ibid.

47. E. Avakame, J. Fyfe, and C. McCoy, "Did You Call the Police? What Did They Do? An Empirical Assessment of Black's

Theory of Mobilization of Law," *Justice Quarterly* 16, no. 4 (1999): 765–92.

48. Antunes and Scott, 1981.

49. See http://news.yahoo.com/blogs/lookout/violence-mars-occupy-wall-street-protests-vermont-elsewhere-163738122.html.

50. G. Cordner, L. Gaines, and V. Kappeler, *Police Operations: Analysis and Evaluation* (Cincinnati, OH: Anderson Publishing, 1996), 157.

51. M. Palmiotto, *Criminal Investigation* (Lanham, MD: University Press of America, 2004), 17–19.

52. See official FBI website at http://www.fbi.gov.

53. Ibid.

54. Ibid.

55. D. Schroeder and M. White, "Exploring the Use of DNA Evidence in Homicide Investigations: Implications for Detective Work and Case Clearance," *Police Quarterly* 12, 3 (2009): 319–42.

56. Ibid.

57. P. Greenwood and J. Petersilia, *The Criminal Investigation Process Volume I: Summary and Policy Implications* (Santa Monica, CA: RAND Corporation, 1975).

58. Ibid.

59. J. Eck, *Solving Crimes: The Investigation of Burglary and Robbery* (Washington, DC: Police Executive Research Forum, 1983).

60. Ibid.

61. J. Liederbach, E. Fritsch, and C. Womack, "Detective Workload and Opportunities for Increased Productivity in Criminal Investigations," *Police Practice and Research* 12, no. 1 (2011): 50–65.

62. Liederbach, Fritsch, and Womack, 2011, 59.

63. K. J. Litwin, "A Multilevel Multivariate Analysis of Factors Affecting Homicide Clearances," *The Journal of Research in Crime and Delinquency* 41, no. 4 (2004): 327–51.

64. Ibid.

65. A. Roberts, "Predictors of Homicide Clearance by Arrest: An Event History Analysis of NIBRS Incidents," *Homicide Studies* 11, no. 2 (2007): 82–93. See also J. L. Puckett and R. J. Lundman, "Factors Affecting Homicide Clearances: Multivariate Analysis of a More Complete Conceptual Framework," *Journal of Research in Crime and Delinquency* 40, no. 2 (2003): 171–93; and also M. R. Gottfredson and M. J. Hindelang, "A Study of the Behavior of Law," *American Sociological Review* 44, no. 1 (1979): 3–18.

66. Roberts, 2007.

67. Kelling and Moore, 1988.

68. B. Reaves, *Census of State and Local Law Enforcement Agencies, 2008* (Washington, DC: Bureau of Justice Statistics, 2011).

69. Ibid.

70. C. Mamalian, N. LaVigne, and the staff of the Crime Mapping Research Center, *The Use of Computerized Crime Mapping by Law Enforcement: Survey Results* (National Institute of Justice, 1999).

71. E. Groff and N. La Vigne, "Mapping an Opportunity Surface of Residential Burglary," *Journal of Research in Crime and Delinquency* 38, no. 3 (2001): 257–78.

72. E. Groff, "Simulation for Theory Testing and Experimentation: An Example Using Routine Activity Theory and Street Robbery," *Journal of Quantitative Criminology* 23, no. 2 (2007): 75–103.

73. E. Groff and J. McEwen, "Disaggregating the Journey to Homicide," In *Geographic Information Systems and Crime Analysis*, ed. Fahui Wang (Chapel Hill: University of North Carolina at Chapel Hill, 2005), 60–83.

74. D. Weisburd, N. Morris, and E. Groff, "Hot Spots of Juvenile Crime: A Longitudinal Study of Arrest Incidents at Street Segments in Seattle, Washington," *Journal of Quantitative Criminology* 25, no. 4 (2009): 443–67.

75. R. Block, "Gang Activity and Overall Levels of Crime: A New Mapping Tool for Defining Areas of Gang Activity Using Police Records," *Journal of Quantitative Criminology* 16, no. 3 (2000): 369–83.

76. Reaves, 2011.

77. Ibid.

78. E. Groff and N. La Vigne, "Forecasting the Future of Predictive Crime Mapping," *Crime Prevention Studies* 13 (2002): 29–57.

79. W. Spelman, "Criminal Careers of Public Places," in *Crime and Place*, ed. D. Weisburd and J. Eck (Crime Prevention Studies, Vol. 4.) (Monsey, NY: Criminal Justice Press, 1995).

80. G. Vilke and T. Chan, "Less Lethal Technology: Medical Issues," *Policing: An International Journal of Police Strategies and Management* 30, no. 3 (2007): 341–57.

81. B. Reaves, *Local Police Departments, 2007* (Washington, DC: Bureau of Justice Statistics, 2010), 38.

82. Ibid.

83. M. White and J. Ready, "The TASER as a Less Lethal Force Alternative: Findings on Use and Effectiveness in a Large Metropolitan Police Agency," *Police Quarterly* 10, no. 2 (2007): 170–91.

84. A. Maroney, "Liability Issues and On-Duty Cellular Phone Use," *Police Chief* 67 (2000): 47–51.

85. K. Adams and V. Jennison, "What We Do Not Know About Police Use of Tasers?" *Policing: An International Journal of Police Strategies and Management* 30, no. 3 (2007): 447–65.

86. S. Hougland, C. Mesloh, and M. Henych, "Use of Force, Civil Litigation, and the Taser: One Agency's Experience," *FBI Bulletin* 74, no. 3 (March 2005).

⊠ **Section 8**

1. See http://archives.clintonpresidentialcenter.org/?u=051299-speech-by-president-on-crime-bill-unveiling.htm.

2. W. Skogan, "Efficiency and Effectiveness in Big-City Police Departments," *Public Administration Review* 36, no. 3 (May/June, 1976): 278–86.

3. Ibid., 278.

4. Ibid., 278.

5. G. Kelling and M. Moore, *Evolving Strategy of Policing* (Washington, DC: U.S. Department of Justice, 1988).

6. Ibid.

7. Ibid.

8. National Research Council, *Fairness and Effectiveness in Policing: The Evidence* (Washington, DC: The National Academies Press, 2004).

9. See http://www.dnainfo.com/20101028/washington-heights-inwood/more-police-officers-patrol-washington-heights-inwood-fight-rise-crime.

10. Eck, J. and E. Maguire, "Have Changes in Policing Reduced Violent Crime? An Assessment of the Evidence," In *The Crime Drop in America*, ed. A. Blumstein and J. Wallman (New York: Cambridge University Press, 2000).

11. See http://www.theiacp.org/LinkClick.aspx?fileticket=LF7xdWl1tPk%3D&tabid=87.

12. B. Reaves, *Census of State and Local Law Enforcement Agencies, 2008* (Washington, DC: U.S. Department of Justice, Office of Justice Programs, Bureau of Justice Statistics, 2011).

13. New York City Police Department, *Operation 25* (New York: Charles C. Thomas, 1970).

14. S. James Press, *Some Effects of an Increase in Manpower in the 20th Precinct of New York City* (Santa Monica, CA: The Rand Corporation, 1971).

15. G. Kelling, T. Pate, D. Dieckman, and C. Brown, *Kansas City Preventive Patrol Experiment: A Technical Report* (Washington, DC: Police Foundation, 1974).

16. Kansas City Police Department, *Response Time Analysis* (Kansas City, MO: Kansas City Police Department, 1977).

17. W. Spelman and D. Brown, *Calling the Police: A Replication of the Citizen Reporting Component of the Kansas City Response Time Analysis* (Washington, DC: Police Executive Research Forum, 1981).

18. National Research Council, 2004, 228–32.

19. C. Maxwell, J. Garner, and J. Fagan, *The Effects of Arrest on Intimate Partner Violence: New Evidence From the Spouse Assault Replication Program* (Washington, DC: National Institute of Justice, 2001).

20. L. Sherman and R. Berk, *Specific Deterrent Effects of Arrest for Domestic Assault, Minneapolis* (Washington, DC: National Institute of Justice, 1984). See also L. Sherman and R. Berk, "Specific Deterrent Effects of Arrest for Domestic Assault," *American Sociological Review* 49, no. 2 (1984): 261–72.

21. L. Sherman and D. Weisburd, "General Deterrent Effects of Police Patrol in Crime 'Hot Spots:' A Randomized, Controlled Trial," *Justice Quarterly* 12, no. 4 (1995): 625–48.

22. L. Green, "Cleaning Up Drug Hot Spots in Oakland, California: The Displacement and Diffusion Effects," *Justice Quarterly* 12, no. 4 (1995): 737–54.

23. L. Sherman and D. Rogan, "Effects of Gun Seizures on Gun Violence: 'Hot Spots' Patrol in Kansas City," *Justice Quarterly* 12, no. 4 (1995): 673–93.

24. D. Weisburd and L. Green, "Policing Drug Hot Spots: The Jersey City Drug Market Analysis Experiment," *Justice Quarterly* 12, no. 4 (1995): 711–35.

25. M. Scott, *Benefits and Consequences of Police Crackdowns* (Washington, DC: U.S. Department of Justice, 2003).

26. L. Sherman, "Police Crackdowns: Initial and Residual Deterrence," in: *Crime and Justice: A Review of Research, Vol. 12,* ed. M. Tonry and N. Morris (Chicago: University of Chicago Press, 1990).

27. New Haven Police Department, *Directed Deterrent Patrol: An Innovative Method of Preventive Patrol* (Washington, DC: United States Department of Justice, 1976).

28. Ibid.

29. G. Cordner, *Pontiac (MI) Police Department—Integrated Criminal Apprehension Project, Final Evaluation Report* (Washington, DC: National Institute of Justice, 1978).

30. J. Boydstun, *San Diego Field Interrogation—Final Report* (Washington, DC: Police Foundation, 1975).

31. National Research Council, 2004.

32. H. Milton, J. Halleck, J. Lardner, and G. Abrecht, *Police Use of Deadly Force* (Washington, DC: Police Foundation, 1977).

33. G. Cordner, L. Gaines, and V. Kappeler. *Police Operations: Analysis and Evaluation* (Cincinnati, OH: Anderson Publishing, 1996), 122.

34. A. Abrahamse, P. Ebener, and P. Greenwood, *Experimental Evaluation of the Phoenix Repeat Offender Program* (Washington, DC: National Institute of Justice, 1991).

35. D. Kennedy, A. Braga, A. Piehl, and E. Waring, *Reducing Gun Violence: The Boston Gun Project's Operation Ceasefire* (Rockville, MD: National Institute of Justice, 2001).

36. J. H. Skolnick and D. H. Bayley, *New Blue Line—Police Innovation in Six American Cities* (New York: Free Press, 1986).

37. National Research Council, 234–35.

38. See http://www.usaonwatch.org/about/neighborhood-watch.aspx.

39. R. Yin, M. Vogel, J. Chaiken, and D. Both, *Patrolling the Neighborhood Beat: Residents and Residential Security* (Santa Monica, CA: Rand, 1976).

40. L. Sherman, D. Gottfredson, D. MacKenzie, J. Eck, P. Reuter, and S. Bushway, *Preventing Crime: What Works, What Doesn't, What's Promising: A Report To the United States Congress* (Washington, DC: National Institute of Justice, 1997).

41. W. Skogan and S. Hartnett, *Community Policing Chicago Style: Year Two* (Chicago: Illinois Criminal Justice Information Authority, 1995).

42. W. Skogan, *Impact of Policing on Social Disorder: Summary of Findings* (Rockville, MD: National Institute of Justice, 1992)

43. Ibid., 3.

44. Ibid.

45. A. Pate, M. Wycoff, W. Skogan, and L. Sherman, *Reducing Fear of Crime in Houston and Newark—A Summary Report* (Washington, DC: Police Foundation, 1986).

46. R. Trojanowicz and B. Bucqueroux, *Community Policing: How To Get Started* (Cincinnati, OH: Anderson Publishing, 1994), 160.

47. M. Wycoff, and W. Skogan, *Community Policing in Madison: Quality From the Inside, Out* (Washington, DC: Police Foundation, 1993). See also Skogan and Hartnett, 1995.

48. Ibid.

49. Skogan and Hartnett, 1995; see also C. Uchida, B. Forst, and O. Sampson, *Modern Policing and the Control of Illegal Drugs: Testing New Strategies in Two American Cities* (Washington, DC: National Institute of Justice, 1992); W. Skogan, *Disorder and Decline* (New York: Free Press, 1990).

50. W. Skogan and M. Wycoff, "Storefront Police Offices: The Houston Field Test," in *Community Crime Prevention: Does It Work?* ed. D. Rosenbaum (Beverly Hills, CA: Sage, 1986).

51. National Research Council, 2004, 233.

52. G. Kelling et al., *The Newark Foot Patrol Experiment* (Washington, DC: Police Foundation, 1981).

53. W. Bowers and J. Hirsch, "The Impact of Foot Patrol Staffing on Crime and Disorder in Boston: An Unmet Promise," *American Journal of Policing* 6, no. 1 (1987): 17–44. See also G. Cordner, "Foot Patrol Without Community Policing: Law and Order in Public Housing," in *The Challenge of Community Policing: Testing the Promises,* ed. D. P. Rosenbaum (London: Sage, 1994), 182–91.

54. R. Trojanowicz, *Job Satisfaction: A Comparison of Foot Patrol Versus Motor Patrol Officers* (East Lansing: Michigan State University, National Neighborhood Foot Patrol Center, 1985).

55. J. Schnelle, R. Kirchner, M. McNees, and J. Lawler, "Social Evaluation Research: The Evaluation of Two Police Patrolling Strategies," *Journal of Applied Behavior Analysis* 8, no. 4 (1975): 353–65.

56. Ibid., 362.

57. National Research Council, 243.

58. National Research Council, 244.

59. J. Eck and W. Spelman, *Problem-Solving: Problem-Oriented Policing in Newport News* (Rockville MD: Police Executive Research Forum, 1987).

60. Ibid.

61. T. Hope, "Problem-Oriented Policing and Drug Market Locations: Three Case Studies," in *Crime Prevention Studies, Vol. 2,* ed. Ronald V. Clarke (Monsey, NY: Criminal Justice Press, 1994).

62. R. Clarke and H. Goldstein, "Reducing Theft at Construction Sites: Lessons From a Problem-Oriented Project," in *Analysis For Crime Prevention,* ed. Nick Tilley (Monsey, NY: Criminal Justice Press, 2002).

63. A. Braga, D. Weisburd, E. Waring, L. Green Mazerolle, W. Spelman, and F. Gajewski, "Problem-Oriented Policing in Violent Crime Places: A Randomized Controlled Experiment," *Criminology* 37, no. 3 (1999): 541–80.

64. G. Cordner, "Fear of Crime and the Police: An Evaluation of a Fear-Reduction Strategy," *Journal of Police Science and Administration* 14, no. 3 (1986): 223–33.

✄ **Section 9**

1. See http://articles.chicagotribune.com/2011-07-27/news/chi-65-million-for-unmarked-car-accident-that-killed-chicago-boy-injured-girl-20110727_1_chicago-boy-police-car-datondra-mitchell.

2. See http://dictionary.law.com/Default.aspx?selected=1151.

3. Ibid.

4. D. Payne, *Police Liability: Lawsuits Against the Police* (Durham, NC: Carolina Academic Press, 2002).

5. V. Kappeler, *Critical Issues in Police Civil Liability, 4th ed.,* (Prospect Heights, IL: Waveland Press, 2006).

6. Payne, 2002.

7. Kappeler, 2006, 5.

8. Ibid.

9. Kappeler, 2006.

10. See http://www.merriam-webster.com/dictionary/tort.

11. Kappeler, 2006.

12. Ibid.

13. Ibid.

14. Ibid.

15. Ibid.

16. Ibid.

17. C. Franklin, *The Police Officer's Guide to Civil Liability* (Springfield, IL: Charles C Thomas, 1993).

18. C. Archbold and E. Maguire, "Studying Civil Suits Against the Police: A Serendipitous Finding of Sample Selection Bias," *Police Quarterly* 5, no. 2 (2002): 222–49.

19. C. Archbold, "Newspaper Accounts of Lawsuits Involving the Police: An Alternative Data Source?" *Journal of Crime and Justice* 29, no. 2 (2006): 1–23.

20. Ibid., 11.

21. C. Archbold, D. Lytle, C. Weatherall, A. Romero, and C. Baumann, "Lawsuits Involving the Police: A Content Analysis of Newspaper Articles," *Policing: An International Journal of Police Strategies and Management* 29, no. 4 (2006): 625–42.

22. M. Vaughn, T. Cooper, and R. del Carmen, "Assessing Legal Liabilities in Law Enforcement: Police Chiefs' Views," *Crime & Delinquency* 47, no. 1 (2001): 3–27.

23. K. Lersch and J. Feagin, "Violent Police–Citizen Encounters: An Analysis of Major Newspaper Accounts," *Critical Sociology* 22, no. 2 (1996): 29–49.

24. Vaughn, Cooper, and del Carmen, 2001.

25. Payne, 2002.

26. F. Scogin and S. Brodsky, "Fear of Litigation Among Law Enforcement Officers," *American Journal of Police* 10, no. 1 (1991): 41–45.

27. Ibid., 43.

28. Vaughn, Cooper, and del Carmen, 2001.

29. Ibid., 17.

30. "Hit Parade: Minneapolis's Ten Most Expensive Cops, Blow by Blow," *City Pages*, August 17, 15 (1994): 6–22.

31. See http://blogs.citypages.com/blotter/2009/09/minneapolis_pay.php.

32. Ibid.

33. See http://articles.latimes.com/2011/may/08/local/la-me-millionaire-lapd-cops-20110508.

34. Ibid.

35. Ibid.

36. See http://www.losangelesemploymentlaws.com/2011/05/lapd-ranked-one-of-the-most-litigious-police-departments-in-us.shtml.

37. See http://www.suntimes.com/news/metro/2308521-418/cases-lawsuits-police-strategy-legal.html.

38. Ibid.

39. S. Walker, *Police Accountability: The Role of Citizen Oversight* (Belmont, CA: Wadsworth Publishing, 2001), 7–8.

40. United States Department of Justice, *Principles for Promoting Police Integrity: Examples of Promising Police Practices and Policies* (Washington, DC: U.S. Department of Justice, 2001).

41. G. Kelling and M. Moore, *Evolving Strategy of Policing* (Washington, DC: U.S. Department of Justice, 1988).

42. A. Vollmer, "Police Progress in the Past Twenty-Five Years," *Journal of Criminal Law and Criminology* 24, no. 1 (May–Jun., 1933): 161–75.

43. Franklin, 1993.

44. S. Walker, G. Alpert, and D. Kenney, "Early Warning Systems for Police: Concept, History, and Issues," *Police Quarterly* 3, no. 2 (2000): 132–52.

45. S. Walker, G. Alpert, and D. Kenney, *Early Warning Systems: Responding to the Problem Police Officer* (Washington, DC: National Institute of Justice, 2001).

46. Ibid.

47. M. Hickman, *Citizen Complaints about Police Use of Force* (Washington, DC: Bureau of Justice Statistics, 2006).

48. See http://www.calea.org/content/accreditation-and-civil-liability.

49. S. Walker, *Police Accountability: Current Issues and Research Needs* (Washington, DC: National Institute of Justice, 2007).

50. T. Oettmeier and M. Wycoff, *Personnel Performance Evaluation in the Community Policing Context* (Washington, DC: United States Department of Justice, 1997).

51. Hickman, 2006.

52. Ibid.

53. Walker, 2007, 19.

54. See http://www.ci.la.ca.us/oig/rirprpt.pdf http://www.ci.la.ca.us/oig/rirprpt.pdf.

55. See http://www.parc.info/client_files/Altus/10-19%20altus%20conf%20paper.pdf.

56. G. Alpert, D. Kenney, R. Dunham, and W. Smith, *Police Pursuits: What We Know* (Washington, DC: Police Executive Research Forum, 2000). See also J. Fyfe, "Police Use of Deadly Force: Research and Reform," *Justice Quarterly* 5, no. 2 (1988): 165–205.

57. G. Alpert and J. MacDonald, "Police Use of Force: An Analysis of Organizational Characteristics," *Justice Quarterly* 18, 2 (2001): 393–409.

58. K. Wong and K. Rakestraw, *The A, B, C's of Risk Management* (Washington, DC: International City/County Management Association, 1991).

59. G. Armitage and H. Knapman, "Adverse Events in Drug Administration: A Literature Review," *Journal of Nursing Management* 11, no. 2 (2003): 130–41; P. Ladebauche, "Lessons in Liability for Pediatric Nurses," *Pediatric Nursing* 27, no. 6 (2001): 581–98; B. Osborne, "Principles of Liability for Athletes Trainers: Managing Sport-Related Concussion," *Journal of Athletic Training* 36, no. 3 (2001): 316–22; D. Baerger, "Risk Management With the Suicidal Patient: Lessons From Case Law," *Professional Psychology: Research and Practice* 32, no. 4 (2001): 359–67; T. Baxter, "Governing the Financial or Bank Holding Company: How Legal Infrastructure

Can Facilitate Consolidated Risk Management," *Current Issues in Economics and Finance* 9, no. 3 (2003): 1–8; F. Reamer, "Malpractice Claims Against Social Workers: First Facts," *Social Work* 40 (1995): 595–602; S. Gelman, "Risk Management Through Client Access to Case Records," *Social Work* 37, no. 1 (1992): 73–80; T. Ichniowski, "There's No Claims Crisis Now, But New Challenges Loom," *Architectural Record* 183 (1995): 22–29; E. Paleologos and I. Lerche, "Option Coverage Techniques for Environmental Projects," *Journal of Management in Engineering* 18, no. 1 (2002): 3–7; J. Harshfield, "Liability Issues of Using Volunteers in Public Schools," *NASSP Bulletin* 80, no. 581 (1996): 61–66; J. Dise, "School Held Liable for Textbook Selection: The Risk of Educational Malpractice," *School & College* 34 (1995): 46–48.

60. G. Gallagher, *Risk Management Behind the Blue Curtain: A Primer on Law Enforcement Liability* (Arlington, VA: Public Risk Management Association, 1992).

61. S. Walker, *Police Accountability: The Role of Citizen Oversight* (Belmont, CA: Wadsworth Publishing, 2001), 100–1.

62. C. Archbold, "Managing the Bottom Line: Risk Management in Policing," *Policing: An International Journal of Police Strategies & Management* 28, no. 1 (2005): 38–50.

63. C. Archbold, *Police Accountability, Risk Management, and Legal Advising* (New York: LFB Scholarly Publishing, 2004).

64. See http://www.calea.org/content/accreditation.

65. Ibid.

66. See http://copwatch.org/.

67. See http://newstandardnews.net/content/index.cfm/items/1507.

68. See http://www.cuapb.org/.

69. See http://minglecity.com/group/batteredbypd.

70. See http://www.detroitcoalition.org/.

71. R. Schanlaub, "Anti-Police Internet Sites," *Law and Order* 53, no. 12 (December 2005).

72. See http://orlandocopwatch.com/group-protests-outside-orlando-police-department/.

73. See http://www.lib.jjay.cuny.edu/len/2002/10.31/.

74. See http://pewresearch.org/pubs/1066/internet-overtakes-newspapers-as-news-source.

75. See http://blog.nielsen.com/nielsenwire/consumer/u-s-homes-add-even-more-tv-sets-in-2010/.

76. C. Archbold, D. Lytle, C. Weatherall, A. Romero, and C. Baumann, "Lawsuits Involving the Police: A Content Analysis of Newspaper Accounts," *Policing: An International Journal of Police Strategies & Management* 29, no. 4 (2006): 625–42. See also C. Archbold, "Newspaper Accounts of Lawsuits Involving the Police: An Alternative Data Source?" *Journal of Crime & Justice* 29, no. 2 (2006): 1–23.

77. D. Livingston, "Police Reform and the Department of Justice: An Essay on Accountability," *Buffalo Criminal Law Review* 2, no. 2 (1999): 817–59.

78. Ibid.

79. See http://www.justice.gov/crt/about/spl/findsettle.php#police.

80. N. Kupferberg, "Transparency: A New Role for Police Consent Decrees," *Columbia Journal of Law and Social Problems* 42 (2008): 129–76.

81. Livingston, 1999.

82. D. Ross and P. Parke, "Policing by Consent Decree: An Analysis of 42 U.S.C. 14141 and the New Model for Police Accountability," *Police Practice and Research* 10, no. 3 (2009): 199–208.

83. S. Walker, *The New World of Police Accountability* (Thousand Oaks, CA: Sage, 2005).

84. See http://www.mlive.com/news/detroit/index.ssf/2010/01/monitor_has_grave_concerns_abo.

85. Ibid.

86. Ibid.

87. A. Pate and L. Fridell, *Police Use of Force: Official Reports, Citizen Complaints, and Legal Consequences. 2 Vols.* (Washington, DC: The Police Foundation, 1993).

88. P. Finn, *Citizen Review of Police: Approaches and Implementation* (Washington, DC: National Institute of Justice, 2001), 7.

89. Walker, 2005, 144.

90. Walker, 2005.

Section 10

1. G. Kelling and M. Moore, *Evolving Strategy of Policing* (Washington, DC: U.S. Department of Justice, 1988).

2. Ibid., 3

3. Ibid., 4

4. Ibid., 4

5. Ibid., 6

6. Ibid., 6

7. Ibid., 12

8. See http://www.gallup.com/poll/148163/Americans-Confident-Military-Least-Congress.aspx.

9. Ibid.

10. S. Smith, G. Steadman, T. Minton, and M. Townsend, *Criminal Victimization and Perceptions of Community Safety in 12 Cities, 1998* (Washington, DC: U. S. Department of Justice, 1999).

11. C. Gallagher, E. Maguire, Stephen Mastrofski, and Michael Reisig, *The Public Image of the Police. A Final Report to the*

International Association of the Chiefs of Police. See http://www.theiacp.org/PoliceServices/ProfessionalAssistance/ThePublicImage ofthePolice/tabid/198/Default.aspx.

12. S. Brandl, J. Frank, R. Worden, & T. Bynum, "Global and Specific Attitudes Toward the Police: Disentangling the Relationship," *Justice Quarterly* 11, no. 1 (1994): 119–34.

13. Ibid.

14. Ibid., 129.

15. D. Easton, *A Systems Analysis of Political Life* (New York: John Wiley & Sons, 1965). See also D. Easton, "A Re-Assessment of the Concept of Political Support," *British Journal of Political Science* 5, no. 4 (1975): 435–37.

16. T. Cox, and S. Falkenberg, "Adolescents' Attitudes Toward Police: An Emphasis on Interactions Between the Delinquency Measure of Alcohol and Marijuana, Police Contacts and Attitudes," *American Journal of Police* 6, no. 2 (1987): 45–62. See also Y. Hurst and J. Frank, "How Kids View Cops: The Nature of Juvenile Attitudes Toward the Police," *Journal of Criminal Justice* 28 (2000): 189–202; D. Walker, R. Richardson, T. Denyer, O. Williams, and S. McGaughey, "Contact and Support: An Empirical Assessment of Public Attitudes Toward the Police and the Courts," *North Carolina Law Review* 51, no. 1 (1972): 43–79; M. White and B. Menke, "On Assessing the Mood of the Public Towards the Police: Some Conceptual Issues," *Journal of Criminal Justice* 10 (1982): 211–30.

17. R. Kaminski and E. Jefferis, "The Effect of a Violent Televised Arrest on Public Perceptions of the Police," *Policing* 21, no. 4 (1998): 683–706.

18. W. Huang and M. Vaughn, "Support and Confidence: Public Attitudes Toward the Police," in *Americas View of Crime and Justice: A National Opinion Survey*, ed. T.J. Flanagan and D.R. Longmire (Thousand Oaks, CA: Sage, 1996), 31–45. See also P. Jesilow, J. Meyer, and N. Namazzi, "Public Attitudes Toward the Police," *American Journal of Police* 14, no. 2 (1995): 67–88.

19. M. Reisig and M. Correia, "Public Evaluations of Police Performance: An Analysis Across Three Levels of Policing," *Policing: An International Journal of Police Strategies and Management* 20, no. 2 (1997): 311–25.

20. M. Reisig and A. Giacomazzi, "Citizen Perceptions of Community Policing: Are Attitudes Toward Police Important?" *Policing: An International Journal of Police Strategies and Management* 21, no. 3 (1998): 547–61. See also M. Reisig and R. Parks, "Experience, Quality of Life, and Neighborhood Context: A Hierarchical Analysis of Satisfaction with Police," *Justice Quarterly* 17, no. 3 (2000): 607–29; J. Schaffer, B. Huebner, and T. Bynum, "Citizen Perceptions of Police Services: Race, Neighborhood Context, and Community Policing," *Police Quarterly* 6, no. 4 (2003): 440–68.

21. M. Correia, M. Reisig, and N. Lovrich, "Public Perceptions of State Police: An Analysis of Individual-Level and Contextual Variables," *Journal of Criminal Justice* 24 (1996): 17–28.

22. J. Frank, B. Smith, and K. Novak, "Citizen Attitudes Toward the Police: Exploring the Basis of Citizen Attitudes," *Police Quarterly* 8, no. 2 (2005): 206–28.

23. S. Decker, "Citizen Attitudes Toward the Police: A Review of Past Findings and Suggestions for Future Policy," *Journal of Police Science and Administration* 9, no. 1 (1981): 80–87. More recently, R. Weitzer and S. Tuch, "Determinants of Public Satisfaction with the Police," *Police Quarterly* 8, no. 3 (2005): 279–97.

24. S. Smith, G. Steadman, and T. Minton, *Criminal Victimization and Perceptions of Community Safety in 12 Cities, 1998* (Washington, DC: Bureau of Justice Statistics. 1999).

25. R. Weitzer and S. Tuch, "Perceptions of Racial Profiling: Race, Class, and Personal Experience," *Criminology* 40, no. 2 (2002): 435–56.

26. W. Skogan, "Citizen Satisfaction with Police Services: Individual and Contextual Effects," *Police Studies* 7 (1978): 469–79.

27. S. Cheurprakobkit, "Police–Citizen Contact and Police Performance: Attitudinal Differences Between Hispanics and Non-Hispanics," *Journal of Criminal Justice* 28, no. 4 (2000): 325–36.

28. I. Sun and Y. Wu, "Arab Americans' Confidence in Police," *Crime and Delinquency* (forthcoming).

29. T. Taylor, K. Turner, F. Esbensen, and L. Winfree Jr. "Coppin' an Attitude: Attitudinal Differences Among Juveniles Toward Police," *Journal of Criminal Justice* 29 (2001): 295–305. See also Cheurprakobkit, 2000.

30. Y. Wu, I. Sun, and B. Smith, "Race, Immigration and Policing: Chinese Immigrants' Satisfaction with Police," *Justice Quarterly*, 28, no. 5 (2011): 745–74.

31. J. Frank, S. Brandl, F. Cullen, and A. Stichman, "Reassessing the Impact of Race on Citizens' Attitudes Toward the Police: A Research Note," *Justice Quarterly* 13, no. 2 (1996): 321–34.

32. R. Weitzer, "Citizens' Perceptions of Police Misconduct: Race and Neighborhood Context," *Justice Quarterly* 16, no. 4 (1999): 819–46.

33. L. Cao, J. Frank, and F. Cullen, "Race, Community Context and Confidence in the Police," *American Journal of Police* 15, no. 1 (1996): 3–22.

34. R. Sampson and D. Bartusch, *Attitudes Toward Crime, Police, and the Law: Individual and Neighborhood Differences* (Washington, DC: National Institute of Justice, 1999).

35. B. Brown and W. Benedict, "Perceptions of the Police: Past Findings, Methodological Issues, Conceptual Issues and Policy Implications," *Policing: An International Journal of Police Strategies & Management* 25, no. 3 (2002): 543–80. See also S. Cheurprakobkit, 2000; Hurst and Frank, 2000; Y. Hurst, J. Frank and S. Browning,

"The Attitudes of Juveniles Toward the Police: A Comparison of Black and White Youth," *Policing: An International Journal of Police Strategies & Management* 23, no. 1 (2000): 37–53; M. Leiber, M. Nalla, and M. Farnworth "Explaining Juveniles' Attitudes Toward the Police," *Justice Quarterly* 15, no. 1 (1998): 151–73.

36. S. Nofziger and L. Williams, "Perceptions of Police and Safety in a Small Town," *Police Quarterly* 8, no. 2 (2005): 248–70.

37. D. Bayley and H. Mendelsohn, *Minorities and the Police: Confrontation in America.* (New York: Free Press, 1969). See also D. Smith, "The Origins of Black Hostility to the Police," *Policing and Society* 2, no. 1 (1991): 1–15; J. Worrall, "Public Perceptions of Police Efficacy and Image: The 'Fuzziness' of Support for the Police," *American Journal of Criminal Justice* 24, no. 1 (1999): 47–66.

38. D. Dean, "Citizen Ratings of the Police: The Difference Contact Makes," *Law and Policy Quarterly* 2, no. 4 (1980): 445–71; H. Jacob, "Black and White Perceptions of Justice in the City," *Law and Society Review* 6, no. 1 (1971): 69–89.

39. M. Reisig and M. Chandek, "The Effects of Expectancy Disconfirmation on Outcome Satisfaction in Police–Citizen Encounters," *Policing: An International Journal of Police Strategies & Management* 24, no. 1 (2001): 87–99; Schafer, Huebner, and Bynum, 2003.

40. D. Carter, "Hispanic Perception of Police Performance: An Empirical Assessment," *Journal of Criminal Justice* 13 (1985): 487–500. See also Cheurprakobkit, 2000.

41. Reisig and Chandek, 2001.

42. Smith, Steadman, Minton, and Townsend, 1999.

43. R. Brunson, "'Police Don't Like Black People'": African American Young Men's Accumulated Police Experiences," *Criminology & Public Policy* 6, no. 1 (2007): 71–102; R. Weitzer and S. Tuch. "Racially Biased Policing: Determinants of Citizen Perceptions," *Social Forces* 83, 3 (2005): 1009–30.

44. Y. Hurst and J. Frank, 2000, 189–202.

45. E. Wentz and K. Schlimgen. "Citizens' Perceptions of Police Service and Police Response to Community Concerns," *Journal of Crime and Justice,* 35, no. 1 (2012): 114–133.

46. Y. Hurst and J. Frank, 200, 189–202.

47. J. Miller, R. Davis, N. Henderson, J. Markovic, and C. Ortiz, *Public Opinions of the Police: The Influence of Friends, Family, and News Media* (New York: Vera Institute of Justice, 2001).

48. S. Eschholz, B. Sims Blackwell, M. Gertz, and T. Chiricos, "Race and Attitudes Towards the Police: Assessing the Effects of Watching 'Reality' Police Programs," *Journal of Criminal Justice* 30 (2002): 327–41.

49. Ibid.

50. E. Jefferis, R. Kaminski, S. Holmes, and D. Hanley, "The Effect of a Videotaped Arrest on Public Perceptions of Police Use of Force," *Journal of Criminal Justice* 25 (1997): 381–95. See also

P. Jesilow and J. Meyer, "The Effect of Police Misconduct on Public Attitudes: A Quasi–Experiment," *Journal of Crime and Justice* 24, no. 1 (2001): 109–21.

51. G. Shaw, R. Shapiro, S. Lock, and L. Jacobs, "The Poll-Trends: Arime, the Police, and Civil Liberties," *Public Opinion Quarterly* 62, no. 3 (1998): 405–7.

52. R. Fox and R. Van Sickel, *Tabloid Justice: Criminal Justice in an Age of Media Frenzy* (Boulder, CO: Lynne Rienner Publishers, 2001).

53. Ibid.

54. M. Sanden and E. Wentz, "Juvenile Perceptions of the Police and Police Services," paper presented at the Academy of Criminal Justice Science meetings in March 2012 (New York, NY).

55. Schaefer, Huebner, and Bynum, 2003.

56. Hurst and Frank, 2000.

57. S. Albrecht and M. Green, "Attitudes Toward the Police and the Larger Attitude Complex: Implications for Police–Community Relationships," *Criminology* 15, no. 1 (1977): 67–86.

58. Schaefer, Huebner, and Bynum, 2003, 447.

59. Cao, Frank, and Cullen, 3–22. See also M. Reisig and A. Giacomazzi, 1998, 547–61; Reisig and Parks, 2000.

60. Decker, 1981, 80–87.

61. Ibid.

62. W. Skogan, S. Hartnett, J. DuBois, J. Comey, M. Kaiser, and J. Lovig, *On the Beat: Police and Community Problem Solving* (Boulder, CO: Westview Press, 1999).

63. Bureau of Justice Assistance, *A Police Guide to Surveying Citizens and Their Environment* (Washington, DC: U.S. Department of Justice, Bureau of Justice Assistance, 1993).

64. G. Kelling, T. Pate, D. Dieckman, and C. Brown, *The Kansas City Preventive Patrol Experiment: A Technical Report* (Washington, DC: Police Foundation, 1975).

65. Cordner, 1986; Williams and Pate, 1987.

66. W. Westley, *Violence and the Police: A Sociological Study of Law, Custom, and Morality* (Cambridge: MIT Press, 1971).

67. J. Skolnick, *Justice Without Trial: Law Enforcement in a Democratic Society* (New York: John Wiley & Sons, 1966).

68. J. Van Maanen, "The Asshole," in *Policing: A View from the Streets,* ed. P. K. Manning and J. Van Maanen (New York: Random House, 1978), 221–38.

69. Kelling and Moore, 1988.

70. S. Mastrofski, M. Reisig, and J. McCluskey, "Police Encounter toward the Public: An Encounter-Based Analysis," *Criminology* 40, no. 3 (2002): 519–52.

71. J. Wilson, "Dilemmas of Police Administration," *Public Administration Review* Sept./Oct. 1968: 407–17.

72. L. Sherman, "Learning Police Ethics," *Criminal Justice Ethics* 1, 1 (1982): 10–19.

73. S. Walker, *The Police in America: An Introduction* (3rd ed.). (New York: McGraw-Hill, 1999), 220.

74. J. Groeger, *Memory and Remembering: Everyday Memory in Context* (Reading, MA: Addison-Wesley, 1997).

75. For more information, see http://nationalpal.org/.

76. Jefferis, Kaminski, Holmes, and Hanley, 1997. See also P. Jesilow and J. Meyer, "The Effect of Police Misconduct on Public Attitudes: A Quasi-Experiment," *Journal of Crime and Justice* 24, no. 1 (2001): 109–21.

77. Schafer, Huebner, and Bynum, 2003, 441.

78. Decker, 1981, 89–105.

79. S. Cox and J. Fitzgerald, *Police in Community Relations: Critical Issues, 3rd ed.* (Dubuque, IA: Brown and Benchmark Publishers, 1996).

80. J. McElvain and A. Kposowa "Police Officer Characteristics and Internal Affairs Investigations for Use of Force Allegations," *Journal of Criminal Justice* 32, no. 3 (2004): 265–79. See also S. Walker, "Complaints Against the Police: A Focus Group Study of Citizen Perceptions, Goals, and Expectations," *Criminal Justice Review* 22, no. 2 (1997): 207–26.

81. Bureau of Justice Assistance, *A Police Guide to Surveying Citizens and Their Environment* (Washington, DC: Bureau of Justice Statistics, 1993). See also D. Weisel, *Conducting Community Surveys: A Practical Guide for Law Enforcement* (Washington, DC: Bureau of Justice Statistics, 1999).

82. K. Beck, N. Boni, and J. Packer, "The Use of Public Attitude Surveys: What Can They Tell Police Managers?" *Policing: An International Journal of Police Strategies & Management* 22, no. 2 (1999): 191–213. See also H. Carlson and M. Sutton, "A Multi-Method Approach to Community Evaluation of Police Performance," *Journal of Criminal Justice* 9 (1981): 227–34; B. Hesketh, "The Police Use of Surveys: Valuable Tools or Misused Distractions?" *Police Studies* 15, no. 2 (1992): 55–61; T. Oettmeir and M. Wycoff, "Personnel Performance Evaluations in the Community Policing Context," in *Community Policing: Contemporary Readings,* ed. G. Alpert and A. Piquero (Prospect Heights, IL: Waveland Press, 1998), 275–305; S. Percy, "In Defense of Citizen Evaluations as Performance Measures," *Urban Affairs Quarterly* 22, no. 1 (1986): 66–83; Q. Thurman and M. Reisig, "Community-Oriented Research in an Era of Community Policing," *American Behavioral Scientist* 39, no. 5 (1996): 570–86; and Weisel, 1999.

83. K. Peak, R. Bradshaw, and R. Glensor, "Improving Citizen Perceptions of the Police: Back to the Basics with a Community Policing Strategy," *Journal of Criminal Justice* 20 (1992): 25–40. See also Jesilow, Meyer, and Namazzi, 2001, 67–88.

84. L. Riechers and R. Roberg, "Community Policing: A Critical Review of Underlying Assumptions," *Journal of Police Science & Administration* 17, no. 2 (1990): 105–14. See also, R. Roberg, "Can Today's Police Organizations Effectively Implement Community Policing?" in *The Challenge of Community Policing: Testing the Promises,* ed. D. Rosenbaum (Thousand Oaks, CA: Sage, 1994), 249–57; J. Greene and S. Decker, "Policy and Community Perceptions of the Community Role in Policing: The Philadelphia Experience," *Howard Journal of Criminal Justice* 28, no. 2 (1989): 105–23; J. Webb and C. Katz, "Citizen Ratings of the Importance of Community Policing Activities," *Policing: An International Journal of Police Strategies & Management* 20, no. 1 (1997): 7–23.

85. J. Baseheart and T. Cox, "Effects of Police Use of Profanity on a Receiver's Perceptions of Credibility," *Journal of Police and Criminal Psychology* 9, no. 2 (1993): 9–19; see 13.

86. G. Carte, "Changes in Public Attitudes Toward the Police: A Comparison of 1938 and 1971 Surveys," *Journal of Police Science and Administration* 1, no. 2 (1973): 182–200; see 200.

87. M. Chandek, "Race, Expectations and Evaluations of Police Performance: An Empirical Assessment," *Policing: An International Journal of Police Strategies & Management* 22, no. 4 (1999): 675–95. See also S. Decker and R. Smith, "Police Minority Recruitment: A Note on its Effectiveness in Improving Black Evaluations of the Police," *Journal of Criminal Justice* 8, no. 6 (1980): 387–93.

88. L. Cao and B. Huang, "Determinants of Citizen Complaints Against Police Abuse of Power," *Journal of Criminal Justice* 28, no. 3 (2000): 203–13.

89. W. Raffel, "Citizen Police Academies: The Importance of Communication," *Policing: An International Journal of Police Strategies & Management* 28, no. 1 (2005): 84–97.

90. M. Palmiotto and N. Unninthan, "The Impact of Citizen Police Academies on Participants: An Exploratory Study," *Journal of Criminal Justice* 30, no. 2 (2002): 101–6.

91. M. Frazier, T. Strickland, and J. Calhoun, "Changing Public Perceptions of Officers by Challenging Irrational Ideas," *Campus Law Enforcement Journal* 16 (1986): 41.

92. P. Parrish, "Police and the Media," *FBI Law Enforcement Bulletin* 62 (1993): 24–25.

93. P. Otto, "The Importance of Building Strong Media Relations: They Will Tell the Story With or Without You," *ACJS Today* 19 (2000): 8–9.

94. Otto, 2000; Parrish, 1993.

95. Jefferis, Kaminski, Holmes, and Hanley, 1997, 392.

 # Section 11

1. W. Flynn and B. McDonough. "Police Work With Juveniles: Discretion, Model Programs, and School Police Resource Officers," in *Juvenile Justice Sourcebook: Past, Present, and Future* by Albert Roberts (New York: Oxford University Press, 2004), 199–215.

2. K. Davis, *Discretionary Justice* (Baton Rouge: Louisiana State University Press, 1969).

3. W. Westley, *Violence and the Police: A Sociological Study of Law, Custom and Morality* (Cambridge: Massachusetts Institute of Technology, 1970).

4. J. Samaha, *Criminal Justice, 7th ed.* (Belmont, CA: Wadsworth Publishing, 2006), 10.

5. L. Weber Brooks, "Police Discretionary Behavior: A Study of Style," in *Critical Issues in Policing: Contemporary Readings, 6th ed.,* ed. R. Dunham and G. Alpert (Long Grove, IL: Waveland Press, 2010), 71–89.

6. D. Ross, "Emerging Trends in Police Failure to Train Liability," *Policing: An International Journal of Police Strategies & Management* 23, no. 2 (2000): 169–93.

7. C. Archbold, "Managing the Bottom Line: Risk Management in Policing," *Policing: An International Journal of Police Strategies and Management* 28, no. 1 (2005): 30–48.

8. Ibid.

9. Ibid.

10. D. Waddington, *Policing Public Disorder: Theory and Practice* (Portland, OR: Willan Publishing, 2007).

11. D. Klepal and C. Andrews, "Stories of 15 Black Men Killed by Police Since 1995," *The Cincinnati Enquirer*, April 15, 2001.

12. R. Anglen, K. Alltucker, T. Bonfield, and D. Horn, "Riot Costs Add Up: The Price in Lost Business, Battered Image and Human Pain is Incalculable," *The Cincinnati Enquirer*, October 07, 2001. See http://www.enquirer.com/editions/2001/10/07/loc_1riot_costs_add_up.html.

13. M. White, "Discretion," in *The Encyclopedia of Police Science, 3rd ed.*, ed. Jack Greene (Taylor and Francis: New York: 2007), 405–11.

14. Ibid.

15. J. Schafer, D. Carter, A. Katz-Bannister, and W. Wells, "Decision Making in Traffic Stop Encounters: A Multivariate Analysis of Police Behavior," *Police Quarterly* 9, no. 2 (2006): 184–209.

16. D. Black, "The Social Organization of Arrest," *Stanford Law Review* 23, no. 6 (1971): 1087–1111.

17. J. Fyfe, "Police Use of Deadly Force: Research and Reform," *Justice Quarterly* 5, no. 2 (1988): 165–205.

18. G. Alpert and P. Anderson, "Most Deadly Force—Police Pursuits," *Justice Quarterly* 3, no. 1 (1986): 1–14.

19. J. Goldstein, "Police Discretion Not to Invoke the Criminal Process; Low-Visibility Decisions in the Administration of Justice," *The Yale Law Journal* 69, no. 4 (1960): 543–94.

20. E. Buzawa, "Police Officer Response to Domestic Violence Legislation in Michigan," *Journal of Police Science and Administration* 10, no. 4 (1982): 415–24.

21. E. Riksheim and S. Chermak, "Causes of Police Behavior Revisited," *Journal of Criminal Justice* 21, no. 4 (1993): 353–82.

22. L. Sherman, "Causes of Police Behavior: The Current State of Quantitative Research," *Crime and Delinquency* 17, no. 1 (1980): 69–100.

23. National Research Council, *Fairness and Effectiveness in Policing: The Evidence* (Washington, DC: The National Academies Press, 2004).

24. J. Fyfe, "Shots Fired: An Examination of New York City Police Firearms Discharges," PhD Dissertation. (School of Criminal Justice, State University of New York at Albany, 1978).

25. National Research Council, 2004.

26. I. Sun and B. Payne, "Racial Differences in Resolving Conflicts: A Comparison Between Black and White Police Officers," *Crime and Delinquency* 50, no. 4 (2004): 516–41.

27. J. Crank, "Legalistic and Order Maintenance Behavior Among Police Patrol Officers: A Survey of Eight Municipal Police Agencies," *American Journal of Police* 13, no. 1 (1993): 103–26.

28. Sherman, 1980.

29. R. Worden, "Situational and Attitudinal Explanations of Police Behavior: A Theoretical Reappraisal and Empirical Assessment," *Law and Society Review* 23, no. 4 (1989): 667–711.

30. E. Bittner, *The Functions of the Police in Modern Society* (Chevy Chase, MD: U.S. Department of Health and Human Services, National Institute of Mental Health, 1970).

31. A. Reiss, *The Police and the Public* (New Haven, CT: Yale University Press, 1971).

32. D. Smith and C. Visher, "Street-Level Justice: Situational Determinants of Police Arrest Decisions," *Social Problems* 29, no. 2 (1981): 167–78.

33. Ibid.

34. R. Friedrich, "Police Use of Force: Individuals, Situations, and Organizations," *Annals of the American Academy of Political and Social Science* 452, no. 1 (1980): 82–97.

35. Ibid.

36. R. Worden, "Situational and Attitudinal Explanations of Police Behavior: A Theoretical Reappraisal and Empirical Assessment," *Law and Society Review* 23, 4 (1989): 667–711. See also J. Garner, J. Buchanan, T. Schade, and J. Hepburn, *Understanding the Use of Force By and Against the Police* (Washington, DC: National Institute of Justice, 1989); W. Terrill and S. Mastrofski, "Situational and Officer-Based Determinants of Police Coercion," *Justice Quarterly* 19, no. 2 (2002): 215–48.

37. D. Bayley, "The Tactical Choices of Police Patrol Officers," *Journal of Criminal Justice* 14, no. 4 (1986): 329–48.

38. J. Skolnick and J. Fyfe, *Above the Law: Police and the Excessive Use of Force* (New York: Free Press, 1993).

39. S. Mastrofski, R. Worden, and J. Snipes, "Law Enforcement in a Time of Community Policing," *Criminology* 33, no. 4 (1995): 539–63.

40. S. Mastrofski, R. Ritti, and D. Hoffmaster, "Organizational Determinants of Police Discretion: The Case of Drunk-Driving," *Journal of Criminal Justice* 15, no. 5 (1987): 387–402.

41. S. Walker, *The New World of Police Accountability* (Thousand Oaks, CA: Sage, 2005).

42. W. Westley, "Violence and the Police," *American Journal of Sociology* 59, no. 1 (1953): 34–41; J. Skolnick, *Justice Without Trial: Law Enforcement in a Democratic Society* (New York: Willan Publishing, 1966).

43. Westley, 1953, 41.

44. White, 2007, 406.

45. J. Wilson, *Varieties of Police Behavior* (Cambridge, MA: Harvard University Press, 1968).

46. J. Wilson and B. Boland, "The Effect of the Police on Crime," *Law & Society Review* 12 (1978): 367–90; see specifically page 379.

47. Ibid.

48. J. Fyfe, "Geographic Correlates of Police Shooting: A Microanalysis," *Crime and Delinquency* 17, no. 1 (1980): 101–13.

49. D. Klinger, "Negotiating Order in Patrol Work: An Ecological Theory of Police Response to Deviance," *Criminology* 35, no. 2 (1997): 277–306.

50. J. Sobol, "Social Ecology and Police Discretion: The Influence of District Crime, Cynicism, and Workload on the Vigor of Police Response," *Journal of Criminal Justice* 38, no. 4 (2010): 481–88. See also K. Hassell, "Variation in Police Patrol Practices: The Precinct as a Sub-Organizational Level of Analysis," *Policing: An International Journal of Police Strategies & Management* 30, no. 2 (2007): 257–76.

51. Skolnick and Fyfe, 1993.

52. *Tennessee v. Garner*, 471 U.S. 1 (1985); *Mapp v. Ohio*, 367 U.S. 643 (1961).

53. Ibid.

54. Weber Brooks, 2010.

55. Ibid.

56. Ibid.

57. M. Buerger and A. Farrell, "The Evidence of Racial Profiling: Interpreting Documented and Unofficial Sources," *Police Quarterly* 5, no. 3 (2002): 272–305.

58. D. Ramirez, J. McDevitt, and A. Farrell, *A Resource Guide on Racial Profiling Data Collection Systems: Promising Practices and Lessons Learned* (Washington, DC: U.S. Department of Justice, 2000). See page 9.

59. Ibid.

60. M. Lampson, "On the Silver Anniversary of *Terry v. Ohio*: The Reasonableness of an Automatic Frisk," *Criminal Law Bulletin* 28, no. 4 (1992): 336–81.

61. H. Mac Donald, "The Myth of Racial Profiling," *City Journal,* Spring 2001.

62. D. Barlow and M. Barlow, "Racial Profiling: A Survey of African American Police Officers," *Police Quarterly* 5, no. 3 (2002): 334–58.

63. L. Ohlin and F. Remington, *Discretion in Criminal Justice: The Tension Between Individualization and Uniformity*. SUNY Series in New Directions in Criminal Justice Studies (Albany: State University of New York Press, 1993).

64. Ibid.

65. S. Walker, *Taming the System: The Control of Discretion in Criminal Justice, 1950–1990* (New York: Oxford University Press, 1993).

66. President's Commission on Law Enforcement and Administration of Justice, *Task Force Report: The Police* (Washington, DC: U.S. Government Printing Office, 1967).

67. W. Muir, *Police: Street Corner Politicians* (Chicago: University of Chicago Press, 1977).

68. J. Van Maanen, "Boss: First Line Supervision in an American Police Agency," in *Control in the police organization,* ed. M. Punch (Cambridge, MA: Massachusetts Institute of Technology Press, 1983).

69. R. Shepard Engel, "The Effects of Supervisory Styles on Patrol Officer Behavior," *Police Quarterly* 3, no. 3 (2000): 262–93.

70. R. Johnson, "Officer Attitudes and Management Influences on Police Work Productivity," *American Journal of Criminal Justice* 36, no. 4 (2011): 293–306.

71. F. Vandall, *Police Training for Tough Calls: Discretionary Situations (limited edition)* (Atlanta, GA: Emory University, 1976).

72. Ibid.

73. United States Department of Justice, *A Problem-Based Learning Manual for Training and Evaluating Police Trainees.* (Washington, DC: United States Department of Justice, 1999). See http://www.cops.usdoj.gov/print.asp?Item+461.

74. National Research Council, 2004.

75. M. Breci and R. Simons, "An Examination of Organizational and Individual Factors That Influence Police Response to Domestic Disturbances," *Journal of Police Science Administration* 15, no. 2 (1987): 93–104. See also R. Berk, D. Loseke, S. Berk, and D. Rauma, "Bringing the Cops Back In: A Study of Efforts to Make the Criminal Justice System More Responsive to Incidents of Family Violence," *Social Science Research* 9, no. 3 (1980): 193–215.

76. National Research Council, 2004.

77. Fyfe, 1988.

78. G. Alpert and L. Fridell, *Police Vehicles and Firearms: Instruments of Deadly Force* (Prospect Heights, IL: Waveland Press, 1992).

79. D. Carn, "Hey Officer, Didn't Someone Teach You to Knock—The Supreme Court Says No Exclusion of Evidence for Knock-and-Announce Violations in *Hudson v. Michigan*," *Mercier Law Review* 58 (2007): 779–98.

80. J. Sparger and D. Giacopassi, "Memphis Revisited: A Reexamination of Police Shootings After the 'Garner' Decision," *Justice Quarterly* 9, no. 2 (1992): 211–26.

81. See http://dictionary.findlaw.com/definition/reasonable-suspicion.html.

82. D. Harris, *Profiles in Injustice: Why Racial Profiling Cannot Work* (New York: The New Press, 2002).

83. See http://www.policyarchive.org/handle/10207/bit-streams/11652.pdf.

84. L. Sherman, *Policing Domestic Violence: Experiments and Dilemmas* (New York: Free Press, 1992).

85. L. Sherman and R. Berk, "Specific Deterrent Effects of Arrest For Domestic Assault," *American Sociological Review* 49, no. 2 (1984): 261–72.

86. F. Dunford, D. Huizinga, and D. Elliott, "The Role of Arrest in Domestic Assault: The Omaha Experiment," *Criminology* 28, no. 2 (1990): 183–206.

87. J. Hirschel, I. Hutchison III, C. Dean, J. Kelley, and C. Pesackis, *Charlotte Spouse Assault Replication Project: Final Report* (Washington, DC: National Institute of Justice, 1990).

88. L. Sherman, J. Schmidt, D. Rogan, P. Gartin, E. Cohn, D. Collins, and A. Bacich, "From Initial Deterrence to Long-Term Escalation: Short-Custody Arrest For Poverty Ghetto Domestic Violence," *Criminology* 29, no. 4 (1991): 821–50.

89. R. Berk, A. Campbell, R. Klap, and B. Western, *A Bayesian Analysis of the Colorado Springs Spouse Abuse Experiment* (Department of Sociology and Program in Social Statistics, University of California, Los Angeles, 1991). See also R. Berk, A. Campbell, R. Klap, and B. Western, "The Deterrent Effect of Arrest in Incidents of Domestic Violence: A Bayesian Analysis of Four Field Experiments," *American Sociological Review* 57, no. 5 (1992): 698–708.

90. A. Pate, E. Hamilton, and A. Sampson, *Metro-Dade Spouse Abuse Replication Project: Final Report* (Washington, DC: National Institute of Justice, 1991).

91. A. Smith, "It's My Decision, Isn't It?: A Research Note on Battered Women's Perceptions of Mandatory Intervention Laws," *Violence Against Women* 6, no. 12 (2000): 1384–402.

92. B. Balos and I. Trotzky, "Enforcement of the Domestic Abuse Act in Minnesota: A Preliminary Study," *Law and Inequality* 6, no. 3 (1988): 83–125. See also K. Ferraro, "Cops, Courts and Woman Battering," in *The Criminal Justice System and Women: Offenders, Victims, and Workers*, ed. B. R. Price & N. J. Sokoloff (New York: McGraw-Hill, 1995), 262–71; F. Lawrenz, J. Lembo, and T. Schade, "Time Series Analysis of the Effect of a Domestic Violence Directive on the Numbers of Arrests Per Day," *Journal of Criminal Justice* 16, no. 6 (1988): 493–98; and C. Maxwell, J. Garner, and J. Fagan, *The Effects of Arrest on Intimate Partner Violence: New Evidence From the Spouse Assault Replication Program Series—Research in Brief* (Washington, DC: National Institute of Justice, 2001).

93. S. Walker and V. Bumphus, "Effectiveness of Civilian Review: Observations on Recent Trends and New Issues Regarding the Civilian Review of the Police," *American Journal of Police* 11, no. 4 (1992): 1–16.

 # Section 12

1. See http://www.injusticeeverywhere.com/.

2. J. Ross, *Policing Issues: Challenges & Controversies* (Burlington, MA: Jones and Bartlett Learning, 2011).

3. T. Barker and D. Carter, *Police Deviance, 3rd ed.* (Cincinnati, OH: Anderson Publishing, 1994).

4. Ibid.

5. R. Roberg and J. Kuykendall, *Police and Society* (Belmont, CA: Wadsworth Publishing Company, 1993).

6. M. Palmiotto, *Police Misconduct: A Reader for the 21st Century* (Upper Saddle River, NJ: Prentice Hall, 2001).

7. D. Carter, "Police Brutality: A Model for Definition, Perspective and Control," in *The Ambivalent Force,* ed. A.S. Blumberg and E. Neiderhoffer (New York: Holt, Rinehart and Winston, 1985).

8. Barker and Carter, 1994, 7–8.

9. Palmiotto, 2001, 32.

10. G. Kelling and M. Moore, *Evolving Strategy of Policing* (Washington, DC: U.S. Department of Justice, 1988).

11. S. Walker, *A Critical History of Police Reform: The Emergence of Professionalism* (Lexington, MA: Lexington Books, 1977).

12. Kelling and Moore, 1988.

13. P. Maas, *Serpico, The Cop who Defied the System* (New York: The Viking Press, 1973).

14. Ibid.

15. See http://www.msnbc.msn.com/id/44035946/ns/us_news-crime_and_courts/t/jury-convicts-officers-katrina-shootings/.

16. See http://cityroom.blogs.nytimes.com/2007/08/09/the-abner-louima-case-10-years-later/.

17. See http://topics.nytimes.com/topics/reference/times topics/people/d/amadou_diallo/index.html.

18. See http://www.injusticeeverywhere.com/?page_id=1858.

19. J. Roebuck and T. Barker, "Typology of Police Corruption," *Social Problems* 21, no. 3 (1974): 423–37.

20. G. Alpert and R. Dunham, *Policing Urban America* (Prospect Heights, IL: Waveland Press, 1997).

21. See http://www.foxnews.com/story/0,2933,384942,00.html.

22. See http://www.baltimoresun.com/news/maryland/baltimore-city/bs-md-ci-eddy-arias-guilty-plea-20110714,0,5151748.story.

23. See http://www.hudsonreporter.com/view/full_story/2360014/article-Sentencing-of-West-New-York-police-officers-brings-closure-to-long-ordeal.

24. See lukemusicfactory.blogspot.com/.../dc-police-officer-charged-with-stealing.

25. See http://www.theindychannel.com/news/14306963/detail.html.

26. See http://www.nytimes.com/2011/10/29/nyregion/in-ticket-fixing-scandal-16-officers-to-be-charged.html.

27. See http://www.nytimes.com/2011/11/01/opinion/the-nypds-ticket-fixing-scandal.html.

28. See http://www.wxyz.com/dpp/news/region/oakland_county/west-bloomfield-police-officer-accused-in-ticket-fixing-case.

29. See http://www.tulsaworld.com/news/article.aspx?subjectid=14&articleid=20110828_11_A9_Brando529037.

30. See http://www.tulsaworld.com/news/article.aspx?subjectid=14&articleid=20111106_11_A1_CUTLIN951360.

31. See http://www.kbtx.com/home/headlines/87465962.html.

32. See http://www.whas11.com/news/local/Police-officer-charged-with-burglary-assault-pleads-guilty-129957673.html.

33. See http://record-bergen.vlex.com/vid/denies-aiding-pols-rank-colleague-paramus-63037731.

34. See http://www.nj.com/news/index.ssf/2010/01/newark_police_officer_accused.html.

35. T. Barker, "An Empirical Study of Police Deviance Other Than Corruption," *Journal of Police Science and Administration* 6, no. 3 (1978): 264–72.

36. J. Hunt and P. Manning, "Social Context for Police Lying," *Symbolic Interaction* 14, no. 1 (1991): 51–70.

37. C. Slobogin, "Testilying: Police Perjury and What To Do About It," *University of Colorado Law Review* 67 (1996): 1037, 1059.

38. See http://www.newhampshire.com/article/20111121/NEWS03/711219963.

39. I. Son and D. Rome, "The Prevalence and Visibility of Police Misconduct: A Survey of Citizens and Police Officers," *Police Quarterly* 7, no. 2 (2004): 179–204.

40. See http://news.cincinnati.com/videonetwork/1149661783001/Cell-Phone-VIdeo-Allegedly-Shows-Sleeping-Cop.

41. A. Sapp, "Sexual Misconduct by Police Officers," in *Police Deviance*, ed. T. Barker and D. L. Carter (Cincinnati, OH: Anderson Publishing, 1994), 187–89.

42. T. Maher, "Police Sexual Misconduct: Female Police Officers' Views Regarding its Nature and Extent," *Women & Criminal Justice* 20, no. 3 (2010): 263–82.

43. T. Maher, "Police Sexual Misconduct: Officers' Perceptions of its Extent and Causality," *Criminal Justice Review* 28, no. 2 (2003):

355–81. See also T. Maher, "Police Chiefs' Views on Police Sexual Misconduct," *Police Practice and Research*, 9, no. 3 (2008): 239–50.

44. See http://getcopsofftheblock.blogspot.com/2011/08/phoenix-mayor-phil-gordons-son-police.html.

45. P. Kraska and V. Kappeler, "Police On-Duty Drug Use: A Theoretical and Descriptive Examination," *American Journal of Police* 7, no. 1 (1988): 1–28.

46. See http://lacrossetribune.com/news/local/state-and-regional/article_abc2e7b4-5258-11df-9362-001cc4c002e0.html.

47. J. Dietrich and J. Smith, "The Non-Medical Use of Drugs Including Alcohol Among Police Personnel: A Critical Literature Review," *Journal of Police Science and Administration* 14, no. 4 (1986): 300–6.

48. R. Van Raalte, "Alcoholism as a Problem Among Officers," *Police Chief* 46 (1979): 38–39.

49. See http://www.journalgazette.net/article/20111115/LOCAL07/311159965/1043/LOCAL07.

50. M. Durose, E. Schmitt, and P. Langan, *Contacts Between Police and the Public: Findings From the 2002 National Survey* (Washington, DC: Bureau of Justice Statistics, Government Printing Office, 2005).

51. R. Worden, "The 'Causes' of Police Brutality: Theory and Evidence on Police Use of Force," in *And Justice For All: Understanding and Controlling Police Abuses of Force,* ed. W.A. Gellar & H. Toch (Washington, DC: Police Executive Research Forum, 1995), 31–60.

52. Human Rights Watch, *Shielded from Justice: Police Brutality and Accountability in the United States* (New York: Human Rights Watch, 1998).

53. K. Adams, "Measuring the Prevalence of Police Abuse of Force," in *And Justice For All: Understanding and Controlling Abuse of Force,* ed. W. Geller and H. Toch (Washington, DC: Police Executive Research Forum, 1995).

54. See http://www.jsonline.com/news/milwaukee/63554812.html.

55. J. Heinonen, "Police Officer Characteristics and the Likelihood of Using Deadly Force," *Policing: An International Journal of Police Strategies & Management* 31, no. 4 (2008).

56. D. Klint, *TASER Device Liability and Litigation Risk* (2007). See http://www.taser.com/images/resources-and-legal/legal-reference/downloads/taser-device-liability-and-litigation-risk.pdf.

57. J. Fyfe, "Blind Justice: Police Shootings in Memphis," *The Journal of Criminal Law and Criminology* 73, no. 2 (1982): 707–22.

58. See http://www.commondreams.org/headlines01/0428-04.htm.

59. See http://www.nytimes.com/2003/05/23/us/cincinnati-settles-suits-against-police.html?ref=timothythomas.

60. M. Palmiotto, *Police Misconduct: A Reader for the 21st Century* (Upper Saddle River, NJ: Prentice Hall, 2001).

61. L. Sherman, *Police Corruption: A Sociological Perspective* (Garden City, NY: Anchor Books, 1974).

62. S. Ivković, "Rotten Apples, Rotten Branches, and Rotten Orchards: A Cautionary Tale of Police Misconduct," *Criminology & Public Policy* 8, no. 4 (2009): 777–85.

63. C. Griffin and J. Ruiz, "The Sociopathic Police Personality: Is It a Product of the Rotten Apple or the Rotten Barrel?" *Journal of Police and Criminal Psychology* 14, no. 1 (1985): 28–37.

64. M. Punch, "Rotten Orchards: 'Pestilence,' Police Misconduct and System Failure," *Policing and Society* 13, no. 2 (2003): 171–96.

65. Sherman, 1974.

66. Knapp Commission Report on Police Corruption, *New York City Commission to Investigate Allegations of Police Corruption.* (New York: Knapp Commission, 1973), 4.

67. Barker, 1977.

68. M. White, *Current Issues and Controversies in Policing* (Upper Saddle River, NJ: Pearson Prentice Hall, 2007), 245.

69. A. Arcuri, M. Gunn, and D. Lester, "Moonlighting By Police Officers: A Way of Life," *Psychological Reports* 60, no. 1 (1987): 210.

70. V. Bryan and E. Taiji, "Police Work Hours, Fatigue and Officer Performance," in *Police and Policing: Contemporary Issues,* ed. D. Kenney and R. McNamara (Westport, CT: Praeger Publishers, 1999), 78–95.

71. See http://www.examiner.com/moderate-in-detroit/thanks-to-a-newly-passed-ordinance-detroit-police-officers-can-now-moonlight.

72. Barker, 1977.

73. Roberg and Kuykendall, 1993.

74. S. Ellwanger., "How Police Officers Learn Ethics," in *Justice, Crime, and Ethics, 7th ed.,* by M. Braswell, B. McCarthy, and B. McCarthy (Cincinnati, OH: Anderson Publishing, 2012), 45–67.

75. Ibid., 53.

76. Ibid., 58.

77. Ibid., 59.

78. Barker, 1977.

79. Ibid.

80. Roberg and Kuykendall, 1993.

81. Ibid.

82. R. Weitzer, "Incidents of Police Misconduct and Public Opinion," *Journal of Criminal Justice* 30, no. 5 (2002): 397–408.

83. J. Greene, "Zero Tolerance: A Case Study of Police Policies and Practices in New York City," *Crime & Delinquency* 45, no. 2 (1999): 171–87.

84. C. Archbold, D. Lytle, C. Weatherall, A. Romero, and C. Baumann, "Lawsuits Involving the Police: A Content Analysis of Newspaper Accounts," *Policing: An International Journal of Police Strategies & Management* 29, no. 4 (2006): 625–42.

85. S. Decker, "The Police and the Public: Perceptions and Policy recommendations," in *Police and Law Enforcement, 1975–1981, Vol. 3,* ed. R. Homant and D. Kennedy (New York: AMS Press, 1985), 89–105.

86. T. Barker and D. Carter, "Fluffing Up the Evidence and Covering Your Ass: Some Conceptual Notes on Policy Lying," *Deviant Behavior* 11, no. 1 (1990): 61–73.

87. R. Hunter, "Officer Opinions on Police Misconduct," *Journal of Contemporary Criminal Justice*, 15, no. 2 (1999): 155–70.

88. H. Goldstein, *Police Corruption: Perspectives on its Nature and Control* (Washington, DC: Police Foundation, 1975).

89. S. Walker, *Police Accountability: The Role of Citizen Oversight* (Belmont, CA: Wadsworth Publishing, 2001), 5.

90. Ibid., 6.

91. See report by Samuel Walker at http://www.unomaha.edu/criminaljustice/PDF/core.pdf.

92. See http://www.observer.com/2011/09/occupy-wall-street-update-alleged-police-brutality-caught-on-film-video/.

93. See http://www.justice.gov/crt/about/spl/nopd.php for an example.

94. V. Kappeler, R. Sluder, and G. Alpert, *Forces of Deviance: The Dark Side of Policing* (Prospect Heights, IL: Waveland Press, 1994), 262.

95. Ibid., 241.

96. Ibid., 245.

97. J. Greene, A. Piquero, M. Hickman, and B. Lawton, *Police Integrity and Accountability in Philadelphia: Predicting and Assessing Police Misconduct* (Rockville, MD: National Institute of Justice, 2004).

98. M. Sellbom, G. Fischler, and Y. Ben-Porath, "Identifying MMPI-2 Predictors of Police Officer Integrity and Misconduct," *Criminal Justice and Behavior* 34, no. 8 (2007): 985–1004.

99. B. Arrigo and N. Claussen, "Police Corruption and Psychological Testing: A Strategy for Preemployment Screening," *International Journal of Offender Therapy and Comparative Criminology* 47, no. 3 (2003): 272–90. See also Sellbom, Fischler, and Ben-Porath, 2007.

100. J. Greene, A. Piquero, M. Hickman, and B. Lawton, *Police Integrity and Accountability in Philadelphia: Predicting and Assessing Police Misconduct* (Rockville, MD: National Institute of Justice, 2004).

101. Ibid.

102. See http://www.llrmi.com/articles/legal_update/le_integrity_tests.shtml.

103. T. Prenzler, "Senior Police Managers' Views on Integrity Testing, and Drug and Alcohol Testing," *Policing: An International Journal of Police Strategies & Management* 29, no. 3 (2006): 394–407.

104. See http://www.nytimes.com/1999/09/24/nyregion/police-used-in-stings-to-weed-out-violent-officers.html?pagewanted=all&src=pm.

105. Prenzler, 2006.

106. L. Sherman, *Scandal and Reform: Controlling Police Corruption* (Berkeley: University of California Press, 1978), 165.

107. H. Goldstein, *Police Corruption—A Perspective on its Nature and Control* (Washington, DC: Police Foundation, 1975).

108. G. Rothwell and J. Baldwin, "Whistle-Blowing and the Code of Silence in Police Agencies Policy and Structural Predictors," *Crime & Delinquency* 53, no. 4 (2007): 605–32.

109. International Association of Chiefs of Police, *Building Trust Between the Police and the Citizens They Serve: An Internal Affairs Promising Practices Guide for Local Law Enforcement* (Washington, DC: United States Department of Justice, Office of Community Oriented Policing Services, 2009).

110. A. Pate, L. Fridell, and E. Hamilton, *Police Use of Force: Official Reports, Citizen Complaints and Legal Consequences, Volumes 1 and 2* (Washington, DC: Police Foundation, 1993).

111. M. Hickman, *Citizen Complaints about Police Use of Force* (Rockville, MD: Bureau of Justice Statistics, 2006).

112. S. Walker, C. Archbold, and L. Herbst, *Mediating Citizen Complaints Against Police Officers: A Guide for Police and Citizens* (Washington, DC: Office of Community Oriented Policing Services, 2002).

113. J. Maxwell, *Dispute Mediation: A Training Manual* (1994).

114. S. Walker and C. Archbold, "Mediating Citizen Complaints Against the Police: An Exploratory Study," *Journal of Dispute Resolution* 2 (2000): 231–44.

115. See http://dictionary.reference.com/browse/ethics.

116. See http://www.theiacp.org/PoliceServices/Executive Services/ProfessionalAssistance/Ethics/ReportsResources/Ethics TraininginLawEnforcement/tabid/194/Default.aspx.

117. B. Reaves, *State and Local Law Enforcement Training Academies, 2006* (Washington, DC: United States Department of Justice, 2009).

118. See http://www.cops.usdoj.gov/Default.asp?Item=2049.

119. L. Miller and M. Braswell, "Police Perceptions of Ethical Decision-Making: The Ideal vs. the Real," *American Journal of Police* 11, no. 4 (1992): 27–46.

120. G. Felkenes, "Attitudes of Police Officers Toward Their Professional Ethics," *Journal of Criminal Justice* 12, no. 3 (1984): 211–20.

121. C. Klockars, S. Ivkovich, and M. Haberfeld, *Enhancing Police Integrity* (Rockville, MD: National Institute of Justice, 2005).

122. Ibid.

 # Section 13

1. See http://quotationsbook.com/quote/5646/.

2. See http://www.bloomberg.com/apps/news?pid=news archive&sid=aNivTjr852TI.

3. See http://cops.usdoj.gov/html/dispatch/06-2011/DirectorMessage.asp.

4. Office of Community Oriented Policing Services, *Impact of the Economic Downturn on American Police Agencies* (Washington, DC: United States Department of Justice, Office of Community Oriented Policing Services, 2011).

5. See http://sanfrancisco.cbslocal.com/2011/04/27/hundreds-of-san-jose-police-officer-jobs-still-on-the-line/.

6. Office of Community Oriented Policing Services, 2011.

7. Ibid.

8. See http://www.talgov.com/tpd/tpd-online.cfm.

9. Office of Community Oriented Policing Services, 2011.

10. B. Forst, "The Privatization and Civilianization of Policing," In *Boundary Changes in Criminal Justice Organizations: Criminal Justice 2000, Vol. 2*, ed. C.M. Friel (Washington, DC: National Institute of Justice, 2000), 19–79.

11. B. Reaves, *Census of State and Local Law Enforcement Agencies, 2008* (Washington, DC: Bureau of Justice Statistics, 2011).

12. Forst, 2000.

13. Office of Community Oriented Policing Services, 2011.

14. B. Reaves, *Census of State and Local Law Enforcement Agencies, 1996* (Washington, DC: United States Department of Justice, 1998).

15. Forst, 2000, 23.

16. Office of Community Oriented Policing Services, 2011.

17. Ibid.

18. Ibid.

19. International Association of Chiefs of Police (IACP), *Policing in the 21st Century: Preliminary Survey Results* (Alexandria, VA: IACP, 2010).

20. See http://www.policevolunteers.org/about/.

21. See http://www.ci.fargo.nd.us/CityInfo/Departments/Police/CitizenResources/CitizenVolunteerProgram/.

22. Office of Community Oriented Policing Services, 2011.

23. New Jersey State Association of Chiefs of Police, *Police Department Regionalization, Consolidation, Merger & Shared Services: Important Considerations for Policy Makers* (West Trenton, NJ: New Jersey State Association of Chiefs of Police, 2007).

24. Julianne J. Duvall, "City County Consolidation: A Matter of Efficiency?" In *Forms of Local Government: A Handbook on City, County and Regional Options,* ed. Roger L. Kemp (Jefferson, NC: McFarland Publishing, 1999).

25. Office of Community Oriented Policing Services, 2011.

26. C. Werner, *The Older Population: 2010* (Census Briefs, November 2011). See http://www.census.gov/prod/cen2010/briefs/c2010br-09.pdf.

27. See http://www.ncea.aoa.gov/ncearoot/Main_Site/pdf/publication/NCEA_WhatIsAbuse-2010.pdf.

28. Ibid.

29. See http://www.ncea.aoa.gov/ncearoot/Main_Site/pdf/publication/FinalStatistics050331.pdf.

30. Ibid.

31. Ibid.

32. W. Bourns, "Police Gerontology Services for the Elderly: A Policy Guide," *The Justice Professional* 13, no. 2 (2000): 179–92.

33. Ibid., 188.

34. See http://www.alz.org/documents_custom/2011_Facts_Figures_Fact_Sheet.pdf.

35. Ibid.

36. C. Heisler, "Elder Abuse and the Criminal Justice System: New Awareness, New Responses," *Generations* 24, no. 2 (2000): 52–58.

37. See http://www.alz.org/safetycenter/we_can_help_safety_medicalert_safereturn.asp.

38. See http://projectlifesaver.org/Lifesaver/resource-center/news-and-press-releases/.

39. S. Lachenmayr, K. Denard Goldman, and F. Brand, "Safe Return: A Community-Based Initiative between Police Officers and the Alzheimer's Association to Increase the Safety of People with Alzheimer's Disease," *Health Promotion Practice* 1 (2000): 268–78.

40. R. Zevitz and D. Marlock, "Senior Citizen Assault Prevention Unit," *FBI Law Enforcement Bulletin* 58, 3 (1989): 10–13.

41. R. Zevitz and A. Gurnack, "Factors Related to Elderly Crime Victims' Satisfaction With Police Service: The Impact of Milwaukee's "Gray Squad," *The Gerontologist*, 31, no. 1 (1991): 92–101.

42. K. Amendola, M. Slipka, E. Hamilton, and J. Whitman, *The Course of Domestic Abuse Among Chicago's Elderly: Risk Factors, Protective Behaviors, and Police Intervention* (Washington, DC: The Police Foundation, December 2010). See http://www.policefoundation.org/pdf/elderabuse.pdf.

43. L. Teplin and N. Pruett, "Police as Street Corner Psychiatrist: Managing the Mentally Ill," *International Journal of Law and Psychiatry* 15, no. 2 (1992): 139–56.

44. M.F. Abramson, "The Criminalization of Mentally Disordered Behavior: Possible Side-Effect of a New Mental Health Law," *Hospital and Community Psychiatry* 23, no. 4 (1972): 1036–45.

45. A. Lurigio, J. Snowden, and A. Watson, "Police Handling of People with Mental Illness," *Law Enforcement Executive Forum* 6 (2006): 87–110.

46. L. Teplin, *Keeping the Peace: Police Discretion and Mentally Ill Persons* (Washington, DC: National Institute of Justice,, July 2000).

47. Ibid.

48. P. Finn and M. Sullivan, "Police Handling of the Mentally Ill: Sharing Responsibility with the Mental Health System," *Journal of Criminal Justice* 17, no. 1 (1989): 1–14.

49. Ibid.

50. Ibid.

51. Ibid., 11.

52. V. Cooper, A. Mclearen, and P. Zapf, "Disposition Decisions with the Mentally Ill: Police Perceptions and Characteristics," *Police Quarterly* 7, no. 3 (2004): 295–310.

53. W. Wells and J. Schafer, "Officer Perceptions of Police Responses to Persons With a Mental Illness," *Policing: An International Journal of Police Strategies and Management*, 29, no. 4 (2006): 578–601.

54. A. Lurigio, J. Snowden, and A. Watson, "Police Handling of People With Mental Illness," *Law Enforcement Executive Forum* 6 (2006): 87–110.

55. J. Hails and R. Borum, "Police Training and Specialized Approaches to Respond to People With Mental Illnesses," *Crime and Delinquency* 49, no. 1 (2003): 52–61.

56. See http://www.slate.com/articles/news_and_politics/explainer/2011/05/too_crazy_for_court.html.

57. J. Monahan, *Mental Illness and Violent Crime* (Washington, DC: United States Department of Justice, Office of Justice Programs, National Institute of Justice, October 1996).

58. S. Fazel, N. Långström, A. Hjern, M. Grann, and P. Lichtenstein, "Schizophrenia, Substance Abuse, and Violent Crime," *Journal of American Medical Association* 301, no. 19 (2009): 2016–23.

59. L. Teplin, G. McClelland, K. Abram, and D. Weiner, "Crime Victimization in Adults With Severe Mental Illness: Comparison With the National Crime Victimization Survey," *Archives of General Psychiatry* 62, no. 8 (2005): 911–21.

60. See http://www.endhomelessness.org/section/about_homelessness/snapshot_of_homelessness.

61. Ibid.

62. D. Carter and A. Sapp. "Police Experiences and Responses Related to the Homeless," *Journal of Crime and Justice* 16, no. 2 (1993): 87–108.

63. T. Zakrison, P. Hamel, and S. Hwang, "Homeless People's Trust and Interactions With Police and Paramedics," *Journal of Urban Health: Bulletin of the New York Academy of Medicine* 81, no. 4 (2004): 596–605.

64. Carter and Sapp, 1993.

65. Ibid.

66. Ibid.

67. J. Strasser, S. Damrosch, and J. Gaines. "Nutrition and the Homeless Person," *Journal of Community Health Nursing* 8, no. 2 (1991): 65–73.

68. Carter and Sapp, 1993.

69. See http://santamonicapd.org/HLP.aspx.

70. See www.stpete.org/socialservices/homelessness/.../StPetePhase1Report.pdf.

71. See http://www.usatoday.com/news/nation/2008-03-04-katrina-health_N.htm.

72. See http://media.al.com/bn/other/Alabama%20 Immigration%20Law%202011.pdf.

73. See http://alisondb.legislature.state.al.us/acas/search ableinstruments/2011rs/bills/hb56.htm.

74. See http://www.azleg.gov/legtext/49leg/2r/summary/s.1070pshs.doc.htm.

75. D. Harris, "The War on Terror, Local Police and Immigration Enforcement: A Curious Tale of Police Power in Post-9/11 America," *Rutgers Law Journal* 38 May (2006): 1–60.

76. Police Foundation, *The Role of Local Police: Striking a Balance Between Immigration Enforcement and Civil Liberties* (Washington, DC: The Police Foundation, April 2009).

77. See http://www.ice.gov/news/library/factsheets/287g .htm#signed-moa.

78. Ibid.

79. Ibid.

80. See http://www.bordc.org/resources/police.pdf.

81. See http://www.msnbc.msn.com/id/38237264/ns/us_ newsimmigration_a_nation_divided/t/arizonas-famed-sheriff-joe-defends-immigration-law/#.TvziXno3HNU.

82. Police Executive Research Forum, *Critical Issues in Policing Series: Police Chiefs and Sheriffs Speak out on Local Immigration Enforcement* (Washington, DC: Police Executive Research Forum, April 2008).

83. Ibid.

84. Ibid.

85. G. Vidales, K. Day, and M. Powe, "Police and Immigration Enforcement: Impacts on Latino(s) Residents' Perceptions of Police," *Policing: An International Journal of Police Strategies and Management* 32, no. 4 (2009): 631–53.

86. See http://terrorism.about.com/od/whatisterroris1/ss/DefineTerrorism_4.htm.

87. A. Larabee, "A Brief History of Terrorism in the United States," *Knowledge, Technology & Policy* 16, no. 1 (2003): 21–38.

88. See http://www.theonlinerocket.com/news/lost-lives-remembered-during-9-11-ceremony-1.2333384#.Tv31Pno3HNU.

89. W. Oliver, "The Fourth Era of Policing: Homeland Security," *International Review of Law, Computers & Technology* 20, no. 1–2 (2006): 49–62.

90. Oliver, 2006.

91. J. Pastor, "Terrorism and Public Safety Policing," *Crime and Justice International* 21, no. 85 (2005): 9–17.

92. M. de Guzman, "The Changing Roles and Strategies of the Police in a Time of Terror," *ACJS Today* (September–October 2002): 8–13.

93. S. Brandl, "Back to the Future: The Implications of September 11, 2001 on Law Enforcement Practice and Policy," *Ohio State Journal of Criminal Law* 1 (2003): 133–54.

94. B. Raymond, L. Hickman, L. Miller, and J. Wong, *Police Personnel Challenges After September 11: Anticipating Expanded Duties and a Changing of Labor Pool* (Santa Monica, CA: RAND, 2005).

95. D. Thacher, "The Local Role in Homeland Security," *Law & Society Review* 39, no. 3 (2005): 635–76.

96. J. Lee, "Policing After 9/11: Community Policing in an Age of Homeland Security," *Police Quarterly* 13, no. 4 (2010): 347–66.

97. A. Chappell and S. Gibson, "Community Policing and Homeland Security: Friend or Foe?" *Criminal Justice Policy Review* 20, no. 3 (2009): 326–43.

98. D. Marks and I. Sun, "The Impact of 9/11 on Organizational Development Among State and Local Law Enforcement Agencies," *Journal of Contemporary Criminal Justice* 23, no. 2 (2007): 159–73.

99. C. Ortiz, N. Hendricks, and N. Sugie, "Policing Terrorism: The Response of Local Police Agencies to Homeland Security Concerns" *Criminal Justice Studies* 20, no. 2 (2007): 91–109.

100. W. Tafoya, *Delphi Forecast of the Future of Law Enforcement* (University of Maryland—doctoral dissertation, 1986).

101. Ibid.

102. See http://www.policefuturists.org/about_pfi.htm.

103. Ibid.

104. See http://fwg.cos.ucf.edu/.

105. J. Schafer, ed., *Policing 2020: Exploring the Future of Crime, Communities, and Policing* (Washington, DC: Federal Bureau of Investigation, 2007).

106. J. Schafer, M. Buerger, R. Myers, C. Jensen, and B. Levin, *The Future of Policing: A Practical Guide for Police Managers and Leaders* (Boca Raton, FL: CRC/Taylor-Francis, 2012).

107. Bureau of Labor Statistics, U.S. Department of Labor, *Occupational Outlook Handbook, 2010–11 Edition, Police and Detectives*. See http://www.bls.gov/oco/ocos160.htm.

108. Ibid.

109. Ibid.

110. J. Schafer, "The Future of Police Image and Ethics," *Police Chief* (December 2011).

111. See http://www.iacpsocialmedia.org/Resources/Publications/2010SurveyResults.aspx.

112. J. Joline Myers, T. Lough, and K. Pawleko, "Off Duty Comments: The Effects of Social Networking on Public Careers," *Law Enforcement Executive Forum* 11 (2011): 1–19.

113. *Thaeter v. Palm Beach County Sheriff's Office*, et al., 449 F.3d 1342 (11th Cir. 2006).

114. W. Tangel and A. Morabito, "Minority Recruitment: A Working Model," *Police Chief* 71 (March 2004).

115. G. Cordner and A. Cordner, "Stuck on a Plateau? Obstacles to Recruitment, Selection, and Retention of Women Police," *Police Quarterly* 14, no. 3 (2011): 207–26; see 208.

116. Ibid., 218.

117. Ibid., 218.

118. See http://blog.discoverpolicing.org/uncategorized/policing-jetson-style/ .

119. Ibid.

120. B. Reaves, *Local Police Departments, 2007* (Washington, DC: Bureau of Justice Statistics, December 2010).

121. See http://www.usatoday.com/news/nation/2010-02-15-head-cameras-police_N.htm.

122. Ibid.

123. Reaves, 2010.

124. See http://www.msnbc.msn.com/id/44124367/ns/technology_and_science-tech_and_gadgets/t/louisville-police-add-computers-mounted-patrol/#.TwDIsXo3HNU.

125. M. Sakiyama, D. Shaffer, and J. Lieberman, "Facebook and the Police: Communication in the Social Networking Era" (April 20, 2011). Graduate Research Symposium (CUA). See http://digitalscholarship.unlv.edu/grad_symposium/2011/april20/5.

126. Ibid.

127. R. Rantala, *Cybercrime Against Businesses, 2005* (Washington, DC: Bureau of Justice Statistics, 2008).

128. C. Hale, "Cybercrime: Facts & Figures Concerning This Global Dilemma," *Crime & Justice International* 5, no. 65 (2002): 5, 6, and 24–26.

129. Rantala, 2008.

130. Ibid., 7.

131. Ibid., 7.

132. T. Aeilts, "Defending Against Cybercrime and Terrorism: A New Role for Universities," *FBI Law Enforcement Bulletin* 74 (2005): 14–20.

133. Ibid., 16.

134. H. Stambaugh, D. Beaupre, D. Icove R. Baker, W. Cassaday, and W. Williams, *State and Local Law Enforcement Needs to Combat Electronic Crime* (Washington, DC: National Institute of Justice, August 2000).

135. Hale, 2002.

136. R. Burns, K. Whitworth, and C. Thompson, "Assessing Law Enforcement Preparedness to Address Internet Fraud," *Journal of Criminal Justice* 32, no. 5 (2004): 477–93.

137. Hale, 2000.

138. See http://abcnews.go.com/Technology/michigan-police-cellphone-data-extraction-devices-aclu-objects/story?id=13428178#.TwDFXno3HNU.

139. See http://duijusticelink.aaa.com/issues/detection/passive-alcohol-sensors.

140. See http://www.droplex.com/safety/alcohol_pasiv.php.

141. See http://www.gizmag.com/go/7024/.

142. See http://projectlifesaver.org/Lifesaver/resource-center/news-and-press-releases/.

143. See http://gcn.com/articles/2010/10/08/sl-baltimore-pd-gps.aspx.

144. See http://www.rmtracking.com/blog/2009/02/11/criminals-beware-police-are-using-gps-to-track-you/.

145. See http://lawblog.legalmatch.com/2011/07/15/exciting-police-technologies-criminal-investigations/.

146. See http://lawblog.legalmatch.com/2011/07/15/exciting-police-technologies-criminal-investigations/.

147. See http://thelede.blogs.nytimes.com/2011/05/18/x-ray-scan-reveals-513-mexican-migrants-in-2-trucks/.

Credits and Sources

Section 1. Photo, page 2: ND State Historical Society. Photo, page 5: ND State Historical Society. Photo, page 6: North Dakota State University. Photo, page 8: Virginia Fire and Police Museum. Photo, page 9: North Dakota State University. Photo, page 10 (top): North Dakota State University. Photo, page 10 (bottom): North Dakota State University. Reading 1, pages 16–29: Philip Reichel. (1988). "Slave patrol as a transitional police type." *American Journal of Police, 7:* 51–77. Reading 2, pages 29–45: Kelling, G. and M. Moore. (1988). "The evolving strategy of policing." National Institute of Justice.

Section 2. Photo, page 46: Carol Archbold. Photo, page 48: Carol Archbold. Photo, page 51: Fargo Police Department. Photo, page 53: Carol Archbold. Reading 3, pages 57–72: Goldstein, Herman. (1979). "Improving policing: A problem-oriented approach." *Crime and Delinquency, 25,* 2: 236–258. Reading 4, pages 73–84: David Carter and Jeremy Carter. (2009). "Intelligence-Led Policing Conceptual and Functional Considerations for Public Policy." *Criminal Justice Policy Review, 20,* 3: 310–325.

Section 3. Photo, page 85: Carol Archbold. Photo, page 88: Carol Archbold. Photo, page 89: Carol Archbold. Photo, page 90: Carol Archbold. Photo, page 99: Lisbon Police Department. Reading 5, pages 103–110: E.M. Luna-Firebaugh. "Women in tribal policing: An examination of their status and experiences." *Social Science Journal, 39,* 4: 583–592. Copyright ©

2002, Elsevier. Reprinted with permission. Reading 6, pages 111–124: Ralph A. Weisheit, L. Edward Wells, and David N. Falcone. "Community Policing in Small Town and Rural America" *Crime & Delinquency* October 1994 40: 549–567.

Section 4. Photo, page 125: Carol Archbold. Photo, page 129: ND State Historical Society. Photo, page 130: Carol Archbold. Photo, page 133: Carol Archbold. Photo, page 136: Carol Archbold. Reading 7, pages 138–153: K. D. Hassell and S. G. Brandl. (2009). "An Examination of the Workplace Experiences of Police Patrol Officers: The Role of Race, Sex, and Sexual Orientation." *Police Quarterly, 12,* 4: 408–430. Reading 8, pages 154–164: Ch. 1, "Culture and Knowledge," from John Crank. *Understanding Police Culture,* 2nd ed. pp. 13–28. Reprinted with permission.

Section 5. Photo, page 165: Carol Archbold. Photo, page 166: Carol Archbold. Photo, page 170: Fargo Police Department. Photo, page 173: Fargo Police Department. Photo, page 175: Fargo Police Department. Reading 9, pages 178–192: Roy Roberg, Scott Bonn, "Higher education and policing: where are we now?" *Policing: An International Journal of Police Strategies & Management,* Vol. 27 Iss: 4, pp.469–486. Copyright © 2004 Emerald Publishing Group. Reprinted with permission. Reading 10, pages 192–208: Robin Haar (2005). "Factors Affecting the Decision of Police Recruits to 'Drop Out' of Police Work." *Police Quarterly,* December 2005; vol. 8, 4: pp. 431–453.

Section 6. Photo, page 210: Carol Archbold. Photo, page 211: Fargo Police Department. Photo, page 217: Carol Archbold. Photo, page 220: Fargo Police Department. Photo, page 223: Carol Archbold. Reading 11, pages 226–240: Willis, James. (2011) "First-Line Supervision and Strategic Decision Making Under Compstat and Community Policing." *Criminal Justice Policy Review* 1–22. Reading 12, pages 241–245: From *Behind the Shield: Police in Urban Society* by Arthur Niederhofer. Copyright © 1967 by Arthur Niederhofer. Used by permission of Doubleday, a division of Random House, Inc.

Section 7. Photo, page 246: Fargo Police Department. Photo, page 248: North Dakota State University. Photo, page 249: Carol Archbold. Photo, page 251: Fargo Police Department. Photo, page 252: Fargo Police Department. Photo, page 255: Fargo Police Department. Reading 13, pages 259–271: M. Alderden and S. Ullman. "Gender Difference or Indifference? Detective Decision Making in Sexual Assault Cases." *Journal of Interpersonal Violence, 27* (2012): pp. 3–22. Reading 14, pages 271–282: Bruce Taylor, Apollo Kowalyk and Rachel Boba. (2007) "The Integration of Crime Analysis Into Law Enforcement Agencies: An Exploratory Study Into the Perceptions of Crime Analysts." *Police Quarterly 10:* 154–169.

Section 8. Photo, page 283: Carol Archbold. Photo, page 285: Fargo Police Department. Photo, page 291: Carol Archbold. Photo, page 293: Carol Archbold. Reading 15, pages 296–308: L. Sherman and Richard Berk. (1984). "The Specific Deterrent Effects of Arrest for Domestic Assault." *American Sociological Review, 49,* 2: 261–272. Reading 16, pages 309–327: Ratcliffe, JH, Taniguchi, T, Groff, ER & Wood, JD (in press). The Philadelphia Foot Patrol Experiment: A randomized controlled trial of police patrol effectiveness in violent crime hotspots. *Criminology.*

Section 9. Photo, page 328: Carol Archbold. Photo, page 329: Fargo Police Department. Photo, page 332: Carol Archbold. Photo, page 335: Fargo Police Department. Photo, page 337: Carol Archbold. Reading 17, pages 341–355: Carol Archbold. (2005). "Managing the bottom line: Risk management in policing." *Policing: An International Journal of Police Strategies and Management.* 28, 1: 30–48. Reading 18, pages 356–367: Samuel Walker, Geoffrey Alpert and Dennis Kenney (2000). "Warning Systems for Police: Concept, History, and Issues" *Police Quarterly,* 3: 132–152.

Section 10. Photo, page 370: Fargo Police Department. Photo, page 375: Fargo Police Department. Photo, page 376: Fargo Police Department. Photo, page 377: Fargo Police Department. Photo, page 381: Fargo Police Department. Reading 19, pages 383–393: Stacey Nofziger and L. Susan Williams. (2005). "Perceptions of Police and Safety in a Small Town." *Police Quarterly,* 8: 248–270. Reading 20, pages 394–401: Ch. 14, "Angels and Assholes: The construction of police morality," from John Crank. *Understanding Police Culture,* 2nd ed. pp. 201–212. Reprinted with permission.

Section 11. Photo, page 402: Carol Archbold. Photo, page 404: Carol Archbold. Photo, page 406: Fargo Police Department. Photo, page 408: Carol Archbold. Photo, page 411: Fargo Police Department. Reading 21, pages 416–424: G. Alpert, R. Dunham, M. Stroshine, K. Bennett and J. McDonald. (2004). *Police officers' decisions making and discretion: Forming suspicion and making a stop—Executive summary.* Research report submitted to the National Institute of Justice, Office of Justice Programs, United States Department of Justice, Washington DC. Reading 22, pages 425–436: D. Barlow and M. Barlow. (2002). "Racial Profiling: A survey of African American police officers." *Police Quarterly 5:* 334–358.

Section 12. Photo, page 437: Carol Archbold. Photo, page 441: Fargo Police Department. Photo, page 443: Carol Archbold. Photo, page 450: Fargo Police Department. Reading 23, pages 453–464: Klockars, Carl. B. "The Dirty Harry problem." *The Annals, 452*

(November 1980), pp. 33–47. Reading 24, pages 464–475: Gennaro F. Vito; Scott Wolfe; George E. Higgins; William F. Walsh. "Police Integrity: Rankings of Scenarios on the Klockars Scale by 'Management Cops.'" *Criminal Justice Review 36* (2011):152–164.

Section 13. Photo, page 476: Carol Archbold. Photo, page 482: Fargo Police Department. Photo, page 486: Fargo Police Department. Photo, page 488: Carol Archbold. Reading 25, pages 493–508: Mary Romero. (2006). "Racial Profiling and Immigration Law Enforcement: Rounding Up of Usual Suspects in the Latino Community." *Critical Sociology, 32:* 447–473. Reading 26, pages 509–520: King, W. and T. Dunn. (2004). "Dumping: Police-initiated Tran jurisdictional transport of troublesome persons." *Police Quarterly, 7, 3:* 339–358.

Index

About the Author

Carol A. Archbold is an Associate Professor of Criminal Justice at North Dakota State University in Fargo, North Dakota. She earned her PhD from the University of Nebraska-Omaha in 2002. Dr. Archbold's research interests include women in policing, police accountability and liability, police handling of sexual assault cases, and police and race issues. She has published articles in such journals as *Police Quarterly, Policing: An International Journal of Police Strategies and Management, International Journal of Police Science and Management, Police Practice and Research: An International Journal, Journal of Criminal Justice,* and the *Journal of Crime and Justice.* In 2004, Dr. Archbold published a book based on the first national study of the use of risk management in law enforcement in the United States, *Police Accountability, Risk Management and Legal Advising* (LFB Scholarly Publishing). This study was the focus of her dissertation. Along with Samuel Walker and Leigh Herbst (Culver), she was a contributing author for "Mediating Citizen Complaints Against Police Officers: A Guide for Police and Citizens," funded by the Office of Community Oriented Policing Services (United States Department of Justice, Washington, DC). In 2011, she was one of three authors of a reader, *Women and Policing in America: Classic and Contemporary Readings* (Aspen Publishing), with Dorothy Moses Schulz and Kimberly Hassell. Future research endeavors include a study of the impact of the oil boom on law enforcement in western North Dakota and research focused on the processing of sexual assault cases by the police.

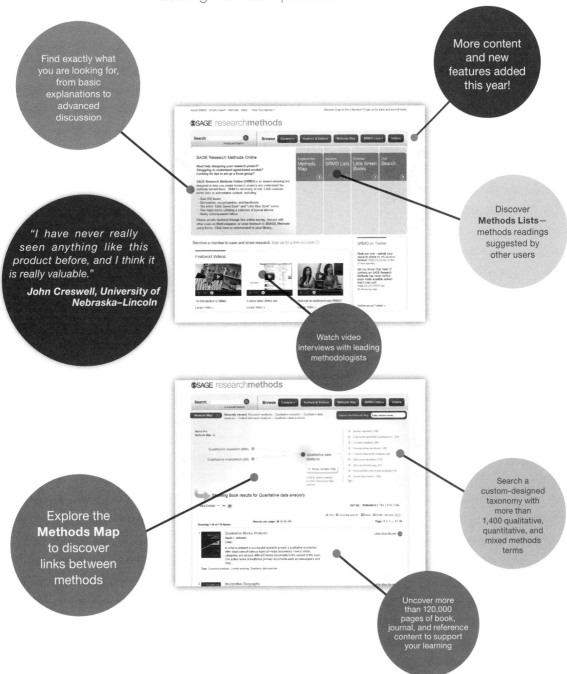